## ACKNOWLEDGEMENTS

**The authors** would like to thank Ann-Marie Shaw and Olivia Eccleshall for their joint effort in editing, as well as all those at Rough Guides who helped in producing the book – Helen Prior, Katie Pringle, Sharon Martins and Maxine Repath in particular – plus the Map Studio, Romsey, Hants, for their work on the maps, Neil Cooper for typesetting and Ken Bell for proofreading; thanks also to everyone at the Mexican Tourist Office in London, to the staff of the Belize High Commission and the embassies of Guatemala, Honduras and El Salvador in London and to Robert A. Jacobsen for his detailed research and numerous emails in compiling the Maya Chronology.

**Peter**: Thanks to all the people who offered help, advice, encouragement and hospitality throughout Chiapas, Petén and Belize. Many of you are mentioned in the *Mexico* and *Belize* guides, but in Guatemala I'd also like to give special thanks to Leticia Bolaños de Martinez of IDAEH for her help in visiting archeological sites in Petén and to Carla Molina for her expert advice on ecotourism in Guatemala; more thanks on conservation issues go to Luis Furlán of PROARCA-CAPAS, to Roan McNab of WCS, to Anne Dix of USAID, to Rolando Montenegro Betancourt of CONAP; in Petén thanks to Placido and Fluvia Castellanos in Machaquilá and Benedicto and Lileana Grijalva in Flores.

**Iain**: In Guatemala, thanks to Lorena Artola, all at Inguat (especially Sandra Monterroso and Migdalia), Tom Lingenfelter, Geo Mendoza,

José and Lucky, Defensores de la Naturaleza, the Proyecto Eco-Quetzal in Cobán, Phillipa Myers, Ileana, Deedle and Dave and Fiona and Bruce for coming along for the ride. In Honduras, thanks to all at the IHT, but especially Kenia Lima de Zapata, and Gracia María Lanza, Captain Sosa, Howard Rosenzweig and his family in Copán, the Posada Arco Iris, Phil and Kaj in West End, the indomitable party girls Claire and Danielle, Alun, Esther, André and all at the Mango Inn and UDC, Mike Wendling, Don Pearly and all the Baymen crew in Guanaja, Ricardo Steiner, Alessandro and Maya Vista in Tela, and all at *Honduras Tips* and *Honduras This Week*. In the UK, thanks to Olivia and Annie for their good-natured professionalism and hard work, Peter Eltringham for his boundless enthusiasm and support, Kate Berens and Martin Dunford, all the Rough Guides production team, Dominique Young, Jamie Marshall and Maya in London and all at the Guatemalan and Honduran embassies in London.

**Gary**: Special thanks to José Antonio Arévalo and Lorena Gomez for their advice and friendship. Thanks also to Lena Johanesson, Ana Beatriz Rivas and the helpful staff at CORSATUR and SalvaNatura.

**Polly**: Thanks to Cesar and all at Budget, to Cameron Boyd, John Cronin, Gorgeous Gary Hodges, Pier Luigi, Sonia Migani, Pepe – and above all to Marina Mike for (possibly) saving my life and to whom all good things are on their way.

## READERS' LETTERS

Thanks to everyone who has taken the time to write or email with suggestions, comments and informaton for this edition, including:

Martine Bruin, Leonardo Carbonara, Martin Crossland, Julian Evans, Macdara Ferris, Matt Hartell, Sarah and Jeannie Hatt Phelps,

Simon Hughes, Robert Jacobsen, Kristi L. Kilbourne and Jeronimo Villalta, Karen and Kristin Hulin, Georgina Jones, Hugo Parkinson, Jeanette Quinn, Felix Riede, David Rosenthal, Howard Rosenzweig, Frances Runnalls, Laura Schmulewitz, Tom Singleton, Julie Tucker

# CONTENTS

# LIST OF MAPS

## MAP SYMBOLS

| | | | | | |
|---|---|---|---|---|---|
| ⌒CA1⌒ | Carretera Interamericana | ★ | Bus stop | Λ̇ | Campground |
| ═══ | Other major highways and roads | 🅿 | Parking | ◉ | Accommodation |
| ═══ | Minor highways and roads (paved) | ♦ | Site of interest | ▣ | Restaurant |
| ------ | Unpaved highways | ⚕ | Spa | @ | Internet access |
| ------ | Footpath | ♥ | Castle | ▮ | Gas station |
| ▨▨▨ | Pedestrianized street | ⚒ | Ruin | 🕯 | Lighthouse |
| ⧟⧟⧟ | Steps | ◠ | Cave | ⓘ | Information centre |
| ┅━┅ | Train line | ⤳ | Mountain range | ⓒ | Telephone |
| — — · | Ferry route | ▲ | Mountain peak | ⊠ | Post office |
| ▪━▪━▪ | International boundary | ⪡ | Viewpoint | ▮ | Building |
| ---- | Chapter division boundary | ⋀ | Volcano | ✚ | Church (town maps) |
| ━━ ··· | District boundary | ⋔ | Escarpment | ⁺⁺ | Cemetery |
| ━━━ | River | ⧜ | Reef | ▨ | Park |
| ▪▪▪▪ | Wall | ⧛ | Waterfall | ▨ | National park |
| ✕ | Airport | ⬥ | Immigration post | ⋯ | Beach |

# INTRODUCTION

Some three thousand years ago, nomadic tribes began to settle deep in the Mesoamerican rainforests, establishing the foundations of the most sophisticated ancient civilization on the American continent. The land they chose, which we know today as the **Maya World**, extends through southern Mexico, Guatemala, Belize and a sliver of El Salvador and Honduras. It's an astonishingly diverse environment, with the hot, scrub-forested plain of the Yucatán peninsula in the north blending gradually into the lowland jungle of the centre, and in the south a spectacular mountainous region, studded with volcanoes and crater lakes and draped with pine and cloudforests. While the southern coastline is pounded by the Pacific Ocean, gentler Caribbean waters lap the white-sand beaches and coral islands that fringe the region's eastern shores.

This is a land whose natural attractions would draw visitors anyway – and indeed the Caribbean coast of Mexico, and to a lesser extent the cayes of Belize and Honduras's Bay Islands, are big resort areas – but it's the chance to visit the **monumental ruins** of ancient Maya cities, some of them stranded in dense, tropical rainforest, that sets the region apart. **Tikal** and **Palenque** are among the most atmospheric sites, dominated by colossal temple pyramids and set in jungle that screeches with toucans, parakeets, and spider and howler monkeys. To the north, the less humid environs of the Yucatán are home to the equally magnificent architecture of **Chichén Itzá** and **Uxmal**; further south, the turbulent history of **Copán** in Honduras is recorded in some of the finest carved monuments and stelae in the Maya World. But these are just a few of the most impressive Maya ruins – scattered throughout the region are the remains of more than a thousand other settlements, for the most part completely unexcavated.

Although all the major cities had been mysteriously abandoned by 1200 AD, the region was never completely depopulated and, despite the depredations of the **Spanish Conquest**, descendants of the great astronomers, architects and calendar-keepers survive in the region today. Of approximately nine million indigenous Maya, Guatemala is home to over six million, with around two million in Mexico, and the rest in smaller communities in Belize and Honduras. For the vast majority of **modern Maya**, Spanish has always been a second language, and their nominally Catholic (but increasingly evangelical) faith is still tempered with traditional religious customs. Inimitable Maya textiles continue to be worn, especially in the highlands of Guatemala and Chiapas, and some isolated communities still observe the 260-day Tzolkin calendar of their ancestors. Having survived almost five hundred years of colonial oppression and political persecution, there are unmistakable signs of a **cultural reawakening**, as Maya throughout the region develop a renewed sense of pride in their unique identity.

This staggering ancient – and modern – cultural heritage is matched by the region's equally rich **natural environment**. Offshore, virtually the entire Caribbean coastline is protected by the second longest **barrier reef** in the world: diving or snorkelling in the warm waters here, amidst a kaleidoscopic world of tropical fish and coral, is an unforgettable experience. Though the smallest of the Maya nations, it's Belize that has the strongest tradition of state environmental protection, which has ensured the preservation of a landscape ranging from the granite peaks of the Maya Mountains, riddled with caves holding Maya artefacts, to the western rivers and jungle, best visited from the ecotourism base of San Ignacio. Throughout the region, however, the network of national parks and reserves is growing, offering protection to some spectacular **wildlife**, including jaguars and other cats, lumbering tapirs, monkeys and an incredible number of **bird species**.

**Travelling** around the Maya World is an adventure in itself. There's an excellent network of roads – of varying quality – almost constantly traversed by buses. This is how most people travel and, though not always comfortable, taking the bus is a quintessential Central American experience – you may find yourself sharing a seat with a Maya woman and her three kids, or even a chicken or two. The countless Caribbean islands of the Yucatán, Belize and Honduras are served by regular boats and ferries; while internal flights can save days of travel and won't necessarily break the bank.

Now that the civil wars in El Salvador and Guatemala are over, the only ongoing **conflict** in the region is in the Chiapas highlands, where a Zapatista-led rebellion has been smouldering since 1994; this has little effect on travellers to the area, though. **Safety** is a real issue, however, and, though it's the usual pickpocketing and bag-snatching that most travellers need to worry about, where risks are more significant we've outlined them in the text.

## Where to go

In **Mexico**'s Yucatán peninsula, the entire Caribbean coastline of Quintana Roo state is blessed with stunning white-sand beaches. The arrival point for most visitors is the manufactured mega-resort of **Cancún**, the region's twenty-first-century temple of the sun; further down the coast, Cozumel and Playa del Carmen have also been heavily developed. If you're in search of somewhere quieter, head for relaxed **Tulum**, with its cliff-perched Maya ruin – many travellers' favourite spot on this coast – or for complete undisturbed peace, there are any number of tiny beaches dotted between the resorts. Further south, the **Sian Ka'an** biosphere reserve and **Laguna Bacalar** offer spectacular scenery and wildlife-spotting possibilities.

**Mérida**, the capital of Yucatán state and the largest city in the region, is a likeable place with a maze-like market and a stately collection of well-preserved colonial buildings. It's an excellent base for visiting most of the well-known sites. **Chichén Itzá**, probably the most visited of them all, is in easy reach, as is **Uxmal** with its vertiginous pyramid temple. A series of lesser sites lie nearby in the Puuc hills. Moving into the neighbouring state, the colonial capital city of **Campeche** makes an enjoyable excursion. From here you can visit the decorative Chenes ruins, of which Edzná is the most accessible. To the south, stretching down towards the Guatemalan border, the largest and most powerful ancient Maya city, **Calakmul**, is surrounded by an immense biosphere reserve.

In Chiapas, modern Maya culture is more in evidence, especially around the delightful highland city of **San Cristóbal del las Casas**, a focal point for the local Tzeltal and Tzotzil Maya. Chiapas also has some first-class ruins. **Palenque** is perhaps the finest, but along the Río Usumacinta lie a number of smaller sites, none with a more splendid location than **Yaxchilán**, situated in a great loop in the river. The exquisite pools and waterfalls of **Agua Azul** and **Misol Ha** are also major attractions, while the unspoilt scenery around the fifty **Lagos de**

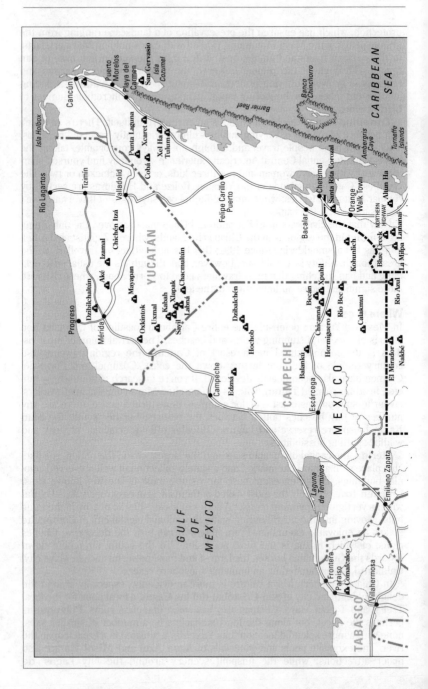

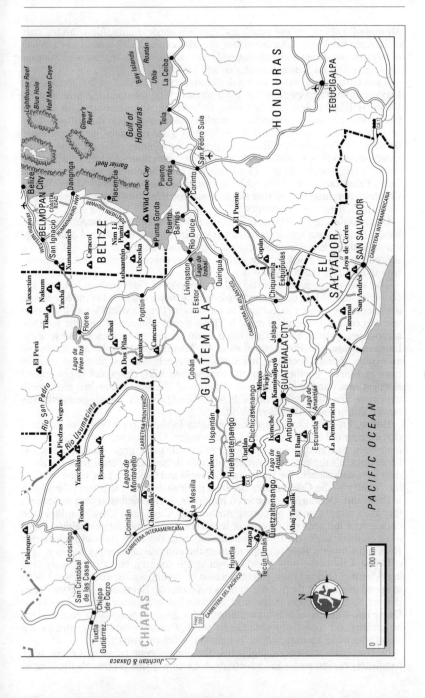

**Montebello** offers endless hiking and camping opportunities. Although the state of Tabasco has less to offer the visitor, the state capital Villahermosa has a wealth of modern museums and galleries and there are some fascinating archeological sites, including **La Venta**, Comalcalco and Malpasito.

It's in **Guatemala**, where over half the country's population is indigenous, that Maya traditions and customs are most obvious. The mesmerizing beauty of the **Western Highlands** is the first place to head for, where the strength of traditional culture is most apparent in the markets and fiestas. **Lago de Atitlán** is postcard picturesque – a vast lake dwarfed by three giant volcanoes, its shores ringed by some of the most traditional villages in the country. The scenery around **Quetzaltenango** is also breathtaking, with more volcanoes and alpine peaks dotted with indigenous villages; it's an easy trip from here to the weekly market at **San Francisco el Alto**, the largest and finest in the Maya World. **Chichicastenango** has another fantastic market: this is the one everyone goes to for textiles, masks and souvenirs.

**Guatemala City**, with poverty and pollution to match most Latin American capitals, is probably not worth spending too long in, especially as the old colonial capital of **Antigua** is just an hour away. Antigua could hardly be more different – a supremely relaxing historic city, with an endless supply of cafés, restaurants and bars to revitalize the jaded traveller.

The sparsely populated north and east region of Guatemala is home to the country's finest Maya ruins, most buried in the dense rainforest of the Maya biosphere reserve, giving you a chance to see some of Petén's **wildlife** too. If you only see one ruin in Guatemala, make it **Tikal**, a vast complex of gigantic temples, acropolises, palaces and plazas. Deep in the protected jungles of the Reserva Biósfera Maya, the Preclassic sites of **El Mirador** and Nakbé are much less accessible, though becoming much easier to reach from the attractive gateway town of **Flores**. Further south, the mist-soaked hills, caves and rivers around sleepy **Cobán** and the jungle-coated gorge of the **Río Dulce** are also worth exploring. The one notable ruin in these parts is **Quiriguá**, whose spectacular stelae are the largest in the Maya World.

**Belize**, the only English-speaking country in the Maya World, also boasts a rich number of Maya sites. Caracol, Xunantunich, Lamanai and Lubaantun are the main ones, though only Caracol compares in scale to the great ruins of Mexico or Guatemala. It's the natural environment that's Belize's main draw, from the abundant flora and fauna of the lagoons at Sarteneja and Crooked Tree in the north of the country to the **Cockscomb Basin**, a reserve designed to protect the jaguar, in the south. Offshore are scattered hundreds of tiny islands known as "cayes", the main targets being upmarket **Ambergris Caye**, and **Caye Caulker**, the choice spot for young independent travellers. Other, mostly uninhabited cayes offer dramatic scuba-diving and snorkelling, with the coral atolls of **Lighthouse Reef** and **Glover's Reef** perhaps offering the ultimate underwater scenery.

**Belize City** is the only sizeable town in the country, but it's no beauty and, apart from changing buses, catching a boat or visiting a museum, you won't need to spend much time there – nor in the sleepy capital, Belmopan. Make your way, instead, to **San Ignacio** in the west, surrounded by forested hills and rivers, or **Dangriga**, a centre of Garífuna culture and a good stepping-stone to the Maya Mountains and central cayes. In the far south, **Punta Gorda** is a centre for the Maya who make up over half the population of Toledo district.

In **Honduras**'s western highlands, the magnificent ruins of **Copán** offer exquisitely carved stelae and a hieroglyphic stairway that represents the longest

## AVERAGE TEMPERATURES AND MONTHLY RAINFALL

|  | Jan | Feb | Mar | Apr | May | Jun | Jul | Aug | Sept | Oct | Nov | Dec |
|---|---|---|---|---|---|---|---|---|---|---|---|---|
| **Mérida, Mexico** | | | | | | | | | | | | |
| Max °C | 28 | 29 | 37 | 41 | 40 | 33 | 33 | 33 | 32 | 31 | 29 | 28 |
| Min °C | 17 | 17 | 19 | 21 | 22 | 23 | 23 | 23 | 23 | 22 | 19 | 18 |
| Rainfall (mm) | 25 | 18 | 28 | 28 | 79 | 173 | 122 | 135 | 155 | 102 | 33 | 31 |
| **Belize City** | | | | | | | | | | | | |
| Max °C | 29 | 29 | 30 | 31 | 31 | 31 | 32 | 32 | 32 | 31 | 28 | 28 |
| Min °C | 19 | 20 | 21 | 24 | 24 | 23 | 23 | 22 | 22 | 22 | 20 | 20 |
| Rainfall (mm) | 136 | 64 | 38 | 58 | 108 | 196 | 164 | 172 | 245 | 305 | 226 | 186 |
| **Guatemala City** | | | | | | | | | | | | |
| Max °C | 23 | 25 | 27 | 28 | 29 | 27 | 26 | 26 | 26 | 24 | 23 | 22 |
| Min °C | 12 | 12 | 14 | 14 | 16 | 16 | 16 | 16 | 16 | 16 | 14 | 13 |
| Rainfall (mm) | 8 | 3 | 13 | 31 | 152 | 274 | 203 | 198 | 231 | 173 | 23 | 8 |
| **Santa Ana, El Salvador** | | | | | | | | | | | | |
| Max °C | 32 | 33 | 34 | 34 | 33 | 31 | 32 | 32 | 31 | 31 | 31 | 32 |
| Min °C | 16 | 16 | 17 | 18 | 19 | 19 | 18 | 19 | 19 | 18 | 17 | 16 |
| Rainfall (mm) | 8 | 5 | 10 | 43 | 196 | 328 | 292 | 297 | 307 | 241 | 41 | 10 |
| **San Pedro Sula, Honduras** | | | | | | | | | | | | |
| Max °C | 25 | 27 | 29 | 30 | 30 | 28 | 27 | 28 | 28 | 27 | 26 | 25 |
| Min °C | 14 | 14 | 15 | 17 | 18 | 18 | 18 | 17 | 17 | 17 | 16 | 15 |
| Rainfall (mm) | 12 | 2 | 1 | 26 | 180 | 177 | 70 | 74 | 151 | 87 | 38 | 14 |

known glyphic text. North of here, the cities of San Pedro Sula and La Ceiba serve as stopping-off points en route to the idyllic **Bay Islands**. Each of the three main islands has its aficionados, but **Utila** is the cheapest and most popular with backpackers, while **Guanaja** and **Roatán** are geared up more for scuba-divers on package holidays.

The Maya slice of **El Salvador** holds some of the most fantastic scenery in the country. One of the biggest attractions is **Lago de Coatepeque**, a pristine crater lake bordered by Cerro Verde and the Izalco volcano. The Maya ruins here are less imposing than further north, though **Tazumal**, and **Joya de Cerén**, where an entire community was buried in volcanic ash, are well worth a look.

### When to go

**Seasons** in the Maya World are less marked by extremes of temperature than Europe or North America. The dominant feature here is the **rainy season**, beginning in May and reaching a crescendo during October and November, when the danger from **hurricanes** is at its greatest. Even during the rainy season days are often sunny, and the rain confined to a brief – if torrential – late afternoon downpour. Travel is rarely affected for very long and, though dirt roads and low bridges can be washed away during heavy storms, local transport is usually up and running as soon as the rain stops. During August there can often be a lull in the rains – known as *la canícula* in Guatemala and the "mauger season" in Belize – and the tourist industry turns the luxuriant vegetation produced by the summer rains to its advantage by promoting this period as the **"green season"**. The hottest time of year is in April and early May, before the first of the rains.

The most important factor determining climate is **altitude**. Much of Guatemala and Chiapas is above 1500m, and these parts enjoy a benign climate with warm days and mild or cool evenings. In the lowlands, temperatures are higher and the increased humidity can be quite uncomfortable – especially if you're exploring the forests of Belize, lowland Chiapas and Petén. The climate of Yucatán is a little different to the rest of the region, and in December and January night-time temperatures here can be unexpectedly cool.

Everywhere, the main **tourist season** is from mid-December to March, and this is when you can expect the luxury hotels to push up their prices, though rates at budget places tend to fluctuate less. The popular resorts are always packed out at Christmas, New Year and Easter – if you're planning a visit then, you'll need to plan and book rooms ahead. There's another surge in visitor numbers from mid-July to early September, during the European and North American holidays.

# PART ONE

## THE

# BASICS

# GETTING THERE FROM NORTH AMERICA

**Reaching the Maya region from the US and Canada is simplest, quickest and usually cheapest by air. The main US, Mexican and Central American airlines all have regular flights to the region's main airports: Mérida and Cancún in Mexico, Guatemala City, Belize City, and San Pedro Sula in Honduras,** in addition to many smaller airports. A vast number of possible destinations, routes and prices make any comprehensive listing virtually impossible but most non-stop flights leave from Miami, Houston, Los Angeles, Atlanta and Dallas. Airlines serving these hubs have excellent connections throughout the US and Canada.

If you live close to the US/Mexican border, a cheap option for getting to southern Mexico is to cross into Mexico and take an internal flight (which you can arrange through your local travel agent) to Cancún or another Mexican airport. This can represent very good value for money: for example, the Tijuana–Mexico City flight costs little more than a first-class bus. In southern Mexico, the main airports are at Cozumel, Tuxtla Gutiérrez, Mérida and Villahermosa, and there are smaller airports at Palenque, San Cristóbal and Chetumal. Another good way from North America to the Maya region (and to get around quickly when you're there) is to buy one of the airpasses outlined on pp.6 & 31.

## AIRLINES IN NORTH AMERICA

In addition to the destinations listed below, many airlines have frequent departures for other cities just outside the Maya region, including San Salvador and Oaxaca. For details of **air passes**, see pp.6 & 31.

**Aeromexico** (☎1-800/237-6639, *aeromexico .com*). Direct flights from many US gateways to Mexico City and Cancún. Tickets can be linked to the "Mexipass" for connections throughout Mexico, and onwards to Central and South America.

**American** (☎1-800/433-7300, *aa.com*). Daily non-stops from Miami and Dallas to Belize City and all Central American capitals.

**Canada 3000** (☎1-866/865-3000, *canada3000.com*). Inexpensive charter flights from Halifax, Montréal, Toronto and Vancouver to Cancún and Cozumel.

**Continental** (☎1-800/231-0856, *continental.com*). The largest number of daily non-stops from Houston to destinations in Mexico, Belize City and all Central American capitals.

**Delta** (☎1-800/241-4141, *delta.com*). Daily flights from Atlanta to Cancún, Guatemala City and San Salvador.

**Méxicana** (☎1-800/531-7921, *mexicana.com*). Frequent flights from Chicago, Denver, LA, New York, San Francisco and Toronto to Mexico City. Tickets can be linked to the "Mexipass" with flights on subsidiary airline Aerocaribe from airports in the Yucatán peninsula to Belize City, Flores, Palenque & Guatemala City.

**Grupo Taca** (☎1-800/535-8780, *grupotaca.com*). Reservations for four of the national airlines of Central America: Aviateca (Guatemala), Nica (Nicaragua), Lacsa (Costa Rica) and Taca (El Salvador). Taca is the biggest airline in the group and between them they have dozens of daily flights from LA, San Francisco, New York, Washington DC, Houston, Miami and Toronto to Mexico City, Cancún and the other main Yucatán airports and to the capitals and many other cities in Central America; tickets can be linked to the "Latin AirFlex" airpass.

**United Airlines** (☎1-800/538-2929, *ual.com*). Daily flights from Chicago, Washington and LA to Guatemala City, as well as services to Mexico City and San Salvador.

You can also travel overland inexpensively **by bus** from the US/Mexico border into Mexico. Some buses are quite luxurious, but the journey can take between two and four days, so most travellers choose to break the journey in Mexico City.

## SHOPPING FOR AIR TICKETS

Prices are higher in the high **seasons** of July and August, and Christmas and Easter, although the price you actually pay for a flight often depends more on with whom you book it than on a particular season. Seat availability can also be a problem in the high seasons: selecting a good flight agent, flying mid-week and booking as far ahead as possible will pay dividends.

If you plan to travel around the region you should consider buying an **open-jaw ticket**, which enables you to fly into one city and out of another and is particularly good value if combined with an airpass (see below). Many airlines offer youth or student fares to under-26s. If you qualify, you'll save perhaps eight to ten percent again but these tickets are subject to availability and can have eccentric booking conditions.

Although the airlines' own **websites** are increasingly useful, and several now have an online booking facility that can save money, they are just as often confusing and frustrating. The best place to begin an Internet search for flights to Central America and Mexico is eXito's website, followed up by a phone call to their expert staff; other flight specialists are listed in the box on

below. It's also definitely worth checking on a couple of the general online travel sites (try *expedia.com*, *travelocity.com* or *travel.yahoo.com*), as they have access to a vast number of fares and masses of other travel services.

There are so many possible permutations of routes, airlines and destinations that the following **fares** can serve only as an approximate guide. Generally, flying to Cancún or Mérida will be the least expensive option (and either would be a good place to begin a trip to the Maya World), with Guatemala City and San Salvador a bit more expensive and Belize City often the most expensive destination. Typical fares **from the USA** to Cancún and Central America are around US$470–520 low season, US$515–575 high season from New York; US$640–665/680–730 from Seattle; US$445–495/475–525 from Houston. **From Canada** your best bet is probably to fly to Miami or Houston on either American or Continental and change there. There are also charter flights with Canada 3000. From Toronto, Montréal and Ottawa expect to pay around C$635 low season/C$850 high season; from Vancouver; C$695/950.

## AIRPASSES

If you want to visit other cities in the region you can cut costs by taking advantage of a couple of airpasses linking gateways in North America and Mexico with other cities in Central America and even onwards to South America. The conditions and costs of airpasses change frequently (and the

---

### NORTH AMERICAN FLIGHT SPECIALISTS AND CONSOLIDATORS

**Air-tech**, 584 Broadway, Suite 1007, New York, NY 10012 (☎1-800/575-TECH or 212/219-7000, *airtech.com*). Standby seat broker and courier flights. Very good deals on their website, if you're prepared to be flexible.

**Council Travel**, 205 E 42nd St, New York, NY 10017 (☎ & fax 1-800/226-8624, *counciltravel.com*). The Council on International Educational Exchange is a nationwide student/budget travel specialist with a range of travel-related services and information.

**eXito**, 1212 Broadway, Suite 910, Oakland, CA 94612 (☎1-800/655-4053, *exitotravel.com*). North America's top specialist for travel to Latin America. Website has a particularly useful airfare finder, with a comparison of the merits of various airpasses in addition to masses of invaluable travel information.

**Now Voyager**, 74 Varick St, Suite 307, New York, NY 10013 (☎212/431-1616, *nowvoyagertravel.com*). Courier flight broker. Check the excellent website first, then call for flight prices, though usually only flights to Mexico on offer.

**STA Travel**, 10 Downing St, New York, NY 10014 (☎1-800/781-4040, *sta.com*; other offices throughout US). Worldwide discount travel specialists in student/youth fares and travel-related services such as student IDs.

**Travel Cuts**, 187 College St, Toronto, ON M5T 1P7 (☎1-800/667-2887, from US ☎416/979-2406, *travelcuts.com*). Foremost Canadian specialists in student fares, IDs, insurance and other travel services. Dozens of branches throughout Canada, often on college campuses.

## SPECIALIST OPERATORS IN THE US

*Prices below don't include flights unless stated.*

**AmeriCan Adventures**, PO Box 1155, Gardenia, CA 90249 (☎310/324-3447 or 1-800/873-5872, *americanadventures.com*). Inexpensive, small-group van-based camping trips (with some hotels), throughout the Americas. Around US$700 for a twelve-day "Mayan Adventure" visiting the beaches and Maya sites of Yucatán and Chiapas, plus around $90 food kitty.

**Ceiba Adventures**, PO Box 2274, Flagstaff, AZ 86003 (☎928/527-0171 or 1-800/217-1060, *ceiba @mindspring.com, ceibaadventures.com*). Multi-sport adventures, including rafting, kayaking and caving, and archeological tours throughout the Maya region, including the Lacandón forest in Chiapas.

**Elderhostel**, 11 Ave de Lafayette, Boston, MA 02111-1746 (☎1-877/426-8056 or 978/323-4141, *elderhostel.org*). A non-profit organization offering upmarket educational programmes for over-55s. A week studying bottlenose dolphins on the Belize atolls is around US$2200; US$2400 for a 10-day birding and archeology trip in Yucatán and Chiapas (both including airfare from much of US).

**Far Horizons**, PO Box 91900, Albuquerque, NM 87199-1900 (☎1-800/552-4575, *farhorizon.com*). Some of the very best archeological trips to all Maya sites in the region, including remote sites where the latest discoveries are being unearthed. About US$3000 for a nine-day expedition.

**Green Tortoise Adventure Travel**, 494 Broadway, San Francisco, CA 94133 (☎1-800/867-8647 or 415/956-7500; *info@greentortoise.com, greentortoise.com*). Tours to "cool places off the beaten-path" on converted buses with sleeping space. The "Southern Migration" is a very popular 23-day journey from San Francisco to Antigua in Guatemala via Baja California and Chiapas. Leaves in December and costs US$900 including food; other, shorter trips in Yucatán.

**Guatemala Unlimited**, 1212 Broadway, Suite 910, Oakland, CA 94612 (☎1-800-733-3350 or 510-496-0631, *guatemala1@aol.com, guatemalaunlimited .com*). Experienced company with an extensive array of custom-arranged tours to obscure and better-known Maya ruins, as well as jungle trekking, river-rafting, mountain-biking and volcano tours; also a good source of discount flights to Guatemala.

**International Expeditions**, One Environs Park, Helena AL 35080 (☎1-800/633-4377, *ietravel.com*). Superbly led, very comfortable natural history tours throughout Guatemala and Belize. A nine-day

"Naturalist's Quest" trip costs US$2500; $3195 for a 10-day tour of the Guatemalan highlands, including airfare from Miami, Dallas or Houston.

**Journeys International**, 107 April Dr, Suite 3, Ann Arbor, MI 48103 (☎1-800/255-8735 or 734/665-4407, *journeys-intl.com*). Superb nature- and culture-oriented tours to Central America, some for women only. Around US$1800–2200 for a week, excluding airfare.

**Peter Hughes Diving**, 1390 South Dixie Hwy, Suite 1109, Coral Gables, FL 33146 (☎1-800/932-6237, *peterhughes.com*). Luxurious, all-inclusive trips on 120-foot live-aboard dive boats based in Belize and the Bay Islands, departing Saturdays. Around US$1500–1800 per week; advanced dive instruction and underwater photography course available.

**Slickrock Adventures**, PO Box 1400, Moab, UT 84532 (☎1-800/390-5715 *slickrock@slickrock.com, slickrock.com*). One of the very best companies, offering sea-kayaking on a Belize atoll, caving, jungle and river (some white-water) expeditions in Belize; US$2095 for an adventure week in Belize; US$1850 for a week kayaking and snorkelling at Glover's Reef.

**Suntrek**, Sun Plaza, 77 West Third St, Santa Rosa CA 95401(☎1-800/SUNTREK or 707/523-1800, *suntrek.com*). Wide range of van-based camping tours throughout USA and Mexico. Excellent two-week "La Ruta Maya" tour through Yucatán and Chiapas from Cancún to San Cristóbal and back for around US$800 plus food kitty.

**Toucan Adventure Tours**, PO Box 1073, Cambria, CA 93428 (☎805/927-5885, *toucanad-ventures.com*). Inexpensive camping tours through the Maya region of Yucatán, Belize and Guatemala. Three-week "Ruta Maya" trip; around US$1150 for land costs.

**Tread Lightly Limited**, PO Box 329, 37 Juniper Meadow Rd, Washington Depot, CT 06794 (☎1-800/643-0060 or 860/868-1710, *info@tread-lightly.com, treadlightly.com*). Wide selection of top-notch "low impact" natural history, archeological and cultural trips to Belize, Guatemala, the Yucatán and Honduras, often including kayaking, rafting and hiking and reaching the less visited Maya sites.

**Victor Emanuel Nature Tours**, PO Box 33008, Austin, TX 78764 (☎1-800/328-VENT or 512/328-5221, *ventbird.com*). The best small-group bird-watching tours you can get, led by dedicated professionals. US$2795 for ten days at Chan Chich, Belize, with a trip to Tikal; also trips to Yucatán and El Triunfo reserve in Chiapas.

## SPECIALIST TOUR OPERATORS IN CANADA

*Note: some of these companies provide quotes in US$ only.*

**Adventures Abroad**, 2148–20800 Westminster Highway, Richmond, BC, V6V 2W3 (☎604/303-1099 or 1-800/665-3998, *adventures-abroad.com*). Excellent small-group tours, focusing on archeology, culture, nature and relaxation throughout the Maya region. Eight days in Honduras including Roatán and Copán for C$1231; a week in Yucatán for C$1417 (excluding air fare).

**Eco-Summer Expeditions** PO Box 1765, Clearwater, BC V0E 1N0 (☎1-800/465-8884 or 250/674-0102, *ecosummer.ca*). Wildlife tours, river rafting and sea-kayaking expeditions in western and southern Belize; US$1395 for six days; US$1995 for 10 days.

**Gap Adventures**, 19 Duncan St, Toronto, ON M5H 3HI (☎1-800/465-5600 or 416/260-0999, *gap.ca*). Offices in Calgary (☎403/251-9266) and Ottawa (☎613/562-3821). Wide range of group trips (some camping) with diving and kayaking in

Yucatán, Belize and throughout Central America. Around US$850 for eight days' sea-kayaking in Belize; US$1600 for a 32-day "Central American Journey" (all trips exclude airfare).

**Global Adventures**, PO Box U49, Bowen Island, BC V0N 1G0 (☎1-800/781-2269, *globaladventures.ca*). Small-group sailing, sea-kayaking and jungle trips, mainly in southern Belize: eight days' sea-kayaking C$1500; 12 days kayak and caves, C$2100.

**Island Expeditions**, 368–916 W Broadway, Vancouver, BC V5Z 1K7 (☎1-800/667-1630 or 604/452-3212, *islandexpeditions.com*). The best foreign outfitters in the region, running expertly led sea- and river-kayaking expeditions in Belize, with inland caving and a Tikal trip. US$1460 for eight days inland and kayaking on Glover's Reef; US$1240 for six nights exploring rainforest rivers in southern Belize.

price you pay will not include internal departure taxes), though you can expect savings of between thirty and fifty percent on the same flights bought separately. The best way to find out if you'll benefit from an airpass is to call a recommended flight specialist and book as far ahead as possible (see boxes on pp.4 & 31).

The "**Latin AirFlex**" programme offered by Grupo Taca consists of pre-booked, pre-paid coupons (minimum 3, maximum 16), valid for 180 days. You'll need to book it outside Central America and there's a US$75 surcharge if you fly into Central America on an airline not a member of Grupo Taca; once booked, a reservation change costs US$50. For example, flying from Belize City to Flores, on to La Ceiba or Roatán, then back to Belize (3 coupons) costs US$195; add in Guatemala City for a further US$65. If you fly to Belize or Guatemala from Toronto, San Francisco or Montréal, for instance, using Grupo Taca, a return flight will add US$530 to the above itinerary.

The "**Mexipass International**" offered by Aeroméxico and Mexicana, both of which have an extensive network throughout the US, Canada and Mexico, can be linked with flights from North America, within Mexico and on to Central America. This pass also consists of pre-booked, pre-paid

coupons (minimum purchase of 3) at discount prices for travellers from outside Mexico, and is particularly good value if you're flying from Canada or Europe. The airpass is valid for ninety days and offers real savings on longer, multi-stop routes: you need to book routes and dates in advance.

### PACKAGES AND ORGANIZED TOURS

The range of **package tours** to the Maya region increases every year. Specialist companies take escorted groups on tours to Maya ruins, colonial towns, markets and beaches, often crossing several borders, and with options including biking, diving, rafting and bird-watching. If time is short, these can be very good value, especially for first-time visitors to the region, and the tour companies often have special arrangements with airlines for seat prices.

Budget tour groups usually travel by van, staying at comfortable, family-run hotels or camping, and calling at the main tourist attractions as well as some lesser-known places. More expensive tours stay at some luxury hotels and lodges, and can offer caving, rafting and sea-kayaking, or take you on expeditions with archeologists and scientists to remote sites and nature reserves.

Though in most cases you could organize the same or very similar itineraries yourself for less money, you'd probably need more time and some knowledge of Spanish. However, sea-kayaking trips, caving and expeditions to remote jungle ruins and rivers are more difficult (or even impossible) to organize on your own, and are best done in an organized group, with expert leaders and emergency back-up.

## ROUTES THROUGH MEXICO

It's a long haul **overland** to the Maya region from the US and Canada, with several possible routes through Mexico. For those needing a **visa** to visit any of the Central American countries, there are Guatemalan consulates in Tapachula and Comitán and a Belize consulate in Chetumal; for more on entry requirements, see p.14.

Greyhound (☎1-800/229-9424, *greyhound.com*) runs regularly to all the major border crossings, and some buses even take you over the frontier and into the Mexican bus station, and in many cases you can reserve tickets with their Mexican counterparts. Mexican buses similarly cross the border into US bus stations. Green Tortoise (see p.5) run cheap and cheerful long-haul trips through Mexico to Guatemala. You can buy all these tickets and the "**Ameripass**" buspass online.

There are constant buses to Mexico City from every Mexican border crossing (roughly 18–22hr), and beyond Mexico City there are good bus connections to Cancún and the main Guatemala and Belize border crossings. The best route **into Guatemala** takes you along the Carretera Interamericana (Pan-American Highway) through Oaxaca and San Cristóbal de las Casas (see p.153), and then on to Huehuetenango. The other **main routes** are along Mexico's Pacific coast to Tapachula, where you can take **international buses** to Guatemala City, and along the Caribbean coast to Chetumal, then into Belize. An interesting option is to travel from the Maya sites of Palenque and Yaxchilán in Chiapas, by boat along the Río Usumacinta (see p.149) to a border crossing in the department of Petén in Guatemala, to visit Tikal.

Driving south may give you a lot of freedom, but it does entail a great deal of bureaucracy. You need a separate insurance policy for Central America (sold at the border). Sanborn's (☎1-800/222-0158) arranges insurance for Mexico and Central America, and also offers legal assistance, road maps and guides, and a 24-hour emergency hotline. The car will also require an entry permit, for which you'll need to show the registration and licence. US, Canadian, EU, Australian and New Zealand driving licences are valid in Mexico and throughout Central America, but it's a good idea to arm yourself with an **International Driving Licence** as well. If you belong to a motoring organization at home you may find they'll offer advice, maps and even help from reciprocal organizations in Mexico. Unleaded petrol/gasoline is widely available in the region.

## GETTING THERE FROM THE UK AND IRELAND

**At the time of writing there is just one direct scheduled flight from the UK to a Maya World destination (on British Airways from London to Cancún, though this service may have been suspended by the time you read this). Generally though, flying there involves changing aircraft (and sometimes airline), usually in the US. That said, it's possible to reach Guatemala City, Cancún, Mérida or San Pedro Sula in one day from London (the best connections are on Continental, Iberia, KLM and American); flying to Belize City always involves an overnight stay en route. Flying to Cancún, served by a vast number of well-priced scheduled and charter flights, is often the least expensive option and is in many ways an ideal arrival point.**

Although flying from London gives you the greatest variety of flights to the US and onwards to Mexico or Central America, you can often get flights from other UK airports for the same or only a slightly higher price. A scheduled flight to Belize City or Guatemala City (with Belize City usually the more expensive option), on American (via Dallas or Miami) or Continental (via Newark or Houston) will cost around £484 low season/£605 high season return.

British Airways flies from London non-stop to Mexico City from around £455 low/£585 high – and there are often good promotional offers beating these fares. Continental's fares to Mexico City are similar, and their fares to Cancún are usually very competitive, at around £378/598.

Several other European airlines fly to Mexico City, with Iberia from London (£465/584, via Madrid and Miami) often good value. You can also reach Cancún, Guatemala City and San Salvador the same day; Iberia flights from Manchester require an overnight stop in Madrid. Lufthansa (via Frankfurt) has very similar fares.

If you want to travel through several countries in Central America, or continue into South America, then it's worth considering an **open-jaw ticket** (which lets you fly into one city and out of another). The low-season price for an open-jaw flying London–Cancún and returning Guatemala City–London can be as little as around £500, and lots of other options are available. For details of the Mexipass International from Aeroméxico /Mexicana and the Latin AirFlex **airpasses**, see p.6.

### SHOPPING FOR TICKETS

Flights to Central America fill up early, so book ahead as far as you can. Official fares, quoted by the airlines, are generally more expensive than those booked through a specialist travel agent. Wherever you book, **peak season rates** apply in July, August, December and at Easter, and the lowest prices will be from October to early December and mid-January to the end of February. Tickets are usually valid for between three and six months – you'll usually pay more for one that allows you to stay for up to a year – and there's always some deal available for young people or students, though don't expect massive reductions.

On the **internet** *cheapflights.co.uk* has one of the best and fastest farefinders, allowing some rapid comparisons and best-buy deals on fares to Mexico and Central America from various UK airports; you don't book flights here though, the site provides a link to the travel agent offering the best price. Frequently, however, no single general travel website is consistently going to give you the best deal, so it's worth shopping around on *travelocity.co.uk* and *expedia.co.uk* as well. The usefulness of the airlines' own websites increases with every re-design, and some (though by no means all) offer real bargains if you book online. Despite the rapid advances of the giant internet travel sites, however, you'll find the **specialist flight agents** (see box, p.9) usually offer the best fares, backed by expert first-hand travel advice. Journey

## AIRLINES IN THE UK

For more details on routes for these and other airlines, see "Airlines in North America" box on p.3.

**American Airlines** ☎08457/789789, *aa.com*

**British Airways** ☎0845/7733377, *britishairways .com*

**Continental** ☎0800/776464, *continental.com*

**Iberia** ☎020/7830 0011, *iberia.com* Daily flights from Heathrow to Mexico City and Cancún, via Madrid.

**KLM** ☎0990/750900, *klmuk.com* Daily flights from Heathrow and London City (via Amsterdam) to Mexico City; partner Northwest flies daily to Cancún.

**Mexicana** ☎020/8492 0000, *sales@mextours .co.uk* Information and reservations only; no Méxicana flights between UK and Mexico, but they do sell the "Mexipass" airpass.

**Groupo Taca** ☎0870/241 0340, *grupotaca.com* Agents for several Central American airlines.

**Virgin Atlantic** ☎01293/747747 for Virgin reservations and flight information (*virgin.co.uk*), or ☎0870/ 876 6111 for Virgin Travelstore, where you can get competitive prices on any flights.

## SPECIALIST FLIGHT AGENTS

**Journey Latin America**, 12 & 13 Heathfield Terrace, London W4 4JE (☎020/8747 3108, fax 8742 1312, *journeylatinamerica.co.uk*); 28–30 Barton Arcade, Deansgate, Manchester (☎0161/832 1441, *man@journeylatinamerica.co.uk*). The acknowledged leaders for airfares and tours to Latin America, with some of the best prices on high-season flights.

**North South Travel**, Moulsham Mill Parkway, Chelmsford, Essex CM2 7PX (☎ & fax 01245/608291, *northsouthtravel.co.uk*). Small, friendly and competitive agency offering worldwide discounted fares. Profits are used to support development projects in Africa, Asia and Latin America.

**South American Experience**, 47 Causton St, London SW1P 4AT (☎020/7976 5511, *southamericanexperience.co.uk*). Flight and tailor-made itinerary specialists, with very good airfare prices on their website and high-quality tours to the Maya region.

**STA Travel**, 85 Shaftesbury Ave, London W1, and offices elsewhere across the UK (national sales enquiries ☎0870/160 6070, *statravel.co.uk*; Manchester ☎0161/834 0668; Edinburgh

☎0131/226 7747). Student/youth travel specialists with 250 branches worldwide, offering flights, tours, accommodation and many travel-related services, including a help desk if you have problems while abroad.

**Trailfinders**, 194 Kensington High St, London W8 7RG (long-haul flights ☎020/7938 3939, *trailfinders .co.uk*); 58 Deansgate, Manchester (☎0161/839 6969); 254–284 Sauchiehall St, Glasgow (☎0141/353 2224); 22–24 The Priory Queensway, Birmingham (☎0121/236 1234); 48 Corn St, Bristol (☎0117/929 9000); other offices in London, Cambridge, Newcastle and Dublin. An independent travel company with a wide range of deals on flights and specializing in tailor-made travel, hotels and car hire; exellent travel health clinic in Kensington High St branch.

**Usit CAMPUS**, 52 Grosvenor Gdns, London (national call centre ☎0870/240 1010, *usitcampus .co.uk*). Student/youth travel specialists, with 40 branches on university campuses, in YHA shops and in cities all over Britain, and dozens worldwide. Good website with tons of travel-related products for sale and information.

Latin America's website leads the field, closely followed by those of Usit CAMPUS, Trailfinders and South American Experience.

## PACKAGES AND INCLUSIVE TOURS

Many companies in the UK offer guided **package tours** to Yucatán, Guatemala and Belize, and they can be especially good value if you're short of time. They're usually led by someone from the UK who knows the area and in many cases you'll have a

local guide too. These itineraries are usually very popular, so you should book well ahead. Transport varies from local buses to comfortable minibuses, fast launches to light aircraft. The box below covers the best and most experienced UK operators going to the Maya area; all can provide detailed information sheets on each trip. Prices given are a guide only; several tours also require local payment for some meals. Some tours operate only through the winter period but many run year-round.

## SPECIALIST TOUR OPERATORS

**Adventure Bound**, 14 Barley Mow Passage, Chiswick, London W4 4PH (☎020/8742 8612, *adventurebound.co.uk*). A range of good budget trips through Mexico and the Maya region of Central America, staying at hotels and using public transport; 22-day "Mayan Circle" for £1150, 9-day "Quetzal Highway" including Tikal and Belize for £590.

**Cathy Matos Mexican Tours**, 75 St Margaret's Ave, London N20 9LD (☎020/8492 0000, *sales@mextours.co.uk, cathymatosmexico.com*). Very experienced company and specialists in little-known resorts, offering a wide variety of tailor-made tours, including archeological sites, colonial cities and haciendas in Yucatán. Also UK agents for Méxicana Airlines.

**Dragoman Camp Green**, Kenton Rd, Debenham, Suffolk IP14 6LA (☎01728/861133, *dragoman.com*). Eight-week overland camping/hotel expeditions through Mexico and Central America to Panamá; around £1600, plus $750 food/hotel kitty; four weeks for around £900 plus $385 kitty.

**Exodus**, 9 Weir Rd, London, SW12 0LT (☎020/8675 5550, *exodus.co.uk*). Sixteen-day escorted hotel-based tours through the Maya region for around £1450, including airfare from London.

**Explore Worldwide**, 1 Frederick St, Aldershot GU11 1LQ (☎01252/760000, *exploreworldwide.com*). Wide range of two- to three-week hotel-based tours to Central America and Mexico. Most tours run year-round. Around £1250 for 15 days in Mexico, Guatemala and Belize, including airfare.

**Global Travel Club**, 1 Kiln Shaw, Langdon Hills, Basildon, Essex SS16 6LE (☎01268/541732, *global-travel.co.uk*). Small company specializing in individually arranged diving and cultural tours to Mexico, Guatemala and Belize.

**Journey Latin America**, 12–13 Heathfield Terrace, London W4 4JE (☎020/8747 8315, *journeylatinamerica.co.uk*). Wide range of high-standard group tours and tailor-made itineraries from the acknowledged experts. Their three-week "Quetzal Journey" through Guatemala, Chiapas, Yucatán and Belize costs around £1820 including airfare and good-quality accommodation, but not meals. Also a nine-night "Adventure Week" with sea-kayaking, rafting and jungle trip in Belize for around £2000.

**Kumuka**, 40 Earls Court Rd, London W8 6EJ (☎020/7397 6664, *kumuka.co.uk*). Several hotel-based group trips (maximum 15) through Mexico and Central America. The seven-week "Central American Explorer" (around £1600, excluding airfare and meals) takes in Guatemala, Chiapas and Yucatán in Mexico before visiting Belize then Honduras, Nicaragua and Costa Rica. A similar five-week trip is around £1250.

**Reef and Rainforest Tours**, 1 The Plains, Totnes, Devon TQ9 5DR (☎01803/866965, *reefrainforest.co.uk*). Individual itineraries from a very experienced company, focusing on nature reserves, research projects and diving in Belize and Honduras.

**Scuba Safaris**, PO Box 8, Edenbridge, Kent TH8 7ZS (☎01342/851196, *scuba-safaris.com*). A knowledgeable, well-organized company, specialists in arranging fully inclusive dive packages. Around £2000 for a week on a live-aboard boat in Belize or the Bay Islands; £200 less for a week in a luxury dive resort. Prices include airfare, overnight accommodation in Houston and six days' diving (tuition about $200 extra).

**Travelbag Adventures**, 15 Turk St, Alton, Hants GU34 1AG (☎01420/541007, *travelbag-adventures.com*). Small-group hotel-based tours through Yucatán and Central America; sixteen-day "Realm of the Maya" trip, from Cancún through Belize and Guatemala for around £1300 including airfare but not meals.

**Trips**, 9 Byron Place, Clifton, Bristol BS8 1JT (☎0117/987 2626, *tripsworldwide.co.uk*). Friendly, experienced company with an inspired range of high-quality tailor-made itineraries and tours to Mexico and all of Central America. A fifteen-day "Ruins and Rainforest" trip taking in Guatemala's Western Highlands, Tikal and Belize's Cayo District and Ambergris Caye for £1920. Also agents for many other recommended tour operators.

**Wildlife Worldwide**, 170 Selsdon Road, South Croydon, Surrey CR2 6PJ (☎020/8667 9158, *wildlifeworldwide.com*). Superb bird-watching trips to Belize and Guatemala led by expert naturalists, visiting some remote protected areas and staying at very comfortable jungle lodge. Around £2500 for 16 days.

## USEFUL ADDRESSES IN IRELAND

### AIRLINES

**Aer Lingus** ☎01/886-8888

**British Airways**: Belfast ☎0854/773-3377, *britishairway.com*; Dublin ☎01-800/626-747

**British Midland**: Belfast ☎0870/6070-555 *flybmi.com*; Dublin ☎01/407-4036

**Iberia** ☎01/407-3017

**KLM** Belfast ☎0990/750-900

**Ryanair** ☎01/609-7800, *ryanair.com*

### FLIGHT AND TOUR AGENTS

**Maxwell's Travel**, D'Olier Chambers, 1 Hawkins St, Dublin 2 (☎01/677-9479, fax 679-3948). Very experienced in travel to Latin America and Ireland's representatives for many of the specialist tour operators in the UK.

**Trailfinders**, 4–5 Dawson St, Dublin 2 (☎01/677-7888, *trailfinders.co.uk*). Irish branch of the air fare and independent travel experts. Very good flight and holiday deals.

**USIT Now**, 19–21 Aston Quay, O'Connell Bridge, Dublin 2 (☎01/602-1700); Fountain Centre, College St, Belfast BT1 6ET (☎028/9032-4073; *usitnow.ie*). All-Ireland student travel agents, with seventeen offices, mainly on campuses. Very useful website.

## BY CARGO SHIP FROM UK AND IRELAND

The days of working as a deck hand for your passage around the world may be over but you can still take the banana boat to Belize and Honduras – though you won't be doing it to save money. A voyage on the MV Auckland Star from Waterford, Southampton, and Flushing to Big Creek, near Placencia, in Belize costs £1000 one way (£1850 return). After Belize the boat calls at Puerto Cortés, Honduras. Passengers (maximum six) stay in comfortable, a/c cabins on the upper deck, and meals are taken with the ship's officers. If you find the idea interesting contact Cargo Ship Voyages, Hemley, Woodbridge, Suffolk IP12 4QF (☎01473/736265, cargovoyager@cargoshipvoyages.com).

## GETTING THERE FROM IRELAND

No airline offers direct **flights from Ireland** to the Maya region and you may find the best value deals involve a connecting flight to London. You can also take a direct flight to the US or Europe and connect easily with flights to Mexico and Central America. Delta has the widest range of direct flights from Dublin (and several from Shannon) to JFK and Atlanta, with daily connections to Mexico City and Guatemala. Aer Lingus from Dublin (and some from Shannon) has same-day connections to Mexico City and Cancún, for example, via New York (JFK).

**Fares** from Belfast to Guatemala (via London and the US) start from IR£545 low season going up to £700 high season; from Dublin to Guatemala City you can expect to pay around IR£525 low season to IR£644 high season, both on American (via Miami). Discount fares from Belfast to Cancún range from £440 to £595 return, with BA, Continental and Iberia often coming out best. Iberia (via Madrid), Lufthansa (via Frankfurt) and United (via Chicago) often have good deals on flights from Dublin to Mexico City and Cancún from IR£366 low season to IR£560 (plus around IR£33–49 tax, depending on route).

# GETTING THERE FROM AUSTRALIA & NEW ZEALAND

There are no direct flights from Australasia to Cancún, Belize, Guatemala, Honduras or El Salvador, so consequently you've little choice but to fly via the US or Mexico City. For most airlines, low season is from mid-January to the end of February and October to the end of November; high season mid-May to the end of August and December to mid-January. Seat availability on international flights out of Australia and New Zealand is often limited, so it's best to book several weeks ahead.

## FLIGHTS AND FARES

Tickets purchased direct from the airlines are usually at fairly expensive published rates; **specialist flight agents** (see box on p.13) offer much better deals on fares and have the latest information on limited special offers. Flight Centre, STA and Trailfinders generally offer the lowest fares; in New Zealand also try Usit Beyond. You might also want to have a look on the **internet**: *travel.com.au* and *travelforless.co.nz* offer discounted fares.

Few **round-the-world tickets** include Central America, however it is possible to visit as a side trip (sometimes at extra cost) with the more flexible mileage-based tickets, such as the "Star Alliance 1" offered by Ansett Australia/Air New Zealand/United/Thai, starting at A$2499/NZ$3289, and "One World Explorer" by Qantas/British Airways/American Airlines/Cathay, which starts at A$2599/NZ$3799, both of which allow side trips, backtracking and open-jaw travel. If you intend to see something of Mexico or other Central American countries you may want to check out the various airpasses on offer that are available with your main ticket (see p.6 for details); most of the discount agents listed on p.13 can help you choose the most suitable one.

## AUSTRALIAN AIRLINES

**Air New Zealand** (Australia ☎13 2476, New Zealand ☎0800 737 000 or 09/357 3000, *airnz.com*). Daily to LA from Sydney, Brisbane, Melbourne, Adelaide and Auckland, either direct or via Honolulu/Tonga/Fiji/Papeete.

**Continental Airlines** (Australia ☎02/9321 9242, New Zealand ☎09/308 3350, *continental.com*). Teams up with Qantas and Air New Zealand to offer a through-service to Mexico and Central America via LA and Houston.

**Grupo Taca** (Australia ☎02/9221 8200, *grupotaca.com*). No NZ office. Alliance of main Central American airlines, with a useful airpass connecting cities in USA, Mexico and Central America.

**JAL** (Australia ☎02/9272 1111, New Zealand ☎09/379 9906, *japanair.com*). Several flights a week to LA and Mexico City from Sydney,

Brisbane, Cairns and Auckland with an overnight stopover in Tokyo included in the fare.

**Korean Airlines** (Australia ☎02/9262 6000, New Zealand ☎09/307 3687, *koreanair.com*). Several flights a week from Sydney, Brisbane and Auckland to LA with an overnight in Seoul included in the fare.

**Qantas** (Australia ☎1313 13, New Zealand ☎09/357 8900 or 0800/808 767, *qantas.com.au*). Daily to LA from major Australian cities, either non-stop or via Honolulu, and daily from Auckland via Sydney.

**United Airlines** (Australia ☎13 1777, New Zealand ☎09/379 3800, *ual.com*). Daily to LA and San Francisco from Sydney, Melbourne and Auckland either direct or via Honolulu.

## AUSTRALASIAN DISCOUNT FLIGHT SPECIALISTS

**Flight Centre**, Australia: 82 Elizabeth St, Sydney, and branches throughout Australia (for nearest branch ☎133 133, bookings ☎1300/733, *flightcentre.com.au*); New Zealand: 205 Queen St, Auckland, and other branches (☎09/358 4310).

**STA Travel**, Australia: 702 Harris St, Ultimo, Sydney, plus other offices in state capitals and major universities throughout Australia ☎1300/360 960, *statravel.com.au*); New Zealand: 267 Queen St, Auckland (☎0800/ 874 773) and other offices elsewhere.

**Student Uni Travel**, 92 Pitt St, Sydney (☎02/9232 8444, *sut.com.au*), plus branches in Brisbane, Cairns, Darwin, Melbourne and Perth. Student/youth discounts and travel advice.

**Thomas Cook**, Australia: 175 Pitt St, Sydney, plus branches in other state capitals (☎13 1771 or ☎1800/801 002, *thomascook.com.au*); New Zealand: 96 Anzac Ave, Auckland (☎09/379 3920).

**Trailfinders**, 8 Spring St, Sydney (☎02/9247 7666, *trailfinders.com.au*), plus branches in Melbourne, Brisbane, Cairns and Perth. Agents for many adventure travel specialists to Mexico and Central America.

**Travel.com**, 76–80 Clarence St, Sydney (☎02/9249 5232 or 1300/130 482, *travel.com.au*). Excellent fare-finder on website and superb links to tours and voluntary work contacts in the Maya region.

**Usit Beyond**, Jean Batten Place, 18 Shortland St, Auckland (☎09/379 4224 or 0800/874 823, *usit-beyond.co.nz*).

From Australia (Sydney), the cheapest fares to LA are direct on United Airlines, Qantas and Air New Zealand at A$1179 low season to A$2499 high season. Via Asia, fares are higher but include an overnight stop in the carrier's home city, with the best deals on All Nippon Airways (ANA) via Osaka, and Korean Airlines via Seoul, for A$1429/1899. The best-value flights to Mexico City are with JAL (via an overnight in Tokyo) for A$1629/1979, however, if you're after a more

## SPECIALIST TRAVEL AND TOUR AGENTS IN AUSTRALIA AND NEW ZEALAND

If you prefer to have all the arrangements made for you before you leave, then the specialist travel agents below can help you plan your trip. Most can do anything from booking a few nights' accommodation to arranging fully escorted archeological–cultural tours. Some of the "adventure" specialists can also help organize activities such as diving, rafting and jungle treks. Note that few of the tour prices include air fares, but the same agents can usually assist with flight arrangements. Many of the US and UK specialist agents (on pp.5 & 10) will accept bookings from Australasia and some below are agents for those companies.

**Adventure Associates**, 197 Oxford St, Bondi Junction (☎02/9389-7466 or 1800/222-141, *adventureassociates.com*). Escorted tours and tailor-made archeological and cultural expeditions to the Maya area from a top company.

**Adventure Specialists**, 69 Liverpool St, Sydney 2000 (☎02/9261-2927 or 1800/634-465). Variety of adventure-travel options to Central America, specializing in Guatemala and Belize.

**The Adventure Travel Company**, 164 Parnell Rd, Parnell, Auckland (☎09/379-9755, *advakl@hot.co.nz*). Agents for many of the UK and US adventure travel specialists organizing tours to Mexico and Central America.

**Adventure World**, Australia: 73 Walker St, North Sydney (☎02/956-7766 or 1800/221-931), plus branches in Melbourne, Brisbane, Adelaide and Perth; New Zealand: 101 Great South Rd, Remuera, Auckland (☎09/524-5118). Variety of tours, including trips to Tikal and Chichicastenango from Guatemala City and reef-river cruises in Belize.

**Contours**, 6th Floor, 310 King St, Melbourne 3000 (☎03/9670-6900 or 1300/135-391, *contourstravel .com.au*). Specialists in cultural and archeological tours to Mexico and Central America ranging from short stays to a 27-day expedition including Mexico, Guatemala, Belize and Honduras.

**Geckos**, Peregrine Travel Centre, 5th Floor, 38 York Street, Sydney (☎02/9290-2770, *geckos.com.au*), plus offices in Brisbane, Melbourne, Adelaide and Perth. Extended overland adventures from southern Mexico through Central America; agents for Exodus in UK.

direct route Air New Zealand can get you there for A$2429/2959, while Qantas' and United Airlines' fares are more expensive at A$2669/3199. Fares from all eastern Australian state capitals are generally the same (with Ansett and Qantas providing a free connecting service between these cities, whereas fares from Perth and Darwin are about A$200 more.

The best deals to Cancún are currently on JAL, via Tokyo and Mexico City, continuing on Aeroméxico, for A$2170/2499. Prices to Guatemala City (via Los Angeles on Air New Zealand continuing on Taca or Mexicana) are from A$2299/NZ$2599 low season to A$2899/NZ$3199 high season, while United have similar prices. Also for roughly the same price, both Qantas and Air New Zealand team up with Continental to provide a through-service via LA and Houston to all the Central American cap-

itals. American Airlines' fares via LA are higher at A$2699/NZ$2899–A$3059/NZ$3299, but still competitive.

From New Zealand (Auckland) one of the cheapest fares to LA is NZ$1729 on Air Tahiti Nui. Qantas Air Pacific flights (either direct or via Pacific island stopovers) are around NZ$1799/$1889 and United fares are around NZ$1825/$1885. Most fares to Mexico City include a stopover in LA. Air Tahiti Nui/Delta Airlines have a fare of NZ$2215 for May to November departures with stopover options on Tahiti and LA; United and American fares are around NZ$2524/$2655. If you want to fly right into a Maya World hub there are some good fares to Guatemala City, though you'll have at least one stopover and another change of flight in the US. Air Tahiti Nui/Continental fares begin at NZ$2440, with United and American working out slightly higher.

# VISA AND ENTRY REQUIREMENTS

Information on the entry requirements for tourist visitors to the five countries covered in this book, while correct at the time of going to press, is liable to change. For citizens of most Western countries and Japan, visas are generally not necessary in any of the countries in the region with the exception of El Salvador – and even then you can obtain one on arrival. If you're a national of any other country (usually including South Africa) it's crucial to contact a consulate

before travelling to check what's required of you. If you intend to work, including voluntary work, or study at an official institution (not a Spanish language school) you'll need to apply to the appropriate consulate well in advance for the relevant visa.

Officially you won't be allowed into any of the countries of the Maya World if you cannot show a **return ticket** and "sufficient funds" (usually estimated to be around US$50 per day), though this is virtually never enforced at land borders and only rarely if you arrive by air. Since you can cross all the borders by land (and thus leave by bus) a ticket back to your home country from anywhere in the region or from the USA and a credit card will usually be sufficient evidence.

The length of time visitors are permitted to stay in the various countries varies considerably – Mexico often grants 90 or 180 days permission (unless you enter the country in Chiapas; see p.139), Guatemala gives 90 days, whereas Belize, Honduras and El Salvador usually give out thirty-day stamps, though these can be extended. Once you get your stamp (and visa/tourist card if required), you should keep your **passport** with you at all times, or at the very least carry a photocopy, as you may be asked to show it.

If travelling overland through **Mexico**, those who need visas for the Central American countries won't necessarily need to get them too far in advance as there are consulates for every country in the capital; there's also a Guatemalan consulate in Comitán, Guatemalan and El Salvadorean consulates in Tapachula, and a Belize consulate in Chetumal. Belize, Guatemala, Honduras and El Salvador all have consulates in each others' capitals (or in Belize City) and sometimes in other towns; these are listed in the text where appropriate.

## MEXICO

Citizens of the US, Canada, Western Europe (including the EU), Australia, New Zealand and Japan don't need a visa to enter Mexico as tourists for up to 180 days. South Africans and citizens of most non-Western countries will need to **apply for a visa**. Anyone under eighteen travelling without parents will generally need their written consent – check with the embassy for the latest on whether a letter from one or both parents is needed. To see a list of all Mexican embassies and consulates check on *precisa.gob.mx* (in Spanish only) and search for *embajadas*.

**US citizens** don't even need a passport to enter Mexico – any official photo ID will do – though immigration will be much quicker and easier if you do have one and you will need one to travel onwards to any of the Central American countries. Every other visitor will need a **valid passport** (and visa if necessary) and a **tourist card** (or FMT — *folleto de migración turística*). The card (actually a paper form) is free at the point of issue but you'll have to pay an **immigration fee** (currently US$18) at one of the many banks named on the form before you leave. Don't leave this too late as there are no banks at the Mexican border posts where you enter Guatemala or Belize – officials *will* turn you back if you've not paid. If you're **flying in** you should be given a tourist card on the plane, or on arrival at the airport (and the immigration fee will probably be included when you buy your ticket). **Travelling overland** into Mexico, you'll be given one at the border crossing. Alternatively, you can apply to any Mexican consulate in advance. Guard your tourist card well – you are legally required to carry it at all times and it must be handed in when you leave the country. Should you lose it you'll need to go through a difficult interview at an immigration office in Mexico to get a replacement.

A tourist card is valid for a single entry only and it's a good idea to apply for a longer length of time than you think you might need as you'll have to pay the immigration fee again and getting an extension is a time-consuming business. **Entering Mexico in Chiapas** – only possible from Guatemala – you'll almost certainly only receive a fifteen-day permit to stay and cards and extensions are difficult to obtain in the state. If you need an extension it may well be worth crossing into a neighbouring state (Campeche, Tabasco, Yucatán or Oaxaca) and applying, or crossing the Guatemalan border and getting a new tourist card on re-entry.

## BELIZE

Citizens of the US, Canada, the EU, Australia and New Zealand do not need visas to enter Belize. **Swiss** citizens, however, do need one (US$25 and not officially obtainable at the border). There is no charge to enter the country and Belizean immigration personnel don't ask for the mysterious payments often demanded in other countries in the region. You'll generally be allowed a stay of **thirty days**, which can be renewed for US$12.50/Bz$25 each month, for a maximum of six months, after which you may have to leave the country for 24 hours. **Leaving Belize** you'll have to pay a US$10 **exit fee** and a US$3.75 **conservation fee**. The box below has details of a few Belizean embassies and consulates around the world; for the complete list visit *belize.gov.bz /diplomats.html*

## GUATEMALA

Citizens of the EU, the US, Canada, Japan, Switzerland, Norway, Mexico, Israel, Brazil, Australia and New Zealand need only a **valid passport** to enter Guatemala. Passport-holders from some countries (including the Czech Republic and South Africa) also need a **tourist card**, available at the point of entry and costing US$5; again valid for up to ninety days. Finally, citizens from a number of countries including most of Africa and Asia need **visas** (US$10), which must be obtained in advance and may take up to a month to process from a Guatemalan consulate. If you're in any doubt about whether you need a visa for Guatemala it's always worth phoning an embassy or consulate to check up on the latest entry requirements; there are embassies in all the regions' capitals.

## EMBASSIES AND CONSULATES

### IN THE US

**Belize** 2535 Massachusetts Ave NW, Washington DC 20009 (☎202/332-9636).

**El Salvador** (Consulate) 1724 20th St, Washington DC 20009 (☎202/331-4032, *elsalvador.org*); plus many other consulates throughout US

**Guatemala** 2220 R St NW, Washington DC 20008 (☎202/745-4952, *embaguat@sysnet.net*). There are also consulates in Chicago, Houston, LA, Miami, New York and San Diego.

**Honduras** 3007 Tilden St NW, Washington DC 20008 (☎202/966-7702, *embhondu@aol.com*), plus many consulates across the US.

**Mexico** 2827 16th St NW, Washington, DC 20036 (☎202/736-1000, *embassyofmexico.org*); and consulates in fifty other US towns and cities; check the website for your nearest office.

### IN CANADA

**Belize** (Honorary Consuls) Suite 3800, South Tower, Royal Bank Plaza, Toronto M5J 2JP (☎416/865-7000); in Quebec (☎514/871-4741); in Vancouver (☎604/730-1224).

**El Salvador** 209 Kent St, Ottawa ON K2P 1Z8 (☎ 613/238 2939); plus several consulates throughout Canada.

**Honduras** 151 Slater St, Suite 805A, Ottawa, ON K1P 5H3 (☎613/233 8900).

**Guatemala** 130 Albert St, Suite 1010, Ottawa ON K1P 5G4 ((☎613/2337188).

**Mexico** 45 O'Connor St, Suite 1500, Ottawa, ON K1P 1A4 (☎613/233 8988, *embamexcan.com*), plus consulates in Toronto, Montréal and Vancouver.

### IN THE UK

**Belize** 22 Harcourt House, 19 Cavendish Square, London W1M 9AD (☎020/7499 9728, *bzhclon@btconnect.com*).

**El Salvador** Mayfair House 3rd Floor, 39 Great Portland St, London W1N 7JZ (☎020/7436 8282, *embasalondres@netscapeonline.co.uk*).

**Guatemala** 13 Fawcett St, London SW10 9HN (☎020/7351 3042, fax 7376 5708, *embaguate_londres@compuserve.com*).

**Honduras** 115 Gloucester Place, London W1V 6JT (☎020/486 4880, *hondurasuk@lineone.net*).

**Mexico** 8 Halkin St, London SW1X 8QR (☎020/7235 6393, *mexicanconsulate.org*)

### IN SOUTH AFRICA

**Mexico** 3rd floor, 1 Hatfield Square, 1101 Burnett St, PO Box 9077, Pretoria 0001 (☎012/362-1437, *sre.gob.mx/sudafrica/*).

### IN SWITZERLAND

**Belize** (Honorary Consul General) 1 Rue Pedro-Meylan, 1211 Geneva 17, CP 106 (☎786-3883, fax 786-9939).

### IN AUSTRALIA AND NEW ZEALAND

**Belize** Australia: British High Commission, Commonwealth Ave, Yarralumla, Canberra (☎06/257-1982); New Zealand: British High Commission, 44 Hill St, Wellington (☎04/495-0889).

**El Salvador** No representatives.

**Guatemala** The nearest representative is in USA.

**Honduras** Australia: Honorary Consulate, Level 7, 19-31 Pitt St, Sydney, NSW 2000 (☎02/9350-8121). New Zealand: contact consulate in Australia.

**Mexico** Australia: 14 Perth Ave, Yarralumla, Canberra, ACT 2600 ☎02/6273-3963); 135 New South Head Rd, Edgecliff, Sydney, NSW 2027 (☎02/9326-1292, *embassyofmexicoinaustralia .org*). New Zealand: 111–115 Customhouse Quay, 8th floor, Wellington (☎04/472-5555).

When you arrive at immigration you may be asked by the official how long you plan to stay, and offered thirty, sixty or ninety days. If you want ninety days make sure you get it. There is no charge to enter Guatemala, though it's common for border officials at land crossings to ask for a fee (typically Q10 = US$1.25), which is destined straight for their back pockets – travellers often avoid payment of this by asking for *un recibo* (a receipt), but be prepared for a lengthy delay before being waved through.

If you want to **extend your visit** by up to ninety days, go to the immigration department (*migración*) in the INGUAT (tourist information) building at 7 Av 1-17, Zone 4 in Guatemala City, or simply cross a border and re-enter.

## HONDURAS

Citizens of the US, EU, Switzerland, Norway, Canada, Japan, Australia and the Central American countries (except Belize) with a valid passport get a thirty-day stamp on arrival, which can be extended to a maximum of ninety days at immigration offices throughout the country. South Africans, New Zealanders and citizens from most developing countries need a visa in advance from a Honduran embassy or consulate. These cost US$10–20 depending on where they are issued and can be extended within Honduras for up to ninety days.

When you enter Honduras there is officially no charge, but as in Guatemala, border officials usually demand a "fee" to enter the country, typically L20 (US$1.50).

A search on the Honduran government website *www.sre.hn* (in Spanish only) will reveal a list of Honduras embassies.

## EL SALVADOR

Citizens of the EU (except Greece and Portugal) and citizens of Switzerland, Norway, Israel and Japan do not need a visa or tourist card to enter El Salvador and are issued with a ninety-day stamp on arrival. Citizens of the US, Canada, Australia, New Zealand, Greece and Portugal can get a tourist card at the point of entry (US$10 and valid up to 90 days). If you need ninety days, make sure you ask for it. Citizens of all African countries, including South Africa, need a visa and will have to write to the embassy in Spain: Calle Serrano 114, Edificio Izquierda 28006, Madrid.

Mexicans and citizens from all other Central American countries (except Belize) do not need a visa or tourist card to enter El Salvador. Most nationalities that are not mentioned above need a visa in advance from an embassy or consulate, which can take a month to process. For a list of all El Salvadorean embassies and consulates check *www.rree.sv*

# INSURANCE

Wherever you go in Central America, medical insurance is essential. Make sure your policy includes provision for repatriation by air ambulance. Some specialist travel policies also offer cover for loss or theft of personal possessions and travel delay, though on most this is optional. Whether you take this part depends on how valuable your belongings are, but be warned that theft is rife in some areas and expensive-looking luggage attracts attention.

Before **buying a policy**, check to see if you're already covered for certain eventualities. **Credit and charge cards** often have certain levels of medical or other insurance included, especially if you use them to pay for your trip. This can be quite comprehensive, anticipating anything from lost or stolen baggage and missed connections to charter companies going bankrupt. That said, however, the medical cover offered is usually insufficient for Central American destinations (you want coverage of US$2,000,000), so check the small print carefully, as you should for any policy.

**Homeowners' or renters' insurance** often covers theft or loss of documents, money and valuables while overseas, and many **private medical schemes** also cover you when abroad – make sure you know the procedure and the helpline number. **Canadian provincial health plans** typically provide some overseas medical

## ROUGH GUIDES TRAVEL INSURANCE

**Rough Guides** offers its own travel insurance, customized for our readers by a leading UK broker and backed by a Lloyds underwriter. It's available for anyone, of any nationality, travelling anywhere in the world.

There are two main Rough Guide insurance plans: **Essential**, for basic, no-frills cover; and **Premier** – with more generous and extensive benefits. Alternatively, you can take out **annual multi-trip insurance**, which covers you for any number of trips throughout the year (with a maximum of 60 days for any one trip). Unlike many policies, the Rough Guides schemes are calculated by the day, so if you're travelling for 27 days rather

than a month, that's all you pay for. If you intend to be away for the whole year, the Adventurer policy will cover you for 365 days. Each plan can be supplemented with a "Hazardous Activities Premium" if you plan to indulge in sports considered dangerous, such as skiing, scuba-diving or trekking. Rough Guides also does good deals for older travellers, and will insure you up to any age, at prices comparable to SAGA's.

For a policy quote, call the Rough Guide Insurance Line on US freefone ☎1-866/220 5588 UK freefone ☎0800/015 09 06, or, if you're calling from elsewhere ☎ +44 1243/621 046. Alternatively, get an online quote at *roughguides.com/insurance*

coverage, although they are unlikely to pick up the full tab in the event of a mishap. Holders of official Canadian and US **student/teacher/youth cards** are also entitled to accident coverage and hospital in-patient benefits – the annual membership is far less than the cost of comparable insurance. Students may also find that their student health coverage extends during the vacations and for one term beyond the date of last enrolment.

Otherwise, comprehensive travel insurance is sold by almost every travel agent (many will offer insurance when you book your flight or holiday), but you'll almost certainly be better off arranging

your own from a specialist company – **Rough Guides' own travel insurance** offers highly competitive rates (see box).

Whichever policy you choose, if you plan to participate in **water-sports**, including scuba-diving and rafting, you'll probably have to pay an extra premium. Note also that very few insurers will arrange on-the-spot payments in the event of a major expense or loss; you will usually be reimbursed only after going home. In all cases of loss or theft of goods, you will have to contact the local police to have a report made out so that your insurer can process the claim.

# HEALTH

It's always easier to become ill in a country with a different climate, different food and different germs – still more so in a poor country with lower standards of sanitation than you might be used to. Most visitors, however, get home again without catching anything more serious than a dose of "traveller's diarrhoea". The most important precaution is to be aware of health risks posed by poor hygiene, untreated water, insect bites, undressed open cuts and unprotected sex.

Above all, it's vital to get the best **health advice** you can before you set off. Pay a visit to your doctor or a **travel clinic** (see p.20) as far in advance of travel as possible (at least eight weeks) and if you're pregnant or likely to become so mention this at the outset. Many clinics also sell the latest travel health products, including mosquito nets, water filters, medical kits and so on. In addition to the Websites mentioned in the box on p.20 there are a number of **books** advising on health precautions and disease prevention; the best and most up-to-date is *The Rough Guide to Travel Health*, a pocket-size volume packed with accurate information for all parts of the world. And, regardless of how well prepared you are medically, you will still want the security of **health insurance** (see "Insurance" on opposite).

## VACCINATIONS, INOCULATIONS AND MALARIA PRECAUTIONS

The only obligatory inoculation for the region is a **yellow fever** vaccination if you're arriving from a "high-risk" area – northern South America and equatorial Africa – in which case you need to carry your vaccination certificate. Up to date **polio**, **tetanus** and **typhoid** vaccinations are considered essential and it's also worth considering **diphtheria**, **hepatitis A** and **tuberculosis (TB)** vaccination. Long-term travellers or anyone spending time in rural areas should consider the combined **hepatitis A and B** and the **rabies** vaccines (though see p.22 for a caveat on that).

**Malaria** is a danger in some parts of the region (particularly in the rural lowlands). It's not a problem in the big cities, anywhere over 1500m and major coastal destinations, including Cozumel and Cancún. If you plan to visit any other lowland areas, particularly anywhere inland and including any Maya sites, a course of tablets is essential.

The recommended prophylactic is **chloroquine** (inexpensive, safe in pregnancy and no prescription needed); you'll need to begin taking

---

## WHAT ABOUT THE WATER

**Contaminated water** is a major cause of sickness in Mexico and Central America, and even if it looks clean, all tap water should be regarded with caution. In most big cities and resorts tap water will be filtered and treated, often using a heavy dose of chlorine. Purified bottled water (check the seal is intact) is widely available in shops, many restaurants use purified water (*agua purificada*) and hotels frequently provide bottles in your room; you'll only need to consider **treating your own water** if you travel to remote areas. Any good outdoor equipment shop will stock a range of water treatment products.

While **boiling water** for ten minutes kills most micro-organisms, it's not the most convenient method. **Water filters** remove visible impurities and larger pathogenic organisms (most bacteria and cysts). **Chemical sterilization** with either chlorine or iodine tablets (or a tincture of iodine liquid) is effective (except in preventing amoebic dysentery or giardiasis), but the resulting liquid doesn't taste very pleasant – though it can be masked with lemon or lime juice. Iodine is unsafe for pregnant women, babies and people with thyroid complaints. **Purification**, involving both filtration and sterilization, gives the most complete treatment, and travel clinics and good outdoor equipment shops will stock a wide range of portable water purifiers. In the UK the "Aqua Pure Traveller" is the best-value portable water filter and purifier, costing under £30 and capable of treating 350 litres of water; it's available from all the UK travel health specialists in the box on p.20, branches of Boots or from the manufacturer's website, *thirstpoint.com* The Swiss-made Katadyn filters are expensive but extremely useful.

## MEDICAL RESOURCES FOR TRAVELLERS

The International Association for Medical Assistance to Travellers (IAMAT, cybermall.co.nz/NZ/IAMAT/) is a non-profit organization open to all; there's no charge for membership, although a donation is requested to help support its work. Membership brings a number of benefits including climate charts, leaflets on various diseases and inoculations, and a list of English-speaking doctors in Central America; the website has excellent links.

The websites of the International Society for Travel Medicine (istm.org) and Travel Health Online (tripprep.com) each provide a comprehensive database of necessary vaccinations fo most countries and allow you to search for travel clinics throughout the world.

### IN NORTH AMERICA

**Canadian Society for International Health** (☎613/230-2654, *csih.org/*). Distributes a free pamphlet "Health Information for Canadian Travellers" containing an extensive list of travel health centres in Canada; very good website links.

**Centers for Disease Control** (☎1-800/311-3435, *cdc.gov/travel/camerica.htm*). Clear, comprehensive and frequently updated Web pages covering Mexico and Central America; check these before any others if you can. Current information on health risks and precautions.

**Health Canada** (*hc-sc.ca/*). An excellent website, in English and French: click on the "Information for Travellers" link. Lots of other useful links, and lists travel health clinics throughout Canada.

**International SOS Assistance** (☎1-800/523-8662, *internationalsos.com*). Members (US and Canadians only) receive pre-trip medical referral info, as well as overseas emergency services designed to complement travel insurance coverage.

**Travel Medicine** (☎1-800/872-8633, *travmed.com*). Sells water filters and all health-related travel products. Lists travel clinics in US and Canada, and you can check their current *Travel Health Guide* online.

### IN THE UK AND IRELAND

British travellers should pick up a copy of the free booklet *Health Advice for Travellers*, published by the Department of Health; it's available from GPs' surgeries, many chemists and most of the agencies listed here.

**British Airways Travel Clinics** 156 Regent St, London W1R (☎020/7439 9584) and Cheapside, EC2 (☎020/7606 2977) and at the BA terminal at Victoria Station (☎020/7233 6661). Excellent medical advice, vaccinations and a comprehensive range of travel health items. No appointments necessary at Regent Street; call ahead at other clinics.

**Hospital for Tropical Diseases Travel Clinic**, Mortimer Market Centre, Capper St, London WC1

---

the pills a week before you enter an area where there's a risk of malaria and continue for four weeks after you return. An alternative (especially if you're only going for a short time) is **malarone**, which you need start only 2 days before you go and continue for a week after you return. Although it's a very effective drug, there are some drawbacks – it's much more expensive than chloroquine, it's available on prescription only, you can only take it for up to 28 days and it's not suitable for pregnant women or babies. Whichever antimalarial you choose, you should still take precautions to **avoid getting bitten** by insects: sleep in screened rooms or under nets, burn mosquito coils containing permethrin (available everywhere), cover up arms and legs, especially around dawn and dusk when the mosqui-

toes are most active, and use insect repellent containing 50 percent DEET on your skin and up to 100 percent on clothing.

Also prevalent in some parts (usually occurring in epidemic outbreaks), **dengue fever** is a viral infection transmitted by mosquitoes which are active during the day. There is no vaccine or specific treatment, so you need to pay great attention to avoiding bites.

**North Americans** can get inoculations at any immunization centre or at most local clinics, and will have to pay a fee. Many GPs in the **UK** have a travel surgery where you can get advice and certain vaccines on prescription, though they may not administer some of the less common immunizations. Note too that though some jabs (diphtheria, typhoid) are free, others will incur quite a

(☎020/7387 9300, *thehtd.org*). Healthline message service on ☎09061/337733 (50p/min) with hints on hygiene, illness prevention and appropriate immunizations (after the brief introduction, key in 68 for Central America; 46 for Mexico); there's also a less expensive fax-back health information service on ☎09061/991992. All travel vaccinations (usually by appointment only) and travel health products available; a visit to a tropical medicine consultant costs £15 – waived if you have vaccinations at HTD.

**MASTA (Medical Advisory Service for Travellers Abroad)** (☎01276/685040 for a list of over 20 MASTA clinics, *masta.org*); leave a message on the Travellers' Health Line (☎ 09068/224100; 60p/min) and you'll be sent information specific to your trip. The website has plenty of practical advice on staying healthy abroad, plus information on diseases you might encounter. Runs clinics in several branches of Boots.

**Nomad Traveller's Store and Medical Centres**, 40 Bernard St, London WC1N (☎020/7833 4114, *nomadtravel.co.uk*; in STA branch); 3–4 Wellington Terrace, London N8 (☎020/8889 7014); 4 Potters Rd, New Barnet, Herts EN5 (☎020/8441 7208); 43 Queens Rd, Clifton, Bristol BS8 1QH (☎0117/922 6567). The Nomad Travel Health Line (☎09068/633 414; 60p per min) lets you speak to a health professional, or you can leave a message and someone will call you back free of charge. One of the best and most experienced travel equipment suppliers in the UK, with a mail and online ordering service. The clinics have some of the best prices for vaccinations, so it's best to call ahead for an appointment.

**Trailfinders Travel Clinic**, 194 Kensington High St, London W8 (☎020/7938 3999). Expert medical advice and a full range of vaccines and travel medical supplies; no appointments necessary and discounts for Trailfinders clients.

**Travel Medicine Services** PO Box 254, 16 College St, Belfast 1 (☎028/9031 5220). Operates a travel clinic (Mon 9–11am & Wed 2–4pm), which can give inoculations after referral from a GP; phone enquiries only answered during these times. too.

**Tropical Medical Bureau** Grafton Medical Centre, 34 Grafton St, Dublin 2 (☎01/671 9200, *tmb.ie*); Dun Laoghaire Medical Centre, 5 Northumberland Ave, Dun Laoghaire, Co. Dublin (☎01/280 4996). Specialist travel medicine clinics can give all immunizations; call for an appointment.

### IN AUSTRALIA AND NEW ZEALAND

**Travellers' Medical and Vaccination Centre (TMVC)** 7/428 George St, Sydney (☎02/9221 7133); 1/170 Queen St, Auckland (☎09/373 3531); plus branches in most other big cities across Australia and New Zealand. Their website, *tmvc.com.au*, has a list of TMVCs throughout Australia, New Zealand, South Africa and Southeast Asia, plus general information on travel health and services for health professionals.

---

hefty charge; it can be worth checking out a travel clinic where you can receive vaccinations almost immediately, often at lower cost. In **Australasia**, vaccination centres are always less expensive than doctors' surgeries.

### OTHER SIMPLE PRECAUTIONS

What you eat or drink while you're travelling is crucial: a poor diet lowers your resistance. Be sure to drink **clean water** (any bottled drinks, including beer and soft drinks, are already purified; for more on water purification see the box on p.19). You should avoid food that has been on display for a while and is not freshly cooked and also steer clear of salads and raw shellfish. In addition to the hazards mentioned under "Intestinal Troubles" below, contaminated food and water can also transmit the hepatitis A virus, which can lay a victim low for several months with exhaustion, fever and diarrhoea, and can even cause liver damage.

Two other common causes of illnesses are **altitude** and the **sun**. The best advice in both cases is to take it easy; allow yourself time to acclimatize before you race up a volcano, and build up exposure to the sun gradually. Use a strong sunscreen and, if you're walking during the day, wear a hat and try to keep in the shade. Avoid dehydration by drinking plenty of water or fruit juice. The most serious result of overheating is heatstroke, which can be potentially fatal. Lowering the body temperature (by taking a tepid shower, for example) is the first step in treatment. Finally, if you're taking **oral contraception** or any other orally administered drug, bear in mind that severe diarrhoea can reduce their efficacy.

## INTESTINAL TROUBLES

Despite all the dire warnings given here, a bout of **diarrhoea** is the medical problem you're most likely to encounter. No one, however cautious, seems to avoid it altogether. Its main cause is simply the change of diet: the food in the region contains a whole new set of bacteria, as well as perhaps rather more of them than you're used to. The best cure is the simplest one: take it easy for a day or two, drink lots of bottled water and eat only the blandest of foods – papaya is good for soothing the stomach and also crammed with vitamins. Only if the symptoms last more than four or five days do you need to worry.

**Cholera** is an acute bacterial infection, recognizable by watery diarrhoea and vomiting. However, risk of infection is considered low, particularly if you're following the health advice above, and symptoms are rapidly relieved by prompt medical attention and clean water. If you're spending any time in rural areas you also run the risk of picking up various **parasitic infections**: protozoa – amoeba and giardia – and intestinal worms. These sound (and can be) hideous, but they're easily treated once detected. If you suspect you may have an infestation, take a stool sample to a good **pathology lab** and go to a doctor or pharmacist with the test results (see "Getting Medical Help" on p.23). More serious is **amoebic dysentery**, which is endemic in many parts of the region. The symptoms are similar to a bad dose of diarrhoea but include bleeding too. On the whole, a course of flagyl (metronidazole or tinidozole) will cure it. If you plan to visit far-flung corners then it's worth getting hold of this before you go, and some advice from a doctor on its use.

## BITES AND STINGS

Taking steps to avoid getting bitten by **insects**, particularly mosquitoes, is always good practice. **Sandflies**, often present on beaches, are tiny, but their bites, usually on feet and ankles, itch like hell and last for days. **Ticks**, which you're likely to pick up if you're walking or riding in areas with domestic livestock (and sometimes in the forests generally), need careful removal with tweezers – those in a Swiss Army knife are ideal. Head or body **lice** can be picked up from people or bedding, and are best treated with medicated soap or shampoo; very occasionally,

they may spread typhus, characterized by fever, muscle aches, headaches and eventually a measles-like rash. If you think you have it, seek treatment from a doctor.

**Scorpions** are common; mostly nocturnal, they hide during the heat of the day – often in thatched roofs. If you're camping, or sleeping in a village cabaña, shake your shoes out before putting them on and try not to wander round barefoot. Their sting is painful (rarely fatal) and can become infected, so you should seek medical treatment if the pain seems significantly worse than a bee sting. You're less likely to be bitten by a **spider**, but the advice is the same as for scorpions and insects: seek medical treatment if the pain persists or increases.

You're unlikely to see a **snake**, and most are harmless in any case. Wearing boots and long pants will go a long way towards preventing a bite – tread heavily and they will usually slither away. If you do get bitten, remember what the snake looked like (kill it if you can), immobilize the bitten limb as far as possible and seek medical help immediately: antivenins are available in most main hospitals.

Swimming and snorkelling might bring you into contact with potentially dangerous or venomous **sea creatures**. You're extremely unlikely to be a victim of a shark attack (though the dubious practice of shark-feeding as a tourist attraction is growing, and could lead to an accidental bite), but **jellyfish** are common and all corals will sting. Some jellyfish, like the Portuguese man-o'-war, with its distinctive purple, bag-like sail, have very long tentacles with stinging cells, and an encounter will result in raw, red weals. If you are stung, clean the wound with vinegar or iodine and seek medical help if the pain persists or infection develops. The spines of sting rays and scorpion fish are all extremely poisonous, so be careful where you put your feet.

Finally, **rabies** is present in the region. The best advice is to give dogs a wide berth and not to play with animals at all, no matter how cuddly they may look. Treat any bite as suspect: wash any wound immediately with soap or detergent and apply alcohol or iodine if possible. Act immediately to get treatment – rabies is fatal once symptoms appear. There is a **vaccine**, (effective for 2 yrs), recommended for anyone visiting for over 30 days or travelling to remote areas.

## GETTING MEDICAL HELP

For minor medical problems, head for a **farmacia** – look for the green cross. Pharmacists are knowledgeable and helpful, and many speak some English. They can also sell drugs over the counter (if necessary) which are only available on prescription at home. Every capital city has **doctors** and dentists, many trained in the US, who are experienced in treating visitors and speak good English. Your embassy will always have a list of recommended doctors, and we've included some in our "Listings" for the main towns. Health insurance (see p.17) is essential and for anything serious you should to go to the best **private hospi-** **tal** you can reach; again, these are located mainly in the capital cities. If you suspect something is amiss with your insides, it might be worth heading straight for the local **pathology lab** (all the main towns have them), before seeing a doctor, as the doctor will send you there anyway. Many rural communities have a **health centre** (*centro de salud* or *puesto de salud*), where health care is free, although there may only be a nurse or health-worker available and you can't rely on finding anyone who speaks English. Should you need an injection or transfusion, make sure that the equipment is **sterile** (it might be worth bringing a sterile kit from home) and ensure any blood you receive is screened.

## COSTS AND MONEY

By European or North American standards, the cost of living in the Maya World is low, and, with most currencies gradually dropping in value against the dollar and pound sterling, it's possible to live quite cheaply here. Belize is the most expensive country, while other areas are all roughly comparable. Of course in some regions (coastal areas of the Yucatán, Guanaja and Roatán especially), where the local economy is tourism-driven, things can be much more expensive.

The **US dollar** is by far the most widely accepted foreign currency. In both El Salvador and Guatemala it ranks as an official currency and is accepted as legal tender, while in Mexico, Belize and Honduras you also can pay for most things in dollars. **Credit cards** are very useful for withdrawing currency from bank ATMs, but don't count on paying with them except in upmarket hotels and restaurants.

It's always a good idea to have some **travellers' cheques**, which you can cash in most towns, and some US dollar bills wherever you are, in case you run short of local currency a long way from the nearest bank. All the international airports have banks for **currency exchange**, while at all the main land border crossings there are usually banks and a swarm of moneychangers who generally give fair rates for cash and sometimes travellers' cheques. Even at the most remote border crossings,

> ### EXCHANGE RATES
> Though the following **exchange rates** were correct at time of going to press, inflation and devaluation in some countries will mean that they may change somewhat over the course of this edition of the guide.
> **Belize** (Belizean dollar) Bz$2=US$1
> **El Salvador** (colón) 8.75c=US$1
> **Guatemala** (quetzal) Q7.80=US$1
> **Honduras** (lempira) L16=US$1
> **Mexico** (peso) $9=US$1

you'll usually find a wad-wielding local or two from whom you can get some local currency.

All the local currencies (with the exceptions of Belize, which has fixed exchange rates of Bz$2 to US$1, and El Salvador, where the Salvadorean colón is fixed at 8.75 against US$1) float against the US dollar. Prices throughout the guide are quoted in US dollars.

## CREDIT CARDS, TRAVELLERS' CHEQUES AND WIRING MONEY

**Credit cards** are becoming increasingly widely accepted in the region, though you shouldn't expect to be able to use them as you would in North America or Europe. They are usually accept-

**VISA TRAVEL MONEY:** *www.visa.com*

This is a disposable debit card pre-paid with dedicated travel funds which you can access from over 457,000 visa ATMs in 120 countries with a PIN that you select yourself. When your funds are depleted, you simply throw the card away. Since you can buy up to nine cards to access the same funds – useful for couples/families travelling together – it's recommended that you buy at least one extra as a back up in case your first is lost or stolen. There is a 24-hour Visa global customer assistance services centre which you can call from any of the 120 countries toll-free. In the UK, many Thomas Cook outlets sell the card.

ed in upmarket shops, hotels and restaurants, but you won't be able to pay for your comedor meal or pensión bill with plastic.

Visa is the most useful brand, followed by Mastercard. You can use your card to get cash over the counter at banks and from ATMs, everywhere (though only from Barclays in Belize, and *only* at ATMs in Mexico). Although most ATMs are in service 24 hours, it's wiser to use them when the bank is open: firstly you can see a bank employee if something goes wrong and the machine keeps your card (though this is very rare), and secondly you benefit from the security of daylight. Using your **debit card** means you don't have to buy and countersign travellers' cheques and, though you pay a handling charge each time you use it, the amount may be less than the commission on cheques and you may benefit from a better exchange rate. Note that Plus and Visa debit cards (see box) are much more widely accepted than the Cirrus brand.

**Travellers' cheques** are a safe way to bring money, as they offer the security of a refund if they're stolen. To facilitate this you want to make sure that you have cheques issued by one of the big names (such as American Express, Visa, Thomas Cook or Citibank), which are more readily accepted. You should also always carry your proof of purchase when trying to change travellers' cheques, as some places will refuse to deal with you otherwise.

Having money **wired from home** is never convenient or cheap, and should be considered a last resort. Funds can be sent via **Western Union** or **American Express MoneyGram**. Both companies' fees depend on the destination and the amount being transferred. The funds should be available for collection at the local branch within minutes of being sent.

It's also possible – for a fee – to have money wired directly from a bank in your home country to a bank in Central America, although this is somewhat less reliable as it involves two separate institutions, and can take from a couple of days to several weeks. If you use this route, the person wiring the funds to you will need to know the routing number of the bank the funds are being wired to.

## COSTS

In most circumstances, the cost of living in the region is much **cheaper** than in North America and Europe (though in Belize and the coastal areas of Quintana Roo, prices are not that different from the US). As a general rule, locally produced goods are cheap and anything imported is overpriced.

What you spend will obviously depend on where, when and how you choose to travel. **Peak tourist seasons**, such as Christmas and Easter, tend to push up hotel prices, and certain tourist centres are notably more expensive at these times. **Public transport**, geared to locals, is invariably a bargain – though bear in mind that in some places (such as Lago de Atitlán in Guatemala) there's a quasi-institutionalized two-tier price system. Travelling by car is expensive, and the cost of renting a car is higher in the Maya region than it is in the US or Canada, as is the cost of fuel – although this is still cheaper than in Europe.

It may be worth carrying a **student card** if you have one, as it sometimes opens the way for a reduction, but it won't save you a great deal and, unless you need one to clinch a deal on air fares, it's not worth buying one for the trip.

**Guatemala** and **Honduras** are two of the cheapest countries to visit, with some very inexpensive budget hotel rooms, though the mid-range accommodation is sometimes only fair value for money. Restaurant meals are inexpensive, but the transport system, though cheap, is crowded, slow and rudimentary. In **El Salvador** food, drink and transport are as cheap as Guatemala and Honduras, though accommodation can run more expensive. Away from the coast, **Mexico** represents very good value for money, especially in Chiapas – you'll find an excellent range of hotels in most areas, at all price levels, superb food and a comfortable, reliable transport system.

The careful **budget traveller** can reckon on getting by on a minimum of **US$15 a day in Mexico, Guatemala, Honduras** or **El Salvador**. Accommodation is typically US$3–5 a night (based on sharing a double room), with food costing perhaps US$5 a day, and another US$5 accounted for by travel costs, entry charges to the sites and museums. Add on a dollar for every beer.

Moving into the **mid-range market**, a couple travelling together sharing hotel rooms and meals might expect to spend US$75 a day. This is based on two people sharing a comfortable double hotel room (usually with air-conditioning, cable TV and private bathroom) costing US$12–25 each a night, eating three good meals a day including some wine or a couple of beers each, costing around US$15–20 each a day, and including first-class bus travel and entry charges, which might add another US$7–10 a day each. Single travellers should reckon on perhaps US$45–50 a day for the same standards.

At the **luxury** end of the market it's possible to really blow out by taking specialized tour excursions, internal flights, scuba-diving and renting a car, but you'll still get excellent value for money compared to the US and Europe.

**Belize** is the most expensive country in the region with prices about forty percent higher than in any other country. The budget hotel that costs US$12 a night in Belize is probably half that price in Guatemala or Mexico. The budget traveller should reckon on a minimum of US$25 a day in Belize, while a couple requiring a little more comfort and some tours should expect to pay more like US$100 a day between them. Travel by public bus is a relative bargain in Belize, probably just a shade more expensive than in the other countries.

# INFORMATION AND MAPS

Information about the Maya World is available from a number of sources, though much of the promotional puff provided by the official tourist offices is pretty to look at, but of little practical use. However, the quality of such information is improving, and if you have specific questions you could try contacting some of the official organizations listed here.

When digging out information on the Maya region, don't forget the **specialist travel agents** (see pp.4–6, 9–10 & 13) and the **embassies** (see p.16). Best of all for practical details are the **internet sites** in the box below.

**TOURIST OFFICE WEBSITES**
See also the list of useful internet sites on pp.27–28.
**Belize** *travelbelize.org*
**El Salvador** *elsalvadorturismo.gob.sv*
**Guatemala** *guatemala.travel.com.gt*
**Honduras** *hondurasinfo.hn*
**Mexico** *mexico-travel.com, wotw.com/mundo-maya*

Current political analysis and an interesting and informative overview of the society, economy and environment of each country is provided by two **specialist publishers**: the Resource Center in the US *(lrc-online.org)*, who produce the *Inside* series covering each country, and the Latin America Bureau *(lab.org.uk)* in the UK, an independent, non-profit research organization, whose *In Focus* series so far covers Belize, Guatemala and Mexico as well as much of South America. Though detailed, the books are not large, around 100–200 pages, and if you're going to spend any length of time in the region it's well worth having a look at these before you go.

The **Latin American Travel Advisor** is a quarterly newsletter with a comprehensive report

## TOURIST INFORMATION

### IN AUSTRALIA AND NEW ZEALAND

It's difficult to find official tourist information about the Maya region in Australia or New Zealand; your best bet is to contact the websites, Bushbooks (see box below), the consulate (listed on p.16) or specialist travel agents (p.13).

### IN NORTH AMERICA

Mexico has numerous tourist offices scattered around North America; the other countries less so. The information lines listed below will be able to send you tourist information or direct you to your nearest office.

**Belize** US ☎212/563-6011 or 1-800/624-0686

**El Salvador** US ☎212/889-3608; Canada: ☎613/238-2939

**Guatemala** US ☎1-800-INGUAT-1; Canada ☎613/233-2339

**Honduras** US ☎1-800/410-9608

**Mexico** US & Canada ☎1-800/44-MEXICO

### IN THE UK

The Mexico and Guatemala offices and the consular representatives of the other countries (addresses are listed on p.16) will send you information on their respective countries if you send an SAE; give them a call first to check what they have and how much postage you'll need to stick on the envelope.

**Guatemala** ☎020/7349 0346, *embaguate_londres@compuserve.com*

**Mexico** ☎020/7488 9392, *info@mexico-travel.co.uk*

**Belize** ☎020/7499 9728, *bzhc-lon@btconnect.com*

**El Salvador** ☎020/7436 8282, *embasalondres@netscapeonline.co.uk*

**Honduras** ☎020/7486 4880, *hondurasuk@lineone.net*

on each country in the region, covering safety, health, politics and the economy, along with a special feature on a relevant topic. One issue costs US$15, or you can pay US$39 for a year's subscription. Send a cheque or moneyorder to Latin American Travel Consultants, PO Box 17-17-908, Quito, Ecuador (fax 593/2-562-566). Headlines and excerpts are published on their website: *amerispan.com/latc/*

While you're in the region you'll find **government tourism offices** in each capital city, in state capitals in Mexico, in the international airports and in the main tourist centres. The information they're able to give is variable, but they can usually provide at the very least a city map, a bus timetable and perhaps a list of hotels (and they may even call them for you). SECTUR (the Mexican tourism department) are probably the best organized, but again the information they dispense varies from office to office. Addresses and phone numbers (and an idea of how useful a particular office will be) are given throughout the guide. In addition, there are some locally run initiatives, often set up by an association of tourism businesses. Many of the tour or travel agents mentioned in the guide should also be reliable sources of information.

### UK RESOURCES

In London you can visit **Canning House Library**, 2 Belgrave Square, SW1X 8PJ (☎020/7235 2303, *canninghouse.com*), which has the UK's largest publicly accessible collection of books and periodicals on Latin America. It's free to use, though you have to be a member to take books out and receive the twice-yearly *Bulletin*, a review of recently published books on Latin America. An excellent resource centre also in London is **Maya – The Guatemalan Indian Centre**, 94A Wandsworth Bridge Rd, London SW6 2TF (☎ & fax 020/7371 5291; closed Jan,

### RESOURCE CENTRE OUTLETS

**UK** Latin America Bureau ☎020/7278 2829, *lab@gn.apc.org, lab.org.uk*

**IRELAND** Trocaire Resource Centre ☎01/874-3875, *trocaire.org*

**USA** The Resource Center, PO Box 2178, Silver City, NM 88062-2178 ☎505/388-0208

**CANADA** Fernwood Books ☎902/422-3302, *fernwoodbooks.ca, fernwood@istar.ca*

**AUSTRALIA** Bushbooks ☎02/4323-3274

## USEFUL WEBSITES

### BELIZE

**belizeaudubon.org** Well respected conservation organization, Belize Audubon Society (BAS), which manages numerous nature reserves, national parks and associated visitor centres and publishes a range of books and guides. Great wildlife pictures.

**belize.gov.bz** Belize government's official news reports and press releases.

**belizeit.com** Good all round site with strong art and music material.

**belizenet.com** Useful site for up-to-date news, business and weather reports. Good maps and photos.

**belizenet.de** German Tour agency, International Belize Travel Marketing's site with plenty of good content and links for German speakers.

**spearbelize.org.bz** Site belonging to the Society for the Promotion of Education and Research (SPEAR), with reliable coverage of social, cultural, political and economic affairs concerning Belize.

**turq.com/belizefirst** Free online magazine, *Belize First*, with accurate hotels, restaurants and destination reviews.

**unbelizeable.com** Informative hotel and restaurant reviews, and the latest archeological fieldwork.

### EL SALVADOR

**elsalvador.com** Spanish-language website attached to the daily newspaper *El Diario de Hoy*.

**elsalvador-magazine.com** Spanish-language tourist information site with useful destination features and information and a good selection of photos.

**elsalvadorturismo.gob.sv** Official government site run by tourist agency Corsatur with information in both English and Spanish.

**laprensa.com.sv** Spanish-language site for the daily newspaper *La Prensa Gráfica*.

**salvanatura.org** Interesting site run by a not-for-profit organization that manages some of El Salvador's national parks and forests, including Bosque El Imposible – site has news, photos and information.

**suchitototurismo.com** Spanish-language site providing tourist information and NGO program activity in and around Suchitoto, El Salvador's finest colonial town.

**www.sv** Multilingual site offering a broad range of information on El Salvador's economy, society, culture and tourism.

### GUATEMALA

**atitlan.com** Well-designed site with encyclopedic coverage of the Atitlán region, rich with cultural content and hotel and restaurant listings.

**ghrc-usa.org** Extensive monitoring of Guatemalan human rights issues, with bi-monthly updates and analysis.

**guatemalantravelmall.com** Comprehensive site with on-line hotel, restaurant, and Spanish school bookings and some interesting ecotourism tours.

**http://mars.cropsoil.uga.edu/tropag/guatem.htm** Despite the misleading domain name, the Guatemalan Web Page Directory is easily the most comprehensive Guatemala portal and the best place to start a search on virtually any topic concerning the country.

**interhuehue.com** Informative site with good links and listings of the Huehue area.

**maya.org.uk** London-based Maya–Guatemalan Indian Centre's useful site has news of forthcoming UK cultural events and good links.

**mayaparadise.com** Useful listings and information about the Río Dulce and Lago de Izabal area.

**revuemag.com** Tourism and travel issues, mainly dealing with Guatemala.

**rigobertamenchu.org** Nobel Peace Prize winner Rigoberta Menchú's site, concentrates on development and human rights matters.

**sigloxxi.com** Leading Guatemalan newspaper, Siglo XXI; Spanish-only website.

**stetson.edu/~rsitter/TodosSantos** Useful cultural content and practical coverage of Todos Santos region.

**theantiguajournal.com** Plenteous facts and links in this colonial city-specific site.

**xelapages.com** Excellent, well-structured site covering the Quetzaltenango area, with comprehensive language school and business listings, plus a decent message board.

### HONDURAS

**bayislands.com** Roatán articles and listings on the *Coconut Telegraph*'s website.

**copanruinas.com** News, reviews, hotels and restaurants in the Copán region.

*continued overleaf*

**divehonduras.com** Dive resorts and sites, plus scuba hotels and schools.

**honduras.com** Background country information plus tourism and travel news.

**honduras-resources.com** Portal with business, news information and links.

**hondurastips.honduras.com** Excellent travel and tourism information.

**honparks.html** National parks, reserves and ecotourism in Honduras.

**iloveutila.com** Some island news, but mainly deals with real estate and property.

**marrder.com/htw** *Honduras This Week*, best English language news source, with reliable national news reports plus interesting content from regions including Copán and the Bay Islands.

**marrder.com/hw/travel** Travel information, hotel and restaurant reviews, Spanish schools, good links.

**projecthonduras.com** US-based site with news and information, an excellent development work page, soccer and more.

**roatanet.com** Excellent, well-designed site with hotels, music, and a superb, very quirky news archive.

**tiempo.hn** National newspaper *El Tiempo*'s Spanish-only site: news, support and business.

**www.hn** Country directory with links to newspapers, ISPs and businesses.

**www2.planeta.com/mader/ecotravel/center /honduras/** National parks, reserves, ecotourism.

### MEXICO

**mexconnect.com** Large and well organized US-based online magazine with good current travel and business information, news, book reviews and much more.

**mexicanwave.com** Clear, easy to navigate pages from a UK-based online magazine ("Europe's Gateway to Mexico"), with travel, news, book and film reviews and listings of Mexican and Latin American events in UK.

**tourbymexico.com** Mexican site with geographical, historical and archeological information about each state of Mexico (and many cities), with good links to tourism-related sites.

Easter and August; *maya.org.uk*). Membership (£5 annually) gives you access to the library (reference only) and video collection, and you receive information of the monthly events and film shows held at the centre. There is a particularly fine textile collection here and the centre's director, Krystyna Deuss, is the acknowledged British authority on historic and contemporary Maya dress and ritual.

For general information on **independent travel**, pick up a copy of the excellent *Everything You Need to Know Before You Go* (Abroadsheet Publications, from specialist bookshops); author Mark Ashton has managed to compile an enormous amount of good, general advice into one amazingly well-organized (large) glossy sheet; if you're planning an expedition from the UK, you should avail yourself of the services of the **Expedition Advisory Centre** at the Royal Geographic Society, 1 Kensington Gore, London SW7 2AR (☎020/7581-2057, *rgs.org/eac*). As well as expedition planning seminars, the EAC also publishes a range of specialist books.

### THE INTERNET

The number of pages on the **internet** devoted to Mexico and Central America is growing daily. The first place to check out is the comprehensive and logically laid-out homepage of the **Latin American Information Center** (LANIC; *lanic.utexas.edu*), which has a seemingly never-ending series of superb links for each country. You can reach almost anywhere and anything in the region connected to the net from here. The best portal for **Central America** is undoubtedly *centramerica.com* while **Planeta** *(planeta.com)* is an excellent resource for ecotourism and independent travel in the region, run by the prolific author and journalist Ron Mader. It's also worth checking the Web page of the **Latin American Travel Advisor** (see p.25). Finally, the ever-helpful members of the **newsgroup** *rec.travel.latin-america* have a huge (and generally accurate) information base and will answer any query about travel in the region.

## MAPS

The best **maps** of the region are produced by International Travel Map Productions (736A Granville St, Vancouver, BC, V62 1G3, Canada). Their range includes individual maps of Southeast Mexico, the Yucatán, Guatemala and El Salvador, Honduras and Belize; there's also a small-scale Central America map. You should be able to find them in specialist map shops or from online bookshops such as Amazon (*amazon.com*), and they are sometimes available in Central American cities, though it's wise to try to get what you need before you go.

If you need a good **road atlas** of Mexico, the Nelles 1:2,500,000 is one of the clearest, though the International Travel Map 1:300,000 also shows relief and has many mileage and driving times. In Mexico, the best maps are those published by Patria, which cover each state individually, and by Guía Roji, who also publish a Mexican Road Atlas. Both makes of map are easy to locate – try branches of Sanborn's or large Pemex stations.

Detailed **hiking and climbing maps** are more difficult to come by. In **Mexico**, INEGI, the governmental cartographers, produce very good topographic maps on various scales; they have an office in every state capital. In **Guatemala** the large-scale maps (1:50,000) produced by the Instituto Geográfico Militar (see p.328) are out of date but are at least accurately contoured. Topographic maps produced by Ordnance Survey in the UK are available for **Belize**: two sheets at 1:250,000 cover the whole country, with 44 sheets at 1:50,000 scale providing greater detail, though many are out of date and not all are readily available. The available sheets are sold in the UK by Stanfords and in Belize at the Land Tax Office in Belmopan (see p.256). In **Honduras**, topographical maps are available in the capital Tegucigalpa from the Instituto Geográfico Nacional, 15 C & 1 Av, Comayagüela (☎225 0752, *http://ns.sdnhon.org.hn/~ihnhon*). In San Pedro Sula there are good detailed maps of all the national parks at Fundación Ecologista, 7 Av and 1 C. Topographic maps seem to be impossible to find in **El Salvador**, but you could try the tourist office.

---

### MAP OUTLETS

#### US
**Rand McNally**, 444 N Michigan Ave, Chicago, IL 60611 (☎312/321-1751); 150 E 52nd St, New York, NY 10022 (☎212/758-7488); 595 Market St, San Francisco, CA 94105 (☎415/777-3131); 1201 Connecticut Ave NW, Washington DC 20003 (☎202/223-6751); and around thirty stores across the US – call ☎1-800/333-0136 ext 2111 for the nearest store or consult their website *randmcnally.com*

#### CANADA
**ITMB**, 530 W Broadway, Vancouver, BC V5Y 1P8, Canada (☎604/879-3621, *itmb.com*).
**World Wide Books and Maps**, 1247 Granville St, Vancouver V6Z 1G3 (☎604/687-3320); 118 Holland Ave, Ottawa, Ontario K1Y 0X6 (☎613/724-6776; *worldofmaps.com*).

#### UK
**Stanfords**, 12–14 Long Acre, WC2E 9LP (☎020/7836 1321, *stanfords.co.uk*); maps by mail or phone order are available on this number and via *sales@stanfords.co.uk* Other branches within British Airways offices at 156 Regent St, W1R 5TA (☎020/7434 4744), and 29 Corn St, Bristol BS1 1HT (☎0117/929 9966).

#### AUSTRALIA AND NEW ZEALAND
**Mapland**, 372 Little Bourke St, Melbourne (☎03/9670 4383, *mapland.com.au*).
**Specialty Maps**, 46 Albert St, Auckland (☎09/307 2217, *ubd-online.co.nz/maps*).

# GETTING AROUND

**Most travellers in the region (and most locals) get around by public bus – with perhaps an occasional flight or boat trip. Because many people don't own cars, the public bus network is generally extremely comprehensive and very cheap. Except in Mexico, local buses tend to be extremely full. If you're travelling independently without your own vehicle you'll have to get used to spending a lot of time in (and waiting for) them.**

Each country has at least one domestic airline, and taking an occasional, inexpensive **flight** can save hours of road travel over difficult terrain. If you're heading for the Tikal ruins from Guatemala City, for example, the hour-long flight (from US$75) will save you an eight- to ten-hour bus journey. Air passes can also be very good value; see pp.6 & 31.

## BY BUS

Public **buses** are cheap, crowded, convenient and sometimes wildly entertaining. There is a huge network, with daily services connecting most towns with the regional and state capitals. Generally, second-class buses will stop anywhere (the concept of bus stops has yet to really catch on) regardless of how many people are already on board.

There are, loosely, two classes of bus, first (*primera*) and second (*segunda*). On a **first-class bus** (also sometimes called a pullman) you can book your seat in advance. Generally, first-class buses ply the main highways and usually stop in

terminals (not at the roadsides), leaving the minor roads to the second-class services. They vary tremendously from country to country, but the best of them, especially on international routes, are air-conditioned and complete with videos and reclining seats. In **Mexico**, buses are extremely comfortable, punctual and speedy, and seats are usually allocated by computer. Travel in Mexico on first-class buses works out around US$2.75 an hour. In **Guatemala** on the other hand, a first-class bus can be a very old Greyhound with cracked windows, ripped seats and bald tyres; travel normally works out around US$1 an hour, though there are also a limited number of better services. The Maya region of **Honduras** is served by an excellent network of buses, including an increasing number of very flash a/c luxury coaches: prices vary between US$1.50 and US$2.25 an hour depending on the comfort level. Buses **in Belize** are mostly old US school buses, though there are some bigger, more comfortable express buses, costing slightly more than the average US$2 per hour. In the north and west of the country hourly or half hourly services operate punctually along the main highways (connecting the main towns and the border posts) every hour; heading south they run every hour or two.

On **second-class buses** (known as *camionetas* in Chiapas and Guatemala) travel works out at around US$0.75 an hour in all the countries. The buses are invariably ramshackle, third-hand, recycled US school buses, easily recognized by their trademark clouds of thick black noxious fumes and rasping exhausts. They're often garishly painted and serve mainly to carry villagers, their shopping and their animals to and from market – the original and ubiquitous "chicken bus". Snack vendors tout for business, and merengue and Mexican ranchero assaults your eardrums from decrepit speakers. The general onboard "etiquette" is three to a bench seat (with no exceptions for gringos), the aisles crammed with another twenty or thirty standing sufferers, and the roof loaded with mountainous baskets of vegetables and fruit from the marketplace. Except in Belize, the driver always seems to be a moustachioed ladino with an eye for the ladies and his helper (*ayudante*) always overworked and underage. It's the *ayundante*'s job alone to scramble up to the roof to retrieve your rucksack, collect the fares and bellow out the destination to all and sundry.

In remote villages and places where buses cannot or do not reach, **pickup** trucks transport passengers. Unless it's raining, or the road is really atrocious, a bumpy pickup ride is often vastly preferable to a crowded bus as you get a chance to see the countryside and breathe fresh air. Expect to pay the driver the same rate as you would for a second-class bus fare – around US$0.75 an hour.

At **land borders**, some buses cross over to the adjacent country's terminal to drop off and pick up passengers. This simplifies transport and immigration, especially if the immigration posts and terminals are some distance apart. Heading further south in Central America, the best **international bus service** is the Ticabus (*ticabus.com*) running from Guatemala City to Panamá City, calling at San Salvador, Managua and San José. The whole journey takes two and a half days, including overnights (at your own expense) at San Salvador and Managua.

## BY PLANE

With the exception of the Yucatán peninsula, most of the areas covered in this book are very mountainous, and though distances between the major sites may not look too lengthy on a map, rudimentary roads and difficult terrain mean that the going can be slow. So if time is tight, or you just can't face another bus journey, it's worth considering a flight – prices are generally very reasonable. Each country has an internal air network, and there are also numerous international flights within the region.

Within **Guatemala** the only flight that is really worth considering is from Guatemala City to Flores (for Tikal). Four airlines fly this route and prices start from a bargain US$75 return. A domestic airline, Inter, operated by the Taca Group, offers numerous other destinations within Guatemala, but as distances are not that great (and cancellations are frequent) few people choose to fly with them. There are also daily international connections from Guatemala to Cancún, Belize City, San Salvador, San Pedro Sula, Mexico City and numerous flights south to Costa Rica (around US$150 return) and South America.

In **Belize** there are two scheduled domestic carriers and a number of charter airlines. The main routes are between Belize City and San Pedro (US$27 one way), Caye Caulker (US$27), Dangriga (US$33), Placencia (US$60) and Punta Gorda (US$78). Popular international destinations include Flores (for Tikal), Guatemala City, Chetumal and Cancún in Mexico, San Pedro Sula, La Ceiba and Roatán in Honduras and San Salvador.

---

## AIR PASSES

The best way to find out how (or if) an air pass will benefit you is to call JLA in the UK (☎020/8747-3018, *sales@journeylatinamerica.co.uk, journeylatinamerica.co.uk*); or contact eXito in the US (☎1-800/655-4053 or 510/655-2154; *exito@ wonderlink.com, wonderlink.com/exito*). In Australia try Trailfinders (☎02/9247 7666, *trailfinders.com.au*); in New Zealand call Usit Beyond (☎09/379 4224, *usitbeyond.co.nz*).

### The Latin AirFlex Airpass
If you want to visit the whole region in a fairly short time, this can cut costs considerably. For example, a routing Miami–Belize City–Guatemala City–Roatán–Miami will cost US$548 low season/US$593 high season (plus taxes) – at least one-third less than flying the same route on a normal ticket. The pass links North American gateways with all the capitals and some other cities in Central America, as well as some destinations in South America and the Caribbean – the possible routes are mind-boggling. You have to buy the pass (in the form of coupons for each flight) before leaving home, book your route in advance and enter the region on one of the Taca Group airlines (Aviateca, Lacsa, Nica and Taca). Free date changes are allowed if space is available (within

the sixty-day validity of the pass), but a change of route will cost US$50.

### The Mexipass International
This combines the extensive networks of Aeroméxico and Mexicana, linking North American gateways with Mexico and onto several Central and South American cities. Houston–Cancún–Guatemala City–Houston is US$695 (plus taxes).

### The Mexipass Domestic
This is a final option if you want to travel extensively within Mexico. It's valid for travel with Aeroméxico and Mexicana airlines and there's a minimum purchase of two flights. The Mexipass fare for Mexico City–Palenque–Mérida–Mexico City is US$315.

In **Honduras** many people fly from San Pedro Sula (US$42 one way) or La Ceiba (US$18 one way) to the Bay Islands. From San Pedro Sula there are numerous international flights within the Maya region (Cancún US$140, Guatemala City and Belize City from US$90 one way) and also plenty of international departures to other Central American destinations, plus North and South America.

## BY BOAT

**Boats** are the main form of transport in many parts of the Maya region. On the Caribbean coast (Isla Mujeres, Cozumel, the Belize cayes and the Honduran Bay Islands), boats, ferries and skiffs are an essential link between the islands and the mainland. There are also daily **sea connections** between Punta Gorda (Belize) and Puerto Barrios (Guatemala), and less regular boats connecting Puerto Cortés (Honduras) with Belize City, Placencia and Dangriga (Belize) and Puerto Barrios (Guatemala).

The isolated Garifúna village of Lívingston in Guatemala is only accessible by boat, either from Puerto Barrios or Río Dulce town, Punta Gorda in Belize or by occasional speedboats from Omoa in Honduras. Within Guatemala, boats will get you around the three large **lakes** of Atitlán, Izabal and Petén Itzá, as well as the Río Dulce area. Finally, between the jungles of Chiapas in Mexico and Petén in Guatemala, the Río Usumacinta that divides the two nations has numerous **river connections** (see pp.149 & 470).

If you're a **canoe** enthusiast, an ideal base to explore Belize's river network is the town of San Ignacio where canoes are readily available to rent, whether for an hour or a week. **Sea kayaks** can be rented in Caye Caulker, Placencia and at a number of resorts in the Belize cayes and Guanaja and Roatán in the Bay Islands.

## BY TAXI

**Taxis** are readily available at every international airport and from virtually every domestic terminal; prices to the city centre are usually fixed. In the main towns, drivers often loiter around the main plazas and transport terminals, but **meters** are a rarity except in Guatemala City – always fix a price before you set off. Taxis can also be a good substitute for a rental car; you have the advantage of your own transport without the responsibility of driving it, and it often works out cheaper for half-day excursions.

## BY CAR

Prices vary a little for **car rental** throughout the region but are generally on the expensive side considering the relatively low cost of hotels and restaurants. In Mexico and Guatemala rates start from around US$230 a week for a standard car, but in Belize, where companies usually only offer sport/utility vehicles, the cheapest rate for a week is around US$400. In Honduras you can expect to pay from US$250 a week, while El Salvador has the cheapest rates – from US$200 a week.

If you plan to rent a car make sure you get a good map (see p.29) and bear in mind the high **accident rates**, and that as a foreigner any collision is likely to be construed as your fault. Always take full-cover insurance and beware that many companies will make you sign a "waiver" document so you are responsible for the first US$1000 of damage in the event of an accident or damage.

If you've succeeded in getting your own car here (see "Getting There", p.7), any further problems you face are likely to seem fairly minor. If you belong to a **motoring organization** at home, it's worth calling to see if they'll offer advice, maps and even help from reciprocal organizations in Mexico and Central America. **Security** is a major headache – always park in a safe place and never leave your car in the street overnight. Traffic is generally light outside the main cities and major routes are paved. **Fuel** is marginally more expensive than in the US but cheaper than in Europe, though filling stations are scarce outside the main cities. Unleaded fuel is now widely available in all countries.

## BY BICYCLE AND MOTORBIKE

**Motorbikes** are not that common in the Maya region, and rental outlets few and far between. Expect to pay around US$25 a day for an old 200cc machine, including insurance and unlimited mileage. You'll find rental outlets in Guatemala at Panajachel and Antigua, in Mexico at the main resorts including Cancún and Cozumel, and in Honduras there are bikes available to explore the island of Roatán.

**Bicycles** are everywhere in Central America, and increasing numbers of visitors bring their own. If you do, you'll find a repair shop in every town, though it will inevitably be difficult to find spare parts for high-tech models. Some buses can carry bikes on the roof, giving greater flexibility. Unfortunately, renting a bike is not usually good value, with prices from US$1 an hour or around US$7–10 a day (which is more than the average daily wage). Consequently few travellers choose to rent bikes here. For real two-wheeled enthusiasts, an excellent contact in Guatemala is Beat at Maya Mountain Bike Tours in Antigua (see p.353).

Membership of the UK's Cyclists' Touring Club (69 Meadrow, Godalming, Surrey GU7 3HS ☎01483/417217, *cycling@ctc.org.uk*; *ctc.org.uk*) means you can access trip reports from cyclists who have taken bikes to Central America, as well as other information.

# ACCOMMODATION

Most countries have some form of price (and in theory, quality) regulation and there's sometimes also a **hotel tax** to pay: always check if this is included in the rate you're quoted. (Prices quoted in this guide include tax, with the exception of Belize, where it's standard practice to quote 7 percent tax as a separate charge.) It's highly advisable to have a look at the room before you take it: make sure the light and fan work, and if you've been told there's hot water, find out what that means – it may only be at certain times of day.

## BUDGET ROOMS

Even if you're travelling through Central America on a tight budget you can expect reasonable levels of comfort and cleanliness in most **budget hotels**. Across the region's **towns** (except in Belize) you should be able to find a clean double room for under US$10 a night, and in many places you'll pay half that. Inevitably, the better deals are often where young travellers congregate in large numbers: there are superb, cheap places around Lago de Atitlán and in San Cristóbal de las Casas and some good options in Utila, Honduras.

A basic room in a **lowland** town will have a light and a fan (*ventilador*) in addition to the bed, though don't expect a reading light or anywhere to put clothes; some places also supply a towel,

Accommodation comes in all shapes and sizes and it's usually not hard to find somewhere reasonable. Places go by a bewildering range of names; hotel, obviously, but you'll frequently see pensión, casa de huéspedes, hospedaje, posada and even parador. The different names don't always mean a great deal: in theory a casa de huéspedes is less formal than a hotel but in reality the main difference will be the price. Rancho and campamento usually refer to some form of camping. In English-speaking Belize and the Honduran Bay Islands you're more likely to find the words hotel, inn, guest house, lodge and resort used.

## ACCOMMODATION PRICE CODES

All the accommodation listed in this book has been categorized into one of nine price bands, as set out below. The prices quoted are in US dollars and refer to the cheapest room available for two people sharing in high season.

| | | |
|---|---|---|
| ① under US$5 | ④ US$15–25 | ⑦ US$60–80 |
| ② US$5–10 | ⑤ US$25–40 | ⑧ US$80–100 |
| ③ US$10–15 | ⑥ US$40–60 | ⑨ over US$100 |

soap and toilet paper. In the **highlands** of Guatemala and Chiapas, a fan is rarely standard – it's much more important to check that there are sufficient blankets to keep out the cold and that there's hot water. Plenty of budget places also give you the option of a private bathroom (ie, a toilet and basic shower), which will typically add US$3–4 to the price of the room. It always works out much cheaper to **share a room** with other travellers; many hotels have rooms with three or four beds that are popular with local families. **Single travellers** will have to get used to paying at least seventy percent of the cost of a double room; we have indicated in the guide the places that offer good deals.

If the **price** seems a little high for the type of establishment, it's worth asking if there's a less expensive room (*¿Tiene un cuarto más barato, por favor?*) – you'll often get the same room at a lower price. It's always better to get a room at the back, away from the noise of the street, and upstairs you're more likely to benefit from a breeze. Most small hotels will be family run, and the owners usually take pride in the cleanliness of the rooms. There will usually be a place to hand-wash clothes (a *pila*); ask first before you use it. The very best cheap hotels in the smaller towns also have beautifully tended garden courtyards – perfect for sitting in the sun and reading.

As a rule, budget hotels in the **big cities** tend to be less attractive and more expensive than those in smaller towns and the tourist areas, though we've listed the exceptions in the relevant chapters. In the bigger cities it's worth paying a little more or even moving to one grade of hotel higher than you might otherwise, to stay in a more secure place – particularly for your first night. Cheap hotels are often crowded around bus stations and markets; some of these can be very dismal, being used by prostitutes and their clients. However, in every capital there are at least one or two hotels where other travellers congregate to offer company and perhaps security.

Budget hotels in **rural areas** or **coastal locations** not geared to the tourist market are usually quite basic: a ramshackle building or perhaps a stick-and-thatch cabaña. These can be delightful – you'll be less of a guest and more like an extra member of the family – but they can also be very uncomfortable, with lumpy mattresses and poor ventilation. This is where serviceable insect proofing can make the difference between misery and a good night's sleep.

**Booking ahead** for a budget room is not usually necessary (and often not possible as many don't have phones), though it might be worth trying at busy times like Christmas and Easter. Otherwise, arriving early at your destination will give you a better selection.

## HOTELS, RESORTS AND LODGES

If you spend around US$20–25 for a double room, you can expect a fairly plain but clean room with a private bathroom with hot water in the highlands, and with a fan or air conditioning in the lowlands. There are plenty of excellent deals in the **mid-range** price bracket and you'll find the better places make an effort to decorate the room attractively, sometimes with wall-hangings or textiles. You can also expect better-quality mattresses and perhaps a reading light or a writing desk. Generally, the differences between a hotel in the **upper mid-range** (US$40–80) and the luxury price bracket come down to facilities: you'll rarely find a swimming pool or gym, the in-house restaurant (if there is one) will be less ambitious, and there may be no service after 10pm. Nevertheless, you'll find there are some very attractive, enjoyable places to stay in the mid-range bracket, many with real colonial character and lovely gardens, and lacking the "corporate" feel of many of the luxury places.

Moving into the **luxury hotel** end of the market (above US$80), certain features become virtually standard. Hotels will usually have a swimming pool and health facilities, a restaurant or two, landscaped gardens, manicured lawns and sometimes a tennis court, and often all sorts of shops offering overpriced touristy trinkets. Many have in-house tourism desks from where you'll be able to organize excursions. Rooms will nearly always have air conditioning (*aire acondicionado*), tea- and coffee-making facilities and often a couple of double beds. Service levels should also be good. The major disadvantage with many of the large hotels at this level is that they can be frighteningly impersonal places where all sense of the region is lost once you're behind the security gates. For this reason we prefer to recommend the smaller-scale luxury options, of which there are many. Service facilities may not be able to match the larger hotels, but the pay-off is that they are often located in wonderfully atmospheric colonial buildings, with individually decorated rooms, delightful mature gardens full of flowering shrubs and shady trees. They are also often locally or foreign (rather than corporation) owned.

Some of the most spectacular accommodation is found in the network of upmarket **jungle lodges**, mainly in Belize, which are often in beautiful, remote locations in or near national parks. Here you'll often have a private thatched cabaña, with a balcony overlooking the forest, lake or other natural attraction. Many of these places charge upwards of US$150 a night, though the experience of a rainforest dawn chorus and the chance of getting close to wildlife can make the cost worthwhile. They are often used by adventure and nature tour operators (see pp.5, 6, 10 & 13), and occupancy varies with the season; if the lodge is open out of season, ask about possible discounts.

There are also an increasing number of luxury **beach resorts** being developed in the Honduran Bay Islands and the Belizean cayes. Many of these are geared to scuba-divers on all-in packages booked in North America or Europe and are often prohibitively expensive for the independent traveller. The best of these places in Guanaja, Roatán, Ambergris Caye and Placencia offer wonderful environments for divers, where almost everything is organized around the reef, tanks, fins and compressed air – non-divers will probably feel alienated by the one topic of conversation.

## YOUTH HOSTELS, CAMPING AND HAMMOCKS

The region is so full of inexpensive hotels that you'll scarcely need to consider staying in a **youth hostel**, which is just as well as they are extremely rare. There are five hostels in southern Mexico (including Campeche and Cancún), but you'll probably pay the same as in a budget hotel and have to sleep in a single-sex dorm and conform to silly curfew rules. There are also woefully few **campsites**, primarily because camping has yet to catch on with the locals. A tent and a sleeping bag are only really necessary if you're hiking right off the beaten track, climbing a volcano or jungle trekking. A **hammock** can be useful, especially by the beach in Quintana Roo or Belize; some of the finest in the world are manufactured in Mérida, and they make great souvenirs too.

# EATING AND DRINKING

Corn and beans, the key essentials of the Maya diet, have been grown in the region for thousands of years. Though there are numerous methods of preparation, most meals are still incomplete without a portion of these two staples, often seasoned with chile. The food in the south of the region is uniformly Central American, with corn tortillas, beans and eggs on almost every menu. Cuisine is not a particular highlight of Belize either, though there are some excellent seafood dishes. Southern Mexico offers the most varied menus, including some superb Yucatecan specialities.

The monotony of the Central American diet can get to travellers after a while. Fortunately, however, there is a tremendous variety of food available in the big cities and main tourist centres, as enterprising locals and foreigners have opened restaurants to cater for gringo tastebuds. In places like San Cristóbal de las Casas, Panajachel, Antigua, Utila and Roatán there is **ethnic food** from all over the world on offer: Thai and Indian curries, vegetarian wholefood, Mediterranean specialities, all-American favourites and even Middle Eastern and Japanese dishes. Much of this culinary smorgasbord may not be very authentic, but if you've spent any time in the wilds subsisting on a diet of eggs, beans and tortillas, this cosmopolitan eating scene will come as quite a relief.

## WHERE TO EAT

Except for the very rich, the people of the Maya world cannot regularly afford to eat out. Most **basic restaurants** reflect this and serve simple, filling food at low prices. The very cheapest place to eat is always the **comedor**, which is a basic eatery with a very simple line-up of dishes costing US$1–2. Often there's no menu (*carta*), so you'll have to ask what's on offer or look inside the bubbling pots. You'll almost always be able to get something to suit **vegetarians**, as any comedor will have eggs, beans and tortillas or tacos. There will also be fried chicken (*pollo frito*), steak (*bistek*) and soups (*caldos*). Many places do a set lunch menu (*comida corrida* or *menú del día*) which is usually an excellent deal, comprising three courses for around US$2, sometimes less. In Belize, you can count on getting rice and beans and fried chicken, but you'll have to pay more: reckon on at least US$5 a meal.

**Upmarket restaurants** only exist in the big cities or the main tourist centres. They tend to be more formal and expensive, but outside the tourist places, the menu will be pretty familiar, dominated by meat dishes. There are also thousands of **fast-food** joints, all modelled on the American originals. Prices are high compared to comedor nosh (around US$3 a meal) and for many locals a trip to *McDonald's* or *Pollo Campero* is a big treat.

Finally, there is some excellent **street food** available, some of the most common offerings being pupusas, tacos, tamales and baleadas (see below), and you'll find *papas fritas* (fried potato chips) almost everywhere. You should exercise a little caution with street food, however, as hygiene standards are variable.

## WHAT TO EAT

**Corn** (*maíz*) is the single most important ingredient in the Maya diet – the ancient Maya even believed that they originated from it – and it's most commonly consumed as a **tortilla**, a thin, flat pancake made from cornflour that accompanies almost every meal in the region (except in Belize). The maize is traditionally ground by hand and shaped by clapping it between two hands – though in Mexico, tortilla presses are now widespread. It is cooked on a **comal**, a hot plate made of metal or clay, and usually brought to the table wrapped in cloth. Tortillas should be eaten while

warm as they don't stay fresh for very long. The very best tortillas have a delicate taste and a pliable texture; if you're served hard, leathery tortillas, you should send them back. The slightly burnt, smoky taste of tortillas will become very much a part of your trip.

Tortillas can be adapted in a multitude of different ways, especially in Mexico where **tacos** (fried, rolled tortillas stuffed with almost anything), **enchiladas** (baked stuffed tortillas) and **quesadillas** (toasted tortillas wrapped around a cheese filing) are ubiquitous. In El Salvador and Guatemala the **pupusa** (a thick, toasted tortilla topped with ingredients including avocado, refried beans, meat and cheese, and served with crunchy cabbage and carrot) is more common, while in Honduras the most popular snack is a **baleada** (tortilla stuffed with beans and cheese, sometimes with a little guacamole). **Tamales** (maize dough, steamed in a banana leaf and stuffed with a little meat or something sweet) are popular throughout the region.

**Beans** (*frijoles*) are the second essential item in the Maya diet. The beans themselves are either of the black or pinto variety and they are usually served in two ways: *volteados* (or *refritos*), where the beans are boiled, mashed, and then refried in a great dollop; or *parados*, which are whole boiled beans, often prepared with a few slices of onion and served in their own black juice. For breakfast, beans are usually served refried with eggs and cream, and at other times of the day they're often offered up on a separate plate to the main dish. Almost all truly Maya meals include a portion of beans, and for many of the region's indigenous people, beans are the only regular source of protein.

**Chiles** are the final essential ingredient of Maya cuisine, sometimes placed raw or pickled in the middle of the table in a jar, but also served as a sauce – *salsa picante*. With more than a hundred different varieties, the strength can vary tremendously, so treat them with caution until you know what you're dealing with. In Mexico the class of the salsa can even give some indication as to the quality of the restaurant – there are some tremendous raw salsas made with tomato, chile, coriander and onion, or cooked salsas made with tomato, onion and chile.

The most commonly eaten **meat** is chicken (*pollo*), with beef (*res*) and pork (*cerdo*) being a little less common. Steak is *bistec de res* and a hamburger is a *hamburguesa*. Every comedor or

## A GLOSSARY OF FOOD AND DRINK TERMS

### Basics

| | | | | | |
|---|---|---|---|---|---|
| *arroz* | rice | *leche* | milk | *sal* | salt |
| *azúcar* | sugar | *mantequilla* | butter | *salsa* | sauce |
| *carne* | meat | *pan* | bread | *verduras/* | vegetables |
| *crema* | cream | *pescado* | fish | *legumbres* | |
| *ensalada* | salad | *pimienta* | pepper | | |
| *huevos* | eggs | *queso* | cheese | | |

### Soups (*sopas*) and starters

| | | | |
|---|---|---|---|
| *caldo* | broth (with bits in) | *entremeses* | hors d'oeuvres |
| | | *sopa* | soup |
| *ceviche* | raw fish salad, marinated in lime juice | *de arroz* | with rice |
| | | *de fideos* | with noodles |
| | | *de lentejas* | lentil |
| *consome* | consommé | *de verduras* | vegetable |

### Eggs (*huevos*)

| | | | |
|---|---|---|---|
| *con jamón* | with ham | *rancheros* | fried and smothered in a hot chile sauce |
| *a la Mexicana* | scrambled with tomato, onion and mild chile sauce | *revueltos* | scrambled |
| *motuleños* | fried, served on a tortilla with ham, cheese and salsa | *tibios* | lightly boiled |
| | | *con tocino* | with bacon |

### Snacks (*antojitos*)

| | | | |
|---|---|---|---|
| *baleada* | tortilla stuffed with cheese and refried beans | *pan de coco* | coconut bread |
| | | *pupusa* | toasted tortilla served with assorted toppings and raw vegetables |
| *burritos* | wheatflour tortillas, rolled and filled | | |
| *chilaquiles* | torn-up tortillas cooked with meat and sauce | *quesadillas* | toasted or fried tortillas with cheese |
| *chiles rellenos* | stuffed peppers | *queso fundido* | melted cheese, served with tortillas and salsa |
| *chuchito* | stuffed maize dumpling | | |
| *enchiladas* | rolled-up tacos, covered in chile sauce and baked | *sopes* | smaller bite-size versions of tostadas |
| *enchiladas suizas* | as above, in sour cream | *tacos* | fried tortillas with filling |
| *flautas* | small rolled tortillas filled with meat or chicken and then fried | *tacos al pastor* | tacos filled with pork |
| | | *tamales* | cornmeal pudding, usually stuffed and steamed in banana leaves |
| *gorditas* | small, fat, stuffed corn tortillas | | |
| *machaca* | shredded dried meat scrambled with eggs | *tlacoyo* | fat tortilla stuffed with beans |
| | | *torta* | filled bread roll |
| *molletes* | split torta covered in beans and melted cheese, often with ham and avocado too | *tostadas* | flat crispy tortillas piled with meat and salad |

### Fish and seafood (*pescados y mariscos*)

| | | | | | |
|---|---|---|---|---|---|
| *anchoas* | anchovies | *filete entero* | whole, filleted fish | *ostión* | oyster |
| *atún* | tuna | | | *pez espada* | swordfish |
| *cabrilla* | sea bass | *huachinango* | red snapper | *pulpo* | octopus |
| *calamares* | squid | *jurel* | yellowtail | *robalo* | bass |
| *camarones* | prawns | *langosta* | crawfish (rock lobster) | *sardinas* | sardines |
| *cangrejo* | crab | | | *tiburón* | shark |
| *corvina blanca* | white sea bass | *langostinos* | king prawns | *trucha* | trout |
| *dorado* | dolphin (mahi mahi) | *lenguado* | sole | | |
| | | *merluza* | hake | | *continued overleaf* |

## A GLOSSARY OF FOOD AND DRINK TERMS contd

### Meat (*carne*) and Poultry (*aves*)

| | | | | | |
|---|---|---|---|---|---|
| alambre | kebab | chorizo | spicy sausage | milanesa | breaded |
| albóndigas | meatballs | chuleta | chop | | escalope |
| barbacoa | barbecued meat | codorniz | quail | pata | feet |
| bistec | steak (not | conejo | rabbit | pato | duck |
| | always beef) | cordero | lamb | pavo/guajolote | turkey |
| cabeza | head | costilla | rib | pechuga | breast |
| cabrito | kid | filete | tenderloin/fillet | pierna | leg |
| carne (de res) | beef | guisado | stew | pollo | chicken |
| carne adobado | barbecued/ | hígado | liver | salchicha | hot dog or |
| | spicily stewed | lengua | tongue | | salami |
| | meat | longaneza | cooked spicy | ternera | veal |
| carnitas | spicy pork | | sausage | tocino | bacon |
| cerdo | pork | lomo | loin (of pork) | tripa/callos | tripe |
| chivo | goat | machaca | shredded meat | venado | venison |

### Vegetables (*verduras, legumbres*)

| | | | | | |
|---|---|---|---|---|---|
| aceitunas | olives | ejotes | green beans | papas | potatoes |
| aguacate | avocado | elote | corn on the cob | pepino | cucumber |
| betabel | beetroot (often | espárragos | asparagus | plátano | plantain |
| | as a juice) | frijoles | beans | rajas | strips of green |
| calabacita | zucchini | hongos | mushrooms | | pepper |
| | (courgette) | jitomate | red tomato | tomate | green tomato |
| calabaza | squash | lechuga | lettuce | zanahoria | carrot |
| cebolla | onion | lentejas | lentils | | |
| champiñones | mushrooms | nopales | prickly pear | | |
| chícharos | peas | | leaves, | | |
| col | cabbage | | something | | |
| coliflor | cauliflower | | like squash | | |

### Fruits (*fruta*) and juices (*jugos*)

| | | | |
|---|---|---|---|
| chabacano | apricot | mamey | like a large zapote, with |
| cherimoya | custard apple (sweetsop) | | sweet pink flesh and a big pip |
| ciruelas | tiny yellow plums | mango | mango |
| coco | coconut | manzana | apple |
| durazno | peach | melón | melon |
| frambuesas | raspberries | naranja | orange |
| fresas | strawberries | papaya | papaya |
| granada | yellow passion fruit | piña | pineapple |
| guanabana | soursop, like a large custard | plátano | banana |
| | apple | sandía | watermelon |
| guayaba | guava | toronja | grapefruit |
| higos | figs | tuna | prickly pear (cactus fruit) |
| limón | lime | uvas | grapes |
| | | zapote | sapodilla (*chicu*), fruit of the |
| | | | chicle tree |

### Sweets (*dulces, postres*)

| | | | | | |
|---|---|---|---|---|---|
| ate | quince paste | crepas | pancakes | helado | ice cream |
| cajeta | caramel confection | ensalada de | fruit salad | nieve | sorbet |
| | often served | frutas | | pastel | cake |
| | with... | flan | crème caramel | | |

## Common terms

| | | | |
|---|---|---|---|
| *asado/a* | roast | | chocolate and spices – |
| *barbacoa/pibil* | wrapped in leaves and herbs | | served with chicken or turkey |
| | and steamed/cooked in a pit | | |
| *empanado/a* | breaded | *a la parrilla* | grilled |
| *frito* | fried | *a la plancha* | grilled |
| *al horno* | baked | *a la Veracruzana* | usually fish, cooked with |
| *al mojo de ajo* | fried in garlic and butter*con* | | tomatoes and onions |
| *con mole* | the most famous of Mexican | *a la tampiqueña* | meat in thin strips served with |
| | sauces containing chile, | | guacamole and enchiladas |

restaurant will have something for the committed carnivore. Meats are fried (*frito*), grilled/broiled (*a la plancha* or *a la parrilla*), roasted (*asado*) or breaded (*empanado*). In basic *comedores* the meat is generally tough, but in steakhouses some choice cuts are available. Other traditional Maya dishes include a superb range of **stews** – known as *caldos* – made with duck, beef, chicken or turkey.

You'll find **eggs** on almost every menu, most commonly fried, scrambled or poached, but there are also some uniquely Mexican combinations: *huevos rancheros* are fried eggs in a rich tomato-based salsa sauce and *huevos motuleños* are eggs cooked with tomato, salsa, cheese and peas on a bed of tortillas.

### CREOLE FOOD

At its best, **Creole** food can be delicious, taking the best from the sea and mixing it with the smooth taste of coconut and mild spices. All along the eastern coast between Belize and Honduras you'll find the influence of Africa and the Caribbean is never far away, with plantain, cassava and breadfruit all part of culinary tradition, but sadly not always present in the region's restaurants. Conch soup, *pan de coco* (coconut bread) and *tapada* (fish, potatoes and vegetables including yucca) are all specialities. **Fish** is an essential part of the Creole diet: you'll find shark steak, red snapper, barracuda and grouper all on the menu.

At its worst, Creole food can be something of a neglected art, conforming to a single recipe – the ubiquitous **rice and beans** – and a few other bland, starchy dishes. If you're lucky, your rice and beans may be injected with a bit more interest in the form of a little fish, chicken or beef and perhaps a side portion of fried plantain.

**Seafood** is almost always excellent, with superb fresh shrimp and crab. On San Pedro and

Caye Caulker in Belize, the food is often exceptional, and the only worry is that you might get bored with **lobster**, which is served in an amazing range of dishes. You may want to avoid eating lobster in Honduras, however: over-collection has led to local divers having to spend more and more time underwater chasing fewer and fewer lobsters – a practice which has caused many deaths.

### VEGETARIAN FOOD

Most people in the region eat as much meat as they can afford (which may be daily or just once a month) and vegetarianism is almost unknown anywhere in the region. To check if something is suitable, ask if it's *sin carne* (without meat); locals may not consider chicken to be a meat, however, so you may want to ask if it's *sin pollo* too. You'll certainly have no problem getting something to eat in any town or village, with eggs, beans, tortillas or rice and beans always available and fresh fruit everywhere. Popular **vegetarian dishes** include *chiles rellenos* (stuffed peppers) and quesadillas.

If things get a bit desperate, head for a Chinese restaurant or a pizzeria – both are common in the region. Mercifully, in the main tourist centres you won't usually have to explain your eating preferences and there will be many more cosmopolitan possibilities to enjoy, including salads, hummus and falafel.

### DRINKING

The basic **drinks** to accompany food are water, fruit juices, fizzy drinks and beer. If you're drinking water, stick to bottled stuff (*agua mineral* or *agua pura*); it comes either plain (*sin gas*) or carbonated (*con gas*). Fizzy drinks (*refrescos* or *aguas*) such as Coca-Cola, Pepsi and Fanta are on sale everywhere.

## JUICES AND SHAKES

Real fruit juices (*jugos*) and fruit shakes (*licuados*) are very common and a good healthy treat. **Juices** can be squeezed from anything that will go through the extractor. Orange (*naranja*) and carrot (*zanahoria*) are the staples, but you should also experiment with some of the more obscure tropical fruits. **Licuados** are made of fruit mixed with water (*con agua*) or milk (*con leche*) in a blender. They are always fantastic, but watch out for the five or six spoons of sugar that the locals normally take – you might want to ask for yours without sugar (*sin azúcar*). You could also try *limonada* (fresh lemonade) or *aguas frescas* – flavoured cold drinks: *agua de arroz*, a delicious drink like iced rice pudding, *agua de jamaica* (hibiscus) or *de tamarindo* (tamarind). The danger is that some of these drinks may not be made with purified water (*agua purificada*) – if you're suspicious, try a licuado made with milk.

## COFFEE AND TEA

**Coffee** is the principal export crop of the Maya region, though, regretfully, this status is seldom reflected in the quality of the cup you'll be served. There are some exceptional coffee blends available, but you'll usually only get an export-quality brew in the very upmarket or foreign-owned establishments.

In its basic form, *café solo* or *negro*, coffee is strong, black, often sweet (ask for it *sin azúcar* for no sugar), and comes in small cups. For weaker black coffee, ask for *café americano*, though be warned that you may be given instant; if you do want instant, ask for Nescafé. White coffee is *café con leche* in most of the region, but known as *café cortado* or *con un pocito de leche* in Mexico. *Café con leche* in Mexico is made with all milk and no water (check if it's *hecho de leche*). Espresso and cappuccino are still relatively rare, but becoming increasingly more common, particularly in Mexico and Guatemala.

**Tea** (*té*) can often be found, and you may well be offered a cup at the end of a comida. Usually it's a herb tea like *manzanilla* (camomile) or *yerbabuena* (mint). If you get the chance to try traditional hot chocolate, "the drink of the Aztecs", then do so – it's an extraordinary, spicy, semi-bitter concoction, quite unlike the milky bedtime drink of your childhood.

## ALCOHOL

**Beer** (*cerveza*) is generally good everywhere in the region. Mostly light, lager-style brews, bottles typically cost a dollar a bottle (US$1.75 in Belize) in bars, less than half that from a supermarket. In Mexico the main **lager** beers are Bohémia, Superior, Dos Equis and Tecate (the last normally served with lemon and salt). The Belizean beer, Belikin, comes in three varieties. In Guatemala, Gallo has a near monopoly but is pretty bland; the premium Montecarlo is better. All the four Honduran beers are made by the same company and tend to be refreshing rather than intoxicating, while El Salvador has maybe the best beers in the region, including Pilsener, Suprema and Regia. **Dark beer** (*cerveza obscura*) is available too. In Mexico there are three main varieties: Indio, Tres Equis and the excellent Negra Modelo. In Belize there is a good Belikin stout and Guinness is brewed under licence, and in Guatemala, Moza beer makes an interesting, flavoursome change from the ubiquitous Gallo.

**Wine** (*vino* – *tinto* for red, *blanco* for white) only makes an appearance in very upmarket restaurants, where a reasonable bottle will cost at least US$10; Chilean wines are usually the best value. In supermarkets, a reasonable bottle of Chilean or Argentinean wine will cost about US$5, though there are litre cartons of cheaper stuff on sale too. Mexico produces a fair number of perfectly good wines. You're safest sticking to the brand names like Hidalgo or Domecq.

As for **spirits**, the most famous is Mexico's **tequila**, derived from the maguey plant, though it is rarely drunk in any other country in the region. The best stuff is aged (*añejo* or *reposado*) for smoothness; try Sauza Hornitos, which is powerful, or Commemorativo, which is unexpectedly gentle on the throat. **Mescal** (often spelt mezcal) is basically the same drink, made from a slightly different type of maguey plant and younger and less refined. **Pulque**, a mildly alcoholic milky beer made from the same cactus, is the traditional drink of the poor and sold in special bars called *pulquerías*. Surprisingly, **margaritas** (tequila, orange liqueur and fresh lime juice) are seldom drunk outside the tourist bars.

**Rum** (*ron*) is the most important spirit outside Mexico and each country has a good brand or two. Prices are low, with a 75cl bottle costing as little as US$3 and a better-quality brand US$5. Flor de Caña from Honduras is many travellers' favourite, while some people favour the Guatemalan Ron Botran Añejo or the very smooth (and expensive) Zacapa Centenario. Guatemala, Honduras and El Salvador all produce **aguardiente**, a fire-water made from sugar cane, whose power is at the heart of many a fiesta; in

Guatemala, Quezalteca is the most popular brand. In Honduras, Yuscarán is a national institution, often blended with herbs and plants. Drinking international liquor brands is extremely expensive anywhere in the Maya area; just ask for *nacional* if you want the local variety.

The best atmosphere for drinking any of these is in hotel bars or tourist areas. Traditional **cantinas** are for serious and excessive drinking, have a thoroughly threatening, macho atmosphere and are barred to women most of the time, though big-city *cantinas* can be more liberal.

## MAIL, PHONES AND THE INTERNET

Mail and telecommunication services in Central America are very variable with services currently undergoing a profound period of change. Generally postal services are very cheap but can be unreliable, and many locals use courier companies to send important packages and documents overseas; in Belize, however, things are more efficient. Local telephone and fax connections are very cheap throughout the region and long-distance national calls are not too pricey. International calls are extremely expensive using state-run phone company facilities whose rates are way above what you'd pay in North America or Europe, but in many towns independently run communications offices offer much better value. Internet cafés and facilities are mushrooming throughout the region wherever foreigners gather, and though rates are generally inexpensive connection speeds can be pedestrian.

### MAIL

When sending mail home, the best way to ensure speedy delivery is to use the **main post office** in a capital city; this will also be the best place to send parcels. **Post boxes** are rare – you'll find them in the lobbies of big hotels and some tourist shops, but the best bet is to take mail to a post office. As a rule of thumb, an airmail letter to the US takes about a week and to Europe from ten days to two weeks. **Receiving mail** is less certain, but you can generally rely on the service in main post offices. Letters (with your surname underlined) should be sent to Lista de Correos (or General Delivery in Belize), Correo Central, name of city, country, and finishing with Central America (or Mexico). When looking to see if mail has arrived, ask to see the Lista de Correos, which is usually typed up each day, and search for your name (check whether mail is being held under your forename or surname). You'll need identification – a passport is best – and there's sometimes a small fee to collect your mail. Note that the Lista de Correos system is no longer operational **in Guatemala** – you'll have to rely on getting your mail sent to a private address like a language school or a travel agent.

Always use some form of registration when sending **parcels**; it won't cost much more than the postage and you'll get a certificate to give you some sort of peace of mind. You can send parcels via surface mail but this takes months. Be prepared for the parcel to undergo some form of inspection, and there may also be some quirky labelling and wrapping regulations to observe.

Specialist **courier companies** (DHL, Federal Express, etc) are establishing more and more offices throughout the region and even small towns now have offices. Obviously the charges involved are way above the standard postal rates, but they do represent the safest method of sending packages or documents home.

## PHONES

Although telephone systems are gradually improving, local technology is still pretty primitive and connections are not always what they should be. **Local calls** are always cheap, but call boxes are not particularly widespread anywhere so it's often better to call from your hotel (some hotels in Mexico won't even charge you). Long-distance domestic calls are not too expensive either. In Mexico it's more cost-effective to use a telephone card for these.

For **international calls** it's well worth avoiding using official (usually state-run – Belize is the exception) company offices such as Telgua in Guatemala, Telecom in El Salvador or Hondutel in Honduras. In Mexico (using cardphones, available almost everywhere) calls cost US$1.70 per minute to USA, US$2.50 to Europe. In many tourist centres businesses such as internet cafés will have services much cheaper then this.

In Belize (using cardphones, available almost everywhere) calls cost US$1.25 per minute to the USA; US$2.25 to Europe. At present there are no private companies, but competition is being introduced so prices may come down. In Honduras, a three-minute call is US$18 to the UK or Australia, and US$8 to the USA. Taking a telephone charge card or calling card with you is a good idea. Most North American cards work throughout the region, but at present UK-issued cards only function in Mexico and Belize.

By far the best international call rates are offered by a growing number of private communication businesses, prevalent in Mexico though still not permitted in Belize. In Guatemala, for example, rates start from US$0.20 to the USA and Canada, US$0.40 to the EU and US$0.60 per minute to Australia and New Zealand at Kall

Shop, who have branches in Antigua and Quetzaltenango. Even cheaper still, internet phone connections are offered in a growing number of places, cutting costs as low as US$0.80 for a 30min call, though the quality of line can be appalling. In Honduras police raided internet cafés offering web-based calls in early 2001, and confiscated equipment, though many were back in business within days.

**Calling home collect** (*llamar por cobrar*) is fairly simple from most countries: North Americans are able to call collect from any country, but you can only call the UK collect from Mexico and Belize. You should be able to send (and receive) a **fax** from any (largish) telephone office in the region, and it's often easier than making a phone call.

## THE INTERNET

**Online services** are becoming more and more widespread in the Maya region. You'll find **cyber-cafés** in the capital cities and most of the major tourist centres, so if you have a service provider which allows you to pick up email anywhere, you can check your mail while abroad. Rates can be as little as US$1.50 in Antigua, **Guatemala** (where there are around twenty cybercafés) or an extortionate US$12 an hour in the **Bay Islands**, where all calls are classified as long distance because they have to be routed via the mainland. In **Belize**, BTL, the country's phone company, controls access to the Internet, and prices to go online are high compared to other places in the region (at least US$2.50 per half-hour) but it's still cheaper than an overseas phone call. In **Mexico** the internet is fantastically popular and almost every town will have a "cybercafé" or ten, often packed with students doing homework or emailing friends, where you can go online very cheaply (from as little as US$1.25 an hour). Many are listed in the guide but you'll come across dozens more. Before you go, look at *netcafeguide.com* and click on the Latin America map to check out the locations.

# THE MEDIA

The press in the Maya region tends to be somewhat limited in international coverage, though there are some English-language publications which provide useful information and are readily available everywhere. Television tends to be dominated by American broadcasts, though you might find some interesting local programmes.

The **BBC World Service** in English can be picked up by radios with short wave on 5975KHz in the 49m band, especially in the evening, on 15,220KHz in the 25m band, especially in the morning, and on 17,840KHz, especially in the afternoon. Other possible frequencies include: 6175KHz, 6195KHz, 9590KHz and 9895KHz. **The Voice of America** broadcasts on 15,210KHz, 11,740KHz, 9815KHz and 6030Khz.

## MEXICO

There are two main **English-language newspapers** in Mexico. *The News* is a frumpy US-oriented organ which you'll find pretty much anywhere with a significant English-speaking presence. Far better is the broadsheet *Mexico City Times,* which has the usual wire stories and incisive pieces from the *New York Times* and Britain's *Economist* and *Independent;* the Saturday issue even includes the Latin American edition of the *Guardian Weekly. Time* and *Newsweek* are easily available too.

Of the **domestic newspapers**, few carry much foreign news, and what there is is mainly Latin American; they are usually lurid scandal sheets, full of violent crime depicted in full colour. While each state has its own press, most are little more than government propaganda. The best national paper if you read Spanish is *La Jornada*, which is quite daringly critical of government policy, especially in Chiapas, and whose journalists regularly face death threats as a result.

On Mexican **TV** you can watch any number of US shows dubbed into Spanish, and cable and satellite are now widespread; even quite downmarket hotels offer numerous cable channels, many of them American.

**Radio** stations in the capital, Guadalajara and other major towns have programmes in English for a couple of hours each day, and in many places US broadcasts can also be picked up.

## GUATEMALA

By far the most useful **English-language newspaper** published in Guatemala is the excellent (and free) *Guatemala Post,* which will give you an authoritative insight into this complicated country and help keep you informed of the current security situation. It covers political affairs consistently well, with articles from *El Periódico*, Guatemala's best campaigning newspaper, and offers interesting cultural comment. Also well worth picking up is the monthly magazine the *Revue*, aimed at the ex-pat and tourist market, which always has an interesting piece or interview, though it tends to be more advertisement-driven. The *Revue* has expanded in the last few years to cover Belize, El Salvador and Honduras. You can pick up copies of both of the above at the major hotels and many restaurants in the region.

Keep an eye out too for *Destination Petén* and *Caribbean View,* two (fairly slimline) free listings magazines which cover the north and east of the country respectively. *Time, Newsweek* and occasionally the *Economist* are all sold in bookstores in Antigua and the top hotels in Guatemala City, and you may find the odd US newspaper too – *USA Today* or the *Miami Herald.* The best domestic **Spanish-language daily newspapers** are the outspoken *El Periódico* and the reliable *Siglo Veintiuno,* but both are less readily available than the mainstream, conservative *Prensa Libre.*

**Television stations** are in plentiful supply. Viewers can choose from six local channels and over a dozen satellite channels, all of them dominated by American programmes. CNN news is readily available. Guatemala has an abundance of **radio stations**, though variety is not their strong point: most transmit a turgid stream of Latin rock, cheesy merengue and evangelical rantings.

## BELIZE

Belize's English-language media can make a welcome break in a world of Spanish, but this doesn't necessarily mean that it's very easy to keep in touch with what's happening in the rest of the world. Local news is reported in a very nationalistic manner but international events get very little attention. In Belize City, Belmopan, San Pedro and occasionally in some other towns, you should be able to get hold of some foreign newspapers. Satellite TV is widespread, and the best source of American news.

The four national **newspapers** – The People's Pulse, The Reporter, The Belize Times and The Amandala (all published weekly on Friday) –mostly stick to a party line, and some are acutely xenophobic, though there's usually an interesting article or two. There are also inexpensive tourist newspapers: the San Pedro Sun and Ambergris Today (Ambergris Caye) and the Placencia Breeze (Placencia).

There are two more-or-less national **television stations**: Channel 5, producing superb news and factual programmes, and the populist Channel 7, which shows an almost uninterrupted stream of imported American shows. Cable TV (mostly pirated from satellite) is the nation's preferred viewing medium, giving saturation coverage of American soaps, talk shows, sports, films and CNN. Most towns in Belize have their own **radio station** and there are also several national ones. Love FM has the most extensive coverage, offering easy listening, news, discussions and often controversial phone-ins. Another major station is KREM, with an emphasis on Belizean culture, talk and punta rock.

### HONDURAS

The most useful **publications for travellers** are Honduras This Week (marrder.com/htw), a good weekly English-language newspaper with in-depth coverage of events in Honduras, plus tourist and business information, and Honduras

Tips, a free tourism magazine with plenty of valuable information and features, plus hotel and restaurant listings. You'll find both in the big hotels in Copán, San Pedro Sula, La Ceiba and the Bay Islands. If you're in Roatán, keep an eye out for the quirky island-based Coconut Telegraph publication.

Of the five daily **Spanish-language newspapers**, El Tiempo, based in San Pedro Sula, is the most liberal and is regularly critical of the government and armed forces. The conservative La Prensa has the biggest circulation and the best international coverage.

There are over 170 **radio** stations in Honduras and numerous cable networks with US programmes, usually broadcast in English with Spanish subtitles.

### EL SALVADOR

In El Salvador you can pick up copies of the Revue (see under Guatemala above), which includes an El Salvador section. There is also a Spanish-language weekly magazine called Ke Pasa which is a great guide to music, cinema and entertainment in the capital – it's available from many bars and restaurants. Of the four national Spanish-language **newspapers**, the morning La Prensa Gráfica and El Diario de Hoy are widely read and very conservative; both do have good entertainment/cultural events sections on Friday and Saturday.

There are over seventy **radio** stations, and seven national **television** channels, plus cable companies which broadcast programmes from the US, Spain and CNN news.

# OPENING HOURS AND HOLIDAYS

**Most offices, shops, post offices, museums and government offices are open Monday to Friday from 8.30am to 5pm throughout the region, though some take a break for lunch. On Saturdays, government offices are closed and some museums and post offices open from 9am until noon, but most shops are open all day.**

**Banking** hours are generally similar, with most branches being open until 4pm (earlier in Mexico) and on Saturday mornings as well. In Guatemala, opening hours are extremely convenient, with many banks staying open until 7pm (and some as late as 8pm) from Monday to Friday and until 1pm on Saturdays. The siesta tradition persists in the Yucatán, where some shops close for the hottest part of the day.

On principal **public holidays** (see box below) almost all businesses close down, and in addition, each village or town will also have its own fiesta or saint's day when everything will be shut. These can last anything from one day to two weeks.

**Archeological sites** are open every day, usually from 8am to 5pm. At Tikal, the hours are even

> It's worth noting that many indigenous communities and some local transport operators refuse to observe the Mexican time change in summer, preferring **la hora vieja** – the old time.

more relaxed (6am to 6pm, or 8pm with permission). Sites in Mexico are free on Sundays.

## FIESTAS

**Traditional fiestas** are one of the great excitements of a trip to the Maya region, and every town and village, however small, devotes at least one day a year to celebration. The date is normally prescribed by the local saint's day and the main day is always marked by a climactic event, though the party often extends to a week or two around that date. On almost every day of the year there's a fiesta in some corner of the region, and with a bit of planning or a stroke of luck you should be able to witness at least one.

The format of fiestas varies between three basic models: ladino, Maya and Creole. In towns with a largely **ladino** population, fairs are usually

## PUBLIC HOLIDAYS

**January**
1  New Year's Day
**February**
5  Anniversary of the Constitution (Mexico)
24  Flag Day (Mexico)
**March**
9  Baron Bliss Day (Belize)
21  Benito Juárez Day (Mexico)
Easter week (*Semana Santa*) in March or April
**April**
14  Day of the Americas (Honduras)
**May**
1  Labour Day
5  Battle of Puebla (Mexico)
24  Commonwealth Day (Belize)
**June**
30  Army Day (Guatemala)
**August**
3-6  El Salvador del Mundo (El Salvador)
**September**
1  Presidential address to the nation (Mexico)

10  National Day (Belize)
15  Independence Day (Guatemala, Honduras, El Salvador)
16  Independence Day (Mexico)
21  Independence Day (Belize)
**October**
3  Birth of Francisco Morazán (Honduras)
12  Discovery of America Day/Pan-America
20  Revolution Day (Guatemala)
21  Armed Forces Day (Honduras)
**November**
1  All Saints' Day (Mexico)
2  Day of the Dead (El Salvador, Mexico)
19  Garífuna Settlement Day (Belize)
20  Anniversary of the Revolution (Mexico)
**December**
12  Virgin of Guadalupe (Mexico)
24  Christmas Eve (Mexico)
25  Christmas Day
26  Boxing Day (Belize)

set up and the days are filled with processions, beauty contests and perhaps the odd marching band and plenty of fireworks, while the nights are dominated by dancing to merengue rhythms. In the Guatemalan and Chiapas highlands (and to a lesser extent in the Maya villages of Belize and Yucatán), where the bulk of the population is **Maya**, it's a different world. Here you'll see traditional dances, costumes and musicians, and a blend of religious and secular celebration that incorporates elements which predate the arrival of the Spanish. **Creole** celebrations are unabashedly hedonistic affairs, much more like a Caribbean carnival, with floats, earth-shaking reggae basslines, rum punch and plenty of grinding hips.

What they all share is an astonishing energy and an unbounded enthusiasm for drink, dance and fireworks, all three of which are virtually impossible to escape during the days of fiesta. One thing you shouldn't expect is anything too organized: fiestas are, above all, chaotic, and the measured rhythms of traditional dance and music are usually obscured by the crush of the crowd and the huge volumes of alcohol consumed by participants. If you join in the mood, there's no doubt that fiestas are wonderfully entertaining and that they offer a real insight into the region's culture, ladino or *indígena*. Guatemala has some of the most spectacular fiestas, and the best include some specifically local element, such as the giant kites at **Santiago Sacatepéquez**, the religious processions in **Antigua** and the horse race in **Todos Santos Cuchumatán**.

At certain times virtually the whole Maya region erupts simultaneously: **Semana Santa** (Easter week) is perhaps the most important, but **November 1 and 2** (All Saints' Day and the Day of the Dead) and **Christmas** are also marked by partying across the area. **Independence Day** in Guatemala, Honduras and El Salvador is September 15 – another huge day for processions and celebrations.

## MUSIC AND DANCE

**Music and dance combine many different influences, but yet again they can be broadly divided between indigenous, ladino and Creole. For the ladinos, it's merengue, salsa and Latin house that get the punters grooving, and for the Creoles it's reggae and soca, but in many indigenous areas, dance is usually confined to fiestas, and in the highland villages this means traditional dances, heavily infused with history and symbolism.**

At Maya fiestas, the drunken dancers may look out of control, but the process is taken very seriously and involves great expense on the part of the participants who have to rent their ornate costumes. The most common dance is the **Baile de la Conquista**, which re-enacts the victory of the Spanish, while at the same time managing to ridicule the conquistadors. According to some studies, the dance is based on pre-Columbian traditions. One of the most impressive dances is the **Palo Volador**, in which men swing by ropes from a thirty-metre pole. Today this is only performed in Chichicastenango, Joyabaj and Cubulco in Guatemala, and in isolated indigenous communities in Mexico, north of the Maya area.

Some of the best dancing you'll ever see is to the hypnotic drum patterns of **punta**, the music of the Garífuna, which betrays a distinctive West African heritage. Most Garífuna live on the Caribbean coast of Honduras, but there are also small communities at Lívingston in Guatemala and in Belize. If you get the chance to attend a punta party, be prepared for some explosively athletic shimmying and provocative hip movements – nineteenth-century Methodists were so outraged they called it "devil dancing". An excellent time to see **Garífuna drumming** and dance is November 19, Garífuna Settlement Day in Belize, and the best places to head for are either Dangriga or Hopkins.

**Traditional music** of either type is dominated by the **marimba**, a type of wooden xylophone that may well have originated in Africa (although some still argue that it developed independently in Central America). The oldest versions use gourds beneath the sounding board and can be played by a single musician, while modern models, using hollow tubes to generate the sound, can need as many as seven players. The marimba is at the heart of traditional music, and marimba orchestras play at every occasion, for both ladino and indigenous communities. In the remotest of villages you sometimes hear them practising well into the night, particularly around market day. Other important instruments, especially in Maya bands, are the *tun*, a drum made from a hollow log; the *tambor*, another drum traditionally covered with the skin of a deer; *los chichines*, a type of maracas made from hollow gourds; the *tzijolaj*, a kind of piccolo; and the *chirimia*, a flute.

**Ladino music** is a blend of North American and Latin sounds, drawing on **merengue**, a rhythm that originally came from the Dominican Republic, which includes elements of Mexican music and the cumbia and salsa of Colombia and Cuba. There are also plenty of local bands producing their own version of the sound. It's fast-moving, easy-going and very rhythmic, and on any bus you'll hear many of the most popular tracks.

In the Bay Islands, **reggae** is the sound you'll hear on the street. Much of the music comes from Jamaica and the Caribbean islands, though Belize does have its own thriving domestic scene.

# CRIME AND PERSONAL SAFETY

While political violence has decreased over recent years, crime rates throughout the region are rising alarmingly, especially in tourist locations. The majority of crime is petty theft – bag-snatching or pickpocketing – but some criminals operate in gangs and are prepared to use extreme violence to rob you.

**Guatemala** tops the list for tourist crime, closely followed by the north of **Honduras** and **El Salvador**; given the relatively small number of tourists in these last two, the probability of coming across trouble is that bit higher. **Mexico** and **Belize** are much safer in general, but incidents are rising in those countries too. Wherever you go you should take common-sense precautions, and if you've got valuables, make sure you insure them properly (see p.17).

## AVOIDING CRIME

You're more likely to be a **victim** of crime when you've just arrived, especially when you're looking for a room after dark – getting to your hotel in daylight will add greatly to your safety. Keep your most valuable possessions in a moneybelt under your outer clothes and don't wear expensive jewellery. Trousers with zipped pockets are a good idea for deterring pickpockets. Surprisingly, border crossings, where you'll often have to change money, aren't that dangerous, as the presence of armed officials generally discourages thieves in the immediate area of the immigration post. If at all possible do the transaction and put your money away out of sight of other people, and once away from the post, be on your guard. You should also beware of people helping you find a bus and offering to carry your luggage; in many cases they will genuinely be offering a service in return for a tip, but at times like this you're easily distracted and might not see your luggage disappear.

Travelling on **public transport**, particularly by bus, you'll usually be separated from your main bag: it will go either in the luggage compartment underneath or in the rack on top. This is usually safe enough (and you have little option in any case), but keep an eye on it whenever you can. Although the theft of the bag itself is uncommon, opportunist thieves may dip their hands into zippers and outer pockets. You can buy small padlocks for backpacks, but for even greater security, put your pack into a coffee or flour sack (*costal*) and put that into a net

## TRAVEL WARNINGS AND SAFETY INFORMATION

For **British travellers**, the **Foreign Office Travel Advice Unit** (☎020/7238-4503, Mon–Fri 9.30am–4pm; ☎01374/500900 for automated service, *foc.gov.uk/*) issues travel advice notices, which give a broadly accurate overview of the dangers facing visitors to Central America. They also produce a worthwhile leaflet for backpackers and independent travellers, which gives good advice and explains what a consul can and cannot do for you when you're abroad.

For **US travellers**, the equivalent is the **State Department's Consular Information Service** (*http://travel.state.gov/travel_warnings.html*), which publishes information sheets about each country, again listing fairly accurately the main dangers to US citizens. If any country is considered particularly dangerous, a travel warning will be issued,

though this may in fact simply indicate an isolated incident involving a US visitor. The advice contained in these pages is worth heeding, but don't be put off travelling completely – you could get into just as much danger in any big city at home.

You can always register at your **embassy** when (or even before) you arrive – phone numbers are listed in the guide. This is advisable if you're spending a long time in, or travelling to, remote areas of the region, though it's not necessary if you're on an organized tour. Always take photocopies of your passport and insurance documents and try to leave them in a secure place; leave a copy with someone at home too. A second credit card, kept in a very safe location and only to be used in emergencies, will be invaluable if your other cards or funds get stolen.

(*red*). It might look a little outlandish but it's the way the locals transport goods and keeps your rucksack clean and dry too. Sacks and nets are sold in any market. Once on the bus it's best to keep your small bag on your lap. If you do put it on the inside luggage rack, keep it in sight and tie it (or preferably clip it with a carabiner) onto the rack to deter thieves who may try to snatch it and throw it out of the window to an accomplice (it happens).

In your **hotel**, make sure the lock on your door works from the inside as well as out: in many budget hotels the lock will be a small padlock (*candado*) on the outside. It's a good idea to buy your own, though, so you're the only one with keys; they're readily available on street stalls. Many hotels will have a safe or secure area for valuables. If you use it, make sure that whatever you put in is securely and tightly wrapped; a spare, lockable moneybelt is good for this.

Muggings and armed robberies are not common, but when they happen there's little you can do about it, so prevention is essential. Avoid obviously dangerous areas – deserted **city centres** and **bus stations** late at night – just like you would at home. Watch out for anyone who surreptitiously throws an obnoxious liquid over your pack or clothes – it's probably a ploy for a "passer-by" to help you clean it up, while another member of the gang snatches your bag. Much more serious are the planned armed robberies on tourist minibuses and luxury buses in Guatemala and Mexico. The robbers will usually go round the passengers collecting money and valuables, but occasionally victims are taken

away and assaulted and even raped. For this reason some tour groups in Guatemala are accompanied by an armed guard.

## POLICE

If you have anything stolen, report the incident immediately to the **police**. If there is a tourist police force, try them first, if only to get a copy of the report (*denuncia*) for insurance purposes (see p.17). The police in these parts are poorly paid and you can't expect them to do much more than make out the report – often you'll have difficulty getting them to do even this. You may have to dictate it to them and sometimes they'll demand a fee for their services. If you don't speak Spanish, try to bring along someone who does. If you can, you should also report the crime to your **embassy** – it helps the consular staff build up a higher-level case for better protection for tourists.

Obviously you want to avoid any **trouble** with the police whatsoever. Practically every capital city has foreigners incarcerated for **drug** offences who'd never do it again if they knew what the punishment was like. Drugs of all kinds are readily available, but if you do indulge, be very discreet – the pusher may have a sideline reporting clients to the police, and catching "international drug smugglers" gives the country concerned brownie points with the DEA. If you are arrested your embassy will probably send someone to visit you and maybe find an English-speaking lawyer, but they certainly can't get you out of jail.

# WORK AND STUDY

There are opportunities to work and study in all the countries of the Maya region, with a huge number of development agencies and language schools based here. It's certainly possible to turn up and find a suitable language school without arranging things in advance, but if you're looking for development work it makes sense to plan ahead; some useful contacts are listed below. You should also check out the websites listed on p.50.

## WORK

There are probably thousands of opportunities for **voluntary workers** in development projects throughout the region. In most cases you'll need to have a useful skill, speak at least basic Spanish and be able to commit yourself for a couple of months.

The best place to look for a placement is on the **internet**: try *gapyear.com*, with a vast amount of information on volunteering generally, plus a huge, invaluable database on travel and living abroad; or check out a large site such as *idealist.org* to get an idea what's on offer – medical and health specialists are always desperately needed, though there are openings in other areas, from work helping to improve the lives of street children to environmental projects and wildlife conservation. Also well worth looking at is the comprehensive range of **books** and information published by *Vacation Work* (☎01865/241978, *vacationwork.co.uk*). Titles include *Directory of Summer Jobs Abroad*, *Taking a Gap Year* and *Work Your Way Around the World*, and there are many more; most are updated annually. The **Central Bureau for Educational Visits**, 10 Spring Gardens, London SW1A 2BN (☎020/7389-4880;*centralbureau .org.uk*) publish *A Year Between*, which contains useful sections on voluntary work placements in Central America. The US-based organization Transitions Abroad (PO Box 1300, Amherst, MA 01004; ☎413-256 3414, *transabroad.com*) publishes the informative *Work Abroad*, while the **Council on International Educational Exchange** (see Council Travel entry on p.50) also arranges and administers worldwide volunteer and study programmes and has information projects in the Maya region.

In the Maya region itself there are some excellent local organizations designed specifically to link voluntary workers with projects. In Guatemala, the **Project Mosaic Guatemala** 1 Av Sur 21, Antigua (☎813 5758, fax 832 7337, *pmg.dk; promigua@yahoo.com*) has links to over sixty groups, including projects to help street children and reforestation work. There's a second good drop-in resource centre in Antigua called **El Arco** at 5 Av Norte 25B (☎832 0162, fax 832-1540, *adventravelguatemala.com*, *elarco@guate.net*). The best place to head for in Quetzaltenango is the language school **Casa Xelajú** (see p.50) which has excellent contacts with dozens of development projects.

Most large organizations based outside the region charge fees to place volunteer workers, including *worldwide.edu* which has dozens of language schools in Mexico and Central America, with email links and student comments about the schools; *afs.org* also have plenty of projects to muse over; *earthwatch.org*, accepting volunteers worldwide, have environmental placements in the region, especially in Belize; while the Ecologic Development Fund (*ecologic.org;* US-based although accepting UK volunteers) also offer internships and volunteer opportunities. In the US, try **Volunteers for Peace**, 43 Tiffany Rd, Belmont, VT 05730 (☎802-259-2759, fax 802-259-2922, *vfp@vermontel.com*, *vermontel.com/~vfp/home.htm*), a non-profit group that organizes work camps in Honduras, Guatemala and Mexico.

## PROJECT WEBSITES AND EMAIL ADDRESSES

**Arcas** *arcaspeten@intelnet.net.gt* Volunteers needed in Guatemala to help rehabilitate animals illegally kept as pets for release back into the wild; and opportunities to help out in a sea turtle reserve on the Pacific coast.

**Ak'Tenamit** *aktenamit.org* Volunteer opportunities in health, education and agriculture in a large established project, working with Q'eqchi' Maya in Río Dulce region of Guatemala.

**Alternatives** *alternatives.ca* Canadian-based organization with development projects in Mexico and El Salvador.

**Amigos de Las Américas** *amigoslink.org* Community health initiatives in Mexico and Honduras.

**Belize Audubon Society** *belizeaudobon.org* Volunteer programme in protected areas and wildlife conservation.

**Belize River Archaeological Settlement Survey** *www.lsweb.sscf.ucsb.edu/projects/pilarweb* Field study programme at El Pilar.

**Casa Alianza** *casa-alianza.org* Charity which helps street children in Guatemala and Honduras; the work is extremely demanding and volunteers need to give a minimum six-month commitment.

**Casa Guatemala** *http://mayaparadise.com/casaguae.htm* Teachers, doctors, nurses and helpers needed to work with street kids and orphans in Río Dulce region.

**Casa Xelajú** *casaxelaju.com/volunteer* Language school which also has myriad opportunities and links to projects – including women's co-operatives and journalism placements – in Guatemala's Quetzaltenango region.

**Coral Cay Conservation** *coralcay.org.* Expeditions in the Bay Islands of Honduras to survey the reefs and establish a database for coastal zone management and proposed marine protected areas. Approximate costs range from £715 for two weeks to £2850 for twelve weeks, including a PADI scuba-diving course but excluding airfare.

**Council on International Educational Exchange** *ciee.org* Large US-based organization with myriad of voluntary programmes.

**Earthwatch** *earthwatch.org* Environmental placements including projects protecting cacti and orchids in Yucatán and manatees in Belize.

**Ecologic** *ecologic.org* Internships and volunteer opportunities in forestry projects in the highlands and Caribbean coast of Guatemala plus habitat protection initiatives in Honduras and Belize.

**Green Reef** *ambergriscaye.com* Volunteers, including divers, to conduct surveys of reef fish and to take part in educational programmes for schools in Belize.

**Guatemala Accompaniment Project** *nisguagap@igc.org* Monitoring the human rights and resettlement of returned refugees in Guatemala; minimum twelve-month commitment.

**Habitat for Humanity** *habitat.org/intl* One- to three-week house-building projects in all five countries of the Maya World.

**Hospital** *hospitaldelafamilia.org* Doctors, nurses and medical staff needed to help out in the Guatemalan highlands.

**Idealist** *idealist.org* Excellent place to start a search, with a massive database of links to a wide range of projects in Mexico and Central America; from ecotourism to human rights work, with both voluntary and paid work opportunities.

**International Voluntary Programs Association** *volunteerinternational.org* Dozens of voluntary opportunities throughout Central America in all fields.

**Peace Corps** *peacecorps.gov* Community-based development work in Belize, Guatemala, Honduras and El Salvador.

**Project Honduras** *projecthonduras.com/projectspage.htm* Dozens of voluntary work opportunities for medical staff, teachers, architects and builders.

**Siwa-Ban Foundation (SBF)** Ellen McRae, PO Box 47, Caye Caulker, Belize (☎022/2178, *sbf@btl.net*). Volunteers needed to work on biological surveys of the Caye Caulker Forest and Marine Reserve.

**Trekforce Expeditions** *trekforce.org.uk.* Runs projects in Belize ranging from surveys of remote Maya sites to infrastructure projects in national parks and village communities. Expeditions last two months (£2350) or five months (£3500); the longer programmes also involve learning Spanish in Guatemala and teaching in rural schools in Belize.

**Volunteers for Peace** *vfp.org* Large US-based non-profit group that organizes work camps in the region.

**Water Partners** *water.org/solution/project.* Work providing clean drinking water for impoverished villages in El Salvador, Honduras and Guatemala.

**Western Belize Regional Cave** *indiana.edu/~belize* Archeological research in Cayo District, Belize. Prior field school or caving experience preferred and volunteers/students must be in excellent physical condition.

**Wildlife Care Center of Belize** *wildlifecarecenter@yahoo.com.* Volunteer opportunities to work with confiscated and rescued native wildlife.

**Belize** has plenty of opportunities for voluntary work – mainly as a fee-paying member of a conservation expedition – or study, at an **archeological field school** (see opposite). These options generally mean raising a considerable sum for the privilege and committing yourself to weeks (or months) of hard work, often in difficult conditions. However, the Belize-based conservation organizations below simply require volunteers to be self-funded and self-motivated – and you may even get food and accommodation while you're volunteering.

There's very little **paid work** available in Central America. Your best bet is to approach language schools in the big cities for English teaching work (typically US$5–6 an hour); look for *academias de idiomas* in the telephone directory. You're much more likely to get employed if you can show previous experience or, ideally a TEFL qualification. Occasional vacancies also turn up in the English language press and on noticeboards in the popular bars and cybercafés in places like Antigua for teachers or people with computer or translation skills. There are some opportunities for scuba-divers qualified to PADI divemaster level to work in the dozens of dive schools and resorts in the region – head for Cozumel, the Belize cayes or the Bay Islands and start asking around. Finally in the main tourist centres there always seems to be the odd position for bartenders; the money's terrible and you'll get very few tips, but as as long as you don't expect to make a living, it can be a lot of fun.

## STUDY

The **Spanish-language-school** industry is a significant employer in a number of towns throughout the region, but especially in Guatemala. This is a superb part of the world to study the language, with dozens of excellent schools with extremely cheap rates. In addition, the Spanish spoken in the region is clearly pronounced and has few local dialects.

Most students opt for a study package that includes four or five hours' one-on-one daily tuition with a teacher and full board with a local family, but if you want to make your own accommodation arrangements or prefer to study for up to eight hours a day, this is usually possible. It's also possible to study in groups, though this is usually pre-arranged through a college or university.

The first consideration to make is **where to study**. If you're a complete beginner, it's best to choose a well-established centre such as Antigua (see p.351) or Quetzaltenango (see p.395) in Guatemala where the culture shock is less extreme. The lakeside Atitlán towns of Panajachel (see p.382) and San Pedro la Laguna (see p.385), San Cristóbal de las Casas in Mexico (see p.161) and Copán Ruinas (p.490) in Honduras, though less well-known, are also becoming important secondary centres. The disadvantage with these towns is that there are significant numbers of foreigners in all of them and it's very easy to find yourself speaking English in your spare time. If you already speak some Spanish and really want to accelerate your learning, consider living somewhere more isolated from gringo influence – good places include Cobán (see p.443), Huehuetenango (see p.401), San Andrés and San José near Flores (see p.455) in Guatemala or La Ceiba in Honduras (see p.508).

**Choosing a school** is the next step. Standards of tuition vary markedly, with some "schools" consisting of little more than a desk in someone's front room and an unqualified, inexperienced teacher, while at the other end of the spectrum there are establishments with superb library and video facilities, and highly experienced and motivated teachers. The schools themselves vary considerably: while some are purely profit-driven, many donate a proportion of profits to local development projects such as funding battered women's shelters, clean water initiatives or providing educational scholarships for poor kids. Often you get the chance to visit and learn about the social projects a proportion of your fees is helping to fund.

Virtually all schools also offer some kind of after-hours **activities**, with everything from salsa dancing classes to museum visits on offer. Usually there's no extra charge for these activities, or you get a discounted rate for more costly excursions like mountain biking or rock climbing trips. As the language school industry gets more and more competitive, many schools are now also offering their students additional incentives such as bargain-priced internet rates, discounted laundry facilities and so on.

Though your choice of school is obviously important, your progress in learning Spanish is more dependent upon your own commitment to study and the relationship with your **teacher**. Teaching standards do vary considerably, even in the best schools, so if you are not happy with the enthusiasm and aptitude of your teacher, ask for another. Another key issue is your choice of **accommodation** while you are studying. Most students choose the "full immersion" option whereby you live in the home of a local family and eat breakfast, lunch and dinner with your hosts six days a week (making your own eating arrangements on Sundays). This is an excellent way to really improve your conversational skills, as there's no escape and you're forced to start thinking in Spanish. Some schools offer a choice of accommodation, but in many places you'll simply be allocated a family house. It's essential to check how many other students will be sharing your house, as some schools pack as many as ten foreigners in with one family. Overcrowded houses are a particular problem in prosperous Antigua (see p.345), which suffers from a shortage of host families, but much less common in the other study centres.

By Western standards it's extremely cheap to study Spanish in the Maya region. Though **prices** vary a lot – between $95 and $180 a week for five hours a day one-on-one tuition, full family-based board and most daily after-classes activities – a majority of schools charge around US$130 a week for the above package. Alternatively, it's always possible to find your own accommodation and still enrol for classes; rates average around US$70 for twenty hours' tuition. Some schools increase their rates by around twenty percent in July and August, the most popular months.

To help you decide, you could consult *guatemala365.com* which rates towns as study centres and recommends schools, detailing facilities and educational standards based on students reports and research, or *spanish-schools.com* which also has a comprehensive list of schools in the region. An international organization with substantial involvement in the Maya area is the US-based **Amerispan**, PO Box 40007, Philadelphia PA 19106 (☎1-800/879-6640, *info@amerispan.com*, *amerispan.com*), which has a wide range of resources as well as information on language schools and volunteer opportunities.

# PART TWO

# SOUTHERN MEXICO

# INTRODUCTION

Southern Mexico, comprising the **Yucatán peninsula** and the states of **Chiapas** and **Tabasco**, is both physically and culturally quite distinct from the rest of Mexico, its unique character reflecting the vast distance that separates it from the administrative centre of the country, both past and present. Throughout the region Maya traditions continue to be observed despite years of oppression and the encroaching demands of tourism. It is also home to some of the most spectacular of the ancient **Maya sites**, with temples bursting through a forest canopy that stretches to the horizon. The natural scenery is equally stunning: rugged mountains and steamy jungles give way to beaches of coral sand as fine as white pepper, warm tropical rivers where crocodiles bask in the sun and gently cascading waterfalls of a hundred different blues.

Sticking out from Central America like a thumb, the Yucatán peninsula comprises three states: touristic Quintana Roo, fringed with some of the world's most beautiful beaches; Yucatán, where most of the famous Maya sites are found; and less developed Campeche to the west, whose fortified capital is one of the peninsula's most picturesque cities. The resort of **Cancún** in northern **Quintana Roo** is where most travellers arrive. Despite the imitation Maya pyramids housing hotels and burger bars, the city owes more to Miami than Mexico, with its string of swanky high-rise hotels. Cancún's real attraction, however, is the twenty kilometres of blinding white sand that fronts the hotels, and the numerous opportunities to have fun in the sun, albeit at a price. Fired by Cancún's success, countless new resorts have sprung up to form a tourist corridor along Hwy-307, which runs south as far as Tulum. Formerly backpacker havens, the tiny island of **Isla Mujeres**, just offshore from Cancún, and the beach town of **Playa del Carmen**, some 100km further south, are becoming more expensive and more crowded every year. **Isla Cozumel**, a short ferry ride from Playa, is similarly pricey and, with fewer beaches than the mainland, it is of real interest only to divers, who gather here in shoals to plunge over its dramatic undersea coral walls. Those on a tight budget shouldn't despair, though, as there are more affordable beach destinations near **Tulum**, the most perfectly situated of all Maya ruins. Perched on shallow cliffs like a sentinel above the aquamarine of the Caribbean, it's at its most magical at dawn, when it catches the rays of the morning sun.

**South of Tulum**, tourism has not yet gained a foothold and the coast is dotted with small fishing villages rather than resorts. Only a few kilometres west of the highway tiny hamlets of plaster and palm are inhabited by indigenous Maya, who continue to practise many of the traditions of their ancestors. The coastline along here remains covered in mangroves, populated by myriad birds, crocodiles, turtles and even the occasional manatee. The main town in these parts is the dusty state capital, **Chetumal**, which in itself has little to offer visitors other than easy access to Belize, though nearby attractions include the vast **Laguna Bacalar**, a lagoon of a thousand shades of green and blue. Further inland, this southern part of the peninsula is covered in lush **tropical forest** that extends into Guatemala. This was once the domain of the lowland Maya, and their great ruined metropolises – notably **Calakmul**, **Ró Bec, Kohunlich** and the moated city of **Becán** – litter the jungle.

The peninsula's **northern interior** is arid and flat, covered in scrubby jungle, with the only source of water being freshwater sinkholes known as **cenotes**. Here the legacy of the Spanish is evident in fine **colonial towns** such as **Mérida** and **Valladolid**, built with wealth generated by the hacienda system, and fortified **Campeche**, capital of the state that bears its name, originally built to protect the city from British and French pirates. Between Campeche and Mérida lies a host of Maya ruins. **Edzná**'s grand and lofty central pyramid looks out over a vast and empty central plaza to the endless flatness of the Yucatán. **Uxmal** and the **Puuc** sites are more subtle; their endlessly repeated intricate geometrical carvings, formed from tens of thousands of precisely positioned pieces of stone, are perhaps the Maya's most aesthetically satisfying architectural achievement. East of Mérida lies one of the best-known and most-visited of all Maya sites – **Chichén Itzá**. Thousands of tourists heave their way up the narrow steps of its perfectly symmetrical main temple every day, but after 4.30pm, when the streams of tour buses have left for Cancún and other Quintana Roo resorts, it's possible to have the place to yourself.

Southwest of the peninsula lies the state of **Chiapas**, home to some of Mexico's most diverse and spectacular landscapes. The great mountain ranges of the Sierra Madre Occidental and the Sierra Madre Oriental converge a little north of Chiapas, forming a ridge of peaks rising to over 2000m, clad with oak and pine and crested with volcanoes near **Tapachula** on the border with Guatemala. The remote slopes of these mountains form part of a protected national park, penetrated by roads only at its extremities, while the fertile soils of the narrow coastal plain create one of the state's richest agricultural areas. The volcanic sands of the **Pacific coast**, relentlessly hot despite being pounded by surf, see few foreign visitors now, though the village of **Puerto Arista** offers clean beaches and good-value accommodation. In ancient times, however, lagoons and canals immediately behind the coast provided a safe inland waterway linking the cultures of Mesoamerica.

Inland, the state capital **Tuxtla Gutiérrez** sprawls across the Central Valley, its mundane modernity a stark contrast to the Chiapas highlands, where rich landowners still practise a form of feudalism. Tuxtla is a major transport hub – the western gateway to the highlands – and boasts some fine museums and an excellent zoo. At the heart of the highlands, the elegant Spanish city of **San Cristóbal de las Casas**, the former state capital brimming with Maya life, is one of the major attractions of Chiapas. Women in multi-coloured *huipiles* and shawls fill the street markets and vats of maize steam into the thin mountain air. A visit to the nearby villages of **San Juan Chamula** or **Zinacantán** may feel to you like a trip back in time, but remember that here, non-indigenous people – Mexican and tourist alike – are considered to be relics of an earlier, failed creation and regarded as primitive by the Maya.

Beyond San Cristóbal, the highland road descends through pine trees into the deep moss green of rainforest, as it heads towards **Ocosingo**, a sleepy, red-tiled, ranchers' town and access point for **Toniná**, a large Maya site containing an astonishingly detailed mural and a breathtaking new museum. Beyond here the road passes hundreds of clear blue waterfalls at **Agua Azul** on its way towards the haunting jungle ruins of **Palenque**. Perched on the side of a ridge overlooking the vast expanse of the Yucatán plain that extends across Tabasco, the ruins are best seen at dawn, when thick cloud evaporating from the rainforest clears to expose the elegant white limestone temples and palaces. Lost in the jungle not far away are the ruins of **Bonampak**, reached through the **Lacandón forest**, and **Yaxchilán**, near the border with Guatemala, on the bank of the lazy **Río Usumacinta**, which winds its way across northern Chiapas into the swamps of Tabasco. These cities were built in the Classic period between 300 and 900 AD, making them contemporary with Calakmul and the Río Bec sites in southern Yucatán. Both Palenque and Yaxchilán are famous for the quality of their paintings, which demonstrate a use of perspective that predates its appearance in Europe by hundreds of years. The sculpture, too, is unequalled in Mesoamerica; though the best pieces have been moved to Mexico City, there is still a beautiful bust in the Palenque site museum.

The state of **Tabasco** is for the most part hot and steamy, very flat, and undeveloped for tourists. Numerous rivers descend from the highlands of Chiapas, meandering through Tabasco's swamps to the Gulf coast. These swamps are a haven for crocodiles and numerous species of bird, best seen by boat. Though the coast has plenty of **deserted beaches**, they border a grey Gulf of Mexico whose charms cannot compete with the turquoise waters of the Yucatecan Caribbean. In the far south of the state, the **Sierra Puana** highlands provide a retreat from the heat and humidity, while further west, in

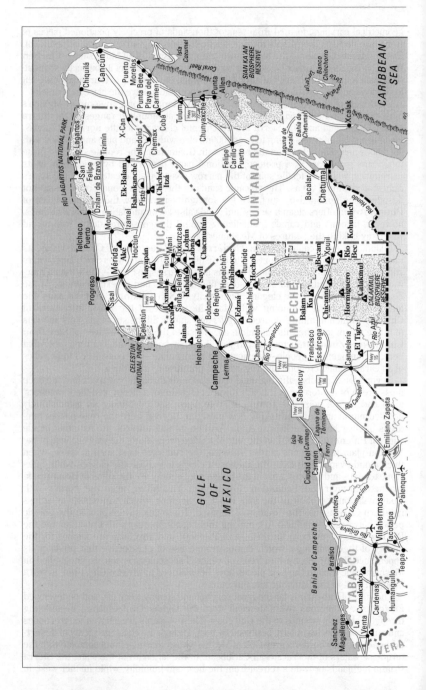

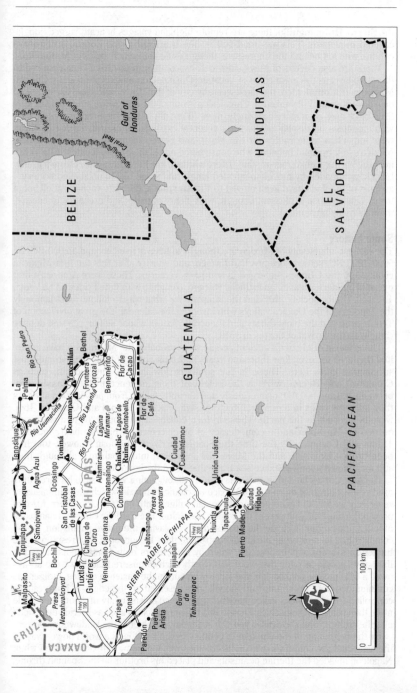

the **Sierra Huimanguillo**, there are remote highland villages beneath jagged, jungle-covered mountains. This was (and still is) the heartland of the **Zoque**, a non-Maya culture, who left behind the impressive, though difficult to reach, ruins of **Malpasito**.

There are also dozens of Maya sites in Tabasco, though few have been restored to the same level as the great cities of Yucatán. The outstanding exception is the Chontal Maya city of **Comalcalco**, the most westerly city of the Maya region and easily visited on a day-trip from Villahermosa. Comalcalco is one of the only Maya cities built of kiln-fired brick and, even more amazingly, most (if not all) of the bricks are works of art – with examples on display in the site's recently expanded museum. Tabasco's rivers were important trade routes for the Maya, and before them, the enigmatic **Olmec**, Mexico's first pyramid builders, who constructed one of their earliest cities at **La Venta** near the border with Veracruz state. There's little to see here now – apart from a grassy hillock surrounded by mosquito-infested jungle and some bits of unlabelled pottery – as most of the finds have been moved to **Villahermosa**, the state capital. An oil-boom town, Villahermosa is pleasant enough, with plenty of parks and greenery to complement its many museums.

## Some history

The earliest inhabitants of Mexico are thought to have arrived around 15,000 BC. By 5000–1500 BC, settled societies had formed, and shortly after this the first Mexican civilization, the **Olmecs**, emerged in southern Veracruz. These were America's first pyramid builders, creating an artificial volcano, complete with fluted sides, at La Venta, Tabasco. Olmec society provided the template for what was to follow, most famously the Zapotecs of the Oaxaca valleys who invented the calendar, the great civilization of Teotihuacán and the bloodthirsty and theocratic Aztecs whose self-prophesied demise came with the arrival of Cortés in 1519.

The greatest of Mexico's ancient people were probably the **Maya**, who have inhabited this area for over four thousand years and built some of their largest and most spectacular cities here. Those in the southern lowlands of the Yucatán, such as **Calakmul** and **Becán**, were at the height of their influence in the **Classic era**, between 300 and 900 AD, mysteriously and abruptly falling from power soon after. As they fell, new cities in a new architectural style, such as **Uxmal** and **Chichén Itzá**, were being built in the north. These in turn collapsed in about 1200 and were succeeded by **Mayapán** and a confederacy of other centres, which probably included Tulum and Cozumel. By the time the Spanish arrived, Mayapán's power, too, had been broken by revolt, and the Maya had splintered into tribalism – although they still maintained a long-distance sea trade that awed the conquistadors.

**Hernan Cortés** landed near Veracruz in 1519, beginning what was to be three hundred years of direct Spanish rule of Mexico (excluding Chiapas, which was administered separately as part of Guatemala until the early nineteenth century). Southern Mexico proved the most difficult part of the region to subdue. The Catholic Church, champions of indigenous rights, forbade the Spanish from enslaving the native population, so the colonists had to seek other means of controlling their labour force. The result was the **hacienda system** of debt peonage, whereby landowners rented small plots of land to the native people at rates that were sufficiently high to ensure that they were always owed a little money, paid back in the form of labour on the hacienda estates. Indigenous communities were broken up and the villagers resettled on the edges of huge estates controlled from mansions called haciendas by the colonists, many of whom were little more than peasants themselves. During this time grand cities such as Mérida developed into the architectural showcases you can see today, redolent of the landowners' power.

By the beginning of the nineteenth century, Spain's status as a world power was on the wane and the country's grip on its colonies was loosening. Mexico rebelled when Napoleon invaded the Iberian peninsula and placed his brother on the Spanish throne,

## FIESTAS IN MEXICO

### JANUARY

**1** New Year's Day: **San Andrés Chamula** (Chiapas) and **San Juan Chamula** (Chis), both near San Cristóbal, have civil ceremonies to install a new government for the year.

**6** Fiesta de Polk Keken in **Lerma** (Campeche), near Campeche, with many traditional dances.

**19** El Pochó dancers perform at **Tenosique** (Tab) dressed as jaguars and men to represent the struggle of good and evil. The celebration concludes on Shrove Tuesday with the burning of an effigy of El Pochó, god of evil.

**20** Día de San Sebastián sees a lot of activity. In **Chiapa de Corzo** (Chis) a large fiesta with traditional dances lasts several days, with a re-enactment on the 21st of a naval battle on the Río Grijalva. A big day too in **Zinacantán** (Chis), near San Cristóbal.

### FEBRUARY

**2** Día de la Candelaria. Colourful Maya celebrations at **Ocosingo** (Chis).

**11** Religious fiesta in **Comitán** (Chis).

**27** In **Villahermosa** (Tabasco), a fiesta commemorates the anniversary of a battle against the French.

**Week before Lent** Carnival is at its most frenzied in the big cities – especially **Villahermosa** (Tab) and **Mérida**, though it's celebrated too in Campeche and Chetumal and on Isla Mujeres and Cozumel and in hundreds of villages throughout the area. **San Juan Chamula** (Chis) has a big fiesta.

### MARCH

**Holy Week** is widely observed – particularly big ceremonies in **San Cristóbal de las Casas**. **Ciudad Hidalgo** (Chis), at the border near Tapachula, has a major week-long market.

**20** Feria de las Hamacas in **Tecoh** (Yuc), a hammock-producing village near Mérida.

**21** Equinox. Huge gathering to see the serpent shadow at **Chichén Itzá**.

### APRIL

**1–7** A feria in **San Cristóbal de las**

**Casas** (Chis) celebrates the town's foundation. A Spring Fair is generally held here later in the month.

**13** The traditional festival of honey and corn in **Hopelchén** (Cam) lasts until the 17th.

**29** Día de San Pedro celebrated in several villages around San Cristóbal, including **Amatenango del Valle** and **Zinacantán**.

### MAY

**3** Día de la Santa Cruz celebrated in **San Juan Chamula** (Chis) and in **Teapa** (Tab), between Villahermosa and San Cristóbal, **Hopelchén** (Cam), **Celestún** (Yuc) and **Felipe Carrillo Puerto** (QR).

**12–18** Fiesta in **Chankán Veracruz** (QR), near Felipe Carillo Puerto, celebrating the Holy Cross which spoke to the Maya here.

**15** Día de San Isidro sees peasant celebrations everywhere – famous and picturesque fiestas in **Huistán** (Chis), near San Cristóbal.

**Variable dates** A four-day nautical marathon from **Tenosique** to **Villahermosa** (Tab), when craft from all over the country race down 600km of the Río Usumacinta.

### JUNE

**24** Día de San Juan is the culmination of several days' celebration in **San Juan Chamula** (Chis).

### JULY

**7** Beautiful religious ceremony in **Comitán** (Chis), with candlelit processions to and around the church.

**25** Día de Santiago provokes widespread celebration – especially in **San Cristóbal de las Casas** (Chis), where they begin a good week earlier (17th is Día de San Cristóbal), and in nearby villages such as **Tenejapa** and **Amatenango del Valle**.

**Variable date** At **Edzná** (Cam) a Maya ceremony to the god Chac is held, to encourage, or celebrate, the arrival of the rains.

*continued overleaf*

**AUGUST**
30 Día de Santa Rosa celebrated in **San Juan Chamula** (Chis).

**SEPTEMBER**
14–16 Throughout Chiapas, celebration of the annexation of the state to Mexico, followed by independence celebrations everywhere.

14 Día de San Roman. In **Dzan** (Yuc), near Ticul, the end of a four-day festival with fireworks, bullfights, dances and processions – in **Campeche** (Cam) the Feria de San Roman lasts until the end of the month.

21 Equinox. Another serpent spectacle at **Chichén Itzá**.

29 Día de San Migual is celebrated with a major festival in **Maxcanu** (Yuc), on the road from Mérida to Campeche and in **Huistán** (Chis).

**OCTOBER**
**First Sunday** Día de la Virgen del Rosario is celebrated in **San Juan Chamula** and **Zinacantán** (Chis).

3 Día de San Francisco in **Amatenango del Valle** (Chis).

**First two weeks** Processions and celebrations associated with the miraculous statue of Cristo de las Ampillas in **Mérida**.

18 A pilgrimage centred on **Izamal** (Yuc) starts ten days of celebration, culminating in dances on the night of the 28th.

**NOVEMBER**
2 Day of the Dead is respected everywhere, with particularly strong traditions in **Chiapa de Corzo** (Chis).

**DECEMBER**
8 Día de la Inmaculada Concepción is widely celebrated, especially in **Izamal** (Yuc) and **Champotón** (Cam), each of which has a fiesta starting several days earlier.

12 Día de la Virgen de Guadalupe is an important one throughout Mexico. There are particularly good fiestas in **Tuxtla Gutiérrez** and **San Cristóbal de las Casas** (Chis), and the following day another in nearby **Amatenango del Valle** (Chis).

using the excuse of loyalty to the deposed king, Fernando. The first leader of the movement for independence was a Catholic priest, Miguel Hidalgo y Costilla, who uttered the famous battle cry – "Mexicanos! Viva Mexico!" However, it was Vicente Guerrero and Agustín de Iturbide who finally secured **independence** in 1821. Little changed for the peasants, however – the hacienda system continued, the land was still in the hands of the small Spanish-born population, and even the **Mexican Revolution** of 1910–17, fought in the name of land redistribution, failed to redress the balance.

The hacienda system has not been altogether unresisted, though: small rebellions pepper the nation's history. The most successful was the 1847 Maya insurrection against plantation owners in the Yucatán peninsula, popularly known as the **Caste Wars**. Outraged at the system of debt peonage and the continued annexation of communal land, a Maya army rose against its oppressors, and within a year the Maya had the Spanish under siege in the peninsula's two largest towns, Campeche and Mérida. Then, as the Maya were on the brink of creating an independent state, swarms of black ants appeared on the horizon, presaging rain, and despite opposition from the Maya generals, each soldier started for home to harvest his cornfield.

History repeated itself in 1994 when a Maya army calling themselves the **Zapatista Army of National Liberation** (EZLN), after Emiliano Zapata, an indigenous hero of the Mexican Revolution, occupied several cities in Chiapas, including San Cristóbal de las Casas. The EZLN demanded an end to debt peonage and the repeal of a law introduced by then President Salinas of the ruling PRI party permitting the sale of government-owned Maya communal land. Protracted negotiations over the intervening period have failed to arrive at a solution, with the legal recognition of indigenous rights acceptable to both the Zapatistas and the PAN government a seemingly perpetual stumbling block. For details see the box on p.139.

# CHAPTER ONE

# YUCATÁN AND CAMPECHE

T he three states that comprise the interminably flat, low-lying plain of the Yucatán peninsula – Yucatán itself, Campeche and Quintana Roo (covered separately in the following chapter) – are among the hottest and most tropical-feeling parts of Mexico, though they in fact lie further north than you might imagine: the sweeping curve of southern Mexico means that Mérida is actually north of the capital. Tourism has made major inroads, of course, especially in the north around the great Maya sites and on the route from Mérida to the resorts of the Quintana Roo coast, but away from the big centres and especially in Campeche state much of the country has been barely touched. And even in and around Mérida, a city large enough to have plenty of life of its own, it's easy to escape the tourist trail and find colonial towns, lesser-known ruins and the beaches the locals use.

Inevitably it is the Maya sites that prompt the most interest, and indeed the extraordinary concentration of superbly preserved centres, their relative ease of access and the variety of different architectural styles are unrivalled. **Mérida**, capital of Yucatán state, is the obvious initial base for exploration, and a vibrant and enjoyable city in its own right, with an attractive colonial centre, excellent market and food of every sort. Lying astride the chief **transport** artery of the region, Hwy-180, which heads east to Cancún via **Chichén Itzá** and southwest to Campeche and Villahermosa, Mérida also offers easy access to the northern coast and to **Uxmal** and a trove of smaller, less visited ruins in the south. Uxmal and Chichén Itzá, certainly, are must-sees, but don't ignore the smaller sites, such as **Kabáh**, **Edzná** near Campeche, or **Dzibilchaltún**, north of Mérida; less carefully cleared and maintained, but also less overrun with tourists, they offer a very different experience.

The road that runs across **the south** of the peninsula, from **Francisco Escárcega** to Chetumal, is relatively new, passing through jungle territory rich in Maya remains, several of which have recently been opened to the public for the first time. Though largely unexplored, these are beginning to see a trickle of visitors as access improves; you can get accommodation and arrange tours at **Xpujil**, a village named after the nearby archeological site, on the border between Campeche and Quintana Roo states.

## ACCOMMODATION PRICE CODES

All the accommodation listed in this book has been categorized into one of nine price bands, as set out below. The prices quoted are in US dollars and refer to the cheapest room available for two people sharing in high season.

| | | |
|---|---|---|
| ① under US$5 | ④ US$15–25 | ⑦ US$60–80 |
| ② US$5–10 | ⑤ US$25–40 | ⑧ US$80–100 |
| ③ US$10–15 | ⑥ US$40–60 | ⑨ over US$100 |

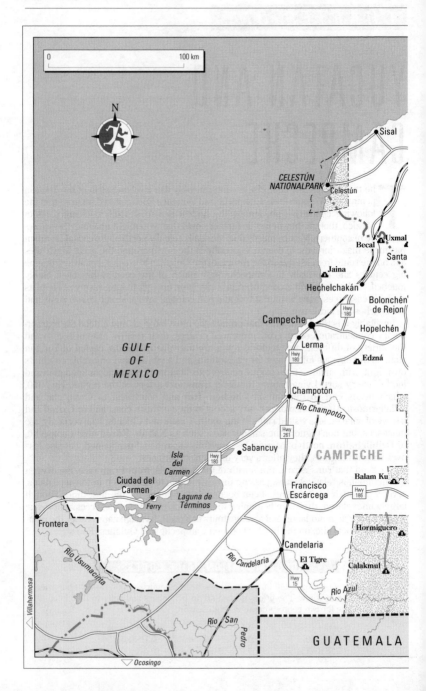

0    100 km

N

CELESTÚN
NATIONALPARK   Celestún

Sisal

Becal   Uxmal

Santa

Jaina

Hechelchakán

Bolonchén
de Rejon

Campeche   Hwy
180   Hopelchén

Lerma

Hwy
180   Edzná

GULF
OF
MEXICO

Champotón

Río Champotón

Hwy
261

Isla
del
Carmen   Hwy
180   Sabancuy   CAMPECHE

Ciudad del
Carmen   Laguna de
Términos   Francisco
Escárcega   Balam Ku

Ferry   Hwy
186

Frontera   Hormiguero

Río Usumacinta   Candelaria

El Tigre   Calakmul

Río Candelaria

Hwy
15   Río Azul

Villahermosa

Río San Pedro

GUATEMALA

Ocosingo

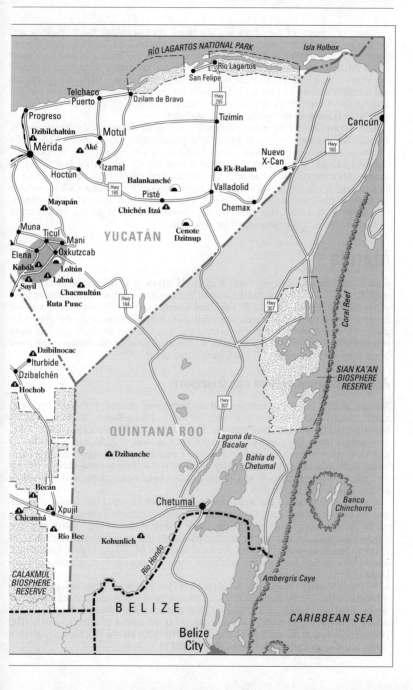

Along with some of the Maya World's finest pre-Columbian ruins, Yucatán and Campeche are scattered with the towns and haciendas built by their Spanish conquerors. This **colonial legacy** is everywhere. Many old haciendas and henequen (sisal) plantations are now open to the public as upmarket hotels, restaurants or simply tourist attractions in their own right, while almost every town and village has its church and arcaded square: Mérida itself is among the most impressive, or check out the impregnable fortifications of **Campeche**, the vast monastery dominating the Maya remains at **Izamal**, or the backwater of **Valladolid**.

As you travel around the peninsula, you'll see marked changes in the **landscape**. In Yucatán, the shallow, rocky earth gives rise to stunted trees – here, underground wells known as **cenotes** are the only source of water. At the opposite end of the scale, Campeche boasts a huge area of **tropical forest**, the Calakmul Biosphere Reserve, though this is steadily shrinking with the growing demand for timber and land for cattle ranching. While the **coastlines** of both states are great for spotting wildlife – notably the flocks of flamingos at Celestún and Río Lagartos – the beaches can't really compare with those in Quintana Roo. Best are the small-scale resorts on the Mérida coast around Progreso, mainly patronized by Mexicans.

# Mérida

Even if practically every road didn't lead to **MÉRIDA**, it would still be an inevitable stop. The "White City", capital of the state of Yucatán, is in every sense the leading town of the peninsula, and remarkably calm and likeable for all its thousands of visitors. Every street in the centre boasts a colonial church or mansion, while the plazas are alive with market stalls and free entertainment. You can live well here and find good beaches within easy reach, but above all it's the ideal base for excursions to the great Maya sites of Uxmal (see p.77) and Chichén Itzá (p.84).

## Arrival, information and city transport

Mérida is laid out on a simple **grid** of numbered streets: even numbers run north–south, odd from east to west, with the zócalo, **Plaza Mayor**, bounded by calles 60, 61, 62 and 63. Mérida's **bus stations** lie around the corner from each other on the west side of town. The relatively new first-class **Cameon**, C 70 55, between calles 69 and 71, is sparkling and air-conditioned, with a guardería. Some short-haul buses use minor terminals, but you're most likely to arrive at the busy **second-class** terminal, on Calle 69 between calles 68 and 70 which has a hotel reservations desk with some perfunctory tourist information.

City buses don't go all the way from the bus stations to the Plaza Mayor. To walk instead (about 20min), turn right outside the second-class bus station and you'll be on the corner of calles 68 and 69; the Plaza Mayor is three blocks north and four blocks east. Colectivos from the smaller places off the main highways terminate in Plaza de San Juan, on Calle 69 between calles 62 and 64. To get to the Plaza Mayor, leave Plaza de San Juan by the northeast corner and walk three blocks north up Calle 62.

Mérida's Manuel Cresencio Rejón **airport** is 7km southwest of the city, and houses a **tourist office** (daily 8am–8pm), post office, long-distance phones and car rental desks. To get downtown, take a colectivo (buy a ticket at the counter in front of the terminal) or bus #79 ("Aviación"), which drops off at the corner of calles 67 and 60.The post office is next to the market at Calle 65 between calles 56 and 56A. Most of Mérida's banks are also on Calle 65, between calles 60 and 64.

**ACCOMMODATION**

| | |
|---|---|
| Los Aluxes | 1 |
| Caribe | 10 |
| Casa Becil | 15 |
| Casa Bowen | 14 |
| Casa de Huéspedes Peniche | 13 |
| Casa del Balam | 4 |
| Casa Mexilio | 18 |
| Dolores Alba | 12 |
| Gran Hotel | 9 |
| Hotel del Parque | 8 |
| Margarita | 11 |
| Mucuy | 6 |
| Pantera Negra | 17 |
| Posada del Angel | 16 |
| Posada Toledo | 5 |
| Reforma | 7 |
| San Juan | 19 |
| Trinidad | 3 |
| Trinidad Galeria | 2 |

CENTRAL MÉRIDA

## Information

Mérida's main **tourist office** is in the Teatro Peón Contreras, on the corner of calles 60 and 57 (daily 8am–8pm; 9/924-9290, *www.cultur.com.mx*). Pick up a copy of the excellent *Yucatán Today* (or consult their Web site: *www.yucatantoday.com*) in English and Spanish, to find out what's going on in and around town; alternatively, *Discover Yucatán* has information on the whole region while *Restaurants of Yucatán* gives detailed reviews of the myriad eating and drinking venues in Mérida and surrounds. There are also plenty of leaflets available on surrounding attractions and you'll usually find some English-speaking staff. Other **tourist information booths** are in the Palacio de Gobierno on the Plaza Mayor, and on calles 59 and 64. Useful websites to check out in advance include *www.cityview.com.mx*, run by *El Diario de Yucatán* newspaper, and *www.merida.gob.mx*

## City transport

As traffic in Mérida is so congested, and most of the places of interest are within walking distance, it really isn't worth the bother of using public transport to get

---

### THE PUUC ROUTE BUS

While at Mérida's second-class bus terminal you may want to buy a ticket for a transport-only **day-trip** by bus around the **Puuc Route**, which can be difficult to visit without your own transport. Ask at the Autotransportes del Sur counter. The trip costs US$7.50 and leaves at 8am every morning, visiting Uxmal, Labná, Sayil, Kabáh and Xlapak. You get just long enough at each site to form a general impression, but there's no guide or lunch included in the price.

---

around in the centre – though it can be fun to hop onto one of the **horse-drawn carriages** that trot up and down the Paseo de Montejo; see p.69. However, to get out to some of the more far-flung sites (Palacio Cantón, for example), you may need to catch a bus. A number of buses leave from Calle 59 just east of the Parque Hidalgo; fares are around US$0.50. **Taxis** can be hailed all around town and from ranks at Parque Hidalgo, the post office, Plaza de San Juan and the airport. **Car rental** offices abound in Mérida, both at the airport and in the city (see "Listings" on p.72).

## Accommodation

There are hundreds of **hotels** in Mérida, many in lovely colonial buildings very near the centre, so that although the city can get crowded at peak times you should always be able to find a room. The very cheapest hotels are concentrated **next to the bus station**, a noisy and grimy part of town, while a string of upmarket hotels line **Paseo de Montejo**, just north of the centre, most of them ultra-modern and lacking in charm or personality; the best hotels lie in between, both geographically and in terms of value. A luxurious alternative is to stay outside town in a colonial hacienda, the closest of which is the seventeenth-century *Hacienda Katanchel*, at C 35 520 (☎9/923-4020, fax 923-4000, *www.hacienda-katanchel.com*), set in 750 acres and boasting individual pavilions and fresh-water wading pools. If you're happy to go further afield, ask at the tourist office for a full list of converted haciendas all over Yucatán (particularly recommended are the four haciendas run by the GMH group – though they do cost several hundred dollars a night; *www.ghmhotels.com*). For those on tight budgets the *Rainbow Maya* **trailer park**, 8km on the road to Progreso (☎9/926-1026; ②–③), has about 100 hook-ups, water and electricity. The head office is in the Canto Farmacía; to book ahead, write to them at C 61 468. Otherwise the best shoestring option in Mérida is the new and very attractive *Nomadas* **youth hostel**, C 62 433 at the junction with C 51 (☎9/924-5223, fax 928-1697, *www.hostels.com.mx*; ②), which is centrally located and run by friendly and helpful, English-speaking staff.

### Near the bus station

**Casa Becil,** C 67 550C, between calles 66 and 68 (☎9/924-6764). Friendly place, popular with North Americans and convenient for the bus station. ③.

**Casa Bowen,** C 66 521B, between calles 65 and 67 (☎9/928-6109). A travellers' favourite for years, this restored colonial house is set around a bright, pleasant courtyard. Spartan but acceptable rooms with baths (some with a/c), and two apartments with kitchens. ④.

**Casa Mexilio,** C 68 495, between calles 59 and 57 (reservations in US ☎1-800/583-6802, *www.mexicoholiday.com*). Quite possibly the most beautiful hotel in Mexico – each of the eight rooms in a restored colonial townhouse is individually decorated; tranquil gardens, sun terraces and pool. Delicious breakfast included in the rates. Highly recommended. ⑥–⑧.

**Pantera Negra,** C 67 547B, between calles 68 and 70 (☎ & fax 9/924-0251, *caractarint@hotmail.com*). One of the most charming hotels in town for any budget, in an intimate and idiosyncratically decorated colonial house, just a block from the bus station. ④.

**Posada del Ángel**, C 67 535, between calles 66 and 68 (☎9/923-2754). Quiet and comfortable, with parking and restaurant. ④.

## In the centre

**Los Aluxes**, C 60 444 (☎9/924-2199, fax 923-3858, *www.aluxes.com.mx*). Big, modern and expensive luxury hotel with all anyone could possible want. ⑨.

**Caribe**, C 59 500, Parque Hidalgo (☎9/924-9022, fax 924-8733, *www.hotelcaribe.com.mx*). In a small plaza a block from the Plaza Mayor, this place has a lovely patio restaurant and views of the cathedral and plaza from the rooftop pool. Travel agency; parking. ⑤.

**Casa del Balam**, C 60 488 (☎9/924-2150, fax 924-5011, *www.yucatanadventure.com.mx*). Luxury, ambience and beautifully furnished rooms, all with a/c, in a central location. The particularly pleasant bar has *mariachi* crooners in the evening. Travel agency and car rental; parking. ⑧.

**Casa de Huéspedes Peniche**, C 62 507, just off the zócalo (☎9/928-5518). Shambling but fascinating once-grand colonial house, with original paintings, a staircase out of *Gone with the Wind* and huge, bare rooms (bring a padlock). All very atmostpheric, if in need of a serious spring clean. ②.

**Dolores Alba**, C 63 464 (☎9/928-5650, fax 928-3163, *www.doloresalba.com*). Popular mid-range hotel arranged around two courtyards and a large swimming pool. Rooms have TV, telephone and a/c. Parking and restaurant. Good value. ⑤.

**Gran Hotel**, C 60 496, Parque Hidalgo (☎9/924-7730, fax 924-7622, *www.granhoteldemerida.com.mx*). Colonnades, fountains, palms and statues all ensure that the *Gran* lives up to its name. Rooms, all with private shower, are well furnished, often with antiques. ⑥.

**Hotel del Parque**, C 60 495, Parque Hidalgo (☎9/924-7844, fax 928-1929). Lovely old building just off the main plaza. Some rooms need improvement and those at the back are quieter. You can dine in intimate little balconies in the restaurant, *La Bella Epoca*. ⑤.

**Margarita**, C 66 506, between calles 61 and 63 (☎9/923-7236). Budget favourite; small but clean rooms and good rates for groups. ②.

**Mucuy**, C 57 481, between calles 56 and 58 (☎9/928-5193, fax 928-7801). Quiet, well-run and pleasant hotel, with clean, good-value rooms. English-speaking staff and a selection of books in English. ③.

**Posada Toledo**, C 58 487 (☎9/923-1690, fax 923-2256; *hptoledo@finred.com.mx*). Superb, beautifully preserved nineteenth-century building. The rooms, all with private shower and some with a/c, are filled with antiques and the courtyard is a delight. Ask for a room downstairs, though – those upstairs are new with low ceilings. ⑤.

**Reforma**, C 59 508 (☎9/924-7922, fax 928-3278, *www.leisureplanet.com*). Long-established, recently restored hotel in a colonial building. Rooms are arranged around a cool courtyard and there's a relaxing poolside bar and parking available. Good prices on guided day-trips to Uxmal and on the *Ruta Puuc*. ⑤.

**San Juan**, C 62 545A, between calles 69 and 71 (☎9/923-6823). A variety of good-value rooms in a listed colonial house, run by a very knowledgeable and friendly Méridan. Free internet, faxes, juice and coffee for guests, plus – for a fee – fascinating tailor-made eco-tourist trips and archeological tours with professional archeologists working in the field. Prices include breakfast. ⑤.

**Trinidad**, C 62 46, between calles 55 and 57 (☎9/923-2033, *ohm@sureste.com*). A wide range of rooms and a plant-filled courtyard. Decorated with modern paintings and antiques. Continental breakfast included and use of pool at *Trinidad Galeria*, run by the same people. ⑤.

**Trinidad Galeria**, C 60 456 at the junction with C 51 (☎9/923-2463, fax 924-2319, *manolor@sureste.com*). Wonderfully eccentric hotel crammed full of interesting artefacts and paintings and favoured by visiting artists. Rooms upstairs are lighter and more spacious. Pool and small breakfast café. Two art galleries on site. ④.

# The City

Founded by Francisco de Montejo (the Younger) in 1542, Mérida is built over, and partly from, the ruins of a Maya city known as **Tihó**. Although, like the rest of the peninsula, it had little effective contact with central Mexico until the completion of road and rail links in the 1960s, trade with Europe brought wealth from the earliest days. In consequence the city looks more European than almost any other in Mexico – many of the older houses, indeed, are built with French bricks and tiles, brought over as tradeable ballast in the ships that exported henequen. Until the advent of artificial fibres, a substantial proportion of the world's rope was manufactured from Yucatecan henequen, a business that reached its peak during World War I.

In 1849, during the Caste Wars, the Maya armies besieging Mérida were within a hair's breadth of capturing the city and thus regaining control of the entire peninsula, when the Maya peasants left the fight in order to return to the fields to plant corn. It was this event, rather than the pleas of the inhabitants for reinforcements, that saved the elite from defeat and brought Yucatán under Mexican control. Around the turn of the twentieth century, Mérida was an extraordinarily wealthy city – or at least a city that had vast numbers of extremely rich landowners riding on the backs of a landless, semi-enslaved peonage – a wealth that went into the building of the grandiose mansions of the outskirts (especially along the Paseo de Montejo) and into European educations for the children of the *haciendados*. Today, with that trade all but dead, Yucatán's capital nevertheless remains elegant and bustling, its streets filled with Maya going about their daily business.

## Plaza Mayor

Any exploration of Mérida begins naturally in the **Plaza Mayor**. The hub of the city's life, it's ringed by some of Mérida's oldest buildings, dominated by the **Catedral de San Idelfonso** (daily 6am–noon & 5–8pm), which was built in the second half of the sixteenth century. Although most of its valuables were looted in the Revolution, the **Cristo de las Ampillas** (Christ of the Blisters), in a chapel to the left of the main altar, remains worth seeing. This statue was carved, according to legend, from a tree in the village of Ichmul that burned for a whole night without showing the least sign of damage; later, the parish church at Ichmul burned down and the statue again survived, though blackened and blistered. The image is the focal point of a local fiesta at the beginning of October. Beside the cathedral, separated from it by the Pasaje San Alvarado, the old bishop's palace has been converted into shops and offices.

Next door to the cathedral is the **MACAY** (Museo de Arte Contemporáneo de Yucatán; daily except Tues 10am–6pm; US$2, free on Sun), the finest art museum in the state, with permanent displays of the work of internationally acclaimed Yucatecan artists such as Fernando Castro Pacheco, Gabriel Ramírez Aznar and Fernando García Ponce. Temporary exhibitions often include ceramics from around the region, Yucatecan embroidery and metallic art. On the south side of the plaza stands the **Casa de Montejo**, a palace built in 1549 by Francisco de Montejo himself and inhabited until 1980 by his descendants. It now belongs to Banamex, and most of the interior is now used as offices and closed to the public. The facade is richly decorated in the Plateresque style, and above the doorway conquistadors are depicted trampling savages underfoot. The **Palacio Municipal**, on the third side of the plaza, is another impressive piece of sixteenth-century design with a fine clock tower, but the nineteenth-century **Palacio de Gobierno** (daily 8am–10pm), completing the square, is more interesting to visit. Inside, murals depict the history of the Yucatán and, on the first floor, there's a large airy room devoted to the same subject.

## North of the Plaza Mayor

Most of the remaining monuments in Mérida lie north of the zócalo, with Calle 60 and later the Paseo de Montejo as their focus. Calle 60 is one of the city's main commercial streets, lined with several of the fancier hotels and restaurants. It also boasts a series of colonial buildings, starting with the seventeenth-century Jesuit **Iglesia de Jesús**, between the Plaza Hidalgo and the Parque de la Madre. Beside it on Calle 59 is the

Cepeda Peraza Library, full of vast nineteenth-century tomes; a little further down Calle 59, the **Pinacoteca Virreinal** houses a rather dull collection of colonial artworks and modern sculptures in a former church. Continuing up Calle 60, you reach the **Teatro Peón Contreras**, a grandiose Neoclassical edifice built by Italian architects in the heady days of Porfirio Díaz and recently restored. The **university** is opposite. One block north of the Teatro Peón Contreras, the sixteenth-century **Iglesia Santa Lucía** stands on the elegant plaza of the same name – a colonnaded square that used to be the town's stage-coach terminal. Three blocks further on, there's the **Plaza Santa Ana**, a modern open space where you turn right and then second left to reach the Paseo de Montejo.

To the east of centre, the **Museo de Arte Popular** (Tues–Sat 9am–8pm, Sun 8am–2pm; free) in the former monastery of La Mejorada, Calle 59 between calles 50 and 48, displays a fine collection of the different styles of indigenous dress found throughout Mexico. The rich wood and glass cases show *huipiles* (the long white dresses embroidered with colourful flowers at the neck, worn by Maya women), jewellery and household items, while old black-and-white photos provide glimpses of village life and ceremonials. At the rear of the museum you can stock up on souvenirs at the really good artesanía shop.

## Paseo de Montejo

The **Paseo de Montejo** is a broad, tree-lined boulevard lined with the magnificent, pompous mansions of the grandees who strove to outdo each other's style (or vulgarity) around the turn of the century. Occupying one of the grandest, the Palacio Canton, at the corner of Calle 43, is Mérida's **Museo de Antropología** (Tues–Sat 9am–8pm, Sun 8am–2pm; US$2.50, free on Sun). The house was built for General Canton, state governor at the turn of the century, in a restrained but costly elegance befitting his position, and has been beautifully restored and maintained. Given the archeological riches that surround the city, the collection is perhaps something of a disappointment, but it's a useful introduction to nearby sites nonetheless, with displays covering everything from prehistoric stone tools to modern Maya life. Obviously there are sculptures and other objects from the main sites, but more interesting are the attempts to fill in the background and give some idea of what it was like to live in a Maya city; unfortunately, most labels are in Spanish only. Topographic maps of the peninsula, for example, show how cenotes are formed and their importance to the ancient population; a collection of skulls demonstrates techniques of deliberate facial and dental deformation to suit Maya tastes (teeth filed into points, foreheads reshaped); and there are displays covering jewellery, ritual offerings and burial practices, as well as a large pictorial representation of the workings of the Maya calendar. The **bookshop** has leaflets and guidebooks in English to dozens of ruins in Yucatán and the rest of Mexico.

The walk out **to the museum** is quite a long one – you can get there on a "Paseo de Montejo" bus from Calle 59 just east of the Parque Hidalgo, or take a **calesa** (horse-drawn taxi; US$10 for a forty-five minute city tour) instead. This is not altogether a bad idea, especially if you fancy the romance of riding about in an open carriage, and if times are slack and you bargain well, it need cost no more than a regular taxi. Unfortunately, however, the horses are not always treated as well as they could be. Take some time to head a little further out on the Paseo de Montejo, to a lovely and very wealthy area where the homes are more modern and interspersed with big new hotels and pavement cafés. The **Monumento a la Patria**, about ten long blocks beyond the museum, is a titan, covered in neo-Maya sculptures relating to Mexican history – you'll also pass it if you take the bus out to Progreso. To do the Grand Tour properly, you should visit the **Parque de las Americas**, on Avenida Colón, which is planted with trees from every country on the American continent, and get back to the centre via the **Parque Centenario**, Av de los Itzaes and C 59, where there's a zoo, botanical gardens and a children's park.

## Markets and handicrafts

Mérida's **market**, a huge place between calles 65, 67, 56 and 54, is for most visitors a major attraction. As far as quality goes, though, you're almost always better off buying in a shop – prices are no great shakes, either, unless you're an unusually skilful and determined haggler. Before buying anything, head for the **Casa de Artesanías** in the Casa de la Cultura del Mayab on Calle 63 west of the zocalo, which also houses the **Museo de la Canción Yucateca** (Tues–Sat 9am–8pm; free), a small collection of photos of Yucatecan composers, with recordings of their music and occasional live performances. Run by the government-sponsored Fonapas organization, the shop sells crafts from the peninsula, which are of a consistently high quality, right down to the cheapest trinkets and toys.

The most popular purchase is a **hammock** – and Mérida is probably the best place in the country to buy one – but if you want something you can realistically sleep in, exercise a degree of care. There are plenty of cheap ones about, but comfort is measured by the tightness of the weave (the closer-packed the threads the better) and the breadth; since you're supposed to lie in them diagonally, in order to be relatively flat, breadth is far more crucial than the length (although obviously the central portion of the hammock should be at least as long as you are tall). A decent-sized hammock (*doble* at least, preferably *matrimonial*) with cotton threads (*hilos de algodon*, more comfortable and less likely to go out of shape than artificial fibres) will set you back at least US$20 – more if you get a fancy multicoloured version. Don't buy a hammock from street vendors or a market stall – they're invariably of poor quality. Far better is to head for a **specialist dealer**, most of which aren't far from the market. Tejidos y Cordeles Nacionales is one of the best, very near the market at C 56 516B. More of a warehouse than a shop, it has hundreds of the things stacked against every wall, divided up according to size, material and cost. Buy several and you can enter into serious negotiations over the price. Similar hammock stores nearby include El Campesino and El Aguacate, both on Calle 58, and La Poblana at C 65 492.

Other good **buys** include tropical shirts (*guayaberas*), panama hats (known here as *jipis*) and *huipiles*, which vary wildly in quality, from factory-made, machine-stitched junk to hand-embroidered, homespun cloth. Even the best, though, rarely compare with the antique dresses that can occasionally be found: identical in style (as they have been for hundreds of years) but far better made and very expensive.

# Eating

Good **restaurants** are plentiful in the centre of Mérida, though those on the Plaza Mayor can be quite expensive. Best head for the historic and atmospheric area around the **Plaza Hidalgo**, just north, along Calle 60 between calles 61 and 59, where you'll find plenty of good restaurants and pavement cafés, lively with crowds of tour groups and locals. Further afield, on **Paseo de Montejo**, are the more expensive and sophisticated restaurants including lots of upmarket places popular with young locals.

There are a number of less expensive places around the junction of calles 62 and 61, at the northwest corner of the Plaza Mayor, but cheapest of all are the *loncherías* in the **market**, where you can get good, filling comidas corridas. Also around the Plaza Mayor several wonderful **juice bars** – notably *Jugos California* – serve all the regular juices and licuados, as well as more unusual local concoctions: try mamey, a fruit with sweet pink flesh, or guanabana, like a large custard apple. Other branches are dotted about the city. Combine these with something from the **bakery** Pan Montejo, at the corner of calles 62 and 63, to make a great breakfast.

**Alberto's Continental Patio**, C 64 482 at the junction with C 57 (☎9/928-5367). Delicious international cuisine including Yucatecan/Mexican and specializing in Lebanese food. The setting in an internal leafy courtyard is very pretty. For special occasions only – the menu is pricey.

## YUCATECAN CUISINE

Yucatecan cuisine is widely considered to be one of Mexico's best, noted for its subtlety and less fiery flavours. Typical **specialities** include *puchero*, a stew of chicken, pork, carrot, squash, cabbage, potato, sweet potato and banana chunks with a delicious stock broth, garnished with radish, coriander and Seville orange; *poc-chuc*, a combination of pork with tomatoes, onions and spices; *sopa de lima* (not lime soup, exactly, but chicken broth with lime and tortilla chips in it); *pollo* or *cochinita pibil* (chicken or suckling pig wrapped in banana leaves and cooked in a *pib*, basically a pit in the ground, though restaurants cheat on this); *papadzules* (tacos stuffed with hard-boiled eggs and covered in red and green pumpkin-seed sauce); and anything *en relleno negro*, a black, burnt-chile sauce. Little of this is hot, but watch out for the *salsa de chile habanero* that most restaurants have on the table – pure fire.

**Las Almendras**, C 50, between calles 57 and 59, in the Plaza Mejorada. One of Mérida's most renowned restaurants, popular with locals and visitors. Delicious, moderately priced Yucatecan food; especially good deal at Sunday lunchtime. The original *Las Almendras*, in Ticul, claims to have invented *poc-chuc* (see box above).

**Restaurante Amaro**, C 59 507, between calles 60 and 62. Set in a lovely stone-flagged tree-shaded courtyard with a fountain. Some vegetarian menus, offering a welcome change for veggies who are tired of endless quesadillas.

**Café La Habana**, C 59 511A, at the junction with C 62. Popular, buzzing 24-hour corner café with excellent coffee and reasonably priced meals.

**El Patio Español**, *Gran Hotel*, C 60, Parque Hidalgo. Historic restaurant offering good, surprisingly well-priced food, and great service. As the name indicates, Spanish dishes are a speciality.

**Café Peón Contreras**, C 60, adjacent to the Teatro Peón Contreras. One of the most pleasant outdoor spots in the city, serving decent Mexican food and pizza. A great place to watch the world go by in relative peace.

**Cafetería Pop**, C 57, between calles 60 and 62. The best breakfast joint in town, which also serves hamburgers, spaghetti and Mexican snacks.

**El Portico del Peregrino**, next door to *Cafeteria Pop*. Classy series of indoor and outdoor patios specializing in Yucatecan cuisine.

**Pizzería de Vito Corleone**, C 59 508, corner of C 62. Inexpensive and friendly pizza restaurant that also does takeaway.

**La Reina**, Parque de Santiago, C 59 between calles 70 and 72. Local café serving excellent home-made Mexican staples at super cheap (US$2.50 for lunch including drink) prices.

**El Rincón**, in the *Hotel Caribe*, C 60, on the corner of Parque Hidalgo. Both this and the cheaper *Cafetería El Meson*, in the same building, are good, central places to eat in pleasant surroundings.

**Restaurant Santa Lucia**, C 60 481, between calles 55 and 57. Atmospheric little restaurant with comprehensive Mexican menu and specializing in steak and fish. Occasional live music.

## Entertainment and nightlife

Mérida is a lively city, and every evening you'll find the streets buzzing with revellers enjoying a variety of **free entertainment**. To find out what's happening, pick up a free copy of *Yucatán Today* from the tourist office or any hotel. **Venues** include the plazas, the garden behind the Palacio Municipal, the Teatro Peón Contreras (next to the tourist office) and the Casa de la Cultura del Mayab, Calle 63 between calles 64 and 66. Things can change, but typical performances might include energetic **vaquerías** (vibrant Mexican folk dances, featuring different regional styles, to the rhythm of a *jaranera* band); Glenn Miller-style **Big Band** music; **marimba** in the Parque Hidalgo; **classical music** concerts; and the very popular **Serenata Yucateca**, an open-air performance of traditional songs and music.

Perhaps the best time to see the Plaza Mayor and the surrounding streets is **Sunday**, when vehicles are banned from the area and day-long music, dancing, markets and festivities take over – a delight after the usual traffic roar. Street markets are set up along Calle 60 as far as the Plaza Santa Ana and there's a **flea market** in the Parque Santa Lucía.

There's plenty to do of a more commercial nature too, from **mariachi nights** in hotel bars to **Maya spectaculars** in nightclubs. Those aimed at tourists will be advertised in hotels, or in brochures available at the tourist office. By far the best of these events is the **Ballet Folklorico de la Universidad de Yucatán**'s wonderful interpretation of traditional Mexican and Maya ceremonies at the Centro Cultural Universitario, at the junction of calles 60 and 57 (Fri only at 9pm; US$2). There are **video bars** and **discos** in most of the big hotels.

Apart from the hard-drinking *cantinas* (and there are plenty of these all over the city – including a couple of good ones on Calle 62, south of the plaza), many of Mérida's **bars** double as restaurants.

### Bars, discos and live music

**Ay Cara!**, C 60, between calles 55 and 57. Popular and noisy upstairs bar with live music, pool table and a younger crowd.

**Azul Picante**, C 60, between calles 55 and C 57. Salsa club with on-site lessons and Mexican- and Caribbean-themed nights.

**La Ciudad Maya**, C 84 502, corner of C 59 (☎9/924-3313). Floor shows with Yucatecan and Cuban music. Daily 1–10pm.

**Estudio 58**, C 58, between calles 55 and 57, next to and underneath the *Hotel Maya Yucatán*. Central disco and nightclub with no cover charge. Live music and a happy hour, 9.30–10.30pm.

**Pancho's**, C 59, opposite the *Hotel Reforma*. A steak restaurant with a pricey Tex-Mex menu and a disco later – it's a magnet for Americans homesick for "Mexican" food. The fun theme, with giant photos of Mexican revolutionaries and bandolier-draped waiters in sombreros, is ridiculously over the top. Try to hit the "happy hour", 6–9pm.

**La Prosperidad**, C 56, corner of C 53. Earthier than the tourist bars, though becoming ever more popular. It's in a huge *palapa*, with live rock music in the afternoons and evenings. The beer's not cheap but it does come with substantial tasty snacks.

**Vatzya**, Paseo Montejo 451 and Av Colon, in the *Hotel Fiesta Americana*. Hotel nightclub with oldies' evening every Wednesday featuring sounds of the 70s and 80s.

## Listings

**Airlines** Aerocaribe/Aerocozumel/Mexicana Inter, Paseo de Montejo 500 (☎9/928-6790; airport ☎9/946-1678; *www.aerocaribe.com*); Aeroméxico, Plaza Americana, *Hotel Fiesta Americana* (☎9/920-1260; airport 946-1400); Aviacsa, Prolongacion Montejo 130 (☎9/926-9087; airport 946-1378); Aviateca, Paseo de Montejo 475C (☎9/925-8059; airport 946-1296); Mexicana, Paseo de Montejo 493 (☎9/924-6633; airport 946-1332).

**American Express** Paseo de Montejo 95, between calles 43 and 45 (Mon–Fri 9am–5pm, Sat 9am–noon; ☎9/928-4222).

**Banks** Most banks are around C 65 between calles 60 and 64, have ATMs and open 9am–4pm. The most centrally located is Banamex in the Casa de Montejo on the south side of the zócalo.

**Books** English-language guidebooks are sold at Dante Touristic Bookstore on the corner of calles 57 and 60. Alternatively borrow English-language books from the Mérida English Library, C 53 between calles 66 and 68, which also functions as a meeting point for the city's ex-pat community.

**Car rental** Budget, at the *Holiday Inn* (☎9/925-6877, airport 946-1393); Hertz, at the airport (☎9/946-13-55); National, C 60 486F (☎9/923-24-93, airport 946-13-94).

## MOVING ON FROM MÉRIDA

Mérida is a major transport hub, especially if you're travelling on **by bus**. Most major destinations are served from the main first- and second-class stations, but some places are better served from the multitude of different little stations dotted around town.

From the first-class **Cameon**, the most important routes run by **ADO** are to Campeche, Mexico City, Palenque and Villahermosa. **Caribe Express** provides a comfortable, a/c service with videos to Campeche and Villahermosa, as well as Cancún, Escárcega, Playa del Carmen and a number of other destinations. There are also services to Akumal, Villahermosa, Tulum and Playa del Carmen run by **Autotransportes del Caribe**. Both Caribe Express and Autotransportes del Caribe also have desks in the main first- and second-class buildings.

Buses from the **second-class** station, on C 69 between calles 68 and 70, leave for **Campeche** (Autotransportes de Sureste; 4hr); **Cancún** (Expreso de Oriente; 6hr); **Escárcega** (Autotransportes de Sureste; 6hr); **Palenque** (Autotransportes de Sureste; 10–11hr); **Playa del Carmen** (Expreso de Oriente; 7hr); **Tuxtla Gutiérrez** (Autotranportes de Sureste; 20hr); **Valladolid** (Expreso de Oriente; 3hr); and **Villahermosa** (Autotransportes de Sureste; 10hr).

Of Mérida's **smaller bus stations**, C 50 on the corner with C 67 serves Autobuses de Occidente en Yucatán, for destinations west of Mérida, and Lineas Unidos del Sur de Yucatán: buses leave for **Celestún** (hourly 5am–8pm; 2hr), **Oxkutzcab** (hourly) and **Sisal** (hourly; 2hr). Autobuses del Noreste en Yucatán leave from C 50 529, between calles 65 and 67, for **Río Lagartos** (6hr), San Felipe (7hr) and Tizimín (4hr). Directly opposite, Autotransportes de Oriente leave for **destinations inland and east of Mérida**, with hourly buses to Cancún (6hr) and to Izamal, Pisté and Valladolid.

In addition, **colectivos** depart Plaza de San Juan, C 69 between calles 62 and 64, for Dzibilchaltún, Oxkutzcab and Ticul, among other destinations. On the northern side of the plaza there are departures to Progreso (1hr) and to Dzibilchaltún, Sierra Papacal, Komchén and Dzitya.

**Flights** from Mérida leave for most Mexican cities and some international destinations; to get out to the airport, catch bus #79 ("Aviacion") going east on Calle 67.

**Consulates** Opening hours are likely to be fairly limited, so it's best to phone ahead and check: UK (also representing Belize), C 58 498 at the junction with C 58 (☎9/928-6152, *dutton@sureste.com*); Cuba, C 1D 320 at C 40 (☎9/944-4216, *consulcuba@yuc.telmex.net.mx*); Spain C 13, 225 (☎9/944-8350); USA, Paseo de Montejo 453 at Av Colón (☎9/925-5011).

**Internet** There are Internet cafés on every street in central Mérida – try Universo, C 63 between calles 62 and 64 (daily 8am–10.30pm) or Oasis, C 57 between calles 62 and 64, both of which are pleasant and good value (US$1.50–2 per hour).

**Laundry** If your hotel doesn't do laundry, try Lavanderia Agua Azul, C 70 505 at C 61 (☎9/924-2581), which offers full-service washes, stain removal and ironing.

**Post office** C 65, between calles 56 and 56A (Mon–Fri 9am–7pm, Sat 9am–2pm). Has a reliable Lista de Correos that keeps mail for 10 days.

**Telephones** Use one of the ubiquitous Ladatels or one of the many casetas dotted around town: Caseta Condesa, C 59 near C 62; Computel, Paseo de Montejo on the corner with C 37; or TelPlus, C 61 497, between calles 58 and 60.

**Travel agencies** Mérida boasts dozens of travel agencies. The best for committed eco-tours is Pronatura, C 17 188A at 10 Col. Garcia Gineres (☎ & fax 9/925-3787 or 920-4647; *ppy@pronatura.org.mx*). Otherwise try Viajes Rotesa, Paseo Montejo 472 at C 39 (☎9/926-2831), or Maya International, C 55 between calles 60 and 62 (☎9/928-3267), both of which offer standard trips to local places of interest.

# North of Mérida: the coast

From Mérida to the port of **Progreso**, the closest point on the coast, is just 36km – an hour on the bus. About halfway between the two, a few kilometres off the main road, lie the ancient ruins of **Dzibilchaltún**, with a cenote at the very middle of the city, fed with a constant supply of fresh water from a small spring, which you can swim in. The drive out of Mérida follows Paseo de Montejo through miles of wealthy suburbs and shopping malls before reaching the flat countryside where the henequen industry seems still to be flourishing. On the outskirts of Mérida there's a giant Cordemex processing plant, and a nearby shop run by the same company sells goods made from the fibre.

It's easy enough to visit both Dzibilchaltún and Progreso in one trip from Mérida if you start early: **buses** to Progreso leave from the terminal on Calle 62 between calles 65 and 67 and combis return to Mérida from the corner of calles 80 and 31 near the post office, on the north side of Progreso's parque central. Once you've visited the ruins, either walk, hitch or wait for the lunchtime bus back to the main road, where you can flag down a Progreso bus. Alternatively, combis for Chablecal stop at Dzibilchaltún; they leave when full (about every half-hour) from the Parque de San Juan at Mérida (corner of calles 62 and 69).

## Dzibilchaltún

The importance for archeologists of the ruins of the ancient city of **Dzibilchaltún** (daily 8am–5pm; US$5, free on Sun) is, unfortunately, hardly reflected in what you actually see. There was, apparently, a settlement here from 1000 BC right through to the Conquest, the longest continuous occupation of any known site; more than eight thousand structures have been mapped and it's known that the city's major points were linked by great causeways – but little has survived, in particular since the ready-dressed stones were a handy building material, used in several local towns and in the Mérida–Progreso road.

In addition to providing the ancient city with water, the 44-metre-deep **Cenote Xlacah** was of ritual importance to the Maya: more than six thousand offerings – including human remains – have been discovered in its depths. A causeway leads from the cenote to a ramshackle group of buildings around the **Templo de las Siete Muñecas** (Temple of the Seven Dolls). The temple itself was originally a simple square pyramid, subsequently built over with a more complex structure. Later still, a passageway was cut through to the original building and seven deformed clay figurines (the dolls) buried, with a tube through which their spirits could commune with the priests. In conjunction with the buildings that surround it, the temple is aligned with various astronomical points and must have served in some form as an observatory. It is also remarkable for being the only known Maya temple to have windows and for having a tower in place of the usual roof-comb. The dolls, and many of the finds from the cenote, can be seen in an excellent museum (8am–4pm; closed Mon) by the site entrance, which presents an overview of Maya culture and history of the region up to the present day. Around Dzibilchaltún, five and half square kilometres have been declared an **Eco-Archeological Park**, partly to protect a unique species of fish found in the cenote. Nature trails take you through the surrounding forest and it's a great place for bird-watching.

## Progreso

First impressions of **PROGRESO** – a working port with a vast concrete pier – are unprepossessing, but the beach is long and broad with fine white sand (though the water's not too clean) and it makes for a pleasant enough day out from Mérida. The shorefront behind the beach is built up all the way to **Puerto Chicxulub**, an unremarkable fishing village some 5km away, and a walk between the two takes you past the mansions of the old henequen exporters, interspersed with modern holiday villas.

Streets in Progreso are confusingly numbered using two overlapping systems: one has numbers in the 70s and 80s, the other in the 20s and 30s. However, it's a small place, and not difficult to find your way around. The **tourist office**, in the Casa de la Cultura on Progreso's main street – Calle 80 – running north–south from the ocean, is not terribly useful though you may be able to pick up copies of free magazines, *Playa Progreso* and *Puerto Progreso*, both of which have useful maps of the town and coastline. There are a couple of **banks** both with ATMs and an **Internet** café also on Calle 80. There are a few moderately priced **places to stay** on Avenida Malecón, which runs along the seafront between the beach and the hotels. The less expensive hotels are a few roads back. Best bets include *Real del Mar*, Av Malecón, near Calle 19 (☎9/935-0798; ④), which has clean simple rooms with bathrooms; *Tropical Suites*, Av Malecón 143 (☎9/935-1263; ④), which has some suites with kitchens; and *Hotel San Miguel*, calles 78 and 28 (☎9/935-1357; ③), which has basic but clean rooms. The nicest hotel in the area, and the closest thing to luxury you'll find out here, is on the beach at Puerto Chicxulub, a half-hour drive north of Progreso – *Margarita's Ville* (☎ & fax 9/944-1434, *www.margaritas.com.mx*; ⑤) – with a lovely sand garden, pool and delicious food on-site. For less expensive **eating**, try the seafood snacks served at *Sol y Mar*, Av Malecón at C 80; *Flamingos*, also on the Malecón; or, for cheap comidas corridas, there are several good comedors in the town's small friendly market.

## Beaches around Progreso

There are stretches of **beach** in either direction from Progreso and, though this coast is the focus of much new tourism development, it's never crowded. Indeed, in winter, when the holiday homes are empty (and the rates come down), you'll have miles of sand to yourself. Check the numbers posted outside the villas and you may find bargain **long-term accommodation**.

The **road east** from Progreso runs through Puerto Chicxulub, where a smart viewing platform (free) over the **Río Uaymitan** is a great place to see flocks of **flamingos**. Go at sunrise or sunset for your best chance of spotting them – the friendly caretakers will lend you binoculars. The coast road continues on to **TELCHACO PUERTO**, one hour away, and the luxury all-inclusive *Reef Club Resort* (in Mérida ☎9/920-4466, *www.reefclubresorts.com*; ⑧). Telchac itself is a laidback seaside village popular in summer with escapees from the city heat of Mérida, and has an excellent small hotel, *Posada Liz* (☎9/917-4125, *posadaliz_telchac@hotmail.com*; ④), as well as several very good seafood restaurants. With more time and a little perseverance, it's possible to get even further east, to **DZILAM DE BRAVO**, a remote fishing village at the end of the road, with no beach because of its ugly, though functional, sea defence wall. Currently there's no hotel in the village but you can stay at the *Hotel Playa Azul* (in Mérida ☎9/923-0794; ③) in nearby **Santa Clara**. From here, though, you can visit **Bocas de Dzilam**, 40km away in the **San Felipe Parque Nacional**; you'll need to track down local guide Javier Nadar, better known as Chacate (ask at the white house with large green gates just past the lighthouse), who charges US$80 for a boatload (4–5hr; up to 7 people) – he also runs trips to nearby cenotes. Set in 620 square kilometres of coastal forests, marshes and dunes, the *bocas* (Spanish for mouths) are freshwater springs on the seabed; the nutrients they provide help to encourage the wide biological diversity found here. Bird- and wildlife-watching is superb: you'll see turtles, tortoises, crocodiles, spider monkeys and dozens of bird species.

A more direct way to get to Dzilam de Bravo is to catch a second-class bus in Mérida from the Autobuses del Noreste terminal. Two buses daily pass through on their way to and from Tizimín and Progreso, and four buses daily leaves for Izamal at 1pm.

**Heading west** from Progreso, there are a number of new hotels and holiday homes along the road to **Yucalpetén**, a busy commercial port and naval base 4km away. Further west, the small but growing resorts of **Chelem** and **Chuburná**, respectively fifteen and thirty minutes from Progreso – and easy day-trips from Mérida – have clean, wide beaches and a few rooms and restaurants.

Beyond Chuburná, the coast road, since damaged by Hurricane Gilbert, is no longer negotiable and you'll have to turn inland. It's not worth making a detour back to the coast at **SISAL** (unbelievably Mérida's chief port in colonial times). These days the place is practically deserted, a shabby knot of dirt tracks. There are a couple of hotels but both are dirty and rundown.

## Celestún

**CELESTÚN**, at the end of a sandbar on the peninsula's northwest coast, would be little more than a one-boat fishing village were it not for its amazing bird-filled lagoon that boasts a large flock of flamingos. To see them – as well as the blue-winged teals and shovellers that migrate here in the winter to take advantage of the plentiful fish in these warm, shallow waters – rent one of the **boats** from the bridge on the main road into town. Get the bus driver to drop you off, as it's a twenty-minute walk from Celestún's main square. The pier from where you'll launch your boat is organized by Mexico's arts and heritage organization Cultur and you'll need to purchase a group ticket (US$36) from the ticket booth and then individual tickets (US$2, max 6 people per boat) for a 1hr 15min tour. Bring your bathers with you as you may get the chance to swim in the rich red waters among the mangroves. Alternatively you could take a longer trip which takes in 7 different ecological sites of interest (two-and-and-half to three-and-a-half hours; US$15 per person) from Celestún's beach with local guide Filiberto Couoh Cavich (known as Ruso) – ask at the *Restaurant Celestún*.

Nominally protected by inclusion in the 600-square-mile **Celestún Natural Park** the flamingos are nevertheless harassed by boats approaching too close in order to give visitors a spectacular flying display, disturbing the birds' feeding. Try to make it clear to your boatman that you don't wish to interrupt the birds' natural behaviour; you will still get good photos from a respectable distance.

There are first-class **buses** from Mérida for Celestún every two hours from the Cameon. Second-class services, which also stop at Sisal, leave from the terminal at the junction of calles 50 and 67. There are half a dozen **lodgings** in the village: the *Hotel Gutiérrez*, C 12 107 (☎9/916-0419; ④), with some a/c rooms; *Hotel Maria Carmen*, C 12 111 (☎9/916-2043; ④); and *Hospedaje Sofia* (no phone; ③) are all fine. Seven kilometres north of the town is a remote eco-lodge, *Eco Paraiso* (☎9/916-2100, fax 916–2111, *www.differentworld.com*; ⑨), with elegant cabañas and miles of deserted beach. The price per room per night is US$192 and includes breakfast and dinner.

Several **seafood restaurants** can be found on the dusty main street and on the beach – ceviche, or raw fish marinated in lime juice, is invariably good here – and there's also a market, a bakery and a filling station, but no bank.

# South of Mérida: Uxmal and the Ruta Puuc

About 80km south of Mérida in the **Puuc hills** lies a group of the peninsula's most important archeological sites. **Uxmal** (pronounced *oosh-mal*) is chief of them, second only to Chichén Itzá in size and significance, but perhaps greater in its initial impact and certainly in the beauty and harmony of its extraordinary architectural style. Lesser sites include **Kabáh**, astride the main road not far beyond; **Sayil**, nearby down a rough side track; and **Labná**, further along this same track. Though related architecturally and each dominated by one major structure, each site is quite distinct from the others. From Labná you could continue to **Oxkutzcab**, on the road from Muna to Felipe Carillo Puerto, and head back to Mérida, via **Ticul** and **Mani**, or else take the longer route past the Maya ruins of **Mayapán**.

Like Chichén Itzá, the Puuc sites are now regarded as being as authentically Maya as Tikal or Palenque, rather than the product of invading Toltecs, as was once believed. Though there are new stylistic themes both in the Puuc sites and at Chichén Itzá, there are also marked continuities of architectural and artefactural technique, religious symbolism, hieroglyphic writing and settlement patterns. The newer themes are now believed to have been introduced by the **Chontal Maya** of the Gulf Coast lowlands, who had become the Yucatán's most important trading partners by the Terminal Classic period (800–1000 AD). The Chontal Maya themselves traded extensively with Oaxaca and central Mexico and are thought to have passed on their architectural styles and themes to the Yucatán.

## Getting to the sites

The sites are far enough apart that it's impractical to do more than a fraction of them by bus, unless you're prepared to spend several days and endure a lot of waiting around. The cheapest and more practical way to visit the sites is to take the **"Ruta Puuc" day-trip bus** (US$7.50), run by Autotransportes del Sur from Mérida's bus station (see box on p.66), and though you don't get much time at the ruins, Uxmal is the last visited and it is possible to stay later and pay for a different bus back. Scores of Mérida travel agencies offer pricier Puuc route trips as well.

It's better still to **rent a car**: in two days you can explore all the key sites, either returning overnight to Mérida or finding a room in Muna, Ticul or, more expensively, at Uxmal itself. This way you could even include the Uxmal son et lumière – better than the one at Chichén Itzá. For details of car rental agencies, see p.72.

# Uxmal

**UXMAL** – "thrice-built" – represents the finest achievement of the **Puuc architectural style**, in which buildings of amazingly classical proportions are decorated with

Uxmal emblem glyph

broad stone mosaic friezes of geometric patterns, or designs so stylized and endlessly repeated as to become almost abstract. As in every Maya site in the Yucatán, the face of **Chac**, the rain god, is everywhere. Chac must have been more crucial here than almost anywhere, for Uxmal and the other Puuc sites, almost uniquely, have no cenote or other natural source of water, relying instead on artificially created underground cisterns, jug-shaped and coated with lime, to collect and store rainwater. In recent years these have all been filled in, to prevent mosquitoes breeding.

Little is known of the city's history, but what is clear is that the chief monuments, and the city's peaks of power and population, fall into the Terminal Classic period, and though there are indications of settlement long before this, most of the buildings that you see date from this period. Some time after 900 AD the city began to decline and by 1200 Uxmal and all the Puuc sites, together with Chichén Itzá, were all but abandoned. The reasons for this are unknown, although political infighting, ecological problems and loss of trade with Tula may have played a part. Later, the **Xiu dynasty** settled at Uxmal, which became one of the central pillars of the League of Mayapán, and from here, in 1441, the rebellion originated that finally overthrew the power of Mayapán and put an end to any form of centralized Maya authority over the Yucatán. All the significant surviving structures, though, date from the Classic period.

## The site

As you enter **the site** (daily 8am–5pm; US$8, free on Sun), the back of the great **Pirámide del Adivino** (Pyramid of the Magician) rises before you. The most remarkable-looking of all Mexican pyramids, it soars at a startling angle from its oval base to a temple some 30m above the ground, with a broad but steep stairway up either side. It takes its name from the legend that it was magically constructed in a single night by a dwarf, though in fact at least five stages of construction have been discovered – six if you count the modern restoration, which may not correspond exactly to any of its earlier incarnations.

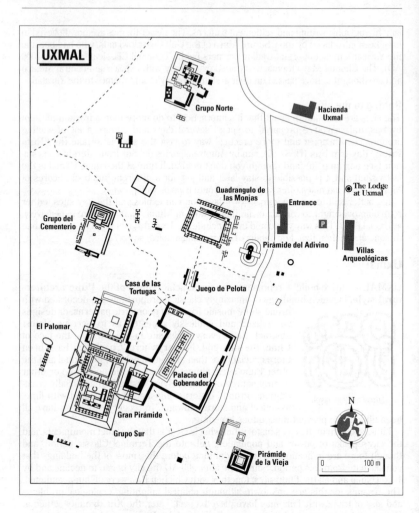

The rear (east) stairway leads, past a tunnel which reveals Templo III, directly to the top, and a platform surrounding the temple that crowns the pyramid. Even with the chain to help you, the climb up the high, thin steps is not for the unfit, nor for anyone who suffers from vertigo. The views, though, are sensational, particularly looking west over the rest of the site and the green unexcavated mounds that surround it. Here you're standing at the front of the summit temple, its facade decorated with interlocking geometric motifs. Below it, the west stairway runs down either side of a second, earlier sanctuary in a distinctly different style. Known as the **Edificio Chenes** (or Templo IV), it does indeed reflect the architecture of the Chenes region (see p.100), the entire front forming a giant mask of Chac. At the bottom of the west face, divided in half by the stairway, you'll find yet another earlier stage of construction (the first) – the long, low facade of a structure apparently similar to the so-called "Nunnery".

The **Quadrangulo de las Monjas** (Nunnery Quadrangle), a beautiful complex of four buildings enclosing a square plaza, is one of many buildings here named quite erroneously by the Spanish, to whom it resembled a convent. Whatever it may have been, it wasn't a convent; theories range from it being a military academy to a sort of earthly paradise where intended sacrificial victims would spend their final months in debauchery. The four buildings are in fact from different periods and, although they blend superbly, each is stylistically distinct. The **north building**, raised higher than the others and even more richly ornamented, is probably also the oldest. Approached up a broad stairway between two colonnaded porches, it has a strip of plain stone facade (from which doors lead into the vaulted chambers within) surmounted by a slightly raised panel of mosaics: geometric patterns and human and animal figures, with representations of Maya huts above the doorways. The **west building** boasts even more varied themes, and the whole of its ornamentation is surrounded by a coiling, feathered rattlesnake with the face of a warrior emerging from its jaws. All four sides display growing Maya architectural skills – the false Maya vaults of the interiors are taken about as wide as they can go without collapsing (wooden crossbeams provided further support), and the frontages are slightly bowed in order to maintain a proper horizontal perspective.

An arched passageway through the middle of the south building provided the square with a monumental entrance directly aligned with the **ball court** outside. Nowadays a path leads through here, between the ruined side walls of the court, and up onto the levelled terrace on which stand the Palacio del Gobernador and the **Casa de las Tortugas** (House of the Turtles). This very simple, elegant building, named for the stone turtles (or tortoises) carved around the cornice, demonstrates well another constant theme of Puuc architecture: stone facades carved to appear like rows of narrow columns. These probably represent the building style of the Maya huts still in use today – walls of bamboo lashed together. The plain bands of masonry that often surround them mirror the cords that tie the hut walls in place.

It is the **Palacio del Gobernador** (Governor's Palace), though, that marks the finest achievement of Uxmal's builders. John L. Stephens, arriving at the then virtually unknown site in June 1840, had no doubts as to its significance: "if it stood this day on its grand artificial terrace in Hyde Park or the Garden of the Tuileries," he later wrote, "it would form a new order . . . not unworthy to stand side by side with the remains of the Egyptian, Grecian and Roman art." The palace faces east, away from the buildings around it, probably for astronomical reasons – its central doorway aligns with the column of the altar outside and the point where Venus rises. Long and low, it is lent a remarkable harmony by the architect's use of light and shade on the facade, and by the strong diagonals that run right through its broad band of mosaic decorations – particularly in the steeply vaulted archways that divide the two wings from the central mass, like giant arrow-heads aimed at the sky. Close up, the mosaic is equally impressive, masks of Chac alternating with grid-and-key patterns and with highly stylized snakes. Inside, the chambers are, as ever, narrow, gloomy and unadorned; but at least the great central room, 20m long and entered by the three closer-set openings in the facade, is grander than most. At the back, the rooms have no natural light source at all.

Behind the palace stand the ruinous buildings of the **Grupo Sur** (South Group), with the partly restored Gran Pirámide (Great Pyramid), and El Palomar (Dovecote or Quadrangle of the Doves). You can climb the rebuilt staircase of the **Gran Pirámide** to see the temple on top, decorated with parrots and more masks of Chac, and look across at the rest of the site. **El Palomar** was originally part of a quadrangle like that of the Nunnery, but the only building to retain any form is this, topped with the great wavy, latticed roof-comb from which it takes its name.

Of the outlying structures, the **Pirámide de la Vieja** (Pyramid of the Old Woman), probably the earliest surviving building at Uxmal, is now little more than a grassy mound with a clearly man-made outline. The **Grupo del Cementerio** (Cemetery

Group), too, is in a state of ruin – low altars in the middle of this square bear traces of carved hieroglyphs and human skulls.

## Practicalities

Several **buses** a day run direct from Mérida to Uxmal, and any bus heading down the main road towards Hopelchén (or between Mérida and Campeche on the longer route) will drop you just a short walk from the entrance. Note that none runs late enough to get you back to Mérida after the son et lumière (a taxi from Mérida costs about US$45 for a round-trip with waiting time). At the modern **entrance to the site** (daily 8am–5pm; US$8, free on Sun) the **tourist centre** includes a small museum, a snack bar and a shop with guides to the site, souvenirs, film and suchlike. Uxmal's son et lumière (daily; US$3) starts at 7pm in winter and 8pm in summer and has a Spanish commentary – you can hire simultaneous translation equipment (US$2.50) – which is pretty crass, but the lighting effects are undeniably impressive.

There are three expensive **hotels** nearby, two of which are right at the site's entrance: *Villas Arqueológicas* (☎ & fax 9/928-0644, *www. clubmed.com*; ⑦), which has a/c rooms, a pool and tennis courts, and *The Lodge at Uxmal* (☎ & fax 9/976-2102, *www.mayaland.com*; ⑨) with similar facilities and a breezy restaurant and bar, *La Palapa,* a convenient spot for a cool drink – a room at the *Lodge* will cost US$194–224. The third and most attractive place to stay is the colonial-style *Hotel Hacienda Uxmal* (☎9/926-2012, fax 926-2011, *www.mayaland.com*; ⑦), slightly further away on the main Merida–Uxmal road.

Travelling from Uxmal to Kabáh, you'll pass the **Sacbe campsite and trailer park** (*sacbebungalow@hotmail.com*; ①–③). It's about fifteen minutes' walk south from the main square in the village of Santa Elena; if you're travelling by bus, ask the driver to drop you off at the entrance. Run by a Mexican–French couple, who have maps and can provide accurate information about the area, the site is a haven for backpackers, with tent sites dotted among the shady fruit trees. There are also some new cabañas, and limited space for your own hammock. For a very small additional charge the owners will cook you a delicious breakfast and supper. There's also a small restaurant in Santa Elena, *El Chac Mool,* which does decent local food and has rooms to rent (③). Note also that you may be able to hitch a ride with Uxmal's workers to Santa Elena after the nightly son et lumière which makes the village a convenient place for basing yourself while seeing the Puuc sites. **SANTA ELENA** itself is worth visiting for the magnificent view from its large **church** (daily except Sat 3–6pm); ask for the sacristan who will open the door to the spiral staircase that leads to the roof. Beside the church is a small **museum** (Tues–Sat 10am–6pm, Sun 10am–2pm; free), which serves as a home for the 200-year-old mummified remains of four children discovered under the church floor in 1980.

## Kabáh

Some 20km south of Uxmal, the extensive site of **KABÁH** (daily 8am–5pm; US$2, free on Sun) stretches across the road. Much of it remains unexplored, but the one great building, the **Codz Poop** or Palace of Masks, lies not far off the highway to the left. The facade of this amazing structure is covered all over, in ludicrous profusion, with goggle-eyed, trunk-nosed masks of Chac. Even in its present state – with most of the long, curved noses broken off – this is the strangest and most striking of all Maya buildings, decorated so obsessively, intricately and repetitively that it seems almost insane. Even the steps by which you reach the doorways and the interior are more Chac noses. There are a couple of lesser buildings grouped around the Codz Poop, and on the other side of the road an unusual circular pyramid – now simply a green, conical mound. Also across the road, a sort of triumphal arch marks the point where the ancient causeway from Uxmal entered the city.

**Leaving Kabáh**, you may have to virtually lie down in the road to persuade a bus to stop for you – ask the guards at the site for the bus times. Hitching a ride with other visitors, though, is generally pretty easy, and with luck you may even meet someone touring all the local sites.

## Sayil

A sober, restrained contrast to the excesses of Kabáh, the ruined site of **SAYIL** (daily 8am–5pm; US$2, free on Sun) lies some 5km along a minor road heading east from the highway, 5km beyond Kabáh. It is again dominated by one major structure, the extensively restored **Gran Palacio** (Great Palace), built on three storeys, each smaller than the one below, and some 80m long. Although there are several large masks of Chac in a frieze around the top of the middle level, the decoration mostly takes the form of bamboo-effect stone pillaring – seen here more extensively than anywhere. The interiors of the middle level, too, are lighter and airier than is usual, thanks to the use of broad openings, their lintels supported on fat columns. The upper and lower storeys are almost entirely unadorned, plain stone surfaces with narrow openings.

Few other structures have been cleared. From the Gran Palacio a path leads to the right to the large temple of **El Mirador**, and in the other direction to a stela, carved with a phallic figure and now protected under a thatched roof. On the opposite side of the road from all this, a small path leads uphill, in about ten minutes, to two more temples.

## Xlapak, Labná and Chacmultún

The minor road continues, paved but in poor condition, past the tiny Puuc site known as **XLAPAK** (daily 8am–5pm; US$1.50, free on Sun). Its proximity to the larger sites of Labná and Sayil means that Xlapak (Maya for "old walls") is seldom visited, but if you have the time, stop to see the recently restored buildings with their carvings of masks and yet more Chac noses. **LABNÁ** (daily 8am–5pm; US$2, free on Sun) is about 3km further. Near the entrance to this ancient city is a palace, similar to but less impressive than that of Sayil, on which you'll see traces of sculptures including the inevitable Chac, and a crocodile (or snake) with a human face emerging from its mouth – symbolizing a god escaping from the jaws of the underworld. Remnants of a raised causeway lead from here to a second group of buildings, of which the most important is the **Arco de Labná**. Originally part of a complex linking two great squares, like the Nunnery at Uxmal, it now stands alone as a sort of triumphal arch. Both sides are richly decorated: on the east with geometric patterns; on the west (the back) with more of these and niches in the form of Maya huts or temples. Nearby is El Mirador, a temple with the well-preserved remains of a tall, elaborate roof-comb.

Signposted from the Ruta Puuc road, just beyond Xlapak, and well worth the 3km detour through orange groves, is the wonderfully romantic **Hacienda Tabi** (US$1.50), an abandoned sugar plantation which was declared a protected ecological reserve by the Mexican government in 1995 and is currently being restored. The plantation's main house is still mostly closed off though you can **stay** in one of three enormous tiled bedrooms upstairs (②; the caretakers will provide meals for an extra charge) and you should have the place with its enormous park, swimming pool and ruined chapel to yourself. For further information contact the *Fundacion Cultural Yucatán,* C 58 429D, Mérida (☎9/923-9453).

**CHACMULTÚN**, 50 km from Labná on a partially paved road off Hwy-184, is another interesting Puuc site, with a series of hilltop buildings built on artificial terraces. One of them, the Edificio de las Pinturas, contains various **wall paintings** of Maya adorned with feathers and brandishing spears or holding trumpets or parasols. Other buildings preserve traces of the deep blues and reds that once covered Maya temples, and the El Palacio building has an intricate columned facade typical of the Puuc style.

## Oxkutzcab and around

From the village of **OXKUTZCAB** (also known as Huerta del Estado) on Hwy-184, 20km from Labna, you can head north back to Mérida via Ticul and Mani. Though there's little reason to overnight in Oxkutzcab, it's as good a place as any to stop for a while, with a huge **fruit market**, bustling and lively in the mornings, selling most of its produce by the crate or sack. Calles 51 and 50 edge the main park and the mercado, with a large Franciscan church at the corner where they meet. There are also some remote Puuc ruins at Kuiuc and Xkichmook, both of which lie off a minor road that runs south from the village.

Buses to Mérida via Ticul (2hr) leave about every hour from the **bus station** at the corner of calles 56 and 51; colectivos come and go from beside the mercado on Calle 51. Of the two basic **hotels**, *Hospedaje Trujeque*, Calle 48, opposite the park (☎9/975-0568; ③), is more comfortable, though *Hospedaje Rosalia*, C 54 103 (☎9/975-0167; ②), is very friendly and has the advantage of being just around the corner from the bus station. The Banamex **bank** on Calle 50, opposite the park, has an ATM. **Restaurants** and cafeterías skirt the market, but if you fancy a long, lazy lunch, try a few blocks back at the *Restaurante Su Cabaña Suiza*, C 54 101, where comidas are served in the tranquillity of a spacious open-sided *palapa*.

### The Grutas de Loltún

Just outside Oxkutzcab, hidden away near the road to Labná, the **Grutas de Loltún** (daily 9am–5pm; US$4, US$2 on Sun), studded with stalactites and stalagmites (one in the shape of a giant corn cob), were revered by the Maya as a source of water from a time long before they built their cities. At the entrance, a huge bas-relief of a jaguar warrior guards the opening to the underworld, and throughout there are traces of ancient paintings and carvings on the walls. Nowadays the caves are lit, and there are spectacular guided tours (officially at 9.30am, 11am, 12.30pm, 2pm, 3pm & 4pm; in practice it depends on who turns up and when). The surrounding jungle is visible through the collapsed floor of the last gallery and ten-metre-long tree roots find an anchor on the cavern floor. There are two decent though pricey **restaurants** near the site entrance, *El Guerrero* and *El Huimic de Loltan*.

Colectivos and trucks from **Oxkutzcab** that pass the caves leave hourly throughout the day from Calle 51 next to the market; if you get there by 8.30am you may be able to catch the truck taking the cave employees to work. Getting back is less easy, as the trucks are full of workers and produce, but, if you wait, something will turn up. The short taxi ride from the village will cost you about US$5.

## Ticul, Mayapán and Mani

Conveniently located 80km south of Mérida on Hwy-184, the town of **TICUL** is, like Mérida, another excellent base for exploring the Puuc region. You can head straight back to Mérida from here or else take the slightly longer route via the Maya sites of **Mani** and **Mayapán**. Ticul is an important centre of Maya shamanism as well as a pottery-producing centre and it's full of shops selling reproduction Maya antiquities, mostly too big to carry home. Visitors are welcome to watch the manufacturing process at the *fabricas*. It is also renowned for its shoes and the streets are lined with shoe-shops. Despite this, Ticul lives life at a slow pace, with more bicycles (and passenger-carrying *triciclos*) than cars.

Located on the main road between Mérida and Felipe Carrillo Puerto in Quintana Roo, Ticul is an important transport centre, well served by **buses** to and from Mérida and with services to Cancún. If you're arriving by bus from Mérida, you'll be dropped in Calle 24 on the corner with Calle 25, behind the church. Buses **from Campeche** don't go through Ticul so you'll have to get off at Santa Elena to catch one of the colectivos that leave from the main square between about 6am and 7pm; the trip takes about thirty minutes. **Trucks** for Oxkutzcab and surrounding villages set off when they're full from the side of the plaza next to the church; **combis** for Mérida leave from further down the same street.

Even-numbered roads run north to south, odd numbers east to west. Calle 23 is the main street, with the plaza at its eastern end at Calle 26. Half a block from the plaza, the *Sierra Sosa*, C 26 199A (☎9/972-0008; ③), has basic **rooms**, with shower and fan (upstairs is better), and a few new a/c rooms with TV. The English-speaking manager, Luis Sierra, is a good source of information, and you can make international calls from reception. Alternatives include the *Hotel Plaza*, C 23 202 (☎9/972-0484, fax 972-0026; *www.hotelplazayucatan.com*; ⑤), the most comfortable and centrally located of the lot with TV, telephone and a/c in all rooms, and the budget *Hotel San Miguel (*no phone; ②), which has plain but very clean rooms at bargain rates.

The best of the **restaurants** is the original (there's another in Mérida) *Los Almendros*, C 23 207, which serves superb local dishes in pleasant surroundings. The *Loncheria Carmelita*, two doors up from *Hotel Sierra Sosa* on Calle 26, does an inexpensive comida and *Los Delfines*, C 27 216, specializes in seafood. As usual, the least expensive places are the *loncherías* near the bus station.

## Mayapán and Mani

Forty-nine kilometres north of Ticul are the ruins of **MAYAPÁN**, the most powerful city in the Yucatán from the eleventh to the fifteenth centuries. Its history is somewhat vague but, according to Maya chronicles, it formed (with Chichén Itzá and Uxmal) one of a triumvirate of cities that as the **League of Mayapán** exercised control over the entire peninsula from around 987 to 1185. However, these dates are controversial, since archeological evidence suggests that Mayapán was not a significant settlement until the thirteenth century. The rival theory has Mayapán founded around 1263, after the fall of Chichén Itzá.

The league broke up when the **Cocom** dynasty of Mayapán attacked and overwhelmed the rulers of an already declining Chichén Itzá, establishing themselves as sole controllers of the peninsula. Mayapán became a huge city by the standards of the day, with a population of some 15,000 in a site covering five square kilometres, in which traces of more than four thousand buildings have been found. Here rulers of subject cities were forced to live where they could be kept under control, perhaps even as hostages. This hegemony was maintained until 1441 when Ah Xupan, a Xiu leader from Uxmal, finally led a rebellion that succeeded in overthrowing the Cocom and destroying their city – thus paving the way for the disunited tribalism that the Spanish found on their arrival, which made their conquest so much easier.

What can be seen today is a disappointment – the buildings anyway were crude and small by Maya standards, at best poor copies of what had gone before. This has led to its widespread dismissal as a "decadent" and failing society, but a powerful case can be made for the fact that it was merely a changing one. Here the priests no longer dominated – hence the lack of great ceremonial centres – and what grew instead was a more genuinely urban society: highly militaristic, no doubt, but also far more centralized and more reliant on trade than anything seen previously.

After the fall of Mayapán, the Xiu abandoned Uxmal and founded **MANI**, 15km east of Ticul. It's hard to believe that what is now simply a small village was, at the time of the Conquest, the largest city the Spanish encountered. Fortunately for the Spanish, its ruler, Ah Kukum Xiu, converted to Christianity and became their ally. Here, in 1548, was founded one of the earliest and largest **Franciscan monasteries** in the Yucatán. This still stands, surrounded now by Maya huts, and just about the only evidence of Mani's past glories are the ancient stones used in its construction. In front of the church, in 1562, Bishop Diego de Landa held the notorious *auto de fe* in which he burned the city's ancient records (because they "contained nothing in which there was not to be seen the superstitions and lies of the devil"), destroying virtually all surviving original Maya literature.

# Chichén Itzá

**Chichén Itzá**, the most famous, the most extensively restored and by far the most visited of all Maya sites, lies conveniently astride the main road from Mérida to Cancún and the

Caribbean, about 120km from Mérida and a little more than 200km from the coast. There's a fast and very regular bus service all along this road, making it perfectly feasible to visit as a day's excursion from Mérida, or en route from Mérida to the coast (or even as a day out from Cancún, as many tour buses do). The site, though, deserves better, and both to do the ruins justice and to see them when they're not entirely overrun by tourists, an overnight stop is well worth considering – either at the site itself or, less extravagantly, at the nearby village of **Pisté** or in Valladolid (see p.90).

Chichén emblem glyph

## The route from Mérida: Izamal and Aké

If your route to Chichén Itzá is fairly leisurely, **IZAMAL**, 72km from Mérida, is the one place that does merit a detour. The town is something of a quiet backwater whose colonial air is denied by its inhabitants' allegiance to their traditional dress and lifestyle. It was formerly an important Maya religious centre, where they worshipped **Itzamna**, mythical founder of the ancient city and one of the gods of creation, at a series of huge pyramid-temples of the same name. Most are now no more than low hillocks in the surrounding country, but two survive in the town itself. One, **Kinich Kakmo** (daily 8am–8pm; free), just a couple of blocks from the central plaza and dedicated to the sun god, has been partly restored. The other had its top lopped off by the Spanish and was replaced with a vast monastery, the **convent of St Anthony of Padua** (daily; free), which was painted a deep yellow, like much of the town, for the pope's visit in 1993. The porticoed atrium is particularly beautiful and photogenic in the late afternoon, and inside it is a statue of the Virgin of Izamal, patron saint of the Yucatán, whose presence draws pilgrims from all over the peninsula.

There are a couple of very basic **hotels** in Izamal, both on the zócalo, where there are also a BanCrecen **bank** with ATM and a **post office**. *Restaurant Portales* on the main square serves good Mexican **food**, as does the *Restaurant El Toro*, next to the bus station, one block back from the main square. **Horse-drawn buggies** lined up around the zócalo will take you for a pleasant *recorrido* of the very pretty town (US$4) and Maya sites. **Buses to Izamal** leave every 45 minutes from Autotransportes de Oriente in Mérida (see p.73). They take a little over an hour and return to Mérida every 45 minutes. It's therefore possible to visit Izamal in a comfortable afternoon trip from Mérida.

The Maya city of **Aké**, which lies halfway between Izamal and Mérida, was probably in alliance with Izamal and is linked to it by one of the peninsula's largest *sacbes* (Maya roads). One of the most impressive structures here is a large, pillared building on a platform, surrounded by a huge plaza of 20,000 square metres. There is also a ruined henequen hacienda, San Lorenzo de Aké, on the same site, whose church is built over one of the temples. The charm of this site lies partly in its tranquillity, as few visitors come here, but you'll need your own transport to get to it. Follow the signs from Tixkobob, the nearest village, which lies on the highway.

## Practicalities

**Arriving at Chichén Itzá** you'll find that the highway, which once cut straight through the middle of the ruins, has been re-routed around the site. If you're on a through bus it may drop you at the junction of the bypass and the old road, about ten minutes' walk from the entrance – most, though, drive right up to the site entrance. Although blocked off by

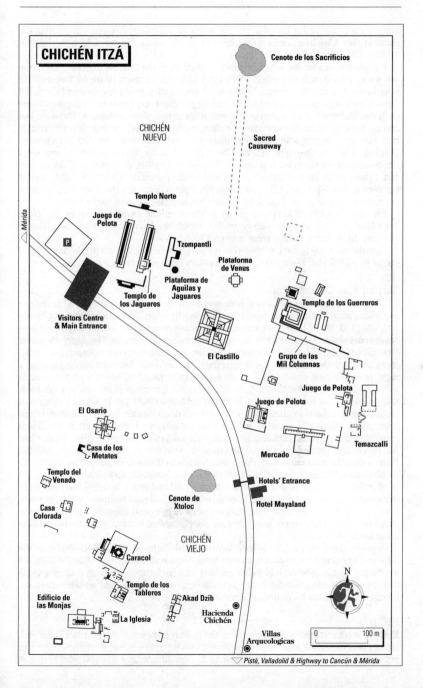

CHICHÉN ITZÁ

Cenote de los Sacrificios

CHICHÉN NUEVO

Sacred Causeway

Templo Norte

Juego de Pelota

Tzompantli

Plataforma de Venus

Plataforma de Aguilas y Jaguares

Templo de los Jaguares

Visitors Centre & Main Entrance

Mérida

P

El Castillo

Templo de los Guerreros

Grupo de las Mil Columnas

Juego de Pelota

Juego de Pelota

El Osario

Casa de los Metates

Temazcalli

Mercado

Templo del Venado

Cenote de Xtoloc

Hotels' Entrance

Hotel Mayaland

Casa Colorada

CHICHÉN VIEJO

Caracol

Templo de los Tableros

Akad Dzib

Edificio de las Monjas

La Iglesia

Hacienda Chichén

Villas Arqueologicas

N

0        100 m

Pisté, Valladolid & Highway to Cancún & Mérida

gates at each side of the fenced-in site, the old road still exists, conveniently dividing the ruins in two: **Chichén Viejo** (Old Chichén) to the south, **Nuevo Chichén** (New or "Toltec" Chichén) to the north.

The main **entry to the site** (daily 8am–5pm, though the process of getting everyone out starts at least an hour earlier; US$8, extra with video camera or tripod, free on Sun) is to the west, at the Mérida end. Keep your ticket, which permits re-entry, and check the timetable for admissions to the various buildings – most open only for a couple of hours each day, and you'll want to plan your wanderings around their schedules. There are bus and car parks here, and a huge **visitor centre** (open until 10pm) with a museum, restaurant, and shops selling souvenirs, film, maps and guides (best are the Panorama series). **Guided tours** of the ruins can also be arranged at the visitor centre. Group tours (9am–3.30pm) for six to eight people, in Spanish or English, cost around US$8 per person. Private tours (8am–2.30pm) cost around US$33 per guide. There's a nightly **son et lumière** in English (9pm; US$4) and Spanish (7pm; US$2), worth seeing if you're staying nearby – it's no great shakes, but there's nothing else to do in the evening.

You can also buy tickets and get in at the **smaller eastern gate** by the *Hotel Mayaland* (see below), where there are fewer facilities. Book at the hotel reception for two-hour **horseback riding trips** around Chichén Viejo.

To make your way to the Caribbean coast from Chichén Itzá, it's best to take any bus you can as far as Valladolid (see p.90), and if necessary change there for a first-class service.

## Staying near Chichén Itzá

Chichén Itzá boasts some excellent **hotels** virtually on site, though they're all in the luxury price range (for cheaper options head for nearby Pisté. The *Hotel Hacienda Chichén* (☎9/924-2150, fax 924-5011; *www.yucatanadventures.com.mx*; ⑧), which has a couple of small ruins within its grounds, is the most charming and friendly. The *Hotel Mayaland* (☎9/651-0127, fax 651-0129, *www.mayaland.com*; ⑨), has a gorgeous colonial-style dining room and attractive rooms, some in luxurious thatched huts dotted about the gardens; a night here will cost US$138–224. Least aesthetically pleasing, but still pretty good, is *Villas Arqueologicas* (☎9/851-0034, fax 851-0018; ⑧), a modern place run by Club Med, with rooms set out round a patio enclosing a pool and cocktail bar: by night, its library of archeological and architectural tomes doubles as a disco (usually empty). All three hotels have pools, which are open to anyone who eats lunch there, though in the *Villas Arqueologicas* you could probably get away with just having a drink at the poolside bar. All three are located in the so-called *zona hotelera*, a right-hand fork off the Pisté–Valladolid road (3km from Pisté) which leads to the eastern gate to the ruins.

Alternatively, the *Dolores Alba* (☎9/928-5650, fax 928-3163; *www.doloresalba.com*; ⑤) is a further 2km away east on the road to Valladolid and much better value. There are two swimming pools, one of which is made from a natural pool complete with rocky bottom, as well as a restaurant. The staff are very helpful and friendly and will provide transport to the site (but not back). Rooms can be booked in advance at the hotel of the same name in Mérida.

Opposite the *Dolores Alba* is the **Parque Ikkil** (8am–6pm; US$3.50) home to the *Sagrado Azul* **cenote** and six very swanky bungalows available for rent (☎9/858-1525; ⑨) at US$120 a night. The park is well organized with landscaped gardens, changing facilities should you wish to swim in the large underground cenote, and on-site restaurant, though on the whole it's rather too sanitized.

## *PISTÉ*

**Pisté** is an unattractive village straddling the main road between Mérida and Valladolid, about twenty minutes' walk from the ruins. Its saving grace is that it enables visitors to get up early enough to miss the teeming hordes of package tourists who arrive at

Chichén Itzá at about 10.30am. You can also stay here without breaking the bank. **Buses** pass Pisté every thirty minutes for Mérida and about every hour for Valladolid. There are also services to Cancún and Playa del Carmen.

Most **hotels** are on the main road, between the village and the ruins, so it's easy to shop around for the best deal. *Hotel Chichén Itzá*, Km 118 (☎9/851-0022, fax 851-0023; ⑤–⑧), has the smartest and most comfortable rooms though not much atmosphere. The *Piramide Inn* (☎9/851-0115; *www.piramideinn.com*; ⑤) is conveniently situated near the bus stop and the western entrance to the ruins and has a pool, *temascal* (traditional sauna) and New Age clientele. Next door the *Stardust Inn* (☎9/851-0122; ⑥) has a slight-ly faded air but the biggest swimming pool in Pisté and an adjacent **trailer park**. The friendly *Posada Olalde* (☎9/851-0086; ③–④), Calle 6, off the main road, has basic, clean rooms with fans and hot water and wonderfully romantic cabañas; coming from the bus terminal, turn left by *El Guayacan Artesenía*. Budget travellers should head for the *Posada El Carrousel* (☎9/851-0078; ③) – the best rooms are at the back, away from the road – or *Posada Chac Mool* (④) the last hotel in Pisté as you head towards the ruins.

There are **restaurants** lining the road, alongside the hotels. The best value are *El Carrousel* and *Las Mestizas*, which both do some good-value regional cuisine. The pricier hotels all have their own restaurants.

## The site

Though in most minds **CHICHÉN ITZÁ** represents the very image of the Maya, in reali-ty it is its very divergence from accepted Maya tradition that makes it so fascinating, and so important to archeologists. Even today, its **history** remains hotly disputed. Archeologists are fairly certain that the city rose to power in the Terminal Classic period (between 800 and 1000 AD), and was probably established about five hundred years before that, but what they are undecided about is exactly who built the city. Much of the evidence at the site – an emphasis on human sacrifice, the presence of a huge ball court and the glorification of military activity – points to a strong Mexican influence; consider-ing the dates of Chichén's ascendancy, it seemed that this was the result of the city's defeat by the Toltecs, a theory reinforced by the resemblance of the Temple of the Warriors to the L-shaped colonnade at Tula, along with numerous depictions of the Toltec god-king, the feathered serpent, **Quetzalcoatl** (Kukulkán to the Maya).

However, recent work here has revealed some continuity between Chichén Itzá and earlier Maya sites in the southern lowlands. It's now thought that Chichén Itzá was never invaded by the Toltecs, but occupied by Maya throughout its history, with the Mexican influence coming via its chief trading partner, the Chontal Maya or Putun of the Gulf Coast lowlands. The Chontal were themselves influenced by Mexico and Oaxaca through a thriving network of trade and political allegiances. This new theory is not without its own puzzles, though, as the **Itzá** kings who ruled Chichén Itzá were referred to by the contemporary Maya as "foreigners". However, they may actually have been Maya who moved north after droughts caused the abandonment of the forest cities, and there is, indeed, a marked continuity of styles with the Maya sites of the southern lowlands.

### Chichén Nuevo

If it's still reasonably early, head first for **El Castillo** (or the Pyramid of Kukulkán), the structure that dominates the site. This should allow you to climb it before the full heat of the day, and get a good overview of the entire area. It is a simple, relatively unadorned square building, with a monumental stairway climbing each face (only two faces of which are restored), rising in nine receding terraces to a temple at the top. The simplicity is deceptive, however, as the building is in fact the **Maya calendar** (see Contexts, p.551) made stone: each staircase has 91 steps, which, when added to the single step at the main entrance to the temple, total 365 steps; other numbers relevant to the Maya calendar recur throughout the construction. Most remarkably, at sunset on the spring and autumn equinoxes, the great serpents' heads at the foot of the main staircase are joined to their tails (at the top) by an undulating body of shadow – an event of just a few hours that draws spectators, and awed worshippers, by the thousand.

Inside the present structure, an earlier pyramid survives almost wholly intact. An entrance has been opened at the bottom of El Castillo, through which you reach a narrow, dank and claustrophobic stairway (formerly the outside of the inner pyramid) that leads steeply to a temple on the top. In its outer room is a rather crude chac-mool, but in the **inner sanctuary**, now railed off, stands one of the greatest finds at the site: an altar, or throne, in the form of a jaguar, painted bright red and inset with jade "spots" and eyes – the teeth are real jaguar teeth. This discovery was one of the first to undermine the Toltec theory: though the sculpture is apparently Toltec in style, it predates their ostensible arrival.

## THE "TOLTEC" PLAZA

The Castillo stands on the edge of the great grassy plaza that formed the focus of Nuevo Chichén Itzá: all its most important buildings are here, and from the northern edge a *sacbe*, or sacred causeway, leads to the great **Cenote de los Sacrificios**. The **Templo de los Guerreros** (Temple of the Warriors), and the adjoining **Grupo de las Mil Columnas** (Group of the Thousand Columns), take up the eastern edge of the plaza. These are the structures that most recall the great Toltec site of Tula, near Mexico City, both in design and in detail – in particular the colonnaded courtyard (which would originally have been roofed with some form of thatch) and the use of atlantean columns, representing warriors in armour, their arms raised above their heads. Throughout, the temple is richly decorated with carvings and sculptures (originally with paintings, too) of jaguars and eagles devouring human hearts, feathered serpents, warriors and, the one undeniably Maya feature, masks of Chac. On top are two superb **chac-mools**: offerings were placed on the stomachs of these reclining figures, representing the messengers who would take the sacrifice to the gods, or perhaps the divinities themselves.

Once again, the Templo de los Guerreros was built over an earlier temple, in which (during set hours) some remnants of faded **murals** can be made out. The "thousand" columns alongside originally formed a square, on the far side of which is the building known as the **Mercado**, although there's no evidence that this actually was a marketplace. Near here, too, is a small, ruinous ball court.

Walking across the plaza towards the main ball court, you pass three small platforms. The **Plataforma de Venus** is a simple, raised, square block, with a stairway up each side guarded by feathered serpents. Here, rites associated with Quetzalcoatl in his role of Venus, the morning star, would have been carried out. Slightly smaller, but otherwise virtually identical in design, is the **Aquilas y Jaguares** platform, on which you'll see relief carvings of eagles and jaguars holding human hearts. Human sacrifices may even have been carried out here, judging by the proximity of the third platform, the **Tzompantli**, where victims' skulls were hung on display. This is carved on every side with grotesquely grinning stone skulls.

## THE BALL COURT

Chichén Itzá's main **Juego de Pelota** (ball court), on the western side of the plaza, is the largest known in existence – some 90m long. Its design is classically Maya: a capital I shape surrounded by temples, with the goals, or target rings, halfway along each side. Along the bottom of each side wall runs a sloping panel decorated in low relief with scenes of the game and its players. Although the rules and full significance of the game remain a mystery, it was clearly not a Saturday afternoon kick-about in the park. The players are shown processing towards a circular central symbol, the symbol of death, and one player (thought to be the winning captain – just right of the centre) has been decapitated, while another (to the left) holds his head and a ritual knife. Along the top runs the stone body of a two-headed snake, whose heads stick out at either end of this "bench".

At each end of the court stand small buildings with open **galleries** overlooking the field of play – the low one at the south may simply have been a grandstand, that at the north (the **Templo Norte**, also known as the Temple of the Bearded Man, after a sculpture inside) was almost certainly a temple – perhaps, too, the umpires' stand. Inside, there are several worn relief carvings and a whispering-gallery effect that enables you to be heard clearly at the far end of the court, and to hear what's going on there.

The **Templo de los Jaguares** also overlooks the playing area, but from the side; to get to it, you have to go back out to the plaza. At the bottom – effectively the outer wall of the ball court – is a little portico supported by two pillars, between which a stone jaguar stands sentinel. Inside are some wonderful, rather worn, relief carvings of Maya priests and warriors, animals, birds and plants. Beside this, a very steep, narrow staircase ascends to a platform overlooking the court and to the **Upper Temple** (restricted opening hours), with its fragments of a mural depicting battle scenes.

The **Cenote de los Sacrificios** lies at the end of the causeway that leads off through the trees from the northern side of the plaza – about 300m away. It's a remarkable phenomenon, an almost perfectly round hole in the limestone surface of the earth, some 60m in diameter and more than 40m deep, the bottom half full of water. It was thanks to the presence of this natural well (and perhaps another in the southern half of the site) that the city could survive at all, and it gives Chichén Itzá its present name "At the Edge of the Well of the Itzá". This well was regarded as a portal to the "other world" and Maya would throw offerings into it – incense, statues, jade and especially metal disks (a few of them gold), engraved and embossed with figures and glyphs – and also human sacrificial victims. People who were thrown in and survived emerged with the power of prophecy, having spoken with the gods. Today a basic cafeteria overlooks the well and serves as a handy viewpoint.

## Chichén Viejo

The southern half of the site is the most sacred part for contemporary Maya, though the buildings here are not, on the whole, in such good condition: less restoration work has been carried out so far, and the ground is not so extensively cleared. A path leads from the road opposite El Castillo to all the major structures, passing first the pyramid known as **El Osario** (also known as the High Priest's Grave), currently undergoing restoration. Externally it is very similar to El Castillo, but inside, most unusually, a series of **tombs** was discovered. A shaft, explored at the end of the last century, drops down from the top through five crypts, in each of which was found a skeleton and a trap door leading to the next. The fifth is at ground level, but here too there was a trap door, and steps cut through the rock to a sixth chamber that opens onto a huge underground cavern – the burial place of the high priest. Sadly the shaft and cavern are not open to the public.

Near here, also very ramshackle, are the **Templo del Venado** (Temple of the Deer) and the **Casa Colorada** (Red House), with a cluster of ruins known as the Southwest Group beyond them. Follow the path round, however, and you arrive at **El Caracol** (the Snail, for its shape; also called the Observatory), a circular, domed tower standing on two rectangular platforms and looking remarkably like a twentieth-century observatory in outline. Its roof has slits aligned with various points of astronomical observation. Four doors at the cardinal points lead into the tower, where there's a circular chamber and a spiral staircase leading to the upper level, from where sightings were made.

El Caracol is something of a Maya–Toltec mix, and, in fact, this was one of the buildings that first led archeologists to postulate the Toltec invasion theory. It has few of the obvious decorative features associated with either, though, and the remaining buildings are pure Maya. The so-called **Edificio de las Monjas** (the Nunnery) is the largest and most important of these – a palace complex showing several stages of construction. It's in rather poor condition, the rooms mostly filled with rubble and inhabited by flocks of swallows, and part of the facade was blasted away by a nineteenth-century explorer, but it is nonetheless a building of grand proportions. Its **annexe** has an elaborate facade in the Chenes style, covered with masks of Chac which combine to make one giant mask, with the door as a mouth. **La Iglesia** (the Church), a small building standing beside the convent, is by contrast a clear demonstration of Puuc design, with a low band of unadorned masonry around the bottom surmounted by an elaborate mosaic frieze and a roof-comb. Hook-nosed masks of Chac again predominate, but above the doorway are also the figures of the four **bacabs**, mythological creatures that held up the sky – a snail and a turtle on one side, an armadillo and a crab on the other.

Beyond Las Monjas, a path leads in about fifteen minutes to a further group of ruins – among the oldest on the site, but unrestored. Nearer at hand is the **Akad Dzib**, a relatively plain block of palace rooms which takes its name ("Obscure Writings") from some undeciphered hieroglyphs found inside. There are, too, red palm prints on the walls of some of the chambers – a sign frequently found in Maya buildings, whose significance is not yet understood. From here you can head back to the road past El Caracol and the Cenote de Xtoloc.

# Valladolid and around

The second town of Yucatán state, **VALLADOLID** is around 40km from Chichén Itzá, still close enough to beat the crowds to the site on an early bus, and of interest in its own right. Although it took a severe bashing in the nineteenth-century Caste Wars, the town has retained a strong colonial feel, and centres on a pretty, peaceful zócalo. The most famous of the surviving churches is sixteenth-century **San Bernardino**, 1km southwest of the zócalo (daily 9am–8pm; mass daily at 6pm). Built over one of the town's **cenotes**, **Sis-Ha**, the church is currently under restoration: the buildings are very impressive, but there's little left inside as, like so many of the Yucatán's churches, San Bernardino was sacked by the local Indians in the wars. Valladolid's other cenote, **Zací**, on Calle 36 between calles 39 and 37 (daily 8am–6pm; US$2), has become a tourist attraction, with a museum and an open-air restaurant at the entrance.

### Arrival and information
First-class buses between Mérida and Cancún don't go into Valladolid, but stop at **La Isleta**, a small bus station on the highway, where you transfer to a local bus for the ten-minute run into town. Valladolid's **bus station** is located on Calle 37 between calles 54 and 56, seven blocks to the west of the zócalo. *De paso* buses run from here at least hourly to both Mérida and Cancún and there are four daily departures for Playa del Carmen, most of which are via Cancún, and one to Cobá and Tulum (see following chapter). Some local second-class buses begin their journey here, too, for the above destinations and the smaller towns, including Tizimín, for Río Lagartos (see p.93).

To get to the centre from the bus station takes about ten minutes. Turn left onto Calle 37, then right after a couple of blocks, then left again, following Calle 39 to the pretty zócalo; you'll pass some of the cheaper **hotels** (see below) on the way. The **tourist office** is on the southeastern corner of the zócalo (Mon–Sat 9am–9pm, Sun 9am–1pm; www.chichen.com.mx/valladolid). Here you can get free maps of Valladolid and visit in-house tour operator Viajes Valladolid (☎9/856-1857; viva@chichen .com.mx), but it's at best a pretty casual set-up and the office may well be unattended.

Best to head for **El Bazaar**, a collection of inexpensive restaurants on the corner of calles 39 and 40 on the zócalo; the souvenir shop here has maps and current information. The **post office** is on the zócalo, near the corner of calles 39 and 40 (Mon–Fri 8am–6pm), as is Bancomer, which changes travellers' cheques and has an **ATM**. Banco de Sureste in Supermaz, a shopping plaza at C 39 229, changes travellers' cheques every weekday until 9pm. In the same plaza you'll find a **supermarket** and **laundry**. For national and international **telephone calls** there are Ladatel casetas at the bus station and on the zócalo (daily 7am–10pm); also on the zócalo is an **Internet** café. You can **rent bikes** from the sports shop owned by the exuberant *"Rei de Beisbol"*, Antonio Negro Aguilar, at C 44 195 – this one-time professional baseball star is also a great source of local information.

## Accommodation

Valladolid's budget hotels lie between the bus station and the centre, but you'd do better heading off toVallodolid's lovely new **hostel**, on the edge of Parque la Candelaria, at calles 44 and 42 (☎9/856-2267; ②), offering a garden, Internet access and tourist information. Antonio Aguilar (see above) also rents out very cheap rooms. For more atmosphere, however, it's worth splashing out a bit while you're here to stay in colonial style on the zócalo.

**Hotel Lily**, C44 192 (☎9/856-2163). Small homely hotel with basic, good-value rooms. ③.

**María de la Luz**, C 42, on the zócalo (☎9/856-2071, fax 856-1181, *maria_luz@chichen.com.mx*). The rooms are less luxurious than the lobby, but comfortable and good value, with a/c; there's also a small pool. ④.

**María Guadalupe**, C 44 198 (☎9/856-2068). The best-value cheap hotel with clean, well-kept rooms with baths. Colectivos for the cenote at Dzitnup leave from outside. ③.

**El Mesón del Marqués**, C 39 203, on the zócalo (☎9/856-2073, fax 856-2280; *h_marques@chichen.com.mx*). Lovely hotel in a former colonial mansion, overlooking a courtyard with fountains and lush plants. There's a wonderful palm-fringed pool, and one of the best restaurants in town. ⑤.

**San Clemente**, C 42, corner of C 41 (☎ & fax 9/856-3161). Just off the zócalo, this very comfortable hotel has a restaurant and pool. Prices are similar to the *María de la Luz*, but the facilities are better. ④.

**Zaci**, C 44 193, between calles 39 and 37 (☎9/856-2167). Pleasant hotel with a lovely, plant-filled courtyard and a small pool. Rooms have either a fan or, for a few dollars more, a/c and cable TV. ④.

## Eating and drinking

Whatever your budget, to eat well in Valladolid you don't have to stray further than the zócalo, where you can get inexpensive snacks or treat yourself without going into debt.

**El Bazaar**, northeastern corner of the zócalo, calles 39 and 40. Inexpensive *loncherías* and pizzerias, always busy and open until late.

**La Cocina de Menyula la Luna**, C 41 opposite the tourist office. Bright and cheerful corner café serving Yucatecan specialities such as *cochinita enterrada* (pork baked in an underground pit).

**Maria de la Luz**, C 42, on the zócalo. Large popular restaurant which opens onto the square and has an extensive Mexican and international menu. Very good-value (approx US$3) breakfast buffet daily.

**El Mesón del Marqués**, C 39 203, on the zócalo. Probably Valladolid's best restaurant, offering tranquillity in the centre of town at tables around the fountain of the hotel courtyard, though it can be packed with tour groups. Yucatecan specialities such as lime soup and *poc-chuc*.

**Restaurante San Bernadino de Siena**, C 49 227, two blocks from Convento San Bernadino (☎9/856-2720). Locally known as *Don Juanito's* and frequented mostly by Mexicans, this highly recommended, mid-price restaurant is a great place for a lazy lunch or dinner away from the hustle and bustle of the town centre.

# Around Valladolid

From Valladolid the vast majority of traffic heads straight on to Cancún and the Caribbean beaches. There are a few places worth taking time out to explore, however, and, if you have more time, an alternative is to head north via Tizimín to **Río Lagartos** or **San Felipe**. You'll need to make an early start if you want to co-ordinate your buses, go on a flamingo trip and get back to Valladolid in the same day – the last bus for Tizimín from Río Lagartos leaves at 5pm and the last bus for Valladolid leaves Tizimín at 6pm. You'll have to return to Valladolid to head on to the Caribbean coast.

## Cenote Dzitnup and Cenote Samulá

Seven kilometres west of Valladolid, the remarkable **Cenote Dzitnup**, or X'Keken (daily 8am–5pm; US$1.50), is reached by descending into a cave, where a nearly circular pool of crystal-clear, turquoise water is illuminated by a shaft of light from an opening in the roof. A swim in the ice-cold water is a fantastic experience, but take a sweater for afterwards as the temperature in the cave is noticeably cooler than outside. Equally, if not more, impressive is the **Cenote Samulá** (daily 8am–5pm; US$1), almost directly across the road – while Dzitnup is frequently crowded and plagued by young boys asking for tips, you may well find yourself alone at Samula, which has the roots of a huge *alamo* tree stretching down into the pool. There are direct colectivos to Dzitnup from outside the *Hotel María Guadalupe* in Valladolid (see above). Alternatively, any westbound second-class bus will drop you at the turn-off, 5km from Valladolid, from where it's a 2km walk down a signed track to both cenotes. You could also take a taxi or, best of all, cycle from Valladolid.

## Balancanché

Thirty-four kilometres from Valladolid, on the way to Chichén Itzá, you can visit the **Caves of Balancanché**, where in 1959 a sealed passageway was discovered leading to a series of caverns in which the ancient population had left offerings to Chac. "Guided tours" in English (daily 11am, 1pm & 3pm; US$4) – in reality, a taped commentary – lead you past the usual stalactites and stalagmites, an underground pool and, most interestingly, many of the original Maya offerings still in situ. Be warned that in places the caves can be cold, damp and thoroughly claustrophobic. Charles Gallenkamp's *Maya* (see "Books" in Contexts) has an excellent chapter devoted to the discovery of the caves, and to the ritual of exorcism that a local *h-man* (traditional priest) insisted on carrying out to placate the ancient gods and disturbed spirits. Buses between Valladolid and Mérida will drop you at *las grutas*.

## Ek-Balam

Twenty-five kilometres north of Valladolid, and a short signposted detour from Hwy-265 to Río Lagartos, **Ek-Balam** (daily 5am–5pm; US$1.70, free on Sun) is a small but unusual Maya site. According to the "Account of Ek-Balam" written by Spanish Commander Juan Gutierrez Picon in 1579, the place was granted to him as a reward for being one of the conquerors of the region. The same account relates that Ek-Balam, meaning "black jaguar", was the name of the great man who founded the city and built most of the five structures at the site. The most important cultural period at Ek-Balam was the Late Classic (700–1000 AD) and what most stands out at the site are the large dimensions of its structures, most of which have yet to be properly restored, as well as the fact that the central part is surrounded by two **walls**, a rare occurrence in Maya cities. Their purpose here is believed to have prohibited (at least symbolically) passage to certain sacred parts of the city in order to maintain their sanctity. The ruins are contained within two large connected plazas and the most impressive building is Structure 1, the **Acropolis**, which stands 33m high and 160m in length – and unfortunately about which very little is known. Influences from the Puuc such as the cut stones and decorative element are evident in Structure 2, the remains of a **palace** 20m high and originally consisting of a double layer of 24 rooms – as well as characteristics of the Peten region in Guatemala, seen in the rounded corners and the sloped walls. Unlike at Uxmal or Chichén Itzá, the facades at Ek-Balam were not decorated with stone-carved figures but rather with stucco modelled into distinct forms and painted. Other interesting structures at the site include an entrance arch and a temple with a walkway curled round it.

There's no public transport to Ek-Balam though there are *combis* to the nearest village, **SANTA RITA**, a shabby little place with no facilities but one or two dusty shops where you can buy cold drinks – and you might be able to persuade a local to take you the five km from here to the site. Otherwise you could join an **organized tour** in Valladolid or Cancún.

## Río Lagartos and Las Coloradas

Travelling by bus from Valladolid north to Río Lagartos, you have to change at the elegant colonial town of **TIZIMÍN**, 51km from Valladolid. There's little to see, but the small **Parque Zoológico de la Reina** has animals from all over the peninsula, and the pretty plaza is peaceful enough for whiling away a few hours. The best of the modest but overpriced **hotels** in the centre is *María Antonia*, Calle 50 (☎9/863-2384; ④) and there's a good **restaurant** in the town's main square, the *Tres Reyes*. Tizimín also has direct bus services to and from Mérida and Cancún.

**RÍO LAGARTOS**, 100km north of Valladolid, stands on a lagoon in marshy coastal flatland, inhabited by vast colonies of **pink flamingos**. Despite talk of turning the area into a new tourist centre, so far it remains a backwater fishing village. It's easy enough to visit on a day-trip from Valladolid, but if you want to **stay**, try *Cabañas dos Hermanos* (☎9/862-0128; ③), at the back of a family home, by the beach, which sleep two or three people and have private bathrooms and pay-as-you-view cable TV; from the bus station, turn right and continue on to the water's edge. Otherwise there are large comfortable rooms at *Posada Leydi* (☎9/862-0005; ③), on Calle 14 at the other end of town, while the smartest option of the lot is *Hotel Villa de Pescadores* on the malecón (☎9/862-0020; ⑤), where all rooms have balconies overlooking the water. A boat trip over to the seaward shore of the spit that encloses the lagoon will bring you to a couple of **beaches**, but they're not up to much, and in the end it's the flamingos alone that make a visit worthwhile.

You're likely to be swamped by offers to take you out to see the flamingos as soon get off the bus or out of your car. If not, the best place to start is the friendly *Restaurante Isla Contoy*, on the waterfront, where you can leaf though a book of photos and visitors' comments while waiting for your boat to turn up. A **boat** to visit the many feeding sites costs around US$35, with a maximum of seven people, but the price and length of the trip are infinitely negotiable. Make sure that your guide understands that you don't want to harass the flamingos, as some will get too close if they think their passengers would prefer to see some action. Recommended is the amiable Marcel Flores (known as *Leche*), who will take you further out than other guides, perhaps as far as Las Coloradas (see below). Ask for him at *Los Negritos* restaurant on the main street as you drive into town. As well as flamingos, you're likely to see fishing eagles, spoonbills and, if you're lucky, one of the very few remaining crocodiles for which Río Lagartos was named.

The most spectacular flamingo colony is at **Las Coloradas**, on the narrow spit that separates the lagoon from the sea about 16km east of Río Lagartos. There's a small village and salt factory here, but you'll need to find your own transport, as the bus timetable does not give you a chance to stay long enough to see anything.

## San Felipe

If it's beaches you're after, **SAN FELIPE**, 12km west of Río Lagartos, is a much better bet – many of the buses from Valladolid to Río Lagartos come out here. There's one good **hotel** in town, *Hotel San Felipe de Jesus*, Calle 9 between calles 14 and 16 (☎9/862-2027; ⑤), which also has a decent **restaurant**. However, most people get a boat (US$5 round trip) across to the offshore spit to set up **camp** on one of a number of beaches. At Mexican holiday times these are positively crowded, the rest of the year quite deserted. If you do camp, be sure to bring protection against mosquitoes; if not, it's easy enough to arrange for the boat to collect you in the evening.

# Isla Holbox

Although most traffic between Mérida and the coast heads directly east to Cancún, it is possible to turn north at Valladolid or Nuevo X-Can to **Chiquilá**, where you can board the ferry for **Isla Holbox**, a 25-kilometre-long island near the easternmost point of the Gulf coast. Sometimes touted as a "new" beach paradise to fill the place that Isla Mujeres once had in travellers' affections, it's still relatively unspoilt. There are miles of empty beaches to enjoy, and anyone who's come from the more touristy resorts will find the island's relaxed, laid-back pace – and the genuinely warm welcome – something of a relief.

## Practicalities

**Buses for Chiquilá** leave Valladolid (2hr 30min) and Tizimín (1hr 30min) a couple of times a day. Catch an early bus to make sure you get the afternoon ferry. Coming from the east, get a bus to the road junction just before Nuevo X-Can and wait for a colectivo (US$1) to Kantunilkin, about halfway to Chiquilá, where you can pick up the bus. The **easiest route** to Chiquilá, though, is the daily direct bus from Cancún which leaves at 8am and returns to the city at 1.30pm (though it always waits for the 1pm Holbox ferry to dock before setting off). The **Chiquilá ferry** for Holbox leaves seven times a day, the first at 6am and the last 5pm (30min; US$2), and returns as many times, from 5am until 4pm. Holbox is also served by a **car ferry**, leaving Chiquilá at 9am and 1pm daily and returning from Holbox at noon (though it often doesn't run, for various reasons). Make sure you don't miss the boat: Chiquilá is not a place you want to get stranded in. There's a restaurant and a store, but little else.

Once on Isla Holbox you'll find a number of lovely **hotels** on the beach and several adequate budget options in town: from the ferry dock, Avenida Juarez, the street directly in front of you, will lead you in several minutes to the main square (if you're carrying heavy luggage tricycle porters charge US$1 per ride), where *Posada Los Arcos*, next to the Tienda Dinorah (☎9/875-2043; ③) has clean and spacious rooms. Try also *Posada Playa Bonita* (②), almost on the seafront. Two recommended mid-range options are the *Hotel Faro Viejo* (☎9/875-2217, fax 875-2186, *www.faroviejoholbox.com.mx*; ⑤), which has pretty rooms overlooking the beach and a very good restaurant, and the lovely *Posada Mawimbi*, 15min further down the beach (☎9/875-2003; ⑤) and run by a friendly Italian couple. There are several upscale hotels still further along the coast (but within walking distance), the best of which are *Hotel Villas Flamingos* (☎9/875-2167, *www.mexicoholiday.com*; ⑧), with six spacious cabañas, four comfortable rooms, all beautifully designed, and a swimming pool on the beach; and *Villas Delfines* (☎9/874-4014, *www.holbox.com*; ⑧), with ten very attractive cabañas and a restaurant which hosts an outdoor barbecue on Saturdays with candlelit tables spread out through the orchid garden.

There are also several very good **restaurants** in the island's village. *La Isla de Colibri*, on the corner of the main square, serves delicious fresh fruit juices and other healthy options; *Zarabanda* is recommended for fresh fish and *Buena Onda* serves delicious Italian dishes. There's also a pizzeria on the main square and one disco–bar, *Las Cariocas*, should you feel the need to party.

There are very few cars in Holbox – the locals use golf carts which are available to rent (US$10 per hour). **Fishing trips** and other sight-seeing tours can be organised through the smarter hotels (which also have kayaks and horses for hire). There's a dive shop at *Posada Mawimbi* – **snorkelling** excursions can be arranged here, too.

# From Mérida to Campeche

From Mérida to Campeche there's a choice of **two routes**. First-class buses, and all *directo* services, take a new fast road which runs parallel to **Hwy-180** – tracing the route of the colonial Camino Real, lined with villages whose plazas are laid out on the traditional plan around a massive old church. The Maya ruins at **Oxkintok**, around halfway on the highway, look fairly unimpressive today, but this was a city with a lifespan of a thousand years or more and was still thriving in the Postclassic – after 1000 AD. The site has some of the oldest hieroglyphs so far found in the Yucatán (dating from between 475 AD and 859 AD), and many of the buildings are earlier, belonging to the upper Preclassic (300 BC–300 AD). Their style, as well as that of ceramics found at the site, suggests a link with the Maya architecture of the Petén. **BECAL**, 10km further south, just inside Campeche state and a short signed detour from the highway, is one of the biggest centres for the manufacture of basketware and the ubiquitous Yucatecan **jipis**, or "Panama" hats (real panama hats come from Ecuador). There's a *Centro Artesanal* by the road where you can buy them, but it's more interesting to go into the village and watch this cottage industry at work. **HECELCHAKAN**, about 80km before Campeche (and also a short detour), has a small **archeology museum** on the main square (Tues–Sat 9am–8pm, Sun 9am–noon; US$1.50), featuring figures from Jaina and objects from other nearby sites.

The longer route **via Muna and Hopelchén**, passing the great sites of **Uxmal**, **Kabáh** and **Sayil** (see pp.77 & 80), offers more to see if you have the time. With a car you could easily visit all three sites, perhaps stopping also at **BOLONCHÉN DE REJON**, with its nine wells (*bolonchén* means nine wells), and the nearby **Grutas de Xtacumbilxunan**, 3km south, and still get to Campeche within the day. By bus it's slightly harder, but with a little planning – and if you set out early – you should be able to get to at least one site. Kabáh is the easiest since the ruins lie right on the main road.

# Campeche

**CAMPECHE**, capital of the state that bears its name, is one of Mexico's colonial gems and has at last been recognized as such, with the designation of the city as a UNESCO World Heritage Site in December 1999. Elegant eighteenth- and nineteenth-century houses painted in pastel shades (1600 facades of which have been recently restored to their former glory), interspersed with the occasional church, give it a distinctly European feel. At its heart, relatively intact, lies a colonial port still surrounded by hefty defensive walls and fortresses; around, you'll find the trappings of a modern city that is once again becoming wealthy. The seafront is a bizarre mixture of ancient and ultra-modern: originally the city defences dropped straight into the sea, but now they face a reclaimed strip of land on which stand the spectacular new Palacio de Gobierno and State Legislature (spectacularly ugly in the eyes of most locals), a series of striking new sculptures representing various aspects of the city – piracy, warfare at sea, fishing – and several big hotels. In the past, few tourists have stopped here, preferring to sweep by en route to Escárcega and Palenque or take Hwy-180 along the beautiful coast route via Ciudad del Carmen to Villahermosa. Though more and more visitors are discovering the immaculately preserved and tranquil streets which compare favourably with Mérida's, for the moment at least Campeche remains unblighted by tourist overkill.

Campeche's colonial **history** was launched with the arrival of a Spanish expedition under Francisco Hernandez, who in 1517 landed outside the Maya town of Ah Kin Pech, only to beat a hasty retreat on seeing the forces lined up to greet them. It wasn't until 1540 that Francisco de Montejo founded the modern town, and from here set out on his mission to conquer the Yucatán. From then until the nineteenth century, it was the chief port in the peninsula, exporting mainly logwood (source of a red dye known as *hematein*) from local forests. It also became an irresistible target for the pirates who operated with relative impunity from bases on the untamed coast round about. Hence the fortifications, built between 1668 and 1704 after a particularly brutal massacre of the population.

## Arrival and information

Campeche's **Central Camionera**, with first- and second-class terminals, is 2km from the colonial centre, along Avenida Gobernadores. To get to the centre, turn left outside, cross the road and take a city bus marked "Centro" or "Gobernadores". Local buses leave from the market, just south of the city wall. If you arrive at the **airport**, about 10km southeast of town, you'll have to take a taxi.

Within the city, even-numbered **streets** run parallel with the sea, starting for some reason with Calle 8, just inside the ramparts; odd-numbered streets run inland. The zócalo, **Parque Principal**, is bordered by calles 8, 10, 55 and 57. Almost everything of interest is gathered within the old walls.

Campeche's **tourist office** (daily 9–3pm & 6–9pm; ☎ & fax 9/816-6767 or 816-5593, *turismo@campeche.gob.mx*), in the Plaza Moch Couoh on Avenida Ruiz Cortines, opposite the unsightly government palace, is helpful and friendly and there's usually someone there who can speak English. Be sure to pick up the free tourist magazines, with articles about what's going on in and around town and in the state. They also have a list of independent **guides** (speaking various languages) who lead tours of the city and archeological zones, though you might be expected to provide the transport; Betty Mena Pacheco is recommended (☎9/811-0733). Other tourist **information booths** (at the bus station and Baluarte de San Pedro at the northwest corner of the walled city) have maps, details of activities and tours, and may offer advice on accommodation.

## Accommodation

Because Campeche is not on the tourist circuit, it boasts plenty of inexpensive **hotels**, though for the same reason they can be rather shabby. Avoid rooms overlooking the street, as Campeche's narrow lanes magnify traffic noise. The best bargains are found within a couple of blocks of the zócalo.

The **youth hostel**, on Avenida Agustín Melgar (☎9/816-1802; ②), is clean and bustling, with single-sex dorms, and camping in the grounds, but it's a long way out. To get there, catch a bus ( "Directo/Universidad") from the Central Camionera, or one marked "Lerma" or "Playa Bonita" heading west through the old walled city.

**America**, C 10 252, between calles 59 and 61 (☎9/816-4588, fax 811-0556, *www.camp.com.mx/hamerica*). Elegant colonial building with comfortable rooms; the best ones overlook the courtyard. ④.

**Baluartes**, Av Ruíz Cortines, just south of the *Hotel del Mar* (☎9/816-3911, fax 816-2410, *baluarte@campeche.sureste.com*). The *Hotel del Mar's* older and slightly cheaper rival, with a pool, TVs and a/c. ⑦.

**Campeche**, C 57 2, opposite the cathedral (☎9/816-5183). Basic rooms in a colonial house; the rooms overlooking the zócalo can be noisy.

**Colonial**, C 14 122 (☎9/816-2222). The best-value place in town, immaculately clean and friendly, in an old colonial building. ③.

**Lopez**, C 12 189 (☎ & fax 9/816-3344). Attractive central hotel with clean, comfortable rooms, TV and a/c. ⑤.

**Hotel del Mar,** Av Ruiz Cortines 51 (☎9/816-2233, fax 811-1618, *delmarcp@camp1.telmex.net.mx*). Formerly the *Ramada Inn*, this comfortable upmarket hotel has a pool, restaurant and car rental facilities. ⑦.

**Posada del Angel**, C 10 307, corner of C 55 (☎9/816-7718). Modern hotel, centrally located by the corner of the cathedral. All rooms have TV and a/c. ④.

**Regis,** C 12 189, between calles 55 and 57 (☎9/816-3175). Seven very large rooms, some with TV and a/c. ⑤.

## The City

A visit to Campeche should begin with a wander through the city's delightful old streets, stopping along the way to visit La Mansión Carvajal on Calle 10 between calles 51 and 53, an elegant colonial house, reminiscent of Andalucian Moorish homes, that once belonged to one of the city's richest families. Next, head for the **Cathedral**, overlooking the zócalo, which was founded in 1540, making it one of the oldest churches on the peninsula – the bulk of the construction, though, took place much later, and what you see is not particularly striking Baroque. Just beyond the zócalo, on C8, the **Museo de las Estelas** (daily 8am–8pm; US$2) is housed in the Baluarte de la Soledad, a bulwark built into the old city walls, and has a small but interesting collection of columns and stelae taken from Edzna and other local Maya sites, depicting religious and civil ceremonies amongst other things; unfortunately all explanations are in Spanish only.

The **Baluarte San Carlos** is the most dramatic of the city's seven surviving bulwarks, with cannons on the battlement roof and, underneath, the beginnings of a network of ancient tunnels that undermines much of the town. The tunnels once provided a place of refuge for the populace from pirate raids and were probably used by the Maya before that. Now they are said to be haunted by evil ghosts who emerge at night through the countless entrances in the old colonial houses to steal children.

Other sights are a little further out. About twenty minutes' walk to the right (northeast) along the seafront is the **Iglesia de San Francisco**, the only surviving remnant of a sixteenth-century Franciscan monastery. On this site, supposedly, the first Mass to be heard in Mexico was celebrated in 1517. Not far beyond lies the **Pozo de la Conquista** (Well of the Conquest), where the same Spanish expedition, under Francisco Hernandez, took on water to fill their leaking casks. In the other direction, again along the waterfront malecón, the **Fort San Miguel** houses Campeche's wonderful **archeological museum** (Tues–Sun 8am–7.30pm; US$2). Objects from Edzná and Jaina predominate – some of the delicate Jaina figurines are cross-eyed, a feature that the Maya considered a mark of beauty. As with straightened noses and flattened foreheads, this was often brought about by deliberate deformation – Bernal Díaz noted that the first two prisoners taken by Hernandez were both cross-eyed. There are also some interesting Olmec and Maya pieces including some fine sculpture and some Prehispanic gold, but the highlight is the treasure from the tombs at Calakmul. The jade death masks are awe-inspiring and every bit as impressive and beautiful as the death masks of Pacal from Palenque. Take a look at the views over the bulwarks, too, which are wonderful at sunset. The **Fort San José**, on a hill on the opposite side of the city, has an armaments museum and a collection of items from the colonial era.

Other than taking a stroll round the city, the most pleasant way to learn a little about Campeche is to take one of two picturesque **tram rides** from their starting point in the zócalo – the **Tranvía de la Ciudad** takes in most sights in the walled city, passing through the narrow streets of the neighbourhood of San Roman, home to the church containing the Black Christ, a 6ft ebony sculpture which was brought from Italy in 1575 and is paraded through the streets on Campeche's feast day, 14 September. The other tram ride, **El Guapo**, runs along the seafront and up to Fort San Miguel (see above). Both 45-minute trips cost US$2 and depart several times a day between 9am and 7pm (though set times are flexible to say the least and trams only go if there are 20 people or more aboard); both also offer informed commentaries in Spanish and English.

If you're desperate to be by the sea, a "Playa Bonita" bus along the waterfront will take you past Fort San Miguel and beyond to the **beaches** at **Playa Bonita** and **Lerma**, a fishing village just beyond the city. It's not a terribly attractive prospect, however, with the port and lots of factories probably spewing out pollutants, and there are better beaches out towards Ciudad del Carmen.

## Eating, drinking and entertainment

Restaurants abound in the centre of Campeche, especially along calles 8 and 10. **Seafood**, served almost everywhere, is a good bet; try the *pan de cazón* (a kind of shark lasagne, made with layers of tortillas) or shrimps in spicy sauce. The café in the centre of the zócalo serves excellent coffee and home-made ice-cream, and Campeche's **market**, just north of the walled city, is surrounded by comedors offering cheap and tasty comidas corridas.

Every Tuesday, Friday and Saturday, Campeche has its own **Son et lumière**, set in front of the city's Land Gate (8.30pm; US$2), which depicts various historical scenes and is heartfelt if not spectacular.

### RESTAURANTS AND BARS

**Casa Viejo**, C 10, above the zócalo's colonnade, Arcos Revolución. Cuban-owned restaurant with well-appointed balcony overlooking the main square and classy international cuisine. Highly recommended, though not for those on a budget.

**Iguana Azul**, C 55, opposite *La Parroquia*. Gorgeously decorated colonial house with small restaurant specializing in Creole and Campechen dishes, and a large bar with leafy courtyard.

**Marganzo**, C 8 262. Overpriced tourist trap with staff in costumes and live music – though the food's decent enough. The place if you're looking for a gringo party atmosphere.

**Restaurant Campeche**, C 57, next door to the *Hotel Campeche*. Large unfussy restaurant with extensive menu – local specialities and Mexican food in general – and reasonable prices.

**La Palapa**, Av Resurgimento (30min stroll along the malecón from the city centre towards Fort San Miguel). Large seafront bar right on the water, where delicious *antojios* are served with every drink.

**La Parroquia**, C 55 8. Traditional, family-run restaurant; good value and very popular with locals. Open 24hr.

**Restaurant Miramar**, calles 8 and 61. Campeche's best seafood; pricey, but worth it.

## Listings

**American Express** Located inside the VIPS – Viajes Programados – Travel Agency, C 59 and Av 16 de Septiembre (☎9/811-1010, fax 816-8333).

**Banks** BanCrecen, calles 10 and 57, and Bital, calles 10 and 55, are both on the main square and have ATMs. Banamex is also on Calle 10, at the corner of Calle 53.

**Car rental** Maya Car Rental (☎9/816-2233) in the *Hotel del Mar.* Viajes Turisticos Xtampak also rent cars(☎9/812-64-85, *www.webcampeche.com/oferta/xtampak*).

**Email and fax**. There are internet cafés on every street in the centre of Campeche, charging approx US$1 per hour. You can fax from the Telecom office on Av 16 de Septiembre (Mon–Fri 9am–8pm, Sat 9am–1pm).

**Laundry** The Tintoria Campeche (Mon–Sat 9am–4pm) on C 55, 26.

**Post office** Av 16 de Septiembre at Calle 53, in the Oficinas del Gobierno Federal (Mon–Fri 8am–8pm, Sat 9am–2pm).

**Tours** *Novia del Mar* (☎9/816-2417) run day-trips to both Edzna (US$25) and Uxmal (US$45). The best way to see the Calakmul biosphere is with Corazon Maya, located in the San Pedro Baluarte, calles 18 and 51 (☎9/811-3788, *www.corazonmaya.cjb.net*), who organize excellent private tours (US$150 for 1–4 people) into the area and can also arrange customized bird-watching or camping trips.

# The Campeche coast

South of Campeche, Hwy 180 sweeps along the mostly deserted coast, passing several small resorts. Thirty minutes from the city, the *Hotel Tucan Siho Playa* (☎9/823-1200, fax 823-1203, *hmtucan@tnet.net.mx*; ⑤) is situated on its own lovely beach overlooking calm turquoise sea and nesting turtles in April and May. Most tourists heading in this direction turn inland at **Champotón**, a growing fishing village and oil port at the mouth of the Río

---

### MOVING ON FROM CAMPECHE

Regular first-class ADO, Colon and second-class Autobuses del Sur **buses** (all from the same terminal – see p.96) leave for Ciudad del Carmen (hourly, 3hr), Mérida (more than 12 daily, 2hr), Chetumal via Escárcega and Xpujil (3 daily, 5–7hr), and Villahermosa (10 daily, 6ú7hr). There are also services to San Cristóbal (via Palenque), Playa del Carmen, Veracruz, Mexico City and Coatzalcoalcos (for southern Veracruz) and second-class buses direct to Uxmal. Minibuses leave from the market just outside the southern end of the old city (C53 and Circuito Baluartes Este), for local villages like the craft centres Becal and Calkini, and for Edzná.

Aeroméxico (☎9/816-6656 or 816-4925) operates a variety of internal **flights**. A taxi out to the **airport** costs around US$8.

---

Champotón (renowned for its delicious seafood cocktails and ceviche), on their way southeast towards Escárcega for Chetumal or Palenque. If you want to get anywhere reasonably quickly, even if you're heading to Villahermosa and beyond, this route is the best option. Alternatively, if you want to head towards Ciudad del Carmen and then into southern Veracruz, you could continue along the coast to **Sabancuy**, 83km before Ciudad del Carmen, a little village which has one of the only half-way decent beaches in Campeche. There are few tourists and only one hotel, the *Posada Bellavista* (②). At **Isla Aguada**, the Puenta de la Unidad, said to be the longest road bridge in Mexico, crosses the eastern entrance to the **Laguna de Terminos**, joining the **Isla del Carmen** to the mainland. If you're driving be careful not to exceed the speed limit; traffic cops posted at either end of the bridge are notorious for demanding heavy on-the-spot fines.

## Ciudad del Carmen

**CIUDAD DEL CARMEN**, the only town of any size on the 35-kilometre-long Isla del Carmen, doesn't merit a special trip except perhaps during its lively **fiesta** in July. It's not unpleasant, but it's hot and crowded and has much less historical atmosphere than Campeche. The conquistadors landed here in 1518, but the first settlers were pirates in 1633. Nowadays it's home to a fishing fleet, catching, among other things, giant prawns for export. The oil boom has created new industries and forced prices up, so you won't find any accommodation bargains here. The town's environs also suffer from oil industry pollution.

Should you be interested, Carmen, as the town is usually known, now has a small **museum**, Calle 22 (daily 8am–8pm; US$0.50), with an imaginative display charting its history.

### Practicalities

ADO (first-class) and Sur (second-class) buses use the same station on Avenida Periferica Ote. To get to the centre, take a taxi or colectivo (5am–11pm; about 20min). The **tourist office**, in the Casa de la Cultura, calles 24 and 27 (Mon–Fri 9am–3pm), has plenty of information (English and Spanish) on Campeche state, but little about Ciudad del Carmen. The **post office** (Mon–Fri 8am–8pm, Sat 9am–1pm) is tucked away at C 22 57, between calles 25 and 27, while Banamex, on the corner of Calle 24 at the edge of the Parque General Ignacio Zaragosa, and Bancomer, C 24 42 at the corner with C 29, both have ATMs and cajeros.

Most of the **accommodation** is on calles 20, 22 and 24 near the waterfront. At fiesta-time places fill up, so book ahead. *Hotel Victoria* (☎9/382-9301; ⑤) and *Hotel Zacarias* (☎9/382-0121; ④), both on Calle 24, are comfortable enough and clean. More luxurious is the *Hotel de Parque*, on the corner of Calle 33 between Parque General Ignacio Zaragosa and the waterfront (☎9/382-3046, fax 382 2437; ⑥), where all rooms have a/c, TV and phone. **Food** in Ciudad del Carmen is a mixture of specialities from the Yucatán peninsula and the state of Tabasco, with a stress on shellfish. Many low-priced restaurants are grouped together along Calle 33 by the busy Parque General Ignacio Zaragosa; recommended is *La Fuente*, at calles 20 and 29, between the waterfront and a small park, which serves cheap Mexican food round the clock. *Los Pelicanos*, Calle 24, has an attractive terrace and its Tex-Mex menu makes it popular with American oilmen. The *Jungle Queen* riverboat leaves from the stretch of malecón opposite the *Hotel del Parque* at 7pm nightly for a four-hour dinner cruise (around US$20–30; book in person on the boat).

# Edzná and the Chenes sites

Some 60km from Campeche lie the impressive ruins of **EDZNÁ** (daily 8am–5pm; US$2.50, free on Sun), the only local site almost accessible by bus. Though this is an area where the **Chenes** style of architecture (closely related to the Puuc of Uxmal – see p.77) dominated – *chen* means "well" and is a fairly common suffix to place names hereabouts – Edzná is far from a pure example of it, also featuring elements of Río Bec, Puuc and Classic Maya design. For the real thing, you have to venture further south.

Edzná was a large city, on the main trade route between the Maya of the highlands and the coast. The most important structure is the great **Templo de los Cinco Pisos** (Temple of the Five Storeys), a stepped palace/pyramid more than 20m high built on a vast acropolis. Unusually, each of the five storeys contains chambered "palace" rooms: while solid temple pyramids and multistorey "apartment" complexes are relatively common, it is rare to see the two combined in one building. At the front, a steep monumental staircase leads to a three-roomed temple, topped by a roof-comb. The view from here is one of the most impressive in the Yucatán. It is easy to imagine the power that the high priest or king commanded as you look out over two plazas, the more distant of which must have been capable of holding tens of thousands of people. Beyond lie the unexcavated remains of other large pyramids, and behind them, the vast flat expanse of the Yucatán shelf. A stela of the god of maize positioned here was illuminated by the sun twice a year, on the dates for the planting and harvesting of maize, and the whole temple is orientated to face to the rising sun.

Lesser buildings surround the ceremonial precinct. The **Casa Grande**, a palace on the northwest side, and some of the buildings alongside it, were cleared by archeologists in late 1986. Some 55m long, the Casa Grande includes a room used as a *temezcal*, with stone benches and hearths over which water could be boiled. There are two haunting stucco masks of the gods of day and night in the **Templo de los Mascarones** and, nearby, a small early Classic ball court in the Petén style and another ball court ring still in place along the west wall. The rest of the site – including a large system of drainage (and possibly irrigation) canals – remains unexcavated.

**Buses** for Pich or Bon Fil leave from the huge market in Campeche (Calle 53 and Circuito Baluartes Este) every half-hour and will take you within 1km of the entrance at Edzná. Getting back is harder: there are passing buses but they are erratic; ask the driver of your bus on the way out. Alternatively, you could join an **organized trip** from Campeche.

## Other Chenes sites

The examples of true Chenes style are accessible only with a car or exceptional determination. The chief sites are reached on a poor road from **HOPELCHÉN**, a village about 100km from Campeche on the long route to Mérida. A bus follows this road as far as **Dzibalchén** and **Iturbide**, but it's not much use for visiting the sites as it turns straight round on arrival. If you choose to **stay** in Hopelchén, *Los Arcos*, Calle 17 on the corner of the plaza, near where the buses stop (☎9/822-0037; ③), is the only option.

The best of the ruins are some way from the paved road and substantially buried in the jungle. **Hochob**, just outside Dzibalchén, has an amazing three-roomed temple (low and fairly small, as are most Chenes buildings), with a facade entirely covered in richly carved, stylized snakes and masks. The central chamber is surmounted by a crumbling roof-comb, and its decoration creates the effect of a huge mask, with the doorway as a gaping mouth. The remains of **Dzibilnocac**, 1km north of Iturbide, demonstrate the ultra-decorative facades typical of the Chenes style and its restored western temple-pyramid makes a trip out here very worthwhile.

# Francisco Escárcega to Xpujil

Heading south from Campeche on the inland route, Hwy-61 meets the east–west Hwy-186 at **FRANCISCO ESCÁRCEGA** (always referred to as Escárcega), a hot, dusty town straggling along the road and old train tracks for a couple of kilometres. There's little to detain you in town and in fact the place has a reputation for being not just ugly but dangerous. However Escárcega does provide a jumping-off point for a number of relatively unexplored **Maya sites** that are now beginning to be developed for tourism. Known as the **Río Bec sites**, many of them are in the **Calakmul Biosphere Reserve**, a vast area of tropical forest, once heavily populated by lowland Maya, which stretches all the way into the Petén region of Guatemala. Though the region's most famous site lies over the border at **Tikal**, others within Mexico, only recently accessible, are every bit as exciting as the sites of the northern Yucatán.

The ADO bus station is at the road junction; from there, walk 1500m east to the centre and the Sur bus station. If you need to **stay**, *Hotel Escárcega* on the town's main drag as you leave towards Campeche (☎9/8240-0187; ④) has clean rooms with private bath. **Getting out of town** is relatively easy: at least ten buses run daily to Mérida, there's an hourly service to Campeche between 4am and 6pm, a 4.30am second-class bus to Palenque, and a couple to San Cristóbal; in addition, Escárcega is on the ADO first-class route between Chetumal and Villahermosa. Services to Xpujil and Chetumal run overnight or in the mornings only – nothing heads out in the afternoon.

However, the far from glamorous village of **XPUJIL** is a better place for exploring the region. Basically a one-street town straddling Hwy-186, it has a few simple places to stay. Try the *Hotel Calakmul* (☎9/832-3304; ④) or the *Restaurant and Cabañas El Mirador Maya* (☎9/871-6005; ④), which has simple, thatched cabañas with hammocks and a money exchange counter. There are a couple of additional restaurants, several Ladatel phones and a small post office.

**Leaving Xpujil**, there are, in theory, three ADO **buses** a day to Chetumal, and an hourly service to Escárcega and onward. It is possible to catch a series of second-class buses through to Mérida via Dzibalchen, Hopelchén and the Ruta Puuc. This rough road passes through the northern half of the Calakmul Biosphere Reserve, and is an interesting and little travelled route north, if you have time to spare.

## The Río Bec sites

The **Río Bec** style, characterized by long buildings with matching towers at each end and narrow roof-combs, can be seen at a number of sites in this region. The most accessible is **Xpujil**, just 1500m back along the highway from Xpujil village (8am–5pm, US$1.50, free on Sun). Dating from the Classic period, it is perhaps the least impressive of all the sites, though its three towers with almost vertical, and purely decorative, stairways are very striking.

The easiest way of taking a **trip to the sites** is with a taxi tour, arranged from the *Hotel Calakmul* in Xpujil. Expect to pay US$40 per head to go to Calakmul/Balam Ku and Kohunlich/Dzibanche and US$30 each for Chicanna/Becan and Xpujil, which includes waiting time. Alternatively you could take an organized tour from Campeche with Corazon Maya or Viajes Turisticos Xtampak, both recommended by the Tourist Board (US$35–50; see Campeche listings for details).

## Becán

**Becán** (8am–5pm, US$2.50, free on Sun), 6km west of Xpujil then 500m north on a signed track, is unique among Maya sites in being entirely surrounded by a dry moat, 15m wide and 4m deep. This moat and the wall on its outer edge form one of the oldest known defensive systems in Mexico, and have led some to believe that this was the site of Tayasal, capital of the Itzá, rather than present-day Flores in Guatemala. The site was first occupied in 600 BC, reaching its peak between 600 and 1000 AD. Unlike many of the sites in the northern Yucatán, many of the buildings here seem to have been residential – note the unusual use of internal staircases. The style is a fusion of Río Bec and Chenes (see p.100), with its profusion of facades with fantastic stone masks.

## Chicanná and Balamku

**Chicanná** (8am–5pm; US$2.50, free on Sun), 3km further west than Becán, south of the highway, hosts the luxurious *Chicanna Ecovillage Resort* (in Campeche ☎9/816-2233, fax 811-1618, *www.chicannaresort.com.mx*). The buildings at the site recall the Chenes style in their elaborate decoration and repetitive masks of Chac; the great doorway in the **House of the Serpent Mouth** is especially impressive. **Balam Ku** (US$1, free on Sun), 50km beyond Chicanná, just after the turn-off to Calakmul, would be completely forgettable were it not for the two huge cross-eyed red masks that adorn its central temple. These are larger than any you'll see in the north, though less impressive than the masks at Kohunlich in nearby Quintana Roo. Their significance is unknown.

## Río Bec and Hormiguero

**Río Bec**, which gives its name to the region's dominant architectural style, and **Hormiguero** are accessible only by dirt road. To see all the scattered buildings of Río Bec (free) you need to go on an organized expedition, but you can see one small group independently: head east 13km from Xpujil, then south 6km to the *ejido* of 20 de Noviembre. The site is protected within the **Reserva de Fauna U'Luum Chac Yuc**, so you need to sign in at the reserve headquarters. You'll see that, as with Xpujil, the "steps" on the twin towers were never meant to be climbed: the risers actually angle outwards. Hormiguero (8am–5pm, US$2, free on Sun), also fuses the Chenes style with the Río Bec. There are only two buildings excavated, the largest having a huge gaping mouth for its central doorway, surrounded by elaborate carving. In Hormiguero, both Margarita Cahuich and Maria Dzib have **rooms** to rent and will help you find a local guide.

## Calakmul

The most impressive of the Río Bec sites, **Calakmul** (8am–5pm, US$1.50 and a further US$2 to enter the protected biosphere reserve) lies 60km off Hwy-186, which cuts across the bottom of the peninsula. Though it is only partially restored, its location in the heart of the jungle and its sheer size make this Classic Maya city irresistible. This is probably the biggest archeological area in Mesoamerica, extending for some 70km. It has seven thousand buildings in the central area alone and more stelae and pyramids than any other Maya city; the great pyramid here is the largest Maya building in existence, with a base covering five acres. The view of the rainforest from the top of the principal pyramids is stunning, bettered only at Tikal, and on a clear day you can even see the tallest Maya pyramid of all, Danta, at El Mirador in Guatemala. You're sure to see some wildlife too, especially if you arrive early – there are peccary, toucan, occasional howler monkeys and even jaguar here.

During the Classic period, the city had a population of about 200,000 people and was the regional capital of the southern part of Petén. A recently discovered *sacbe* (Maya road) running between Calakmul and El Mirador (another leads on to Tikal) has confirmed that these cities were in regular communication, as archeologists had long suspected. Calakmul reached its zenith between 500 and 850 AD but, like most cities in the area, it was abandoned about fifty years later. The site was discovered in 1931, but excavations only started taking place in 1982 and only a fraction of the buildings have been excavated so far, the rest being earthen mounds.

The treasures of Calakmul are on display in the archeological museum at Campeche (see p.97) and include two hauntingly beautiful jade masks. Another, also on display, was found in a tomb in the main pyramid as recently as January 1998. You can also see the first mummified body to be found in Mesoamerica, from inside Structure 15, which was unearthed in 1995.

## El Tigre

Another site worth visiting in this region is the Classic Maya city of **El Tigre**, 140km to the west of Calakmul on the **Río Candelaria**, though it is only accessible by launch – negotiate prices for the four- to six-hour journey with fishermen on the river in **Candelaria** town, which itself is connected by bus or train from either Escárcega or Campeche. Much of the forest on the banks of the Río Candelaria has been cleared by cattle ranchers, but the area is still excellent for birdlife, and if you're lucky you might see a crocodile. The ruins are only partially cleared and there are no tourists. Accommodation is very basic in Candelaria town and non-existent at the ruins, so bring a tent if you want to try to spend the night here. The tourist office in Campeche will have the latest details about camping possibilities.

## travel details

### Buses

There aren't many places that you can't get to by bus on the peninsula. Sometimes the timetabling isn't totally convenient but the service is generally efficient. Some places aren't served by first-class buses, but second-class buses and combis will get you around locally and to the nearest major centre. Such places include: Oxkutzcab, Progreso, Ticul and Tizimín. The following frequencies and times are for first-class services. Second-class buses usually cover the same routes running 10–20 percent slower.

**Campeche** to: Ciudad del Carmen (hourly, 3hr), Mérida (more then 12 daily, 2hr), Chetumal via Escárcega and Xpujil (3 daily, 5–7hr), Villahermosa (10 daily, 6–7hr). There are also services to San Cristóbal (via Palenque), Cancún, Playa del Carmen, Veracruz, Mexico City and Coatzalcoalcos (for southern Veracruz).

**Mérida** to: Campeche (every 30min; 4hr); Cancún (frequently; 6hr); Chetumal (7 daily; 9hr); Mexico City (6 daily; 28hr+); Palenque (2 daily; 10–11hr); Playa del Carmen (frequently daily; 7hr); Progreso (frequently; 1hr); Tizimín (3 daily; 4hr); Tulum (8 daily; 6hr); Uxmal (13 daily; 2hr); Valladolid (hourly; 3hr); Villahermosa (6 daily; 10hr).

**Tizimín** to: Mérida (3 daily; 4hr); Río Lagartos (5 daily; 1hr); Valladolid (hourly; 1hr).

**Valladolid** to: Cancún (6 daily; 2hr); Chetumal (3 daily; 5hr); Cobá (4 daily; 2hr); Mérida (hourly; 3hr); Playa del Carmen (3 daily; 4hr); Tizimín (hourly; 1hr); Tulum (4 daily; 4hr).

### Planes

Mérida has a busy **international airport** with several daily flights to Mexico City and regular connections to Miami and many other cities in the southern US. Campeche and Chetumal also have daily direct services to Mexico City.

# CHAPTER TWO

# QUINTANA ROO

The coastal state of Quintana Roo was a forgotten frontier for most of modern Mexican history – its lush tropical forests exploited for their mahogany and chicle (from which chewing gum is made), but otherwise unsettled, a haven for outlaws and pirates, and for Maya living beyond the reach of central government. In the 1970s, however, the stunning palm-fringed white-sand **beaches** of the Caribbean coast and its magnificent offshore **coral reefs** began to attract **tourists**: the first highways were built, new townships settled, and the place finally became a full state (as opposed to an externally administered Federal Territory) in 1974.

The stretch of **coast** beween Cancún and **Tulum** is the most heavily visited – and the focus of much recent, rapid hotel construction. Modern development is centred on the resorts of **Cancún** and **Playa del Carmen**, along with the islands of **Isla Mujeres** and **Cozumel**, which have become some of the world's most desirable package-tour destinations and increasingly overdeveloped as a result. You'll see images of the Maya everywhere here, but while their culture is shamelessly used to promote tourism, little of this money ever reaches the Maya themselves, and where they haven't been forced out by developers, they continue to live in poverty in small communal villages in the scrub forest, growing maize and carving or weaving a few trinkets for tourists.

Further south things get quieter: the beaches within the **Sian Ka'an Biosphere Reserve** are nesting sites for turtles, and behind them are areas of mangrove swamp, home to numerous animals including jaguar and even manatee. The vast and beautiful **Laguna de Bacalar** was an important stop on the Maya's pre-Columbian trade routes and was later used as an outpost for arms shipment from Belize during the Caste Wars. **Chetumal**, the state capital and a dull, duty-free border town, is of chief importance as a gateway to and from Belize. The southern coast, while rewarding for naturalists and adventurers, is difficult to visit, with only a couple of roads and minimal public transport.

**Inland**, Quintana Roo is little visited. There are some spectacular **Maya sites** here, though they are not as accessible or as well restored as the pristine open-air museums of Yucatán. **Cobá**, a lakeside Maya city just off the road to Valladolid, has some of the Maya World's tallest temples, but is only partially excavated, hidden in jungle swarming with mosquitoes. The Early Classic site of **Kohunlich**, famous for its giant sculpted faces of the Maya sun god, lies in the heart of the Petén jungle that stretches into Guatemala and Belize; even more remote are the ruins of **Kinichna**, **Chacchoben** and **Dzibanche**.

---

## ACCOMMODATION PRICE CODES

All the accommodation listed in this book has been categorized into one of nine price bands, as set out below. The prices quoted are in US dollars and refer to the cheapest room available for two people sharing in high season.

| | | |
|---|---|---|
| ① under US$5 | ④ US$15–25 | ⑦ US$60–80 |
| ② US$5–10 | ⑤ US$25–40 | ⑧ US$80–100 |
| ③ US$10–15 | ⑥ US$40–60 | ⑨ over US$100 |

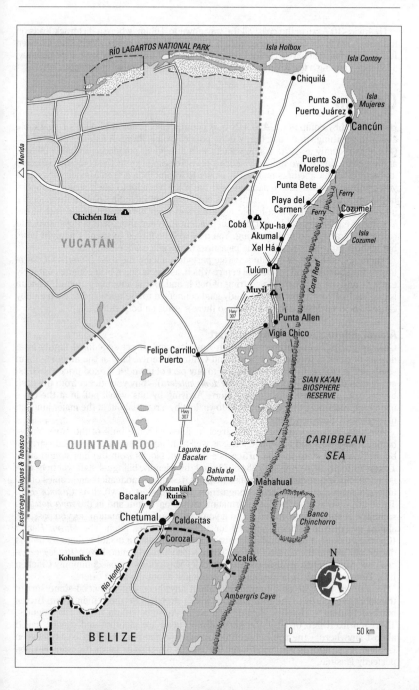

**Highway-307** skirts the coast all the way down to Tulum, where a dirt track leads on to Punta Allen in the Sian Ka'an Biosphere Reserve. Heading west to Valladolid, Chichén Itzá and Mérida, you have a choice between the old road (*viejo*) or the new *cuota* highway, a toll road running a few kilometres north of the old road for most of its length.

# Cancún

Hand-picked by computer, **CANCÚN** is, if nothing else, proof of Mexico's remarkable ability to get things done in a hurry if the political will is there. A fishing village of 120 people as recently as 1970, it's now a city with a resident population of half a million, and receives almost two million visitors a year. To some extent the computer selected its location well. Cancún is marginally closer to Miami than it is to Mexico City, and if you come on an all-inclusive package tour the place has a lot to offer: striking modern hotels on white-sand beaches; high-class entertainment including parachuting, jet-skiing, scuba-diving and golf, a hectic nightlife, and from here much of the rest of the Yucatán is easily accessible. For the independent traveller, though, it is expensive, and can be frustrating and unwelcoming. You may well be forced to spend the night here, but without pots of money the true pleasures of the place will elude you.

There are, in effect, two quite separate parts to Cancún: the *zona commercial* downtown – the shopping and residential centre which, as it gets older, is becoming genuinely earthy – and the *zona hotelera*, a string of hotels and tourist amenities around "Cancún island", actually a narrow strip of sandy land connected to the mainland at each end by causeways. It encloses a huge lagoon, so there's water on both sides.

### Arrival, information and city transport

Charter flights from Europe and South America, and direct scheduled flights from dozens of cities in Mexico and North and Central America, land at the **airport**, 15km south of the centre. Colectivos take you to any part of town for a fixed price (US$7.50 per person to downtown, US$9.50 to the *zona hotelera*) – buy your ticket from the desk by the exit. Taxis cost considerably more. Arriving by bus, you'll pull in at the city's main **bus station**, in the heart of downtown, just by a roundabout at the major junction of avenidas Tulum and Uxmal.

**Avenida Tulum**, Cancún's main street, is lined with the bulk of the city's shops, banks, restaurants and travel agencies, as well as many of the hotels – up side streets, but in view. The **state tourist office** is a couple of blocks from the bus station at Av Tulum 26 (daily 9am–9pm; ☎9/884-8073) and the friendly, bilingual staff will help with even the smallest enquiries. They also dish out free maps and leaflets and copies of the ubiquitous promotional listings **magazines**, the glossiest of which is *Cancún Tips*. There are several other tourist information kiosks on Tulum and in the *zona hotelera*; some are genuine, but if you're asked if you want "tourist information" as you pass, it's almost certain you're being selected for a timeshare sales pitch. The *Miami Herald* (Cancún edition), a daily English-language newspaper with a useful listings section, is dished out free in the smarter hotels. There's also a good general **Website**, *www.cancun.com*. Many hotels arrange **trips** to the chief Maya ruins – most commonly Chichén Itzá, Tulum and Cobá; check with the receptionist about the latest offers.

Downtown you'll be able to walk just about anywhere, but you need some sort of transport to get around the *zona hotelera*, which stretches for more than 20km. **Buses** marked "Tulum – Hoteles, Ruta 1" run along Avenida Tulum every few minutes. There's a fixed fare of US$0.50. Alternatively, **taxis** are plentiful and can be hailed almost anywhere – the trip between downtown and the *zona hotelera* costs between US$5–8. A car affords you more scope and makes day-trips as far as the ruins at Cobá perfectly feasible.

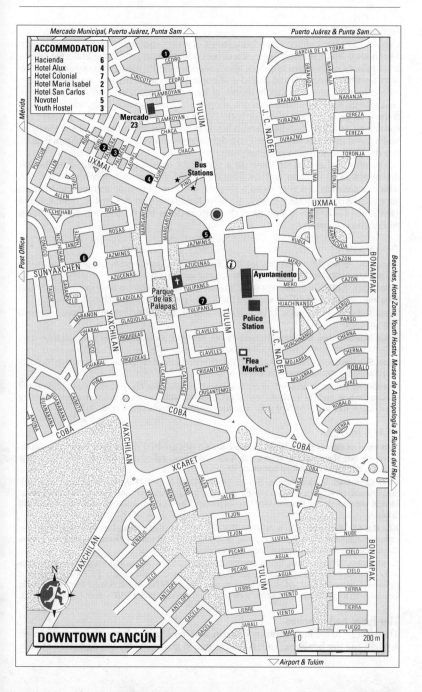

Mercado Municipal, Puerto Juárez, Punta Sam △          Puerto Juárez & Punta Sam △

**ACCOMMODATION**
Hacienda           6
Hotel Alux         4
Hotel Colonial     7
Hotel Maria Isabel 2
Hotel San Carlos   1
Novotel            5
Youth Hostel       3

△ Mérida

△ Post Office

GARCIA DE LA TORRE

CEDRO
CIRICOTE
CEDRO
FLAMBOYAN
TULUM
GRANADA
NARANJA
GRANADA
NARANJA
CEREZA
DURAZNO
DURAZNO
CEREZA
J. C. NADER
LIMA
TORONJA
TORONJA

Mercado 23
FLAMBOYAN
CHACA
CHACA
CHACA

ROBLE
TAZTA
TAZTA
PALMERA
LAUREL
LAUREL
UXMAL

Bus Stations
PINO ★

UXMAL

POLLICUB
ALLEN
ALLEN
TUPAC
NICCHEHABI
CONGO
NICCHEHABI
TANCH
SUNYAXCHEN
TAUCH
SARAMULLO
TAUCH

RUBIA
RUBIA
BARRACUDA
BONAMPAK

ROSAS
ROSAS
JAZMINES
AZUCENAS
MARGARITAS
MARGARITAS
MARGARITAS

JAZMINES
AZUCENAS
TULIPANES

MERO
MERO
CAZON
CAZON
HUACHINANGO
HUACHINANGO
MOJARRA
MOJARRA

Parque de las Palapas
GLADIOLAS
TULIPANES
CLAVELES
CLAVELES
CRISANTEMOS
CRISANTEMOS

*i*
Ayuntamiento

Police Station

J. C. NADER
PARGO
PARGO
CHERNA
CHERNA
ROBALO
JUREL

MABAÑON
GUANABANA
ANONA
COBA
CAIMITO
GUANABANA
PIÑA
COCO
CHIABAL
COBA
YAXCHILAN
GLADIOLAS
ORQUIDEAS
ORQUIDEAS
ALCATRACES
ALCATRACES

"Flea Market"

ROBALO
SIERRA
COBÁ

COBA
XCARET
YAXCHILAN
JALEB
RENO
RENO
VENADO
JALEB

BRISA
NUBE
COBA

TEJON
TEJON
PECARI
PECARI
LIEBRE
LIEBRE
TULUM
ALCE
ALCE
ANTILOPE
ANTILOPE
GACELA
GACELA
JABALI

LLUVIA
AGUA
AGUA
VIENTO
VIENTO
MAR

NUBE
CIELO
CIELO
TIERRA
TIERRA
FUEGO
BONAMPAK

N

**DOWNTOWN CANCÚN**

0        200 m

Beaches, Hotel Zone, Youth Hostel, Museo de Antropología & Ruinas del Rey ▷

▽ Airport & Tulúm

## Accommodation

Cancún has plenty of accommodation, most of it very expensive for the casual visitor. **Downtown** holds the only hope of a decent budget room, while the glittering beach-front palaces of the **zona hotelera** offer exclusive luxury, many with extravagant interiors featuring waterfalls and cascades of tropical vegetation. All have excellent service, with colour TV and minibars in rooms, at least one immaculate pool, glitzy bars and restaurants, and, more often than not, shops and a travel agency. Many will also put on a show in the evening, a disco, or both. While **room rates** are still high if you're not coming on a package holiday, Cancún hoteliers are currently suffering as mass tourism shifts down the coast to prettier Playa del Carmen and you may well find much more reasonable prices than in previous years.

The only real option for those on a very tight budget is the small **youth hostel** downtown at C Palmera and Av Uxmal (☎9/887-0191, *www.mexicohostels.com*; ②), which is pleasant and very clean with several dorms, a rooftop terrace and Internet access. There is another hostel on Blvd Kukulkan, Km 3.2 in the *zona hotelera* (☎9/9/883-1337; ③) – it's rather dirty and run-down but it's the only place in town where you can **camp**.

### DOWNTOWN

**Hacienda**, Av Sunyaxchen 39 (☎9/884-3672, fax 884-1208). Quiet location and good value; rooms all have a/c and colour TV and there's a pool, pretty garden and café. ⑤.

**Hotel Alux**, Av Uxmal 21 (☎9/884-6613). Comfortable and popular hotel; all rooms have TV and telephone, and there's a café on site and a travel agency next door. Good value. ⑤.

**Hotel Colonial**, C Tulipanes 22 (☎ & fax 9/884-1535). Light, simple rooms set round a central courtyard. ⑤.

**Hotel Maria Isabel**, C Retorno Palmera 59 (☎9/884-9015). Cosy small hotel in a quiet side street with cheerful decor and a friendly atmosphere. ⑤.

**Hotel San Carlos**, C Cedro 40 (☎9/884-0602). Newly renovated budget hotel overlooking Mercado 23. Basic, clean rooms, some with balconies. ③.

**Novotel**, Av Tulum 27, across from the bus station (☎9/884-2999, fax 884-3162). Central, clean and secure; the best hotel in its class (book ahead). Rooms, with fan or a/c, are very comfortable; try to get one at the back. The cool patio restaurant overlooks a small garden. ⑥.

### BEACH HOTELS

**Aquamarina Beach Hotel**, Blvd Kukulkán, Km 4.5 (☎9/849-4606, fax 849-4600, *www.aquamarina-beach.com.mx*). Large family resort with kids' club, pool, volleyball, miniature golf and nightly karaoke. Rates include all food and drink. ⑥.

**Club Carrousel**, Blvd Kukulkán, Km 3.5 (☎9/848-7170, fax 848-7179, *www.hotelsescarrousel.com*). Small rooms, all with sea view, on a lovely stretch of beach. Attractions include two swimming pools, Jacuzzi, watersports and thrice-weekly themed parties. The very reasonable rates include all food and drink. ⑥.

**Kin Há**, Blvd Kukulkán, Km 8 (☎9/883-2377, fax 883-2147, *kinha3@mail.caribe.net.mx*). Near the main shopping and entertainment centres. Beautiful rooms and suites with spacious balconies, a full range of facilities and continental breakfast included in the price. ⑥.

**Le Meridien**, Blvd Kukulkán, Km 14 (☎9/881-2200, fax 812-2201, *www.meridiencancun.com.mx*). State-of-the-art luxury hotel with 213 rooms, all with marble bathrooms and satellite TV. Facilities include a three-level swimming pool and rooftop tennis courts. The hotel's beauty spa, *Spa del Mar*, is the best in Cancún, with hydrotherapy treatments, body wraps and massage from US$60 – open to non-guests. ⑨.

## The Town and beaches

There's little to see in **downtown Cancún**, and most visitors head straight for the *zona hotelera* and the **beaches**. Though you're free to go anywhere, and sign-posted public walkways lead down to the sea at regular intervals, some of the hotels do their best to make you feel like a trespasser, and staff will certainly move you off the beach furniture if you're not a guest. To avoid being eyed suspiciously by hotel heavies, head for one of the dozen or so **public beaches**: all are free but you may have to pay a small charge for showers. Entertainment and expensive watersports are laid on all around the big hotels; if you venture further, where more sites await construction, you can find surprisingly empty sand and often small groups of nude sunbathers.

To catch a bit of culture while you're out here, the *Sheraton*, at Blvd Kukulkán, Km 12.5, boasts a small Maya ruin in its grounds, above the pool, while the **Museo de Antropología**, located behind the Convention Centre, Blvd Kukulkán, Km 9 (Mon–Sat 9am–8pm, Sun 10am–7pm; US$2, free on Sun), has a small but absorbing outline of Mesoamerican and Maya culture and history, with information in English and Spanish. Cancún's largest Maya remains, the **Ruinas del Rey** (daily 8am– 5pm; US$1.70, free on Sun), are at Km 17, overlooking the Nichupté Lagoon. They're not especially impressive – and, if you decide not to take one of the guides at the entrance, there's no information available to explain them – but the area is peaceful and very good for bird- and iguana-watching.

The best **snorkelling** in Cancún is at Punta Nizuc, next to *Club Med* territory. You aren't allowed to cross the grounds unless you're staying there, so you have to get off the bus at the *Westin Regina Resort*, cross their grounds to the beach, then turn right and walk for about twenty minutes until you reach the rocky point. Walk across the rocks and snorkel to your heart's content. To join a **snorkelling tour** or go diving, contact Aqua Tours (☎9/9/883-0440) or Aquaworld (☎9/885-2288, *www .aquaworld.com.mx*). A one-tank dive costs about US$50 and a full PADI open-water certification course around US$400. To view the colourful underwater life in a more leisurely fashion, take a trip on the *Sub See Explorer*, a **glass-bottomed boat** that leaves from the Aquaworld centre at Blvd Kukulkán, Km 15.2 hourly from 9am until 3pm (US$35).

Both **jet-ski-ing** (US$50 for 30min) and **parasailing** (US$40 for 10min) are very popular in Cancún and operators are dotted in front of the big hotels on the beach.

## *EATING*

Cancún's **restaurants** outnumber its hotels many times over, and competition is fierce. The bulk of the **tourist restaurants** line Avenida Tulum and its side streets: eat here and you can enjoy "fun" disco sounds with your meal. Though seafood and steak form the mainstay of many menus, you can also eat Arabic, Yucatecan, Italian, Chinese, French, Cajun and Polynesian, not to mention international fast food plus some local chains. Almost all of the restaurants in the *zona hotelera* are geared towards parting ignorant tourists from large amounts of cash – and none can be particularly recommended. If you are staying on the beach, you'd be much better off taking a cab or the convenient *hoteles* bus into downtown Cancún (see below) where you'll find good food at reasonable prices and lots of genuine atmosphere. Otherwise, all the **hotels** in the *zona* have at least one formal restaurant, some of which are very elegant indeed, surrounded by tropical foliage with fountains and music. Many also feature a relaxing beach or poolside dining room.

For **budget food**, follow the locals and make for the markets. The biggest is **Mercado 28**, close to the city's main post office at the western end of Avenida Sunyaxchen, with plenty of food stalls and tiny cheap restaurants. **Mercado 23** is much smaller but makes a relatively peaceful venue for a decent Mexican lunch (see "Listings", p.111). Further along, at the junction of avenidas Tulum and López Portillo, is a small plaza, complete with fountain, at the edge of another market. The little cafés here are packed with Mexican families and it's the nearest Cancún comes to having a zócalo.

## DOWNTOWN

**100 Percent Natural**, Av Sunyaxchen 26, at the junction with Yaxchilán. Not entirely vegetarian, but it serves fruit drinks, salads, yoghurt and granola, as well as Mexican dishes, seafood and burgers. A pleasant enough place, if a little overpriced. Other branches in Plazas Terramar and Kukulkán in the *zona hotelera*.

**Los Almendros**, Av Bonampak 60, opposite the Plaza de Toros. This is the Cancún branch of the famous restaurant that originated in Ticul, and is justly renowned for its good-value Yucatecan specialities.

**D'Pa**, Gladiolas, Parque las Palapas. Chic little French crêperie with pretty outdoor tables and decent wine by the glass.

**Gory Tacos**, C Tulipanes 26. Don't be put off by the name: this spotless and very friendly place serves good, inexpensive Mexican food, steaks, hamburgers and sandwiches, and a range of vegetarian meals.

**La Habichuela**, C Margaritas 25, in front of the Parque las Palapas. Long-established and fairly expensive restaurant set in a walled garden. The menu is excellent, featuring such dishes as *cocobichuela*: half a coconut filled with lobster and shrimp in a curry sauce, accompanied by tropical fruits. Live jazz adds to the atmosphere.

**El Marisquero**, Av Nader and C Mojarra. Friendly seafood restaurant behind the popular souvenir market (known as the flea market) on Avenida Tulum. Good *ceviche* and fresh fish.

**El Meson de Novotel**, Av Tulum 75. Pavement café in front of the *Novotel*, with good breakfasts and special lunchtime offers. A great people-watching spot.

**El Pabila**, inside *Hotel Xbalamque*, Av Yaxchilán 31. Classy coffee shop serving very good cappuccino, espresso and so on in a peaceful and sophisticated environment.

**La Parilla**, Av Yaxchilán 51. Very popular Mexican restaurant specializing in flame-grilled meat. It's a bit of a tourist trap but the food's tasty, and there's a buzzing atmosphere with nightly live music.

**Pericos**, Av Yaxchilán 71. Famous Mexican restaurant with live entertainment, strolling magicians, stilt-walkers, juggling barmen and more. Although patronized almost exclusively by tourists (and very popular – arrive early to avoid queuing) it might well provide the most unforgettable evening of your stay and is defintely worth paying a bit extra for. Not to be missed.

## Entertainment and nightlife

Since Cancún's whole rationale is to encourage almost two million visitors each year to have fun, the entertainment scene is lavish – or remorseless, depending on which way you look at it. There's everything from sports and gambling **bars** to romantic piano bars and fun bars, even just plain drinking bars: enough choice to ensure that you can find a place to have a good time without being ripped off. Most of the **nightclubs**, on the other hand, are pricey, with a "no shorts or sandals" dress code. A couple of **cinemas** show new American releases subtitled in Spanish: the largest downtown is the multi-screen *Cineapolis*, Plaza Las Americas on Avenida Tulum, south of Avenida Coba; in the *zona hotelera*, there's a cinema in the Plaza Kukulkán and two screens in the Forum by the Sea shopping centre, Blvd Kukulkán, Km 9.5.

## BARS AND NIGHTCLUBS

**La Boom**, Blvd Kukulkán, Km 3.5, at the front of the *Hotel Aquamarina Beach*. High-tech disco in an "English setting" with continuous videos. No cover charge Mon, "Ladies' Night" Wed and Sun.

**Christine**, in the *Krystal*, Blvd Kukulkán, Km 9 (☎9/883-1793). The most sophisticated and expensive nightclub in town, famed for its light show. Thursday is 1970s and 1980s night: look in the free magazines or phone to check other weekly events. Don't turn up in shorts, jeans, sandals or without a shirt.

**Coco Bongo**, in the Forum by the Sea centre, Blvd Kukulkán, Km 9.5. Vast state-of-the-art rock and pop disco popular with Spring-Breakers. Cover charge at weekends only; open until 5am.

**Dady O**, Blvd Kukulkán, Km 9.5, opposite the Convention Centre. A 21st-century nightclub with a high-tech sound system and a light and laser show. Casual dress but no shorts. The adjacent Dady Rock bar has all-you-can-drink deals for US$25.

**Fat Tuesday**, Blvd Kukulkán, Km 6.5, and in the Terramar Plaza in the *zona hotelera*. Restaurant-bar with an outside dance floor and a choice of sixty flavours of frozen drinks. Cover charge after 9pm; open until 4am.

**Pat O'Brien's**, Flamingo Plaza in the *zona hotelera*. Live rock, blues and jazz in a larger-than-life version of the famous New Orleans bar. Three bars: a piano bar, a video lounge and an outdoor patio. Open until 2am.

**Roots**, C Tulipanes 26. Funky little jazz and blues club.

**Señor Frogs**, Blvd Kukulkán, Km 5.5. Live reggae bands and karaoke nights.

## SHOWS AND DINNER CRUISES

**Ballet Folklórico Nacional de México**, at Cancún's Convention Centre, Blvd Kukulkán, Km 9 (☎9/881-0400). Buffet dinner nightly at 7pm followed by a professional ballet show featuring 35 artists. Tickets cost around US$50.

**Cancún Queen**, Aquaworld Marina, Blvd Kukulkán, Km 15.2 (☎9/885-2288). Lobster, fish or chicken dinners on a traditional Mississippi paddle boat. Live music followed by a fiesta and a variety of party games with prizes. Nightly departure at 6pm, returning at 9pm. US$39/59.

**Captain Hook**, El Embarcadero, Blvd Kukulkán, Km 4.5 (☎9/883-3736). Spanish Galleon-style boat with piratical sword fighting and lobster/steak dinner. Departs nightly at 7pm, returning at 10.30pm. US$60.

**Columbus**, the Royal Maya Marina at Blvd Kukulkán, Km 16.5 (☎9/883-1488). Romantic cruise with lobster and steak dinner. Departs daily 4pm in winter, 5pm in summer, returning at 7.30pm or 8.30pm respectively. Around US$60 per person.

**Teatro de Cancún**, El Embarcadero, Blvd Kukulkán, Km 4 (☎9/849-4848). Two nightly song and dance shows, *Songs and Dances of Mexico* at 7pm, *Tradición del Caribe* at 9pm. The ticket price of US$30 includes a welcome cocktail.

**Toros**, Plaza de Toros, Av Bonampak and Av Sayil. Weekly bullfights with tacked-on folkloric show; Wed at 3.30pm. US$30.

# Listings

**American Express** Av Tulum 208, two blocks beyond the *Hotel America* (☎9/884-4000).

**Banks** Most banks (generally Mon–Fri 9am–5pm, Sat 9am–1pm) are along Avenida Tulum between avenidas Uxmal and Coba and in the biggest shopping malls – such as the Plaza Caracol, Blvd Kukulkán, Km 8.5 – in the *zona hotelera*. Most now have ATMs with US dollars as well as pesos. The Bital bank, Av Tulum 192, stays open until 7pm on weekdays.

**Car rental** Available at most hotels and at the airport, or try Budget, Av Tulum 231 (☎9/884-0204), or Europcar, Av Nader 27 (☎9/887-3272).

**Consulates** Canada, Plaza Caracol, Blvd Kukulkán, Km 8.5 (Mon–Fri 9am–5pm; ☎9/883-3060); UK, *Hotel Royal Caribbean*, Blvd Kukulkán, Km 16.5 (Mon–Fri 8am–5pm; ☎9/881-0100); US, Plaza Caracol, Blvd Kukulkán Km 8.5 (Mon–Fri 9am–1pm; ☎9/883-0272).

**Laundry** Lavandería Las Palapas, on Gladiolas, at the far side of the park (Mon–Sat 7am–8pm, Sun 8am–2pm); Lavandería Tulum, Av Tulum 213 (Mon–Sat 7am–8pm, Sun 9am–6pm).

**Post office** Avenida Sunyaxchen at the junction with Av Xel-Ha (Mon–Fri 8am–7pm, Sat 9am–1pm), with a reliable Lista de Correos (postcode 77501).

**Shopping** The flea market on Avenida Tulum has an abundance of souvenir-suitable merchandise – the usual blankets, ceramics and silver – but the sales pitch is rather heavy. Mercado 23 (turn left off Avenida Tulum, three blocks north of the bus station) has a small range of arts and crafts from all over the country and is a more relaxed place to pick up reasonably priced mementos.

**Travel agents** There's an abundance of tour operators and travel agency desks at most hotels, which can easily fix you up with the standard trips to Xel-Ha or the main ruins, or sell tickets for a cruise. *EcoloMex Tours*, Plaza Mexico, Av Tulum 200 (☎9/887-1776, *marand@cancun.rece.com.mx*), is the best agency if you want to see the wildlife of the Yucatán.

## MOVING ON FROM CANCÚN

If you're heading west **by car** to Valladolid, Chichén Itzá and Mérida, you have a choice between the old road (*viejo*) or the new (*cuota*) highway, running a few kilometres north of the old road for most of its length. Drive north on Avenida Tulum then turn left to join Avenida López Portillo: after a few kilometres you will have the choice of which road to join. You pay in advance, at the booths on the highway, for the sections you intend to travel along. The trip all the way to Mérida costs US$25.

First and second-class **buses** go from the same well-organised terminal on the corner of avenidas Tulum and Uxmal. Destinations include Mérida, first-class (4 daily; 4hr) and second-class (hourly; 5hr); Campeche, on the deluxe ADO GL service (daily at 3pm; 9hr) and second-class (daily at midnight; 10hr); Chetumal on first-class (daily at 4.30pm; 6hr) and second-class (hourly 5am-12.45pm; 6hr); Mexico City on first-class (2 daily at 10am and 1pm; 18 hr) and second-class (4 daily; 20hr); Playa del Carmen on first-class (6 daily; 1hr) and second-class (every 30min; 1hr); Tizimin (6 daily; 4hr); Tulum on first-class (5 daily; 2hr) and second-class (5 daily; 2hr); and Valladolid (hourly; 3hr).

International **flights** leave regularly from Cancún; from downtown and the *zona hotelera* a taxi to the airport costs about US$10.

### THE FERRY TO ISLA MUJERES

The **passenger ferry** for Isla Mujeres (see below) officially leaves from Puerto Juárez every thirty minutes between 6am and 8pm with both fast (15min; US$3.50) and slow (45min; US$1.80) services. However, in reality they simply leave when full, often at the same time. To get to the ferry terminal, catch a bus ("Ruta 13") heading north from the stop on Tulum, opposite the bus station (20min), or take a taxi from Tulum (around US$3.50).

The **car ferry** (US$13 for car, plus US$2 for each passenger) leaves from Punta Sam, a few kilometres north of Puerto Juárez. There are five departures daily between 8am and 8.15pm, returning from Isla Mujeres between 6.30am and 7.15pm. However, it isn't really worth taking a car over to the island, which is small enough to cycle around and has plenty of bicycles, mopeds and even golf carts for rent.

# Isla Mujeres

**ISLA MUJERES**, just a couple of kilometres off the easternmost tip of Mexico in the startlingly clear Caribbean sea, is an infinitely more appealing prospect than Cancún. Its attractions are simple: first there's the beach, then there's the sea. And when you've tired of those, you can rent a bike, moped or even golf cart to carry you around the island to more sea, more beaches, a coral reef and the tiny Maya temple that the conquistadors chanced upon, full of female figures, which gave the place its name. Unfortunately, however, Mujeres is no longer the desert island you may have heard about, and its natural attractions have been recognized and developed considerably in the last few years. There are now several large hotels and thousands of day-trippers from Cancún, and the once beautiful El Garrafón coral reef is now almost completely dead. Inevitably, too, prices have risen and standards (in many cases) have fallen. All that said, it can still seem a respite to those who've been slogging their way down through Mexico and around the Yucatán – everyone you've met along the way seems to turn up here eventually.

### Arrival, information and getting around

The passenger **ferry** arrives downtown, at the main pier at the end of Avenida Morelos on Avenida Rueda Medina, which runs northeast to southwest; the car ferry comes in further east on Medina at the end of Avenida Bravo. Avenida Madero, one block north from the passenger ferry dock, cuts northeast straight across the island; as you walk away from the dock, the first street you cross is Juárez, the second Hidalgo and the third Guerrero, all of which lead north to the North Beach and south to the zócalo. The boats leave from Puerto Juárez (10min in a taxi from central Cancún) every half-hour, the last at 8pm. Aerocaribe and other airlines also occasionally fly out to Cancún or Cozumel from the small airstrip at the centre of the island.

The zócalo is skirted by Morelos, N Bravo, Guerrero and Hidalgo. The **tourist office** (Mon–Fri 8am–8pm, Sat & Sun 9am–2pm; ☎9/877-0767, *www.isla-mujeres-mexico.com*) is on Avenida Rueda Medina, almost opposite the passenger ferry pier. Here you can pick up leaflets, maps and copies of the free *Isla Mujeres* magazine (in Spanish and English). The **post office** (Mon–Fri 8am–7pm, Sat 9am–1pm) is at the corner of C Guerrero and Av Mateos, about ten minutes' walk from the centre; mail is held at the Lista de Correos for up to ten days (postcode 77400). There are **long-distance phones** at Av Medina 6B (daily 9am–9pm) and an **Internet** café on C Hidalgo and Av Abasolo (daily 10am–8pm). **Banks** are few: Banco del Atlántico, opposite the passenger ferry dock on Avenida Rueda Medina 3 (Mon–Fri 9am–5pm, Sat 9am–2pm), and Bital, further along the same road at Av Rueda Medina 3 (Mon–Fri 8.30am–6pm, Sat 9am–2pm); both have ATMs. There's a **laundry** at C Juárez and Av Abasolo.

The island is a very manageable size with few hills, and the best way of getting around it is by **moped** (US$6 per hour), **bicycle** (US$5 per hour) or **golf cart** (US$10 per hour): at least a dozen places rent out all three forms of transport. There are several **dive shops** on the island – recommended is Coral, Av Matamoros 13A (☎9/877-0763), which offers a range of trips including some to the "Cave of the Sleeping Sharks", where tiger, bull, grey reef, lemon and nurse sharks are regularly encountered.

## Accommodation

Isla Mujeres is short on good-value **budget places to stay**, and, though prices are lower than at Cozumel, so is the quality. Most of the reasonably priced options are on the northern edge of the island.

There is no official **campsite** on Isla Mujeres, but you can pitch your tent or sling up a hammock in the grounds of the *Poc-Na* **youth hostel**, Av Matamoros and C Carlos Lazo (☎9/877-0090, fax 877-0059; ②).

**Casa Maya Guest House**, C Zazil-Ha and Playa Norte (☎ & fax 9/877-0045). Charming small hotel with a friendly owner and individually decorated rooms. ⑥.

**El Caracol**, Av Matamoros 5 (☎9/877-0150). Two blocks from Playa Norte; rooms with or without a/c and a restaurant serving typical Mexican food. ⑤.

**Caribe Maya**, Av Francisco I Madero 9 (☎9/877-0684). More character than the average budget hotel and good value, with some a/c rooms. ④.

**Hotel Cabañas María del Mar**, Av Carlos Lazo 1 (☎9/877-0179, fax 877-0156,*www.cabaña sdel-mar.com*). Next to Playa Norte, with deluxe cabañas on the beach or hotel rooms with a/c, refrigerator and private balcony or terrace. Lively restaurant, tours and car rental. ⑧.

**María José**, Av Madero 25 (☎9/877-0245). Well-kept family-run hotel. Some of the back rooms open onto next-door's roof, where you can hang your hammock. ④.

**Na-Balam**, C Zazil-Ha 118 (☎9/877-0279, fax 877-0446, *www.nabalam.com*). One of the island's most chic hotels with pool, tropical garden on the beach and elegant rooms. ⑧.

**Osorio**, Av Madero; turn left from the ferry, take the first right, and the hotel is on your left (☎9/877-0294). No frills, but it's clean and near the sea. ③.

**Las Palmas**, C Guerrero 20 (☎9/877-0965). The cheapest option on the island; basic but acceptable. ③.

**Perla del Caribe**, Av Madero 2 (☎9/877-0120, fax 877-0011). At the opposite side of town to the ferry, one of the smartest hotels on the island, with a pool, restaurant and sea-view rooms with verandahs. Car rental is available. ⑦.

**Posada del Mar**, Av Medina 15A (☎9/877-0044, fax 877-0266, *www.posadadelmar.com*). Spacious rooms or bungalows with a/c, plus a restaurant and a poolside bar. ⑥.

**Roca Mar**, corner of C Guerrero and Av Bravo, behind the church by the zócalo (☎ & fax 9/877-0101). One of the island's oldest hotels, well maintained, with a restaurant overlooking the Caribbean. ⑥.

**Vistalmar**, avenidas Rueda Medina and Matamoros (☎9/877-0209). Pleasant, very pink hotel opposite the ferry pier. Good value. ④.

**Xul-ha**, C Hidalgo 23 Nte (☎9/877-0075). Relatively new hotel with spacious, clean and comfortable rooms. ⑤.

## The island

Isla Mujeres is no more than 8km long, and, at its widest point, barely a kilometre across. A lone road runs its length, past the dead calm waters of the landward coast – the other side, east-facing, is windswept and exposed. There's a small beach on this side in the town, but the currents even here can be dangerous. The most popular beach, just five minutes' walk from the town plaza, is **Playa Norte** – at the northern tip of the island, but protected from the open sea by a little promontory on which stands what was the lone luxury hotel, the *El Presidente Zazil-Ha*. The hotel now stands abandoned, ravaged by one of the hurricanes that periodically wreck this coast.

If you've had enough of the beach, windsurfing and wandering round town (the Grand Tour takes little more than thirty minutes), rent a bike or moped to explore the south of the island. **El Garrafón National Park** (daily 8am–5pm; US$6), almost at the southernmost tip, is a tropical reef just a few metres offshore, though, unfortunately, the crowds of day-trippers have frightened away a lot of the fish and the coral is virtually dead as a result of damage from divers and the anchors of the tourist boats. Beyond El Garrafón, the road continues to the lighthouse, and from there a short rough track leads to the **Maya temple** at the southernmost tip. It's not much of a ruin, but it is very dramatically situated on low rocky cliffs, below which you can often spot large fish basking.

On the way back, stop at **Playa Lancheros**, a palm-fringed beach that is virtually deserted except at lunchtimes when the day-trippers pile in. There's a small restaurant here, specializing in seafood, and a clutch of souvenir stalls. Inland, in the jungly undergrowth, lurk the decaying remains of the **Hacienda Mundaca**: an old house and garden to which scores of romantic (and quite untrue) pirate legends are attached.

You could also take a day-long boat trip to the island bird sanctuary of **Contoy** (some, with special permission, stay overnight), where you can see colonies of pelicans and cormorants and occasionally more exotic sea birds, as well as a sunken Spanish galleon.

## Eating

The area along and around Calle Hidalgo between avenidas Morelos and Abasolo, lined with **restaurants** and crafts shops, is the best place to spend an evening on Isla Mujeres. Simply wander through the laid-back music-filled streets and see what takes your fancy. For inexpensive, basic Mexican food and great low-priced fruit salads, head for the **loncherías** opposite *Las Palmas* hotel.

**Le Bistro**, Av Matamoros 29. Pseudo-French café with a varied menu at reasonable prices. Good breakfasts.

**Buho's**, Playa Norte. Very popular beach bar with loud rock music, swinging hammock chairs and a happy hour (5–6pm).

**Café Cito**, C Juarez and Av Matamoros. Healthy New-Age breakfasts with good coffee and fruit/yoghurt combos.

**Restaurant Gomar**, C Hidalgo 5 and Av Madero. Good seafood, chicken and Mexican specialities, though rather pricey.

**Miramar**, Av Medina, next to the pier. Attractive place on the seafront, away from the centre. Seafood and meat dishes, a little on the expensive side.

**Pizza Rolandis**, C Hidalgo, between avenidas Madero and Abasolo. One of a chain serving pizza, lobster, fresh fish and other Italian dishes with salads.

# The east coast: Cancún to Playa del Carmen

Resort development along the spectacular white-sand beaches south from Cancún to the marvellous seaside ruins of Tulum proceeds rapidly as landowners cash in on Cancún's popularity. The **Caribbean Barrier Reef** begins off **Puerto Morelos**, a quiet, though expensive, town with excellent beaches. Further south is **Punta Bete**, which is smaller and quieter, while the phenomenal growth of **Playa del Carmen**, the departure point for boats to Cozumel, has transformed a village with a ferry dock into a major holiday destination.

Finding a relatively deserted stretch of beach is increasingly difficult, though not impossible, and many visitors based in Cancún rent a car to explore the coast. Although a moped is feasible as far as Puerto Morelos, where the divided highway ends (and there's a filling station), it's a long trip for the underpowered bikes, and bus and truck drivers show scant respect as they pass. The bus is probably a better idea as the service along Hwy-307 is cheap and efficient.

## Puerto Morelos and around

Leaving Cancún behind, the first town on the coast is **PUERTO MORELOS**, 20km south. Formerly of little interest except as the departure point for the car ferry to Cozumel, in recent years Puerto has seen a surge in popularity, becoming a base for tours and **diving trips**. Although the taxi ride from Cancún airport to Puerto Morelos is a whopping US$40, a number of visitors on international flights bypass the city altogether and make Puerto Morelos their first stop. It's as good a place as any to hang out for a while: despite a rash of new hotel and condo construction, it is a relaxing, laid-back alternative to the bustle of Cancún with some lovely beaches and pristine reef offshore. It's also the only working fishing village between Cancún to Tulum that hasn't been entirely consumed by tourism.

### Arrival and information

Interplaya **buses** leave Cancún's bus station every thirty to forty-five minutes between 5am and 10pm and drop you at the highway junction, where taxis wait to take you the 2km into town. There are several **long-distance telephones** by the police station on the corner of the plaza, a **supermarket**, several **cambios** (daily 7am–10pm) and an **ATM**, though no actual bank. The **car ferry to Cozumel** (around US$40 per car and US$5 per passenger) officially departs three times daily, at 5am, 10.30am and 4pm, returning from Cozumel at 8am, 1.30pm and 7pm. The service is erratic, however, and it's best to check the times either in Cozumel or with the tourist office in Cancún. Although tourist vehicles are given priority you'll need to be at the pier at least an hour before departure to ensure a place.

### Accommodation

Almost all of the hotels in Puerto Morelos are right on the beach, but many of them are overpriced. The only place to **camp** is the *Acamaya Reef Trailer Park* (☎9/871-0132), a couple of kilometres out of the centre, down the first turning on the left, 2km after the turn-off from the main highway, near the entrance to Crococun.

**Amar Inn**, north of the plaza, 500m along the seafront (☎9/871-0026). Very friendly family-run hotel with pretty rooms and cabañas with kitchenettes around a shaded garden. Delicious breakfast included in rates. ⑤.

**Casa Caribe**, north of the plaza, 500m along the seafront and opposite the beach (☎9/871-0459, *casacaribe@puertomorelos.com.mx*). A large peaceful house with four gorgeous, enormous rooms, kitchen facilities and sundecks. Wonderful. ⑦.

**Hotel Inglaterra**, Av Ninos Heroes 29, 200m north of the plaza and two blocks back from the sea (☎9/ & fax 871-0418, *michael@hotelinglaterra.freeserve.co.uk*). Basic but clean and decent rooms at budget prices. ⑤.

**Hacienda Morelos**, on the front, south of the plaza (☎9/ & fax 871-0015). Bright, airy rooms, all right on the beach. ⑦.

**Posada Amor**, C Rojo Romez, just south of the plaza (☎9/871-0033, fax 871-0178, *poséamor@hotmail.com*). The least expensive option in Puerto Morelos. It's not on the beach, but it's friendly and comfortable, with plenty of character. ④.

**Rancho Libertad**, 15min south of the plaza, beyond the car ferry dock (☎9/ & fax 871-0181,*www.rancholibertad.com*). Two-storey thatched cabañas in a tranquil beach and garden setting. Rates include substantial fruit and cereal breakfasts. Guest kitchen facilities and massage available (US$45 per hour). No children. ⑦.

## The Town

The turn-off from Hwy-307 ends at the small, modern **plaza** in the centre of Puerto Morelos: the only proper streets lead north and south for a few blocks, parallel to the beach. The plaza hosts a weekend *tyanguis* or crafts fair, has a baseball court and taxi rank, and is home to *Alma Libre* (Oct–April Tues–Sat 9am–noon & 6–9pm), Mexico's most extensive second-hand English language bookshop. Ahead of the plaza lies the **beach**, a wooden **dock** (the car ferry terminal is a few hundred metres south) and the **lighthouse**.

With the reef only 600m offshore and in a very healthy condition, Puerto Morelos is a great place to learn to **dive**. Both *Almost Heaven Adventures* (☎9/871-0230) and *Nito's Divers* (☎9/871-0012), either side of the plaza, offer certification courses and one- and two-tank dives (US$40–55), as well as sportsfishing charters (around US$200; 5–6hr; up to 4 people) and snorkelling trips (US$20; 2hr).

There are several opportunities to learn more about the **natural and social history** of the area. Maya Echo, a group dedicated to the conservation of the area's natural beauty and the preservation of Maya culture and spirituality, organizes tailor-made, one-day tours into the forest and to local Maya villages (contact Sandra Dayton on ☎9/871-0136, *starseed@prodigy.net*). Goyo Martin of Goyo's Jungle Adventures, on Avenida Ninos Heroes, one block north of the plaza (cellphone ☎0198/106179), also takes people into the forest and to a local cenote (US$40 including lunch; 9am–2pm; 5hr), while friendly guide Marco Riha offers day-trips further afield to major Maya sites Chichén Itzá and Ek-Balam (☎9/895-9632, *www.relaxedalternative.com* – or leave a message at *Rancho Libertad*; from US$90 including tranport, guide, lunch and all entrance fees).

Just south of the turn-off for the *Acamaya Reef Trailer Park* (see above), the **Jardín Botanico Dr Alfredo Barrera** (daily 9am–5pm; US$2.50) features the native flora of Quintana Roo and is definitely worth a visit if you have the time. Exhibits are labelled in Spanish and English and there are also guides who can explain the medicinal uses of the plants. Trails lead to a small Maya site and a reconstruction showing how *chicle* was tapped from the sap of the *zapote* (sapodilla) tree before being used in the production of chewing gum.

## Eating and drinking

Most of Puerto Morelos' **nightlife** centres around the town plaza, a cheerful and laid-back spot for a cold beer or an evening stroll. The best **tacos** in town – and possibly the entire Yucatán – are served up (evenings only) in an unnamed seafront garden on the plaza's northeast corner, while the *Hotel Ojo de Agua*, north of the plaza, occasionally hosts **live music** events and parties.

**El Café**, south side of the plaza. Vegetarian café with salads, healthy breakfasts and fresh juices.

**Casita del Mar**, north of the plaza, 600m along the seafront. This small hotel has a popular Argentinian restaurant with delicious grilled meat and home-made empanadas. Busy at the weekends.

**Johnny Cairos**, south of the plaza on the beach. Very popular all-you-can-eat Sunday barbecue (US$10) with chicken, ribs, guacamole, salads and so on.

**Los Pelicanos**, south corner of the plaza. Great seafood and immaculate service, but it's not cheap.

**El Pirata**, north side of the plaza. Open-air joint with Mexican staples – enchiladas, tacos, burritos and more – at economical prices. Great hanging-out spot.

**Posada Amor**, just south of the plaza. Friendly restaurant with tasty fresh fish, Mexican dishes and Sunday breakfast buffet. Good value.

## Punta Bete

Tucked away between the more touristed resorts of Puerto Morelos and Playa del Carmen, the sedate **PUNTA BETE** is little more than a beach, a few restaurants and a couple of small hotels, though there's now a big, expensive resort just along the shore. Of the hotels, *Paradise Point Resort* (reservations in the US by fax 651-762-8284, *www.knowAmerica.com/Paradise*; ⑤) has pretty beachfront rooms and a small restaurant, while *Coco's Cabañas* (☎9/874-7056, *cchr@caribe.net.mx*; ⑤) is a block back from the sea but has individual cabañas, a small pool and a restaurant serving good international cuisine. The *Playa Xcalacoco* **restaurant** (☎9/872-0026) dishes up reasonably priced basic Mexican food and superb fish from 7.30am until 8pm; it also offers clean, simple but electricity-free rooms (④) and **camping**. Punta Bete's **beach** is nowhere near as beautiful as those in Cancún or Playa del Carmen though it does have the advantage of being uncrowded and for the most part undeveloped. To get here, it's a slow, careful drive or a hot, dusty 4km walk down the pot-holed dirt track (signposted, at Km 296) from the highway.

# Playa del Carmen

**PLAYA DEL CARMEN** (known simply as Playa), once a soporific, very Mexican fishing village, has mushroomed in recent years and now has the dubious distinction of being the world's fastest growing town (its population is expanding by 26 percent a year, according to the *Guinness Book of Records*). It's expensive and overcrowded with holidaymakers, thousands of day-trippers from Cancún and the passengers of passing Caribbean cruise ships. As a result the town's main centre of activity, **Avenida 5** or *Quinta*, a long pedestrianized strip one block back from the sea, is generally packed to capacity with visitors rapidly emptying their wallets in pavement cafes, souvenir and silver jewellery outlets and designer clothes shops. Additionally, with the arrival of US fast-food giants *McDonald's*, *Burger King* and *TGI Friday*, Playa's rather chic European atmosphere is giving way to a blander, more homogenized scene. The **beach**, however, is one of the prettiest on the coast with unfeasibly white sand and gloriously clear sea and the town is compact and easily covered on foot – and boasts the best **nightlife** on the Riviera Maya. The reef offshore is almost as spectacular here as in Cozumel and there are scores of professional **scuba-diving** operations in Playa – recommended is Tank-Ha, Av 5 between calles 8 and 10 (☎9/873-0302, *www.tankha.com*), which offers certification courses (US$350), one- and two-tank dives (US$45–65) and dive packages (from US$175) as well as twice-daily snorkelling tours (9.30am & 1.30pm; US$25; 3hr). If you're a real thrill-seeker, you can sky-dive from Playa with Sky-Dive Playa del Carmen, Plaza Marina (☎9/873-0192, *www.skydive.com.mx*; US$200 for a tandem dive with a certified instructor).

## Arrival and information

**Buses** pull in at the corner of avenidas 5 and Juárez, the main street running east–west from the highway to the beach; some second-class buses stop one or two blocks further inland on Juárez. The **tourist information centre**, on Avenida Juarez between avenidas 15 and 20 (daily 9am–9pm), has helpful, bilingual staff and stocks the useful *Destination Playa del Carmen*, which has a very good map, hotel and restaurant listings. Beware the other tourist information booths scattered around town, as they're mostly

tied up with some ulterior motive – selling timeshares, for example. The best way to **visit local sites** is to hire a taxi driver who'll take you on a round-trip including waiting time for as little as half the price of any tour company.

## Accommodation

You'll have no difficulty finding a room in Playa del Carmen – hotels are being built all the time – and the ever-increasing competition means that rooms are becoming more and more reasonably priced. The town has two hotels with camping facilities and several decent budget hotels (generally, the further from the sea the cheaper the accommodation).

**Baal Nah Kah**, C 12 between the beach and Av 5 (☎9/873-0110, fax 873-0050). Very popular and relaxed Italian-run bed and breakfast. Individual and charming. ⑦.

**Blue Parrot Inn**, on and slightly back from the beach between calles 12 and 14 (☎9/873-0083, fax 873-0049). A wide range of cabañas and rooms; the *Tucan* annexe has elegant suites with one or two bedrooms and kitchenettes. Home to the popular beachfront *Dragon* bar, the hotel has a lively central location. ⑤–⑦.

**Campamiento La Ruina**, C 2 Nte, between Av 5 and the sea (☎9/873-0405). Playa's most sociable and economical place to stay, on the beach with its own ruin in the grounds. There are a variety of options: a few hook-ups; cabañas with or without private bath; camping space, and a huge *palapa* with lockers and room for 34 hammocks. ②–④.

**Cabañas Sofia**, C 2 Nte, between Av 5 and the sea (☎9/873-3112). Another cheap option, smaller and quieter than the Ruina opposite, with similar cabañas and camping space. ②–④.

**Delfin**, Av 5 and C 6 Nte (☎ & fax 9/873-0176, *www.hoteldelfin.com*). Very central downtown hotel. Large, immaculate rooms with fans and private bathrooms. Good value. ④–⑤.

**Kinbe**, C 10 between avenidas 5 and 1 (☎9/873-0441, fax 873-2215, *www.kinbe.com*). Small Italian-run hotel with beautifully designed rooms set around a courtyard. ⑥.

**Hotel Lunata**, Av 5 between calles 6 and 8 (☎9/873-0884, fax 873-1240, *www.lunata.com*). Gorgeous town house with lovely rooms including a honeymoon suite, though as it overlooks the main street the rooms at front can be noisy. Continental breakfast served in a walled garden. ⑦.

**Hotel La Paz**, Av 20 between calles 2 and 4 (☎9/873-0467, fax 873-3178, *www.xaac.com/playacar/paz.htm*). Clean, no-frills budget option two blocks from the sea. ④.

**Posada Freud**, Av 5 between calles 8 and 10 (☎ & fax 9/873-0601, *www.xaac.com/playacar/freud.htm*). Pretty rooms smack in the middle of the action at reasonable – and negotiable – rates. ⑦.

**La Rana Cansada**, C 10 Nte 132 (☎9/873-0389, *www.ranacansada.com*). Friendly hotel with communal living space, kitchen facilities and a laid-back atmosphere. ⑤.

**Urban Hostel**, Av 10 between calles 4 and 6 (☎9/879-9342, *urbanhostel@yahoo.com*). Probably the best bet for budget accommodation, with dorms in a brightly decorated *palapa* and full kitchen facilities for US$10 per person.

## Eating

Playa del Carmen is heaving with **restaurants** of every kind. The pedestrianized section of **Avenida 5** is edged end-to-end with dining tables where you can eat pizza, pasta, French food, burgers and chips, veggie – you name it. The quality of food is usually very good (particularly Italian), but it's rarely reasonably priced – if you're on a budget you'll need to search out where locals go for tacos and *comida corriente* (as a rule of thumb in Playa, the further from the sea, the cheaper the food – and everything else). Probably the nicest places, though, are the **beach restaurants** and bars, where your can sift sand between your toes while eating fresh fish and sipping icy margaritas. Keep an eye open for the various happy hours.

**Los Almendras**, Av 10 and C 6. Traditional Mexican restaurant with outdoor grill and delicious tacos which you fill yourself from a buffet. Good value and unpretentious.

**Andale**, Av 5 between calles 4 and 6. Coffee shop with really good Italian espresso and cappuccino.

**Buenos Aires**, Av 5 between calles 4 and 6. Tucked away in a side street, this Argentinian steakhouse is the best place in town for delicious grilled meat.

**The Coffee Press**, C 2 between Av 5 and the beach. Chilled-out pavement café with good coffee, homemade cakes, soup and sandwiches.

**La Grotta di Bacco**, Av 15 between calles 4 and 6. Superb Italian restaurant with home-made pasta, grilled fish and meat dishes and a classy Italian wine list.

**Hot**, C 10 between avenidas 5 and 10. Bakery with a small, laid-back café serving fresh muffins, bagels and brownies as well as omelettes and sandwiches.

**Media Luna**, Av 5 between calles 8 and 10. Vegetarian and seafood restaurant with good pasta and veggie dishes. Huge delicious breakfasts – fruit salad, French toast, pancakes.

**La Parrilla**, Av 5 between calles 6 and 8. Branch of the very good Mexican grill chain. Live music nightly.

**Lo Sfizio**, C 4 between avenidas 10 and 15. Friendly and noisy Sicilian restaurant with good pasta, the best pizza in town and a long wine list.

**Xtabentum**, C 2 between avenidas 10 and 15. Local family-run Mexican restaurant with tasty *comida corriente*, bean soup, burritos and so on. Very good value.

## Bars and nightlife

You can wander through Playa well into the night, following the happy-hour trail and listening to all sorts of music from salsa and reggae to 1970s classics. Drinks aren't cheap if you pay the full price, but it's a great way to meet people.

**Calypso**, Av 5 between calles 4 and 6. Cosy local atmosphere and a busy dance floor, with live Caribbean music on Fri and Sat evenings.

**Capitan Tutix**, on the beach between calles 2 and 4. Jam-packed bar and disco with live music every night (10pm–midnight) and a predominantly young party crowd. It's *the* pick-up joint in town, and stays open until the last customer leaves.

**Dragon Bar**, on the beach in front of the *Blue Parrot Inn*, calles 12 and 14. Popular, friendly open-air bar with live music in the afternoons and tables on the sand. Open until 2am.

**Requiem**, C 6 between avenidas 5 and 10. Techno dance club which opens nightly at 10pm. Not very Mexican but if techno's your thing, this is the place for you.

## Listings

**Banks** Bital is on Av Juárez between avenidas 10 and 15 (Mon–Fri 8am–4pm) and Bancomer is on Av Juárez between avenidas 25 and 30 (Mon–Fri 9am– 4pm); both have ATMs.

**Car and bike rental** All the large car rental companies have outlets in Playa – most are situated on the main coastal highway at the turn-off into town or Plaza Marina near the Cozumel ferry pier. Try Budget, Plaza Marina (☎9/873-2772), or Localiza, Av Juarez between avenidas 5 and 10 (☎9/873-05-80). Universal, Av 10 between calles 12 and 14 (☎9/876-5960), rents out motorbikes (US$30 per day), bicycles (US$7 per day) and foot scooters.

**Email and fax** There are a number of shops with Internet facilities on or around Avenida 5, including Supersonicos, Av 10 between calles 2 and 4 (daily 8am–2am).

**Post office** on Av Juárez, four blocks back from the beach (Mon–Fri 8am–7pm, Sat 9am–2pm); geared to dealing with tourists and with a stamp machine outside. The Lista de Correos (postcode 77710) keeps mail for ten days.

**Telephones** There are plenty of Ladatel phones and you can call long distance at Computel caseta (daily 7am– 10pm) next to the bus station.

**Travel agents and tours** The small airstrip just south of town handles short jaunts, chiefly to Cozumel, but also to Chichén Itzá and other key Maya sites; operators include Aeroferinco (☎9/873-0636) and Aeroméxico (☎9/873-0350). Eurotravel at Rincon del Sol, Av 5 near C 8, can organize tours to Maya ruins, horse-riding, boat trips, sky-diving and national and international flights. Cenote Sam (☎1/987-64969) takes groups on off-the-beaten-track tours of the jungle.

# Cozumel

**ISLA COZUMEL** is far larger than Mujeres and has, unfortunately, been developed way beyond its potential. However, it offers the best **diving** in Mexico, with spectacular drop-offs, walls and swim-throughs, some beautiful **coral gardens** and a number of little-visited remote reefs where you can see larger pelagic fish and dolphins. The island is also good for **bird-watching** as it's a stopover on migration routes and has several species or variants endemic to Cozumel.

Before the Spanish arrived, the island appears to have been a major Maya centre, carrying on sea trade around the coasts of Mexico and as far south as Honduras and perhaps Panamá; after the Conquest it was virtually deserted for four hundred years. This ancient community – one of several around the Yucatán coast that survived the collapse of Classic Maya civilization – is usually dismissed as being the decadent remnant of a moribund society. But that was not the impression the Spanish received when they arrived, nor is it necessarily the right one. Architecture might have declined in the years from 1200 AD to the Conquest, but large-scale trade, specialization between centres and even a degree of mass production are all in evidence. Cozumel's rulers enjoyed a less grand style than their forebears, but the rest of an increasingly commercialized population were probably better off. And Cozumel itself may even have been an early free-trade zone, where merchants from competing cities could trade peaceably.

Whatever the truth, you get little opportunity to judge for yourself. A US air base, built here during World War II, has erased all trace of the ancient city, and the lesser ruins scattered across the roadless interior are mostly unrestored and inaccessible. The airfield did, at least, bring new prosperity – converted to civilian use, it remains the means by which most visitors arrive.

## Arrival and information

**Arriving** by boat, you'll be right in the centre of town (officially **San Miguel**, but always known simply as Cozumel) with the zócalo just one block inland along Juárez; from the airport you have to take the VW combi service. The **tourist office** (Mon–Fri 9am–3pm & 6–8pm) is upstairs inside the Plaza del Sol shopping centre on the zócalo, but the staff are not very helpful and there's nothing here that you can't get at hotels, restaurants and shop counters throughout the island. The ubiquitous *Free Blue Guide to Cozumel* is particularly useful and packed full of information, maps and handy tips. The **post office** (Mon–Fri 9am–6pm, Sat 9am–noon) is about fifteen minutes' walk from the centre, on Av Melgar at the corner with C 7 Sur; for the Lista de Correos use the postcode 77600. Cozumel has many **banks** (generally Mon–Fri 9am–4pm), most of them with ATMs. Bital, Av 5 and C 1, stays open until 7pm on weekdays; otherwise there are several **casas de cambio** around the main square (daily 9am–10pm).

There are dozens of **dive shops** in town. The better ones use experienced instructors and small, fast boats. Deep Blue, Av 10 at C Salas (☎ & fax 9/872-5653, *www.deepbluecozumel.com*) is one of the best on the island, offering tailor-made small-group tours to some of the most interesting and remote reefs on the island, and a full range of certification courses including PADI and IANTD (Nitrox). They can also help find accommodation, including house rental. **Snorkelling** and **sportfishing** tours are both readily available from most of the diveshops in town; the best snorkelling trips take you right out onto the reef (around US$20 for several hours). An exhilarating – if bumpy - way to see the island is on an **ATV (All Terrain Vehicle** or four-wheel motorbike**)** tour of the uninhabited northeast coast (see below). Wild Tours, Av 15 and C 6 (☎9/872-6747, *wildtour@prodigy.net.mx*; US$65; 2hr 30min), are recommended.

## Getting around

**Cozumel town** has been modernized and is easy enough to get around on foot – there's even a pedestrian zone. There's a distinct lack of buses, however, so to get further afield you'll have to go on a tour, take a taxi or rent a vehicle. **Cycling** is feasible on the tarmacked roads, but it can be a bit of an endurance test if you aren't used to long-distance pedalling, and positively unpleasant if you get caught in a sudden storm, likely from around July to October. **Mopeds** give you a bit more freedom and are easier to handle, and **jeeps** are available from numerous outlets (be sure to check the restrictions of your insurance if you want to go onto the dirt tracks).

There is no shortage of places on Cozumel to **rent vehicles**. Try Aguilar, in the lobby of the *Hotel Aguilar*, C 3 Sur 98 (☎9/872-0307), which also rents out scooters. Prices vary little, but it's worth shopping around for special offers; bikes cost around US$9, mopeds US$25–30 and jeeps around US$45.

## Accommodation

Most **hotels** in Cozumel are expensive all-inclusive resorts strung out along the coast; the rest are lower-priced places in the centre of town, all some way from the island's beaches and none with rooms for less than US$20 per night. Virtually all hotels offer some kind of dive package.

**Aguilar**, C 3 Sur 98, near the corner of Av 5 Sur (☎9/872-0307, fax 872-0769, *haguilar@cozumel .finred.com.mx*). Quiet, slightly kitsch rooms away from the road set around a garden with a small pool. Scooters and car rental available. ④.

**Amigo's B&B**, C 7 Sur 571 between avenidas 25 and 30 (☎ & fax 9/872-3868, *www .cozumelbedandbreakfast.net*). Three separate cottages in a lovely garden with fruit trees. Continental breakfast is included in the rate, served in a communal area which also has TV, video and games. ⑥.

**Casa Mexicana**, Melgar 457 between calles 5 and 7 (☎9/872-0209, fax 872-1387, *www.casamexi-canacozumel.com*). Glamorous, state-of-the-art hotel overlooking the water with pool, travel agency and on-site business centre and gym. ⑨.

**Lorena**, Costera Sur, Km 2.2 (☎9/872-0188, *www.lorenaHotel.com*). Small new hotel just out of town and right on the ocean. All rooms have private balconies with sea view. Pool, beach access and excellent dive packages. ⑦.

**Maya Cozumel**, C 5 Sur 4 (☎9/872-0011, fax 872-0781). Less expensive than the seafront hotels, but just as good, with spacious garden and pool. The a/c rooms have TV, fridges and phones. ⑤.

**Pepita**, Av 15 Sur and C 1 Sur (☎9/872-0098). By far the best of the budget options with clean attractive rooms, a pretty courtyard and complimentary coffee in the mornings. ④.

**Playa Azul**, *zona hotelera* norte, Km 4 (☎9/872-0043, fax 872-0110, *www.playa-azul.com*). Swanky resort on a lovely stretch of beach north of town. Elegant rooms and all facilities on site. ⑨.

**Saolima**, C Salas 260 (☎9/872-0886). Basic but clean rooms away from the road. ④.

**Suites Bahia**, Av Melgar and C 3 Sur (☎9/872-0209, fax 872-1387, *www.dicoz.com/suitesbahia.html*). Waterfront hotel with spacious and comfortable rooms, some with kitchenettes. ⑦.

**Suites Colonial**, Av 5 Sur 9 (☎9/872-0542, fax 872-1387, *www.dicoz.com/suitescolonial.html*). Rooms with a/c, bath, kitchenette, cable TV and phone. ⑦.

**Suites Villa Las Anclas**, Av 5 Sur 325 (☎9/ & fax 872-5476). Elegant two-storey apartments, each sleeping two people, with kitchenettes and peaceful garden. ⑦.

## The island

**Downtown Cozumel** is almost entirely devoted to tourism, packed with restaurants, souvenir shops, tour agencies and "craft markets" – almost exclusively set up to cater for a huge cruise-ship market. During the high season (Nov–April) up to twenty cruise liners a week, each carrying several thousand passengers, disembark at one of the island's five purpose-built piers. Except at the weekend, when the cruise ships don't usually call in, the *malecón* is all too often an uncomfortably crowded throng of day-trippers and you may be hassled by aggressive sales pitches.

**Black coral**, a rare and beautiful product of the reefs, is sold everywhere: until Jacques Cousteau discovered it off the island about twenty years ago, it was thought to be extinct. Even now there's not a great deal (it grows at little more than an inch every fifty years), so it's expensive and heavily protected – don't, under any circumstances, go breaking it off the reefs.

There's an attractive **museum** on the *malecón*, between avenidas 4 and 6 (daily 9am–5pm; US$3), with small displays of the flora, fauna and marine life of the island, as well as Maya artefacts and old photos. It hosts occasional live music or theatre events here – check with the tourist office.

Cozumel's eastern shoreline is often impressively wild but, as on Isla Mujeres, only the west coast is really suitable for **swimming**, protected as it is by a line of reefs and the mainland. The easiest **beaches** to get to are north of the town in front of the older resort hotels. Far better, though, to rent a vehicle and head off down to the less exploited places to the south.

Heading **south**, you pass first a clutch of modern hotels by the car ferry dock; offshore here, at the end of the Paraiso Reef, you can see a rather alarming wrecked airliner on the bottom – it's a movie prop. There's accessible snorkelling by *Hotel Barracuda* and further along opposite the *Villablanca Garden Beach Hotel*. Carry on to the **Parque Chankanaab** or "Little Sea", recently designated a National Park (daily 7am–5pm; US$10), a beautiful if rather over-exploited lagoon full of turtles and lurid fish surrounded by botanical gardens. There's a beach and a tiny reef just offshore, with changing rooms, showers, diving and snorkelling equipment for rent, an expensive restaurant and a protected children's beach. Further south, **Playa San Francisco** is the best spot for lounging and swimming, while at the southern tip, the **Laguna de Colombia** offers interesting snorkelling.

From here you can complete a circuit of the southern half of the island by following the road up the windswept eastern shoreline. There are a couple of good restaurants at **Punta Chiqueros** and **Punta Morena** and, on calm days, excellent deserted sands. The main road cuts back across the middle of the island to town, but if you have a jeep (not a moped, which probably won't have enough gas anyway) you could continue up a rough track (turn off by the *Mescalitos* restaurant) to the northern point; you'll pass **La Palma**, the remains of a small Maya temple dedicated to Ixchel, the goddess of fertility, and the ruin of **Castillo Real**, where potential Maya leaders allegedly went to sit out 365 days and nights alone to test their fortitude and strength of character.

More accessible – halfway across the island from town, on the northern side of the road – the only excavated Maya site on the island, **San Gervasio** (daily 8am–5pm; US$4), was built to honour Ixchel. Apparently modelled on Chitchén Itzá, with several small temples connected by *sacbes* or long white roads, San Gervasio was, between 1200 and 1650 AD, one of the most important centres of pilgrimage in Mesoamerica – though it's not particularly impressive now. On the southern part of the island, the village of **CEDRAL** has a tiny Maya site near the old Spanish church and several **cenotes** reachable only on horseback (US$20 for 2hr); turn inland on the road shortly after passing San Francisco beach. In May, the village hosts a huge *fiesta* with bull fights, prize-winning livestock and dancing.

The southernmost point of the island is now a protected reserve, the **Parque Punta Sur** (daily 8am–5pm; US$10). The thousand-acre site includes several lovely beaches, the **Templo El Caracol** – a small, low-level ruined building which may have been built by the Maya as a lighthouse, and is worth visiting to hear the music produced when the wind whistles through the shells encrusted in its walls – and the Punta Celarain **lighthouse**, with amazing views from the top and an interesting maritime **museum** in the former lightkeeper's house. Viewing towers dotted throughout the park let you survey a large network of lagoons, and a creaking wooden bus transports you between various sites (or you can rent a bicycle); there's also a beach restaurant serving good fried fish.

## Eating and drinking

**Eating** tends to be expensive wherever you go on Cozumel but there's plenty of choice if you've got money to spend. The **zocalo** downtown is a central focus for **nightlife** and although it's a very pleasant spot with foodstalls, frequent live music and strolling mariachis, its restaurants are for the most part overpriced tourist traps. You're better off wandering several blocks back from the seafront for good food and local colour. For a more laid-back atmosphere you can enjoy long, lazy lunches in the **palapas** dotted every few kilometres along the rugged eastern coast.

**Azul Cobalito**, avenidas Juarez and 10. Really good Italian restaurant with wood-fired pizzas and home-made pasta, and fish specialities. Live jazz nightly.

**La Choza**, Av 10 and C Salas. Busy and popular mid-priced restaurant serving Mexican home cooking. Good service and a buzzing atmosphere.

**Con Mil Amores**, Av 10 198. Pretty Spanish café with good Italian coffee, sandwiches and light, healthy meals. It also has book exchange and Internet facilities.

**Diamond Bakery**, Av 15 and C 1 Sur. Excellent bakery with an extensive breakfast menu, home-made ice-cream and pastries.

**Joe's Lobster Pub**, Av 10, between calles Salas and 3. Touristy but fun restaurant serving Mexican dishes; the house speciality is lobster in garlic sauce. Nightly live music. Open daily 6pm– 2am.

**Mi Chabelita**, Av 10, between calles 1 and Salas. Delicious and very cheap Mexican food in simple surroundings. Highly recommended.

**Paradise Café**, on an anticlockwise circuit of the island, it's where the tarmac road meets the east coast. *Palapa*-roofed restaurant/bar in the middle of nowhere, dishing up moderately priced Mexican food to the accompaniment of reggae. Good place to swing in a hammock, sipping a margarita. Daily 10.30am–6.30pm.

**Pepe's Grill**, Av Melgar and C Salas (☎9/872-0213). Seafood and steak in an elegant and relaxed atmosphere. Expensive but worth it. Open daily 5–11pm.

**Prima**, C Salas between avenidas 5 and 10. Very popular Italian restaurant with roof-top terrace, good pizza and pasta.

**Tony Rome's**, C Salas between avenidas 5 and 10. Hilarious karaoke venue with the larger-than-life Tony Rome entertaining the crowds nightly. Loads of fun.

# From Playa south to Tulum

Almost the entire stretch of coast **south of Playa del Carmen**, which includes a number of exquisite **beaches**, has been developed into a string of luxury **all-inclusive resorts** – or condominium "villages" (principally **Puerto Aventuras**, 20km south of Playa, and **Akumal**, 15km still further; both are expensive, sterile and best avoided) – with private gated entrances and consequently little or no access for non-residents to the sea.

Otherwise, the first place of note, 6km south of Playa, is **Xcaret**, tagged the "Incredible Eco-Archeological Park", but in fact a huge, somewhat bizarre **theme park** (Mon–Sat 8.30am–9.45pm, Sun 8.30am–6pm; US$45, US$22 for children under 12). There's a museum, tropical aquarium, aviary, "Maya village", botanical garden, small archeological ruins, pools and beaches, and more than a kilometre of subterranean rivers down which you can swim, snorkel or simply float – along with scores of others – with the help of neon rubber rings.

Twenty-five kilometres further south, **XPU-HA** is the only piece of (relatively) unspoilt beach on this coast. Despite the presence of one all-inclusive resort, *Hotel Copacabaña* (⑧), it's a laid-back place with a long strip of gloriously white sand and clear turquoise sea. If you're on a budget you can stay in basic cabañas or camp on the beach at *Bonanza Xpu-ha* (①/④). Otherwise there's a small hotel, *Villas del Caribe* (☎9/873-2194; ⑤), adjacent to the excellent *Café de Mar* restaurant and bar which is the only real focus of Xpu-ha's small community and serves healthy breakfasts and lunches and delicious Italian food. To get to Xpu-Ha take the exit signposted X-4 from the main coastal highway.

Forty-five kilometres south of Playa, 13km north of Tulum, **Xel-Ha**, or "place where water is born" (daily 8.30am– 6pm; US$19, or US$45 with all food and drink included), is a theme park billed as "the world's largest natural aquarium" and built around an extensive natural formation of lagoons, inlets and caves. It's a beautiful place, but like Xcaret it's usually crowded with day-trippers; get here early – after 9.30am you'll be fighting for space. You can rent snorkelling equipment on the spot and lockers are available. Across the other side of the highway, the small and only partly excavated **ruins** of Xel-Ha are of little interest but for the Temple of the Birds, where faded paintings are still visible in places.

# Tulum

**TULUM**, 130km south of Cancún, is one of the most picturesque of all Maya sites – small, but exquisitely poised on fifteen-metre-high cliffs above the turquoise Caribbean. When the Spanish first set eyes on the place in 1518, they considered it as large and beautiful a city as Seville. They were, perhaps, misled by their dreams of Eldorado, by the glory of the setting and by the brightly painted facades of the buildings, for architecturally Tulum

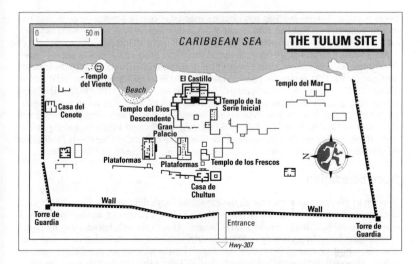

is no match for the great cities. Nevertheless, thanks to the setting, it sticks in the memory like no other. It is also an important Maya spiritual and cultural centre, and is one of the villages in the **Zona Maya**.

If you want to take time out for a **swim**, you can plunge into the Caribbean straight from the beach on site. There are limitless further possibilities strung out along the sandy road that runs south along the beautiful and deserted coastline. This track continues, though practicable only in a sturdy (and preferably four-wheel drive) vehicle, all the way to Punta Allen at the tip of the peninsula. The beginning of the old road has been blocked to protect the ruins from traffic damage, so you have to join it further south.

## Arrival and information

Arriving in Tulum can be confusing because there are two distinct parts of the community. The main coastal highway from Cancún turns slightly inland here and while the village proper, an ugly concrete sprawl, straddles either side of this main road, the **ruins** and most of the local **accommodation** are right on the sea and connected to each other by the badly potholed Boca Paila/Punta Allen road. There's a special well-marked exit to the ruins; otherwise you reach the sea via a 2km turn-off at the Pemex gas station as you enter the village from the north.

The **bus station** is at the southern end of the village. If you're heading to the ruins or the beach you'll need to get off before the terminal at the relevant turn-off and walk or take a **taxi** – there's no public transport. It's worth knowing that Tulum's taxi drivers are particularly cut-throat, intimidating locals who pick up hitchhikers (consequently most don't) and denying the existence of hotels which don't pay them commission - if you've been given the name of a particular hotel, insist on being taken there.

Almost opposite the bus station is *The Weary Traveller* (daily 8am–11pm; ☎9/871-2461, *www.everycontinent.com*), a backpacker information centre with Internet access, noticeboards and free maps of the area; the staff are helpful, the coffee's very good and it's a great place to meet other tourists. There's no bank in town (the nearest ATM is

13km north at Xel-ha) but you can **change money** at one of several casas de cambio on the main street. You can **rent a car** from *Ana y Jose* (☎9/871-2030, *www.tulumre-sorts.com*); the office is opposite the bus station in Tulum village.

Most visitors to Tulum are happy to spend their days lying on the beach, but for something more energetic, the Cenote Dive Centre (*www.cenotedive.com*), close to the turn-off for Cobá (see p.128), organizes cavern snorkelling tours (US$30) as well as PADI scuba-diving (US$35–60) and specialized cave-diving courses (US$300–1100). On the other side of the road, Sian Ka'an Tours (☎9/871-2363) runs trips into the Sian Ka'an reserve (see p.128 for details). The nearby *Restaurante Crocodilo* takes reservations for horseback rides to the Maya ruins at Muyil (US$65 including snacks and English-speaking guide; 5hr). There are several dive shops along the beach; the one at *Cabañas Punta Piedra* also runs hiking trips into the jungle (US$20; 6hr) and rents bicycles for US$6 per day.

## Accommodation

Though by no means as dramatic as the growth of Playa del Carmen, there has been a sizeable increase in the number of hotels along Tulum's 10km of gorgeous white sand – and a related shift in the whole Tulum "scene". Once famously popular among hippy backpackers lured by its beauty and dirt-cheap beachfront accommodation, Tulum now also plays host to several very ritzy "boutique" hotels with jet-set guests and rates to match. Although until recently it was a truism in Tulum that the further from the ruins the more expensive the hotel, there are now a number of reasonably priced cabañas and even small **campsites** dotted all the way to the end of the *zona hotelera*. Bear in mind, though, that the cabañas close to the ruins are not only very basic and none too clean, but attract constant rumours of theft and even rape (nonetheless you'll have to arrive early in the day to be in with a good chance of getting a space). The hotels below are listed in order of their distance from the ruins, beginning with the closest.

**Cabañas El Mirador**, 1km from the ruins along the old Punta Allen road (no phone). Basic sandy-floor cabañas with beds or hammock hooks (bring your own hammock or rent one of theirs). Shared cold-water bathroom. The restaurant is perched on the cliff, giving an idyllic view and wonderful cooling breezes. ③.

**Cabañas Don Armando's**, next door to *El Mirador* (☎9/874-4539). Sturdy, sandy-floored cabañas with security guards. Easily the most popular of the inexpensive places near the ruins (get there early) with a buzzing restaurant/disco bar on site, constant party scene and scuba dive shop. ③.

**Diamante K**, 1.2km from ruins (☎9/871-2283, *www.diamantek.com*). Beautifully decorated eco-hotel run on solar energy with a funky vegetarian restaurant, massage and sauna. ⑧.

**Cabañas Papaya Playa**, just south of the road connecting Tulum beach and town (☎9/871-2091). Range of accommodation – from spacious rooms with private hot-water bath to simple bamboo cabañas perched above the beach, plus teepees and camping spaces. There's a small restaurant and bar with a fun atmosphere. ②–⑤.

**Cabañas Punta Piedra**, 4km from the ruins, halfway along the beach road (☎9/876-9167). Four pretty rooms, all with small private terrace. ⑤.

**Zamas**, 5km from the ruins (fax 9/871-2067, *www.zamas.com*). Enormous rooms, some right on one of Tulum's prettiest stretches of beach, with a great Italian restaurant and a starry clientele. ⑧.

**Rancho Hemingway**, 500m from Zamas (*hemingwaytulum@hotmail.com*). Range of cabañas with no electricity but a friendly atmosphere. ④–⑥.

**Los Arrecifes**, 500m further south along the road (☎9/879-7307). Established twenty years ago, this is one of the oldest places on this coast. Cabañas with or without private bath in an idyllic place with its own stretch of palm-fringed beach and a restaurant. ④/⑤.

**Hotel Nueva Vida de Ramiro**, 8.5km from the ruins (fax 9/871-2092, *www.nuevavida.com.mx*). Peaceful eco-hotel with attractive, comfortable wooden cabañas on stilts set in cool leafy gardens. ⑧.

**Zacil-Ha**, 200m further on. Simple clean cabañas and camping space, run by a very friendly Maya family. No electricity or hot water but shared outdoor cooking facilities. Great for those on a budget. ②–④.

**Dos Ceibas**, 9km from the ruins (☎9/877-6024, fax 871-2335, *www.dosceibas.com*). Small, beautiful hotel with spacious cabañas in front of a turtle egg-laying beach, with a meditation room and classy restaurant. ⑧.

**Las Ranitas**, next door (☎ & fax 9/877-8554, *www.lasranitas.com*). The fanciest hotel on this coast with tennis courts, swimming pool, lovely rooms and an elegant restaurant and bar. In high season rooms start at US$200. ⑨.

## The site

The **Tulum site** (daily 8am–5pm; US$3, free on Sun) is about 1km from the main road – be sure to get off the bus at the turn-off to the ruins and not at the village. **Entrance** is through a breach in the wall that protected the city on three sides; the fourth was defended by the sea. This wall, some five metres high with a walkway around the top, may have been defensive, but more likely its prime purpose was to delineate the ceremonial and administrative precinct (the site you see today) from the residential enclaves spread out along the coast in each direction. These houses – by far the bulk of the ancient city – were mostly constructed of perishable material, so little or no trace of them remains.

As you go through the walls, the chief structures lie directly ahead of you, with the Castillo rising on its rocky prominence above the sea. You pass first the tumbledown **Casa de Chultun**, a porticoed dwelling whose roof collapsed only in the middle of this century, and immediately beyond it the **Templo de los Frescos**. The partly restored murals inside the temple depict Maya gods and symbols of nature's fertility: rain, corn and fish. They originally adorned an earlier structure and have been preserved by the construction around them of a gallery and still later (in the fifteenth century) by the addition of a second temple on top, with walls which, characteristically, slope outwards at the top. On the corners of the gallery are carved masks of Chac, or perhaps of the creator god Itzamna.

The **Castillo**, on the highest part of the site, commands imposing views in every direction. It may have served, as well as a temple, as a beacon or lighthouse – even without a light, it would have been an important landmark for mariners along an otherwise monotonously featureless coastline. You climb first to a small square, in the midst of which stood an altar, before tackling the broad stairway to the top of the castle itself. To the left of this plaza stands the **Templo del Dios Descendente**. The diving or descending god – depicted here above the narrow entrance of the temple – appears all over Tulum as a small, upside-down figure. His exact meaning is not known: he may represent the setting sun, or rain or lightning, or he may be the Bee God, since honey was one of the Maya's most important exports. Opposite is the **Templo de la Serie Inicial** (Temple of the Initial Series) – so called because in it was found a stela (now in the British Museum) bearing a date well before the foundation of the city, and presumably brought here from elsewhere. Right below the castle to the north is a tiny cove with a beautiful white beach, and on the promontory beyond it the **Templo del Viento** (Temple of the Wind), a small, single-roomed structure. This is mirrored by a similar chamber – the **Templo del Mar** – overlooking the water at the southern edge of the site.

## Eating

Because the accommodation in Tulum is spread over 10km and the village is 2km from the beach, almost every hotel in the place has its own **restaurant** – fittingly they range from cheap and grungy to very chic indeed – and guests tend to stick to these. Still, there are several places along the coast road worth making a trip to: *Gringo Dave's*, 3km from the ruins, which serves delicious fish and grilled meat in a lovely clifftop setting, and *Que Fresco*, at the *Zamas* hotel, a very good Italian restaurant with wood-fired pizzas and fresh pasta. In the village, there are a number of cheap cafés serving *comida corriente* and spit-roasted chicken to the locals, while *Charlie's*, opposite the bus stop, serves up good

Mexican food, and *Il giardino di Tony e Simone*, behind the post office at the northern end of Tulum, is widely considered the best Italian restaurant for miles around. *Helen's*, opposite the post office, has excellent cappuccino and home-made pastries.

# Cobá

Set in muggy rainforest 50km northwest of Tulum, the crumbling city of **COBÁ** (7am–6pm; US$3) is a fascinating and increasingly popular site. As it's scattered between two lakes and linked by a network of causeways, you'll need at least a couple of hours to see it all, although once inside you can rent bikes (US$2.50 per hour) – but it's well worth the effort, as much for the **wildlife** as for the ruins. The jungle around Cobá is home to toucans, egrets, herons and myriad tropical butterflies including the giant electric blue morphidae. There are plenty of vicious mosquitoes too, so bring lots of repellent.

The city's most surprising characteristic is a resemblance not to the great ruins of the Yucatán, but to those of the Maya in lowland Guatemala and Honduras. Ceramic studies indicate that the city was occupied from about 100 AD, up until the advent of the Spanish, and the site is even mentioned in the *Chilam Balam*, a book of Maya prophecy written in the eighteenth century and drawn from earlier oral sources. Its zenith, however, was in the Classic and Late Classic (up until about 800 AD). Most of the larger pyramids were built in this period, including the giant, **Nocoh Mul**, tallest in the Yucatán and strikingly similar in its long, narrow and precipitous stairway to the famous Guatemalan ruins of Tikal. The city's influence and wealth during this period was derived from close links with the great cities of Petén, to the south, as the plethora of stelae, which are associated with Petén sites, and the style of almost all of the buildings and ceramics attest. Later, when the city maintained trade links with the Puuc cities to the west, the production of stelae ceased. In the Early Postclassic, from about 1000 AD, Cobá went into a brief decline, recovering in 1200 AD with a resurgence of new building which included the construction of the temple that crowns the Nocoh Mul pyramid.

### Practicalities

There are four **buses** a day to Cobá from Tulum that continue on to Valladolid; the first leaves Tulum at 6.15am and arrives at the site at 7am. There are also four buses back from Cobá to Tulum, the last leaving at 5.30pm. Otherwise a taxi from Tulum to Cobá costs US$20 each way.

The **village** of Cobá, where the bus stops, is little more than a collection of shacks a few hundred metres from the site entrance. The only really decent **hotel** anywhere near the site is *Villas Arqueologicas* (☎ & fax 9/874-2087; ⑦), a wonderful bit of tropical luxury complete with swimming pool and archeological library. On the less expensive side, there are basic rooms at *El Bocadito* (③). There's a good **restaurant** at the end of the village, *La Piramide*, which sits right on the lake and serves Yucatecan specialities as well as Mexican dishes. Other than this, there are several no-frills cafés by the entrance to the site. Don't swim in the lake here – it's full of crocodiles.

# The Sian Ka'an Biosphere Reserve

Created by presidential decree in 1986, the 13,675-square-kilometre **Sian Ka'an Biosphere Reserve** is one of the largest protected areas in Mexico. The name means "the place where the sky is born" in the Maya language, and seems utterly appropriate when you experience the sunrise on this stunningly beautiful coast. It's a huge, sparsely populated region, with only around a thousand permanent inhabitants, mainly fishermen, *chicleros* and *milpa* farmers.

Approximately one-third of the area is **tropical forest**, one-third **fresh- and salt-water marshes and mangroves**, and one-third is marine environment, including a section of the longest **barrier reef** in the western hemisphere. The coastal forests and wetlands are particularly important feeding and wintering areas for North American migratory birds. Sian Ka'an contains examples of the principal ecosystems found in the Yucatán peninsula and the Caribbean: an astonishing variety of flora and fauna. All five species of Mexican **cat** – jaguar, puma, ocelot, margay and jaguarundi – are present, along with spider and howler **monkeys**, tapir, deer and the West Indian manatee. More than three hundred species of **birds** have been recorded, including flamingo, roseate spoonbill, white ibis, crested guan, wood stork, osprey and fifteen species of heron. The Caribbean beaches provide nesting grounds for four endangered species of **marine turtle**: the green, loggerhead, hawksbill and leatherback, while Morelet's and mangrove **crocodiles** inhabit the swamps and lagoons.

The Biosphere Reserve concept, developed since 1974 by UNESCO, is an ambitious attempt to combine protection of natural areas and the conservation of their genetic diversity with scientific research and sustainable development. Reserves consist of a strictly protected **core area**, a designated **buffer zone** used for non-destructive activities and an outer **transition zone**, merging with unprotected land, where traditional land use and experimental research take place. The success of the reserve depends to a great extent on the co-operation and involvement of local people, and the Sian Ka'an management plan incorporates several income-generating projects, such as improved fishing techniques, ornamental plant nurseries and, of course, tourism.

You can enter the reserve on your own (and at present there is no entrance fee) and there is accommodation at **Punta Allen**, the largest village here, but by far the best way to explore is on a **day-trip** with the **Centro Ecologico Sian Ka'an** (*www.siankaan.org*) run by American ecologist Cameron Boyd. Cameron lives in the biosphere and funds his research and educational programmes with two standard tours, daytime and sunset, around the fringes of the reserve's vast open spaces, with excellent opportunities for birdwatching. You can reserve a place on either trip at Sian Ka'an Tours in Tulum (see p.126).

For further information on the biosphere, contact the **Amigos de Sian Ka'an**, a Cancún-based, non-profit organization formed to promote the aims for which the reserve was established. The Amigos support scientific research and produce a series of guide and reference books on the natural history of Sian Ka'an. Their office in Cancún is at Av Cobá 5 between calles Nube and Brisa, on the third floor of the Plaza America (☎9/884-9583, fax 887-3080, *sian@cancun.com*), or write to Apartado Postal 770, Cancún 77500, Quintana Roo, Mexico.

## Muyil

The little-visited site of **Muyil** (daily 8am–5pm; US$1.70, free on Sun) lies to the north of the reserve, about 25km south of Tulum. To **get there** catch any second-class bus heading between Tulum and Chetumal and ask to be dropped at the entrance. A sign on the left of the highway points to the modest entrance; for now this consists solely of a ticket booth, though there are plans to add a gift shop and snack bar at some point.

Despite its size – probably the largest on the Quintana Roo coast – and proximity to Hwy-307, Muyil is hardly developed for tourism, and you'll probably have the place to yourself. Archeological evidence indicates that Muyil (also known as Chunyaxche) was continuously occupied from the Preclassic period until after the arrival of the Spanish in the sixteenth century. There is no record of the inhabitants coming into direct contact with the conquistadors, but they were probably victims of depopulation caused by introduced diseases. Most of the buildings you see today date from the Postclassic period, between 1200 and 1500 AD. The tops of the tallest structures, just visible from the road, rise 20m from the forest floor. There are more than one hundred mounds and temples, none of them completely clear of vegetation, and it's easy to wander around and find dozens of buildings buried in the jungle; climbing them is forbidden, however.

The centre of the site is connected by a *sacbe* – a Maya road – to the small **Muyil lagoon** 500m away. This lagoon is joined to the large Chunyaxche lagoon and ultimately to the sea at **Boca Paila** by an amazing **canalized river**: the route used by Maya traders. If you travel along the river today you'll come across even less explored sites, some of which appear to be connected to the lagoon or river by **underwater caves**.

**Leaving the site**, particularly if you're making your way up to Tulum, should be easy enough, provided you don't leave it too late; continuing south could prove a little more difficult.

## Punta Allen

Right at the tip of the peninsula, with a lighthouse guarding the northern entrance to the **Bahía de la Ascensión**, the Maya lobster-fishing village of **PUNTA ALLEN** is not a place you'd stumble across by accident. Some tourists from Cancún do get down this far in rented cars, but if you've only got one day virtually all you can do is turn around and head back.

Despite having a population of just four hundred, Punta Allen is the largest village within the reserve and is a focus of initiatives by both government departments and non-governmental organizations promoting sustainable development. During the summer, Earthwatch volunteers (see p.50) come here to assist scientists gathering data.

Entering the village, past the tiny naval station on the right and beached fishing boats on the left, you come to the first of the **accommodation** options: the *Curzan Guest House* (☎9/834-0358, fax 834-0383; ⑤), with tall conical cabañas and teepees, some with hot water. There's a **bar** and **restaurant** with information about the reserve, though you'll need to book meals if you're not staying there. On the beach, the *Let It Be Inn* (☎9/871-2092, *www.letitbeinn.com*; ⑦) has three cabañas with private bath and a separate large thatched cabaña with a self-catering kitchen and dining room. *Chen Chomac Resort* (☎9/877-8678; ⑦), a few kilometres north of the village, has some comfortable, modern thatched cabañas on the beach. There are only a couple of small **restaurants**, the *Punta Allen* and the *Candy*, but a **mobile shop** travels the length of the peninsula on Thursdays and Saturdays, selling meat, bread, fruit and vegetables, reaching Punta Allen about 2pm: useful if you're camping. Note that there's no cash facility in the village, and no petrol station beyond Tulum.

There's a **long-distance phone** (☎9/871-2424) in the village shop which also serves the community. Although there's no **dive shop**, the hotels generally have some form of watersport equipment for their guests and may let non-residents rent it. The *Let It Be Inn* offers all-inclusive fishing packages (US$1000 for 2 days/3 nights), while local fishermen can be persuaded to take you out into the reserve for a fee; they also go across the bay to the even tinier village of **Vigia Chico**, on the mainland. Captain Victor Barrera for instance, takes people fishing out on the salt flats and organizes eco-tours (☎9/871-2424, *www.siankaanflats.com*).

# From Tulum to Chetumal

The road from Tulum to Chetumal skirts around the Sian Ka'an Biosphere Reserve and heads inland, past Felipe Carrillo Puerto, a major crossroads on the routes to Valladolid and Mérida, the beautiful **Laguna Bacalar**, and on to **Chetumal**, the gateway to Belize and a good point from which to explore **Kohunlich** and other Maya sites.

## Felipe Carillo Puerto

**FELIPE CARILLO PUERTO**, formerly known as **Chan Santa Cruz**, is the capital of the "Zona Maya" and an important spiritual centre for the Maya. During the Caste Wars, Maya from the north gathered forces here and looked for guidance from a miraculous talking cross that told them to fight on against their oppressors. (Such talking crosses and statues are common in Maya mythology as conduits through which disincarnate spirits speak, or as manifestations of a soul, usually that of a shaman, when it has left the body during the state of trance; they are known as *way'ob* by the Yucatek Maya.) Presumably as an attempt to disguise its rebellious past, the town was renamed after a former governor of the Yucatán who was assassinated in 1924. However, a monument to the martyrs of the Caste Wars still stands in the town. There are several reasonable **hotels** around the main plaza – try the *Hotel Esquivel* (☎9/834-0344; ③) on the zócalo, only 100m from the small bus station, but check the rooms first as some are significantly better than others.

## Laguna Bacalar

Further south, some 35km north of Chetumal, is the beautiful **Laguna Bacalar**, the second largest lake in Mexico; 45km long and, on average, 1km wide, it links with a series of other lakes and eventually the Río Hondo and the sea. The village of Bacalar was a key point on the pre-Columbian trade route and unexcavated **Maya remains** surround the lake shore. The *Chilam Balam* of Chumayel, one of the Maya's sacred books, mentions it as the first settlement of the Itza, a Maya tribe originally from central Mexico. Near the village, there's a semi-ruinous **fort** built by the Spanish for protection against British pirates from Belize (then British Honduras), it became a Maya stronghold in the Caste Wars, and was the last place to be subdued by the government, in 1901. There's a wide variety of **birdlife**, as well as huge fish that reach nearly two metres in length. Nearby is the **Cenote Azul**, an inky-blue "bottomless" well that is crowded with swimmers and picnickers at weekends.

There are several lakeshore **restaurants** in the village and a small range of options if you want to **stay**. Aside from the wonderfully kitsch and comfortable *Hotel Laguna* (☎ & fax 9/834-2206; ⑤), *Amigos B&B* (reservations in Cozumel ☎ & fax 9/872-3868, *www.bacalar.net*; ⑤)has four lovely rooms overlooking the lake and breakfast is included in the rates. Several kilometres north of town *Rancho Encantado* (☎9/831-0037, *www.encantado.com*; ⑨ including breakfast and dinner) is a small New Age resort on the lakeshore, with a dozen very pretty cabañas and resident massage therapist; it also organizes trips to Kohunlich and other Maya sites.

# Chetumal and around

If you're heading south to Belize or Guatemala, you can't avoid **CHETUMAL**, capital of the state of Quintana Roo. The city is beginning to assert itself after decades of virtual stagnation, but there are still no "sights" to speak of. The best is the new **Museo de la Cultura Maya** (Tues–Sun 9am–7pm; US$5) on Héroes, near the corner of Mahatma Gandhi. Although it has very few original artefacts, the numerous interactive displays and models provide a fascinating insight into ancient Maya society, mathematics and cosmology. Chetumal's broad, modern streets (the town was levelled by Hurricane Janet just over thirty years ago) are lined with rather dull, overpriced hotels and restaurants, and with shops doing a brisk trade in **low-duty goods** – Dutch cheese, Taiwanese hi-fis, American peanuts, reproduction Levis from the Far East, Scotch whisky – to be smuggled into Belize or back into Mexico. Chetumal's surroundings, however, do offer the opportunity for some beautiful excursions, and the **waterfront**, enlivened by free music in the plaza, has a certain sleazy tropical charm.

## Practicalities

Chetumal's main **bus station** is a short taxi ride out of town and the **airport** is only 2km west of the centre, at the end of Avenida Revolución. **Avenida de los Héroes**, the town's main street, runs down from a big electricity-generating plant to the waterfront. The **information kiosk** (look for the small glass pyramid opposite the archeological

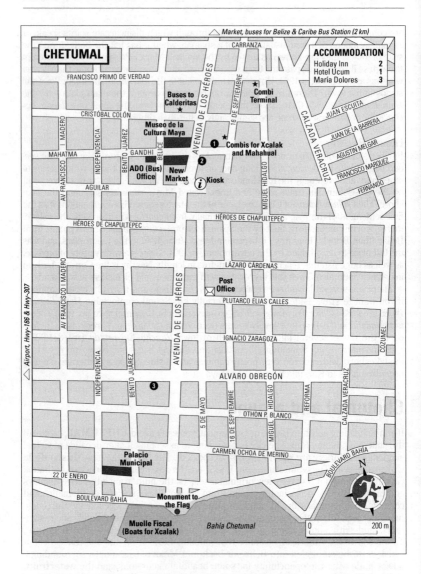

museum) is very helpful with information on buses, hotels and maps; they can also give information on Belize. The **bus ticket office** in town is on Av Belice at C Mahatma Gandhi. There's a **Guatemalan consulate** at Av de los Héroes 358 (Mon–Fri 9am–4pm; ☎9/832-6565), which issues visas (not necessary for citizens of the EU or the US).

Most of Chetumal's **hotels** are on Avenida de los Héroes, especially around the information kiosk and at the junction with Calle Obregón. One of the best in town, with private showers and a good restaurant, is the *Hotel Ucum*, C Mahatma Gandhi 167

(☎9/832-0711; ③), while the nicest luxury option is the *Holiday Inn*, Av de los Héroes 171 (☎9/832-1100; ⑧), which has a/c rooms, a pool and a travel agency. Calle Obregón, which cuts east–west along Avenida de los Héroes, also has some good deals, such as the *María Dolores*, C Obrégon 206 (☎9/832-0508; ④), with one of the best budget restaurants in town.

Chetumal has nothing special in the way of restaurants, though there are **places to eat** all along Avenida de los Héroes, especially around Calle Obregón – try *Sosilmar* at the *María Dolores* for good meat and fish. The café next to the *Hotel Ucum* serves a good comida corrida – a favourite with the locals. For budget food, stick to the area around the **markets**, opposite the museum. Vegetarians, as is so often the case, have few options. The best is *Sergio's* at C Obregon 182, which serves some veggie soups, pizzas and salads. There's a good **bakery** next to the *María Dolores*.

## Around Chetumal

Near Chetumal are any number of refreshing escapes from the heat and dull modernity. At weekends, the town descends en masse on **CALDERITAS**, a small seaside resort just 6km north around the bay; there's only one **place to stay**, an unnamed trailer park which has simple rooms (②) and a large, picturesque garden right on the seafront. The **Laguna Milagros**, off the road towards Francisco Escárcega, is less spectacular than Bacalar, but is superb for bird-watching.

Seven kilometres north of Calderitas is the small Maya site of **Oxtankah** (daily 8am–5pm; US$2.20, free on Sun), the remains of a maritime city developed to exploit ocean resources, specifically salt for trade purposes. The site was occupied principally between the Early Classic period of 300–600 AD, and while the ordinary populace spread throughout the Chetumal Bay area, the nobility and close associates lived in palaces and other important buildings centred around the site's two principal squares, *Plaza de las Abejas* (Plaza of the Bees) and *Plaza de las Columnas* (Plaza of the Columns). Though the remains of these buildings – which are architecturally similar to those in Petén, Guatemala – are not especially impressive, the site also contains a ruined chapel built by the Spanish conquerors and is a peaceful wooded place with trees – *ceiba, yaxche* – and other flora neatly labelled.

**XCALAK** is a tiny, very sleepy fishing community at the tip of the isthmus that stretches like a finger towards Belize on the other side of the huge Bahía de Chetumal. Flattened by a hurricane in 1955, the village still looks half-abandoned, with no electricity or phone lines.

---

### MOVING ON FROM CHETUMAL

From Chetumal's main bus station you'll be able to travel to most destinations on first- or second-class buses. First-class services include: **Cancún** (8 daily via **Tulum**, **Playa Del Carmen**); **Campeche** (6 daily, via **Escarcega** and **Xpujil**); **Mérida** (11 daily); **Mexico City** (2 daily); **Palenque and San Cristóbal** (1 daily); and **Villahermosa** (3 daily). There are second-class services that follow the same routes. Buses to **Flores in Guatemala** (1 daily) also leave from the main terminal. Buses for towns in **Belize** leave hourly from **Lázaro Cárdenas** market, north of the city centre. Combis for **Bacalar** (every 30min), **Río Hondo** (2 daily at 6am & 3.30pm) and **Mahahual/Xcalak** (1 daily at 7am) leave from the Terminal de Combis on Av Hidalgo at Primo de Verdad. Other, smaller combis are scheduled to depart for Mahahual/Xcalak from C 16 de Septiembre at Av Mahatma Gandhi at 7am, but their departures are whimsical.

Taesa, Aviasca and Aeromexico have daily **flights** to Mérida, Cancún and Mexico City; if you want to fly to Belize, you have to cross to Corozal, twenty minutes from the border, and take an internal flight. Crossing into Belize is straightforward: hand in your Mexican tourist card at the immigration office at the border and re-board the bus to Belizean immigration; there's no charge. Moneychangers at the border offer fair rates and take travellers' cheques.

There are no spectacular beaches and nothing much to do in the village, yet Xcalak is increasingly popular with visitors thanks to the superb **snorkelling**, **fishing** and **diving** around the (as yet) pristine offshore reef as well as the vast atoll of **Banco Chinchorro**. Consequently, the village has been staked for development and is set to change rapidly. There are growing facilities for tourists: if you're on a strict budget there's one basic and uncomfortable **hotel**, the *Caracol* (②) – far better to splash out and stay at *Marina Mike's* (*www.xcalak.com*; ⑦) at the northern end of the village, which has four gorgeous rooms with fully fitted kitchens, huge balconies overlooking the sea and its own tiny beach. Further north, up an appallingly potholed road to Mahahual, is a series of rather chic small hotels – the best of these are *Tierra Maya*, 2km from Xcalak (☎9/831-0404, *www.tierra-maya.net*; ⑥), *Sin Duda Villas*, 8km further north (☎9/831-0006, *www.sindudavillas.com*; ⑦–⑨), and neighbouring *Villa La Guacamaya* (*www.villalaguacamaya.com*; ⑦). All three are attractive, comfortable and right on the sea. There's a very good **restaurant** in Xcalak, *Conchitas*, specializing in fresh fish, and a **bar**, *San Jordi*, where you can pick up information on bird-watching and boat trips. Also in the village is a PADI-approved **dive shop** (☎9/831-0461, *divextc@pocketmail.com*) which offers snorkelling trips (US$25; 2hr) and open water certification courses (US$325).

**MAHAHUAL**, 55km north of Xcalak and now connected to it by a fast new road, has a small European ex-pat community (Xcalak's is almost exclusively North American), and a tiny beach. It too is set to change considerably with the construction of a cruise-ship pier and all the attendant services – principally a large shopping mall. It's slightly closer to the Chinchorro atoll and has a wider range of **budget accommodation**. *Cabanas Doctor* (④) and *Cabanas Tio Fil* (⑤) both have comfortable rooms and can organize snorkelling and boat trips, while 7km south along the bumpy old road to Xcalak, *Garza Azul* (④) and *Kabah-Na*, 2km further on (*kabahna@yahoo.com*; ④), are attractive, good-value cabañas and will provide meals on request. Another 2km on is *Paytocal Diving*, a small dive centre run by a friendly French couple with lovely bed-and-breakfast accommodation (⑤), and very reasonably priced scuba-diving courses (US$190 for a PADI open-water course, or US$30 for one dive, US$50 for two). The coast's other dive outfit, very well-equipped with boats large enough to reach the Banco Chinchorro, is at the nearby *Maya-Ha* resort (☎9/831-0065, *www.mayaharesort.com*; ⑨). Foodwise, there's a great breakfast **café** in Mahahual, *Café del Mar*, serving home-made bread, fruit salads and egg dishes, and several decent fish restaurants.

Local buses and combis run from Chetumal to Xcalak via Mahahual along the initial 18km of the old coastal route and then turn onto the new fast road. They leave Chetumal at 6am and 3.30pm daily from the terminal at the junction of avenidas Verdad and Hidalgo. Coming from Cancún you can connect with this service at Limones (7.30am and 4.30pm). Buses to Calderitas leave from Cristóbal Colón, near the junction with Héroes. Travelling around this area, keep your passport and tourist card with you – as in all border zones, there are checkpoints on the roads.

## Kohunlich and other Maya sites in the south

The most direct route from Chetumal back towards central Mexico is across the bottom of the peninsula via Francisco Escárcega along Hwy-186. Though the road enters the forests of the Calakmul Biosphere reserve in Campeche state, in Quintana Roo most of the trees have been felled to ranch cattle for the beefburger industry. The only worthwhile stop along the road is the Classic Maya city of **KOHUNLICH**, set some 60km from Chetumal, then another 9km off the road from the village of Fco Villa (daily 8am–5pm; US$3, free on Sun).

The ruins which are seldom visited by anyone other than butterflies and birds, are beautifully situated, peering above the trees. The buildings date from the late Preclassic to the Terminal Classic (100-900 AD) and the majority are in the Rio Bec architectural style characteristic of the region, featuring long rectangular buildings between towers decorated with (mostly) non-functional stairways. Foliage has reclaimed most of them, and those which are cleared are little more than pyramid-shaped piles of rubble, looted by grave-robbers before archeologists could preserve them. A notable exception is the Temple of Masks, named after the four two-metre-high stucco masks which decorate its facade. Disturbing enough now, these wide-eyed, open-mouthed gods once stared out from a background of smooth, bright red-painted stucco. Other exceptions, following recent reconstruction efforts, include a ball court, the Pixa'an palace and an area called Ya'axna which was a residential compound with a ceremonial centre and now offers wonderful views over the jungle canopy from its tall temples.

You can also visit other Maya sites in the south of Quintana Roo including the impressive Río Bec ruins at **Dzibanche**, **Chacchoben** and **Kinichna**. At present there is no public transport to any of these ruins (or to Kohunlich); if you're without a car the best way to see them is to take a taxi tour from **Xpujil** (see Yucatan chapter; p.101), though it's worth checking with the tourist office in Chetumal about alternative options.

## travel details

### Buses

The most useful bus services are between Mérida and Cancún and those provided by Mayab, which run at least every thirty minutes between Cancún and Playa del Carmen. Some places aren't served by first-class buses but second-class buses and combis will get you around locally and to the nearest major centre. The following frequencies and times are for both first and second class services.

**Cancún** to: Campeche (2 daily at 3pm & midnight; 9–10hr); Chetumal (hourly 5am–midnight: 6hr); Mérida (hourly; 4–5hr); Playa del Carmen (every 30min; 1hr); Puerto Morelos (every 30min; 30min); Tizimín (6 daily; 4hr); Tulum (10 daily; 2hr); Valladolid (hourly; 3hr); Villahermosa (1 daily; 14hr).

**Chetumal** to: Bacalar (every 30min; 30min); Belize City via Orange Walk (hourly; 4hr); Campeche (6 daily via Escarcega and Xpujil; 7hr); Cancún (8 daily via Tulum and Playa del Carmen; 6hr); Guatemala (1 daily; 12hr); Mahahual/Xcalak (2 daily at 6am and 3.30pm; 3hr 30min–4hr 30min); Mérida (11 daily; 7hr); Mexico City (2 daily; 24hr); Palenque and San Cristóbal (3 daily; 7–10hr); Playa del Carmen (10 daily; 5–7hr); Villahermosa (5 daily; 9–11hr).

**Playa del Carmen** to: Cancún (every 30min; 1 hr); Chetumal (10 daily; 5–7hr); Cobá (2 daily; 2hr); Mérida (10 daily; 8hr); Mexico City (3 daily; 30hr+); Palenque and San Cristóbal (3 daily; 11–16hr); Tulum (frequently; 1hr); Tuxtla Gutiérrez (2 daily; 20hr); Valladolid (5 daily; 3–4hr); Villahermosa (4 daily; 13hr).

**Tulum** to: Cancún (frequently; 1hr); Chetumal (8 daily via Bacalar; 4–5hr); Cobá (4 daily; 1hr); Mérida (6 daily; 4–7 hr); Playa del Carmen (frequently; 1hr); Valladolid (5 daily; 4hr); San Cristóbal (3 daily via Palenque; 10hr).

### Planes

Cancún and Cozumel both have busy **international airports** with several daily flights to Mexico City and regular connections to Miami and many other cities in the southern US. Chetumal also has daily direct services to Mexico City. Around the Caribbean coast various small companies fly light planes – very frequently between Cancún and Cozumel, less often from these places to Isla Mujeres, Playa del Carmen and Tulum.

### Ferries

There are frequent ferry services to **Isla Mujeres** and **Cozumel**. Although there are car ferries to both islands, it's hardly worth taking a vehicle to Isla Mujeres as the island is so small.

### Passenger Ferries

**Playa del Carmen** to: Cozumel (hourly; 50min).
**Punta Juárez, Cancún** to: Isla Mujeres (every 30min; 30min).

### Car Ferries

**Puerto Morelos** to: Cozumel – erratic, so check (3 daily; 2hr 30min).
**Punta Sam** to: Isla Mujeres (5 daily; 40min).

# CHAPTER THREE

# CHIAPAS AND TABASCO

**E**ndowed with a stunning variety of cultures, landscapes and wildlife, **Chiapas**, Mexico's southernmost state, has much to tempt visitors. Deserted Pacific beaches, rugged mountains and ruined cities buried in steamy jungle offer a bewildering choice, added to which **indigenous traditions** continue to be observed – albeit with a struggle – almost everywhere. Chiapas was actually administered by the Spanish as part of Guatemala until the early nineteenth century, when it seceded to join newly independent Mexico, and today it has a higher proportion of indigenous people than any state except Oaxaca.

The villages around **San Cristóbal de las Casas**, in the geographic centre of the state, are the stronghold of indigenous culture. A visit here is an entry to another age and, though tolerated, your presence is barely acknowledged. There is, of course, a darker side to this: picturesque as their life may seem to tourists, the indigenous population has long been bypassed or ignored by the political system, their land and their livelihood under constant threat from modernization or straightforward seizure.

The **Zapatista** rebellion, which broke out on New Year's Day 1994 and centred in this area, did not appear from nowhere: a revived Zapatista peasant movement had long been carrying out attacks on army patrols and, despite official denials of armed insurrection, the army had raided training camps in search of "subversives". News of such happenings was successfully suppressed, however, until the situation burst into the world's consciousness. One continuing legacy of the rebellion is a heavy army presence in what the Mexican authorities refer to as the "**conflict zone**", an area occupied (nominally at least) by the Zapatistas in the southeastern corner of the state. At its widest extent this could be anywhere east of the road from San Cristóbal via Ocosingo to Palenque, though in essence it means the Lacandón region (often referred to as el monte or la selva), now encircled by the **Carretera Fronteriza** (The Frontier Highway), running roughly parallel with the Guatemalan border. In fact you're extremely unlikely to stumble into trouble visiting the main attractions in this region, such as the **Lagos de Montebello** or the ruins of **Yaxchilán** or **Bonampak**, and the army will always treat genuine tourists with respect.

## ACCOMMODATION PRICE CODES

All the accommodation listed in this book has been categorized into one of nine price bands, as set out below. The prices quoted are in US dollars and refer to the cheapest room available for two people sharing in high season.

| | | |
|---|---|---|
| ① under US$5 | ④ US$15–25 | ⑦ US$60–80 |
| ② US$5–10 | ⑤ US$25–40 | ⑧ US$80–100 |
| ③ US$10–15 | ⑥ US$40–60 | ⑨ over US$100 |

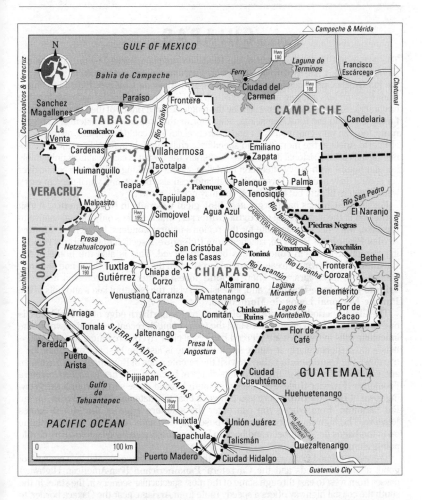

The state of **Tabasco** is less obviously attractive than its neighbour – steamy and low-lying for the most part, with a major oil industry marring the landscape. Recently, however, the state has been seeking to encourage tourism, above all pushing the legacy of the **Olmecs**, Mexico's earliest developed civilization. The vibrant, modern capital, **Villahermosa**, on a bend in the mighty Río Grijalva, has a wealth of parks and museums, the best-known of which, the **Parque La Venta**, displays the original massive Olmec heads discovered at the site of La Venta, in western Tabasco. In the extreme southwest, bordered by Veracruz or Chiapas, a section of Tabasco reaches into the mountains up to 1000m high. Here, in a region almost never visited by outsiders, a low-impact tourism initiative allows you to splash in pristine rivers and waterfalls and explore the astonishing ruins of **Malpasito**, a city of the Zoque culture, about which little is known.

# CHIAPAS

The terrain of Chiapas ranges from the Pacific coastal plain, backed by the peaks of the Sierra Madre de Chiapas, through the mainly agricultural Central Depression, irrigated by the Río Grijalva, rising again to the highlands, **Los Altos de Chiapas**. Beyond the highlands the land falls away again: in the north to the Gulf coast plain of Tabasco, while to the east a series of great rivers, separated by the jungle-covered ridges of the **Lacandón rainforest**, flow into the Río Usumacinta, which forms the border with Guatemala. The **climate**, too, can vary enormously. In one theoretical day you could be basking on the beach at Puerto Arista in the morning, and spending a chilly night by a fireside in the old colonial capital of San Cristóbal de las Casas. Generally the lowlands can be almost unbearably hot and humid, with heavy afternoon rainfall in summer, making a dip in the sea or river (or pool) a daily necessity. Days in the highlands can also be hot, and you'll need to carry water if you're hiking, but by evening you may need a sweater.

For its size Chiapas has the greatest **biological diversity** in North America. A visit to the **zoo** in the state capital of **Tuxtla Gutiérrez**, which houses only animals native to the state, will whet your appetite for the region's natural wonders. In the huge **Montes Azules Biosphere Reserve**, reached from **Palenque**, a section of the largest remaining rainforest in North America has been preserved. This is also the home of the **Lacandón Maya**, who retreated into the forest when the Spanish arrived, and shunned contact until fifty years ago. There's **cloud forest** in the south, protected in the **El Triunfo Biosphere Reserve**, and, far easier to visit, the beautiful lakes and hills of the **Parque Nacional Lagos de Montebello**.

The Classic-period Maya site of **Palenque**, on the northern edge of the highlands, is one of Mexico's finest ancient sites and the focus of much recent restoration work. The limestone hills in this area are pierced by crystal-clear rivers, creating exquisite waterfalls – most spectacularly at **Agua Azul**. Palenque is also the best starting point for a trip down the **Usumacinta valley**, to visit the remote ruins of Bonampak and Yaxchilán and you can stay nearby in the Lacandón village of **Lacanjá**. The newly paved Carretera Fronteriza (Frontier Highway) pushes on south beyond these sites, through the growing town of **Benemérito**, where you can get a boat to Guatemala, or visit Ixcán, on the Río Lacantún, from where you can enter the southern edge of the Monte Azules Reserve. The highway is now served by buses day and night, enabling you to continue on to the Lagos de Montebello and back to San Cristóbal, passing frequent army checkpoints along the route.

Travelling around Chiapas is not difficult: the main cities are connected by a network of good, all-weather roads and the **Carretera Panamericana** (Pan-American Highway) passes from west to east through some of the most spectacular scenery in the state. In the south the coastal highway offers a speedy route from **Arriaga**, near the Oaxaca border, to **Tapachula**, almost on the frontier with Guatemala. In the out-of-the-way places, particularly in the jungle, travel is by dirt roads, which, though generally well maintained, can cause problems in the rainy season. These more remote places are also fairly well served by public transport, though it's more likely to be combis and trucks taking people and produce to and from markets than the comfortable buses of the main roads.

# Palenque

Perched on top of an escarpment at the northern edge of the Chiapas highlands, **PALENQUE** is for many people the most extraordinary of the major Maya sites. It's not large – you can see everything in a morning – but it is hauntingly beautiful, set in thick jungle screeching with insects. The town itself (officially Santo Domingo de

## THE LEGACY OF THE ZAPATISTA REBELLION

On **January 1, 1994**, the day the NAFTA treaty came into effect (see p.559), several thousand lightly armed rebels, wearing their uniform of green or black army-style tunics and black *pasamontañas* (balaclavas), occupied **San Cristóbal de las Casas**, the former state capital and Chiapas' major tourist destination. During their brief occupation of the Municipal Palace, **Subcomandante Marcos**, the Zapatistas' enigmatic leader, or at least main spokesperson, read *La Declaración de la Selva Lacandona*, declaring war on the "seventy-year-old dictatorship . . . of traitors", and demanded the resignation of the Mexican president. Witty, erudite and penetrating communiqués signed by Marcos, sent from a secret destination in the Lacandón rainforest and published in the Mexican and international press, kept the struggle in the world spotlight. The war was being waged by the Zapatistas with the pen and the **Internet** – and they were winning the vital public opinion battle. An unprecedented level of international solidarity made the Mexican government wary of attempting a brutal suppression of the guerrillas.

Today, despite years of on/off negotiations and with the PRI no longer in power, no lasting peace treaty has been signed. Although the rebellion itself now belongs more to history than to current affairs, Marcos retains his enigmatic charisma as champion of the underprivileged and the Zapatistas continue to benefit from immense popular support. Throughout the rebellion tourists have visited Chiapas without problems other than delays due to army checks. In San Cristóbal Zapatista dolls and Marcos souvenirs, emblazoned with his masked features, sell in their thousands.

A word of warning, though, if your sympathies extend beyond giving economic assistance to the indigenous souvenir makers: at the time of writing there is still a concerted anti-foreigner campaign in Chiapas. Government officials, citing the "infestation of foreign activists who stir up and manipulate many indigenous groups contrary to constitutional order", claim that the presence of simpatico foreigners influences and even controls political opposition in the state. Although there are foreign observers in "civil peace camps" in the Zapatista areas, they are not recognized as such by the Mexican authorities. Being in (or even near) the **conflict zone** invites suspicion of taking part in political activities – illegal for foreigners – and can lead to deportation.

If you do go be as fully informed as you can: SIPAZ, the International Service for Peace, does have a volunteer programme in Chiapas and its Web site – www.nonviolence.org/sipaz – provides more information. The extremely well-organized Zapatista Web site – www.ezln.org – has superb links, and is also an excellent source of information.

### ENTERING MEXICO VIA CHIAPAS

It's worth noting that if you're **entering Mexico via Chiapas** (only possible from Guatemala) you'll almost certainly be given a maximum of fifteen days' stay – and **to renew your entry stamp** in the state, you'll have to undergo a lengthy interview with an immigration official during which you'll need to convince them that you're neither a journalist nor going anywhere in the conflict zone. The best bet if you want to stay longer in Chiapas (or Mexico) is to renew your tourist card in another state capital (say in Campeche or Mérida).

Palenque) is of little intrinsic interest and is best viewed simply as a base for exploring the ruins and the waterfalls in the nearby hills. And, since there are a number of new camping and cabaña places near the ruins, you may prefer not to stay in town at all.

## Arrival, orientation and information

Arriving at any of the **bus terminals**, you'll be on Avenida Juárez, where the highway comes into town. If you plan to leave the same day, particularly on a first-class bus, get your onward or return ticket on arrival. The **airport** is 5km north, in a dusty settlement

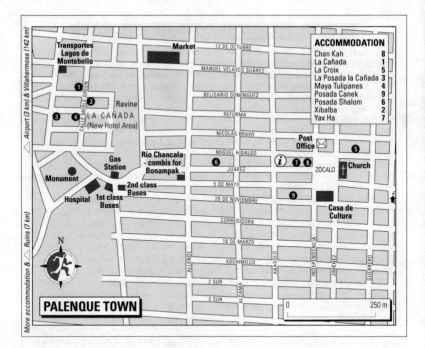

Palenque Town

**ACCOMMODATION**

| | |
|---|---|
| Chan Kah | 8 |
| La Cañada | 1 |
| La Croix | 5 |
| La Posada la Cañada | 3 |
| Maya Tulipanes | 4 |
| Posada Canek | 9 |
| Posada Shalom | 6 |
| Xibalba | 2 |
| Yax Ha | 7 |

called Pakal Ná. Walk less than 100m to the highway to flag down a passing cab (US$2) to town – the airport taxis themselves will charge three times this.

Palenque's three **main streets**, avenidas Juárez, 5 de Mayo and Hidalgo, all run parallel to each other and lead straight up to the zócalo, the Parque Central. There is a **tourist office** in the Plaza de Artesanías on Avenida Juárez, a block below the zócalo, but all the staff can do is hand out a street map and some tour leaflets. You'll get better **information** from one of the recommended travel agents (below) or from Palenque's own **Web site**, *www.palenquemx.com* – it's slow to load but interesting and very informative. The **post office** is on Independencia, a block from the plaza; and there's a **laundry** on Avenida 5 de Mayo, opposite the *Hotel Kashlan*. Several places offer **Internet connection**; try Cibernet, on Independencia, near 20 de Noviembre, or Red Maya on Avenida Juárez near the *Posada Shalom*.

The **banks** on Avenida Juárez are well used to changing travellers' cheques, but service is as slow as ever – you're better off using the **ATMs**. Alternatively, many of the **travel agencies**, also on Juárez, will change dollars or travellers' cheques; commission varies but service is considerably quicker than at the banks.

## Accommodation

Palenque has seen a massive boom in **hotel** construction in recent years. There are plenty of places on the streets leading from the **bus stations** to the zócalo, especially Juárez (though the traffic noise means these are best avoided). **La Cañada rainforest area**, west of the town centre, set among the relative quiet of the remaining trees, is generally

## TOUR AND TRAVEL AGENCIES IN PALENQUE

The surge in the numbers of tourists visiting Palenque has encouraged a dozen or so travel agencies to offer **tours** to the surrounding attractions. None can sell you an international air ticket, nor is there anywhere in town to rent a car. However, any of them can take you to the waterfalls at **Agua Azul** and **Misol-Há** (see p.151) and further afield to the ruins of **Bonampak** (see p.146) and **Yaxchilán** (see p.149). Bear in mind that since the paving of the Frontier Highway, leading to Bonampak and Yaxchilán, and the opening of inexpensive accommodation and restaurants nearby, the sites are easy enough to **visit independently**. See pp.146–149 for details of how to get to Bonampak and Yaxchilán on your own.

If you do go on a tour check what's included in the price: entry to the sites, for example, meals or an English-speaking guide. **Sample prices** are: US$10 per person for an all-day trip to Misol-Há and Agua Azul; US$55 for a one-day van-based trip to the Maya ruins at Yaxchilán and Bonampak; and US$85 for an overnight trip to both sites, including camping near Bonampak. To visit both sites by plane will cost around US$130. A **taxi to Bonampak** costs around US$70. Guided **horse-riding** is also on offer, and some agencies can organize rafting and light aircraft flights. The agencies also like to arrange travel **to Guatemala** via Bethél on the Río Usumacinta – about US$30 to Flores – but you can do the trip on your own *and* visit Yaxchilán on the way for less.

The best **tour agency** in Palenque is Na Chan Kan (☎9/345-0263, *nachan@tnet.net.mx*), with a small office on Avenida Juárez just up from the bus terminals and a main office behind the restaurant of the same name, on the corner of Hidalgo and Jiménez, on the corner of the zócalo; manager Rosy Bacelis Lacroix speaks good English. Other recommended agencies are Viajes Yax-Ha, Juárez 123 (☎9/345-0798, *yax_ha@tnet.net.mx*), and Kichan Bahlum, on Juárez, near the corner with Abasolo (☎9/345-0511). Two rival companies, Colectivos Chambalu and Transportes Otolum, run combis and buses **to Palenque ruins** (every 15min 6am–6pm; US$0.80) from their depots on Allende, either side of the junction with Juárez. They each also have two daily trips to **Agua Azul** (US$9).

more upmarket, though with a couple of excellent budget hotels. You'll also find a host of really good new places, in addition to the long-established *Mayabell* **campsite**, lining the **road to the ruins**. Note that some places will try to charge higher prices at times of peak demand: July and August and Easter and Christmas.

### IN TOWN

**Chan Kah**, Juárez and Independencia (☎9/345-0318). A touch of luxury right on the zócalo, this very comfortable small hotel is under the same ownership as the *Chan Kah Resort Village* near the ruins. ⑥.

**La Croix**, Hidalgo, on the corner of the zócalo (☎9/345-0014). A long-established favourite and, though past its best, still worth trying. Rooms are arranged around a large, jungle-like courtyard whose walls are decorated with murals of Palenque. Popular with motorcyclists. ④.

**Posada Canek**, 20 de Noviembre 43 (☎9/345-0150). One of the best-value hotels if you're travelling alone, and a popular travellers' place, with dorms (US$5 per person) and rooms, some with private bath, and hot water in the shared showers. There's luggage storage, and good views from the balcony. ③.

**Posada Shalom**, Juárez 156 (☎9/345-0944). One of two allied hotels with this name; the other is a few blocks away on Corregidora, near the corner with Abasolo. Both have clean rooms and tiled private bath: the best value in town at this price. Luggage storage. ④.

**Yax Ha**, Juárez 13, just below the zócalo (☎9/345-0856). Another good-value place, with comfortable rooms with private bath and TV; some with a/c. ④.

## LA CAÑADA RAINFOREST AREA

**La Cañada**, Merle Green 14 (☎9/345-0102, fax 345-1302). Spacious hotel rooms (some with a/c) and private cottages in quiet, tree-shaded grounds; excellent value at this price. Very good restaurant. ⑤.

**Maya Tulipanes**, Merle Green 6 (☎9/345-0201, *mtulipan@tnet.net.mx*). Luxury hotel, with very comfortable, a/c rooms. Shady grounds, a small pool and a good restaurant. ⑥.

**La Posada Cañada**, behind the *Maya Tulipanes* (☎9/345-0968). A very friendly place, popular with backpackers, and owner Doña Patty Gómez knows guides who can take you on trips into the jungle. Rooms are in a brightly painted two-storey building, and come with private bath, hot water, bedside lights and free drinking water. Good bar and restaurant with live music most nights. Discount for *Rough Guide* readers if staying more than one night. ④.

**Xibalba**, Merle Green 9 (☎9/345-0411, *shivalva@tnet.net.mx*). Lovely, tiled rooms with private bath in an A-frame building with a wooden deck upstairs; cable TV and a/c available. Good restaurant and travel agency downstairs. ④/⑤.

## ON THE ROAD TO THE RUINS

The following hotels and campsites are listed in order of their distance from town.

**Cabañas Safari**, 1.5km from town, on the left (☎9/345-1145, *nachan@tnet.net.mx*). Good-value, very comfortable, thatched, A-frame cabañas and suites with a deck and hammocks outside and beautiful decor inside, run by the very friendly Uscanga family. ⑤.

**Camping Chaac**, at the roadside 2km from the site entrance (*vtdeviaje@starmedia.com*). Rustic, very inexpensive, thatched, screened cabañas, plus camping (①) and a small restaurant on the banks of two streams. The shared showers are clean, there's a river pool to bathe in and a *temezcal* – sweat bath – built by friendly owner Alfredo Tello. Prices include breakfast. ③.

**Mayabell Camping and Trailer Park**, at the roadside 2km from the site entrance (☎9/345-0597, *mayabell82@hotmail.com*). A great favourite with backpackers and adventure tour groups, with *palapa* shelters for hammocks and tents, a number of vehicle pads with electricity and water, and some very comfortable private cabañas with hot water. The tiled shared showers have hot water and the site isn't crowded, so you'll usually get a space. The path to the ruins through the back of the campsite is now closed, but magic mushroom aficionados continue to scour the fields in the morning mist. Lockers available. Hammock rental or tent camping (①, per person), RV with two people (②), cabaña (④).

**El Panchan**, at the national park entrance, down a 200m track (3km from the ruins). A cluster of separate, great-value budget cabins and camping places, set in the forest with clear streams flowing through the grounds, with something of a "New Age" atmosphere. *Chato's Cabañas* (☎9/345-2073, *elpanchan@yahoo.com*; ③), built by the man behind El Panchan, Moises "Chato" Morales, has neat, thatched cabañas and two-storey houses, some with private bath; there's also a pool and an observation deck for birdwatching. *Don Mucho's* restaurant serves Italian, Mexican and vegetarian dishes at reasonable prices, with some live music. Nearby, *Rashita* (*rashita@yahoo.com*; ②/③) has brightly painted, very comfortable cabañas, some with private bath, and a deck with hammocks, in a lovely garden with a maze. There's a great vegetarian restaurant and the owner offers massage and meditation. *Ed and Margarita's* (*edcabanas@yahoo.com*; ④) has comfortable, inexpensive thatched cabins, while *Beto's Cabins and camping* (①/②) is the least expensive place here, with shelters for hammocks (with lockers) and simple, shared-bath cabins, a laundry and a very inexpensive café.

## Eating and drinking

Food in Palenque town is fairly basic, and most restaurants serve up similar dishes, often pasta and pizza, to customers who've really only come for the ruins; some of the best places are actually in *El Panchan* (see "Accommodation", above). Despite this, there are bargains available from the many **set menus** on boards outside most restaurants. Avenida **Juárez** has several **budget places** between the bus stations and the zócalo; *Pizzeria Palenque*, near the corner with Allende, is a good bet. Avenida **Hidalgo** has more Mexican-style food, with several taco places and even a couple of seafood restaurants. At the top of Hidalgo, on the corner of the zócalo, the *Restaurant Maya* has a wide choice and is popular though overpriced; *Virgo's* across the street is better value.

Further along, opposite the church on the corner with Jiménez, *Na Chan Kan* serves good-value breakfasts and set meals; tables outside allow you to watch life on the zócalo. *Las Tinajas*, on 20 de Noviembre across from *Posada Canek*, is a pleasant, family-run restaurant, with good food at fair prices. There's a good Mexican **bakery**, *Flor de Palenque*, on Allende next to the Chambalu colectivo terminal.

## Palenque ruins

Superficially, Palenque's style bears a close resemblance to the Maya cities of the Usumacinta valley, but its **towered palace** is unique. The **setting**, too, is remarkable, surrounded by hills covered in jungle, while at the same time being right at the edge of the great Yucatán plain – climb to the top of any of the structures and you overlook an endless stretch of low pale-green flatland across the dark green of the hills. The city

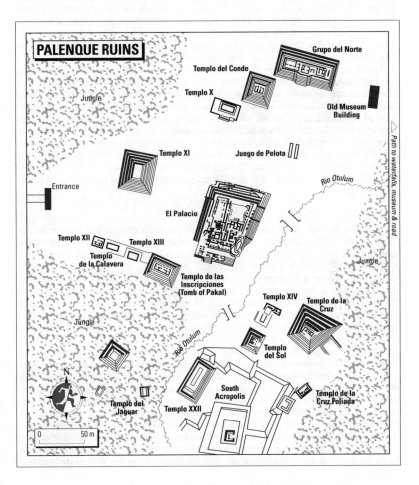

PALENQUE RUINS

flourished during the Classic period from around 300 to 900 AD, but its peak apparently came during a relatively short period of the seventh century, under two rulers – **Hanab Pakal** and **Chan Bahlum**. Almost everything you can see (and that's only a tiny, central part of the original city) dates from this era.

## Practicalities

**Getting to the site** is no problem. Two *combi* services, Chambalu and Otolum, both leaving from termini on Allende either side of Avenida Hidalgo, run at least every fifteen minutes from 6am to 6pm, and will stop anywhere along the road, useful if you're staying at one of the hotels or campsites near the ruins. After 6pm, you'll either have to walk or take a taxi.

The ruins are in a **national park** (daily 8am–6pm; archeological zone daily 8am–5pm; US$3 including museum, free on Sun). If you want to avoid the worst of the heat it's best to arrive early and climb the temples in the morning mist, but the crowds are inescapable whenever you arrive. There's a small **café** by the entrance (and some expensive lockers), and a toilet by the ticket office. There are also ranks of souvenir stalls here and you'll usually find a group of Lacandón in white robes selling arrows and other artefacts. Ask them about visiting their communities in the forest – most now have basic camping facilities (see Bonampak, p.146).

A prior visit to the **museum** (Tues–Sun 10am–4.30pm), on the road 1.5km before the site entrance, will give you a good idea of the scale of Palenque. The map of the site shows that only a quarter of the structures have been excavated and an intricate model of the palace complex shows how it would have appeared in the Classic period, with the tops of the buildings adorned with roof combs. There are several carved panels removed from the site, and a good number of incense burners – large urns with elaborately stuccoed gods and mythological creatures. You can also view a copy of Hanab Pakal's famous sarcophagus lid – worthwhile before you see the real thing in the Temple of the Inscriptions. Signs in the museum and throughout site are in English, Spanish and Tzeltal, though Chol is the language spoken by most modern Maya in this part of Chiapas.

## The site

As you enter **the site** itself, the great palace, with its extraordinary watch-tower, stands ahead of you. To the right, at the end of a row of smaller structures, is the **Temple of the Inscriptions**, an eight-stepped pyramid, 26m high, built up against a thickly overgrown hillside. The broad, steep stairway up the front, and paths up the hill, lead to a sanctuary on top that contains a series of stone panels carved with hieroglyphic inscriptions relating to Palenque's dynastic history. Most remarkable, though, is the **tomb of Hanab Pakal** that lies at the heart of this pyramid. Discovered in 1952, this was the first such pyramid burial found in the Americas, and is still the most important and impressive. The **burial chamber** (10am–4pm), reached by a narrow, vaulted stairway, is uncomfortably dank and eerie, but well worth the steep, slippery descent. You may not feel able to linger long at the bottom, however, as a long line of hot, claustrophobic visitors waits impatiently behind you. The smaller objects – including the skeleton and the jade death mask – have been moved to the Anthropology Museum in Mexico City, but the massive, intricately carved stone **sarcophagus** is still here. One of the most renowned iconographic monuments in the Maya World, the sarcophagus lid depicts Pakal at the moment of his death, falling into the Underworld, symbolized by a monster's jaws. Above the dead king rises the **Wakah Kan** – the World Tree and the centre of the universe – with **Itzam-Ye**, the Celestial Bird, perched on top representing the heavens. In order that the deified king buried here should not be cut off from the world of the living, a psychduct – a hollow tube in the form of a snake – runs up the side of the staircase, from the tomb to the temple.

In June 1994 another remarkable tomb was discovered, in **Temple XIII**, in a pyramid similar to the Temple of the Inscriptions, located just to the west. This burial, of a man around forty years of age, is considered by archeologists to date from a similar period to that of Pakal. In addition to a number of jade and obsidian grave goods and food and drink vessels to sustain the deceased on his way to *Xibalba*, the Maya Underworld, the sarcophagus also contained the remains of two females, one adult and one adolescent. More recent excavations in the **South Acropolis** have revealed a painted tomb and a stone throne inscribed with over two hundred glyphs, among other rich grave goods. Although neither of these tombs is available for viewing at the time of writing, preparations are under way to open them to the public in the near future.

The centrepiece of the site, **The Palace**, is in fact a complex of buildings constructed at different times to form a rambling administrative and residential block. Its square **tower** (whose top floor was reconstructed in 1930) is quite unique, and no one knows exactly what its purpose was – perhaps a look-out post or an astronomical observatory. Bizarrely, the narrow staircase that winds up inside it starts only at the second level, though you're no longer allowed to climb it. Throughout you'll find delicately executed relief carvings, the most remarkable of which are the giant human figures on stone panels in the grassy courtyard.

From here, the lesser buildings of the **Grupo del Norte**, and the **Juego de Pelota** (ball court), are slightly downhill across a cleared grassy area. On higher ground in the other direction, across the Río Otulúm – lined with stone and used as an aqueduct in the city's heyday – and half-obscured by the dense vegetation around them, lie the **Templo del Sol**, the **Templo de la Cruz** and the **Templo de la Cruz Foliada**. All are tall, narrow pyramids surmounted by a temple with an elaborate stone roof comb. Each, too, contains carved panels representing sacred rites – the cross found here is as important an image in Maya iconography as it is in Christian, representing the meeting of the heavens and the underworld with the land of the living.

The **Templo del Jaguar** is reached by a small path that follows the brook upstream – a delightful shaded walk. Beyond, more temples are being wrested from the jungle. If you want to penetrate a bit further, follow the path along the stream behind the Templo de las Inscripciones and you're in the jungle – or at least a pleasantly tame version of it. Tarzan creepers hang from giant trees, while all around there's the din of howler monkeys, strange

---

### MOVING ON FROM PALENQUE

Leaving Palenque by **bus**, there are surprisingly few direct services **to Mérida** (9hr): ADO has departures via **Campeche** at 8am, 7pm and 9pm, Maya de Oro at 10pm, and there are a couple of second-class services. There's a first-class departure for **Oaxaca** (14hr) at 5.30pm; there are two first-class departures (via **Chetumal** and **Playa del Carmen**) to **Cancún** (12hr), at 5pm and 8pm, and a couple of overnight buses to **Mexico City** (17hr). There are first- and second-class departures to **Tuxtla** (7hr) at least hourly, all calling at **Ocosingo** and **San Cristóbal** (5hr). ADO has plenty of buses to the main transport hub of **Villahermosa** (2hr 30min), and you may find it easier to get there and change for your onward journey.

Transportes Comitán y Lagos de Montebello, on Velasco Suárez, just past the market, has services down the Usumacinta valley for **Bonampak**, and **Frontera Corozal** (for **Yaxchilán**, and **Bethél** in Guatemala); some services continue all round the Frontier Highway to **Comitán**. Combis Río Chancala, on 5 de Mayo, also have services along the Usumacinta valley as far as **Bememérito**. Aerocaribe flies to Mérida, Cancún and Villahermosa, and to **Flores** in Guatemala. Check with one of the recommended travel agents on p.141.

bird calls and mysterious chatterings. The path leads to the *ejido* of Naranjo, a little over an hour's walk away. It's easy to believe you're walking over unexcavated pyramids: the ground is very rocky and some of the stones certainly don't look naturally formed.

Downstream, the river cascades through the forest and flows over beautiful limestone curtains and terraces into a series of gorgeous pools – the aptly named **Bathing Pool of the Queen** is the most exquisite. The path leading down beside the river, past more recently excavated buildings and across the river over a suspension bridge, eventually comes out on the main road opposite the museum and is an official **exit**; you can enter here if you already have a ticket, though you'll have to buy it from the main entrance.

# The Usumacinta valley and the Carretera Fronteriza south

The valley of the **Río Usumacinta** and the **Lacandón forest** form Mexico's last frontier, and the recently completed **Carretera Fronteriza** (Frontier Highway) serves a number of new settlements whose inhabitants are rapidly changing the rainforest to farmland. The highway is now paved all the way round to Comitán (see p.169), and numerous buses from Palenque cover the route though the Mexican army may still discourage you from travelling beyond **Benemérito**, and there is a real danger of armed robbery in this wild region. The first section of the road also provides easy access for visits to the sites of **Bonampak** and **Yaxchilán**, both still surrounded by jungle, and to the Lacandón village of Lacanhá. Several tour agencies in Palenque offer trips to the sites (see box on p.141) – though you can also easily organize your own trip. If you do decide to head out on your own, you'll need to be prepared to walk, and possibly also to camp, though **accommodation** is increasingly available.

Exploring this route presents other options beyond Bonampak and Yaxchilán. From the riverbank settlement of Frontera Corozal, you can get a boat a short distance upstream to **Bethél** in Guatemala (see p.470), and from the fast-expanding town of Benemérito you can occasionally take a longer trip on a trading boat upstream to **Sayaxché** (also in Guatemala; see p.467), on the Río de la Pasión. The interior of this remote corner of Chiapas is the home of the **Lacandón Maya** and fortunately has some form of protection as the **Montes Azules Biosphere Reserve**.

## Lacanhá and Bonampak

The outside world first heard of the existence of **Bonampak** in 1946, when Charles Frey, an American conscientious objector taking refuge in the forest, was shown the site by the Lacandón, who apparently still worshipped at the ancient temples. Shortly after this, American photographer Giles Healey was also led to the site by the Lacandón, and was shown the famous **murals** –the first non-Maya ever to see these astonishing examples of Classic Maya art.

It's quite possible to visit Bonampak independently on a day-trip **from Palenque**, and, as always, it's best to get an early start: Transportes Lagos de Montebello, on Avenida Velasco Suárez, and Combis Río Chancala, on Avenida 5 de Mayo, have numerous departures to destinations along the Carretera Fronteriza, beginning at 4.30am. If you want to stay nearby, several families in **Lancanhá** offer simple camping places and dorms.

## Practicalities

For both Lacanhá and Bonampak, you need to get off the bus at **San Javier** (about 3hr), where there's an abandoned government control hut on the left and a basic comedor on the right. Lacandón taxi driver Chan Kin will probably be waiting here to

## THE LACANDÓN

You may already have encountered the impressively wild-looking **Lacandón Maya** selling exquisite (and apparently effective) bows and arrows at Palenque. Still wearing their simple, hanging white robes and with their hair uncut, the Lacandón were until recently the most isolated of all the Mexican tribes. The ancestors of today's Lacandón are believed to have migrated to Chiapas from the Petén of Guatemala during the eighteenth century. Prior to that the Spanish had enslaved, killed or relocated the original inhabitants of the forest. The Lacandón refer to themselves as *Hach Winik* (true people); "Lacandón" was a label used by the Spanish to describe any native group living in the Usumacinta valley and western Petén outside colonial control. Appearances notwithstanding, some Lacandón families are (or were) quite wealthy, having sold timber rights in the jungle, though most of the timber money has now gone. This change has led to a division in their society, and today most Lacandón live in one of two main communities: Lacanhá Chansayab, near Bonampak, with a village population predominantly made up of evangelical Protestants, some of whom are keenly developing low-impact tourist facilities (see below); and Nahá, where a small group still attempt to live a traditional life.

The best **source of information** on the Lacandón is the Casa Na Bolom in San Cristóbal de las Casas (see p.158), where you can find a manuscript of *Last Lords of Palenque* by Victor Perera and Robert Bruce (Little Brown & Co, 1982). *Hach Winik* by Didier Boermanse (University of Albany, 1998) is an excellent recent study of Lacandón life and history.

drive you to Bonampak for under US$10. Otherwise, it's a two-hour walk – head along the paved side road bearing right. After 4km, at a right-hand bend, you'll find *Camping Margarito* (①, tents available), run by the friendly Chan Kayun family who also have a small **restaurant**. This is where most tours camp for the night. The road to Bonampak branches off left here, while continuing on the side road for a few kilometres, past *Camping Carmelo* (①), brings you to **LACANHA CHANSAYAB**. The road enters Lacanhá at its tiny airstrip, where signs point to several purpose-built **campsites**, **cabins** and **hammock shelters** (①–②). A few places also have simple dorm **rooms** (②), with mosquito-netted beds and electric light. The best one, *Camping Don Vicente*, in a grassy area on the bank of a clear, fast-flowing river, is run by Vicente Kin Paniagua and his family, who produce some of the best artesanía in the village. The villagers are eager to show you the gorgeous rivers and waterfalls in the forest and you can reach the **Lacanhá ruins** in under two hours from here. Ask for Kin Bor or Carlos Chan Bor, at the house where the paved road enters the village, either of whom will be able to fix you up with knowledgeable Lacandón guides to lead you. If you're coming from San Cristóbal, pick up an information sheet in the Casa Na Bolom (see p.158) before you set off.

Taking the **road to Bonampak**, you pass through the new site entrance, complete with mock corbelled arch across the road, a **visitor centre** and a café with clean toilets, a few hundred metres past *Camping Margarito*; this is where you'll pay the **entrance fee** (daily 8am–4pm; US$2.50). Lacandón boys may offer to guide you to the ruins (US$5) though it's perfectly possible to follow the gravel road on your own. There's also a **hiking trail** to the site (with some interpretive labels), though with this one you'll have a less apprehensive trip through the forest if you *do* have a guide. The hike is wonderful in the dry season (Jan to late-April) – be prepared for mud at other times.

Once you've seen the ruins, head back to The San Javier junction, where you'll be able to catch a **bus** or combi to Palenque at virtually any time – the road sees enough traffic to make hitching possible, too.

## The site

After crossing the airstrip, still used by some tour groups, you enter the site at the northwest corner of the main plaza, bounded by low walls. Note that during your visit the guards will not let you out of their sight – they're particularly vigilant near the Temple of the Frescoes (see below). In the centre of the plaza **Stela 1** shows a larger-than-life **Chan Muan**, the last king of Bonampak, dressed for battle; his image is depicted everywhere here. Ahead, atop several steep flights of steps, lies the **Acropolis**. On the lower steps more well-preserved stelae show Chan Muan, the king of Bonampak, preparing himself for bloodletting and apparently about to sacrifice a prisoner.

Splendid though these scenes are, the highlight of this superb site is the famed **Temple of the Frescoes**, on the hillside just beyond the plaza. Inside three separate chambers, on the temple walls and roof, the renowned **Bonampak murals** depict vivid scenes of haughty Maya lords, splendidly attired in jaguar-skin robes and quetzal-plume headdresses, their equally well-dressed ladies, and bound prisoners, one with his fingernails ripped out, spurting blood. Musicians play drums, pipes and trumpets in what is clearly a celebration of victory. Dated to around 790 AD, these murals show the Bonampak elite at the height of their power. However, unknown to them, the collapse of the Classic Maya civilization was imminent: some details on the murals were never finished and Bonampak was abandoned shortly after the scenes in the temple were painted.

In **Room** 1, an infant wrapped in white cloth (the heir apparent?), is presented to assembled nobility under the supervision of the lord of Yaxchilán, while musicians play trumpets in the background. **Room 2** contains a vivid, even gruesome, exhibition of power over Bonampak's enemies: tortured prisoners lie on temple steps, while above them lords in jaguar robes are indifferent to their agony. A severed head has rolled down the stairs and Chan Muan grasps a prisoner (who appears to be pleading for mercy) by the hair – clearly about to deal him the same fate. **Room 3** shows the price paid for victory: Chan Muan's wife, **Lady Rabbit**, prepares to prick her tongue to let blood fall onto the paper in a clay pot in front of her. The smoke from burning the blood-soaked paper will carry messages to ancestor-gods. Other gorgeously dressed figures, their senses probably heightened by hallucinogenic drugs, dance on the temple steps.

Though time and early cleaning attempts have taken their toll on the murals, work in the 1990s has restored some of their glory. Sadly, you're no longer allowed to enter the rooms completely – you have to be content with peering in from just inside the doorway – though you can still see all the paintings.

# Frontera Corozal and Yaxchilán

Twenty kilometres beyond San Javiér, the turning for **FRONTERA COROZAL** is marked by a comedor and shop selling basic supplies. Corozal itself, another 19km down the paved side road, and served by regular buses and combis from Palenque (last one back at 4pm), is on the bank of Río Usumacinta; to get to Yaxchilán, you need to catch a **boat** here. There's a Mexican **immigration post** here: visitors to Yaxchilán will always be asked to show their passports, despite the fact that the site is in Mexico. On the right, past the immigration post, are the thatched and brightly painted **cabañas** of *Escudo Jaguar* (☎5/147-9300 in México; ④/⑤). These spacious rooms have comfortable beds with mosquito nets, hot water in the tiled bathrooms and full-length windows opening onto the porch – a touch of luxury at a bargain price. There's also a good **restaurant**, and you can **camp** nearby for less than US$3. More basic accommodation is available at Corozal's two **posadas** – the *Yhani* (with fan; ②), on the right before the immigration post, is marginally the better – while the *Usumacinta* is the best of Corozal's **comedores**.

Entering Guatemala is relatively easy, with plenty of lanchas – narrow riverboats with benches along the side and a thatched roof for shade – between Corozal and Bethél, thirty minutes upstream, though you might have to wait for the boat to fill up; set fares usually apply, working out at about US$7 per person. There's a Guatemalan immigration post in Bethél and buses leave at 4am and 1pm for Flores (see p.451). The lancheros here or in Corozal can arrange trips downriver to the impressive ruins of Piedras Negras (see p.470), in Guatemala, though you'll need to get a group together as a two- to-three-day trip will cost anything from US$75 to US$150 each, depending on the number. Below the site the river speeds through two massive canyons: the Cañon de San José, with fearsome rapids between cliffs 300m high, then the slightly less dramatic Cañon de las Iguanas.

## Yaxchilán: the site

To reach the site, you need to get a ride in a lancha; officially tickets are only sold at *Escudo Jaguar* but it's worth asking around at the waterfront. Increasingly, however, fares are set by the lanchero co-operatives in Corozal and Bethél, and work out around US$12 per person, with little scope for bargaining. The journey downstream usually takes under an hour and when you arrive you'll have to scramble up the steep bank or climb a flight of rickety steps.

A larger site than Bonampak, Yaxchilán (daily 8am–4pm; US$2.50, free on Sun), strategically built on a bend in the river, was an important centre in the Classic period. When the water is low, you can see (and climb) a pyramid built on a rock shelf on the river bed. Some archeologists suggest this was a bridge support, though this is unlikely as no corresponding structure has been found on the opposite bank, and the altar on top may indicate that it was used for religious ritual.

The first groups of numbered buildings and those around the main plaza, built on fairly level river terraces, are easy to view. The temples bear massive honeycombed roofs, now home to dozens of bats, and everywhere there are superb, well-preserved stucco carvings. These panels, on lintels above doorways and on stelae, depict rulers performing ritual events, often involving bloodletting to conjure up spirit visions of ancestors. Some of the very best lintels have been removed to the British Museum in London, but the number and quality of the remaining panels are unequalled at any other Maya site in Mexico. Yaxchilán's most famous kings (identified by their name-glyphs) were Shield Jaguar II and his son Bird Jaguar IV, who ruled at the height of the city's power, from around 680 AD to 760 AD. Under their command Yaxchilán began the campaign of conquest that extended its sphere of influence over the other Usumacinta centres and enabled alliances with Tikal and Palenque.

A path behind Building 42 leads through the jungle, over several unrestored mounds, to three more tall temples. The guards won't always take you back here, as it's out of their way (and they insist you begin to return well before the 4pm closing time), but the climb is worth the effort for the view of distant mountain ridges. There's a real sense of a lost city as you explore the ancient, moss-covered stones, watched from the trees by toucans and monkeys. Butterflies flit around the forest glades, and so, unfortunately, do mosquitoes.

## The southern Usumacinta

Continuing south a further 35km brings you to **BOCA LACANTÚN**, where a bridge carries the road over the enormous Río Lacantún. You can expect any bus along this road to be stopped by immigration officials or army checkpoints, so keep your passport handy. Nearby, at the confluence of the Lacantún and Usumacinta rivers, is the **Planchón de Figuras**, a massive limestone carved with Maya glyphs, birds, animals and temples. If you're travelling by river, you'll see the beautiful **Chorro cascades** just downstream.

## Benemérito and onwards

The sprawling frontier town of **BENEMÉRITO**, 2km beyond Boca Lacantún, is the largest settlement in the Chiapas section of the Usumacinta valley, and an important centre for both river and road traffic. If you're **arriving by boat** from Guatemala you'll be met by Mexican soldiers who'll check your passport – the immigration office here is not always open, so you may be sent onward to Frontera Corozal (see p.148) to complete the paperwork. There's a hospital, market, shops, comedores and a few desperately basic **hotels**; you're better off heading on to Corozal (see p.148), to Lacanhá (see p.147) or even on to Palenque. The highway is the town's main street and in the centre, at the Farmacía Arco Iris, is the main road leading to the river, less than 2km away. **Heading north** is no problem: buses from Transportes Lagos de Montebello pull in opposite the *Hospedaje Montanero* and combis wait across from the *Hospedaje El Tapanco*. **Heading south** around the Frontier Highway buses from Palenque pass through every couple of hours, eventually reaching the Lagos de Montebello and Comitán.

## By river to Guatemala

If you hope to get by boat **from Benemérito to Sayaxché** (see p.467) you'll need patience or a good deal of money. **Trading boats** (12hr) are the cheapest method, but with no proper schedule you just have to ask. Fast boats sometimes make the trip, in less than three hours, stopping at the various sites en route, but you'll have to charter them at a cost of at least US$250. **Entering Guatemala**, you'll get your passport stamped at the army post at **Pipiles**, at the confluence with the Río de la Pasión. There's no Mexican immigration here (and probably not at Benemérito): **entering or leaving Mexico** make sure you get your passport stamped (your best bet is Frontera Corozal) and be prepared for army checkpoints along the highway.

# The Chiapas highlands

There is nowhere in Mexico so rich in scenery or indigenous life as highland Chiapas. Forested uplands and jungly valleys are studded with rivers and lakes, waterfalls and unexpected gorges, and flush with the rich flora and fauna of the tropics – wild orchids, brilliantly coloured birds, and monkeys. For much of its history the isolation of the state allowed the **indigenous population** to carry on their lives little affected. In the villages, you'll see the trappings of Catholicism and of economic progress, but in most cases these go no deeper than the surface: daily life is still run in accordance with ancient customs and beliefs. It's worth noting that many indigenous communities and some local transport operators refuse to observe the time change in summer, preferring *la hora vieja* – the old time.

Strong and colourful as the traditions are, away from the big towns, Spanish is still very much a second language and the economic and social lot of the Maya population remains greatly inferior to that of ladinos. The oppressive exploitation of the *encomienda* system (see p.557) existed here far longer than in parts of Mexico more directly in the government eye. There were **local rebellions**, quickly suppressed, from colonial times to the late nineteenth century, and despite some post-revolutionary land redistribution, most small villages still operate at the barest subsistence level. Not surprisingly, the Zapatista leadership found willing recruits in highland villages.

Nowadays, however, many of the old customs are disappearing, and it's comparatively rare to see men in traditional clothing, though many women still wear it. Conversely, such traditions as do survive are clung to fiercely, and you should be extremely sensitive about **photography** – especially of anything that might have religious significance – and donning **native clothing**, the patterns on which convey subtle social and geographic meaning.

# Palenque to San Cristóbal

The journey from Palenque to San Cristóbal through the Chiapas highlands is an impressive and beautiful one, as the road winds up and around the spectacular mountain valleys, lush with greenery. Many people do the five-hour trip in one go, but there are some wonderful attractions to see (and stay at) along the way. The exquisite **waterfall** at Misol Há and the awesome cascades at **Agua Azul** deserve more than the quick glimpses offered on tours from Palenque; both places have some accommodation and it's more rewarding when the crowds have gone.

The only large town on the route, **Ocosingo** (and the surrounding area) was the heartland of the **Zapatista rebellion**, so be prepared to be searched by the Mexican army on as you travel around. In the largely Tzeltal villages around here all of the women, if none of the men, still wear traditional clothing; something you'll see a lot more of later. You'll need to pass through Ocosingo if you want to visit either the near-by ruins of **Toniná** or the beautiful **Laguna Miramar**, the largest lake in southeast Mexico.

## Misol-Há and Agua Azul

At **Misol-Há**, 20km from Palenque, a 30m waterfall provides a stunning backdrop to a pool that's safe for swimming (US$0.70). A fern-lined trail through lush rainforest filled with bird calls leads along a ledge behind the wide cascade – and you can enjoy the refreshing spray as you stroll along. It's an easy 1500-metre walk from the road, and there's inexpensive **accommodation** in some of the most beautiful wooden cabañas anywhere in Mexico (☎ & fax in Palenque 9/345-1210; ⑤). The cabins, and the **restaurant** catering to tour groups, are owned and run by the San Miguel *ejido*; each cabin has a private bathroom and electricity and some have kitchens.

Thirty-five kilometres beyond here, the series of beautiful waterfalls on the Río Shumulhá in the **Parque Nacional Agua Azul** is now a major tour-bus destination, with microlight flights over the falls, or horse-riding tours for the less foolhardy. If you come by bus (not on a tour), you'll be dropped at the crossroads, where there are usually taxis waiting to take you the 4km to the base of the falls; otherwise it's a 45-minute walk. At the end of the track you pay to enter the park (US$0.75), and there are several **restaurants** and a campsite with hammock space. You can stay and eat better at *Comedor & Camping Casa Blanca*, at the top of the main fall, where there are also simple beds and hammock space in a large barn-like building (①), and the owners hire out horses. Be sure to keep a close eye on your belongings, though, and be warned that **violent attacks** on tourists have occurred away from the main area. It's hard to resist the temptation to take a swim but watch out for signs warning of **dangerous currents**, as there are several extremely perilous spots, and people drown here every year. The whole area is exceptionally beautiful, with dozens of less-er falls above the developed area, and at the right times of year the valley is alive with butterflies. If it's safe to walk upstream you'll come across a perilous-looking bridge over the river and eventually you'll reach an impressive gorge where the river explodes out of the jungle-covered mountain.

## Ocosingo and around

**OCOSINGO** makes a good place to escape the tourist crowds of San Cristóbal or Palenque. It's not as pretty as San Cristóbal, but it's certainly a great deal more attractive than Palenque, its streets lined with single-storey, red-tiled houses and thick with the scent of wood smoke. It's a town that has stayed close to its country roots, with plenty of farmers in from the ranches in their cowboy hats and pick-ups. It's also the jumping-off point for the amazing Maya site of **Toniná**.

**Buses** all stop on or near the main road: walk down the hill and you'll find the zócalo. It's surrounded by elegant *portales* and a big old country church, as well as an *Ayuntamiento* with a thoroughly incongruous modern first floor, complete with tinted-glass office windows. The best of the **hotels** are the *Hotel Central* (☎9/673-0024; ④), under a modern section of the *portales* by the *Restaurante La Montura*, and the *Margarita* (☎9/673-0280; ④), down the side street by the *Montura*, which has some a/c rooms, and the *Agua Azul*, 1 Ote Sur (head right at the church; ☎9/673-0302; ③), with comfortable rooms around a courtyard. The *Hospedaje San José* (☎9/673-0002; ③), off to the left at the bottom of the zócalo, is the best of the budget places.

Several **places to eat** face the square – *Los Arcos* is the best – and the *Rahsa*, the best restaurant in town, is on 3 Sur Ote, a side street southwest of the plaza. The *Cafetería El Candil*, opposite the *Hospedaje San José*, is a great budget restaurant, with neat tables on a garden terrace, and the *Hotel Agua Azul* has a good comida corrida. The **food market**, or *tianguis*, straight down Avenida Central from the zócalo, is where indigenous women sell fruit and vegetables and locally produced cheeses, including a round waxy variety and delicious cream cheese.

There's a **travel agent**, Viajes Xanav, C Central Nte 40C (☎9/673-0094), where you can book domestic and international flights. **Leaving Ocosingo** by road is easy enough until mid-evening, with frequent buses and combis to San Cristóbal and buses to Palenque. The last ATG buses in either direction leave at 7.30pm – though they're *de paso* and so likely to be later.

## Toniná

Though it receives few visitors, the Classic period Maya site of **TONINÁ** (daily 9am–4pm; US$2.50, including museum), some 14km east of Ocosingo, is surprisingly big. It centres on an enormous grassy plaza, once surrounded by buildings, and a series of seven artificial terraces climbing the hillside above it. At the bottom are two restored ball-courts and an overgrown pyramid mound; as you climb the hill, passing corbel-arched entrances to two vaulted rooms on the right, you begin to get an impression of Toniná's vastness. The sixth and seventh terraces each have a number of small temples, while beyond are more huge mounds, currently under excavation. From the top there are fine views of the surrounding countryside.

There are also tombs on both the fifth and sixth levels, one of which contains an enormous mask of the Earth Monster, a powerful force in Maya cosmology. The most striking feature, however, is the enormous **Mural of the Four Suns**, on the sixth platform. This amazingly well-preserved stucco codex tells the story of Maya cosmology by following the four suns (or eras of the world) as they were created and destroyed. The worlds are depicted as decapitated heads surrounded by flowers; a grinning, skeletal Lord of Death presents a particularly graphic image as he grasps a defleshed human head.

In ancient times Toniná was known as "the place of (celestial) captives " and in the stunning new **museum** (closed Mon) several carved panels and sculptures depict many bound (and sometimes headless) captives. Glyphs on the panels record the place the prisoners were captured, while those on the loincloths of the captives may tell who they were.

The **road from Ocosingo** to Toniná is now paved, and combis leave frequently from the market area, heading either for the site itself or the large army base by the turn-off to the site – look for the destination signs "Predio" or "Ruinas"; alternatively, a taxi will only cost US$5. At the entrance to the site the *Restaurant Toniná* serves simple food, cold beer and soft drinks, and also sells good t-shirts and postcards. There's also extremely comfortable **accommodation** nearby, in the neat wooden **cabins** of *Rancho Esmeralda*, signed just before the turn-off (fax only 019/673-07-11, *ranchoes@mundomaya.com.mx*; (④/⑤), a ten-minute walk from the ruins. The cabins have no electricity (they're lit with oil lamps) and no private bath, but the spacious, thatched shared bathroom has hot water. You can also **camp** and park RVs. It's in a wonderful, tranquil setting, and the food is both superb and plentiful. American owners Glen and Ellen will make you very welcome, even if you turn up without booking, and can arrange great, guided horseback trips through the beautiful Ocosingo valley and a spectacular **overflight** of the ruins (with Servicios Aéreos de San Cristóbal; also available through Viajes Xanav in Ocosingo, see opposite).

## Laguna Miramar

A much more remote excursion is a visit to **Laguna Miramar**, over 100km southeast of Ocosingo, in the heart of the Lacandón forest. It's now a pristine part of the **Montes Azules Biosphere Reserve**, and staying here enables you to experience the largest surviving area of rainforest in North America. There are no settlements on the lakeshore, and no motor boats are allowed. An island in the lake has traces of a fortress, a stronghold of the Maya until it was finally conquered in 1559. The high canopy forest is home to abundant wildlife, including howler and spider monkeys, tapirs and jaguars, and there are rivers and caves to explore.

A trip here is a unique chance to visit one of the last truly remote corners of Mexico, and you can visit on your own or as part of an organized group. To **travel independently** you'll need to get a combi from the market in Ocosingo (leaving around 9am or 10am) to the *ejido* of **San Quintín**, about five hours down the mostly unpaved road, following the valley of the Río Jataté. Here you'll be checked by the army and you'll need a guide from the community to lead you to **Emiliano Zapata**, another *ejido* a few kilometres away; some combis continue all the way. Alternatively you can take a fascinating **flight** to San Quintín from Ocosingo for around US$30 one way. It's still a 9km hike to the lake and you'll need to carry supplies and hire a guide – around US$12 per day. Fernando Ochoa at the *Casa de Pan* in San Cristóbal (☎9/678-0465, *miramar@mundomaya.com.mx*), arranges superb, fully equipped three-day **expeditions** to Laguna Miramar for around US$300, including transport from San Cristóbal, flights from Ocosingo, guides, camping and meals.

# San Cristóbal de las Casas

Surrounded by rocky peaks and pine-forested mountains slashed by horrendous erosion gullies, **SAN CRISTÓBAL DE LAS CASAS** nestles in a valley at an elevation of over 2000 metres. Its low, whitewashed red-tiled houses seem huddled together as if to keep out enemies, and indeed, the town was designed as a Spanish stronghold in a hostile area; the attack by Zapatista rebels in January 1994 (see p.139) was the latest in a long series of uprisings by the indigenous population. It took the Spanish four years to pacify the area sufficiently to establish a town here in 1528. Officially named Ciudad Real ("Royal City"), it was more widely known as Villaviciosa ("Evil City") for the oppressive exploitation exercised by its colonists. In 1544, **Bartolomé de las Casas** was appointed bishop, and promptly took an energetic stance in defence of the native population. His name – added to that of the patron saint of the town – was held in something close to reverence by the Maya. Throughout the colonial era, San Cristóbal was the capital of Chiapas, which was then administered as part of Guatemala; it lost this rank in 1892 as a result of its reluctance to accept the union with Mexico. Today it offers visitors a refreshing climate and an unrivalled provincial colonial charm, as well as a chance to visit Maya villages and buy unique souvenirs at great prices.

Though it's the local crafts and the indigenous way of life that draw people to San Cristóbal, this romanticization is not always appreciated by the Indians themselves, who not

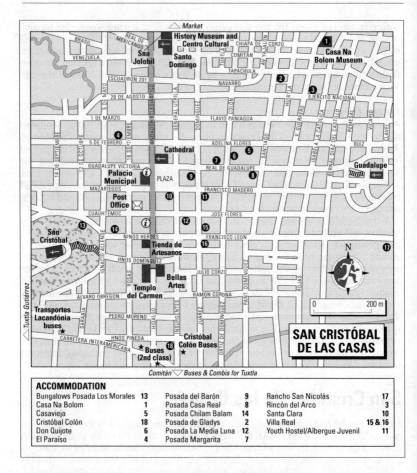

△ *Market*

△ *Tuxtla Gutiérrez*

*Comitán* ▽ *Buses & Combis for Tuxtla*

**SAN CRISTÓBAL DE LAS CASAS**

0       200 m

### ACCOMMODATION

| | | | | | | | |
|---|---|---|---|---|---|---|---|
| Bungalows Posada Los Morales | 13 | Posada del Barón | 9 | Rancho San Nicolás | 17 |
| Casa Na Bolom | 1 | Posada Casa Real | 8 | Rincón del Arco | 3 |
| Casavieja | 5 | Posada Chilam Balam | 14 | Santa Clara | 10 |
| Cristóbal Colón | 18 | Posada de Gladys | 2 | Villa Real | 15 & 16 |
| Don Quijote | 6 | Posada La Media Luna | 12 | Youth Hostel/Albergue Juvenil | 11 |
| El Paraíso | 4 | Posada Margarita | 7 | | |

surprisingly resent being treated as tourist attractions or objects of amateur anthropology. Nevertheless, the life of the town depends on the people from surrounding villages, who fill its streets and dominate its trade. Many of the salespeople are **expulsados** – converts to evangelical Protestantism expelled by the village leaders – now living in shanties on the edge of town and unable to make a living from farming. The women make crafts to sell to tourists and have taken advantage of the publicity generated by the Zapatistas: the most popular souvenirs they sell are now hand-made **Marcos dolls**, complete with ski mask, rifle and bandoliers. There's even a female Zapatista doll of Romana, who is reputed to be in a position of command in the movement.

Despite being the main focus of the Zapatista attack, the town was only occupied for thirty hours, and no tourists were harmed; many, in fact, took advantage of the opportunity to be photographed with the rebels. Today, San Cristóbal remains one of the most restful and enjoyable places in the republic to spend a few days doing very little, with an infrastructure set to cater for its young, predominantly European visitors.

## Arrival and information

First impressions of San Cristóbal, with the modern parts of the city sprawling unattractively along the highway, are not the best. In the centre, though, there is none of this thoughtless development. Whether you come by first- or second-class **bus**, you'll almost certainly arrive just off the Carretera Interamericana (Hwy-190) at the southern edge of town. From the Cristóbal Colón **first-class terminal** walk straight up Avenida Insurgentes for about seven blocks up to the plaza. There's no **left-luggage** service at the bus station, but you can rent lockers at the Tienda El Paso, one block up Insurgentes on the left. The **airport** is 18km east of the town; a taxi into the centre costs US$6, and taxi journeys within town cost about US$1.

The helpful **state tourist office**, just off the southwest corner of the zócalo at Av Hidalgo 3 (Mon–Fri 9am–9pm, Sat 9am–8pm, Sun 9am–2pm; ☎9/678-6570), is one of the best in the country, with good free city maps, up-to-date lists of hotels in all price ranges, and details of bus times and events. Staff know Chiapas well, and there's usually someone who speaks English (and possibly other European languages). Free **listings** magazines with information on hotels, restaurants and excursions are also usually available. There are more bulletin boards in and around the **municipal tourist office** in the Palacio Municipal, on the northeast corner of the zócalo.

## Accommodation

San Cristóbal boasts some of the best-value **budget and mid-price hotels** in Mexico. Walking up Insurgentes from the bus station you'll pass examples in all price ranges. Press on a little further along Calle Real de Guadalupe, off the northeast corner of the zócalo, and you'll find many more. All but the most basic places have hot water, though not necessarily all the time. Nights can be pleasantly cool in summer, but cold in winter, so make sure there are enough blankets. For **longer stays**, check out the many noticeboards in the popular cafés, where you'll find rooms and houses for rent. The closest official **campsite** is *Rancho San Nicolás* (see below).

### Budget and mid-price accommodation

**Bungalows Posada Los Morales**, Ignacio Allende 17 (☎9/678-1472). Whitewashed stone cabins, each with a living room with fireplace, bath (generally with hot water) and stove, in a hillside garden four blocks west of the zócalo. Authentic colonial atmosphere, right down to the ancient wooden furniture and flagstones, and wonderful views of the town. ④.

**Cristóbal Colón**, Av Insurgentes 81, just across from the first-class terminal (☎9/678-56-89). Very handy if you've arrived late or have an early departure, it's actually a good-value place, with clean rooms above a reasonable, inexpensive restaurant. ②.

**Posada del Barón**, Av Belisario Domínguez 2 (☎ & fax 9/678-0881). Well-run, modern hotel one block east of the zócalo. Each room has a spotless tiled bathroom with plenty of hot water. ④.

**Posada Casa Real**, C Real de Guadalupe 51 (☎9/678-1303). Large rooms with very comfortable double beds, run by the welcoming Amparo Salazar. No private baths, but there is hot water and a *pila* for washing clothes on the sunny, flower-filled rooftop terrace. Prices are under US$5 per person, so good value for singles. ②.

**Posada Chilam Balam**, C Niños Heroes 9 (☎9/678-4340). Small, simple hotel a few blocks west of the zócalo, run by the friendly Gutiérrez family. Single-storey red-tiled rooms around a courtyard, and a *pila* in the tiny garden. Hot water but no private bathrooms. ②.

**Posada de Gladys**, C Cintalapa 6A (☎9/678-8733). A long way from the zócalo and a little difficult to find at first, this is a deservedly popular, well-run travellers' hang-out with dorm beds in small rooms (US$3.50) and private rooms. The clean, tiled, shared bathrooms have hot water, and there's a sitting area with couches and a communal kitchen. ②.

**Posada Margarita**, C Real de Guadalupe 34 (☎9/678-0957). Long-standing budget favourite and there's usually someone here who speaks English. Rooms are a little bare but comfortable; no private showers though the communal ones are clean, with plenty of hot water. Good, inexpensive café in the blue-and-white tiled courtyard, and the more expensive restaurant (next door) has live music most nights. Good travel agency and luggage storage, too. ②.

**Posada La Media Luna**, C Felipe Flores 1 (☎ & fax 019/678-1658, *paint49@hotmail.com*). Wonderful place to stay with five simply but beautifully furnished rooms with bedside lights (some with private bath, TV and video) around a shady courtyard. It's run by artist Luciana Tamayo Lizama, who teaches art and Spanish and also speaks French and English; she also has another small hotel on María Adelina Flores. Rates include breakfast. ③/④.

**Rancho San Nicolás**, 2km east of the centre, on the extension of C Francisco León (☎9/678-0057). Primarily a campsite (②) and trailer park, but with a few rooms in a pleasant country setting. ④.

**Villa Real**, two locations on Av Benito Juárez, 8 and 24A (☎9/678-2930). New hotels, with comfortable, well-furnished, carpeted rooms, all with private bath, at very good rates; good views over the town. ④.

**Youth Hostel/Albergue Juvenil**, Av Benito Juárez 2, near the corner with C Madero (☎9/678-7655, *youth@sancristobal.com.mx*). Dorm beds (mostly only four in a room) with shared baths in a friendly hostel that's not part of the YHI system. US$3.50 per person.

## More expensive accommodation

**Casa Na Bolom**, Av Vicente Guerrero 33 (☎9/678-1418, fax 678-5586, *nabolom@sclc.ecosur.mx*). Very comfortable rooms and lovely private cottages with fireplaces and private bath, all decorated with textiles, artefacts and original photos taken by Gertrude Blom in this famous museum and research centre (see p.158). Delicious meals are served, made with organically grown vegetables from the garden; if you're not staying here you can book ahead for dinner – call by 5pm – or just turn up for breakfast (7.30–10am). ⑤/⑥.

**Casavieja**, C María Adelina Flores 27 (☎ & fax 9/678-6868, *hcvieja@casavieja.com.mx*). Modern hotel with well-furnished, carpeted colonial-style rooms and suites with balconies and beautiful bathrooms arranged around small patios. Very good-value restaurant. ⑥.

**Don Quijote**, C Cristóbal Colón 7; turn left where Colón crosses Real de Guadalupe (☎9/678-0920, *hquiote@mundomay.com.mx*). Quiet, comfortable rooms with shower and constant hot water. The lobby is decorated with original costumes from Chiapas villages collected by the owner, Joaquín Hernánz, who speaks English and French. Free morning coffee. ④.

**El Paraíso**, C 5 de Febrero 19 (☎ & fax 9/678-0085). A wonderfully restored colonial-style house. Rooms are smallish but very comfortable, and the restaurant is excellent. Great value at this price. English and German spoken. ⑤.

**Rincón del Arco**, Ejército Nacional 66, corner of Av Vicente Guerrero (☎9/678-1313, fax 678-1568). Large rooms and suites with antique furniture, fireplaces and beautifully tiled bathrooms, set in delightful gardens with views of the surrounding hills. Restaurant and parking. ⑤/⑥.

**Santa Clara**, Av Insurgentes 1, corner of the zócalo (☎9/678-1140, fax 678-1041). A former colonial mansion, with rooms and suites surrounding a spacious, plant-filled patio; public areas are adorned with colonial weapons and suits of armour. Heated pool and good restaurant. ⑤/⑦.

# The City

With a wealth of colonial **churches** and many interesting little **museums**, the true pleasure of a visit to San Cristóbal lies in simply wandering the streets and absorbing the atmosphere. It's also a great base for visiting nearby villages, studying Spanish or buying inexpensive textiles, weavings and jewellery, including silver and amber. Several shops and museums offer the chance to preview indigenous crafts.

In the centre, the **zócalo**, Plaza 31 de Marzo, usually referred to simply as **el parque**, is worth seeing, not so much for the relatively ordinary sixteenth-century cathedral (though it does have a nice *artesonado* ceiling and elaborate pulpit) as for some of the colonial mansions that surround it. For a full description of the city's colonial churches and monuments, pick up a copy of Richard Perry's excellent book *More Maya Missions: Exploring Colonial Chiapas*, available in the bookstores listed on p.160. The finest of the mansions is **La Casa de la Sirena**, now the *Hotel Santa Clara*, dating from the mid-sixteenth century, with a very elaborate doorway around the corner on Avenida Insurgentes. In the middle of the zócalo there's a bandstand and a café, and even when no band is playing the city authorities provide piped music. If you haven't already come across them, this is probably where you'll first encounter some of San Cristóbal's insistent **salespeople**, mostly women and girls from the villages, traditionally dressed and in no mood to take no for an answer. You must either learn to say no as if you really mean it, or else accept that they'll break your resistance eventually. Bear in mind that they really do need the income: many have been expelled from their villages for converting to Protestantism and often live in desperate hardship.

The most attractive new development in the centre is the **Andador Eclesiástico**, a tree-lined pedestrian walkway tiled with geometric designs, connecting the Templo del Carmen on Hidalgo, via the zócalo, to the church of Santo Domingo at the north end of Avenida 20 de Noviembre; other pedestrian streets are planned.

## Templo del Carmen
From the zócalo, Hidalgo leads south to the **Templo del Carmen**, by the Moorish-style (*mudéjar*) tower and arch across the road, which once served as the gateway to the city. The church is not particularly inspiring architecturally, but you can also visit the adjoining cultural complex, including the Casa de la Cultura and **Instituto de Bellas Artes**. Considering the amount of artistic activity in and around San Cristóbal, these are pretty disappointing – especially since a serious fire in 1993 destroyed several eighteenth-century religious paintings – but sometimes there's an interesting temporary exhibition, concert or recital. On the way here, at the corner with Niños Heroes, you pass the **Tienda de los Artesanos de Chiapas** (Tues–Sun 9am–2pm & 5–8pm), a state-run venture which provides an outlet for Chiapas textiles and crafts at fair prices. The **displays of weaving** and embroidery styles in the exhibitions here are as good as in any museum and if you're planning to visit any of the villages have a look in here first to get an idea of what's on offer.

## Santo Domingo and nearby museums
In the other direction, Avenida General Utrilla leads north from the zócalo towards the market. At no. 10 (Plaza Siván), the small **Museo del Ambar** (daily 10am–6pm; free) displays and sells authentic amber found in the Simojovel Valley.

**Santo Domingo**, further up, is perhaps the most intrinsically interesting of San Cristóbal's churches, with a lovely pinkish Baroque facade embellished with Habsburg eagles. Inside, it's huge and gilded everywhere, with a wonderfully ornate pulpit – see it in the evening, by the dim light of candles, and you can believe it's all solid gold. Being so close to the market, Santo Domingo is often full of traders and villagers, and the area in front of the church is filled with **craft stalls** – often the best place to buy souvenirs; there's even a **Zapatista** stall near the corner of Utrilla and Escuadrón 201. Part of the former *convento* next to Santo Domingo has been converted into a craft co-operative, **Sna Jolobil**, selling textiles and other village products. The quality here is generally good, and prices correspondingly higher than outside. A block behind the church, in another part of the monastery, the **Museo Etnografía y Historia**, in the Centro Cultural de los Altos de Chiapas (Tues–Sun 10am–5pm; US$1.50), has gorgeous displays of textiles as well as vivid portrayals of how the Indians fared under colonial rule. For scholars, the **library** at the rear is a fascinating place to study old books and records of Chiapas, and the gardens are a relaxing place to rest.

## The market and other shops

San Cristóbal's daily **market** lies beyond Santo Domingo along General Utrilla. It's a fascinating place, if only because here you can observe indigenous life and custom without causing undue offence. What's on sale is mostly local produce and household goods, although there are also good tyre-soled leather *huaraches* and rough but warm sweaters, which you might well feel the need of. The market is far bigger than at first you suspect, so make sure you see it all (though beware that the main covered part is full of really gross, bloody butchers' stalls). For other high-quality **crafts**, try the stores in town, especially on Real de Guadalupe – those furthest from the zócalo, like Artesanías Real at 44 and Artesanías Chiapanecas at 46C, are the best. La Pared, on Hidalgo, also has a very good selection of genuine, good-quality amber and silver jewellery, which you can see on *www.laparedmexico.com*; it also sells books and has long-distance telephone facilities (see p.160). A visit to Taller Leñateros, C Flavio Paniagua 54, allows you to observe the fascinating process of making paper by hand from such diverse items as banana leaves, cornstalks, coconut fibre and bamboo, mixed with waste paper and rags and coloured with natural dyes. The finished products are then printed with traditional indigenous and modern designs to become beautiful cards and notebooks. Leñateros is Spanish for "woodcutters" and many workers here formerly cut firewood from the pine forests surrounding San Cristóbal. Now, in addition to creative paper goods, they also produce *La jícara* (*The Gourd*) – a **literary magazine** in the folded-bark book design of a Maya codex.

## Casa Na Bolom

Behind Santo Domingo, Chiapa de Corzo leads east towards the **Casa Na Bolom** at Vicente Guerrero 33, not only a private home and hotel (see "Accommodation", above), but also a **museum and library** of local anthropology (library open daily 10am—2pm; free), particularly of the isolated Lacandón Maya (see box on p.147). This was the home of Danish explorer and anthropologist Frans Blom, who died in 1963, and his Swiss wife Gertrude (Duby), an anthropologist and photographer who died in 1993, and is renowned as a centre for the study of the region's indigenous cultures. The whole centre is overseen by the Asociación Cultural Na Bolom, and also arranges some small-scale volunteer cultural and agricultural projects. You'll need to speak Spanish; write or email for details (address in "Accommodation").

A **tour** of the house, grounds and the **Museo Moxviquil** (in English or Spanish daily at 11.30am & 4.30pm, US$2.75 including a film) is the best way to get to know Na Bolom and the story of its founders. The museum exhibits discoveries from the site of Moxviquil (see p.163), and other rooms explain the history and culture of the Chiapas Highlands and the Lacandón Forest. There's also a collection of items belonging to Frans Blom, including the detailed maps he made of Chiapas. Beyond the main buildings, arranged around beautiful, flower-filled courtyards, is Na Bolom's **garden**, with flowers and vegetables set among towering pine trees. After the tour, a film about the life of the Bloms and specific ecological, cultural and political aspects of life in Chiapas is shown. Across the street from the entrance Na Bolom also has a small **café**, the *Jaguar Garden* (see "Eating", below). In one corner is a replica of a traditional house of the highlands, constructed using wooden walls covered with mud and a roof thatched with grass. There's also a good **gift shop** and information about San Cristóbal's many other small museums.

## Guadalupe and San Cristóbal

Further afield, two churches dominate views of the town from their hilltop sites: **Guadalupe** to the east and **San Cristóbal** to the west. Neither offers a great deal architecturally, but the climbs are worth it for the views – especially San Cristóbal, at the top of a dauntingly long and steep flight of steps. Be warned, though, that women have been subjected to harassment at both of these relatively isolated spots (especially San Cristóbal): don't climb up here alone or after dark.

# Eating, drinking and entertainment

There's a huge variety of good **restaurants** along Insurgentes and in the streets immediately around the zócalo, especially on Calle Madero. Where San Cristóbal really scores, however, is in lively places that cater to a disparate, somewhat bohemian crowd, made up of university and language-school students, a cosmopolitan expatriate population and a constant stream of travellers. Lots of the places are vaguely arty, with a coffee-house atmosphere and interesting menus that feature plenty of **vegetarian** options. There are a couple of good **bakeries** on Diego de Mazariegos, two blocks west of the zócalo.

As for **nightlife**, many of these same places host **live music** in the evenings, only rarely imposing a cover charge. There's a **cinema** in the Centro Cultural El Puente, on Real de Guadalupe, showing Latin American and foreign films. As always, check current venues and listings in the tourist office on Hidalgo.

## Cafés and restaurants

**Los Anafres**, C Flavio de Paniagua 2, near the corner with Utrilla. Friendly little Mexican restaurant where you can eat indoors or in a sunny courtyard. The speciality is grilled meats brought to your table on the *anafre* (a tiny barbecue grill) but there are also good vegetarian choices and it's good for breakfast too.

**Café Museo Café**, C María Adelina Flores 10. Delicious coffee served in a small museum. The walls are adorned with beautiful illustrations depicting the history of the coffee trade in Mexico and you can buy locally produced beans or even visit the communities where they're grown.

**Café El Puente**, Real de Guadalupe 55. Popular café serving inexpensive salads, soups, sandwiches and cakes; also acts as a cultural centre, with Internet access, newspapers and magazines, lectures, film shows and a good noticeboard. Closed Sun.

**Casa de Pan**, Dr Navarro 10. Superb range of vegetarian food and baked goods, including bagels, made with locally grown organic ingredients and at very reasonable prices. Owners Kip and Ronald Nigh are active in development projects for indigenous women and organic agriculture. Live music nightly and there's a cookbook available. Closed Mon.

**La Creación**, C 1 de Marzo, near 5 de Mayo. Good breakfasts, sandwiches, salads and tacos. Really livens up in the evenings, with DJs in the week and live Latin jazz on weekends.

**Emiliano's Moustache**, Cresencio Rosas 7, near Cuauhtémoc. Vast range of authentic tacos – the *especiál* is big enough for two – with some vegetarian chioces. Live music in the evening.

**El Gato Gordo**, Madero 28. Good, clean, inexpensive and deservedly popular place serving Mexican and international dishes with great-value specials; read the newspapers, watch TV and listen to music. Closed Mon.

**Jaguar Garden**, Casa Na Bolom. A small café set in a lovely garden across the street from the entrance to the Casa Na Bolom.

**Latinos**, Madero and Juárez. More of a late-night music venue, but with good Mexican, vegetarian and international food. Many types of music: Latin, of course, with salsa, reggae, jazz and rock.

**Madre Tierra**, Insurgentes 19, corner of Hermanos Domínguez. European-style restaurant in a colonial house, often with live salsa or classical music. Great, healthy food includes home-made soup, salad and pasta. The next-door bakery and deli sells wholewheat bread and carrot cake. The upstairs terrace bar has good views of ancient walls and red-tiled roofs.

**El Mirador II**, Madero 16. The best inexpensive Mexican restaurant on Madero; good tortas and comidas corridas.

**Naturalissimo**, 20 de Noviembre 4. One of the city's best vegetarian restaurants, spotlessly clean, with a great-value daily special.

**Paris-Mexico**, Madero 20. Authentic French and Mexican cuisine, expertly cooked and not overpriced – try the daily lunch special, a three-course meal of soup, crêpe and dessert, always with a vegetarian option.

**Plaza Mirador**, Plaza 31 de Marzo 2. Surprisingly inexpensive considering the location overlooking the zócalo, and serving tasty filling meals, usually with a vegetarian choice.

**Restaurante Tuluc**, Insurgentes 5. Justifiably popular, with a good comida corrida and dinner specials, this is the first place to open in the morning (6am); ideal if you have to catch an early bus.

**El Teatro Café**, 1 de Marzo 8. Superb, moderately priced French and Italian food. Boasts the only rooftop dining area in San Cristóbal – definitely the best place to enjoy the sunset as you eat. French and English spoken.

## Listings

**Banks and exchange** Most banks are around the zócalo; they usually exchange dollars and give cash advances (mornings only) and most have 24hr ATMs. Casa de Cambio Lacantún, Real de Guadalupe 12 (Mon–Sat 8am–2pm & 4–8pm, Sun 9am–1pm) offers a quicker service and will exchange currencies other than US dollars.

**Bike rental** Los Pinguinos, 5 de Mayo 10B (☎9/678-0202, *pinguino@hotmail.com*), is the best place. Well-maintained bikes for about US$2 per hour, US$8 per day, and takes tours to local attractions. English and German spoken.

**Bookstores** Librería Chilam Balam, on General Utrilla near Dr Navarro, has a wide selection, including academic and educational books, plus guides and topographic maps of Chiapas. Librería La Pared, Hidalgo 2, next to the tourist office, has new guidebooks (including *Rough Guides*) and the largest selection of new and second-hand books in English and other European languages in southern Mexico; you can rent, trade or buy books. Accepts Visa and Mastercard. Other useful bookshops are Librería Soluna, Real de Guadalupe 13B, with a fair choice of books and guides, and Librería La Quimera, Real de Guadalupe 24B. Casa Na Bolom, Vicente Guerrero 33, also has an excellent library (daily 10am–2pm, free) and sells some books and maps of the Lacandón forest.

**Email and Internet access** San Cristóbal boasts at least a dozen rapidly changing places where you can go online. Currently there's a good clutch around the junction of Madero with Domínguez and Juárez, just one block from the zócalo, with *Chisnet*, at Juárez 2, being the best value. Ask anyone who's been here for more than a day where the best place is now.

---

### MOVING ON FROM SAN CRISTÓBAL

San Cristóbal is pretty well connected, and you can get directly to most destinations in the state and throughout the Yucatán. The **tourist office** maintains an accurate and up-to-date list of all bus times – check first. Ticket lines are long, so try to buy your onward ticket in advance; you might find that TRF (across the highway), running first- and second-class buses to most main destinations, has a quicker ticket service.

**Tuxtla Gutiérrez** (2hr) is served frequently by most companies, and in addition combis tout for customers outside the bus stations on the Carretera Panamericana. **Villahermosa** (7hr) is not so well served, though there are a few first-class services daily with Cristóbal Colón; it's easier to get any bus to Tuxtla and change there. For **Palenque** (5hr), there are plenty of first- and second-class departures, day or night. All buses going to Palenque call at **Ocosingo** (2hr 30min), and there's also plenty of passenger-van traffic: just go to the highway and someone will call out to you. Cristóbal Colón has the best service to **Ciudad Cuauhtémoc** (3hr 30min; all via Comitán; 2hr) on the Guatemalan border, and on the highway you'll also find any number of combis to Comitán.

For **Oaxaca** (12hr) there are two overnight services at 5pm and 8pm; other departures are from Tuxtla. The first-class companies all have at least two daily overnight services to **Mexico City** (19hr). For **Campeche** (10hr) and **Mérida** (13hr), there's a first-class service at 9.30pm. For the **Yucatán coast**, Maya de Oro has a luxury service at 9.30pm, calling at **Chetumal** (10hr; for Belize) **Playa del Carmen** (14hr), **Tulum** (15hr) and **Cancún** (16hr).

Currently the only **flights** from San Cristóbal are two daily services on Aeromar to Mexico City, though others are planned; check with Santa Ana Tours, above.

**Immigration office** (☎9/678-6594). The office itself is a couple of kilometres west of the centre, at the junction of the Carretera Panamericana and Diagonal Centenario – best get a taxi.

**Language courses** Centro Bilingüe, in Centro Cultural El Puente, Real de Guadalupe 55 (☎ & fax 9/678-3723, *spanish@sancristobal.podernet.com.mx*), is the longest-established language school in San Cristóbal. Instituto Jovel, María Adelina Flores 21 (☎ & fax 9/678-4069, *www.mexonline.com/jovel.htm*), is newer but very highly recommended. Both offer Spanish courses at various levels, and can arrange accommodation with local families.

**Laundry** Lava Sec, Crescencio Rosas 12; Lavorama, Guadalupe Victoria 20A; Lavendaría Mixtli, corner of 1 de Marzo and 16 de Septiembre; and many more.

**Post office** Corner of Cuauhtémoc and Crescencio Rosas, southwest of the zócalo (Mon–Fri 8am–7pm, Sat 9am–1pm). In addition, most hotels also have Mexipost boxes.

**Telephones** The best-value place in town to make long-distance calls and calls abroad is Librería La Pared, Hidalgo 2, costing under US$1 per minute to North America, Europe, and Japan. Additionally, there are plenty of Ladatel cardphones around, including under the arches of the Palacio Municipal and in the Cristóbal Colón terminal, and many shops have casetas.

**Travel and tour agencies** San Cristóbal has dozens of tour agencies, most doing very much the same thing: tours to local villages (recommended ones are listed on p.162) and perhaps further afield to the Sumidero Cañon (see p.165). The best for international and domestic air tickets is Santa Ana Tours, Madero 9A (☎9/678-0298); for local and national adventure tours try Viajes Pakal, Cuauhtémoc 6B (☎9/678-2818, *pakal@sancristobal.podernet.com.mx*). The best and most experienced of the local tour operators is Viajes Chincultik, Real de Guadalupe 34, in the Posada Margarita (☎ & fax 9/678-0957, *viajeschincultik@latinmail.com*).

# Around San Cristóbal

**Excursions** to the villages around San Cristóbal should be treated with extreme sensitivity. Quite simply, you are an intruder, and will be made to feel so – be very careful about taking photographs, and certainly never do so inside churches (theoretically you need a permit from the tourist authorities in Tuxtla Gutiérrez for any photography in the villages; in practice you should always get permission locally). There's a well-worn travellers' tale, true in its essentials, of two gringos being severely beaten up for photographing the interior of the church at San Juan Chamula. You should also be careful about what you wear: cover your legs, and don't wear native clothing – it may have some meaning or badge of rank for the people you are visiting.

The best time to make your visit is on a Sunday, when most villages have a market, or during a fiesta. At such times you will be regarded as having a legitimate reason to come, and you'll also find some life – most villages are merely supply points and meeting places for a rural community and have only a very small permanent population.

Some kind of trip out of San Cristóbal is definitely worth it, though, if only for the ride into the countryside, even if on finally reaching a village you find doors shut in your face and absolutely nothing to do (or, conversely, you are mobbed by begging kids). The indigenous people in the immediate vicinity of San Cristóbal and to the west are generally **Tzotzil** speaking, while those a little further to the east are **Tzeltal**, but each village has also developed its own identity in terms of costumes, craft specialities and linguistic differences: as a result, the people are often subdivided by village or groups of villages and referred to as Chamulas, Zinacantecos, Huistecos (from Huistán) and so on.

It's a good idea to find out about village life before you go; the **Tienda de los Artesanos** on Hidalgo (see p.157) has a good display on the villages, with examples of the local dress in each, and the tourist office can supply details of tours and bus timetables where relevant.

**THE SAN CRISTÓBAL AREA**

## Transport and tours

Inexpensive combis leave frequently for Chamula and Zinacantán, less often but still several times a day for other villages, from the end of Utrilla, just north of the market in San Cristóbal. If you'd rather take an **organized tour** (around US$8–9 per person), there are several to choose from. Among the best are those led by Mercedes Hernández Gómez, who grew up in Zinacantán – her knowledge is so extensive that she never gives the same tour twice. Meet by the kiosk in the zócalo at 9am; she'll be carrying her distinctive umbrella. Alex and Raul's "Culturally Responsible Excursions" leave from outside the municipal tourist office on the zócalo at 9.30am, while the Casa Na Bolom (see p.158) also offers tours to nearby villages and to Lacandón communities. From the tourist office, you can also get details on **horseback tours** into the surrounding area; the *Posada Margarita* is one of several places organizing them.

Some organized tours go to the **Grutas de San Cristóbal** (also called "Rancho Nuevo" caves; daily 9am–5pm; US$0.65), an enormous cavern extending deep into a mountain about 10km to the southeast, but it's easy enough to do it by bus or bike since they're well-signed, on the right just off the highway to Comitán. A track leads for about 1km from the road through a pine-forested park with hiking trails often used by the army. If you want to go by **bike** it's about a fifty-minute ride, uphill most of the way from San Cristóbal.

Another favourite trip is to **El Arcotete**, a large, natural limestone arch that forms a bridge over a river. To get there, follow Real de Guadalupe out of town, past the Guadalupe church, where it then becomes the road to Tenejapa; El Arcotete is down a signed track to the right about 3.5km past the church.

## Moxviquil

**Moxviquil**, a completely deserted ruined **ancient site**, is a pleasant excursion from San Cristóbal of a few hours on foot; it's best, however, to study the plans at the Casa Na Bolom first, as all you can see when you get there are piles of rough limestone. To get there, find Av Yajalon, a few blocks east of Santo Domingo, and follow it north to the end (about 30min) at the foot of tree-covered hills, in a little settlement called Ojo de Agua. Head for the highest buildings you can see, two timber shacks with red roofs. The tracks are at times indistinct as you clamber over the rocks, but after about 300m a lovely side valley opens up on your left – suitable for camping. The main path veers gradually to the right, becoming quite wide and leading up through a high basin ringed by pine forest. After 3km you reach the village of **Pozeula**; the ruins are ahead of you across a valley, built on top of and into the sides of a hill.

## San Juan Chamula

**SAN JUAN CHAMULA** is the closest of the villages to San Cristóbal and the most frequently visited, though it is little more than a collection of civic and religious buildings with a few houses – most of its population actually lives on isolated farms or *ejidos* in the countryside. It is also very commercialized – prices in the market are certainly no bargain, and local kids will pester you for "presents", chanting *"regaleme"*, the whole time. The best way to deal with the situation is to select just one or two children and buy a couple of the painted clay animals or braided bracelets they're selling, then tell all the others you've bought all you're going to and hope they'll go to someone else. To get the most out of a visit you really need to go on one of the organized tours (see above); questions are answered honestly and in full.

Before you enter Chamula's **church** be sure to obtain permission (and buy a ticket; US$0.65) from the "tourist office", in the Palacio Municipal to the right-hand side of the plaza as you face the church. The rituals observed here – a mixture of Catholic and traditional Maya practice – are extraordinary, and the church itself is a glorious sight, both outside and in, where worshippers and tourists shuffle about in the flickering light of a thousand candles. Protestant converts among the villagers are driven out and only some of the Catholic sacraments are accepted. Do *not* take **photographs** inside, or even write notes. Your ticket also allows you to enter the interesting little **Museo Etnográfico**, behind the Palacio. Thatched rooms with mud and straw walls display artefacts of village life, musical instruments and costumes from Chamula and other villages.

Several **comedores** around the plaza provide simple, filling meals and in the cantina you can buy *posh*, a wickedly strong cane alcohol used as an offering in the church and also simply to get celebrants blind drunk. Combis depart regularly from San Cristóbal's market for Chamula, especially frequent for the Sunday market. If you take a bus up, the 10km back is an easy and delightful walk, almost all downhill.

## San Lorenzo Zinacantán and other villages

**SAN LORENZO ZINACANTÁN** is also reasonably close, some 15km southwest, and readily accessible on public transport. Surrounded by steep, pine-forested hills, it's even a relatively easy walk from Chamula (about 1hr 30min). The Zinacantecos are much friendlier than Chamulans, and you'll not encounter many pushy kids selling souvenirs here. The men wear wonderful rose-pink ponchos with silver threads (called *pok'ul*), decorated with tassels and embroidered flowers, and the same colours and designs feature in the women's costumes. Beautiful table-mats decorated with large embroidered flowers are made here, and some tours include a visit to a house where you can meet the women who weave them.

If you reach Zinacantán early enough on Sunday morning you'll have time to visit the large, whitewashed church with red pantile roof, look around the market, and still get to Chamula before the market there has packed up. Zinacantán also has a **museum**, called Museo Ik'al Ojov ("Our Great Lord"), with displays of costumes from different hierarchical groups and a tableau of a house interior (daily 8am–6pm; donation).

A number of other villages can be reached by early morning combis from the market area, although you may have difficulty getting back. **TENEJAPA**, about 28km northeast of San Cristóbal through some superb mountain scenery, is the closest easily accessible Tzeltal village, and has a reasonably good Sunday market, and there are wonderful **hikes** into the surrounding mountains. Combis leave for Tenejapa from Bermudas, an unmarked side street running east from the market, near the corner with Yajalon, about hourly or when full (1hr). Last one back to San Cristóbal leaves Tenejapa at 3pm. **HUISTÁN**, some 36km out, just off the road to Ocosingo, is Tzotzil-speaking, and with more than the usual amount of villagers in traditional dress.

# San Cristóbal to Tuxtla Gutiérrez

The two-hour journey from San Cristóbal to **Tuxtla Gutiérrez** is one of the most spectacular in Mexico, as the road twists through the mountains, breaking through the cloud into cool pine forests to offer sweeping views of highland valleys, before descending into the heat of the Grijalva valley. Most people come this way simply to take the boat trip through the astonishing **Cañon del Sumidero**, but the town of **Chiapa de Corzo**, on the riverbank from which the boats depart, has some colonial monuments as well as some little-visited but easily accessible **Maya ruins**. Tour agents in San Cristóbal offer good-value **day-trips** to the canyon (doing it on your own is only fractionally cheaper), but Tuxtla does have some sights worth seeing – **museums** and a fascinating **zoo** – so you might want to consider staying overnight.

## Chiapa de Corzo

**CHIAPA DE CORZO** is an elegant little town overlooking the river, barely twenty minutes from Tuxtla. An important centre in Preclassic times, it's the place where the oldest Long Count date, corresponding to December 7, 36 BC, has been found on a stela (the remaining ruins are on private land behind the Nestlé plant, beyond the far end of 21 de Octubre). There are at least a dozen **places to eat** on the riverside here, and plenty to see: the most striking feature is an amazingly elaborate **sixteenth-century fountain**, which dominates the plaza. A blend of Spanish and Moorish architecture, it is built of brick in the *mudéjar* style in the shape of the Spanish crown. A tribute to its painstaking restoration, it is one of the most spectacular surviving early colonial monuments in Mexico. The small **museum of regional handicrafts**, in a cobbled courtyard surrounded by the ancient brick arches of the Convento Santo Domingo (Tues–Sun 10am–4pm; US$0.50), features the local painted and lacquered gourds.

There are two **hotels** in town: the basic *Los Angeles*, on the southeast corner of the plaza (③); and the newer, more upmarket **Hotel La Ceiba**, Domingo Ruíz 300 (☎ & fax 9/616-0389, *laceiba5@prodigy.net.mx*; ⑤), three blocks west from the plaza, very quiet and comfortable, with a/c rooms and a small pool.

**To get to Chiapa** from San Cristóbal, take any second-class bus or combi (few first-class services stop in the town), though you're likely to be dropped off by the highway; there's a steady stream of *microbuses* from Tuxtla passing to take you to the centre.

## The ruins of Chiapa de Corzo

Strategically located on an ancient trade route high above the Río Grijalva, the ruins of **Chiapa de Corzo** comprise some two hundred structures scattered over a wide area of private property, shared among several different owners and sliced in two by the Carretera Interamericana. Mound 32, a small flat-topped pyramid, is clearly visible at the road junction as you head east of town. This is the longest continually occupied site in Chiapas, beginning life as a farming settlement in the early Preclassic period (1400–850 BC). By the late Preclassic (250 BC–250 AD), it was the largest centre of population in the region, trading all over Mesoamerica. What you see today are mainly low pyramids, walls and courtyards.

To **get to the site** from town, take any *microbús* heading east from the plaza, get off at the junction with Hidalgo and follow the signs. After about ten minutes you'll come to an unmarked gate in a fence on the right; go to the house (officially closed Mon) and pay the US$0.75 **fee** to the family who farm among the ruins. Walking, it's about 3km northeast from the plaza in Chiapa de Corzo, passing the beautifully located sixteenth-century church ruin of San Sebastián on the way.

## The Cañon del Sumidero

Just downstream from Chiapa de Corzo, the Río Grijalva has carved the **Cañon del Sumidero**, a spectacular cleft through cliffs that in places reach almost 1500m in height. The most popular way to see the canyon is to take a boat from the *embarcadero*, just below the plaza; **boats** leave when full and charge US$8 per person. The trip lasts a couple of hours, passing several waterfalls (best during the rains) and entering caves in the cliffs, enlivened by glimpses of quite large **crocodiles** and a commentary that points out the spot where hundreds of Chiapanec warriors flung themselves off the cliff rather than submit to the Spanish. Before the Chicoasen Dam was built at the end of the canyon, tremendous rapids made the river unnavigable and it still flows rapidly during the rainy season.

To appreciate the view from above, take the road that runs north from Tuxtla past a series of miradores, in a **national park** that includes the most scenic sections of the canyon. The best views are from the mirador known as **La Coyota**, or at the end of the road near the restaurant *La Atalaya*. There's no public transport other than tours, but to see at least the lower reaches you could take a "Km 4" combi from Tuxtla heading north along 11 Ote Nte, past the Parque Madero, and get off at the turnaround point. From here it's a 25-minute walk to the first mirador, **La Ceiba**, for stunning views of the canyon and river. There's usually sufficient traffic to make hitching a possibility, though be sure to take water along.

## Bochil, Simojovel and around

Just beyond Chiapa de Corzo, the **road to Villahermosa** (see p.180) – a spectacular wind down to the Gulf plain – cuts off to the north. Few tourists take this route, but it offers an interesting excursion to some little-visited highland villages; you can also return to San Cristóbal this way.

The road climbs through mountains wreathed in cloud to **BOCHIL**, some 60km from Tuxtla, where some buses pull over for a rest stop. It's a pleasant small town, a centre for the **Tzotzil Maya**, and a good base from which to explore the surrounding hills and villages. Most people still wear the traditional dress or *traje*, the women in white *huipiles* with red embroidery, pink ribbons in their hair and dark blue skirts, and maybe a few men in the white smock and trousers rolled up to the knee. You'll be stared at, usually covertly, and, as always, should be *very* wary of taking photographs.

There are a couple of simple **places to stay**, including the *Posada San Pedro* (b), whose basic rooms are set out around a courtyard on 1 Pte Nte, a block from the plaza; head for Banamex at the top of the plaza and turn right. Bochil has a frequent second-class bus service to Tuxtla, with Autotransportes Tuxtla–Bochil. Five kilometres beyond Bochil at **Puerto Cate**, a side road leads down to the right to **San Andrés Larráinzar**, a Tzotzil village 23km down the dirt track; trucks cover the route. From San Andrés you can reach **San Juan Chamula** (p.163), 18km away, which is well connected by combis **to San Cristóbal**. This makes for an interesting route to or from San Cristóbal – but you'll need to check the current political situation and set off fairly early.

Combis run regularly up the minor road to **SIMOJOVEL**, 40km from Tuxtla at the head of a spectacular valley, the source of most of the amber you'll find sold in local markets. Should you want **to stay**, the *Casa de Huéspedes Simojovel*, one block south of the plaza on Independencia (b), has basic rooms around a flower-filled courtyard.

# Tuxtla Gutiérrez

**TUXTLA GUTIÉRREZ**, the capital of the state and a fast-growing, modern city, does its best to deny most of Chiapas's attraction and tradition, but you may well end up having to stay the night here as it's the main gateway to central Mexico and a major transport hub. It's not a bad place anyway – there are a fascinating **zoo** and some excellent **museums**.

The centre of town is arranged in the usual Chiapas grid of numbered streets fanning out from Avenida Central, which runs east–west, and C Central, which runs north–south; often you'll see the streets named not just as 3 Av Nte, but as 3 Av Nte Pte, which defines which quarter of the city you're in – it can be extremely confusing if you're looking for the junction of 3 Nte Pte with 3 Pte Nte. **Avenida Central** (also known as Av 14 de Septiembre and Blvd Belisario Domínguez) is the town's focus, with the **zócalo** right at the centre.

## Arrival and information

Tuxtla has two **airports**. The Aeropuerto San Juan, near Ocozocuautla on a hilltop often shrouded in fog, 28km to the west of town, is generally used only in summer; colectivos run from here into the city. Aeropuerto Francisco Sarabia is a more convenient 7km west of the city; taxis or colectivos will bring you into the centre. First-class **buses** pull in to the ADO/Cristóbal Colón station on 2 Av Nte at 2 C Pte; you can leave luggage at the juice bar *Miroslava* opposite.

The main second-class terminal, used by Autotransportes Tuxtla Gutiérrez (ATG) and a couple of smaller companies, takes up half a block of 3 Sur Ote, near 7 Ote, 1km southeast of the centre: for the zócalo, follow 2 Calle Sur west past the market area until you hit Calle Central Sur, then turn right.

The most central place to pick up maps and information is at the **municipal tourist office**, conveniently located in the underpass at C Central Nte and 2 Av Nte Ote; unfortunately opening hours are erratic. Tuxtla's state **tourist office** is a good way west of the zócalo, across from the *Hotel Bonampak* in the Edificio Plaza de las Instituciones at Blvd Belisario Domínguez 950 (Mon–Fri 9am–3pm & 6–9pm; ☎9/613-9396), but the staff have a good selection of maps and leaflets about all Chiapas's attractions. The **post office** (Mon–Fri 8am–7pm, Sat 9am–1pm) is just off the east side of the zócalo.

**Banks** are everywhere; Banamex on 1 Sur Pte and Bancomer on Avenida Central Pte are both within a couple of blocks of the zócalo. A good **travel agent** is Viajes Miramar (☎9/612-3930), off the northeast corner of the zócalo at 1 Av Ote Nte 310. You can obtain **topographic maps** of the state from the Hacienda and INEGI offices (government departments), on the fourth floor of the Edificio Plaza, corner of Av Central and 2 C Ote Sur – useful if you're travelling in out-of-the-way places. Crazy Web, at 2 Avenida Nte (two doors from the *Hotel Casablanca*) is one of the best places in Tuxtla for **Internet and email**.

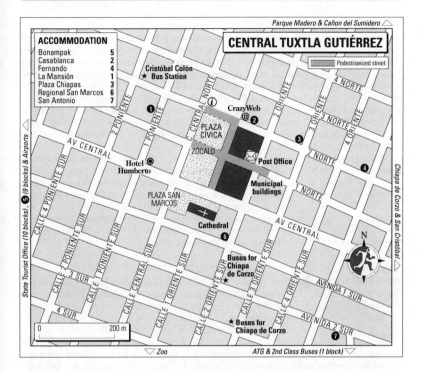

## Accommodation

Tuxtla has no shortage of decent **places to stay**, with plenty of budget options. Most hotels have hot water, but there are occasional shortages. Though inexpensive, the hotels near the bus stations are noisy. If you want the convenience of being central with less noise, head a few blocks east (left out of the first-class bus station, crossing the zócalo by the underpass) to find a clutch of hotels in all price ranges along 2 Avenida Nte Ote.

**Bonampak**, Belisario Domínguez 180 (☎9/613-2047, *hotbonam@prodigy.net.mx*). Fourteen blocks west of the zócalo, where Av Central becomes Blvd Domínguez, and part of the Best Western chain. Rooms are all a/c, and there's a pool, restaurant, travel agency and car rental. ⑦.

**Casablanca**, 2 Av Nte Ote 25 (☎ & fax 9/611-0305, *amhm_chis@chiapas.net*). Friendly place offering good-value rooms, some with a/c and TV. Luggage storage. ③/⑤.

**Fernando**, 2 Av Nte Ote 515 (☎9/613-1740). The best value in this area: large, comfortable rooms and helpful staff. Parking available. ③.

**La Mansión**, 1 C Pte Nte 221 (☎9/612-2151). Only a block west of the zócalo and a block from Cristóbal Colón, this comfortable, affordable hotel has a lift and a good-value restaurant. ④.

**Plaza Chiapas**, 2 Av Nte Ote 299 (☎9/613-8365). Modern hotel with good prices. All rooms have private bath, some have balcony. ③.

**Regional San Marcos**, 2 C Ote 176 at 1 Av Sur (☎ & fax 9/613-1940, *sanmarcos@chiapas.net*). Good-value well-run modern hotel, a block south of the zócalo and a block east of the cathedral with some a/c rooms. There's also a good restaurant and bar. ④/⑤.

**San Antonio**, 2 Av Sur Ote 540 (☎9/612-2713). Clean, friendly, inexpensive hotel near the ATG terminal. Rooms are large with private bath. ②.

## The City

Sights downtown are few: the **zócalo**, or Plaza Cívica, is the chief of them, recently refurbished with much ostentatious marble, fountains and the very restrained, whitewashed **Catedral de San Marcos**. Its bell tower is one of the leading local entertainments: every hour a mechanical procession of the twelve apostles goes through a complicated routine accompanied by a carillon of 48 bells. At the side of the cathedral, the **Plaza San Marcos** is full of life, its ever-growing **handicraft market** bustling with vendors from all over Chiapas. In the zócalo, across Avenida Central, there's often free live music, especially at weekends. West of the zócalo, between 9 and 10 calles, you pass the clean and very popular **Parque la Marimba**, a favourite evening gathering place for families to stroll and listen to the marimba bands.

Slightly further afield, you could also head out to the **Parque Madero**, northeast of the centre, where the small **Museo Regional de Chiapas** (Tues–Sun 9am–4pm; US$1.50) displays artefacts and maps detailing the pre-Columbian groups living in Chiapas – highlights include intricately carved human bones from the ruins of Chiapa de Corzo (see p.165). Botanical gardens and an *Orquideario* full of blooms native to the Chiapas jungle are in the same complex, reached along a shaded walkway. To get there, head north from the zócalo and then turn right onto 5 Avenida Nte Ote for 2km, or take a combi marked "Parque Madero" along Avenida Central.

## The zoo

If you have half a day to spare, you could spend it at the **Zoológico Miguel Alvárez del Toro** or **ZOOMAT** (Tues–Sun 8.30am–5.30pm; free but donations welcome), on a forested hillside south of the city. There's a **bus** out there, #60, marked "Cerro Hueco" or "Zoológico", which you can catch on 1 Calle Ote between avenidas 6 and 7 Sur – it's very slow and roundabout, though, and a taxi (US$1.45) is a great deal easier.

The zoo claims to have every species native to Chiapas, from spiders to jaguars, and, by any standards, it's excellent, with good-sized cages, complete with natural vegetation and freshwater streams, and a conservationist approach. There is, for example, one dark cage with a label that announces the most destructive and dangerous species of all: peer in and you're confronted with a reflection of yourself. A number of animals, including *guaqueques negros* (agoutis) – rodents about the size of a domestic cat – and some very large birds, are free to roam the zoo grounds. Occasionally you'll witness bizarre meetings, as these creatures confront their caged relatives through the wire. This is particularly true of some of the pheasants – *ocofaisan* and *cojalita* – where the descendants of the caged birds are freed but make no attempt to leave because they naturally live in family groups. People of nervous disposition should avoid the *vivario*, which contains a vast and stomach-turning collection of all the snakes, insects and spiders you might meet on your travels.

## Eating and drinking

The centre of Tuxtla has dozens of **restaurants**, and you need never wander more than a block or so either side of Avenida Central to find something in every price range. Juice bars are everywhere and there are also some great bakeries along Avenida Central. The very **cheapest** places are on 2 Sur, while between the second-class bus area and the centre you'll pass several tiny, family-run restaurants, each serving an excellent-value comida corrida – for a really good one try the *Restaurante del Centro*, 2 C Ote Sur. More inexpensive places to eat can be found in the Mercado Díaz Ordáz, C Central Sur, between avenidas 3 and 4 Sur. *Gringo's Chicken*, on C 2 Ote just south of Av Central, may satisfy a yen for cooking *estilo Americano*, though the combination of southern-fried chicken with chile, tortillas and southern-fried potatoes is uniquely Mexican. Most popular for socializing and people-watching are the swish restaurants behind the cathedral, always packed with smartly dressed locals. Prices for the Mexican food at *La Parroquia* are not too high and there's a good

---

**MOVING ON FROM TUXTLA**

Cristóbal Colón, ADO and Maya de Oro buses all depart from the **first-class station** at the corner of 2 Av Nte Ote and 2 C Pte Nte; Rapidos del Sur (RdS), a good second-class line, is adjacent. Cristóbal Colón has departures every couple of hours for **San Cristóbal** (2hr) and other destinations include **Mexico City**(16hr), **Veracruz** (11hr), and **Oaxaca** (9hr). RdS serve the Chiapas coast; and Maya de Oro run luxury services to Mexico, **Mérida** (14hr) and **Cancún** (18hr). The various **second-class terminals** are dotted around the city. The main one, at the junction of 3 Av Sur Ote and 6 C Ote Sur, is used by Autotransportes Tuxtla Gutiérrez (ATG), and serves San Cristóbal, Oaxaca, Villahermosa, Mérida, Palenque and Cancún. Other local buses operate from the street outside.

It's only a short taxi-ride to the **Aeropuerto Franciso Sarabia**; if you're flying from the San Juan airport check with your airline about a combi.

---

breakfast buffet. Next door, the *Trattoria San Marco* serves good portions of pizza, Mexican food, and great gateaux at slightly higher prices. For **vegetarian** food, try *Naturalissimo*, just off Avenida Central at 6 Pte Nte, west of the zócalo; it's clean and modern, with a great daily special. Opposite there's a good bread and cheese shop. The *Café Avenida*, next to the *Hotel Avenida*, at Av Central 224, is an authentic Mexican coffee shop and there's a **bakery** in the block west of the café.

# San Cristóbal to Guatemala: Comitán and Montebello

Southeast of San Cristóbal, the Carretera Interamericana continues to the border through some of Chiapas's most scintillating scenery. You'll pass through **Amatenango del Valle**, a Tzeltal-speaking village with a reputation for good unglazed pottery, and **Comitán**, the only place of any size, which is the jumping-off point not only for Guatemala and the **Lagos de Montebello National Park**, but for the Classic period **Maya sites** of Junchavín and Tenam Puente. Beyond the Montebello lakes, the Carretera Fronteriza runs past **Tziscao** and over forested ridges to the Usumacinta valley and on to **Palenque**.

## Comitán and around

An attractive town in its own right, **COMITÁN** is spectacularly poised on a rocky hillside and surrounded by country in which wild orchids bloom freely. Once a major **Maya centre** of population, Comitán was originally known as Balún Canán (Nine Stars, or Guardians), renamed Comitlán (Place of Potters) when it came under Aztec control. The final place of any note before the border (Ciudad Cuauhtémoc is no more than a customs and immigration post), today Comitán is a market and supply centre for the surrounding agricultural area. There's a **Guatemalan consulate** and a collection of reasonable **hotels**, and it's a good place to rest if you've some hard travelling through the Lacandón forest or into Guatemala ahead of you.

Comitán's zócalo, on several levels and with plenty of shady places to rest, is surrounded by municipal buildings, the Santo Domingo church, shops, restaurants and the theatre. The *portales* on the west side and several other buildings are painted in an attractive orange and brown style. Opposite the Palacio Municipal, adjoining the church on the corner of the zócalo, the **Casa de Cultura** (daily 9am–8pm; free) features murals on the walls of its courtyard and has exhibits on local history, while the splendid little **Museo Arqueológico**

(Tues–Sun 10am–5pm; free) presents an easily understandable chronology of the local Maya sites. The town also boasts a wealth of beautiful churches, many of historical and architectural interest, including the colonial Santo Domingo and San Sebastián.

## Arrival and information

**Buses** stop along the Carretera Interamericana, a long six or seven blocks from the centre. Only Cristóbal Colón has a terminal (and a guardería); all other buses just pull in at the roadside.

Comitán's layout can be confusing at first; pick up a free map from the **tourist office** in the side street just past the Palacio Municipal (Mon–Fri 9am–6.30pm, ☎9/632-2640). They will also have the latest information on who needs Guatemalan visas. The **consulate** itself is at the corner of 1 C Sur Pte and 2 Av Pte Sur, a couple of blocks southwest of the zócalo (Mon–Fri 8am–4.30pm; ☎ & fax 9/632-2979; US$10 fee for visa). If you need only a tourist card pick one up at the border. Bancomer, for **currency exchange**, plus dollar cash advances and ATM, is on the zócalo, and the **post office** is one and a half blocks south on Central Sur (Mon–Fri 8am–7pm, Sat 8am–1pm). The best **travel agent** is Viajes Tenam, behind the Palacio Municipal at Pasaje Morales 8A (☎019/632-1654), and can arrange domestic and international flights. Check your **email** nearby, in *Café Internet*, at Pasaje Morales 12.

**Moving on from Comitán**, there are plenty of first- and second-class buses and combis to Ciudad Cuauhtémoc for the border, and San Cristóbal and Tuxtla to the west. Head out to the highway along Calle Central and you'll be near several bus stops; the Cristóbal Colón terminal is four blocks south. Heading for the **Lagos de Montebello** and the **Frontier Highway** buses or combis of Transportes Lagos de Montebello leave about every fifteen minutes from their terminal on 2 Av Pte Sur, between 2 and 3 Calles Sur, three blocks southwest of the zócalo. Comitán's **airport**, a few kilometres south of town, has two daily departures on Aeromar for Mexico City.

## Accommodation

Comitán has plenty of good-value **hotels** in all price ranges and all those below are close to the centre. Nights here are much cooler than days, so you'll need at least one blanket.

**Hospedaje Colonial**, 1 C Nte Ote 13 (☎9/632-5067). Very good value, with basic, clean rooms, private bath and secure parking. ③.

**Hospedaje Montebello**, 1 Nte Pte 10, a block northwest of the zócalo (☎9/632-3572). Great budget hotel. Large, clean rooms around a courtyard, some with private bath, and the communal shower is really hot. Clothes-washing facilities. ②.

**Hospedaje Primavera**, C Central Pte 4, just west from the zócalo (☎9/632-2041). Basic but clean rooms round a courtyard, with several budget places to eat nearby. ②.

**Posada el Castellano**, 3 C Nte Pte, a couple of blocks north of the zócalo (☎9/632-3347, fax 632-0117). Comfortable, friendly modern hotel. Well-furnished rooms with private bath, cable TV and phone around a courtyard with a fountain; secure parking and a very good restaurant. ④.

**Pensíon Delfín**, Av Central 19A, right on the zócalo (☎9/632-0013). Good value, with modern rooms, dependable hot water, safe parking and a quiet courtyard at the back. ④.

**Posada del Virrey**, Av Central Nte 13 (☎9/632-1811). Bright, modern, tiled rooms with private bath and TV set around a courtyard with a fountain. ④.

## Eating and drinking

Most of the best **places to eat** in Comitán are on the zócalo. For really good-value Mexican food in clean surroundings, try *Helen's Enrique*, with tables under the arches, or the *Restaurant Nevelandia*, and there are a couple of cheaper places. The *Café Quiptic*, next to the Casa de Cultura, serves good breakfasts, with very good coffee. The **market**, two blocks east of the zócalo, is filled with fruit stands and has some very good comedores. Finally, if you drink alcohol you should try **Comiteco**, a rich-tasting local speciality and virtually unobtainable elsewhere; it's made from *agave*, like tequila, but is smoother and a good deal cheaper. There's a wide range to choose from and you can taste before you buy at the distillery shop, *Aguardientes de Comitán*, 1 Pte Sur 14, just a block southwest of the zócalo.

## The ruins of Junchavín and Tenam Puente

The little-visited site of **Junchavín** (daily 7am–5pm; free) is about a 45-minute walk northwest from Comitán's zócalo: follow Avenida Central Nte for about 2km until you reach the church of Santa Teresita on the right, recognizable by its two tall bell towers. The road immediately past the church to the right, signposted **Quija**, will lead you out of town into hilly farming country. The entrance to the site is on the left after 1500m. Hundreds of steps lead up to a flat-topped pyramid, flanked by two smaller structures. The best time to visit is early or late in the day to avoid the heat. Views are superb and it is said you can see Chinkultic (see p.172), 45km to the southeast. Combis from the zócalo run along the road to Quija; ask at the tourist office for times.

   **Tenam Puente** (daily 8am–5pm; free) is a much larger site, a few kilometres off the Carretera Interamericana, 15km to the south of Comitán. A bus leaves for the *ejido* of **Francisco Sarabia** from 3 Ote Nte in Comitán at 8.30am, but you can take any bus heading south and get off at the junction 11km further on, then hitch or walk the 3km to the village. People here are friendly and will direct you to the ruins, which lie 1km beyond the school and playground. The path is sometimes difficult to find among the bushes and cornfields, but you'll soon see stone terraces and mounds, and eventually several large structures, including a 20m pyramid. There are pleasant walks in the forested hills around here, but you'll need to take water.

# Comitán to Lagos de Montebello

The **Parque Nacional Lagos de Montebello** stretches along the border with Guatemala down to the southeast of Comitán, beautiful wooded country in which there are more than fifty lakes, sixteen of them very large. The combination of pine forest and lakes is reminiscent of Scotland or Maine, with miles of hiking potential. You could see quite a bit of the park in a long day-trip – buses cover the route all day from 5am, with the last bus leaving the park entrance around 7.30pm – but to really enjoy the beautiful lakes and forest, and to visit the small but spectacular **ruins of Chinkultic**, you're better off staying in or near the park.

   The road leading to the national park turns off the Carretera Interamericana 16km from Comitán at the village of **La Trinitaria**, with the park entrance 36km further on. Once in the park this road becomes the **Carretera Fronteriza** – roughly following the line of the Guatemalan border and paved all the way to **Palenque**. Transportes Lagos de Montebello buses from Comitán cover the whole route in about ten hours and you can visit Yaxchilán and Bonampak (see pp.149 & 146) on the way. In the recent past, there were frequent **army checkpoints** along this road and you may still be asked for your passport at any time. The soldiers are invariably polite but make sure your tourist card is valid.

## Accommodation along the road to the park

The most comfortable of the several **places to stay** along the road is the *Parador Museo Santa María*, about 18km from the Trinitaria junction then 2km along a dirt track on the right (☎ & fax 9/678-0988; ⑥). A former hacienda, it's a lovely place furnished with antiques and oil paintings and full of period atmosphere, but with hot water and electricity. Another 12km brings you to a cluster of budget accommodation – buses and combis will stop right outside. First, just a kilometre or so past the turning for

Chinkultic (below), there's the *Hospedaje La Orquidea* (②), better known simply as *Doña María's*. Here half a dozen simple cabins with electric light and very basic shared cold showers are set among the pines. It's a very *simpatico* place, run by Doña María Domínguez, who gave a lot of help and support to the Guatemalan refugees who fled here in the 1980s. Next door, and a step above in comfort, *Pino Feliz* (③) has rooms in wooden cabins with shared, hot-water showers. Owner Roberta Alborres cooks good, simple meals and César Castellanos can guide you on foot or on horseback to lakes and caves you'd never find on your own. Half a kilometre past here on the right, the *Restaurant and Cabañas La Palapa* (③) has a couple of pleasant cabañas and rooms in an A-frame house, all with shared hot showers.

## The ruins of Chinkultic

Just before *Doña María's* on the Lagos de Montebello road, a 2km track leads off to the left to the Classic period Maya ruins of **CHINKULTIC** (US$2). So far only a relatively small proportion of the site has been cleared and restored, but it's well worth a visit if only for the dramatic setting. Climb the first large mound, and you're rewarded with a view of a small lake, with fields of maize beyond and forested mountain ridges in the background. Birds, butterflies and dragonflies abound, and small lizards dart at every step. A ball-court and several *stelae* have been uncovered, but the highlight is undoubtedly the view from the top of the tallest structure, **El Mirador**. Set on top of a steep hill, with rugged cliffs dropping straight down to a cenote, the temple occupies a commanding position; though peaceful now, this was clearly an important hub in ancient times.

## Park practicalities

The park entrance is less than 4km past the budget cabaña places, and most combis terminate a few kilometres beyond the entrance at the **park headquarters**. On the way you'll pass some of the more accessible and picturesque lakes including the **Laguna de Siete Colores**, lent different tints by natural mineral deposits. At the headquarters, overlooking Laguna Bosque Azul, the **restaurant**, *Bosque Azul*, has a very basic cabaña (②) and there's a free **campsite** on the lakeshore. The small river flowing out of the lake (head for the bridge signed "paso de soldaldo") passes through an exquisitely beautiful, jungle-lined gorge and under a massive natural **limestone arch** before disappearing into a cave beneath a cliff face. Small boys will greet you and offer to guide you to the *grutas*; though you won't really need their help, they are friendly and do have a genuine interest in showing the caves to visitors. Scrawny **horses** are available for hire from behind the restaurant.

## Tziscao and the Carretera Fronteriza east

Just inside the park entrance, the paved Carretera Fronteriza turns off to the right. Still inside the park boundaries, it passes the village of **TZISCAO**, a tiny settlement on the shore of Laguna Tziscao. On the lake's edge here is the *Hotel and Restaurant Tziscao* (③), with simple, good-value rooms and wooden cabins. You can rent boats on the lake and follow the foot trail around the water. Along the way you pass **Laguna Internacional**, where the border is marked by a white obelisk at either end of the lake: **entering Guatemala** here is *not* recommended. Beyond Tziscao, the Carretera Fronteriza (served by buses from Comitán) winds through mountains with some spectacular views and precipitous drops, but the jungle has now all been cut down and burnt and the area is becoming heavily settled. After several hours the road climbs a steep limestone ridge and passes through an impressive tunnel before dropping down to the village of **Ixcán**, at the confluence of the Ixcán and Jataté rivers; downstream of here they form the Río Lacantún, eventually flowing into the Usumacinta.

A new tourism project here, *Estación Ixcán* (⑥, ② for camping), enables you to visit the southern **Montes Azules Bisophere Reserve**. The brainchild of US-based Conservation International, the project aims to promote conservation by developing economic alternatives to cutting down the forest. The *Estación* is beautifully located on the far bank of the Río Jataté, above some rapids in the turquoise river. **Accommodation** is in screened, shared-bath rooms (some with balcony) in a large thatched building and there's also limited space for **camping**. Meals are taken in the unscreened dining room overlooking the river – and you'll be swatting insects as you eat. Local guides can take you along the impressive, jungle-lined rivers and show you the forest wildlife. Though you could just turn up in Ixcán and find a boat to take you downstream from the village (ask for Don Oscar, who heads the tourism committee), it's best to book ahead by calling the office in Tuxtla (☎ & fax 9/613-9776, *cimextg@prodigy.net.mx*).

Beyond Ixcán the highway crosses the Río Ixcán on a new bridge high above the river and continues to **Benemérito** (3hr; see p.150). Be aware that this route traverses the "conflict zone" (see p.139) and you may well be stopped by the army or even forbidden to proceed.

## Ciudad Cuauhtémoc and the Guatemalan border

A visit to the Lagos de Montebello is a good introduction to the landscapes of Guatemala, but if you want to see the real thing, it's only another 60km or so from the La Trinitaria junction (plenty of passing buses) to the **Mexican border post** at CIUDAD CUAUHTÉMOC. There's little here but a few houses, the immigration post, a restaurant and the Cristóbal Colón bus station; the two **hotels** are not recommended. Make sure you've been to a bank in Mexico to pay the Mexican **immigration fee** (see below) before you leave the country, otherwise the officials will turn you back. There's nowhere to change money on the Mexican side (though you could try asking a taxi driver); **moneychangers** on the Guatemalan side will give you reasonable rates for travellers' cheques or US dollars, not as good for pesos.

The **Guatemalan border post** is at **La Mesilla**, a 3km taxi ride away (about US$0.50 per person in a shared taxi). As always, the crossing is best attempted in daylight and you may not be able to get your passport stamped after 8pm. If you require a **visa**, you should really have got one before now: chances are you'll be let in if you agree to pay the entry charge, which could be as much as US$10. And the La Mesilla border post has been one of the worst in the country for exacting illegal charges from tourists. For information about **onward transport** and **hotels** see p.406.

# The Chiapas Coast

Highway 200 provides a fast route from the Oaxaca border to Guatemala, with little to detain you on the way. **Arriaga**, the first town on the Chiapas coast road, is a dusty, totally uninteresting place, but its location at the junction of Hwy-195 (the road over the mountains to Tuxtla) means you may have to change buses here. **Tonalá**, larger and marginally more inviting, is just a thirty-minute bus ride away down Hwy-200, though if you want to break your journey you're better off heading to the beach at **Puerto Arista**.

Continuing south, the highway traverses the steamy coastal plain of the **Soconusco**, running about 20km inland, with the 2400m peaks of the **Sierra Madre de Chiapas** always in view. The plain itself is a fertile agricultural area, mainly given over to coffee and bananas, though there are also many ranches, where cattle grow fat on the lush grass.

**Tapachula** is the main city along this part of the coast, and with good connections to the border you can speed straight on, pausing only to change buses, or possibly to visit the ruins of **Izapa**, right by the roadside. It's not a bad place to spend the night, however, with several inexpensive hotels, and from here you can easily reach the cool coffee country around the delightful hill town of **Unión Juárez**, nestled at the foot of **Volcán Tacaná**, the highest peak in Chiapas.

## Puerto Arista

Although this quiet village may not be everyone's idea of a perfect beach resort, **PUERTO ARISTA**, with its miles of clean sand and invigorating surf, does offer a chance to escape the unrelenting heat of the inland towns. There's little to see, and you have to stay under the shade of a *palapa* near the shore to benefit from the breezes, but it's a worthwhile stop if you've been travelling. While the waves are definitely refreshing, you need to be aware of the potentially dangerous **rip tides** that sweep along the coast – never get out of your depth. Combis and taxis to Puerto Arista (US$0.50) leave Tonalá at least every twenty minutes (or when full) from the corner of 5 de Mayo and Matamoros, a couple of blocks south of the zócalo in the market area, where the streets are crammed with fruit and vegetable stalls.

The road from Tonalá joins Puerto Arista's only street at the **lighthouse**, which is the centre of town. Walk a couple of kilometres left or right and you'll be on a deserted shoreline; ahead lies the beach, with **hotels** and inexpensive *palapa* **restaurants** packed closely together. It won't feel crowded, though, unless you arrive in Semana Santa, as there seem to be at least as many buildings abandoned or boarded up as there are occupied. **Prices** are difficult to determine and most places try to overcharge. The best bet is to have a *refresco* or a cold beer at a restaurant and ask if you can leave your bags while you have a good look around. The cheaper places are basic and not particularly good value; bargain with the owner and you may be able to knock the price down.

### Accommodation

Turn right at the lighthouse to find *La Puesta del Sol* (④), the *Brisas del Mar* (④) and the *Agua Marina* (④). These don't have phones but they are clean and well run, with some private bathrooms, but the best hotel here is the *Arista Bugambilias* (☎ & fax 9/663-0767 ext. 116; ⑦), with rooms and suites around a pool and private garden right on the beach. Turn left at the lighthouse, and you'll see signs for more hotels and basic cabaña places. The *Lucero* (☎9/663-01827 ext. 152; ⑥), just back from the beach, is a relative bargain, with tiled rooms and suites with a/c and a pool. Walk a few hundred metres beyond here and you'll come to *José's Camping and Cabañas*, (☎9/664-9982, ④) the friendliest place in Puerto Arista and a great place for budget travellers. Run by José (originally from Canada) and his wife Petriy, the well-built brick and thatched bungalows, each with comfortable beds, electric light and a flower-filled patio with hammocks, are a perfect place to relax; the food is wonderful and there's a pool. The shared bathrooms are great. There are also several **camping** places (①) among the coconut trees.

### Tonalá to Tapachula

With your own vehicle, you can explore some of the side roads leading from Hwy-200 in the 220km between Tonalá and Tapachula, further south: either up into the mountains, where the heavy rain gives rise to dozens of rivers and waterfalls, or down to almost deserted beaches. Travelling by bus, it's much more difficult (though still possible) to take in destinations off the main road, and you need to be prepared to hitch and camp. At **HUIXTLA**, 42km before Tapachula, Hwy-211 snakes over the mountains via Motozintla to join the Carretera Interamericana near Ciudad Cuauhtémoc and the Guatemalan border at **La Mesilla** (see p.406). This boneshaking road offers stupendous mountain views and is covered by buses running between Tapachula, Comitán and San Cristóbal.

Most coastal villages are actually on the landward side of a narrow lagoon, separated from the ocean by a sandbar. These sandbars block many rivers' access to the sea, causing marshes to form and providing a superb wetland habitat, the highlight of which is an **ecological reserve** protecting 45km of coastline near **Acacoyagua**. For thousands of years, from at least 3000 BC until the Spanish Conquest, these estuaries and lagoons, connected by canals, formed a safe inland waterway stretching from Oaxaca to western Guatemala; one of the richest trade routes in Mesoamerica.

## Tapachula

Though most travellers see it as no more than an overnight stop en route to or from Guatemala, **TAPACHULA** does actually have something to offer, being a gateway to both the coast and the mountains, with a lovely setting at the foot of the 4000m Volcán Tacaná. A busy commercial centre, known as the capital of the Soconusco, the southeastern region of the state, it grew in importance in the nineteenth century with the increasing demand for coffee and bananas. Being a border city, it has a lively cultural mix, including not just immigrants from Central America, but also small German and Chinese communities. The **Museo Regional de Soconusco** (Tues–Sun 10am–5pm; US$0.50), in the same building as the tourist office, tells their story, as well as displaying scraps of excavated finds from local ruins.

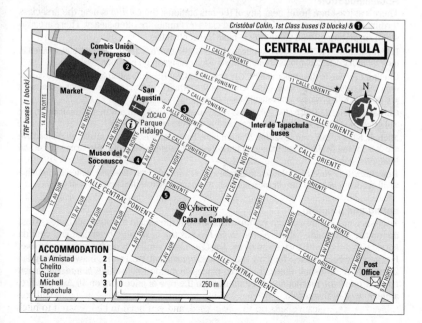

CENTRAL TAPACHULA

Cristóbal Colón, 1st Class buses (3 blocks) & ➊

Combis Unión y Progreso ➋

Market

San Agustín ➌

ZÓCALO
Parque Hidalgo

Inter de Tapachula buses

Museo del Soconusco ➍

@ Cybercity
Casa de Cambio ➎

TRF buses (1 block)

11 CALLE PONIENTE
9 CALLE PONIENTE
7 CALLE PONIENTE
5 CALLE PONIENTE
3 CALLE PONIENTE
1 CALLE PONIENTE
CALLE CENTRAL PONIENTE

11 CALLE ORIENTE
9 CALLE ORIENTE
7 CALLE ORIENTE
5 CALLE ORIENTE
3 CALLE ORIENTE
1 CALLE ORIENTE
CALLE CENTRAL ORIENTE

14 AV NORTE
12 AV NORTE
10 AV NORTE
8 AV NORTE
6 AV NORTE
4 AV NORTE
2 AV NORTE
AV CENTRAL NORTE

12 AV SUR
10 AV SUR
8 AV SUR
6 AV SUR
4 AV SUR
2 AV SUR

Post Office

**ACCOMMODATION**

| | |
|---|---|
| La Amistad | 2 |
| Chelito | 1 |
| Guizar | 5 |
| Michell | 3 |
| Tapachula | 4 |

0    250 m

## Arrival and information

The city's layout is a little confusing, for while the streets are laid out in the regular numbered grid common in Chiapas, the zócalo, **Parque Hidalgo**, is not at its centre. It's not too far away, though: Calle Central meets Avenida Central three blocks east and a block south of the zócalo. All the main **bus stations** are north of the centre; the various second-class companies have their terminals within walking distance of the zócalo, while first-class Cristóbal Colón (also the terminal for international buses from Guatemala) is further out at 17 C Ote between avenidas 1 and 3 Nte. A taxi to the centre costs US$1.25 and walking takes about twenty minutes. Tapachula's **airport**, 18km south on the road to Puerto Madero, is served by several national airlines with flights to México.

The **tourist office** (daily 9am–3pm & 6–9pm; ☎9/626-1884, ext. 100) is on the ground floor of the old Palacio Municipal, on the west side of the zócalo. There's usually someone who speaks English and the helpful staff will give you a city map, call a hotel for you and advise on tour guides to local attractions. The **post office** (Mon–Fri 8am–6pm, Sat 8am–1pm) is a long way southeast of the zócalo at 1 C Ote, between avenidas 7 and 9 Nte. The main **banks** are one block east of the zócalo, but for **changing cash** and travellers' cheques you'll get a much quicker service from Casa de Cambio Santa, 2 Av Nte 9, between Calle Central and 1 C Pte (Mon–Fri 9am–5pm, Sat 9am–2pm); you can also get Guatemalan quetzales here. Nearby, at 2 Av Nte 7, is *Cybercity*, one the best **Internet and email** locations in Tapachula. If you need a **Guatemalan visa**, the **consulate** is at 2 C Ote 33, between avenidas 7 and 9 Sur (Mon–Fri 8am–4pm; ☎9/626-1252). And for tickets on the international buses to Guatemala try Viajes Tapachula at Av Central Nte 42 (☎9/625-1345).

## Accommodation

There's at least one **hotel** near any of the bus stations; the *Chelito* is near the first-class terminal but the ones around the second-class terminals are often sleazy. There are also some surprisingly good-value hotels near the centre, too.

**La Amistad**, 7 C Pte 34, between avenidas 10 and 12 Nte (☎9/626-2293). The best budget hotel in the city, with clean, cool rooms around a flower-filled courtyard. Free drinking water. ③.

**Chelito**, 1 Av Nte at the corner of 17 C Ote (☎9/626-2428). Handy location just around the corner from the Cristóbal Colón buses (head left out of the terminal), with clean tiled rooms (some with a/c and TV) with private bath; restaurant and parking. ④.

**Guizar**, 4 Av Nte 27 (☎9/62/6-1400). Good-value, modern rooms with private bath, some with a/c and cable TV. There's an elevator, a breezy sitting area upstairs and a bar. ④.

**Michell**, 5 C Pte 23A (☎9/625-2640). Modern hotel half a block east of the zócalo; all rooms have a/c and TV and doubles have balconies, but access is up a steep flight of stairs. Accepts Visa and Mastercard. ⑤.

**Tapachula**, 6 Av Nte 18, off the southwest corner of the zócalo (☎9/626-4370). Entered through a small shop, this is one of the cheapest places in town; the rooms at the back are best. ②.

## Eating and drinking

There are more than enough **restaurants** around the zócalo to satisfy all tastes. Most are on the south side, where *Nuevo Doña Leo* has the best-value breakfast and comida corrida, together with tortas and tacos; *Los Comales* is similar, but a bit more expensive. For genuine **Soconusco** food try the *Fonda Tapachol*, at 1 C Pte 11, between avenidas 2 and 4 Nte. As usual, there are cheap places to eat and some fine *panaderías* to be found around the market area, beginning with the row of juice bars on 10 Avenida Pte, a block west of the zócalo.

PETER WILSON

JERRY DENNIS

Tulum, Quintana Roo, Mexico

El Caracol observatory, Chichén Itzá, Mexico

JERRY DENNIS

El Castillo, Chichén Itzá, Mexico

Coral and diver, Caribbean coast, Mexico

Belltower, Izamal, Mexico

Maize harvest, Chajul, Guatemala

Pyramid of the Magician, Uxmal, Mexico

Fiesta costume, Guatemala

Temple of Five Storeys, Edzná, Mexico

Main plaza and Agua volcano, Antigua, Guatemala

Maya fiddle player, Mexico

House of the Serpent Mouth, Chicanná

Vallodolid cenote, Yucatán, Mexico

---

**MOVING ON FROM TAPACHULA**

**First-class buses** for destinations throughout Mexico leave from the Cristóbal Colón terminal; any bus or combi from the centre to Talismán passes the entrance. Some of the better second-class services also leave from here. If you're heading directly to Guatemala City you can take advantage of the daily luxury Galgos (10am & 3pm) or Línea Dorada (2pm) services which leave from here and take you right through the border (US$24; 5–6hr) and you can buy tickets from most travel agencies. To save you going back to the terminal, you can buy most first-class bus tickets from Multi Pack, 8 Av Nte 4 (☎9/626-6982). All first-class and most second-class buses to Tuxtla (for San Cristóbal) head up the coast via Arriaga.

The main **second-class bus operators** are TRF, at the corner of 16 Av Nte Pte and 3 C Nte Pte, for the coast as far as Salina Cruz and Tuxtla; Inter de Tapachula, 7 Pte between 2 Calle and Central Nte, for the coast road and Ciudad Hidalgo on the Guatemalan border. Unión y Progreso, 5 C Pte between avenidas 12 and 14 Nte, runs frequent combis to Unión Juárez and to the Talismán Bridge for the Guatemalan border.

---

## The ruins of Izapa

Though the road to the border passes right through the archeological site of **IZAPA** (daily 9am—5pm, US$1), few visitors bother to stop, which is a pity, since as well as being easy to get to, the site is large – with more than eighty temple mounds – and important for its evidence of both the Olmec and early Maya cultures. Izapa culture, in fact, is seen as a transitional stage between the Olmecs and the glories of the Classic Maya period. Even though many of the best carved monuments have been removed to museums, including the Anthropology Museum in Mexico City, you can still see early versions of the rain god Chac and others in elaborate bas-relief on altars. Founded before 1250 BC, Izapa continued to flourish throughout the Maya Preclassic period, until around 300 AD; most of what remains is from the later period, perhaps around 200 AD, and the site continued to be occupied until the Postclassic.

The **northern side** of the site (left of the road as you head to the border) is more accessible than the southern half. There's a ball court, and several *stelae*, which, though not Olmec in origin, are carved in a recognizable Olmec style, similar to monuments at other early Maya sites. The **southern side**, down a track about 1km back along the main road, is a good deal more overgrown, but you can spot altars with animal carvings – frogs, snakes and jaguars – and several unexcavated mounds. To **get there**, take any bus or combi to the Talismán border and ask the driver to drop you at the site, which is signposted from the road.

## Unión Juárez

The small town of **UNIÓN JUÁREZ**, 43km from Tapachula and perched on the flank of the Volcán Tacaná at a height of over 1100m, offers a chance to escape the heat of the lowlands. Unión Juárez is almost on the Guatemalan border and hikers can obtain permission here to cross on foot at Talquián, 10km north. There are also some excellent **day-hikes** to waterfalls and, with a guide, you can even reach the volcano's summit, at 4092m the highest point in Chiapas. This is a two- to three-day trip, with a cabin to sleep in at the top, though you'll need to bring a warm sleeping bag at least. The journey from Tapachula follows the valley of the **Río Suchiate**, which forms the border with Guatemala.

**Buses** and combis for Unión Juárez leave at least every twenty minutes from the Unión y Progreso terminal in Tapachula. As the road climbs up the lush green valley the bananas and *cacao* give way to coffee and you begin to enjoy good views of two majestic volcanoes; Tacaná itself, and the 4220 metre peak of Tajumulco, the highest mountain in Guatemala. At **CACAHOATÁN**, the halfway point, you change to a *combi* run by Transportes Tacaná, across the street from the Unión y Progreso station – the whole journey takes around one hour twenty minutes and costs about US$1.50.

The area around Unión Juárez is of the best coffee-growing areas in Chiapas and on the way up, a few kilometres before Unión Juárez, you pass the restored coffee plantation house of **Santo Domingo**, built in the 1920s. The three-storey wooden house with balconies all around and set in a beautiful garden with a pool was the home of the coffee baron Enrique Braun Hansen, whose German origins are reflected in the building's architectural style – early American meets Alpine hotel, with predominantly Art Nouveau interiors. Now part of a successful community tourism project, there's a good restaurant on the ground floor and above is a (free) **museum of coffee**. Across the road the *Hotel Santo Domingo* (☎9/629-9073, *fonmicro.rtn.net.mx*; ④) is a really good-value **place to stay**, with spacious rooms with comfortable beds and private bath around a patio garden.

Unión Juárez itself has two **hotels**: the budget but comfortable *Posada Aljoad*, half a block off the west side of the zócalo (☎9/647-2025; ④), which has neat rooms with private bath around a courtyard and a good inexpensive restaurant; and the larger, good-value *Hotel Colonial Campestre*, which you pass as you enter the town (☎9/647-2000, fax 647-2015; ⑤). Rooms and suites here are comfortable and spacious, with solid wooden furniture, en-suite bathrooms and TV. Ask the owner, Don José Antonio Valera, about his autobiography *Aroma de Café Armargo*; he'll be happy to discuss it over local coffee and cake. His son, Fernando, is an excellent guide if you want to tackle the track to the summit. The *Campestre* has a good **restaurant**, *La Suiza Chiapaneca*, while on the north side of the attractive plaza, the *Carmelita* and *La Montaña* are also good, inexpensive places where you can sit outside and enjoy views of **Pico de Loro**, a steep, rocky outcrop looking indeed like a parrot's beak. Combis leave for Cacahoatán (and Tapachula) from the east side of the plaza (every 15min until 8pm; 9pm from Cacahoatán).

## The Guatemalan border: the Talismán Bridge and Ciudad Hidalgo

Both of these southern crossing points are easy places to enter Guatemala, but the **Talismán Bridge** is closer to Tapachula and better for onward connections. From Tapachula, combis (operated by Unión y Progreso) run frequently (taking about 30min), passing the Cristóbal Colón bus station on the way. **Leaving Mexico** the officials will check if you've paid your **immigration fee** at a bank – if not you'll be sent back as they don't accept payment.

In theory there's a small toll to pay to cross the bridge, but the **Guatemalan immigration** procedure is generally trouble-free. For those who need a visa, there's a **Guatemalan consulate** in Tapachula. **Changing money** is best done in Tapachula (see p.175), but there's no shortage of moneychangers at the border, and you'll get only a slightly less favourable rate.

There are several basic **hotels** and **restaurants** at the border, though there's much better accommodation in Tapachula. Heading **onwards**, Guatemala City is about five to six hours away: there's usually a bus waiting, otherwise, take a bus or van to **Malacatán** and continue from there. The best way though is to take one of the international bus services from Tapachula to Guatemala City. Travelling **into Mexico** you'll be given a tourist card at immigration and there's no shortage of combis to Tapachula and plenty of first-class buses from Tapachula onwards. You'll probably have your passport checked many times along Hwy-200, so be prepared.

Further south, the border town of **CIUDAD HIDALGO** is a very busy road crossing and the point where the railway enters Guatemala, but it's less convenient if you're travelling by bus. There's a **casa de cambio** (and freelance moneychangers) at the corner of Av Central and C Central Sur, and several **hotels**; the *Hospedaje La Favorita*, Calle Central Ote (③), is best. Plenty of willing locals offer to pedal you across the Puente Rodolfo Robles to **Ciudad Tecún Umán** in Guatemala (see p.408), but it's an easy walk. Cristóbal Colón runs a **bus** from Ciudad Hidalgo to Mexico City daily at 6pm, but it's much easier to take a bus or combi to Tapuchula (45min) and change there – there's almost always one waiting by the casa de cambio.

# TABASCO

The state of **Tabasco**, crossed by numerous slow-moving tropical rivers on their way to the Gulf, is at last making determined efforts to attract tourists. These rivers were used as trade highways by the ancient **Olmec**, **Maya** and **Zoque** cultures, and the state boasts dozens of **archeological sites**. Few of these pre-Columbian cities have been fully excavated, though **Comalcalco**, a Maya site north of Villahermosa, and the Olmec site of **La Venta** northwest of the capital have been expertly restored and are certainly worth visiting. A trip to the restored Zoque site of **Malpasito**, in the remote Sierra Huimanguillo and easily the most attractive ancient city in the state, is perhaps more difficult on your own but even more rewarding.

Tabasco's **coast**, alternating between estuaries and sandbars, salt marshes and lagoons, is off the beaten track to most visitors. A road runs very close to the shore, however, enabling you to reach the deserted beaches, which as yet have somewhat limited facilities. Much of inland Tabasco is very flat, consisting of the flood plains of a dozen or so major rivers; indeed, most of the state's borders are waterways. You can travel by river into the Petén in **Guatemala**, leaving from La Palma, near **Tenosique**, in the far eastern corner of the state and near the Classic Maya site of **Pomoná**.

**Villahermosa**, the state capital and an almost unavoidable stop, has undergone an amazing transformation in recent decades, with oil wealth financing the creation of spacious parks and several museums – the city at last lives up to its name. One excellent example is the **Parque Museo La Venta**, an outdoor archeological exhibition on the bank of a lagoon, which provides the most accessible glimpse of the Olmec civilization.

In the far south of the state, around **Teapa** and Villa Luz, the Chiapas highlands make their presence known in the foothills of the **Sierra Puana**. Waterfalls spill down from the mountains, and village tracks provide some great **hiking trails**. A few small spas (*balnearios*) have developed and, despite the proximity to Villahermosa, you can enjoy a respite from the well-travelled tourist circuit.

## Some history

Little is know about the **Olmec culture**, referred to by many archeologists as the mother culture of Mesoamerica. Its legacy of the Long Count calendar, glyphic writing, a rain god deity – and probably also the concept of zero and the ball game – influenced all subsequent civilizations in ancient Mexico, and the fact that it developed and flourished in the unpromising environment of the Gulf coast swamps 3200 years ago only adds to its mystery.

The Spanish conquistador **Hernan Cortés** landed at the mouth of the Río Grijalva in 1519, and at first easily defeated the local **Chontal Maya**. However, the town he founded, Santa María de la Victoria, was beset first by indigenous attacks and then by pirates, eventually forcing a move to the present site and a change of name to Villahermosa de San Juan Bautista in 1596. For most of the colonial period, Tabasco remained a relative backwater, since the Spanish found the humid, insect-ridden swamps distinctly inhospitable. **Independence** did little to improve matters as local leaders fought among themselves, and it took the **French invasion** of 1862 and Napoleon III's imposition of the unfortunate Maximilian as emperor of Mexico to bring some form of unity, with Tabasco offering fierce resistance to this foreign intrusion.

The industrialization of the country during the dictatorship of Porfirio Díaz passed agricultural Tabasco by, and even after the **Revolution** it was still a poor state, dependent on cacao and bananas. Though **Tomás Garrido Canabal**, Tabasco's governor in the 1920s and 1930s, is still respected as a reforming socialist whose implementation of laws regarding workers' rights and women's suffrage was decades ahead of the rest of the country, his period in office was also marked by intense **anticlericalism**. Priests were killed or driven out, all the churches were closed, and many of them, including the cathedral in Villahermosa, torn down. The region's **oil**, discovered in the 1930s but not fully exploited until the 1970s, provided the impetus to bring Tabasco into the modern world, enabling capital to be invested in the agricultural sector and Villahermosa to be transformed into the cultural centre it is today.

# Villahermosa and around

**VILLAHERMOSA**, the state capital, is a major and virtually unavoidable road junction: you're almost bound to pass through here on the way from central Mexico to the Yucatán or back, especially if you hope to see Palenque (see p.138), and it's a good base from which to visit the ruins of **Comalcalco** and **La Venta** (see pp.184 and 186).

It's a large and prosperous city, and at first impression it can seem as bad a case of urban blight as any in Mexico. However, the longer you stay, the more compensations you discover: quite apart from the **Parque La Venta** and sudden vistas of the broad sweep of the **Río Grijalva**, there are attractive plazas and quiet ancient streets, impressive ultra-modern buildings and several new art galleries and museums. In the evening, as the traffic disperses and the city cools down, its appeal is heightened, and strolling the pedestrianized streets around the *Zona Remodelada*, where everything stays open late, becomes a genuine pleasure. This lively area, between the two main squares, the **Parque Juárez** and the **Plaza de Armas**, is also known as *Zona Luz* – or simply *La Zona*.

## Arrival, orientation and information

The Aeropuerto Carlos A. Rovirosa, east of the centre at Carretera Villahermosa–Palenque, Km 13, is a very busy regional **airport**, the nearest one to Palenque. No buses run to the centre; a taxi will cost around US$8. Arriving **by bus** you'll find things are pretty hectic as the highway thunders through the concrete outskirts of town, past the two stations. They are fairly close to each other: second-class a busy, ramshackle affair actually on the highway with constant departures to main destinations; first-class (known simply as El ADO – pronounced *El ah-day-oh*) an efficient modern building just off the highway on Javiér Mina. There's a guardería here (daily 7am–8pm), and you'd be well advised to buy your outward ticket on arrival, partly because it can be hard to get a seat on some departing buses, partly to avoid having to come back here more than necessary. Villahermosa's humidity might make you consider taking **taxis** more frequently – worthwhile as the set fare in the city is only US$1.25 and plenty of combis ply the main streets. The city seems confusing at first, but you soon get to know the destinations, and the drivers and fellow passengers are helpful.

The easiest way **from El ADO to the centre** is to take a colectivo taxi from outside the terminal. There are also combis aplenty – look out for those labelled "Parque Juárez" or "Malecón". Otherwise, it's at least twenty minutes' walk to town: head up Merino or

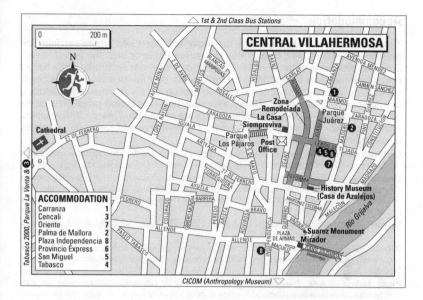

Fuentes, opposite the station, for six or seven long blocks, and then turn right at Madero, past most of the budget hotels. To get from El ADO to the second-class terminal, turn left on Mina, walk three blocks down to the highway, Blvd Adolfo Ruíz Cortines, turn right and cross it on the overpass – you can't miss the terminal. There are fewer taxis from **the second-class terminal** but combis are plentiful; it's not easy to work out where they're going – you want one heading along Madero, for example, or to CICOM – but asking a local is the best way to find out. If you want to walk, cross the road by the footbridge, turn left and follow the highway to its junction with Madero, then head right.

### Information

Despite the growth in visitor numbers Villahermosa's **tourist information** remains inadequate. The small booths at the airport and at El ADO can offer only a jumble of hotel leaflets, and the main state and federal **tourist office** (Mon–Fri 9am–3pm & 6–9pm; ☎9/316-3633), near the modern **Tabasco 2000** shopping and business complex at the junction of Paseo Tabasco and Avenida de los Ríos, is too far away from the centre to be of much use. It does have some excellent booklets and maps, though, but you're often charged for stuff usually given away free elsewhere. There's also a small tourist information office at the entrance to the Parque La Venta – again you might have to pay.

There are branches of all major **banks** at the airport and in the centre, on Madero or Juárez, and you can easily change cash and travellers' cheques. The main **post office** is in the *Zona Remodelada* at the corner of Sáenz and Lerdo (Mon–Fri 8am–7.30pm). **Internet cafés** are a boom industry here, with at least ten in the *Zona Luz*. Most are a great bargain – try *Naveghalia*, run by the friendly Marín family at Lerdo 608, up the steps past the Casa Siempreviva. There's no shortage of **travel agencies** in *La Zona* either, and all the big hotels have a tour desk to arrange domestic flights and trips to Palenque. Creatur, Paseo Tabasco 715 (☎9/315-3999, *creatur@inforedmx.com.mx*), is the best in the region, with multilingual staff.

# Accommodation

There are plenty of **budget hotels** in the centre and, if you look around carefully, you can find somewhere both comfortable and reasonable in or near the pedestrianized *Zona Luz*, with some of the best options on Madero or Lerdo de Tejada. Many budget places have rooms on several floors but often no lift; bear this in mind as you're sweating with the humidity. Several now have an a/c option and it's always worth checking if free drinking water is available. There's a very good selection of **mid-range** hotels in the centre too, though the most **upmarket** hotels are around the Tabasco 2000 complex. Along Constitución, a block from the river, it's possible to find rooms for very little, though the very cheapest are distinctly dodgy.

**Carranza**, Carranza 806, just off Parque Juárez (☎9/315-9522). Worth checking out as most rooms are modern, with tiled private baths, and some have a/c and TV. Café and parking. ⑤.

**Cencali**, Paseo Tabasco and Juárez (☎9/315-1999, *www.cencali.com.mx*). The best-value hotel in this upmarket area, set in luxuriant gardens on the shore of a lagoon, the *Cencali* has a quiet location and an inviting pool. Comfortable, well-furnished a/c rooms and suites with beautiful tiled bathrooms; upstairs rooms have balconies. ⑧.

**Oriente**, Madero 425 (☎9/312-1101). Good-value, clean, tiled rooms with private bath, some with a/c and TV; drinking water available. ③/④.

**Palma de Mallorca**, Madero 510 (☎9/312-0144). Good budget option, with large rooms, some with a/c, clean private bathrooms with hot water, bedside lights and comfortable sitting areas on the landings. ③/④.

**Plaza Independencia**, Independencia 123 (☎9/312-1299, *villahermosa@hotelesplaza.com.mx*). Comfortable, well-furnished rooms and suites at good prices in a quiet area just off the zócalo. There's a lift, a pool, a good restaurant, a bar with live music and secure parking. ⑥/⑦.

**Provincio Express**, Lerdo de Tejada 303 (☎9/314-5376, *villaop@prodigy.net*). New, very clean hotel right in the *Zona Luz*. All rooms have a/c, private bath, TV and phone. ⑤.

**San Miguel**, Lerdo de Tejada 315 (☎9/312-1500). Battered but serviceable rooms (some with a/c and TV) with clean sheets, private bath and bedside lights. ③/④.

**Tabasco**, Lerdo de Tejada 317 (☎9/312-0077). Basic but good value, and plenty of room. ②.

# The City

Though most visitors quite rightly head straight out to the **Parque La Venta**, the centre of Villahermosa warrants some exploration. The pedestrianized **Zona Remodelada**, with some vestiges of the nineteenth-century city, is as good a place as any to start your wandering. At its northern end the bustling **Parque Juárez**, at the junction of Madero and Zaragoza, is lively in the evenings as crowds swirl around watching the street entertainers. Opposite, on Madero, the **Centro Cultural de Villahermosa** (daily 10am–9pm; free) has changing exhibitions of art, photography and costume, as well as being a venue for films and concerts, with a good café too. The zócalo, the **Plaza de Armas**, with its river views, is a pleasant place to while away some time, especially in the cool of the evening when there may also be some music on offer. Here, the imposing white-painted **Palacio del Gobierno**, with classical columns, turreted corners and an attractive clock tower, faces the pretty little church of La Concepción. On the corner of the zócalo the **Puente Solidaridad** footbridge over the Grijalva has an enormous mirador for splendid views at sunset.

### The city-centre museums

In the centre of the *Zona*, on the corner of Sáenz and Lerdo, the distinctive pink and purple paintwork of **La Casa Siempreviva**, dating from the early 1900s, immediately catches the eye. Now a free gallery with a small café, it's one of the few fully restored houses from that era, with tiled floors, stained-glass arched windows and some later Art

Deco features. In the 1930s it was home to journalist and women's rights activist Isabel Rullan, and in the 1940s it became Villahermosa's first hotel with private bathrooms. The side streets here boast a number of other small **art galleries** – look around for advertisements for current exhibitions. The steps at the far end of Lerdo lead up to the small, tree-shaded **Parque Los Pájaros**, where budgerigars sing in a large, wrought-iron arched cage and water flows through a series of blue-tiled fountains and pools.

Villahermosa's small **history museum**, at the corner of 27 de Febrero and Juárez (Tues–Sat 9am–8pm; US$0.75), gives a quirky, detailed account of Tabasco's history, illustrated by such diverse objects as an early X-ray machine, the printing press of *El Disidente* newspaper from 1863 and archeological pieces from Comalcalco and other information on the Maya sites. The turn-of-the-century museum building is popularly known as the "**Casa de Azulejos**" – and indeed there are tiles everywhere, forming an optical illusion in the lobby, with examples of patterns from all over Europe and the Middle East. Upstairs, wrought-iron balconies overlook the *Zona* – look up to see the statues of nymphs and classical figures perched on the railings around the roof.

## The CICOM complex

An easy walk along the riverbank from the *Zona Remodelada* brings you to Villahermosa's cultural centre, **CICOM** – Centro de Investigaciones de las Culturas Olmeca y Maya. The complex includes a concert hall, a beautiful theatre, a research library and a fine restaurant, along with the **Centro de Estudios y Investigación de los Belles Artes** (Tues–Sun 10am–4pm; free), which hosts art and costume displays. The highlight for most visitors is undoubtedly the **Museo Regional de Antropología Carlos Pellicer Cámara** (Tues–Sun 9am–6pm; US$1.50), with artefacts and models displayed on four levels, proceeding chronologically downwards from the top floor. In addition to the displays of Olmec and Maya ceramics and other artefacts (including a fascinating toy jaguar with wheels), you can also view a reproduction of the Bonampak murals. Carlos Pellicer, a poet and anthropologist born in Villahermosa, and the driving force behind the rescue of the stone carvings from the original La Venta, is commemorated by a bronze statue outside the complex. His house, at C Sáenz 203, in the *Zona Remodelada*, has also been turned into a museum – the **Carlos Pellicer Casa Museo** (daily 9am–8pm; free).

## Parque la Venta and the Museo de Historia Natural

Soon after they were discovered by Pemex engineers draining a marsh, most of the important finds from the Olmec **site of La Venta** (p.186) – some 120km west of Villahermosa – were transferred to the **Parque la Venta** (daily 9am–5pm; US$2, including **zoo**). Although hardly the exact reproduction it claims to be, Parque la Venta does give you a chance to see a superb collection of artefacts from the earliest Mexican civilization, on the shores of the Laguna de Ilusiones, in the beautiful jungly setting of the Parque Tomás Garrido Canabal.

You should visit the **museum** first, under an enormous thatched roof, to familiarize yourself with the known facts of the Olmec culture. The most significant and famous items are, of course, the gigantic **basalt heads**, which present such a curious puzzle with their flattened, negroid features. There's a whole series of other Olmec stone sculptures; follow the numbers as the path winds through the park. In their zeal to re-create an authentic jungle setting, the designers have deer and coatis (members of the raccoon family) wandering around freely, while crocodiles, jaguars, monkeys and others exist in sizeable enclosures. The mosquitoes are an authentic but unplanned touch.

Also in the park, opposite the entrance, the excellent **Museo de Historia Natural** (daily 9am–8pm; US$1) has displays on geography, geology, animals and plants. **Combis** run to the park from along Madero in the city centre ("Tabasco 2000", "Circuito 1", "Parque Linda Vista" among others) and also along the highway from the second-class bus terminal. Beyond La Venta, many of the buses continue to Tabasco 2000.

# Eating and drinking

The number of **restaurants** in Villahermosa has grown over the last few years, and some of the new ones are truly cosmopolitan. Most of the better hotels have good dining rooms and, if you're staying near Tabasco 2000, your hotel restaurant will be among the best in the city.

Both **bus stations** have plenty of food joints nearby. Inside the second-class there are juice and coffee bars, a good bread shop and a less good restaurant. Across the street from El ADO, there's a row of inexpensive places including the 24-hour *Noche y Día*. As ever, the **market** is good for fruit, bread and cheap tacos: you'll find it several blocks northeast of the *Zona Remodelada*, at Pino Suárez and Zaragoza.

The pedestrianized *Zona Luz* is filled with window-shoppers enjoying frozen yoghurts or eating out at open-fronted restaurants or one of the many *coctelerias*. There are plenty of places to enjoy a good cup of **coffee** here too: the *Café La Cabaña*, at the south end of Juárez near the Casa de los Azulejos, is good but pricey. In the opposite direction along Juárez, near the corner with Zaragoza, the *Café Casino* is almost as good and less expensive. In the centre, the *portales* on the west side of Madero house several good, inexpensive **taco restaurants**, while beyond here, at the junction of Paseo Tabasco and the malecón, are some more upmarket ones.

## Restaurants

**Aquarius**, Zaragoza 513, behind the Parque Juárez. Excellent vegetarian restaurant and health-food shop, with delicious fresh wholemeal sandwiches and daily specials.

**La Bodegita del Centro**, Lerdo, near the corner with Madero. The buffet here is one of the best options in the centre for an inexpensive, filling meal at lunchtime; select from a variety of taco fillings, washed down with *horchata*, a vanilla- or almond-flavoured rice drink.

**Bruno's**, corner of Lerdo and 5 de Mayo, facing the Parque los Pájaros. Authentic Mexican food and drink in a popular, often crowded, bar and restaurant whose walls are lined with fascinating old photographs.

**Café del Portal**, Independencia, facing the Plaza de Armas. Originally a theatre which first became a café in the 1940s, it's now a beautifully restored restaurant serving great coffee and complete meals under blue arches framed by bright yellow columns. Good breakfasts and a great Sunday brunch.

**Guaraguao**, corner of 27 de Febrero and Javiér Mina. The place to sample the best of *comida Tabasqueña*, serving specialities from the coasts and rivers of Tabasco. These include *pejelagarto*, a type of alligator gar (a pike-like freshwater fish), and great seafood. It closes early, though, about 8.30 or 9pm.

**El Torito Valenzuela**, corner of 27 de Febrero and Madero. Deservedly popular for filling tacos and tortas.

# Comalcalco

The Classic-period site of **Comalcalco** (daily 10am–5pm; US$2.50, including museum) is an easy, very worthwhile trip from Villahermosa, and you can be fairly sure of having the carefully tended ruins virtually to yourself. The westernmost Maya site, Comalcalco was occupied around the same time as Palenque (see p.138), with which it shares some features, and may even have been ruled by some of the same kings. The area's lack of building stone forced the Chontal Maya to adopt a distinctive, almost unique, form of construction – kiln-fired brick. As if the bricks themselves were not sufficient to mark this site as different, the builders added mystery to technology: each brick was stamped or moulded with a geometric or representational design before firing, with the design face deliberately placed facing inwards, so that it could not be seen in the finished building.

## MOVING ON FROM VILLAHERMOSA

Villahermosa being the state capital, you should have no problems getting an onward bus. To get to the first-class terminal take a "Chedraui" *combi* – they go to a huge department store behind the terminal and generally also go past the second-class terminal.

Between them, ADO and Cristóbal Colón operate dozens of services to all the main destinations: **Tuxtla** (7hr), Veracruz (7hr), **Tenosique** (3hr), Mérida (9hr), Campeche (6hr), Cancún (12hr), Chetumal (7hr), Oaxaca (9hr), Mexico City (12hr), even the US border and Pacific coast, costing little more than to the capital. From El ADO there are several departures to **Palenque** (2hr 30min), and you can also easily get there from the second-class terminal, from where there are constant departures to all the same destinations, plus **Comalcalco**, Paraíso and Frontera. For **San Cristóbal** (8–9hr), there are a few direct services, including a convenient one at 7.30am; otherwise change at either Tuxtla or Palenque.

## The museum and the site

You can now see the astonishing designs on the bricks in Comalcalco's marvellous new **museum** (closed Mon), though the labels are in Spanish only. Animals depicted include crocodiles, turtles, frogs, lizards, dogs and mice, while those portraying the sculpted faces of rulers display an advanced level of artistic development. The most amazing figure, however, is of a skeleton which appears to be leaping out at you from the surface of the brick. The abundant clay that provided such a versatile medium for architects and artists here also formed the basis for many more mundane artefacts. Comalcalco means "place of the *comales*" – fired clay griddles for cooking tortillas — in Nauhatl, and these and other clay vessels have been found in great numbers. Some of the largest jars were used as **funerary urns** and several are on display here, including one with an intact skeleton.

There's usually a **guide** available to show you around the site – Eugene Martinez Torres has collaborated on a book about Comalcalco's bricks, and he speaks excellent English. The accessible area is not large but you'll need to take water with you, as the humidity is extremely high, and if you're going to venture into the long grass or bushes, insect repellent is a must. Though there are dozens of structures, only around ten or so of the larger buildings have been subjected to any restoration, though more work is in progress. Due to the fragile nature of the brickwork you're not allowed to climb many of the buildings, though you can follow a path up to Structure III and around the Palacio.

The first one you come to is the main structure of the **North Plaza Cluster**: Temple I, a tiered pyramid with a massive central stairway. Originally, the whole building (along with all of the structures here) would have been covered with stucco, sculpted into masks and reliefs of rulers and deities, and brightly painted. Only a few of these features remain, with exposed ones protected from further erosion by thatched shelters, while some are deliberately left buried. Opposite Temple I is the **Great Acropolis**: eighty metres long with more buildings being excavated, and there's a fine stucco mask of Kinich Ahau, the Maya sun god. At the far end of the site you'll come to **El Palacio**, where you can climb the mound and get a close view of the brickwork. There's a series of massive brick piers and arches here, faintly reminiscent of English Victorian railway architecture. These once formed an enormous double corbelled vault, eighty metres long and over eight metres wide – one of the largest enclosed spaces the Maya ever built. At the side of Temple V a small, corbelled room contains stucco reliefs of nine, richly dressed, half life-size figures apparently in conversation or even argument – they may represent the **Lords of Xibalba**, the Maya underworld.

You'll also get a good overview of the whole site from up here, including many other mounds in the surrounding forest and farmland. **Cacao**, used as money by the Maya, and the main ingredient of their drinking chocolate, is grown in the area (Tabasco is Mexico's biggest producer of the crop), and you'll see cacao bushes on the way in, with huge green bean pods sprouting straight from their trunks.

## Practicalities

The **bus from Villahermosa** takes an hour and a quarter: ADO has several departures a day, and Transportes Somellera runs an hourly service from the second-class station. Both bus stations in Comalcalco are on Gregorio Méndez; walk the 150m back to the highway and catch a combi heading north (left) towards Paraíso. The ruins are on the right after about five minutes, along a newly paved road; some combis go all the way there, otherwise it's a fifteen-minute walk. There's a small **restaurant** and toilets at the site, and plenty of buses back to Villahermosa; should you get stuck in Comalcalco, there are a few basic **hotels** near the bus stations.

## La Venta

The small town of **LA VENTA**, on the border between Tabasco and Veracruz, would be of little interest were it not for the **archeological site** (daily 10am–4.30pm; US$2.50, free on Sun) where the huge Olmec heads displayed in Villahermosa were discovered. In the **museum** at the entrance, models show where the site was located, in a swamp surrounded by rivers, while glass cases are filled with unlabelled bits of pottery. Information panels on the wall give a good explanation of Olmec culture and history. The site itself has a few weathered stelae or monuments, but the highlight is the huge grass-covered mound, about 30m high, clearly a pyramid, with fluted sides believed to represent the ravines on the flanks of a sacred volcano. The climb up is worth the effort for the views and the breeze. Paths below take you through the jungle – fascinating for its plants and butterflies but haunted by ferocious mosquitoes.

La Venta is served by a steady stream of **buses** to Villahermosa and Coatzalcoalcos, so there's no need **to stay**; the *Hotel del Sol* (④), on the corner of the small plaza, is a friendly, pleasant option if you get stuck.

## The Zoque ruins of Malpasito

More than 100km southwest of Villahermosa, between the borders of Veracruz and Chiapas, a narrow triangle of Tabasco thrusts into the mountains. Known as the **Sierra Huimanguillo**, from the town in the lowlands just to the north, they're not that high, only up to 1000m, but they are rugged. To appreciate them at their best you have to hike; not only to caves, canyons and waterfalls, but also to the **Zoque ruins of Malpasito**, with their astonishing **petroglyphs**. The ruins are not that easy to reach independently and you may have to camp when you get there. First you'll have to pass through **HUIMANGUILLO**, a mid-sized town 70km southwest of Villahermosa.

### Practicalities

Buses leave Villahermosa for Huimanguillo frequently during the day; if there isn't a direct one, go second-class to **Cárdenas** and change there. ADO buses stop right in the centre, on Escobar, half a block south of the plaza. Second-class buses arrive at the terminal on Gutiérrez, near the market, five blocks west from the centre along Libertad. If you need to **stay** here try the *Hotel del Carmen* on Morelos 39, two blocks south of the plaza (☎ & fax 9/375-0915; ④). The owner, George Pagole del Valle, knows the site well and can provide worthwhile information. If you're not staying, get a bus heading to **Malpaso** and get off at the village of **Rómulo Calzada**, 70km south. Here you'll need to head west 5km to the *ejido* of **MALPASITO** – there may be a combi or a truck going. By now you can see the peaks, with the great jungle-covered plateau of El Mono Pelón ("the bald monkey") dominating the skyline. This is the highest point in Tabasco, and the sheer sides look impossible to climb. In Malpasito ask for the Peréz Rincón family; they might have a room to rent and you can eat with them.

### The site

A walk of just over 1km from Malpasito brings you to the Late Classic **Zoque ruins of Malpasito** (daily 10am—5pm; US$1.75), overlooked by jagged, jungle-covered mountains and reminiscent of Palenque (see p.138). Though the architectural style resembles that of the Maya, the Zoque were a separate culture, and little is known about them today. On the way in you pass terraces and grass-covered mounds, eventually leading to the unique **ball court**. At the top of the stone terraces forming the south side of the court, a flight of steps leads down to a narrow room, with stone benches lining either side. Beyond this, and separate from the chamber, is a square pit more than 2m deep and 1.5m square. This room may have been used by the ball players, or at least one team, to effect a spectacular entrance as they emerged onto the top of the ball court. Beyond the ball court a grass-covered plaza leads to two flights of wide steps with another small plaza at the top, with stunning views of mountains all around.

Perhaps the most amazing feature of this site are the **petroglyphs**. More than three hundred have been discovered so far: animals, birds, houses and what are presumably religious symbols etched into the rock. One large boulder has the most enigmatic of all: flat-topped triangles surmounted by a square or rectangle, and shown above what look like ladders or steps – possibly stylized houses. The trail leads on to a clear pool beneath a twelve-metre waterfall – too good to miss if the hike around the ruins has left you hot and dirty. More trails lead up into the mountains; a relatively easy one leads to the base of **La Pava**, an almost perpendicular pillar of rock, the top of which is said to resemble the head of a turkey.

Higher up the valley the **La Pava waterfalls** are an hour's hike along the side of the gorge, stepping between moss-covered boulders, and crossing the river on a suspension bridge. This is an utterly beautiful, tranquil place, perfect for enjoying the abundant wildlife.

# Teapa and the southern hills

An hour's bus ride through banana country to the south of Villahermosa, the small, friendly town of **TEAPA** is a lovely base for the spas and caves nearby. Cristóbal Colón **buses** leave Villahermosa for Tuxtla every couple of hours, calling at Teapa, though buses back are *de paso* and it may be difficult to get a seat. Though some second-class buses stop at the terminal on Méndez, right in the centre, most pull in at the **market** (plenty of good fruit stalls) near the edge of town. To get to the centre, walk a couple of blocks down the hill and turn left at the green clock onto Méndez, which takes you past the hotels and onto the plaza.

Teapa's **hotels** are good value: try the *Casa de Huéspedes Miye* (☎9/322-0420; ③), a clean, family-run place with private showers and (usually) hot water, with rooms round a tiny plant-filled courtyard.

There's **swimming** in the Río Teapa here, but it's better at the *balneario* on the Río Puyacatengo, a few kilometres east (walk or take the bus for Tacotalpa). Colectivos run from the plaza in Teapa to the spectacular **Grutas de Coconá** (daily 8am–4pm; US$0.75). Eight chambers are open to tourists, and some for spelunking only. A stroll through the caves takes about 45 minutes; in one chamber there's a supposedly miraculous representation of the face of Christ, carved by nature into the rock. You could also walk (45min) to the caves from Teapa: from Méndez, head for the Pemex station and turn right, following the sign. When you get near the forested hills, the road divides; head left over the railway track.

## The Sierra Puana: Tapijulapa and Oxolotán

Southeast from Teapa, you can get further away from the humidity of the lowlands by taking day-trips up the valley of the Río Oxolotán to Tabasco's "hill country". This is an extraordinarily picturesque area, with unspoilt colonial towns set in beautiful wooded valleys, and a turquoise river laden with sulphur cascading over terraced cliffs. You'll need to make a fairly early start to get the most out of the day. The 6.30am bus to **Tacotalpa** from the second-class station on Méndez in Teapa (20min) connects with one to **TAPIJULAPA**, the main settlement (45min), in time to have breakfast in the *Restaurant Mariquita*, in the corner of the shady plaza. The town is tiny, with narrow cobbled streets, red-tiled roofs and, unfortunately, no accommodation. Turn right at the end of the main street, Av López Portillo, where steps lead down to the Río Oxolotán. Here you may find boats to take you upstream to visit the **Parque Natural Villa Luz**, with its spa pools, rivers, cascades and caves. There are more boats during holidays, but it's easy enough to **walk** to the park: cross the tributary river on the suspension bridge, head left on the concrete path, across the football field, then follow the track over the hill, keeping close to the main river – about 35 minutes in all.

In the park (open daily; free), signed trails lead to caves, but the outstanding feature – not least for its powerful aroma – is the river, which owes both its smell and its colour to dissolved minerals, especially sulphur. The Río Oxolotán exits from a cave and meanders for 1km or so until it reaches the cliff marking the river valley. Here it breaks up into dozens of cascades and semicircular pools. Thousands of butterflies settle on the riverbanks, taking nourishment from dissolved minerals, and jungle trees and creepers grow wherever they find a foothold: a truly primeval sight. The **caves** are not really open to the public, but you can peer into their precipitous entrances; in Maya cosmology the openings are believed to lead to the Underworld (*Xibalba*) and abode of the Lords of Death. Beyond the caves are a couple of open-air **swimming pools** said to have therapeutic properties.

Trucks and combis frequently make the 25-minute trip from Tapijulapa to **OXOLOTÁN**. Here the ruins of a seventeenth-century Franciscan monastery host performances by the *Teatro Campesino y Indígena* (The Peasant and Indian Theatre), a company that has taken part in cultural festivals throughout Mexico and abroad. If you're in the area when a performance is scheduled, it's worth making an effort to go. **To get there from Tapijulapa**, climb the hill to the church, then descend to the road beyond, where there's a bus stop. The last bus back leaves at 6pm, but you're probably better off catching the 3pm bus if you're heading to Teapa.

# East to the Usumacinta and Guatemala

Heading east from Villahermosa, Hwy-186 cuts across a salient of northern Chiapas before swinging north into **Campeche** to Francisco Escárcega, then east again as the only road across the base of the Yucatán peninsula to **Chetumal**. At Catazajá, in Chiapas, 110km from Villahermosa, is the junction for **Palenque**. If you've already been there and want to see **Tikal**, you can go via **Tenosique** and La Palma (opposite), but it's quicker and cheaper to go from Frontera Corozal (see p.148), though you could visit the nearby ruins of **Pomoná**.

Coming from either Palenque or Villahermosa, you'll pass through the dull town of **EMILIANO ZAPATA**, hopefully only to change buses. The **bus stations** are in the same building on the edge of the town, and there are plenty of first- and second-class services to Villahermosa and Tenosique, tailing off rapidly in the evening. If you do get stuck, try the *Hotel Ramos* (☎9/343-0744; ⑤), opposite the bus station, which is at least comfortable and saves you going into town, and has Creatur, the only proper **travel agent** for a long way.

## Tenosique

The Río Usumacinta is crossed by the road and railway at Boca del Cerro, a few kilometres from **TENOSIQUE**, where the now placid river leaves some pretty impressive hills. **Buses** arrive at a small terminal close to the highway, just out of town. Inexpensive colectivos run frequently to the centre; get off when you see a large white church with blue trim on the right of the main street, Calle 26 (also known as Calle "Pino Suárez"). If you have **to stay**, the *Azulejos* (③), opposite the church, has friendly staff; slightly better is the *Rome* (☎9/342-0151; ④), a block closer to the plaza, on Calle 28.

If you're staying overnight and you've exhausted what limited sightseeing Tenosique has to offer (such as visiting the house where Pino Suárez was born and admiring his bust and monument), you'll want to head for the zócalo and calles 26 and 28, the main areas for shopping and **eating**. The juice bar on the corner of the plaza prepares good licuados; there's also a good coffee shop just past the plaza on Calle 28, and the **market**, with a row of inexpensive comedores, is opposite. *La Palapa* restaurant overlooks the broad river, where the boat traffic heads constantly back and forth.

If you're going **to Guatemala** you'd be wise to stock up on provisions: there's a good **bakery** opposite the *Hotel Rome* and fruit stalls everywhere. The banks in Tenosique aren't interested in changing **money**, but Bancomer has an ATM. For Guatemalan quetzales ask around in the shops on Calle 28 where you should find someone who will give better rates than the boatmen. **Moving on**, there are plenty of bus services to Villahermosa during the day, a first-class service to Mexico City at 5pm and a 6pm bus to Escárcega and points east, with services finishing off around 7pm.

## Pomoná

On the road from Emiliano Zapata, about 30km west of Tenosique, the ruins of **Pomoná** (daily 8am–4pm) are reached 4km down a signed track. Although the site, located in rolling countryside with views of forested hills to the south, makes a pleasant diversion, a visit is really only for the dedicated. The restored structures date from the Late Classic period; the site's largest building is a stepped pyramid with six levels. Pomoná was a subject site of the much larger city of Piedras Negras in Guatemala, further up the valley of the Usumacinta. The modern little **museum** houses some interesting carved panels and stelae, made even more mysterious by the omission of any explanations as to what you're seeing.

## La Palma and the Río San Pedro to Guatemala

**Buses** for **LA PALMA** leave Tenosique every two hours from 4.30am to 4.30pm; there's no terminal, just follow Calle 31 down the side of the church for five blocks. They head due east through flat farming and ranching country and after an hour reach the Río San Pedro, stopping at the *Parador Turístico* restaurant, by the dock, for the **boat-trip to El Naranjo** in Guatemala (see p.470). The usual departure time is 8am, returning at 1pm from El Naranjo (4hr; US$24), but you may have to wait until sufficient passengers turn up. The trip is, frankly, overpriced, and you'll have a much more interesting time crossing from Frontera Corozal to **Bethél** (see p.470), visiting Bonampak and Yaxchilán en route. There are some very basic **rooms** at La Palma; ask at the restaurant.

**Leaving for Guatemala**, you hand in your Mexican tourist card at the immigration post at El Pedregal (make sure you've already paid the fee at a bank), about halfway through the journey.

# travel details

## Buses

Departures given are for direct first-class services; there are likely to be at least as many second-class buses (and often combis as well) to the same destinations.

**Palenque** to: Campeche (3 daily; 6hr); Cancún (3 daily; 12hr); Mérida (3 daily; 9hr); Mexico City (2 daily; 17hr); San Cristóbal (hourly; 5hr); Tuxtla Gutiérrez (hourly; 7hr); Villahermosa (at least 8 daily; 2hr 30min). Plenty of second-class buses run along the Carretera Fronteriza for the junctions to **Bonampak** and **Yaxchilán**.

**San Cristóbal** to: Ciudad Cuauhtémoc, for Guatemala (at least 8 daily; 3hr 30min); Comitán, for Lagos de Montebello or the Guatemalan border (at least hourly; 2hr); Mexico City (5 daily; 18hr); Palenque (9 daily; 5hr); Tapachula (4 daily; 9hr); Tuxtla Gutiérrez (constantly; 2hr); Villahermosa, some direct, otherwise via Tuxtla or Palenque (6 daily; 8–9hr).

**Tapachula** to: Arriaga (at least 12 daily; 4hr); Mexico City (12 daily; 18hr); Oaxaca (1 daily; 12hr); San Cristóbal (2 daily; 9hr); Tuxtla Gutiérrez (15 daily; 7hr); Veracruz (1 daily; 14hr); Villahermosa (2 daily; 13hr); Guatemala City (2 daily; 5–6hr).

**Tuxtla Gutiérrez** to: Ciudad Cuauhtémoc, for Guatemala (6 daily; 6hr); Comitán, for Lagos de Montebello or the Guatemalan border (hourly; 4hr); Mérida (4 daily; 14hr) Mexico City (at least 9 daily; 16hr); Palenque (hourly; 7hr); San Cristóbal (first-class hourly, others constantly; 2hr); Tapachula (15 daily; 7hr); Tonalá (hourly; 3hr 30min); Villahermosa (9 daily; 7hr).

**Villahermosa** to: Campeche (at least 12 daily; 6hr); Cancún (5 daily; 12hr); Chetumal (5 daily; 7hr), Mérida (at least 12 daily; 9hr), Mexico City (at least hourly; 11hr); Palenque (8 daily; 2hr 30min); San Cristóbal, some direct, otherwise via Tuxtla or Palenque (6 daily; 8–9hr); Tapachula (2 daily; 13hr); Tuxtla Gutiérrez (9 daily; 7hr); Veracruz (12 daily; 7hr).

## International buses

**Tapachula** to: Guatemala (3–4 daily; 5–6hr).

## International boats

**La Palma** (near Tenosique) to: El Naranjo, Guatemala (1 daily; 4hr)

**Frontera Corozal** (Yaxchilán) to: Bethél, Guatemala (several daily, no schedule; 30min)

## Planes

Air services throughout the region are expanding as new airports open up, and services will almost certainly have increased from those listed in the text. For the latest information check with one of the recommended travel agents.

**Villahermosa** has several daily flights to the capital, but there are also daily direct services from Tuxtla Gutiérrez, Comitán and Tapachula. Aerocaribe has scheduled services between Palenque and Cancún.

Servicios Aéreos San Cristóbal, based in **Ocosingo** (☎9/673-1088), operate light aircraft – from Palenque or San Cristóbal to Yaxchilán or Bonampak, or Ocosingo to Laguna Miramar for example.

# PART THREE

# BELIZE

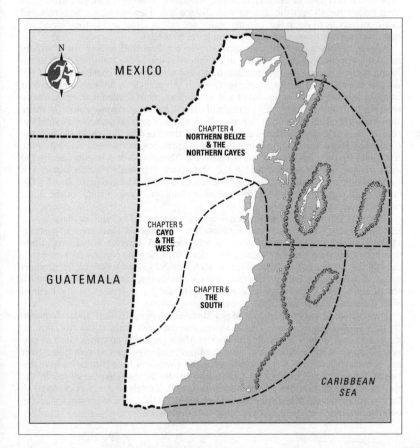

**MEXICO**

**CHAPTER 4**
**NORTHERN BELIZE & THE NORTHERN CAYES**

**GUATEMALA**

**CHAPTER 5**
**CAYO & THE WEST**

**CHAPTER 6**
**THE SOUTH**

**CARIBBEAN SEA**

# INTRODUCTION

Wedged in by the Yucatán peninsula to the north and the forests of Petén to the west, **Belize** offers some of the most breathtaking coastal scenery – both above and below water – anywhere in the Maya World. Add to this magnificent inland landscapes, Maya ruins and wildlife to rival any destination in the region, and it's easy to see why the number of visitors to this tiny country increases every year. Despite its small size – roughly that of Wales or Massachusetts – Belize has the lowest population density in Central America, a fact that contributes to its easygoing, friendly and, with the exception of bustling Belize City, noticeably uncrowded character. With far less of a language barrier to overcome than elsewhere in the region, Belize's numerous small hotels and restaurants, and reliable public transport, make it an ideal place to travel independently, offering visitors plenty of scope to explore the heartland of the ancient Maya. Substantial evidence of **Maya culture** has been discovered all over the country and, though only a few sites have been restored as extensively as those in the Yucatán, many are just as large, and in their forest settings you're likely to see more wildlife and fewer tour buses.

Belizean territory comprises marginally more sea than land, and for many visitors the sea is the main attraction. Lying just offshore is one of the country's most astonishing natural wonders – the dazzling turquoise shallows and cobalt depths of the longest **barrier reef** in the Americas. Beneath the surface, a brilliant, technicolour world of fish and corals awaits divers and snorkellers, while scattered along the entire reef, like emeralds set in sapphire, a chain of islands, known as **cayes**, protect the mainland from the ocean swell and offer more than a hint of tropical paradise. Beyond the reef lie the real jewels in Belize's natural crown – three of only four **coral atolls** in the Caribbean. Dawn here is a truly unforgettable experience, as the red-gold disk of the sun glides up over the foaming white reef crest. These reefs and islands, among the most diverse marine ecosystems on the planet, are increasingly under threat, but Belize is at the forefront of practical research to develop effective protection for the entire coastal zone; for visitors, this means a chance to explore some of the finest **marine reserves** in the world.

Belizeans' recognition of the importance of conserving their natural heritage means that the country now has the greatest proportion of **protected land** (over 40 percent) in the hemisphere. As a result, the **densely forested interior** remains relatively untouched, boasting abundant natural attractions, including the region's highest waterfall and the world's only **jaguar reserve**. Rich tropical forests support a tremendous range of **wildlife**, including howler and spider monkeys, tapirs and pumas, jabiru storks and scarlet macaws; spend any time inland and you're sure to see the national bird, the unmistakable keel-billed toucan.

The rugged, almost impenetrable **Maya Mountains**, rising to over 1100m, dominate Belize's south-central region. This is where the country's main rivers rise, flowing north and east to the Caribbean. The ancient Maya grew rich on cacao (used as currency) grown in these valleys and developed powerful city-states by controlling river and coastal trade routes. Over the millennia, the rivers and their tributaries have dissolved the limestone bedrock to form some of the largest **cave systems** in the Americas. Few of these have been fully investigated, though all the ones explored so far contain numerous **Maya ceremonial artefacts**. All the caves are registered archeological sites and each year more become accessible to visitors.

Almost every visitor will have to spend at least some time in **Belize City**, even if only passing through, as it's the hub of the country's transport system. First-time visitors may be shocked initially by the decaying buildings and the pollution of the river, but it is nonetheless possible to spend several pleasant hours in this former outpost of the British Empire. In contrast, Belize's capital, **Belmopan**, is primarily an administrative centre, with little to offer visitors.

Northern Belize is relatively flat and often swampy, with a large proportion of agricultural land, though as everywhere in Belize there are **Maya ruins** and **nature reserves**. In the northwest, adjacent to the Guatemalan border, is the vast **Rio Bravo Conservation Area**, where hunting has been banned for over a decade, allowing unusually close encounters with the wildlife. The forests here hide dozens of Maya sites, the largest of which, **La Milpa**, is just one of many in the country currently being examined by archeological teams. **Lamanai**, near Orange Walk, is one of the most impressive Maya sites in the country, while the lagoons at **Sarteneja** (Shipstern Nature Reserve) on the northeast coast and inland at **Crooked Tree** provide superb protected habitats for wildlife, particularly birds.

The mainland coast is almost entirely low-lying and swampy – wonderful for wildlife, but for swimming and underwater activities you need to visit the **cayes**, the largest of which, **Ambergris Caye**, draws over half of all tourists to Belize, with the small resort town of **San Pedro** their main destination. Here, in **Bacalar Chico National Park**, you can wander around the ports of the ancient Maya. **Caye Caulker**, to the south, is the most popular of the islands with independent travellers. Many of the other cayes are becoming easier to reach, and organized day-trips are available for divers and snorkellers to **Turneffe Islands** and **Lighthouse Reef** atolls.

In the west, **San Ignacio** has everything the ecotourist could want: Maya ruins and rainforest, rivers and caves, and excellent accommodation in every price range. On the way here you should make every effort to visit what is one of the two best **zoos** in the Maya region (the other being in Tuxtla Gutiérrez, Chiapas). **Caracol**, the largest Maya site in Belize, is now a routine day-trip from San Ignacio, and the magnificent ruin of **Xunantunich** is just to the west, on the way to the Guatemalan border. Right on the border (and extending across it) is **El Pilar**, the largest Maya site in the Belize River valley.

**Dangriga**, the main town of the south-central region, serves as a jumping-off point for visitors to the central cayes and atolls (little developed at present, but becoming more accessible every year) and for trips to the **Cockscomb Basin Wildlife Sanctuary**. Further down the coast, the quiet Garífuna village of **Hopkins** sees more visitors every year, and the delightful, laid-back **Placencia**, at the tip of a long, curving peninsula, has some of the country's best **beaches**. Most visitors to **Punta Gorda**, the main town of Toledo District, are on their way to or from **Puerto Barrios** in Guatemala by boat. Venture inland, however, and you'll find the villages of the **Mopan** and **Kekchí Maya**, set in some of the most stunning countryside in Belize and surrounded by the only true **rainforest** in the country. Here are yet more caves, rivers and ruins, including **Lubaantun**, source of the enigmatic Crystal Skull.

Exactly how Belize came by its name is something of a mystery; it could be a corruption of "Wallace", the name either of a notorious English pirate who is reputed to have landed here in 1638, or of Peter Wallace, a Scotsman who may have founded a colony here in 1620. However, those preferring a more ancient origin believe the name to be derived from the **Maya** term *belekin*, meaning "towards the east". Today, Belize is the only **English-speaking** country in the Maya World, as much a Caribbean nation as a Latin one, with a blend of cultures and races that includes Maya, Mestizo, African and European. The **modern Maya** in Belize form around eleven percent of the population and are descended from three separate groups, all relatively recent arrivals.

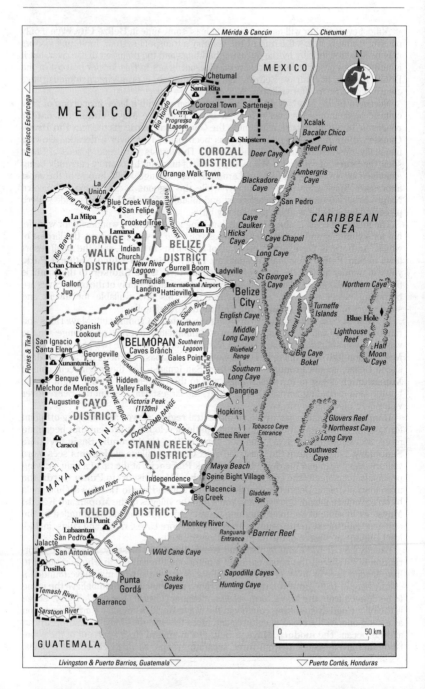

△ Mérida & Cancún    △ Chetumal

MEXICO

Chetumal

Santa Rita

Rio Hondo

Cerros

Corozal Town    Sarteneja

Progresso
Lagoon

Xcalak
Bacalar Chico

Shipstern

Reef Point

Deer Caye

CorozAL
DISTRICT

La
Unión

Blue Creek

Orange Walk Town

Blackadore
Caye

Ambergris
Caye

Blue Creek Village
San Felipe

San Pedro

La Milpa

Crooked Tree

NORTHERN HIGHWAY

Rio Bravo

Lamanai

Altun Ha

Caye
Caulker

CARIBBEAN
SEA

ORANGE
WALK
DISTRICT

Indian
Church

BELIZE
DISTRICT

Hicks'
Caye

Caye Chapel

Chan Chich

New River
Lagoon

Burrell Boom

Ladyville

Long Caye

Gallon
Jug

Bermudian
Landing

International Airport

St George's
Caye

Northern Caye

Hattieville

Belize
City

Belize River

WESTERN HIGHWAY

Sibun River

Turneffe
Islands

Blue Hole

Spanish
Lookout

Northern
Lagoon

English Caye

Lighthouse
Reef

San Ignacio
Santa Elena

BELMOPAN

Central Lagoon

Half
Moon
Caye

Georgeville

Caves Branch

Southern
Lagoon

Middle
Long Caye

Big Caye
Bokel

Xunantunich

HUMMINGBIRD HIGHWAY

Gales Point

Bluefield
Range

Benque Viejo
Melchor de Mencos

Hidden
Valley Falls

MOUNTAIN PINE RIDGE

Southern
Long Caye

Augustine

CAYO
DISTRICT

Stann Creek

Dangriga

Victoria Peak
(1120m)

COCKSCOMB RANGE

Hopkins

Glovers Reef

Caracol

South Stann Creek

Sittee River

Tobacco Caye
Entrance

Northeast Caye
Long Caye

STANN CREEK
DISTRICT

Southwest
Caye

MAYA MOUNTAINS

Maya Beach

Seine Bight Village

Monkey River

Independence

Placencia

SOUTHERN HIGHWAY

Big Creek

Gladden
Spit

TOLEDO DISTRICT

Nim Li Punit

Monkey River

Lubaantun
San Pedro

Rio Grande

Ranguana
Entrance

Barrier Reef

Jalacte

San Antonio

Wild Cane Caye

Pusilhá

Moho River

Snake
Cayes

Sapodilla Cayes

Punta
Gordá

Hunting Caye

Temash River

Barranco

Sarstoon River

GUATEMALA

0    50 km

△ Francisco Escárcega

△ Flores & Tikal

▽ Livingston & Puerto Barrios, Guatemala    ▽ Puerto Cortés, Honduras

N

These are the **Yucatec**, who fled from the peninsula's **Caste Wars** in the mid-nineteenth century and live mainly in the north; the **Mopan**, who arrived in southern and western Belize from Petén in the late 1800s; and the **Kekchí**, who came to Toledo in southern Belize from Alta Verapaz around the same time. Belize's **official language** is English, though **Spanish** is at least as widely spoken, but it's the rich, lilting **Creole**, based on English but typically Caribbean, which is the language understood and spoken by every Belizean, whatever their native tongue. In addition to English and Creole, the Maya of Belize all speak at least one Maya language and, for English speakers at least, Belize is probably the best place to pick up some Maya words and experience Maya culture first-hand.

## Some history

Belize is the youngest nation in the Maya World, only gaining full independence from Britain in 1981, and its history has been markedly different from the surrounding Latin American republics since at least the mid-seventeenth century. Although the whole region, including Belize, was (to a greater or lesser degree) colonized by Spain in the sixteenth century, it was the colonial entanglement with Britain that gave Belize its present cultural, social and political structures. Belize's early history is impossible to separate from that of the surrounding areas in Mexico and Guatemala and from the **Early Postclassic** (around 950 AD) to the time of the **Spanish Conquest** in the 1540s the Yucatán peninsula and northern Belize consisted of over a dozen rival provinces, bound up in a cycle of competition and conflict. And, far from being practically deserted when the Spanish arrived, as had formerly been suggested, the Maya population is now estimated to have been around 200,000 by 1500 AD — almost as high as it is today. Never part of a single empire, the Maya towns and provinces here were still vigorously independent, as the Spanish found to their cost on several occasions. Northern Belize was part of the wealthy, independent Maya province of **Chactemal** (later Chetumal), with its capital probably located at Santa Rita, near Corozal. Chetumal was a wealthy province producing cacao and honey, while trade, alliances and wars kept it in contact with surrounding Maya states up to and beyond the Spanish conquest of Aztec Mexico. **Lamanai**, on the New River south of Orange Walk, also remained occupied throughout the Postclassic and beyond. Further south in Belize was the province known to the Maya of Chetumal as **Dzuluinicob** ("Land of Foreigners"), whose capital, **Tipu**, lay on the Macal River south of San Ignacio.

The first contact with **Europeans** was in 1511, when shipwrecked Spanish sailors landed on the southern coast of Yucatán: five were immediately sacrificed, and the others taken as slaves. When Spanish envoys came to ask for the release of their countrymen, one of them, **Gonzalo Guerrero**, refused to go, preferring life among his former captors. He had married the daughter of the chief of Chetumal, adopting Maya ways, and later became a crucial military adviser to the Maya in their resistance to the Spanish. His knowledge of Spanish tactics meant that attempts in the 1520s and 1530s to subdue the Maya of Chetumal were disastrous failures.

Late in 1543, however, Gasper Pacheco began another chapter in the sickeningly familiar tale of Spanish atrocities; advancing on Chetumal, he destroyed crops and food stores and ruthlessly slaughtered the inhabitants. By 1544, Pacheco had subdued Maya resistance sufficiently to found a town on Lake Bacalar and claim **encomienda** (tribute) from villages around Chetumal. It is likely that he also conquered parts of Dzuluinicob, though the Maya still strenuously resisted Spanish domination. During the second half of the sixteenth century, the Spanish gradually strengthened their hold over northern Belize, establishing missions at Lamanai and Tipu. The Maya resentment that was always present beneath the surface boiled over into total **rebellion** in 1638, forcing Spain to abandon Chetumal and Tipu completely. However, it is likely that the Maya of Belize were under some form of Spanish influence even if they were not under direct rule. The Maya struggle to remain independent was to continue with simmering resentment until 1707, when the population of Tipu was forcibly removed to Lago de Petén Itzá. This act effectively ended Spanish attempts to settle the west of Belize, as it was impossible to establish a successful colony without people to work for the Spanish *encomenderos*.

The failure of the Spanish to occupy southern Yucatán allowed buccaneers or **pirates** (primarily British) preying on the Spanish treasure fleets to find refuge along the coast of Belize. Spanish forces mounted several expeditions to dislodge the buccaneers (or **Baymen** as they called themselves), but these were never more than partially successful. These expeditions continued until in 1798, when the settlers (with British naval help) achieved victory in the **Battle of St George's Caye** – a success that reinforced the bond with the British government. In 1862, Belize became a colony of **British Honduras** and in 1871 it was officially declared a Crown Colony, becoming an integral, though minor part of the British empire.

Although **Mexico's independence** in 1821 signalled the end of the Spanish empire on the mainland of the Americas, Mexico's claim to at least the northern part of British Honduras (as an extension of Yucatán) was not resolved until 1897. **Guatemala's claim**, however, has been the source of much more belligerent disagreement with Britain, and there's no doubt that the British government shared much of the blame for the confusion. In a vain attempt to reach a settlement Britain and Guatemala signed the **Anglo-Guatemalan Treaty** in 1859: the interpretation of this treaty and its various clauses has been the source of controversy and dispute ever since. Essentially, under Article 7 of the treaty, Britain agreed to fund and build a road from Guatemala City to the Atlantic coast and in return Guatemala would drop its claim to Belize. Britain never built the road and in 1940 Guatemala repudiated the treaty, and its new constitution of 1945 declared Belize – *Belice* in Spanish – to be the 23rd department of Guatemala. In 1948 Guatemala made the first of several **threats to invade** Belize to "recover" the territory: Britain responded by sending cruisers and troops, the first of many military deployments over the next four decades.

For the people of Belize, the twentieth century was dominated by uncertainty over their relationship with Britain – still regarded as the "mother country" by many colonial peoples. In both 1914 and 1939, thousands of Belizeans volunteered to assist the war effort, but each time the returning soldiers faced poverty and humiliation – events which marked the onset of black consciousness and the beginning of the **independence movement**. By the 1950s, the days of the British empire were numbered and the 1954 general election, in which all literate adults could vote, was won with an overwhelming majority by the People's United Party (PUP), led by George Price, with a manifesto to achieve independence from Britain.

**Guatemala**, however, as inheritor of the Spanish colonial jurisdiction of the same name, had never entirely let go of its claim to Belize, though the British government paid only scant attention to what it regarded as minor dispute in an insignificant corner of the empire.

Accordingly, Belize was granted **internal self-government** in 1964 – the first step on the road to full independence. The prospect of an independent Belize outraged Guatemalan national pride and the government moved troops to the border several times, threatening an invasion to recover the department of "Belice". Throughout the 1970s, the situation remained tense, but gradually international opinion shifted in favour of Belizean independence, underlined most significantly by a **UN resolution** passed in 1980 which demanded Belize's independence with all territory intact by the following year. Although further negotiations with Guatemala did not fully resolve the territorial dispute, Belize achieved full **independence** on September 21, 1981, with Queen Elizabeth II as head of state. The present Guatemalan government, while restating its historic claim to at least some of Belize's territory, claims to be committed to solving any dispute through negotiation, and the two countries continue to exchange ambassadors.

Belize's **democratic credentials** are beyond dispute: at each general election since independence, the voters have kicked out the incumbent government and replaced it with the opposition. In practice, this has meant that the left-of-centre PUP has alternated with the more market-led United Democratic Party (UDP). This pattern was dramatically illustrated in 1998, when the UDP government's neo-liberal economic policies (under pressure from the World Bank) resulted in thousands of public sector redundancies – and a catastrophic defeat in the 1998 general election, with even Prime Minister Manuel Esquivel losing his seat. The PUP, with Said Musa as prime minister, now forms Belize's government.

Despite a booming **tourist industry** that brings in over US$115 million a year, **agriculture** remains the mainstay of Belize's **economy**, accounting for over sixty percent of foreign exchange earnings and almost a third of employment. Sugar is the most important agro-export, followed by bananas and citrus products. Figures are obviously not available for Belize's income from the lucrative drug transhipment business, but this illicit economy is almost as large as the official one. **Per capita** income is high for Central America, at over US$3000, boosted by the remittances many Belizeans receive from relatives abroad, mainly in the US. This apparent advantage is offset by the fact that many of the brightest and most highly trained citizens leave Belize, assimilating easily into English-speaking North America.

Though Belize's traditional links with Britain and the Commonwealth countries in the West Indies remain strong, the United States is now its largest trading partner, and supplies much of the foreign aid on which it still depends. Britain's position as the former colonial power and a major aid-provider following independence is gradually being replaced by aid channelled through multilateral organizations, including the EU.

Belize is currently participating in the negotiations for a **Free Trade Area of the Americas**, with December 2005 set as the target date for the agreement to come into force. This agreement would establish the largest free trade area in the world, an idea viewed with alarm by many Belizean workers, who fear that an end to all tariffs will further depress agricultural prices and drive the small manufacturing base into bankruptcy. Even worse in many people's eyes, such proposals might signal an end to the **fixed rate of exchange** with the US$, leading to potentially catastrophic devaluation of the Belize dollar. Regardless of the domestic popular sentiment, however, Belize is firmly linked to the US-dominated international financial structures, and will have to face increasing challenges from global competition in the early years of this century.

# CHAPTER FOUR

# NORTHERN BELIZE AND THE NORTHERN CAYES

I n ancient times, northern Belize was one of the wealthiest regions of the Maya World. The rulers of the city-states controlled the trade along the Hondo, Belize and New rivers, and the seaborne coastal trade along the Caribbean coast. Many visitors to Belize are drawn here today by the natural and cultural attractions of the region – the impressive Maya sites and several large expanses of strictly protected land – but, without doubt, the most appealing and popular features of the country lie offshore along the Belize Barrier Reef. Here the islands of the generally upmarket Ambergris Caye and the more budget-oriented Caye Caulker offer relaxing bases to enjoy the reef. They also provide a springboard to the two northern atolls, Turneffe Islands and Lighthouse Reef, each boasting world-renowned dive sites. The astonishingly diverse ecosystems of the reef and the cayes are protected in a network of marine reserves and national parks stretching from the border with Mexico. Belize City, the country's largest urban area and former capital, is also the nation's transport hub. You'll certainly pass through here at some point, and should allow time to visit some of its historic buildings and the new museums and galleries.

Physically, the northern half of the country is relatively low-lying, with large areas of swamp in the east. The only towns in the north are **Orange Walk** on the New River, jumping-off point for trips to the ruins of **Lamanai**, and **Corozal**, a peaceful settlement on the shore of Corozal Bay, a short distance from the Mexican border. Although much of the land is given over to agriculture, there are also extensive nature reserves. All the nature reserves have accommodation, and a stay in one of these offers a much more enjoyable experience than you'll get on a brief day-visit. In the villages of **Bermudian Landing** and **Crooked Tree** community-based projects combine conservation and tourism. In the extreme northeastern corner of Belize **Shipstern Nature Reserve** protects a system of lagoons and lowland forest, and in the far northwest, the **Rio Bravo Conservation Area** covers a range of habitats from lagoons and savannah to higher, forested ridges. The area is well connected by roads inland and an ever more frequent and reliable boat service to the cayes. There are also some superb **tours** on offer, though most places are very easy to visit independently.

## ACCOMMODATION PRICE CODES

All the accommodation listed in this book has been categorized into one of nine price bands, as set out below. The prices quoted are in US dollars and refer to the cheapest room available for two people sharing in high season.

| | | |
|---|---|---|
| ① under US$5 | ④ US$15–25 | ⑦ US$60–80 |
| ② US$5–10 | ⑤ US$25–40 | ⑧ US$80–100 |
| ③ US$10–15 | ⑥ US$40–60 | ⑨ over US$100 |

# BELIZE CITY

The narrow, congested streets of **Belize City** can seem daunting to anyone at first, especially if they have been prepared by the usual travellers' tales of crime-ridden urban decay. Admittedly, at first glance, the city can be unprepossessing and chaotic. Its buildings – many of them dilapidated wooden structures – stand right at the edge of the road or on the banks of stagnant canals (still used for much of the city's drainage), and there are few sidewalks to offer refuge to pedestrians from the ever-increasing numbers of cars and trucks. The hazards of Belize City, however, are often reported by those who have never been here.

Most visitors hurry through on their way to catch their next bus or a boat out to the cayes, but the city has a distinguished history, a handful of sights and an astonishing energy. The 70,000 people of Belize City represent every ethnic group in the country, with the **Creole** descendants of former slaves and Baymen forming the dominant element, generating an easy-going Caribbean atmosphere. One of the very best times to visit is in fact during the "low season", when the **September Celebrations** fill the streets with music, dancing and parades, and the highlight, **Carnival**, sees gorgeously costumed dancers shimmer and gyrate through the city to electrifying Caribbean rhythms. Whenever you come, if you approach the city with an open mind, meet the inhabitants, and take in the new museums and galleries, you may well be pleasantly surprised.

Belize City is divided neatly into two halves – north and south – by the **Haulover Creek**, a delta branch of the Belize River. The pivotal point of the city centre is the **Swing Bridge**, always busy with traffic and opened twice a day to allow larger vessels up and down the river. **North** of the Swing Bridge things tend to be slightly more upmarket; here you'll find expensive hotels, most of the embassies and consulates and some very luxurious homes. **South** of the Swing Bridge is the commercial zone, with banks, offices and supermarkets; the foreshore here is the city's most prestigious district, home to the colonial governor's residence, now an arts centre and museum. Belize City is small enough to make **walking** the easiest way to get around, at least in daylight.

---

### HASSLE

Walking in Belize City **in daylight** is perfectly safe if you observe common-sense rules. The introduction of specially trained **tourism police** in 1995 made an immediate impact on the level of hassle and this, coupled with the legal requirement for all tour guides to be licensed, drove away the hustlers and really reduced street crime. You'll soon learn to spot dangerous situations and in the city centre you can always ask the tourism police (☎72222, ext 401) for advice or directions; they'll even walk you back to your hotel if it's near their patrol route. That said, it's still sensible to proceed with caution: most people are friendly and chatty, but quite a few may want to sell you drugs or bum a dollar or two. The best advice is to stay cool. Be civil, don't provoke trouble by arguing too forcefully, and never show large sums of money on the street, especially US dollars. Women wearing short shorts or skirts will attract verbal abuse from local studs.

The virtual absence of nightlife apart from the bars and discos in a few of the more expensive hotels means there's little reason to walk the streets **after dark**; if you do venture out, bear in mind that anyone alone is in danger of being mugged. It's a good idea to travel by taxi at night, especially if you've just arrived by bus. For more on security and avoiding trouble see p.47.

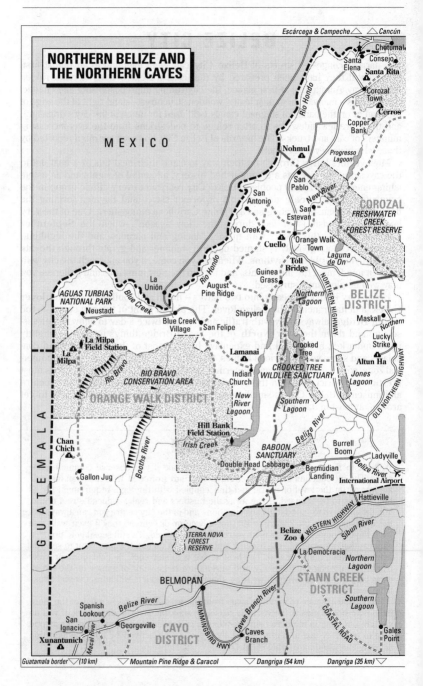

## NORTHERN BELIZE AND THE NORTHERN CAYES

Escárcega & Campeche △ △ Cancún

MEXICO

Chetumal
Santa Elena
Consejo
Santa Rita
Corozal Town
Cerros
Copper Bank

Nohmul
Progresso Lagoon

San Pablo
San Antonio
San Estevan
New River
COROZAL FRESHWATER CREEK FOREST RESERVE

Yo Creek
Cuello
Orange Walk Town
Laguna de On

Rio Hondo

La Unión
August Pine Ridge
Guinea Grass
Toll Bridge
Northern Lagoon
BELIZE DISTRICT

AGUAS TURBIAS NATIONAL PARK
Neustadt
Shipyard
Maskall
Lucky Strike
Northern

Blue Creek
Blue Creek Village
San Felipe
Lamanai
Crooked Tree
CROOKED TREE WILDLIFE SANCTUARY
Altun Ha
Jones Lagoon

La Milpa Field Station
La Milpa
Rio Bravo
RIO BRAVO CONSERVATION AREA
ORANGE WALK DISTRICT
Indian Church
New River Lagoon
Southern Lagoon

Chan Chich
Booths River
Hill Bank Field Station
Irish Creek
BABOON SANCTUARY
Burrell Boom
Ladyville

Gallon Jug
Double Head Cabbage
Bermudian Landing
Belize River
International Airport

Hattieville

TERRA NOVA FOREST RESERVE
Belize Zoo
WESTERN HIGHWAY
Sibun River
La Democracia
Northern Lagoon
STANN CREEK DISTRICT

BELMOPAN

Spanish Lookout
San Ignacio
Belize River
Georgeville
CAYO DISTRICT
HUMMINGBIRD HWY
Caves Branch River
Caves Branch
Southern Lagoon
COASTAL ROAD
Gales Point

Xunantunich

GUATEMALA

Guatamala border ▽ (10 km)   ▽ Mountain Pine Ridge & Caracol   ▽ Dangriga (54 km)   Dangriga (35 km) ▽

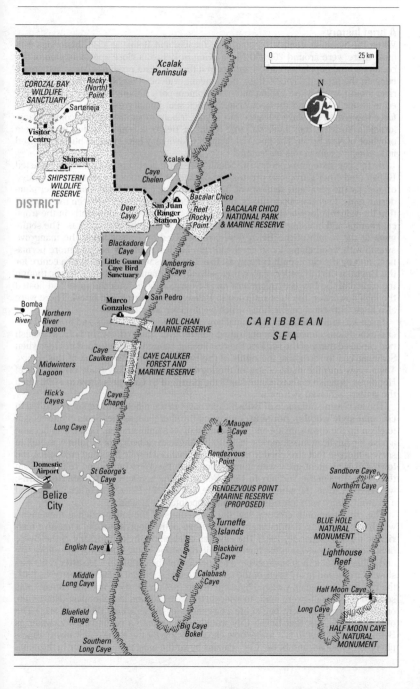

## A brief history

When the **Spanish** conquered southern Yucatán and Belize in 1544, historians estimate there were around 200,000 Maya living in Belize (a close approximation of the
country's total population today) and, even if there is scant proof of a Maya settlement
beneath the present-day city, there is abundant evidence that Moho Caye, just off the
river mouth, was a Maya fishing and transhipment port. Although Spanish friars founded missions inland and the secular authorities sent military expeditions upstream to
force the scattered Maya villages into paying tribute to *encomenderos* (colonial land-
lords) in Yucatán, they built no large towns in Belize, a remote region in a remote
province of New Spain. The imperial Spanish Crown may have reigned but it exercised
little effective rule in this far frontier.

By the late sixteenth century the Spanish treasure fleets in the Caribbean attracted
British (and other European) **pirates**, or buccaneers, who took advantage of the refuge
offered by the reefs and shallows of Belize, using the cayes as bases for further plundering raids. Ever the opportunists, the buccaneers made money between raids by cutting the valuable **logwood** (used for textile dyes) which grew abundantly in the tropical swamps and building a number of camps from Campeche to Honduras. The settlement at the mouth of the Belize River, constructed by consolidating the mangrove
swamp with wood chips, loose coral and rum bottles, gradually became more permanent, and by the eighteenth century **Belize Town** was well established as a centre for
the **Baymen** (as the settlers called themselves), their families and their slaves, though
the capital of the Bay settlement was on St George's Caye. After the rains had floated
the logs downriver, the men returned to Belize Town to drink and brawl. There were
also huge Christmas celebrations which went on for weeks.

Spain was still the dominant colonial power in the region, however, and mounted several expeditions aimed at demonstrating control over the territory. In 1779, a Spanish
raid captured many of the settlers, the rest fleeing, though most returned in 1783, when
Spain agreed to recognize the rights of the British settlers. As a result of this, Belize
Town grew into the main centre of the logwood and mahogany trade on the Bay of
Honduras. Spanish raids continued until the **Battle of St George's Caye** in 1798, when
the settlers achieved victory.

The increasing influence of British expatriates in the nineteenth century resulted in
**colonial-style wooden housing** dominating the shoreline, as the "Scots clique" began
to clean up the town's image and take control of its administration. Belize also became
a base for Anglican missionaries: in 1812 the Anglican cathedral of St John was built to
serve a diocese that stretched from Belize to Panamá. Despite fires and epidemics, the
town and settlement grew with immigration from the West Indies and refugees from
the Caste Wars in the Yucatán. In 1862, Belize became a colony of **British Honduras**,
with Belize City as the administrative centre, and in 1871, Belize was officially declared
a Crown Colony, with a resident governor appointed by Britain.

The early twentieth century saw the beginnings of the independence movement,
which was given added momentum by the effects of the Depression and a massive **hurricane** on September 10, 1931. The city was celebrating the anniversary of the Battle
of St George's Caye when the hurricane hit, uprooting houses, flooding the entire city
and killing about a thousand people – ten percent of the population. Disaster relief was
slow to arrive and many parts of the city were left in a state of squalid poverty. In 1961,
the city was once again ravaged by a hurricane: 262 people died, and the damage was
so serious that plans were made to relocate the capital inland to Belmopan. (Hattieville,
on the Western Highway, began life as a refuge for those fleeing the hurricane.) The
official attitude was that Belize City would soon become a redundant backwater as
Belmopan grew, but in fact few people chose to leave for the sterile "new town" atmosphere of Belmopan, and Belize City remains by far the most populous place in the coun-

try. Since **independence** in 1981, the rise of foreign investment and tourism has made an impact, and since then Belize City has been experiencing a construction boom.

## Arrival and information

Although Belize City is by far the largest urban area in the country (the capital, Belmopan is less than one tenth the size), getting from the transport terminals to the centre is very easy, and once you get downtown you'll find that almost everything you need is within a kilometre of the Swing Bridge. **Taxis**, identified by their green licence plates, charge Bz$5 (US$2.50) for one or two passengers within the city. A **city bus** operates to a few residential areas, but is of little use to the visitor.

Belize City has two **airports**. International flights land at the **Philip Goldson International Airport**, 17km northwest of the city at Ladyville, just off the Northern Highway. Belize's **domestic airlines** also make stops at the international airport, so you might want to pick up an onward flight right away: prices to all destinations are US$15 more than from the main domestic base at the **municipal airport**, on the edge of the sea a few kilometres north of the centre. There's no bus service from either airport to Belize City. From the international airport a taxi into the city is US$15 (or it's a 25-min walk to the Northern Highway to flag down one of the frequent passing buses); from the municipal airport, a taxi costs US$2.50 and walking takes 25 minutes.

The main **bus companies** in Belize have their terminals in the same western area of the city, around the Collet Canal and Magazine Road, a fairly derelict part of town known as Mesopotamia. It's only 1km from the centre and you can easily walk – or, especially at night, take a taxi – to any of the hotels listed below. Most scheduled **boats returning from the cayes** pull in at the Marine Terminal on the north side of the Swing Bridge, though some use Courthouse Wharf on the south side; from either it's a fairly short walk or taxi ride to any of the hotels or bus depots.

The **Belize Tourist Board** (BTB) office is some distance from the centre, at Gabourel Lane in front of the Central Bank building (Mon–Fri 8am–5pm; ☎02/77213). Although it's not an essential visit you can pick up free bus timetables, a hotel guide and city map, nature reserve brochures and copies of the (sometimes free) **tourist newspapers**. In the city centre the **Marine Terminal** ticket office (p.208) next to the Swing Bridge has reliable information on **bus and boat schedules**.

Should you want to escape the city for a while, you can take a **day tour** inland. Most visit at least two of the following: the Belize Zoo, Bermudian Landing Baboon Sanctuary, Crooked Tree Wildlife Sanctuary, Altun Ha ruins and Lamanai ruins. All but the last two are very easy to visit independently, though, with the exception of the zoo, you'll need to stay overnight. However, even with the extra cost of accommodation, it's still likely to work out less expensive and more rewarding than a tour. If time is short and you'd prefer a **guided tour** contact Belize Travel Adventures, 168 N Front St (☎02/33064, *bzetravel@btl.net*). David Cunningham (☎014/9828) and Mary Avila (☎31270) are superb **independent tour guides**.

## Accommodation

There are about fifty **hotels** in Belize City, around a third of which cost US$15–25 double, with at least another half-dozen in the US$25–40 range; the selection below covers all price ranges. There's usually no need to book (unless you're eager to stay in a particular hotel) as you'll almost always find something in the price range you're looking for. To make finding a particular hotel easier, the listings below have been divided into accommodation north and south of **Haulover Creek**.

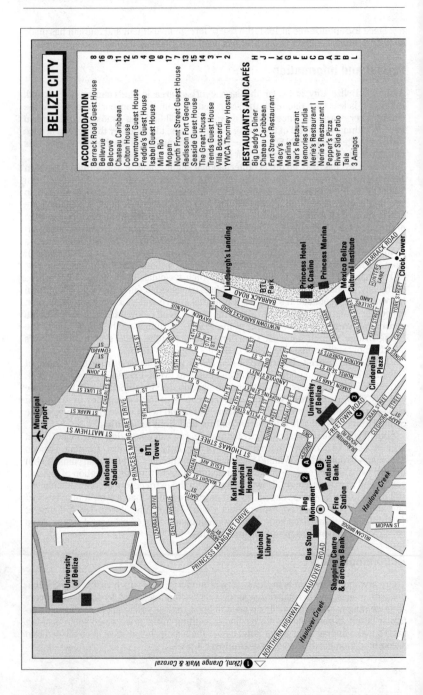

# BELIZE CITY

## ACCOMMODATION

| | |
|---|---|
| Barrack Road Guest House | 8 |
| Bellevue | 16 |
| Belcove | 9 |
| Chateau Caribbean | 11 |
| Colton House | 12 |
| Downtown Guest House | 5 |
| Freddie's Guest House | 4 |
| Isabel Guest House | 10 |
| Mira Rio | 6 |
| Mopan | 17 |
| North Front Street Guest House | 7 |
| Radisson Fort George | 13 |
| Seaside Guest House | 15 |
| The Great House | 14 |
| Trends Guest House | 3 |
| Villa Boscardi | 1 |
| YWCA Thornley Hostel | 2 |

## RESTAURANTS AND CAFÉS

| | |
|---|---|
| Big Daddy's Diner | H |
| Chateau Caribbean | J |
| Fort Street Restaurant | I |
| Macy's | K |
| Marlins | G |
| Mar's Restaurant | F |
| Memories of India | E |
| Nerie's Restaurant I | C |
| Nerie's Restaurant II | D |
| Pepper's Pizza | A |
| River Side Patio | H |
| Tala | B |
| 3 Amigos | L |

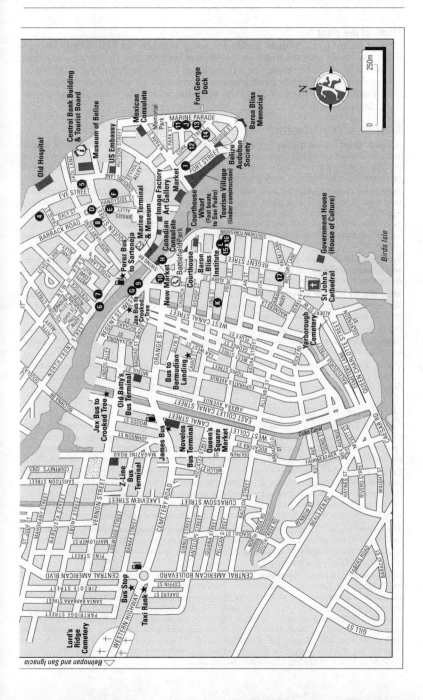

## North of the river

Most of Belize City's **budget hotels** are north of the Swing Bridge, and the ones listed have been selected firstly on the basis of security, and then price – anything cheaper is likely to be unsafe – and those listed below also have good single rates. The more upmarket hotels (most take credit cards) are generally located in the historic **Fort George area** or along the **seafront**, where the residents can benefit from the sea breezes.

*BUDGET ACCOMMODATION*

**Barrack Road Guest House**, 8 Barrack Rd (☎02/36671). Just two blocks from the Marine Terminal and set back from the main road, this quiet, clean and very secure guest house, run by the helpful Molly and Leo Castillo, is great value. Rooms (some have private bath) around a tiled courtyard and rates include a small breakfast. ④.

**Downtown Guest House**, 5 Eve St, near the end of Queen St (☎ & fax 02/32057, *calista89@hotmail.com*). Best-value budget place in the city. Small rooms (some with private bath), but very friendly, clean and secure, with a balcony over the street at the front, TV and fridge in the sitting room downstairs. Cook your own food in the small kitchen or the owner, Miss Kenny, will cook a bargain breakfast and other vegetarian meals; she has the shop next door for cold beer, drinks and snacks. ③.

**Freddie's Guest House**, 86 Eve St, on the city edge near the waterfront (☎02/33851). Three clean, secure and peaceful rooms with comfortable beds with bedside lamps; the best value in this price range. One room has immaculate private bath and the shared bathroom gleams. ④.

**Mira Rio**, 59 N Front St (☎02/34147), across the road from the *North Front Street Guest House*. Recently renovated rooms, some with private bath, overlooking the river. The bar below is good for information, as boat owners often call in for a beer, but there's no late-night noise. ④.

**North Front Street Guest House**, 124 N Front St (☎02/77595, *thoth@btl.net*). A budget travellers' favourite: friendly, helpful and just two blocks from the Marine Terminal. Simple shared-bath rooms and a balcony overlooking the street. ③.

**YWCA Thornley Hostel**, corner of Freetown Rd and St Thomas St (☎02/44971, *ywca@btl.net*). Comfortable beds (not bunks) in dorm rooms with shared bathrooms. The YWCA runs a school for disadvantaged children and operates a volunteer programme. US$10 per person.

*MODERATE TO EXPENSIVE*

**Chateau Caribbean**, 6 Marine Parade (☎02/30800, fax 30900, *www.chateaucaribbean.com*). Comfortable, colonial-style hotel with recently renovated a/c rooms, some with sea views. The spacious public areas, with wicker furniture and balconies overlooking the sea, are a favourite of visiting film crews, and the *Chateau* has often been used as a movie set. Good restaurant. ⑧.

**Colton House**, 9 Cork St (☎02/44666, fax 30451, *www.coltonhouse.com*). Beautifully kept colonial house with shaded gardens in the Fort George area; the best guest house in Belize. The six a/c rooms are individually decorated in English country-house style, each with an immaculate bathroom and balcony. Owners Alan and Ondina Colton keep an extensive book and video library on Belize and offer free coffee in the mornings though no meals are served. No children under nine. ⑦.

**The Great House**, 13 Cork St (☎02/33400, fax 33444, *www.greathousebelize.com*). Twelve spacious, well-equipped and well-run rooms in a modernized and expanded private house (originally built in 1927) in the prestigious Fort George area. All rooms have a/c, a balcony, private bath, coffee-maker, TV, phone and dedicated fax line. ⑨.

**Radisson Fort George Hotel and Marina**, 2 Marine Parade, north side of the harbour mouth (☎02/33333, fax 73820, *www.radissonbelize.com*). Luxurious flagship of the city's hotels, and by far the most expensive at around US$150, though you can expect discounts on the "rack rates" when it's not full. All rooms have a huge cable TV, fridge and minibar and many have extra electrical and telephone sockets for business travellers. Rooms in the Club Wing, reached by the only glass elevator in Belize, have marble floors and unbeatable sea views. Some rooms have bathrooms specially adapted for wheelchair users. There's an excellent restaurant and the grounds are an oasis of calm on the edge of the sea, with a sea-facing pool and a huge private dock, used by the larger live-aboard dive boats. ⑨.

**Trends Guest House**, 91 Freetown Rd (☎02/36066, fax 36065, *edsan@btl.net*). Five very comfortable, carpeted, no-smoking, a/c rooms, with private bath and cable TV in a secure new hotel a couple of kilometres west of the centre. Run by the friendly Edward Felix, who offers guests a free beer, soft drink or bottled water on arrival and coffee or tea in the morning. No credit cards or travellers' cheques accepted. There's another *Trends* on Caye Caulker (see p.240). ⑤.

**Villa Boscardi**, 6043 Manatee Drive (☎ & fax 02/31691, or ☎014/7734, *www.villaboscardi.com*). Beautiful, spacious, well-equipped and immaculately clean no-smoking rooms with a/c, private bath, TV and telephone in a private house 4km from the city centre, just off the Northern Highway. Friendly owners Franco and Francoise Boscardi (originally from Italy) offer guests free pick-up from anywhere in the city and will do all they can to help you enjoy your stay. Breakfast is included in the room rate (other meals can be delivered) and there's a full kitchen for guests. No service charge and no extra charge for using credit cards. ⑦.

## The south side

**Belcove Hotel**, 9 Regent St West (☎02/73054, *belcove@hotmail.com*). Recently renovated rooms, some with a/c and most with private bath. There's a certain thrill of being on the edge of the dangerous part of town, though the hotel itself is quite secure. ④/⑤.

**Bellevue Hotel**, 5 Southern Foreshore (☎02/77051, fax 72353, *fins@btl.net*). The top hotel on the south side of the Swing Bridge, right on the seafront. Modern, a/c rooms in a converted colonial house with a relaxing courtyard, adorned with palms and pool. The upstairs *Harbour Room* bar is a popular meeting place; especially during the evening happy hour (5–8pm), and the *Maya Tavern* disco is a focal point of the city's nightlife, with live music on Friday and Saturday nights. ⑦.

**Isabel Guest House**, across the Swing Bridge, above and behind Central Drug Store (☎02/73139). Small, friendly, mainly Spanish-speaking guest house, with large rooms and private showers. Good for a group sharing. ④.

**Mopan Hotel**, 55 Regent St (☎02/77351, *www.hotelmopan.com*). A large wood-fronted building at the quiet end of the street near the colonial House of Culture and popular with naturalists, writers and scientists. All rooms have private bath, some have a/c; the best rooms are in the bright, breezy new extension. ⑥.

**Seaside Guest House**, 3 Prince St, half a block from the southern foreshore (☎02/78339, *friends@btl.net*). A clean, well-run and very secure hotel, and a renowned meeting place for budget travellers. One room has seven hostel-style dorm beds (US$10) and there are some private rooms. Good hot shared showers, a payphone, accurate information and breakfast can be ordered. You get a key for access at all times – a rarity in budget hotels. ③.

# The City

Richard Davies, a British traveller in the mid-nineteenth century, wrote of the city: "There is much to be said for Belize, for in its way it was one of the prettiest ports at which we touched, and its cleanliness and order . . . were in great contrast to the ports we visited later as to make them most remarkable." Many of the features that elicited this praise have now gone, though some of the distinctive **wooden colonial buildings** have been preserved as heritage showpieces, converted into hotels, restaurants or museums. Even in cases where the decay is too advanced for the paintwork, balconies and carved railings to be restored, the old wooden structures remain more pleasing than the concrete blocks that have replaced so many of them.

Before the construction of the first wooden bridge in the early 1800s, cattle were winched over the waterway that divides the city – hence the name Haulover Creek. Its replacement, the present **Swing Bridge**, made in Liverpool and opened in 1923, is the only manually operated swing bridge left in the Americas. Every day at 5.30am and 5.30pm the endless parade of vehicles and people is halted and the process of turning begins. Using long poles inserted into a capstan, four men gradually lever the bridge around until it's pointing in the direction of the harbour mouth. During the few minutes that the bridge is open, the river traffic is busier than that on the roads, and traffic is snarled up across the whole city.

## The north side

Immediately on the **north side** of the Swing Bridge is the **Marine Terminal**, the beautifully restored former Belize City Fire Station, built in 1923 and the place to catch **boats for the northern cayes**. Inside there's a small restaurant, reasonably clean toilets, (expensive) luggage lockers and some shops. One of them, Sunny's, has pesos and quetzales for anyone headed to Mexico or Guatemala, sells tickets to Flores and beyond, and stocks maps and guide books, including *Rough Guides*. The same building also houses two of Belize's superbly designed new museums (both daily 8am–4.30pm; US$2). The **Coastal Zone Museum** contains displays and explanations of reef ecology, and upstairs, the **Maritime Museum** exhibits a fascinating collection of models and documents relating to Belize's seafaring heritage.

Opposite the Marine Terminal is the three-storey **Paslow Building**, the largest wooden building in the country, with the **post office** on the ground floor. A block east of the Marine Terminal, at 91 N Front St, **The Image Factory** (Mon–Fri 9am–6pm; ☎02/34151; free but donations welcome) is host to Belize's hottest contemporary artists. The gallery puts on outstanding and often provocative exhibitions and you often get a chance to discuss the work with the artists themselves. Continuing east along N Front Street, past the "temporary" market (which often has a greater variety of produce than the official market south of the Swing Bridge), you pass the **National Handicraft Centre** (Mon–Fri 8am–5pm), which sells high-quality Belizean crafts at fair prices. This area is now undergoing development as a "tourism village", ready to present an ersatz view of Belizean culture to hordes of cruise ship passengers.

Beyond here the road follows the north shore of the river mouth – an area that was Fort George Island until 1924, when the narrow strait was filled in – reaching the point marked by **Bliss Lighthouse**, a memorial to Baron Bliss, Belize's greatest benefactor (see below). Walking around the shoreline you pass **Memorial Park**, which honours the Belizean dead of the two World Wars. In this area you'll find several **colonial mansions**, many of the best-preserved now taken over by embassies and upmarket hotels; a fine example is the Mexican embassy on the north corner of the park.

Natural history enthusiasts will benefit from a visit to two of Belize's foremost conservation organizations in the Fort George area. The **Programme for Belize**, at 1 Eyre St (☎02/75616; *www.pfb.org*), manages the Rio Bravo Conservation Area (p.223); call in for news on access and progress from the enthusiastic staff. Further along, at 12 Fort St, the **Belize Audubon Society** (☎02/35004) has information, books, maps and posters relating to all the country's wildlife reserves, and is very prominent in conservation education. North of here, at the corner of Hutson Street and Gabourel Lane, is the **US Embassy**; this superb "colonial" building was actually constructed in New England in the nineteenth century from American timber, before being dismantled and shipped to Belize. It's also notable for being the only US embassy in the world not guarded by US Marines. Just beyond here, in front of the Central Bank building, the Victorian former colonial prison is undergoing conversion into the **Museum of Belize** and will house colonial and Maya artefacts. About 750m north along the shore, at the far end of Eve Street, a new sea wall and promenade have been built, leading to the enormous *Princess Hotel*. The attractive new park (**BTL Park**) beyond was built on reclaimed land and it was in this area that Charles Lindbergh landed the *Spirit of St Louis* in 1927, the first aeroplane to touch down in Belize.

## The south side

The **south side** is generally the older section of Belize City: in the early days the elite lived in the seafront houses while the backstreets were home to the slaves and labourers. These days it's the city's commercial centre, containing the main shopping streets, banks and travel agencies. Right by the Swing Bridge is the three-storey **indoor mar-**

**ket**, built on the site of the rather decrepit old colonial market, dating from 1820. **Albert Street**, running south from the Swing Bridge, is the main commercial thoroughfare, with banks, supermarkets and good-value T-shirt and souvenir shops – Sings, at number 35, has some of the best bargains. On the parallel **Regent Street**, a block closer to the sea, are the former colonial administration and court buildings, known together as the **Courthouse**. These well-preserved examples of colonial architecture, with their columns and fine wrought iron, were completed in 1926 after an earlier building on the same site was destroyed by fire. The Courthouse overlooks **Battlefield Park**, a patch of grass and trees with a (usually dry) ornamental fountain in the centre, named to commemorate the heated political meetings which took place there before independence.

A block south of the Courthouse, on the waterfront and resembling a squat airport control tower, the **Bliss Institute** is in fact a **performing arts centre** hosting exhibitions, concerts and plays. The Institute was funded by the legacy of Baron Bliss, a moderately eccentric Englishman with a Portuguese title – visit the Maritime Museum to find out more about him. A keen fisherman, he arrived off the coast of Belize in his yacht *Sea King* in 1926 after hearing about the tremendous amount of game fish in local waters. Unfortunately, he became ill and died without ever having been ashore, but he must have been impressed by whatever fish he did catch, as he left most of his considerable estate (which became The Bliss Trust) to benefit the people of the colony. In gratitude, the authorities declared March 9 (the date of his death) an official public holiday – **Baron Bliss Day** – commemorated by boat races funded partly by his legacy.

At the southern end of Albert Street is **St John's Cathedral**, the oldest Anglican cathedral in Central America and one of the oldest buildings in Belize. Work began in 1812 and was completed in 1820, the red bricks for its construction brought over as ballast in British ships. With its square, battlemented tower, it looks more like a large English parish church than anything you might expect to find in Central America. Here, between 1815 and 1845, the kings of the Mosquito Coast were crowned amid great pomp, taking the title to a British Protectorate that extended along the coast of Honduras and Nicaragua.

Opposite the cathedral, in a breezy seafront setting, shaded by Royal palms and complete with beautiful green lawn, is the well-preserved, white-painted colonial Government House, now renamed the **House of Culture** (daily 8.30am–4.30pm; entrance to grounds free, US$2.50 to the house). Built in 1814, it was the governor's residence when Belize was a British colony: at midnight on September 20, 1981 the Belize flag was hoisted here for the first time as the country celebrated independence. The present governor general, Sir Colville Young, wanted to make this superb example of Belize's colonial heritage open to everyone, with the result that in 1996 it was designated a **museum**. A plush red carpet leads down the hall to the great mahogany staircase, the walls lined with prints of sombre past governors. Much of the collection of silverware, glasses and furniture used during the colonial period may well have moved to the Museum of Belize (see opposite) by the time you read this, as in its new role as House of Culture the building hosts painting and dance workshops, art exhibitions and musical performances. In the grounds, the carefully restored *Sea King*, the tender of Baron Bliss's yacht of the same name, stands as testimony to the craftsmanship of Belizean boatbuilders.

**Yarborough Cemetery**, just west of the cathedral, was named after the magistrate who owned the land and permitted the burial of prominent people here from 1781 – commoners were admitted only after 1870. Although the graves have fallen into disrepair, a browse among the stones will turn up fascinating snippets of history. At the seaward end of this strip of land, connected to the mainland by a narrow wooden causeway, **Bird's Isle** is a venue for reggae concerts and parties.

# Eating, drinking and nightlife

The multitude of **restaurants** in Belize City are beginning to offer some variety, though the tasty but monotonous **Creole** fare of rice and beans still predominates. There's also plenty of seafood and steaks, and a preponderance of **Chinese** restaurants — usually the best bet for **vegetarians** — and some very good **Lebanese** and **Indian** restaurants. Greasy fried chicken is available as a takeaway from small restaurants all over the city: a Belizean favourite known as "dollar chicken", whatever the price. If you're really in a hurry, try *HL's Burger*, Belize City's answer to *McDonald's*, which has a growing number of outlets. The big hotels have their own restaurants, naturally quite expensive, but with much more varied menus and good service.

If you're shopping for food, the main **supermarkets** – Brodie's and Romac's – are worth a look; they're on Albert Street, just past the park, and their selection of food is good if expensive, reflecting the fact that much is imported. Milk and dairy products, produced locally by Mennonite farmers (see p.220), are delicious and of good quality. Naturally enough, local **fruit** is cheap and plentiful, though highly seasonal; Belizean citrus fruits are among the best in the world.

In the listings below we have quoted a phone number in places where it is recommended you should **reserve a table**, or for those places which offer a **delivery service**.

## Restaurants and cafés north of the river

**Chateau Caribbean**, 6 Marine Parade. Undisturbed views of blue sea and offshore islands from this cool first-floor restaurant, above the hotel of the same name. Prices are more reasonable than you'd guess from the gleaming white linen and cutlery.

**Fort Street Restaurant**, 4 Fort St (☎02/30116). High-quality Creole and American food in the relaxed surroundings of a restored colonial house. Pricey, though the daily lunch special remains reasonable value.

**Mar's Belizean Restaurant**, 11 Handyside St. Tasty Belizean food at great prices in spacious, clean surroundings run by Maria "Mar" Evans. Karaoke, and other music, on some Fridays.

**Memories of India**, corner of Queen and Handyside streets (☎02/31172). The only Indian restaurant in the city centre and very good, with chicken, lamb and lots of vegetarian curries. Free deliveries.

**Nerie's Restaurant II**, corner of Queen and Daly streets. The best Belizean food north of the river, and fantastically good value, served in clean, well-run and brightly lit surroundings. Very busy at lunchtimes, when there's always a special. *Nerie's I*, on Freetown Road just past Cinderella Plaza, opposite the Belize Technical College, is just as good.

**Pepper's Pizza**, 4 St Thomas St (☎02/35000). Decent pizza restaurant with reliable deliveries. Open Mon–Thurs 10am–10pm, Fri & Sat 10am–11.30pm, Sun noon–9pm.

**Princess Hotel Restaurant**, Newtown Barracks Road. All-you-can-eat buffet at lunch and dinner for only US$7.50 at the biggest hotel in Belize. The food theme varies daily: Italian, Oriental, Mexican and so on. Free buffets for gamblers at the casino.

**Tala**, 164 Freetown Rd (☎02/45841). The best Lebanese food in the country, with delicious tahini, falafel, hummus and kebabs — try the Lebanese plate. Will deliver.

**The Smoky Mermaid**, 13 Cork St, below the *Great House*. One of the city's best new restaurants, with tables around a courtyard fountain and a popular Friday evening happy hour.

## Restaurants and cafés south of the river

**Big Daddy's Diner**, upstairs in the new market, south side of the Swing Bridge. Great breakfasts and Belizean dishes, with a daily lunch special, served in clean, bright surroundings with the best harbour and bridge views in the city. Open Mon–Sat 7am–4pm.

**Macy's**, 18 Bishop St (☎02/73419). Long-established and very reasonably priced Creole restaurant that's popular with locals; very busy at lunchtimes.

**Marlins**, 11 Regent St West, next to the *Belcove Hotel*. Good, inexpensive, local food in large portions, with some tables on the verandah overlooking the river. Closes early, around 7.30pm.

**River Side Patio**, at the rear of the market. Good place to relax with a drink as you watch the bridge swing. Mexican-style food, and early-evening entertainment on Friday and Saturday.

**3 Amigos**, 2B King St (☎02/79936). A team of friendly professionals – chef Edward and waiters Franz and Sherman, the three amigos – prepare and serve what is consistently the best food in the city at great prices. All dishes are exquisitely prepared and if you can't make up your mind from the extensive menu just go for the daily special. Always vegetarian alternatives to the mainly seafood, salad and steak entrées. Open Mon–Sat 11am–11pm.

## Drinking, nightlife and entertainment

Belize City's more sophisticated, air-conditioned **bars** are found in the most expensive establishments, and several, particularly the *Bellevue*, the *Great House* and the *Radisson*, generally have Friday evening **happy hours** where you can chat with city professionals enjoying a drink after work. At the lowest end of the scale are dimly lit dives, effectively men-only, where, though there's the possibility that you'll be offered drugs or be robbed, it's more likely that you'll have a thoroughly enjoyable time meeting easy-going, hard-drinking locals. There are several places between the two extremes, some of them in restaurants and hotels – for example, the early-closing *Marlins* restaurant (see above), *Mira Rio* hotel (see "Accommodation", p.206) and *Nu Fenders*, a bar on the corner of Queen and Handyside streets.

**Nightlife**, though not as wild as it used to be, is becoming more reliable and the quality of live bands is improving all the time. If you're after **live music** the *Radisson Fort George* and the *Calypso Bar* at the *Princess Hotel* hold regular dances and frequently host top local bands, while Santino's Messengers usually play the *Maya Tavern* at the *Bellevue Hotel*, on Friday and Saturday nights. There's **punta and reggae** at *Planet Hollywood* (not part of the chain), on the corner of Queen and Handyside streets, while *Nerie's Restaurant*, opposite, has local band Davonix (no cover charge) in the upstairs *La Bodega Lounge* on Friday evenings. A bit further afield the *Lumba Yard Bar*, on the riverbank just out of town on the Northern Highway, hosts some of the best bands. The newest addition to Belize City's nightlife scene is the **casino** at the *Princess Hotel*. You'll need a passport or photo ID to gain temporary membership (free) and officially you have to change **US$25 minimum** into tokens for the slot machines — any you don't use are changed back. You don't have to be a really high roller to play here though, and the drinks and buffet are free while you're dropping money into the slots and sitting at the poker and roulette tables.

## Listings

**Airlines** Aerocaribe and TACA, Belize Global Travel, 41 Albert St (☎02/77363); Aerovias, Mopan Travels, 55 Regent St (☎02/75446); American, corner of New Rd and Queen St (☎02/32522); Continental, 80 Regent St (☎02/78309); Maya Island Air, Municipal Airport (☎02/31140 or 026/2345); Tropic Air, Municipal Airport (☎02/45671 or 026/2012).

**American Express** in Belize Global Travel, 41 Albert St (☎02/77363).

**Banks and exchange** The main branches of Atlantic, Barclays, Belize and Scotia banks are on Albert Street (Mon–Thurs 8am–2pm, Fri 8am–4.30pm). Barclays, opposite the park, does cash advances on Visa (Belize Bank charges US$7.50), and has the only ATM which accepts foreign-issued cards. Cash in US$ is usually readily available from the banks. Shops, hotels and restaurants accept US$ bills (giving change in Bz$) and many also accept travellers' cheques and plastic. Guatemalan and Mexican currency is often difficult to obtain, except at the borders, but Sunny's in the Marine Terminal usually has quetzales and pesos.

**Books** In addition to the shops listed here, many of the larger hotels also sell books, magazines and papers (including Caribbean editions of US newspapers and *Time*, *Newsweek* etc.), and some budget hotels operate book exchanges. Both the Book Center, 2 Church St, opposite the BTL office (☎02/77457), and Angelus Press, 10 Queen St (☎02/35777) have a wide range of books on Belize, maps and guides including *Rough Guides*.

## MOVING ON FROM BELIZE CITY

Moving on from Belize City **to all towns** in the country, across the borders **to Chetumal** in Mexico and **to Melchor** in Guatemala, and **to the main northern cayes** is very simple during daylight. While a few buses continue to run on the main routes during the evening, there are no **night flights** (international or domestic) in Belize, nor do any **scheduled boats** operate at night.

Most of the **bus departure points** are in the same area, along the Collet Canal and Magazine Road, a short walk from the centre of town. While the main bus companies have their own depots, there are numerous smaller operators with regular departures but no contact address or telephone number – all those listed below are marked on the Belize City map. Where **express services** are available (currently on Northern and Western highways only) these are faster and a fraction more expensive than regular services, stopping only in main towns.

At the time of writing, Novelo's, the largest bus company in Belize and covering the northern and western routes, had recently taken over Batty's and Venus buses, and was about to consolidate its operations from a new depot, very near the two existing stations. This is likely to be at the junction of Cemetery Road and West Collet Canal, and is also marked on the city map (pp.204–205).

### BUS COMPANIES AND DEPOTS

**James Bus** leaves daily for **Dangriga** (3hr) and **Punta Gorda** (8hr) (via Belmopan) from Shell station, Cemetery Road, near Collet Canal; 4 departures beginning at 7am.

**Jex Bus** (☎025/7017) leaves for **Crooked Tree** (1hr 30min) from Regent Street West and Pound Yard, Collet Canal. Mon–Sat 10.30am, 4.30pm & 5.30pm

**McFadzean's Bus** leaves for **Bermudian Landing** (1hr 15min) (via Burrell Boom) from the corner of Cemetery Rd and Mosul St, near the Batty bus depot, at noon & 5pm.

**Novelos**, 19 West Collet Canal (☎02/77372); for the **Western Highway** including Belmopan, **San Ignacio** (2hr 30min and **Benque Viejo** (for Guatemalan border, 3hr). Daily, every 30min from 5am–9pm. For services along the Northern Highway and to Chetumal, Mexico, see Venus entry, below.

**Perez Bus** leaves for **Sarteneja** (4hr) from the Texaco station on North Front St at noon & 1pm.

**Car rental** The following companies are in Belize City and will arrange vehicle pick-up and drop-off anywhere in the city or at the Municipal or International airports at no extra charge: Avis ☎02/34619; Budget ☎02/23435; Crystal (which allows you to take vehicles over the Guatemalan border) ☎02/31600; IBTM ☎02/32668 or 016/2997. For more information see "Getting Around" in Basics p.32.

**Embassies and consulates** Though the official capital is Belmopan, some embassies remain in Belize City and are normally open Monday to Friday mornings. Several EU countries have (mainly honorary) consulates in Belize City; current addresses and phone numbers are in the Diplomatic Listings, at the back of the green pages in the telephone directory. Canada (cannot issue passports), 83 N Front St (☎02/31060); Guatemala, 8 A St, Kings Park (☎02/33150); Honduras, 91 N Front St (☎02/45889); Mexico, 18 N Park St (☎02/31388); USA, 29 Gabourel Lane (☎02/77161).

**Film developing** For prints, slides and fast passport photos, try Spooners, 89 N Front St, or Titos, 9 Barrack Rd.

**Immigration** The Belize Immigration Office is in the Government Complex on Mahogany Street, near the junction of Central American Blvd and the Western Highway (Mon–Thurs 8.30am–4pm, Fri closes 3.30pm; ☎02/24620). Thirty-day extensions of stay (the maximum allowed) cost Bz$25.

**Russell's Bus** leaves for **Bermudian Landing** from Cairo St, near the corner of Cemetery Rd and Euphrates Ave at noon & 4.30pm.

**Venus**, Magazine Road (☎02/73354); the **Northern Highway**, including **Orange Walk** (1hr 30min), **Corozal** (2hr 30min) and to **Chetumal**, Mexico (3hr 30min). Every day, hourly from 6am–6pm.

**Z-Line (ZL)**, Magazine Road (☎02/73937); the main company for daily services along the **Hummingbird and Southern highways** and Coastal Rd to **Dangriga** (2–3hr), **Placencia** (2 daily services; 5–6hr) and **Punta Gorda** (8hr). Approximately hourly from 7am–5pm.

## BY AIR

See "Listings" p.211 for details of international and domestic airlines.

### Domestic flights
Domestic flights originate from Belize City's Municipal Airport, with dozens of scheduled flights to many destinations. Maya Island Air and Tropic Air operate flights to: Caye Caulker (15–20min) and San Pedro (10min from Caye Caulker), at least hourly from 7am–5pm; Dangriga (8–10 daily; 25min), Placencia (a further 20min) and Punta Gorda (another 25min).

### International flights
Belize City International Airport to: Cancún (3–4 weekly; 1hr 30min), San Salvador (1 daily; 1hr 30min), Guatemala City (at least 1 daily; 1hr 30min), Flores (3 daily; 45min), Roatán (1 daily; 1hr 45min), San Pedro Sula (1 daily; 1hr). See "Basics" p.4 for further information.

## BY BOAT

Scheduled **boats to Caye Caulker** leave from the Marine Terminal (☎02/31969) on N Front Street, by the Swing Bridge (every 2hr 9am–5pm; 45min; US$7.50 one way, day return US$12.50); also at least 3 daily to Ambergris Caye (1hr 25min; US$12.50 one way, open return US$22.50). For **San Pedro on Ambergris Caye**, other scheduled boats leave from Courthouse Wharf, south of the Swing Bridge (3 daily, calling at Caye Caulker). Any scheduled boat will also stop on request at **St George's Caye**. For more information see the boxes on pp.231 and 241. The *Gulf Cruzer* (☎02/24506) departs Fridays at 6am for Placencia (2hr; US$25) and Puerto Cortés, Honduras (a further 3hr and another US$50).

**Laundry** Central America Coin Laundry, 114 Barrack Rd (Mon–Sat 8.30am–9pm; reduced hours Sun), and in many hotels.

**Medical care** Dr Gamero, Myo-On Clinic, 40 Eve St (☎02/45616); Karl Heusner Memorial Hospital, Princess Margaret Drive, near the junction with the Northern Highway (☎02/31548).

**Police** The main police station is on Queen Street, a block north of the Swing Bridge (☎02/72210; Emergency ☎90 nationwide). Alternatively, contact the Tourism Police (☎02/72222, ext 401; see p.199).

**Post office** The main post office is in the Paslow Building, on the corner of Queen Street, immediately north of the Swing Bridge (Mon–Fri 8am–noon & 1–4.30pm).

**Telecommunications and email** There are payphones and cardphones dotted around the city; or use the main BTL office, 1 Church St (Mon–Sat 8am–6pm), which also has fax facilities and the best-priced email service. *Karol's Internet Café*, 9 Barrack Rd, has a few connected computers, but is more expensive than BTL and there's no support.

**Travel and tour agents** The following travel agents are the best for information and bookings on flights and connections throughout the region; all can arrange tours and car rental within Belize: Belize Global Travel, 41 Albert St (☎77363, *bzadventur@btl.net* ); JAL's Travel and Tours, 184 North Front St (☎02/45407).

# THE NORTH

**Northern Belize** is an expanse of relatively level land, where lagoons, swamps and savannahs are mixed with rainforest and farmland. The largest town in the north is **Orange Walk**, the country's main centre for sugar production. Further to the north, **Corozal**, just fifteen minutes from the border, is a small and peaceful Caribbean town with a strong Mexican element. Most of the original settlers here were refugees from the Caste Wars in Yucatán, and as a result, Spanish is as common as Creole throughout the north.

Most visitors to northern Belize are here to see the **Maya ruins** and **wildlife reserves**. The ruins of **Altun Ha**, reached by the old Northern Highway, are usually visited as part of a day-trip from Belize City or San Pedro, and the largest site, **Lamanai**, features some of the most impressive pyramids in the country. Other sites include **Cuello** and **Nohmul**, respectively west and north of Orange Walk, and **Santa Rita** and **Cerros**, both near Corozal.

The four main **wildlife reserves** in the region each offer a different approach to conservation and an insight into different environments. At the **Bermudian Landing Community Baboon Sanctuary** in the Belize River valley, a group of farmers have combined agriculture with conservation, much to the benefit of the black howler monkey, while at the **Crooked Tree Wildlife Sanctuary** a network of rivers and lagoons offers protection to a range of resident and migratory birds, including the endangered jabiru stork. By far the largest and most ambitious conservation project, however, is the vast **Rio Bravo Conservation Area**: 1000 square kilometres of tropical forest and river systems in the west of Orange Walk district, adjoining the border with Guatemala. The most northerly protected area is the **Shipstern Nature Reserve**, preserving a large area of tropical forest and wetland.

**Travelling around** the north is fairly straightforward if you stick to the main roads, with buses running at least hourly along the Northern Highway between Belize City and Santa Elena on the Mexican border, calling at Orange Walk and Corozal, and continuing across the border to the market in **Chetumal**.

## Belize City to Orange Walk

Regular, fast buses run the 88km along the **Northern Highway** from Belize City to Orange Walk in less than an hour and a half. To get to the **Bermudian Landing Baboon Sanctuary**, **Crooked Tree Wildlife Sanctuary** or the ruins of **Altun Ha** by public transport, you'll need to take one of the local buses detailed in the text.

Leaving Belize City you pass spreading suburbs, where expensive houses are constructed on reclaimed mangrove swamps; look to the east and you'll get a glimpse of the sea. Seven kilometres from the city a metal-framed bridge carries the road over the mouth of the Belize River at the point where the Haulover Creek branches away to the south. For the next few kilometres the road stays very close to the river and is prone to flooding after heavy rain. At **Ladyville**, 15km from Belize City, you pass the turning to the international airport.

### The Bermudian Landing Community Baboon Sanctuary and Burrell Boom

The **Community Baboon Sanctuary**, established in 1985 as a collaboration between primate biologist Rob Horwich and a group of local farmers (with help from the World

Wide Fund for Nature), is one of the most interesting conservation projects in Belize. A mixture of farmland and broadleaved forest, the sanctuary stretches along 30km of the Belize River valley – from Flowers Bank to Big Falls – and comprises a total of eight villages and over a hundred landowners. Farmers here have adopted a voluntary code of practice to harmonize their own needs with those of the wildlife in a project combining conservation, education and tourism.

The main focus of attention is the **black howler monkey** (locally known as a baboon), the largest monkey in the New World. The baboons live in troops of between four and eight, and spend the day wandering through the leafy canopy feasting on leaves, flowers and fruits. At dawn and dusk they let rip with the famous howl, a deep and rasping roar that carries for miles. The sanctuary is also home to around two hundred bird species, plus anteaters, deer, peccaries, coatis, iguanas and the endangered Central American river turtle. Special **trails** are cut through the forest so that visitors can see it at its best; you can wander these alone or with a guide from the village and you can also take a guided **canoe trip** along the river.

The village of **BERMUDIAN LANDING**, 43km northwest of Belize City, lies at the heart of the area, a Creole village and former logging centre that dates back to the seventeenth century. The turn-off to the village is 23km along the Northern Highway; the rest of the journey is along a road that's paved as far as Burrell Boom (see below), and is also used to access Hill Bank Field Station (see p.224). Regular buses run from Belize City to the village, daily except Sunday (see p.212), and some of the other villages in the sanctuary now have their own bus services. Bear in mind that returning **buses for Belize City** leave Bermudian Landing early – between 5.30 and 6.30am.

On the way to Bermudian Landing, 6km after the Northern Highway turn-off, you'll pass **BURRELL BOOM**, also on the Belize River. It's named for the boom — a huge, heavy metal chain placed across the river during logging days to catch the logs floating down, and you can see the chain and the anchors that held it by the roadside on the right as you pass through the village. There's a good hotel in Burrell Boom, *El Chiclero* (☎028/2005, *soffitt@io.com*; ⑦), with large, tiled, a/c rooms, very comfortable beds, a good restaurant and a pool. The owner, Carl Faulkner, an American ex-pat, can regale you with amazing tales of life in Belize. If you have your own vehicle and are heading directly west you can save time by cutting down through Burrell Boom to Hattieville, on the Western Highway (see p.249).

## Bermudian Landing Practicalities

Visitors to Bermudian Landing are asked to register at the **visitor centre** (daily 8am–4pm; US$5) at the western end of the village. The fee includes a short guided trail walk and inside the centre is Belize's first natural history museum, with exhibits and information on the riverside habitats and animals you're likely to see. You can **camp** at the visitor centre (US$5; check in with manager Iola Joseph). Alternatively, a number of local families offer **bed and breakfast** rooms (④), a wonderful way to experience village life; check at the visitor centre or ask the sanctuary manager, Fallet Young, who lives nearby, though you'll always get somewhere to stay if you just turn up. *Nature Resort*, behind the visitor centre (☎014/9286, *naturer@btl.net*; ⑤), has two beautiful cabins, each with private bath, electric lights, fan and coffee maker, and hammocks on the porch; **budget rooms** in the nearby wooden house share a separate, clean tiled bathroom. The resort is managed by Alvin Young, who can arrange canoe or horse rental for around US$25 a day; a guide will cost more but the trails are easy to follow on your own. There are a few simple **restaurants and bars** in the village: *Russell's Restaurant*, in the centre on the left-hand side (also the place where the bus parks for the night), has tables under the thatch overlooking the river.

# The ruins of Altun Ha

Fifty-five kilometres north of Belize City and just 9km from the sea is the impressive Maya site of **Altun Ha** (daily 8am–4pm; US$5), occupied for around twelve hundred years until the Classic Maya collapse in 900–950 AD. Its position close to the Caribbean coast suggests that it was sustained as much by trade as agriculture – a theory upheld by the discovery of trade objects such as jade from the Motagua valley in Guatemala and obsidian from the Mexican and Guatemalan highlands – both very important in Maya ceremony. The jade would have come from the Motagua valley in Guatemala and much of it would probably have been shipped onwards to the north.

Around five hundred buildings have been recorded at Altun Ha, but the core of the site is clustered around two Classic period plazas. Entering from the road, you come first to **Plaza A**, enclosed by large temples on all four sides. A magnificent tomb has been discovered beneath Temple A-1, the **Temple of the Green Tomb**. Dating from 550 AD, this yielded a total of three hundred items of grave goods, including jade, jewellery, stingray spines, skin, flints and the remains of a Maya book. Temple A-6, which has been particularly badly damaged, contains two parallel rooms, each about 48m long and with thirteen doorways along an exterior wall.

The adjacent **Plaza B** is dominated by the site's largest temple, B-4, the **Temple of the Masonry Altars**, the last in a sequence of buildings raised on this spot. If it seems familiar, it's because you might already have seen it on the Belikin beer label. Several tombs have been uncovered within the main structure but only two were found intact; most of the others were probably desecrated during the political turmoil that preceded the abandonment of the site. In 1968, archeologists discovered a carved jade head of **Kinich Ahau**, the Maya sun god, in one of the tombs. Standing just under 15cm high, it is the largest carved jade found anywhere in the Maya World. At the moment it's kept hidden away in the vaults of the Belize Bank, as there's no national museum to display it; this may change when the Museum of Belize opens (see p.208).

Outside these two main plazas are several other areas of interest, though little else has been restored. A short trail through the B Group leads south to **Rockstone Pond**,

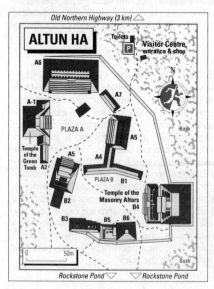

a literal translation of the Maya name of the site and also the present-day name of a nearby village. The pond was dammed in Maya times to form a reservoir (today it's home to a large crocodile); at the eastern edge stands Structure F-8 (Reservoir Temple), the oldest building at Altun Ha. Built in the second century AD, it housed a cache that contained obsidian blades and other offerings imported from the great city of Teotihuacán in the Valley of Mexico. These artefacts have been dated to around 150 AD, evidence of early contact between the lowland Maya and Teotihuacán.

## Practicalities

Altun Ha is fairly difficult to reach independently (though it can be done in a day from Belize City) as the track to the site is located along the Old Northern Highway — turn off the Northern

Highway at Mile 18. There are **buses** (Mon–Sat) from Mosul Street in Belize City (call the community phone ☎031/2058 to check times) to the village of **MASKALL,** passing the turn-off to the site at the village of **LUCKY STRIKE** (community phone ☎021/2017), 3km from Altun Ha. You'll probably have to walk in from here and should only do it this way if you're really dedicated: Altun Ha is probably the least interesting of the major sites in Belize, and Lamanai (see p.221) is better architecturally and easier to reach independently.

There's no **accommodation** at the site but you can ask the caretaker for permission to camp nearby, or press on 15km to Maskall, where you may be able to get a room. Any travel agent in Belize City will arrange a tour (see "Listings" p.213) and increasing numbers make the visit as part of a day-trip from San Pedro (p.240). If money's no object, however, you can submit to the hedonistic (and undoubtedly therapeutic) pleasures of the outrageously Californian-style *Maruba Resort and Jungle Spa,* near Maskall at Mile 40, Old Northern Highway (☎03/22199, in US ☎713/799-2031, *www.maruba-spa.com*; ⑨). Rates start at US$155 for a room and go up to US$425 for a suite. Each room and cabin is luxurious, verging on the opulent, with hand-built wooden furniture and feather beds (there are alternatives if you're allergic). All are decorated individually; one does boast larger-than-life carved wooden penises for door handles, but they're not obtrusive. The food is excellent though the menu includes wild game; there's also a small collection of wild animals, held in doubtful legality and in unsatisfactory cages. On the purely therapeutic side you'd need to stay a week to take advantage of all the health and beauty treatments.

## Crooked Tree Wildlife Sanctuary and village

Further along the Northern Highway, roughly midway between Belize City and Orange Walk, a well-signed branch road heads west 5km to **Crooked Tree Wildlife Sanctuary,** a reserve that takes in a vast area of inland waterways, logwood swamps and lagoons. The sanctuary's greatest treasure are the tens of thousands of migrating and resident birds; over 300 species have been recorded, including snail kites, tiger herons, snowy egrets, ospreys and black-collared hawks. The sanctuary was designated Belize's first **Ramsar site** (after the Ramsar conference on wetlands in Iran) in 1998, as a "wetland habitat of international importance for waterfowl" and it's an ideal nesting and resting place for the sanctuary's greatest treasure: the tens of thousands of migrating and resident **birds,** including snail kites, tiger herons, snowy egrets, ospreys and black-collared hawks. The most famous visitor is the **jabiru stork,** the largest flying bird in the New World, with a wingspan of 2.5m. Belize has the biggest nesting population of jabiru storks at one site; they arrive in November, the young hatch in April or May, and they leave just before the summer rainy season gets under way. The **best time to visit** for bird-watchers is from late February to June, when the lagoons shrink to a string of pools, forcing wildlife to congregate for food and water. Visitors are welcome to participate in the May jabiru census; contact the Belize Audubon Society (see p.572) for details. If you set off to explore the lagoons you might also catch a glimpse of howler monkeys, crocodiles, coatis, turtles or iguanas.

In the middle of the reserve, connected to the mainland by a causeway, the village of **CROOKED TREE** straggles over a low island in the wetlands. Over three hundred years old, it's possibly the oldest community in Belize, with an economy based on fishing, farming and, more recently, tourism. Although the main attraction at Crooked Tree – taking guided boat trips through the lagoon and along sluggish, forest-lined creeks – can work out quite expensive (upwards of US$35 per person, even in a group), it's worth coming just to enjoy the unbelievably tranquil pace of life. Some of the mango and cashew trees here are reckoned to be more than a hundred years old, and during January and February the air is heavy with the scent of cashew blossom. Even without going on a boat trip through the lagoons you'll see plenty of birds as you stroll through the sandy, tree-lined lanes and along the lakeshore. Guides here are supremely knowledgeable, imparting their expertise with understated enthusiasm.

## Practicalities

There are four daily **buses** to Crooked Tree from Belize City. The Jex service (☎025/7017) leaves once daily from Regent Street West (Mon–Sat 10.30am), and twice daily from the Pound Yard bridge (Mon–Fri 4.30pm & 5.30pm); there's also a daily Novelo's service (Mon–Fri 4pm, Sat noon & Sun 9am). As always it's a good idea to check the times with the company (details on p.212), or by calling the village community phone on ☎021/2084. There's enough traffic along the side road from the Northern Highway to make hitching an option; any non-express bus along the highway will drop you off at the junction. Returning buses leave daily for Belize City (Mon–Sat between 6am & 7am; Sun 4pm). The US$4 visitor fee is payable in the **Sanctuary Visitor Centre** near the end of the causeway. The reserve wardens, Steve and Donald Tillett and Rennie Jones, are excellent **guides**, as is Randy Gillett; all are extremely knowledgeable about the area's flora, fauna and rural culture. If you're planning your trip from Belize City, contact David Cunningham, a superb naturalist and avid birder (☎02/4400 or 014/9828) who'll take you to Crooked Tree in his air-conditioned van.

Many villagers now have private telephones (all fixed cellular). You can use the **telephone** at the Jex store – the best stocked in the village – just past the end of the causeway, and there's a payphone in the centre of the village. There are a number of quiet, friendly **restaurants** and **bars** in the village – the liveliest is the *Riverview*, on the side of the lagoon, which has a disco most weekends and sometimes live music.

### ACCOMMODATION

Most of the accommodation at Crooked Tree is in resort-type lodgings, and there's also reasonably priced **bed and breakfast** accommodation (*Molly's* is recommended; ④). Otherwise, there's a dorm room at *Bird's Eye View Lodge* (see below), and most of the resort lodges also have space for camping (US$5 per person). All the places listed can arrange superb guided boat tours through the reserve.

**Bird's Eye View Lodge** (☎02/32040, *birdseye@btl.net*). Comfortable, if incongruous-looking concrete building, right on the lakeshore. All rooms have private bath and there's a dorm room (US$12.50 per person) and camping available. The food is excellent and the tiny bar on the upstairs deck is a good place to catch the evening breeze. Room rates include breakfast. ⑦.

**Chau Hiix Lodge** (☎02/73787, *www.belize-travel.com/chauhiix.htm*). Very well-appointed wooden cottages with a/c and duplex rooms with fan, set in comfortable isolation amid 4000 acres of forest and wetlands at Sapodilla lagoon on the southern edge of the sanctuary. Just getting here is an adventure, as the boat (there's no road access) navigates broad lagoons and tiny creeks. Book in advance; packages include transport from the airport, meals, guided trips and use of boats and canoes. US$535 per person for three nights. ⑨.

**Crooked Tree Resort** (☎02/77745). The once-neat wood-and-thatch cabins on the lakeshore are now getting a bit run-down, but are still a bargain. ⑤.

**Paradise Inn** (☎025/7044, *www.adventurecamera.com/paradise*). Simple but beautiful thatched cabins at the north end of the village just paces from the lake, built by the owner Rudy Crawford; if you call ahead someone will meet you where the bus stops. Rudy's sons, Glen and Robert, are two of the best guides in the village. The hospitality is wonderful and the home-cooked food is great. Camping available. ⑥.

**Sam Tillett's Hotel** (☎ & fax 021/2026 or ☎014/7920, *samhotel@btl.net*). Near the village centre, on the bus route. Though not on the lagoon, this is the best-value hotel in the village. Rooms (including the comfortable Jabiru suite and an inexpensive budget room) are in thatched cabañas and each has a private bath. Sam, known throughout Belize as the "king of birds" for his knowledge, is a great host. The deck is a good place to relax in the evenings, the garden attracts an amazing variety of birds and there's a shelter for camping. Sam's wife, Rita, runs the restaurant, serving superb Belizean food. ③–⑤.

## Around Crooked Tree: Chau Hiix

Visitors to Crooked Tree can benefit from a couple of projects carried out nearby by volunteers from two British-based conservation development organizations, each aiming to promote bird-watching around the lagoon. Both are accessible by boat only. The first,

3km north of the village, is an amazing 700m-long **boardwalk** supported 1.5m above the swamp on strong logwood posts. You'll need to get there **by boat** most of the year but in the dry season it's possible to drive. Built in 1997 by a Raleigh team, the walkway allows access through the otherwise impenetrable low forest at the edge of the lagoon and a 7m high observation tower affords panoramic **views** – a great place to enjoy the sunset.

**Chau Hiix** ("small cat"), a Maya site on the western shore of the lagoon, has escaped looting and therefore offers potentially revolutionary discoveries to the University of Indiana team currently excavating here. Climbing the nearby **observation tower** (also with a boardwalk, built by Trekforce volunteers), will give you a clearer idea of the site, though admittedly much of what you see are just great, forested mounds. A number of burials have been discovered and the findings are currently being analysed. You experience a real thrill of discovery as you wander around the site, particularly if you're with a guide from the village (many have worked on the excavations) as they point out sites of recent finds. Most exposed stonework is covered over at the end of the season, but there are plans to consolidate the structures, and make them more accessible to visitors.

# Orange Walk and around

With a population approaching 20,000, **ORANGE WALK** is the largest town in the north of Belize and the centre of a busy agricultural region. Like Corozal to the north, Orange Walk was founded by Mestizo refugees fleeing from the Caste Wars in Yucatán in 1849, who chose as their site an area that had long been used for logging camps and was already occupied by the local Icaiché (Chichanha) Maya. Throughout the 1850s and 1860s the Icaiché, led by Marcos Canul, were in conflict both with the Cruzob Maya, who were themselves rebelling against Mestizo rule in Yucatán, and with the British settlers and colonial authorities in Belize. Canul organized successful raids against British mahogany camps and even briefly occupied Corozal in 1870. In 1872 the Icaiché launched an attack on the barracks in Orange Walk. The West India Regiment, which had earlier retreated in disarray after a skirmish with Canul's troops, this time forced the Icaiché to flee across the Rio Hondo, taking the fatally wounded Canul with them. A small monument opposite the park in Orange Walk commemorates the last (officially the only) battle fought on Belizean soil.

Though not unattractive, the town boasts few tourist attractions and Corozal (see p.226), less than an hour to the north, is a preferable place to spend the night. The centre of town is marked by a distinctly Mexican-style formal plaza and the town hall is called the Palacio Municipal, reinforcing the strong historic links to Mexico. The tranquil, slow-moving **New River**, a few blocks east of the centre, was a busy commercial waterway during the logging days; now it provides a lovely starting point for a visit to the ruins of **Lamanai**, to which several local operators offer tours (see p.221). The land around Blue Creek and Shipyard (on the riverbank on the way to Lamanai) has been developed by **Mennonite** settlers, members of a Protestant religious group, many of whom choose to farm without the assistance of modern technology (see box on p.220).

## Practicalities

Hourly **buses** from Belize City and Corozal pull up on the main road in the centre of town. Officially Queen Victoria Avenue but always referred to as the Belize–Corozal Road, it's lined with hotels, restaurants and filling stations. Services to and from Sarteneja (see p.225) stop at Zeta's store on Main Street, two blocks to the east, while local buses to the surrounding villages (including Indian Church, for Lamanai) leave from the crossroads by the fire station in the centre of town.

---

### MENNONITES IN BELIZE

The **Mennonites** arose from the radical Anabaptist movement of the sixteenth century and are named after the Dutch priest Menno Simons, leader of the community in its formative years. Recurring government restrictions on their lifestyle, especially regarding their pacifist objection to military service, forced them to move repeatedly. Having removed to Switzerland they travelled on to Prussia, then in 1663 to Russia, until the government revoked their exemption from military service, whereupon some groups emigrated to North America, settling in the prairies of Saskatchewan. World War I brought more government restrictions, this time on the teaching of German (the Mennonites' language). This, together with more widespread anti-German sentiments in the Dominion and the prospect of conscription, drove them from Canada to Mexico, where they settled in the arid northern state of Chihuahua. When the Mexican government required them to be included in its social security programme it was time to move on again. An investigation into the possibility of settling on their own land brought them to the colony of British Honduras in 1958.

They were welcomed enthusiastically by the colonial authorities, eager to have willing workers to clear the jungle for agriculture. Perseverance and hard work made them successful farmers, and in recent years prosperity has caused drastic changes in their lives. The Mennonite Church in Belize is increasingly split between the *Kleine Gemeinde* – a modernist section who use electricity and power tools, and drive trucks, tractors and even cars – and the *Altkolonier* – traditionalists who prefer a stricter interpretation of their beliefs. Members of the community, easily recognizable in their denim dungarees and straw hats, can be seen trading their produce and buying supplies every day in Orange Walk and Belize City.

---

There are no recommended budget **hotels**; if you do have to stay, then the best option is the mid-priced *St Christopher's*, 10 Main St (☎ & fax 03/21064; ⑤/⑥), which has beautiful rooms (some a/c) with private bath, set in grounds sweeping down to the river. The majority of **restaurants** in Orange Walk are Chinese, though there are a few Belizean-style places serving simple Creole or "Mexican" food. *Lover's Restaurant*, tucked away in the far corner of the park at 20 Lover's Lane, offers the best Belizean food and is the meeting place for the Novelo's Jungle River Tours (see p.222).

The best place to **change money** and get cash advances is the Scotia Bank, just east of the plaza. The **post office** is on the right of the main road at the north end of town.

# Maya sites around Orange Walk

Although the **Maya sites** in northern Belize have been the source of a number of the most important archeological finds anywhere in the Maya world, they are not (with the notable exception of Lamanai) as monumentally spectacular as some in the Yucatán. Today, the area around Orange Walk has some of the most productive arable farmland in Belize, and this was also the case in Maya times – aerial surveys in the late 1970s revealed evidence of raised fields and a network of irrigation canals, showing that the Maya practised skilful intensive agriculture. In the Postclassic era this region became part of the powerful Maya state of Chactemal (or Chetumal), controlling the trade in cacao beans (used as currency) grown in the valleys of the Hondo and New rivers. For a while the Maya here were even able to resist the conquistadors, and long after nominal Spanish rule had been established in 1544 there were frequent Maya rebellions, including one in 1638 when they drove the Spanish out and burned the church at Lamanai.

## Cuello and Nohmul

**Cuello**, a small site 5km west of Orange Walk, dates back to 1000 BC, making it one of the earliest sites in the Middle Preclassic Maya lowlands. However, the site is more interesting to archeologists than to the casual visitor; there's not much to look at except a single small stepped pyramid (structure 350), rising in nine tiers – a common feature of Maya temples – and several earth-covered mounds. The ruins are behind a factory where Cuello rum is made and the site is on the Cuello family land, so you should ask permission to visit by phoning ☎03/22141; you can also get a tour of the distillery if you ask. A taxi from Orange Walk costs about US$5 each way.

**Nohmul** (Great Mound), 17km north of Orange Walk and just west of the village of San Pablo, was a major ceremonial centre with origins in the early Preclassic period, perhaps as early as 900 BC. The city was abandoned before the end of the Classic period, to be reoccupied by a Yucatecan elite during the Early Postclassic (known here as the Tecep phase, around 800–1000 AD). The ruins cover a large area, comprising the east and west groups, connected by a *sacbe* (causeway), with several plazas around them. The main feature (structure 2) is an acropolis platform surmounted by a later pyramid which, owing to the site's position on a limestone ridge, is the highest point in northern Belize. As at so many of Belize's Maya sites, looters have plundered the ruins and, tragically, at least one structure has been demolished for road fill. That said, some structural restoration has taken place as it is a site earmarked for tourism.

Nohmul lies amid sugar-cane fields, 2km west of **San Pablo**, on the Northern Highway; any bus between Corozal and Orange Walk goes through the village. To visit the site, contact Estevan Itzab, whose land it's on and who lives in the house on the west side of the highway, across from the village water tower at the north end of the village; his son Guillermo will probably be your guide.

## Lamanai

Though they can't match the scale of the great sites in Mexico and Guatemala, the **ruins of Lamanai** (daily 8am–4pm; US$5) are among the most impressive in Belize, and their setting on the New River Lagoon, in a 950-acre archeological reserve, gives them a special quality that is long gone from the sites that are served by a torrent of tourist buses.

Lamanai is one of only a few sites whose original Maya name *Lamanyan* is known; it translates as "Submerged Crocodile", hence the numerous representations of crocodiles. *Lamanai*, however, is a seventeenth-century mistranslation of *Lamanyan*, and actually means "Drowned Insect". The site was continually occupied from around 500 BC up until the sixteenth century, when Spanish missionaries built a church – the location of Indian Church village. More than seven hundred structures have been mapped here by teams led by David Pendergast of the Royal Ontario Museum, the majority of them still buried beneath mounds of earth. Seven troops of black howler monkeys make Lamanai their home and you'll certainly see a couple of them peering down through the branches as you wander the trails.

### The site

The most impressive feature at Lamanai, prosaically named N10-43, but informally called "El Castillo", is a massive **Late Preclassic temple**, towering 35m above the forest floor. When first built, around 100 BC, it was the largest structure in the entire Maya World, though it was extensively modified later. The view across the surrounding forest from the top of the temple is magnificent. On the way to El Castillo you pass N10-27, a much smaller, unreconstructed pyramid, at the base of which lies **Stela 9**, bearing some of the best-preserved carvings at Lamanai. Dated to 625 AD, it shows the magnificently attired Lord Smoking Shell participating in a ceremony – probably his accession. This glyph has become emblematic of Lamanai and features on many of the T-shirts on sale here. At the northern end of the site, structure N9-56 is a sixth-century pyramid with two stucco masks of a deity (probably Kinich Ahau, the sun god) carved on different levels. The lower mask, 4m high, is particularly well preserved, showing a clearly humanized face wearing a crocodile headdress and bordered by decorative columns. The temple overlies several smaller, older buildings, the oldest of which is a superbly preserved temple from around 100 BC, and there are a number of other well-preserved and clearly defined glyphs.

Traces of later settlers can be seen around the nearby village of **INDIAN CHURCH**: to the south of the village are the ruins of two churches built by Spanish missionaries, and to the west are the remains of a nineteenth-century sugar mill, built by Confederate refugees from the American Civil War.

The small **archeological museum** at the site houses an amazing collection of artefacts, arranged in chronological order, mostly figurines depicting gods and animals, particularly crocodiles. The most beautiful exhibits are the delicate eccentric flints – star and sceptre-shaped symbols of office – skilfully chipped from a single piece. The most unusual item is a drum the size and shape of a pair of binoculars. Nazario Ku, the friendly head caretaker at the site, is very knowledgeable about Maya culture and is the best guide at the site.

## Practicalities

**Getting to Lamanai** is relatively easy. Three buses a week (Mon, Wed & Fri; 2hr) leave at 4pm from the side of the fire station in Orange Walk for **Indian Church**. The bus is based in the village, leaving for Orange Walk at 6am on the same days, so you'll have to stay overnight; you can check bus times by calling the community phone in Indian Church on ☎031/2015. The most pleasant way to get here, though, is by river, and a number of operators organize **day-trips** for US$30–50 per person. By far the most informative are those of Jungle River Tours, run by Antonio, Wilfrido and Herminio Novelo at the *Lover's Restaurant* in Orange Walk (☎03/22293, fax 23749). In addition to their extensive knowledge of Maya sites, the Novelos are also wildlife experts, and will point out the lurking crocodiles and dozens of species of bird, including snail kites, that you might otherwise miss. Another good (though more expensive, at around US$85) regular tour is aboard the *Lamanai Lady*, which departs daily at 9am from the **Tower Hill Toll Bridge**, 11km south of Orange Walk: book through Discovery Expeditions in Belize City (☎02/30748).

**To get to the bridge** independently take the Novelo's bus that leaves Belize City at 7am for Chetumal (the driver will drop you at the right place in good time for the 9am start); doing this part on your own saves you at least US$30. By road in **your own vehicle**, head west at the south end of Orange Walk, by Dave's Store, and continue along the Yo Creek road as far as San Felipe, where you should bear left for the village of Indian Church, 2km from the ruins.

If you want **to stay** in Indian Church (and you'll have to if you're travelling by bus), there are a couple of places offering **rooms** (④), though they're rather overpriced. Speak to Nazario Ku at the site and he'll let you **camp** at his house or rent you a hammock very cheaply; you can eat with the family. You can also visit the Xochil Ku (Sacred Flower) project in his grounds (daily; donation), a butterfly-breeding educational centre where you can see the butterflies develop through the stages of their life cycle.

More **upmarket accommodation** is available nearby in the comfortable, wooden, thatched cabañas at *Lamanai Outpost Lodge* (☎ & fax 02/33578, *www.lamanai.com*; ⑧), set in extensive gardens sweeping down to the lagoon. Guests can use canoes or take a "moonlight safari" to spot nocturnal wildlife, or even take part in some Maya research under the supervision of archeologist Laura Howard, the director of the **Lamanai Field Research Center** (LFRC) which is based at the lodge. Since students stay at the *Lodge* these are fairly expensive, working out around US$1300–2000 for two weeks; the *Lodge's* Web site has full details.

# The Rio Bravo Conservation Area

In the far northwest of Orange Walk district, the **Rio Bravo Conservation Management Area** is a tract of over 1000 square kilometres designated for tropical forest conservation, research and sustained-yield forest harvests. This conservation success story actually began with a disastrous plan in the mid-1980s to clear the forest, initially to fuel a wood-fired power station and later to provide Coca-Cola with frost-free land to grow citrus crops. Environmentalists were alarmed, and their strenuous objections forced Coca-Cola to drop the plan, though the forest remained threatened by agriculture.

An imaginative project to save the threatened forest, the **Programme for Belize**, was initiated by the Massachusetts Audubon Society in 1988. Funds were raised from corporate donors and conservation organizations, but the most widespread support was generated through an ambitious "adopt-an-acre" scheme, enthusiastically taken up by schools and individuals in the UK and North America. Coca-Cola itself, anxious to distance itself from the charge of rainforest destruction, has donated more than nine square kilometres. Today, rangers with powers of arrest patrol the area to prevent illegal hunting and logging and to stop farmers encroaching onto the reserve with their *milpas*. The guarded boundaries also protect dozens of Maya sites, most of them unexcavated and unrestored, though many have been looted.

The **landscape** ranges from forest-covered limestone escarpments in the northwest, near the Guatemalan border, eastwards through the valleys of several rivers, to palmetto savannah, pine ridge and swamp in the southeast around the New River Lagoon. The Rio Bravo area has 240 endemic tree species, and the forest teems with **wildlife**, with seventy mammal species, including all five of Belize's large cats, tapirs, monkeys and crocodiles, plus four hundred bird species. The strict ban on hunting, enforced for over ten years now, makes the Rio Bravo and Gallon Jug area the best place in Belize to actually see these beasts; even pumas and jaguars are fairly frequently spotted. Adjoining the Rio Bravo to the south, the privately owned land of **Gallon Jug** also contains a large area of protected land, in the centre of which is the fabulous *Chan Chich Lodge* (below) – regarded as one of the best eco-lodges in the world – an incredibly beautiful place to stay.

There's no **public transport** to the Rio Bravo Conservation Management Area, but if you want to visit or stay at either of the **field stations** see overleaf. Getting here from Orange Walk means you have to pass through the very modern Mennonite settlement of **Blue Creek**, high up on the Rio Bravo escarpment. Here you'll find one of the most astonishing artefacts in Belize: the fuselage and more of a **Super Constellation**, the world's first airliner. How it reached its final resting place is a fascinating story and if you're an aviation buff call in at Abe Dyck's house, next to the still powerfully evocative remains of the airliner, and someone will show you around and fill you in on the details. In the valley below, the Rio Hondo forms the boundary with Mexico and the border crossing here is only for use by Belizeans, who pole canoes over to the Mexican village of **La Unión**, where a brisk trade in cigarettes and beer fuels the local economy. There's a customs post but no immigration, though if you stroll down to the riverbank you can join in the negotiations if you have some pesos.

## La Milpa and Hill Bank field stations

One of the aims of the Programme for Belize is environmental education and **field stations** have been built at La Milpa and Hill Bank to accommodate both visitors and students. Each field station has comfortable (though expensive) **dorms** (US$77 per person), and the facilities utilize the latest "green" technology, including solar power and composting toilets; La Milpa also has beautiful thatched **cabañas** (US$93 per person;

sleep up to six). Prices, though high (there are discounts for student groups), include three meals and two excursions or lectures a day and each station also has a natural history library. To visit or stay at either station contact the appropriate station manager (Ramon Pacheco at La Milpa, Roberto Pott at Hill Bank) through the PFB office, 1 Eyre St, Belize City (☎02/75616, fax 75635, *pfbel@btl.net*), who will arrange transport.

### La Milpa: the field station and Maya site

Set in a former *milpa* clearing in the higher, northwestern forest, **La Milpa Field Station** has a tranquil, studious atmosphere; deer and ocellated turkeys feed contentedly around the cabins and there are binoculars and telescopes for spotting birds. A day-visit to the field station, which includes a guided tour of La Milpa ruins or one of the trails costs US$20, but getting there on public transport is not easy; you'll have to get a bus from Orange Walk to San Felipe, 37km away, and arrange to be picked up there – the PFB office will give details.

Five kilometres west of the field station is the huge, Classic Maya city of **La Milpa**, the third largest site in Belize. After centuries of expansion, La Milpa was abandoned in the ninth century, though Postclassic groups subsequently occupied the site and the Maya here resisted both the Spanish conquest in the sixteenth century and British mahogany cutters in the nineteenth century. The site is currently being investigated as part of a long-term archeological survey by Boston University; recent finds include major elite burials with many jade grave goods. The **ceremonial centre**, built on top of a limestone ridge, is one of the most impressive anywhere, with at least 24 courtyards and two ball courts. The **Great Plaza**, flanked by four temple-pyramids (the tallest stands 24m above the plaza floor), is one of the largest public spaces in the Maya world.

### Hill Bank Field Station

At the southern end of the New River Lagoon and 70km west of Belize City, **Hill Bank Field Station** is a former logging camp which has been adapted to undertake scientific forestry research and development. **Selective logging** is allowed on carefully monitored plots, and there's a tree nursery. There's plenty of wildlife around too, particularly birds and crocodiles, and butterflies abound. The **dorms** here (identical to those at La Milpa, above) have a screened verandah with table and chairs, overlooking the lagoon; for an even better view climb the twelve-metre **fire tower** outside. With your **own vehicle** you can follow the road west and north from Bermudian Landing (see p.215).

## Gallon Jug and Chan Chich Lodge

Forty kilometres south of the La Milpa field station, the former logging camp of **GALLON JUG**, set in the neat fenced pastures of the Gallon Jug Estate, is the home of Barry Bowen, reportedly the richest man in Belize. In the 1980s, his speculative land deals led to an international outcry against threatened rainforest clearance. The experience apparently proved cathartic: Bowen is now an ardent conservationist and most of the 500 square kilometres here are strictly protected. The focal point is the luxurious, world-class **Chan Chich Lodge** (☎ & fax 02/34419, in US ☎1-800/343-8009, *www.chanchich.com*; ⑨), which regularly wins awards in the travel press. Set in the plaza of the Classic Maya site of Chan Chich ("little bird"), the spacious thatched cabañas are surrounded by superb forest and there's a refreshing, fully screened pool. The construction of the lodge on this spot (all Maya sites are technically under government control) was controversial at the time, but received Archeology Department approval as it was designed to cause minimal disturbance. Certainly the year-round presence of visitors and staff does prevent looting – a real problem in the past. It is a truly awe-inspiring setting; grass-covered temple walls crowned with jungle tower up from the lodge and the forest explodes with a cacophony of bird calls at dawn. The **guided trails** are incomparable; day or night wildlife sightings are consistently high, with around seventy jaguar sightings a year, half of them during daylight. You can drive here from Orange Walk (through Blue Creek and La Milpa, see above), but most guests fly in to the airstrip at Gallon Jug.

# Sarteneja and the Shipstern Nature Reserve

The largely uninhabited **Sarteneja peninsula**, jutting out towards the Yucatán in the northeast of Belize, is covered with dense forests, swamps and lagoons that support an amazing array of wildlife. The only village here is **Sarteneja**, a mainly Spanish-speaking lobster-fishing centre that's just beginning to experience tourism. A couple of new hotels have been built, there's also accommodation at the reserve headquarters (see practicalities, below), and guides are available to take you to the lagoons and beyond. Although Sarteneja itself, and especially its shoreline, are pretty enough, it's the **Shipstern Nature Reserve**, 5km before the village (daily 8am–5pm; US$5 including guided walk), owned and managed by the Swiss-based International Tropical Conservation Foundation and covering eighty square kilometres, which is the main attraction. All **buses** to Sarteneja pass the entrance to the reserve; the headquarters and **visitor centre** are just 100m from the road.

The bulk of the reserve is made up of what's technically known as "tropical moist forest", although it contains only a few mature trees as the area was wiped clean by Hurricane Janet in 1955. It also includes some wide belts of savannah – covered in coarse grasses, palms and broad-leaved trees – and the shallow Shipstern Lagoon, dotted with mangrove islands. Taking the superb guided walk along the **Chiclero Trail** from the visitor centre, you'll encounter more named plant species in one hour than on any other trail in Belize. It's also a bird-watcher's paradise: the lagoon system supports blue-winged teal, American coot, several species of egret and huge flocks of lesser scaup, while the forest is home to fly-catchers, warblers, keel-billed toucans, collared aracari and at least five species of parrot. In addition, there are crocodiles, manatees, coatis, jaguars, peccaries, deer, raccoons, pumas and an abundance of insects, particularly butterflies. Though the reserve's butterfly farm didn't prove as lucrative as hoped, the wardens still tend the butterflies carefully, releasing them into the forest when mature. You can **stay** here in neat four-bed dorms (US$10 per person) with cooking facilities, and there's a two-roomed house for rent (US$40 per day). For information, call the Belize Audubon Society (BAS) in Belize City (☎02/34987), though there will almost certainly be room if you just turn up.

## Sarteneja village practicalities

The Perez **bus** leaves Belize City from the Texaco station on North Front Street at noon & 1.30pm, and Venus (may be using the Novelo's name now) at 12.30pm (all times Mon–Sat; US$6). They all pass through Orange Walk ninety minutes later, stopping at Zeta's store on Main Street; it's a further ninety minutes to Sarteneja. Buses return to Belize City from Sarteneja at 4am, 5am and 6am. If you're **heading for Mexico**, you may be able to get a ride in a sailboat or skiff from Sarteneja to Consejo, 13km north of Corozal, and just a few kilometres across the bay from Chetumal; ask for Pablo Canul, who runs a skiff. Make sure you get your passport stamped (in Consejo or Corozal) before you leave Belize.

There's **accommodation** in Sarteneja, or you can stay in the reserve (see above). In the village *Fernando's Seaside Guest House* (☎04/32085; ⑤), on the seafront, an excellent **fishing guide** and can take you across to Bacalar Chico National Park, on Ambergris Caye (see p.238).

# Corozal and around

**COROZAL,** 45km north of Orange Walk along the Northern Highway, is Belize's most northerly town, just twenty minutes from the Mexican border. Corozal's location near the mouth of the New River enabled the ancient Maya to prosper here by controlling river- and seaborne trade, and two sites – Santa Rita and Cerros – are within easy reach. The present town was founded in 1849 by refugees from the massacre in Bacalar, Mexico, who were hounded south by the Caste Wars.

Today, Corozal is a neat mix of Mexican and Caribbean styles, its grid pattern largely due to reconstruction in the wake of Hurricane Janet in 1955. Quiet and hassle-free, even at night, it has a breezy shoreline park shaded by palm trees, while on the tree-shaded main plaza, the **town hall** is worth a look inside for the vivid depiction of local history in a mural by Manuel Villamar Reyes. In two of the plaza's corners you can see the remains of small forts, built to ward off Maya attacks. On October 12, **Columbus Day** – or

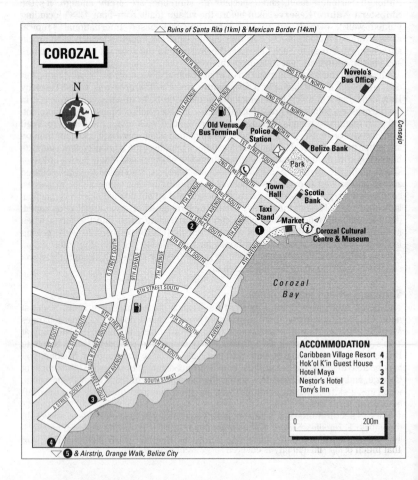

△ Ruins of Santa Rita (1km) & Mexican Border (14km)

**COROZAL**

N

SANTA RITA ROAD

3RD STREET NORTH

Novelo's Bus Office

11TH AVENUE

10TH AVENUE

2ND STREET NORTH

1ST STREET NORTH

△ Consejo

Old Venus Bus Terminal

Police Station

Belize Bank

1ST STREET SOUTH

Park

2ND STREET SOUTH

7TH AVENUE

3RD STREET SOUTH

Town Hall

Scotia Bank

4TH STREET SOUTH

5TH AVENUE

Taxi Stand

Market

**②**

**①**

Corozal Cultural Centre & Museum

6TH STREET SOUTH

G STREET SOUTH

9TH AVENUE

7TH AVENUE

*Corozal Bay*

6TH STREET SOUTH

7TH ST. SOUTH

**⊞**

1ST AVENUE

8TH ST. SOUTH

9TH ST. SOUTH

D STREET SOUTH

C STREET SOUTH

B STREET SOUTH

8TH STREET SOUTH

**③**

A STREET SOUTH

SOUTH STREET

**ACCOMMODATION**

| | |
|---|---|
| Caribbean Village Resort | **4** |
| Hok'ol K'in Guest House | **1** |
| Hotel Maya | **3** |
| Nestor's Hotel | **2** |
| Tony's Inn | **5** |

| 0 | 200m |
|---|---|

**④**

▽ **⑤** & Airstrip, Orange Walk, Belize City

PanAmerica Day, as it is now known – celebrations in Corozal are particularly lively, a combination of Mexican fiesta and Caribbean carnival.

## Arrival and information

All **buses** between Belize City and Chetumal pass through Corozal, roughly hourly in each direction. The airstrip is alongside the highway a few kilometres south of the centre; Maya Island Air and Tropic Air operate daily **flights** between Corozal and San Pedro on Ambergris Caye. Jal's travel agency (☎04/22163) at the south of town, beyond *Tony's Inn*, can organize both domestic and international flights. For reliable tourist **information**, visit the **Corozal Cultural Centre** (Tues–Sat 9am–noon & 1–4.30pm; ☎04/23176), housed in the restored colonial market building in the water-front park, just past the new market. Inside, there's a museum (US$1.50) with imaginative displays depicting episodes in Corozal's history. Scotia Bank, on the plaza, is the best place for **cash advances**, and the **post office** is on the west side of the plaza.

For organized **tours** to nature reserves and archeological sites on both sides of the border, contact Henry Menzies at *Caribbean Village* (☎04/22725). Stephan Moerman (☎04/22833 or 22539), a French biologist and naturalist, arranges superb guided tours to Cerros (see below) and Bacalar Chico National Park (see p.238).

## Accommodation, eating and drinking

Corozal has plenty of hotel **rooms** in all price ranges and you'll always be able to find something suitable. Most of the best **meals** are also to be found in the hotels. The popular bar at *Nestor's* serves American and Belizean food, while the *Hotel Maya* serves good Belizean and Jamaican food in a quieter environment. There's a wonderful restaurant at *Tony's*, and *Haley's* in *Caribbean Village* is renowned locally for its inexpensive Creole food. Corozal also has the usual complement of Chinese restaurants. Amazingly, *Le Café Kela*, run by Stephan and Marguerite Moerman on the seafront just north of the centre, serves authentic, great-value French meals and pastries in a lovely garden.

**Caribbean Village Resort**, south end of town, across from the sea (☎04/22045, fax 23414). Good-value, whitewashed, thatched cabins, with hot water, among the palms. Plus an inexpensive restaurant, trailer park (US$12) and camping (US$5). ④.

**Hok'ol K'in Guest House**, facing the sea a block south of the market (☎04/23329, fax 23569, *maya@btl.net*). Large, tiled rooms and suites with hammocks on the balcony and private bath. The ground floor is completely wheelchair-accessible, and there's a restaurant, gardens and a guest lounge with TV. ⑤.

**Hotel Maya**, south end of town, facing the sea (☎04/22082, fax 22827, *stay@hotelmaya.com*). Clean, friendly, well-run rooms, all with private bath and some with a/c and cable TV, and a one-bedroom furnished apartment. Good restaurant downstairs and owner Rosita May is an agent for Maya Island Air and Aerocaribe. ⑤/⑥.

**Nestor's**, 5th Avenue South, between 4th and 5th streets (☎04/22354, *nestors@btl.net*). Reasonable budget hotel with private bathrooms. Popular sports bar and restaurant downstairs. ④.

**Tony's Inn and Beach Resort**, on the seafront, about 1km south of the plaza (☎04/22055, *www.tonysinn.com*). A touch of well-run luxury in a superb location with secure parking. The spacious rooms (most a/c) with king-sized beds overlook landscaped gardens and a pristine beach bar, and the hotel's *Vista del Sol* restaurant is excellent. ⑦/⑧.

# Around Corozal: Santa Rita, Cerros and Copper Bank

Of the two small Maya sites within reach of Corozal (both daily 8am–4pm; US$2.50), the closest is **Santa Rita**, about fifteen minutes' walk northwest of the town. To get there, follow the main road in the direction of the border and when it divides take the left-hand fork; the caretaker will show you around once you've signed in. It's thought that much of the ancient city is covered by present-day Corozal.

Founded around 1800 BC, Santa Rita appears to have been continuously occupied until the arrival of the Spanish, by which time it was in all probability the powerful Maya city known as **Chactemal** (Chetumal), which dominated the trade of the area. It was certainly still a thriving settlement in 1531 AD, when the conquistador Alonso Dávila entered the city, only to be driven out almost immediately by Na Chan Kan, the Maya chief, and his Spanish adviser Gonzalo Guerrero. Structure 1 contained superb Postclassic Mixtec-style murals similar to those found at Tulum, in Quintana Roo (see p.124), but the building was bulldozed in the late 1970s.The main remaining building, Structure 7, is a small but attractive stepped pyramid. Burials excavated here include that of an elaborately jewelled elderly woman, dated to the Early Classic period, and the tomb of a Classic period lord.

The remains of the Preclassic centre of **Cerros**, on a peninsula jutting from the southern shore of Corozal Bay, are best reached by boat in the company of a guide (easy enough to organize in Corozal; see above). A new chain-winched ferry (daily 6am–9pm, free) at **Pueblo Nuevo** crosses the New River a few kilometres south of Corozal (the turn-off is signed), allowing access to the site through **COPPER BANK** village; a **bus** (Mon–Sat 11.30am, also 4pm Mon, Wed & Fri; 30 min) leaves for the village from behind the Venus terminal in Corozal.

Its strategic position at the mouth of the New River enabled Cerros to dominate the regional water-borne trade, and it was one of the earliest places in the Maya world to adopt the rule of kings. Beginning around 50 BC it grew explosively from a small fishing village to a major city in only two generations. A kilometre-long canal bordered the central area, providing drainage to the town and the raised field system that supported it. Despite initial success, however, Cerros was abandoned by the Classic period, eclipsed by shifting trade routes. The site includes three large acropolis structures, ball courts and plazas flanked by pyramids. The largest building is a 22-metre high temple – its intricate stucco masks, representing the rising and setting sun, and Venus as morning star and evening star, are presently covered to prevent erosion, but restoration schemes are planned and the small new **visitor centre** has displays. **Mosquitoes** can be a problem here any time of the year, so bring repellent.

In Copper Bank, *The Last Resort* (☎041/2009, *rickz@btl.net*; ③) offers excellent **budget accommodation** on the shores of Laguna Seca. Friendly owners Enrique Flores and Donna Noland have clean, simple, whitewashed thatched cabins with electricity, mosquito-netted beds and shared showers and toilet; some cabins have kitchen facilities. They also have a good restaurant, space for **camping and Rvs** and can arrange trips to Cerros.

## The Mexican border crossing

Heading **into Mexico**, all northbound Novelo's and Venus buses will take you to either the **bus terminal** in Chetumal (plenty of onward express buses; see p.133 for more details) or the nearby market. Novelo's has an office in the Chetumal terminal, and as their buses leave Belize City in the morning you'll have a head start on travelling through Mexico. The whole journey takes under an hour, including the border crossing. The route takes you to the **Santa Elena border crossing** on the Rio Hondo. After you've cleared Belize immigration (paying the Bz$20 exit and the Bz$7.50 PACT conservation tax), the bus carries you over the bridge to the Mexican side. Border formalities are very straightforward and few Western nationalities need a visa; simply pick up and fill out your **Mexican tourist card** – at the bottom of which is a section stating how much (in pesos) you'll have to pay at a bank in Mexico before you leave. For visa advice, check with the Mexican consulate in Belize City (see "Listings", p.212). **Entering Belize** you'll have to fill out an immigration card but there's no fee to pay. **Moneychangers** on the Belize side will give good rates changing US or Belize dollars for pesos; there aren't any on the Mexican side, though most banks in Mexico have ATMs you can use.

# THE NORTHERN CAYES
# AND ATOLLS

Belize's spectacular **barrier reef**, with its dazzling variety of underwater life and string of exquisite islands – known as **cayes** – is the main attraction for most first-time visitors to the country. Part of the **Western Caribbean Barrier Reef** stretching from just south of Cancún to Honduras – the longest barrier reef in the western hemisphere – it runs the entire length of the coastline at a distance of 15–40km from the mainland. Most of the cayes (pronounced "keys") lie in shallow water behind the shelter of the reef, with a limestone ridge forming larger, low-lying islands to the north, and smaller, less frequently visited outcrops – often merely a stand of palms and a strip of sand – clustered toward the southern end of the chain. A paradise for **scuba-divers** and **snorkellers**, who can experience sites of almost unbelievable beauty and isolation, a visit to the cayes is supremely relaxing, tempting you to take it easy in a hammock, feast on seafood and sip rum punch as the sun sets.

Beyond the chain of islands and the coral reef are two of Belize's three **atolls**: the **Turneffe Islands** and **Lighthouse Reef**, where you'll find some of the most spectacular diving and snorkelling sites in the Caribbean. Lighthouse Reef encompasses the protected Half Moon Caye and Blue Hole Natural Monuments – the latter an enormous collapsed cave that attracts divers from all over the world – and both are regularly visited by dive boats from San Pedro or Caye Caulker. Such is the importance of this astonishing marine ecosystem that much of the reef and most of Belize's marine reserves were declared a World Heritage Site in December 1996. Several conservation organizations have projects on the cayes, requiring self-funded **volunteers**; these are mentioned in the text below, and there's more information on pp.50 & 572.

In recent years the town of **San Pedro**, on **Ambergris Caye**, the largest and most developed of the cayes, has undergone a transition from a predominantly fishing economy to one geared to commercial tourism. There are still some beautiful spots here, however, notably the protected areas at either end of the caye: **Bacalar Chico National Park** and **Hol Chan Marine Reserve**. South of Ambergris Caye, **Caye Caulker**, which also has a marine reserve, is the most accessible and least expensive of the islands, popular with budget travellers. **St George's Caye**, Belize's first capital, occupies a celebrated niche in the nation's history and still has some fine colonial houses as well as a couple of resorts.

**Bird-watching**, as anywhere in Belize, is fascinating. Around two hundred species live in or visit the coastal areas and cayes, from ospreys to sandpipers and flamingos to finches. Many otherwise rare birds are relatively common here; for instance, the preservation of the red-footed booby on Half Moon Caye was the main reason for establishing a Natural Monument there in 1982. Fishing trips for species such as snapper, barracuda and grouper are easily arranged, and a local guide can take you to the best spots. Some snorkelling trips can include a chance of fishing using a handline.

Finally, if you enjoyed the breathtaking aerial view afforded when flying into Ambergris Caye, you might like to take Tropic Air's **Deep Reef Flying** tour, a spectacular flight over the northern cayes and atolls that's a perfect way to appreciate your surroundings (departs Wed 10am; US$99).

## A brief history of the cayes

The earliest inhabitants of the cayes were **Maya** peoples or their ancestors. By the Classic period the Maya had developed an extensive trade network stretching from the Yucatán to Honduras, with settlements and transhipment centres on several of the islands. Traces of Maya civilization remain on some of the cayes today, especially

Ambergris Caye, which boasts the site of **Marco Gonzalez**, near the southern tip, and the remains of a number of ports and trading centres on the northwestern shores. Evidence of coastal trade, such as shell mounds, has been found on many other islands.

Probably the most infamous residents of the cayes were the **buccaneers**, usually British, who lived here in the sixteenth and seventeenth centuries, taking refuge in the shallow waters after plundering Spanish treasure ships. In time the pirates, now calling themselves **Baymen**, settled more or less permanently on some of the northern and central cayes, establishing the settlement's first capital on **St George's Caye**. In 1779 a Spanish force sacked the caye and imprisoned the Baymen and slaves, but the Baymen returned in 1783 and took revenge on the Spanish fleet in the celebrated **Battle of St George's Caye** in 1798.

Fishermen and turtlers continued to use the cayes as a base for their operations, and refugees fleeing the Caste Wars in the Yucatán towards the end of the last century also settled on the islands in small numbers. During the last century the island's population increased steadily, while establishment of the **fishing co-operatives** in the 1960s brought improved traps, ice plants and access to the export market. Although there's a **closed season** for lobster, from 15 February to 15 June, overfishing could still severely damage the industry. At around the same time came another boom, as the cayes of Belize, particularly Caye Caulker, became a hangout on the hippy trail, and then began to attract more lucrative custom. The islanders generally welcomed these new visitors: rooms were rented and hotels built, and a new prosperity began to transform island life.

## HURRICANE KEITH

On September 29, 2000 **tropical storm Keith** developed in the western Caribbean, heading for Belize. Within 36 hours the storm had become a Category 4 hurricane, with winds of 200km/hr – a virtually unprecedented rate of increase – and presented a terrible danger to the northern half of the country. The speed of the hurricane's development meant that few people managed to escape from the northern cayes, and thousands of locals and many tourists braced themselves for a direct hit. Keith struck Ambergris Caye from the west with tremendous force, tearing down hundreds of flimsy wooden houses, ripping roofs off hotels, flinging boats onto the shore and toppling coconut trees. The storm then proceeded to do the same to Caye Caulker, where damage was even more extensive, before returning once more to Ambergris Caye. For 48 hours the eye of the hurricane oscillated between the two cayes and, because the main wind direction was from the west, an enormous quantity of thick, reeking mud was dredged up from the San Pedro lagoon. The storm also struck Turneffe Atoll and other northern cayes and was on course for Belize City. But, after three days blasting the cayes the windspeed was reduced and Keith was downgraded to a tropical storm, and the expected landfall between Belize City and Corozal didn't materialize. Nobody actually on the cayes died as a result of the hurricane but three people were killed in boats as they attempted to flee the storm. The mainland escaped the devastating winds but over 75cm of rain caused **tremendous flooding** in the northern districts.

Keith was the second devastating hurricane to strike the northern cayes in under two years – Hurricane Mitch in 1998 destroyed all the docks at the front of both Ambergris Caye and Caye Caulker, though it did little structural damage to buildings. At the time of writing most of the damage to hotels and tourist infrastructure had been repaired and all the places mentioned in the *Guide* are back in business. In fact the most noticeable effect might be the loss of coconut trees and other vegetation. However, if you are on the cayes or coast during the hurricane season (officially June–Nov), listen to **tropical storm warnings** on the radio and keep an eye on the Weather Channel's "Tropical Update". If one is approaching get to the mainland and head west as quickly as you can.

# Ambergris Caye and San Pedro

Geographically part of Yucatán's Xcalak Peninsula, **Ambergris Caye**, the most northerly and by far the largest of the cayes, is separated from Mexico by the narrow **Bacalar Chico** channel, dug by the ancient Maya. The island's main destination and point of arrival is the former fishing village of **SAN PEDRO**, facing the reef just a few kilometres from the southern tip, 58km northeast of Belize City. If you fly into San Pedro, which is the way most visitors arrive, the views are breathtaking: the water appears so clear and shallow as to barely cover the sandy seabed. The most memorable sight is the pure white line of the reef crest, dramatically separating the vivid blue of the open sea from the turquoise water on its leeward side.

As you land at the tiny airport, with the sea to one side and the lagoon to the other, a glimpse at San Pedro shows it taking up the whole width of the island. It's not a large town – you're never more than a stone's throw from the sea – but its population of five thousand is the highest on any of the cayes. Development is spreading north from the town, with a number of beach resorts already established and plans for hotels and even another airport near the northern end. San Pedro is the target for over half the visitors to Belize, most of whom are here on North American package tours – almost all prices on the caye are quoted in US dollars. Some of the country's most exclusive hotels, restaurants and bars are here; the few budget places are in the original village of San Pedro. Despite development, the town just about manages to retain elements of its Caribbean charm with two-storey, clapboard buildings still predominating in the centre. However, more lofty concrete structures are an increasingly common feature, and in the built-up area most of the coconut palms have been cut down. More were destroyed by Hurricane Keith in 2000 and many of the remainder are dying from the "lethal yellowing" disease, sweeping down from the north.

One of the most interesting (and hectic) times to be in San Pedro is during the **International Costa Maya Festival**, a week-long celebration featuring cultural and musical presentations from the five Mundo Maya countries, held annually in August. The festival began as a way to drum up visitors during the off season; it's now so popular you may need to book rooms.

---

### GETTING TO AND FROM AMBERGRIS CAYE

**Flying** to San Pedro is the easiest and most popular approach: from Belize City Municipal and Belize International airports. Maya Island Air (☎02/31140, 026/2345 in San Pedro) and Tropic Air (☎02/45671, 026/2012 in San Pedro) between them have flights at least hourly from 7am to 5pm (25min). Both airlines also fly from **San Pedro to Corozal**, so you could head into Mexico without returning to Belize City.

Though **boats** from Belize City to San Pedro (1hr 15min; US$12.50 one way) are less frequent than those to Caye Caulker (see box on p.241), there are a few regular fast services, almost all calling at Caye Caulker first. Note that some boats may not run on Sundays, or during the low season, though at least three direct boats will be operating every day of the year. The *Triple J* (☎02/44375) is the best boat on the run and one of the first to leave, at 9am from Courthouse Wharf, returning at 3pm. The Caye Caulker Water Taxis Association (☎02/31969) also runs regular boats, leaving from the **Marine Terminal** by the Swing Bridge in Belize City at 9am, noon & 3pm, with the last return trip leaving San Pedro at 2.30pm. In the afternoons the *Thunderbolt* leaves the Swing Bridge at 1pm, returning at 7am the next morning, and the *Andrea* (☎026/2578) leaves Courthouse Wharf at 3pm, again returning at 7am. Travelling **from San Pedro to other cayes**, any of the above scheduled boats also stop at **Caye Caulker** (and there are regular departures from San Pedro to Caye Caulker from 8am to 3pm weekdays, up to 4.30pm at weekends), and they'll also call at **St George's Caye** or **Caye Chapel** on request.

## Arrival and information

**Arriving** in San Pedro, boats usually dock at the *Coral Beach* or Texaco piers on the front (reef) side of the island. Both are within a block of the centre of town, marked by the seafront **Central Park**. Landing at San Pedro's **airport**, only 500m south of the centre at the north end of Coconut Drive, is almost as convenient. It's within easy walking distance of any of the hotels in town, though **golf buggies** and **taxis** will be waiting for your custom. A taxi in town costs US$2.50 but *always* check the fare first and *never* let a taxi driver take you to a hotel of their choosing. Even if you arrive with a booking call first if you can as a common **taxi driver scam** is to tell you the hotel you've booked is actually full so the driver will take you to one where he earns (or extorts) a fat commission. If you want to, you can **leave luggage** at the airport while you look for somewhere to stay – see the staff in the Travel and Tour Belize office a few steps north of the airstrip; they give good advice and information on hotels (including budget options), or indeed anything else in San Pedro.

San Pedro's official **tourist office** (daily 9am–5pm; ☎026/2298) shares its location with the **Ambergris Museum** (see p.235) in the Island Plaza Mall on Barrier Reef Drive; the travel or tour agencies recommended on p.240 can also provide accurate information. It's always worth picking up a copy of the island's free tourist newspaper, the *San Pedro Sun*, available from most hotels and restaurants. Finally, as befits Belize's premier tourist destination, Ambergris Caye has one of the best Belizean **Web sites** – *www.ambergriscaye.com*.

## Orientation and getting around the island

The three **main streets** of the town centre run parallel to the beach. Formerly (and more prosaically) called Front, Middle and Back streets, they now have names more in keeping with an upmarket image – Barrier Reef Drive, Pescador Drive and Angel Coral Street. Most locals stick to the old names; in any case it's impossible to get lost.

The **town centre** is small enough to get around on foot; pleasant enough at any time, it's particularly enjoyable on weekend evenings, when Barrier Reef Drive is closed to vehicles. However, in recent years, the town has expanded rapidly to the north and south, so you might want to **rent a bike**, a **moped** (or a very expensive **golf cart**) from one of the travel agencies to explore the sometimes rough roads further out. Several hotels some distance from the centre have **courtesy bikes** for guests – something you might want to consider when choosing a place to stay. You can also **rent a bike** from Joe's Bike Rental, at the south end of Pescador (☎026/4371); US$6 for a half-day, US$40 for a week, including a lock and lights – and the police here are vigilant at spotting unlit bikes and booking the rider.

On some occasions you might need a **water taxi**, especially to the northern resorts. It's always best to ask at your hotel for a recommended boat and you can also often find them by the dock in front of **Fido's Courtyard**, a group of shops and restaurants on Barrier Reef Drive just north of the park. There's also a **fast ferry** to and from the north – the comfortable *Island Express* (☎014/5678; US$5 each way), with regular departures from Fido's during daylight hours.

## Accommodation

Most of the **hotels**, including all the budget options, are in San Pedro itself, though there are increasing numbers of more expensive places north and south of the town. You shouldn't have any problem finding somewhere to stay in the high season

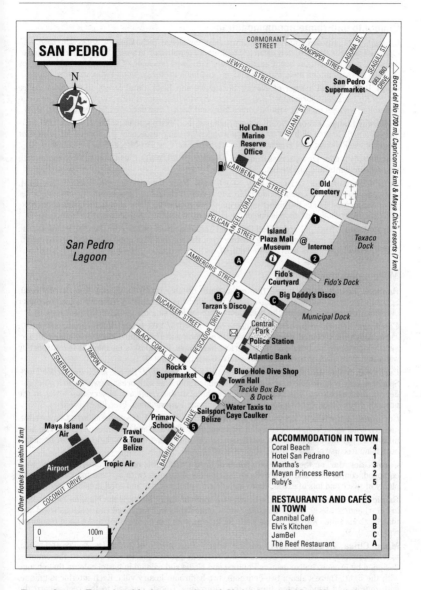

**SAN PEDRO**

N

CORMORANT STREET

SANDPIPER STREET

LAGUNA ST

SEAGULL ST

DEL RIO DRIVE

JEWFISH STREET

*Boca del Rio (700 m), Capricorn (5 km) & Maya Chica resorts (7 km)*

San Pedro Supermarket

IGUANA ST.

Hol Chan Marine Reserve Office

CARIBENA STREET

CORAL STREET

ANGEL STREET

Old Cemetery

PELICAN STREET

Island Plaza Mall Museum

@ Internet

Texaco Dock

*San Pedro Lagoon*

AMBERGRIS STREET

Fido's Courtyard

*Fido's Dock*

BUCANEER STREET

Tarzan's Disco

Big Daddy's Disco

*Municipal Dock*

BLACK CORAL ST.

PESCADOR DRIVE

Central Park

Police Station

TARPON ST.

ESMERALDA ST.

Rock's Supermarket

Atlantic Bank

Blue Hole Dive Shop

Town Hall

*Tackle Box Bar & Dock*

Water Taxis to Caye Caulker

Primary School

Sailsport Belize

*Other Hotels (all within 3 km)*

Maya Island Air

Travel & Tour Belize

BARRIER REEF DRIVE

Airport

Tropic Air

COCONUT DRIVE

0    100m

**ACCOMMODATION IN TOWN**

| | |
|---|---|
| Coral Beach | 4 |
| Hotel San Pedrano | 1 |
| Martha's | 3 |
| Mayan Princess Resort | 2 |
| Ruby's | 5 |

**RESTAURANTS AND CAFÉS IN TOWN**

| | |
|---|---|
| Cannibal Café | D |
| Elvi's Kitchen | B |
| JamBel | C |
| The Reef Restaurant | A |

(December to Easter), with the exception of Christmas and New Year (when many places hike up the rates even further) and booking ahead is definitely advisable. **Prices** are higher in general than in the rest of Belize but **discounts** on the quoted rates are often available, especially in the low season, so it's worth calling ahead to ask. Almost everywhere takes credit cards.

## Budget to mid-range accommodation

**Changes in Latitudes**, 1km south of town, near the Belize Yacht Club (☎ & fax 026/2986, *latitudes@btl.net*). Six immaculately clean a/c rooms with private bath in a very friendly B&B, set in gardens half a block from the sea. Canadian owner Lori Reed is a mine of information, and arranges the best tours. Common area, with full kitchen, and book exchange; good low-season discounts. ⑦.

**Coral Beach Hotel**, corner of Barrier Reef Drive and Black Coral Street, in the town centre (☎026/2013, fax 2864, *forman@btl.net*). Nineteen comfortable rooms with private bath, fan or a/c in a rambling wooden building with balconies front and back. Good packages for dive groups. ⑥/⑦.

**Hideaway Lodge**, 1km or so south of town, just past the Texaco station (☎026/2141, fax 2269, *hideaway@btl.net*). Rooms with fan or a/c in a wooden building; especially good value for groups or longer stays. Relaxing pool area and on-site restaurant serving Tex-Mex and Belizean dishes. ⑥.

**Martha's**, Pescador Drive, across from *Elvi's Kitchen* (☎026/2053). Clean, comfortable rooms with fan, bedside lights, and private bath. ⑥.

**Ruby's**, Barrier Reef Drive, a very short walk from the airstrip (☎026/2063, fax 2434, *wamcg@cowichan.com*). Clean, comfortable, family-run hotel right on the seafront. Rooms have better views and increased rates the higher up you go; all are good value, those with shared bathrooms especially so. *Ruby's Café*, next door, is one of the first to open and the hotel organizes good trips. ④–⑥.

**San Pedrano**, corner of Barrier Reef Drive and Caribeña Street (☎026/2054, fax 2093). Quiet, clean hotel, in a wooden building, set back slightly from the sea, but with good views and breezy verandahs. Comfortable rooms with private bath. ⑥.

## More expensive hotels

**Bananas Resort**, on the beach 1km or so south of town (☎026/3890, *www.bananabeach.com*). Spacious, well-run, fully equipped a/c suites with kitchens and cable TV. All have balconies, either overlooking the pool or facing the ocean. Rates are for four sharing; good weekly packages. ⑧.

**Capricorn Resort**, on the beach 5km north of town (☎026/2809, fax 021/2091, *capricorn@btl.net*). Three delightful, secluded, wooden cabins with porches, and a beautiful upper-storey suite with a/c, overlooking a pristine beach; all make perfect hideaways. Breakfast is included as is transport by water taxi from town on arrival and departure. Good restaurant. ⑧.

**Caribbean Villas Hotel**, just over 1km south of town (☎026/2715, fax 2885, *c-v-hotel@btl.net*). Spacious, very comfortable rooms and well-equipped suites, all with ocean views, set in a quiet garden on the beachfront. The best-value smaller hotel in this range. An observation tower in the grounds gives views of the lagoon and there's fantastic bird-watching. Free bikes. ⑧/⑨.

**Coconuts**, on the beach 1km south of town (☎026/3500, fax 3501, *coconuts@btl.net*). Comfortable, modern hotel with clean, well-decorated tiled rooms, all with a/c, and balconies all round. The helpful owners pay the taxi fare when you arrive, so call ahead first. Rates include a decent breakfast buffet and free use of bikes. Good, shaded beach bar. ⑧.

**Corona del Mar**, on the beach 1km south of town (☎026/2055, *corona@btl.net*). Beautiful, well-equipped, comfortable and very well-run apartments and suites (with a/c and full kitchens) with plenty of space and lots of extras. Rates include rum punch all day and a full breakfast. ⑧/⑨.

**Exotic Caye Beach Resort**, on the beach 1km south of town – formerly the *Playador* (☎026/2870, in US ☎1-800/201-9389, *www.belizeisfun.com*). Comfortable, well-furnished and spacious wood-and-thatch cabaña suites with a/c. Great value for groups, with a pool, dive shop and a good restaurant and bar. ⑧/⑨.

**Mata Chica Beach Resort**, on the beach 7km north of town (☎ & fax 021/3012, *matachica@btl.net*). The most beautiful and spacious beach cabañas and suites in the country, designed by French/Italian owners Philippe and Nadia and painted in pastel colours that change with the light. There's also a two-bedroom, two-bathroom luxury villa. Each interior is unique, with murals and hand-painted tiles in the bathrooms. Guests can sail to the reef aboard the resort's luxurious catamaran. Good restaurant: see *Mambo*, p.239. US$225 for a double cabaña, US$475 for the villa. ⑨.

**Mayan Princess Resort**, Barrier Reef Drive, just north of the centre (☎026/2778, *mayanprin@btl.net*). Very comfortable, spacious, well-equipped beachfront suites, each with a large balcony overlooking the sea; the best-value suites in town for the price. Free taxi shuttle from the airport. ⑧.

**Tropica Beach Resort**, on the beach 1km south of town (☎026/2701, in US ☎1-888/778-9776, *www.tropicabelize.com*). Large, comfortable wood-and-thatch cabañas on a lovely beach with great pool and a friendly bar and restaurant. Each room has a wooden deck and inside there's wooden floors, wicker furniture, a tiled bathroom and plenty of storage space. ⑧.

**Victoria House**, 3km south of town (☎026/2067, in US ☎1-800/247-5159, *www.victoria-house.com*). A range of luxury rooms, cabañas and villas in a stunning beachfront location, set in spacious grounds resembling a botanical garden – an obvious hit with honeymooners. Service is excellent and there's a pool and a fine restaurant. Prices start at US$135 for a double room in high season, and go up to US$625 for a two-bed villa; you get the best overall value on an all-in package. ⑨.

## Exploring the caye and the reef

Although there are a few places you can visit on land, it's the **water** which is the focus of daytime entertainment on Ambergris Caye, from sunbathing on the docks to windsurfing, sailing, kayaking, fishing, **diving** and **snorkelling**. A word of **warning**: there have been a number of accidents in San Pedro in which speeding boats have hit people swimming off the piers. A line of buoys, not always clearly visible, indicates the "**safe area**", but speed-boat drivers can be a bit macho; be careful when choosing where to swim.

Before going snorkelling or diving, whet your appetite for the wonders of the reef with a visit to the excellent **Hol Chan Marine Reserve office and visitor centre** (Mon–Fri 8am–noon & 1–5pm; ☎026/2247) on Caribeña Street. They have photographs, maps and other displays on the marine reserves (see pp.237 & 238), and the staff will be pleased to answer your questions. Equally worthwhile is a visit to the **Ambergris Museum** in the Island Plaza Mall on Barrier Reef Drive (daily 2–6pm; US$2.50), run by the Ambergris Historical Society. Maya pottery comprises some of the oldest exhibits, with colonial weapons and old photographs illustrating the island's history up to the 1960s.

**South of San Pedro**, the road continues for several kilometres to the Maya site of Marco Gonzalez, though the terrain becomes swampier and more mosquito-infested the further you go. The site is hard to find and there's not a lot to see, but studies have shown that it was once an important trade centre, with close links to Lamanai (see p.221). At the southernmost tip of the island is the impressive Hol Chan Marine Reserve (see p.237).

A kilometre **north of the centre** the **Boca del Rio** (usually referred to simply as "The River") is a narrow but widening erosion channel crossed during daylight hours by a tiny ferry (US$0.50 per person), just big enough to take a golf cart (US2.50. On the other side, a rudimentary road (navigable by golf cart, and possibly upgraded by now) leads to **Tres Cocos** and the northern resorts. The northernmost section of the caye, now accessible on organized day-trips, boasts the spectacular **Bacalar Chico National Park and Marine Reserve** and several **Maya sites**. All of the trips described below can be booked from your hotel or any tour or travel agent.

### Diving

For anyone who has never dived in the tropics before, the **reefs near San Pedro** are fine, but experienced divers looking for high-voltage excitement will be disappointed. This is a heavily used area which has long been subjected to intensive fishing, and much of the reef has been plundered by souvenir hunters. To experience the best diving in Belize you need to take a trip out to one of the **atolls** (see pp.247–248).

**Dive instruction** and **local dives** are best done with smaller, independent **operators** rather than the bigger dive shops as both the instruction and guiding will be more tailored to your needs. A a two-tank dive costs around US$50, including tanks, weights, air and boat. In general, a PADI or NAUI **open water certification** costs around US$350; a more basic, introductory **resort course** costs around US$125. Among the best local dive operators are Amigos del Mar, at the dock just north of the centre (☎026/2706, *amigosdive@btl.net*).

For comfortable **day visits to the Blue Hole** and the atolls there's the *Blue Hole Express* (☎026/2982), a fast twelve-metre boat charging US$165 for divers, US$110 for snorkellers, or the *Miss Gina* (☎026/2071), a very fast Pro-42 dive boat that's slightly more expensive at US$185 for divers, US$125 for snorkellers. The *Offshore Express* (☎026/2817) is a fifteen-metre **live-aboard dive boat**, sleeping five or six, and gives you the opportunity to stay out at the atolls for two to three days. The crew run a couple of two-day trips per week, costing US$250 for five dives, including all food, and you can **camp** on Lighthouse Reef. Snorkellers can usually go along as well, paying slightly less than divers. The boats are popular and space is limited, so book well in advance if possible. Any of the above boats picks up passengers at Caye Caulker on request, at no extra charge.

For the best **advice** on any aspect of diving from San Pedro, or to **book** the dive boats recommended below, contact the Blue Hole Dive Center on Barrier Reef Drive (☎ & fax 026/2982, *bluehole@btl.net*). The best dive shops in San Pedro recommend you make a voluntary contribution of US$1 per tank to help fund the town's **hyperbaric chamber**: this covers you for treatment if you need it, so make sure you fill out the agreement when you sign on to dive. If you want to capture the **underwater wildlife** on film but don't have a suitable camera you can rent one from the Blue Hole Dive Shop; a Nikon MX-10 including a 36-exposure film costs US$38 for one or two days.

## Snorkelling, windsurfing, kayaking and other trips

Just about every hotel in San Pedro offers **snorkelling** trips, costing around US$20 for about three hours, plus about US$5 to rent equipment. If you've never used a snorkel before, practise the technique from a dock first; you might also prefer to snorkel in a life-jacket – this will give you greater buoyancy, and help to stop you bumping into the coral. **Snorkelling guides** here (who must also be licensed tour guides) have a great deal of experience with visitors, and they'll show you how to use the equipment before you set off. **Night snorkelling**, a truly amazing experience, is also available, and usually costs a little more than a daytime trip.

---

### SAFEGUARDING THE BELIZE CORAL REEF

**Coral reefs** are among the most complex and fragile ecosystems on earth. Colonies have been growing at a rate of less than 5cm a year for thousands of years; once damaged, the coral is far more susceptible to bacteria, which can quickly lead to large-scale irreversible damage. All snorkelling **tour guides** in Belize are schooled in reef ecology before being granted a licence (which must be displayed as they guide), and if you go on an organized trip, as most people do, he or she will brief you on the following **precautions to avoid damage** to the reef.

• Never anchor boats on the reef – use the permanently secured buoys.
• Never touch or stand on corals – protective cells are easily stripped away from the living polyps on their surface, destroying them and thereby allowing algae to enter.
• Don't remove shells, sponges or other creatures from the reef, or buy reef products from souvenir shops.
• Avoid disturbing the seabed around corals – quite apart from spoiling visibility, clouds of sand settle over corals, smothering them.
• If you're either a beginner or an out-of-practice diver, practise away from the reef first.
• Don't use suntan lotion in reef areas – the oils remain on the water's surface.
• Check you're not in one of the marine reserves before fishing.
• Don't feed or interfere with fish or marine life; this can harm not only sea creatures and the food chain, but snorkellers too – large fish may attack, trying to get their share!

Generally, the options available mean you can either head north to the spectacular **Mexico Rocks** or Rocky Point or, more commonly, south to the **Hol Chan Marine Reserve** (see p.237) and **Shark-Ray Alley** where you can swim in shallow water with three-metre **nurse sharks** and enormous **stingrays** – an extremely popular (but controversial) attraction. Watching these creatures glide effortlessly beneath you is an exhilarating experience and, despite their reputations, swimming here poses almost no danger to snorkellers. Biologists, however, claim that the practice of **feeding the fish** to attract them alters their natural behaviour, exposing both the fish and humans to danger. At times the area is so crowded that any hope of communing with nature is completely lost and there's also the possibility that a shark could accidentally bite a hand – as has already happened.

Two of the best local **snorkel guides** are Alfonso Graniel (☎014/5450) and Dino Gonzalez (☎026/2422). Several boats take snorkellers out for a **day-trip to Caye Caulker**, employing a mix of motor and sail, and comprising two or more leisurely snorkel stops, snacks and drink on board (lunch on the caye is not included), returning to San Pedro around sunset. A day aboard either the sailboat *Rum Punch II* (US$45, **sunset cruise** US$15; ☎026/2340), or the 22-metre, motor-powered *Winnie Estelle* (US$55; ☎026/2982), with a spacious, shaded deck to spread out on, is supremely relaxing.

The best **windsurfing and sailing** rental and instruction on the caye is offered by Sailsports Belize (☎026/4488, *sailsports@btl.net*), on the beach in front of the *Holiday Hotel*, run by an English couple, Chris Beaumont and Jo Sayer, both qualified Royal Yachting Association instructors. Sailboard rental costs US$20—25 an hour, US$65–75 for a seven-hour day, depending on the style of board. Sailboat rental is US$30 an hour. Seaduced By Belize, run by superb naturalist guide Elito Arceo (☎026/3221 or 014/6049, *seabelize@btl.net*), has the best guided **kayak tours** (US$40 a half-day), visiting the lagoons and mangroves to spot birds and other wildlife.

In addition to the boat trips to **Caye Caulker** (see above), there are increasingly popular **day-trips** inland from San Pedro to the ruins of **Altun Ha** (aroundUS$60, see p.216) and even **Lamanai** (US$175, see p.221). Rounding the southern tip of the island in a fast skiff, you head for the mainland at the mouth of the **Northern River**, cross the lagoon and travel up the river to the tiny village of **Bomba**, where good wood carvings are made. With a good guide this is an excellent way to spot wildlife, including **crocodiles** and **manatees**, and the riverbank trees are often adorned with **orchids**. The best **guide** is Daniel Nuñez, who runs Tanisha Tours (☎026/2314), and Carlos Alejos (☎026/3219) is also highly recommended.

## The south: Hol Chan Marine Reserve

The **Hol Chan Marine Reserve**, 8km south of San Pedro, at the southern tip of the caye, takes its name from the Maya for "little channel", and it is this break in the reef that forms the focus of the reserve. Established in 1987, its three zones – covering a total of around thirteen square kilometres – preserve a comprehensive cross-section of the marine environment, from **coral reef** through **seagrass beds** to **mangroves**. All three habitats are closely linked: many reef fish feed on the seagrass beds, and the mangroves are a nursery area for the juveniles. As your boat approaches, you'll be met by a warden who explains the rules and collects the entry fee (US$2.50). You'll see plenty of marine life here, including some very large **snappers**, **groupers** and **barracuda**. However, its very popularity brings problems, and much damage has already been caused by snorkellers standing on the coral or holding onto outcrops for a better look – on all the easily accessible areas of the reef you will see the white, dead patches, especially on the large brain coral heads. **Never touch** the coral – not only will that damage the delicate ecosystem, but it can also cause you agonizing burns; even brushing against the razor-sharp ridges on the reef top can cause cuts that are slow to heal. Near Hol Chan, and now regarded as part of the reserve, is the extremely popular (but controversial) **Shark-Ray Alley** (see above) where you can swim with **nurse sharks** and **stingrays**.

## The north: Bacalar Chico National Park and the Maya sites

A visit to the remote and virtually pristine northern section of Ambergris Caye is an unmissable highlight, not only for the obvious attractions of the **Bacalar Chico Marine Reserve and National Park**, but also for the chance to see a number of previously inaccessible **Maya sites** on the northern coast. On a day-trip from San Pedro you can visit several areas of the reserve and take in two or three of the ten or more Maya sites; the best **guide** to Bacalar Chico is Daniel Nuñez (☎026/2314). Travelling by boat through Boca del Rio and up the west coast, you might briefly stop to observe colonies of seabirds roosting on some small, uninhabited cayes; there are several species of herons and egrets and you might even spot the **roseate spoonbill**.

Travelling by boat through Boca del Rio and up the west coast, you might briefly stop to observe colonies of seabirds roosting on some small, uninhabited cayes; **Little Guana Caye** is a bird sanctuary. The reserve itself covers the entire northern tip of Ambergris Caye – the largest protected area in the northern cayes. Its 110 square kilometres extend from the reef, across the seagrass beds to the coastal mangroves and **caye littoral forest**, and over to the salt marsh and lagoon behind. The reserve is patrolled by rangers based at the headquarters and **visitor centre** at San Juan, on the northwest coast, where you register and pay the US$2.50 park fee. There's a surprising amount of **wildlife** up here, including crocodiles, deer, peccary and, prowling around the thick forests, several of the wild cats of Belize. Birdlife is abundant and **turtles** nest on some beaches: contact the Belize Audubon Society (see p.208) or the Hol Chan Reserve office (see p.237) if you want to help patrol the beaches during the turtle nesting season.

Some of the **Maya sites** in the north of the caye are undergoing archeological investigation and there's a real air of adventure and discovery as you explore the ancient ruins now buried in thick bush and jungle. **Santa Cruz**, about two-thirds of the way up the west coast of Ambergris Caye, is a very large site, known to have been used for the shipment of trade goods in the Postclassic era, though the true function of most of the stone mounds here remains uncertain. Further north, the beach at **San Juan** was another transhipment centre for the ancient Maya; here you'll be crunching over literally thousands of pieces of Maya pottery. But perhaps the most spectacular site is **Chac Balam**, a ceremonial and administrative centre; getting there entails a walk through mangroves to view deep burial chambers, scattered with thousands more pottery shards.

On the way back, you navigate **Bacalar Chico**, the narrow channel dug by the Maya about 1500 years ago to allow a shorter paddling route for their trading canoes between their cities in Chetumal Bay and the coast of Yucatán. At the mouth of the channel the reef is close to the shore; the boat has to cross into the open sea, re-entering the leeward side of the reef as you approach San Pedro, so completing a circumnavigation of the island.

## Eating, drinking and entertainment

There are plenty of places to eat in San Pedro, including some of the best restaurants in the country, and at the very top of the range, the quality of food and wine compares favourably with resorts anywhere in the world, though **prices** are higher than elsewhere in Belize. **Seafood** is prominent at most restaurants, which tend to reflect the tastes of the town's predominantly North American guests; thus you can also rely on plenty of steak, shrimp, chicken, pizza and salads. Many **hotels** have their own dining room, and often also do **beach barbecues**. There are several **Chinese** restaurants, too, the cheaper ones representing the best value on the island. In the evening several **fast-food stands** open for business along the front of Central Park.

**Buying your own food** isn't particularly cheap here: there's no market and the **supermarkets** are stocked with imported canned goods. However, the range and quality of groceries is improving all the time. Unless you're staying in an apartment, cooking your food might also be a problem – it's not as easy in San Pedro as it is on other islands to improvise your own beach barbecue. At the luxury end of the scale, there's the Sweet Basil **deli**, just north of Boca del Rio, with a great selection of imported cheeses, wine and paté. La Popular **bakery**, on Buccaneer Street, has a wide selection of breads, including Mexican-style *pan dulces*, and there are some **fruit and vegetable stalls** dotted around the centre. Manelly's Ice Cream Parlour, on Pescador, is the best place in town for a sit-down **ice-cream** treat.

## Restaurants

**Cannibal Café**, on the front, just past the *Holiday Hotel*. Tasty, well-priced snacks and light meals on a palm-shaded deck overlooking the sea. Good seafood, and very good fish and chips.

**Capricorn Restaurant**, on the beach in the *Capricorn Resort* (see p.234) 5km north of town (☎026/2809). Chef Clarence is in his element serving unbeatable gourmet food in a beautiful location; try the stone-crab cakes or filet mignon/seafood combo. You'll need to book for dinner in high season. Closed Wed.

**Elvi's Kitchen**, on Pescador, across the road from *Martha's* hotel (☎026/2176). Long an institution in San Pedro, and always serving good burgers and fries, *Elvi's* has zoomed upmarket, with an expanded menu featuring soups, Caesar salad, steaks, chicken and, of course, lobster and all manner of seafood. Slick service with prices to match and gentle live music in the evenings.

**Jade Garden**, Coconut Drive, south of town. The best Chinese restaurant on the island, and good value too.

**JamBel**, on the park, next to *Big Daddy's*. A friendly, good-value place serving a very tasty blend of Jamaican and Belizean specialities, such as jerk chicken, pork and fish, coconut curry, shrimp and lobster (and always a vegetarian option), washed down with Belikin or Red Stripe.

**Mambo**, on the beach 7km north of town (☎021/3010). The dining room of the *Mata Chica Beach Resort* (see p.234) and one of Ambergris Caye's top restaurants, with superb food and wine and a classy, romantic atmosphere. Nadia, in charge of the cooking, is Italian and the menu changes daily but it's always fabulous; try the exquisite home-made fettuccini or the original paella. Dinner reservations are essential.

**El Patio**, a couple of kilometres south of the centre, next to Rock's supermarket. Fine dining at very reasonable prices in a lovely courtyard with fountains. Open for all meals.

**The Reef**, near the north end of Pescador. Really good Belizean food, including delicious seafood, at great prices in a simple restaurant cooled by a battery of fans.

**Rendezvous**, on the beach 5.5km north of town (☎026/3426). A new venue serving a delicious and unique fusion of Thai-French cuisine, accompanied by wines from the restaurant's own estate in California. Expensive by Belize standards at aroundUS$15–20 for an entrée, but well worth it.

**Ruby's Café**, Barrier Reef Drive, next to the entrance to *Ruby's Hotel*. Delicious home-made cakes, pies and sandwiches, and freshly brewed coffee. Open at 6am, so it's a good place to order a packed lunch if you're going on a trip.

**Sweet Basil**, 500m north of Boca del Rio (☎026/3869). A gem of a café and deli, run by Mary Ellen Stevens, and well worth making the effort to visit. Great pasta, seafood, salads, Italian specialities and the best selection of cheeses in Belize, all accompanied by fine wines. Closed Mon.

**Woody's Wharf**, south of town, behind *Corona del Mar*. Large portions of good seafood, Tex-Mex and Belizean dishes, and always a great daily special, served in a small *palapa* with a sand floor. A bargain for the island.

## Bars and nightlife

**Entertainment** in San Pedro becomes more sophisticated every year, and the best way to find out what's on (and what's hot) is to ask at your hotel or check the listings in the local press; what follows is a brief mention of a few highlights. Many of the hotels have bars, several of which offer **happy hours** while back from the main street are a couple of small **cantinas** where you can buy a beer or a bottle of rum and drink with the locals. For the best beachside happy hour (5–7pm), head for *Crazy Canuk Bar* at the *Exotic Caye Resort* where the resident band will get you in the party mood. *Big Daddy's* **disco**, in and around a beach bar just past the park, has early evening piano, and a lively reggae band later on. Happy hour here runs from 5 to 9pm and there's a daily beach barbecue. The extremely popular *Tarzan's Disco and Nite Club*, opposite the park, has a lively, popular dance floor. San Pedro's biggest disco is the new, a/c *Barefoot Iguana*, on Coconut Drive just south of the Yacht Club. Beyond here and to the right the tiny *Black and White Reggae Bar* (no cover) is the focal point for the island's Garífuna community; you'll be welcome to enjoy the drumming and punta rock.

## Listings

**Airlines** Maya Island Air (☎026/2345) and Tropic Air (☎026/2012) each have flights at least every hour to Belize Municipal and International airports, calling at Caye Caulker. Most hotels can arrange flights.

**Books** Many of the larger hotels have gift shops for books on Belize; the *Sunbreeze* has a particularly good selection of other titles as well, and the Book Center on Barrier Reef Drive has a reasonable selection, including guide books and maps. Any of these places, or Belizean Arts in Fido's Courtyard, are likely to stock *Rough Guides*.

**Banks and Exchange** You needn't worry about changing money, as travellers' cheques and US dollars are accepted – even preferred – everywhere. The Atlantic Bank on Barrier Reef Drive (Mon–Fri 8am–2pm, Sat 8.30am–noon) is the best place for cash advances, despite the US$5 charge.

**Conservation** Apart from the Hol Chan office (see p.237) you can contact Green Reef (☎026/2838, *greenreef@btl.net*) for information on the marine reserves and ecology of Ambergris Caye. Founded in 1996 to provide environmental education, it also provides opportunities for self-funded volunteers in education and biological monitoring.

**Laundry** Two places in Pescador Drive; washing costs US$3, drying another US$3.

**Police** Emergency ☎90; police station ☎026/2022.

**Post office** Barrier Reef Drive, in the Alijua Building (Mon–Thurs 8am–noon & 1–5pm, Fri 1–4.30pm).

**Shopping and souvenirs** In a resort destination like San Pedro you're never far from a souvenir or T-shirt shop, but if you're in the mood to enjoy some selective gift shopping, then the best place to visit is Belizean Arts in Fido's Courtyard, with an unparalleled range of Belizean and Central American arts and crafts. You'll also find some excellent wood carvings on the beach in front of the *Sunbreeze*.

**Travel and tour agencies** Your hotel will be able to book any of the tours mentioned in the text; for local trips around the caye and to the mainland, Tanisha Tours (☎026/2314, *www.tanishatours.com*) is the best. For international and regional flights the best place to check is Travel and Tour Belize, on Coconut Drive, near the airport (☎026/2031, *www.traveltourbelize.com*); owner Iraida Gonzalez is Belize's undisputed expert in arranging weddings in Belize.

# Caye Caulker

South of Ambergris Caye and 35km northeast of Belize City, **Caye Caulker**, a little over 7km long, is the most accessible and affordable island for the independent traveller. The island's name derives from that of a wild fruit and a local delicacy, the *hicaco* or coco plum. In 1961 Hurricane Hattie destroyed most of the houses and tore a gash through the island at a point just north of the village. Now widened by mangrove destruction and erosion, "The Split", as it's known, is a popular spot for swimming. Caye Caulker was hit badly by Hurricane Mitch in 1998, which destroyed all the docks on the front of the island, but **Hurricane Keith** in 2000 caused far worse damage (see box on p.230). The storm struck from the west, destroying numerous houses and boats. Many hotels suffered structural damage and most of the coconut trees in the village were toppled. Recovery here took longer than on Ambergris Caye, but all the places listed below were fully open within two months of the hurricane and there are certain to be more by now.

Until relatively recently, tourism existed almost as a sideline to the island's main source of income, **lobster fishing**, which has kept the place going for decades. And, despite the present decline in catches, there are always plenty of lobsters around for the annual **Lobster Fest**, held in the third weekend of June to celebrate the opening of the season. Fishermen have now become hoteliers, and fishing boats now offer snorkelling trips; new hotels and bars are being built, older ones improved, and prices – low for years – have begun to rise. For the moment, however, Caye Caulker remains relaxed and easy-going. As yet there is little air-conditioning on the island, which is fine most of the time when a cooling breeze blows in from the sea, but it can mean some very sticky moments if the breeze dies. **Sandflies and mosquitoes** can cause almost unbearable irritation on calm days, making a good insect repellent essential.

The success of a lengthy campaign by many islanders and others in Belize's environmental community has resulted in the protection of the northern tip of the island and a section of the barrier reef as the **Caye Caulker Forest and Marine Reserve**, upholding the country's reputation as a leader in the field of natural area conservation.

## Arrival and information

The **airstrip** is 1km south of the centre. Golf cart taxis can take you to your hotel, though hotels south of the main dock are only a 10–15-minute walk. **By boat** you'll be dropped off at one of the main piers on the island; either the "Front" (east) Dock or the "Back" (west) Dock – easily recognizable as they're longer than the others. Note: the Back Dock was completely **destroyed** by Hurricane Keith and had not been rebuilt at the time of writing. From either dock you simply walk straight ahead to the **water taxi office**, effectively the centre of the village. Staff here can give **information** and will probably hold your luggage while you look for a place to stay. The recommended snorkelling and tour offices also provide reliable information and can arrange **domestic and international flights**, tours and trips to other islands. They may also have **books** (including *Rough Guides*) and **maps**. If you get a chance, look at the **Website** *www.gocayecaulker.com* before you arrive; it lists most businesses on the caye and is well maintained.

---

### GETTING TO AND FROM CAYE CAULKER

For more detailed information on getting to Caye Caulker see p.213; below is a summary.

**Flights** on the San Pedro run stop at the Caye Caulker airstrip, 1.5km south of the village centre; call the airlines' main offices (see p.211) for information. On the island the offices are at the airstrip (Maya Island Air ☎026/2345; Tropic Air ☎026/2102). However, most visitors to Caye Caulker still arrive by **boat**. There are departures every two hours from 9am to 5pm (45min; US$7.50) from the Marine Terminal in Belize City (☎02/31969). All scheduled boats to San Pedro also call at Caye Caulker.

Boats **from Caye Caulker to San Pedro** depart every three hours from 7am to 4pm (check at the Caye Caulker Water Taxi office; ☎022/2992) and return roughly every two to three hours from 7am to 2.30pm (later on weekends and public holidays). If you're heading for one of the small or uninhabited islands you may have to hire someone to take you there.

**Leaving for Belize City**, boats depart roughly every two hours from 6.30am to 3pm (5pm on weekends and public holidays). It's best to check in at the water taxi office and book a place in a boat the day before you leave; the staff will also know the times that the boats on the San Pedro–Belize City run call at Caye Caulker; make sure it's clear which dock the boat is leaving from.

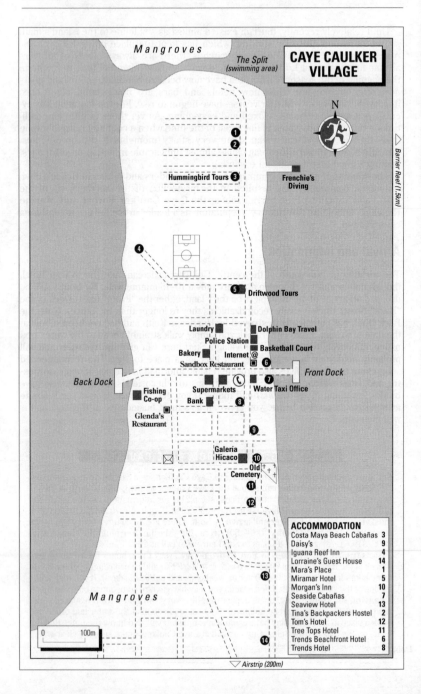

**CAYE CAULKER VILLAGE**

*Mangroves*

*The Split (swimming area)*

N

▷ *Barrier Reef (1.5km)*

Hummingbird Tours ❸

Frenchie's Diving

❹

❺ Driftwood Tours

Laundry
Police Station
Bakery
Sandbox Restaurant

Dolphin Bay Travel
Basketball Court
Internet @ ❻

*Back Dock*

Supermarkets
Bank

☎
Water Taxi Office ❼

*Front Dock*

Fishing Co-op
Glenda's Restaurant

❽

❾

Galeria Hicaco ❿
Old Cemetery
⓫

⓬

*Mangroves*

⓭

**ACCOMMODATION**

| | |
|---|---|
| Costa Maya Beach Cabañas | 3 |
| Daisy's | 9 |
| Iguana Reef Inn | 4 |
| Lorraine's Guest House | 14 |
| Mara's Place | 1 |
| Miramar Hotel | 5 |
| Morgan's Inn | 10 |
| Seaside Cabañas | 7 |
| Seaview Hotel | 13 |
| Tina's Backpackers Hostel | 2 |
| Tom's Hotel | 12 |
| Tree Tops Hotel | 11 |
| Trends Beachfront Hotel | 6 |
| Trends Hotel | 8 |

0    100m

⓮

▽ *Airstrip (200m)*

There are no street names on the caye, but the street running along the shore at the front of the island is effectively "**Front Street**", with just one or two streets running behind it in the centre of the village. Tina Auxillou, who runs Caye Caulker's **travel agency**, Dolphin Bay Travel (☎ & fax 022/2214, *dolphinbay@btl.net*), has outstanding local knowledge and can book domestic and international flights.

There are several **payphones** in the centre and the BTL office is opposite the water taxi office. The **post office** is on the back street, south of the village centre. **Email** and Internet services are offered by *CyberCafé*, just north of the *Sandbox Restaurant*. The Atlantic Bank (Mon–Fri 8am–2pm, Sat 8.30am–noon) gives **cash advances** (US$5 fee) and can sometimes give US dollars in cash, and an increasing number of businesses accept plastic for payment.

One thing to be aware of in Caye Caulker is the **tap water**; it sometimes smells sulphurous, giving off a rotting odour. This may be the result of natural chemicals in the groundwater, but most places simply use septic tanks for waste disposal, and effluent does seep into the water table. Tap water on the caye should be regarded as **unfit to drink**; make sure your hotel gives you rainwater or buy bottled water.

# Accommodation

Most of the year it's easy enough to find an inexpensive room in one of the small, mostly clapboard **hotels**, but to arrive at Christmas or New Year without a **reservation** could leave you stranded. Even the furthest hotels are no more than fifteen minutes' walk from the Front Dock and places are easy to find: the listings below are given roughly in the order you'd come to them walking from the dock. Most places now have hot water and many accept credit cards. There are also a growing number of houses or **apartments for rent**. Most will have a small stove, fridge, hot water and cable TV; try M&M Apartments (☎022/2229), or Heredia's Apartments (☎022/2132), both near the football field. You'll come across other places as you walk around; prices start at about US$165 per week.

## North from the "Front" Dock

**Trends Beachfront Hotel**, on the beach, immediately right of the Front Dock (☎022/2094, *trends-bze@btl.net*). Large rooms in a new wooden building with comfortable beds and a deck with hammocks; also a private beachfront cabaña with fridge. Round the corner on Front Street (left at BTL office) there's another *Trends* with less expensive rooms; both are linked to the one in Belize City (p.207). ④–⑤.

**Miramar Hotel**, Front Street, past the basketball court (☎022/2357). Good-value budget rooms with shared bath in a wooden building with a large balcony, overlooking the sea, at the front. ④.

**Iguana Reef Inn**, at the back (west) of the caye, on the far side of the football field (☎022/2213, *www.iguanareefinn.com*). The most luxurious place on the island, with twelve well-furnished, a/c suites with queen-sized beds and fridge, and great sunset views. Excellent Web site. ⑧.

**Costa Maya Beach Cabañas**, towards the Split (☎022/2432, *www.costamaya–belize.com*). New, clean rooms with bedside lights and private bath in hexagonal cabins, run by a friendly family. ⑤.

**Tina's Backpackers Hostel**, 20m past *Costa Maya*, facing the sea (☎022/2214, *dolphinbay@btl.net*). Nineteen dorm beds in a wooden house, with kitchen and common area; US$10 high season per person, camping US$5.

**Mara's Place**, towards the Split (☎022/2156). Six simple, comfortable and very good value wooden cabins with private bath, TV and porch. ⑤.

## South from the "Front" Dock

**Seaside Cabañas**, on the left of the Front Dock (☎022/2498, *seasidecabanas@btl.net*). Very well built, spacious and well-furnished wood-and-thatch rooms and cabañas, with private bath, comfortable beds, fans, TV, fridge and coffee maker, and outside a deck with hammocks. ⑥/⑦.

**Daisy's** (☎022/2150). Simple, budget rooms, just back from the sea and run by a friendly family. ④.

**Morgan's Inn**, opposite Galería Hicaco (where you enquire; ☎022/2178, *sbf@btl.net*). Three quiet, roomy cabins, one with private cold-water bath, set just back from the beach; each sleeps at least three, though only one cabin has cooking facilities. ⑤/⑥.

**Tree Tops Hotel**, just beyond the cemetery (☎022/2008, fax 2115, *treetops@btl.net*). Easily the best hotel on the island (indeed the country) at this price, just 50m from the water. Five comfortable rooms, with fridge, cable TV and powerful ceiling fan; most have private bath and the shared bathroom is immaculate. Owners Terry and Doris Creasey are extremely helpful, giving reliable tourist information, and will book flights and tours for you. Booking advisable. ⑤.

**Tom's Hotel** (☎022/2102, *toms@btl.net*). A large hotel for Caye Caulker, with twenty bargain, clean, tiled rooms (most with private bath) in a concrete building with all-round balcony, and five cabins. ⑤.

**Seaview Hotel**, (☎022/2205, *seaview@btl.net*). On the beach, south of the centre. Four very comfortable rooms with private bath and fridge in a concrete house; also a one-bedroom wooden cottage with private bath for rent (US$225 a week). ⑥.

**Lorraine's Guest House**, just past the *Anchorage* (☎022/2002). A bargain near the beach, with simple but comfortable cabins, run by the friendly Alamilla family; Orlando makes great wooden souvenirs. ④.

# Exploring the reef and the caye

To the east **the Barrier Reef** lies only 1.5km from the shore and the white foam of the reef crest is always visible. It's certainly an experience not to be missed: swimming along coral canyons surrounded by an astonishing range of fish, with perhaps even a shark or two (almost certainly harmless nurse sharks). Here, as everywhere, snorkellers should be aware of the fragility of the reef and be careful not to touch any coral – even sand stirred up by fins can cause damage (see box on p.236).

The northern part of the island is long and narrow, covered in mangroves and thick vegetation that extends right down to the shore: the rare and threatened **caye littoral forest** habitat. In 1998 the northernmost forty hectares were declared the **Caye Caulker Forest Reserve**, contiguous with the **Marine Reserve**. As the leaves fall and mud accumulates some areas rise just above sea level, at least in the dry season. Between these areas are lagoons that remain year-round; excellent habitats for crocodiles, turtles and water birds. Other native inhabitants of the littoral forest include boa constrictors, scaly-tailed iguanas (locally called "wish willies"), geckos, land and hermit crabs and lizards.

As always, your trip to the reef or the littoral forest will be more enjoyable if you have some idea of what you're seeing. At the Galería Hicaco (☎022/2178, *sbf@btl.net*), toward the south end of Front Street, marine biologist Ellen McRae can explain exactly what it is you're seeing in this amazing underwater world. As a naturalist guide she can also take you for a really **well-informed tour** of the reef, or an early-morning **Audubon bird walk**, an introduction to the dozens of bird species of the caye – waders from herons to sandpipers, with pelicans, spoonbills and the ever-present frigate birds swooping down with pinpoint accuracy on morsels of fish. The Galería also acts as a centre for environmental information and as the base of the Siwa-Ban Foundation formed to protect the home of the **black catbird**, in the terrestrial section of the Caye Caulker reserves.

## Swimming, snorkelling and diving

**Swimming** isn't really possible from the shore as the water's too shallow. You have to leap off the end of piers or go to "The Split" at the north end of the village. Snorkelling **trips to the reef** from Caye Caulker are easily arranged and cost around US$10–25 per person, depending on where you go. Most last several hours and take in a number of sites, often going to **Hol Chan Marine Reserve** and **Shark-Ray Alley** (see p.237). You can usually rent decent **equipment** (US$3.50 for snorkel, mask and fins) from the place where you book your trip; always check it fits well and try to practise from a dock before you go to the reef.

The best trips and guides are generally offered by Meldie Rosado of Driftwood Snorkelling (☎2011), near the *Miramar Hotel*; Meldie is very reliable, has good snorkelling equipment and can advise on trips into Guatemala. Also recommended are Barbara and Heather of Hummingbird Tours, in *Costa Maya Cabañas* (☎2432, *www.hummingbirdtours.com*). Carlos Miller is one of the best independent tour guides on the caye, and Carlos Ayala, of Carlos Tours (☎014/9986), is a very conscientious guide who takes small groups on snorkelling or sailing trips. One of the best **independent trips** is offered by Ras Creek in his dory *Rice 'n' Beans* (US$12.50). Ras leaves from the Front Dock around 11am (check in the *Sandbox*) and takes you out to the reef right in front of the caye. Rum punch is provided, and guests help prepare lunch, arriving back as the sun is setting – the perfect end to an utterly relaxing day.

Frenchie's (☎022/2234, *frenchies@btl.net*), at the northern end of the village, is the longest-established **dive shop** on the caye and offers safe and very knowledgeable trips, with some great reef diving (two-tank dive, US$55), and **night dives** (US$40). A day-trip to **Lighthouse Reef** and the **Blue Hole** (see p.248), leaving at 7am, (three dives, US$165, snorkellers US$65) is an unforgettable experience. After the unique, slightly spooky, splendour of diving over 35m into the depths of the Blue Hole there's the fantastic 80-metre wall off **Half Moon Caye**, where you can meet the red-footed booby birds and the huge hermit crabs face to face. PADI **instruction** is cheaper than on Ambergris Caye, at US$250, or US$540 for a **dive master** course. Frenchie's can book you a place on the bigger dive boats from San Pedro (see p.236), and you'll be picked up from Caye Caulker at no extra charge. Disposable **underwater cameras** are available from the snorkel here, but higher-quality photographic equipment is not generally available for rent. If you'd like to learn **underwater photography** get in touch with James Beveridge of Seaing is Belizing (☎022/2079).

## Other activities and trips to other islands

Belize has the largest surviving population of the West Indian manatee, and trips can take you **manatee-watching at Swallow Caye** (US$28), south of Caye Caulker, where the gentle animals congregate around a hole in the shallows just offshore; the skipper turns off the motor and poles toward the hole in order not to disturb them. You're almost certainly guaranteed a sighting, often of whole family groups, though you're not allowed to get into the water with them. These trips also usually include a visit to **Goff's Caye**, **English Caye** or **Sergeant's Caye** – tiny specks of sand and coral with a few palm trees.

You'll also see signs for **fishing trips** as you walk around. Some of the best are operated by Porfilio Guzman (☎022/2152) and Roly Rosado (☎2058), who both live near the north end of the village; ask for them by name – any of the locals will direct you. If you want to go around the southern section of the caye on your own you can rent a **kayak** for around US$13–20; try *Daisy's* hotel or ask at the Galería Hicaco, where you can also rent a **sailboard** and receive instruction.

## Eating, drinking and entertainment

Good cooking, large portions and very reasonable prices are features of all the island's **restaurants**, half of which you'll pass while looking for a room. **Lobster** (in season) is served in every imaginable dish, from curry to chow mein; other **seafood** is generally good value, accompanied by rice or potatoes and sometimes salad. Along Front Street are a couple of **fast food** stands, serving *tacos* and *burritos*. There's a good **bakery** on the street leading to the football field, which does great cinnamon buns, and many houses advertise banana bread, coconut cakes and other home-baked goodies. As you walk around you might see children selling bread or pastries from bowls balanced on their heads; it's always worth seeing what snacks are on offer. You can also buy food at several well-stocked **shops and supermarkets** on the island.

## Restaurants and cafés

**Coco Plum Gardens Café**, south of the centre, towards the airstrip. Wholefood café serving great breakfasts – crepes and home-made granola – sandwiches, pizza and desserts in a lush garden setting, with an art gallery. Also has delicious Belizean fruit jams and wines. Open Tues–Sun 7am–3.30pm.

**Glenda's**, at the back of the island. Justly famous for delicious cinnamon rolls and fresh orange juice, this is a favourite breakfast meeting place.

**Happy Lobster**, on Front Street, north of the centre. Good, inexpensive local restaurant that offers the best value on the caye.

**Marin's Restaurant**, towards the south end of middle street. A very long-established restaurant, serving really good seafood either indoors or in a shady courtyard. Pricier than it used to be.

**Martinez Restaurant**, on the front, just past the *Miramar Hotel*. Reasonable Belizean food at very good prices; might also have some very basic rooms available.

**Oceanside**, next to *Martinez*. One of the best places on the island, serving tasty, well-presented seafood at good prices.

**The Sand Box**, by the Front Dock. The best restaurant on the island, serving great Italian/American food and local dishes in large portions. Open from 7am for a coffee and roll before the boat. Closed Thurs.

**Sobre Las Olas**, on the front, beyond the *Rainbow*. Good seafood and steaks in a beach barbecue atmosphere.

**Tropical Paradise**, at the southern end of Front Street. Good-quality Belizean and American-style food at reasonable prices in a comfortable a/c dining room.

## Bars and nightlife

Caye Caulker's **social scene** oscillates around the various bars and restaurants, and frequently nowadays there's **live music** to add atmosphere to the evening, especially in the busier places along Front Street. Few places are strictly bars, though the three-storey *I&I's*, between *Tropical Paradise* and *Edith's*, is more bar than restaurant – take care negotiating the stairs on the way down. Most people are friendly enough, but as the evening wears on and drink takes its toll things can get rowdy. Be careful with your money too – Caye Caulker has a criminal element and a drug problem, but only three policemen. Away from the music, evening entertainment mostly consists of relaxing in a restaurant over dinner or a drink.

# Other northern cayes and the atolls

Although Caye Caulker and San Pedro are the only villages anywhere on the reef, there are several other islands that can be visited. Caye Caulker is within day-trip distance of some of these and there are a few superbly isolated hotels – called **lodges** – on some reefs and cayes. The attraction of these lodges is the "simple life", usually focusing on diving or fishing; staying at them is generally part of a package that includes transfers from the airport, accommodation, all meals and the sports on offer. Buildings are low-key, wooden and sometimes thatched, and the group you're with will probably be the only people staying there. Views of palm trees curving over turquoise water reinforce the sense of isolation.

## St George's Caye

Tiny **St George's Caye**, around 15km from Belize City, was the capital of the Baymen in the eighteenth century and still manages to exude an air of colonial grandeur; its beautifully restored colonial houses face east to catch the breeze and their lush green lawns are enclosed by white picket fences. The sense of history is reinforced by the eighteenth-century cannons mounted in front of some of the finer houses; for another glimpse into the past you could head for the small graveyard of the early settlers on the southern tip of the island. Today, the island is home to the villas of Belize's elite, an adventure training centre for British forces in Belize and a few fishermen, who live toward the north end in an area known, appropriately enough, as "Fishermen Town".

There's not much here for the casual visitor but some fishing and snorkelling trips do call at St George's Caye. If you come you may meet Austrian Karl Bishof, who runs Bela Carib (☎02/49435), a company that carefully collects and exports tropical fish. The tanks contain a fascinating display of reef creatures and you're welcome to look around. After your visit take a look at the great T-shirts in Karl's Fisherman Town Gift Shop.

**Accommodation** on the caye is luxurious, expensive and generally sold as a package. *Cottage Colony* (☎02/77051 or 021/2020, *fins@btl.net*; ⑧) has rooms in comfortable, colonial-style, wooden houses with modern facilities set in palm-shaded grounds, and the dining room overlooks the Caribbean. It's usually a great place for fishing and diving, and perfect for relaxation but transport and services can be unreliable: if the boat taking you out doesn't leave on time then other things may not be as they should. *St George's Lodge* (☎02/44190, fax 31460, *fred@gooddiving.com*; ⑨), is an all-inclusive diving resort — the first in Belize, and with rave reviews in the diving press — comprising a ten-room main lodge and six luxury, wood-and-thatch cottages with private verandahs. Rates begin at US$200; you can get a better deal by paying in advance for a package, which includes airport transfer, diving and meals. There's no drinks licence but guests can bring their own alcohol.

## The Bluefield Range

In the **Bluefield Range**, a group of mangrove cayes 35km southeast of Belize City, you can stay on a remote **fishing camp**. *Ricardo's Beach Huts* (☎02/31609, *fabianbeck@btl.net*) offer simple, comfortable accommodation (minimum 2 nights) right on the water, in huts built on stilts. At US$170 per person for three days/two nights it's not cheap, but the price includes transport to and from Belize City, all meals – including, as you might imagine, fresh fish and lobster – and a fishing or snorkelling trip to Rendezvous Caye, right on the reef; *Rough Guide* readers get a discount. Ricardo Castillo is a reliable, expert fishing guide, scrupulously practising conservation of the reef. For more information ask at *Mira Rio* bar, 59 N Front St, Belize City (☎02/44970), where the trips start.

## The Turneffe Islands

The virtually uninhabited **Turneffe Islands**, 40km from Belize City, are an oval archipelago of low-lying mangrove islands 60km long, enclosed by a beautiful coral reef. **Fishing** here, for bonefish and permit on the shallow flats, is world class, and dedicated anglers can expect to fish at least six hours every day, with most of the sport-fishing on a "catch and release" basis. **Diving** is sublime and there's any amount of simply wonderful **snorkelling**. Currently there is no protected land at Turneffe, but there is a proposal for a new marine reserve at **Rendezvous Point**, on the northwest edge of the atoll.

The reefs can be visited on day-trips from San Pedro or Caye Caulker and a few places offer all-inclusive **accommodation**; you'll need to book ahead and, though they are expensive, most places will offer discounts if you book through their Web sites. On **Blackbird Caye**, halfway down the eastern side, *Blackbird Caye Resort* (☎02/32772, in US ☎1-800/346-6116, *www.islandream.com/island.blackbrd.htm*) has luxury wood-and-thatch cabañas. A week's package, including transfers, all meals, diving/snorkelling and perhaps fishing, costs US$1200–1500. On **Caye Bokel** at the southern tip of the archipelago, *Turneffe Island Lodge* (☎ & fax 021/2011, in US ☎1-800/874-0118, *www.turneffelodge.com*), has luxurious cabins on a twelve-acre private island. A package costs US$1250–2000 for a week, depending on the main activity.

## Lighthouse Reef, the Blue Hole and Half Moon Caye

About 80km east of Belize City is Belize's outermost atoll, **Lighthouse Reef**, with the Blue Hole and Half Moon Caye natural monuments forming the main attractions. You can visit the atoll as either a day- or overnight trip from San Pedro (p.236) or Caye Caulker (p.245), and **camp** on Half Moon Caye (below). The **Blue Hole** is technically a "karst-eroded sink-hole", a shaft about 300m in diameter and 135m deep, which opens out into a complex network of **caves and crevices**, complete with stalactites and stalagmites. It was formed over a million years ago when Lighthouse Reef was a sizeable island – or even part of the mainland. Its great depth gives it a peculiar deep blue colour, and even swimming across is disorienting as there's no sense of anything beneath you. Unsurprisingly, Lighthouse Reef and the Blue Hole are major magnets for **divers**, offering incredible walls and drop-offs. Several **shipwrecks** form artificial reefs; the most prominent is the *Ermlund*, which ran aground in 1971 and looms over the reef just north of Half Moon Caye.

The **Half Moon Caye Natural Monument**, the first marine conservation area in Belize, was declared a national park in 1982 and became a World Heritage Site in 1996. Visitors must register with the ranger on arrival, and pay the US$5 **fee**, which includes entry to the Blue Hole. The **visitor centre**, built by volunteers from Raleigh and Trekforce expeditions, has displays on the ecology of the caye.

The 45-acre caye is divided into two distinct ecosystems: in the west, guano from thousands of seabirds fertilizes the soil, allowing the growth of dense vegetation, while the eastern half has mostly coconut palms growing in the sand. A total of 98 bird species has been recorded here, including frigate birds, ospreys, mangrove warblers, white-crowned pigeons and – most important of all – a resident population of four thousand **red-footed boobies**, one of only two nesting colonies in the Caribbean. The boobies came by their name because they displayed no fear of humans, enabling sailors to kill them in their thousands, and they still move only reluctantly when visitors stroll among them. Their nesting area is accessible from a platform and the birds are not in the least bothered by your presence. Apart from birds, the island supports iguanas and lizards, and both **loggerhead and hawksbill turtles** nest on the beaches, which also attract the biggest hermit and land crabs in Belize.

There's no accommodation on the caye, but **camping** is allowed with the permission of the Belize Audubon Society (see p.208), who manage the reserve; many of the overnight diving expeditions camp here.

## travel details

### Buses

Bus company addresses and details of **services from Belize City** are given in the box on pp.212–3.

**Bermudian Landing** to: Belize City (Mon–Sat 2–3 daily; 1hr 15min), via Burrell Boom.

**Chetumal** to: Belize City (hourly; 3hr 30min, express services 3hr), via Corozal and Orange Walk.

**Corozal** to: Belize City (hourly; 2hr 30min), via Orange Walk (1hr); to Chetumal (hourly; 1hr including border crossing).

**Crooked Tree** to: Belize City (4 daily; 1hr 30min).

**Orange Walk** to: Belize City (hourly; 1hr 30min); to Corozal (hourly; 1hr); Indian Church, for Lamanai (3 weekly on Mon, Wed & Fri at 4pm; 2hr).

**Sarteneja** to: Belize City (Mon–Sat 2–3 daily; 3hr 30min).

### Planes

Maya Island Air (☎026/2345) and Tropic Air (☎026/2012) each operate three daily flights between Corozal and San Pedro, Ambergris Caye. Each airline also operates flights at least hourly from 7am–5pm between Belize City and San Pedro, calling at Caye Caulker. There are no domestic flights from Belize City to either Orange Walk or Corozal.

### Boats

For a rundown of **boats** to the northern cayes from Belize City and between the cayes themselves, see the boxes on pp.231 & 241.

# CHAPTER FIVE

# CAYO AND THE WEST

H eading west from Belize City to the Guatemalan border, you travel through a wide range of landscapes, from open grassland and rolling hills to dense tropical forest. A fast paved road, the Western Highway, covers the 130km from Belize City to the Guatemalan border, a route that takes you from the heat and humidity of the coast to the lush foothills of the Maya Mountains. Before reaching Belize's tiny capital, Belmopan, the road passes several places of interest: the Belize Zoo, the Monkey Bay Wildlife Sanctuary, and Guanacaste National Park. Heading further west, following the Belize River valley, the road skirts the northern foothills of the Maya Mountains. You're now in Cayo District, the largest of Belize's six districts and arguably the most beautiful – a sentiment enthusiastically endorsed by the inhabitants.

South of the highway most of the landscape, including the entire mountain range, is under official protection in a vast network of national parks, wildlife sanctuaries and forest and archeological reserves. One of the most-visited protected areas, the **Mountain Pine Ridge Forest Reserve**, is a pleasantly cool region of hills and pine woods boasting some of the finest lodge accommodation in the country. The ruins of **Caracol**, the largest Maya site in Belize and a focus for current archeological research, lie deep in the jungle south of here. **San Ignacio**, on the Macal River, and only 15km from the Guatemalan border, is the busy main town of Cayo District and the ideal base for exploring the forests, rivers and ruins of western Belize.

Between San Ignacio and the Guatemalan border, the road climbs past the hilltop ruin of **Cahal Pech**, then descends, following the valley of the **Mopan River** to the frontier bridge. A few kilometres before the frontier itself, at the village of **San José Succotz**, an ancient ferry crosses the river, allowing access to another hilltop Maya site, **Xunantunich**, whose highest structures offer stunning views over to Guatemala's department of Petén. Belize's westernmost Maya site, **El Pilar**, 18km northwest of San Ignacio, actually extends into Guatemala, and is the first **International Archeological Reserve** anywhere in the Maya World.

## Belize City to San Ignacio

Served by frequent buses between Belize City and San Ignacio, the Western Highway leaves the city through the middle of the Lord's Ridge cemetery, then skirts the shoreline, running behind a tangle of mangrove swamps. After 10km the road crosses the **Sir John Burden Canal**, an inland waterway, now a nature reserve and valuable wildlife corridor, that connects the Belize River with the **Sibun River**. At HATTIEVILLE, 26km further on, named after the 1961 hurricane that created the refugees who initially populated it, there's a turning north to **Burrell Boom** and **Bermudian Landing** (see p.215), a short cut to the Northern Highway. If time permits you should allow an hour or two to visit the **Belize Zoo**, probably the finest zoo in Central America. Just beyond the zoo, the unpaved **Coastal Road** to Dangriga offers a short cut to the south (see p.281). At **Monkey Bay Wildlife Sanctuary** you'd need to stay at least a day or two to fully appreciate what's on offer, but **Guanacaste National Park** is a worthwhile stop right by the roadside just before Belmopan.

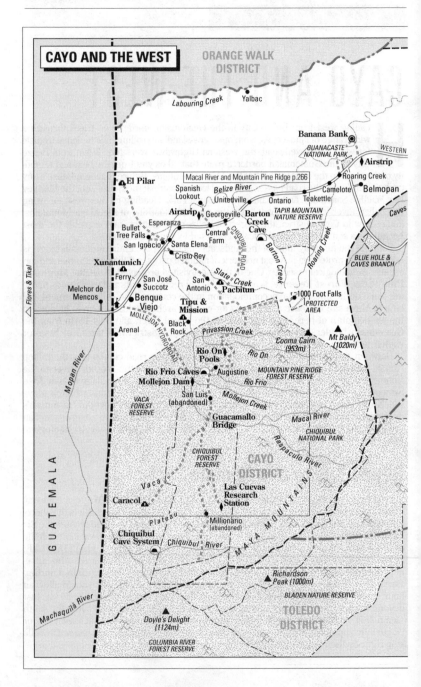

## CAYO AND THE WEST

ORANGE WALK
DISTRICT

Labouring Creek
Yalbac

Banana Bank
GUANACASTE
NATIONAL PARK
WESTERN
Airstrip
Roaring Creek
Belmopan
Camelote
Teakettle

El Pilar
Macal River and Mountain Pine Ridge p.266
Spanish
Lookout
Belize River
Unitedville
Ontario
Airstrip
Georgeville
Barton
Creek
Cave
TAPIR MOUNTAIN
NATURE RESERVE
Esperanza
Bullet
Tree Falls
San Ignacio
Central
Farm
Barton Creek
Roaring Creek
Santa Elena
Cristo Rey
Slate Creek
CHIQUIBUL ROAD
BLUE HOLE &
CAVES BRANCH
Caves

Xunantunich
Ferry
San José
Succotz
San
Antonio
Pacbitun
1000 Foot Falls
PROTECTED
AREA

Melchor de
Mencos
Benque
Viejo
Tipu &
Mission
Cooma Cairn
(953m)
Mt Baldy
(1020m)
MOLLEJON HYDRO ROAD
Black
Rock
Privassion Creek
Rio On
Arenal
Rio On
Pools
Augustine
MOUNTAIN PINE RIDGE
FOREST RESERVE
Rio Frio
Rio Frio Caves
Mollejon Dam
San Luis
(abandoned)
Mollejon Creek
Macal River
VACA
FOREST
RESERVE
Guacamallo
Bridge
CHIQUIBUL
NATIONAL PARK
Raspaculo River
CHIQUIBUL
FOREST
RESERVE
CAYO
DISTRICT
Vaca
Las Cuevas
Research
Station
Caracol
plateau
Millionario
(abandoned)
Chiquibul
Cave System
Chiquibul River
MAYA MOUNTAINS
Richardson
Peak (1000m)
Machaquila River
BLADEN NATURE RESERVE
TOLEDO
DISTRICT
Doyle's Delight
(1124m)
COLUMBIA RIVER
FOREST RESERVE

GUATEMALA

△ Flores & Tikal

Mopan River

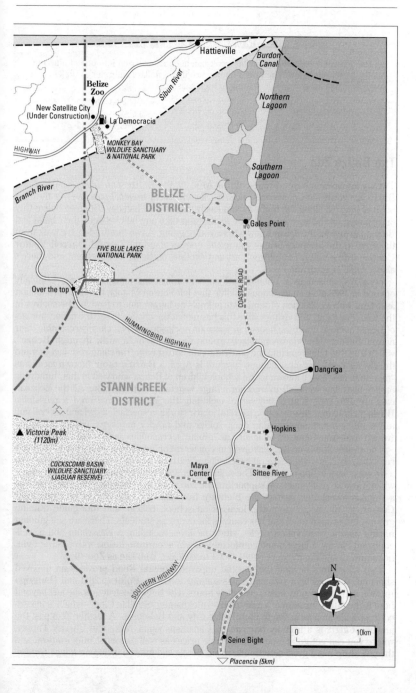

Hattieville

Burdon Canal

Sibun River

Belize Zoo

Northern Lagoon

New Satellite City (Under Construction)

La Democracia

HIGHWAY

MONKEY BAY WILDLIFE SANCTUARY & NATIONAL PARK

Southern Lagoon

Branch River

BELIZE DISTRICT

Gales Point

FIVE BLUE LAKES NATIONAL PARK

COASTAL ROAD

Over the top

HUMMINGBIRD HIGHWAY

Dangriga

STANN CREEK DISTRICT

Hopkins

▲ Victoria Peak (1120m)

COCKSCOMB BASIN WILDLIFE SANCTUARY (JAGUAR RESERVE)

Maya Center

Sittee River

N

SOUTHERN HIGHWAY

0        10km

Seine Bight

▽ Placencia (5km)

# The Belize Zoo

Twenty kilometres beyond Hattieville, at Mile 29, the **Belize Zoo** (daily 8.30am–5pm; Bz$15 for adult foreign visitors, Bz$7.50 for children, *www.belizezoo.org*) is the first point of interest along the highway and easily visited on a half-day trip from Belize City or as a stop on the way west. To **get to the zoo** take any bus between the capital and Belmopan and let the driver know where you're going. A two-hundred-metre walk from the sign on the highway brings you to the entrance and the **Gerald Durrell Visitor Centre**, with displays of children's art and exhibits on Belize's ecosystems and there's also a small **restaurant**.

Long recognized as a phenomenal conservation achievement, the zoo originally opened in 1983 after an ambitious wildlife film left Sharon Matola, the film's production assistant, with a collection of semi-tame animals no longer able to fend for themselves in the wild. For locals and visitors alike this has meant the chance to see the native animals of Belize at close quarters, housed in spacious enclosures which closely resemble their natural habitat. The zoo is organized around the theme of "**a walk through Belize**", with a trail that takes you into the pine ridge, the forest edge, the rainforest, lagoons and the river forest. The most famous resident is April, a **Baird's tapir** (known locally as "mountain cow") well known to the schoolchildren of Belize, who visit in their hundreds on her birthday (in April) to feed her a huge vegetable birthday cake. All the Belizean cats are also represented and some, including the **jaguars**, have bred successfully. **Birds** include toucans, macaws, parrots, jabiru storks, a spectacled owl and several vultures; other inhabitants include deer, spider and howler monkeys, peccaries, agouti (which sometimes appears on menus as "gibnut"), crocodiles and various snakes.

The Belize Zoo is actively involved in conservation education and Sharon, who still runs the zoo, has written several excellent and extremely popular children's books with a strong conservation message. These and other souvenirs are on sale in the **gift shop**, while if you're really keen on supporting the zoo you can become a Friend and receive a regular newsletter. Across the highway from the zoo, the **Tropical Education Center**, as the name suggests, focuses on school, college and tour-guide training groups, but is open to all and has courses for overseas students. There are self-guiding **nature trails**, observation decks, study facilities including a classroom and a well-equipped library, a lagoon and comfortable dorm **accommodation** with electric light, hot showers and flush toilets (☎081/3003 *tec@btl.net*, Web site as Zoo; ③).

Two kilometres beyond the zoo the unpaved **Coastal Road** provides an unpaved short cut (marked by a sign and a gas station) to **Gales Point** (p.281) and **Dangriga** (p.286), and is served by buses every few hours. The huge construction site just beyond here is the future location of a new town — nicknamed "Satellite City" – which is intended to provide an alternative to both Belize City and Belmopan. A further 2km past the junction *Cheers* is a friendly **bar** run by Canadians Anita, Mike and Chrissy Tupper, where you can get good food at reasonable prices as well as tourist **information,** and the **gift shop** has a good selection of maps, books and guides, including *Rough Guides*.

## Monkey Bay Wildlife Sanctuary

Half a kilometre past *Cheers* and 400m off to the left of the highway (signposted at Mile 31½), the **Monkey Bay Wildlife Sanctuary** (☎081/3032, *mbay@btl.net*) is a 44-square-kilometre protected area extending to the Sibun River and offering birding and nature **trails** through five distinct habitat types. Adjoining the sanctuary across the river is the nine-square-kilometre **Monkey Bay National Park**. The two protected areas serve as a wildlife corridor spanning the Sibun valley south through karst limestone hills to the Manatee Forest Reserve. Government agencies and NGOs are currently working on an ambitious project to extend this corridor to connect protected areas in northern Belize, across the rapidly developing Western Highway, with those in the south.

The sanctuary headquarters includes a **field research station**, which serves as library, museum and classroom and specializes in hosting academic programmes in natural history; it's also a wonderfully relaxing **place to stay** for anyone, either in the bunkhouse (US$7.50) or camping (US$5). Monkey Bay is a viable experiment in "off the grid" sustainable living, utilizing solar power and rainwater catchment, and the food, some of it grown in the station's organic gardens, is delicious and plentiful. From Monkey Bay you can arrange guided **canoe, caving and birding trips** on the Sibun River and explore little-visited **caves** in the Sibun Hills to the south, all of which have evidence of use by the ancient Maya. Monkey Bay is also the contact point for visits to **Cox Lagoon Crocodile Sanctuary**, a 120 square-kilometre private nature reserve north of the highway that's home to around one hundred Morelet's crocodiles. Visitors can camp and canoe here: contact the directors, Matt and Marga Miller, at Monkey Bay.

## Onward to Guanacaste Park

Five hundred metres beyond Monkey Bay, **JB's Bar** is an old favourite with the British Army, whose mementos deck the walls. The bar has an early evening happy hour, plus a **restaurant** serving good Belizean and Tex-Mex food, and there's a range of comfortable, well-priced **accommodation** (☎081/3025, *www.jbbelize.com*; ⑤): three rooms, a thatched cabaña, a house and space for RVs. *JB's* marks the boundary between the Belize and Cayo Districts, and here the open expanse of pine and savannah begins to give way to rich pastures and citrus groves.

Twenty-five kilometres beyond *JB's*, and 2km before the turning for Belmopan, opposite the airstrip at Mile 46, a track leads off to the right to **Banana Bank Lodge** (☎081/2020, fax 2026, *www.bananabank.com*; ⑦–⑧ including breakfast; no service charge). This 4000-acre working cattle ranch, half of which is still primary forest, is on the north bank of the Belize River, which you cross by foot-passenger boat; an alternative route, marked at the turn-off to the right just beyond **Roaring Creek** village, allows you to drive all the way, crossing the river on an old chain-driven ferry. The **accommodation**, with views sweeping down to the river, consists of five very spacious, beautifully furnished, wood-and-thatch cabañas with large bathrooms, and seven rooms in the lodge. The food, all home-cooked and mostly home-grown, is superb and plentiful. The *Lodge* is owned by Americans John and Carolyn Carr, who offer great **horse-riding**, with sixty well-trained horses, a new stable block and a training arena. The ranch's natural history is astonishing: over two hundred bird species have been recorded here, and there's a beautiful **lagoon** with resident Morelet's crocodiles and an observation tower for bird-watching. Carolyn is also an accomplished artist and her work is exhibited all over the country. She's also very proud of her **"mini observatory"** on the riverbank; the twelve-inch Meade telescope here is the best in the country.

## Guanacaste National Park

Right by the highway, at the junction for Belmopan and the Hummingbird Highway, **Guanacaste National Park** (daily 8am–4.30pm; US$2.50) is Belize's smallest national park and the easiest to visit; **buses** stop right outside. The **visitor centre** has maps and information on the park ecology (including a superb exhibit on the life cycle of the leaf-cutter ants, which you'll see all over Belize), and there's an orchid display in the courtyard. Outside, four or five short **trails** take you through the park and along the banks of the Belize River: you can wander through a superb area of lush tropical forest at the confluence of the river and Roaring Creek.

The main attraction is a huge **guanacaste** or tubroos tree, a forty-metre-high, spreading hardwood that supports some 35 species; hanging from its limbs are a huge range of bromeliads, orchids, ferns, cacti and strangler figs, which blossom spectacularly at the end of the rainy season. Other botanical attractions include young mahogany trees, *cohune* palms, a cotton tree and quamwood, while the forest floor is a mass of ferns, mosses and vines. As the park is so close to the road, your chances of seeing any four-footed **wildlife** are fairly slim, but recently a small number of howler monkeys have used the park as a feeding ground. **Birds**, however, abound, with over fifty species, among them blue-crowned motmots, black-faced ant-thrushes, black-headed trogons and squirrel cuckoos.

# Belmopan

From Guanacaste Park the Western Highway pushes on towards San Ignacio and the Guatemalan border, while a paved branch road turns south 2km towards Belize's capital, **BELMOPAN**, beyond which it becomes the Hummingbird Highway, continuing all the way to the coast at Dangriga. For most people the capital is no more than a break in the bus ride to San Ignacio, though if you're heading to Dangriga or Placencia this is the place to change buses.

Belmopan was founded in 1970 after Hurricane Hattie swept much of Belize City into the sea. The government decided to use the disaster as a chance to move to higher ground and, in a Brasília-style bid to focus development on the interior, chose a site in the geographical heart of the country. The name of the city combines the words Belize and **Mopan**, the language spoken by the Maya of Cayo. The layout of the main government buildings, designed in the 1960s, is supposedly modelled on a Maya city, with structures grouped around a central plaza. Belmopan was meant to be a classic New Town, symbolizing the dawn of a new era, with tree-lined avenues, banks, embassies and telecommunications worthy of a world centre. Today it has all the essential ingredients of a successful town bar one – people. The majority of Belizeans still prefer the congestion of Belize City to the boredom of Belmopan, though scares caused by recent **hurricanes** – Mitch in 1998 and Keith in 2000 – are prompting a re-think by those who can afford to buy or build a house here.

Unless you've come to visit a government department, there's no particular reason to stay any longer in Belmopan than it takes your bus to leave. The former theatre opposite the market square sometimes has temporary displays of Belizean archeological artefacts, which once formed the basis of the collection in the now-closed Archeological Vault, and a new exhibition area is currently under construction; to find out what's available for viewing call the **Archeology Department** on ☎08/22106. The **Archives Department** (Mon–Fri 8am–5pm, free; ☎08/22247, *www.pro.gov.uk/belize*), 26–28 Unity Blvd, also welcomes visitors: its photographs, documents, newspapers and sound archives provide a fascinating glimpse of old Belize.

## Practicalities

**Buses from Belize City** to San Ignacio and Dangriga all pass through Belmopan, and Western Transport (connecting with Z-Line services to Dangriga, Placencia and Punta

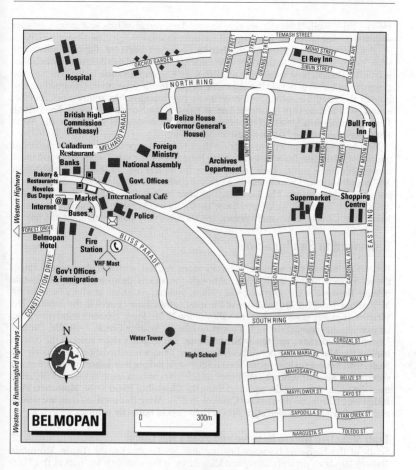

**BELMOPAN**

0        300m

Gorda) runs a frequent service between Belmopan and **San Ignacio**. The last bus from Belmopan to Belize City leaves at 7pm, to San Ignacio at 10.30pm. **Heading south** along the Hummingbird Highway, the first to leave is the James Bus at 7am, with other services roughly hourly until 6pm. Currently only Novelo's has a terminal and ticket office though there's usually a parked Z-Line bus for tickets and information. At the moment all buses pull up in front of the small **market**, where only Novelo's has a terminal and ticket office, though there's usually a parked Z-line bus for tickets and information; a new terminal is planned, however, so some changes may have taken place by the time you read this.

The market itself has several good food and fruit stands and vendors will come aboard buses to sell snacks and drinks. The nearest **restaurant** is the *Caladium*, in front of the Novelo's terminal, serving inexpensive Belizean dishes including a daily special; with air conditioning, clean toilets and a no-smoking policy, it's the best in the centre. Nearby, to the left of the market, the Canadian-run *International Café*

(Mon—Fri 7.30am–3.30pm), serving sandwiches, soups, salads and snacks (always with vegetarian choices), is also good for **information**.

Just beyond the market are the **banks** (including Barclays, for cash advances), while the **post office** is to the right of the market square and the BTL **telephone** office is on Bliss Parade, beside the large satellite dish. The **immigration** office is in the main government building beside the old movie theatre by the fire station; this building also houses the Land Tax office, where you can buy **topographic maps** of Belize. For **email** go to Techno Hub (Mon–Sat 8am–8.30pm) in the Novelo's terminal. The **British High Commission** (☎08/22146), equivalent to the embassy, is situated on the North Ring Road, behind the National Assembly building.

**Hotels** in Belmopan tend to cater for the needs and expense accounts of diplomats and aid officials; San Ignacio, less than an hour away, is far more interesting and much less expensive. If you do have to stay here, the *El Rey Inn*, 23 Moho St (☎08/23438; ④), is a pleasant and reasonably inexpensive option, with clean rooms, bedside lights and private bathrooms. The best place in town is *Bull Frog Inn*, 25 Half Moon Ave (☎08/22111, fax 23155, *bullfrog@btl.net*; ⑥–⑦). Its comfortable, air-conditioned rooms have cable TV, telephone and balcony, and there's a very good restaurant and bar.

# Belmopan to San Ignacio

Beyond Belmopan the scenery becomes more rugged, with thickly forested ridges always in view to the south. Here, although the strictly protected **Tapir Mountain Nature Reserve** is not open to casual visitors, you can get a taste of what's there by visiting **Actun Tunichil Muknal**, one of the most extraordinary **caves** in the country. The Western Highway stays close to the valley of the Belize River, crossing numerous tributary creeks and passing through a series of villages: Roaring Creek, Teakettle, Ontario, Unitedville, Esperanza, and finally **Santa Elena**, San Ignacio's sister town on the eastern bank of the Macal River. There's been something of an accommodation boom along this route, with a couple of long-established cottage-style **lodges** now joined by several newer enterprises. Alternatively, with your own vehicle you can turn south at Georgeville, 26km from the Belmopan junction, and head along the **Chiquibul Road** to the **Mountain Pine Ridge** (see p.270) and the ruins of **Caracol** (p.273). Along this unpaved road are several places to stay and the added attraction of Belize's best **butterfly exhibit.**

## Tapir Mountain Nature Reserve and Pook's Hill Lodge

South of the highway, between Roaring and Barton creeks, the **Tapir Mountain Nature Reserve** protects 28 square kilometres of the northern foothills of the Maya Mountains, a rich habitat covered in high-canopy tropical forest and home to all of Belize's **national symbols**: Baird's tapir, the keel-billed toucan, the black orchid and the mahogany tree. The reserve is accorded Belize's highest category of protected land and, as one criterion of this is to "maintain natural processes in an undisturbed state", Tapir Mountain can only be visited by accredited researchers.

Although you cannot enter the reserve, you can enjoy spectacular views of it by staying nearby at one of the best new lodges, **Pook's Hill Jungle Lodge** (☎081/2017, fax 08/23361, *pookshill@btl.net*; ⑧–⑨), run by the extremely hospitable Ray and Vicky Snaddon. The turning to the lodge is clearly signposted at Mile 52, at the village of **Teakettle**, 8km west of Belmopan. The nine-kilometre track up to the lodge is bumpy but in good condition; if you're travelling by bus call ahead from the junction, where there's a payphone, and someone will pick you up. **Accommodation** is in nine thatched cabañas, grouped in a small clearing overlooking the thickly forested Roaring Creek valley and with breathtaking views across the Reserve to the Mountain Pine Ridge beyond. Delicious meals are served in the dining room at the edge of the forest and upstairs a thatched, open-sided deck doubles as a bar in the evenings.

This spectacular location clearly held attractions for the ancient Maya too: the lodge sits on a Maya platform and immediately behind the cabañas there's a *plazuela* (small plaza) group with house mounds and an ancestor shrine. There are wonderful **nature trails** and superb **horse-riding trails**, and you can hike or ride to more substantial ruins and caves further up the valley. You don't have to go far to see the **wildlife** either – bird-watching here is in a league of its own and there will almost always be a raptor of some kind, perhaps a bat falcon hunting or feeding. To cool off, you can go **tubing** in the river.

## Actun Tunichil Muknal

A few kilometres higher up Roaring Creek valley, south of the *Pook's Hill Lodge* and upstream along Roaring Creek, lies **Actun Tunichil Muknal** ("Cave of the Stone Sepulchre"). Astonishingly well-preserved skeletons of Maya human sacrifices discovered here make it one of the most spectacular **caves** in the country open to visitors. Although looting has occurred in one chamber, the main chamber, which sits much higher up the cave wall, was not touched and the artefacts here are spellbinding: an enormous stingray spine and a huge obsidian blade lean upright against each other, encircled by stones. Carved in slate, these metre-long representations of bloodletting implements are an indisputable indication of the sacred ceremonies performed here over 1000 years ago. Perhaps the most dramatic sight, however, is the skeleton of a young woman lying below a rock wall – and nearby the stone axe that may have killed her.

Currently only two trained guides are allowed to lead groups into the cave — and you'll need to be pretty fit and able to swim to do the trip, and for much of the time you're wading knee- or even chest-deep in water. See p.264 for details of the trips run by Aaron Juan, of Mayawalk Adventures in San Ignacio.

## Warrie Head Lodge and Caesar's Place

Beyond Teakettle, at Mile 54, just over the Warrie Head Creek bridge, is **Warrie Head Ranch and Lodge** (☎08/723826 or 02/77185, fax 75213, *www.belizenet.com/warrie*; ⑦), formerly a logging camp and now a working farm offering very comfortable wooden cabins and rooms set back a few hundred metres from the road. Owners Johnny and Elvira Searle have gone to great lengths to provide visitors with a glimpse of Belize's colonial heritage – the rooms have modern facilities but are filled with authentic period furniture, and colonial artefacts abound, including a restored 1904 steam engine once used to haul logs. The grounds, filled with fruit and native trees, slope down to the creek, where an exquisite series of travertine terraces forms turquoise pools – perfect for swimming.

On the bank of Barton Creek to the right of the highway at Mile 60, **Caesar's Place** (☎09/22341, fax 23449; *blackrock@btl.net*; ⑥) is Caesar and Antonieta Sherrard's café and guest house, with comfortable, attractive rooms, trailer hookups (US$7.50) and space for camping (US$3.75). The *Patio Café* is a good place to stop for lunch and serves delicious **home cooking**, with Belizean and American dishes mingling with the flavours of other Central American countries. The **gift shop** is one of the best in Belize: Caesar makes great carvings using wood properly dried in a solar kiln, and there are slate carvings reproducing Maya art and Guatemalan textiles. There's also a **mini museum**, authorized by the Archeology Department, exhibiting Maya artefacts from Belize, and the **bookshop** is a good place to pick up information about the Maya, and about travelling in Guatemala and Mexico, with maps and guides, including *Rough Guides*. Caesar's son Julian can organize canoe or caving trips along the Macal River, with accommodation at *Black Rock*, on the Macal River (see p.268). Beyond *Caesar's*, just over the Barton Creek bridge, the two prominent, grass-covered **pyramids** mark the Maya site of **Floral Park**; you'll see virtually all there is to see as you pass by in the bus.

## The Chiquibul Road

Six kilometres beyond Barton Creek, at the **Georgeville** junction, an unpaved road leads south to the **Mountain Pine Ridge** (see p.270). This is the **Chiquibul Road** – well used by villagers, foresters and tourists – which reaches deep into the forest, and heads for Caracol (see p.273). You could get off at this junction if you're hitching to **Augustine/Douglas Silva**, headquarters of the Mountain Pine Ridge Forest Reserve, though you really need 4WD, or a mountain bike, to explore this fascinating and exciting area of hills, waterfalls, caves and jungle properly. Nevertheless, the road itself, usually in good condition anyway, is being upgraded to enable easier and faster access to Caracol.

## Mountain Equestrian Trails

Eleven kilometres along the road, **Mountain Equestrian Trails** (☎09/23310 or 014/4764, in US ☎1-800/838-3918, *www.metbelize.com*; ⑨) is Belize's premier **horse-riding** vacation centre, with superb riding on nearly 100km of forest trails encompassing various ecosystems. It also offers very comfortable **accommodation** (US$120) on the edge of the Pine Ridge: ten rooms in thatched, oil-lamp-lit cabañas and a villa. The *Cantina* restaurant here dishes out tasty Belizean and Mexican-style meals in large portions. If you want to get even closer to nature there's also an idyllic **tented camp**, *Chiclero Trails* (⑨), the base for low-impact wildlife safaris deep into the Chiquibul forest.

## Green Hills Butterfly Ranch

On the opposite side of the road to *MET*, the **Green Hills Butterfly Ranch and Botanic Garden** (daily 8am–5pm; ☎091/2017, *www.belizex.com/greenhills.htm*; US$4), run by Dutch biologists Jan Meerman and Tineke Boomsma, is Belize's biggest and best butterfly exhibit. The main attraction is the enclosed **flight area**, where scores of gorgeous tropical butterflies flutter around, settling periodically on the flowers to sip nectar. Over 35 different species are bred here, though you'll usually see around twenty to 25, depending on the breeding cycle, and, particularly in the early morning, you can watch one of nature's wonders as the butterflies emerge from jewelled chrysalises.There's also an amazing botanical garden here, home to **Belize's National Passionflower Collection** and a renowned collection of **epiphytes** (air plants).

## On to San Ignacio: Santa Elena

A few kilometres along the Western Highway beyond Georgeville you pass **Central Farm**, the Belize College of Agriculture research station. Beyond here a road to the right leads to **Spanish Lookout**, one of Belize's most successful Mennonite farming settlements; its neat, well-maintained farmhouses, white-fenced fields, paved roads and tractor showrooms replicating the American Midwest. The Mennonites here have embraced modern technology enthusiastically – and have the best-stocked auto parts shops in the country.

Before reaching San Ignacio the Western Highway passes through its sister town of **SANTA ELENA**, on the eastern bank of the Macal River. Though quite a large town, Santa Elena has few of the attractions of San Ignacio, but it is the site of the turn-off to the **Cristo Rey road** (see p.271) to the Mountain Pine Ridge (see p.270). Most visitors choose to stay in San Ignacio, but there are a couple of very good-value **hotels** here. The *Aguada* (☎09/23609, *aguada@btl.net*; ④), signed on the right near the town entrance and run by the very welcoming Bill and Cathie Butcher, has neat, clean, comfortable rooms (some with a/c) with private bath. A little further on, the *Snooty Fox Guest House* (☎09/22150, *evas@btl.net*; ④–⑥), high above the Macal River at 64 George Price Ave, has spotless rooms and a sizeable furnished **apartment** – a comparative rarity in Cayo. Guests can use the kitchen and the restaurant and bar have great views over the river to San Ignacio. There's secure parking and owner Michael Waight offers the best-value **canoe rental** in the area – just US$22.50 per day, including life-jacket and ice chest. At Santa Elena the Macal River is crossed by the **Hawksworth Bridge**, built in 1949 and still the only road suspension bridge in Belize. Traffic from Belize City crosses the river on a low bridge (covered in high water) a little downstream; the suspension bridge is used only by westbound traffic.

# San Ignacio and Cayo District

On the west bank of the Macal River, 35km from Belmopan, **SAN IGNACIO** is a friendly, relaxed town that draws together much of the best in inland Belize. The main town of Cayo District and the focus of tourism in west-central Belize, it offers good food, inexpensive hotels and restaurants, and frequent bus connections. It's an excellent base for day- and overnight-trips to the surrounding hills, streams, ruins, caves and forests. Several local tour operators (see the box on p.264) run trips south into the **Mountain Pine Ridge** and beyond there to the ruins of **Caracol**. Heading west to the border you pass through the village of **San José Succotz**, where a hand-cranked ferry across the Mopan River allows access to the Maya site **Xunantunich**. A couple of kilometres beyond Succotz, **Benque Viejo** is the last town in Belize and focus of several contemporary art projects, of which the earth sculpture park of **Poustinia** is perhaps the most intriguing. The main rivers tumbling down the western slopes of the Maya Mountains, the **Macal River** and the **Mopan River**, join to form the Belize River just downstream from San Ignacio, and the forested hills that begin here roll all the way across Guatemala and south to Toledo District. The evenings are cool and the days fresh, and there's a virtual absence of mosquitoes and other biting insects. The **population** is typically varied: most people are Mestizos – of mixed Spanish and Maya descent – but you'll also see Creoles, Mopan and Yucatec Maya, Mennonites, Lebanese, Chinese and even Sri Lankans.

Although you can easily use San Ignacio as a base for day-trips, numerous guest houses and ranches in the surrounding countryside offer **cottage-style accommodation** and organized trips; all are covered in the text. Most offer a comfortable night's sleep and good home cooking – even gourmet dining – as well as horse-riding, bird-watching, canoeing and caving. All can be reached by road and are well signposted from San Ignacio, though to get to a couple of them you'll also have to cross the river in a canoe.

## Some history

San Ignacio town is usually referred to as Cayo by locals (and this is what you'll often see indicated on buses), a name coined by Spanish colonists, who called this area "El Cayo", the same word they used to describe the offshore islands. It's an apt description of the area, in a peninsula between two converging rivers, and also a measure of how isolated the early settlers felt, surrounded by the forest. It wasn't just the jungle they had to fear; the forest was also home to a Maya group who valued their independence. **Tipu**, a Maya city that stood at Negroman on the Macal River, about 9km south of the present town, was the capital of the province of Dzuluinicob, where for years the Maya resisted attempts to Christianize them. The early wave of conquest, in 1544, made only a little impact here, and the area was a centre of rebellion in the following decades. Two **Spanish friars** arrived in 1618, but a year later the entire population was still practising idolatry. Outraged, the friars smashed the idols and ordered the native priests flogged, but by the end of the year the Maya had once again driven out the Spaniards. Four years later, Maya from

Tipú guided a Spanish expedition against the Itzá and in 1641 the friars returned, determined to Christianize the inhabitants. To express their defiance of the Spanish clerics the Maya priests conducted a mock mass, using tortillas as communion wafers, and threw out the friars. From then on Tipú remained an outpost of Maya culture, providing refuge to other Maya fleeing Spanish rule, apparently retaining a good measure of independence until 1707, when the population was forcibly removed to Lake Petén Itzá in Guatemala.

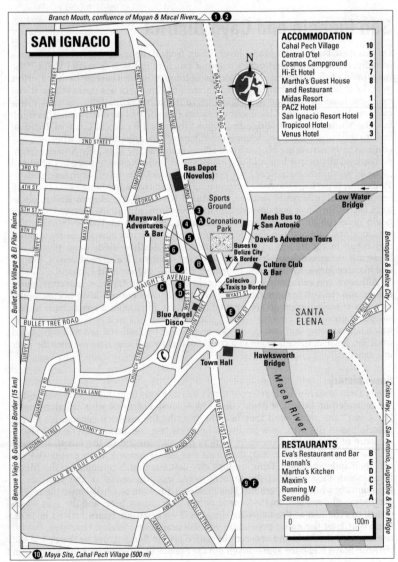

# SAN IGNACIO

Branch Mouth, confluence of Mopan & Macal Rivers, △ ❶ ❷

**ACCOMMODATION**

| | |
|---|---|
| Cahal Pech Village | 10 |
| Central O'tel | 5 |
| Cosmos Campground | 2 |
| Hi-Et Hotel | 7 |
| Martha's Guest House and Restaurant | 8 |
| Midas Resort | 1 |
| PACZ Hotel | 6 |
| San Ignacio Resort Hotel | 9 |
| Tropicool Hotel | 4 |
| Venus Hotel | 3 |

**RESTAURANTS**

| | |
|---|---|
| Eva's Restaurant and Bar | B |
| Hannah's | E |
| Martha's Kitchen | D |
| Maxim's | C |
| Running W | F |
| Serendib | A |

Bus Depot (Novelos)

Sports Ground

Mayawalk Adventures & Bar

Coronation Park

Mesh Bus to San Antonio

David's Adventure Tours

Buses to Belize City & Border

Culture Club & Bar

Colecivo Taxis to Border

Blue Angel Disco

Town Hall

Hawksworth Bridge

Low Water Bridge

SANTA ELENA

Macal River

0 100m

△ Bullet Tree Village & El Pilar Ruins

△ Belmopan & Belize City

△ Benque Viejo & Guatemala Border (15 km)

△ Cristo Rey, △ San Antonio, Augustine & Pine Ridge

▽ ❿, Maya Site, Cahal Pech Village (500 m)

Like many places in Belize, San Ignacio probably started its present life as a logging camp. A map drawn up in 1787 simply states that the Indians of this general area were "in friendship with the Baymen". Later it was a centre for the shipment of chicle, the sap of the sapodilla tree and basis of chewing gum. The self-reliant *chicleros*, as the collectors of chicle were called, knew the forest intimately, including the location of most, if not all, Maya ruins. When the demand for Maya artefacts sent black-market prices rocketing, many of them turned to looting.

Until the Western Highway was built in the 1930s, local transport was by mule or water. It could take ten days of paddling to reach San Ignacio from Belize City, though later small steamers made the trip. Nowadays, river traffic, having almost died out, is enjoying something of a revival as increasing numbers of tourists take river trips. Indeed, a good time to visit San Ignacio is at the start of *La Ruta Maya* **canoe race**, held annually in early March, when teams of paddlers race all the way to Belize City. Anyone can enter but local guides always win.

## San Ignacio: arrival and information

San Ignacio's main street is **Burns Avenue**; along here, or nearby, you'll find almost everything you need, including the best produce market in Belize. **Buses** stop in the marketplace just behind Burns Avenue. To check times of onward services ask at the Novelo's office in the market area. You can **leave luggage** at Novelo's too, or at *Mayawalk Bar*, easily visible from the bus stop and also good for **information**. If you have time before you arrive visit the Cayo district's superb website, *www.belizex.com/cayo.htm*; on arrival, although there's no official tourist office here, you can call in at several other places providing first-class information on trips and tours. See Bob Jones, at the long-established *Eva's Bar*, 22 Burns Ave, or any member of Martha August's family at *Martha's Kitchen*, on West Street, while some of the best **independent tour guides** in San Ignacio are listed in the box on p.264. For a long time *Eva's* was also the only **internet café** in Belize (*evas@btl.net*), but a few rivals have opened lately; the best is *Top Cat*, 8 Hudson St.

All the **banks** are on Burns Avenue, though there's no reliable ATM (you can easily buy Guatemalan quetzales at the border). The **BTL office** (Mon–Fri 8am–noon & 1–4pm, Sat 8am–noon) is above the St Martin's Credit Union on Far West Street; you'll find the **post office** right in the centre, next to Courts furniture store. **Car rental** is available at Western Auto Rental (☎09/23181). For domestic and international **air tickets** go to Exodus Travel, 2 Burns Ave (☎09/24400). Arts and Crafts of Central America, two doors from *Eva's*, sells reasonably priced Guatemalan *típica* **gifts**, books (including *Rough Guides*) and maps. Past here, Caesar's Gift Shop sells the same jewellery and wood carvings as at his place on the Western Highway (see p.257); you can also find out about *Black Rock River Lodge*, in the Macal River valley (see p.268). **Laundry** can be dropped off at *Martha's*, on West Street.

## Accommodation

The **hotels** in San Ignacio offer the best-value budget accommodation in the country, and are improving in quality and services all the time. You'll almost always find space but you should book if you want to stay at a particular place during busy periods. For **camping** near town see the *Cosmos* and *Midas* entries, and for accommodation in the **Cayo countryside** see the listings under The Macal River (p.267), The Mopan River (p.270) and the Mountain Pine Ridge (p.273).

**Cahal Pech Village**, Cahal Pech Hill, just across from the Maya site (☎09/23740, *daniels@btl.net*), 2km from the town centre. A well-designed and good-value "village" of comfortable wood-and-thatch cabañas on a hillside overlooking San Ignacio. Each cabaña – named after a Belizean Maya site – has a private bath, and the interiors are decorated with Guatemalan textiles. The sixteen-room hotel, with a/c rooms and suites, is equally comfortable; for details ask at *Venus* in town. ⑥/⑦.

**Central O'tel**, 24 Burns Ave (☎09/23734, *easyrider@btl.net*). Simple, clean, good-value hotel with shared bath, and the balcony with hammocks is great for watching the street below. Good local information. ③.

**Cosmos Campground**, a 15-min walk from town along the road to Branch Mouth (☎09/22116, *cosmoscamping@btl.net*). Full camping facilities, including decent showers, flush toilets and a kitchen area. As well as tent space (US\$3.50), there are eight clean, simple cabins, some with private bath.. ①–③.

**Green Heaven Lodge**, 10km out of town, just off the Western Highway, signed 1km along the Chial Road to *Chaa Creek* (☎091/2023, *www.ghlodgebelize.com*). Run by a young French couple, Sebastian and Anne-Karine, four comfortable, private-bath cabins with tiled roofs overlook the pool. The couple also operate *La Vie en Rose*, the only French restaurant in Cayo, serving first-class French cuisine as well as a tasty snack menu. ⑤.

**Hi-Et Hotel**, West St, behind *Eva's* (☎09/22828). Friendly, family-run budget hotel, recently renovated. Four upstairs rooms, each with a tiny balcony, sharing a bathroom. The least-expensive hotel in town, and phenomenally popular.③.

**Martha's Guest House**, West St, behind Eva's (☎09/23647, *marthas@btl.net*). Recent renovations have made the best hotel in San Ignacio even better. Friendly owners, Martha and John August, have kept the homely atmosphere that makes it very popular and you're advised to book. The new rooms are very comfortable and well furnished, and several have beautiful tiled bathrooms and balconies. It's also good for information and the restaurant below is a favourite meeting place. There's a range of good books on Belize (and *Rough Guides* for sale) and a good drop-off laundry. Accepts Visa. ④/⑤.

**Midas Resort**, Branch Mouth Rd (☎09/23172, *midas@btl.net*). Run by the friendly Alvin and Emelda Reimer, *Midas* is the only resort actually in town and the best-value cabaña place in Cayo. Very comfortable Maya-style thatched cabañas and newer wooden cabins, all with private bath, set above the riverbank; camping and trailer hook-ups also available. Within walking distance of the centre but with the peace and quiet of the countryside. Accepts Visa. ④/⑤.

**PACZ Hotel**, 4 Far West St, two blocks behind *Eva's* (☎09/24538). Five clean, comfortable rooms with shared baths. A great bargain, especially for three sharing (no single rates), with a good restaurant below. ③.

**San Ignacio Resort Hotel**, 18 Buena Vista St (☎09/22034, *sanighot@btl.net*), a ten-minute walk uphill from town centre. San Ignacio's premier hotel has comfortable rooms, some with balcony and a/c, a very good restaurant – with a terrace overlooking the pool and Macal River valley – and the *Stork Club* bar has a happy hour on Fridays. Well-signed trails lead down to the river and up to a forested hilltop; ideal for early morning bird-watching. It's expensive though – see if you can get a discount. ⑧/⑨.

**Tropicool Hotel**, Burns Ave, 75m past *Eva's* (☎09/23052). The best-value budget place in town, with bright, clean, shared bathrooms, bedside lights and a sitting room with TV. Laundry area and bike rental available. ③.

**Venus Hotel**, 29 Burns Ave (☎09/23203, fax 22225, *venus@btl.net*). Two-storey hotel, the biggest in town, with good rates – the best deal around if you want to stay a few days. Most rooms have new tiled bathrooms, a/c and TV, and there are still some real bargain rooms in the original wooden building. Accepts Visa/MC. ④/⑤.

## Eating, drinking and nightlife

Along with its budget hotels, San Ignacio has several good, inexpensive **restaurants** (see *Green Heaven* entry above for a recommended French restaurant), and there are a number of reliable **fast food stalls** in the market area. If you have anywhere to cook, then the Saturday **market** is worth a visit; it's the best in Belize, with local farmers bringing in fresh-picked produce. It's also a good place to stock up on provisions for trips; see Chris Lowe at the market for his *Fruit-A-Plenty* trail mix and granola bars. For general groceries, Celina's Store, two blocks from the *Venus Hotel* down Burns Avenue, has the widest selection. In the centre of town there are plenty of **fruit stands** laden with bananas, oranges and papayas. You can pick up good fresh **bread** and baked goods from Torres bakery, at the end of Far West Street.

Most of the restaurants listed below double as **bars** and in this *Eva's* is probably the best. San Ignacio is a popular weekend spot for Belizeans and there's a range of **live music and dancing** on offer. The *Western Bar*, overlooking the market, is a typically Belizean **club**: dark and very loud. Next door and overlooking the river, the *Culture Club* (above *El Cenote* **sports bar**) is a much better bet, with Latin and Afro-Cuban sounds mixing with Belizean beat — and with an open balcony you can enjoy the tropical evening as well. The *Blue Angel* **disco**, on Hudson Street, often has bands at weekends, but has lost its pre-eminent position in the local music scene to *Cahal Pech Tavern*, a huge thatched structure dominating the hilltop next to *Cahal Pech Village* that's a regular venue for some of the best bands in Belize.

## Restaurants

**Eva's Restaurant and Bar**, 22 Burns Ave. Usually very busy in the evenings, it's the information centre of Cayo and a great place to meet fellow travellers and local tour operators. Food quality is variable though, and the service often indifferent. Email and internet service are available.

**Hannah's**, 5 Burns Ave. Delicious, authentic Indian cuisine, freshly prepared and worth the wait.

**Martha's Kitchen and Pizza Parlour**, West St, behind *Eva's*. Under the guest house of the same name and just as well run. Great breakfasts with strong, locally grown coffee, and main dishes of traditional Creole food and pizza with delicious cakes for dessert and always a vegetarian choice. The patio tables are a popular place to meet for breakfast, and a good place to meet your tour guides.

**Maxim's**, Far West St, behind *Martha's*. The best of San Ignacio's Chinese restaurants, serving large portions.

**The Running W Restaurant**, at the *San Ignacio Resort Hotel*, 18 Buena Vista St. Excellent food in tranquil surroundings; breakfasts are especially good value.

**Serendib Restaurant**, 27 Burns Ave. Tasty Sri Lankan curries and seafood at very reasonable prices. Good service.

# Around San Ignacio

The people of San Ignacio are justifiably proud of their beautiful river valley and the surrounding countryside, and there's plenty of outdoor action on offer – from relaxing **canoe trips** along the mostly gentle Macal River to tubing or **kayaking** along the faster Mopan River. **Cahal Pech** ruins are (just) within walking distance, on top a steep hill though, so you might prefer to take a taxi. The nearby farmland and forest is ideal for exploring on **horseback** or **mountain bike** (you can take a bike on the bus to San Antonio, for the Pine Ridge). **Caving** is increasingly popular, but make sure you go with a licensed guide who's qualified in cave rescue. Finally, there are several other **Maya sites** further afield in Cayo that are well worth exploring, particularly with a knowledgeable local guide; you can also join expertly guided daily trips to **Tikal** (see p.457) here.

Most of the bigger hotels and lodges have their own tour desk but there are a number of small-scale, **independent local operators** who offer good-value trips to the many attractions around San Ignacio (see box overleaf). Many of these places are difficult, even impossible, to visit on your own and it's usually easy enough to get a group together.

## Branch Mouth

Perhaps the easiest introduction to this region is to take the twenty-minute walk to **Branch Mouth**, where the Macal and Mopan rivers merge to form the Belize River. The track leads north from the football field, past rich farmland, with thick vegetation, tropical flowers and butterflies on either side. At the confluence of the rivers is a huge tree, with branches arching over the jade water. A rusting iron mooring ring in the trunk is a reminder of the past importance of river transport; now there are swallows

## INDEPENDENT TOUR OPERATORS IN SAN IGNACIO

The list below covers many of the best operators covering a wide range of adventurous options. As always in Belize, make sure anyone offering you a guided trip is a **licensed tour guide** – they should display their photo-card guide licence. Each of the guides named below is either in San Ignacio or will pick you up there. For **bike rental** check at the *Crystal Paradise* office, across from the marketplace (☎09/22772), or see Wally at the *Tropicool Hotel* (☎09/23052).

**Caves Branch Adventure Company**, Ian Anderson, Caves Branch, on the Hummingbird Highway (☎08/22800, *caves@pobox.com*; see p.285), offers superb caving, rappelling and jungle trips (US$65–95).

**David's Adventure Tours**, David Simpson, office at far side of marketplace (☎09/23674, *davidstours@hotmail.com*). Tours to Barton Creek Cave (opposite) and along the Macal River; around US$23. See also *Guacamallo Jungle Camp*, p.268.

**Easy Rider**, Charlie Collins, contact at Arts and Crafts on Burns Ave, where staff will phone her as she lives out of town (☎23734, *easyrider@btl.net*). The best-value horse-riding trips in San Ignacio – US$25 for a half day and US$40 for a full day. Charlie knows the area well, her horses are looked after, and she carefully matches riders to the right mount.

**Eco Jungle Tours**, Orlando Madrid, Hudson Street, across from the post office (☎09/23425, *ecojungletours@hotmail.com*). Canoe floats on the Macal River and jungle trips; around US$23. Also see *Hummingbird Cabañas*, p.267.

**Everald's Caracol Shuttle**, Everald Tut, *Crystal Paradise Resort* (☎09/22772, *cparadise@btl.net*). Daily trips to Caracol and the Mountain Pine Ridge; US$50 per person.

**International Archeological Tours**, Ramón Silva, West Street, next to *Martha's* (☎09/23391, *iatours@btl.net*). Ramón is an expert Mayanist, with extensive knowledge of practically all Maya sites, and can take you to sites in Guatemala other than Tikal. Tours are expensive: US$65–125.

**Mayawalk Adventures**, Aaron Juan, 19 Burns Ave (☎09/23070, *www.belizex.com.mayawalk/*). Aaron, a very experienced caving guide who leads truly amazing trips into the Maya underworld, is one of only two guides with permission to take tours into Actun Tunichil Muknal (see p.257) and can organize overnight caving and rock-climbing expeditions (from US$65).

**River Rat**, Gonzalo Pleitez (☎09/37013, *riverratbelize@btl.net*). Gonzalo lives way up the Macal River and arranges excellent white-water kayak floats and jungle trips (US$45–80).

**Toni's River Adventures**, Toni Santiago, who lives out of town (☎09/23292 or contact Toni at *Eva's*). Toni runs by far the longest-established and best-value guided canoe trip on the Macal River. For US$12.5 per person he or one of the guides will paddle you expertly upriver to the Rainforest Medicine Trail (see opposite). Also organizes overnight camping trips along the river.

skimming the surface, parrots flying overhead and scores of tiny fish in the water. The scar of raw earth on the opposite bank is evidence of the severe flooding of recent years, when the river rose within metres of the suspension bridge and even inundated the streets of San Ignacio.

## Cahal Pech

Twenty minutes' walk uphill out of town to the southwest, clearly signposted along the Benque road, lie the ruins of **Cahal Pech** (daily 8am–5pm; US$5, including **museum** with a model of the site). Cahal Pech means "place of ticks" in Mopan Maya, but that's certainly not how the elite families who ruled here in Classic times would have known it. Cahal Pech was the royal acropolis-palace of an elite Maya family during the Classic period, and there's evidence of monumental construction from at least as early as the

Middle Preclassic, 400 BC, when the city probably dominated the central Belize River valley. Studies of the buildings and ceramics show that the site was continuously occupied from 900 BC to at least 800 AD, though most of what you see dates from the eighth century AD.

Entering the site through the forest you arrive at Plaza B, surrounded by temple platforms and the remains of dwellings; your gaze is soon drawn to **Structure 1**, the Audiencia. If you're used to seeing finely executed, exposed stonework at reconstructed Maya sites then the thick overcoat of lime-mortar on buildings here may come as a bit of a shock. The ancient Maya, however, viewed bare stone facings as ugly and unfinished, and covered all surfaces with a thick coat of brightly painted plaster or stucco.

You can stroll across to the adjacent hilltop for a **drink** at the *Cahal Pech Tavern* for a cultural experience of an entirely different nature.

### Barton Creek Cave

Of the many **cave trips** available in Cayo, one of the most fascinating is to **Barton Creek Cave**, accessible only by river, and only on a tour (around 4hr; US$25 per person; minimum three people). The original and **best guide** to the cave is David Simpson, a multi-lingual Belizean who runs David's Adventure Tours in San Ignacio (✆09/23574) and who will carefully and responsibly show you the astonishing Maya artefacts in the cave. A trip here also usually includes a visit to Green Hills Butterfly Ranch, see p.258). Seven kilometres along the Chiquibul Road, you turn off through farmland, passing the traditional Mennonite settlement of **Upper Barton Creek**, to reach the cave entrance. Framed by jungle, it's at the far side of a jade-green pool, which is where you board a canoe. The river is navigable for about 1600m, and in a couple of places the roof comes so low you have to crouch right down, before ending in a gallery blocked by a huge rockfall. The clear, slow-moving river fills most of the cave width, though the roof soars 100m above your head in places, the way ahead illuminated by a powerful lamp. Several **Maya burials** line the banks; the most awe-inspiring is indicated by a skull set in a natural rock bridge used by the Maya to reach the sacred site. Like all caves in Belize, Barton Creek Cave is a registered archeological site, and nothing must be touched or removed. If it's been raining a subterranean waterfall cascades over the rocks – a truly unforgettable sight. Beyond lie many more miles of passageways, only accessible on a fully equipped expedition.

## The Macal River

Upstream from San Ignacio steep limestone cliffs, farmland and forested hills line the lower **Macal River valley**, and if the idea of a gentle day or more on a river appeals, then any of the resorts can rent canoes to paddle on your own. Another very popular choice is to take a **guided canoe trip** upriver to *Chaa Creek*, with an excellent **Natural History Centre** and the **Rainforest Medicine Trail** next door (both covered below); you'll see far more wildlife with a guide than you ever would alone. Further upsteam there's the new and rapidly growing **Belize Botanic Garden**, at *duPlooy's*, and there's plenty of accommodation in all price ranges along the river; see p.267 for details.

### The Rainforest Medicine Trail

A canoe trip is the best way to visit the **Rainforest Medicine Trail**, next to *Chaa Creek* (daily 8am–noon & 1–4pm; US$5; ✆09/23870, *www.rainforestremedies.com*). The trail is dedicated to Don Eligio Panti, a Maya bush doctor (*curandero*) from San Antonio village who, before dying at the age of 103, passed on his skills to Dr Rosita Arvigo, director and founder of the **Ix Chel Tropical Research Station**, where the trail begins.

The medical knowledge of the Maya was extensive, and the trail takes in a wide range of **traditional healing plants**, many of them now used in modern medicine. Walking the trail is a fascinating experience; there are vines that provide fresh water like a tap; poisonwood, with oozing black sap, its antidote always growing nearby; and

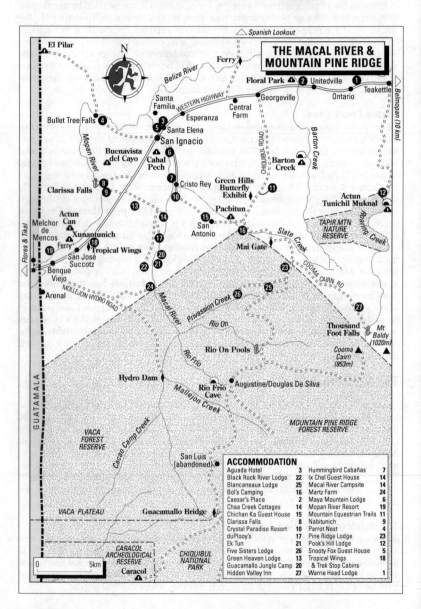

**THE MACAL RIVER & MOUNTAIN PINE RIDGE**

| ACCOMMODATION | | | |
|---|---|---|---|
| Aguada Hotel | 3 | Hummingbird Cabañas | 7 |
| Black Rock River Lodge | 22 | Ix Chel Guest House | 14 |
| Blancaneaux Lodge | 25 | Macal River Campsite | 14 |
| Bol's Camping | 16 | Martz Farm | 24 |
| Caesar's Place | 2 | Maya Mountain Lodge | 6 |
| Chaa Creek Cottages | 14 | Mopan River Resort | 19 |
| Chichan Ka Guest House | 15 | Mountain Equestrian Trails | 11 |
| Clarissa Falls | 8 | Nabitunich | 9 |
| Crystal Paradise Resort | 10 | Parrot Nest | 4 |
| duPlooy's | 17 | Pine Ridge Lodge | 23 |
| Ek Tun | 21 | Pook's Hill Lodge | 12 |
| Five Sisters Lodge | 26 | Snooty Fox Guest House | 5 |
| Green Heaven Lodge | 13 | Tropical Wings | 18 |
| Guacamallo Jungle Camp | 20 | & Trek Stop Cabins | |
| Hidden Valley Inn | 27 | Warrie Head Lodge | 1 |

the bark of the negrito tree, once sold for its weight in gold in Europe as a cure for dysentery. You'll also see specimens of the tropical hardwoods of the jungle that have been exploited for economic reasons. The more mundane, but very welcome, products of the forest range from herbal teas to blood tonic: Traveller's Tonic, a preventative for diarrhoea, really works, as does Jungle Salve for insect bites, and there are many more cures and tonics available in the **gift shop**. Rosita has written about her apprenticeship to the famous *curandero* (see *Sastun*, in "Books", p.584) and is a founder member of the Belize Association of Traditional Healers; you can buy a copy of their excellent newsletter, *Tree of Life*, and any of Rosita's books also in the shop.

## Chaa Creek Natural History Centre

A visit to the marvellous **Chaa Creek Natural History Centre** (daily 8am–5pm; US$6), in the grounds of *Chaa Creek Cottages*, is the best introduction to Cayo's history, geography and wildlife; if you're spending more than a couple of days in the area, try to see this first. With fascinating and accurate displays of the region's flora and fauna, vivid archeological and geological maps, and a scale model of the Macal valley, it's worth a visit in its own right; it also has the **Butterfly Breeding Centre** (included in entry fee) where you can admire the magnificent blue morpho. Call to check on the current events programme (☎09/22037).

## The Belize Botanic Gardens

Located at *duPlooy's* (see p.268), upstream from *Chaa Creek*, the **Belize Botanic Gardens** (daily 8am–5pm; US$5; ☎09/23101) are an ambitious and ongoing project established in 1997 on fifty acres of former farmland and forest. The garden is the brainchild of *duPlooy's* owners and avid plant lovers, Ken and Judy duPlooy. There are already around four hundred tree species, a nursery with over a thousand seedlings, a magnificent, specially designed **orchid house**, with 160 species, ponds with bird hides and several interpretive **trails**. The aim is to create a first-class biological educational and study resource for Belizean and overseas researchers, and to conserve many of Belize's native plant species in small areas representative of their natural habitats. You approach through an avenue of fruit-bearing trees, designed to encourage wild **birds**, and you can be guided around the gardens by **expert naturalist** guide Philip Mai; call ahead if you need a guided tour.

## Accommodation on the Macal River

Most accommodation along the Macal River is in upmarket **cabaña-style resorts**, beautifully set in the forest above the riverbank, though some do have slightly cheaper options, and will even give discounts to *Rough Guide* readers. There are also a couple of **budget places** in wonderful locations. The listings below are in the order that you approach them travelling upriver, though all are accessible by road; for a couple you also have to cross the river by boat. Any of these places can organize **canoe floats** and superb **horseback tours** to nearby Maya ruins, and some also have **mountain bikes** for rent.

**Hummingbird Cabañas**, at the entrance to Cristo Rey village (☎09/23425, *ecojungletours@hotmail.com*). Simple thatched cabins with private bath run by the friendly Madrid family. Good, inexpensive restaurant and canoes for rent. For here and *Crystal Paradise* (below) you can get the San Antonio bus along the Cristo Rey road; a taxi costs about US$12.50. ④.

**Crystal Paradise Resort**, just past the village of Cristo Rey, on the east bank of the river, and on the bus route to San Antonio (☎ & fax 09/22772, *cparadise@btl.net*). A friendly place with a range of accommodation, including private thatched cabañas and simple rooms, owned and built by the Belizean Tut family. Victor built the thatch-roofed dining room overlooking the valley and his sons Jeronie and Everald arrange tours throughout Cayo and to Tikal. You can be picked up free in San Ignacio if you call before 4.30pm. Cabaña price includes two delicious meals. ⑤–⑨.

**Ix Chel Guest House**, just downstream from *Chaa Creek* (☎09/23870, *ixchel@btl.net*) and reached along the same road. Very comfortable rooms with shared bath in a wooden house next to the renowned Rainforest Medicine Trail, and popular with students of alternative medicine. ⑤.

**The Lodge at Chaa Creek**, on the unpaved Chial turn-off, 10km along the road to Benque (☎09/22037, fax 22501, *www.chaacreek.com*). Beautiful, whitewashed wood-and-stucco cabañas in gorgeous grounds high above the Macal River, with a justly deserved reputation for luxury and ambience. The cottages range from delightful cabins to a luxury Jacuzzi suite with four-poster bed. There's a fine restaurant and bar with spacious outdoor deck and an amazing new conference centre and spa. A trail map guides you through the forest and over the hills to several nearby Maya sites. Cabañas US$165 in high season, with good off-season discounts. ⑨.

**Macal River Safari Camp**, on the east bank, just below *Chaa Creek* (same contact details). The brainchild of Mick Flemming of *Chaa Creek*, with roomy tents under thatched roofs on raised wooden bases. It's camping in comfort, with hot water in clean, tiled bathrooms, and oil lamps in the evening; plus there's access to all the *Chaa Creek* trails. US$50 per person, including meals.

**duPlooy's**, further along the *Chaa Creek* track (☎09/23101, fax 23301, *www.duplooys.com*). Spacious bungalows (US$150) beautifully located in farmland and forest on the west bank of the Macal River, and home to the Belize Botanic Garden (see above). *La Casita* (US$250) is a two-storey house with queen-size beds and luxurious bathroom with Jacuzzi and all-round balcony overlooking the river; rooms in the *Pink House* are less expensive at US$40. The deck, extending from the bar, overlooks the river cliffs, providing a walkway into the forest. Getting here without a vehicle is difficult, but there's a shuttle service from the airport leaving at 2pm; free if you're staying for three nights, US$25 if not. ⑥–⑨.

**Guacamallo Jungle Camp**, on the east bank of the river; contact David's Adventure Tours in San Ignacio for transport (☎09/23674, *davidstours@hotmail.com*). Simple cabins high above the river (which you cross in a canoe), located on the edge of a huge and mysterious Maya site; you'll have the pleasure of exploring this on your own. Lots of good food and a wonderful sense of timelessness at night as you sit on a Maya mound outside your cabin watching the stars. US$25 per person, including transport, dinner and breakfast.

**Ek Tun**, in a remote location on the east bank of the Macal River, not directly accessible by road (☎091/2002, in US ☎303/442-6150, *www.ektunbelize.com*). The most luxurious stick-and-thatch cabañas in the country, and there are only two, to preserve the sublime isolation. Both cottages have two bedrooms (one in the loft), shower and deck overlooking the garden. Gourmet dinner is served overlooking the river. Trails lead through the forest and along the river cliffs dotted with cave entrances, and high above you can see the rare orange-breasted falcon. Swimming in the river or the secluded natural pool is idyllic, and there is much evidence of Maya occupation in the area. US$220 including breakfast and dinner. ⑨.

**Black Rock River Lodge** (☎09/22341, fax 23449, *www.blackrocklodge.com*); it's possible to drive here, or call at *Caesar's Place* on the Western Highway (see p.257) or the gift shop in San Ignacio (see p.261) to make transport arrangements. Set high above the west bank of the Macal River with stunning views of the jungle-clad limestone cliffs of the upper Macal valley, the solidly built deluxe cabañas have a private hot shower and floors made of smooth stones from the river. Solar power provides electricity. From the open-sided, thatched dining room you can see the river rushing over the black slate that gives its name to the lodge. It's a fairly easy hike from here up to Vaca Falls, or to caves containing some amazing Maya pottery, and there are fine horses to ride. ⑥–⑧.

**Martz Farm**, 13km along the Arenal/Mollejon Hydro Road in Benque Viejo (☎09/23742). This is further upriver from the other places on the Macal, and difficult to reach on your own; contact through *Eva's* or *Martha's* in San Ignacio – José or Doris, who run the cabins, call in town daily. It's well worth the effort though, with comfortable thatched cabins perched in trees above a rushing, crystal-clear creek, inexpensive rooms and plenty of home-cooked food. Reaching the river involves a climb down a gorgeous 30-metre waterfall (there's also a steep trail) to a remote beach; across the river the forest beckons and there's great horse riding. ④/⑤.

# The Mopan River

The main tributary creeks of the **Mopan River** rise in the Maya Mountains, then flow into Guatemala, re-entering Belize at the village of **Arenal**, 5km south of the border. The river then leaves Belize briefly, rushing under the bridge at the frontier, before the final (and perhaps most picturesque) 25km stretch to its confluence with the Macal

River at Branch Mouth (see p.263). There are some attractive and not too serious **white-water rapids** along this stretch, and it's easy enough to arrange kayak or rafting trips on the Mopan; check at any of the resorts listed below; *Clarissa Falls* or *Trek Stop* are best. As with the Macal River, there are **Maya ruins** in the vicinity: **El Pilar** (best visited from the burgeoning village of Bullet Tree Falls, below) and **Buenavista del Cayo** are described below; Xunantunich, the easiest of Belize's major sites to visit, is covered on p.276.

## Bullet Tree Falls

Five kilometres west of San Ignacio (leaving town along the Bullet Tree road) is the small but growing village of **BULLET TREE FALLS**, a predominately Spanish-speaking *mestizo* village and a good base from which to visit El Pilar. A bridge crosses the Mopan River at the falls – really just a set of rapids — and nearby there are some very pleasant cabins on the riverbank. In the middle of the village, immediately before the bridge, is the new **El Pilar Cultural Centre**, *Be Pukte* in Mayan (opening hours vary; call Teresa Garcia on ☎09/37003 to check), established by the Amigos de El Pilar. Inside there's a good model of El Pilar and information booklets on sale. A **medicinal trail** has recently been established, and you can join a guided tour (US$5). A shared taxi from San Ignacio costs US$1 per person and it's easy enough to hitch. There are a couple of good **places to stay** in the village, listed with other river "Accommodation", below.

## El Pilar and Buenavista del Cayo

**El Pilar**, the largest Maya site in the Belize River valley, is reached along a rough (motorable) road climbing the escarpment, 14km northwest of Bullet Tree Falls. Bullet Tree taxis charge US$25 for a carload and the driver will wait for two hours while you visit. The site is open daily (no admission charge at present); caretakers Marcos Garcia or Carmen Cruz will show you around. The weekend caretaker, Teo Williams, has a fascinating account of his life and work published as *Teo's Way*, written largely in Creole and available from him or from the cultural centre in Bullet Tree.

El Pilar's long sequence of construction began in the Preclassic period, around 450 BC, and continued right through to the Terminal Classic, around 1000 AD, when some of the largest existing temples were completely rebuilt. The site covers 40 hectares and includes 70 major structures grouped around 25 plazas. The most impressive structures – four large pyramids between fifteen and twenty metres high and a ball court – are grouped around **Plaza Copal**, from whose west side a flight of steps leads down to a thirty-metre-wide causeway running to **Pilar Poniente** in Guatemala.

The site's position on the frontier with Guatemala might have led to difficulties of access, or even curtailed further study, but the respective governments, urged on by concerned local leaders and the international archeological community, have overcome generations of mutual suspicion to create the **El Pilar Archeological Reserve for Maya Flora and Fauna**, covering an area of nine square kilometres on both sides of the border. One theory under investigation at El Pilar is that the Maya grew a number of different food crops on the same plot, a method known as "forest garden" agriculture, and researchers are attempting to re-create this technique in an experimental and educational exhibit.

Several **hiking trails** lead you around, focusing on both the archeology and natural history of El Pilar, and the site is considered one of the finest bird-watching areas in Cayo. If you're in the area in April or May, check out the one-day **El Pilar Fiesta** held annually and well worth attending (check dates at *elpilar@btl.net*).

On the east bank of the Mopan River, halfway between San Ignacio and the border, the small Maya site of **Buenavista del Cayo** was once the centre of a wider political region of which Cahal Pech is known to have been a satellite. The ruins are on private land and you need permission from the owner to visit; perhaps the best way to get there is on horseback – Easy Rider (see p.264) runs tours. Archeologists have uncovered a palace, ball courts, carved stelae, plazas and courtyards. A number of important burial items were also found here, including the famous Jauncy vase, now in Belmopan. There's also evidence that the Maya established workshops to mass-produce pottery on the site. Since excavation most of the structures have been covered over, but there is a charming palace and courtyard in a glade.

## Accommodation on the Mopan River

There is less accommodation along the Mopan River than there is along the Macal, but what's available is more within the reach of the budget traveller and no less special for it. The resorts below are listed in order of increasing distance from San Ignacio (see map on p.266 for locations, and see Benque Viejo entry for details of another resort).

**Parrot Nest**, just past Bullet Tree Falls at the end of the track just before the bridge (☎09/37008, *www.parrot-nest.com*). Six simple, clean thatched cabins (two sitting very securely up a Guanacaste tree), set in beautiful gardens on the riverbank. One cabin has private bathroom and the shared bathrooms are immaculate, with hot showers. Owners Chris and Theo Cocchi are very welcoming and serve good, filling meals, and Chris runs free shuttles for guests from *Eva's* in San Ignacio. ⑤.

**Clarissa Falls**, along a signed track to the right off the Benque road, just before the *Chaa Creek* turn (☎09/23916, *clarissafalls@btl.net*). A very restful place right by a set of rapids, with some of the nicest riverside cabins in the country. Owner Chena Gálvez has improved the cabins and all are now wheelchair accessible with a private bath, and some have a full kitchen. There's also a "bunkhouse" cabin with shared hot-water showers (US$7.50 per person) and space for camping (US$4 per person) and hookups for RVs. Great home-cooking and a quiet bar overlooking the falls. Horse-riding, canoeing, rafting and tubing at reasonable rates. ④–⑥.

**Nabitunich**, a couple of kilometres past the *Clarissa*, along another track on the right, at Mile 71 (☎09/32309, *rudijuan@btl.net*). Comfortable rooms in charming thatched stone cottages (Mayan for "Little Stone House"), set in 400 acres of forest and farmland run by the hospitable Rudy and Margaret Juan and their family. The gardens have spectacular views of El Castillo at Xunantunich (see p.276) and horse-riding, canoeing and tours are available. Good, filling meals are served in the thatched restaurant, much of it grown organically on the farm. There's a fantastically good-value **student** rate (US$12.50, including breakfast) but you'll need your student card, and **camping** (①) is available. Cottage rates include breakfast and dinner. ⑦.

# The Mountain Pine Ridge

South of San Ignacio, the **Mountain Pine Ridge Forest Reserve** is a spectacular range of rolling hills and jagged peaks formed from some of the oldest rocks in Central America. In amongst these granite outcrops there are also some sections of limestone, riddled with caves, the most accessible of which are the **Rio Frio Caves** in Augustine/Douglas Silva. For the most part the landscape is semi-open, a mixture of grassland and pine forest growing in nutrient-poor, sandy soil, although in the warmth of the river valleys the vegetation is thicker gallery forest, giving way to rainforest south of the **Guacamallo Bridge**. The rains feed a number of small streams, most of which run off into the Macal and Belize rivers. One of the most scenic rivers is the **Rio On**, rushing over cataracts and forming a gorge – a sight of tremendous natural beauty within view of the picnic shelter. On the northern side of the ridge are the **Thousand-Foot Falls** (actually over 1600ft (490m) and the highest in Central America).

The Pine Ridge is virtually uninhabited but for some tourist lodges and one small settlement, **Augustine/Douglas Silva**, site of the forest reserve headquarters. The whole area is perfect for **hiking** and **mountain biking**, but **camping** is allowed only at Augustine/Douglas Silva and at the Mai Gate, beyond San Antonio village (see *Bol's*, p.272). It's fairly hard – though rewarding – to explore this part of the country on your own, and unless you have a car, a mountain bike or come on an organized tour, you may have to rely on hitching. To explore the many forestry roads branching off the main reserve road, you need the 1:50,000 topographic maps sold in the Land Tax office in Belmopan (see p.256).

## Getting to the reserve

There are two **entrance roads** to the reserve, one from the village of **Georgeville**, on the Western Highway (see p.258), and the other from **Santa Elena**, along the **Cristo Rey Road** and through the village of **San Antonio** (four Mesh **buses** a day head out to San Antonio from San Ignacio). If you're up to it, the best way to get around is to rent a **mountain bike** in San Ignacio; the bus to San Antonio takes bikes, or you could put them in the back of a passing pickup truck. Any travel agent or resort can arrange **organized tours**: if you're staying at any of the Cayo resorts, a full-day tour of the Pine Ridge costs around US$45–50 per person for a group of four; more if you want to go to Caracol. If you're **on a budget**, contact Rafael August of Western Adventure Tours through *Martha's*, or Tommy of Tommy's Tours through *Eva's*, who can take you on a superb tour for less. Recent road improvements in the Pine Ridge, particularly on the road to Caracol, make a trip in a **rental jeep** perfectly feasible (most of the year), but always check road conditions first and heed the advice of the forestry officials.

## The Cristo Rey Road

The **road to Cristo Rey** village begins in Santa Elena, 450m west of the Hawksworth Bridge and served by all the Mesh buses to San Antonio (below). Two kilometres along this road is the excellent **Maya Mountain Lodge** (☎09/22164, *www.mayamountain.com*; ⑥–⑧), run by Bart and Suzi Mickler. Set in rich tropical forest, it provides a fascinating introduction to the wildlife of Belize. Accommodation is in colourfully decorated individual cabañas, each with a private bath and electricity; the larger and less expensive *Parrot's Perch* cabin is ideal for groups. Delicious meals are served in an open-sided dining room. The lodge sometimes hosts student groups and has a well-stocked library and a lecture area; after dinner most evenings there's an informed cultural or educational presentation. Families are especially welcome and there are plenty of activities for kids, including a new pool and the best illustrated trail guide in Belize. If there's space, independent travellers might be eligible for a fifty-percent discount (no groups, no rented cars) if carrying this guide.

After another few kilometres you come to **CRISTO REY**, a pretty village of scattered wooden houses and gardens on a high bank above the Macal River. Near the beginning of the village Orlando and Lillette Madrid run *Sandals Restaurant* and a few simple, inexpensive **cabins** (see p.267). Orlando also runs Eco Jungle Tours (☎014/7446) and he can take you on guided canoe or cave trips; he also **rents canoes** at good rates. At the other end of the village *Crystal Paradise Resort* offers a wider range of accommodation and tours (see p.267).

## San Antonio and Pacbitún ruins

In **SAN ANTONIO**, 10km further on from Cristo Rey, the villagers are descendants of Maya (Uxcawal is their name, in their own language) refugees, who fled the Caste Wars in Yucatán in 1847, and most people still speak Yucatec as well as Spanish and English. Their story is told in a fascinating written account of San Antonio's oral history, *After 100 Years*, by Alfonso Antonio Tzul. Nestled in the Macal River valley, surrounded by scattered *milpa* farms, with the forested Maya Mountains in the background, the village is poised to become a base for hiking and horseback tours along old *chiclero* trails. The home of the late **Don Eligio Panti**, the famous *curandero* who died in 1996 (see p.265) and who now has a national park named after him (see below), it's an ideal place to learn about traditional Maya healing methods, not least by going to see the Garcia sisters, who grew up in the village determined not to let their Maya culture be swamped by outside influence. The sisters run the *Chichan Ka Guest House* (☎091/2023, *tanah-info@awrem.com*; ④) at the approach to the village (the bus stops right outside). Rooms (some with private bath) are simple but comfortable and the balcony has panoramic views of the Maya Mountains. Meals are prepared in the traditional way – often using organic produce from the garden – and courses are offered in slate carving, for which the sisters are renowned, and the gathering and use of medicinal plants. Their **gift shop** has become a favourite tour-group stop. Maria Garcia is also president of the Itzamna Society, a local organization formed to protect the Maya environment and culture and promote community development. There may be placement for suitably qualified volunteers to assist with the programme; contact Maria at the above address. Next door is the small **Tanah Museum** (US$3), the proceeds from which go towards the establishment of a 500-acre **Botanical Garden and Maya Reserve**. At the time of writing the land for this had just been allocated and the area will be known as the **Elijio Panti National Park**. Guides from the village can take you on trails to caves and waterfalls and there are plans for a campsite. The Mesh **bus to San Antonio** (Mon–Sat only; 1hr) departs from the market in San Ignacio four times a day between 10.30am and 5pm, returning from San Antonio between 6am and 3pm.

Three kilometres east of San Antonio, on the road to the Pine Ridge, lie the **ruins of Pacbitún**, a major ceremonial centre. One of the oldest known Preclassic sites in Belize (around 1000 BC), it continued to flourish throughout the Classic period, and Maya farming terraces and farmhouse mounds can be seen in the hills all around. Pacbitún, meaning "stones set in the earth", has at least 24 temple pyramids, a ball court and several raised causeways, though only Plaza A and the surrounding structures are cleared. The tombs of two elite women yielded the largest haul of Maya musical instruments ever found in one place: drums, flutes, ocarinas (wind instruments) and the first discovery of Maya maracas. Though the site is not always open to casual visitors, José Tzul, who lives on the right just before the entrance, runs Blue Ridge Mountain Rider (☎09/22322) and can arrange wonderful **horseback tours** of the area, taking in Pacbitún (US$50 per day), and can even guide you through little-known trails to the lodges in the Mountain Pine Ridge.

## The forest reserve

Not far beyond Pacbitún, and 25km before Augustine, the entrance roads meet and begin a steady climb towards the **entrance to the reserve** proper. One kilometre beyond the junction is a **campsite** (①) run by Fidencio and Petronila Bol, a delightful couple and owners of Bol's Nature Tours. Fidencio used to work as a caretaker at several Maya sites, including Pacbitún and Caracol, and Petronila has compiled *A Book of Maya Herbs*. Fidencio can guide you to several nearby **caves** – the aptly named Museum Cave holds dozens of artefacts, including intact bowls. About 5km uphill from the campsite is the **Mai Gate**, a forestry checkpoint (where visitors register), which has reserve information as well as toilets and drinking water. Once you've entered the reserve, the dense, leafy forest is quickly replaced by pine trees.

After 3km a branch road heads off to the left, running for 7km to a point overlooking the **Thousand-Foot Falls** (US$1.50). The setting is spectacular, with rugged, thickly forested slopes across the steep valley – almost a gorge. The long, slender plume of water becomes lost in the valley below, giving rise to their other, more poetic name – Hidden Valley Falls. The waterfall itself is about 1km from the viewpoint, but try to resist the temptation to climb around for a closer look: the slope is a lot steeper than it first appears and, if you do get down, the ascent is very difficult indeed.

One of the reserve's main attractions has to be the **Rio On Pools**, a gorgeous spot for a swim, 11km further on. Here the river forms pools between huge granite boulders before plunging into a gorge, right beside the main road. Another 8km from here and you reach the reserve headquarters at **AUGUSTINE**. This small settlement, now housing only a few forestry workers, was renamed **DOUGLAS SILVA** (after a local politician), but only some of the signs have been changed. If you're heading for **Caracol**, this is where you can get advice on road conditions from the Forest Department. You can camp here but you'll probably need to bring all your own supplies as the village store appears to have permanently closed.

The **Rio Frio Cave** is a twenty-minute walk from Augustine, following the signposted track from the parking area through the forest to the main cave, beneath a small hill. The Rio Frio flows right through and out of the other side of the hill here and if you enter the foliage-framed cave mouth, you can scramble over limestone terraces the entire way along and into the open again. Sandy beaches and rocky cliffs line the river on both sides.

### Accommodation in the Mountain Pine Ridge

The **resorts** in the Pine Ridge include some of the most exclusive accommodation in the interior of Belize. These lodges, mostly cabins set amongst pines, surrounded by the undisturbed natural beauty of the forest reserve, and with quiet paths to secluded waterfalls, are ideal places to stay if you're visiting Caracol. The listings below are in the order in which you approach them from the entrance road.

**Hidden Valley Inn**, signed on the Cooma Cairn road to Thousand-Foot Falls (☎08/23320, fax 23334, in US ☎1-800/334-7942, *www.hiddenvalleyinn.com*). Twelve roomy, well-designed cottages with fireplaces stacked with logs to ward off the evening chill, at the highest elevation of any accommodation in Belize, and set in a seventy-square-kilometre private reserve which includes Thousand-Foot Falls. Meals are in the spacious main house where guests enjoy the ambience of a mountain lodge, with wood-panelled walls and a well-stocked library. Prices (US$180 double) include breakfast, dinner, tax and service charge. ⑨.

**Pine Ridge Lodge**, on the road to Augustine, just past the Cooma Cairn junction to Thousand-Foot Falls (☎09/23180, in US ☎1-800/316-0706, *www.pineridgelodge.com*). A small resort on the banks of Little Vaqueros Creek, with a choice of simple Maya-style thatched cabins and more modern ones with red-tiled roofs. The grounds and trees are full of orchids and trails lead to pristine waterfalls. The restaurant is a favourite refreshment stop on tours of the Pine Ridge. Continental breakfast included. ⑧.

**Blancaneaux Lodge**, 1km beyond Pine Ridge Lodge, then 2km down a track to the right, by the airstrip (☎09/23878, in US ☎1-800/746-3743, *www.blancaneauxlodge.com*). Owned by Francis Ford Coppola, *Blancaneaux* is the most sumptuous lodge in the Pine Ridge and features a few Hollywood luxuries — reflected in the prices, though these are considerably lower during the off season. Guests stay in comfortable and very spacious hardwood, thatched cabañas and villas overlooking Privassion Creek, set in landscaped grounds. Villas (up to US$450) have two enormous, beautifully decorated rooms with varnished hardwood floors, and there's a huge, private screened porch. The restaurant boasts a wood-fired pizza oven and an espresso machine, and meals feature Italian specialities served with home-grown organic vegetables and fine Italian wines. At the time of writing Coppola had recently purchased *Turtle Inn*, in Placencia (p.298). ⑨.

**Five Sisters Lodge**, at the end of the road past *Blancaneaux* (☎091/2005, fax 09/23081, *www.fivesisterslodge.com*). Set on the hillside among the granite and pines, this has the best location in the Pine Ridge. It's also the only Belizean-owned resort here and is the pride and joy of owner Carlos Popper. There are fourteen very comfortable palmetto-and-thatch cabañas and suites, each with hot showers and a deck with hammocks, and less expensive rooms (some with shared bath) in the main building. Electricity is provided by a small, unobtrusive hydro but the oil lamps are wonderfully romantic and the resort is popular with honeymooners. The dining-room deck gives tremendous views of the Five Sisters waterfalls cascading over the granite rocks of Privassion Creek – you can ride down in the only funicular lift in Belize. Rates include breakfast; other meals are good value if you're on a day-trip. ⑦–⑨.

# Caracol and around

Beyond Augustine the main ridges of the Maya Mountains rise up to the south, while to the west is the Vaca plateau, a fantastically isolated wilderness. Sixteen km past Augustine the road crosses the Macal River on the low **Guacamallo Bridge** and you enter the Chiquibul Forest. The turning for Caracol is 2.5km past the bridge, and may not be well signed. A further 18km brings you to the **visitor centre**, where you sign in with caretaker Bruce Cadle and his crew, who know a great deal about the site. Officially, you still need a **permit** from the Archeology Department to visit; check

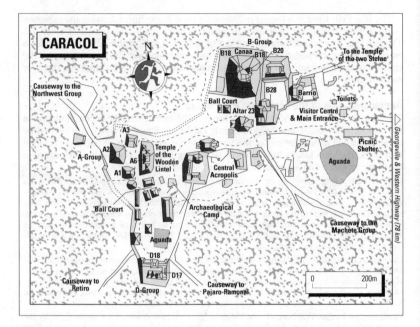

CARACOL

N

B-Group
B18 Canaa B18 B20
To the Temple of the two Stelae

B28
Barrio
Toilets

Causeway to the Northwest Group

Ball Court
Altar 23
Visitor Centre & Main Entrance

Picnic Shelter

A3

A2
A-Group
A6
Temple of the Wooden Lintel
A1
Central Acropolis
Aguada

Ball Court
Archaeological Camp

Causeway to the Machete Group

Aguada
D18
D17
Causeway to Retiro
D-Group
Causeway to Pajaro-Ramonal

0        200m

Georgeville & Western Highway (78 km)

with them on ☎08/22106 to see if this is still the case. Many tour operators in San Ignacio run trips to Caracol (see box on p.264): Everald Tut (☎091/2014) has a daily van **shuttle**, US$50 per person.

The ruins of **Caracol** (daily 8am–4pm; US$5), the largest known Maya site in Belize, were lost in the rainforest for several centuries until their rediscovery by *chiclero* Rosa Mai in 1937. They were first systematically explored by A.H. Anderson in 1938: he named the site Caracol – Spanish for "snail" – because of the large numbers of snail shells found there. Anderson was accompanied by Linton Satterthwaite of the University of Pennsylvania in the 1950s, but much of their work and other early records were destroyed by Hurricane Hattie in 1961. In 1985 the first detailed, full-scale excavation of the site, the "Caracol Project", began under the auspices of Drs Arlen and Diane Chase of the University of Central Florida. Initially expected to take at least ten years, research continues to unearth a tremendous amount of material on the everyday life of all levels of Maya society. Over 100 **tombs** have been found and ceremonially buried caches contain items as diverse as a quantity of mercury and amputated human fingers. There are also many hieroglyphic inscriptions, enabling epigraphers to piece together a virtually complete dynastic record of Caracol's rulers from 599 AD.

Apparently there was a large and wealthy middle class among the Maya of Caracol and dates on stelae and tombs suggest an extremely long occupation, beginning around 600 BC. The last recorded date, carved on stela 10, is 859 AD, during the Terminal Classic, and evidence points to a great fire around 895 AD. At its greatest extent, around 700 AD during the Late Classic period, Caracol covered 88 square kilometres and had a population estimated to be around 150,000, with over 30,000 structures – a far greater density than at Tikal. So far only around ten percent of greater Caracol's full extent has been mapped and research continues each field season. What continues to puzzle archeologists is why the Maya built such a large city on a plateau with no permanent water source – and how they managed to maintain it for so long. The reservoir the Maya built is still used when the archeolologists are in residence.

## The site

The **visitor centre** (built by Raleigh volunteers) is the best at any Maya site in Belize and an essential first stop. There's a map of the epicentre and some very informative display panels as well as artefacts from the site. There's also a large, thatched picnic shelter and clean toilets. Only the city's core, covering 38 square kilometres and containing at least 32 large structures and twelve smaller ones around five main plazas, is currently open to visitors – though this is far more than you can effectively see in a day.

It's an amazing experience to be virtually alone in this great abandoned city, the horizon bounded by jungle-covered hills, through which it's only three hours on foot to Guatemala. Caracol is also a **Natural Monument Reserve**, a haven for wildlife as well as archeologists, and you may catch sight of ocellated turkeys feeding in the plazas, and tapirs dine at night on the succulent shoots growing on cleared areas. The site is so isolated that in the past it was badly looted; today, a permanent team of caretakers is on guard and the Belize Defence Force make frequent patrolling visits. During your visit you'll be guided by one of the guards, or, if excavation is in progress, by one of the researchers. Caracol's largest structure **Caana** – "Sky Palace" – towers above the forest and, at 42m, is the tallest Maya building in Belize (and still one of the tallest buildings in the country). At the top of this immense restored structure is a small plaza, with three more sizeable pyramids above this; an altar here has revealed signs of a female ruler. Beneath Caana a series of looted tombs still have traces of the original painted glyphs on the walls.In the plaza below, Altar 23 – the largest at Caracol – clearly depicts two bound captive lords from subdued cities probably located in present-day Petén; the glyphs above and between them date it to 810 AD. Other glyphs and altars tell of war between Caracol and **Tikal** (see p.457), with power over a huge area alternating between the two great cities. One altar dates Caracol's victory over Tikal at 562 AD – a victory that set the seal on the Caracol's rise to power. Several altars and stelae were deliberately broken by logging tractors in the 1930s, including Altar 23 above. One of the most awe-inspiring sights in this fantastic city is an immense, ancient **ceiba tree** – sacred to the Maya – with enormous buttress roots twice as high as a human being.

## The Chiquibul Cave System

Fifteen kilometres beyond the Caracol turn the Chiquibul Road continues to reach the vast **Chiquibul Cave System**, the longest cave system in Central America, containing what is probably the largest cave chamber in the western hemisphere. The entire area is dotted with caves and sinkholes, which were certainly known to the ancient Maya and probably used for ceremonies; as yet there has been no cave found in Belize which does not contain Maya artefacts. At present the area is impossible to reach on your own – you'll need to come on a properly organized expedition, with permission from the Forest Department in Belmopan — but some tour operators are planning to run trips in the future, so it's worth checking with those recommended in the *Guide*. Further south **Puente Natural** is an enormous natural limestone arch and the *Las Cuevas* **rainforest research station** is nearby. Although not generally open to the public, visitors on organized tours can stay here in the wooden cabins.

## Succotz and the ruins of Xunantunich

Back on the Western Highway, the village of **SAN JOSÉ SUCCOTZ** lies about 12km west of San Ignacio, right beside the Mopan River, just before Benque Viejo. It's a very traditional village in many ways, inhabited largely by Mopan Maya, who celebrate fiestas here on March 19 and May 3. Under colonial administration the Maya of Succotz sided with the British, a stance that angered other groups, such as the Icaiché (see p.219), who burnt it to the ground in 1867. The villagers here still identify strongly with their Maya culture, and many of the men work as caretakers of other Maya sites in Belize. The Magaña family's art gallery and **gift shop** (signed from the main road) sells superb wood and slate carvings.

Outside fiesta times, Succotz is a quiet village, and the main reason most people visit is to see the Classic period ruins of **Xunantunich** (pronounced Shun-an-tun-ich), "the Stone Maiden", up the hill across the river. Any bus or shared taxi running between San Ignacio and the border will drop you by the venerable, hand-winched **cable ferry** (8am–5pm, Mon–Sat free, Sun US$1.50) which carries foot passengers and vehicles across the river. From the riverbank, you have to walk or drive up a steep, 2km track to the site. If you're carrying luggage you can safely leave it in the *Plaza Café* opposite the ferry; owners Edward and Virginia Jenkins provide good **information**.

### Trek Stop and Tropical Wings Butterfly House

Just before the village (signed on the left) there's a wonderful budget **place to stay**, *Trek Stop Cabins* (☎09/32265, *www.thetrekstop.com*; ④). Set in a quiet forest clearing near the road, the eight simple, clean non-smoking cabins with comfortable beds, mosquito nets and a porch cost US$10 per person and there's also a **campsite** (①). Run by American biologists John and Judy Yaeger and Succotz resident Tino Penados, it's an environmentally friendly place, with shared composting toilets and solar-heated showers. Plants here replicate those in a Maya medicinal garden and the library focuses on the Maya and natural history. The restaurant serves some of the best-value food and largest portions in Cayo, always with good vegetarian choices, and there's a self-catering kitchen. Bikes (US$7.50 a day), kayaks (US$15 a day for one or two people), and tubes (US$5 a day) are available for rent, and guided river and nature trips can be arranged.

Visit the well-designed **Tropical Wings Butterfly House and Nature Center** (daily 8am–5pm; US$2.50, including an excellent guided tour) on the site, and you're in a delicate, enchanting world full of tropical colour. About two dozen species of butterflies successfully breed here, and outside in the Nature Center you can see the caterpillars and chrysalises at all stages of development.

### Xunantunich

**Xunantunich** (Mon–Fri 8am–5pm; weekends and holidays 8am–4pm; US$5) was explored in the 1890s by Dr Thomas Gann, a British medical officer, and in 1904 Teobalt Maler of the Peabody Museum took photographs and made a plan of the largest structure, A–6, commonly known as El Castillo. Gann returned in 1924, excavated large numbers of burial goods and removed the carved glyphs of Altar 1, the whereabouts of which are now unknown. British archeologist J. Eric S. Thompson excavated a residential group in 1938, unearthing pottery, obsidian, jade, a spindle, seashells, stingray spines and hammers. Recent excavations have found evidence of Xunantunich's role in the power politics of the Classic period – it was probably allied as a subordinate partner, along with Caracol, to the regional superpower Calakmul, against Tikal. By the Terminal Classic, Xunantunich was already in decline, though still

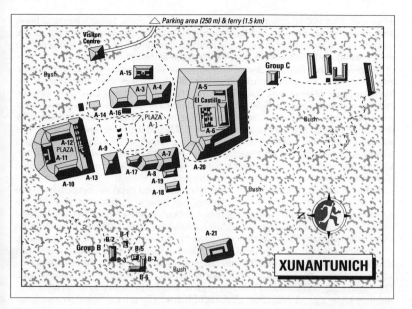

△ Parking area (250 m) & ferry (1.5 km)

XUNANTUNICH

apparently populated until around 1000 AD, after the so-called Classic Maya "collapse".

Your first stop should be the marvellous **visitor centre**, with a superb scale-model of the city and other well-labelled exhibits. One of the highlights is a fibreglass replica of the famous hieroglyphic frieze, from which you get a much better idea of the significance of the real thing. Nearby, the original small museum has several well-preserved stelae from the site.

**The site** is built on top of an artificially flattened hill and includes five plazas, although the remaining structures are grouped around just three of them. The track brings you out into Plaza A–2, with large structures on three sides. Plaza A–3, to the right, is almost completely enclosed by a low, acropolis-like building, and Plaza A–1, to the left, is dominated by **El Castillo**, the city's largest structure, 40m high, and a prominent symbol of Belize's national identity. As is so often the case, the building is layered, with later versions built on top of earlier ones. It was once ringed by a decorative **stucco frieze** carved with abstract designs, human faces and jaguar heads, depicting a king performing rituals associated with assuming authority, and has been extensively restored. The climb up El Castillo is daunting, but the views from the top are superb, with the forest stretching out all around and the rest of the ancient city mapped out beneath you. The Preclassic ruins of **Actuncan** are a couple of kilometres north.

## Benque Viejo and the border

The final town before the Guatemalan border is **BENQUE VIEJO DEL CARMEN**, thirteen kilometres from San Ignacio. Here Belize and Guatemala combine in almost equal proportions and Spanish is certainly the dominant language. Benque, as it's usually known, is a pleasant, quiet place – home to several artists, musicians and writers, it has seen a fascinating cultural revival in recent years. Cubola, Belize's foremost **book and music publishers**, at 35 Elizabeth St (☎09/32241), produce recordings of the country's top bands and anthologies of Belizean literature. The village also produces superb **wood and slate carvings**; you'll see them for sale at Xunantunich.

The most recent manifestation of this flowering of the town's arts, however, is an astonishing new **sculpture park**, Poustinia, five kilometres from the town on the Mollejon Hydro/Arenal road. Established by brothers David and Luis Ruiz, with the assistance of some British artists, it was originally part of the family's cattle ranch. Forty acres have been transformed into a collection of surreal **earth art** sculptures by Belizean, European and Caribbean artists, and it is hoped that, over time, the sculptures will merge into, and become one with, their surrounding environment. Admission (US$5) is by appointment only; contact David (☎09/32084, *david–ruiz@hotmail.com*). Visitors are provided with maps for a self-guided tour, and self-catering accommodation is available for visitors who want to stay in the park.

Budget **hotels** in Benque are basic at best and if you need an inexpensive room you're much better off staying in Succotz or San Ignacio. If, however, you're in the mood for some luxurious pampering, then the new *Mopan River Resort*, on the west bank of the Mopan River opposite the town (☎09/32047, fax 33272, *www.mopanriver-resort.com*; ⑨), might be just what you need. It's Belize's first **all-inclusive resort**, with luxurious and beautifully furnished hardwood thatched cabañas and suites with private baths, electricity, cable TV and rattan furniture. These are the most spacious wooden cabañas in the country, with enormous screened porches and a lovely pool. The owners, Jay and Pamella Picon, go to great lengths to ensure a comfortable stay, and they know a great deal about all parts of Belize. The price is based on a package (minimum stay 3 nights; closed from July to early November) costing around US$850 per person per week, including accommodation, meals, drinks, tours (including Tikal) and transfers from the International Airport – quite possibly the best deal in the country at this level.

**Crossing the border**, 2km beyond Benque, is straightforward, as there's a constant stream of taxis to and from the border post (US$1 per person). Leaving Belize, you'll have to pay the **exit tax** of US$10 and the PACT **conservation fee** of US$3.75; **arriving in Belize** there's nothing to pay – just fill in the immigration form.

---

## ENTERING GUATEMALA FROM BELIZE

**Visas to enter Guatemala** are not needed by most nationalities but you'll usually be asked to pay a semi-official **entry fee** – about Q10 (about US$1.50) or even US$10, and be given a 30-day stamp. You'll be swamped by **moneychangers** who'll pester you on either side of the border; bargain with a couple and you'll get a fair rate. There's a LADATEL (long distance) **telephone** just past Guatemalan immigration, though the cards it takes are not easy to find.

**Buses and minibuses to Flores** and El Remate (see p.456) will be waiting at the border; the bus station itself is in the market in Melchor – a shared taxi from the border will cost a couple of *quetzales* or it's a fifteen-minute walk over the bridge and up the hill to the right. The official bus **fare** to Flores is Q15 (under US$2). Buses depart from the border at 8am and 10am; thereafter every 2–3hr until 5pm. At the border you'll also be approached by **taxi** and **minibus** drivers; they'll charge about US$10 per person ( for a group of four) to Flores or Tikal – after some bargaining – and leave whenever they have a load. The best minibus deals are offered by Manuel Sandoval, who runs Transportes Memita (he aims to have a regular departure from the border to Tikal, leaving at 9am), and Hugo Mayén; both are friendly, honest and reliable.

## travel details

**Belize City to:** destinations along the Western Highway and the Guatemalan border (3hr 30min). The Western Highway is served by half-hourly Novelo's buses (5am–9pm). Some continue over the border to Melchor de Mencos, others stop in Benque. There is an express service, stopping only in Belmopan, every 2–3hr, saving an hour on the journey time above.

**Belmopan to:** San Ignacio and Benque. Western Transport runs at least an hourly service (Mon–Fri 7am–5pm; fewer services on weekends) and some services continue to Melchor.

**Benque and the border to:** Belize City. Novelo's buses half-hourly daily 4am–5pm, express service every 2–3hr.

**San Antonio to:** San Ignacio. Mon–Sat 6am, 7am, 1pm & 3pm; 1hr.

**San Ignacio to:** Belmopan and Belize City. Novelo's run half-hourly services, including expresses from 4.30am; last bus to Belize at 6pm.

**San Ignacio to:** San Antonio, Mesh bus from marketplace (Mon–Sat 4 daily 10am–5pm; 1hr); **to the border**, frequent services at least every 30min during peak times 7.30am– 4pm; 30min). Some only go as far as Benque – shared taxi to border costs US$1pp from Benque, though if you're headed to the border it's often easier and quicker to take a shared taxi for US$2 per person from the market in San Ignacio.

# CHAPTER SIX

# THE SOUTH

To the **south of Belmopan Belize** is at its wildest. Here the central area is dominated by the **Maya Mountains**, sloping down towards the coast through a series of forested ridges and valleys carved by sparkling rivers. As you head further south the climate becomes more humid, promoting the growth of dense **rainforest**, rich in wildlife. The forests here have evolved to cope with periodic hurricanes sweeping in from the Caribbean and have in the past been selectively logged for mahogany. Among the broadleaf forests there are also large stands of Caribbean pine, looking strangely out of place in the tropics. The **coastal strip** south of Belize City is a band of savannah, swamp and lagoon, while beyond Dangriga the shoreline is composed of sandy bays, peninsulas and mangrove lagoons. In the far south the estuaries of the slow-moving Temash and Sarstoon rivers, lined with the tallest **mangrove forest** in Belize, form the country's southernmost national park.

Population density in this part of Belize is low, with most of the towns and villages located on the coast. **Dangriga**, the largest settlement, is the home of the **Garífuna** people – descended from Carib Indians and shipwrecked, enslaved Africans. The villages of **Gales Point**, on Southern Lagoon, north of Dangriga, and **Hopkins**, on the coast to the south, are worth visiting to experience their tranquil way of life. Further south, the **Placencia peninsula** has become established as the focus of coastal tourism in southern Belize; from here and Dangriga you can visit a number of idyllic **cayes** sitting right on top of the reef. Many snorkelling trips visit **Laughing Bird Caye** or the beautiful **Silk Cayes** just inside the reef, while beyond them is the unique **Gladden Spit Marine Reserve**, a sanctuary established specifically to protect **whale sharks** – the largest fish in the world. Further out, pristine **Glover's Reef** provides a perfect base for sea-kayaking, with the bonus of both budget and luxury accommodation on a remote atoll.

**Inland**, the Maya Mountains remain unpenetrated by roads, forming a solid barrier to land travel except on foot or horseback. Successive Belize governments, showing supreme foresight, have placed practically all of the mountain massif under some form of legal protection, whether as national park, nature reserve, wildlife sanctuary or forest reserve. The most accessible area of this rainforest, though still little visited by tourists, is the **Cockscomb Basin Wildlife Sanctuary**, a reserve designed to protect the sizeable jaguar population and an ideal base for exploring the forest. You'll come across plenty of tracks – but don't count on seeing a jaguar. The sanctuary is also starting point for the **Victoria Peak Trail** – an arduous but rewarding trek to the summit of the second highest mountain in Belize.

The Southern Highway, now mostly paved and the only road heading south of Dangriga, comes to an end in the small town of **Punta Gorda**, connected by daily skiffs to **Puerto Barrios** in Guatemala. Inland, in the lush southern foothills of the Maya Mountains, you can visit and stay in Kekchí and Mopan **Maya villages**. Maya sites in the south are just as numerous as in the rest of the country, though generally smaller and certainly less well-known; recent restoration and the new visitor centres make a visit to the main ones very worthwhile. **Nim Li Punit**, just off the highway, has the largest and one of the best-preserved stelae in the country, and **Lubaantun**, near San Pedro Columbia, was where the enigmatic **Crystal Skull** came to light in 1926. Offshore, the **Sapodilla Cayes**, now protected as a marine reserve, are perhaps the most beautiful of all Belize's islands.

---

### ACCOMMODATION PRICE CODES

All the accommodation listed in this book has been categorized into one of nine price bands, as set out below. The prices quoted are in US dollars and refer to the cheapest room available for two people sharing in high season.

① under US$5      ④ US$15–25      ⑦ US$60–80
② US$5–10        ⑤ US$25–40      ⑧ US$80–100
③ US$10–15       ⑥ US$40–60      ⑨ over US$100

---

# The Coastal Road and Gales Point

To head south from Belize City you first need to go west; either to Belmopan for the Hummingbird Highway (see p.284), or to the start of the unpaved **Coastal Road shortcut to Dangriga**, heading southeast from Mile 30 on the Western Highway. The road is usually in good condition and is served by several Z-Line buses a day on the Belize City–Dangriga route. Along the way the scenery is typical of southern Belize: citrus plantations, pine ridge and steep limestone hills covered in broadleaf forest.

### Gales Point

The tranquil Creole village of **GALES POINT** straggles along a narrow peninsula jutting into the shallow, placid **Southern Lagoon**, connected by creeks to **Northern Lagoon**, an even larger body of water. All **buses** heading along the unpaved Coastal Road to Dangriga pass the junction to Gales Point, 4km from the village itself, and most go all the way into the village. There is also a route to Gales Point **by boat** from Belize City, used by some tour groups, which takes you along some amazing **inland waterways**, travelling upstream on the Haulover Creek, then along the Burdon Canal Nature Reserve, across the Sibun River and through the Northern and Southern lagoons; if you get a chance to travel this way to Gales Point you should take it.

The mangrove-cloaked lagoons, linked to the sea by the Manatee River, are such an essential breeding area for rare wildlife, including jabiru storks, manatee, crocodiles and both freshwater and marine turtles, that the government has established the **Manatee Special Development Area** to encourage sensitive conservation-oriented development and local people have trained to become tour guides. The lagoon system is the largest manatee breeding ground in the entire Caribbean basin, and Belize's main nesting beaches of the endangered **hawksbill** and **loggerhead turtles** lie either side of the mouth of the Manatee River.

With help from international conservation organizations and volunteers, several villagers guard the turtles' nesting beaches and have installed signs and buoys warning boatmen to slow down to avoid harming the manatees. Leroy Andrewin, who grew up here hunting turtles but now spends most of his time, and practically all his money, protecting turtle nests from predators, is a real conservation hero; he'll take you out on a night patrol – or you could **volunteer** for a longer stay. Renting a dory (traditionally a dugout canoe) for about US$10 per day allows you to explore the waterways, or you can take a trip with a local **guide**. Gales Point is also a centre of **traditional drum-making**; you can learn to make and play drums at Emett Young's Creole Drum School. Emett often performs elsewhere so it's best to check ahead to see if he's at home. You'll also learn a lot about local history and culture – made even more enjoyable while sipping the home-produced cashew wine in the evenings.

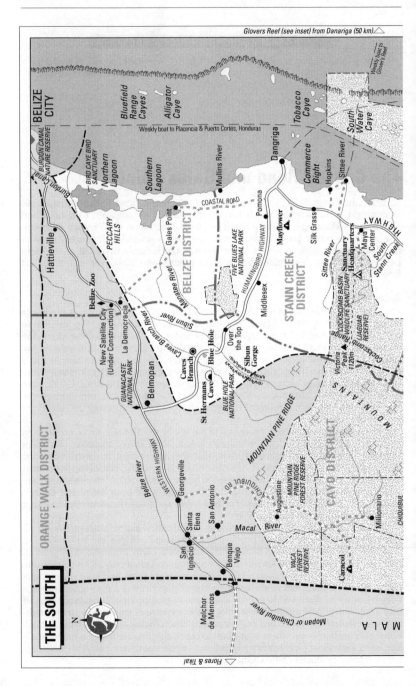

Glovers Reef (see inset) from Danariga (50 km) △

Weekly boat to Glover's Reef

BELIZE CITY

Bluefield Range Cayes

Alligator Cave

Tobacco Cave

South Water Cave

BURDON CANAL NATURE RESERVE

BIRD CAVE BIRD SANCTUARY

Northern Lagoon

Southern Lagoon

Mullins River

Dangriga

Commerce Bight

Hopkins

Sittee River

Weekly boat to Placencia & Puerto Cortés, Honduras

Burdon Canal

Hattieville

PECCARY HILLS

Gales Point

COASTAL ROAD

Pomona

Mayflower

Silk Grass

Sittee River

HIGHWAY

BELIZE DISTRICT

Manatee River

FIVE BLUES LAKE NATIONAL PARK

HUMMINGBIRD HIGHWAY

STANN CREEK DISTRICT

Maya Center

South Stann Creek

Belize Zoo

New Satellite City (Under Construction)

La Democracia

Caves Branch River

Sibun River

Middlesex

COCKSCOMB BASIN WILDLIFE SANCTUARY

Headquarters

GUANACASTE NATIONAL PARK

Belmopan

Over the Top

Blue Hole

Sibun Gorge

Cockscomb Range

Victoria Peak 1120m

JAGUAR RESERVE

Caves Branch

St Hermans Cave

BLUE HOLE NATIONAL PARK

MOUNTAINS

WESTERN HIGHWAY

Belize River

Georgeville

San Antonio

CHIQUIBUL RD

Augustine

MOUNTAIN PINE RIDGE

MOUNTAIN PINE RIDGE FOREST RESERVE

CAYO DISTRICT

ORANGE WALK DISTRICT

Santa Elena

San Ignacio

Benque Viejo

Macal River

Millionario

CHIQUIBUL

VACA FOREST RESERVE

Caracol

THE SOUTH

Melchor de Mencos

Mopan or Chiquibul River

MALA

N

Flores & Tikal △

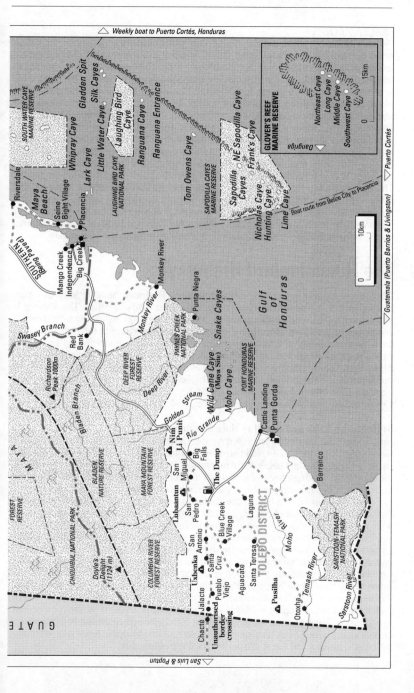

*PRACTICALITIES*

Deborah Callender, who runs the *Orchid Café* (☎014/5621), also publishes the village newsletter, and if you're serious about staying or taking a tour here you should call her for **information** first. Walking along the village's only street, you'll see several signs pointing to houses offering simple bed and breakfast **accommodation** (④); to book call the *Orchid Café* or try the community telephone on ☎021/2031. *Gentle's Cool Spot*, a small bar at the point where the buses turn around, also has a few simple, clean, though very basic rooms (③), and recently a couple of **campsites** have opened – *Metho's Coconut Camping* (☎021/2031; ①) has space in a sandy spot and you can rent a tent from *Yvette's Store* (☎014/5621). The most luxurious accommodation is *Manatee Lodge* (☎ & fax 021/2040, in US ☎877/462-6283, *www.manateelodge.com*; ⑦; no service charge), a two-storey, white-painted colonial-style building with green trim, set in lush lawns lined with coconut trees right at the tip of the peninsula. Rooms (all non-smoking) are spacious and comfortable and the meals are superb. The wooden deck on the upper floor is an ideal spot for watching sunrise or sunset, and guests can use the lodge's canoes and small sailboats to enjoy the lagoon. The bed and breakfast places offer tasty Creole food, as do a couple of other houses, though apart from *Manatee Lodge* the only real **restaurant** is the *Orchid Café*, serving great local and international dishes, including vegetarian meals, on a breezy deck festooned with orchids.

# The Hummingbird Highway

After recent resurfacing work, the **Hummingbird Highway**, heading southeast from Belmopan (see p.254) to Dangriga, is one of the best roads in Belize. The scenery is magnificent as the road heads steadily over the hills through lush forest with the eastern slopes of the **Maya Mountains**, coated in greenery, rising to the right. The hills form part of a ridge of limestone mountains, riddled with underground rivers and caves, many of which you can visit on guided trips to explore the Maya underworld. About 19km out of Belmopan the road crosses the **Caves Branch River**, a tributary of the Sibun River. Further on, just past the highest point on the road is the stunningly beautiful **Five Blues Lake National Park**; beyond here the road follows the **Stann Creek valley**, lined with citrus groves, virtually all the way to Dangriga.

## St Herman's Cave and the Blue Hole National Park

Just beyond the Caves Branch River, by the roadside on the right, is **St Herman's Cave** (daily 8am–4pm; US$4, valid also for the Blue Hole), one of the most accessible caves in Belize. Any bus between Belmopan and Dangriga will drop you at the cave or the Blue Hole, making an easy day-trip, but to really appreciate the mysteries of caving in Belize you need to stay nearby, at the *Caves Branch Jungle Lodge* (see below).

Follow the marked trail behind the **visitor centre** (with good displays of the plant, bird and animal life found here, particularly bats), for ten minutes to the cave entrance, beneath a dripping rock face. To enter, down steps that were originally cut by the Maya, you'll need a flashlight. Inside, you clamber over the rocks and splash through the river for about twenty minutes, admiring the stunning formations, before the cave appears to end. A new **interpretive trail**, with a spectacular observation platform, leads over the cave for 4km to a **campsite** (①). Another signed trail leads 3km from the cave, over the ridge, to the **Blue Hole National Park**, which you can also reach by continuing along the highway for 2km. The Blue Hole is actually a short, ten-metre deep stretch of underground river – cenote in Mayan – whose course is revealed by the collapse of a karst cavern, flowing on the surface for about 50m before disappearing beneath another rock face. Its cool, fresh turquoise waters, surrounded by dense forest and overhung with vines, mosses and ferns, are perfect for a refreshing dip.

*CAVES BRANCH JUNGLE LODGE*
The best place to stay near the Blue Hole (and indeed along the whole Hummingbird Highway) is **Caves Branch Jungle Lodge** (☎ & fax 08/22800, *www.cavesbranch.com*), at Mile 41½. It's well-signed, 1.5km beyond St Herman's Cave and a few hundred metres before the Blue Hole, 1km in from the main road along a level track; all passing buses will stop at the entrance.

Set in a huge area of superb, high canopy forest on the banks of the beautiful **Caves Branch River**, the lodge offers a range of comfortable, rustic **accommodation** to suit all budgets. The highlights are the spacious, screened cabaña suites, with a king-size bed, private bathroom with hot shower and a living room with wicker furniture (⑧); there are great private cabañas too (⑦). For budget travellers even the **bunkhouse** (US$15 per person) has showers and flush toilets, and finally there's **camping** and hammock space (US$5); all prices include tax and there's no service charge. Delicious, filling buffet-style meals are served in a simple dining room above the river. Try to plan at least two nights here; even if you don't take any of the trips on offer, one day just won't seem long enough and the birding is superb.

*Caves Branch* is run by Canadian Ian Anderson, who, together with some of the most experienced local guides in the country, leads truly amazing **guided tours** through some of the area's most spectacular caves and along crystal-clear rivers running through the limestone hills. All the caves contain **Maya artefacts** – ceramics, carvings and the like – with abundant evidence of Classic period ceremonies. You can float on inner tubes 10km along a subterranean river, your headlamp piercing the intense darkness, or even ascend an underground river several kilometres upstream as it cuts through a limestone ridge, climbing stupendous waterfalls thundering through crystal caverns. Some caves are dry, and you must take great care not to touch the glittering crystal formations as you climb over rocks and around stalagmites. Newer and perhaps more challenging activities are **rappelling** – descending over the sheer wall of a sink-hole and through the forest canopy – and **rock climbing**, with walls graded according to your level of experience.

The guides are re-certified each year in Cave and Wilderness Rescue and Wilderness First Aid (*Caves Branch* were the founders of the Belize Cave and Wilderness Rescue Team), and all trips have back-up support. Participants on all expeditions need good hiking boots (and climbing shoes, where applicable). The expeditions are not cheap (on average about US$75 per person), but they're well worth the cost, as the guest book entries testify.

## Over the Top and Five Blues Lake National Park

Beyond the Blue Hole, the Hummingbird Highway undulates smoothly through the increasingly hilly landscape, eventually crossing a low pass. This is the highest point on the road, and the downhill slope is appropriately called **Over the Top**. On the way down, the road passes through **ST MARGARET'S VILLAGE**, where a women's co-operative arranges bed-and-breakfast **accommodation** in private houses (☎081/2005; ④). A few kilometres past the village, the *Over the Top Restaurant* stands on a hill at Mile 32, overlooking the junction of the track to **Five Blues Lake National Park**, seventeen square kilometres of luxuriantly forested karst scenery, centred around a beautiful lake. Named for its constantly changing colours, the lake is another cenote or "blue hole", caused by a cavern's collapse. It's about an hour's walk to the lake and the road is passable in a good vehicle; trails enable you to explore the practically deserted park. Continuing south for 3km on the highway from Over the Top, there's cabaña and bed-and-breakfast **accommodation** at *Palacio's Mountain Retreat* (⑤), overlooking a river; buses stop right outside.

## On towards Dangriga

*Palacio's* marks the start of the **Stann Creek valley**, the centre of the Belizean citrus fruit industry. Bananas were the first crop to be grown here, and by 1891 half a million stems were being exported through Stann Creek (now Dangriga) every year. However, this banana boom came to an abrupt end in 1906, when disease destroyed the crop, and afterwards the government set out to foster the growth of **citrus fruits**. Between 1908 and 1937 the valley was even served by a small railway – some of the highway bridges were originally rail bridges – and by 1945 the citrus industry was well established. Today it accounts for about thirteen percent of the country's exports and, despite widely fluctuating prices, is heralded as one of the nation's great success stories – although for the largely Guatemalan labour force, housed in rows of scruffy huts, conditions are little better than on the oppressive coffee fincas at home. Ten kilometres before Dangriga, the filling station is a useful place to refuel without going into town; just beyond this is the junction with the **Southern Highway** (now mostly paved) heading to Punta Gorda.

# Dangriga

**DANGRIGA**, formerly called Stann Creek, is the district capital and the largest town in southern Belize. It's also the cultural centre of the **Garífuna**, a people of mixed indigenous Caribbean and African descent. Since the early 1980s Garífuna culture has undergone a tremendous revival; as a part of this movement the town was renamed Dangriga, a Garífuna word meaning "sweet waters" – applied to the North Stann Creek flowing through the centre.

The most important day in the Garífuna calendar is November 19, **Garífuna Settlement Day**, when Dangriga is packed solid with expatriate Belizeans returning to their roots, and the town erupts into wild celebration. The party begins the evening before, and the drumming and punta dancing pulsate all night long. In the morning there's a re-enactment of the arrival from Honduras, with people landing on the beach in dugout canoes decorated with palm leaves. Christmas and New Year are also celebrated in unique Garífuna style. At this time you might see the *wanaragu* or *Jonkunu* (John Canoe) dance, where **masked and costumed dancers** represent figures consisting of elements of eighteenth-century naval officers and Amerindian tribal chiefs wearing feathered headdresses and with shell rattles on their knees. Dangriga is also home to some of the country's most popular artists and performers, including painter Benjamin Nicolas, painter and guitarist Pen Cayetano, drum-maker Austin Rodríguez, and the Warribagaga Dancers and Turtle Shell Band; the artists have small galleries here, and you may catch a live dance performance. Fine **crafts** are produced as well; distinctive brown and white basketware, woven palm- hats and baskets and dolls in Garífuna costume.

During quieter times the atmosphere is enjoyably laid-back, though there's little to do during the day. As the south of the country becomes more accessible, however, Dangriga is becoming increasingly useful as a base for visiting south-central Belize, the cayes offshore and the mountains, ruins and jaguar reserve inland.

## Arrival, orientation and information

In addition to **buses** heading just for Dangriga, all buses between Belize City and Punta Gorda call here (see p.212 for details of bus companies and services in Belize City). Generally there will be a service every hour or so from 8am to 5pm; a few of these (only from Z-Line) will use the Coastal Road (see p.281). Arriving, buses enter Dangriga at the south end of town and most continue to the centre. Z-Line has a modern terminal

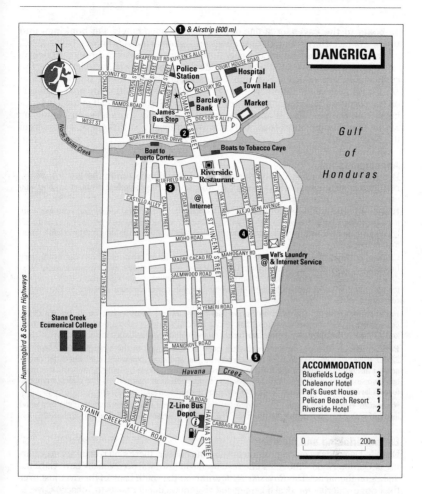

**DANGRIGA**

N

△ ❶ & Airstrip (600 m)

GRAPEFRUIT RD KUYLEN'S ALLEY
COURT HOUSE ROAD
**Police Station** ■ **Hospital**
COCONUT RD
COCHANS AVE
RECTORY RD ■ **Town Hall**
RAMOS ROAD **Barclay's Bank** ■ **Market**
WEST ST **James Bus Stop** DOCTOR'S ALLEY
North Stann Creek
NORTH RIVERSIDE DRIVE
**Boat to Puerto Cortés** ❷ **Boats to Tobacco Caye**

*Gulf*

*of*

*Honduras*

**Riverside Restaurant**
BLUEFIELD ROAD
❸
CASTILLO ALLEY
@ **Internet**
CEDAR STREET
CANAL STREET
REAR PINE ST
PINE STREET
ST VINCENT STREET
OAK STREET
ALEJO BENI AVENUE
MAGOON ST
KNOPP'S STREET
CHATUYE ST
MAGOON'S ST
GANEY STREET
HOWARD STREET
❹
MOHO ROAD
MADRE CACAO RD
MAHOGANY RD
Val's Laundry
@ **& Internet Service**
SALMWOOD ROAD
TUBROOSE STREET
SHARP STREET
POLACK STREET
YEMERI ROAD
ECUMENICAL DRIVE

Hummingbird & Southern Highways

**Stann Creek Ecumenical College**
■■
ZERICOTE STREET
MANGROVE ROAD
❺
*Havana Creek*

STANN CREEK VALLEY ROAD
SAMPSON'S ST
DANIEL'S ST
UNITY STREET
ISLA ROAD
**Z-Line Bus Depot**
ℹ
HAVANA STREET
CABBAGE ROAD

**ACCOMMODATION**
Bluefields Lodge          3
Chaleanor Hotel          4
Pal's Guest House        5
Pelican Beach Resort    1
Riverside Hotel           2

0                    200m

---

(with luggage storage) about 1km south of the centre, while James buses stop on the street outside the police station. Dangriga's **airstrip**, served by regular flights from Belize City (continuing to Placencia and Punta Gorda), is by the shore, just north of the *Pelican Beach Hotel*; you'll need a taxi into town.

The centre of town is marked by the **road bridge** over the South Stann Creek, with the main thoroughfare leading north as Commerce Street and south as St Vincent Street. Almost everything you're likely to need, including **hotels, restaurants, banks** and **boat transport**, is on or very near this road; Barclays Bank, near the BTL office a block north of the bridge, has the only ATM that accepts foreign cards. Dangriga's official **tourist office** is in the Z-Line terminal (Mon–Fri 8am–5pm, ☎22277), though the quality of information is patchy; you'll generally be better off checking in the *Riverside Restaurant*, especially if you need information on **boats to the cayes**, or at one of the recommended hotels. For **bookings and tours** contact Derek and Debbie Jones of *Aquamarine Adventures* (☎05/23262, *djones@btl.net*), independent tour operators dealing with resorts throughout Belize, or Godfrey Young, of C&G Tours (☎05/23641; *cgtours@btl.net*), who has a range of comfortable, a/c vehicles. For both domestic and **international flights** check at *D's Travel Service*, 64 Commerce St (☎05/22709, *kit@btl.net*). **The post office** is on the corner of Mahogany and Caney streets, in the southern half of town, a block back from the sea. **Email** access is available from *Val's Laundry*, on Mahogany Street, opposite the post office, and from *WorldCom*, 15 St Vincent St, across from the Belize Bank.

## Accommodation

Dangriga has experienced something of a hotel-building boom in the last few years, resulting in an ample choice of **places to stay** and – with some real bargains on offer – no need to stay in a cheap dive.

**Bluefield Lodge**, 6 Bluefield Rd (☎05/22742, *bluefield@btl.net*). Clean, secure and very well run, it's everything a budget hotel should be, with good-value rooms (some with private bath) and really comfortable beds with bedside lights. Owner Louise Belisle also maintains a very reliable information board. ④.

**Chaleanor Hotel**, 35 Magoon St (%05/22587, fax 23038). A large, great-value hotel run by the very hospitable Chadwick and Eleanor Usher, with spotless, spacious rooms, all with private bath. Next door are some equally clean budget rooms in a wooden building, some with private bath. Free coffee and purified water are available in the lobby, and you can enjoy your meals from the rooftop restaurant. ③/⑤.

**Pal's Guest House**, 868 Magoon St, by the bridge over Havana Creek (☎ & fax 05/22095, *palbze@btl.net*). Good-value accommodation in two buildings: budget rooms (some with private bath and TV) are in the older part; newer beachfront rooms all have private bath and TV. ④–⑥.

**Pelican Beach Resort**, on the beach 2km north of town, next to the airstrip (☎05/22024, fax 22570, *www.pelicanbeachbelize.com*). Dangriga's largest and most expensive hotel; check for out-of-season discounts. Rooms at the front are in a wooden colonial-style building; at the rear is a modern, two-storey concrete building with spacious rooms and large bathrooms. The dining room features a large marine aquarium. Top-class tours inland and to the cayes. ⑧/⑨.

**Riverside Hotel**, right beside the bridge (☎05/22168). Clean rooms (some with bath) in a good location with a vantage point over the river. Prices are per person; a good deal for singles. ③.

## Eating, drinking and nightlife

Despite Dangriga's central position in Garífuna culture, there's no restaurant specializing in Garífuna food – though some restaurants in town will occasionally have Garífuna dishes on the menu. The *Riverside Restaurant*, on the south bank of the river just over the bridge, catering for local boatmen and visitors waiting for boats to Tobacco Caye, is easily the best place in the town centre, serving tasty Creole food, including great breakfasts and a daily special. *King Burger* (not what you might think) under the *Riverside Hotel* serves good rice, chicken, burgers, fruit juices, fish and conch soup (a Belizean delicacy). The *Starlight* is the best value of several Chinese restaurants on the main street, and *Dangriga Pizza* opposite the side of the police station delivers (☎05/237860). For picnic supplies you could try the **market** on the north bank of the river, by the sea, but it's very small – for other groceries it's best to head for the supermarket just south of the bridge.

There's no shortage of **bars** in Dangriga, though some are particularly dubious-looking, both inside and out. The best local nightspots are the *Round House Reggae Bar* and *Malibu Beach Club*, along the beach to the north of the centre, just before the *Pelican Beach*. Both are good places to meet the locals and dance on the sand, though they're likely to be open only at weekends.

### A BRIEF HISTORY OF THE GARÍFUNA

**The Garífuna** trace their history back to the island of **St Vincent**, one of the Windward Islands in the eastern Caribbean. At the time of Columbus's landing in the Americas the islands of the Lesser Antilles had recently been settled by people calling themselves *Kalípuna*, or *Kwaib* (from which we get the terms Garífuna and Carib) from the South American mainland, who had subdued the previous inhabitants, the Arawaks. The admixture of African blood came in 1635 when two Spanish ships, carrying slaves from Nigeria to their colonies in America, were wrecked off St Vincent and the survivors took refuge on the island. At first there was conflict between the Caribs and the Africans, but the Caribs had been weakened by wars and disease and eventually the predominant race was Black, with some Carib blood, becoming known by the English as the **Black Caribs** – in their own language they were *Garinagu*, or *Garífuna*.

For most of the seventeenth and eighteenth centuries St Vincent was nominally under British control, but in practice it belonged to the Caribs (Garífuna), who successfully fended off British attempts to gain full control of the island until 1796. The colonial authorities could not allow a free Black society to survive amongst slave-owning European settlers, and the Garífuna population was hunted down and transported to **Roatán**, one of the Bay Islands (see p.517), where the British abandoned them. Perhaps in response to pleas for help from the Garífuna, who continued to die on Roatán, the Spanish commandante of Trujillo, on the Honduran mainland, took the 1700 survivors to Trujillo where they were in demand as labourers. The Spanish had never made a success of agriculture here and the arrival of the Garífuna, who were proficient at growing crops, benefited the colony considerably. The boys were conscripted and the Garífuna men gained a reputation as sailors, soldiers and mercenaries.

In the early nineteenth century small numbers of Garífuna moved up the coast to **Belize**, and although in 1811, Superintendent Barrow of Belize ordered their expulsion, it had little effect. When European settlers arrived in Stann Creek in 1823, the Garífuna were already there and were hired to clear land. The largest single migration to Belize took place in 1832 when vast numbers, under the leadership of Alejo Benji, fled from Honduras (by then part of the Central American Republic) after they had supported the wrong side in a failed revolution to overthrow the republican government. It is this arrival which is today celebrated as **Garífuna Settlement Day**, though it seems likely many arrived both before and after.

Throughout the nineteenth and twentieth centuries the Garífuna travelled widely in search of work. To start with they confined themselves to Central America (where they can still be found all along the Caribbean coast from Belize to Nicaragua), but in World War II Garífuna men supplied crews for both British and US merchant ships. Since then trips to the US have become an important part of the local economy, and there are small Garífuna communities in New York, New Orleans, Los Angeles and even in London. Belize has a National Garífuna Council, and its scholars are attempting to create a written language. The council has already published *The People's Garífuna Dictionary* and some school textbooks. *The First Primer on a People Called Garífuna* by Myrtle Palacio is in English and available in Belize. There's an excellent US-based Garífuna **Web** site (*www.garifuna-world.com*) listing cultural events and current developments in the entire Garífuna community.

## Offshore: Tobacco Range Cayes and Columbus Reef

The **Tobacco Range** is a group of mangrove cayes (a couple of which have accommodation planned) just behind the beautiful **Columbus** and **Tobacco reefs**, about 16km east of Dangriga. The largest caye in the range, **Man-O'-War Caye**, is a **bird sanctuary** named after the frigate or man-o'-war birds you'll see hanging on the breeze with outstretched wings. In the breeding season the males develop an immense, bright red balloon on their throats and the island is full of nesting birds; watching the birds from a boat

## MOVING ON FROM DANGRIGA

Returning **to Belize City**, Z-Line buses (☎05/22732) leave roughly every hour from 5am to 5pm. Most head up the Hummingbird Highway (3hr, via **Belmopan**), though two or three will travel along the Coastal Road (2hr). James Bus Line doesn't have a terminal, but departing buses (currently 4 daily in each direction) will pass along the main street; those heading north do not use the Coastal Road. Z-line has at least five daily buses between Dangriga and **Punta Gorda** (4–5hr), from 10.30am to 5.30pm. All buses to Punta Gorda stop at **Independence** – also known as **Mango Creek** – (2hr) where you can pick up boats to Placencia (see p.301).

There are usually two daily Z-Line services from Dangriga to **Placencia** (2hr 30min), but departure times are continually changing: currently they are 12.30pm and 4.30pm; at least one bus calls at **Hopkins** (40min) and **Sittee River**, and these villages also have a dedicated Z-Line service at 11am.

Dangriga is served by **flights** on Tropic Air (☎05/22129) and Maya Island Air (☎05/22659) every couple of hours to and from Belize City, continuing south to Placencia and Punta Gorda.

For **Puerto Cortés in Honduras** a fast **skiff** leaves each Saturday at 9am (US$50; around 3hr) from the north bank of the river, two blocks from the bridge; be there an hour before departure with your passport so that the skipper, Carlos Reyes (☎05/23227), can take care of the formalities.

is fine but you can't land on the island. Beyond the superb Columbus Reef, with a scattering of small cayes along its length, including the tiny **Tobacco Caye** perched on its southern tip, lies Tobacco Reef with slightly larger **South Water Caye** on the southern end. Each caye has a number of delightful places to stay – sunsets out here can be breathtakingly beautiful, outlining the distant Maya Mountains with a purple and orange aura.

### Tobacco Caye

**Tobacco Caye**, ideally situated right on the reef, is easy to reach and has the least expensive accommodation. **Boats** (US$15; 40min) leave every day from near the bridge, but there are no regular departures; check for information at the *Riverside Restaurant* in Dangriga. The most prompt and reliable service is operated by Captain Buck, though any of the hotel owners on the island will take you, and maybe arrange a package deal. Tobacco Caye is tiny – if you stand in the centre you're only a couple of minutes from the shore in any direction, with the unbroken reef stretching north for miles. The island's **dive shop**, *Tobacco Caye Diving* (☎014/9907, *www.tobaccocayediving.com*), has a good selection of equipment, including snorkel gear, and owner Andy Muha offers PADI courses and trips to the atolls. A single-tank local dive (without a boat but including equipment) costsUS$25; a dive course is US$230.

**Accommodation** here is simple but comfortable, and generally good value; you'll be staying either in wooden buildings on the sand or cabins right over the sea. The places below include all meals in the price but here more than anywhere it's essential to check what you're paying for – and whether the price is quoted in US or Belize dollars. *Gaviota Coral Reef Resort* (☎ & fax 051/2032; ⑥/⑦) is the least expensive place to stay, with cabins on the sand and over the water, and budget rooms in the main building, all with shared bath. Meals are wonderful and there's discounted transport for guests if you call ahead. *Lana's on the Reef* (☎051/2036 or 05/22571; ⑦) has four simple rooms with shared bath in a lovely wooden house, and the best food on the island. At *Reef's End Lodge* (☎05/22419, fax 22828, *www.reefsendlodge.com*; ⑦/⑧) you stay right on the shore in a cabin room or in one of a pair of spacious private cabañas, all with private bath, hot water and a deck. The restaurant is built over the sea on the tip of the reef, and the bar is a fantastic place to enjoy the sunset. **Tobacco Caye Lodge** (☎ 051/2033 or 02/76247, *tclodgebelize@yahoo.com*; ⑧)) used to be *Island Camps* until the small cabins were destroyed by Hurricane Mitch in 1998. Now completely rebuilt and more upmarket, the lodge has the largest area of any hotel on the island, stretching from the reef at the front to the lagoon at the back. Accommodation comprises three spacious, comfortable, two-room houses with deck and hammocks, and there's a good beach bar by the dock.

### South Water Caye

Eight kilometres south of Tobacco Caye and about three times the size, **South Water Caye** is arguably one of the most beautiful islands in Belize. Like Tobacco Caye it sits right on the reef and offers fantastic, very accessible snorkelling and scuba-diving in crystal-clear water. South Water Caye is now the focus of a large new **marine reserve**, and the southern end of the island is part of a small nature reserve. Turtles sometimes nest in the sand here, and the reef curves around offshore protecting the pristine beach. With one exception – the very low-key *Bernie's Snacks and Cabins* (☎014/6553; ⑥), a couple of small, brightly painted wooden cabins with shared bath – **accommodation** on the caye is upmarket and expensive and has to be booked in advance as part of a package. The *Pelican Beach Resort* in Dangriga (☎05/22024, *www.pelicanbeachbelize.com*) has a range of idyllic options in a stunning location at the south end of the island, including some beautiful wooden houses and a two-storey wooden hotel; rates (including meals) are in the range of US$185–220. They also operate *The Pelican's University*, which houses groups, often students, in a two-storey building with five bunk-bedded rooms – definitely a fine place to study: US$68 per person per day including meals. *Leslie Cottages* (☎ & fax 051/2030 or 05/37076, in US ☎1-800/548-5843, *izebelize@btl.net*; ⑨) has very comfortable wooden cabins with private bath, electricity, wide decks, and dorm rooms, in a tropical field research station. Although many guests here are on study trips, it's a wonderful place for anyone to stay.

# The Southern Highway to Placencia

To the south of Dangriga the country becomes more mountainous, with settlements mainly restricted to the coastal lowlands. The **Southern Highway**, running from Dangriga to Punta Gorda, is now mostly paved, with the remainder frequently graded. Strong bridges have been built high above the river levels, making the entire highway passable except during the worst rainstorms. For its entire length the highway is set back from the coast, running beneath the peaks of the Maya Mountains, often passing through pine forest and vast citrus and banana plantations. Your first reason to pull off the Southern Highway might be to visit the Late Classic Maya **Mayflower Ruins**, while further along, several branch roads lead off to settlements, such as **Hopkins**, a Garífuna village on the coast, and the nearby Creole village of **Sittee River**, where you can catch the boat to the idyllic cayes of **Glover's Reef**. From the village of **Maya Centre**, 36km south of Dangriga, a road leads west into the Cockscomb Basin Wildlife Sanctuary – the **Jaguar Reserve**.

## Mayflower ruins and Mama Noots Resort

Ten kilometres south of the junction with the Stann Creek Valley Road, an unpaved six-kilometre branch road twists through citrus groves and forest to the foothills of the Maya Mountains and the Late Classic site of **Mayflower**. There are really three Maya sites here; Mayflower, which is near the end of the branch road, and Maintzunun and

T'au Witz, each a short distance through the forest. Apart from a few medium-sized stone mounds and areas which are clearly plazas there's not much to see architecturally but the location, on a creek where the coastal plain meets the forested mountains, is sublime, rich in tremendous bird and animal life. To really appreciate the area you can **stay nearby**, at *Mama Noots Resort* (☎051/2050, *mamanoots@btl.net*; ⑧), set in a large grassy clearing surrounded on three sides by forest-covered hills. Owners Kevin and Nanette Denny have left most of their fifty acres of primary and secondary forest intact (much of the land is steep hillside anyway), though some fruits and vegetables are grown organically. The accommodation consists of a large, two-room wood and thatch house and six rooms in a wheelchair-accessible concrete building. All the rooms have private bath, fans, 24-hour electricity and balconies with hammocks. Trails lead to nearby waterfalls and even the occasional visits by a jaguar only add to the natural atmosphere. All buses heading south from Dangriga pass the side road; call ahead and a horse-drawn Mennonite buggy will pick you up from the junction.

# Hopkins and Sittee River

Stretching for more than 3km along a shallow, gently curving bay, and thickly shaded by palm trees, **HOPKINS** is home to around a thousand Garífuna people, who, until recently, made their living from small-scale farming and fishing, often paddling dugout canoes to pull up fish traps, or using baited handlines. Garífuna Settlement Day on November 19 is celebrated enthusiastically with singing, dancing and above all the beating of drums – an integral part of the Garífuna culture. A few kilometres south of the Hopkins turn-off is the junction of the road to the Creole village of **Sittee River**, a pleasant place in its own right, but most useful as a jumping-off point for Glover's Reef (see p.294).

## Hopkins practicalities

Hopkins is a pleasant place to spend a few days relaxing, with food and accommodation in all price ranges, and you can rent kayaks, windsurf boards and bicycles. Many hotels can arrange trips to the reef and cayes further out; for **diving** check with Second Nature Divers (☎ & fax 05/37038, *divers@btl.net*), based in Sittee River. The view back towards the village from the sea, with the high ridges of the Maya Mountains in the background, is breathtaking. Unfortunately, the water immediately offshore, while clean, is silty and the coconut trees which used to shade the whole village have been wiped out by the "lethal yellowing" disease advancing inexorably down the coast from Mexico; the disease-resistant variety planted to replace them will take a while to mature.

The **bus** service to Hopkins is a little unpredictable, but there's at least one daily run to and from the village; currently the 11am Z-Line service from Dangriga to Placencia calls in en route – check at your hotel for the current situation. As there are no street names in Hopkins, the best way to locate anything is to describe its position in relation to the point where the road from the Southern Highway enters the village, dividing it roughly into northern and southern halves. The main road heading south through the village is paved, though the asphalt gives way to sand at the southern end; this road continues 5km to **Sittee River** (see opposite). The central road junction is increasingly becoming the village **information centre**: boards and signs point the way to hotels and restaurants and at the *King Casava* restaurant Mark Nuñez welcomes visitors with good information and also runs a **taxi service**. Hopkins is changing fast and there will inevitably be new places and services that we have not been able to mention here.

The *Jabiru Restaurant and Bar*, on the left just before the road from the highway enters the village, is one of the most reliable **places to eat**, with good Creole and Garífuna dishes; owner Anselma Christiana also runs *Over the Waves* restaurant, on the beach in the centre. *Tyson's Diner*, north of the centre, is a tiny, friendly place also serving good, simple Garífuna and Creole meals, while *Iris's Restaurant*, south of the centre, serves great breakfasts, seafood and rice and beans meals. Some of the village bars now have **happy hours** and **live music** — look out for the Hopkins Ayumahani Band — and the *King Casava* restaurant also offers live entertainment at weekends.

## ACCOMMODATION

Hopkins has plenty of **accommodation** in all price ranges, and booking ahead is only really necessary around Christmas, Easter and November 19, Garífuna Settlement Day. There are also several **houses for rent**. An increasing number of hotels also have **bicycles** for guests to use; useful as the village extends so far along the beach.

**Hopkins Inn**, on the beach, south of the centre (☎05/37013, *www.hopkinsinn.com*). Friendly place with four immaculate whitewashed cabins with showers, fridge and coffee-maker. Owners Rita and Greg Duke offer trips on their Super-cat, run snorkel and boat trips and help arrange other activities. Ample continental breakfast included. German spoken. ⑥.

**Ransom's Seaside Garden Cabaña**, south of the centre (☎05/22889). Wonderful, very comfortable two-bedroom cabaña with full kitchen– usually a three-night minimum stay required. Kayaks and bicycles are free for guests and owner Barry Swan also has a one-bedroom furnished wooden house for rent at US$35 per day. ⑨.

**Sandy Beach Lodge**, on the beach, at the south end (☎05/37006). Six simple, spacious, good-value rooms in wood-and-thatch cabins with fan (most with private bath), run by Belize's only women's cooperative. Meals, served at set times, feature seafood cooked in Creole and Garífuna style. ④.

**Seagull's Nest Guest House**, on the beach, south of the centre (☎05/37015). Bargain shared rooms in a wooden house, some with bunk beds for US$10 per person, and a separate, two-room, concrete house with kitchen and balcony. ⑥.

**Swinging Armadillos**, on the beach, 150m north of the centre (☎05/37016). A collection of small, simple bunk rooms (US$10 per person) and one private room, perched over the sea above the small bar and restaurant of the same name. Friendly owner Mike Flores has a boat and a truck for trips and also rents bikes. ④.

**Tania's Guest House**, south of the centre, on the right of the road (☎05/37058 or 014/8829). Although not directly on the beach, this small, friendly hotel is a great bargain. Some rooms have private bath, fan, bedside light and cable TV – and the price quoted includes tax. ③/④.

**Tipple Tree Beya**, on the beach, near the south end (☎051/2006, *tipple@btl.net*). Good-value, neat, clean rooms in a wooden building, one with private bath. A very friendly place, with good information. There's also a furnished wooden house to rent, with fridge and cooker, for US$40 per day or you can camp for US$5 per person. ④/⑤.

**Yugadah Inn**, near the south end, on the beach side of the road (☎05/37089). Four simple, bargain rooms with fan and shared cold-water bath, upstairs in a wooden house run by the friendly Nuñez family. ④.

## Sittee River

**Sittee River** and its banks offer great opportunities for spotting wildlife; apart from the dozens of bird species there are freshwater turtles and crocodiles. It is served by the same buses as Hopkins on the Dangriga/Placencia route, the road from Hopkins passing through the village to connect with the Southern Highway. Most visitors here are on their way to *Glover's Atoll Resort* (see below), but there are a few **places to stay**. The great-value *Toucan Sittee* (☎05/37039; ④), owned by the extremely hospitable Neville and Yoli Collins and set in a beautiful riverbank location, is by far the best accommodation option. The solidly built, well-furnished, wooden cabins have electric light and hot showers, and there are also very comfortable dorm beds (US$9) and camping (US$4). The food is really good, with lots of fresh fruit and vegetables, and they rent **canoes** and **bikes**. Nearby, *Glover's Guest House* (☎051/2016, *glovers@btl.net*; ④), where you check in for the Glover's Reef trip, has dorm beds forUS$8 as well as double rooms. The guest house's restaurant is right on the river-bank and the boat to the atoll ties up outside. If you need to get **supplies** for your trip to Glover's Reef there's Hill Top Farm for vegetables and the well-stocked Reynold's Store for groceries.

# Glover's Reef

The southernmost of Belize's three coral atolls, **Glover's Reef** lies between forty and fifty kilometres off Dangriga. Named after British pirate John Glover, the atoll is roughly oval in shape, about 35km north to south, and its only cayes are in the south-eastern section. Glover's Reef is the best developed and most biologically diverse atoll in the Caribbean, rising from ocean depths of over 600m, with some of the best **wall diving** in the world. Inside the beautiful aquamarine lagoon are hundreds of **patch reefs** – a snorkelling wonderland. All the cayes have nesting ospreys, and Belize's marine turtles nest on the beaches. There are also vitally important grouper spawning grounds on the northeast of the atoll, and immense **whale sharks** – the largest fish in the world – pass through in spring and autumn. These unique features helped to bring about the decision in 1993 to declare the whole atoll a protected area – **Glover's Reef Marine Reserve** – and in 1996 it was designated a World Heritage Site. The atoll is divided into management zones, and no fishing is allowed from any of the cayes. All of the cayes here offer some **accommodation**, mostly in purpose-built camps and cab-ins for **sea-kayaking** groups, though there is one upmarket diving lodge, and on Northeast Caye there are cabins within the reach of budget travellers.

## The cayes

Covered in thick coconut and broadleaf forest, and with evidence of Maya fishing camps, **Northeast Caye** is home to *Glover's Atoll Resort* (☎051/2016 or 014/8351, *www.belizemall.com/gloversatoll*). Owned by the Lomont family, who have lived here for over thirty years, the resort has ten simple, self-catering **beach cabins** overlooking the reef (US$149 per person per week), a dorm room in a wooden house (US$99 per week) and spaces for **camping** (US$80 per week). Rates include transport from Sittee River in the resort's motor/sail boat, *Christmas Bird*, which picks up guests each Sunday morning and leaves the caye the following Saturday; the trip takes up to four hours, longer if under sail. Unless you're in a pre-booked group (in which case you can arrange to be catered for), you'll generally have to bring your own food and make your own meals. Cooking is done on a kerosene stove, or on the barbecue pit nearby, though you can order some meals and basic supplies are available. Five gallons of drinking water (stored rainwater) per person is provided free – you pay if you use more – but **coconuts** are free and contain delicious water. **Activities** (paid for separately) include sea kayaking, fishing, snorkelling, scuba-diving with PADI or NAUI certification, and sailing to the other cayes.

**Long Caye**, just across the channel from Northeast Caye, is the base for the sea-kayak expeditions run by Slickrock Adventures (see *Basics*, p.5). **Accommodation** is in sturdy, comfortable, wooden thatched cabins on stilts, each boasting a deck with ham-mock overlooking the reef, and wonderful meals are served in the spacious new dining room. **Diving** on the caye is provided by Jim Schofield, who runs Off the Wall Diving (☎014/6348, *offthewall@btl.net*), and also has some cabins available for guests. Four kilo-metres to the southwest, **Middle Caye** is in the wilderness zone of the reserve. It's the base for the Fisheries Department **conservation officers**, who rigorously patrol the reserve, and has a marine research and monitoring station and laboratory run by the Wildlife Conservation Society (see p.572 in *Contexts*). You can visit with permission, and there are some interesting displays on the ecology of the atoll.

Southwest Caye, 5km beyond Middle Caye, is the base for the **sea-kayak groups** of Vancouver-based Island Expeditions (see p.6 in *Basics*), with superb guides and an exemplary environmental record. Guests stay in spacious, comfortable white tents and eat gourmet meals in the new, screened dining room. Training is given in paddling and sailing the kayaks, and you can visit the other cayes or even take part in overnight camping expeditions to uninhabited islands. The original caye was sliced into two twelve-acre islands by Hurricane Hattie and on the other part, divided by a narrow channel, is the luxurious *Manta Resort* (in the US ☎1-800/326-1724, *www.mantaresort.com*; ⑨), one of the best-managed resorts in the country, offering **accommodation** in twelve very comfortable a/c wooden cabins, each with private bath and a deck outside with hammocks. **Diving** is the resort's speciality, with three dedicated dive boats and several skiffs available. Packages include boat transfer from Belize City (3hr) and cost around US$1495 for a week's diving, US$1995 for fishing.

# The Cockscomb Basin Wildlife Sanctuary and Maya Center Village

Back on the mainland, the jagged peaks of the **Maya Mountains** rise to the west of the Southern Highway, their lower slopes covered in dense rainforest. The tallest summits are those of the Cockscomb range, which includes **Victoria Peak**, at 1120m the second highest mountain in Belize and a dramatic sight on a clear day. In 1888 the Goldsworthy Expedition made the first recorded successful attempt on the summit of Victoria Peak, though it's reasonably certain that the ancient Maya were first to make it to the top. Beneath the sharp ridges is a sweeping bowl, part of which was declared a **jaguar reserve** in 1986. It has since been expanded to cover an area of over four hundred square kilometres – the **Cockscomb Basin Wildlife Sanctuary**.

Technically, this is a **tropical moist forest**, with an annual rainfall of up to 300cm that feeds a complex network of wonderfully clear streams and rivers, most of which eventually run into the Swasey River and the South Stann Creek; the sanctuary also performs a vital role in watershed protection. The forest is home to a sizeable percentage of **Belize's plant and animal species**. Among the mammals are tapir, otter, coati, deer, anteater, armadillo and, of course, jaguar, as well as all other cat species. Over 290 species of bird have also been recorded, including the endangered scarlet macaw, the great curassow, the keel-billed toucan and the king vulture. It is particularly important as a refuge for the largest raptors, including the solitary eagle and the white hawk eagle. There's also an abundance of reptiles and amphibians, including the red-eyed tree frog, the boa constrictor and the deadly fer-de-lance snake (known as "tommy-goff" in Belize). The forest itself is made up of a fantastic range of plant species, including orchids, giant tree ferns, air plants (epiphytes) and trees such as *banak*, *cohune*, mahogany and ceiba. The sanctuary is managed by the Belize Audubon Society, with some financial assistance from WWF, WCS and Jaguar cars.

The area was inhabited in Maya times, and the ruins of **Kuchil Balam**, a Classic-period ceremonial centre, still lie hidden in the forest. It was also exploited by the mahogany loggers; the names of their abandoned camps, such as Leave If You Can and Go to Hell, illustrate how they felt about life in the forest. In more recent times the residents of Quam Bank, a logging camp and Mopan Maya village, moved out of the Cockscomb when the reserve was established, relocating to the village of Maya Center on the Southern Highway.

## Maya Center practicalities

All buses heading south from Dangriga pass **MAYA CENTER** village (45min), from where a rough ten-kilometre track leads to the sanctuary headquarters. You need to sign in and pay the reserve entrance fee (US$5) at the thatched **craft centre** at the road junction. Run by the village women's group, there's **information** about accommodation in the reserve and good, well-priced slate carvings and embroidery. Just beyond, the small **shop** run by Julio Saqui (see also below) sells basic supplies and cold drinks, including beer. The families in Maya Center are a few of the totally genuine proponents of the concept of "eco-tourism", and staying here is a perfect way to learn about the life of the forest and experience Maya culture. You can also spot lots of wildlife along the adjacent **Cabbage Haul Creek** – it's particularly good for bird-watching.

Although many tour operators will tell you that you can't get into the Jaguar Reserve without going on a tour, you can easily walk in from Maya Center – it takes a couple of hours or so along the gentle uphill slope, and you can leave any excess luggage with Julio at his shop. For the best experience, though, don't go it alone – the people of Maya Center know the reserve intimately, and are by far the best **guides** around. If you've come by bus and don't fancy the walk you can **ride in** with *Julio's Cultural and Jungle Tours* (☎051/2020), or check with his brothers Ernesto and Liberato, each of whom also offers accommodation and guide services (see below). A pick-up ride is aroundUS$15, and you can share the cost.

There are a couple of friendly, inexpensive and good-value **places to stay** in Maya Center, and sometimes houses available to rent. Just behind the craft centre Liberato and Yoli Saqui run *Mejen Tz'il Lodge* (☎051/2020, *lsaqui@btl.net*), a large, wooden cabin with dorm rooms for US$8 per person. Yoli serves great **meals** and you can rent **tents** here for use on the Victoria Peak Trail. At the end of the village, 500m up the track to the reserve, Ernesto and Aurora Saqui run *Nu'uk Che'il* (Mayan for "in the middle of the forest") *Cottages* (☎ & fax 051/2021, *nuukcheil@btl.net*, ④), simple but delightful thatched cabañas, with electric light, fan and shared shower; there's also a dorm room with beds for US$8. The **restaurant**, serving Maya and Belizean food, is a great place to get a filling meal on your way to or from the reserve. Aurora is one of the Garcia sisters from San Antonio, Cayo (see p.271), and has developed a medicinal trail (US$2) in the forest next to the cottages; she also makes **traditional herbal medicines**, for sale in the H'men Herbal Center. Owners of either of the above places can arrange **guides** and supplies for the Victoria Peak Trail, as can Greg Sho, the most experienced guide in Maya Center, and one of the best bush and river kayak guides in the country. Greg and his wife Celestina run *Greg's Bar*, on the highway, just before the reserve entrance: the bar is a great place to wait for buses. Finally, Raul Balona is another very experienced guide.

## The Jaguar Reserve

At the sanctuary headquarters, in a cleared grassy area surrounded by beautiful tropical foliage, there's an excellent **visitor centre**, with a model of the Cockscomb Basin, displays on the area's ecology, and maps and trail guides; you can also pick up a copy of *Cockscomb Basin Wildlife Sanctuary*, a superb and detailed guide to the history, flora and fauna of the reserve. There's comfortable dorm **accommodation** here in two styles: the old huts for US$7.50, and a newer, purpose-built dorm (US$17 per person) behind the main buildings; there are also comfortable rooms (⑤) and a **campground** (US$2.50) a little further on. If you're not on a group tour you'll have to bring your own food and cook it on the gas stove.

Although the basin could be home to as many as fifty of Belize's six-hundred-strong **jaguar population**, your chances of seeing one are very slim. However, it's an ideal environment for plant-spotting, serious bird-watching or for seeking out other elusive wildlife, and the trail system in the Cockscomb is the best developed in any of Belize's protected areas. **Inner tubes** are available from the ranger's office; walk upstream and float down for an amazingly tranquil view of the forest. The **Ben's Bluff Trail** is a strenuous but worthwhile four-kilometre hike from the riverside to the crest of a forested ridge – where there's a great view of the entire Cockscomb Basin – with a chance to cool off in a delightful rocky pool on the way back. If you're suitably prepared, you can climb Victoria Peak – a two-day hike each way – with backcountry **campsites** prepared by Trekforce volunteers.

# The Placencia peninsula

Sixteen kilometres south of Maya Center, a good dirt road heads east from the Southern Highway through pine forest and banana plantations for 13km, reaching the sea at the tiny settlement of **Riversdale**. This marks the start of the **PLACENCIA PENINSULA**, a narrow, sandy finger of land separating the Caribbean and Placencia Lagoon and curving down 26km to **Placencia**, a small, laid-back fishing village, light years from the hassle of Belize City, and now catering to an increasing number of tourists. As you travel south down the peninsula you'll pass a dozen or so (mostly upscale) **resorts and hotels**, most of them owned and operated by expatriate North Americans. Accommodation is usually in cabins with private bathrooms and electricity. In addition to the pleasures of a Caribbean beach just a few steps away, most of the resorts also have access to Placencia Lagoon, and can arrange diving trips and tours inland to the Jaguar Reserve and several Maya ruins.

## Maya Beach and Seine Bight

The first of the peninsula's resorts are in **MAYA BEACH**, a beautiful stretch of coast with white sand beaches, halfway to Placencia. All the hotels here, listed below in the order you approach them from the north, are right by the road and have mains electricity; more details can be found on Maya Beach's own **website**: *www.gotobelize.com*

*Maya Beach Hotel* (☎06/12040; *mayabch@btl.net*; ⑦) has spacious, modern rooms overlooking the beach, with queen-sized beds, private bath and tiled floors. This is also the location of the *Maya Beach Sports Bar and Grill*, and hotel prices include breakfast. *Barnacle Bill's Beach Bungalows* (☎06/37010, *taylors@btl.net*; ⑧) are two large, very well-equipped wooden houses on stilts on a beautiful sandy beach, run by friendly US expats Bill and Adriane Taylor. Each house has a double bedroom, bathroom with tub, living room with sofa bed and a great kitchen. A kilometre south of *Barnacle Bill's* are the six lovely, wood-and-thatch cabins of *Singing Sands Inn* (☎ & fax 06/22243, in the US 1-800/649-3007, *ssi@btl.net*; ⑧). There's a good restaurant here, especially for vegetarians, as well as a bar, a pool and bikes for guests. Owner Marti Cottrell offers a massage service and also has an apartment for longer rentals. Another kilometre south brings you to *Maya Playa* (☎06/37010, *mayaplaya@btl.net*; ⑦), four palmetto and thatch A-frame cabañas in a beautiful beachfront location. Friendly owner Chuck Meares has built a very tall *palapa* on the beach for his kitchen and dining room and guests are welcome to cook and eat their meals there.

Three kilometres beyond Maya Beach the Garífuna village of **SEINE BIGHT** now has several resorts and hotels, some of which look out of place alongside the often dilapidated shacks in the village, though the main road has now been paved. If you do plan to **stay overnight** the budget *Effie's Guest House* (☎06/24056; ④) is the nicest place in the village, with clean, simple rooms with shared bath in a wooden house on the beach; friendly owner Effie Hill prepares delicious meals in her house across the road. There are several **bars and restaurants** to choose between: you can play pool in the *Sunshine Bar* or listen to Garífuna music and drumming in the *Kulcha Shak* (which also has basic but overpriced rooms). Further south, at the back of the soccer field, are *Lola's Art Gallery* and *Laguñedu Café and Cat's Claw Bar*, where Lola Delgado displays her superb (and affordable) oil and acrylic paintings of village life. Lola is a great cook and her superb Creole or Garífuna dinners are followed by drumming, singing and dancing, with Lola's husband, Eddy V, playing keyboards in his Banana Patch Sound Machine. It's a good evening but you'll need to check when she's cooking – call ☎014/2435 first.

## Resorts from Seine Bight to Placencia

Beyond Seine Bight another series of resorts offers upscale **accommodation**, listed below in the order you approach them from the north. Even though they're pricey, most places will give *Rough Guide* readers worthwhile discounts. All the places listed also have **restaurants** that are among the best in the country, and you'll usually need to book for dinner.

**The Inn at Robert's Grove** (☎06/23565, *www.robertsgrove.com*), 1km south of Seine Bight. Luxury resort with spacious, well-designed, a/c rooms and suites overlooking the beach, the sea and the pool. The top-class international restaurant has the only temperature-controlled wine cellar in Belize. Doubles US$150, including breakfast. ⑨.

**Serenity Resort**, on the beach 2km south of Seine Bight (☎06/23232, *serenity@btl.net*). Twelve large, comfortable, sky-blue cabins with patio, and a 10-bedroom hotel with a conference centre. There's a good restaurant, with panoramic views from the roof, and the lagoon-side *Bamboo Room Bar* features live music. ⑧.

**Rum Point Inn**, just north of the airstrip, 4km from Placencia (☎06/23239, fax 23240, in US ☎1-800/747-1381, *www.rumpoint.com*). Expert naturalists Corol and George Bevier offer some of the most sumptuous (and expensive) rooms on the peninsula. The unique, giant mushroom-shaped whitewashed cabins, with windows cut into the roof and plants growing inside, are spacious, cool and very comfortable, and the enormous suites have the biggest bathrooms in the country. There's also a pool, to help with dive instruction, and the library, with an emphasis on archeology, science and natural history, is the best of any hotel in Belize. Doubles US$175. ⑨.

**Kitty's Place**, just south of the airstrip (☎06/23227, *www.kittysplace.com*). Conveniently near the village and one of the nicest options in this area, with a variety of really comfortable accommodation including apartments, beach cabañas and rooms in a couple of colonial-style houses on the beach. The grounds and views are unbeatable and the atmosphere is sublime. Kitty also has several fully equipped houses and apartments, from US$300–800 per week. The *Sand Bar*, on the beach, has a Friday evening happy hour, and the restaurant serves delicious Belizean and international food. ⑥–⑨.

**Blancaneaux Turtle Inn**, 1km north of the village (☎06/23244, in US ☎1-800/746-3743, *www.blan-caneauxlodge.com*). Luxurious and spacious wood-and-thatch cabañas and villas with tiled bathrooms and kitchen, on a gorgeous, palm-lined beach. This superb, upscale resort has just been purchased by Francis Ford Coppola, who owns *Blancaneaux Lodge* in Cayo (see p.273), and some changes are planned – already renowned for diving, fishing and jungle tours, it's likely to move even more upmarket. Cabañas US$145. ⑨.

## Placencia

Perched on the tip of the peninsula, shaded by palm trees and cooled by the sea breeze, **PLACENCIA** is a welcome stop after the bus ride from Belize City or Dangriga. It is also one of the few places in mainland Belize with proper beaches, and this, together with the abundant, inexpensive accommodation, makes it a great place to relax. Unfortunately the distance from the reef puts many of the tours out of the reach of travellers on a low budget, though more options are becoming available.

The easiest way to reach Placencia is on one of the regular Maya Island or Tropic Air **flights** from the international or municipal airports (about 45min). Much cheaper are the direct **buses from Dangriga**, which leave at 11.30am and 5.30pm. You can also hop over easily on the regular **boat service** from **Independence/Mango Creek**, the small town just across the lagoon, where residents come to buy supplies and the older children go to school. For full transport details in Independence, see p.301.

### Arrival, orientation and information

**Buses** from Dangriga end up at the beachfront gas station, right at the end of the peninsula (they return between 5am and 7am – but check locally for times of next morning's departures). If you're **flying** in, there's usually a taxi (US$10, and you can share the cost) waiting to take you to the village; if not it's only a three-minute walk to

*Kitty's* where you can call BJ's Taxi (☎06/23131) or check when the next **Placencia Shuttle** bus service, which stops on the road outside (☎014/3928; US$2.50 one way, US$4 return), is heading in. **Boats** from Independence (see p.301), Belize City and Puerto Cortés arrive at the main dock, by the gas station; walk to the end of the dock and the sidewalk (see below) will be to your right. The *Gulf Cruza*, a large fast covered skiff, leaves Placencia for **Puerto Cortés**, Honduras (4hr, US$50; see p.502), each Friday at 9.30am, going first to **Big Creek**, where you clear immigration: the onward journey from Big Creek to Puerto Cortés is only two hours and thirty minutes. The *Cruza* returns to Placencia on Monday, leaving for Belize City (3hr; Bz$50) at 2.30pm. If you're looking for **budget rooms** you should get off the bus when you see the sign for the *Seaspray Hotel*, about halfway through the village, on the left-hand side of the road. Head for **the sidewalk**, a concrete walkway that winds through the palms like an elongated garden path, and you'll be at the centre of a cluster of hotels and restaurants.

The **Placencia tourism center** (Mon–Fri 8.30–11.30am & 1–5pm, Sat 8.30–11.30am; ☎06/24045, *placencia@btl.net*) is the best place to check anything on offer locally – from scuba diving to Garifuna drumming – and you can call hotels from here. For a full listing of everything in the village and the peninsula, pick up a copy of *Placencia Breeze* (US$0.25), the best tourist newspaper in Belize, or visit the peninsula's excellent **website**, *www.placencia.com*. The Atlantic **bank** (Mon–Thurs 8am–2pm, Fri 8am–4pm), across from the main dock by the gas station, can deal swiftly with cash advances. The **post office** is upstairs in the wooden building at the end of the sidewalk; the **BTL office** is by the sidewalk in the centre of the village and there are several payphones around. The *Purple Space Monkey* (also a restaurant), in a large thatched building on the roadside opposite the soccer field, provides first-class **email and Internet** connections. There's no travel agent as such in the village, but many of the hotels and all the tour operators can book **domestic flights**. The best self-service **shops** in the village are Wallen's Market, by the soccer field, and Olga's, just before the gas station, and if your hotel doesn't offer **laundry service**, then follow the signs to Cara's Laundry. Several **gift shops** provide souvenir opportunities and One World, next to the sidewalk south of the centre, sells *Rough Guides*.

## Accommodation

There's a wide choice of **accommodation** in the village, and you should have no problem finding a room provided you don't arrive at Christmas, New Year or Easter without a booking. If you want a **house to rent** bear in mind that plenty of the hotels below (and along the peninsula) also manage houses and self-catering apartments. One of the best-value places is offered by Ted Berlin (☎06/23172), who, in addition to being a qualified acupuncturist, has a couple of simple but charming places to rent for around US$125 per week; also worth trying are *Be Back Cabins* (☎06/23143; ④), on the left just before the end of the road, comprising three small houses on stilts with basic kitchen, including fridge. For more upmarket houses, see the entry for *Kitty's Place* on p.298.

### BUDGET ACCOMMODATION

**Cozy Corner Hotel** (☎06/23280, *www.cozycornerhotel.com*), on the beach in the centre of the village. Good-value, spacious ground-floor rooms with tiled floors and private bath and a big wooden deck all round. There's a good restaurant here, too. ④.

**Deb & Dave's Last Resort**, on the road, the bus will stop outside (☎06/23207, *debanddave@btl.net*). The nicest budget place in the village: lovely, very comfortable wooden rooms with a shared, clean bathroom. You can rent bikes and kayaks here and Dave is a superb tour guide. ④.

**Julia's Guest House**, in the centre of the village, just south of the *Seaspray* (☎06/23185). Simple, very clean rooms with shared bath in the older building with porch near the sidewalk, and newer rooms with private bath on the beach. ③–④.

**Lydia's Guest House**, near the north end of the sidewalk (☎06/23354, *lydias@btl.net*). Great-value, quiet, clean, secure rooms in two wooden houses, run by the very friendly Lydia Villanueva, who'll cook breakfast on request. Also a good house for rent. ④.

**Paradise Vacation Resort**, follow the path to the right from the end of the sidewalk, at the main dock (☎06/23260, *glenmar@btl.net*). Very good value, two-storey hotel. Most rooms have private bath, and there's a large deck upstairs where you can enjoy the breeze. ③.

**Seaspray Hotel**, on the beach in the centre of the village (☎ & fax 06/23148, *seaspray@btl.net*). A popular, well-run hotel with a range of accommodation, from budget rooms to a private cabin, all with private bath and some with refrigerator and balcony. Owners Jodie and Norman Leslie can arrange tours and give reliable information. ③–⑤.

**Traveller's Inn**, signed from the sidewalk, just south of the centre (☎06/23190). Five basic but comfortable rooms – the cheapest in the village – with shared bath and tiny communal porch under Maurice and Lucille Villanueva's house, plus some with private bath in a separate building. Also a house for rent. ③–⑤.

## MID-RANGE AND ABOVE

**Barracuda and Jaguar Inn**, signed just past the market, towards the south end of the village (☎06/23330, fax 23250, *www.barracudajaguarinn.com*). Two varnished wooden cabins with double beds, private bath, fridge and coffee-maker, set in luxuriant tropical gardens. It's Placencia's best value in this range and has good information. Rates include breakfast, there's no credit card surcharge and a discount if you book using the *Rough Guide*. Also a spacious, fully furnished two-bedroom apartment for rent. ⑤–⑦.

**Coconut Cottage**, on the beach, just south of the centre (☎06/23155, *kwplacencia@yahoo.com*). Two gorgeous, well-decorated and immaculately clean cabins in a quiet location, equipped with fridge, coffee-maker and hot-water shower; very popular, so you'll need to book in advance. ⑥.

**Harry's Cozy Cabañas**, 300m west from the south dock, turn right at the gas station (☎ & fax 06/23155, *harbaks@yahoo.com*). Spacious wooden cabins on stilts with a screened porch on a lovely, quiet little beach. Each cabin has a double and single bed, a fridge and coffee-maker, and one has a small kitchen. The plant-filled gardens are an iguana sanctuary – and according to Harry, relaxing with a Belikin under his "Tree of Knowledge" actually does impart wisdom. ⑥.

**Merlene's Apartment**, west from the south dock, turn right at the gas station (☎06/23210). The best studio apartment in the village, with a double and a single bed and a kitchen with a huge fridge and stove. The balcony along the front lets you watch the sunrise over Placencia Caye. Rates include breakfast. ⑥.

**Ranguana Lodge**, on the beach in the centre of the village (☎ & fax 06/23112, *www.ranguanabelize.com*). Five beautiful white cabañas with porches and hammocks, with a hardwood interior. All have comfortable beds, a fridge and coffee-maker. This is the place to book for Ranguana Caye, an idyllic island on the reef. ⑥.

**Serenade Guest House**, (☎06/23163, fax 24074, *wwwbelizecayes.com*), on the sidewalk south of the centre. Good-value rooms with private bath, some with a/c, in a large, white-painted concrete building. This is where you book for Frank's Caye (see p.309). ⑥.

**Trade Winds Cabañas**, on the south point (☎06/23122, fax 23201, *trdewndpla@btl.net*). Six brightly painted cabins and three rooms with private bath, fridge, coffee-maker, and deck with hammocks, on the largest and sandiest beach in the village. Run by Janice Leslie, Placencia's former postmistress and owner of the *J-Byrd Bar* who's a mine of local knowledge. ⑤/⑥.

## Eating, drinking and nightlife

There are plenty of good **restaurants** in Placencia, though even more than elsewhere in Belize, places change management fast, so it's always worth asking a resident's advice first. There are also a number of good restaurants at the resorts along the peninsula, and it may be worth sharing a cab to try somewhere different. Most places close early; you'll certainly have a better choice if you're at the table by 8pm. Fresh **bread** is available from John The Bakerman, just north of the market, and from a number of local women who bake jonny cakes, Creole bread and buns. The best-value food counter in Placencia, serving fried chicken and rice and beans, doesn't even have a name but it's easy to find: just turn left at the end of the road and ask for Pearl.

The **evenings** in Placencia are as relaxed as the days and there are plenty of **bars**, ideal for drinking rum and watching the sun set; an increasing number have **live music** to enhance the party mood. The *J-Byrd Bar* (with adjacent gift shop) run by Janice Leslie of *Trade Winds*, by the south dock, is open all day and often has live music at weekends. One of the best beachfront locations is the *Cozy Corner* (in front of the hotel of the same name), with a deck and tables under the palms, while nearby, on the sidewalk, the *Sunrise* has a band at weekends. Turn right at the sign by the soccer field for *Lagoon Saloon*, a favourite meeting place at the south end of the village; it closes early though, so is best for an early evening drink.

## RESTAURANTS

**BJ's Restaurant**, by the road junction just past the soccer field. The best value Belizean food in the village at genuine Belizean prices, with friendly service in clean surroundings.

**Daisy's Ice Cream Parlour**, set back from the sidewalk, just south of the *Seaspray*. Long-established and deservedly popular place for ice cream, cakes and snacks, also serving complete meals.

**Merlene's Restaurant**, beneath her apartment (see "Accommodation", opposite; ☎06/23210). Great for breakfast (usually the first to open), serving good coffee and fantastic home-made bread and fry-jacks. Lunch and dinner are equally good, especially for fish, but it's tiny so you may have to book. Merlene is exuberantly friendly and is renowned for her cakes – if you have a birthday to celebrate, ask if she can make one for you.

**Pickled Parrot Bar & Grill**, at the *Barracuda and Jaguar Inn*. Very friendly place under a big thatched roof. Consistently the best restaurant in the village and deservedly popular, serving fresh seafood, great pizza, pastas and salads with a daily special. The bar has wonderful tropical blender drinks. Closed Sun.

**Purple Space Monkey Internet Café** (*psmonkey@yahoo.co.uk*), opposite the soccer field. Well-connected computers and good coffee, breakfasts and burgers under a huge thatched roof. Opens early and closes late.

**Tentacles**, built over the water at the south end of the village, in front of the *Dockside Bar*. The large deck on stilts is a superb spot to enjoy the sunset. Good steaks, pasta, seafood and a weekend barbecue. Closed Thurs.

---

### INDEPENDENCE TRAVEL CONNECTIONS

Just across the lagoon from Placencia, **Independence**, though of little intrinsic interest, is a useful travel hub, served by all **buses** between Dangriga and Punta Gorda. There's a regular **boat to Placencia** – the *Hokey Pokey* (☎06/22376; 35min; Bz$10 one way) – which leaves Independence at 8.30am and 2.30pm, returning from Placencia at 10am and 4pm; the boatman usually meets the arriving buses. Otherwise, if you wait around for a while, you may be able to get a lift on a boat with a Placencia local. The fare depends on what you're willing to pay – reckon on around US$7.50 if you're sharing. A charter costs at least US$18.

**Heading north** from Independence, Z-Line buses leave for **Dangriga** (2hr) at 7am, 10am and 1pm, and south to **Punta Gorda** (2hr 30min) at 1pm, 6pm and 8pm. The James bus also passes through three or four times daily in each direction; it's always best to check times first: ☎05/22160 for Z-Line and ☎07/22049 for James. Z-Line buses take a rest/meal stop at the *Café Hello* in Independence; the James bus stops at *Marita's* across the way on Hercules Avenue.

With all these transport connections you should be able to avoid getting stuck **overnight** here. If you do, the *Hello Hotel* (☎06/22428; ⑥), mainly used by banana business people, has some a/c rooms; you could also try the clean, simple *Ursula's Guest House* (③) on Gran Main Street.

# Around Placencia, offshore and inland

Trips from Placencia can be tailor-made to your preference and perhaps your pocket, and you can arrange anything from an afternoon on the water to a week of camping, fishing, snorkelling and sailing. The main reef lies about 30km offshore; this distance means that snorkelling and diving trips are more expensive here than at many other places in Belize. Here are the exquisitely beautiful **Silk Cayes**, now a marine reserve, where the Barrier Reef begins to break into several smaller reefs and cayes. There are also many smaller islands and coral heads closer to the shore. Among them are the **Bugle Cayes** and **Lark Caye**, while many trips take in uninhabited **Laughing Bird Caye National Park**. **Gladden Spit**, a promontory on the reef east of the Silk Cayes, has been designated a **marine reserve** to protect the seasonal visitation of the enormous yet graceful **whale shark**, attracted here during the late spring full moons by huge numbers of spawning snappers.

**Day-boat-trips** to the cayes are offered by several operators (the best are listed below) and cost around US$33–45, depending on the location; usually this includes lunch and sometimes snorkelling equipment. All **tour guides** in Belize are licensed and anyone taking you to see whale sharks will have undergone special training in how to approach the sharks without harming them or disturbing their feeding. **Diving or snorkelling** at the cayes or along the reef is excellent, with shallow fringing and patch reefs, and some fantastic wall diving. In the village Aquatic Adventures (☎ & fax 06/23182, *glenmar@btl.net*), run by Glen and Martha Eiley from the dock in front of the *Paradise Hotel*, offers the best diving instruction, excursions and equipment rental. PADI or NAUI open-water certification costs US$350, and a two-tank dive trip is US$65. For snorkelling trips to the cayes or **manatee-watching** check with Nite Wind Guides at the end of the sidewalk (☎06/23487).

**Placencia Lagoon** is ideal for exploring in a **canoe or kayak**, available at some hotels (US$15 per day, and sometimes included in the room price). Dave Vernon, who runs Toadal Adventure (☎06/23207, *www.toadaladventure.com*), is one of the best tour guides in Belize. In addition to his natural history trips he's also a superb river and ocean kayak guide; tours cost between US$20 and US$50 and you can rent a top-range double kayak for US$40 per day. Dave also rents **mountain bikes** and an increasing number of hotels also rent bikes to guests. Other very good kayak and fishing guides are Jimmy and Ali Westby, of Deja Vu Charters (☎06/23300, *pladejavu@btl.net*). Check with *Kitty's Place* (which also has good-quality kayaks and bikes for rent) about **live-aboard sailing** on the *Ocean Gypsy*, a comfortable 34-foot **catamaran**.

The waters off Placencia are rich in fish, and the village boasts a number of renowned **fishing guides**. Among the best are Bernard Leslie who runs Ocean Motion (☎06/23162), from a small office near the southern end of the sidewalk, and Earl and Kurt Godfey of Southern Guide (☎06/23433). It's also worth **heading inland** from Placencia – up the thickly forested banks of the **Monkey River** (see below) or to the **Jaguar Reserve** (see p.296). Incidentally, although many tour operators offer day-trips to the Jaguar Reserve, it's quite feasible to do the trip independently by bus, leaving Placencia in the early morning and returning on the afternoon bus from Dangriga as it passes Maya Center (see p.295).

## The Monkey River

One of the best inland day-trips from Placencia takes you by boat 20km southwest to the almost pristine **Monkey River**, teeming with fish, birdlife, turtles and, naturally enough, **howler monkeys**. Monkey River Magic (☎06/23330 or 014/4452) runs the best **tours** (US$45, minimum two people), led by Evaristo Muschamp, a very experienced local guide. Tours from Placencia leave from the dock by the gas station at

7.30am. A thirty-minute dash through the waves is followed by a leisurely glide up the river and a walk along forest trails. Binoculars are essential if you want to make the most of the amazing **bird-watching** here and on the journey.

Lunch is taken on a sandbank in the river if you're bringing a picnic, or you can get a meal in *Alice's Restaurant* in **MONKEY RIVER TOWN** (in reality a tiny village). There's also time to enjoy a stroll around the village and have a drink at one of three **bars**. If you want **to stay**, there's *Enna's Hotel* (☎061/2033; ④), which has decent basic rooms, shared bathrooms and 24-hour electricity, or the *Sunset Inn* (☎061/2028; ④) with rooms in a two-storey wooden building with comfortable beds, private bath and fan, overlooking the river. Owner Martha Garbutt serves tasty Creole food in the restaurant and her son Clive is an excellent guide. Another good guide from the village is Eloy Cuevas (☎06/22014), who's also one of the best **fly-fishing guides** in Belize.

On the coast just north of the mouth of the Monkey River, a couple of places offer **accommodation**. The best is *The Monkey House* (☎061/2032, in US ☎409/755-1659, *www.belizemonkeyhouse.com*; ⑦), on the shore only 300m north of the village. Run by Americans Sam and Martha Scott, there are two very pleasant wooden cabins with private bath, each with a screened porch; the dining room is just yards from the sea and the food is great.

# The far south: Toledo District

South of the Placencia and Independence junctions, the Southern Highway leaves the banana plants and the grim settlements squashed beside the plantation roads, twisting at first through pine forests, and crossing numerous creeks and rivers. There are only a few villages along the way, and new citrus plantations are frequently in view, the neat ranks of trees marching over the hills. The mountains to the west are all part of the country's system of forest reserves, national parks and nature reserves, though conflicts over the status of some protected areas are emerging as **Toledo District** (whose residents often feel they live in Belize's "forgotten district") becomes more developed. Wildlife is abundant but the reserves are often inaccessible, though on the northern border of Toledo, at **RED BANK**, you can see one of the largest concentrations of **scarlet macaws** in Central America. There's currently no regular transport to Red Bank; for details on staying or visiting contact the Programme for Belize or the Belize Audubon Society in Belize City (see p.208), or call the Red Bank **community telephone** (☎06/22233).

Although the Maya of Belize are a fairly small minority within the country as a whole, in Toledo the two main groups – Mopan and Kekchí – make up about half the population. For the most part they live in simple villages, very similar in appearance to their Guatemalan counterparts; the verdant, mountainous landscape of the far south resembles that of Guatemala's Alta Verapaz and southern Petén, where the ancestors of many of Belize's modern-day Maya came from. The biggest of the Maya villages are **San Antonio** and **San Pedro Columbia**, reached by a good side road heading west from the highway.

There's plenty of evidence that the ancient Maya lived here too, with ruins scattered in the hills around the villages. The best-known site is **Lubaantun**, where the famous Crystal Skull was "discovered", but **Nim Li Punit**, with some impressive stelae, is an easy visit from the highway. The Southern Highway ends in **Punta Gorda**, the southernmost town in Belize and the only town in Toledo. It's the base for visits to both the inland villages and the southernmost cayes, and is connected to **Puerto Barrios** in Guatemala (see p.422) by several daily skiffs.

## South to Punta Gorda: Nim Li Punit

About 73km from the Placencia junction, near the Maya village of **Indian Creek**, are the ruins of **Nim Li Punit** (daily 8am–4pm; US$2.50), a Late Classic period Maya site probably allied to nearby Lubaantun. It's an easy, very worthwhile visit from the road, only a kilometre west of the highway and well signposted, so it's often included on tour itineraries and any passing bus will stop by the entrance; ask caretakers Placido Ash or Pedro Sam to show you around. The site is home to the largest and one of the best-preserved stelae in Belize and recent restoration work has revealed many more features. The new **Stela House and Visitor Centre** protects some of the best stelae and provides explanations – in Kekchí and English – of some of the texts carved on them.

The site lies on a ridge with views over the maize fields of the village to the entire southern coastal plain beyond – a scene largely unchanged since ancient times. A total of 25 stelae were found here, eight of them carved. **Stela 14**, at almost 10m high, is the tallest in Belize, and one of the tallest anywhere in the Maya World – although it was never erected. You enter the site through a plaza surrounded by walls and buildings of cut stones held together without mortar, a characteristic of sites in southern Belize, and pass through the ball court to the South Group, which holds most of the carved stelae. Although Stela 14 is now in the Stela House, it's still an impressive sight, with panels of glyphs above and a richly attired ruler below: it's his elaborate headdress that gives Nim Li Punit its name, being Kekchí for "big hat". **Stela 15**, dated to 721 AD and the earliest stela here, is slightly smaller yet even more impressive. Carvings on this great sandstone slab depict a larger-than-life figure in the act of dropping an offering – perhaps *copal* incense or kernels of corn – into an elaborately carved burning brazier supported on the back of a monster. To his right, a much smaller figure also makes an offering into the brazier, while on his left side a column of very clear glyphs separates the main figure from an attendant, or guard; all three figures are almost entirely surrounded by panels of glyphs.

Across the road from the track to the site, and a short distance south, *Nim Li Punit Cabins and Guesthouse* (☎02/36324 or 071/2004, *www.belizelodge.com*; ⑧✉ has **accommodation** in shared-bath rooms (US$28 per person) and private rooms in wooden cabins. From here you can take **hiking** trips into the forest and **boat trips** along the river and into Port Honduras Marine Reserve with naturalist guides. The junction from the Southern Highway to **San Antonio and the Maya villages** is 17km south of Indian Creek – marked by a gas station at a place called "The Dump"; beyond here the road is smooth and fast all the way into Punta Gorda, 21km to the south.

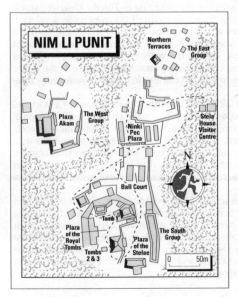

## Punta Gorda

The Southern Highway eventually comes to an end in **PUNTA GORDA** (commonly known as PG), the heart of the isolated Toledo District. The few visitors who make it out here are rewarded by spending a few days at the Maya villages inland (see pp.309–313), where you can experience a way of life far removed from the rest of Belize. Punta Gorda's position on low sea cliffs allows cooling breezes to reduce the worst of the heat but there's no denying that this is the wettest part of Belize. The trees are heavy with mosses and bromeliads, their lush growth encouraged by heavy rains which can last for days. Offshore, the **Sapodilla Cayes** and **Port**

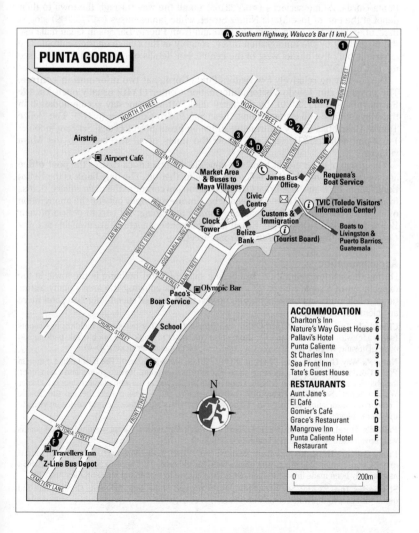

**PUNTA GORDA**

A. *Southern Highway, Waluco's Bar (1 km)*

NORTH STREET
NORTH STREET
Bakery
B

Airstrip
Airport Café
C
2
3
King Street
4 D
5

Market Area
& Buses to
Maya Villages

James Bus
Office

Requena's
Boat Service

Civic
Centre

Customs &
Immigration

TVIC (Toledo Visitors'
Information Center)

E
Clock
Tower

Belize
Bank

(Tourist Board)

Boats to
Livingston &
Puerto Barrios,
Guatemala

Paco's
Boat Service

Olympic Bar

School

6

N

Travellers Inn
Z-Line Bus Depot

**ACCOMMODATION**
Charlton's Inn                    2
Nature's Way Guest House    6
Pallavi's Hotel                     4
Punta Caliente                     7
St Charles Inn                      3
Sea Front Inn                       1
Tate's Guest House             5

**RESTAURANTS**
Aunt Jane's                         E
El Café                                 C
Gomier's Café                     A
Grace's Restaurant             D
Mangrove Inn                      B
Punta Caliente Hotel           F
Restaurant

0                    200m

**Honduras** form the focus of Belize's newest **marine reserves**. Punta Gorda's population of around four thousand is a mixture of Mestizos, Garífuna, Maya and Creoles, with a few Lebanese and Chinese as well – and is the focal point for a large number of villages and farming settlements. Saturday is the busiest day, when people from the surrounding villages come in to trade. Despite the recent minor building boom, Punta Gorda remains a small, unhurried, friendly town and you won't encounter any hassle.

## Arrival and information

**Buses** from Belize City, all via Dangriga, take around seven or eight hours to reach Punta Gorda; Z-Line services (☎07/22165) go all the way through the town to their depot at the end of José María Nuñez Street, while James buses (☎07/22049) stop at their office near the main dock. Skiffs to and from Puerto Barrios in Guatemala use the main dock by the immigration office, roughly in the centre on the seafront. The airstrip is only five blocks west of the centre. For details of moving on from PG, see the box on p.307.

Despite having relatively few visitors Punta Gorda has two **information centres**. The privately run Toledo Visitors Information Center (TVIC; usually open Tues & Fri mornings; ☎07/22470), by the ferry dock, offers homestay accommodation in the Maya village and a guest house near San Pedro Columbia (p.312). The Belize Tourist Board has a very informative office on Front Street (Tues–Sat 8am–noon & 1–5.30pm; ☎07/22531); staff will know the times of all the buses to the Maya villages.

The group of government buildings opposite the main dock houses the **post office** and a **public phone**; the BTL office is a block further on. The only **bank** is the Belize Bank (Mon–Fri 8am–1pm, Fri also 2–4pm) at the top corner of the main square, across from the Civic Center. There will usually be a **moneychanger** outside the immigration office when the international boats are coming and going; it's best to get rid of your Belize dollars before you leave. **Email and Internet** connections are available at *Cyber Café*, just past the *Sea Front Inn* on Front Street.

## Accommodation

During the last few years there has been a spate of **hotel** building in the town, in the expectation of a rapid rise in the number of visitors enjoying the area's many attractions. While numbers have increased, however, few people spend long here, and there are plenty of bargains.

**Charlton's Inn**, 9 Main St (☎07/22197, *charlstin@btl.net*). This two-storey building has rooms (some a/c) with private bath and TV; there's also cold water to drink. The *Inn* has safe parking and owner Duwane Wagner can arrange car rental and sell domestic air tickets. ④–⑥.

**Nature's Way Guest House**, 65 Front St (☎07/22119, *beowulf@btl.net*). The best budget option in Punta Gorda; renowned as a meeting place and information point. Private rooms and clean, comfortable dorm accommodation (US$9). Good meals are served in the wholefood restaurant. Owner William "Chet" Schmidt, a committed environmentalist and a driving force behind the Toledo Ecotourism Association, has been in PG for over thirty years and offers the best advice on visits to the Maya villages. ③.

**Pallavi's Hotel**, 19 Main St (☎22414), next to *Grace's Restaurant*. Clean, good-value tiled rooms with private bath in a two-storey concrete building. ③.

**Punta Caliente Hotel**, 108 José María Nuñez St (☎07/22561, *puntacal@btl.net*), next to the Z-Line terminal. Clean, comfortable rooms with private bath, fan and cable TV. There's a good restaurant, which has virtually been made into a museum of Garífuna culture by owner and historian Alex Arzú. ④.

**St Charles Inn**, 23 King St (☎07/22149). At the top end of the scale for Punta Gorda, clean and quiet, with carpeted private rooms with TV. ⑤.

**Sea Front Inn**, Front Street, north of the centre (☎07/22300, fax 22682, *seafront@btl.net*). Strikingly different from anything else in PG, this four-storey stone-and-wood-fronted building has spacious rooms with tiled floors, a/c, TV and balcony. ⑦.

**Tate's Guest House**, 34 José María Nuñez St, two blocks west of the town centre (☎07/22196, *teach@btl.net*). A quiet, friendly, family-run hotel with some a/c rooms. ④/⑤.

## Eating and drinking

**Restaurants** in Punta Gorda are improving and it's certainly easy to get a filling meal at a reasonable price. The *Punta Caliente Hotel* has one of the best restaurants in town, serving Creole and Garífuna dishes and a daily special. In the centre of town *Grace's Restaurant*, opposite the BTL office, serves inexpensive Belizean dishes in very clean surroundings, and further south, opposite the clock tower, *Aunt Jane's* also serves bargain Creole meals. To the north along Front Street the *Mangrove Inn* is a bright place serving seafood, burgers, steaks, Chinese dishes and vegetarian options (not open for breakfast). A few hundred metres further north, past the *Sea Front Inn*, *Gomier's Café* serves delicious organic and soy meals, with a daily special; it's closed at weekends. *El Café*, behind *Charlton's Inn*, does the **best coffee** in town and opens for breakfast at 6am. Visitors wanting a quiet chat with the locals will get a warm welcome from Olympia Vernon in her tiny *Olympic Bar*, near the corner of Main and Clements streets. Another good place to enjoy an early evening drink is *Waluco's*, though it's 2km from the centre; follow Front Street north over the metal bridge. It's popular with ex-pats (there's a surprising number in PG), with a deck to enjoy the breeze. On the way you'll pass *360 Degrees*, a small new bar and restaurant serving Belizean food.

## Staying around Punta Gorda: Toledo's ecotourism projects

Ecotourism is a buzzword throughout Belize, and several projects in Toledo are poised to reap the benefits. Their aim is to achieve a balance between the need for economic development and the need to preserve the rich natural and cultural heritage of the area. It is hoped that small numbers of "low-impact" visitors will provide additional income to

## MOVING ON FROM PUNTA GORDA

Z-Line **buses** (☎07/22165) leave for Dangriga and Belize City (7–8hr) at 4am, 5am and 10am; the James bus (☎07/22049) departs 6am, 8am, 11am and noon. Buses for the **Maya villages** leave around noon on the days they run from the streets next to the Civic Center. **San Antonio** is the biggest village and has daily bus services – Leonardo Cal in the tourist office will have full details. There are departures at noon (Mon, Wed, Fri & Sat) for **San Pedro Columbia** (for Lubaantun, see p.312). Most other villages have just one bus, which travels at least on **market days** (Wed & Sat) and sometimes other days as well. Returning from the villages all buses leave early – around 3.30–5.30am.

To **Puerto Barrios** in Guatemala there are several regular daily **skiffs** (US$12; 1hr in good weather). There's no need to buy your ticket in advance (though you can); just turn up at the dock half an hour or so before departure so the skipper can get the paperwork ready. The best boats are Paco's (leaves at 8.30am; ☎07/22246), Requena's (leaves at 9am; ☎07/22070), and Carlos Carcamo's (leaves at 4pm). You will have to pay the **exit tax** (US$10) and the PACT fee (US$3.75). Some boats will call at **Lívingston** if there's sufficient demand and there are usually boats going there on Tuesday and Friday. Returning, boats leave Barrios at 8am or 10am, 1pm & 2pm.

Each domestic airline has four or five daily **flights** from 7am to 4pm, calling at Placencia and Dangriga on the way to Belize City; check the airlines' offices at the airstrip: Maya Island Air (☎07/22856); Tropic Air (☎07/22008).

villages without destroying the communities' traditional way of life. The **Punta Gorda Eco-Trail** incorporates both public and privately owned land in the immediate vicinity of the town, taking in **howler monkey** habitat on nearby forested hilltops, a **green iguana** breeding project and a **medicinal plant** trail; check at *Nature's Way* (see p.306) for details. One interesting project is the cultivation of cacao beans, to produce **chocolate**; almost all of the crop around here is used to make the delicious Maya Gold organic chocolate sold abroad. Belize was a great centre of cacao production in ancient times and the Maya used cacao beans as money, which were traded over great distances. You'll often see cacao beans drying on special concrete pads as you travel through the villages.

Many Maya villages in Toledo are sited in **Indian Reservations**, designated as such in colonial times to protect the Maya subsistence lands. Title, however, remained with the government (which leases logging concessions), not the Maya who actually occupied the reserves. Recent developments in forestry policy have alarmed community leaders, who fear that so-called "conversion forestry", which allows all trees over a certain size on the reservations to be cut down for timber production, will cause further severe erosion and silt up previously clear streams used for drinking. The **Toledo Ecotourism Association**, 65 Front St, Punta Gorda (☎07/22680), aims to combat the destruction of the forest where the participants make their livelihood by offering visitors a **Guest House and Eco Trail Program**. Thirteen villages in southern Toledo are involved in the project; each has an eight-bed guest house (US$9 per person) and meals are taken at different houses to allow distribution of the income. Each village has its own attraction, be it a cave, waterfall, river or ruin, and there are guided walks or horse rides (around US$3.50 per hour; 4hr minimum); there may also be canoes to rent. The villagers have an extensive cultural knowledge of the medicinal uses of plants and the ancient Maya myths and this can be an excellent way to find out about Maya culture and experience village life without feeling like an intruder. The programme has also raised the consciousness of the villagers themselves as they learn to use both the concept of ecotourism and the political process to protect their forest; its efforts were recognized in 1997 with a tourism industry award for "Socially Responsible Ecotourism". The guest houses detailed in the text on pp.309–311 are part of the programme. Though most villages have community telephones, operating on a solar panel, you'll find few other modern conveniences (such as electricity and flush toilets), but if you go with an open mind you'll have a fascinating and rewarding experience and the villagers will be happy to teach you some Maya words.

**Tours** of the PG interior, the coast and the cayes are available from local and international operators. Green Iguana Adventures (☎07/22475, *wilfred@belizehome.com*) offer bird-watching, fishing, **camping and kayaking** trips. Island Expeditions (see p.6 in *Basics*) organize amazing kayak trips along the Moho River. TIDE, the Toledo Institute for Development and Environment (☎07/22129, *www.belizeecotours.org*), a local NGO, is involved with many practical development and conservation projects, including training net fishermen to become fly-fishing guides. They also offer **mountain bike** tours and camping trips to **Payne's Creek National Park**. If you are interested in **volunteering** in TIDE's conservation programme contact the director, Will Maheia.

## Out to sea: the cayes and the coast

From Punta Gorda you can see range upon range of mountains in Guatemala and Honduras, but the Belizean **coastline south** of here is flat and sparsely populated. Tidal rivers meander across a coastal plain covered with thick tropical rainforest that receives over 350mm of rain a year, forming a unique ecosystem in Belize. The Temash River is lined with the tallest mangrove forest in the country, the black mangroves towering over 30m above the riverbanks, while in the far south, the Sarstoon River, navigable by small boats, forms the border with Guatemala; the land between these rivers is now the **Sarstoon-Temash National Park**. These rivers are sometimes paddled on tours run by both local guides (covered above) and international sea-kayaking companies (see *Basics*, pp.5 & 6), this time using inflatable river kayaks. The only village on the coast down here is **BARRANCO** (community phone (☎07/22138), a small, traditional Garífuna settlement of two hundred people, which you can visit through the village guest house programme (see opposite). A rough seasonal road connects the village with the Southern Highway, but most people rely on traditional dories, now motor-powered, to get to Punta Gorda.

The cayes and reefs off Punta Gorda mark the southern tip of Belize's Barrier Reef. The closest cayes to Punta Gorda consist of about 130 low-lying mangrove islands in the mouth of a large bay to the north of town, where the shoreline is a complex maze of mangrove islands and swamps. Four hundred square kilometres of the bay and adjacent coast are now protected in the **Port Honduras Marine Reserve**. On **Wild Cane Caye** archeologists, with the assistance of Earthwatch volunteers, have found evidence of a Maya coastal trade centre. The first real coral sand beaches are found on the **Snake Cayes,** a group of four islands 27km northeast of Punta Gorda, and the easiest to visit from the town. Beyond here the main reef is fragmented into several clusters of cayes, each surrounded by a small independent reef.

The largest and most easterly group of cayes are the stunningly beautiful **Sapodilla Cayes**, a chain of five main islands — each almost encircled by coral and with gorgeous soft-sand beaches — and several rocky outcrops. The islands form the focus of the **Sapodilla Cayes Marine Reserve** and some cayes already have accommodation and more resorts are planned; all will face increasing visitor pressure in the near future. **Northeast Caye**, uninhabited, thickly covered with coconut trees and under government ownership, has been proposed as a **core zone** of the reserve, to be left undeveloped. **Frank's Caye**, a small island flanked by two even tinier ones, currently has the only tourist resort, the idyllic *Serenade Island Resort* (☎06/23163, *www.belizecayes.com*; ⑧), with three simple, comfortable wooden cabins with deck and hammock. **Hunting Caye** has an immigration post to deal with foreign visitors (mainly from Honduras and Guatemala at the moment) and has limited camping possibilities; the sand at the incredibly beautiful **Crescent Moon Beach** on the east side attracts hawksbill turtles to nest.

## Towards the mountains: Maya villages and ruins

Heading inland from Punta Gorda towards the foothills of the Maya Mountains, you meet yet another uniquely Belizean culture. Here **Mopan Maya** are mixed with **Kekchí** speakers from the Verapaz highlands of Guatemala. For the most part each group keeps to its own villages, language and traditions, although both groups are largely integrated into modern Belizean life and most people speak English and Creole. Guatemalan families have been arriving here for the last hundred years or so, escaping repression and a shortage of land at home, and founding new settlements deep in the forest. Several families a year still cross the border to settle in land-rich Belize – a source of contention between authorities on both sides of the border. The villages are connected by roads and most have a basic bus service from Punta Gorda (see box on p.307), although moving around isn't that easy and in many places you'll have to rely on hitching, despite the fact that there isn't much traffic. A good option is to **rent a bike** from Punta Gorda (ask at *Nature's Way* or TIDE). The people here are of course used to walking, and the villages are also connected by an intricate network of footpaths. And, if the development plan for Toledo is implemented, then the road from the Southern Highway at the "Dump" junction will be paved, to the Guatemalan border. This is a controversial proposition, as some Maya communities feel they will be further marginalized as international developers follow in the wake of the highway.

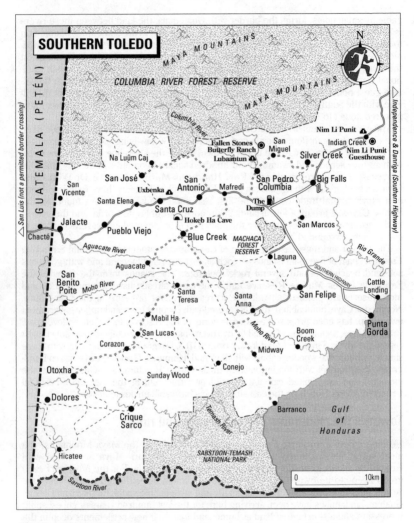

**SOUTHERN TOLEDO**

MAYA MOUNTAINS

COLUMBIA RIVER FOREST RESERVE

MAYA MOUNTAINS

Columbia River

Nim Li Punit

Fallen Stones
Butterfly Ranch
Lubaantun

San
Miguel

Indian Creek
Silver Creek

Nim Li Punit
Guesthouse

Na Luúm Caj

San José

Uxbenka

San
Antonio

Mafredi

San Pedro
Columbia

Big Falls

San
Vicente

Santa Elena

Santa Cruz

Hokeb Ha Cave

The
Dump

Jalacte

Pueblo Viejo

Blue Creek

MACHACA
FOREST
RESERVE

San Marcos

Chacté

Aguacate River

Laguna

SOUTHERN HIGHWAY

Rio Grande

San
Benito
Poite

Aguacate

Moho River

Santa
Teresa

Santa
Anna

San Felipe

Cattle
Landing

Mabil Ha

San Lucas

Moho River

Punta
Gorda

Corazon

Boom
Creek

Otoxha

Sunday Wood

Conejo

Midway

Dolores

Crique
Sarco

Barranco

Gulf
of
Honduras

Hicatee

Temash River

SARSTOON-TEMASH
NATIONAL PARK

Sarstoon River

0        10km

GUATEMALA (PETÉN)

San Luis (not a permitted border crossing)

Independence & Dangriga (Southern Highway)

## San Antonio and Uxbenka

The Mopan Maya village of **SAN ANTONIO**, perched on a small hilltop, is the easiest
settlement to reach, as it's served by daily buses from Punta Gorda. It also has the benefit of *Bol's Hill Top Hotel* (community phone ☎07/22124; ③), which has simple **rooms**
with electric light and superb views. There are a couple of shops in the village and you
can get **meals** at Theodora's or Clara's houses, behind *Bol's*. The area is rich in wildlife,
surrounded by jungle-clad hills and swift-flowing rivers. Further south and west are the
villages of the Kekchí Maya, relatively recent immigrants who still retain strong cultural links with Guatemala.

The founders of San Antonio were from the Guatemalan town of San Luis just across
the border, and they maintain many age-old traditions. Among other things the Indians

of San Luis brought with them their patron saint – opposite *Bol's Hotel* is the beautiful **stone-built church** of San Luis Rey, with a set of superb **stained-glass windows** depicting the twelve apostles and other saints donated by the people of St Louis, Missouri. The villagers also adhere to their own pre-Columbian traditions and fiestas – the main one takes place on June 13, and features marimba music, masked dances and much heavy drinking.

Seven kilometres west from San Antonio, 1km before the village of **Santa Cruz**, are the ruins of **Uxbenka**, a fairly small Maya site, superbly positioned on an exposed hilltop, with great views towards the coast. Uxbenka's existence only became known to archeologists in 1984 after reports of looting in the area. As you climb the hill before the village you'll be able to make out the shape of two tree-covered mounds to your left. Though the site has not been fully excavated, you can still discern a couple of pyramids and a plaza, and there are several badly eroded stelae, protected by thatched shelters. There's a **guest house** at the entrance to the village, and several buses a week, some of which continue to **Jalacté** on the border. All around are **trails** through the forest to rivers and waterfalls, and you can walk over to **San José** (with a guest house and on a bus route; community phone ☎07/22972) in about three hours.

## Blue Creek and Pusilha

At Mafredi, about 4km before San Antonio, a branch road (served by buses from PG) heads off south and west to **BLUE CREEK**, where the main attraction is the village's namesake – a beautiful stretch of water that runs through magnificent rainforest. The junction is marked by *Roy's Cool Spot*, a well-stocked shop where you can get a meal, a drink and possibly a room to stay. Four kilometres along the road to Blue Creek you can **stay** in the simple bamboo and wood cabins of *Roots and Herbs* (④), where Pablo and Sonia Bouchub can teach you about the medicinal plants of Toledo. There's good food and Pablo is a great **guide**; the bird-watching is fantastic and he knows routes to ruins, lagoons and caves.

Another 3km brings you to Blue Creek itself, with the river flowing through the middle of the village; the **guest house** is across the bridge and to the left. To get to the best **swimming** spot, walk upriver along the right-hand bank (facing upstream), and in about ten minutes you'll come to a lovely turquoise pool and the wooden cabins of *Blue Creek Rainforest Lodge* (*bluecreek@btl.net*; ⑨, including meals) set among the trees. The lodge, used by both student groups and adventure tourists, is under the same ownership as *Leslie Cottages* on South Water Caye (see p.291), where you make reservations. Another fifteen minutes' walk upriver is the impressive entrance to **Hokeb Ha cave**, the source of Blue Creek, where the river gushes from beneath a mossy rock face. The entire area is made up of limestone bedrock honeycombed with caves, many of which were sacred to the Maya, and doubtless there are still plenty of others waiting to be rediscovered. If you want to explore the cave contact Sylvano Sho, who lives by the bridge at the entrance to the trail. He's the best **guide** in Blue Creek and can take you to Maya altars deep in the cave, though you may have to swim to reach them; his wife Delphina serves simple, tasty meals in their house.

About 7km west of Blue Creek is the Kekchí village of **Aguacate**, beyond where the road climbs a ridge leading to the valley of the Moho River, near the border with Guatemala. Further up the valley are the ruins of **Pusilha**, a large Maya centre. The city is built alongside the river on a small hilltop and although many of the buildings are quite extensive, none is very tall, reaching a maximum height of just five or six metres. The site has yielded an astonishing number of carved monuments and stelae, including zoomorphs in a style similar to those at Quiriguá in Guatemala, leading archeologists to suggest that at some stage Pusilha may have been under Quiriguá's control. The site's most unusual feature is the remains of a stone bridge. The ruins are accessible by boat, on foot or on horseback, and you'll need a local guide to show you the way.

## San Pedro Columbia and Lubaantun

To visit the ruins of **Lubaantun** (daily 8am–5pm; US$4) from San Antonio, get a lift along the road to the Southern Highway and turn left at the side road leading **to SAN PEDRO COLUMBIA**, a mainly Kekchí village 4km away; the village also has its own bus service from Punta Gorda on market days. To **get to the site** head through the village and cross the bridge over the Columbia River, just beyond which you'll see the track to the ruins, a few hundred metres on the left; the ruins are about a twenty-minute walk. Lubaantun – "Place of the Fallen Stones" in modern Mayan though not its original name – is a major Late Classic centre which at one time covered a large area. It's possible that Lubaantun was a regional administrative centre while Nim Li Punit, only 17km away, had a more ceremonial or religious function for the same political unit, though it appears that Lubaantun was only occupied briefly, from 700 AD and abandoned before 880 AD, very near the end of the Classic period.

Sign in at the new **Visitor Center** where glass cases display some of the finds made at the site – astonishing eccentric flints (symbols of a ruler's power) and ceramics; wall panels give accounts of the site's discovery and excavation and show life in a modern Maya village. Dozens of mass-produced ceramic figurines, often depicting ball-players – items found nowhere else in such quantities – were found here, as were many **ocarinas** – clay whistles in the shape of animal effigies. Caretaker Santiago Coc makes wonderful working replicas; when you hear their evocative notes floating through the ruins you can perhaps imagine the sounds which may have accompanied Maya ceremonies; ask Santiago if he has time to give you a guided tour.

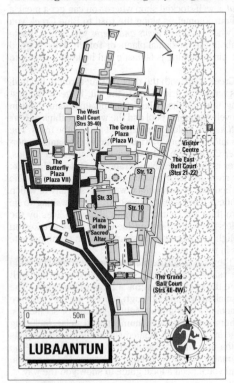

The site is on a high ridge and from the top of the tallest building you could once (just) see the Caribbean, over 30km away, though climbing on the high pyramids is now not allowed. However, it's still an impressive site, as is the surrounding forest. There are five main plazas with eleven major structures and three ball courts with ball-court markers; the whole site is essentially a single acropolis. Maya architects shaped and filled the hillside, with retaining walls as much as 10m high. Buildings here were constructed by layering stone blocks carved with particular precision and fitted together, Inca-style, with nothing to bind them. This technique, and the fact that most of the main buildings have rounded corners, give Lubaantun an elegance sometimes missing from larger, more manicured sites. The relative plainness and monumentality of Lubaantun's architecture is also similar to the later buildings at Quiriguá (see p.420) which, like Nim Li Punit, has numerous stelae, and there may have been some political connection between these sites.

## THE CRYSTAL SKULL OF LUBAANTUN

Perhaps Lubaantun's most enigmatic find came in 1926, when the famous **Crystal Skull** was unearthed here. The skull, made from pure rock crystal, was found beneath an altar by Anna Mitchell-Hedges, the adopted daughter of the British Museum expedition's leader, F.A. Mitchell-Hedges. By a stroke of luck the find coincided with her seventeenth birthday, and the skull was then given to the local Maya, who in turn presented it to Anna's father as a token of their gratitude for the help he had given them. It is possible that the "discovery" was a birthday gift for Anna, placed there by her father who had acquired it on his previous travels, although she strenuously denies the possiblity. Anna Mitchell-Hedges still owns the skull; she recalls how she spotted sunlight glinting off it during the excavation of a rubble-filled shaft and promises to reveal more in the course of time.

While mystery and controversy still surround the original skull, London's British Museum has another crystal skull which – according to Dr G.M. Morant, an anthropologist who examined both skulls in 1936 – is an exact copy of the one found at Lubaantun. He also concluded that both of the life-size crystal skulls are modelled on the same original human head but could give no answer as to their true age and origin. While on display in the Museum of Mankind (now closed), its label was suitably vague: "Possibly from Mexico, age uncertain . . . resembles in style the Mixtec carving of fifteenth-century Mexico, though some lines on the teeth appear to be cut with a jeweller's wheel. If so it may have been made after the Spanish Conquest." There is a similar, smaller crystal skull in the Musée de l'Homme in Paris, and others exist too; all attract great interest from "New Age" mystics, who believe that crystal has supernatural properties.

Lubaantun was brought to the attention of the colonial authorities in 1903 and the governor sent Thomas Gann to investigate. A survey in 1915 revealed many structures, and three ball-court markers were removed and taken to the Peabody Museum. The British Museum expedition of 1926 was joined in 1927 by J. Eric S. Thompson, who was to become the most renowned Maya expert of his time. No further excavations took place for over forty years until Norman Hammond mapped the site in 1970, producing a reconstruction of life in Lubaantun which showed the inhabitants' links with communities on the coast and inland. Lubaantun's wealth was created by the production of cacao beans, used as money by the civilizations of Mesoamerica.

### SAN PEDRO PRACTICALITIES

Several places in and around San Pedro (community phone ☎07/22303) offer **accommodation**. Alfredo and Yvonne Villoria, who run *Dem Dats Doin'* (☎07/22470; ④), on the right a kilometre before the village, have a bright, clean **bed and breakfast** room on their sustainable technology farm which grows an astonishing range of organic fruits and vegetables. Through the village and 3km beyond the turn-off to the ruins (follow the signs), a steeply undulating road leads to *Fallen Stones Butterfly Ranch* (☎07/22167, *www.fallenstones.co.uk*; ⑨ including breakfast and service charge), which has comfortable, private-bath wooden cabins on a hilltop with superb views over the Columbia River Forest Reserve to the Maya Mountains beyond. The dining room juts over a ridge, offering good food and gorgeous views at dawn and dusk. The **butterflies** are reared in what amounts to a tiny (and charming) industrial process; every step, from the mating and egg-laying, through the stages of caterpillar development, to the critical packing of the chrysalis for shipping, is governed by meticulous timing – all carefully supervised by the "ranch" workers, who look after their insect babies with tender loving care.

## travel details

The Southern Highway doesn't have as many buses running along it as the Northern and Western highways, and bus schedules are not quite as reliable. However, as road improvements take effect journey times will shorten and timetable reliability will improve. The main routes are listed below; other buses to the smaller villages are covered in the text. Bus company offices and departure frequencies from Belize City to Dangriga, Placencia and Punta Gorda are covered in the box on pp.212–214.

### Buses

**Dangriga to:** Belize City (12 daily; 2–3hr); Hopkins and Sittee River (1–2 daily; 45min); Placencia (2 daily; 2hr); Punta Gorda (8 daily; 5hr). All buses between Dangriga and Punta Gorda stop at Independence/Mango Creek.

**Hopkins and Sittee River to:** Dangriga (1 daily around 7am; 45min).

**Placencia to:** Dangriga (2 daily; 2hr); both connect with departures to Belize City.

**Punta Gorda to:** Belize City (5 daily; 8–9hr); Dangriga (5 daily; 5hr).

### Flights

Maya Island Air (☎02/35371 in Belize City) and Tropic Air (☎02/45671) each have at least four daily flights from **Belize City to Dangriga** (25min); most continue to **Placencia** (a further 20min) and **Punta Gorda** (20min beyond Placencia).

### International boats

**Dangriga to Puerto Cortés**, Honduras (weekly skiff, on Sat; 3hr)

**Placencia and Big Creek to Puerto Cortés**, Honduras (weekly skiff, on Fri; 3hr)

**Punta Gorda to Puerto Barrios**, Guatemala (at least 3 daily; 1hr)

# PART FOUR

# GUATEMALA

MEXICO

BELIZE

**CHAPTER 9**
**THE NORTH & EAST**

**CHAPTER 8**
**THE WESTERN HIGHLANDS & PACIFIC COAST**

HONDURAS

**CHAPTER 7**
**GUATEMALA CITY & ANTIGUA**

EL SALVADOR

# INTRODUCTION

At one time the heart of the ancient Maya World, Guatemala has an exceptional wealth of archeological remains, with giant temples and rainforest cities scattered around the country, and it is this outstanding legacy that makes the country so compelling for visitors. Though the cities have long been abandoned, the descendants of the ancient **Maya** remain, having survived almost five hundred years of cultural attack. Today, they comprise over half of Guatemala's thirteen million population and it is their vibrant culture, perhaps the strongest in Latin America, that is Guatemala's most definitive characteristic. Countering this is a powerful **ladino** society, a blend of Latin machismo that is decidedly urban and commercial in its outlook.

The Guatemalan landscape is astonishingly diverse. Separated from the steamy flatlands of the Pacific coast by a spiky backbone of volcanoes, the Maya **highlands** offer some of the most beautiful scenery. High ridges, pine forests, sweeping valleys, tiny cornfields and gurgling streams provide a backdrop for sleepy, traditional villages where amazing fiestas and markets take place. Traditional weavings and handicrafts are made in this region by the Maya and one of the best places to buy them is at the famous twice-weekly market at **Chichicastenango**. The huge highland lake, **Lago de Atitlán**, is unmissable: ringed by sentinel-like volcanoes, its shores are dotted with some of the most traditional indigenous villages in the country. **Panajachel**, on the northern shore, is the principal resort, home to some excellent restaurants, cafés and textile stores, but there are a number of alternative bases around the lake if you're searching for some real solitude. Bohemian **San Pedro La Laguna**, on the opposite shore of the lake, has a real travellers' scene, while Santiago Atitlán, San Marcos La Laguna, Santa Cruz La Laguna and Jaibalito all boast blissfully tranquil guest houses.

There is more bewitching scenery around the country's second city of **Quetzaltenango** (also called Xela), an excellent place for a series of day-trips to nearby hot springs, market towns and volcanoes. Further north, deep in the mountains of the **Cuchumatanes**, there are scores of extremely traditional and isolated villages. Perhaps the two best places to head for are **Nebaj**, in the Ixil triangle, and **Todos Santos Cuchumatán** to the north of Huehuetenango; both are intensely rewarding places to visit, with excellent walking amidst superb scenery, and plenty of cheap pensions.

The **Pacific coast** is generally hot and dull – a strip of black volcanic sand and a smattering of mangrove swamps that blend into the country's most productive farmland. The beaches here are not as you imagine a Pacific beach to be, except at the wildlife reserve of **Monterrico**, which boasts a maze of swamps to explore and a fine stretch of sand where three species of turtle nest.

If it's real adventure and exploration you seek, nothing can compete with the hidden archeological wonders of **Petén**. This unique lowland area, which makes up about a third of the country, is covered with dense rainforest – only recently threatened by development – that harbours the remains of vast Maya cities and a tremendous array of wildlife, including jaguar, howler and spider monkeys, the lumbering tapir, toucans and scarlet macaws. The only town of any size here is **Flores**, from where you can easily reach **Tikal**, the most impressive of all Maya sites. Other dramatic ruins, such as the monumental triadic temples of Preclassic **El Mirador**, require days of tough travel to reach.

To the east of the Petén is another highland region, the **Verapaces**, with stunning alpine scenery and the sleepy coffee centre of **Cobán**, while further east are the spectacular gorge systems of the **Río Dulce**, the ruins of **Quiriguá** and, on the Caribbean coast, the funky town of **Lívingston**, home to Guatemala's only black community.

**Guatemala City** is of little interest to travellers except for a couple of museums: it's much better to stay in the quintessentially colonial city of **Antigua**, just an hour away, which has a unique architectural heritage and the country's best selection of hotels, restaurants and cafés. Antigua also has a number of good language schools and is an ideal place to **study Spanish**.

## Some history

By the time the Spanish arrived in Guatemala in 1523, **the Maya** were in crisis. The Classic Maya culture, which had reached degrees of sophistication in architecture, astronomy and art unequalled by any other pre-Columbian society, had collapsed over six hundred years previously. The spectacular cities of Petén – Tikal, Ceibal, Piedras Negras and Río Azul – had been long abandoned to the jungle and most Maya lived in the highlands to the south. When the conquistadors entered the Guatemalan region, the situation could not have been more favourable to them: the highland Maya tribes were warring amongst themselves and an exploding population had outstripped its food supply.

**Pedro de Alvarado**, the conquistador despatched by Cortés to explore Guatemala, could hardly have been better suited to the job – ambitious, cunning, intelligent, dashingly handsome and brutally cruel. By 1525, just two years after his arrival, he had conquered all the main tribes with a series of utterly ruthless military manoeuvres and savvy tactical alliances. At the most significant battle, near modern-day Quetzaltenango, the Spanish defeated a 30,000-strong K'iche' force with a few hundred horsemen, soldiers and Mexican allies. Legend has it that Alvarado himself slew the K'iche' leader **Tecún Umán** in hand-to-hand combat. After being driven from Iximché, the capital of their Kaqchikel Maya allies, the Spanish moved to a site (now called Ciudad Vieja), near Antigua, where they established their first permanent capital on November 22, 1527.

The early years of **colonial rule** were marked by a catalogue of uprisings, natural disasters and disease, with waves of plague, typhoid and smallpox killing around ninety percent of the Maya population. In 1541, following a massive earthquake, the capital was devastated by a mud slide. A new city was established at nearby **Antigua**, which grew to control the provinces of Guatemala (present-day Costa Rica, Nicaragua, El Salvador, Honduras, Guatemala and Chiapas) and was the region's centre of political and religious power for two hundred years, until another catastrophic earthquake in 1773 forced the capital to move again to its present-day site of **Guatemala City**. With no gold or silver to plunder, colonial society was based on agriculture: livestock, cacao, tobacco, cotton and, most valuable of all, indigo and cochineal, were all farmed using indentured indigenous labour and presided over by a Spanish-born ruling class and the Catholic Church.

Two centuries of colonial rule totally reshaped Guatemalan society, giving it new cities, a new religion, a transformed economy and a racist hierarchy. Nevertheless, the indigenous culture was never completely eradicated as in other parts of the continent. In the relative isolation of the highlands, the Maya simply absorbed the symbols and ideas of the new regime, fusing Maya and Catholic traditions to create a unique synthesis of old and new world beliefs.

The event that precipitated **independence** was Napoleon's invasion of Spain, after which a mood of reform swept through the colonies, leading to the signing of the Act of Independence in 1821. Guatemala soon joined the liberal **Central American federation**, which had a US-style constitution and set about abolishing religious orders, the death penalty and slavery. This era was brought to a swift end, however, by a religious revolt from the mountains, led by a charismatic, conservative 23-year-old, Rafael Carrera, who would accept no authority other than the Catholic Church. There was another major turning-point in Guatemalan politics, with the election of president Rufino Barrios in 1871, an arrogant man with tyrannical tendencies, who revolutionized the country's agriculture, encouraging **coffee** farming, and increasing foreign trade twenty-fold as a result.

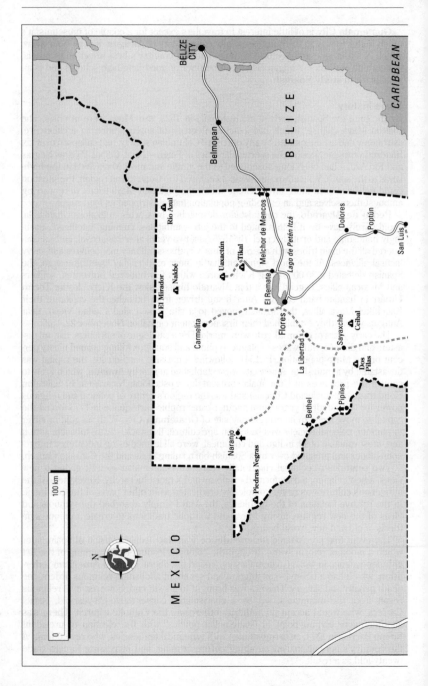

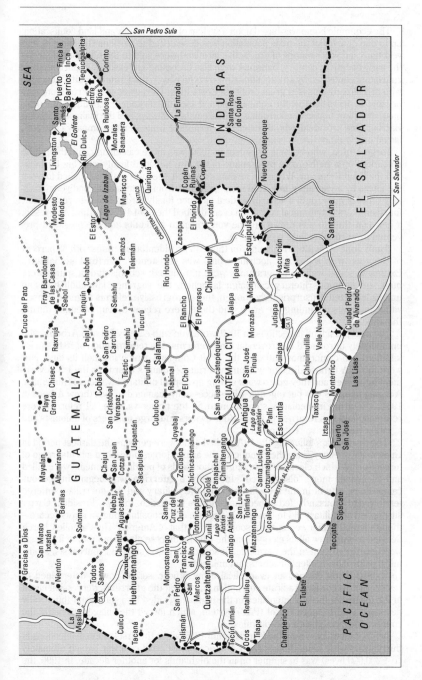

The economic boom was based upon a system of forced labour and land confiscation: up to one quarter of the male population was despatched to work on the fincas at harvest time and vast swathes of productive farmland were sold to the highest bidder. By the early twentieth century, **bananas** were also becoming increasingly important, their cultivation controlled by an exceptionally powerful player, the **United Fruit Company**, who had already amassed great profits in Costa Rica. The power of the Fruit Company became so pervasive that the company earned itself the nickname "El Pulpo" (the octopus), its yellow tentacles controlling all Guatemala's railways and the main port, Puerto Barrios. One president, who threatened to terminate United Fruit Company contracts, lasted barely more than a year.

**Jorge Ubico**, who became president in 1930, was more calculating, and though he embarked on a high-profile programme of reform, he sided firmly with big business and the Fruit Company. When the peasants revolted, they were still compelled to work the fincas by a **vagrancy law**. However, opposition from professionals and young military officers grew, until a wave of student violence finally forced Ubico to resign after fourteen years of tyrannical rule, in an event dubbed the **1944 revolution**. As a result, a new constitution was drawn up, the vote given to all adults and the president prevented from running for a second term.

**Juan José Arévalo**, a teacher, won the 1945 presidential elections with 85 percent of the vote, with a political doctrine which was christened "**spiritual socialism**". Extensive social welfare programmes were introduced: schools and hospitals were built, an ambitious literary campaign launched, the vagrancy law abolished and unions legalized. Unsurprisingly, though, these progressive reforms angered conservative interests, including the army, and there were repeated coup attempts during this time.

The next presidential elections, in 1950, were won with ease by **Jacobo Arbenz**, who immediately introduced controversial **land reforms**. His redistribution of 8840 square kilometres to campesinos outraged the Fruit Company, which lost half its land. Nor were the CIA (whose director was on the Fruit Company's board) or the US government impressed and they got to work setting up a small military invasion of Guatemala. A ragtag of exiles was put together who successfully managed to overthrow Arbenz in 1954. The army immediately stepped in to fill the power vacuum, all reforms were reversed, land was returned to its previous owners and large numbers of unionists and agrarian reformers were executed.

The thirty years following the CIA-backed coup were perhaps the darkest period in Guatemala's history since the Conquest. The armed forces unleashed a brutal reign of terror during which elections were rigged, thousands of political opponents were killed and thousands more "disappeared". Inevitably, a **guerrilla war** began. Indigenous campesinos, caught in the crossfire between the military and the guerrillas, suffered terribly, and thousands fled to become refugees in Mexico. In 1977, President Carter suspended all military aid to Guatemala because of its appalling human rights record – though Israeli military equipment soon replaced that of America. The Catholic Church decided to withdraw all its clergy from the Quiché diocese after a number of its priests were murdered, and in the towns, death squads targeted students, journalists, academics, politicians, lawyers, teachers and unionists.

In 1982, **Ríos Montt**, an evangelical army officer, seized power, determined to restore law and order, eradicate corruption and defeat the guerrillas. Repression eased in the towns but the war intensified in the highlands, aided by a successful (but locally detested) Civil Defence Patrol (PAC) system, which forced the villagers to patrol the countryside, armed with ancient rifles.

Democratic reform remained elusive until 1985, when the first legitimate elections in thirty years were held, though Latin America's most acrid civil war (which ultimately cost 200,000 lives) was to simmer on in the highlands for another decade. In 1996, the

**Peace Accords** signed by the new president, **Álvaro Arzú**, and the guerrilla leaders brought to an end the 36-year conflict with a fanfare of promises of indigenous rights, human rights investigations and socio-economic development for all Guatemalans. Frustratingly, only limited progress was made towards these objectives during the Arzú administration, as the president pushed through minor reforms that did little to challenge the interests of the dominant political and military elite.

State-sponsored violence, however, seemed to have become a thing of the past, until, in April 1998, Guatemala was stunned by the murder of **Bishop Juan Geradi**. Under the auspices of the Catholic church, Geradi had just published an exhaustive investigation into the human rights abuses of the civil war, blaming the army for eighty percent of the atrocities. Most Guatemalans immediately recognized the hand of the military behind the bishop's assassination, though the army intelligence chiefs responsible were only brought to trial in 2001, after an epochal investigation and court case debased by bomb blasts and incessant witness and prosecutor intimidation.

Despite this horrific killing, political violence did fall in the Arzú years, though there was an alarming upsurge in the crime rate. Petty theft, muggings, robberies, drug- and gang-related incidents and murders soared. In 1997, despite its relatively small population, Guatemala had the fourth-highest incidence of kidnapping in the world, when over 1000 people were abducted. A new police force, the PNC, trained by experts from Spain, Chile and the USA, quickly gained a reputation as bad as its predecessor for endemic corruption and ineffectualness. Not surprisingly, law and order became the key issue of the 1999 election campaign.

Former lawyer and professor **Alfonso Portillo** won Guatemala's 1999 presidential elections with a mandate to implement the Peace Accords and tackle impunity among the criminal gangs. In the grossest of ironies, Portillo sought to boost his ratings during the presidential campaign by confessing to killing two men during a brawl in Mexico in 1982, declaring "a man who defends his life will defend the lives of his people". The tactic paid off handsomely, as Portillo, leader of the right-wing FRG (Guatemalan Republican Front), won by a landslide after a second round of voting. Portillo campaigned on a populist platform to cut poverty by tackling corruption and tax evasion, though perhaps the conclusive factor was the support of his political mentor, FRG founder and former general Ríos Montt. Montt, Guatemala's most controversial politician, had been ruled illegible to stand for the presidency because of his role in an earlier coup, but was widely perceived to be in control behind the scenes.

Initially, there was a positive groundswell of optimism as Portillo unveiled a diverse cabinet which included academics, indigenous activists and human rights advocates. Nevertheless, many of the key institutions – including the Bank of Guatemala and the Ministries of the Economy, Communications and Interior – were placed under the control of right-wing FRG politicians and pro-business monetarists. In a bold move Portillo broke the military chain of command by appointing a moderate colonel, Juan de Dios Estrada, instead of a general as Minister of Defence, an action which infuriated the army top brass. Credibly, he also moved quickly to solve the Geradi murder – another key campaign pledge.

This success aside, Portillo's popularity ratings quickly plummeted. The new president lurched from crisis to crisis as a series of corruption scandals were unearthed, the **crime rate** continued to soar and criminal impunity persisted. Portillo even dispatched his family to Canada in June 2000 after threats from a kidnapping gang, a savage indictment of the security situation. By early 2001, barely a week seemed to pass without an armed bank robbery or a public lynching, as rural Guatemalans, frustrated with the country's bankrupt justice system, administered mob rule, killing suspected culprits. Confidence in Portillo reached an all-time low in June 2001 following a mass breakout from Guatemala's main maximum-security prison. Seventy of the country's most notorious convicts – murderers, rapists, kidnappers and gang lords – blasted their way out of

## FIESTAS IN GUATEMALA

*JANUARY*

1–5 **Santa María de Jesús**, near Antigua (main action on the 1st and 2nd).

19–25 **Rabinal**, in the Verapaces (main days 23rd and 24th). Dances performed include the epic pre-Columbian Rabinal Achi.

22–26 **San Pablo La Laguna**, Lago de Atitlán (main day 25th).

*MARCH*

Second Friday in Lent **Chajul**, in the Ixil triangle.

*APRIL*

24 **San Jorge La Laguna**, Lago de Atitlán.

25 **San Marcos La Laguna**, Lago de Atitlán.

*MAY*

6–10 **Uspantán** (main day 8th).

8–10 **Santa Cruz La Laguna** (main day 10th).

*JUNE*

12–14 **San Antonio Palopó**, near Panajachel (main day 13th).

21–25 **Olintepeque**, near Quetzaltenango.

22–25 **San Juan Cotzal**, near Nebaj.

22–26 **San Juan Atitlán** (main day 24th).

27–30 **San Pedro La Laguna** (main day 29th).

28–30 **Almolongo**, near Quetzaltenango (main day 29th).

*JULY*

21–Aug 4 **Momostenango** (most interesting on July 25 and Aug 1). Plenty of interesting celebrations and traditional rituals in this centre of costumbres.

23–27 **Santiago Atitlán** (main day 25th).

25 **Antigua**. Live bands and salsa and merengue in the main plaza.

25 **Cubulco**, in the Verapaces. Riotous fiesta with spectacular dances including the Palo Volador.

31–Aug 6 **Cobán**. City celebrations followed by the national folklore festival.

*AUGUST*

1–4 **Sacapulas** (main day 4th).

9–15 **Joyabaj**, west of Santa Cruz del Quiché (main day 15th). Very unusual fiesta with many pre-Columbian dances including the Palo Volador.

12–15 **Nebaj** (main day 15th).

15 **Guatemala City**. Bank holiday in the capital celebrated with marching bands and city-wide indulgence.

*SEPTEMBER*

12–18 **Quetzaltenango** (main day 15th).

17–21 **Salamá** (main day 17th).

24–30 **Totonicapán** (main day 29th).

*OCTOBER*

1–6 **San Francisco el Alto** (main day 4th).

2–6 **Panajachel** (main day 4th).

29–Nov 1 **Todos Santos Cuchumatán**.

*NOVEMBER*

1 (All Saints Day) Celebrations all over the country, but most dramatic in **Todos Santos Cuchumatán** with the epic drunken horse race and in **Santiago Sacatepéquez**, where massive paper kites are flown.

23–26 **Nahualá** (main day 25th).

22–26 **Zunil** (main day 25th).

25 **Santa Catarina Palopó**, Lago de Atitlán.

30 **San Andrés Xecul**, near Quetzaltenango.

30 **San Andrés Itzapa**, near Antigua.

*DECEMBER*

7 Bonfires (the Burning of the Devil) throughout the country

7 **Ciudad Vieja**, near Antigua.

13–21 **Chichicastenango** (main day 21st). Many interesting dances in this well-attended fiesta.

jail, armed with a smuggled arsenal of sub-machine-guns and grenade launchers, with obvious internal connivance. Many media figures expressed doubt that Portillo would be permitted to finish his presidential term, as persistent rumours of a military-backed coup swept through the country.

Guatemala under Portillo has also suffered from a faltering **economy**, as traditional exports (principally coffee, sugar and bananas) have been hit by low commodity prices and the nation's high interest rates affected investment. The quetzal remained weak against international currencies, prompting the government to introduce dollarization in May 2001, and to sign up for a customs union with Honduras, El Salvador and Nicaragua by 2003 in an effort to boost the economy. Efforts to improve tax collection, a key part of the Peace Accords, failed to materialize. According to MINUGUA, the United Nations mission to oversee the Accords, only 36 percent of the government's commitments had been met by 2001.

Guatemala remains a seismically divided country, with racism endemic and the Maya subject to institutionalized discrimination. Political and economic power remains very much concentrated in the hands of the **ladino** half of the population, with politicians severely restricted by the shadow of the dominant Guatemalan oligarchy of landowners, generals and big business. Income distribution remains woefully skewed, with only Sierra Leone and Brazil having more unequal tax structures according to World Development Report figures. Land reform is still untackled (it's estimated that close to seventy percent of the cultivable land is owned by less than five percent of the population) and some 85 percent of the population – most of them Maya – remains in poverty, with little affordable access to health care or education.

Fighting these fundamental inequalities is an increasingly well-organized and confident opposition. One of the most prominent activists fighting for change is the K'iche' Maya woman, **Rigoberta Menchú**, who won the Nobel Peace Prize in 1992 for her work on behalf of indigenous people. Today, the stirrings of a cultural reawakening are unmistakable: hundreds of new schools are being established so that indigenous children can learn in their own language, and there is a resurgence of interest in *costumbres* (traditional religious ways).

In many ways, the years since the Peace Accords have been a bitter disappointment to many Guatemalans. Though the peace has held, political violence has been replaced by random acts of criminal thuggery and the unreformed justice system is seemingly moribund. The economic outlook remains weak, with low living standards and the highest population growth rate in the hemisphere (almost three percent per annum). More and more poor Guatemalans are fleeing to the USA as illegal migrants, seeking opportunities denied them at home. Increasingly more marginal plots are being farmed as campesinos, loggers and cattle ranchers continue to butcher rapidly diminishing forests and threaten protected reserves and national parks. Though there is ground for optimism in some areas, including a vibrant tourism industry, the key points of the Peace Accords have not been addressed and the immediate future looks unstable, as Guatemala faces many more difficult years ahead.

# GUATEMALA CITY, ANTIGUA AND AROUND

**S**ituated just forty kilometres apart in Guatemala's highlands, the two cities of **Guatemala City** and **Antigua** could hardly be more different. The capital, Guatemala City, fume-filled and concrete-clad, is a maelstrom of industry and commerce. There are few attractions or sights here to detain the traveller,

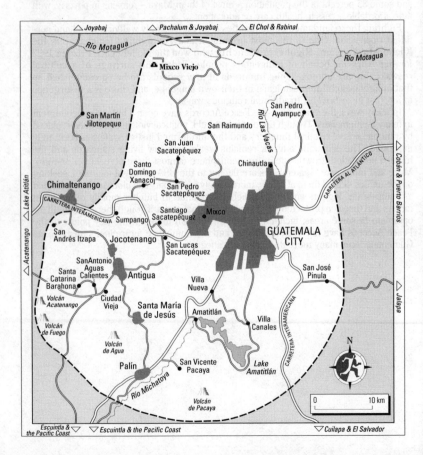

though a day or two spent visiting the museums and exploring the markets and shops won't be wasted. Antigua is everything the capital is not: tranquil, urbane and resplendent with spectacular colonial buildings and myriad cosmopolitan cafés, restaurants and hotels. Unsurprisingly, it is the town where most travellers choose to base themselves, finding the relaxed atmosphere a welcome break after the frenzied pace of life in Guatemala City.

Guatemala City is actually the fourth capital of the country. The Spanish conquistadors made their first base at Iximché in 1523, but when they were driven out by the Kaqchikel tribe, they retreated to another site close to today's village of Ciudad Vieja. In 1541, however, this was destroyed by a cataclysmic flood, and the capital was moved to Antigua. The new site grew steadily from small beginnings to become the centre of Spanish colonial power and one of the most important cities in the Americas, but when a series of devastating earthquakes all but destroyed it in 1773, it was decided to move the capital to present-day Guatemala City. The new capital, although slow to develop at first, began growing at an unbelievable rate at the start of the twentieth century and now dominates the country, forming the political and economical heart of the nation.

The countryside around Antigua and Guatemala City – an astonishing landscape of volcanoes, pine forests, meadows, milpas and coffee farms, punctuated with villages – is well worth exploring. Looming over the capital is the **Volcán de Pacaya**, one of the most active volcanoes in Latin America. Recently, it has been spewing a spectacular fountain of sulphurous gas and molten rock and every year or so an eruption douses Guatemala City in ash, closing the airport for a day or two. However, it's usually possible to climb a secondary peak that overlooks the main cone of Pacaya, as well as the volcanoes of **Agua** and **Acatenango**, close to Antigua.

There are countless interesting villages to visit in this area, including **San Andrés Itzapa**, where there is a pagan shrine to the "evil saint" Maximón, **Jocotenango** which boasts two new museums dedicated to coffee and Maya music, and **Santa María de Jesús**, a Maya village where the trail to the Volcán de Agua begins, The one **Maya ruin** in the region that can compete with the lowland sites further north is **Mixco Viejo**; it's tricky to get to unless you have your own transport, but its setting, in splendid isolation, is tremendous. Little evidence remains of the former magnificence of **Kaminaljuyú**, today almost buried in the capital's suburbs, but this was once one of the largest and most important cities of the Maya World.

# Guatemala City

**GUATEMALA CITY** sprawls across a sweeping highland basin, surrounded on three sides by low hills and volcanic cones. Congested and polluted, it is, in many ways, the antithesis of the rest of the country. The capital was moved here in 1776 after the seismic destruction of Antigua, but the site had been of importance long before the arrival of the Spanish. These days, its shapeless and swelling mass, ringed by shanty towns,

---

## ACCOMMODATION PRICE CODES

All the accommodation listed in this book has been categorized into one of nine price bands, as set out below. The prices quoted are in US dollars and refer to the cheapest room available for two people sharing in high season.

| | | |
|---|---|---|
| ① under US$5 | ④ US$15–25 | ⑦ US$60–80 |
| ② US$5–10 | ⑤ US$25–40 | ⑧ US$80–100 |
| ③ US$10–15 | ⑥ US$40–60 | ⑨ over US$100 |

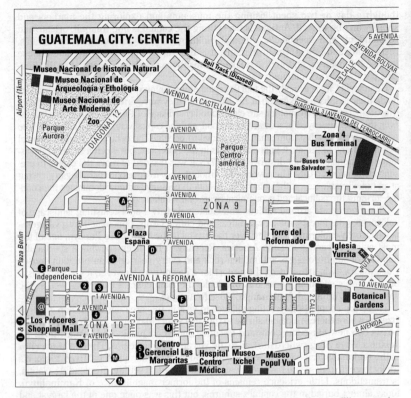

GUATEMALA CITY: CENTRE

ranks as the largest city in Central America. It is home to over three million people, almost a quarter of Guatemala's population, and is the undisputed centre of politics, power and wealth.

The city has an intensity and vibrancy that are both its fascination and its horror, and for many travellers a trip to the capital is an exercise in damage limitation, as they struggle through a swirling mass of bus fumes and crowds. For decades, the centre has been run-down and polluted, abandoned by the affluent middle classes and blue-chip businesses who long ago fled to the suburbs. However, after all these years of neglect and decay, efforts are being made by a small group of conservationists to preserve what's left of the historic centre, Zona 1, and a smattering of fashionable new cafes and bars, popular with students, have opened in restored buildings the heart of the city.

Like it or not – and many travellers don't – Guatemala City is the crossroads of the country, and you'll certainly end up here at some time, if only to hurry between bus terminals or negotiate a visa extension. Once you get used to the pace, it can offer a welcome break from life on the road, with cosmopolitan restaurants, cinemas, shopping plazas, a couple of good museums and metropolitan culture. And if you really can't take the pace, it's easy enough to escape: buses leave every few minutes, day and night.

## Some history

The pre-conquest Maya city of **Kaminaljuyú**, whose ruins are still scattered amongst the western suburbs, was well established here two thousand years ago. As a result of

ZONAS 9 & 10
ACCOMMODATION
Camino Real                    2
Holiday Inn                    3
Hotel Casa Santa Clara         5
Hotel Inter-Continental        4
Hotel Princess Reforma         1

RESTAURANTS AND CAFÉS
Café Restaurant Pereira        B
El Gran Pavo                A & M
Jake's                         I
La Lancha                      N
Los Alpes                      F
Los Antojitos                  E
Luigi's Pizza                  K
Olivadda                       L
Palace                         H
Piccadilly                     C
Puerto Barrios                 D
Tamarindos                     G
Vesuvio Pizza                  J

an alliance with the great northern power of Teotihuacán (near present-day Mexico City) in early Classic times (250–550 AD), Kaminaljuyú came to dominate the highlands and eventually provided the political and commercial backing that fostered the rise of Tikal (see p.457). The city was situated at the crossroads of the north–south and east–west trade routes and at the height of its prosperity it was home to a population of some 50,000. However, following the decline of Teotihuacán around 600 AD, Kaminaljuyú was surpassed by the great lowland centres that it had helped to establish, and soon after their rise, some time between 600 and 900 AD, the city was abandoned.

Seven centuries later, when Alvarado entered the country, the fractured tribes of the west controlled the highlands and preoccupied the conquistadors. The Spanish ignored the possibility of settling here until the devastating 1773 earthquake that forced them to flee disease-ridden Antigua and establish a new capital. The new city was named **Nueva Guatemala de la Asunción** by royal decree and was officially inaugurated on January 1, 1776.

The new city's growth was initially slow, as many chose not to flee Antigua, despite endless decrees and repeated waves of smallpox and cholera. An 1863 census listed just 1206 residences and the earliest photographs show the city was still little more than a large village with a theatre, a government palace and a fort. Another factor retarding the city's growth was the existence of a major rival, Quetzaltenango, but when it too was razed to the ground by a massive earthquake in 1902, many wealthy families moved to the capital, finally establishing it as the country's primary city.

BUS COMPANIES IN THE CAPITAL

The main bus companies, their addresses and departure times, are all given in the box on p.341.

Just fifteen years after the Quetzaltenango earthquake, the capital itself was badly hit by a series of **earthquakes** in 1917 and 1918, which caused widespread devastation and necessitated substantial reconstruction. However, since these tremors, Guatemala City has grown at an incredible rate, mainly due to an influx of rural immigrants. The steady flight from the fields, characteristic of all developing countries, was aided and abetted by a chronic shortage of land and, in the 1970s and 1980s, by internal refugees escaping the military's "scorched earth" offensives and widespread rural violence. Many of these displaced people, for the most part Maya, feel unwanted and unwelcome in the city and the divisions that cleave Guatemalan society are at their most acute in the capital's crumbling streets. While the wealthy elite sip coffee in air-conditioned shopping malls and plan their next visit to Miami, swathes of the city have been left to disintegrate into a threatening tangle of fume-choked streets, largely devoid of any kind of life after dark. A small army of **street children** lives rough, scratching a living from begging, prostitution and petty crime, and there is strong evidence of "social cleansing" by the security forces. The disparities of life in the city are glaringly extreme, as glass skyscrapers tower over sprawling shanty towns, and shoeless widows peddle cigarettes and chewing gum to designer-clad nightclubbers.

## Arrival and information

Arriving in Guatemala City for the first time, it's easy to feel overwhelmed by its scale, with suburbs sprawled across some 21 **zones**, but you'll find that the central area, which is all that you need to worry about, is really quite small.

Broadly speaking, the city divides into two distinct halves. The northern section, centred on **Zona 1**, is the old part of town, containing the parque central, most of the budget hotels, shops, restaurants, cinemas, the post office and many of the bus companies. This part of the city is cramped, congested and polluted, but bustling with activity. The two main streets are 5 and 6 avenidas, both thick with street traders, fast-food joints and copious neon. Directly north of the parque central is **Zona 2**, a largely residential suburb, with the sole attraction of the **Parque Minerva**, where there is a relief map of the country, a popular local attraction.

South of Zona 1, acting as a buffer between the two halves of town, is **Zona 4**, home of the administrative centre or Centro Cívico, the national theatre and the **tourist office**, Inguat, at 7 Av 1–17 (Mon–Fri 8am–4pm, ☎331 1333, fax 331 8893). The information desk, on the ground floor, sells a half-decent map of the country and city and there's always someone who speaks English. For detailed hiking maps, go to the Instituto Geográfico Militar, Av Las Américas 5–76, Zona 13 (Mon–Fri 8am–4pm). The other great "landmark" in Zona 4 is the **bus terminal**, a crazy world of peripatetic humanity, exhaust fumes and the city's largest fruit and vegetable market.

The southern half of the city, **Zona 9** and **Zona 10**, is the modern, wealthy part of town, split in two by Avenida la Reforma. Here you'll find exclusive offices, apartment blocks, hotels and shops and Guatemala's most expensive nightclubs, restaurants and cafés. Many of the embassies and two of the country's finest museums are also here. Continuing south, the neighbouring Zonas 13 and 14 are rich, leafy suburbs and home to the airport, zoo and more museums and cinemas.

There is little of interest in the west side of the city except the landmark Tikal Futura shopping mall and the sparse remains of the ruins of **Kaminaljuyú**, which have been mostly erased by the city's suburbs.

## ADDRESSES IN GUATEMALA CITY

The system of street numbering in the capital may seem a little confusing at first and it is complicated by the fact that the same calles and avenidas can exist in several different zones. Always check the zone first and then the street. For example "4 Av 9–14, Zona 1" is in Zona 1, on 4 Avenida between 9 and 10 calles, house number 14.

## By air

**Aurora airport** is on the edge of the city in Zona 13, some way from the centre, but close to Zona 10. The domestic terminal, though in the same complex, is separate, and entered by Avenida Hincapié. In the complex, you'll also find a Banco del Quetzal for exchange (Mon–Fri 6am–8pm, Sat & Sun 6am–6pm) plus 24-hour **cashpoints** which accept Visa, Mastercard, Cirrus and Plus cards. There's also a **tourist information** office (daily 6am–9pm; ☎331 4256,) on the upper (departures) floor, a Telgua phone office and a post office (both Mon–Sat 7am–9pm).

Much the easiest way to get to and from the airport is by taxi: you'll find plenty of them waiting outside the terminal. The fare to or from Zona 1 is around US$10, to Zona 10 around US$7. Otherwise, city bus #83 leaves from directly outside the terminal, across the concrete plaza, dropping you in Zona 1, either on 5 Avenida or 9 Avenida, though services do not run after 8pm. Virtually all Guatemala City's four- and five-star hotels, and Zona 13 guest houses, offer free pick-ups from the airport if you inform them first.

If, like many travellers, you're **heading for Antigua**, there are regular shuttle bus services from the airport (US$10) though they don't run to a fixed schedule and only leave if there's a minimum of three passengers. A taxi from the airport is US$25. In daylight hours, you can get to Antigua cheaply and fairly conveniently by taking a taxi to the Tikal Futura shopping mall on the Calzada Roosevelt highway (US$5), crossing the road via the pedestrian bridge and catching an Antigua-bound bus (US$0.60) from the bus stop beside the bridge.

## By bus

If you're travelling by **first-class** (Pullman) bus, you'll arrive at the company's own private terminal – virtually all of them are in Zona 1, including all services from the Mexican border and Petén. If you've arrived by **second-class** "chicken bus" from Antigua, you'll arrive in Zona 1 at the junction of 18 Calle, between 4 and 5 avenidas. The Zona 4 terminal operates second-class buses to the western highlands, the Pacific coast and some towns in the eastern highlands and you'll find the main terminal for San Salvador very close by on 3 Avenida and 1 Calle.

## City transport

As in any big city, coping with the public transport system takes time. Even locals can be bamboozled by Guatemala's seemingly anarchic web of **bus routes**. In Zona 1 buses #82 and #83 stop on 10 Avenida, while buses to many different parts of the city run along 4 Avenida. Destinations are posted on the front of the bus. Buses run from around 6 or 7am until about 9.30pm. Guatemala City has a ferocious rush hour and many roads throughout the city are jammed between 7.30am and 9am and from 4 to 7.30pm.

If you can't face the complexities of the bus system or it's late at night, it's well worth calling for a metered **taxi**, a comfortable and fairly cheap option. Amarillo Taxis (☎332 1515; 24hr) are highly recommended; all cabs are equipped with state-of-the-art navigation systems and will pick you up from anywhere in the city; the fare from Zona 1 to Zona 10 is US$4–5. There are plenty of non-metered taxis around too – you'll have to use your bargaining skills with these and fix the price beforehand.

## USEFUL BUS ROUTES

**#71** Starts on 10 Av, Zona 1, and goes to the Centro Cívico.

**#82** Starts in Zona 2 and continues through Zona 1 along 10 Avenida, then past the Centro Cívico in Zona 4 and on to Avenida la Reforma before turning left at the Obelisco. The route passes many of the embassies, the American Express office, the Popol Vuh and Ixchel museums and the Los Próceres shopping centre.

**#83** Starts on 10 Avenida, Zona 1, and goes via the Centro Cívico to the airport.

Any bus marked **"terminal"**, and there are plenty of these on 4 Avenida in Zona 1, will take you to the main bus terminal in Zona 4.

Any bus with **"Bolívar"** or **"Trébol"** written on will take you along the western side of the city, down Avenida Bolívar and to the Trébol junction for connections to the western highlands.

## Accommodation

The majority of the budget and mid-range hotels are grouped in noisy central and eastern **Zona 1**; it's not the safest neighbourhood at night and not a great place for wandering around in search of a room. Many travellers are now choosing to stay close to the airport, in **Zona 13**, where there are a number of good new options – all offer free airport pick-ups and drop-offs, though be sure to book ahead. The disadvantage with this quiet, sub-urban location is that there are very few restaurants and cafés close by, and the bus service is infrequent. Guatemala City's luxury hotels are clustered in a relatively safe part of town, **Zona 10**, where the "Zona Viva" boasts a glut of dining options, bars and nightclubs.

### Zona 1

**Chalet Suizo**, 14 C 6–82 (☎251 3786, fax 232 0429). Friendly, comfortable and, as it's right opposite the police headquarters, very safe. Nicely designed, spotlessly clean and all very Swiss and organized, with left luggage and a new café that's open all day. Private or shared bath. No double beds. ④/⑤.

**Hotel Colonial**, 7 Av 14–19 (☎232 6722, fax 232 8671, *colonial@infovia.com.gt*). Well-situated colonial-style hotel with dark wood, wrought iron and an attractive tiled lobby. Tasteful and comfortable, but slightly old-fashioned; the rooms come with or without private bathroom. ④.

**Hotel Fénix**, 7 Av 15–81 (☎251 6625). Safe, friendly and vaguely atmospheric, set in an old, warped, wooden building. There's a quirky café downstairs and some rooms have private bath, though it can be noisy early in the morning. ②.

**Hotel Hernani**, corner 15 C and 6Av A (☎232 2839). Comfortable old building with good, clean rooms, all with their own shower. One of the better budget deals in town. ②.

**Hotel Monteleone**, 18 C 4–63 (☎238 2600, fax 238 2509). Rooms are attractively decorated, with quality mattresses and bedside lamps, and some have private bath. Very decent value – clean, safe and right by the Antigua terminal – but not the best area to be in after dark. ②/③.

**Hotel PanAmerican**, 9 C 5–63 (☎232 6807, fax 251 8749, *www.hotelpanamerican.com*). The city's oldest smart hotel, very formal and civilized, with a strong emphasis on Guatemalan tradition. Cable TV, continental breakfast and airport transfer included. Brilliant for Sunday breakfast. ⑥.

**Hotel Posada Belén**, 13 C A 10–30 (☎253 4530, fax 251 3478, *www.guateweb.com*). Tucked down a side street in a beautiful old building. Supremely quiet, safe and very homely, with its own restaurant. No children under five. ⑥.

**Hotel Royal Palace**, 6 Av 12–66 (☎ & fax 332 4036). Very comfortable, landmark right in the heart of Zona 1 with well appointed, spacious rooms and good service, but be sure to avoid the noisy streetside rooms. Seasonal bargain rates. ⑦.

**Hotel San Martín**, 16 C 7–65 (☎238 0319). Very cheap, clean and friendly, this is among the best deals at the lower end of the scale. Some rooms with private bath. ②.

**Hotel Spring**, 8 Av 12–65 (☎232 2858, fax 232 0107). An excellent deal here and a safe location, though it's often full of Peace Corps volunteers. The fairly spacious rooms, with or without private bath, are set around a pretty colonial courtyard and some have private bath; there's also a new block where all rooms have cable TV. Breakfast available and free mineral water. ②/③.

**Pensión Meza**, 10 C 10–17 (☎232 3177 or 253 4576). Infamous budget travellers' hangout; cheap and laid-back, with plenty of 1960s-style decadence. Fidel Castro and Che Guevara stayed here – the latter in room 21. Pretty dilapidated dorms (US$2.50) and doubles, some with private shower. Noticeboard, ping-pong, music all day, and the helpful owner, Mario, speaks good English. ①.

## Zona 13

**El Aeropuerto Guest House**, 15 C A 7–32 (☎332 3086, fax 362 1264, *hotairpt@guate.net*). Five minutes' walk from the international airport. Call for a free pick-up or walk across the grass outside and follow the road to the left. A pleasant, convenient and comfortable place: rooms have cable TV, private showers and fluffy towels. Continental breakfast is included and there are email and fax facilities for guests. ⑤.

**Dos Lunas**, 21 C 10-92 (☎ & fax 334 5264, *www.xelapages.com/doslunas*). Clean, secure and friendly guest house set in quiet suburban surrounds a short drive from the airport. Free pick-up, drop-off and breakfast, plus excellent travel information and tips from the dynamic young Guatemalan owner. Very popular, so essential to book well ahead. US$10 per person.

**Economy Dorms**, 8 Av 17-74, Col Aurora I (☎331 8029). Basic dormitory accommodation with free continental breakfast and transfers from the airport. US$10 per person.

**Hotel Hincapié**, Av Hincapié 18–77 (☎332 7771, fax 337 4469, *aruedap@infovia.com.gt*). Under the same management as the *El Aeropuerto* and conveniently located for the domestic terminal. Rates include local calls, continental breakfast, and transport to and from the airport. ④.

**Patricia's Bed and Breakfast**, 19 C 10-65, Col Aurora II (☎331 0470; *www.geocities.com/xela-ju2001*). Small, family-run guest house with pleasant rooms and friendly atmosphere a short distance from the airport. US$10 per person. ④.

## Zonas 9 and 10

**Camino Real**, Av la Reforma and 14 C, Zona 10 (☎333 4633, fax 337 4313, *www.quetzalnet.com/caminoreal*). Landmark hotel, long favoured by visiting heads of state and anyone on expenses, though the chintz-heavy decor is beginning to look rather dated. Excellent location in the heart of the Zona Viva, plus bars, shops and sports facilities – including two pools. Rooms from US$167. ⑨.

**Holiday Inn**, 1 Av 13–22, Zona 10 (☎332 2555, fax 332 2584, *www.guatered.com/holidayinn*). First-class hotel, within walking distance of the city's best upmarket shops, bars and restaurants. Commodious rooms and suites, plus a fully equipped business centre and an in-house Internet café. Rooms from US$140. ⑨.

**Hotel Casa Santa Clara**, 12 C 4–51, Zona 10 (☎339 1811, fax 332 0775, *www.hotelcasasantaclara.com*). Small, beautifully appointed hotel in the Zona Viva, with tastefully decorated modern rooms. Also boasts a quality in-house Mediterranean restaurant. ⑦.

**Hotel Inter-Continental**, 14 C 2–51 Zona 10 (☎379 4444, fax 379 4447, *www.interconti.com*). This spectacular new Zona Viva hotel is now the city's most stylish five-star address. Among its many charms are a monumental lobby featuring fine art, modern sculpture and a modish bar, sumptuous bedrooms, a fine French restaurant and a wonderful outdoor pool. Rooms from US$145. ⑨.

**Hotel Princess Reforma**, 13 C 7–65, Zona 9 (☎334 4545, fax 334 4546, *www.hotelesprincess.com*). Pleasant mid-sized hotel with very comfortable rooms, and high standards of service. There's a small pool, sauna, gym and tennis courts. Rooms from US$134. ⑨.

# The City

Guatemala City is hardly over-endowed with sights, but there are some places that are worth visiting while you're here. The Ixchel, Popol Vuh and Archeological museums are particularly good, and there are a few impressive buildings in Zona 1 as well as some more outlandish modern structures dotted across the southern half of the city.

If you're interested to see how the rich let their hair down, head for the Zona Viva in Zona 10, while Zona 1 is the place to see the big city streetlife – hawkers, market vendors, evangelical preachers and prostitutes are all here in abundance.

## The old city: Zona 1

The hub of the old city is **Zona 1**, which is also the busiest and most claustrophobic part of town. This is the run-down historic centre, a squalid world of low-slung, crumbling nineteenth-century town houses and faceless concrete blocks, broken pavements, car parking lots and plenty of noise and dirt. Though the city authorities largely left Zona 1 to rot for decades, tentative signs of regeneration are beginning to emerge, as a committed group of planners and architects attempt to preserve the capital's heritage, and clusters of new bars and cafés are opening in historic buildings. It's a process that will take decades to achieve, as the area remains plagued by pollution and noise from thundering fume-belching buses and beset by social problems, but the streets, thick with street vendors and urban bustle, do harbour a certain brutal fascination and are undeniably the most exciting part of the capital.

The heart of the capital, the windswept plaza called the **parque central**, is also the country's political and religious centre and the point from which all distances in Guatemala are measured. It's a strangely soulless place, patronized by bored taxi-drivers, *lustradores* (shoeshiners) and pigeons, that only really comes alive on Sundays and public holidays when a tide of Guatemalans descend on the square to stroll, chat and snack or to visit the *huipil* market. There is a new national spirit detectable here now, as soldiers chat with Maya girls, and you may even hear politics being discussed – something almost unthinkable a decade or so ago. Next to the giant Guatemalan flag in the centre of the square is a small box containing an **eternal flame** dedicated to "the anonymous heroes for peace", which has made the parque a place of pilgrimage for many Guatemalans.

The most striking building here is the **Palacio Nacional**, a grandiose stone-faced structure started in 1939 under President Ubico. For decades it housed the executive branch of the government, and from time to time its steps have been fought over by assorted coupsters. The palace is currently undergoing conversion into an interactive museum of the history of Guatemala. If you can get inside, it's worth a look at its most imposing features – two Moorish-style interior courtyards and the stained glass windows of the former **Salas de Recepción** on the second floor.

On the east side of the plaza, the blue tile-domed **Catedral** (daily 8am–1pm & 3–7pm) was completed in 1868. Its solid, squat design was intended to resist the force of earthquakes and has, for the most part, succeeded. Inside there are three main aisles, all lined with arching pillars, austere colonial paintings and intricate altars supporting an array of saints. The cathedral's most poignant aspect is outside, however: etched into the twelve pillars that support the entrance railings are the names of thousands of the dead and disappeared, victims of the civil war – children, parents and priests – including an astounding number from the department of Quiché.

Opposite the cathedral, the western side of the parque central merges into the **Parque del Centenario**, former site of the Palacio de los Capitanes Generales, which was destroyed by the 1917 earthquake. The parque is unremarkable in the extreme, with an ugly, concrete, shell-shaped bandstand which is occasionally used for live concerts and evangelical get-togethers. Looming over the Parque del Centenario is a modern block housing the **Biblioteca Nacional** (National Library), which holds the archives of Central America.

Heading to the east, around the back of the cathedral, there's the sunken concrete bulk of the **Mercado Central** (Mon–Sat 6am–6pm, Sun 9am–noon), painted sickly blue and yellow, with a miserable mini-plaza and car park on its roof. Taking no chances, the architect of this building apparently modelled the structure on a nuclear bunker, sacrificing any aesthetic concerns to the need for strength. Inside, you'll find

**GUATEMALA CITY: ZONA 1**

Centro Cívico

Parque Minerva

La Bodeguita del Centro

National Library

Buses to Antigua

Parque Concordia

4 AVENIDA

5 AVENIDA

Parque del Centenario

Police HQ

6 AVENIDA

Palacio Nacional

Iglesia de San Francisco

Parque Central

7 AVENIDA

Buses to Esquipulas & Chiquimula

Casa Mima

Cathedral

Buses to Cobán

8 AVENIDA

9 AVENIDA

Mercado Central

Buses to Mexican Border

Buses to Petén

Train Station (Disused)

10 AVENIDA

Buses to Puerto Barrios

11 AVENIDA

0     200 m

N

**RESTAURANTS & CAFÉS**

| | |
|---|---|
| Altuna | E |
| Cafebreria | C |
| Café de Centro Histórico | H |
| Café Gran Pavo | B |
| Europa Bar | F |
| Fu Lu Sho | D |
| Las Cien Puertes | I |
| Long Wah | A |
| Rey Sol | G |
| Tao Restaurant | J |

**ACCOMMODATION**

| | |
|---|---|
| Chalet Suizo | 5 |
| Hotel Colonial | 7 |
| Hotel Fénix | 6 |
| Hotel Hernani | 4 |
| Hotel Monteleone | 1 |
| Hotel PanAmerican | 3 |
| Hotel Posada Belén | 10 |
| Hotel Royal Palace | 2 |
| Hotel San Martín | 8 |
| Hotel Spring | 9 |
| Pensión Meza | 11 |

textiles, leatherware and jewellery on the top floor; fruit, vegetables, snacks, flowers and plants in the middle; and **handicrafts**, mainly basketry and *típica*, in the basement. Unexpectedly, the market is a pretty good spot to buy traditional weaving, with an astonishing range of cloth from all over the country on offer.

To the south of the parque central are **6 and 7 avenidas**, thick with clothes shops, street traders, fast-food joints and neon signs. On the corner of 6 Avenida and 13 Calle is the **Iglesia de San Francisco**, dating from 1780, a church famous for its carving of the Sacred Heart. It's said that when it was built, the mortar was mixed with cane syrup, egg whites and cow's milk to enhance its strength against earthquakes. Another block to the south is the **police headquarters**, an outlandish-looking mock castle complete with imitation medieval battlements.

Just 300m east of the police headquarters along 14 Calle, at the corner with 8 Avenida, **Casa Mima** (Mon–Sat 9am–12.30pm & 2–5pm; US$2) is an immaculately restored late nineteenth-century town house, with original Moderne, Art Deco and French neo-Roccoco furnishings, offering a fascinating glimpse of a wealthy middle-class household. There are excellent explanatory leaflets, and usually an English-speaking guide, plus a delightful little café, with good coffee and cookies, on the rear patio. As you head south from Casa Mima, along 8 Avenida, things go into a slow but steady decline, until you finally emerge in the madness of **18 Calle**, a distinctly sleazy part of town probably best avoided day or night. An assorted collection of grimy nightclubs and "streap-tease" joints, this is the street that most of the city's petty thieves, prostitutes and low-life seem to call home. At the junction of 18 Calle and 9 Avenida is the wooden shell of the former **train station**, from which regular passenger services used to leave for Tecún Umán and Puerto Barrios. It was badly damaged by a fire in 1996, days before an audit was due to start, and currently there are only sporadic cargo trains running in Guatemala.

At the southern end of the old city, separating it from the newer parts of town, the distinctively 1960s architecture of the **Centro Cívico** marks the boundary between Zonas 1 and 4. Looming over 7 Avenida is the Banco de Guatemala building, bedecked with bold modern murals and stylized glyphs designed by Dagoberto Vásquez – the images recount the history of Guatemala and the conflict between Spanish and Maya. Just to the south you'll find the main office of **Inguat** (see p.328) and opposite is the lofty landmark **Teatro Nacional**, also referred to as the Miguel Asturias cultural centre, one of the city's most prominent and unusual structures, completed in 1978. Designed along the lines of an ocean liner, painted blue and white with portholes as windows, it has superb views across the city. Cultural events are regularly staged in the theatre's auditorium and an adjoining open-air space, and there's also a little-visited museum dedicated to the Guatemalan military that's really only of interest to would-be *comandantes*.

## The new city
The southern half of the city is far more spacious, with broader streets, and is, roughly speaking, divided into two by **7 Avenida**. To the south of the Centro Cívico over in Zona 4, at the junction of 7 Avenida and 2 Calle, is the landmark **Torre del Reformador**, Guatemala's answer to the Eiffel Tower. This was built in honour of President Barrios, whose liberal reforms transformed the country between 1871 and 1885. Unfortunately you can't go up it. Just to the south on the junction with Ruta 6 is the **Yurrita Church**, built in an outlandish neo-Gothic style more reminiscent of a horror movie set than the streets of Guatemala City.

Continuing southeast down Ruta 6 from the Yurrita church, you approach **Avenida la Reforma**, the new city's main transport artery, which divides Zonas 9 and 10. Many of the new city's important sites and buildings are to be found on or just off this tree-lined boulevard, including the **Botanical Gardens** (Mon–Fri 8am–3.30pm, US$1.20) of the San Carlos University; the entrance is on 0 Calle. Inside you'll find a beautiful small garden with quite a selection of species, all neatly labelled in Spanish and Latin. There's also a small, not terribly exciting natural history museum, with a collection of stuffed birds, including a quetzal and an ostrich, as well as geological samples, wood types, live snakes and some horrific pickled rodents.

Far more worthwhile are the two privately owned museums in the campus of the University Francisco Marroquín, reached by following 6 Calle Final off Avenida la Reforma to the east. **Museo Ixchel** (Mon–Fri 8am–5.50pm, Sat 9am–12.50pm; US$2.50, students US$1) is strikingly housed in its own purpose-built cultural centre. Probably the capital's best museum, the Ixchel is dedicated to Maya culture, with particular emphasis on traditional weaving. There's a stunning collection of hand-woven fabrics, including some very impressive examples of ceremonial costumes, with explanations in English. There's also information about the techniques, dyes, fibres and weaving tools used, and the way in which costumes have changed over the years. Don't miss the very good miniature *huipil* collection in the basement..

Right next door, on the third floor of the *auditorio* building, is the city's other private museum, the excellent **Popol Vuh** archeological museum (Mon–Fri 9am–5pm, Sat 9am–1pm; US$2.50), boasting an outstanding collection of artefacts from sites all over the country. The small museum is divided into Preclassic, Classic, Postclassic and Colonial rooms, and all the exhibits are top quality. In the Preclassic room are some stunning ceramics, stone masks and *hongo zoomorfo* (mushroom heads); the Classic room has an altar from Naranjo, some lovely incense burners and a model of Tikal; the Postclassic contains a replica of the Dresden Codex; and the colonial era is represented by various ecclesiastical relics and processional crosses.

Back on Avenida la Reforma, the smart part of town is to the south, a collection of leafy streets filled with boutiques and travel agents, the American embassy, banks, office blocks and sleek hotels. This part of town has clearly escaped the Third World. A little to the east, around 10 Calle and 3 Avenida, is the so-called **Zona Viva**, a tight bunch of upmarket hotels, restaurants and nightclubs and, at the bottom of La Reforma, the upmarket Los Próceres shopping mall. If you've spent some time in the impoverished highland villages, the ostentation on show in this little enclave will come as quite a shock to the system. To get to Avenida la Reforma from Zona 1, take bus #82, which runs along 10 Avenida in Zona 1, past the Yurrita Church and all the way along Avenida la Reforma, which is a two-way street so you can return by the same means.

## WEST OF 7 AVENIDA

Out to the west of 7 Avenida it's quite another story, and while there are still small enclaves of upmarket housing, and several expensive shopping areas, things are really dominated by commerce and transport, including the infamous **Zona 4 bus terminal**, at 1 Calle and 4 Avenida. This area is probably the country's most impenetrable and intimidating jungle – a brutish swirl of petty thieves, hardware stores, bus fumes and sleeping vagrants. Around the terminal the largest **market** in the city spreads across several blocks. To get to the bus terminal from Zona 1, take any of the buses marked "terminal" from 4 Avenida or 9 Avenida, all of which pass within a block or two.

Further to the south, in Zona 13, the **Parque Aurora** houses the city's remodelled **zoo** (Tues–Sun 9am–5pm; US$1.20), with a collection that includes African lions, Bengal tigers, crocodiles, giraffes, Indian elephants, hippos, monkeys and all the Central and South American big cats, including some well-fed jaguar. Most of the larger animals have a reasonable amount of space, many smaller animals do not.

On the other side of the Parque Aurora is a collection of state-run museums (all Tues–Fri 9am–4pm, Sat & Sun 9am–noon & 1.30–4pm). The best of these is the **Museo Nacional de Arqueología y Etnología** (US$5), which has a world-class selection of Maya artefacts, though the design and displays are somewhat antiquated. The collection has sections on prehistoric archeology and ethnology and includes some wonderful stelae and panels from Machaquila and Dos Pilas, spectacular jade masks from Abaj Takalik and a stunning wooden temple-top lintel from Tikal. However it's the exhibits collected from Piedras Negras, one of the remotest sites in Petén, that are most impressive. Stela 12, dating from 672 AD, brilliantly depicts a cowering captive king begging for mercy and there's a monumental carved stone throne from the same site, richly engraved with superb glyphs and decorated with a twin-faced head. Right opposite the archeological museum, the city's **Museo Nacional de Arte Moderno** (US$1.70) also suffers from poor presentation and layout but can boast some imaginative geometric paintings by Dagoberto Vásquez, vibrant semi-abstract work by the indigenous artist Rolando Ixquiac Xicará and a collection of startling exhibits by Efraín Recinos including a colossal marimba-tank (a sculpture that is part indigenous musical instrument, part tank). There's also a permanent collection of the bold Cubist art and massive murals of Carlos Mérida, Guatemala's most celebrated artist, which draws strongly on ancient Maya tradition. Finally, the **Museo Nacional de Historia Natural** (US$1.70) is probably the most neglected of the trio of museums, featuring a range of mouldy-looking stuffed animals from Guatemala and elsewhere and a few mineral samples. Close by, on 11 Avenida, is a touristy handicraft market, while to the south is Aurora airport. To get here, take bus #63 from 4 Avenida or #83 from 10 Avenida.

## Kaminaljuyú

Way out west on the edge of the city, beyond the stench of the city rubbish dump, is the long thin arm of Zona 7, which wraps around the ruins of **Kaminaljuyú** (daily 9am–4pm; US$4). Archeological digs on this side of the city have revealed the astonishing proportions of a Maya city that once housed around 50,000 people and includes more than three hundred mounds and thirteen ball courts. Unlike the massive temples of the lowlands, these structures were built of adobe, and most of them have been lost to centuries of erosion and a few decades of urban sprawl. Today, the archeological site, incorporating only a tiny fraction of the original city, is little more than a series of earth-covered mounds, a favourite spot for football and romance, and it's virtually impossible to get any impression of Kaminaljuyú's former scale and splendour.

To get to the ruins, take bus #35 from 4 Avenida in Zona 1; alternatively, any bus with a small "Kaminaljuyú" sign in the windscreen passes within a block or two.

# Eating, drinking and entertainment

Despite its status as the capital and the largest city in Central America, Guatemala City isn't a great place for indulging. Most of the population hurry home after dark and it's only the very rich who eat, drink and dance until the small hours. There are, however, restaurants everywhere in the city, invariably reflecting the type of neighbourhood they're in. Nightclubs and bars are concentrated in Zona 10.

Movie-watching is also popular and there is a good selection of cinemas. Most movies are shown in English with Spanish subtitles. There are four cinemas on 6 Avenida south of the main plaza. Of the others, the very best for sound quality is the Magic Place on Avenida las Américas, Zona 13. Also recommended are Cine Las Américas, Avenida las Américas, between 8 and 9 calles, Zona 13, and Cine Tikal Futura, in the Tikal Futura shopping mall, Calzada Roosevelt, Zona 11. Programmes are listed in the two main newspapers, *El Gráfico* and *Prensa Libre*.

### Restaurants and cafés

When it comes to eating cheaply in Guatemala City, stick to Zona 1, where there are some good comedores and dozens of fast-food chains. In the smarter parts of town, particularly Zonas 9 and 10, the emphasis is more on upmarket cafés and glitzy dining, though the choice is wider here than elsewhere, taking in Mexican, Middle Eastern, Chinese and Japanese options.

#### ZONA 1

**Altuna**, 5 Av 12–31. Spanish/Basque food in a wonderfully civilized old colonial mansion. Very strong on fish and seafood, but also pasta and Castilian treats like Manchego cheese and *jamón serrano*. Not cheap, but worth a splurge for the elegant ambience.

**Cafebreria**, 5 Av 13–32. Part bookshop, part Internet café, serving coffee, snacks and more substantial dishes on a quiet covered patio. The owner also plans to open a budget hotel upstairs.

**Café de Centro Histórico**, 6 Av 9–50. Stylish café on the upper floor of a beautifully restored 1930s building replete with original tiles, wood panelling and evocative monochrome photographs. Simple menu of inexpensive Guatemalan dishes, pies and salads, plus great coffee.

**Europa Bar**, 11 C 5–16. The most popular expat hangout in Zona 1, set inauspiciously beneath a multistorey car park. Primarily a bar, with CNN and sports on screen, but there are also cheapish eats. Owner Judy is a mine of local information. You can trade US dollars here and make local calls. Closed Sun.

**Fu Lu Sho**, 6 Av and 12 C. Popular, inexpensive Chinese restaurant with an Art Deco interior, opening onto the bustle of 6 Avenida.

**El Gran Pavo**, 13 C 4–41. Massive portions of genuinely Mexican, moderately priced food. It's riotous on the weekend when mariachi bands prowl the tables. Also at 6 C 3–09, Zona 9; 15 Av 16–72, Zona 10; 13C and 6 Av, Zona 10

**Long Wah**, 6 C 3–75, west of the Palacio Nacional. One of the best of the many Chinese restaurants in this neighbourhood, with a good inexpensive menu.

**Rey Sol**, south side of Parque Centenario. "Aerobic" breakfasts (sic), very good selection of vegetarian dishes and licuados. The shop sells wholemeal bread, granola and veggie snacks.

**Tao Restaurant**, 5 C 9–70. The city's best-value three-course veggie lunch. There's no menu; you just eat the meal of the day at tiny tables around a plant-filled courtyard.

## ZONA 4

**Cafe Restaurant Pereira**, inside the Gran Centro Comercial mall, 6 Av and 24 C. Just a couple of blocks west of Inguat, this is a very popular comedor with excellent set meals of typical Guatemalan food. Also at Av la Reforma 14–43, Zona 9.

## ZONAS 9 AND 10

**Los Alpes**, 10 C 1–09, Zona 10. A haven of peace, this garden café has superb pastries, pies and crêpes and a relatively inexpensive breakfast menu considering the smart location. Closed Mon.

**Los Antojitos**, Av la Reforma 15–02, Zona 9. Good, moderately priced Central American food – try the *chiles rellenos* or guacamole.

**Jake's**, 17 C 10–40, Zona 10. Lunch and dinner from an international menu, very strong on fish and with terrific sweets. Pleasant, candle-lit atmosphere, excellent service and correspondingly high prices. Closed Sun & Mon.

**La Lancha**, 13 C 7–98, Zona 10. French-owned restaurant, with a superb menu of very reasonably priced traditional Gallic dishes, plus a daily special, and a tremendous wine list. Open for lunch Mon–Fri, dinner Thurs & Fri only.

**Luigi's Pizza**, 4 Av 14–20, Zona 10. Very popular, moderately priced Italian restaurant, serving delicious pizza, pasta and baked potatoes.

**Olivadda**, 12 C 4–51, Zona 10. Very smart restaurant with a stylish interior and a leafy terrace garden, majoring in authentic, moderately priced Mediterranean fare.

**Palace**, 10 C 4–40, Zona 10. Pasta and snacks, cakes and pastries in a cafeteria atmosphere.

**Piccadilly**, Plaza España, 7 Av 12–00, Zona 9. One of the most popular continental restaurants with tourists and Guatemalans alike. Decent range of pastas and pizzas, served along with huge jugs of beer. Moderate prices. Also in Zona 1 on 6 Av and 11 C.

**Puerto Barrios**, 7 Av 10–65, Zona 9. Excellent, but pricey, seafood restaurant in a slightly comical boat-like building.

**Tamarindos**, 11 C 2–19A, Zona 10. Uber-chic bar-restaurant with modish Italian furniture, sensitive lighting, European chillout music and a very hip, moneyed clientele. The pan-Asian menu matches the site with delicious, beautifully presented Thai, Malay and Chinese influenced dishes set at far from outrageous prices – expect to pay around $15 a head.

**Vesuvio Pizza**, 18 C 3–36, Zona 10. Huge pizzas with plenty of mouth-watering toppings, cooked in a traditional, wood-burning oven.

## Bars and clubs

The best bet for a night out in **Zona 1** is to start somewhere like *Las Cien Puertes* or *El Tiempo* and then head to *Altos del Cairo* close by to see a band, or check out what's on at *La Bodeguita* Alternatively, if you crave the low life, then stroll on down 18 Calle, to the junction with 9 Avenida, and you're in the heart of the red-light district, where the bars and clubs are truly sleazy.

Zona 10 is where the wealthy go to have fun and it's anything but an egalitarian experience. *Sento Senso* is a good place to head for, while there's a strip of bars along 1 and 2 avenidas in the Zona Viva, plus plenty of dance clubs. House music is firmly established in Guatemala, though you'll be lucky to get anything other than the commercial "handbag" strain; most DJs spin a mix of pan-Latin sounds and rave hits, with the merengue of the Caribbean often spiced up with raggamuffin vocals; plus there are specialist clubs for salsa fanatics. The city's premier reggae bar is *La Gran Comal* on Via 4 between 6 Avenida and Ruta 6, Zona 4. Radiating rhythm, it's relaxed, but not as worn-out as the clubs of Zona 1. It's a favourite haunt of black Guatemalans from Lívingston and the Caribbean coast, and well worth a visit.

**Altos del Cairo**, first floor, 9 C 6–10, Zona 1. Raucous drinking den with simple bench seating, draught beer, and rock, pop and salsa nights.

**La Bodeguita del Centro**, 12 C 3–55, Zona 1 (☎230 2976). Large, left-field venue with live music, comedy, poetry and all manner of arty events. Free entry in the week, around US$4 at weekends. Definitely worth a visit for the Che Guevara memorabilia alone.

**Las Cien Puertes**, Pasaje Aycinena, 9 C between 6 and 7 Av, Zone 1. Funky, artistic bar in a beautiful run-down colonial arcade. Good Latin sounds, very moderate prices and some imaginative Guatemalan cooking. Recommended.

**Crocodilo's**, 16 C and 2 Av, in the Los Próceres shopping mall in Zona 10. A restaurant that doubles up as a cocktail bar, with a happy hour between 6 and 9pm.

**El Establo**, 14 C 5–08, Zona 10. Large, stylish European-owned bar with polished wood interior, good food and a soundtrack of decent jazz and Western music.

**Kahlua**, 15 C and 1 Av, Zona 10. Currently one of the most happening clubs in town with two dance floors and a chill-out room. Attracts a young crowd with a reasonable mix of dance and Latin pop.

**Sesto Senso**, 2 Av 12–81, Zona 10. Hip, lively bar-restaurant venue with superb menu of global food, plus great coffee and snacks, and often some live music in the evening.

**Shakespeare's Pub**, 13 C 1–51, Zona 10. Small basement bar, with friendly staff, mainly catering to middle-aged expat North Americans.

**El Tiempo**, Pasaje Aycinema, 9 C between 6 and 7 Av, Zona 1. Very lively bar in the heart of the historic centre that's a magnet for the city's bohemian youth, hedonists and thinkers, where there are sporadic musical jams, protest poetry readings and the like.

**Xtreme**, 3 Av and 13 C, Zona 10. Industrial decor, with a dark interior full of steel and aluminium, plus a tooth-loosening sound system, make this club one of the coolest places in town. The Latin dance, house and chart pop attracts a rich, young crowd.

## Listings

**Airlines** Airline offices are scattered throughout the city, with many along Avenida la Reforma. It is fairly straightforward to phone them and there will almost always be someone in the office who speaks English. Aerocaribe (see Mexicana, below); Aerovías, Av Hincapié 18 C, Zona 13 (☎332 5686, airport ☎332 7470); Air Canada, 12 C 1–25, Zona 10 (☎335 3341, *www.aircanada.ca*); American Airlines, *Hotel El Dorado*, Av la Reforma 15-45, Zona 9 (☎334 7379, *www.americanair.com*); Aviateca (see Taca, below); British Airways, 1 Av 10–81, Zona 10, 6th floor of Edificio Inexa (☎332 7402; *www.british-airways.com*); Continental, 12 C 1–25, Zona 10, Edificio Géminis 10, 12th floor of Torre Norte (☎331 3341, *www.continental.com*); Copa, 1 Av 10–1, Zona 10 (☎361 1567, *www.copaair.com*); Delta, 15 C 3–20, Zona 10, Centro Ejecutivo building (☎337 0642, *www.delta-air.com*); Iberia, Av la Reforma 8–60, Zona 9 (☎334 3816, airport ☎332 5517, *www.iberia.com*); Inter (see Taca, below); Lacsa (see Taca, below); Jungle Flying, Av Hincapié & 18 C, domestic terminal, Hangar 21, Zona 13 (☎360 4917, *jungleflying@guate.net*); Mexicana, 13 C 8–44, Zona 10, Edificio Edyma (☎333 6048, *www.mexicana.com*); Nica (see Taca, below); Taca Group (Aviateca, Inter, Lacsa, Nica), Av Hincapié 12–22, Zona 13 (☎334 7722, *www.grupotaca.com*); Tikal Jets, La Aurora airport, international terminal (☎334 5631); United Airlines, Av la Reforma 1–50, Zona 9, Edificio el Reformador (☎332 2995, *www.ual.com*).

**American Express** Diagonal 6 10–01, Centro Gerencial Las Margaritas, Zona 10 (Mon–Fri 8.30am–5pm; ☎339 2877, fax 339 2882).

**Banks and exchange** At the airport, Banco Del Quetzal (Mon–Fri 6am–8pm, Sat & Sun 6am–6pm) gives a good rate, takes most European currencies, and has a 24-hr Mastercard and Cirrus cashpoint; Visa and Plus cardholders should head for the nearby 24-hr Bancared cashpoint. In Zona 1,

Credomatic, on the corner of 5 Av and 11 C, gives Visa and Mastercard cash advances (Mon–Fri 8.30am–7pm, Sat 9am–1pm) and will cash travellers' cheques. In Zona 10, head for the Centro Gerencial Las Margaritas, at Diagonal 6 10–01, where there are numerous banks where you can cash travellers' cheques, three 24-hr cashpoints for Visa and Plus cards and another, inside the Banco de Central América (Mon–Fri 9am–5pm, Sat 9am–1pm), that accepts Mastercard and Cirrus cards.

**Books** The pleasantest bookshop in town is Sopho's, Av la Reforma 13–89, Zona 10, where there's a decent selection of English language fiction and literature – you can also get good coffee here. Over the road in Zona 9 the Librería del Pensativo, 7 Av and 13 C, Edificio La Cúpula, is worth a browse, while in Zona 1 try Arnel, in the basement of the Edificio El Centro on 9 C, corner of 7 Av. Finally Géminis, 3 Av 17–05, Zona 14, is also worth a visit if you're in the south of the city.

**Car rental** Renting a car in Guatemala is quite expensive and you should always keep a sharp eye on the terms, there are usually large penalties if you damage the vehicle. Jeeps can be rented for a little under US$55 a day and cars start from US$35. Adaesa Renta Autos, 4 C A 16–57, Zona 1 (☎220 2180, *masifre@hotmail.com*); Americar, 6 Av 3–95, Zona 10 (☎361 8641, *www.america.com*); Autorrentas (Budget agent), Av Hincapié 11–01, Zona 13 (☎332 2024, *budget@infovia.com*); Avis, 6 Av 11–24, Zona 9 (☎334 1057, *avis@guate.net*); Hertz, 7 Av 14–76, Zona 9 (☎334 2540, *rentauto@guate.net*); Rental, 12 C 2–62, Zona 10 (☎361 0672, fax 334 2739) – the only company to rent motorbikes; Tabarini, 2 C A 7–30, Zona 10 (☎332 2161, fax 334 1925); Thrifty, Av la Reforma 8–33, Zona 10 (☎332 1220, *thrifty@guate.net*).

**Embassies** Most of the embassies are in the southeastern quarter of the city, along Avenida la Reforma and Avenida las Américas, and they tend to open weekday mornings only unless otherwise indicated. Belize, Av la Reforma 1–50, 8th Floor, Suite 803, Edificio el Reformador, Zona 9 (Mon–Fri 9am–1pm & 2–5pm; ☎334 5531 or 331 1137); Brazil, 18 C 2–22, Zona 14 (☎337 0949); Canada, 13 C 8–44, 8th Floor, Edificio Edyma Plaza, Zona 10 (Mon–Thurs 8am–4.30pm, Fri 8am–1.30pm; ☎333 6102); Chile, 14 C 15–21, Zona 13 (☎332 1149); Colombia, 12 C 1–25, Zona 10 (☎335 3602); Costa Rica, Av la Reforma 8–60, 3rd floor, Torre 1, Edificio Galerías Reforma, Zona 9 (☎ & fax 332 0531); Ecuador, 4 Av 12–04, Zona 14 (☎337 2902); El Salvador, 4 Av 13–60, Zona 10 (☎366 2240); Germany, 20 C 6–20, Edificio Plaza Marítima, Zona 10 (☎338 0028); Honduras, 12 C 1–25, 12th floor, Edificio Géminis, Zona 10 (☎338 2068); Mexico, 15 C 3–20, Zona 10 (Mon–Fri 9am–1pm & 3–5pm; ☎333 7254 or 333 7255); Netherlands 16 C 0–55, 13th floor, Torre Internacional, Zona 10 (☎367 4761); Nicaragua, 10 Av 14–72, Zona 10 (☎368 0785); Panama, 5 Av 15–45, Torre 2, Edificio Centro Empresarial, Zona 10 (☎333 7176); Peru, 2 Av 9–67, Zona 9 (☎331 8558); United Kingdom, 16 C 0–55, 11th floor, Torre Internacional, Zona 10 (Mon–Fri 9am–noon & 2–4pm; ☎367 5425); United States, Av la Reforma, 7–01, Zona 10 (Mon–Fri 8am–5pm; ☎331 1541); Venezuela, 8 C 0–56, Zona 9 (☎331 6505).

**Immigration** The main immigration office (*Migración*) is conveniently located on the second floor of the Inguat HQ at 7 Av 1–17, Zona 4 (☎634 8476, Mon–Fri 9am–3pm). For more details about visa extensions see p.16.

**Internet** Guatemala City is under-endowed with Internet cafés compared to Antigua, and rates are much higher, typically around US$5 an hour. In Zona 1, Cafebreria at 5 Av 13–32 is well set up, while in Zona 10 head for the Próceres shopping mall at 16 C and 2 Av where you can surf at Café Virtual at ground level or Wizards on the third floor.

**Laundry** Lavandería Obelisco, Av la Reforma 16–30, next to the Samaritana supermarket (Mon–Fri 8am–6.45pm, Sat 8am–5.30pm), charges around US$3 for a self-service wash and dry, and there's also a self-service laundry at 4 Av 13–89, Zona 1.

**Libraries** The best library for English books is in the IGA (Guatemalan American Institute) at Ruta 1 and Via 4, Zona 4. There's also the National Library on the west side of the Parque del Centenario, and specialist collections at the Ixchel and Popol Vuh museums.

**Medical care** Your embassy should have a list of bilingual doctors, but for emergency medical assistance dial ☎125 for the Red Cross, or head for the Centro Médico, a private hospital with 24-hr cover, at 6 Av 3–47, Zona 10 (☎332 3555). Central Dentista de Especialistas, 20 C 11–17, Zona 10 (☎337 1773), is the best dental clinic in the country, and superb in emergencies.

**Pharmacies** Farmacia Osco, 16 C and 4 Av, Zona 10.

**Photography** Colour transparency and both colour and monochrome print film is easy to buy, though expensive. There are several camera shops on 6 Avenida in Zona 1. Foto Sittler, 12 C 6–20, Zona 1, and La Perla, 9 C and 6 Av, Zona 1, repair cameras and offer a three-month guarantee on their work.

## MOVING ON FROM GUATEMALA CITY

To get to the **international terminal** of **Aurora airport** from Zona 1, either take bus #83 from 10 Avenida (30min) or take a taxi (around US$10); from Zona 10 a taxi is around US$6. There's a US$30 departure tax on all international flights, payable in either quetzals or dollars. The **domestic terminal** is in the same complex but only reached via Avenida Hincapié, you'll need to take a taxi. Note that all Taca and Tikal Jets internal flights leave from the international terminal. The domestic departure tax is US$0.80.

If you're leaving by **first-class bus**, departures are from the bus company offices. Most are spread around the streets surrounding the old train station at 18 C and 9 Av in **Zona 1**, where there are first-class departures to Puerto Barrios, Cobán, the Pacific highway, eastern highlands, the Mexican border and Petén.

Moving on by **second-class bus**, the main centre is the chaotic **Zona 4 terminal**, where services run to all parts of the country. To get there, take any city bus marked "terminal"; you'll find these heading south along 4 Avenida in Zona 1.

**Police** The main police station is in a bizarre castle-like structure on the corner of 6 Av and 14 C, Zona 1. In an emergency dial ☎120.

**Post office** The main post office, 7 Av and 12 C (Mon–Fri 8.30am–6.30pm, Sat 8.30am–4.30pm), has a Lista de Correos, where they will hold mail for you.

**Telephone** You can make long-distance phone calls and send faxes from Telgua, one block east of the post office (daily 7am–midnight).

**City Tours** Excellent walking tours of the historic centre of the city are organized by Antañona, 11 Av 5–59, Zona 1 (☎238 1751, *walkingtour@hotmail.com*); tours leave from their offices Mon–Fri at 9.30am and cost US$10 per person. Plenty of agencies offer guided city tours that usually include the main museums and sites and transport, including Clark Tours (see "Travel agents", below).

**Travel agents** There are plenty in the centre and along Avenida la Reforma in Zonas 9 and 10, flights to Petén can be booked through all of them. Clark Tours, Diagonal 6 10–01, 7th floor, Torre 2, Las Margaritas, Zona 10 (☎339 2888, fax 339 2909, *www.clarktours.com*), organizes trips to many parts of the country; Ecotourism & Adventure Specialists, 4 Av A 7–95, Zona 14, (☎337 0009, *www.ecotourism-adventure.com*), offers well co-ordinated trips to Petén and many remote parts of the country; Maya Expeditions, 15 C 1–91, Zona 10 (☎363 4955, fax 363 4164, www.mayaexpeditions.com), specializes in ecotourism adventure and rafting trips. Viajes Tivoli, 6 Av 8–41, Zona 9 (☎339 2260, *viajes@tivoli.com.gt*), or 12 C 4–55, Zona 1 (☎238 4771) is a good all-round agent with competitive rates for international flights.

**Work** Hard to come by. The best bet is teaching at one of the English schools, most of which are grouped on 10 and 18 calles in Zona 1. Check the classified sections of the *Guatemala Post* and *Revue*.

# Around Guatemala City

Escaping from the urban extremes of the capital is fairly straightforward and, fortunately, there is some superb scenery and some interesting villages within a hour or two of the centre. If you can, avoid travelling on a Sunday when everyone else seems to be day-tripping too.

## South of the capital

Heading south towards the Pacific, just 25km south of Guatemala City, is **Lago de Amatitlán**. The lake, nestled at the foot of the Volcán de Pacaya and encircled by forested hills, enjoys an undeniably superb setting, though its waters are now very polluted. Amatitlán's very proximity to the capital has been its downfall and every weekend its shores are swamped by day-trippers and holiday-home owners. However, there are some **thermal baths**, where you can take a revitalizing dip, and boats, which can be rented for around US$2 an hour. Buses run every fifteen minutes or so to the village of **Amatitlán**, 1km off the highway, from 20 Calle and 3 Avenida , Zona 1 (45min).

### BUSES FROM GUATEMALA CITY

The abbreviations we've used for the bus companies are as follows:

| | | | | | |
|---|---|---|---|---|---|
| **KQ** | King Quality | **RO** | Rutas Orientales | **TE** | Transportes Escobar y Monja Blanca |
| **L** | Lituega | **RZ** | Rápidos Zacaleu | | |
| **LA** | Líneas Américas | **SJ** | San Juanera | **TG** | Transportes Galgos |
| **LD** | Línea Dorada | **TB** | Ticabus | **TM** | Transportes Marquensita |
| **LH** | Los Halcones | **TA** | Transportes Alamo | | |
| **MI** | Melva Internacional | **TD** | Transportes Dulce María | **TR** | Transportes Rebuli |
| **P** | Pulmantur | | | **TV** | Transportes Velásquez |

| To | Company | Bus stop | Frequency | Journey time |
|---|---|---|---|---|
| **Antigua** | various (2nd) | 18 C & 4 Av, Zona 1 | 15min | 1hr |
| **Chichicastenango** | various (2nd) | Zona 4 terminal | 30min | 3hr 30min |
| **Chiquimula** | RO | 19 C & 9 Av, Zona 1 | 15 daily | 3hr 30min |
| **Cobán** | TE | 8 Av 15–16, Zona 1 | 14 daily | 4hr 30min |
| **Cubulco** | TD (2nd) | 19 C & 9 Av, Zona 1 | 10 daily | 5hr |
| **Escuintla** | various (2nd) | Zona 4 terminal | 30min | 1hr 15min |
| **Esquipulas** | RO | 19 C & 9 Av, Zona 1 | 15 daily | 4hr |
| **Flores** | various (1st/2nd) | 17 C & 8 Av, Zona 1 | 16 daily | 9hr |
| | LD (1st) | 16 C 10–55, Zona 1 | 3 daily | 9hr |
| **Huehuetenango** | LH (1st) | 7 Av 15–27, Zona 1 | 3 daily | 5hr 30min |
| | TV (1st) | 20 C 1–37, Zona 1 | 9 daily | 5hr 30min |
| | RZ(1st) | 9C 11–42,Zona 1 | 3 daily | 5hr 30min |
| **La Mesilla** | TV (1st) | 20 C 1–37, Zona 1 | 9 daily | 7hr |
| **Monterrico** | various (2nd) | Zona 4 terminal | 5 daily | 4hr |
| **Panajachel** | TR (2nd) | 21 C 1–54, Zona 1 | 11 daily | 3hr |
| **Puerto Barrios** | L (1st) | 15 C 10–40, Zona 1 | 18 daily | 5hr 30min |
| **Quetzaltenango** | LA (1st) | 2 Av 18–74, Zona 1 | 6 daily | 4hr |
| | TA (1st) | 21 C 1–14, Zona 1 | 5 daily | 4hr |
| | TM (1st) | 1 Av 21–31, Zona 1 | 8 daily | 4hr |
| | TG (1st) | 7 Av 19–44, Zona 1 | 6 daily | 4hr |
| | SJ (2nd) | Zona 4 terminal | 10 daily | 4hr 30min |
| **Rabinal** | TD (2nd) | 19 C & 9 Av, Zona 1 | 10 daily | 4hr 30min |
| **Salamá** | TD (2nd) | 19 C & 9 Av, Zona 1 | 10 daily | 3hr 30min |
| **San Salvador** | MI (1st) | 3 Av 1–38, Zona 9 | 11 daily | 5hr |
| | TB (1st) | 11 C 2–72, Zona 9 | 1 daily | 5hr |
| | KQ (1st) | Col.Vista Hermosa II, Zona 15 | 2 daily | 5hr |
| | P(1st) | Hotel Raddison Suites, Zona 10 1Av 12–43, | | 2 daily 5hr |
| **Santa Cruz del Quiché** | various (2nd) | Zona 4 terminal | 30min | 4hr |
| **Tecún Umán** | various (1st) | 19 Av & 8 C, Zona 1 | 30min | 5hr |
| **Talismán** | various (1st) | 19 Av & 8 C, Zona 1 | 30min | 5hr 30min |
| **Tapacula** | LD (1st) | 16 C 10–55, Zona 1 | 2 daily | 7hr |
| | TG (1st) | 7 Av 19–44, Zona 1 | 2 daily | 7hr |
| **Zacapa** | RO | 19 C & 9 Av, Zona 1 | 15 daily | 3hr |

---

### SAFETY ON THE VOLCÁN DE PACAYA

Before setting out on the climb to the peak of Pacaya, you should bear in mind that the volcano has been the scene of a number of **attacks**, rapes, murders and robberies. Though incidents have decreased in recent years, tours now come complete with armed guards. While most people climb the volcano without encountering any trouble, it is worth checking the current security situation with your embassy or at the tourist offices in Guatemala City or Antigua and keeping an eye on the Antigua noticeboards, where recent incidents are usually publicized. Virtually all the daily tours (no matter who you book with) leave Antigua around 1.30pm and return by around 10.30pm; try Gran Jaguar Tours, 4 C Poniente 30 (☎832 2712, *www.granjaguar.com*) in Antigua.

---

A further 10km down the highway, a turn-off heads into the hills through an aromatic network of coffee and tobacco plantations to the small village of **SAN VICENTE PACAYA**, from where trails lead to the **Volcán de Pacaya**. This volcano has been in a constant state of eruption since 1965 and is the most active in the Maya region. A trip to the smoking cone is an unforgettable experience, but as there have been a number of attacks around Pacaya in recent years (see box above) and given the volcano's extremely active nature, witnessing the spectacle does involve a degree of risk.

The best time to watch the eruptions is **at night**, when the sludge that the volcano spouts can be seen in its full glory as a plume of brilliant orange. Though it is possible to climb the cone independently, virtually everyone now chooses to join a group with a guide and an armed guard. Antigua is the best place to organize a trip, most of which cost around US$7 a head.

### Northwest of the capital

Leaving the city through Zona 7 and a suburb called El Florida, the road starts to climb into the hills, through an area that, apart from one or two luxury mansions, is oddly uninhabited. The first village you come to is **SAN PEDRO SACATEPÉQUEZ**, where the impact of the earthquake is still painfully felt. The Friday market here is small, but still worth a browse. Another six kilometres takes you over a ridge and into the village of **SAN JUAN SACATEPÉQUEZ**. As you approach, the road passes a number of makeshift greenhouses where flowers are grown, an industry that has become the local speciality. By far the best time to visit is for the Friday market, when the whole place springs into action and the village is packed. Keep an eye out for the *huipiles* worn in San Juan, which are unusual and impressive, with bold geometric designs of yellow, purple and green. **Buses** to both villages run every half-hour or so from the Zona 4 terminal in Guatemala City.

Beyond San Juan the road divides. If you follow the branch heading for **MIXCO VIEJO**, the scenery changes dramatically, leaving behind the pine forests and entering a huge dry valley scattered with small farms. Mixco Viejo was the capital of the Poqomam Maya, one of the main pre-conquest tribes, whose language has all but died out. The site, thought to date from the thirteenth century, is in a magnificent position: protected on all sides by deep ravines, it can be entered only along a single-file causeway. When the Spanish arrived in 1525, this was one of the largest highland centres, with nine temples, two ball courts and a population of around nine thousand. After an initial failure by the Spanish to gain control here, Alvarado attacked the city himself with the aid of two hundred Mexican allies, but his armies were attacked from behind by a force of Poqomam warriors who arrived from nearby Chinautla. The ensuing battle was won by the Spanish cavalry, but the city remained impenetrable. According to legend, Alvarado then learned of a secret entrance to the city; he entered Mixco virtually unopposed and then massacred all the inhabitants.

Today the site has been impressively restored, with its plazas and temples laid out across several flat-topped ridges. Like all the highland sites the structures are fairly low – the largest temple reaches only about ten metres in height – and devoid of decoration. It is, however, an interesting site in a spectacular setting and, during the week, you'll probably have the ruins to yourself, which gives the place all the more atmosphere.

Mixco Viejo is by no means an easy place to reach, and if you can muster enough people it's worth **renting a car** (see p.339). Alternatively, Swiss Travel, in the *Chalet Suizo* in Guatemala City (see p.330), can organize **tours** of the site, or contact one of the travel agents listed on p.340.

# Antigua

Superbly sited in a sweeping highland valley and suspended between the cones of Agua, Acatenango and Fuego volcanoes is one of the Guatemala's most enchanting colonial cities – **ANTIGUA**. In its day, it was one of the great cities of the Spanish empire, ranking alongside Lima and Mexico City, and serving as the administrative centre for all of Central America and Mexican Chiapas. Built by Spanish architects and Maya labourers, it is a classically designed city of elegant squares, churches, monasteries and grand houses, and this magnificent colonial legacy has ensured Antigua's continuing prosperity as one of Guatemala's premier tourist attractions.

Antigua was actually the third capital of Guatemala. The Spanish settled first at the site of **Iximché** (see p.364) in July 1524 and then at a site a few kilometres from Antigua, now called Ciudad Vieja, but when this was devastated by a massive mud slide from the Volcán de Agua in 1541, the capital was moved to Antigua. Antigua grew slowly but steadily as religious orders established themselves one by one, competing in the construction of schools, churches, monasteries and hospitals, all largely built by the sweat and blood of the conscripted Maya.

The city reached its peak in the middle of the eighteenth century, after the **1717 earthquake** prompted an unprecedented building boom, and the population rose to around fifty thousand. By this stage, Antigua was a genuinely impressive place, with a university, a printing press and a newspaper. But, as is so often the case in Guatemala, earthquakes brought all of this to an abrupt end. For the best part of a year the city was shaken by tremors, with the final blows delivered by two severe shocks on September 7 and December 13, 1773. The damage was so bad that the decision was made to abandon the city in favour of the modern capital. Fortunately, despite endless official decrees and epidemics of disease, many refused to leave and Antigua was never completely deserted.

Since then, the city has been gradually repopulated, particularly in the last hundred years or so, and as Guatemala City has become increasingly congested, many of the city's middle classes have moved to Antigua. They've been joined by a large number of resident and visiting foreigners, attracted by its relaxed and sophisticated atmosphere, lively cultural life, benign climate and largely traffic-free streets.

Efforts have been made to preserve the architectural grandeur of the past, especially after Antigua was listed as a UNESCO World Heritage site in 1979 – local conservation laws protect the streets from the intrusion of overhanging signs and house extensions are severely restricted. Though many colonial buildings lie in splendidly atmospheric ruin or else are steadily decaying, many more have been impeccably restored and sympathetically converted into hotels or restaurants.

Because of its relaxed atmosphere and beauty, Antigua is a favoured hangout for jaded travellers to refuel and recharge. The bar scene is always lively and there's an extraordinarily cosmopolitan choice of restaurants. If you can make it here for **Semana Santa** (Easter week), you'll witness the most extravagant and impressive

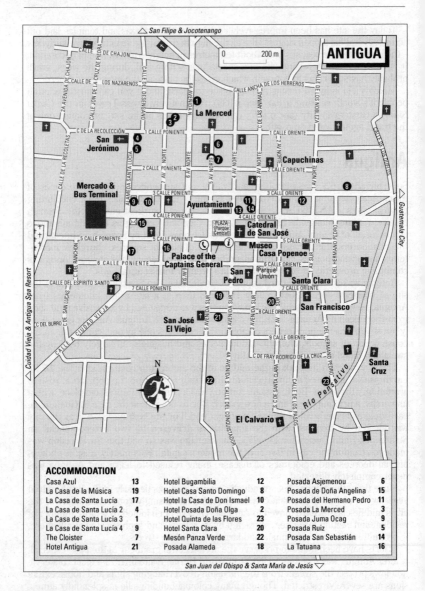

△ San Filipe & Jocotenango

**ANTIGUA**

0        200 m

La Merced

San Jerónimo

Capuchinas

Mercado & Bus Terminal

Ayuntamiento

Catedral de San José

Museo Casa Popenoe

Palace of the Captains General

San Pedro

Santa Clara

San José El Viejo

San Francisco

Santa Cruz

El Calvario

Río Pensativo

◁ Cuidad Vieja & Antigua Spa Resort

Guatemala City ▷

### ACCOMMODATION

| | | | | | | | |
|---|---|---|---|---|---|---|---|
| Casa Azul | 13 | Hotel Bugambilia | 12 | Posada Asjemenou | 6 |
| La Casa de la Música | 19 | Hotel Casa Santo Domingo | 8 | Posada de Doña Angelina | 15 |
| La Casa de Santa Lucía | 17 | Hotel la Casa de Don Ismael | 10 | Posada del Hermano Pedro | 11 |
| La Casa de Santa Lucía 2 | 4 | Hotel Posada Doña Olga | 2 | Posada La Merced | 3 |
| La Casa de Santa Lucía 3 | 1 | Hotel Quinta de las Flores | 23 | Posada Juma Ocag | 9 |
| La Casa de Santa Lucía 4 | 9 | Hotel Santa Clara | 20 | Posada Ruiz | 5 |
| The Cloister | 7 | Mesón Panza Verde | 22 | Posada San Sebastián | 14 |
| Hotel Antigua | 21 | Posada Alameda | 18 | La Tatuana | 16 |

San Juan del Obispo & Santa María de Jesús ▽

processions in all Latin America. Another attraction is the city's **language schools**, some of the best and cheapest in the continent, drawing students from around the globe. Expats from Europe, North and South America and even Asia contribute to the town's cosmopolitan air, mingling with the Guatemalans who come here at weekends to eat, drink and enjoy themselves.

The downside of this settled, comfortable affluence is perhaps a loss of vitality – this civilized, isolated world can seem almost a little too smug and comfortable. After a few days of sipping cappuccinos and eating cake, it's easy to forget that you're in Central America at all.

## Arrival and information

Antigua is laid out on the traditional Spanish grid system, with avenidas running north–south, and calles east–west. Each street is numbered and has two halves, either a north and south (*norte/sur*) or an east and west (*oriente/poniente*), with the plaza, the parque central, regarded as the centre. Despite this apparent simplicity, poor street lighting and the lack of street signs combine to ensure that most people get lost here at some stage. If you get confused, remember that the Volcán de Agua, the one that looms most immediately over the town, is to the south.

**Arriving by bus**, you'll end up in the main bus terminal, a large open space beside the market. The street opposite (4 C Poniente) leads directly to the plaza. The **tourist office** (daily 8am–6pm; ☎ & fax 832 0763) on the south side of the plaza dispenses excellent, if occasionally overly cautious, information. You'll find the **tourist police** just off the parque central on 4 Avenida Norte (☎832 7290), who will help you with any difficulties; twice daily, officers escort visitors up to the Cerro de la Cruz, which offers a panoramic view of Antigua and the surrounding volcanoes.

Antigua is one of the most popular places in Latin America to **study Spanish**. For a full list of recommended schools see p.351, or consult the noticeboards in various tourist venues which advertise private language tuition – as well as apartments, flights home and shared rides. Probably the most read are those at *Doña Luisa's* restaurant, 4 C Ote 12, and the *Rainbow Reading Room*, 7 Av Sur 8.

For **tours** of the city, contact Geovany at Monarcas, 7 Av Nte 15a (☎832 4779, *www.angelfire.com/mt/monarcastravel*), who looks at Maya influence on Antiguan architecture and the flora around the city, or Elizabeth Bell's Antigua Tours, at 3 C Ote 28 (☎832 0140 ext 341, *www.antiguatours.com*), for excellent historical walking tours.

## Accommodation

Hotels in Antigua are in plentiful supply although, like everything else, they can be a bit hard to find due to the absence of overhanging signs. Be warned that rooms get extremely scarce (and prices increase) around Holy Week.

**Casa Azul**, 4 Av Nte 5 (☎832 0961, fax 832 0944, *www.infoguate.com/casazul*). Choice location, just off the plaza, with huge, very stylish rooms in a converted colonial mansion. Facilities include sauna, Jacuzzi and a delightful small rooftop pool. ⑧.

**La Casa de la Música**, 7 C Pte 3 (☎832 0335, *www.lacasadelamusica.centroamerica.com*). Sumptuous guest house with a selection of very attractive bedrooms and characterful suites, all with fireplaces and antique furniture. There's a large garden, with plenty of space for children to play, a guests' lounge with an extensive library and plenty of family games. Very friendly and efficient service, breakfast is included and additional meals are also available. ⑥/⑦.

**La Casa de Santa Lucía**, Alameda Santa Lucía Sur 5 (☎832 6133). Recently refurbished hotel with secure, spacious rooms with dark wood furnishings, all with private hot-water bath, hence it's very popular. You'll have to ring the bell to get in; guests are given a key. ②.

**La Casa de Santa Lucía 2**, Alameda Santa Lucía Nte 21, **La Casa de Santa Lucía 3**, 6 Av Norte 43 A, and **La Casa de Santa Lucía 4**, Alameda Santa Lucía 5 (no phones). Almost carbon copies of the original. Spacious rooms with twin beds and private hot showers, and extremely well priced. Ring the bell for entry. ②.

**The Cloister**, 5 Av Nte 23 (☎ & fax 832 0712, *www.thecloister.com*). Small, elegant hotel, set almost under Antigua's famous arch, with beautifully furnished rooms around a flowering courtyard. There's a real air of tranquillity here, plus a well-stocked private library and reading room. ⑧/⑨.

**Hotel Antigua**, 8 C Pte 1 (☎832 0288, fax 832 0807, *www.hotelantigua.com.gt*). Venerable establishment, popular with Guatemala's elite families, and decorated with tasteful colonial-style furniture. There's a large swimming pool set in expansive gardens, and the pleasant rooms have open fires to ward off the winter chill. US$112 including breakfast. ⑨.

**Hotel Bugambilia**, 3 C Ote 19 (☎832 5780, *www.theantiguajournal.com*). Clean, safe place in a quiet location with parking, but rooms are a little plain. The owners are very helpful and hospitable. Snacks available. ③.

**Hotel Casa Santo Domingo**, 3 C Ote 28 (☎832 0140, fax 832 0102, *www.casasantodomingo.com.gt*). Spectacular colonial convent, sympathetically converted into a hotel and restaurant at a cost of several million dollars. Rooms and corridors are bedecked in ecclesiastical art and paraphernalia and there's no lack of luxury. Probably the most atmospheric hotel in Guatemala. High-season rates start at US$132, but there are substantial discounts at quiet times of the year. ⑨.

**Hotel la Casa de Don Ismael**, 3 C Pte 6 (☎832 1939). Attractively presented rooms with towels and soap provided, a lovely little garden, free mineral water and free tea or coffee in the morning. Communal bathrooms are brightly painted and kept spotless. Very fair prices. ②.

**Hotel Posada Doña Olga**, Callejón Campo Seco 3A (☎832 0623). Exceptionally good value new guest house, with very clean rooms, all with private bath, and a rooftop sun terrace. ②.

**Hotel Quinta de las Flores**, C del Hermano Pedro 6 (☎832 3721, fax 832 3726 ). A little out of town, but the attractive, tastefully decorated rooms and the spectacular garden, with a swimming pool and many rare plants, shrubs and trees, make it a wonderful place to relax. ⑦.

**Hotel Santa Clara**, 2 Av Sur 20 (☎ & fax 832 0342). Tranquil location on the east side of town and very spacious, comfortable rooms, most with two double beds and all with private bath, set around a pleasant little courtyard. Parking. ③.

**Mesón Panza Verde**, 5 Av Sur 19 (☎ & fax 832 2925, *mpv@infovia.com.gt*). Small, immaculately furnished hotel in a colonial-style building that is also home to one of Antigua's premier restaurants. Supremely comfortable suites, some with four-poster beds, plus good-value doubles. Small swimming pool, faultless service and a healthy breakfast included in the price. ⑥/⑧.

**Posada Alameda**, Alameda Santa Lucía Sur 18 (☎832 7349, *alameda@intelnet.net.gt*). Good new hotel close to the bus terminal, with six comfortable rooms, all with cable TV, plus baggage storage and security boxes. ③.

**Posada Asjemenou**, 5 Av Nte 31 (☎832 2670, *cangeletti@hotmail.com*). Comfortable rooms with a colonial feel, set around a courtyard with or without private bath. ④/⑤.

**Posada de Doña Angelina**, 4 C Pte 33 (☎8325173). Popular budget option. Many of the 42 rooms are a bit gloomy, but there's usually space here. Close to the bus terminal, so not the most tranquil place in town. Run by a dynamic señora and there's a secure store room where you can leave your baggage. ②/③.

**Posada del Hermano Pedro**, 3 C Ote 3 (☎832 2089, fax 832 2090). Comfortable hotel in a huge, tastefully converted colonial mansion just behind the main square. The pleasant rooms all have cable TV. ⑥.

**Posada La Merced**, 7 Av Nte 43a (☎832 3197, *posadalamerced@hotmail.com*). Large refurbished hotel with a good choice of attractive rooms (some set around a pretty garden patio at the rear) that all enjoy spotless private bathrooms and nice decorative touches. The very helpful Kiwi owner is a good source of local information. ④.

**Posada Juma Ocag**, Alameda Santa Lucía Nte 13 (☎832 3109). Superb, very well managed new place. The nine cheery, comfortable rooms represent excellent value: all have wardrobes and private bath, and are draped with local fabrics. Book ahead. ③.

**Posada Ruiz**, Alameda Santa Lucía Nte 17 and **Posada Ruiz 2**, 2 C Pte 25 (no phones). Pretty grim, small rooms with no frills, but rates are extremely cheap and both are a short stumble from the bus terminal. ①.

**Posada San Sebastián**, 3 Av Nte 4 (☎ & fax 832 2621). Very quiet, charming establishment. Each room is individually decorated with antiques, there's a gorgeous little bar and the location is very convenient. Excellent value. ⑥.

**La Tatuana**, 6 Av Sur 3 (☎832 1223, *latatuana@micro.com.gt*). Small hotel with bright, imaginatively decorated rooms, all with private bath, and comfortable beds. Extremely good value for the price. ④.

## SEMANA SANTA IN ANTIGUA

Antigua's Semana Santa (Holy Week) celebrations are perhaps the most extravagant and impressive in all Latin America. The celebrations start with a procession on Palm Sunday, representing Christ's entry into Jerusalem, and continue through to the really big processions and pageants on Good Friday. On Thursday night the streets are carpeted with meticulously drawn patterns of coloured sawdust, and on Friday morning a series of processions re-enacts the progress of Christ to the Cross accompanied by sombre music from local brass bands. Setting out from La Merced, Escuela de Cristo and the village of San Felipe, teams of penitents wearing peaked hoods and accompanied by solemn dirges and clouds of incense carry images of Christ and the Cross on massive platforms. The pageants set off at around at 8am, the penitents dressed in either white or purple. After 3pm, the hour of the Crucifixion, they change into black.

It is a great honour to be involved in the procession, but no easy task as the great cedar block carried from La Merced weighs some 3.5 tonnes, and needs eighty men to lift it. Some of the images displayed date from the seventeenth century and the procession itself is thought to have been introduced by Alvarado in the early years of the Conquest, imported directly from Spain.

Check the exact details of events with the tourist office who should be able to provide you with a map detailing the routes of the processions. During Holy Week hotels in Antigua are often full, and the entire town is always packed on Good Friday. But even if you have to make the trip from Guatemala City or Panajachel, it's well worth coming here for, especially on the Friday.

## The City

Antigua has an incredible number of ruined and restored colonial buildings, and although these constitute only a fraction of the city's original architectural splendour, they do give an idea of its former extravagance. However, the prospect of visiting them all can seem overwhelming; if you'd rather just see the gems, make **La Merced**, **Las Capuchinas**, **Casa Popenoe** and **San Francisco** your targets.

If Antigua seems to you a little too sanitized and over-oriented to the tourist dollar, head for the area around the bus terminal and the **marketplace**, which has a little more *Guatemalteco* character and myriad cheap stalls selling snacks, juices and licuados, flowers, fruit and vegetables and secondhand clothes and shoes.

### The parque central

The shady **parque central** is a favoured meeting place and civic focal point – though its calm atmosphere is relatively recent. For centuries the central plaza was the focus of the colonial city, bustling with constant activity. A huge market spilled out across it, which was cleared only for bullfights, military parades, floggings and public hangings.

The most imposing of the surrounding structures is the **Catedral de San José**, on the eastern side, its richly carved facade brilliantly illuminated at night. The first cathedral was begun in 1545, but an earthquake brought down much of the roof and, in 1670, it was decided to start on a new cathedral worthy of the town's role as a capital city. The scale was astounding: a vast dome, five naves, eighteen chapels and an altar inlaid with mother-of-pearl, ivory and silver. But in 1773, it was destroyed yet again by an earthquake. Today, two of the chapels have been restored, and inside is a figure of Christ by the colonial sculptor, Quirio Cataño. Behind the church, entered from 5 C Oriente, are the remains (entrance fee US$0.40) of the rest of the original structure – a mass of fallen masonry and some rotting beams, broken arches and hefty pillars. Buried beneath the floor are some of the great names of the Conquest, including Alvarado, his wife Beatriz de la Cueva, Bishop Marroquín and the historian Bernal

Díaz del Castillo. At the very rear of the original nave, steps lead down to a burial vault that's regularly used for Maya religious ceremonies, an example of the coexistence of pagan and Catholic beliefs that's so characteristic of Guatemala.

Along the entire south side of the square runs the squat two-storey facade of the **Palace of the Captains General**, with a row of 27 arches along each floor. It was originally constructed in 1558, but rebuilt after earthquake damage. The palace was home to the colonial rulers and also housed the barracks of the dragoons, the stables, the royal mint, law courts, tax offices, great ballrooms, a large bureaucracy, and a lot more besides. Today it contains the local government offices, the headquarters of the Sacatepéquez police department and the tourist office. Directly opposite is the **Ayuntamiento**, the city hall, which dates from 1740 and remained undamaged until the 1976 earthquake. It holds a couple of minor museums, the Museo de Santiago (daily 9am–6pm; US$1.30), which contains a collection of colonial artefacts in the old city jail, and the Museo del Libro Antiguo (same hours, US$1.30), in the rooms that held the first printing press in Central America. A replica of the press is on display, alongside some copies of the works produced on it. From the upper floor of the Ayuntamiento there's a wonderful vista of the three volcanoes that ring the city, especially fine at sunset.

## South and east of the parque central

Across the street from the ruined cathedral, in 5 C Oriente, is the **Museo de Arte Colonial** (Tues–Fri 9am–4pm, Sat & Sun 9am–noon & 2–4pm; US$3.20), formerly the site of a university. The deep-set windows and beautifully ornate cloisters make it one of the finest architectural survivors in Antigua. The museum contains a good collection of dark and brooding religious art, sculpture, furniture and murals depicting life on the colonial campus.

Moving down 5 Calle Oriente, at the corner with 1 Avenida Sur is the **Casa Popenoe** (Mon–Sat 2–4pm; US$0.90), a superbly restored colonial mansion that gives an interesting insight into domestic life in colonial times. Originally owned by a Spanish judge, it was abandoned for some time until its painstaking restoration by Dr Wilson Popenoe, a United Fruit Company scientist. Among the paintings are portraits of Bishop Marroquín and the menacing-looking Alvarado himself. The kitchen and servants' quarters have also been carefully renovated: you can see the original bread ovens, the herb garden and the pigeon loft, which would have provided the mansion's occupants with their mail service. Go up to the roof for great views of the city and Volcán de Agua.

A little further down 1 Avenida Sur is the imposing church of **San Francisco** (daily 8am–6pm). One of the oldest churches in Antigua, dating from 1579, it grew into a vast religious and cultural centre that included a school, a hospital, music rooms, a printing press and a monastery. All of it was lost, though, in the 1773 earthquake. Inside the church are buried the remains of Hermano Pedro de Betancourt (a Franciscan from the Canary Islands who founded the Hospital of Belén in Antigua). Pilgrims come here from all over Central America to ask for the benefit of his powers of miraculous intervention. The ruins of the monastery, which are among the most impressive in Antigua, have pleasant grassy verges with good picnic potential.

One block west and one block north of San Francisco, two churches face each other at opposite ends of **Parque Unión**, a pretty palm-tree lined plaza, which doubles as an open-air típica textile street market. Women travel from as far away as Lago de Atitlán and the Ixil triangle to sell their wares here, returning home after a day or two, hopefully with a little cash gained. At the western end is the **San Pedro Church** dating from 1680, and at the eastern end **Santa Clara**, a former convent. In colonial times it was popular for aristocratic ladies to take the veil here; the hardships were not too

For a list of **language schools** in Antigua, see p.351.

extreme and the nuns gained a reputation for their fine cooking. The convent was twice destroyed in the earthquakes of 1717 and 1773, but the current building with its ornate facade survived the 1976 tremors intact. In front of Santa Clara is a large *pila* or wash-house where village women gather to scrub, rinse and gossip.

## North and west of the parque central

At the junction of 2 C Ote and 2 Av Nte is the site of **Las Capuchinas** (Tues–Sun 9am–5pm; US$ 1.30), the largest and most impressive of the city's convents, dating from 1726, whose ruins are some of the best preserved but least understood in Antigua. The Capuchin nuns who lived here were not allowed any visual contact with the outside world: food was passed to them by means of a turntable and they could only speak to visitors through a grille. The ruins are the most beautiful in Antigua, with fountains, courtyards and massive earthquake-proof pillars. The most unusual point is the unique tower or "retreat", with eighteen tiny cells set into the walls on the top floor and a cellar supported by a massive pillar that probably functioned as a meat storage room. The exterior of this architectural curiosity is also interesting, ringed with small stone recesses that represent the Stations of the Cross.

A couple of blocks to the west, spanning 5 Avenida Norte, the arch of **Santa Catalina** is all that remains of the original convent founded here in 1609. The arch was built so that the nuns could walk between the two halves of the establishment without being exposed to the pollution of the outside world. Somehow it has managed to defy the constant onslaught of earthquakes and is now a favoured, if clichéd, spot for photographers as the view to the Volcán de Agua is unobstructed from here.

Walking under the arch and to the end of the street, you reach the church of **La Merced**, which boasts one of the most intricate facades in the entire city. Look closely and you'll see the outline of a corn cob, a motif not normally used by the Catholic Church and probably added by the original Maya labourers. The church is still in use, but the cloisters and gardens (entrance US$0.25), including a monumental tiered fountain, lie in ruins exposed to the sky.

Continue west down 1 Calle Poniente to the junction of the tree-lined street, Alameda Santa Lucía, and you reach the spectacular remains of **San Jerónimo**, (daily 9am–5.30pm; US$1.30) a school built in 1739. Well-kept gardens are woven between the huge blocks of fallen masonry and crumbling walls and the site is regularly used as a spectacular site for classical music concerts. On the other side of the bus station is an imposing monument to Rafael Landívar (1731–93), a Jesuit composer who is generally considered to be the finest poet of the colonial era.

# Eating and drinking

In Antigua the choice of food is even more cosmopolitan than the population. You can eat your way around the world in a number of reasonably authentic restaurants for a few dollars a time, or dine in real style for around US$10 a head. The only thing that seems hard to come by is authentic Guatemalan comedor food – which will be quite a relief if you've been subsisting on eggs and beans in the mountains.

## Cafés

**Café Sol**, 1 C Pte 9. Simple courtyard café that bakes its own bread. Healthy snacks and tasty sandwiches and cakes. Also has in-house email, fax and phone facilities.

**Café Condesa**, west side of plaza; pass through the Casa del Conde bookshop. Extremely civilized, though pricey, place to enjoy an excellent breakfast, coffee and cake or full lunch. The gurgling fountain and period charm create a nice tone for the long, lazy Sunday brunches favoured by Antiguan society. Alternatively, grab a *latte* from the adjoining take-away window.

**Café la Fuente**, in La Fuente, 4 C Ote 14. Vegetarian restaurant/café where you can eat stuffed aubergine and falafel or sip good coffee in one of the most attractive restored courtyards in town. On Saturdays village women set up a *huipil* market around the fountain.

**Fernando's Kaffee**, 7 C Pte 11. Simple premises but unquestionably the finest coffee in town – ground, roasted and served by a perfectionist – plus delicious home-made pastries.

**Pasteleria Okrassa**, 6 Av Nte 29. Great for croissants, cinnamon rolls and healthy drinks – try the raspberry juice.

**Jugocentre Peroleto**, Alameda Santa Lucía Nte 36. Excellent budget hole-in-the-wall cabin with cheap, healthy breakfasts, fruit juices and yummy cakes.

**Rainbow Café**, 7 Av Sur 8. Relaxed bohemian atmosphere in this favourite travellers' hangout. Great vegetarian menu of creative salads and pasta dishes, epic smoothies and decent cappuccinos matched by friendly, prompt service. Also home to one of Antigua's best travel agents, a good secondhand bookshop, and regular musical jams.

**Destino**, 1 Av Sur 8. Diminutive café pit-stop, popular with language students, that's ideal for a caffeine hit or a slab of home-made cake, though the convivial American owner will rustle up a bacon sandwich for those in need.

## Restaurants

**El Sereno**, 4 Av Nte 16. Superb colonial setting with beautiful dining rooms and a lovely roof terrace with some of the finest views in Antigua. Extensive, expensive menu with many seasonal specialities plus a decent wine list.

**Beijing**, 6 Av Sur and 5 C Pte. Antigua's best Chinese and East Asian food, prepared with a few imaginative twists. Good noodle dishes, soups and Vietnamese spring rolls. Fairly expensive.

**Café Panchoy**, 6 Av Norte 1B. Good-value cooking with a real Guatemalan flavour – top steaks and some traditional favourites like chiles rellenos served around an open kitchen. Excellent margaritas. Closed Tues.

**Café-Pizzeria Asjemenou**, 5 C Pte 4. A favourite for its legendary breakfasts. Also very strong on pizza and calzone, but the service can be erratic. Daily 9am–10pm.

**Casa de las Mixtas**, 1 Callejón, off 3 C Poniente. A basic comedor, but nicely set up with attractive decor and cooking that's executed with more flair than most. Open early until 7.30pm.

**Comedor Típico Antigüeño**, Alameda Santa Lucía Sur 5. Excellent canteen-like comedor, opposite the bus terminal and market, with bargain set lunches and meals; all include a soup starter.

**Doña Luisa's**, 4 C Ote 12. One of the most popular places in town. The setting is relaxed but the menu could do with a revamp – the basic line-up of chile con carne, baked potatoes, salads and hamburgers is a little uninspired. An adjoining shop sells bread and pastries baked on the premises.

**Frida's**, 5 Av Nte 29. Lively atmosphere and the best Mexican food in town – a tasty selection of enchiladas, fajitas etc. Decorated with 1950s Americana.

**La Casserole**, Callejón de la Concepción 7. This elegant, expensive restaurant, in a pretty patio location, serves the finest French cooking in Antigua. Leave room for the epic desserts. Closed Mon.

**La Escudilla**, 4 Av Nte 4. Tremendous courtyard restaurant, in the same premises as *Riki's Bar*, that's usually extremely busy on account of the excellent-value, good-quality food. The pasta is good, the US$3 all-day, all-night set meal is exceptional value, salads are delicious and vegetarians have plenty of tasty choices. You may have a wait, though, when it's busy.

**La Fonda de la Calle Real**, upstairs at 5 Av Nte 5, over the road at 5 Av Nte 12 and a third restaurant (the nicest location) at 3 C Pte 7. Probably the most famous restaurant in Antigua, and patronized by Bill Clinton during his 2000 visit. Try the excellent Guatemalan specialities, including *pepián* (spicy meat stew) and *caldo real* (chicken soup) or the sizzling grilled meats. Prices are moderate to expensive. Closed Wed.

**Panza Verde**, 5 Av Sur 19. One of Antigua's most exclusive restaurants. Exemplary European cuisine, professional service and a nice setting, with well-spaced tables grouped around a courtyard garden. Try the trout or sea bass meunière.

**Quesos y Vinos**, 5 Av Norte 32. Very stylish Italian-owned restaurant with a reliable reputation for good home-made pasta and pizza, and wines from Europe and South America. Moderate.

## STUDYING SPANISH IN ANTIGUA

Antigua's **language-school** industry is big business, with a couple of dozen established schools, and many more less reliable set-ups, some operating in the front room of someone's house. Whether you're just stopping for a week or two to learn the basics, or settling in for several months in pursuit of total fluency, there can be no doubt that this is one of the best places in Latin America to learn Spanish: it's a beautiful, relaxed town, lessons are cheap and there are several superb schools. The only major drawback is that there are so many other students and tourists here that you'll probably end up spending your evenings speaking English. If this worries you then you might want to consider studying in a less touristy town – Quetzaltenango, Huehuetenango, Cobán and San Andrés and San José on Lago de Petén Itzá all have Spanish schools and fewer visitors.

Before making any decisions, you could drop into **Amerispan**, 6 Av Nte 40 (☎ & fax 832 0164; in US ☎1-800/879-6640, fax 215/985-4524, *www.amerispan.com*), which selects schools throughout Latin America to match the needs and requirements of students, and provides advice and support.

### CHOOSING A SCHOOL

The tourist office in Antigua has a list of "approved schools", but this is as much a product of bribery and influence as a reflection of professional integrity. Note that the Rigoberta Menchú school has no connection at all with the Rigoberta or her foundation. The following schools are well-established, recommended and towards the top end of the price scale:

**Academia Antigüeña de Español**, 1 C Pte 33 (☎832 2685; *www.granjaguar.com/antiguena*).

**APPE**, 6 C Pte 40 (☎832 0720, *www.guacalling.com/appe*).

**Centro America Spanish Academy** inside La Fuente, 4 C Ote 14 (☎ & fax 832 6268, *www.quik.guate.com/spanishacademy*).

**Centro Lingüístico de la Fuente**, 1 C Pte 27 (☎ & fax 832 2711, *www.delafuenteschool.com*).

**Centro Lingüístico Maya**, 5 C Poniente 20 (☎ & fax 832 0656, *www.travellog.com/guatemala/antigua/clmaya/school.html*).

**Christian Spanish Academy**, 6 Av Nte 15 (☎ 832 3922, fax 832 3760, *www.learncsa.com*).

**Probigua**, 6 Av Nte 41B (☎ & fax 832 0860, *http://probigua.conexion.com*).

**Projecto Lingüístico Francisco Marroquín**, 7 C Pte 31 (☎832 2886, *www.plfm-antigua.org*). Also teaches Maya languages.

**San José El Viejo**, 5 Av Sur 34 (☎832 3028, fax 832 3029, *www.guate.net/spanish*).

**Sevilla**, 1 Av Sur 8 (☎ & fax 832 0442, *www.sevillantigua.com*).

**Tecún Umán Linguistic School**, 6 C Pte 34 A (☎ & fax 831 2792, *www.tecunuman.centramerica.com*).

**La Unión**, 1 Av Sur 21 (☎ & fax 832 7337, *www.launion.conexion.com*).

**San Jerónimo**, Alameda Santa Lucía Nte and 1 C Pte. As it opens at 7am, this pleasant, simple patio-based comedor is a good bet for an early breakfast, though the friendly owners also serve tasty, very inexpensive lunches and snacks.

**Weiner**, Alameda Santa Lucía Sur 8. Especially good for a well-priced, filling breakfast, this restaurant also does lunchtime specials for US$2.50, serves good coffee and herbal teas and has a fair selection of bottled beers.

# Drinking and nightlife

Evening activity is officially curtailed in Antigua by a "dry law" which forbids the sale of alcohol after 1am. The places listed below on 5 and 7 Avenidas Norte are particularly popular with the gringo crowd and all open at around 7pm. Antigua's **dance scene** is burgeoning, drawing a big crowd from Guatemala City. The venues tend to be very quiet Monday to Wednesday, busy Thursday and heaving at weekends.

There are a number of small video **cinemas** that show a range of Western films on a daily basis – *Trainspotting*, *Salvador* and *Buena Vista Social Club* are on almost permanently. Fliers with weekly listings are posted on noticeboards all over town. The main cinemas are: Cinema Bistro, 5 Av Sur 14; Cinemaya, 6 C Pte 7, and Maya Moon, 6 Av Nte 1A, while the Proyecto Cultural El Sitio, 5 C Pte 15, also shows a good choice of Latin American and art-house movies.

## Bars and clubs

**El Afro**, 6 C Pte 9. Funky sociable bar, usually crammed at weekends with a salsa-stepping crowd, though space is tight for really serious dancing.

**La Canoa**, 5 C Pte between 4 and 5 avenidas. A small, unpretentious club where people come to dance to mainly Latin sounds. Merengue is the main ingredient, spiked with a dash of salsa and reggae; they also play a few tracks of western and Latin pop/rock. Good mix of locals and foreigners and reasonable drink prices, though perennial licensing problems mean it is shut down from time to time. US$2 at weekends, free in the week.

**La Casbah**, 5 Av Nte 30. The most controversial place in town, attracting a well-heeled crowd from Antigua and Guatemala City. The venue, in the ruins of an ancient church, is spectacular and the music can occasionally match the site, with deep bassline-driven dance mixes. Gay night on Thurs. Drinks are expensive. Mon–Wed free, Thurs, Fri & Sat around US$3.50.

**La Chimanea**, 7 Av Nte 7. One of the more popular bars, though the music selection is disturbingly eclectic – expect everything from Rod Stewart to Black Sabbath.

**Dante's**, 7 C Pte 6B. Arguably the hippest place in town, this large, stylish bar hosts live bands and regular Cuban and house music club nights.

**Equinoccio**, 7 Av Nte and 2 C Pte. Bar-cum-club that's *the* place to groove to Latin music – predominantly merengue and salsa, but occasionally a little Cuban hip hop – with a dark bar zone and a large dance floor. Moderate drink prices.

**Macondo's**, 5 Av Nte and 2 C Pte. Probably the closest thing Antigua has to a pub, though the themed nights (Wed is ladies' night) and constant visual barrage of music videos spoil things somewhat.

**Mono Loco**, 2 Av Nte 6B. Popular gringo bar, with full US and some EU sports coverage, though the music selection can be banal.

**Picasso's**, 7 Av Nrte 16. No-nonsense drinking-hole that can get quite lively in high season. Usually closed Sun.

**Riki's Bar**, 4 Av Nte 4. Unquestionably the most happening place in town due to the excellent site inside *La Escudilla*, the eclectic funk, nu jazz and downbeat music policy and the unrivalled happy hour (7–9pm), which means this place is packed most nights.

# Listings

**Adventure sports** Maya Mountain Bike Tours, 3 C Pte and 7 Av Nte (☎832 3743, *www.mayanbike*.com), has an excellent range of two-wheeler trips, and offers bike rental, plus white-water rafting; Old Town Outfitters, 6 C Pte 7 (☎832 4243, *www.bikeguatemala.com*), runs mountain bike excursions and rock-climbing trips for all levels, and offers tent, sleeping bag, pack and bike rental.

**Art workshops** Artguat, Callejón López 22 (☎832 6403, fax 832 6925, *www.artguat.org*). Well-structured courses in painting, back-strap weaving, natural dye techniques and photography.

**Banks and exchange** Banco Industrial, 5 Av Sur 4, just south of the plaza (Mon–Fri 8.30am–7pm, Sat 8am–5pm), with a 24-hr ATM for Visa and Plus cardholders; Banco del Agro, north side of the plaza (Mon–Fri 9am–8pm, Sat 9am–6pm); Lloyds, in the northeast corner of the plaza (Mon–Fri 9am–5pm), which changes sterling travellers' cheques. Note that the Banco del Quetzal Mastercard/Cirrus cashpoint on the north side of the plaza routinely accepts cards but fails to dispense money.

**Bookstores** Casa Andinista, 4 C Ote 5A (☎832 0161); Casa del Conde, on the west side of the plaza (☎832 3322); Un Poco de Todo, also on the west side of the plaza. The Rainbow Reading Room, 7 Av Sur 8, has by far the largest selection of secondhand books.

**Car and bike rental** Avis, 5 Av Nte 22 (☎ & fax 832 2692), and Tabarini, 2 C Pte 19A (☎ & fax 832 3091,*www.centroamerica.com/tabarini*), both have similar prices with cars from around US$45 a day and jeeps from US$60, including unlimited mileage and insurance. La Ceiba, 6 C Pte 15 (☎832 0077), rents out motorbikes from US$25 a day. Aviatur, 5 Av Norte 35 (☎ & fax 832 2642), and Maya Mountain Bike Tours and Old Town Outfitters (see "Adventure sports", above) rent mountain bikes for around US$8 a day or US$25 weekly.

**Horse riding** Ravenscroft Stables, 2 Av Sur 3, in the village of San Juan del Obispo, on the road up to Santa María de Jesús (☎832 6229).

**Internet** There are over twenty places where you can send and receive email; rates are set at around US$1.50 an hour though there are discounts for heavy users. The best set-up places include La Ventana, 5 Av Sur 24 (daily 8am–9pm), and Enlaces, 6 Av Nte 1 (daily 9am–9.30pm). Conexión, in the La Fuente cultural centre at 4 C Ote 14 (daily 8am–8pm), is probably the best place to head for real computer queries and techie expertise.

**Laundry** Rainbow Laundry, 6 Av Sur 15 (Mon–Sat 7am–7pm). A wash typically costs around US$2.

**Libraries and cultural institutes** El Sitio, 5 C Pte 15 (☎832 3037), has an active theatre, library and art gallery, and regularly hosts exhibitions and concerts; see the *Revue* or *Guatemala Post* for listings.

**Medical care** There's a 24-hour emergency service at the Santa Lucía Hospital, Calzada Santa Lucía Sur 7 (☎832 3122). Also, Dr Aceituno, who speaks good English, has his surgery at 2 C Pte 7 (☎832 0512).

**Pharmacies** Farmacia Santa María, west side of the plaza (daily 8am–10pm).

**Police** The police HQ is on the south side of the plaza, next to the tourist office (☎ & fax 832 0572). The tourist police are just off the plaza on 4 Avenida Norte (☎832 7290).

**Post office** Alameda de Santa Lucía opposite the bus terminal (Mon–Fri 8am–4.30pm). DHL are at 6 Av Sur 16 (☎832 3718, fax 832 3732, *ecastill@gtl-co.gt.dhl.com*), and Quick Shipping is at 3 Av Nte 26 (☎832 2595).

**Supermarket** La Bodegona at 4 C Pte and Alameda Santa Lucía.

**Taxis** On the east side of the plaza close to the cathedral, or call ☎832 0479.

**Telephones** The Telgua office is just south of the plaza on 5 Avenida Sur (7am–10pm), but rates are higher here than anywhere else and you'll have to queue. Several places now offer Internet-linked phone facilities, including La Ventana (see "Internet", above) enabling you to call North America for US$0.25 a minute or Europe and the rest of the world for a little more, though lines can be fuzzy. The cheapest conventional phone connections are at Kall Shop, 6 Av Sur 12A (daily 8am–8pm), where you can call North America for US$0.25 a minute, Western Europe for US$0.45, and Australia and New Zealand for US$0.64 a minute.

**Travel agents** There are dozens of travel agents in Antigua; the following are the most professional and reliable. The Rainbow Travel Center, 7 Av Sur 8 (daily 9am–6pm; ☎832 4202, fax 832 4206, *rainbowtravel@gua.gbm.net*), is fully computerized and has some of the best deals in town, as well as friendly and efficient staff. Viajes Tivoli, at 4 C Ote 10, on the west side of the plaza (Mon–Sat 9am–6pm; ☎832 4274, fax 832 5690, *antigua@tivoli.com.gt*) is another recommended all-rounder. Monarcas, 7 Av Nte 15A (☎ & fax 832 4779, *www.angelfire.com/mt/monarcastravel*), is a highly recommended specialist agency with some fascinating Maya culture and ecology tours and daily connections to Copán, Honduras. Adventure Travel Center Viareal, 5 Av Nte 25B (☎ & fax 832 0162, *viareal@guate.net*), is particularly good for adventure and sailing trips and shuttle bus services. Perfect for backpackers, Quetzalventures, 1 C Pte 12 A (☎832 5827, *www.quetzal-ventures.com*), offers a number of good, inexpensive trips to Petén and the Verapaz highlands; all profits aid Guatemalan street children. Vision Travel, 3 Av Nte 3 (☎832 3293, fax 832 1955, *www.guatemalainfo.com*), has very high standards of service and is consistently recommended.

# Around Antigua

The countryside around Antigua is superbly fertile and breathtakingly beautiful. The valley is dotted with small villages, ranging from the ladino coffee centre of Alotenango to the traditional indígena village of Santa María de Jesús. None of them is more than an hour away and all make interesting day-trips. For the more adventurous, the volcanic peaks of Agua, Acatenango and the active Fuego (if conditions permit) offer strenuous but superb hiking, best done through a specialist agency. For details on climbing Pacaya, near Guatemala City, see p.342.

## Santa María de Jesús and the Volcán de Agua

Up above Antigua, a smooth new sealed road snakes through the coffee bushes and past the village of San Juan del Obispo before arriving in **SANTA MARÍA DE JESÚS**, starting point for the ascent of the Volcán de Agua. Perched high on the shoulder of the volcano, this large, scruffy village is some 500m above Antigua, with magnificent views over the Panchoy valley and east towards the smoking cone of Pacaya. The village was founded at the end of the sixteenth century and is of little interest, though the women wear beautiful purple *huipiles*. There's a good little hospedaje here, *El Oasis* (☎832 0130; ①) just below the plaza, if you want an early start. Buses run from Antigua to Santa María every hour or so from 6am to 5pm, and the trip takes thirty minutes.

**Agua** is the easiest and by far the most popular of Guatemala's big cones to climb: on some Saturday nights hundreds of people spend the night at the top. It's an exciting ascent with a fantastic view to reward you at the summit. The trail starts in Santa María de Jesús (see above). To reach it, head straight across the plaza, between the two ageing pillars, and up the street opposite the church doors. Take a right turn just before the end and then continue past the cemetery and out of the village. From here on it's a fairly simple climb on a clear path, cutting across the road that goes some of the way up. The climb can take anything from four to six hours and the peak, at 3766m, is always cold at night. There is shelter (though not always room) in a small chapel at the summit, however, and the views certainly make it worth the struggle.

## Ciudad Vieja and San Antonio Aguas Calientes

To the south of Antigua, the Panchoy valley is a broad sweep of farmland, overshadowed by three volcanic cones and covered with olive-green coffee bushes. A single road runs out this way, eventually reaching Escuintla and the Pacific coast, and passing a string of villages as it goes. **Minibuses** from the terminal in Antigua run a regular service to Ciudad Vieja, San Antonio and Santa Catarina.

The first place of interest, 5km from Antigua, is **CIUDAD VIEJA**, a scruffy and unhurried village with a distinguished past: it was near here that the Spanish established their second capital, **Santiago de los Caballeros**, in 1527. Within twenty years the new capital had a cathedral, monasteries, farms and a school, but while the rest of the conquistadors were settling in, their leader, Alvarado, was off seeking wealth in Mexico, Peru and Spain. In 1541 he set out for the Spice Islands, travelling via Jalisco where he met his end, crushed to death beneath a rolling horse. When news of his death reached his wife **Doña Beatriz**, at home in Santiago, she plunged the capital into an extended period of mourning, staining the entire palace with black clay, inside and out. On the morning of September 9, 1541, she became the first woman to govern in the Americas, but before the night of her inauguration was out, an earthquake struck, and from the crater of the Volcán de Agua a great wave of mud and water slid down, sweeping away the capital and killing Doña Beatriz.

Today there's no trace of the original city, and all that remains from that time is a solitary tree, in a corner of the plaza, which bears a plaque commemorating the site of the first mass ever held in Guatemala. The plaza also boasts an eighteenth-century colonial church that has recently been restored. The exact centre of the original city is still the subject of some debate, but the general consensus puts it about 2km to the east of Ciudad Vieja.

Down a branch road, 3km west from Ciudad Vieja, the indigenous village of **SAN ANTONIO AGUAS CALIENTES** is set to one side of a steep-sided bowl beneath the peak of Acatenango. San Antonio is famous for its weaving, characterized by complex floral and geometric patterns; there's a new indoor textile market next to the plaza where you can find a complete range of the local output. This is also a good place to learn the traditional craft of back-strap weaving; if you're interested, the best way to find out about possible tuition is by simply asking the women in the market.

A kilometre further along the road, merging into San Antonio, is the village of **SANTA CATARINA BARAHONA**, where there's a modest ruined colonial church, and signposted out on the edge of the village, a small concrete **swimming pool** (Tues–Sun 9am–6pm) – the perfect place for a chilly dip.

## Jocotenango and San Andrés Itzapa

Just 2km north of Antigua, the unappealing suburb of **JOCOTENANGO**, "place of bitter fruit", set around a huge, dusty plaza and long notorious for its sleazy bars, now boasts a couple of interesting new attractions. **Casa K'ojom** (daily 9am–5pm; US$2.50 including tour, *www.kojom.com*) is a purpose-built museum dedicated to Maya culture, especially music. The history of indigenous musical traditions is logically presented from its pre-Columbian origins, through sixteenth-century Spanish and African influences – which brought the marimba, bugles and drums – to the present day, with audio-visual documentaries of fiestas and ceremonies. Other rooms are dedicated to the village weavings of the Sacatepéquez department and the cult of Maximón (see below). Next door, the **Museum of Coffee** (daily 9am–5pm; US$2.50), based in the Finca la Azotea, a 34-hectare plantation dating from 1883, offers a look around a working organic coffee farm. All the technicalities of husking, sieving and roasting are clearly explained and you're served a cup of the aromatic home-grown brew after your tour. Buses from the Antigua terminal pass Jocotenango every thirty minutes on their way to Chimaltenango; the museums are 500m west of the plaza, down a dirt road.

The road from Antigua to Chimaltenango continues beyond Jocotenango, ascending the Panchoy valley, past dusty farming villages, before a dirt track branches off to **SAN ANDRÉS ITZAPA**, one of the many villages badly hit by the 1976 earthquake. San Andrés is home to the cult of **San Simón** (or Maximón), the "evil saint", who is housed in his own pagan chapel. Despite San Andrés being just 18km from Antigua, few tourists visit this shrine, and you may feel less intrusive and more welcome here than his other places of abode which include Zunil (see p.396) and Santiago Atitlán (p.384). Once you've tracked him down, you'll find that Maximón lives in a fairly strange world, his image surrounded by drunken men, cigar-smoking women and hundreds of burning candles, each symbolizing a request: red for love, white for health, and so on. Local stores stock candles and incense and there are also books on witchcraft for sale. Uniquely in Guatemala, this San Simón attracts a largely ladino congregation and he is particularly popular with prostitutes.

If you want to visit San Simón you have to do so between sunrise and sunset, as the Maya believe he sleeps at other times. Head for the central plaza from the dirt road into the village, turn right when you reach the church, walk two blocks, then up a little hill and you should spot street vendors selling charms, incense and candles. If you get lost, just about any child will direct to the "Casa de San Simón" for a quetzal tip.

Inside the dimly lit shrine, the walls are adorned with hundreds of plaques from all over Guatemala and Central America, thanking San Simón for his help. You may be offered a *limpia*, or soul cleansing, which, for a small fee, involves being beaten by one of the resident women workers with a bushel of herbs. A bottle of the firewater *aguadiente* is also demolished: some is offered to San Simón, some of it you'll have to drink yourself and the rest is consumed by the attendant, who sprays you with alcohol (from her mouth) for your sins – all in all, quite an experience.

To get to **San Andrés Itzapa** from Antigua, take any bus heading to Chimaltenango from the terminal (every 20min, 5.30am–7pm) and get the driver to drop you off where the dirt road leaves the highway. From there you can hitch or else it's a thirty-minute walk.

## Santiago Sacatepéquez and Sumpango

Just north of the Carretera Interamerica highway, some 16km above Antigua, the otherwise uninteresting village of **SANTIAGO SACATEPÉQUEZ** is well worth a visit if you're in Guatemala on November 1. On this day a local fiesta honours the **Day of the Dead** and massive kites made from paper and tobacco are flown in the cemetery to release the souls of the deceased from their agony. The festival is immensely popular, and hundreds of Guatemalans and tourists come every year to watch the spectacle. Teams of young men struggle to get the kites aloft while the crowd looks on with bated breath, rushing for cover if a kite comes crashing to the ground. The neighbouring village of **SUMPANGO**, 6km west along the Interamericana, has an identical tradition – so every few years, when there's not enough wind and the kites at Santiago fail to rise to the occasion, everyone heads there in the hope of better weather. You'll have no problem reaching either Santiago Sacatepéquez or Sumpango on fiesta day, when travel agencies and language schools send fleets of minibuses up to the villages; to get there by public transport take any bus as far as San Lucas Sacatepéquez on the Interamericana and catch a connection there.

---

### MOVING ON FROM ANTIGUA

Because of its small size, and its position off the Interamericana, few bus routes originate in Antigua. If you're heading to anywhere in the east of the country, take the first bus to Guatemala City and change there. If you're heading into the western highlands, except Panajachel, it's usually best to catch the first bus to Chimaltenango (see p.362) and get another connection there. The main bus destinations are as follows:

**Guatemala City** (1hr). A constant flow of buses leaves for the capital (Mon–Sat 4am–7.30pm, Sun 6am–8pm)

**Ciudad Vieja** (hourly; 20min)

**Chimaltenango** (every 30min; 40min)

**Escuintla via El Rodeo** (6 daily; 1 hr 30min)

**Panajachel** (1 daily at 7am; 2hr 30 min)

**San Antonio Aguas Calientes** (every 30min; 20min)

**Santa María de Jesús** (every 30 min; 30 min)

#### SHUTTLES

Minibus shuttle services run from Antigua to many parts of the country, and can be booked through most travel agents, including Adventure Travel Center Viareal (see "Listings", p.353). Shuttles are a lot more expensive than public buses but much more comfortable and quicker. There are frequent airport and Guatemala City shuttles for US$7–10 depending on the time of day; Chichicastanango (around US$12) is well served on market days (Thurs & Sun); and there's usually a daily service to Panajachel (around US$12). For Copán in Honduras (around US$30), try Monarcas (see p.353). Shuttles to the Rio Dulce (around US$25) and Monterrico (around US$20) run at weekends and when there is enough demand – normally three people is sufficient.

# CHAPTER EIGHT

# THE WESTERN HIGHLANDS AND PACIFIC COAST

The **western highlands** are considered by most visitors – and most Guatemalans – to be the most beautiful and captivating part of the entire country. Stretching from the outskirts of the capital to the Mexican border, the area is defined by two main features: the awesome chain of sentinel-like volcanoes that define the southern side and the towering bulk of the **Cuchumatanes** mountain range that rises from the tropical plains to the north. Between the two is a bewitching pattern of twisting, pine-forested ridges, lakes, gushing streams and deep valleys. These highlands are the heartland of the **Maya**, who have lived here for over two thousand years, and it is their incredibly rich culture that gives the region its unique identity.

Beneath the volcanoes, a world away from the cool mountain air and unhurried pace of the highlands, is the steamy **Pacific coast**, known to Guatemalans as La Costa Sur. This is ladino country, a flat featureless landscape of huge farm plantations, bustling towns and largely disappointing beach resorts. The sticky lowland climate, dangerous sea currents and poor facilities unsurprisingly attract few tourists, but there are a couple of important archeological sites and also one pleasant resort, **Monterrico**, with a network of swamps, home to all kinds of wildlife including sea turtles.

The western highlands and Pacific coast may be poles apart climatically and culturally, but historically both regions have been interlinked since the earliest times. With the lofty peaks of the highlands blocking an easy entry route into Guatemala to the north, anyone trying to invade the country, from the first hunter-gatherers to the **Spanish conquistadors**, entered to the south, along the coast. The early ancestors of the Maya moved down the narrow Pacific coastal plain from Mexico and settled in villages along the coast before heading inland and establishing the first city of the Maya World, **Kaminaljuyú**, at a site close to Guatemala City. Alvarado and the conquistadors followed a similar path into Guatemala in 1523, before defeating the K'iche' Maya near the highland town of Quetzaltenango.

The Spanish had little time for the hostile climate of the Pacific coast and the region remained largely undeveloped until independence, when the land was cleared for farming and huge agricultural **fincas** were established. Coffee bushes were planted on the lower slopes of the mountains and cotton and sugar cane in the lowlands. With insufficient local labour to work the fincas, thousands of highland Maya were forcibly recruited (by presidential decree) to toil in the coastal heat in appalling conditions. Today their descendants still migrate to the Pacific coast for seasonal work out of economic necessity, and many are debilitated by malaria and pesticide poisoning.

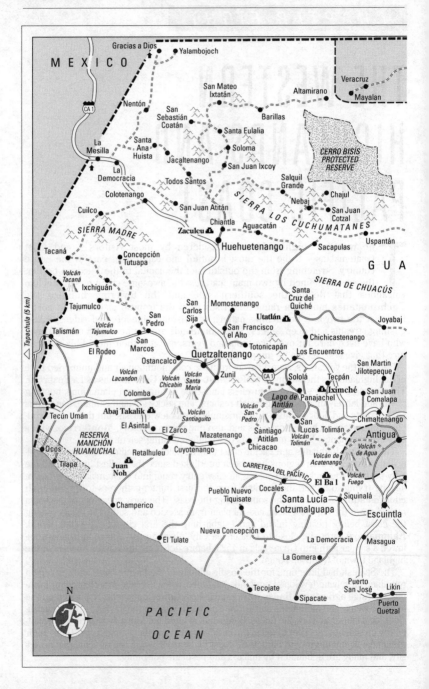

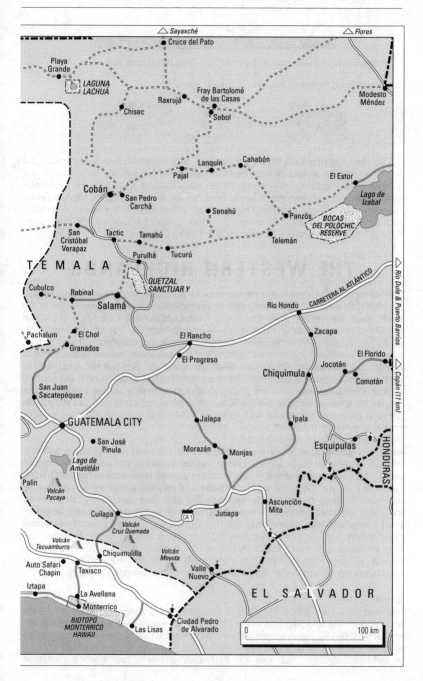

---

**ACCOMMODATION PRICE CODES**

All the accommodation listed in this book has been categorized into one of nine price bands, as set out below. The prices quoted are in US dollars and refer to the cheapest room available for two people sharing in high season.

| ① under US$5 | ④ US$15–25 | ⑦ US$60–80 |
|---|---|---|
| ② US$5–10 | ⑤ US$25–40 | ⑧ US$80–100 |
| ③ US$10–15 | ⑥ US$40–60 | ⑨ over US$100 |

---

Two main **highways** cut through the region, both thick with thundering trucks and buses, so getting around is very easy. In the south, the nation's fastest route, the **Carretera al Pacífico**, runs close to all the major lowland towns between the border with El Salvador and the town of Tecún Umán on the Mexican frontier. The **Carretera Interamericana** to the north is of more interest to travellers as it scythes a serpentine path through some spectacular mountain scenery, passing on the way the major junctions of Chimaltenango, Los Encuentros and Cuatro Caminos.

# THE WESTERN HIGHLANDS

The strength of the Maya culture in the western highlands and its outstanding beauty, studded with volcanoes, deep river valleys and possibly the most beautiful lake in the world, **Lago de Atitlán**, make this region Guatemala's primary attraction. It's a land blessed with tremendous fertility but cursed by instability: the hills are regularly shaken by earthquakes and occasionally showered by volcanic eruptions. Of the thirteen cones that loom over the western highlands, three volcanoes are still active: **Pacaya**, **Fuego** and **Santiaguito**. Two major **fault lines** also cut through the area, making earthquakes a regular occurrence. The most recent major quake in 1976 was centred around **Chimaltenango** – it left 25,000 dead and around a million homeless. But despite its sporadic ferocity, the landscape is outstandingly beautiful and the atmosphere is calm and welcoming, with irrigated valleys and terraced hillsides carefully crafted to yield the maximum potential farmland.

The highland landscape is controlled by many factors, all of which affect its appearance. Perhaps the most important is **altitude**. At lower levels the vegetation is almost tropical, supporting dense forests, **coffee**, **cotton**, **bananas** and **cacao**, while higher up, the hills are often wrapped in cloud and the ground is sometimes hard with frost. Here trees are stunted by the cold, and **maize** and potatoes are grown alongside grazing herds of sheep and goats. The **seasons** also play their part. In the rainy season, from May to October, the land is superbly green, with young crops and lush forests of **pine**, **cedar** and **oak**, while during the dry months the hillsides gradually turn to a dusty yellow. You'll find no matter what the time of year that the climate is benign: the days are pleasurably warm, but rarely hot, and the evenings are mild. In a few spots the climate is decidedly different, though, such as in the high-altitude town of Quetzaltenango, where it gets very chilly between November and February.

## Some history

The earliest known people to settle in the western highlands are thought to have arrived from the arid Mexican lands to the north, establishing small villages in the region by 2500 BC. These people were farmers, who cultivated the same basic staples as today's **Maya** – corn, beans, squash and chiles – and who almost certainly spoke a proto-Maya language. This area was to remain peripheral and sparsely populated throughout the Classic era, while in the northern lowlands (today's Petén), glorious monuments were constructed and scientific and artistic achievements accomplished.

The highlands were undoubtedly dominated by **Kaminaljuyú** (see p.336), just outside today's Guatemala City, which controlled trade routes and was closely aligned with the mighty city of Teotihuacán to the north. Towards the end of the eleventh century, the highlands were invaded by **Toltecs** from the north, who established themselves as an elite ruling class. Under Toltec domination, a number of rival centres emerged, based on tribal and linguistic divisions. The most powerful tribes were the **K'iche'**, with their capital at Utatlán; the **Mam** centred at Zaculeu and the **Kaqchikel**, based at Iximché.

Though pre-conquest life was certainly hard, the **arrival of the Spanish** in 1523 was a total disaster for the Maya population. In the early stages, **Alvarado** and his army met with a force of K'iche' warriors in the Quetzaltenango basin and defeated them in open warfare. Alvarado is said to have slain the great K'iche' warrior, **Tecún Umán**, himself. The Spanish made their first permanent base at **Iximché**, the capital of their Kaqchikel Maya allies, but this uneasy alliance was to last only a few years. Alvarado then moved to a site near the modern town of Antigua, today called Ciudad Vieja, from where the Spanish gradually brought the rest of the highlands under a degree of control. The damage done by Spanish swords, however, was nothing when compared to that of the **diseases** they introduced. Waves of smallpox, typhus, plague and measles swept through the indigenous population, reducing their numbers by as much as ninety percent in the worst-hit areas.

In the long term, the **Spanish administration** of the western highlands was no gentler than the Conquest, as indigenous labour became the backbone of the Spanish empire. Guatemala offered little of the gold and silver that was available in Peru or Mexico, but there was still money to be made from **cacao** and **indigo**. As well as being the heart of Spanish Guatemala, Antigua served as the administrative centre for the whole of Central America and Chiapas (now in Mexico). In 1773, however, it was destroyed by a massive earthquake and the capital was subsequently moved to its modern site.

The departure of the Spanish in 1821 and subsequent **independence** brought little change at village level. Ladino authority replaced that of the Spanish, but Maya were still required to work the coastal plantations, and when labour supplies dropped off they were simply press-ganged and forced to work, often in horrific conditions. It's a state of affairs that has changed little even today, and remains a major burden on the indígena population.

In the late 1970s, **guerrilla movements** began to develop in opposition to military rule, seeking support from the indigenous population and establishing themselves in the western highlands. The Maya became the victims in this process, caught between the guerrillas and the army. A total of 440 villages were destroyed; around 200,000 people died and thousands more fled the country, seeking refuge in Mexico. In recent years indigenous society has also been besieged by a tidal wave of American **evangelical churches** whose influence undermines local hierarchies, dividing communities and threatening to destroy Maya culture.

Today, with the signing of the 1996 **Peace Accords**, tensions have lifted and there is evidence of a new spirit of self-confidence within the highland Maya population. Fundamental problems remain – poverty, racism and the still unsettled issue of **land reform** – but there is a reawakened sense of pride in Maya identity. Despite intense pressure – and an increasing migration of young Maya men north into the United States to look for work – the traditional structures of society are largely still in place. Rejecting ladino commercialism, the Maya see trade as a social function as much as an economic one. Conservative and inward-looking, they live in a world centred on the village, with its own civil and religious hierarchy. Subsistence farming of maize and beans remains at its heart, and the land its life-blood.

## Where to go

Almost everywhere in the western highlands is of interest to the traveller. The landscape is exceptionally beautiful, dotted with highland villages of adobe houses and whitewashed colonial churches. **Lago de Atitlán** is unmissable – a lake of astounding natural beauty ringed by volcanoes and some of the most traditional Maya villages in all Guatemala. **Chichicastenango**, a sleepy highland town steeped in Maya/Catholic tradition, has perhaps the most famous market in the country. At the **markets** of **Sololá** and **San Francisco el Alto** there is little for the Western traveller to buy, but the pleasure is in the sights and smells and in soaking up the atmosphere. It's also worth trying to check out a few of the smaller-scale markets throughout the region (see box above), if only to buy some fruit, take a photograph or two and enjoy the relaxed atmosphere.

For real adventure, spectacular scenery and myriad hiking possibilities, the **Ixil triangle** in northern Quiché and the countryside around **Todos Santos Cuchumatán** are unmatched. Both are remote, intensely traditional areas that lie at the end of tortuous bus journeys; both suffered terribly in the civil war. Much easier to get to are the villages around **Quetzaltenango** (Xela), Guatemala's second city. Though Xela itself is a relatively unexciting provincial centre, it has some first-class **Spanish schools** and, within easy reach, you'll find the villages of Zunil and San Francisco el Alto, the amazing hot springs of Fuentes Georginas and the climbable, near-perfect cone of the Santa María volcano. Trekking trips to the beautiful crater lake on top of the Chicabal volcano and to Tajumulco, Guatemala's highest peak, can also be arranged in Quetzaltenango.

The scenery, villages and Maya culture are the main attractions in the highlands, but there are also interesting **historical Maya ruins**: Iximché, the pre-conquest city of the Kaqchikel, the K'iche' stronghold of **Utatlán**, and the Mam city of **Zaculeu**. There are also hundreds of assorted smaller sites, many still actively used for Maya religious ritual and ceremony. These ancient cities don't bear comparison to Tikal, Copán and the lowland centres, but they're fascinating nevertheless.

The **Carretera Interamericana** is the main transport artery, served by a constant flow of buses. If you want to get to more remote areas, however, you'll have to use the slow and uncomfortable dirt roads, especially in northern Quiché and Huehuetenango. Fortunately there is always the the mountain scenery to help cushion the ride. The most practical plan of action is to base yourself in one of the larger places and then make a series of day-trips to markets and fiestas, although even the smallest of villages will usually offer some kind of accommodation.

# The Carretera Interamericana

Leaving Guatemala City, the serpentine **Carretera Interamericana** cuts right through the western highlands as far as the border with Mexico. In its entirety this road stretches from Alaska to Chile (with a short break in southern Panamá), and here in Guatemala it forms the main artery of transport in the highlands. As you travel around, the highway and its junctions will inevitably become familiar since, wherever you're going, it's invariably easiest to catch the first local bus to the Carretera Interamericana and then flag down one of the buses heading along the highway. Along the route you'll see kerbside stalls set up by subsistence farmers selling surplus fruit and vegetables and you'll pass giant billboards brandishing tobacco company slogans – *"Para ganadores"* (For winners) – and assorted political graffiti.

Heading west from the capital, you'll climb steadily up a three-laned highway to San Lucas Sacatepéquez, from where a well-maintained side road descends to Antigua.

## TOURIST CRIME

While there is no need to be paranoid, visitors to the highlands, especially the heavily touristed areas, should be aware that **crime against tourists** – including robbery and rape – is a problem. Pay close attention to security reports from your embassy and follow the usual precautions with extra care. Though attacks on hikers in the Lago de Atitlán area are very unusual, it's still safer to walk in a group. In the more remote highlands, where foreigners are a much rarer sight, attacks are extremely uncommon.

There are three further major junctions on the Carretera Interamericana, which you'll soon get to know well. The first of these is **Chimaltenango**, an important town and capital of its own department; from its ugly sprawl along the highway you can also make connections to or from Antigua. Continuing west, **Los Encuentros** is the next main junction, where one road heads off to the north for Chichicastenango and Santa Cruz del Quiché and another branches south to Panajachel and Lago de Atitlán. Beyond this the highway climbs high over a mountainous ridge before dropping to **Cuatro Caminos**, from where side roads lead to Quetzaltenango, Totonicapán and San Francisco el Alto. The Carretera Interamericana continues on to Huehuetenango before it reaches the Mexican border at La Mesilla. Virtually every bus travelling along the highway will stop at all of these junctions and you'll be able to buy fruit, drink and fast food from a resident army of vendors, some of whom will storm the bus looking for business, while others are content to dangle their wares in front of your window.

## Chimaltenango

Founded by Pedro de Portocarrero in 1526, on the site of the Kaqchikel centre of Bokoh, **CHIMALTENANGO** was later considered as a possible site for the new capital. It has the misfortune, however, of being positioned on the continental divide and it suffered terribly from the earthquake in 1976, which shook and flattened much of the surrounding area. Today's town, its centre just to the north of the main road, is dominated by that fact, with dirt streets, breeze-block walls and an air of weary desperation. The town extracts what little business it can from the stream of traffic on the Carretera Interamericana, and the roadside is crowded with cheap comedores, mechanics' workshops, and sleazy bars that become brothels by night. "Chimal" is also home to a good new **Spanish school** where you can live and study away from the gringo scene of Antigua, but within firing range if you need to catch a film or have a meal. The Spanish and Maya Language School of Chimaltenango, 9 C final, Lote 23, Quintas Los Aposentos 1 (☎ & fax 839 1492), is staffed by ex-Peace Corps teachers and supports good local causes. Chimal can also boast a suprisingly decent community **website** (*www.chimaltenango.com*), with plenty of information in Spanish about the central highlands and the town itself. **Buses** passing through Chimaltenango run to all points along the Carretera Interamericana. For Antigua they leave every twenty minutes between 5.30am and 7pm from the market in town – though you can also wait at the turn-off on the highway.

To the north of Chimaltenango a road continues north through 19km of plunging ravines and pine forests to the village of **SAN MARTÍN JILOTEPEQUE**. The village remains badly scarred by the 1976 disaster, but the sprawling Sunday market is well worth a visit and the weaving here, the women's *huipiles* especially, is some of the finest you'll see – with intricate and ornate patterning, predominantly in reds and purples. **Buses** to San Martín leave the market in Chimaltenango every hour or so from 4am to 2pm, the last one returning at about 3pm, and the trip takes around forty minutes.

## Tecpán and the ruins of Iximché

Continuing west along a fast section of the Carretera Interamericana, the next site of interest lies close to the small town of **TECPÁN**, ninety minutes or so from Guatemala City. This may well have been the site chosen by Alvarado as the first Spanish capital, to which the Spanish forces retreated in August 1524 after they'd been driven out of Iximché. Today it's a place of no great interest, though it has a substantial number of restaurants and guest houses. It caters for a mainly Guatemalan clientele who come to picnic at the ruins and drink and eat in town.

The **ruins of Iximché** (daily 8am–5pm; US$3.50), the pre-conquest capital of the Kaqchikel, are about 5km south of Tecpán on a beautiful exposed hillside, protected on three sides by steep slopes and surrounded by pine forests. From the early days of the Conquest, the Kaqchikel allied themselves with the conquistadors, so the structures here suffered less than most at the hands of the Spanish. Since then, however, time and weather have taken their toll and the majority of the buildings that housed a population of 10,000 have disappeared, leaving only a few stone-built pyramids, clearly defined plazas and a couple of ball courts. Nevertheless, the site is strongly atmospheric and its grassy plazas, ringed with pine trees, are marvellously peaceful, especially during the week, when you may well have the place to yourself. The ruins are still actively used as a focus for Maya worship: sacrifices and offerings take place down a small trail through the pine trees behind the final plaza. There is also a small **museum** (same hours, no additional charge) at the entrance to the site with a jumbled collection of stone carvings, photographs and information (in Spanish only) about Iximché.

**To get here**, you can take any bus travelling along the Carretera Interamericana between Chimaltenango and Los Encuentros and ask to be dropped at Tecpán; the centre of the town is about 1km from the main highway. To get to the ruins, simply walk through Tecpán and out the other side of the plaza, passing the *Centro de Salud*, and follow the road through the fields for 5.5km – in all, an hour or so on foot from the Interamericana. With any luck you'll be able to hitch some of the way, particularly at weekends when the road can be fairly busy. There's **camping** at the site, but bring your own food as the small shop sells little other than drinks. Iximché's shady location is perfect for a picnic or barbecue. If you're not planning to camp, be back on the Carretera Interamericana before 6pm to be sure of a bus onwards.

# Chichicastenango

The road for Chichicastenango and the **department of El Quiché** leaves the Carretera Interamericana at the **Los Encuentros** junction at km127.3, another 34km past the Iximché turn-off. Heading north from Los Encuentros, the highway drops down through dense, aromatic pine forests, plunging into a deep ravine before bottoming out by a tributary of the Motagua river.

Continuing upwards around endless switchbacks, the road eventually reaches **CHICHICASTENANGO** (or "Chichi" for short), "Guatemala's *"mecca del turismo"*. If it's market day, you may get embroiled in one of the country's very few traffic jams – a rare event outside the capital – as traders, tourists and locals all struggle to reach the town centre. In this compact and traditional town of cobbled streets, adobe houses and red-tiled roofs, the calm of day-to-day life is shattered on a twice-weekly basis by the **Sunday and Thursday markets** – Sunday is the busiest. The market attracts hordes of tourists and commercial traders, as well as Maya weavers from throughout the central highlands.

The market is by no means all that sets Chichicastenango apart however. For the local Maya population it's an important centre of culture and religion. The area was

△ Santa Cruz del Quiché (19km)

**CHICHICASTENANGO**

Buses to
Santa Cruz del Quiché
★ Buses to Interamericana
& Guatemala City

Banco
Industrial

Centro
Comercial

El Calvario    Plaza
                Santo
Museo Rossbach  Tomás
Former Monastery

Mask
Shop

Pascual Abaj

0        200 m

**ACCOMMODATION**

| | |
|---|---|
| Colonial El Centro | 7 |
| Hospedaje El Salvador | 8 |
| Hospedaje Girón | 3 |
| Hotel Chalet House | 1 |
| Hotel Chugüilá | 4 |
| Hotel Posada Belen | 9 |
| Hotel Santo Tomás | 5 |
| Maya Inn | 6 |
| Posada El Arco | 2 |

**RESTAURANTS AND CAFÉS**

| | |
|---|---|
| Buenadventura | C |
| Café-Restaurant La Villa de Los Cofrades | A |
| Casa San Juan | E |
| Comedor Gumarcaj | B |
| La Fonda del Tzijolaj | D |

▽ Los Encuentros & Guatemala City

inhabited by the Kaqchikel long before the arrival of the Spanish and, over the years, Maya culture and folk-Catholicism have been treated with a rare degree of respect – although inevitably this blessing has been mixed with waves of arbitrary persecution and exploitation. Today, the town has an incredible collection of Maya artefacts, parallel indígena and ladino governments and a church that makes no effort to disguise its acceptance of unconventional pagan worship. Traditional weaving is also adhered to here, the women favouring superb, heavily embroidered *huipiles*. The men's costume of short trousers and jackets of black wool embroidered with silk is highly distinguished, although it's very expensive to make and these days most men opt for Western dress.

However, for the town's **fiesta** (December 14–21), at Easter and on Sundays, a handful of *cofrades* (elders of the religious hierarchy) still wear traditional clothing and carry spectacular silver processional crosses and incense burners. The fiesta, while not the most spontaneous, is certainly one of the most spectacular, and has attractions including a massive procession, live bands, traditional dances, clouds of incense, gallons of *chicha* (home-brewed alcohol), endless deafening fireworks. The highlight however is the *Palo Volador*, a spectacle with pre-Columbian roots, in which men (usually blind drunk) throw themselves off a twenty-metre pole, supported by ropes tied round their waists, and spin to the ground. On the final day, all babies born in the previous year are brought to the church for christening.

## Arrival and information

There's no bus station in Chichi, but the corner of 5 C and 5 Av operates loosely as a terminal. **Buses** leaving Guatemala City for Santa Cruz del Quiché, Joyabaj and Nebaj pass through Chichicastenango every twenty minutes or so, stopping in town for a few minutes to load up with passengers. In Guatemala City, buses leave from the terminal in Zona 4, from 4am to about 5pm. Coming from Antigua, you can pick up a bus easily in Chimaltenango on the Carreterra Interamericana. From Panajachel, you can take any bus up to Los Encuentros and change there; or on market days there are several direct buses, supplemented by a steady flow of special tourist shuttles run by various companies. There are also special shuttle services from Antigua on market days.

There a small **tourist information** office (daily 8am–noon & 2-6pm; ☎756 1015) beside Santo Tomás church on 8 Calle; they usually have a good stock of leaflets about the department. If you're bitten by market fever and need to **change money**, there's no problem in Chichi, even on a Sunday. Try Banco Ejército on 6 Calle (Tues–Sun 9am–5pm) or, almost opposite, Banco Industrial (Mon 10am–2pm, Wed–Sun 10am–5pm) for Visa card holders. *Hotel Santo Tomás* also offers exchange. The **post office** (Mon–Fri 9am–5.30pm) is behind the church on 7 Avenida, and **Telgua** (Mon–Fri 8am–6pm, Sat 9am–1pm) is on 6 Avenida. Try Acses at 6 C 4–52 for **Internet** connections, where rates are set at US$4 per hour.

## Accommodation

Hotels can be in short supply on Saturday nights, but you shouldn't have a problem on other days. Prices can also be inflated on market days, but at other times you can usually negotiate a good deal.

**Colonial El Centro**, 8 C and 6 Av (☎756 1249). Friendly, family-owned guest house, very close to the plaza, with clean inexpensive rooms, some with private bath. ②.

**Hospedaje Girón**, 6 C 4–52 (☎756 1156, fax 756 1226). Pretty, well-priced pine-trimmed rooms, with or without private bath, plus parking. Good value for single travellers. ③/④.

**Hospedaje El Salvador**, 5 Av 10–09 (☎756 1329). Decent budget hotel, with a vast warren of bare but cleanish rooms, a bizarre external colour scheme, and cheap prices. Insist that the owners turn on the hot water. ②.

**Hotel Chalet House**, 3C C 7–44 (☎756 1360, *multiple@concyt.gob.gt*). Excellent new hotel in a quiet street on the north side of town. The ten rooms are all very clean and have nice touches like highland wool blankets and textiles, plus comfortable beds and private bathrooms. There's also a tiny dining room where you can get breakfast, and a rooftop terrace. ④.

**Hotel Chugüilá**, 5 Av 5–24 (☎756 1134, fax 756 1279). Attractive, if rather old-fashioned rooms, all on different levels and some with fireplaces. Lovely greenery and pot plants everywhere. Secure parking. ⑤.

**Hotel Posada Belen**, 12 C 5–55 (☎ & fax 756 1244). Not the most attractive rooms, though half have private bath and many have good views. Cable TV available for a little extra. ②/③.

**Hotel Santo Tomás**, 7 Av 5–32 (☎756 1061, fax 756 1306). Very comfortable, well-appointed rooms set around two colonial-style courtyards. Rooms 29–37 are the ones to book if you can – they have great mountain views. Restaurant, swimming pool, sauna and Jacuzzi. ⑦.

**Maya Inn**, 8 C and 3 Av (☎756 1176, fax 756 1212). Chichi's oldest tourist hotel offers very comfortable rooms with old-fashioned period furnishings and fireplaces. Though its character is undeniable, prices are a bit steep, and you pity the staff decked out in mock-traditional dress. ⑧.

**Posada El Arco**, 4 C 4–36 (☎756 1255). Superb new guest house, run by friendly English-speaking brothers. Seven huge, attractive rooms with good wooden beds, reading lights and attractive decor, including local Maya fabrics. Rooms 6 and 7 have access to a pleasant terrace. Beautiful garden, with grassy lawn and avocado trees, and stunning countryside views. ④.

## The Town

Though most visitors come here for the market, Chichicastenango also offers an unusual insight into traditional religious practices in the highlands. At the main **Santo Tomás Church**, in the southeast corner of the plaza, the K'iche' Maya have been left to adopt their own style of worship, blending pre-Columbian and Catholic rituals. The church was built in 1540 on the site of a Maya altar, and rebuilt in the eighteenth century. It's said that the indigenous *maxeños* became interested in worshipping here after Francisco Ximénez, the priest from 1701 to 1703, started reading their holy book, the **Popol Vuh**.

Don't enter the building by the front door, which is reserved for *cofrades* and senior church officials; use the **side door** instead and be warned that taking **photographs** inside the building is considered deeply offensive – don't even contemplate it. Before entering the church, it's customary to make offerings in a fire at the base of the steps or to burn incense in perforated cans, a practice that leaves a cloud of thin, sweet smoke hanging over the entrance. Inside is an astonishing scene of avid worship. A soft hum of constant murmuring fills the air as the faithful kneel to place candles on low-level stone platforms for their ancestors and the saints. For these people, the entire building is alive with the souls of the dead, each located in a specific part of the church. Ronald Wright described the scene in his illuminating book, *Time Among the Maya*:

> *A large semicircular flight of stone steps leads to the front door; and these steps are a sacred stage like the huge stairways of the ancient pyramids. Here the senior shaman-priests burn clouds of incense and arrangements of candles to Mundo and the ancestors. These men are "chuchkahau" (mother-fathers), heads of their lineages, guardians of calendrical knowledge, and rememberers of the dead. Many of their forebears are buried beneath this church: every portion of the steps and the floor inside is dedicated to the founders of families, going back in some cases to the ancient Quiché [K'iche'] kings.*

Beside the church is a former monastery, now used by the parish administration. It was here that the Spanish priest Francisco Ximénez became the first outsider to be shown the Popol Vuh. His copy of the manuscript is now housed in the Newberry Library in Chicago: the original was lost some time later in the eighteenth century. The text itself was written just to the north of here, in Utatlán, shortly after the arrival of the Spanish, and is a brilliant poem of over nine thousand lines that details the cosmology, mythology and traditional history of the K'iche'.

On the south side of the plaza, on market day often hidden by stalls, the newly renovated **Rossbach Museum** (Tues, Wed, Fri & Sat 8am–noon & 2–4pm, Thurs & Sun 8am–1pm & 2–4pm, US$0.15) houses a broad-ranging collection of pre-Columbian artefacts, mostly small pieces of ceramics (including some demonic-looking incense burners), jade jewellery and stone carvings, some as old as two thousand years, that had been kept by local people in their homes. A second room, due to open in 2002, will be dedicated to local artesanías, including weavings, masks and carvings.

Facing Santo Tomás across on the west side of the plaza, the whitewashed **El Calvario** chapel is like a miniature version of Chichi's main church. Inside, the atmosphere is equally reverential as prayers are recited around the smoke-blackened wooden altar, and women offer flowers and stoop to kiss a supine image of Christ, entombed inside a glass cabinet.

## THE CEMETERY AND THE SHRINE OF PASCUAL ABAJ

The town **cemetery**, down the hill behind El Calvario, offers further evidence of the strange mix of religions that characterizes Chichicastenango. The graves are marked by anything from a grand tomb to a small earth mound and in the centre is a Maya shrine where the usual offerings of incense and alcohol are made.

The church and cemetery are certainly not the only scenes of Maya religious activity: the hills that surround the town, like so many throughout the country, are topped with shrines. The closest of these, less than a kilometre from the plaza, is known as **Pascual Abaj**. Although the site is regularly visited by tourists, it's important to remember that any ceremony you witness is deeply serious and you should keep your distance and be sensitive about taking any photographs. The shrine is laid out in a typical pattern with several small altars facing a stern pre-Columbian sculpture. Offerings are usually overseen by a *brujo* (a type of shaman) and range from flowers to sacrificed chickens, always incorporating plenty of incense, alcohol and incantations.

To get to Pascual Abaj, walk down the hill beside the Santo Tomás church, take the first right, 9 Calle, and follow this as it winds its way out of town. You'll soon cross a stream and then a well-signposted route takes you through the courtyard of a workshop that churns out wooden masks. If you look up, you might see a thin plume of smoke if there's a ceremony in progress. The path continues uphill for ten minutes through a dense pine forest.

## Eating

If you've come from Panajachel or Antigua, the dining scene here may come as a bit of a shock to the system. You won't find sushi or Thai curries in Chichi, just good-value Guatemalan comedor food. The plaza on **market day** is the place to come for authentic highland eating: try one of the makeshift food stalls, where you'll find cauldrons of stew, rice and beans.

**Buenadventura**, upper floor, inside the Centro Comercial. Bird's-eye view of the vegetable market; simple, no-nonsense food and the breakfasts are the cheapest in town.

**Café-Restaurant La Villa de Los Cofrades**, 6 C and 5 Av, first floor. Good set meals – soup, a main dish and salad, fries and bread – for under US$4, superb breakfasts and real coffee.

**Casa San Juan**, west side of plaza, beside the El Calvario chapel. Stylish bar-restaurant with a brightly painted interior and plenty of artwork, with good, imaginative Guatemelan cooking, including a US$2.50 set meal. Live music some nights.

**Comedor Gumarcaj**, opposite the *Hotel Santo Tomás*. Simple, scruffy but cheap and friendly comedor that serves up a mean chicken and chips and lush licuados.

**La Fonda del Tzijolaj**, upper floor in the Centro Comercial. Yes, the name's unpronounceable, but the food is probably the best in town and the balcony views of the church of Santo Tomás and the market are excellent. Try the delicious chiles rellenos.

# Santa Cruz del Quiché and around

The capital of the Department of El Quiché, **SANTA CRUZ DEL QUICHÉ** lies half an hour north of Chichicastenango. A good paved road connects the two towns, running through pine forests and ravines, and past the **Laguna Lemoa**, a lake which, according to local legend, was originally filled with tears wept by the wives of K'iche' kings after their husbands had been slaughtered by the Spanish. Santa Cruz del Quiché itself is a fairly uneventful place where not a lot happens. It is, however, the transport hub for the department and the most direct route to the Ixil triangle, as well as being the only practical place to base yourself for a visit to the nearby ruins of **Utatlán**.

On the central plaza, there's a large colonial church, built by the Dominicans with stone from the ruins of Utatlán. The Catholic Church suffered terribly in El Quiché in the late 1970s and early 1980s, when priests, who were often connected with the cooperative movement, were singled out and murdered. The situation was so serious that Bishop Juan Gerardi withdrew all his priests from the department in 1981. They have since returned to their posts, but the bishop himself was later assassinated in April 1998.

Beside the church, the large clock tower is also said to have been built from Utatlán stone, stripped from the temple of Tohil. In the middle of the plaza, a defiant statue of the K'iche' hero, Tecún Umán, stands prepared for battle, though his position is undermined somewhat by an ugly urban tangle of hardware stores, *panaderías* and trash that surrounds this corner of the square and the spectacularly ugly, looming presence of the tin-roof-topped, breeze-block-built mercado.

## Arrival and information

The **bus terminal**, a large, open affair, is about four blocks south and a couple east of the central plaza. Connections are generally excellent from Quiché. There's a constant stream of second-class **buses** to Guatemala City, going every twenty minutes between 3.30am and 5pm; all pass through Chichicastenango and Los Encuentros. There are also regular services to Nebaj between 8.30am and 4pm, to Uspantán, four times a day between 9am and 2pm (5hr), and to Quetzaltenango, regularly between 3am and 1pm.

The street directly north of the terminal is **1 Avenida**, which takes you up into the heart of the town. Two **banks** will change your travellers' cheques: Banco Industrial at the northwest corner of the plaza (Mon–Fri 8.30am–5.30pm, Sat 8.30am–12.30pm), which also advances cash on Visa, and Banco G&T Continental, 6 A 3–00 (Mon–Fri 9am–7pm, Sat 9am–1pm), where Mastercard holders can obtain cash. If you're heading into the Ixil Triangle (see p.372), you may want to stock up on **film**: try Kodak or Fuji, both one block northeast of the central church.

## Accommodation

There's a limited range of **hotels** in Quiché, none of them luxurious. The cheapest are very grim and right beside the bus terminal; most of the others are between the terminal and the plaza.

**Hospedaje Tropical**, 1 Av and 9 C. Extremely basic place; no hot water but dirt cheap. ①.

**Hotel Maya Quiché**, 3 Av 4–19, Zona 1 (☎755 1464). A friendly place with big clean rooms, some with bathroom. ②/③.

**Hotel Rey K'iche**, 8 C 0–39, Zona 5 (☎755 0824). Two blocks north, one east from the terminal. Well-run, extremely clean and welcoming place with 26 rooms, most with cable TV and private bath, plus a good comedor. ②/③.

**Hotel San Pascual**, 7 C 0–43, Zona 1(☎755 1107). Walk up 1 Avenida, and turn left into 7 Calle. Large, clean rooms and equally well-kept communal bathrooms. ②–③.

**Posada Calle Real**, 2 Av 7–36, two blocks from the terminal. Good-value budget deal: rooms are smallish but clean and the bathrooms (with reliable hot water) are well scrubbed. ②.

## Eating and drinking

There's very little to get excited about in Quiché. Most **restaurants** and **cafés** are grouped around the plaza. *El Torito Steakhouse*, 7 C 1–73, just southwest of the plaza, is the smartest place in town, with kitsch cowboy decor and a menu that's a real carnivore's delight – try the tasty sausages and fried chicken. On the west side of the plaza is *La Pizza de Ciro*, which dispenses reasonable pizzas that taste fine if you've come from remote Nebaj and pretty poor if you've journeyed from cosmopolitan Antigua. Close by are several uninspiring bakeries, with dry pastries and cakes, and also *Café La Torré*, a friendly place for a coffee, snack or a delicious piece of cheesecake. For a no-nonsense comedor meal try *Restaurante Las Rosas*, 1 Av, 1–28.

# The ruins of Utatlán (K'umarkaaj)

Early in the fifteenth century, riding on the wave of successful conquest, the K'iche' king Gucumatz (Feathered Serpent) founded a new capital, K'umarkaaj. A hundred years later, the Spanish arrived, renamed the city **Utatlán**, and then destroyed it. Today you can visit the ruins, about 4km to the west of Santa Cruz del Quiché.

According to the Popol Vuh, Gucumatz was a lord of great genius, assisted by powerful spirits, and there's no doubt that his capital was once a great city, with several separate citadels spread across neighbouring hilltops. It housed the nine dynasties of the tribal elite, including the four main K'iche' lords, and contained a total of 23 palaces. The splendour of the city embodied the strength of the K'iche' empire, which at its height boasted a population of around a million.

By the time of the Conquest, however, the K'iche' had been severely weakened and their empire fractured. They first made contact with the Spanish on the Pacific coast, suffering a heavy defeat at the hands of Alvarado's forces near Quetzaltenango, with the loss of their hero, Tecún Umán. The K'iche' then invited the Spanish to their capital, but the suspicious Alvarado captured the K'iche' leaders, burnt them alive and then destroyed the city.

**The site** (daily 8am–5pm; US$2) is not as dramatic as some of the ruins in Petén, but is impressive nonetheless, surrounded by deep ravines and pine forests. This setting and the fascinating historical significance of the site make up for the lack of huge pyramids and stelae. There has been little restoration since the Spanish destroyed the city and only a few of the main structures are still recognizable; most are buried beneath grassy mounds and shaded by pine trees. The small **museum** has a scale model of what the original city may once have looked like.

The central plaza is almost certainly where Alvarado burned alive the two K'iche' leaders in 1524. Nowadays, it's where you'll find all the remaining three **temple buildings**, the great monuments of Tohil, Auilix and Hacauaitz, all of which were simple pyramids topped by thatched shelters. In the middle of the plaza there used to be a circular **tower**, the Temple of the Sovereign Plumed Serpent, and its foundations can still be made out. The only other feature that is still vaguely recognizable is the **ball court**, which lies beneath grassy banks to the south of the plaza.

Perhaps the most interesting thing about the site today is that *brujos*, the traditional Maya priests, still come here to perform religious rituals, practices that predate the arrival of the Spanish by thousands of years. The entire area is covered in small burnt circles – the ashes of incense – and chickens are regularly sacrificed in and around the plaza. Beneath the plaza is a long **tunnel** that runs underground for about a hundred metres. Inside are nine **shrines**, coincidentally or not, the same number as there are levels of the Maya underworld, *Xibalbá*. Each is the subject of prayer and attention, but it is the ninth, housed inside a chamber, that is the most actively used for sacrifice, incense and alcohol offerings. Why the tunnel was constructed remains uncertain, but some local legends have it that it was dug by the K'iche' to hide their women and children from the advancing Spanish whom they planned to ambush at Utatlán. Others believe it represents the seven caves of Tula mentioned in the K'iche' masterpiece, the Popol Vuh (see p.552). Whatever the truth, today the tunnel is the focus for active Maya rituals and a favourite spot for sacrifice, the floor carpeted with chicken feathers, and candles burning in the alcoves at the end. To get to the tunnel follow the signs to *la cueva* (the cave); the entrance is usually littered with empty incense wrappings and *aguardiente* liquor bottles. If there is a ceremony taking place, you'll hear the mumbling of prayers and smell incense smoke as you enter the tunnel, in which case it's wise not to disturb the proceedings by approaching too closely. Tread carefully inside the tunnel, as some of the side passages end abruptly with precipitous drops.

**To get to Utatlán**, you can walk or take a taxi there from Santa Cruz del Quiché. To walk, head south from the plaza along 2 Avenida, and then turn right down 10 Calle, which will take you all the way out to the site – it's a pleasant forty-minute hike. You're welcome to **camp** close to the ruins, but there are no facilities or food. A taxi there and back, with an hour at the ruins, costs around US$7.

## East to Joyabaj

An astonishingly good paved road runs east from Santa Cruz del Quiché, beneath the impressive peaks of the **Sierra de Chuacús**, through a series of interesting villages set in beautiful rolling farmland. The first of the villages is **CHICHÉ**, a sister village to Chichicastenango, with which it shares costumes and traditions, though the market here is on Wednesday. Next is **CHINIQUE**, followed by the larger village of **ZACUAL-**

**PA**, which has Thursday and Sunday markets in its beautiful broad plaza. The village's name means "where they make fine walls", and in the hills to the north are the remains of a pre-conquest settlement. There's a pensión down the street beside the church, should you want to stay.

The last place out this way is the small town of **JOYABAJ**, again with a small archeological site to its north. During the colonial period, Joyabaj was an important staging post on the royal route to Mexico, but all evidence of its former splendour was lost when the earthquake in 1976 almost totally flattened the town and hundreds of people lost their lives: the crumbling facade of the colonial church that stands in front of the new prefabricated version is one of the few physical remains. In recent years the town has staged a miraculous recovery, however, and is now once again a prosperous traditional centre: the Sunday **market**, which starts up on Saturday afternoon, is a huge affair well worth visiting, as is the **fiesta** in the second week of August – five days of unrelenting celebration that includes some fantastic traditional dancing and the spectacular *Palo Volador*, in which "flying" men or *ángeles* spin to the ground from a huge wooden pole, a pre-conquest ritual now performed in only three places in the entire country. The pole represents the Maya world tree, with its top in the heavens and its base in *Xibalbá*, the underworld. Though the fiesta is in many ways a hybrid of Maya and Christian traditions, the *ángeles* symbolize none other than the wizard twins of the Popol Vuh (see p.522), who descend into the underworld to do battle with the Lords of Death.

It's possible to **walk** from Joyabaj, over the Sierra de Chuacús, to Cubulco in Baja Verapaz (see p.437). It's a superb but exhausting hike, taking at least a day, though it's perhaps better done in reverse as transport connections are far better in Joyabaj.

## Practicalities

**Buses** run between Guatemala City and Joyabaj, passing through Santa Cruz del Quiché, every hour or so (from 8am to 3pm from the capital and 5am to 3pm from Joyabaj). There's a good but very basic **pensión**, the *Hospedaje Mejia* (①), on the plaza in Joyabaj, and plenty of scattered **comedores** – one of the best is just off the main street beside the petrol station.

For Panajachel and connections to the Pacific coast, **buses leave Joyabaj** at 5am, 8am and noon, heading for Cocales. It's also possible to get back to the capital along a rough and seldom-travelled route via **San Martín Jilotepeque** (see p.362) on the daily bus that leaves Joyabaj at 2am.

# To the Cuchumatanes: Sacapulas and Uspantán

The land to the north of Santa Cruz del Quiché is sparsely inhabited and dauntingly hilly. About 10km out of town, the road passes through San Pedro Jocopilas, and from there presses on through parched mountains, eventually dropping to the isolated town of **SACAPULAS**, an hour and a half from Quiché. In a spectacular position on the Río Negro, beneath the foothills of the Cuchumatanes, Sacapulas has a small colonial church and a good market every Thursday and Sunday beneath a huge ceiba tree in the plaza.

With its strategic position, Sacapulas should be a transport hub but, alas, it's not. To **get to Sacapulas** is not too difficult; you can catch any of the buses that leave Santa Cruz del Quiché for Uspantán or Nebaj. **Leaving Sacapulas** can be difficult: the four daily buses for Quiché leave between 2am and 6am so you may have to **hitch**. Wait by the bridge as traffic heading for Quiché can turn left or right after crossing the river. There's a daily Transportes Rivas bus to Huehuetenango at 5am (4hr) and four buses to Uspantán (2hr 30min) between 1pm and 5pm but all services in this remote region are erratic and subject to delays and cancellations. Hitchhike by truck or pick-up whenever possible and expect to pay the same rate as you would on the bus.

At least if you get stuck there's a half-decent place to **stay**: the *Restaurant Río Negro* offers basic but clean rooms (①). The cook, Manuela, serves up good **meals** and excellent banana, pineapple and papaya milkshakes.

East of Sacapulas, a dirt road rises steeply, clinging to the mountainside and quickly leaving the Río Negro far below. As it climbs, the views are superb, with tiny Sacapulas dwarfed by the sheer scale of the landscape. Eventually the road reaches a high valley and arrives in **USPANTÁN**, a small town lodged in a chilly gap in the mountains, and often soaked in steady drizzle. Rigoberta Menchú (see p.554), the Maya woman who won the 1992 Nobel Peace prize is from Chimel, a tiny village in this region, but probably the only reason you'll end up here is in order to get somewhere else. With the bus for Cobán and San Pedro Carchá leaving at 3am, the best thing to do is go to bed, or try and hitch a lift. There are three friendly pensiones – all are basic but clean and very cheap – *Casa del Viajero* (①) just southeast of the plaza, *Galindo* on 5 Calle (①) and *La Uspanteka* (①) on 4 Calle. **Buses** for Uspantán, via Sacapulas, leave Quiché at 9am, 11am, noon and 2pm, returning at 11.30pm, 1am, 2am and 3am – a five-hour trip.

# The Ixil triangle

High up on the spine of the Cuchumatanes, in a landscape of steep hills, bowl-shaped valleys and gushing rivers, is the **Ixil triangle**. Here the three small towns of Nebaj, Chajul and Cotzal, remote and extremely traditional, share a language spoken nowhere else in the country. This triangle of towns forms the hub of the **Ixil-speaking region**, a massive highland area which drops away towards the Mexican border and contains at least 100,000 inhabitants. These lush and rain-drenched hills are hard to reach and notoriously difficult to control, and today's relaxed atmosphere and highland charm conceal a bitter history of protracted conflict. It's an area that embodies some of the very best and the very worst characteristics of the Guatemalan highlands.

On the positive side is the beauty of the landscape and the strength of indigenous culture, both of which are overwhelming. When Church leaders moved into the area in the 1970s, they found very strong communities with women included in the process of communal decision-making. The people were reluctant to accept new authority for fear that it would disrupt the age-old structures. Counterbalancing these strengths are the horrors of the human rights abuses that took place here until the mid-1990s, which must rate as some of the worst anywhere in Central America.

Before the **Conquest**, the town of Nebaj was a sizeable centre, producing large quantities of jade and possibly allied in some way to Zaculeu (see p.401). The Spanish Conquest was particularly brutal in these parts, however. After many setbacks, the Spaniards managed to take Nebaj in 1530 and by then they were so enraged that not only was the town burnt to the ground, but the survivors were condemned to slavery as punishment for their resistance. Things didn't improve with the coming of independence, when the Ixil people were regarded as a source of cheap labour and forced to work on the coastal plantations; many never returned. Even today large numbers of local people are forced to migrate in search of work and conditions on many of the plantations remain appalling. In the late 1970s and early 1980s, the area was hit by waves of horrific violence as it became the main theatre of operation for the **EGP** (the Guerrilla Army of the Poor). Caught up in the conflict, the people suffered enormous losses, with the majority of the smaller villages destroyed by the army and their inhabitants herded into "protected" settlements. With the peace accords, a degree of normality has returned to the area and new villages are being rebuilt on the old sites.

Despite this terrible legacy, the fresh green hills are some of the most beautiful in the country and the three towns are friendly and accommodating, with a relaxed and distinctive atmosphere.

# Nebaj

NEBAJ is the centre of Ixil country, a beautiful old town, by far the largest of the three, with white adobe walls and cobbled streets. The weaving done here is unusual and intricate, its greatest feature being the women's *huipiles*, which are an artistic tangle of complex geometrical designs in superb greens, yellows, reds and oranges, worn with brilliant red *cortes* (skirts). On their heads, the women wear superb headcloths decorated with pompom tassles that they pile up above their heads; most men no longer wear traditional dress. You'll find an excellent shop selling goods produced by the Ixil weaving co-op on the main square.

The small **market** is worth investigation, a block to the east of the church. On Thursday and Sunday numbers swell and traders from out of town visit with second-hand clothing from the US, stereos from Taiwan and Korea and chickens, eggs, fruit and vegetables from the Guatemalan highlands. The town church is also worth a look, although it's fairly bare inside. If you're here for the second week in August, you'll witness the **Nebaj fiesta**, which includes processions, dances, drinking, fireworks and marathon marimba-playing.

## Arrival and information

The **plaza** is the focal point for the community, with the major shops, municipal buildings and police station all encircling the square. The market and **bus terminal** are on 7 C nearby. There is a **bank**, Bancafé, 2 Av 46, near the market (Mon–Fri 8.30am–4pm, Sat 9am–1pm), which exchanges both cash and travellers' cheques; and next door a new **Internet café** with modern terminals, good rates and discounted international call facilities.

**Getting to** Nebaj is straightforward with **buses** from Santa Cruz del Quiché every hour and a half between 8.30am and 4pm (4hr), plus a daily service from Huehuetenango every morning (6hr), or you can take a bus to Sacapulas and change there. **Leaving Nebaj** is more problematic, with the schedules being subject to frequent changes (though the Huehuetenango bus generally leaves at 5am and departures for Quiché in the early hours), so check at the terminal before you want to leave. **Pick-ups and trucks** supplement the buses; the best place to hitch south is on the road out of town, a little further past the *Hotel Ixil*.

## Accommodation

You'll find little in the way of luxury in Nebaj, although what there is does have an inimitable charm and prices here are some of the lowest in the country. There are few street signs, so you'll probably have to rely on the gang of children who act as guides – none of the hotels in town is more than a few minutes' walk from the terminal.

**Hospedaje Esperanza**, northwest of the plaza. Friendly, simple but very basic for the price and you'll have to pay extra for a hot shower. Not the best deal in town but a good place to stay if you're interested in learning to weave – ask the owner's daughter for lessons. ②.

**Hospedaje Ilebal Tenam**, three minutes from the plaza on the road to Chajul/Cotzal. Tremendous hospedaje with two floors of simple but very clean rooms, exhilaratingly hot showers and safe parking. ①.

**Hospedaje Las Tres Hermanas**, a block northwest of the plaza. Despite its damp rooms, ancient mattresses and shabby appearance, this is one of the most famous hotels in Guatemala. During the troubles of the 1970s and 1980s this place put up a virtual who's who of international and Guatemalan journalists including Victor Perera, George Lovell and Ronald Wright (see p.579). It is still run by two of the original three sisters, who must have some stories to tell. ③.

**Hotel Ixil**, on the main road south out of town. The large, bare rooms are a little on the damp side, though the setting is pleasant, around a courtyard in a nice old colonial house, and there's a warmish shower. Better quality rooms, with private bath and hot showers, are available in a nearby house if you ask the friendly staff. ①–②.

**Hotel Posada de Don Pablo**, one block west of the plaza, opposite *Irene's* comedor. Attractive hotel, with smallish but spotless, pine-trimmed rooms, comfortable beds, private bathrooms and safe parking. ③.

**Nuevo Hotel Ixal**, three blocks south of the plaza. Good, secure little hotel with a charming court-yard. The pleasing rooms have private baths, and those on the upper floor enjoy mountain views. ②.

**Posada Maya Ixil**, four minutes northwest of the plaza, just off the road to Chajul/Cotzal. Excellent new hotel, easily the smartest in town, with real character. Large, comfortable rooms, decorated with vibrant local textiles and rustic furniture and pottery, with private bath. ③.

## Eating

As for **eating**, the best comedors in town, serving cheap, tasty Guatemalan food, are *Irene's*, just off the main plaza, and *Pasabien* by the bus terminal, with several others in the plaza itself. The *Maya-Inca* on 5 Calle is owned by a friendly Peruvian/Guatemalan couple and serves delicious Peruvian and local dishes, though the portions are small; there are also reasonable pizzas at *Cesar's* on 2 Avenida opposite Bancafé. Alternatively, some village women offer home-cooked Ixil-style meals for tourists for around US$2 per person, or there's always something to eat at the market. For entertainment, most of the raving in town is courtesy of Nebaj's burgeoning neo-Pentecostal church scene, with four-hour services involving much wailing and gnashing of teeth.

## Walks around Nebaj

In the hills that surround Nebaj there are several beautiful **walks**, with one of the most interesting taking you to the village of **ACUL**, two hours away. Starting from the church in Nebaj, cross the plaza and turn to the left, taking the road that goes downhill between a shop and a comedor. At the bottom of the dip it divides and here you take the right-hand fork and head out of town along a dirt track. The track switchbacks up a steep hill-side, and heads over a narrow pass into the next valley, where it drops down into Acul.

The village was one of the original so-called "model villages" into which people were herded after their homes had been destroyed by the army. If you walk on through the village and out the other side, you arrive at the Finca San Antonio, run by an Italian-Guatemalan family who have lived here for more than fifty years and make some of the country's best cheese, which they sell at pretty reasonable prices.

A second, shorter walk takes you to a beautiful little **waterfall**, La Cascada de Plata, about an hour from Nebaj. Take the road to Chajul and turn left just before it crosses the bridge, a kilometre or two outside Nebaj. Don't be fooled by the smaller version you'll come to shortly before the main set of falls.

# San Juan Cotzal and Chajul

To visit the other two towns in the Ixil triangle, it's best to coincide your visit with **market days** when there is more traffic on the move: Cotzal is on Wednesday and Saturday, Chajul on Tuesday and Friday, Nebaj on Thursday and Sunday. **Buses** run to an irregular schedule, but on Thurday and Sunday transport returns to both the other towns from Nebaj after 10am. Pick-ups supplement the buses. Look out, too, for aid agency and MINUGUA (United Nations) four-wheel drives. It's certainly possible to visit both towns as part of an interesting day-trip from Nebaj if you get an early start.

**SAN JUAN COTZAL** is closer to Nebaj, up to an hour and a half away, depending on the state of the road. The town is set in a gentle dip in the valley, sheltered some-what beneath the Cuchumatanes and often wrapped in a damp blanket of mist. Cotzal attracts very few Western travellers so you may find many people assume you're an aid worker or attached to a fundamentalist church.

Intricate turquoise *huipiles* are worn by the Maya women in Cotzal, who also weave bags and rope from the fibres of the maguey plant. There is little to do in the town itself, but there is some great hill-walking close by. If you want to **stay**, there is a small, very basic pensión called *Don Polo* (②), two blocks from the church, or you may find the *farmacia* in the corner of the plaza will rent you a room. *La Maguey* **restaurant**, in someone's front room, a block behind the church, serves up reasonable, if bland, food. **Buses** should return to Nebaj daily at 6am and 1am; you'll have to hitch at other times.

Last but by no means least of the Ixil settlements is **CHAJUL**. Made up almost entirely of old adobe houses, with wooden beams and red-tiled roofs blackened by the smoke of cooking fires, it is also the most determinedly traditional and least bilingual of the three towns. The women of Chajul wear earrings made of old coins strung up on lengths of wool and dress entirely in red, filling the streets with colour – you'll see them washing their scarlet *cortes* and *huipiles* at the stream that cuts through the middle of the village. Here boys still use blowpipes to hunt small birds, a skill that dates from the earliest of times but is now little used elsewhere.

The colonial church, a massive structure with huge wooden beams and gold leaf decoration, is home to the **Christ of Golgotha** and the target of a large pilgrimage on the second Friday of Lent – a particularly good time to be here. The *Hospedaje Cristina* (①) initially looks a pretty depressing option if you want somewhere to **stay** for the night, though it has some good rooms on the upper floor. Alternatively, the new *Hospedaje Esperanza* (①), close to the church, is basic but clean, or you could ask at the post office where one of the workers rents out rooms. Some other families also rent out beds in their houses to the steady trickle of travellers now coming to Chajul; you won't have to look for them, they will find you. For **eating**, there's an assortment of simple comedores and food stalls scattered around the marketplace.

If you want to walk off your lunch, it's possible to **hike from Cotzal to Chajul**, two to three hours away through the spectacular Ixil countryside. Retrace your steps down the Nebaj–Cotzal road to the edge of town and follow the dirt road that branches off to the right; the road is in good condition and it's impossible to get lost. The final uphill part of the walk is quite tough, especially if the sun is shining.

A number of unscheduled trucks bump along the two-hour route between Nebaj and Chajul on **market** days (Tues & Fri) and there are regular morning **buses** from 4am. Return buses leave at 11.30am and 12.30pm and there's usually a **truck** at 3.30pm. (You'll share the covered trailer with firewood and vegetables – not recommended for anyone who is claustrophobic.)

# Lago de Atitlán

*Lake Como, it seems to me, touches the limit of the permissibly picturesque; but Atitlán is Como with the additional embellishments of several immense volcanoes. It is really too much of a good thing. After a few days of this impossible landscape one finds oneself thinking nostalgically of the English Home Counties.*

Aldous Huxley, *Beyond the Mexique Bay* (1934)

Whether or not you share Huxley's refined sensibilities, there's no doubt that **LAGO DE ATITLÁN** is astonishingly beautiful and most people find themselves captivated by its scenic excesses. Indeed, the effect is so overwhelming that a handful of gringo devotees have been rooted to its shores since the 1960s.

The lake itself is an irregular shape, with three main inlets. It measures 18km by 12km at its widest point and shifts through an astonishing range of blues, steely greys and greens as the sun moves across the sky. Hemmed in on all sides by steep hills and massive volcanoes, it's at least 320m (nearly 1000ft) deep.

Another astonishing aspect of Atitlán is the strength of Maya culture still evident in the lakeside villages. Despite the thousands of tourists that pour in from Europe and North America every year, you can still find some of the most intensely traditional villages in Guatemala here. **San Antonio Palopó**, **Santiago Atitlán** and, above the lake, **Sololá** are

some of the very few villages in the entire country where Maya men still wear *traje* – traditional costume. Two languages, **Tz'utujil** and **Kaqchikel**, are spoken on the shores, and a third, **K'iche'**, a few kilometres away.

There are thirteen villages on the shores of the lake, with many more in the hills behind, ranging from the cosmopolitan resort-style **Panajachel** to tiny, isolated **Tzununá**. The villages are mostly subsistence farming communities and it's easy to hike and boat around the lake staying in a different one each night. The area has only recently attracted large numbers of tourists and for the moment things are still fairly undisturbed, but some of the new pressures are decidedly threatening. The increase in population has also had a damaging impact on the shores of the lake, as the desperate need to cultivate more land leads to deforestation and accompanying soil erosion.

You'll probably reach the lake through Panajachel, which makes a good base for exploring the surrounding area. "Pana" has an abundance of cheap hotels and restaurants and is well served by buses. To get a real sense of a more typical Atitlán village, however, travel by boat to Santiago Atitlán or San Antonio Polopó. **San Pedro La Laguna** is now the village that marijuana smokers and party people head for, with the most active travellers' "scene" and a surplus of extremely cheap hotels. **Santa Cruz** and **San Marcos** are the places to go if you're seeking real peace and quiet and there are good hikes on this side of the lake.

All things Atitlán seem to be covered in the excellent lake **website** *www.atitlan.com* including good accommodation options, and plenty of historical and cultural information.

## Sololá

Perched on a natural balcony overlooking the lake, **SOLOLÁ** is a fascinating place, ignored by the majority of travellers. In common with only a few other towns, it has parallel indígena and ladino governments and is probably the largest Maya town in the country, with the vast majority of the people still wearing traditional costume.

The town itself isn't much to look at: a wide central plaza with a recently restored clock tower on one side and a modern church on the other. However, its **Friday market** is one of Central America's finest – a mesmeric display of colour and commerce. From as early as 5am the plaza is packed, drawing traders from all over the highlands, as well as thousands of local Sololá Maya, the women covered in striped red cloth and the men in their outlandish **"space cowboy"** shirts, woollen aprons and wildly embroidered trousers. The town's symbol, an abstraction of a bat, can still be seen on the back of the men's jackets; it refers to the royal house of Xahil, who were the rulers of the Kaqchikel at the time of the Conquest. The pre-conquest site of **Tecpán-Atitlán**, which was abandoned in 1547 when Sololá was founded by the Spanish, is to the north of town.

If you can't make it for the Friday market, there's another smaller version on Tuesdays. Another interesting time to visit Sololá is on Sunday, when the **cofradres**, Maya religious brotherhoods, parade through the streets in ceremonial costume to attend the 10am Mass.

## Panajachel

Ten kilometres beyond Sololá and separated by a precipitous descent is **PANAJACHEL**. Over the years, what was once a small Maya village has become something of a resort, with a sizeable population of long-term foreign residents whose numbers are swollen in the winter by North American seasonal migrants and tourists. Panajachel was a premier hippie hangout back in the 1960s and 1970s and developed a bad reputation amongst some sections of Guatemalan society as a haven for drug-taking gringo drop-outs. Today "Pana" is much more integrated into the tourism mainstream and is as popular with Guatemalans, Mexicans and Salvadoreans as Westerners. The lotus-eaters and crystal-gazers have not all deserted Panajachel however. Many have reinvented themselves as (vaguely) conscientious capitalists who own restaurants and export típica clothing. Today there is much talk about the lake being one of the world's few "vortex energy fields", along with the Egyptian pyramids and Machu Pichu. Though you are unlikely to see fish swimming backwards or buses rolling uphill to Sololá, the lake does have an undeniable power and attracts a perennial population of healers, therapists and masseurs to Panajachel. In many ways it's this **gringo** crowd that gives the town its modern character and identity – vortex energy centre or not.

Not so long ago (although it seems an entirely different age), Panajachel was a quiet little village of **Kaqchikel** Maya, whose ancestors were settled here after the Spanish crushed a force of Tz'utujil warriors on the site. Today the old village has been enveloped by the new building boom, but it still retains a traditional feel, and most of the Maya continue to farm in the river delta behind the town. The Sunday market, bustling with people from all around the lake, remains oblivious to the tourist invasion.

For travellers, Panajachel is one of those inevitable destinations and, although no one ever owns up to actually liking it, everyone seems to stay for a while, particularly as it's a comfortable base for exploring the lake and the central highlands. The old village is still attractive and although most of the new building is fairly nondescript, its lakeside setting is superb. The main **daytime activity** is either shopping – weaving from all over Guatemala is sold with daunting persistence in the streets here, but you'll need to bargain hard as prices can be high – or simply hanging out. There's an amazing selection of places to eat and drink or surf the Net, plus reasonable swimming and sunbathing at the

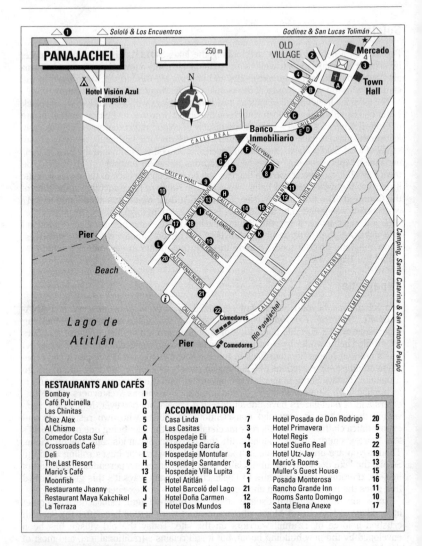

## RESTAURANTS AND CAFÉS

| | |
|---|---|
| Bombay | I |
| Café Pulcinella | D |
| Las Chinitas | G |
| Chez Alex | 5 |
| Al Chisme | C |
| Comedor Costa Sur | A |
| Crossroads Café | B |
| Deli | L |
| The Last Resort | H |
| Mario's Café | 13 |
| Moonfish | E |
| Restaurante Jhanny | K |
| Restaurant Maya Kakchikel | J |
| La Terraza | F |

## ACCOMMODATION

| | | | |
|---|---|---|---|
| Casa Linda | 7 | Hotel Posada de Don Rodrigo | 20 |
| Las Casitas | 3 | Hotel Primavera | 5 |
| Hospedaje Eli | 4 | Hotel Regis | 9 |
| Hospedaje García | 14 | Hotel Sueño Real | 22 |
| Hospedaje Montufar | 8 | Hotel Utz-Jay | 19 |
| Hospedaje Santander | 6 | Mario's Rooms | 13 |
| Hospedaje Villa Lupita | 2 | Muller's Guest House | 15 |
| Hotel Atitlán | 1 | Posada Monterosa | 16 |
| Hotel Barceló del Lago | 21 | Rancho Grande Inn | 11 |
| Hotel Doña Carmen | 12 | Rooms Santo Domingo | 10 |
| Hotel Dos Mundos | 18 | Santa Elena Anexe | 17 |

**public beach**, where you can also rent a kayak for a few hours (mornings are usually much calmer) or scuba-dive with ATI Divers (see p.389). Alternatively, if you're seduced by the bohemiam ambience and easy-going pace of lakeside life, Panajachel now boasts a number of new language schools where you can **study Spanish** (see p.382).

## Arrival, information and accommodation

The bus drops you beside the Banco Inmobiliario, very close to the main drag, Calle Santander, which runs down to the lakeshore. Straight ahead, up Calle Principal, is the old village. The **tourist office** is on the lakeshore (Mon–Sat 9am–5pm; ☎762 1392), with English-speaking staff, basic hotel information, and boat and bus schedules. **Taxis** usually wait outside the post office, or you can call one on ☎762 1571.

The streets of Panajachel are overflowing with cheap **hotels**, and there are plenty of "**rooms**". If you have a tent, first choice is the *Campaña* **campsite** (☎762 2479; US$2 per person), on the corner of the road to Santa Catarina and Calle del Cementerio over the river bridge (just off the map). Here happy campers will find kitchen and storage facilities and there are also sleeping bags and tents for rent. Don't bother camping at the public beach: your stuff will be ripped off.

There are a dozen or so **Internet** cafés in Pana and rates are very inexpensive, at around US$1.40 an hour. Amongst the best are the *Green Earth,* midway along Calle Santander, and *Café Pulcinella* at C Principal 0–72, which also bakes a mean pizza and sells Chianti by the glass.

## BUDGET ACCOMMODATION

**Casa Linda**, down an alley off the top of Calle Santander. Popular backpackers' retreat where the central garden is undeniably beautiful but the rooms, some with private bath, are a shade pricey for a hospedaje. ②/③.

**Las Casitas**, Calle Principal, near the market (☎ & fax 762 1224, *hotelcasitas@yahoo.com*). Very clean, friendly and safe, plus free email access for guests. Rooms are tastefully decorated and have good-quality beds and reading lamps; most have private bath. An upstairs dormitory is planned. ③.

**Hospedaje Eli**, Callejón del Pozo, off Calle de los Arboles (☎762 0148). Ten clean, cheap rooms overlooking a pretty little garden in a quiet location. ①.

**Hospedaje García**, Calle el Chali (☎762 2187). An abundance of featureless but perfectly reasonable budget rooms. ②.

**Hospedaje Montufar**, down an alley off the top of Calle Santander (☎762 0406). Quiet location and the rooms are cleaned with true evangelical zeal by a very accommodating family. Doubles and triples available. ②.

**Hospedaje Santander**, Calle Santander (☎762 1304, *www.atitlan.com/roomssantander.htm*). Leafy courtyard, friendly owners and clean, cheap rooms, some with private bath, though hot showers are a little extra. ①/②.

**Hospedaje Villa Lupita**, Callejón El Tino (☎762 1201). Impressive new family-run hotel, on a quiet alley close to the church. Fourteen excellent-value rooms, all with bedside lights, rugs and mirrors, some with private bath. There's a sun terrace and free purified water for guests. ②/③.

---

### BOATS

All lakeside villages are served by small fast boats called **lanchas**, which have largely replaced larger, slower ferry boats. Lanchas do not run to a fixed schedule but depart when the driver has enough passengers to cover his fuel costs, so you may have to wait around a while, sometimes up to an hour at quiet times of the year.

There are two **piers** in Panajachel. The pier at the end of Calle Rancho Grande is for Santa Catarina, San Antonio, San Lucas, Santiago Atitlán and lake tours. The second pier at the end of Calle del Embarcadero is for all villages on the northern side of the lake: Santa Cruz (10min), Jaibalito, Tzununá and San Marcos (20min); some services continue on to San Pablo, San Juan and San Pedro (30min). There are also direct lanchas to San Pedro which cut straight across the lake in a white-knuckle twenty-minute ride. The last boats on all these routes leave around 6.30pm.

Unfortunately, **rip-offs** are the rule for tourists, you'll be asked for two or three times what locals normally pay, so unless you can convince the boat owners that you're a resident, expect to pay around US$1.30 per trip. Another scam is charging more for the last boat of the day. **Tours of the lake**, visting San Pedro, Santiago Atitlán and San Antonio Palopó, can be booked in virtually any travel agent (see below); all leave around 9am and return by 4pm, they cost US$8–10 per person.

**Hotel Doña Carmen**, just off Calle Rancho Grande (☎762 2035, *losgarcia10@hotmail.com*). Nicely situated in a quiet corner of town, this pleasant family-run place offers simple, clean budget rooms, some with private bath, set off a huge shady garden. ②.

**Hotel Sueño Real**, Calle Ramós (☎762 0608, fax 762 1097). Excellent new hotel, very close to the lakeshore in a quiet location, owned by a friendly, helpful family. The seven attractive, secure rooms – all with private bath – represent superb value for money. ③.

**Mario's Rooms**, Calle Santander (☎762 1313). Good choice of pleasant, very clean rooms, some airy and light with private bath, others are more basic. Hot water on request for a few quetzales. ②/③.

**Posada Monterosa**, Calle Monterrey (☎762 0055). Attractive little hotel, with ten spotless rooms, all with pine furnishings and private bath, and safe car parking. ③.

**Rooms Santo Domingo**, down a path off Calle Monterrey (☎762 0236). One of the cheapest places in town, set well away from the hustle. Very simple wooden rooms all face a charming little garden, and more expensive options upstairs with private bath. ①/③.

**Santa Elena Anexe**, Calle Monterey 3–06 (☎ 762 1114). Safe, pleasant, ramshackle place with an abundance of children and parrots. Very cheap for single travellers, though hot showers are extra. ①.

## MID-RANGE ACCOMMODATION

**Hotel Dos Mundos**, Calle Santander (☎762 2078, fax 762 0127, *www.atitlan.com/dos_mundos.htm*). Italian-owned hotel, just off the main drag, offering comfortable rooms set in a private garden, where there's also a small swimming pool; breakfast is included. The attached *Lanterna* restaurant is recommended for authentic Italian cuisine at moderate prices. ⑥.

**Hotel Primavera**, Calle Santander (☎762 2052, fax 762 0171, *www.atitlan.com/primavera.htm*). Stylistically, the design of this minimalist hotel is almost revolutionary for Guatemala – all blond wood, magnolia walls and a notable absence of típica textiles or rustic clichés. Elegant rooms, a tiny Zen-like garden zone and a classy restaurant, *Chez Alex*, downstairs. Very good value, too. ⑤.

**Hotel Regis**, Calle Santander 3–47 (☎762 1149, fax 762 1152, *www.atitlan.com/regis.htm*). Age-old colonial-style establishment with attractive individual bungalows and rooms, all with cable TV, though the real attraction is the wonderful natural hot spring. ⑥.

**Hotel Utz-Jay**, Calle 15 de Febrero (☎762 0217, fax 762 1358, *www.atitlan.com/utz-jay.htm*). Oustanding new hotel set in a large, tranquil garden, with five very stylish adobe-and-stone houses (all sleep up to four and have private bath), decorated with nice homely touches. In-house *tuj* herbal sauna, plus a selection of excellent tours available. Book ahead, though there may be more rooms shortly as the owners are busy constructing accommodation next door. ④.

**Muller's Guest House**, Calle Rancho Grande (☎762 2442, *www.atitlan.com/muller.htm*). Swiss-owned guest house where the tasteful rooms, with quality modern European furnishings, are set around a grassy garden. Breakfast is included. ⑤–⑥.

**Rancho Grande Inn**, Calle Rancho Grande (☎762 2255, fax 762 2247, *www.atitlan.com/ranchogrande.htm*). A long-standing Panajachel institution with very attractive, nicely appointed bungalows, superbly kept gardens and helpful staff. Breakfast included. ⑥.

## LUXURY ACCOMMODATION

**Hotel Atitlán**, on the lakeside, 1km west of the centre (☎ & fax 762 1441 or 762 1416, *www.atitlan.com/hotelatitlan.htm*). The swankiest hotel in the Panajachel area with a stunning lakeside location, lovely gardens and a swimming pool. Rooms are very comfortable and tastefully decorated. A double costs US$120. ⑨.

**Hotel Barceló del Lago**, right on the lakeshore (☎762 1555, fax 762 1562 *www.atitlan.com/barcelo.htm*). Opulent, all-inclusive colossus complete with pool, Jacuzzi and gym. Very corporate, "international" flavour – only the great volcano views remind you you're in Guatemala. Doubles US$110 low season, US$162 high season. ⑨.

**Hotel Posada de Don Rodrigo**, Calle Santander, facing the lake (☎ & fax 762 2322 or 762 2329, *www.centramerica.com/posadadedondodrigo*). Colonial-style hotel by the lakeside, with a large outdoor pool, sauna and squash court. Most of the accommodation in the main block is on the small side, so try to book a room in the new superb wing (301–311) – they're supremely spacious and boast bathtubs and stunning volcano views. ⑧.

## Eating, drinking and entertainment

Panajachel has an abundance of **restaurants**, all catering to the cosmopolitan tastes of its floating population. You'll have no trouble finding tasty Chinese, Italian, Mexican and Mediterranean dishes. For really cheap and authentically Guatemalan food there are plenty of comedores on and just off the new beach promenade and close to the market in the old village.

### CAFÉS AND RESTAURANTS

**Bombay**, halfway down Calle Santander. Eclectic vegetarian food which, despite the name, has little Indian about it. Indonesian *gado-gado,* epic pitta-bread sandwiches (try the falafel), and organic coffee, plus a US$3 daily set menu.

**Las Chinitas**, towards the northern end of Calle Santander. Excellent pan-Asian cuisine in a pretty patio setting. Nonyan (Malay-Chinese) cooking is the main draw, with Thai and Japanese dishes at moderate prices. Closed Mon.

**Chez Alex**, halfway along Calle Santander. Unquestionably the flashest place in town, with an over-designed peach interior and gilt plates and cutlery. Heavyweight menu, majoring in European classics – the food's good, though not outstanding. Expensive.

**Al Chisme**, Calle de los Árboles. A smart, European-style restaurant and bar adorned with black and white photographs of former customers. Delicious food including bagels, sandwiches, crêpes and pasta, but all a little pricey. Closed Wed.

**Comedor Costa Sur**, near the church in the old town. Clean and attractive comedor, loudly bedecked with Mexican blankets. Great breakfasts, lunchtime dishes and licuados.

**Crossroads Café**, Calle del Campanario 0–27. Easily the finest coffee in town; selected, blended and roasted by perfectionists. A multitude of combinations and flavourings possible, including lattes and mochas, plus real hot chocolate and fresh pastries. Closed Mon and for siesta 1–2pm.

**Deli**, southern end of Calle Santander. Excellent range of healthy meals and snacks: salads, sandwiches, pastries, bagels, cakes, wine and tea in a pretty garden setting. Service is friendly, but often lethargic.

**The Last Resort**, Calle el Chali. Looks vaguely like an English pub, but does the best American buffet breakfasts in town. Also pasta, steaks and vegetarian dishes, served in huge portions.

**Mario's Café**, halfway down Calle Santander. A limited range of low-cost food: huge salads, delicious yoghurt and pancakes.

**Moonfish**, upper floor, C Principal 0–72. Scruffy-chic bohemian dive popular with travelling scenesters, with a fine line-up of inexpensive tempe burritos and sandwiches, plus yoghurt licuados. Eclectic sounds – drum 'n' bass, reggae, rock – plus live music some nights.

**Restaurante Jhanny**, halfway down Calle Rancho Grande. Ignore the fairylights and head inside for a superb Guatemalan-style *menú del día* (US$2.50); tables are nicely arranged around a little garden.

**Restaurant Maya Kakchikel**, C el Chali 2–25. Bright little comedor, great for Guatemalan food, though the owners also serve up excellent filling breakfasts and crêpes.

**La Terraza**, northern end of Calle Santander. One of the finest restaurants on the lake, with a classy European menu plus a few Asian-influenced dishes. Quite formal, and expensive.

### NIGHTLIFE

Panajachel has a gregarious party spirit at weekends and during the main holiday season, when many young Guatemalans head to the lake to drink and flirt, though things are less lively at other times. Pana's prime bar and dance scene is centred around the southern end of Calle de los Árboles, where there's a cluster of busy places including the long-running *Circus Bar, Porque No* and *El Aleph* for **live music**, plus the *Chapiteau* **nightclub**. For a less frenetic environment head for *Moonfish* or *The Last Resort* (see "Cafés and Restaurants", above), or *Ubu's Cosmic Cantina*, on Calle de los Árboles, where there's a big screen for sports fans, movie buffs and news addicts. Finally, there are occasional **poetry** recitals at *Delante's Bookshop* off Calle Buenas Nuevas, video **movies** at Carrot Chic and Turquoise Buffalo on Calle de los Árboles, and a **pool hall** in the old village, near the post office.

## Listings

**Banks and exchange** Banco Inmobiliario, at C Santander and C Principal (Mon–Fri 9am–7pm, Sat 9am–12.30pm), or Banco Industrial, on Calle Santander, which has a 24-hr ATM for Visa card holders. Try the AT travel agency or *Hotel Regis*, both on Calle Santander, for Mastercard transactions.

**Bicycle rental** Moto Servicio Queche, C de los Árboles and C Principal, rents mountain bikes for US$1 an hour, US$5 a day.

**Bookstores** Delante, down an alley off Calle Buenas Vistas, has a friendly atmosphere and a very comprehensive selection of secondhand books. The Gallery on Calle de los Árboles stocks a reasonable choice of secondhand titles and a few interesting new books in English.

**Language schools** Escuela Jabel Tinamit, off Calle Santander (☎762 0238, *http://members.nbci.com/ learnspanish*), and Jardín de América, Calle 14 de Febrero (☎ & fax 762 2637, *www.atitlan.com/ jardin.htm*).

**Laundry** Lavandería Automatico, C de los Árboles 0–15 (Mon–Sat 7.30am–6pm), US$3.50 for a full load washed, dried and folded.

**Medical care** Dr Edgar Barreno speaks good English; his surgery is down the first street that branches to the right off Calle de los Árboles (☎762 1008).

**Motorbike rental** Moto Servicio Queche, C de los Árboles and C Principal (☎762 2089), rents 185cc bikes for US$6 an hour, US$25 for 24 hours, US$100 for the week.

**Pharmacy** Farmacia La Unión, Calle Santander.

**Police** On the plaza in the old village (☎762 1120).

**Post office** In the old village, down a side street beside the church (Mon–Fri 8am–4.30pm), or try Get Guated Out on Calle de los Árboles (☎762 0595, *gguated@c.net.gt*) for bigger shipments.

**Telephone** To make a phone call or send a fax, check first with businesses in Calle Santander for the best rates; many advertise discounted calls. Otherwise, Telgua (daily 7am–midnight) is near the junction of C Santander and C 15 de Febrero.

**Travel agents** Rainbow Travel, C Principal near the junction with C Santander (☎762 1302), is a good all-rounder, with competitive international flight prices; Sevicios Turisticos Atitlán, C Santander, near C 14 de Febrero (☎762 2075, fax 762 2246, *www.atitlan.com*), is another recomended agent.

# The eastern shore

On the eastern shore, backed up against the slopes of the crater, are a couple of villages, the first of which, **SANTA CATARINA PALOPÓ**, is just 4km from Panajachel. The people of Santa Catarina used to live almost entirely by fishing and trapping crabs, but the introduction of black bass into the lake to create a sport-fishing industry has put an end to all that as the bass eat the smaller fish. They've now turned to farming and migratory work, with many of the women travelling to Panajachel and Antigua to peddle their weaving, though you'll have no problem finding someone to sell you one of the stunning *huipiles* – made with vibrant turquoise and purple zigzags – in the village itself.

Much of the shoreline as you leave Santa Catarina has been bought and developed, and great villas, ringed by impenetrable walls and razor wire, have come to dominate the environment. Here you'll find the landmark *Hotel Villa Santa Catarina* (☎762 1291, fax 762 2013, *villasdeguatemala.com*; ⑦) which enjoys a prime lakeside plot, with 31 very comfortable rooms, two banqueting halls, a pool and restaurant. Beyond here, the road winds around the shore for another 3km until you reach the upmarket *San Tomas Bella Vista Retreat* (☎762 1566, *www.santomasatitlanlodge.guate.com*; ⑦), with fourteen attractive bungalows, all boasting great views, plus a pool and restaurant. Another 2km brings you to **SAN ANTONIO PALOPÓ**, a large, traditional village, squeezed in beneath a steep hillside. It is on the tour-group itinerary, so the locals have become a bit pushy in selling their weavings, but despite this, the village is quite interesting and the situation is beautiful. The hillsides above San Antonio are well irrigated and terraced, reminiscent of rice paddies, and most men wear the village *traje* of red shirts with vertical stripes and short woollen kilts. Women wear almost identical shirts, made of the same fabric with subtle variations to the collar design. The whitewashed central church is also worth a look; just to the left of the entrance are two ancient bells.

Regular pick-ups ply this route from Panajachel, leaving approximately every thirty minutes (the last one returns to Panajachel from San Antonio at 5pm) and of course there are **boats** (see p.379). If you decide **to stay**, there are two options: the fairly upmarket *Hotel Terrazas del Lago* (☎762 1288, fax 762 0157; ⑤), down by the water, which has comfortable rooms and beautiful views, or the very simple but clean pensión (①) owned by Juan López Sánchez, near the entrance to the village. Try the comedor below the church for a cheap **meal**.

If you want to continue to circumnavigate the lake from San Antonio, you'll have to catch a boat, as shortly beyond the village a steep section of the Atitlán crater prevents the construction of a road. The next village, **SAN LUCAS TOLIMÁN**, is probably the least attractive of the lot, a busy ladino-dominated coffee production centre. Though the setting under the Volcán de Tolimán is tremendous, in San Lucas the easygoing atmosphere of the lake is tempered by the influence of the Pacific coast. Both the Tolimán and Atitlán **volcanoes** can be climbed from here, though taking a guide is recommended as the trails are difficult to locate; ask at your hotel or the town hall. The main **market day** here is on Friday, which is certainly the best time to drop by, although it unfortunately clashes with the market in Santiago.

If you need somewhere to **stay**, head for the *Hotel Villa Real Internacional* on 7 Av 1–84 (☎722 0102; ③–④), with reliable hot showers, safe parking and a restaurant, or the *Hotel Brisas del Lago* (③), down by the lake, which has similar facilities. By far the most luxurious place in San Lucas is the *Pak'ok Marina and Resort* (☎206 7561 & 334 6076, fax 334 6075, *www.virtualguatemala.com/patok*; ⑦), a spectacular new hotel located in the grounds of an old coffee finca, with lovely gardens, colonial-style rooms and apartments and a pool. For good, inexpensive food, the best place is the *Café Tolimán* by the lake, or *La Fonda* close to the plaza.

San Lucas is at the junction of the coast road and the road to Santiago Atitlán, and **buses** regularly thunder through in both directions. On the whole, they head out towards Cocales and the coast and on to Guatemala City in the early morning, with the last bus at about 3pm, while there are hourly buses to Santiago between 5am and 6pm. There are also five daily buses between here and Panajachel (1hr) running mostly in the morning; the last one leaves at 4pm. Lanchas, which don't run to a fixed schedule, also connect San Lucas with Panajachel (30min; US$2), some calling in at San Antonio and Santa Catarina on the way.

## Santiago Atitlán

On the other side of the Tolimán volcano, **SANTIAGO ATITLÁN** is set to one side of a sheltered horseshoe inlet, overshadowed by the twin cones of Atitlán and Tolimán. It's the largest and most important of the lakeside villages, and also one of the most traditional, being the main centre of the Tz'utujil-speaking Maya. At the time of the Conquest, the Tz'utujil had their fortified capital, **Chuitinamit-Atitlán**, on the slopes of the San Pedro volcano, while the bulk of the population lived spread out around the site of today's village. Alvarado and his crew, needless to say, destroyed the capital and massacred its inhabitants, assisted this time by a force of Kaqchikel Maya, who arrived at the scene in some three hundred canoes.

Today, Santiago is an industrious but relaxed sort of place. During the day the town becomes fairly commercial, its **main street**, which runs from the dock to the plaza, lined with weaving shops and art galleries. There's nothing like the Panajachel overkill, but the persistence of underage gangs here can still be a bit much. By mid-afternoon, once the tour groups have left, things revert to normal and the whole village becomes a lot more friendly. There's not a lot to do in Santiago other than stroll around soaking up the atmosphere, or enjoying the **market** – Friday is the main day, though there's also a smaller event on Sundays.

The old colonial Catholic **church** is well worth a look, however. The huge altarpiece, which was carved when the church was under *cofradía* control, culminates in the shape of a mountain peak and a cross. The cross symbolizes the Maya world tree, which supports the source of all life, including people, animals and the corn ears that you can see on the cross. In the middle of the floor is a small hole which Atitecos believe to be the centre of the world. The church is also home to a memorial plaque commemorating Father Stanley Rother, an American priest who served in the parish from 1968 to 1981. Father Rother was a committed defender of his parishioners in an era when, in his own words, "shaking hands with an Indian has become a political act". Branded a Communist by President García, he was assassinated by a paramilitary death squad like hundreds of his parishoners before and after him. His body was returned to his native Oklahoma for burial, but his heart was removed and buried in the church.

As is the case in many other parts of the Guatemalan highlands, the Catholic Church in Santiago is locked in bitter rivalry with several evangelical sects, who are building churches here at an astonishing rate. Their latest construction, right beside the lake, is the largest structure in town. Folk-Catholicism also plays an important role in the life of Santiago and the town is well known as a key centre of the cult of **Maximón**, the drinking and smoking saint (see pp.355 and 396). Any child will take you to see him; just ask for the "Casa de Maximón". If you can get to Santiago at **Easter**, there's a huge religious procession through the town culminating in a symbolic and highly charged confrontation between an effigy of Christ, borne by the town's Catholics, and the image of Maximón, complete with a cigar in his mouth.

The traditional **costume** of Santiago, still worn a fair amount, is both striking and unusual. The men wear long shorts which, like the women's *huipiles*, are striped white and purple and intricately embroidered with birds and flowers. The women also wear a *xk'ap*, a band of red cloth approximately 10m long, wrapped around their heads, which has the honour of being depicted on the 25-centavo coin. Sadly this headcloth is going out of use and on the whole you'll probably only see it at fiestas and on market days, worn by the older women.

## Practicalities

**Boats** to Santiago leave from the beach in Panajachel at 5.45am, 9.30am, 11.30am and 3pm – the trip takes about an hour – but there are also unscheduled lancha services at other times. The village is also astonishingly well connected by **bus** with almost everywhere except Panajachel (see below).

As for **accommodation**, a backpackers' favourite is the *Hotel Chi-Nim-Ya* (☎721 7131; ①/②) where some rooms have private bath, on the left as you enter the village from the lake. The good-value *Hotel Tzutuhil*, in the centre of town (☎721 7174; ②), is a five-storey concrete building with spectacular views from the top floor and a restaurant. For something special, there are a number of good options; all can be reached by water taxi from the dock, or by road. The *Posada de Santiago*, on the lakeshore 1km south of the town (☎ & fax 721 7167; *www.atitlan.com/posada.htm*; ⑥), is a luxury, American-owned bed and breakfast, with rooms in stone cabins, each with its own log fire, a few budget rooms and a fine restaurant. A kilometre north of the dock, the *Bird House* (☎716 7440, *thebirdhousetk@hotmail.com*; ③/④) is another excellent place to stay, with attractive rooms and apartments, nice lakeside gardens, a library and great home-made food. About 500m further north, *Hotel*

*Bambú* (☎416 2122; ⑤) has beautiful thatch-roofed stone bungalows and rooms, plus an excellent restaurant with Spanish specialities. Next door, there's quite a scene developing at *Las Milpas* (☎416 3395, *las_milpas@hotmail.com*; ③), a great new bohemiam retreat-cum-hotel run by an ex-Grateful Dead roadie, with four comfortable cabañas, camping (US$4 per person), a hot tub and sauna, tasty vegetarian food, plenty of live music and full moon cruises.

There are three **restaurants** at the entrance to the village, just up from the dock, all fairly similar. In the centre of the village you can eat at the *Hotel Tzutuhil* or, if you really want to dine in style, head out to the restaurant in the *Posada de Santiago* or *Hotel Bambú*.

**Leaving Santiago**, buses depart from the central plaza and head to San Lucas Tolimán (hourly between 2.30am & 4.30pm) and, via Cocales, to Guatemala City (6 daily between 2.30am & 2pm). For San Pedro, nine boats leave Santiago every day from 6am until 3pm (40min).

# San Pedro La Laguna

Around the other side of the Volcán de San Pedro is the village of **SAN PEDRO LA LAGUNA**, which has now usurped Panajachel to become the pivotal centre of Guatemala's travelling "scene". Generally, this status involves little more than playing host to the few dozen colourful foreigners who have set up home here and providing a plentiful supply of marijuana to keep the young gringo visitors happy. This isn't Goa, but San Pedro does have a distinctively bohemian flavour. Things certainly seem very mellow here but it hasn't always been so. Crack cocaine arrived in San Pedro in the early 1990s and the locals got so fed up with the wasted gringos in their midst that they wrote to a national newspaper demanding that the freaks get out of town. Today things seem to have settled down again and, despite the obvious culture clash between locals (most of whom are evangelical) and travellers, everyone seems to get on reasonably well. San Pedro has also started to establish itself as a **language school** centre in recent years, the beautiful location drawing increasing numbers of students, though the quality of tuition is pretty variable at present (see p.51). Try Casa Rosario, south of Santiago Atitlán dock (☎7675795), and San Pedro Spanish School, between the piers (☎703 1100).

Again, the lakeside setting is undeniably spectacular, with the San Pedro volcano rising to the east and a ridge of steep hills running behind the village. To the left of the main beach, as you look towards the lake, a line of huge white boulders juts out into the water – an ideal spot for an afternoon of swimming and sunbathing. Two **thermal pools**, adjacent to each other halfway between the two docks, offer further opportunities to relax. The best of these, Thermal Waters (☎206 9658, *thermalwaters@hotmail.com*; open late afternoon only; US$2.50 per person), run by Antonio, a long-term Canadian resident, also offers fine organic vegetarian food and camping spots (see below).

The **Volcán de San Pedro**, which towers above the village to a height of some 3020m, is largely coated with coffee plantations and tropical forest and can be climbed in four to five hours. Most of the village guides are reliable – including Samuel Cumatz Batzin (☎762 2487) who can often be found at *Casa Elena* (see below) – and it's well worth utilizing their services, as the foliage is dense and the route can be tricky to find. Get an early start in order to see the views at their best and avoid the worst of the heat. If you'd rather do something a little more relaxing, Excursion Big Foot (☎204 6267), just left of the Panajachel dock, rents out **horses** for US$2.50 an hour, **bicycles** for US$10 a day and **canoes** for US$2 for two hours.

## Arrival and information

There are two docks in San Pedro. All boats from Panajachel and villages on the north side of the lake, including Santa Cruz and San Marcos, arrive and depart from the Panajachel dock on the north side of town, while boats from Santiago Atitlán use a separate dock a ten-minute walk away. Most of the village is centred around the Catholic church in the centre of town, where you'll find the marketplace (busiest on Thurs and Sun), post office and, a block to the south, Banrural (Mon–Fri 9am–5.30pm, Sat 9am–12.30pm), which will change travellers' cheques. There are very few phone lines in town, and consequently just one place, Solar Pools, between the docks, currently offering international call and **email** facilities – most visitors head into Panajachel where there are much speedier and cheaper connections.

## Accommodation

San Pedro has some of the cheapest accommodation in all Latin America, with a number of basic, clean **guest houses** that almost all charge less than US$3 a person per night, plus **camping** at Thermal Waters, halfway between the docks (US$1.30 per person; see above). There's nothing in the way of luxury, but there are a few new comfortable options. If you plan to stay around for a while then you might want to consider **renting a house**, which works out incredibly cheap; try the noticeboard in *D' Noz* bar above *Nick's Place*. To locate any of the hotels listed below, let one of the local children guide you through the coffee bushes; a tip of a quetzal or two is appropriate.

**Casa Elena**, left after *Nick's Place*. Nine tidy rooms with twin beds, some right on the lakeshore. Owned by a friendly Maya family. ①.

**Hotel Bella Vista**, turn left after *Nick's Place*, by the docks. Pretty decent budget hotel with really cheap rates and clean, bare rooms. The mattresses are foam slabs, though. ①.

**Hotelito El Amanecer Sakcari**, between the docks (☎812 1113). Friendly, family-run place with ten attractive tiled rooms, all with private bath. Most of the rooms have wonderful lake views. ②.

**Hotel Mansión del Lago**, right above the Panajachel dock (☎811 8172). Bulky, somewhat obtrusive new place, with spotless, excellent-value rooms that are unquestionably the smartest in town: all have nice pine beds, private bath and balcony areas with lake outlooks. ②–③.

**Hotel San Pedro**, close to the Santiago Atitlán dock, next door to the *Villa Sol*. Set above the police station, this should be be the safest place in town. Clean rooms, some with private bath. ②.

**Hotel Ti'Kaaj**, near the Santiago Atitlán dock. Very basic rooms, but the lovely shady garden, replete with orange trees and hammocks, certainly helps compensate. ①.

**Hotel Valle Azul**, turn right at the Panajachel dock (☎207 7292). Hulking concrete monster of a hotel, but the views are excellent and the good-value rooms, some with private bath, are reasonable enough. ①/②.

**Hotel Villa Sol**, beside the Santiago Atitlán dock (☎334 0327, fax 360 0994). Plenty of space here, but the 42 clean, perfunctory rooms are set in somewhat souless twin-deck blocks. Bizarrely – despite the location – none enjoy lake views. ①/②.

## Eating and drinking

The steady flow of gringo travellers has given San Pedro's **cafés** and **restaurants** a decidedly international flavour and most places are excellent value for money. Vegetarians are well catered for, though there are also a few typical Guatemalan comedores in the centre of the village and by the Santiago Atitlán dock. The San Pedro **drinking** scene is centred around the English-owned *D'Noz* bar, above *Nick's Place*, where you'll find an eclectic musical selection including a good slice of techno and drum 'n' bass, plus free video movies (nightly, at 7pm) and tasty food. Between the docks there are more drinking holes, including the Dutch-run *Tony's Sports Bar* and *Torj's Bar* over the pathway. The guys at *D'Noz* also organize DJ-driven **full moon parties** on the lakeside close to San Pedro most months of the year, though events are sometimes cancelled in the rainy season.

### *CAFÉS AND RESTAURANTS*

**Café Luna Azul**, 400m west of the Panajachel dock. Wonderful lakeside location, with a good dock for swimming and sunning, plus great breakfasts, lunches and treats – try the chocolate fudge cake. Open daily 9am–4pm.

**Comedor Francés**, between the docks. Reasonably priced Gallic fare – coq-au-vin at less than US$2 and yummy crêpes.

**Matahari**, turn right from the Santiago Atitlán dock. The best comedor in San Pedro, with tasty line-up of Guatemalan dishes and amazingly good fries.

**Nick's Place**, by the Panajachel dock. Great-value grub (chicken and chips at US$2) and a lake-front location make this the most popular place in town. There's another branch serving Italian food beside the Santiago dock.

**Pinocchio**, between the two docks. Consistently good Italian, where you can feast on bruschetta and pasta in a pretty garden setting.

**Restaurante Rosalinda**, a short walk uphill from the Santiago Atitlán dock. Excellent comedor – fresh lake fish, grilled meats and a warm welcome.

**Restaurante Ti'Kaaj**, opposite the eponymous hotel. Stunning views of the lake and volcanoes from the upper floor and a lovely garden out front too. Famous for its burgers, though it also does great breakfasts and pasta.

**Restaurante Valle Azul**, overlooking the lake. Popular for daytime chilling and tasty snacks and drinks.

**Tintin**, between the docks. Pleasant patio setting and a delicious menu of pitta bread sandwiches, Thai and Indonesian dishes.

# The northern shore

The **northern side** of the lake harbours a string of isolated villages, including some of the most traditional settlements of the Central Highlands. From San Pedro, a rough road runs as far as Tzununá and from there a spectacular path continues all the way to Sololá. Non-direct lanchas to Panajachel will call in at any village en route, but the best way to see this string of isolated settlements is **on foot**: it makes a fantastic day's walk. A narrow strip of level land is wedged between the water and the steep hills most of the way, but where this disappears the path is cut into the slope providing dizzying views of the lake below. To walk from San Pedro to Santa Cruz takes between five and six hours and if you want some really rewarding hiking, this is the section of the lake to head for. There's a good choice of accommodation along the way in San Marcos, Jaibalito and Santa Cruz.

From San Pedro you follow a dirt road to **SAN JUAN LA LAGUNA**, just 2km or so away at the back of a sweeping bay surrounded by shallow beaches. The village specializes in the weaving of *petates*, mats made from lake reeds, and there's a large weaving co-op, *Las Artesanas de San Juan*, where they welcome visitors and have plenty of goods for sale – if you walk from the dock it's signposted on the left. On the other side of the street is the simple *Hospedaje Estrella del Lago* (①) with eleven secure rooms, none with private bath, while uphill, in the centre of the village, you'll find a quiet comedor, *Restaurant Chi'nimaya*, and a very under-used branch of *Nick's Place* for American-style sandwiches and meals. Behind the church and basketball court, there's a shrine to **Maximón** (see p.355). San Juan's evil saint, dressed here in local garb, attracts fewer visitors here than elsewhere, so you may want to bring him some liquor or a cigar. Leaving San Juan, you'll pass below the Tz'utujil settlement of **San Pablo La Laguna**, perched high above the lake a fifteen-minute walk away, and connected to the Pan-American highway by a tortuous road. After this, the villages start shrinking considerably.

## San Marcos La Laguna

Guatemala's premier New Age centre, the tiny village of **SAN MARCOS LA LAGUNA**, is about a two-hour walk from San Pedro, or a twenty-minute ride in one of the regular pick-ups that bump along the road between the villages. The land close to the lakeshore, densely wooded with banana, mango, jocote and avocado trees, is where San Marcos' bohemian hotels and guest houses have been senstively established, while the Maya village is centred on higher ground away from the shore. Apart from a huge new stone church, built to replace a colonial original destroyed in the 1976 earthquake, there are no sights in the Maya village. Though distinctly polarized, relationships between the two communities remain reasonably good.

San Marcos has a decidedly tranquil appeal – there's little in the way of partying and no bar scene at all. The main draw is the *Las Pirámides* yoga and meditation retreat (see "Accommodation", below), with a surplus of auxiliary practitioners and masseurs, plus the requisite organic bakery and healing centre. There's excellent swimming from a number of wooden jetties by the lakeshore, and a mesmerizing view of Atitlán's three volcanoes, including a perspective of the double-coned summit of Tolimán, plus a glimpse of the grey 3975m peak of Acatenango, over 50km to the east.

## ACCOMMODATION

To **get to** any of the places listed below, disembark at the westernmost of San Marcos' two docks where *Posada Schumann* and *Las Pirámides* have jetties (look out for the mini pyramid) and all accommodation is signposted from there.

**El Paco Real** (☎801 2297). Attractive French-owned place, with pleasant, well-constructed stone bungalows, some sleeping up to four, set in a garden dotted with chairs. No private bathrooms, but the communal facilities are kept spotless. Terrific in-house restaurant. ③.

**Las Pirámides** (☎205 7151, *www.laspiramides.com.gt*). Meditation retreat centre set in leafy grounds, where monthly courses beginning the day after full moon (though you can also enrol on a daily or weekly basis) include hatha yoga, healing and meditation techniques, plus days of fasting and silence and plenty of esoteric pursuits. All accommodation is in comfortable pyramid cabañas, and there's delicious vegetarian food. US$10–12 per person per day including all courses but not food.

**Posada Schumann** (cell phone ☎202 2216). Stylish, solar-powered hotel with a wonderful lakeside plot and accommodation in rooms or stone bungalows (sleeping between two and six); numbers 8 and 10 have stupendous volcano views. Very friendly management, decent restaurant, private wooden jetty for sunbathing and swimming, plus a Maya sauna. ④/⑤.

**Hotel San Marcos**. Six cheap and perfunctory but clean rooms in a concrete block, none with private bath. ②.

**Hotel Quetzal** (☎306 5039). Good-value private rooms and a small dormitory in a sturdy-looking two-storey house. Children welcome. ②.

**Unicornio**. Quirky English-Guatemalan-owned set-up with small A-frame huts in a nice garden, with a kitchen and a sauna. Massages available. ②.

## EATING

There's a limited choice of places to eat in San Marcos, with inexpensive Guatemalan food available at the *Comedor Marquensita* and *Sonoma* close to the church and pretty decent pizza and pasta at *Rudy's Place* at the back of the village, though it's best to order in advance. Otherwise, any of the hotels closer to the lakeshore have restaurants attached, with superb but pricey French food at *El Paco Real*. There's also excellent healthy eating (including delicious sandwiches and salads) at *Las Pirámides*, while *Posada Schumann* also has a good menu.

## Tzununá to Paxanax

Continuing east from San Marcos, it's a thirty-minute walk along a dirt road to the next lakeside village, **TZUNUNÁ**, where the women often run from oncoming strangers, sheltering behind the nearest tree in giggling groups. Here the road indisputably ends, giving way to a narrow path cut out of the steep hillside, which can be a little hard to follow as it descends to cross small streams and then climbs up again around the rocky outcrops. The next, slightly ragged-looking place is **JAIBALITO**, an isolated lakeside settlement nestled between soaring *milpa*-clad slopes. Though the village remains resolutely Kaqchikel – very little Spanish is spoken and few women have ever journeyed beyond Lago de Atitlán

– the opening of two new hotels means that outside influence is growing. Almost lost amongst the coffee bushes, 70m north of the main pathway, the Norwegian-owned *Vulcano Lodge* (☎410 2237, *www.atitlan.com/vulcano.htm*; ④/⑥) is tranquil and beautifully maintained, its well-tended garden bursting with bougainvillea and flowering shrubs and scattered with sun loungers and hammocks. There's a bright little restaurant decorated with antique *huipiles*, and a choice of spotless, comfortable double rooms and very stylish two-bedroomed suites with balconies, ideal for families. Heading west, it's a steep five-minute walk up along the cliff path to the spectacularly sited *La Casa del Mundo* (☎204 5558, fax 762 2333, *www.atitlan.com/casamundo.htm*; rooms ④/⑤, suite ⑨). It's a simply magnificent place, the culmination of twelve years' work by the warm North American host family, with a range of atmospheric accommodation including a budget room, doubles (rooms 1 and 3 have the best views), detached stone cabins, and a glorious suite with private Jacuzzi, kitchen and balcony. Guests can rent kayaks – the hotel boasts its own dock – and use the lakeside hot tub.

From Jaibalito it's around an hour to Santa Cruz along a stunning, easy-to-follow path gripping the steep hillside. Set well back from the lake on a shelf 100m or so above the water, **SANTA CRUZ LA LAGUNA** is the largest in this line of villages with a population of around 4000. If you arrive here by boat it may appear to be just a collection of **hotels**, as the village is higher up above the lake. There isn't much to see in Santa Cruz, apart from a fine sixteenth-century church, and most people spend their time here walking, swimming or just chilling out with a book. Alternatively, there's some excellent **hiking**, including a walk to a waterfall above the village football pitch, and another to Sololá along a spectacular path that takes around three hours – from there it's easy to catch a bus back to Panajachel.

On the shore, opposite a line of wooden jetties, you'll find the *Iguana Perdida* (*www.atitlan.com/iguana.htm*; ②/③), owned by English-American couple Dave and Deedle, with undoubtedly the most convivial atmosphere in Lago de Atitlán. The rooms are fairly basic, ranging from dorms (US$2.75) to twin-bedded doubles, but it's the gorgeous, peaceful site overlooking the lake and volcanoes that really makes the place. Dinner is a wholesome three-course communal affair (US$4.50) and the *Iguana* is also home to Lago de Atitlán's only **dive school**, ATI Divers (in Panajachel ☎762 2646, *www.atitlan.com*), a professional PADI outfit that can train all levels up to assistant instructor. Next door is another good place, the slightly more expensive and comfortable *Hotel Arca de Noé* (cell phone ☎306 4352, *www.atitlan.com/arcadenoe.htm*; ③–⑤), with a selection of attractive rooms, most with private bath, and uninterrupted views of the lake from the spacious terraced gardens. There's good home cooking here as well, with large breakfasts for US$4 and dinner for US$7. On the other side of the main dock, the *Posada Abaj* (*www.atitlan.com/abaj*; ④) offers beautiful, peaceful gardens, decent, though unexceptional, rooms and a restaurant. However, service standards are not always the highest, and perhaps consequently the hotel is less popular than the others and much more subdued.

Beyond Santa Cruz a lakeside path wriggles past luxury villas for a kilometre to the small bay of **PAXANAX**, ringed by about twenty holiday homes, where a magnificent and superb-value luxury guest house, *Villa Sumaya* (☎762 0488; *www.villasumaya.com*; ⑤/⑥), enjoys a prime site with stupendous lake views. All the seven rooms, and one suite, have stylish decor and balconies with hammocks, and there's a fine Mediterranean restaurant, a hot tub and sauna and a warm welcome from the young owners. Beyond Paxanax the path that runs directly to Panajachel is very hard to follow, and distraught walkers have been known to spend as long as seven hours scrambling through the undergrowth. Lanchas will call in at Paxanax if they see you waving from the pier beside *Villa Sumaya*, but as there's very little traffic from here it's often best to retreat back to Santa Cruz to move on.

# Quetzaltenango (Xela) and around

To the west of Lago de Atitlán, the highlands rise to form a steep-sided ridge topped by a string of forested peaks. On the far side of this is the **Quetzaltenango basin**, a sweeping expanse of level ground that forms the natural hub of the western highlands. It was here that the conquistador Pedro de Alvarado first struggled up into the highlands from the Pacific coast and came upon the abandoned city of Xelajú (near Quetzaltenango), entering it without any resistance. Six days later, he and his troops fought the K'iche' in a decisive battle on the nearby plain, massacring the Maya warriors.

Totally unlike the capital and only a fraction of its size, Guatemala's second city, **QUETZALTENANGO**, has the subdued provincial atmosphere that you might expect in the highlands, its edges gently giving way to corn and maize fields. Bizarre though it may seem, its character and appearance are vaguely reminiscent of an industrial town in northern England – grey, cool and culturally conservative. Ringed by high mountains and bitterly cold in the early mornings, the city wakes slowly, only getting going once the warmth of the sun has made its mark.

## Some history

Under colonial rule, Quetzaltenango flourished as a commercial centre, benefiting from the fertility of the surrounding farmland and good connections to the port at Champerico. When the prospect of independence eventually arose, the city was set

on deciding its own destiny and Quetzaltenango declared itself the capital of the independent state of **Los Altos**. But the separatist movement was unsuccessful and the city has had to accept provincial status ever since. During the coffee boom at the end of the last century, Quetzaltenango's wealth and population grew so rapidly that it began to rival the capital in status.

All this, however, came to an abrupt end when the city was almost totally destroyed by the massive **1902 earthquake**. Rebuilding took place in a mood of high optimism: all the grand Neoclassical architecture dates from this period. A new rail line was built to connect the city with the coast but after this was washed out in 1932–33 the town never regained its former glory, gradually falling further and further behind the capital.

Today, Quetzaltenango has all the trappings of wealth and self-importance: the grand imperial architecture, the great banks and a list of famous sons. But it is completely devoid of the rampant energy that binds Guatemala City to the all-American twenty-first century. The city has a calm and dignified air and Quetzaltecos have a reputation for formality and politeness; if the chaos of Guatemala City gets you down then Quetzaltenango is an ideal antidote.

## Arrival and information

Unhelpfully for the traveller, virtually all buses arrive and depart Quetzaltenango from nowhere near the centre of town. If you arrive by **second-class bus** you'll almost certainly end up in the chaotic **Minerva bus terminal** on the western edge of Xela. Walk through the covered marketplace to 4 Calle and catch a local bus marked "parque" to get to the plaza from there. An extremely useful transport hub is a roundabout called the **rotunda** at the far end of Calzada Independencia, where virtually all long-distance buses stop on their way to and from the city. Three main companies operate **first-class** buses to and from the capital, each with their own private terminal: Líneas Américas terminal is just off Calzada Independencia at 7 Av 3–33, Zona 2, Quetzaltenango (☎761 2063), Alamo is at 4 C 14–04, Zona 3 (☎767 7117), and Galgos is at C Rodolfo Robles 17–43, Zona 1 (☎761 2248).

Quetzaltenango is laid out on a standard grid pattern, somewhat complicated by a number of steep hills. The oldest part of the city, focused around the plaza, is made up of narrow streets, while in the newer part, reaching out towards the Minerva terminal, the blocks are larger. The city is also divided up into **zones**, although for the most part you'll only be interested in 1 and 3, which contain the plaza area and the bus terminal respectively. Most places are within easy walking distance. To get to the Minerva terminal you can take any bus that runs along 13 Avenida between 8 Calle and 4 Calle in Zona 1. For the eastern half of town, along 7 Avenida, catch one of the buses that stops in front of the Casa de la Cultura, at the bottom end of the plaza.

The official **tourist office** is on the main plaza (Mon–Fri 8am–1pm & 2–5pm, Sat 8am–noon; ☎761 4931), with maps, local information and helpful staff. Quetzaltenango is an excellent place to **study Spanish**, with dozens of schools, many of a high standard.

## Accommodation

Most accommodation in Quetzaltenango tends to be a little dour, but several bright new places have opened in recent years. Once you've made it to the plaza, all the places (but one) listed below are within ten minutes' walk.

**Casa Argentina**, 12 Diagonal 8–37 (☎761 2470, *casaargentina@trafficman.com*). The most popular budget place in town with 25 very comfortable single rooms, two dorms (US$3 per bed), a kitchen and very friendly owners who are an excellent source of information. Home of Quetzaltrekkers (see p.396) and assorted resident gringos. ②.

CENTRAL QUETZALTENANGO

△ Minerva Bus Terminal    △ Mercado La Democracia

**RESTAURANTS & CAFÉS**

| | |
|---|---|
| Artura's Restaurant | A |
| Blue Angel Video Café | L |
| Café Baviera | G |
| Café Colonial | M |
| Café El Mana | H |
| Café La Luna | K |
| Cardinali's | D |
| Deli Crêpe | C |
| El Rincón de los Antojitos | E |
| La Polonesa | F |
| La Salida | O |
| La Taquería | J |
| Royal Paris | B |
| Sagrado Corazón | N |
| Salón Tecún | I |

**ACCOMMODATION**

| | |
|---|---|
| Casa Argentina | 9 |
| Casa Kaehler | 3 |
| Casa Mañen | 7 |
| Hotel Casa Florencia | 4 |
| Hotel Modelo | 1 |
| Hotel Occidental | 8 |
| Hotel Río Azul | 2 |
| Hotel Villa Real Plaza | 5 |
| Pensión Altense | 11 |
| Pensión Andina | 10 |
| Pensión Bonifaz | 6 |

**Casa Kaehler**, 13 Av 3–33 (☎761 2091). Attractive place with spotless rooms set around a patio, some with private bath. Decent value, secure and very central, but be sure to book ahead as it's always popular. ②.

**Casa Mañen**, 9 Av 4–11 (☎765 0786, fax 765 0678, *www.comeseeit.com*). Very stylish luxury boutique hotel, with helpful owners, that's also exceptional value for money. Beautifully presented rooms, some with fireplaces, all with *ikat* fabrics and rugs and cable TV, plus two huge split-level suites with sofas and fridges. Wonderful rooftop terrace with Jacuzzi. Breakfast is included in the price. ⑥/⑦.

**Hotel del Campo**, Carretera al Pacífico Km 224, Zona 5, 4km from the town centre (☎ 761 1663, fax 761 0074). Huge, modern, three-star hotel with a swimming pool and a decent restaurant. Though it's good value, it's only really an option if you have your own transport. ⑤.

**Hotel Casa Florencia**, 12 Av 3–61 (☎761 2811, *www.xelapages.com/florencia/index.htm*). The lobby isn't going to win any design awards, but the large nine rooms with wood-panelled walls and fitted carpets are comfortable enough, and all come with private bath. ④.

**Hotel Modelo**, 14 Av A 2–31 (☎761 2529, fax 763 1376, *www.xelapages.com/modelo/index.htm.*). Civilized and quiet, but a bit gloomy for the price and decidedly old-fashioned. The nicest rooms face a small garden courtyard, or try the separate annexe which is better value. ④/⑤.

**Hotel Occidental**, 7 C 12–23 (☎765 4069). In a good location just off the plaza, large plain rooms with good beds, some with private bath. ②/③.

**Hotel Río Azul**, 2 C 12–15 (☎ & fax 763 0654, *rioazul@c.net.gt*). Very reminiscent of an English boarding house, but spotless and welcoming. All rooms have private bath. ③.

**Hotel Villa Real Plaza**, 4 C 12–22 (☎761 4045, fax 761 6780). Comfortable modern hotel across the plaza from the *Bonifaz*, to which it is a modern(ish) rival, but the decor and ambience are a little soulless. ⑤.

**Pensión Altense**, 9 C 8–48 (☎761 2811). Just above the budget range, this place has plenty of clean spacious rooms, all with private bath. Safe parking. ③.

**Pensión Andina**, 8 Av 6–07 (☎761 4012). Very cheap and centrally located, the rooms are pretty plain but fairly clean – some have private bath. Hot water between 6–9am only. ①/②.

**Pensión Bonifaz**, northeast corner of the plaza (☎761 2182, fax 761 2850). The hotel, founded in 1935, has character and comfort, a reasonable (though overpriced) restaurant and a quirky bar. Very much the backbone of Quetzaltenango society, with an air of faded upper-class pomposity, but still one of the best places in town. ⑤.

## The City

There aren't many things to do or see in Quetzaltenango, but if you have an hour or two to spare then it's well worth wandering through the streets, soaking up the atmosphere and taking in the museum. The hub of the place is the **central plaza**, officially known as the **Parque Centro América**. A mass of mock-Greek columns and imposing banks, it has an atmosphere of dignified calm. The buildings have a look of defiant authority, although there's none of the buzz of business that you'd expect, except on the first Sunday of the month when the plaza hosts a good arte-sanías market with blankets, basketry and piles of *típica* weavings for sale.

The northern end of the plaza is dominated by the grand Banco del Occidente, com-plete with sculptured flaming torches. On the west side is Bancafé and the impressive but crumbling **Pasaje Enríquez**, which was planned as a sparkling arcade of upmar-ket shops. It was derelict for many years but has now been partially revived. Inside you'll find the *Salón Tecún*, the hippest place in town, and a good place for meeting other travellers (see "Drinking and nightlife", below).

At the bottom end of the plaza, next to the tourist office, is the **Casa de la Cultura** (Mon–Fri 8am–noon & 2–6pm, Sat 9am–1pm; US$1), the city's most blatant imper-sonation of a Greek temple, with a bold grey frontage. The main part of the building is given over to an odd mixture of local exhibits. On the ground floor, to the left-hand side, you'll find a display of assorted documents, photographs and pistols from the lib-eral revolution and the State of Los Altos (see p.391), sports trophies and a room ded-icated to the marimba. Upstairs there are some modest Maya artefacts, historic pho-tographs and a bizarre natural history room. Amongst the dusty displays of stuffed bats, pickled snakes and animal skins are the macabre remains of assorted freaks of nature, including a sheep born with eight legs and a four-horned goat.

Along the other side of the plaza is the **Cathedral**, with the new cement version set behind the spectacular crumbling front of the original. There's another piece of classi-cal grandeur, the **Municipalidad** or town hall, a little further up. Take a look inside at the courtyard, which has a neat little garden set out around a single palm tree. Back in the centre of the plaza are rows and circles of redundant columns, a few flowerbeds, and a monument to Rufino Barrios, president of Guatemala from 1873 to 1885.

Away from the plaza, the city spreads out, a mixture of the old and new – 14 Avenida is the commercial heart, complete with pizza restaurants and neon signs. At the top of 14 Avenida, at the junction with 1 Calle, stands the restored **Teatro Municipal**, anoth-er spectacular Neoclassical edifice from where there's a wonderful view of the Santa María volcano.

Out in Zona 3 is the **Mercado la Democracia**, a vast covered complex with stalls spilling out onto the streets. There's another Greek-style structure right out on the edge of town, the **Templo de Minerva**. It was built to honour President Barrios's enthusiasm for education and makes no pretence at serving any practical purpose. Beside the temple is the fairly miserable **zoo** (Tues–Sun 9am–5pm; free), where there is also a children's playground. Below the temple are the sprawling **market** and **bus terminal** and it's here that you can really sense the city's role as the centre of the western highlands, with indígena traders from all over the area doing business.

## Eating, drinking and entertainment

There are more than enough **restaurants** to choose from in Quetzaltenango, with a strip of reasonable pizza places on 14 Avenida and a number of new cafés spread across the city. Note that almost nowhere opens before 8am in the morning, so forget early **breakfasts**. After dark, things are generally quiet in the week, but there are a number of lively **bars** that fill up at the weekend, plus a small **club** scene, with a couple of venues in the centre of town, and other alternatives in the suburbs.

### Cafés and restaurants

**Artura's Restaurant**, 14 Av 3–09, Zona 1. Dark, cosy atmosphere, with traditional, moderately priced food and a separate, fairly civilized bar for drinking.

**Blue Angel Video Café**, 7 C 15–22, Zona 1. Popular gringo hangout with a daily video programme. An intimate, friendly place where you can eat great vegetarian food. Daily 2.15–11pm.

**Café Baviera**, 5 C 12-50, Zona 1, a block from the plaza. Spacious pine-panelled coffee house, dripping with photographic nostalgia. Quality cakes and decent coffee, though the set breakfasts are a little pricey. Open daily 8am–8pm.

**Café Colonial**, 13 Av and 7 C, Zona 1. Large café-cum-restaurant with tasty barbecued meats, decent sandwiches and rich licuados.

**Café El Mana**, 13 Av and 5 C, Zona 1. Tiny, very friendly, family-run café with an excellent selection of inexpensive breakfasts (including *mosh* porridge, pancakes and granola), lunches and real coffee. Closed Sun.

**Cardinali's**, 14 Av 3–41, Zona 1. Without doubt the best Italian food outside the capital, at reasonable prices. Make sure you are starving when you eat here because the portions are huge. For a delivery dial ☎761 0924.

**Deli Crêpe**, 14 Av and 3 C, Zona 1. Looks a bit gloomy from the outside, but wait till you try the licuados, pancakes and delicious sandwiches.

**La Luna**, 8 Av 4–11, Zona 1. Stylish new place, ideal for a relaxing cup of coffee and a yummy cake. They also do very fine chocolates.

**Pan y Pasteles**, 18 Av and 1 C, Zona 1. The best bakery in town, run by Mennonites whose fresh pastries and breads are used by all the finest restaurants. Tues & Fri only, 9am–6pm.

**Pensión Bonifaz**, corner of the plaza, Zona 1. Always a sedate and civilized spot for a cup of tea and a cake and for rubbing shoulders with the town's elite, though the restaurant is overrated and best avoided. Expensive.

**La Polonesa**, 14 Av 4–55, Zona 1. Great little place with an unbeatable selection of set lunches (with daily specials) all at under US$2, served on nice solid wooden tables.

**El Rincón de los Antojitos**, 15 Av and 5 C, Zona 1. Despite being run by a French–Guatemalan couple, this friendly little restaurant has a purely Guatemalan menu, with specialities such as *pepián* (spicy chicken stew) and *hilachas* (beef in tomato sauce).

**Royal Paris**, 14 Av A 3–06, Zona 1. Superb, moderately priced French-owned restaurant with a winsome menu of really flavoursome dishes including cassoulet and onion soup, plus snacks like croque monsieur. Special weekdays lunches are a steal at US$2.

**Sagrado Corazón**, 9 C 9–00, Zona 1. Excellent little comedor, with great-value breakfasts, filling meals and very friendly service.

**La Salida**, 9 Av and 10 Av Zona 1. Diminutive vegetarian café, with delicious food including tempe and tofu, Oriental treats like *pad thai*, wholesome soups, and lassis. No alcohol. Closed Wed.

**La Taquería**, 8 Av 5 C, Zona 1. Best Mexican food in town, served in a pleasant courtyard patio setting. Try the enchiladas or the *caldo Tlalpeño* soup. Moderate prices and cheap litres of beer.

## Drinking and nightlife

Considering the size of Quetzaltenango, there's not that much going on in the evenings and the streets are generally quiet by about 9pm. There are a few **bars** worth visiting, however. At the popular *Salón Tecún*, on the west side of the plaza, you can down *cuba libres*, enjoy draught beer and great bar food, and listen to the latest sounds imported by the gringo bar staff. At the more sedate but classy *Don Rodrigo*, 1 C and 14 Av, you'll find leather-topped bar stools, more draught beer and good, but pricey sandwiches. The *Casa Verde* (also known as the *Green House*) at 12 Av 1–40 (☎763 0271) has a lively cultural programme including theatre, dance and poetry readings plus salsa nights at weekends. Close to the Teatro Municipal, there are a cluster of new hip places including the bar *El Zaguan*, at 14 Av A and 1 C, Zona 1, and the club *Bukana's*, almost next door, for salsa and merengue. Of the clubs on the outskirts of town, the *Music Center* attracts a loyal young local clientele, while *Loro's* appeals to an older crowd.

Quetzaltenango is a good place to catch movies, with a number of **cinemas**, though you shouldn't have to stray further than the excellent Cine Paraíso on 14 Avenida A, near the Teatro Municipal, which shows a very varied selection of independent movies from all over the world, plus the odd quality Hollywood production. For **theatre** head for the refurbished Teatro Roma, also on 14 Avenida A, **which** often stages interesting productions. To find **what's on** in Xela, pick up a copy of the free listings magazine *Fin de Semana*, available in many of the popular bars and cafés.

## Listings

**Banks and exchange** Banco Inmobiliario, Banco del Occidente and Bancafé (with the longest opening hours – Mon–Fri 8.30am–8pm, Sat 10am–1.30pm) are all in the vicinity of the plaza and will change travellers' cheques. Banco Industrial, also in the plaza, has an ATM that takes Visa.

**Bike and car rental** Guatemala Unlimited, 12 Av and 1 C, Zona 1 (☎761 6043), has mountain bikes for around US$6 a day; or try the Vrisa bookstore (see below).

**Bookstore** Vrisa, 15 Av 3–64, opposite Telgua and the post office, has over 4000 used titles, plus a newsroom with *Newsweek* and *The Economist*, a message board, espresso coffee and bike rental.

**Consulates** Mexican Consulate, 9 Av 6–19, Zona 1 (Mon–Fri 8–11am & 2.30–3.30pm). A Mexican tourist card costs US$1. Hand in your paperwork in the morning and collect in the afternoon.

**Internet** There are at least a dozen places in Xela where you can surf the Net (all open roughly 9am–9.30pm), including Maya Communications, above Salón Tecún in the Plaza Central; Casa Verde, 12 Av 1–40, Zona 1; and Alternativas at 16 Av 3–35, Zona 3. Prices hover around US$1.40 an hour.

**Language schools** Lots of places offer Spanish lessons; the Centro Maya de Idiomas, 21 Av 5–69 Zona 3 (☎767 0352, *www.centromaya.org*), also offers classes in six Maya languages.

**Laundry** MiniMax, 4 Av and 1 C, Zona 1 (Mon–Sat 7am–7pm). US$2 for a full-load wash and dry.

**Medical care** Doctor de León at the San Rafael hospital, 9 C 10–41 (☎761 4414) speaks English. For emergencies, the Hospital Privado is at C Rudolfo Robles 23–51, Zona 1 (☎761 4381).

**Photography** For camera repairs try Fotocolor, 15 Av 3–25, or one of the several shops on 14 Av.

**Post office** At the junction of 15 Av and 4 C.

**Telephone office** The best rates in town are at Kall Shop, 8 Av 4–24 Zona 1, where calls to the USA and Canada are US$0.25 and Europe US$0.45 per minute. Maya Communications (see "Internet", above) is also competitive. You'll pay much more at the main Telgua office, 15Av and 4C (daily 7am–10pm).

**Tours and travel agencies** Adrenalina Tours, inside Pasaje Enríquez, Plaza Central (☎761 0924, *http://adrenalinatours.xelaenlinca.com*), offers city tours, daily transport to Fuentes Georginas and volcano climbing. Casa Iximulew, 15 Av and 5 C, Zona 1 (☎765 1308, *iximulew@trafficman.com*) runs organized trips to most of the volcanoes and sights around Xela. The Guatemalan Birding Resource Center, 7 Av 19–18, Zona 1 (☎767 7339), offers excellent guided tours to the surrounding countryside. Guatemala Unlimited, 12 Av and C 35, Zona 1 (☎ & fax 761 6043, *www.guatemalaunlimited .centroamerica.com*), has tours all over the country. Quetzaltrekkers, inside *Casa Argentina* (see "Accommodation", p.391), offers hiking trips to volcanoes and to Lago de Atitlán, with all profits going to a street children charity.

**Weaving School** For textile weaving classes contact the Ixchel school at 8Av 4–24, Zona 1 (☎765 3790).

# Around Quetzaltenango

Quetzaltenango (Xela) is the obvious place to base yourself to explore the surrounding countryside, with bus connections to all parts of the western highlands. It's easy to spend a week or two here, making day-trips to the markets and fiestas, basking in hot springs or hiking in the mountains. The valley is heavily populated and there are numerous small towns and villages in the surrounding hills, mostly indigenous agricultural communities and weaving centres. If you want to go **hiking**, the most obvious climb is the **Santa María volcano**, towering above Quetzaltenango itself, but there's also **Laguna Chicabal**, a small lake set in the cone of an extinct volcano, and **Tajumulco**, the highest peak in Central America.

To the south, straddling the coast road, lie **Zunil** and the breathtaking hot springs of **Fuentes Georginas**, 18km away, overshadowed by volcanic peaks. To the north are **San Andrés Xecul**, **Totonicapán**, capital of the department of the same name, and **San Francisco el Alto**, a small town perched on an outcrop overlooking the valley. Thirty-five kilometres beyond lies **Momostenango**, the country's principal wool-producing centre and a focus of Maya culture.

Between them, the Quetzaltenango **tour operators** listed above run trips to everywhere you might wish to go.

## Volcán de Santa María

Due south of Quetzaltenango, the perfect cone of the **Santa María volcano** rises to a height of 3772m. From the town only the peak is visible, but seen from the rest of the valley the entire cone seems to tower over everything around. The view from the top is, as you might expect, spectacular, and if you're prepared to sweat out the climb you certainly won't regret it. It's possible to climb the volcano as a day-trip, but to really see it at its best you need to be on top at dawn, either sleeping on the freezing peak, or camping at the site below and climbing the final section in the dark by torchlight. Either way you need to bring enough food, water and stamina for the entire trip; and you should be acclimatized to the altitude before attempting it.

Take a local bus from the Minerva terminal to the village of **Llanos del Pinal** (hourly, 30min), get off at the crossroads and walk down the dirt road towards the volcano's base. After 45 minutes a marked path leads to the left, soon becoming a rocky trail, and another hour later you'll reach a flat grassy area ideal for **camping.** From here the trail cuts to the right and then straight up the side of the cone; it's another two to three hours to the top. At the summit the views are incredible if you get a clear day, with the Xela valley below, the volcanoes of Tacaná and Tajumulco to the west and four more to the east. Immediately to the south is the (very) active cone of **Santiaguito**, which has been in a state of constant eruption since 1902.

## Zunil and Fuentes Georginas

Heading southwards to the Pacific, you come to the traditional village of **ZUNIL**, a vegetable-growing market town surrounded by steep hills and a sleeping volcano. The plaza is dominated by a beautiful white colonial church with a richly decorated façade, inside of which an intricate silver altar is protected behind bars. The women of Zunil wear vivid purple *huipiles* and carry bright shawls, and for the Monday market the plaza is awash with colour. Just below the plaza is a **textile co-op** where hundreds of women market their beautiful weavings. Zunil is a hotbed of **Maximón** (the evil saint; see p.355) worship. In the face of disapproval from the Catholic Church, the Maya are reluctant to display their Judas, who also goes by the name Alvarado, but his image is usually paraded through the streets during Holy Week, dressed in Western clothes and smoking a cigar. Virtually any child in town will take you to his abode for a quetzal.

In the hills above Zunil are the **Fuentes Georginas**, a spectacular set of luxuriant hot springs. A turning to the left off the main road, just beyond the entrance to the village, leads up into the hills to the baths, 8km away. You can walk it in a couple of hours, or rent a pick-up from the plaza in Zunil. Prices are officially set at US$5 for the trip, no matter how many passengers hitch a ride – it's an exhilarating journey up a smooth paved road which switchbacks through magnificent volcanic scenery. If you're not staying the night you'll have to arrange the return trip (another US$5) a few hours later with the driver. The baths (US$1.30) are surrounded by fresh green ferns, thick moss and lush forest, and to top it all there's a restaurant and a well-stocked bar (with decent wine) beside the main pool. It's easy to spend an afternoon or more here soaking up the scene, though you can also rent one of the very pleasant rustic stone **bungalows** for the night (no phone; ③) complete with bathtub, two double beds, fireplace and barbecue.

**Buses** to Zunil run from Quetzaltenango's Minerva bus terminal every half-hour or so, though you can also catch a bus from the centre of town beside the Shell gas station at 10 C and 9 Av in Zona 1. The last bus back from Zunil leaves at around 6.30pm.

## San Andrés Xecul

Heading to the Interamericana from Quetzaltenango, a kilometre before you reach the junction of Cuatro Caminos, is a branch road that leads to possibly the wildest church in the Maya World. Bypassed by almost everything, **SAN ANDRÉS XECUL** is to all appearances an unremarkable farming village but for the **village church**, a beautiful old building with incredibly thick walls. Its facade is painted an outrageous mustard yellow, with vines dripping plump, purple fruit and podgy little angels scrambling across the surface. The village is also rumoured to act as a "university" for students of shamanism, though there is little evidence of this save the scores of small altars in the hills around. Buses leave for San Andrés from the Minerva terminal in Quetzaltenango several times daily, or take any bus bound for Cuatro Caminos and get the driver to drop you off at the dirt access road to San Andrés and either hitch or walk the 4km.

## San Francisco el Alto

The small market town of **SAN FRANCISCO EL ALTO** overlooks the Quetzaltenango valley from a magnificent hillside setting. It's worth a visit for the view alone, with the great plateau stretching out below and the cone of the Santa María volcano marking the opposite side of the valley. But another good reason for visiting the village is the **Friday market**, which is possibly the biggest in Central America. Traders from every corner of Guatemala make the trip, many arriving the night before, and some starting to sell as early as 4am, by candlelight. Throughout the morning a steady stream of buses and trucks fill the town to bursting; by noon the market is at its height, buzzing with activity.

The town is set into the hillside, with steep cobbled streets connecting the different levels. Two areas in particular are monopolized by specific trades. At the very top is an open field used as an **animal market**, where everything from pigs to parrots changes hands. The teeth and tongues of animals are inspected by the buyers and at times the scene degenerates into a chaotic wrestling match, with pigs and men rolling in the dirt. Below this is the town's plaza, dominated by textiles. On the lower level, the streets are filled with vegetables, fruit, pottery, furniture, cheap comedores, and plenty more. These days most of the stalls deal in imported denim, but under the arches and in the covered area opposite the church you'll find a superb selection of traditional cloth. For a really good **photographic** angle and for views of the market and the surrounding countryside, pay the church caretaker a quetzal and climb up to the **church roof**. By early afternoon the numbers start to thin out, and by sunset it's all over – until the following Friday.

There are plenty of **buses** from Quetzaltenango to San Francisco, leaving every twenty minutes or so from the Minerva terminal, passing the rotunda; the first is at 6am, and the last bus back leaves at about 5pm (45min).

## Momostenango

A further 22km from San Francisco, down a paved road that continues over a ridge behind the town then drops down through lush pine forests, is **MOMOSTENANGO**, a small, isolated town and the centre of wool production in the highlands. Momostecos travel throughout the country peddling their blankets, scarves and rugs; years of experience have made them experts in the hard sell and given them a sharp eye for tourists. The wool is also used in a range of traditional costumes, including the short skirts worn by the men of Nahualá and San Antonio Palopó and the jackets of Sololá. The ideal place to buy Momostenango blankets is in the **Sunday market**, which fills the town's two plazas.

A visit at this time will also give you a glimpse of Momostenango's other feature: its rigid adherence to tradition. Opposite the entrance to the church, people make offerings of incense and alcohol on a small fire, muttering their appeals to the gods. The town is famous for this unconventional folk-Catholicism, and it has been claimed that there are as many as three hundred Maya **shamans** working here. Momostenango's religious **calendar**, like that of only one or two other villages, is still based on the 260-day *Tzolkin* year – made up of thirteen twenty-day months – that has been in use since ancient times.

A good time to visit Momostenango is for the fiesta on August 1, or else for the start of the Maya new year. If you decide to stay for a day or two then you can take a walk to the *riscos*, a set of bizarre sandstone pillars, or beyond to the **hot springs** of Pala Chiquito, about 3km away to the north.

The best **place to stay** in Momostenango is the *Hotel Estiver*, 1C 4–15, Zona 1 (☎736 5036; ②), with clean rooms, some with private bath, great views from the roof and safe parking. For **eating**, there are plenty of small comedores on the main plaza or try the one inside the *Hospedaje Paglóm*, for a good feed. There's a Bancafé **bank** at 1C and 1 Av (Mon–Fri 9am–4pm) which accepts Visa, cash and travellers' cheques.

**Buses** run here from Quetzaltenango, passing through Cuatro Caminos and San Francisco el Alto on the way. They leave the Minerva terminal in Quetzaltenango every hour or so from 9am to 4pm (1hr 15min) and from Momostenango between 6am and 3pm. On Sunday, special early-morning buses leave Quetzaltenango from 6am: you can catch them at the rotunda.

## Totonicapán

Capital of one of the smaller departments, **TOTONICAPÁN** is reached down a direct road leading east from Cuatro Caminos. Surrounded by rolling hills and pine forests, the town stands at the heart of a heavily populated and intensely farmed little region. There is only one point of access and the valley has always held out against outside influence, shut off in a world of its own. Totonicapán is a quiet place, ruffled only by the Tuesday and Saturday **markets**, which fill the two plazas to bursting. Until fairly recently a highly ornate traditional costume was worn here, but this has now disappeared and the town has instead become one of the chief centres of commercial weaving. To take a closer look at the work of local artisans, head for the town's **visitor centre**, called the Casa de la Cultura, on 8 Av 2–17 (Mon–Sat 9.30am–5pm;

*http://larutamayaonline.com/aventura.html*It organizes pricey tours of the town (US$6–14) and classes in weaving and wood carving (US$21–49 per person, depending on class size); the funds raised help benefit the community. The only other sight is located in the northern of the two plazas: a grand, though somewhat faded municipal **theatre**, currently undergoing restoration, a Neoclassical structure echoing the one in Quetzaltenango.

There are good connections between Totonicapán and Quetzaltenango, with buses shuttling back and forth every half-hour or so. Totonicapán is very quiet after dark, but if you want to stay, the best **hotel** is the *Hospedaje San Miguel*, a block from the plaza at 8 Av and 3 C (☎766 1452; ②/③). It is pretty comfortable and some rooms have bathrooms, but beware price rises before market days. The *Pensión Blanquita* (①) is a friendly and basic alternative opposite the petrol station at 13 Av and 4 C. **Buses** for Totonicapán leave Quetzaltenango between 6am and 5pm, passing the rotunda and Cuatros Caminos, or else take any bus to Cuatros Caminos and change there.

# Huehuetenango

**HUEHUETENANGO**, capital of the department of the same name, lies in the corner of a small agricultural plain, 5km from the Carretera Interamericana at the foot of the mighty Cuchumatanes. Though Huehue, as it's known, is the focus of trade and transport for a vast area, its atmosphere is provincial and relaxed. Before the arrival of the Spanish, it was the site of one of the residential suburbs that surrounded the Mam capital of Zaculeu (see p.401). Under colonial rule, it was a small regional centre with little to offer other than a steady trickle of silver and a stretch or two of grazing land and, though the supply of silver dried up long ago, other minerals are still mined, and coffee and sugar have been added to the area's produce.

Today's Huehuetenango has two quite distinct functions – and two contrasting halves – each serving a separate section of the population. The large majority of the people are ladinos, and for them Huehuetenango is an unimportant regional centre far from the hub of things. Here the mood is summed up in the unhurried atmosphere of the attractive **plaza** at the heart of the ladino half of town, where shaded walkways are surrounded by administrative offices. Overlooking it, perched above the pavements, are a shell-shaped bandstand, a clock tower and a grandiose Neoclassical church, a solid whitewashed structure with a facade that's crammed with Doric pillars and Grecian urns.

A few blocks to the east, the town's atmosphere could hardly be more different. Around the **market**, the hub of the Maya part of town, the streets are crowded with traders, drunks and travellers from Mexico and all over Central America. This part of Huehuetenango, centred on 1 Avenida, is always alive with activity, its streets packed with people from every corner of the department and littered with rotten vegetables.

### Arrival, information and accommodation
Huehue is fairly small so you shouldn't have any real problems finding your way around, particularly once you've located the plaza. You'll arrive at the purpose-built **bus terminal** halfway between the Carretera Interamericana and town. Minibuses make constant trips between the town centre and the bus terminal.

Virtually all Huehue's **hotels** are within a short stroll of the plaza and tend to be good value for money, though there's nothing at the top end of the scale.

**Casa Blanca**, 7 Av 3–41 (☎ & fax 769 0777). Modern upmarket hotel, though built in colonial style; all rooms have private bath and cable TV. The fine restaurant and spacious garden terrace are well worth a visit too. ⑤.

**Hotel Central**, 5 Av 1–33 (☎764 1202) Classic budget hotel, with large, scruffy rooms in a creaking old wooden building, though it does have a fantastic comedor. No singles or private baths. ①.

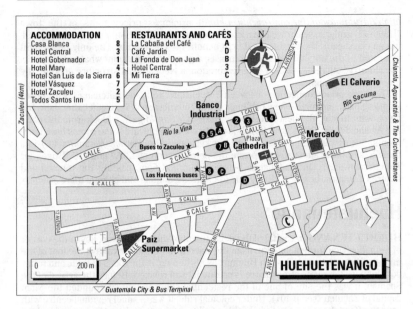

**Hotel Gobernador**, 4 Av 1–45 (☎ & fax 764 1197). Excellent budget hotel run by a very friendly family, with attractive rooms, some with bath, and reliable hot showers. ②.

**Hotel Mary**, 2 C 3–52 (☎764 1618, fax 764 7412). Centrally located with small but pleasant rooms, most with private shower, and loads of steaming hot water. ②/③.

**Hotel San Luis de la Sierra**, 2C 7–00 (☎ & fax 764 1103). Spotless modern hotel with small but very attractive rooms, all with good showers and cable TV; some have wonderful views of the mountains. ④.

**Hotel Vásquez**, 2 C 6–67 (☎764 1338). Cell-sized rooms around a bare courtyard, but clean and safe, with secure parking. ②.

**Hotel Zaculeu**, 5 Av 1–14 (☎764 1086, fax 764 1575). Large, comfortable hotel, something of an institution. Some of the older rooms surrounding a leafy courtyard are a bit musty and gloomy, while those in the more expensive new section are larger and more spacious. All come with cable TV and private bath. There's also parking and a reasonable restaurant. ④/⑤.

**Todos Santos Inn**, 2 C 6–74 (☎7641241). Good, secure budget hotel though the rooms do vary in quality – some are bright and cheery with bedside lights, others are less attractive. Excellent deal for single travellers. ②.

## Eating, drinking and entertainment

Most of the better **restaurants** are, like the accommodation, in the central area, around the plaza. **Films** are shown at the cinema on 3 Calle, half a block west of the plaza.

**La Cabaña del Café**, 2 Calle, opposite *Hotel Vásquez*. Logwood café with an excellent range of coffees (including cappuccino), great cakes and a few snacks.

**Café Jardín**, 4 C and 6 Av. Friendly place serving inexpensive but excellent breakfasts, milkshakes, pancakes and the usual chicken and beef dishes. Open daily 6am–11pm.

**La Fonda de Don Juan**, 2 C 5–35. Attractive place with gingham tablecloths, serving good, if slightly pricey, pizza and pasta, and a reasonable range of beers.

**Hotel Central**, 5 Av 1–33. Very tasty, inexpensive set meals. Particularly good breakfast.

**Mi Tierra**, 4 C 6–46. Attractive little restaurant set in a covered patio with nice decor and a good atmosphere. The flavoursome menu is more imaginative than most – great for house salads, *churrascos* (barbecued meat) and cheesecake – plus very cheap healthy breakfasts. Also has Internet facilities and a good noticeboard.

## Listings

**Banks** Banco G&T Continental is on the plaza (Mon–Fri 9am–8pm, Sat 10am–1pm), Bancafé is a block to the south (Mon–Fri 8.30am–8pm, Sat 9am–3pm), and there's a Banco Industrial on 6 Av 1-42 (Mon–Fri 9am–7pm, Sat 9am–1pm) with a Visa and Plus network ATM.

**Language schools** Huehuetenango is a good place to learn Spanish as you don't rub shoulders with many other gringos. As almost everywhere, schools offer a package of tuition and accommodation with a family for around US$110 a week. One of the best is Instituto El Portal, 1 C 1–64, Zona 3 (☎ & fax 764 1987), closely rivalled by Fundación XXIII, 6 Av 6–126, Zona 1 (☎764 1478), and Xinabajul, 6 Av 0–69 (☎ & fax 764 1518). Abesaida Guevara de López gives good private lessons (☎764 2917).

**Internet** Génesis at 2 C 6–37 and *Mi Tierra* at 4 C 6–46 both charge around US$3.80 an hour.

**Laundry** The best is in the Turismundo Commercial Centre at 3 Av 0–15 (Mon–Sat 9.30am–6.30pm).

**Mexican consulate** In the Farmacia El Cid, on the plaza at 5 Av and 4 C (daily 8am–noon & 2–7pm). They'll charge you US$1.30 for a tourist card that's usually free at the border though few nationalities now need one at all.

**Post office** 2 C 3–54 (Mon–Fri 8am–4.30pm).

**Shopping** Superb weaving is produced throughout the department and can be bought in the market here or at Artesanías Ixquil, on 5 Av 1–56, opposite the *Hotel Central*, where both the prices and quality are high. If you have time, though, you'd be better advised to travel to the villages and buy direct from the producers.

**Telephone** Telgua is at 4 Av 6-54 (daily 7am–10pm), though it may move back to its former location next to the post office.

## Zaculeu

A few kilometres to the west of Huehuetenango are the ruins of **ZACULEU** (daily 8am–6pm; US$3.20), capital of the **Mam**, who were one of the principal pre-conquest highland tribes. The site includes several large temples, plazas and a ball court, but unfortunately it has been restored with an astounding lack of subtlety (or accuracy). Its appearance – more like an ageing film set than an ancient ruin – is owed to a latter-day colonial power, the **United Fruit Company**, under whose auspices the ruins were reconstructed in 1946–7. The walls and surfaces have been levelled off with a layer of thick white plaster, leaving them stark and undecorated. There are no roofcombs, carvings or stucco mouldings, and only in a few places does the original stonework show through. Even so, the site does have a peculiar atmosphere of its own. Surrounded by trees and neatly mown grass, with fantastic views of the mountains, it's also an excellent spot for a picnic. There's a small **museum** on site (daily 8am–noon & 1–6pm), with examples of some of the unusual burial techniques used and some interesting ceramics found during excavation.

The site is thought to have been a religious and administrative centre housing the elite, while the bulk of the population lived in small surrounding settlements or else scattered in the hills. Zaculeu was the hub of a large area of Mam-speakers, its boundaries reaching into the mountains as far as Todos Santos Cuchumatán. However, to put together a history of the site means relying on the records of the K'iche', their more powerful neighbours. According to their mythology, the K'iche' conquered most of the other highland tribes, including the Mam, some time between 1400 and 1475. Following the death of the K'iche' leader, Quicab, in 1475, the Mam managed to reassert their independence, but no sooner had they escaped the clutches of one expansionist empire than the Spanish arrived with a yet more brutal alternative.

Pedro de Alvarado despatched an army under the command of his brother, Gonzalo, which was met by about five thousand Mam warriors. The Mam leader, Caibal Balam,

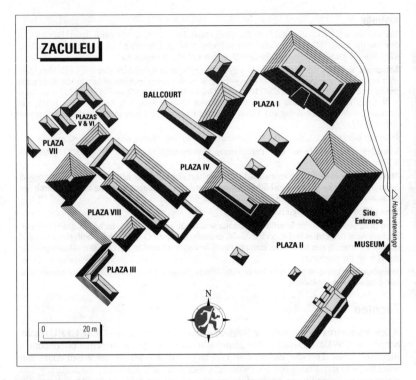

quickly saw that his troops were no match for the Spanish and withdrew them to the safety of Zaculeu, where they were protected on three sides by deep ravines and on the other by a series of walls and ditches. The Spanish army settled outside the city and besieged the citadel for six weeks until starvation forced Caibal Balam to surrender.

**To get to Zaculeu** from Huehuetenango, take one of the pick-ups or buses that leave from close to the school on 7 Avenida between 2 and 3 calles – make sure it's a Ruta 3 heading for Ruinas Zaculeu (not Zaculeu Central).

# The Cuchumatanes

The largest non-volcanic peaks in Central America, the **Cuchumatanes** rise from a limestone plateau close to the Mexican border and reach their full height above Huehuetenango. This area is bypassed by the majority of visitors, though the mountain scenery is magnificent, ranging from wild, exposed craggy outcrops to lush, tranquil river valleys. The upper parts of the slopes are almost barren, scattered with boulders and shrivelled cypress trees, while the lower levels, by contrast, are richly fertile and cultivated with corn, coffee and sugar. Between the peaks, in the deep-cut valleys, are hundreds of tiny villages, isolated by the scale of the landscape. A visit to these mountain villages, either for a market or fiesta (and there are plenty of both), offers one of the best opportunities to see Maya life at close quarters.

The arrival of the Spanish had surprisingly little impact in these highlands, despite the initial devastation, and some of the communities here are amongst the most traditional in the Maya World. More recently, the mountains were the scene of bitter fighting between the army and guerrillas. In the late 1970s and early 1980s, a wave of violence and terror in this area sent thousands fleeing across the border to Mexico, but nowadays, with the fighting over, things are much calmer.

The most accessible of the villages in the vicinity, and the only one yet to receive a steady trickle of tourists, is **Todos Santos Cuchumatán**. The horse-race fiesta on November 1 is one of the most interesting and outrageous in Guatemala. To the east a road struggles through the mountains, past the interesting village of **Aguacatán**, on its way to Cobán in Alta Verapaz. If you seek a real adventure, a remote road leads north to the ladino town of **Barillas** via some of the least visited, most traditional villages in the country.

## Aguacatán

To the east of Huehuetenango, a dirt road turns off at Chiantla to weave through dusty foothills along the base of the Cuchumatanes to **AGUACATÁN**. This small agricultural town is strung out along two main streets, shaped entirely by the dip in which it's built. The language of Akateko is spoken only in this village and its immediate surrounds by a population of around 15,000. During the colonial period, gold and silver were mined in the nearby hills and the Maya are said to have made bricks of solid gold for the king of Spain to persuade him to let them keep their lands. Today, the town is steeped in tradition and the people survive by growing vegetables, including huge quantities of garlic, much of it for export.

Aguacatán's huge Sunday **market** gets under way on Saturday afternoon, when traders arrive early to claim the best sites. On Sunday morning a steady stream of people pours down the main street, cramming into the market and plaza and soon spilling out into the surrounding area. Around noon the tide turns as the crowds start to drift back to their villages, with donkeys leading their drunken drivers. Despite the scale of the market, its atmosphere is subdued and the pace unhurried; for many it's as much a social event as a commercial one. The scaled-down Thursday market is nothing like as compelling a spectacle.

The traditional costume worn by the women of Aguacatán is unusually simple: their skirts are made of dark blue cotton and the *huipiles*, which hang loose, are decorated with bands of coloured ribbon on a plain white background. This plainness, though, is set off by the local speciality – the *cinta*, or headdress, in which they wrap their hair, an intricately embroidered piece of cloth combining blues, reds, yellows and greens, and finished off with pompom tassels.

Aguacatán's other attraction is the source of the Río San Juan, which emerges fresh and cool from beneath a nearby hill, making a good place for a chilly dip. To get there, walk east along the main street out of the village for about a kilometre, until you see the sign. From the village it takes about twenty minutes.

Eight daily **buses** run from Huehuetenango to Aguacatán between 6am and about 2.45pm (1hr). Stay at either the *Nuevo Amanecer* (②) or the *Hospedaje Aguateco* (①), both of which are small and very simple. **Beyond Aguacatán** the road runs out along a ridge, with fantastic views stretching out below, eventually dropping down to the riverside town of **Sacapulas** (see p.371).

## Huehuetenango to Barillas

It's an eight-hour bus trip to Barillas, travelling through beautiful scenery and stopping at several villages en route. Heading north out of Huehuetenango, the road for the mountains passes through the suburb of Chiantla before starting to climb the arid hillside and, as the bus sways around the switchbacks, the view across the valley is superb. In the distance you can sometimes make out the perfect cone of the Volcán de Santa

María, towering above Quetzaltenango some 60km to the south. At the top of the slope the road slips through a pass into the *región andina*, a desolate grassy plateau suspended between the peaks; you'll find the *Comedor de los Cuchumatanes* here, where buses stop for a chilly lunch before pressing on through **Paquix**, the junction for the road to Todos Santos.

Beyond Paquix the road runs through a couple of magical valleys, grazed by sheep and populated by a few hardy highlanders. Great grey boulders lie scattered among ancient-looking oak and cypress trees, their trunks gnarled by the bitter winds. The road emerges at the top of an incredibly steep valley, where it clings to the hillside, cut out of the sheer rock face that drops hundreds of metres to the valley floor. This northern side of the Cuchumatanes contains some of the most dramatic scenery in the entire country, and the road is certainly the most spine-chillingly precipitous.

The first village reached by the road is **SAN JUAN IXCOY**, an apple-growing centre drawn out along the valley floor. There's no particular reason for breaking the journey here, but there is a small **pensión** (①), where you can get a bed and a meal. In season, around the end of August, passing buses are besieged by an army of fruit-sellers. Over another range of hills and down in the next valley is **SOLOMA**, largest, busiest and richest of the villages in the northern Cuchumatanes, with a population of around three thousand – a good place to break the trip. Its flat valley-floor was once the bed of a lake, and the steep hillsides still come sliding down at every earthquake or cloudburst. Soloma translates (from Q'anjob'al, the dominant language on this side of the mountains) as "without security", and its history is blackened by disaster: it was destroyed by earthquakes in 1773 and 1902, half burnt down in 1884, and decimated by smallpox in 1885. The long white *huipiles* worn by the women of Soloma are similar to those of San Mateo Ixtatán and the Lacandones, and are probably as close as any in the country to the style worn before the Conquest. These days they are on the whole donned only for the **market** on Thursday and Sunday, which again is by far the best time to visit, or on fiesta days. The *Hotel Caucaso* is first choice here: an excellent, moderately priced **hotel** (②/③) where some rooms have private bath and cable TV, though there are other options including the less pleasant *Hotel San Antonio* (☎780 6191; ②) at the edge of town, or as a last resort, the scruffy *Hospedaje San Juan* (①).

Leaving Soloma the road climbs again, on a steadily deteriorating surface, over another range of hills, to the hillside village of Santa Eulalia. Beyond, past the junction to San Rafael La Independencia, it heads through another misty, rock-strewn forest and emerges on the other side at **SAN MATEO IXTATÁN**, the most traditional, and quite possibly the most interesting, of this string of villages. Little more than a thin sprawl of wooden-tiled houses on an exposed hillside, it's strung out beneath a belt of ancient forest and craggy mountains. The people here speak **Chuj** and form part of a Maya group who occupy the extreme northwest corner of the highlands and some of the jungle beyond, bordering that of the Lacandón (see p.147).

The only time to visit, other than for the fiesta on September 21, is on a market day, Thursday or Sunday. The rest of the week the village is virtually deserted. The women here wear unusual and striking *huipiles*, long white gowns embroidered in brilliant reds, yellows and blues, radiating out from a star-like centre. The men wear short woollen tunics called *capixay*, often embroidered with flowers around the collar and quetzales on the back. Below the village is a beautiful Maya ruin, the unrestored remains of a small pyramid and ball court, shaded by a couple of cypress trees. If you decide to **stay**, there are several extremely basic pensiones, the best of which is the *El Aguila* (①), run by the very friendly family who also operate the *Comedor Ixateco*.

Beyond San Mateo the road drops steadily east to **BARILLAS**, a ladino frontier town in the relative warmth of the lowlands. Further on still, the land slopes into the Usumacinta basin through thick, uninhabited jungle. Rough tracks penetrate a short distance into this wilderness (and a local bus runs out as far as San Ramón), opening it up for farming, and eventually a road will run east across the **Ixcán** (the wilderness area that stretches between here and the jungles of Petén) to Playa Grande (see p.448). The cheapest place **to stay** in Barillas is the *Tienda las Tres Rosas* (①), and the best, the *Pensión Terraza* (①), costs not much more.

**Buses to Barillas**, passing through all the villages en route, are operated by a number of different companies, leaving Huehuetenango at 7am and between 10pm and midnight, taking around four hours to reach Soloma and at least eight hours to Barillas. San Pedrito, Autobuses del Norte, Transjosue and Rutas Barillenses also run services; check at the bus terminal for details. All buses leave from Huehue main bus terminal, and it's well worth buying your ticket in advance as they operate a vague system of seat allocation. It's a rough and tortuous trip, the buses usually filled to bursting and the road, despite improvements, invariably appalling. Buses leave Barillas for Huehuetenango six times a day.

## Todos Santos Cuchumatán

Backtracking towards Huehuetenango, a road veers to the west from the **Paquix** junction, through high-altitude ladino-farmed land. After 12km or so the road starts to drop, the temperature slowly rises, and you'll start to see the explosively coloured *traje* costume of the Todosanteros. The road continues to decline, gripping the mountains, and you'll soon get a glimpse of the magical village of Todos Santos.

Spectacularly sited in its own remote deep-cut river valley, **TODOS SANTOS CUCHUMATÁN** is many travellers' favourite place in Guatemala. Though the sheer beauty of the alpine surroundings is one attraction, it's the unique culture that is really astounding. The *traje* worn here is startling: the men wear red-and-white candy striped trousers, black woollen breeches and pinstripe shirts, decorated with dayglo pink collars, while the women wear dark blue *cortes* and superbly intricate purple *huipiles*. It's the tradition and isolation that have made the village so attractive to visitors, photographers in particular, though such attention has not always been welcome. In April 2000, an angry mob attacked and killed a Japanese tourist and his Guatemalan guide, believing that the former, who was taking pictures of local children, was a Satanist baby stealer. Though the perpetrators have been jailed, and the community as a whole was stunned and deeply remorseful, the depth of misunderstanding serves to highlight the cultural chasm between this remote, highly susperstitious mountain community and the developed world. There have been no incidents since, but obviously it's very important to respect local sensitivities and be very judicious about taking photographs, particularly of children.

The Todosanteros are perhaps the proudest of all Guatemala's Maya people – there is a distinctive swagger in the step of the men – and the **fiesta** (on November 1) is one of the most famous in the country. For three days the village is taken over by unrestrained drinking, dancing and marimba music. The whole event opens with an all-day horse race and there is a massive stampede as the inebriated riders tear up the course, thrashing their horses with live chickens, their capes flowing out behind them. On the second day, "The Day of the Dead", the action moves to the cemetery, with marimba bands and drink stalls set up amongst the graves. It is a day of intense ritual that combines grief and celebration. On the final day of the fiesta, the streets are littered with bodies and the jail packed with brawlers. The Saturday **market**, although nothing like as riotous, also fills the village.

The village itself is pretty – a modest main street with a few shops, a plaza and a church – but it is totally overshadowed by the looming presence of the Cuchumatanes mountains, insulating Todos Santos from the rest of the world. Above the village – follow the track that goes up behind the *Comedor Katy* – is the small Maya site of **Tojcunanchén**, where you'll find a couple of mounds sprouting pine trees. The site is occasionally used by *brujos* for the ritual sacrifice of animals.

Todos Santos is home to three interesting **language schools**, where you can study Spanish or Mam: Hispano Maya (*www.personal.umich.edu/~kakenned*); Nuevo Amanacer (contact Centro Maya de Idiomas, see p.395), and Proyecto Lingüístico Mam (contact Proyecto Lingüístico Quetzalteco de Español, 5 C 2–40, Zona 1 – or Apdo Postal 114 – Quetzaltenango (☎761 2620). A percentage of the profits from all schools goes to local development projects. There's an excellent community **website** – *www.stetson.edu/~rsitler/TodosSantos* – dedicated to the Todos Santos region.

## Practicalities

**Buses** leave Huehuetenango for Todos Santos from the main bus terminal four times a day at 5.45am, 10am, 1pm and 2pm – get there early to mark your seat and buy a ticket. Some carry on through the village, heading further down the valley to Jacaltenango, and pass through Todos Santos on the way back to Huehuetenango; ask around for the latest schedule.

The best places **to stay** are *Hospedaje Casa Familiar* (②), 30m above the main road past *Comedor Katy*, where views from the terrace café are breathtaking, and *Hospedaje Las Ruinas* (①), further up the track on the right, which has four large rooms in a large twin-storey concrete structure. Turning left just before you reach the *Casa Familiar* brings you to the orange *Hotel Mam*, another good option with hot showers (①), while the new *Hotelito Todos Santos* (②), just east of the plaza, is a fairly decent choice with cleanish rooms. There are two other very cheap "hotels" in Todos Santos, *Hospedaje La Paz* (①) and *Las Olguitas* (①), but both are extremely rough.

*Comedor Katy* does tasty, cheap **meals**, though you can also find good food at the *Casa Familiar* or try the gringo-geared restaurant/cafés *Cuchumatán* or *Tzolkin* nearby. There's a **post office** and a Banrural **bank** (Mon–Fri 8.30am-5pm & Sat 9am–1pm) in the plaza that will change travellers' cheques.

Though most of the fun of Todos Santos is in simply hanging out, it would be a shame not to indulge in a traditional smoke sauna (*chuc*) while you're here. Most of the guest houses will prepare one for you. If you want to take a shirt, pair of trousers or *huipil* home with you, you'll find an excellent co-op selling quality weavings next to the *Casa Familiar*.

## Walks around Todos Santos

The village of **SAN JUAN ATITÁN** is around five hours from Todos Santos across a beautiful isolated valley. Follow the path that bears up behind the *Comedor Katy*, past the ruins and high above the village through endless muddy switchbacks, until you get to the ridge overlooking the valley where, if the skies are clear, you'll be rewarded by an awesome view of the Tajumulco and Tacaná volcanoes. Take the central track from here, heading downhill past some ancient cloud forest to San Juan Atitán, four to five hours further on; it's easy to follow. There's are two **hospedajes** (both ①) if you want to stay and morning **pick-ups** return to Huehue from 6am (1hr). Market days are Monday and Thursday.

Alternatively, you can walk down the valley along the road from Todos Santos to **San Martín** and on to **JACALTENANGO**, a route which also offers superb views. There's a basic hospedaje (①) in Jacaltenango, so you can stay the night and then catch a bus back to Huehuetenango in the morning. Some buses from Huehue also continue down this route.

# West to the Mexico border

From Huehuetenango the Carretera Interamericana runs for 79km to the Mexican border at **La Mesilla**. There are hourly buses between 5am and 6pm (2hr). If you do get stuck at the border there's **accommodation** at the *Hotel Maricruz* (②–③), a clean place with private bathrooms and a restaurant, or the cheaper *Hospedaje Marisol* (②). The two sets of customs and immigration are 3km apart. There are taxis, and on the

Mexican side you can pick up buses running through the border settlement of **Ciudad Cuauhtemoc** to **Comitán** or even direct to **San Cristóbal de las Casas**. Heading into Guatemala, the last bus leaves La Mesilla for Huehuetenango at around 5pm, and there's a pullman to Guatemala City at midnight.

# THE PACIFIC COAST

Beneath the chain of volcanoes that mark the southern side of the highlands is a strip of sweltering, low-lying land, some 300km long and on average 50km wide, known by Guatemalans simply as **La Costa Sur**. This featureless yet supremely fertile coastal plain – once a wilderness of swamp, forest and savannah – is today a land of vast fincas, scattered with indifferent commercial towns and small seaside resorts.

The Pacific coast was once as rich in wildlife as the jungles of Petén, but while Petén has lain largely undisturbed, the Pacific coast has been ravaged by development. Its large-scale agriculture – including sugar cane, palm oil, cotton and rubber plantations – accounts for a substantial proportion of the country's exports. Only in some isolated sections, where mangrove swamps have been spared the plough, can you still get a sense of the way it once looked: a maze of tropical vegetation. The **Monterrico Reserve** is the most accessible protected area, a swampy refuge for sea turtles, iguanas, crocodiles and an abundance of bird life.

As for the archeological sites, they too have largely disappeared, though you can glimpse the extraordinary art of the **Pipil** (see below) around the town of **Santa Lucía Cotzumalguapa**. These small ceremonial centres, almost lost in fields of sugar-cane, reveal a wealth of carvings, and some of them are still regularly used for religious rituals. The one site that ranks with those elsewhere in the country is **Abaj Takalik**, outside Retalhuleu, where the ruins are well worth a detour on your way to or from Mexico, or as a day away from Quetzaltenango (or Retalhuleu).

Unfortunately, nature has cursed the coast here with mosquitoes, unpredictable undertows and currents and man has added filthy palm huts, pig pens and garbage, so that the **beach** is not the attraction it should be. The hotels are also some of the country's worst, so if you're desperate for a dip and a fresh shrimp feast, it's far better to visit on a day-trip from the capital or Quetzaltenango. The one glorious exception to this rule is the nature reserve of **Monterrico**, harbouring a fairly attractive village and possibly the country's finest beach, with a superb stretch of clear, clean sand.

The main transport route in this region is the Carretera al Pacífico that runs between the border with Mexico at Tecún Umán and El Salvador at Ciudad Pedro de Alvarado. There's a regular flow of buses along the highway and you shouldn't have to wait long for a ride.

## Some history

Before the arrival of the **Ocós** and **Itzapa** tribes from the west, little is known of the history of the Pacific coast. By 1500 BC, however, these Mesoamerican tribes had developed village-based societies with considerable skills in the working of stone and pottery. Between 400 and 900 AD, the whole coastal plain was again overrun by Mexicans; this time it was the **Pipil**, who brought with them sophisticated architectural and artistic skills and built ceremonial centres.

The first Spaniards in Guatemala arrived here on the Pacific coast, having travelled overland from the north, and their first confrontation with the Maya occurred in the heat of the lowlands. Once they had established themselves to the north in Quetzaltenango, the Spanish despatched a handful of Franciscans to convert the Pipil coastal population. In **colonial times**, the land was a miserable disease-ridden backwater used for the production of indigo and cacao, or for cattle ranching. It was only after **independence** that commercial agriculture began to dominate this part of the country.

Today the coastal strip is the country's most intensely farmed region – where entire villages are effectively owned by vast fincas, and coffee is grown on the volcanic slopes. Much of the nation's income is generated here, and the main towns are alive with commercial activity and dominated by the assertive machismo of ladino culture. Since the development of large-scale agriculture, the highland Maya have performed much of the hard physical labour: though no longer forcibly recruited, many thousands still come to the coast for seasonal work and continue to be exploited by the fincas.

## From the Mexican border to Coatepeque

The coastal border with Mexico is the busiest of Guatemala's frontiers, with two crossings, Talismán and Tecún Umán, open 24 hours. The northernmost of the two border posts is the **Talismán Bridge**, also referred to as **El Carmen**, where there's little more than a few huts, a couple of basic pensiones (both ①) and a round-the-clock flow of buses to Guatemala City. If you're heading towards Quetzaltenango or the western highlands, take the first bus to **Malacatán** and change there. On the Mexican side, over the bridge, there's a constant flow of minibuses leaving for Tapachula.

The **Tecún Umán** crossing is favoured by most Guatemalans and all commercial traffic. It has an authentic frontier flavour, with all-night bars, lost souls, contraband and moneychangers, plus a choice of banks. There are some cheap hotels: the *Hotel Vanessa 2* (②) and the *Hotel Don José, 2 C 3–42* (☎776 8164; ②) are two of the best, but it's probably a much better idea to get straight out of town – everyone else is. Once again, there's a steady stream of buses to Guatemala City along the Pacific Highway via Coatepeque and Retalhuleu. If you're Mexico-bound, once you're over the border, there are very frequent bus services to Tapachula (30min).

As you head east from the Mexican border, **COATEPEQUE** is the first place of any importance on the main road, a town that's in many ways typical of the coastal strip. A furiously busy, purely commercial centre, this is where most of the coffee produced locally is processed. The action is centred on the **bus terminal**, an intimidating maelstrom of sweat, mud and energetic chaos. Buses run every thirty minutes from here to the two border crossings, hourly between 4am and 6pm to Quetzaltenango and hourly from 2am to 6pm to Guatemala City.

The best place to **stay** in Coatepeque is the *Hotel Villa Real*, 6 C 6–57 (☎775 1308, fax 775 1939; ④), a modern hotel with clean rooms and secure parking. A bit cheaper is the family-run *Hotel Baechli*, 6 C 5–35 (☎775 1483; ④), which has plain rooms with fan and TV, plus secure parking. There are two banks that will change travellers' cheques on the plaza and a Telgua office (daily 7am–10pm) at 5 Av and 7 C.

## Retalhuleu to Cocales

About 40km beyond Coatepeque is the largest town in the region, **RETALHULEU**, usually referred to as **Reu**, pronounced "Ray-oo". Set away from the highway and surrounded by the walled homes of the wealthy, Retalhuleu has managed to avoid the worst excesses of the coast and has a relaxed easy-going air. It was founded by the Spanish in the early years of the Conquest and remains something of an oasis of civilization, with a plaza featuring towering Greek columns, statues of Eros and Venus and an attractive whitewashed colonial church, dating from 1627, with soaring tiered belltowers. If you have time to kill, pop into the local **Museum of Archeology and Ethnology** in the plaza (Tues–Sun 8am–1pm & 2–5pm; US$0.20), where you'll find an amazing collection of anthropomorphic figurines, mostly heads, and some photographs of the town dating back to the 1880s.

Budget **accommodation** is in short supply in Retalhuleu. The best hospedaje is *Hotel Hillman* at 7 Av 7–99 (②) where most rooms have a private bath, otherwise rates go up steeply: the *Hotel Modelo*, 5 C 4–53 (☎771 0256; ③), has decent basic but clean rooms with private bath, while over the road the good-value *Hotel Astor*, 5 C 4–60 (☎771 0475; *hotelastor@infovia.com.gt*; ④), has rooms with fan, TV and bath, set around a pleasant courtyard. If you want a bit more luxury, try the modern *Hotel Posada de Don José*, 5 C 3–67 (☎771 0180; *www.don-jose.com*; ④), which has good a/c rooms, a reasonable restaurant and a pool.

The **plaza** is the hub of activity. Here you'll find three **banks**, including the Banco del Agro and, close by, the Banco Industrial with a 24-hour Visa ATM and the **post office** (Mon–Fri 8am–4.30pm); the **Telgua** office (daily 7am–10pm) is just around the corner. The best **restaurants** are also on the plaza: try the *Cafetería la Luna*, or, for cakes and pastries, *El Volován*.

**Buses** running along the coastal highway almost always pull in at the Retalhuleu terminal on 7 Av and 10 C, a ten-minute walk from the plaza. There's an hourly service to and from Guatemala City, the Mexican border and Quetzaltenango and there are also regular buses to Champerico and El Tulate. Retalhuleu has the only **Mexican consulate** on the Pacific coast, at 5 C and 3 Av (Mon–Fri 4–6pm).

## Abaj Takalik

Near El Asintal, a small village 15km to the east of Retalhuleu, the site of **Abaj Takalik** (daily 9am–4pm; US$3.20) is currently being excavated and has already provided firm evidence of an **Olmec** influence reaching the area in the first century AD. Excavations have so far unearthed enormous stelae, several of them very well preserved, dating the earliest monuments to around 126 AD. This is a large site, with four main groups of ruins and around seventy mounds in the main part of the site. The remains of two large **temple platforms** have also been cleared, and what makes a visit to this obscure site really worthwhile are the carved sculptures and stelae and altars found around their base. In particular, you will find rare and unusual representations of frogs and toads (monument 68) – and even an alligator (monument 66). Amongst the finest carving is stela 5, which features two standing figures separated by a hieroglyphic panel, dated to 126 AD. Look out for a giant Olmec head, too, showing a man of obvious wealth with great hamster cheeks.

There is a small building which acts as the site **museum** containing a model of Abaj Takalik and assorted carvings and ceramics. You should be able to get a warm *agua* near the entrance, but there is no food available.

To **get to Abaj Takalik**, take a local bus from Reu to **El Asintal**, from where it's a 4km walk through coffee and cacao plantations. If using your own transport, take the highway towards Mexico from Reu, and turn right at the sign. Drive through the village of El Astinal passing the entrance to Finca Santa Margarita, where there is a stone carving.

## Champerico, Mazatenango and Cocales

Some 42km south of Retalhuleu, a paved road reaches to the beach at **CHAM-PERICO**, which, though it certainly doesn't feel like it, is the country's third port. The town enjoyed a brief period of prosperity when it was connected to Quetzaltenango by rail, but there's little left now apart from a rusting pier. The **beach** is much the same as anywhere else, and although its sheer scale is impressive and there are lifeguards, it's essential to watch out for the dangerous undertow. Delicious **meals** are widely available: try the *Restaurant Monte Limar* or the *Alcatraz* for fried shrimp and fish, or, for a treat, feast on paella at the *Hotel Miramar* at 2 C and Av Coatepeque (☎773 7231; ②), which also has a fantastic wooden bar and dark, windowless rooms. **Buses** run between Champerico and Quetzaltenango every hour or so, passing through Retalhuleu. The last bus for Retalhuleu leaves Champerico at 6pm.

Back on the highway, heading east, the next place of any size is the unremarkable town of Cuyotenango, where a side road heads off to the sweeping, almost uncommercialized beach of **El Tulate** where the surf is less dangerous and there's a handful of very simple fried fish 'n' shrimp cookshacks, but no hotels. Infrequent buses struggle down to Tulate from Cuyotenango at weekends from Reu and Mazatenango. The next stop on the highway is **MAZATENANGO**, another seething commercial town, which also has a quieter, calmer side centred around the plaza. *Maxim's*, at 6 Av 9–23, serves excellent Chinese food and barbecued meats, or try *Croissants Pastelería* on the plaza for coffee and cakes. There are also a couple of cinemas, plenty of **banks**, a few run-down pensiones and, on the main highway, the decent, clean *Hotel Alba* (☎872 0264; ④), which has secure parking.

About 30km beyond Mazatenango is **COCALES**, a crossroads from where a road runs north to Santiago Atitlán, San Lucas Tolimán and Lago de Atitlán. If you're heading this way you can wait for a connection at the junction, but don't expect to make it all the way to Panajachel unless you get here by midday. The best bet is to take the first pick-up or bus for Santiago and catch a boat from there to other points on the lake. The last transport to Santiago Atitlán leaves Cocales at around 5pm.

## Santa Lucía Cotzumalguapa and around

Another 23km brings you to **SANTA LUCÍA COTZUMALGUAPA**, another uninspiring Pacific town a short distance north of the highway. The main reason to visit is to explore the **archeological sites** that are scattered in the surrounding cane fields. Pullman **buses** passing along the highway will drop you at the entrance road to town, ten minutes' walk from the town centre, while second-class buses from Guatemala City go straight into the terminal, a few blocks from the plaza. Buses to the capital leave the terminal hourly until 4pm, or you can catch a pullman from the highway.

As usual, the **plaza** is at the centre of things. Santa Lucía's shady square is disgraced by possibly one of the ugliest buildings in the country (in a very competitive league), a memorably horrific green and white concrete municipal structure. Just off the plaza you'll find several cheap and scruffy **hotels** including the *Pensión Reforma*, 4 Av 4–71 (①), and the *Hospedaje El Carmen*, around the corner at 5 C 4–35 (①). The nearest upmarket place is the *Caminotel Santiaguito* (☎882 5435, fax 882 2285; ④), a slick motel at Km 90.5 on the main highway, which has a swimming pool and restaurant.

Back in town at least three **banks** will change your travellers' cheques. Try Banco Corporativo in the plaza which accepts most varieties. For **food**, the *Comedor Lau* on 3 Avenida does reasonable Chinese meals or there's a huge *Pollo Campero* on the north side of the square and *Sarita* ice creams on 3 Avenida. For a drink, *Cevichería La Española* on 4 Avenida, south of the plaza, is the best bet.

### Pipil sites around Santa Lucía Cotzumalguapa

**Getting to the sites** isn't easy unless have your own transport or rent a taxi. Drivers loiter with intent in the main plaza – you should reckon on US$10 to visit all the sites. Children will guide on foot as well – ask in your pensión or in the plaza – though a walking tour can be an exhausting and frustrating process, taking you through a sweltering maze of cane fields. If you want to see just one of the sites, choose Bilbao, just 1km or so from the centre of town, which features some of the best carving. If you get lost at any stage, ask for "*las piedras*", as they tend to be known locally.

In 1880, more than thirty Late Classic stone monuments were removed from the Pipil site of **Bilbao**, and nine of the very best were shipped to Germany. Four sets of stones are still visible in situ, however, and two of them perfectly illustrate the magnificent precision of the carving, beautifully preserved in slabs of black volcanic rock. To **get to** the site, walk uphill from the plaza, along 4 Avenida, and bear right at the end, where a dirt track takes you past a small red-brick house and along the side of a cane field. About

200m further on is a fairly wide path leading left into the cane for about 20m. This brings you to two large stones carved in bird-like patterns, with strange circular glyphs arranged in groups of three: the majority of the glyphs are recognizable as the names for days once used by the people of southern Mexico. In the same cane field, further along the same path, is another badly eroded stone, and a final set with a superbly preserved set of figures and interwoven motifs.

The second site is about 5km further afield in the grounds of the **Finca El Baúl**, down the only tarmacked road (3 Avenida) that heads north out of town. The hilltop site has two huge stones that date from the Classic period. The first is propped against a tree, carved in low relief, and depicts a standing figure wearing a skirt. The skirted figure bears a spectacular headdress, possibly that of Huhuetéotl, the fire god of the Mexicans, who supported the sun. Surrounding the figure are a number of carved circles, one seemingly bearing the date 8 deer. The second stone is a massive half-buried head, in superb condition, with wrinkled brow, huge cheesy grin and patterned headdress, which probably again represents Huehuetéotl. The site itself is still actively used for pagan ceremonies, particularly by women hoping for children or safe childbirth. In front of the stones is a set of small altars on which local people make animal sacrifices, burn incense and leave offerings of flowers.

The next place of interest is the **finca** itself, a few kilometres further away from town, where the carvings include more superb heads, a stone skull, a massive jaguar and an extremely well-preserved stela of a ball-court player (monument 27) that dates from the Late Classic period. Alongside all this antiquity is the finca's old steam engine, a miniature machine that used to haul the cane along a system of private tracks. As the finca has its own bus service you may be able to get a ride there. Buses leave from the *Tienda El Baúl*, a few blocks uphill from the plaza, four or five times a day, the first at around 7am and the last either way at about 6pm.

On the other side of town is the final site at **Finca las Ilusiones**, where there's another private collection of artefacts and some stone carvings. To get there, walk east along the highway for about 1km and turn left by the second Esso station. Perhaps the most striking figure here is a pot-bellied statue (monument 58) that is probably from the middle Preclassic era. There are several other original carvings, including some fantastic stelae, plus some copies and a small museum crammed with literally thousands of small stone carvings and pottery fragments.

## La Democracia

Continuing down the highway to Siquinalá, a run-down sort of place, there's another branch road that heads to the coast. Nine kilometres south, on the branch road, **LA DEMOCRACIA** is of particular interest as the home of another collection of archeological relics. To the east of town lies the site of **Monte Alto**, many of whose best pieces are now spread around the town plaza under a vast ceiba tree. These so-called "fat boys" are massive stone heads with simple, almost childlike faces, carved in an Olmec style (see p.183), thought to date from the Mid-Preclassic period, possibly from as far back as 500 BC. Some are attached to smaller rounded bodies and rolled over on their backs clutching their swollen stomachs like stricken Teletubbies. Also on the plaza, the town **museum** (Tues–Sun 8am–noon & 2–5pm) houses carvings, a wonderful jade mask, yokes worn by ball-game players, pottery, grinding stones and a few more carved heads.

## Escuintla and south to the coast

At the junction of the two principal coastal roads from the capital, **ESCUINTLA** is the largest and most important of the Pacific towns. There's nothing to do here, but you do get a good sense of life on the coast, its pace and energy and the frenetic commercial activity that drives it. Escuintla lies at the heart of the country's most productive region, both industrially and agriculturally, and the department's resources include cattle, sugar, cotton, light industry and even a small Texaco oil refinery.

Below the plaza a huge, chaotic **market** sprawls across several blocks, spilling out into 4 Avenida, the main commercial thoroughfare, which is also notable for a lurid blue mock castle that functions as the town's police station.

There are plenty of cheap **hotels** near 4 Avenida, most of them sharing in the general air of dilapidation. The *Hospedaje Oriente*, 4 Av 11–30 (①), is cheap and pretty clean, or for a/c and secure parking head for the recommended *Hotel Costa Sur*, 4 Av and 12 C (☎888 1819; ③). For **changing money**, there's a Banco Industrial at 4 Av and 6 C, and Lloyds at 7 C 3–07. The best deal for **eating** is at *Pizzeria al Macarone*, 4 Av 6–103, which has US$1.50 lunch specials. There are also two **consulates** in town, Honduras at 6 Av 8–24 and El Salvador at 16 C 3–20.

**Buses** to Escuintla leave from the Trébol junction in Guatemala City frequently until 7pm, returning from 8 C and 2 Av in Escuintla. For other destinations there are two terminals: for places **en route to the Mexican border**, buses run through the north of town and stop by the Esso station opposite the Banco Uno (take a local bus up 3 Avenida); buses for the **coast road and inland route to El Salvador** are best caught at the main terminal on the south side of town, at the bottom of 4 Avenida. From the latter, buses leave every thirty minutes for Puerto San José, hourly for the eastern border, and six times daily for Antigua, via El Rodeo.

## Puerto San José

South from Escuintla an excellent smooth highway heads through acres of cattle pasture to **PUERTO SAN JOSÉ**, which, in its prime, was Guatemala's main shipping terminal, funnelling goods to and from the capital. It has now been made virtually redundant by Puerto Quetzal, a container port a few kilometres to the east. Today both town and port are somewhat sleazy and the main business is local tourism: what used to be rough sailors' bars pander to the needs of the day-trippers from the capital who fill the beaches at weekends.

The shoreline is separated from the mainland by the **Canal de Chiquimulilla**, which starts near Sipacate, west of San José, and runs as far as the border with El Salvador, cutting off all the beaches in between. Here in San José, the main resort area is on the other side of the canal, directly behind the beach. This is where all the bars and restaurants are, most of them crowded at weekends with big ladino groups feasting on seafood. The **hotels** nearby are not so enjoyable, catering as they do to a largely drunken clientele, but try *Casa San José Hotel* on Avenida del Comercio (☎776 5587; ③), where you'll find a pool and restaurant. Or, for a really cheap option, *Hospedaje Viñas de Mar* (②), which is basic but right by the beach.

**Buses** between San José and Guatemala City run every thirty minutes or so all day. From Guatemala City they leave from the terminal in Zona 4 and from the plaza in San José.

## Monterrico

The setting of **MONTERRICO**, further east along the coast, is one of the finest on the Pacific coast, with the scenery reduced to its basic elements: a strip of dead straight sand, a line of powerful surf, a huge empty ocean and an enormous curving horizon. The village is friendly and relaxed, separated from the mainland by the waters of the Chiquimulilla canal, which in this case weaves through a fantastic network of mangrove **swamps**. Mosquitoes can be a problem during the wet season.

Beach apart, Monterrico's chief attraction is the **nature reserve**, which embraces the village, the beach – an important **turtle** nesting ground – and a large slice of the swamps behind, forming a total area of some 72 square kilometres. Sadly, however, the protected status the reserve officially enjoys does not stop the dumping of domestic rubbish and the widespread theft of turtle eggs. That said, it's well worth making your way to Monterrico, if only for the fantastically beautiful ocean. This is certainly the best place on the coast to spend time by the sea, though take care in the waves as there's a vicious undertow – lifeguards are on duty at weekends.

You can also visit the **Biotopo Monterrico-Hawaii**, a mangrove swamp with dark, nutrient-rich waters and four distinct types of mangrove that form a dense mat of branches, interspersed with narrow canals, open lagoons, bullrushes and water lilies. The tangle of roots acts as a kind of marine nursery, offering small fish protection from their natural predators, while above the surface the dense vegetation and ready food supply provide an ideal home for hundreds of species of birds, a handful of mammals, including racoons, opossums, ant-eaters and armadillos; plus iguanas, caimans and alligators. The best way to travel is in a small *cayuco*; ask around at the dock for a boatman or organize a trip through *Iguana Tours* (☎238 4690), located on the main street close to the football field. At the reserve's **visitor centre** (daily 8.30am–noon & 2–5pm), just off the beach between *Hotel Mangle* and the *Pez d'Oro*, there's plenty of information about the environment (Spanish only) and an important turtle hatchery; caimans and iguanas are also bred for release.

Monterrico, like most places on the Pacific coast, is very quiet during the week but fills up at **weekends** with Guatemalans from the capital and increasing numbers of language-school students from Antigua. Though the beach is far too expansive to get packed, the atmosphere tends to be get raucous when some of the more frenzied visitors see fit to rip their motorbikes and quad bikes up and down the sands.

## Arrival

The best way to **get to Monterrico** is via the coastal highway at **Taxisco**. From here trucks and buses run the 17km paved road to **LA AVELLANA**, a couple of kilometres from Monterrico on the opposite side of the mangrove swamp, where boats shuttle passengers and cars back and forth. There's a steady flow of traffic between Taxisco and La Avellana, the last bus leaving Taxisco at 6pm and La Avellana at 4.30pm; you'll find the latest schedules posted in several hotels including the *Baule Beach*. Several direct **buses** run between La Avellana and the Zona 4 bus terminal in Guatemala City, taking around three and a half hours; alternatively, get on any bus heading for Taxisco and change there. An altogether easier, though pricey, option if you're staying in Antigua is to use one of the **shuttle bus** services, see p.356, which leave every Friday afternoon and return on Sundays around 3pm.

## Accommodation

Most of Monterrico's **accommodation** is concentrated in the mid-range, with few good budget rooms available. Everything is concentrated right on or just off the beach. As there are **no phones** it isn't that easy to book in advance, though many places have reservation numbers in Guatemala City and others use cellular phones. As elsewhere on the coast, prices can increase by up to fifty percent at weekends, when it's best to book ahead.

**Eco Beach Place**, turn left at the beach, walk for 250m (cell phone ☎309 2505, Guatemala City ☎369 1116 & 365 7217). Very attractive new guest house, set away from the others, run by a friendly Italian-Guatemalan guy with large comfortable doubles – all but one have private bath. There's good grub, a nice lounge and bar area and stunning Pacific vistas from the verandah. ④.

**Hotel Baule Beach**, next door to the *Kaiman* (Guatemala City ☎478 3088, *baulebeach@hotmail.com*). For many years this was a very popular place, but a recent change in management has seen service levels plummet and a general air of decay set in. All rooms have private bath and mosquito net and there's a tiny pool. Avoid the food. ③.

**Hotel El Mangle**, beside the *Baule Beach* (Guatemala City ☎369 8958 & 514 6517, fax 369 7631). Friendly place with thirteen very pleasant but small budget rooms – all have private shower, fan, nice wooden furniture and little terrace with hammocks – and there's a small pool. ④.

**Hotel La Sirena**, turn right at the beach, walk for 100m. Huge, unattractive concrete hotel which nonetheless offers a decent choice of digs: from tiny twin-bed rooms to larger apartments. There's also a pool and a reasonable restaurant. ②–④.

**Johnny's Place**, turn left when you reach the ocean and it's the first place you'll come to (☎cell phone 206 4702, *www.backpackamericas.com/johnnys.htm*). Selection of reasonable, though not wildly attractive, self-catering bungalows sleeping between two and four, each with little bathing pools, plus four gloomy, though cheap, rooms. The new management team promises substantial renovation. ③/⑤.

**Kaiman Inn**, turn left at beach and walk for 200m. The large rooms have mosquito nets and fans but are a little run-down and it can be noisy here. There's a pool and a variable, overpriced Italian restaurant. ④.

**Pez de Oro**, the last place as you head east down the beach (☎cell phone 204 5249, Guatemala City ☎368 3684, *laelegancia@guate.net*). The nicest cottages in Monterrico – well-spaced, comfortable and tastefully decorated. Most are detached and all have ceiling fans and balconies with hammocks. The pretty swimming pool is shaded by coconut palms and there's a good Italian restaurant with excellent pasta and wine by the glass. ⑤.

## Eating and drinking

When it comes to **eating** in Monterrico, you can either dine at one of the hotels on the beach, though menus are pricey, or at one of the comedores in the village, the best being the *Divino Maestro*, where they do a superb shark steak with rosemary. For a relaxing **drink**, head for the *Caracol* bar, which boasts a lethal cocktail list and good tunes; it's run by a friendly Norwegian and Swiss team who can recommend local guides.

## travel details

### Buses

**Chichicastenango** to: Guatemala City (every 30min 5am–4.30pm; 3hr); Quetzaltenango (7 daily; 2hr 30min); Santa Cruz del Quiché (every 30min; 30min).

**Coatepeque** to: Retalhuleu (every 30min; 50min); Talismán and Tecún Umán (12 daily; 40min).

**Cocales** to: Escuintla (14 daily; 30min).

**Escuintla** to: Antigua (6 daily; 1hr 30min); Guatemala City (18 daily; 1hr 30min).

**Guatemala City** to: La Avellena (4 daily; 4hr); Mexican border at Tecún Umán and Talismán via all towns on Pacific Highway (19 daily; 5hr); Puerto San José (15 daily; 2hr); Tapachula, Mexico (3 daily; 6hr).

**Huehuetenango** to: Aguacatán (8 daily; 1hr); Guatemala City (14 daily, 6hr); La Mesilla (10 daily; 2hr); Todos Santos Cuchumatán (3–4 daily; 2hr 30min).

**Joyabaj** to: Guatemala City (11 daily; 4hr 30min); San Martín Jilotepeque (1 daily; 2hr).

**La Avellana** to: Guatemala City (3 daily; 3hr 30min).

**Monterrico** to: Pueblo Viejo, for Itzapa (3 daily; 1hr 30min).

**Panajachel** to: Antigua (1 daily; 3hr); Chichicastenango (5 buses Thurs & Sun, 1–2 on other days; 1hr 30min); Cocales (9 daily; 2hr 30min); Guatemala City (8 daily; 3hr 30min); Quetzaltenango (6 daily; 2hr 30min); Sololá (every 20min; 30min). There are also tourist shuttles to Antigua, Chichicastenango, Guatemala City, Quetzaltenango, and the Mexican border at La Mesilla and Tecún Umán for Mexico City.

**Quetzaltenango** to: Chichicastenango (6 daily; 2hr 30min); Guatemala City (19 daily; 4hr); Huehuetenango (14 daily; 2hr); Momostenango (hourly; 1hr 15min); Panajachel (6 daily; 2hr 30min); Retalhuleu (10 daily; 1hr); San Francisco el Alto (every 30min; 45min); San Pedro la Laguna (3 daily,

2hr 30min); Totonicapán (every 30min; 45min; Santa Cruz del Quiché (7 daily; 3hr); Tecún Umán (10 daily; 2hr 30min); Zunil (every 30min; 25min).

**Retalhuleu** to: Cocales (14 daily; 50min); Champerico (8 daily; 1hr); Guatemala City (10 daily; 4hr); Mazatenango (12 daily; 30min); Quetzaltenango (10 daily; 1hr 15min).

**Santa Cruz del Quiché** to: Guatemala City (every 30min; 3hr 30min); Nebaj (5 daily; 3hr 30min); Quetzaltenango (7 daily; 3hr); Sacapulas (9 daily; 1hr 45min); Uspantán (4 daily; 5hr).

**Talismán** to: Guatemala City (10 daily; 5hr).

**Tecún Umán** to: Guatemala City (14 daily; 5hr); Quetzaltenango (10 daily; 2hr 30min).

## Boats

There are no schedules around Atitlán except these:

**San Pedro la Laguna** to: Santiago Atitlán (9 daily; 40min) plus regular direct lanchas to Panajachel (20min).

**Santiago Atitlán** to: San Pedro la Laguna (9 daily; 40min); Panajachel (4 daily; 1hr).

**Panajachel** to: Santiago Atitlán (4 daily; 1hr) plus regular lanchas to all other lakeside towns.

**La Avellana** to: Monterrico (10 daily, 30 min).

**Monterrico** to: La Avellana (10 daily, 30 min).

# CHAPTER NINE

# THE NORTH AND EAST

The area to the north and east of the capital is an incredibly diverse and beautiful area, where you'll find some of Guatemala's most spectacular Maya sites. The vast northern department of **Petén** is largely lowland jungle, abundant with wildlife and harbouring the ruins of ancient cities with their towering ceremonial centres of temples, pyramids and stelae. Further south, the spectacular alpine scenery of the **Verapaces** offers outstanding hiking possibilities, vast networks of caves to explore and the sublime tranquillity of the pools at Semuc Champey to enjoy. The far south is the most diverse area, comprising both arid and rain-sodden mountain ranges, the near-desert of the central **Motagua valley** and a permanently humid, tropical Caribbean coastline.

This is a very sparsely populated land – there isn't one city in the entire region and no town has a population above fifty thousand – but its lack of people has enabled dozens of **national parks** and reserves to be established. Some are small-scale, designed to safeguard the habitat of a particular species, such as the manatee or the quetzal, while others, such as the Maya Biosphere Reserve, which covers the whole of northern Petén, are gigantic. It's this vast rainforest, much of it still intact despite the attentions of loggers, which offers the ultimate challenge for would-be pioneers in search of some serious adventure. If you're after some less demanding exploration, however, the aquatic splendour of **Lago de Izabal** and the **Río Dulce** gorge area are much more accessible, and have plenty of comfortable accommodation options.

For all the scenic delights of this region, its greatest attraction is the cultural legacy of the **Maya**. Vast temple-rich cities remain buried in the jungles of Petén, some, such as Nakbé, first settled as long as three thousand years ago. The most rewarding site to visit is **Tikal**, perhaps the most magnificent of all Maya ruins, which has been partially cleared and is easily reached by air or road. There are scores of other huge temple cities which remain almost unexcavated, such as Río Azul and El Mirador, and which doubtless conceal secrets about the continent's greatest pre-Columbian culture – a civilization able to construct seventy-metre-high buildings long before the birth of Christ.

Today the region's culture is largely **ladino** and, though there are pockets of people speaking Maya languages, they mostly adhere much less strictly to traditional customs and dress than in the western highlands. Guatemala's black Carib population, known as the Garífuna, also live in this region, near **Lívingston**.

---

## ACCOMMODATION PRICE CODES

All the accommodation listed in this book has been categorized into one of nine price bands, as set out below. The prices quoted are in US dollars and refer to the cheapest room available for two people sharing in high season.

| | | |
|---|---|---|
| ① under US$5 | ④ US$15–25 | ⑦ US$60–80 |
| ② US$5–10 | ⑤ US$25–40 | ⑧ US$80–100 |
| ③ US$10–15 | ⑥ US$40–60 | ⑨ over US$100 |

Zunil market, Guatemala

Basketball, San Juan Atitán, Guatemala

Huipil, San Mateo Ixtatán, Guatemala

Sololá man, Guatemala

Scarlet Macaw

Creole man, Lívingston, Guatemala

Stela H, Copán, Honduras

Lake Atitlán, Guatemala

Santo Tomás Church, Chichicastenango, Guatemala

Tikal, Guatemala

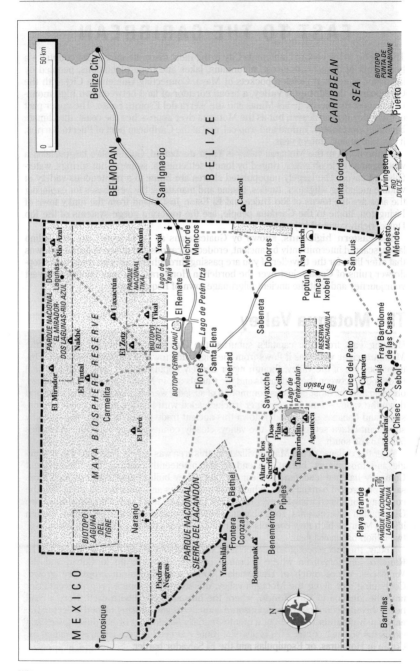

# EAST TO THE CARIBBEAN

The region to the east of Guatemala City is the most disparate part of the country – a heady mix of desert, rainforest, mountains, lakes and huge plantations, peopled by ladinos, Creoles and isolated pockets of Maya. Connecting Guatemala City with the Caribbean is the **Motagua valley**, a broad corridor of land between two high mountain ranges: the Sierra de las Minas and the Sierra del Espíritu Santo. The upper part of the valley is near-desert, but as the Motagua river approaches the coast, the climate becomes increasingly humid and tropical, and at the Caribbean port of Puerto Barrios, it can rain at any time of year.

To the north of the Motagua valley is **Lago de Izabal**, Guatemala's largest lake, a vast expanse of fresh water, ringed by lonely settlements, swamps, hot springs, waterfalls and caves. The largely unpopulated shores are home to a tremendous variety of wildlife including alligators, turtles, iguana and manatees; the best bases for exploring the area are the towns of Río Dulce and El Estor. Just inland from the funky town of Lívingston, home to the Garífuna people, are the towering gorge systems of the Río Dulce, richly covered in jungle.

The **eastern highlands**, known by Guatemalans as "el Oriente", are dry ladino lands, scarred intermittently by ancient, eroded volcanoes and dusty, featureless towns that offer little for the traveller. If you are passing through this area en route to the top-drawer ruins of **Copán**, just over the border in Honduras, you may choose to divert your journey and visit the ancient pilgrimage town of Esquipulas.

# The Motagua Valley

Heading east from the capital's suburbs, the Carretera al Atlántico shadows the **Motagua river valley** as it flows from the highlands towards the Caribbean sea. This upper section of the valley, though never densely populated, has long been a pivotal trade route between the highlands and the Caribbean. In Maya days, salt, shells, cacao, obsidian and the most precious commodity of all, jade, were humped and floated up and down the valley – now it's container trucks loaded with textiles, coffee beans, cotton, sugar and bananas that thunder down this ancient trade route. Quiriguá was the only significant Maya settlement in the valley, closely connected with Copán, which lies 50km to the south.

After the collapse of the Maya civilization, this area was largely abandoned to the jungle and mosquitoes, but at the end of the nineteenth century, the United Fruit Company hatched a scheme to clear the land. They built a railway and planted thousands of acres of banana trees, which spawned profits and influence so great that the company dominated trade for over fifty years and even had a hand in bringing down two Guatemalan governments. Today bananas still dominate the region's economy, though it's Del Monte which now controls the Fruit Company's yellow empire, exporting over two billion bananas a year.

Today, the first place of any concern as you head east along the highway is the **El Rancho** junction, from where a branch road heads north up to Cobán and the Verapaces, where much of Guatemala's coffee and cardamom crops are grown. Continuing east along the Motagua valley, the scenery becomes progressively drier until the junction of **Río Hondo**, where the hills are spiked with cacti. Here a road heads through countless Pepsi-sponsored comedores and an army of food sellers to the **eastern highlands** (see p.432), a quintessentially ladino land of hot dusty towns and expended volcanic cones. This is also the route you need to take if you're heading for Copán in Honduras, or Esquipulas and the El Salvador border.

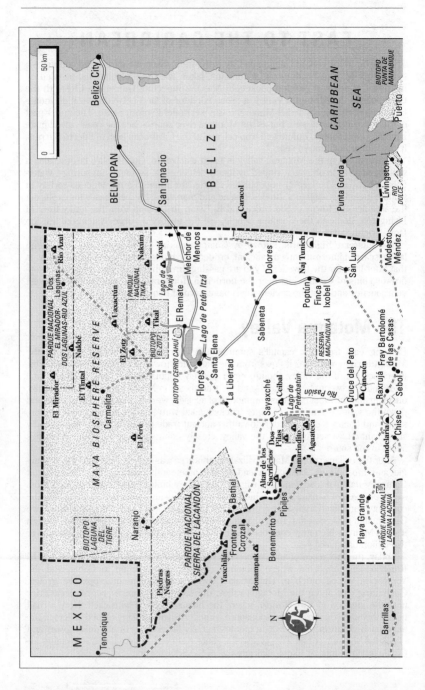

Santo Tomás Church, Chichicastenango, Guatemala

Tikal, Guatemala

Hunting Caye, South Belize

Lubaantun, Belize

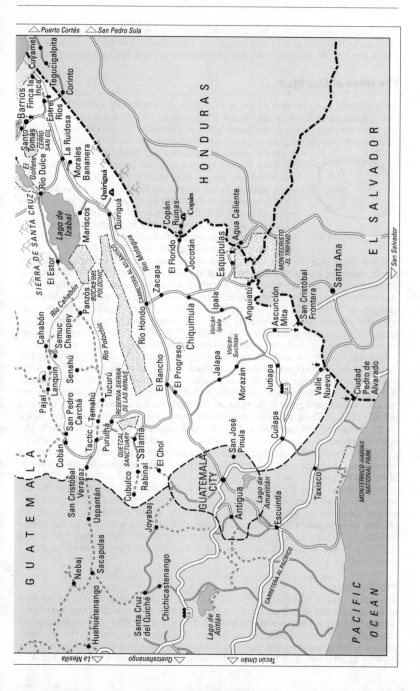

Continuing east along the Carretera al Atlántico, the terrain starts to gather moisture again as the influence of the Caribbean is felt. The ruins of **Quiriguá**, just off the highway at Km 205, are the first really worthwhile place to break the long journey east.

## The ruins of Quiriguá

Set splendidly in an isolated pocket of rainforest, surrounded by an ocean of banana trees, **Quiriguá** may not be able to match the scale of Tikal, but it does have some of the finest carvings in the Maya World. Only neighbouring Copán (see p.486) comes close to matching the magnificent stelae and altars (called zoomorphs), covered in well-preserved and superbly intricate glyphs and portraits.

Quiriguá emblem glyph

The **early history** of Quiriguá is still fairly vague, but during the Late Preclassic period (250 BC–250 AD), migrants from the north, possibly Putun Maya from the Yucatán peninsula, established themselves as the rulers here. Later, in the Early Classic period (250–600 AD), the centre was dominated by Copán, just 50km away, and doubtless valued for its position on the banks of the Río Motagua, an important trade route, and as a source of jade, which is found throughout the valley.

It was the during the rule of the great leader **Cauac Sky** that Quiriguá challenged Copán, capturing its leader Eighteen Rabbit in 737. Dominating the lower Motagua valley and its highly prized resources for a century, it was able to assert its independence and embark on an unprecedented building boom: the bulk of the great stelae date from this period. Under **Jade Sky**, who took the throne in 790, Quiriguá reached its peak, with fifty years of extensive building work, including a radical reconstruction of the acropolis. At the end of Jade Sky's rule, in the middle of the ninth century, the historical record fades out, as does the period of prosperity and power.

Entering the site beneath the ever-dripping ceiba, jocote, palm and fig trees, you emerge at the northern end of the **Great Plaza**. To the left of the path from the ticket office and new museum is a badly ruined pyramid, with the untidy bulk of the **acropolis** dominating the site from the southern end of the plaza. Liberally scattered around the luxuriant tropical grass of the plaza are the finely carved **stelae** for which Quiriguá is justly famous. The nine stelae are among the tallest in the Maya world, and all are similarly studded with portraits and glyphs, and topped by thatched palm roofs. The figures represent the city's rulers, with Cauac Sky depicted on no fewer than seven (A, C, D, E, F, H and J). Two unusual features are particularly clear: the vast headdresses, which dwarf the faces, and the beards. Largest of the stelae is E, which rises to a height of 8m and weighs 65 tons.

As you head down the path towards the acropolis, you can just make out the remains of a **ball court** on your right before you reach the other features that have earned Quiriguá its fame. Squatting at the base of the raised acropolis are six bizarre **zoomorphs**: globular-shaped stone altars carved with interlacing animal and human figures; look out for the turtle, frog, crocodile and jaguar. The best of the lot is P, which shows a figure seated in Buddha-like pose, interwoven with a maze of other detail.

### Practicalities

The **ruins** (daily 7.30am–5pm; US$3.20) are situated some 70km beyond the junction of Río Hondo, and 4km from the main road, reached by a side road that serves the banana industry. All **buses** running between Puerto Barrios (2hr) and Guatemala City (4hr) pass by. There's a fairly regular bus service from the highway to the site itself, plus assorted motorbikes and pick-ups. Leaving the ruins, you shouldn't have to wait too long to get a ride back to the main highway, or you can walk it in forty minutes.

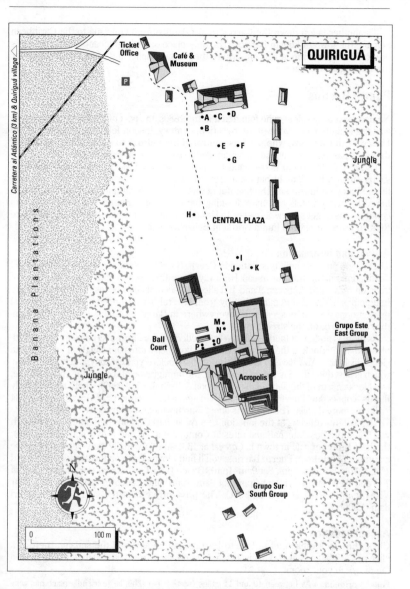

**QUIRIGUÁ**

Carretera al Atlántico (3 km) & Quiriguá village

Ticket Office

Café & Museum

P

• A • C • D
• B

• E • F
• G

H •

CENTRAL PLAZA

Jungle

• I
J • • K

Banana Plantations

M •
N •
• O
Ball Court
P •

Grupo Este East Group

Jungle

Acropolis

N

Grupo Sur South Group

0            100 m

There are a couple of simple places to **stay** in the village of **QUIRIGUÁ**, 5km from the ruins, reached either by following the old railtrack west for 3km or heading back to the highway and getting a ride from there. Alongside the old hospital for tropical diseases is the pleasant *Hotel y Restaurante Royal* (☎947 3639; ②/③) with large old rooms downstairs and modern rooms on the upper floor, while the *Hotel el Eden* (☎947 3281; ②), next to the old station, just off the tracks, is another reasonable budget option, which also serves **meals**.

It's another 90km down the Carretera al Atlántico from Quiriguá to the Caribbean Sea and the town of Puerto Barrios. The only place of any significance on the route is the **Ruidosa junction** at Km 245, where the highway splits and a road turns north for the Río Dulce and Petén.

# Puerto Barrios

Named for the president, who founded it in the 1880s, the port of **PUERTO BARRIOS** was the main port for most of the twentieth century. It soon fell into the hands of the United Fruit Company, who used its control of the railroad to ensure that the bulk of the trade passed this way and also managed to exempt itself from almost all tax.

These days the boom is over and the town distinctly forlorn, with a smattering of sleazy strip clubs, all-night bars and brothels. The streets are wide, but they're poorly lit and badly potholed, and the handful of fine old Caribbean houses are now outnumbered by grimy hotels and hard-drinking bars. The only reason that most travellers come here is to get somewhere else: to Honduras via the new border crossing via Entre Ríos, to Lívingston, or to Punta Gorda in Belize by boat.

### Arrival and information

There is no purpose-built bus station in Puerto Barrios. Litegua **buses**, which serve all destinations along the Caribbean Highway, have their own terminal in the centre of town on 6 Avenida, between 9 and 10 calles. All second-class buses to Chiquimula and Esquipulas arrive and depart close by from several bays grouped around the central market opposite. **Taxis** seem to be everywhere in Barrios – drivers toot for custom as they drive through the streets.

As there is no Inguat tourist office in town, check at the Litegua terminal for bus schedules and at the **dock** at the end of 12 Calle for boat departures to Lívingston and to Punta Gorda in Belize. You have to clear **immigration** before you can buy a ticket to Belize, which is best done the day before departure: the immigration office is at the end of 9 Calle, two blocks north of the dock (daily 7am–noon & 2–5pm; ☎948 0802). There are also daily **flights** connecting Puerto Barrios with Guatemala City (1hr; US$54); call Taca (☎334 7722) for more details. The airstrip is about 3km northeast of the centre of town.

The **Telgua** office is at the junction of 8 Av and 10 C (daily 7am–midnight) though you'll find the best international rates at Comunitel at 7C and 5 Av (daily 8am–10pm); the best **Internet** café in town is *Cafenet* at 13 C and 6 Av (daily 9am–9pm). There are a number of **banks** in Puerto Barrios: you'll find Lloyds Bank on the corner of 7 Av and 15 C (Mon–Fri 9am–4pm, Sat 9am–1pm), Banco G&T Continental (for Mastercard) at 7 C and 6 Av (Mon–Fri 9am–7pm, Sat 9am–1pm), and Banco Industrial (with a 24hr Visa-friendly ATM) at 7 Av and 7 C. The **post office** is at 6 C and 6 Av (Mon–Fri 8am–4.30pm).

### Accommodation

Cheap **hotels** are plentiful in Puerto Barrios and, in amongst the squalor, there is a slice of Caribbean charm. This is a very hot and sticky town so you'll definitely need a fan or a/c in your room.

**Hotel Caribeña**, 4 Av between 10 and 11 calles (☎948 0384). This large friendly place has very good value rooms, with doubles, triples and quadruples available. Friendly management and a quality seafood restaurant which also does cheap breakfasts. ②.

**Hotel Cayos del Diablo**, across the bay, reached by a regular free boat service from the jetty (in Guatemala City ☎333 4633). Lovely Best Western owned hideaway hotel, discreetly set above a secluded beach. Beautiful thatched cabaña accommodation, swimming pool, a good restaurant, tennis courts and kayaks available for rent. The definitive luxury option on this stretch of coastline, with special packages available. ⑨.

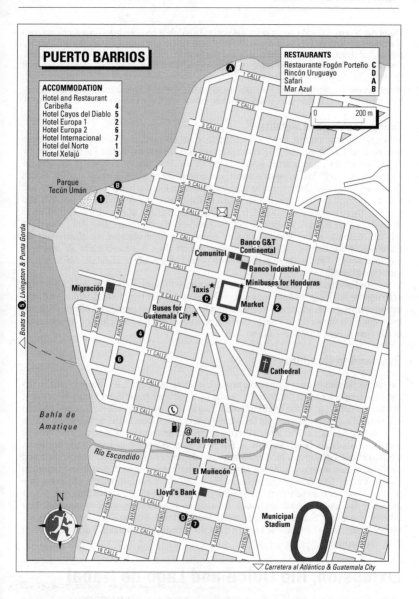

**PUERTO BARRIOS**

**ACCOMMODATION**
| | |
|---|---|
| Hotel and Restaurant Caribeña | 4 |
| Hotel Cayos del Diablo | 5 |
| Hotel Europa 1 | 2 |
| Hotel Europa 2 | 6 |
| Hotel Internacional | 7 |
| Hotel del Norte | 1 |
| Hotel Xelajú | 3 |

**RESTAURANTS**
| | |
|---|---|
| Restaurante Fogón Porteño | C |
| Rincón Uruguayo | D |
| Safari | A |
| Mar Azul | B |

0    200 m

Parque Tecún Umán

Boats to Lívingston & Punta Gorda

Banco G&T Continental

Comunitel

Banco Industrial

Migración

Taxis

Minibuses for Honduras

Buses for Guatemala City

Market

Cathedral

Bahía de Amatique

Café Internet

Río Escondido

El Muñecón

Lloyd's Bank

Municipal Stadium

N

Carretera al Atlántico & Guatemala City

**Hotel Europa 2**, 3 Av and 12 C (☎948 1292). Ideally placed for the ferry to Lívingston, this is a clean, safe, friendly place and all rooms have fan and private shower. Good prices for single travellers. An almost identical twin, *Hotel Europa 1*, is at 8 Av and 8 C (☎948 0127). Both ③.

**Hotel Internacional**, 7 Av and 16 C (☎948 0367). Very well priced motel-style set-up, with a small, heat-busting swimming pool. Rooms all have private shower and TV, and come with a choice of either a/c or fan. ③/④.

**Hotel del Norte**, 7 C and 1 Av (☎ & fax 948 0087). An absolute gem of a hotel – a magnificent colonial time-warp built entirely from wood. The clapboard rooms aren't especially comfortable or very private, but there is a nice swimming pool, and the location, overlooking the Caribbean, is magnificent. Best of all is the incredibly classy, mahogany-panelled restaurant and bar – though the food doesn't quite match the decor. ③–⑤.

**Hotel Xelajú**, 9 C, between 6 and 7 avenidas (☎948 0482). Though it looks a little rough from the outside, this reasonable budget place is safe, has clean rooms, and doesn't allow visiting señoritas. ②/③.

### Eating, drinking and nightlife

When it comes to **eating**, there is an abundance of cheap **comedores** around the market, such as *Cafesama* and *El Punto*, although the *Restaurant Fogón Porteño*, close by on 6 Av and 9 C, has a nicer setting. One of the best places in town is the *Rincón Uruguayo* (closed Mon), where meat is cooked on a giant *parrilla* (grill), South American style, and there are also vegetarian dishes like barbecued spring onions and *papas asados*. It's a ten-minute walk south of the centre at 7 Av and 16 C. For fish and seafood there's plenty of choice: try *Safari*, ten minutes north of the centre on 5 Avenida, which is good, if a little pricey, and serves huge portions; *Mar Azul*, also right on the seafront, at the end of 6 Calle, which is a little cheaper; or *Restaurant La Caribeña*, 4 Av between 10 and 11 calles, which does a superb *caldo de mariscos* (seafood soup). Finally, there is the unique period charm of the *Hotel del Norte* restaurant (see above).

Puerto Barrios also has more than its fair share of **bars**, pool halls and nightclubs, offering the full range of late-night sleaze. None of these is hard to find, with a lot of the action centring around 6 and 7 avenidas and 6 and 7 calles. **Reggae** and **punta rock** are the sounds on the street in Puerto Barrios, and you'll catch a fair selection at weekends in the *Bric a Brac Disco* on 7 C and 7 Av.

## Overland to Honduras

Getting to Honduras from Puerto Barrios is now straightforward, and the previous struggle (the jungle route) through the swamps of Caribbean coast is no longer necessary. Minibuses depart from the marketplace in Puerto Barrios every half-hour or so between 6.30am and 4.30pm, and head, via the small town of Entre Ríos, to the new Arizona bridge over the Río Motagua (1hr) where there's a new Guatemalan **immigration** point (where there's an unofficial US$1 "exit tax"). You then have to catch a pick-up to the border at Corinto inside Honduras a further 8km away, where there's Honduran immigration and plenty of money changers offering fairly reasonable rates. Buses depart from Corinto to Puerto Cortés (2hr 30min) every hour and a half via the pretty village of Omoa (see p.503). If you set out early from Puerto Barrios, you'll get to San Pedro Sula (see p.496) the same day, and it's certainly possible to make an afternoon flight out to one of the Bay Islands. San Pedro Sula is extremely well connected with Puerto Cortés by Citul buses (every 30min 5am–7.30pm; 1hr 15min); the Citul terminal is located just across the plaza from immigration.

# Lívingston, Río Dulce and Lago de Izabal

At the mouth of the Río Dulce and only accessible by boat, **LÍVINGSTON** is a very funky town that not only enjoys a superb setting but also offers a unique fusion of Guatemalan and Caribbean culture, where marimba mixes with Marley. Along with several other villages in Central America, Lívingston provides the focus for the displaced **Garífuna** or black Carib people, who are now strung out along the Caribbean coast between southern Belize and northern Nicaragua. Their history begins on the island of

△ Siete Altares

**LÍVINGSTON**

0    100 m

**ACCOMMODATION**
Hotel California       2
Hotel Caribe          7
Hotel Casa Rosada     6
Hotel Doña Alida      3
Hotel Garífuna        1
Hotel El Viajero      8
Hotel Vista al Mar    4
Tucán Dugú            5

**RESTAURANTS & CAFÉS**
Tiburón Gato          C
Margot                B
Bahía Azul            D
Happy Fish            E
Ubafu                 A

Río Crique

Misión
Popular

Barique's
Place

Bancafé

Immigration

St Vincent in 1635, where their shipwrecked African slave ancestors intermarried with native Carib islanders. In 1795 they rebelled against British rule, and were resettled on the island of Roatán, off Honduras, from where they migrated to the mainland (see p.289). To a lesser extent, Lívingston also acts as a focal point for the Q'eqchi' Maya, many of whom moved into the area to escape the fighting during the guerrilla war.

Lívingston is undoubtedly one of the most fascinating places in Guatemala and many visitors find the languid rhythm of life here hypnotic. The town is just as popular with weekending Guatemalans as it is with international travellers, and offers a welcome break from mainstream Guatemalan culture. Carib **food** is generally excellent and more varied than the usual comedor dishes, and Garífuna punta rock and reggae make a pleasant listening diversion from the standard merengue beat.

While there's not really that much to do in town itself other than relaxing in local style, there are a few places nearby that are worth a visit. The local **beaches**, though safe for swimming, are not of the Caribbean dream variety, but the wonderful white-sand **Playa Blanca**, fringed with coconut palms, is a short trip away, visitable only on a tour (US$10 per person, see travel agents below). Women should note that it is not safe to walk alone along the local beaches, as a number of rapes have been reported in recent years.

The most popular trip out of town is to **Las Siete Altares**, a group of waterfalls about 5km to the northeast. There have been sporadic **attacks on tourists** walking to the falls, and though incidents have diminished in recent years, you should ask about the current situation before setting out; if you decide to go, don't take anything of value. The safest option is to hire a local guide or visit as part of a tour (see below). If you decide to go it alone, continue down the street past the *Ubafu* bar and turn right by the *African Place* hotel to the beach, then follow the sand away from town. After a couple of kilometres, wade across a small river and, just before the beach eventually peters out, take a path to the left. Follow this inland and you'll soon reach the first of the falls; to reach the others, scramble up, and follow the water. All of the falls are idyllic places to swim, but the highest one is the best of all.

## Arrival and information

The only way to get to Lívingston is **by boat**, either from Puerto Barrios, the Río Dulce, Belize, or, occasionally, from Omoa in Honduras. Lívingston is a small place with only a handful of streets, and you can see most of what there is to see in an hour or so. You'll arrive at the main dock on the south side of town; straight ahead, up the hill, is the main drag with most of the restaurants, bars and shops. The **immigration office** (daily 7am–9pm) is on the left as you walk up the hill, a block or so before the *Hotel Río Dulce*.

Exotic Travel (☎947 0049; *kjchew@hotmail.com*), in the same building as the *Bahía Azul* restaurant, and Happy Fish (☎ 902 7143) just down the road, are the best **travel agents** in town. The helpful owners will arrange a variety of **trips** around the area: up the Río Dulce (US$9); along the coast to the lovely white-sand beach of Playa Blanca (US$10); to the Sapodilla Cayes off Belize (see p.309) for **snorkelling** (US$30); and to the Punta Manabique reserve for game **fishing** (US$14). All these trips only depart if there are sufficient people; sign up early and be prepared to wait a day or two.

For **changing money**, try the Banco de Comercio, down the road to the left as you walk up the hill from the docks; Bancafé on the main drag, or the Almacen Koo Wong in the centre of town on Sundays. **Telgua** is on the right, up the main street from the docks (daily 7am–midnight), and the **post office** is next door. There are several **Internet** facilities in Lívingston, try @ or Happy Fish on the main drag, or Explorer Travel which is just west of the dock – rates hover around US$6 an hour.

Scheduled **boats** leave for Puerto Barrios daily at 5am and 2pm (1hr 30min), supplemented by **speedboats**, which leave when full – roughly half-hourly between 6.30am and 5.30pm (25 min). There are also boats to Punta Gorda in **Belize** on Tuesdays and Fridays at 8am (1hr) or to Omoa in **Honduras** when there are sufficient numbers (US$35 per person, min 6 persons; 2hr 30min). Several companies, among them Exotic Travel and Happy Fish, run morning boat trips (US$9 per person) up the Río Dulce, but Explorer Travels are a little more leisurely than most, with greater opportunities to soak up the scenery.

## Accommodation

There is a pretty decent selection of **hotels** in town and though rooms fill up at weekends and during holidays, you should always be able to find a bed.

**Hotel California**, turn left just before the *Bahía Azul* restaurant. Clean hotel painted a very vivid green. Reasonable rooms all with private bath. ②.

**Hotel Caribe**, along the shore to the left of the dock as you face the town (☎948 0053). Basic, budget hotel with bare rooms, some with private shower and fan. ①/②.

**Hotel Casa Rosada**, about 300m left of the dock (☎ & fax 947 0303, fax 947 0304, *info@hotelcasarosada.com*). Very relaxing and charming American-owned establishment, with a harbourfront plot and lush, spacious grounds. The small but cheery wooden cabins have nice hand-painted touches but are a little overpriced (and lack private bath); alternatively there are newly built, very smart duplex bungalows with private bath. Excellent vegetarian meals. ④–⑥.

**Hotel Doña Alida**, turn right immediately after the *Tucán Dugú*, 250m to the north (☎ & fax 947 0027, *hotelalida@hotmail.com*). Selection of spacious modern rooms, some with excellent sea views, in a quiet cliffside location, with a little beach below. Very welcoming owners. ④.

**Hotel Garífuna**, turn left off the main street towards the *Ubafu* bar, then first right (☎948 1091, fax 948 0184). Squeaky-clean, locally owned guest house with good-value, secure and spotless rooms, all with fan and private shower. ②.

**Hotel El Viajero**, turn left after the dock, past the *Hotel Caribe*. A good choice for backpackers, this is a safe budget hotel with clean if slightly shabby rooms, all with fan and some with private bath, set off a thin strip of garden. There's a shoreside snack bar, too. ②.

**Hotel Vista al Mar**, about 350m left of the dock (☎947 0131, fax 947 0134). Secure, simple wooden huts, three with private bath, set close to sea and run by amiable locals. ②/③.

**Tucán Dugú**, first on the right, uphill from the jetty (☎947 0072, fax 947 0614, *www.tukanis.com.gt*). Lívingston's only luxury hotel, with attractive modern rooms set above the bay, a pleasant bar, swimming pool and gardens. ⑦/⑧.

## Eating and drinking

There are plenty of places to **eat** in Lívingston, two of the best for local food being *Tiburón Gato* and *Margot* (where Mama Helén serves up a mean tapado). For a memorable **vegetarian** meal, check out the *Casa Rosada* (see above), though it's not priced for budget travellers. The *Bahía Azul*, on the main street, is probably the most popular place in town, with an excellent terrace for watching Lívingston streetlife. There are also plenty of cheap, small comedores on the main street, all selling decent **fried fish**: try *Comedor Coni* or the *Lívingston*.

For evening **entertainment** there are lots of groovy bars, of which *Ubafu* is usually the most lively, movies at the *Black Sheep* next to the *Bahía Azul*, and a disco on the beach where you'll hear the deep bass rhythms of Jamaican reggae and pure Garífuna punta rock.

# The Río Dulce

Another very good reason for coming to Lívingston is to venture up the **Río Dulce**, a truly spectacular trip that eventually leads to the town of the same name about 30km upriver. From Lívingston the river heads into a system of **gorges**, between sheer rock faces 100m or so in height, with a wall of tropical vegetation and cascading vines clinging to the sides. Here and there you might see some white herons or flocks of squawking parakeets. Six kilometres from Lívingston there's a delightful river tributary, the Río Tatín, which some boatmen will venture up if you pressurize them, where there's a good guest house, the *Finca Tatín* (☎902 0831, *www.geocities.com/fincatatin/index.htm*; ②), set in dense shoreside jungle. Run by hospitable Italians, the four wooden huts are very basic, but the remote, peaceful location is the real draw, and there's excellent healthy food, kayaks for hire, walking trails and Spanish classes available.

Continuing up the Río Dulce for another kilometre or so to the west, you'll pass an excellent place for a swim, where warm sulphurous waters emerge from the base of the cliff. Past here, the river opens up into the **Golfete** lake, surrounded by swampy lowlands, the north shore of which has been designated the **Biotopo de Chocón Machacas** (daily 7am–4pm; US$5), designed to protect the **manatee** – though the huge mammals are extremely timid and you'll be very lucky to see one. The reserve also protects the forest that still covers much of the lake's shore, and there are some specially cut trails where you might catch sight of a bird or two, or, if you've plenty of time and patience, even a tapir or jaguar. Heading on upstream, the river closes in again and passes the marina and bridge at the squalid town known as **Río Dulce** (or sometimes Fronteras). This part of the Río Dulce is a favourite playground for wealthy Guatemalans, with boats and hotels that would put parts of California to shame. The area is also popular with European and North American yachties because of its sheltered waters, its stores and its repair workshops. The road for Petén crosses the river here and the boat trip comes to an end, although you should certainly include a stop at the *castillo*, on the other side of the bridge, if it's re-opened. West of here is the **Lago de Izabal**, a vast freshwater expanse bordered by isolated villages, swamps, hot springs, waterfalls, caves, and the Bocas del Polochic reserve (see p.431). There a useful **website** covering the Río Dulce region, *www.mayaparadise.com;* with good links and listings.

## Río Dulce town

The town of **RÍO DULCE** is little more than a truck stop, where traffic for Petén pauses before the long stretch to Flores. Río Dulce is actually the new name for a couple of older settlements, Fronteras to the north and El Relleno to the south, which have been connected by a monstrous concrete road bridge, obliterating almost any sense of tranquillity in this formerly beautiful area. The road is lined with cheap comedores and stores and you can pick up buses here in either direction. Though the urban ugliness of Río Dulce is initially very offputting, if you escape the immediate area around the bridge you'll find plenty to explore: the Río Dulce gorge itself, the *castillo* close by, the Biotopo Chocón Machacas nature reserve and, venturing further west, Lago de Izabal.

A good **place to stay** for those on a tight budget is *Hotel Backpackers* (☎208 1779, fax 331 9408, *casaguatemala@guate.net*; ①–③), a budget set-up underneath the bridge, on the south side, with dorm beds, private doubles and hammock space. The hotel is owned by the nearby Casa Guatemala children's home, and many of the young staff are former residents. It's a good place to pick up information, and there's a noticeboard with lots of good stuff about yacht crewing opportunities and sailing courses; they also rent canoes. *Hotel Río Dulce*, on the north side of the bridge (☎930 3179; ③), is a comfortable place with spotless double rooms with fans and showers. Very close by, under the bridge, *Bruno's* (☎930 5174, *rio@guate.net*; ④–⑥) offers either modern, comfortable, overpriced rooms with terraces, or less attractive, but cheaper accommodation; there's also a swimming pool and bar-restaurant. *Hacienda Tijax*, two minutes by water taxi from the bus stop on the north side of the bridge (☎902 0858, *www.tijax.com*; camping US$2 per person, rooms ③, cabins ④, bungalows ⑥), is a working teak and rubber farm with a pleasant lakeside plot and tasty, slightly pricey food, hiking trails and horse riding.

As for **restaurants**, *Río Bravo*, on the north side of the bridge, is the best place to meet other travellers (and yachties), eat pizza or pasta and drink the night away – you can also make radio contact with most places around the river and lake from here. *Bruno's* serves up international food and offers the chance to catch up with the latest news and North American sports events – it's very popular with sailing fraternity – they have **Internet** facilities here too. For cheap grub, there's a strip of pretty undistinguished comedores on the main road close to the bus stop. There are three **banks** in Río Dulce that will change travellers' cheques.

**Moving on** from Río Dulce, there are buses every half-hour or so to Guatemala City, and to Flores via Poptún until around 6pm. If you're heading towards Puerto Barrios, take the first bus or minibus to La Ruidosa junction (every 30 min) and pick up a connection there. Heading to El Estor, there are buses around the lakeshore every two hours (1hr 45min) between 6am and 4pm; they all pass the hot springs and Boquerón canyon en route, and some continue on up the Polochic valley towards Cobán and the Verapaces. If you're heading for Lívingston via the Río Dulce gorge, the lancha **boat**

captains will quickly find you; services do not run to a fixed schedules but there are several daily (US$10), mostly in the afternoon. Finally, there are **flights** connecting Río Dulce with Guatemala City on Fridays, Saturdays and Sundays. Telephone Taca (☎334 7722) for details, but be warned that cancellations are frequent.

Río Dulce is also the base for *That*, a remarkable nineteen-metre (62ft) trimaran operated by ATI Divers (☎ & fax 762 2646, *atidivers@yahoo.com*) of Santa Cruz, Lago de Atitlán (see p.389). Wonderful seven-day sailing trips through the Río Dulce gorge to the Belize cayes cost US$390 for snorkellers and US$490 for divers, including all equipment rental, tanks and meals.

## Castillo de San Felipe

Structurally damaged by a large earthquake in July 1997, the **Castillo de San Felipe**, 1km upstream from the bridge, was closed to visitors at the time of writing, but should reopen in the next few years. Looking like a miniature medieval castle and marking the entrance to Lago de Izabal, the *castillo* is a tribute to the audacity of British pirates, who used to sail up the Río Dulce to raid supplies and harass mule trains. The Spanish were so infuriated by this that they built the fortress to seal off the entrance to the lake, and a chain was strung across the river. If it's open (entrance will be US$1.30) you'll find there's a maze of tiny rooms and staircases, plenty of canons and panoramic views of the lake.

A kilometre from the castle, close to the waterside village of **SAN FELIPE**, is the *Rancho Escondido* (☎ & fax 369 2681; ②/③), a friendly American-Guatemalan guest house and backpackers' retreat, with hammock space and a restaurant. If you call or radio from the *Río Bravo* or *Bruno's*, they'll come and pick you up.

# Lago de Izabal

Beyond the *castillo*, the broad expanse of **Lago de Izabal** opens up before you, with great views of the highlands beyond the distant shores. Most guest houses can arrange a tour around the lake with a local boatman from Río Dulce town, or you can explore the north shore easily along the new road to El Estor. Some 25km from Río Dulce, the **hot spring waterfall** (daily 8am–6pm, US$0.65) 300m north of the road is one of Guatemala's most remarkable natural phenomena. Bathtub-temperature spring water cascades into pools cooled by a chilly flow of fresh river water, creating a sublime steamy spa-like environment where it's easy to soak and bathe away an afternoon. Above the waterfall are a series of caves whose interiors are crowded with extraordinary shapes and colours – made even more memorable by the fact that you have to swim by torchlight to see them (bring your own torch). Two kilometres south of the waterfall, the *Finca el Paraíso* **hotel** (☎949 7122; ⑤/⑥) sits on the waterfront, with two rows of large, comfortable, but rarely occupied cabañas and a reasonable, if pricey restaurant. The hotel enjoys a delightfully peaceful location and there's good swimming from the black-sand beach. Buses and pick ups between Río Dulce and El Estor pass the hot springs and hotel hourly in both directions.

Continuing west along the lakeshore it's a further 7km to the **Boquerón canyon**, completely hidden yet just 500m from the road. Near-vertical cliffs soar to over 250m above the Río Sauce which flows through the bottom of the startling jungle-clad gorge, the river bed plotted with colossal boulders. To see Boquerón, you'll have to employ Hugo, a campesino-cum-boatman who lives at the base of the canyon, at the end of a signposted track from the main road, who will paddle you upstream in his logwood canoe for a small fee. The return trip takes around thirty minutes, though it's possible to continue exploring Boquerón – which extends for a further 5km – on foot if you have sturdy footwear and don't mind a scramble.

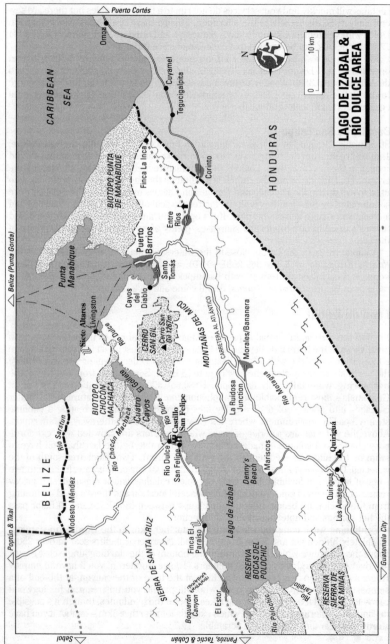

LAGO DE IZABAL &
RÍO DULCE AREA

## El Estor

Heading west beyond Boquerón, it's just 6km to the sleepy lakeside town of **EL ESTOR**. Allegedly named by English pirates who came up the Río Dulce to buy supplies at "The Store" of Lago de Izabal, it's an easy-going, friendly place which was briefly energized in the 1970s when a vast nickel plant flourished just to the west, but quickly settled back into provincial stupor when the commodity price plummeted. Though El Estor remains off the tourist trail, the completion of the paved road to Río Dulce has helped revive local optimism that the town can now capitalize on the vast ecotourism potential of the region.

Considering the size of the place, there's an excellent choice of quality budget and mid-range **accommodation**. The most atmospheric hotel is undoubtedly *Hotel Vista del Lago* (☎949 7205; ③), a beautiful colonial-style wooden building by the dock, claimed by the owners to be the original store that gave the town its name; it offers clean rooms with private bath, the second-floor ones boasting superb views of the lake. A block up, the *Hotel Villela* at 6 Av 2–06 (②) is a reasonable budget deal, its rooms, some with private shower, surrounding a pretty garden. On the east side of the plaza, the *Posada de Don Juan* (②) has large rooms around a grassy courtyard and well-maintained bathrooms, while just north of the plaza, *Hotel Central* (☎949 7244; ②) has pleasant, clean, modern rooms, each with private bath and fan. For a really cheap deal, the *Hospedaje Santa Clara* at 5 Av 2–11 (☎948 7244; ①/②) has basic, clean rooms, some with their own shower. Finally, a kilometre east of the centre, in a prime, tranquil lakeside plot, the bungalows at the *Hotel Ecológico Cabañas del Lago* (☎ & fax 949 7245; ④) are very comfortable, spacious and attractive – Hugo, the owner, will take you there if you drop in at his restaurant in the plaza.

For good inexpensive snacks and breakfasts try the friendly, clean *Cafeteria Santa Clave*, three blocks west of the plaza at 3C 7–75, or *Hugo's Restaurant*, on the main plaza, for steaks and burgers. For something a little more substantial head for the lakeside *Restaurant Chaabil* where you'll pay extra for the location. There's not a lot to do in El Estor, although it does have a friendly, relaxed atmosphere, particularly in the warmth of the evening when the streets are full of activity. Don't miss the pool in the plaza, which harbours fish, turtles and alligators. You could spend a delightful few days exploring the surrounding area, much of which remains undisturbed. There are **bikes** to rent at 6 Av 4–26. The best contacts for **tours** of the area are Hugo at *Hugo's Restaurant*, or Oscar Paz, who runs the *Hotel Vista del Lago*, an enthusiastic promoter of the area who will arrange a boat and guide to explore any of the surrounding countryside, go fishing in the lake or visit the hot springs at *Finca Paraíso*.

## Reserva Bocas del Polochic

Encompassing a substantial slice of lowland jungle on the west side of the lake, the **Bocas del Polochic** nature reserve is one of the richest wetland habitats in Guatemala. The green maze of swamp, marsh and forest harbours at least 224 different species of birds, including golden-fronted woodpeckers, Aztec parakeets and keel-billed toucans. It's also rich in mammals, including howler monkeys, which you're virtually guaranteed to see (and hear), plus rarely encountered manatees and tapirs. There's good accommodation next to the tiny Q'eqchi' village of **SELEMPÍM** in the heart of the reserve – the large mosquito-screened wooden house with bunk beds is managed by the project (US$12 per person per day including three substantial meals) and provides villagers with employment. Locals also lead walking trails up into the foothills of the Sierra de Las Minas and conduct kayak tours of the river delta. The drawback is that visitors wanting to get to the reserve have to pay for the fuel costs of the lancha boat – there's no road system. This can amount to US$35 for a day trip, or as much as US$80 (return) to get to Selempím, though costs are reduced considerably if you can get a group together. To **get to** the reserve contact Defensores de la

Naturaleza at 5 Av and 2 C, El Estor (☎949 7237, *rbocas@defensores.org.gt*), which orga-nizes excellent tours into the heart of the refuge and manages the accommodation at Selempím. To visit the zone nearest to El Estor, contact Hugo or Oscar in El Estor (see above), both of whom run good excursions.

# The eastern highlands

The **eastern highlands**, lying to the southeast of the capital, have to rank as the least-visited part of Guatemala. The population is almost entirely latinized, speaking Spanish and wearing Western clothes, although many are pure Maya by blood. The ladinos of the east have a reputation for behaving like cowboys and supporting right-wing politics – violent demonstrations of macho pride are not uncommon. Not surprisingly, the mil-itary has traditionally recruited much of its key personnel here.

The landscape here lacks the immediate appeal of the western highlands: the moun-tains are lower and the volcanoes less symmetrical. There are plenty of blunted peaks to explore, however, and if you want to climb one, the **Volcán de Ipala** is the best to make for, with an idyllic crater lake at its summit. The region's towns are almost all pret-ty featureless and perennially hot and dusty, so you're unlikely to want to hang around for long. **Esquipulas** is worth a visit, though, for its colossal church, the most impor-tant pilgrimage site in Central America. You can head into either Honduras and El Salvador from here, though if you're making your way to the ruins of Copán there's a quicker route via neighbouring **Chiquimula**.

## Chiquimula

Set to one side of the broad Río San José valley, the town of **CHIQUIMULA** is an unat-tractive, bustling ladino stronghold surrounded by parched near-desert cacti-pierced terrain. If you've just arrived from Honduras, things only get better from here. The town has long been an important transport terminal, but there is little to see here apart from a massive ruined colonial church on the edge of town beside the highway. Most travellers are in town to get to Honduras via the top-drawer Maya site of Copán, just over the border (see p.486).

Everything you're likely to need in Chiquimula is east of the **plaza**, and close to the bus terminal, on 3 Calle, which leads towards the main highway. Of the **hotels**, *Pensión Hernández* at 3 C 7–41 (☎ & fax 942 0708, *hotelh@guate.net*; ②/③) is the first place to try, with plenty of very clean, simple rooms, all with fan and some with television and private shower. It has safe parking, a small pool and the owner speaks good English. A little further down the road, at 3 C 8–30, *Hotel Central* (☎942 6352; ③) has five pleasant rooms all with private bath and cable TV, while *Pensión España*, at 3 C 7–81 (①), is very cheap and basic. A couple of blocks south from here, *Hotel Posada Don Adán* at 8 Av 4–30 (☎942 0549; ③) is comfortable, if old-fashioned; most of its eighteen large rooms have a/c and cable TV and there's parking here too.

When it comes to **eating**, there are plenty of good, inexpensive comedores in and around the **market**, which is centred on 3 C and 8 Av, as well as *Magic Burger* and *Cafe Paíz*, both on 3 Calle, for predictable fast food and good fruit juices. For something a little more ambitious, try *Bella Roma*, 7 Av 5–31, which specializes in pizza and pasta. *Las Vegas*, on 7 Avenida off the plaza, with fairly high prices and garish decor, is where the town's upwardly mobile gather – you can forget the cocktails here, but the food's reasonable. Otherwise the only evening entertainment in Chiquimula is at the Cine Liv on the plaza.

For **changing money** there's a branch of the Banco G&T Continental at 7 Av 4–75 (Mon–Fri 9am–7pm, Sat 10am–2pm) and a Bancafé on the north side of the plaza (Mon–Fri 9am–7pm, Sat 9.30am–1.30pm) with a cashpoint that accepts Visa cards. You can also cash dollars safely at Azujey, the largest of the sombrero shops in the daily market, which is always worth a browse in its own right for its kitsch selection of cowboy gear and leather-ware. There's an **Internet** café, *Email Center* at 6 Av 4–51 (daily 9am–9pm) and Telgua is on the corner of the plaza (daily 7am–midnight). The **bus terminal** is at 1A C, between 10 and 11 avenidas, midway between the plaza and the highway. There are frequent **buses** from here to Guatemala City (every 30min 3.30am–6pm; 3hr 30min), Esquipulas (every 15min 5am–7pm; 1hr), Jalapa via Ipala (hourly 6am–4pm; 3hr) and Puerto Barrios (hourly; 3hr). For Copán, there are hourly buses to the border at El Florido (1hr 30min).

## The Volcán de Ipala

Reached down a side road off the main highway between Chiquimula and Esquipulas, the **Ipala volcano** (1650m) may seem a little disappointing at first, as it looks rather like a rounded hill, unlike the near-perfect conical peaks of the western highlands. However, it's well worth heading for if you yearn for some real solitude. Very few visitors make it out this way and the chances are that if you visit on a weekday you'll have the place to yourself. The eroded cone, inactive for millennia, is now filled by a beautiful little **crater lake**, ringed by dense tropical forest. You can walk round the entire lake in a couple of hours. The lake waters are said to contain a unique species of fish, the *mojarra*, with six prominent spines on its back. It's very peaceful up here and the lake makes a wonderful place to **camp**, though you'll have to bring all your own supplies as there are no shops or other facilities. To **get to** the lake it is possible to climb the volcano from the village of Ipala itself, a distance of around 10km, but the easiest ascent (2hr) is from the south, setting out from close to the village of Agua Blanca (see below). If you have your own transport, head for the tiny settlement of Sauce, at Km 26.5 on the Ipala–Agua Blanca road, park close to the small store and follow the dirt track up to the summit.

**AGUA BLANCA** is a ladino moustache-and-cowboy-hat kind of place, with a good little hospedaje, the *Maylin* (①), and a couple of comedores, the best of which is the *El Viajero*. It's a pretty straightforward route to the lake; ask the way to the Finca el Paxte and continue to the top from there. The village of **IPALA**, 20km to the north of Agua Blanca down a new sealed road, is connected by bus with Jutiapa to the south, Jalapa to the west, Chiquimula to the north and Esquipulas to the east. The village itself is a pretty forlorn place with a few shops and three hotels, the best of which is the basic *Hotel Ipala Real* (☎923 7107; ②), where rooms have en-suite showers and toilets; cable TV is available too.

## Esquipulas

The final town on this eastern highway, **ESQUIPULAS**, has a single point of interest: it harbours the most important Catholic shrine in Central America, a carving of the **Black Christ** that dates from colonial times. It's a beautiful ride from Chiquimula through the hills, beneath craggy outcrops and forested peaks, emerging suddenly at the lip of a huge bowl-shaped valley, with Esquipulas itself below.

The town is entirely dominated by the four perfectly white domes of the **church**, brilliantly floodlit at night. Beneath these the rest of the town is a messy sprawl of cheap hotels, souvenir stalls and restaurants. The year-round pilgrimage has generated numerous sidelines, creating a booming resort where people from all over Central America come to worship, eat, drink and relax, in a bizarre combination of holy devotion and indulgence. The principal day of **pilgrimage**, when the religious significance of the shrine is at its most potent, is January 15. Even the smallest villages will save enough money to send a representative or two on this occasion, filling the town to bursting point. The town has also played an important role in modern-day politics: it was here that the first **peace accord** initiatives to end the civil wars in El Salvador, Nicaragua and Guatemala were signed in 1987.

As a religious shrine, Esquipulas probably predates the Conquest. When the Spanish arrived, the Maya chief surrendered rather than risk bloodshed; the grateful Spaniards named the town in his honour and commissioned the famed colonial sculptor Quirio Cataño to carve an image of Christ for the church. Perhaps in order to make it more appealing to the local Maya, he chose to carve it from balsam, a dark wood. In 1737, the bishop of Guatemala, Pardo de Figueroa, was cured of a chronic ailment on a trip to Esquipulas, and consequently ordered the construction of a new church. This was completed in 1758, and his body was buried beneath the altar.

Inside the church today there's a constant scurry of hushed devotion amid clouds of smoke and incense. In the nave, pilgrims approach the image on their knees, while others light candles, mouth supplications or simply stand in silent groups. The image itself is approached by a side entrance; join the queue to shuffle past beneath it and pause briefly in front before being shoved on by the crowds behind. Back outside you'll find yourself among swarms of souvenir and relic hawkers, and pilgrims who, duty done, are ready to head off to eat and drink away the rest of their stay.

## Practicalities

When it comes to staying in Esquipulas, you'll find yourself amongst hundreds of visitors whatever the time of year. **Hotels** probably outnumber private homes but bargains are in short supply and the bulk of the budget places are grubby and bare. Prices are rarely quoted in writing and are always negotiable, depending on the flow of pilgrims. Avoid Saturday nights, when room prices double.

Many of the **budget** options are clustered together in the streets off the main road, 11 C. The family-run *Hotel Villa Edelmira* (②–③) is one of the best, or look for a room at *La Favorita* on 10 C and 2 Av (②). For a touch more luxury, head for 2 Avenida, beside the church, where you'll find the *Hotel Los Ángeles* (☎943 1254; ③), whose rooms have private bath and cable TV, and the *Hotel Esquipulao* (④), a cheaper annexe of the *Hotel Payaquí* (☎943 1143, fax 943 1371; ⑤), which has rooms with TV and fan, and a pool.

There are also dozens of **restaurants** and **bars**, most of them overpriced by Guatemalan standards. Breakfast is a bargain in Esquipulas; you shouldn't have to pay more than US$1.50 for a good feed. There's a decent range of lunch specials later on, though dinner can be expensive. The *Hacienda Steak House*, a block from the plaza at 2 Av and 10 C, is one of the smartest places in town, while many of the cheaper places are on 11 Calle and the surrounding streets. Banco Industrial has a branch with a 24-hour ATM at 9 C and 3 Av, and there's also a Banco G&T Continental (Mon–Fri 9am–7pm, Sat 10am–2pm) almost opposite.

Rutas Orientales runs a superb hourly **bus** service between Guatemala City and Esquipulas; its office is on the main street at 11 C and 1 Av. There are also buses across the highlands to Ipala and regular minibuses to the borders with **El Salvador** (every 30min; 6am–4pm; 1hr) and **Honduras** at Aguacaliente (every 30min 6am–5.30pm; 30min). If you want to get to the ruins of Copán, you'll need to catch a bus to Chiquimula and change there for the El Florido border post (see p.485). There's a **Honduran consulate** (Mon–Fri 8am–1pm & 3–6pm) in the *Hotel Payaquí*, beside the church.

# THE VERAPACES

The twin departments of the Verapaces presently attract only a trickle of tourists, yet they harbour some of the most spectacular mountain scenery and highland towns in Guatemala. Though both Alta (upper) and Baja (lower) Verapaz border the western highlands, their climates are distinctly different. In the south, the low-altitude terrain of **Baja Verapaz** gets very little rainfall and largely consists of sparsely populated cactus country. To the north, the increasing altitude gradually traps more moisture and the mist-soaked hills around Cobán in **Alta Verapaz** are the wettest, greenest mountains in Guatemala. Locals say it rains for thirteen months a year.

Though Maya traditions and costume are less evident than in the mountains further west, if you've time to spare you'll find these highlands are astonishingly beautiful, with their unique limestone structure, moist, misty atmosphere and boundless fertility. The hub of the area and the capital of Alta Verapaz is **Cobán**, an attractive mountain town with some good accommodation, coffee houses and restaurants. It is a little subdued once the rain really settles in but it's still the best base for exploring the area, particularly in August, when it hosts the National Folklore Festival. In **Baja Verapaz**, the towns of **Salamá**, **Rabinal** and **Cubulco** also have famous fiestas where incredible costumes are worn and traditional dances performed. If you head out to the north of Cobán, you can reach the exquisite natural bathing pools of **Semuc Champey**, surrounded by lush tropical forest and fed by the azure waters of the Río Cahabón.

The **history** of the Verapaces is in many ways quite distinct from the rest of Guatemala. Long before the Conquest, local **Achi Maya** had earned themselves a unique reputation as the most bloodthirsty of all the tribes, said to sacrifice every prisoner that they took. Their greatest enemies were the **K'iche'**, with whom they were at war for a century. So ferocious were the Achi that not even the Spanish could contain them by force. Alvarado's army was unable to make any headway against them, and eventually he gave up trying to control the area, naming it *tierra de guerra*, the "land of war".

The Church, however, couldn't allow so many heathen souls to go to waste, and, under the leadership of **Fray Bartolomé de Las Casas**, they made a deal with the conquistadors. If Alvarado would agree to keep all armed men out of the area for five years, the priests would bring it under control. In 1537 Las Casas and three Dominican friars set out into the highlands, befriended the Achi chiefs, learnt the local dialects and translated devotional hymns. By 1538 they had made considerable progress and had converted large numbers of Maya. At the end of the five years, the famous and invincible Achi were transformed into Spanish subjects, and the king of Spain renamed the province Verapaz (True Peace).

Since the colonial era the Verapaces have remained isolated and, in many ways, independent. All their trade bypassed the capital, taking a direct route to the Caribbean along the Río Polochic and out through Lago de Izabal. The area really started to develop with the **coffee boom** at the turn of the century, when German immigrants flooded into the country to buy and run fincas, particularly around Cobán in Alta Verapaz. The Germans quickly prospered, exporting huge quantities of coffee back to Europe, until their expulsion during World War II, when the US insisted that Guatemala remove the enemy presence. Today, the Verapaces are still dominated by the huge coffee fincas and the wealthy families that own them, and there are also architectural hints of the Germanic influence here and there. Taken as a whole, however, the Verapaces remain very much indígena country: Baja Verapaz has a big **Achi** and a small **K'iche'** population around Rabinal, and in Alta Verapaz the Maya population is largely **Poqomchi'** and **Q'eqchi'**. The production of coffee and more recently the spice **cardamom** for the Middle Eastern market has cut deep into their land and their way of life, the fincas driving many people off prime territory and on to marginal plots. Though the people are predominantly Maya, traditional costume is worn less here than in the western highlands.

The northern, flat section of Alta Verapaz includes a slice of Petén rainforest, and in recent years Q'eqchi' Maya and landless Mestizos from the south have expanded into this region. Here they carve out sections of the forest and attempt to farm, a process which offers little security for the migrants and also threatens the future of the rainforest.

---

**MARKET DAYS IN THE VERAPACES**

| | |
|---|---|
| **Monday** | **Saturday** |
| Senahú; Tucurú. | Senahú. |
| **Tuesday** | **Sunday** |
| Chisec; El Chol; Cubulco; Lanquín; Purulhá; Rabinal; San Cristóbal Verapaz; San Jerónimo. | Chisec; Cubulco; Lanquín; Purulhá; Rabinal; Salamá; San Jerónimo; Santa Cruz; Tactic. |

---

The main **transport** route into the Verapaces climbs up from the El Rancho junction on the Carretera al Atlántico, past the turn-off at La Cumbre and skirts the Quetzal Sanctuary before arriving at Cobán – a journey very well served by frequent pullman buses. As all other routes in the region are unsealed and only covered by a limited service of second-class buses and pick-ups, the going can be slow.

# Baja Verapaz

The main approach to both departments is from the Carretera al Atlántico, where the road to the Verapaz highlands branches off at the **El Rancho** junction. This road, lined with scrub bush and cacti, climbs steadily into the hills, the dusty browns and dry yellows of the Motagua valley soon giving way to an explosion of greens as dense pine forests and alpine meadows grip the mountains. Some 48km beyond the junction is **La Cumbre de Santa Elena**, where the road for the main towns of Baja Verapaz turns off to the west, immediately starting to drop towards the floor of the **Salamá valley**. Surrounded by steep hillsides, with a level flood plain at its base, the valley appears entirely cut off from the outside world.

## Salamá, Rabinal and Cubulco

At the western end of the valley is **SALAMÁ**, capital of the department of Baja Verapaz. The town has a relaxed and prosperous air and, like many of the places out this way, its population is largely ladino. There's not much to do here other than browse in the Sunday market, though the crumbling colonial bridge on the edge of town and the fine old church, with its huge altars, darkened by age, are worth a look. The **fiesta** in Salamá runs from September 17 to 21. If you decide **to stay**, the pick of the hotels is the modern *Hotel Real Legendario* at 8 Av 3–57 (☎940 0187; ③), with very clean rooms, all with private bath, good beds and cable TV, or you could try the *Hotel Tezulutlán* just south of the plaza (☎940 1643; ③) as a reasonable alternative, though the rooms, set round a courtyard, are less attractive. *Pensión Juárez* (☎940 0055; ②), a good budget hotel at the end of 5 Calle, past the police station, is cheaper. For **eating**, try one of the places around the plaza: *El Ganadero* is the best restaurant and *Deli-Donus* scores for coffee and snacks. There's also a Bancafé (Mon–Fri 9am–5pm, Sat 9am–1pm) opposite the church that will cash dollars and travellers' cheques.

**RABINAL** is an hour or so from Salamá, another isolated farming town that's also dominated by a large colonial Baroque church. Here the proportion of indígena inhabitants is considerably higher, making both the Sunday market and the fiesta well worth a visit. Founded in 1537 by Bartolomé de Las Casas himself, Rabinal was the first of the settlements established during his peaceful conquest of the Achi nation. Sights are few in Rabinal itself, but beside the church the town's small **museum** (Mon–Fri

9am–4pm; free) is worth a visit, with exhibits on traditional medicinal practices, local arts and crafts and the impact of the civil war in the region – there were four massacres in 1982 alone in the Río Negro region north of the town. The hills around Rabinal are scattered with Maya ruins, including the remains of Cahyup 3km northwest of the plaza, a thirty-minute hike away.

Rabinal's **fiesta**, running from January 19 to 24, is renowned for its dances, many of them pre-colonial in origin. The most famous of these, an extended dance drama known as the "Rabinal Achí", re-enacts a battle between the Achí and the K'iche' tribes and is unique to the town, performed annually on January 23. Others include the *patzca*, a ceremony to call for good harvests, using masks that portray a swelling below the jaw, and wooden sticks engraved with serpents, birds and human heads. If you can't make it for the fiesta, the Sunday market is a good second-best. Rabinal has a reputation for producing high-quality artesanía, including carvings made from the *árbol del morro* (calabash tree) and traditional pottery. Of the several fairly basic **hotels** in Rabinal, the best is the *Posada San Pablo* at 3 Av 1–50 (①/②), a decent budget hotel with immaculate rooms, some with private bath. If it's full, try the *Hospedaje Caballeros*, 1 C 4–02 (①), or for somewhere really comfortable see if the new three-storey *Gran Hotel Rabinal Achí*, also on 1 Calle, due to open in late 2001, is operational yet; if it is, you'll find 36 comfortable rooms, a pool and a café. For an inexpensive **meal** try *Cafetería Mishell del Rosario* on 1 Calle behind the church. The Banrural at 1 C and 3 Av (Mon–Fri 8.30am–5pm, Sat 9am–1pm) will only cash dollars.

Another hour of rough road brings you down into the next valley and to **CUBULCO**, an isolated ladino town, surrounded on all sides by steep, forested mountains. Cubulco is again best visited for its **fiesta**, this being one of the few places where you can still see the **Palo Volador**, a pre-conquest ritual in which men throw themselves from a thirty-metre pole with a rope tied around their legs, spinning down towards the ground as the rope unravels, and hopefully landing on their feet. It's as dangerous as it looks: most of the dancers are blind drunk and deaths are not uncommon. The fiesta still goes on, though, as riotous as ever, with the main action taking place on July 25. The best place to stay is the *Hospedaje Pías* (①) next to the large *farmacia* in the centre of town, where some rooms have private bath. Avoid the smelly *Posada Morales* ①. There are several good **comedores** in the market, but the best place to eat is *La Fonda del Viajero* which serves up big portions of Guatemalan food at reasonable prices.

There are hourly **buses** from Guatemala City to Salamá and Rabinal from 17C and 11 Av in the capital, five daily continuing on to Cubulco. If you're only going as far as Salamá, there's a steady shuttle of minibuses to and from La Cumbre for connections with Pullman buses between Cobán and Guatemala City.

If you'd rather not leave the valley the same way that you arrived, there is another option. One bus a day, leaving Cubulco at around 9am, heads back to Rabinal and then, instead of heading for La Cumbre and the main road, turns to the south, crossing the spine of the Sierra de Chuacús and dropping directly down towards Guatemala City. The trip takes you over rough roads for at least eight hours, but the mountain views and the sense of leaving the beaten track help to take the pain out of it all.

# The Biotopo del Quetzal

Back on the main highway towards Alta Verapaz and Cobán, the road sweeps around endless tight curves below forested hillsides. Just before the village of Purulhá (Km 161) is the **Biotopo del Quetzal** (daily 7am–4pm; US$3.85), an eleven square kilometre nature reserve designed to protect the habitat of this endangered bird. The forest is also known as the Mario Dary Reserve, in honour of one of the founders of Guatemala's environmental movement, a lecturer from San Carlos University in

## THE RESPLENDENT QUETZAL

The **quetzal**, Guatemala's national symbol – and with the honour of lending its name to the currency – has a distinguished past but an uncertain future. The feathers of the quetzal were sacred from the earliest of times, and in the strange cult of Quetzalcoatl, whose influence spread throughout Mesoamerica, the quetzal was incorporated into the plumed serpent, a supremely powerful deity. To the Maya the quetzal was so sacred that killing one was a capital offence, and the bird is also thought to have been the *nahual*, or spiritual protector, of the Indian chiefs. When Tecún Umán faced Alvarado in hand-to-hand combat his headdress sprouted the long green feathers of the quetzal, and when the conquistadors founded a city adjacent to the battleground they named it **Quetzaltenango**, the place of the quetzals.

In modern Guatemala the quetzal's image saturates the entire country, appearing in every imaginable context. Citizens honoured by the president are awarded the Order of the Quetzal, and the bird is also considered a symbol of freedom, since caged quetzals die from the rigours of confinement. Despite all this, the sweeping tide of deforestation threatens the existence of the bird, and the sanctuary is about the only concrete step that has been taken to save it.

The more resplendent of the birds, and the source of the famed feathers, is the male. Their heads are crowned with a plume of brilliant green, the chest and lower belly is a rich crimson, and trailing behind are the unmistakable oversized, golden-green tail feathers, though these are only really evident in the mating season. The females, on the other hand, are an unremarkable brownish colour. The birds nest in holes drilled into dead trees, laying one or two eggs at the start of the rainy season, usually in April or May. They can also be quite easily identified by their strange jerky, undulating flight.

Guatemala City, who pioneered the establishment of nature reserves in Guatemala and campaigned for years for a cloudforest sanctuary to protect the quetzal. He was murdered in 1981, possibly as a result of his upsetting powerful timber interests. The reserve he instituted is a steep and dense rain- and cloudforest, pierced by waterfalls, natural pools and the Río Colorado, which cascades through the reserve towards the valley floor. **Buses** from Cobán pass the entrance hourly, but make sure they know you want to be dropped at the reserve as it's easy to miss.

Paths through the undergrowth from the road complete a circuit that takes you up into the woods and around above the reserve headquarters (maps available). There are reasonable numbers of quetzals hidden in the forest but they're extremely elusive. The **best time** to visit is around sunrise, just before or just after nesting season (March–June). A favoured feeding tree of the quetzals is the broad-leaved *aguacatillo* which produces a small avocado-like fruit. Whether or not you see a quetzal, the forest itself, usually damp with a perpetual mist the locals call *chipi-chipi*, is well worth a visit: a profusion of lichens, ferns, mosses, bromeliads and orchids spreads out beneath a towering canopy of cypress, oak, walnut and pepper trees.

Less than a kilometre or so past the entrance to the reserve is the rustic *Hospedaje Ranchito del Quetzal* (☎953 9235; ②/③), with clean basic accommodation with or without private bath, and a simple comedor with a menu usually limited to eggs and beans. Compensating for the no-frills facilities are the quetzals often seen in the patch of forest around the hotel; staff sometimes insist on charging an entrance fee even if you just want to come in and look around. For more luxurious accommodation, try the *Hotel Posada Montaña del Quetzal* at Km 156.5 (☎331 0929, *www.medianet.com.gt/quetzal*; ⑤/⑥), which offers very attractive stone and timber bungalows with fireplaces and pleasant rooms with warm private showers and great forest views – there's a restaurant, bar and swimming pool here.

# Alta Verapaz

Beyond the quetzal sanctuary, the main road crosses into the department of Alta Verapaz, and another 13km takes you beyond the forests and into a luxuriant alpine valley of cattle pastures, hemmed in by steep, perpetually green hillsides. The first place of any size is **TACTIC**, a small, mainly Poqomchi'-speaking town adjacent to the main road, which most buses pass straight by.

The colonial **church** in the centre of town, boasting a baroque facade decorated with mermaids and jaguars, is worth a look, as is the Chi-ixim chapel, high above the town. If you fancy a cool swim, head for the *Balneario Cham-che*, a crystal-clear spring-fed **pool**, on the other side of the main road, opposite the centre of town. The simple *Pensión Central*, on the main street north of the plaza (①), is a reasonable budget bet, or for a little more comfort try *Hotel Villa Linda* close by (☎953 9216; ③), where the rooms have private baths.

Continuing towards Cobán, about 10km past Tactic is the turn-off for San Cristóbal Verapaz, a pretty town almost engulfed by fields of coffee and sugar cane, set on the banks of the Lago de Cristóbal. From here a rough road continues to **Uspantán** in the western highlands (see p.372), from where buses run to Santa Cruz del Quiché, via Sacapulas, for connections to Nebaj and Huehuetenango. To head out this way you can either hitch from San Cristóbal or catch one of the buses that leaves San Pedro Carchá (see p.443) at 10am and noon, passing just above the terminal in Cobán ten minutes later, and reaching San Cristóbal after about another half-hour.

## Cobán and around

The heart of this misty alpine land and the capital of the department is **COBÁN**, where the paved highway comes to an end. If you're heading up this way, stay in town for a night or two and sample some of the finest coffee in the world in one of Cobán's genteel cafés. Cobán is not a large place; suburbs fuse gently with nearby meadows and pine forests, giving the town the air of an overgrown mountain village. When the rain settles in, it can have something of a subdued atmosphere and in the evenings the air is usually damp and cool. That said, the sun does put in an appearance most days, and the town makes a useful base to recharge, eat well and sleep well. It also acts as a hub for all kinds of **ecotourism** possibilities in the spectacular mountains and rivers nearby.

### Arrival and information

Transportes Escobar Monja Blanca, one of Guatemala's best **bus** services, operates half-hourly departures between Guatemala City and Cobán, a journey of four to five hours; its office is on the corner of 2 C and 4 Av, Zona 4 (☎952 1536 or 952 1498). Buses to **local destinations** such as Senahú, El Estor, Lanquín and Cahabón leave from the terminal down the hill behind the town hall. There are also regular long-distance departures to and from San Pedro Carchá (see p.443), a few kilometres away.

It's also possible to **fly** between Guatemala City and Cobán: Inter Airlines, operated by Taca, has daily flights (30min) to and from the capital from the small airstrip a few kilometres southeast of the centre of town. There are also occasional charter flights to the remote departmental airstrips of Playa Grande (Ixcán), Chisec and Fray Bartolomé de Las Casas.

Inexcusably, Inguat currently choose not to grace Cobán with a tourist office, but luckily a couple of hotels more than adequately fill the **information** gap. First place to try is the *Hostal d'Acuña* (see below), which has helpful staff, a good folder with maps and bus times and also a useful noticeboard. *Hostal Doña Victoria* also provides good

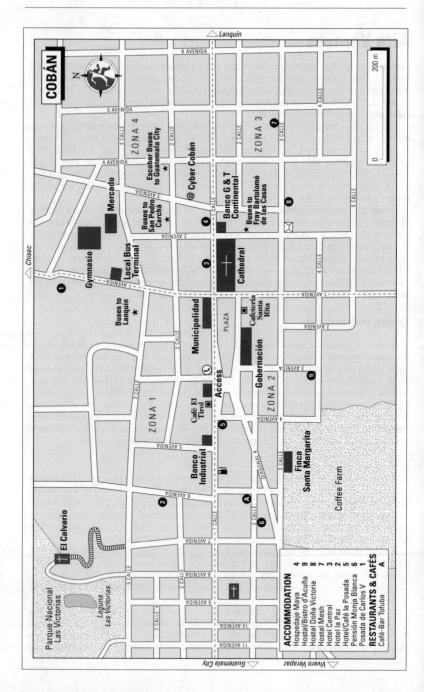

**COBÁN**

△ Lanquín

△ Chisec

△ Guatemala City

△ Vivero Verapaz

Parque Nacional Las Victorias

Laguna Las Victorias

El Calvario

Coffee Farm

Finca Santa Margarita

ZONA 1
ZONA 2
ZONA 3
ZONA 4

Mercado

Gymnasio

Local Bus Terminal

Buses to Lanquín

Municipalidad

Café El Tirol

Banco Industrial

Escobar Buses to Guatemala City

Buses to San Pedro Carchá

@ Cyber Cobán

Banco G & T Continental

Buses to Fray Bartolomé de las Casas

Cathedral

Cafetería Santa Rita

PLAZA

Access

Gobernación

Access

200 m

**ACCOMMODATION**
Hospedaje Maya          4
Hostal/Bistro d'Acuña   9
Hostal Doña Victoria    8
Hostal Mesh             7
Hotel Central           3
Hotel la Paz            2
Hotel/Café la Posada    5
Pensión Monja Blanca    6
Posada de Carlos V      1

**RESTAURANTS & CAFÉS**
Café-Bar Tofuba         A

information. Another source is the Access office, in the same complex as *Café Tirol,* where both the owners are bilingual and there are plenty of terminals where you can surf the **Internet** and check your email.

Cobán is divided into a number of **zonas** like many other Guatemalan towns, with the northeast corner of the plaza at 1 C and 1 Av as the dividing point. Zona 1 is in the north-west, Zona 2 in the southwest, Zona 3 to the southeast and Zona 4 to the northeast.

## Accommodation

Unless you're here for one of the August fiestas you'll probably only pause for a day or two before heading off into the hills, out to the villages, or on to some other part of the country. There are, however, plenty of **hotels** in town, and there's **camping** (US$2.50 per person) at the Parque las Victorias on the northwest side of town, which lacks showers, though there are toilets and running water.

**Hospedaje Maya,** 1 C 2–33, Zona 4, opposite the Cine Norte (☎952 2380). Large, basic hotel used by local travellers and traders. Bargain rates, warm showers and friendly staff but smelly toilets. ①.

**Hostal d'Acuña,** 4 C 3–17, Zona 2 (☎951 0482, fax 952 1547, *uisa@amigo.net.gt*). Undoubtedly the most popular budget choice, offering spotless rooms with comfortable bunks. Dorms (US$5 per bed) are in the garden of a colonial house and guests can enjoy excellent home cooking on the verandah. Highly recommended. ②.

**Hostal Doña Victoria,** 3 C 2–38, Zona 3 (☎951 4213, fax 952 2213, *aventour@intelnet.com.gt*). Beautiful refurbished colonial house dripping with antiques and oozing character. Commodious bedrooms are individually furnished and all come with private bath; the streetside rooms are rather noisy, though. Good café/bar and restaurant. The owners also have a second premises at 1 Av 5–34, Zona 1, which is equally as comfortable though the location is not as good. ⑤.

**Hostal Mesh,** 3C 4–27, Zona 3 (☎ & fax 952 1605, *hostalmesh@hotmail.com*). Small hostel with two clean dormitories, with bunk beds (US$4.50) and safety boxes. Breakfast is included, there's a café-bar at the rear and the owners also organize tours of the region. ②.

**Hotel Central,** 1 C 1–79, Zona 4 (☎ & fax 952 1442). Germanic decor and friendly staff, but the rooms, set round a nice little garden, are a little gloomy for the price – though they do have reliable hot water and private bath. ③.

**Hotel la Paz,** 6 Av 2–19, Zona 1 (☎952 1358). Safe, pleasant budget hotel run by a very vigilant *seño-ra*. Some rooms have private bath. ②.

**Hotel la Posada,** 1 C 4–12, Zona 2, at the west end of the plaza (☎ & fax 952 1495, fax 951 0646, *laposada@c.net.gt*). Probably the city's finest hotel, in an elegant colonial building, with a beautiful, antique-furnished interior. The rooms, many with wooden Moorish-style screens and some with four-poster beds, are set around two leafy courtyards and offer all the usual luxuries, though traffic noise can be a problem. Excellent restaurant and café. ⑥.

**Pensión Monja Blanca,** 2 C 6–30, Zona 2 (☎951 1900 or 952 0531, fax 951 1899, *www.sitio.de/hotel-monjablanca*). A wonderfully old-fashioned atmosphere and a variety of rooms, all set around two stunning courtyard gardens. The older ones are a little run-down but the others have been nicely refurbished and come with private bath; all are very quiet. Don't miss the almost Victorian-style tearoom. ②/③.

**Posada de Carlos V,** 1 Av 3–44, Zona 1 (☎952 3502, fax 951 3501). Mountain chalet-style hotel close to the market, with pine-trimmed rooms and modern amenities including cable TV. Comfortable if not memorable. Check out the lobby photographs of old Cobán. ④.

## The Town

Cobán's imperial heyday, when it stood at the centre of its own isolated world, is long gone, and the glory faded. The elevated **plaza**, however, remains an impressive triangle, dominated by the cathedral, from which the town drops away on all sides. Check inside to see the remains of a massive, ancient, cracked church bell. A block behind, the **market** bustles with trade during the day and is surrounded by food stalls at night. Hints of the days of German control can also be found here and there in the architecture, incorporating the occasional suggestion of Bavarian grandeur. Life in Cobán revolves around **coffee**: the sedate restaurants, tearooms, trendy bars and nightclubs and overflowing supermarket can be attributed to the town's affluent elite, while the crowds that sleep in the market and plaza, assembling in the bus terminal to search for work, are migrant labourers heading for the plantations. For a closer look at Cobán's principal crop, take the guided tour offered by the **Finca Santa Margarita**, a coffee plantation just south of the centre of town at 3C 4–12, Zona 2 (Mon–Fri 8am–12.30pm & 1.30–5pm, Sat 8am–noon; US$2). The interesting tour (an English-speaking guide is usually available) covers the history of the finca, founded by the Dieseldorff family in 1888, and examines all the stages of cultivation and production, and a walk through the grounds. You also get a chance to sample the crop and, of course, purchase some beans.

One of Cobán's most attractive sights is the church of **El Calvario**, a short stroll from the town centre. Head west out of town on 1 Avenida and turn right up 7 Avenida until you reach a steep cobbled path. You'll pass a number of tiny **Maya shrines** on the way up – crosses blackened by candle smoke and decorated with scattered offerings. There's a commanding view over the town from the whitewashed church, which has a distinctly pagan identity, including both Christian and Maya crosses; inside hundreds of corn cobs (sacred in indigenous religion) hang from the roof. Another place worth a look is just outside town: the **Vivero Verapaz** (Mon–Sat 9am–noon & 2–5pm; US$0.75) is a former coffee finca now dedicated to the growing of orchids, which flourish in these sodden mountains. The plants are carefully grown in a shaded environment, and a farmworker will show you around and point out the most spectacular blooms, which are at their best between November and January. The farm is on the old road to Guatemala City, which you reach by leaving the plaza on Diagonal 4, the road that runs past the *Pensión Familiar*; at the bottom of the hill, turn left, go across the bridge and follow the road for 3km. Any taxi driver will be able to take you.

## Eating, drinking and entertainment

When it comes to **eating** in Cobán you have a choice between fancy European-style restaurants and very basic, cheap comedores. For really cheap food, your best bet, as always, is the **market**, but remember that it's closed by dusk, after which street stalls set up in the plaza selling barbecued meat and warm tortillas.

**Bistro Acuña**, 4 C 3–17, Zona 2. The most relaxed place to eat in town – stunning period setting, uplifting classical music, attentive service and a good place to meet other travellers. A full-scale blow-out will cost around US$8 a head but there are many cheaper options, including great cannelloni. Make sure you leave room to sample something from the cake cabinet.

**Café Tirol**, 1 Calle, on the north side of the plaza. Relatively upmarket by Guatemalan standards, though cheaper than the *Posada* (see below). Serves 52 different types of coffee, pretty good breakfasts, hot chocolate, pancakes and sandwiches. Service can be distracted. Open Tues–Sun 7am–8.30pm.

**Cafetería Santa Rita**, 2 Calle, on the plaza, close to the cathedral. Good comedor with friendly service and decent nosh. Very Guatemalan, in the unlikely event you're sick of all those European-style cafés.

**Café and Restaurant la Posada**, 1 C 4–12, Zona 2, at the sharp end of the plaza inside *Hotel la Posada*. The smartest restaurant in town with traditional Guatemalan specialities as well as international cuisine. The café on the verandah outside serves superb breakfasts, bagels and muffins.

**Kam Mun**, 1 C and 9 Av, Zona 2. Excellent, hyper-hygienic Chinese restaurant, with a good line-up of economical Oriental choices. Open daily noon–9.30pm.

*NIGHTLIFE*

Generally speaking Cobán is a pretty quiet place, particularly so in the evenings. In addition to the usual cantinas, however, there are some half-decent **bars**: *Tofuba* at 2 C and 6 Av is one of the trendiest places with a cosmopolitan atmosphere, modern Latin sounds and good snacks, while *Tacobán* at 1 Av and 4 C can get lively at weekends with a sociable crowd and house music. The best **club** in town is *Keops*, 5 Av and 3 C, where the merengue and Latin dance draw a funky bunch of groovers. There are two **cinemas**, the CineTuria in the plaza, and the Cine Norte, on 1 Calle.

## Listings

**Banks and exchange** Banco Industrial at 1 C and 2 Av (Mon–Fri 8.30am–7pm, Sat 8.30am–5.30pm) with Visa facilities, or Banco G&T Continental, 1 C and 2 Av (Mon–Fri 9am–7pm, Sat 9am–1pm) for Mastercard.

**Car rental** Tabarini, 7 Av 2–27, Zona 2 (☎952 1504, fax 951 3282), and Geo Rentals, a local company, in the same building as *Café Tirol* and Access (☎952 1650).

**Email and Internet** Cobán is well wired with email facilities. Access, in the same building as the *Café Tirol*, is very central, but for the best rates and speeds head to *Cybercoban* at 3Av 1–11, Zone 4.

**Laundry** La Providence, at the west end of the plaza on Diagonal 4 (Mon–Sat 8am–noon & 2–5pm).

**Post office** 2 C and 2 Av (Mon–Fri 8am–4.30pm).

**Spanish schools** If you enjoy Cobán's slightly subdued atmosphere you could spend some time studying Spanish at the Instituto Cobán Internacional (INCO Int) at 6 Av 3–03, Zona 3 (☎ & fax 951 2459). Alternatively, there is also the Muq'b'ilbe School close by at 6 Av 5–39, Zona 3, which also offers tuition in the Q'eqchi' language. Both schools offers free excursions, rates start at US$120 a week for 20 hours' tuition and full board.

**Telephones** Telgua has its main office in the plaza (daily 7am–midnight).

**Tours** The *Hostal d'Acuña* and Aventuras Turísticas inside the *Hostal Doña Victoria* both run trips to Semuc Champey, Lanquín, the Rey Marco caves and other destinations in the Verapaces. Projecto Eco Quetzal, at 2 C 14–36, Zona 1 (☎ & fax 952–1047, *bidaspeq@guate.net*), is a highly recommended adventure and cultural tourism specialist, enables visitors to get off the beaten track and visit beautiful remote areas of the Verapaces. Trips, all using local guides, include a three-day hike into the Chicacnab cloud forest (US$55) where quetzals are abundant, and two day-trips to Laguna Lachuá (US$17 per day).

## San Pedro Carchá

Six kilometres away, connected by regular buses, **SAN PEDRO CARCHÁ** is a smaller version of Cobán, with a stronger Maya character and silver instead of coffee money firing the economy. These days the two towns are merging into a single urban sprawl, and many of the buses that go on towards Petén, or even over to Uspantán, leave from Carchá before passing through Cobán. Local buses between the two leave from the terminal in Cobán and from the plaza in Carchá.

If you've an hour to spare, the **regional museum** in a street beside the church (Mon–Fri 9am–noon & 2–5pm; small charge) is worth a look. There's a collection of Maya artefacts and dolls dressed in local costumes, as well as a mouldy collection of stuffed birds and animals including the inevitable moulting quetzal. A little further afield, the **Balneario las Islas** is a stretch of cool water that's popular for swimming; you can also **camp** here. It's a couple of kilometres from the town centre: walk along the main street beside the church and take the third turning on the right, then follow the street for about 1km and take the right-hand fork at the end.

If you want **to stay** here, the *Hotel la Reforma*, 4 C 8–45 (☎9521448; ②), is a good option. For **changing money**, there's a branch of the Banco del Ejército on the plaza (Mon–Fri 9am–1pm & 2.30–5.30pm, Sat 10am–2pm). **Buses** to local destinations such as Senahú, El Estor, Lanquín and Cahabón leave from the plaza. Two buses a day (10am & noon) leave from beside the fire station **to Uspantán**, for connections (via Cobán) to Sacapulas, Nebaj and Quiché.

## San Juan Chamelco

A few kilometres southeast of Cobán, easily reached by regular local buses from the terminal, **SAN JUAN CHAMELCO** is the most important Q'eqchi' settlement in the area. Most of your fellow bus passengers are likely to be women dressed in traditional costume, wearing beautiful cascades of old coins for earrings and speaking Q'eqchi' rather than Spanish. Chamelco's focal point is a large colonial **church**, whose facade is rather unexpectedly decorated with twin Maya versions of the Habsburg double eagle – undoubtedly a result of earlier German presence in the region. Inside the belfry is hidden the village's most significant treasure: a church bell that was given to the Maya leader Juan Matalbatz by the Holy Roman Emperor Charles V.

The best time to visit the village is for its annual **fiesta** on June 16. Participants in the wild processions dress up in a variety of outfits including pre-conquest Maya costumes and representations of local wildlife in celebration of the local Q'eqchi' culture and environment.

Not far from Chamelco is a great **place to stay**, *Don Jerónimo's* (☎308 2255, *www.dearbrutus.com/donjeronimo*; ④ for full board), a vegetarian guest house/retreat in sublime countryside, run by a friendly American who has been living off the land for a good twenty years. Just 500m from here are there are a series of **caves**, the Grutas de Rey Marcos (daily 9am–5pm, US$3 including the services of a guide, plus hard hat and boot rental). Discovered in May 1998, the cave system is over a kilometre long, though the tour only takes you a little way into the complex – you have to wade across an underground river at one stage to see some of the best stalactites and stalagmites, including one that's a dead ringer for the leaning tower of Pisa. To get here, it's a pleasant 5km walk from Chamelco down a signposted road 150m west of the plaza; alternatively you can catch a pick-up from 0 C and 0 Av heading for the village of Chamíl.

## Lanquín and Semuc Champey

Northeast of Cobán, a rough, badly maintained road heads off into the hills, connecting a string of coffee fincas. The road soon drops down into rich land to the north as the valleys open out; their precipitous sides are patched with cornfields and the level central land is saved for the all-important coffee bushes. As the bus lurches along, clinging to the sides of the ridges, there are fantastic views of the valleys below.

The road divides after 43km at the **Pajal** junction, three hours from Cobán, where one branch turns north to Sebol and Fray Bartolomé de Las Casas and the other cuts down deep into the valley to **LANQUÍN**, 12km away (45min), a very sleepy, modest Q'eqchi' village sheltered beneath towering green hills. Don't count on practising your Spanish here – the language has yet to gain much influence. Of the several pensiones, the good, cheap hospedaje-cum-store-cum-comedor, *Divina Providencia* (①), is the best, offering good grub, steaming hot showers and the only cold beers in town. The clapboard-built rooms are comfortable enough, though you'll probably get to know all about your neighbours' nocturnal pursuits. More luxurious is the *Hotel El Recreo* (☎952 2160, fax 952 2333; ④), on the entrance road, with a choice of rooms in wooden huts, a restaurant and a pool. There is electricity only between 6pm and 9pm, though, and prices rise at weekends. Perhaps the best place to stay, however, is a ten-minute walk from the village, along the road to Cahabón. *El Retiro* (*elretirolodge@hotmail*.com; ②) is a wonderful English/Q'eqchi'-owned lodge by the Lanquín river, with camping, palm leaf-thatched cabañas with mosquito screens and hammock space. There's a camp fire and music most nights, and the owners run tours to sights in the region and plan to offer rafting excursions.

Just a couple of kilometres from the village on the road back to Cobán are the **Lanquín caves** (US$1.30), a maze of dripping, bat-infested chambers stretching for at least 3km underground. An illuminated walkway, complete with ladders and chains, cuts through the first few hundred metres, but it's very slippery so take care. It's also well worth dropping by at dusk when thousands of bats emerge from the mouth of the cave and flutter off into the night. A small car park near the entrance to the caves has a covered shelter where you're welcome to **camp** or sling your hammock.

## Semuc Champey

The other attraction around Lanquín are the extraordinary pools of **Semuc Champey** (US$2.50, parking US$0.75), which are a great deal more spectacular than the caves. The problem can be **getting there**, however. If you're very lucky and there are enough tourists in town, you can catch a pickup at about 8am, returning around noon. Otherwise you can book a tour from Cobán (around US$30 per person) or take the *Hostal d'Acuña* shuttle bus (Wed & Sat, when sufficient demand). Hiring Rigoberto Fernández's pick-up for US$10 return trip, including two hours at the pools, is another option. You can find him in the unnamed shop painted vivid green beneath the central park.

The hard way is to walk. It takes nearly three hours and can be extremely tough going if the sun is shining, so take plenty of water. Leave the village along the gravel road that climbs the hill to the south, then drops into another valley. From here the track wanders through thick tropical vegetation where bananas, coffee and the spear-leafed cardamom plants grow beside scruffy thatched huts. After crossing a suspension bridge, the road climbs uphill again to the car park where you may be asked for the entry fee. Finally, follow the muddy track that brings you, at long last, to the pools. The effort of getting here is rewarded by a natural staircase of turquoise waters suspended on a limestone bridge, with a series of idyllic **pools** in which you can swim. The bulk of the Río Cahabón runs underground beneath this natural bridge, and by walking a few hundred metres upstream over a slippery obstacle course of rocks and roots you can see the aquatic frenzy for yourself. The river water plunges furiously into a cavern, cutting under the pools to emerge downstream. If you have a tent or a hammock it makes sense to **stay** the night. There's a thatched shelter here and the altitude is sufficiently low to keep the air warm in the evenings. Be warned, though, it is not safe to leave your belongings unattended.

## Beyond Lanquín

Beyond Lanquín the road continues to **Cahabón** – which has two basic pensiones, the best being *Hospedaje Carolina* (①) – another 24km to the east, and from there a very rough road heads south towards Panzós (see p.446), cutting high over the mountains through superb scenery.

Two daily **buses** leave at 4am and 12.30pm for the three-hour trip to El Estor (see p.431), while pick-ups ply the route more frequently. Buses to Cahabón, passing through Lanquín, leave Cobán five times daily (6am, 12.30pm, 1pm, 2pm & 3pm; 4hr; returning at 2am, 3am, 4am, noon and 3pm). On Sundays there may only be three buses, the last being the 3pm service to Cobán, which is always packed. Heading north, buses pass Pajal for **Fray Bartolomé de Las Casas** (from where you can head northeast to Poptún) and **Raxrujá** (see p.447) twice each morning (around 6.30am & 8.30am).

# The Polochic valley

If you're planning to head out towards the Caribbean from Cobán, or simply interested in taking a short trip along backroads, then the **Polochic valley** is an ideal place to spend the day being bounced around inside a bus. Hourly buses leave Cobán for El Estor, trundling slowly down the valley along a dirt road passing several towns and villages on the way. Travelling the length of the valley, you witness an immense transformation as you drop down through the coffee-coated mountains and emerge in the lush, tropical lowlands. The scenery is pure Alta Verapaz: V-shaped valleys where coffee commands the best land and fields of maize cling to the upper slopes wherever they can. The villages are untidy-looking places where the Q'eqchi' and Poqomchi' Maya are largely latinized and seldom wear the brilliant red *huipiles* that are traditional here.

The first village at the upper end of the valley is **Tamahú**, and below it is **TUCURÚ**. High above Tucurú in the mountains to the north is the **Chelemá Reserve**, a large protected area of pristine cloudforest which contains one of the highest concentrations of quetzals anywhere in the world, not to mention an array of other birds and beasts, including some very vocal howler monkeys. The forest is extremely difficult to reach; to visit, contact Projecto Eco Quetzal in Cobán (see p.443), who can arrange accommodation with local families in the village of Chicacnab.

Beyond Tucurú the road plunges abruptly and cattle pastures start to take the place of the coffee bushes. Both the villages and the people here have a more tropical look about them. Next comes **La Tinta**, and then **Telemán**, the largest of the squalid trading centres in this lower section of the valley. From Telemán a side road branches off to the north to **SENAHÚ**, climbing high into the lush hills past row upon row of neatly ranked coffee bushes. Set behind the first ridge of hills, Senahú is a small coffee centre set in a verdant, steep-sided bowl and an ideal starting point for a short wander in the Alta Verapaz hills. Three **buses** a day run from Cobán to Senahú, the first returning at 4pm (check with the drivers for the latest times); or you could easily hitch a ride on a pick-up or truck from Telemán. There are a couple of simple pensiones, and also the *Hotel El Recreo* in the centre of the village on the plaza (☎952 2160; ③), with twelve pleasant rooms. From here, you can **trek** to some nearby caves, Cuevas de Seamay, used by Maya shamen for ceremonies, and to Semuc Champey and Lanquín in a couple of days – ask for a guide at the *Hotel El Recreo*. Another stunning hike is to Cahabón, which you can also do in a four-wheel drive, weather permitting.

Heading on down the Polochic valley you reach **PANZÓS**, the largest of the valley villages. Its name means "place of the green waters", a reference to the swamps that surround the river, swarming with alligators and birdlife. In 1978, Panzós made the international headlines when a group of campesinos attending a meeting to settle land disputes were gunned down by the army and local police in one of the earliest and most brutal massacres of General Lucas García's military regime. García had a personal interest in the matter, since he owned 78,000 acres of land around Panzós. Over 100,000 people attended a protest rally in Guatemala City after news of the massacre broke and the event is generally regarded as a landmark in the history of political violence in Guatemala. Ten daily buses from Cobán pass through Panzós, while two buses a day and sporadic pick-ups struggle from Panzós up to Cahabón, from where you can easily get to Lanquín. Beyond Panzós the road pushes on towards Lago de Izabal, passing a huge and deserted nickel plant, yet another monument to disastrous foreign investment, just before you come to El Estor (see p.431).

## North towards Petén

In the far northern section of Alta Verapaz, the lush hills drop away steeply onto the limestone plain that marks the frontier with the department of Petén. At present, two rough roads head north: the first from Cobán via **Chisec** and the second from San Pedro Carchá via Pajal, which passes the turn-off for Lanquín and Semuc Champey. From the **Pajal** junction it's a very slow, very beautiful journey north through typical Verapaz scenery – a verdant green landscape of impossibly green mountains, tiny adobe-built hamlets, pasture and pine forests. After three hours or more of twists and turns, you'll reach **Sebol**, an attractive spot on the Río Pasión where tributary waterfalls cascade into the main channel; here a road heads off for Poptún and **FRAY BARTOLOMÉ DE LAS CASAS**. This featureless town has been left off many maps, though it boasts several **hospedajes** – the best are the clean *Hotel Diamelas* (②) and the basic *Pensión Ralíos* (①) – and a couple of banks. Buses leave Las Casas to Cobán (7hr) six times daily and also head northeast to Poptún (see p.450) daily at 3am (5hr 30min). There are also regular flights from the airstrip (US$16); check in the *municipalidad* for details of the next departures. Back on the main road north, the next stop is the small settlement of **Raxrujá**, where the buses from Cobán finish; currently only pick-ups and trucks head north for **Cruce del Pato** and beyond, either up to Sayaxché and Petén or west into the Ixcán.

## Raxrujá and the Candelaria caves

**RAXRUJÁ** is the best place to get a pick-up, truck or, if you're very lucky, a bus north to Sayaxché and Flores or west to Playa Grande and the Ixcán. Little more than a few streets and an army base straggling round the bridge over the Río Escondido, a tributary of the Pasión, it has the only **accommodation** for miles around, so you may end up staying here. *Hotel Raxruhá* (①), next to the Texaco garage, is the best on offer and there are plenty of quite reasonable places to **eat** in town, including the *Comedor Vidalia*. There's a Banrural (Mon–Fri 8am–5pm, Sat 9am–1pm) next to *Hotel Raxruhá* which will cash dollars and travellers' cheques. Buses leave for Cobán at 4am, 9am and 1pm. Heading north, there are occasional buses but expect to have to travel by pick-up or minibus.

The limestone mountains to the west of Raxrujá are full of caves, including the spectacular **Candelaria** complex 10km out of town, off the road to Chisec. This series of caverns, stretching for around 18km and including some truly monumental chambers – "Tzul Tacca" is over 200m long – is located on private property, a short walk from the road, and is jealously guarded by Daniel Dreux, who has set up the **Complejo Cultural de Candelaria** conservation area. Entrance to the complex, including a two-hour tour and a guide to the first cave system, costs US$4 per person, while a two-day tour by lancha boat costs US$35 per person. Alternatively contact one of the Cobán travel agents (see p.443) or the official agents, PTP, 15 C 3–20, Zona 10 in Guatemala City (☎363 4404, www.ptpmayas.com), to organize a trip. The wonderful **accommodation** in the complex (US$50 a day per person including two meals) is often block-booked by French tour groups, but you can **camp** close to the entrance at the *Rancho Ríos Escondidos*.

The area beyond Raxrujá, where the rolling foothills of the highlands give way to the flat expanse of southern Petén, is known as the **Northern Transversal Strip**, dubbed the "Generals' Strip" as huge parcels of land, complete with their valuable mineral resources, were dispensed to military top brass instead of to needy campesinos in the

---

### THE "DISCOVERY" OF CANCUÉN

In September 2000 newspapers across the world proclaimed that an ancient Maya city, lost for 1300 years, called **Cancuén**, "place of serpents", had been discovered by an American-Guatemalan team of archeologists on the banks of the river Pasión. While the actuality was very different – Cancuén had been discovered in 1907 and was even plotted on tourism-board maps of the country – the sheer size of the ruins had certainly been underestimated and new investigations revealed the site to be enigmatic in other ways. Uniquely, Cancuén seems to lack the usual religious and defensive structures so characteristic of Maya cities and appears to have existed as an essentially secular, trading city. For most of the twentieth century, the absence of soaring temple-pyramids led archeologists to assume that Cancuén was a very minor site, and it was ignored for decades. However the vast amounts of jade, pyrite, obsidian and fine ceramics found recently indicate that this was one of the greatest trading centres of the Maya world, with a paved plaza (which may have been a marketplace) covering two square kilometres. Cancuén is thought to have flourished because of its strategic position between the great cities of the lowlands, like Tikal and Calakmul, and the mineral-rich highlands of southern Guatemala. The vast, almost ostentatious, **palace** complex, with 170 rooms and 11 courtyards, is Cancuén's most arresting feature and it's hoped that investigations by Guatemala's Institute of Anthropology and the National Geographic Society will help uncover much about Classic period life.

1970s. In the heart of this region, 11km north of Raxrujá, is the large Maya site of **Cancuén** (see box) where a huge Classic period palace has been unearthed. At the moment the only way to visit the site is with the specialist tour operator Maya Expeditions (see p.340); don't be tempted to hike over to the site as you'll have to dodge past fields of grazing water buffalo, through land owned by the ex-military dictator Lucas García.

## Playa Grande and around

Continuing west from Raxrujá, trucks make the 90km journey to **PLAYA GRANDE** (at least 6hr), the bridging point of the Río Negro. The town is an authentic frontier settlement with cheap hotels, rough bars and brothels plus a smattering of development agencies. If you need to **stay**, the best options are the basic but clean *Hospedaje Torre Visión* or *Reyna* (both ①).

One point of interest in this area is the **Parque Nacional Laguna Lachuá**, a beautiful little lake 4km off the main road east of Playa Grande. One of the least-visited national parks in Central America, this is a beautiful, tranquil spot, the clear, almost circular lake completely surrounded by dense tropical forest. Though it smells slightly sulphurous, the water is good for swimming, with curious horseshoe-shaped limestone formations by the edge that make perfect individual bathing pools. You'll see otters and an abundance of birdlife, but watch out for mosquitoes. There's a large thatched *rancho* (shelter) by the shore, ideal for camping or slinging a hammock. Fireplaces and wood are provided, but you'll need to bring food and drinking water. You can also rent canoes.

You can get to Playa Grande **from Cobán** on one of a stream of trucks and pick-ups setting out from the corner of the bus terminal – a journey of at least six hours. Heading south **from Sayaxché** you need to catch a bus or pick-up to Playitas via Cruce del Pato and take another pick-up or truck from there. There are also charter **flights** from the airstrip in Cobán.

## Into the Ixcán

The Río Negro marks the boundary between the departments of Alta Verapaz and Quiché; the land to the west is known as the **Ixcán**. This huge swampy forest, some of which was settled in the 1960s and 1970s by peasants migrating from the highlands, became a bloody battleground in the 1980s. In the past few years the Ixcán has become a focus for repatriado settlement, as **refugees** who fled to Mexico have been resettled in a string of "temporary" camps west of the river.

Travelling further west across the Ixcán and into northern Huehuetenango, though no longer hazardous, is still very arduous – it can take between two and three days to get from Playa Grande to Barillas (see p.404). **Veracruz**, 20km (1hr 30min) from Playa Grande, is the first place of note, a settlement at the crossroads beyond the Río Xalbal. Some buses continue to Mayalan, 12km away, across the now bridged Río Piedras Blancas. If the road isn't finished yet, you may have to walk 15km (4–5hr) to **Altamira** on the far bank of the Río Ixcán, past several tiny villages; the path is easy to follow. At the last village, **Rancho Palmeras**, ask for directions to the crossing point on the Ixcán, where boys will pole you across the flowing river. Once across, Altamira is still a few kilometres away, up the hill. From here a regular flow of trucks make the 30km (4hr) journey to Barillas over some of the worst roads in the country. It's a spectacular journey, though, especially as you watch the growing bulk of the Cuchumatanes rising ever higher on the horizon. You can also get trucks over the border into **Mexico**, taking you along the Carretera Fronteriza in Chiapas (see p.172), but you need a Guatemalan exit stamp first, probably best obtained in Cobán or Flores.

# PETÉN

The vast northern department of **Petén** covers about a third of Guatemala but contains less than three percent of the country's population. This huge expanse of swamps, dry savannahs and tropical rainforest forms part of an untamed wilderness that stretches into the Lacandón forest of southern Mexico and across the Maya Mountains to Belize. Totally unlike any other part of the country, much of it is all but untouched, with ancient ceiba and mahogany trees that tower 50m above the forest floor. Undisturbed for so long, the area is also extraordinarily rich in **wildlife**. Some 285 species of bird have been sighted at Tikal alone, including a great range of hummingbirds, toucans, blue and white herons, hawks, buzzards, wild turkeys, motmot (a bird of paradise) and even the elusive quetzal, revered since Maya times. Beneath the forest canopy are many other species that are far harder to locate. Among the mammals are the massive tapir or mountain cow, ocelots, deer, coatis, jaguars, monkeys, plus crocodiles and thousands of species of plants, snakes, insects and butterflies.

Recently, however, this position of privileged isolation has been threatened by moves to colonize the country's final frontier. Waves of **settlers**, lured by offers of free land, have cleared enormous tracts of jungle, while oil exploration and commercial logging have cut new roads deep into the forest. The population of Petén, just 15,000 in 1950, is today estimated at over 400,000, a number which puts enormous pressure on the remaining forest. Various attempts have been made to halt the tide of destruction, and in 1990, the government declared that forty percent of Petén would be protected by the **Maya Biosphere Reserve**, although little has been done to enforce this.

The new interest in the region is in fact something of a reawakening as Petén was once the heartland of the **Maya civilization**, which reached here from the highlands some 2500 years ago. Maya culture reached the height of its architectural, scientific and artistic achievement during the Classic period (roughly 250–925 AD), when great cities rose out of the forest. The ruins at Tikal and El Mirador, among the most spectacular of all **Maya sites**, represent only a fraction of what was once here. At the close of the tenth century the cities were mysteriously abandoned, and many of the people moved north to the Yucatán where Maya civilization continued to flourish until the twelfth century.

By the time the Spanish arrived, the area had been partially recolonized by the **Itzá**, a group of Toltec-Maya who inhabited the land around Lago de Petén Itzá. The forest proved so impenetrable that it wasn't brought under Spanish control until 1697, more than 150 years after they had conquered the rest of the country. The Spanish had little enthusiasm for Petén, however, and under their rule it remained a backwater. Independence saw no great change and it wasn't until 1970 that Petén became genuinely accessible by car. Even today the network of roads is skeletal, and many routes are impassable in the wet season.

The hub of the department are the twin lakeside towns of **Flores** and **Santa Elena**. You'll probably arrive here, if only to head straight out to the ruins of **Tikal**, Petén's prime attraction, though the town is also the starting point for adventures to more distant ruins – **El Mirador**, **Nakbé** and **Río Azul**. **El Remate** is a tranquil alternative location, halfway between Flores and Tikal on the eastern shore of Lago de Petén Itzá. The caves and scenery around **Poptún**, on the main highway south, justify exploration, while down the other road south, **Sayaxché** is surrounded by yet more Maya sites. From Sayaxché you can set off down the Río Pasión to **Mexico** and the ruins of **Yaxchilán** (see p.149), or take an alternative route back to Guatemala City – via Cobán in Alta Verapaz.

## Getting to Petén

Many visitors arrive in Petén by bus or plane directly from **Guatemala City**: **by air** it's a short fifty-minute hop to Flores; **by bus** it can take anywhere between eight and ten hours. A number of domestic airlines fly the route daily and **tickets** can be bought from virtually any travel agent in the country; prices range between US$70 and US$120 depending on the airline. Flights are heavily in demand and overbooking is common. Numerous **bus companies** provide around twenty services a day from Guatemala City to Flores, including some very luxurious options. If you don't want to do the 554km trip in one go, it's easy enough to do it in stages – the best places to break the journey are at **Quiriguá** (see p.420), **Río Dulce** (see p.427) and **Poptún** (see below).

Coming from the Guatemalan highlands, you can reach Petén along the backroads **from Cobán** in Alta Verapaz, which is a long, adventurous route. **From Belize or Mexico**, you can enter the country through Petén. The most obvious route is from Belize through the border at Melchor de Mencos, but there are also two river routes that bring you through from Palenque or Tenosique in Mexico. All of these routes are described on pp.469–471.

# Poptún and around

Heading north from the Río Dulce, the main route to Flores cuts through a degraded landscape of small milpa farms and cattle ranches that were untouched jungle a decade or two ago. Some 95km from the Río Dulce, at an altitude of 500m, the first settlement of any interest is the small town of **POPTÚN**. For many travellers this dusty frontier settlement is the unlikely embodiment of rustic bliss and organic food, thanks to the proximity of the *Finca Ixobel* (see below). There's no particular reason to stay in the town itself, but you may well stop by to use the Telgua office or banks. If you do get stuck here, you can **stay** at the friendly *Hotel Posada de los Castellanos* (☎927 7222; ②), where you get a bathroom and hot water. The best food in town can be had at the *Fonda Ixobel 2*, which bakes good bread and cakes.

For a more rural setting, head 4km north of Poptún, to *Cocay Camping* (☎927 7024; ①), set in peaceful isolation on the banks of the river just past the village of **Machaquilá**. The site provides camping space, very simple huts and vegetarian food. Over the bridge to the right, set in a patch of forest on the bank of the Río Machaquilá, are the comfortable thatched cabañas of *Villa de los Castellanos* (☎927 7541, fax 927 7307, *www.ecovilla.com*; ⑤, but ask about special backpacker rates), offering a friendly, comfortable base for adventurous visitors to explore the forests, rivers and caves of central Petén. The Castellanos family have been in Petén since 1720 and Don Placido, the owner, is an excellent source of information — botanical, historical and logistical.

## Finca Ixobel

A couple of kilometres' walk south of Poptún, surrounded by aromatic pine forests in the cool foothills of the Maya Mountains, the *Finca Ixobel* (☎ & fax 927 7363, *www.fincaixobel.conexion.com*) is a working farm that provides **accommodation** to passing tourists. The farm was originally run by Americans Mike and Carole DeVine, but on June 8, 1990, Mike was murdered by the army. This prompted the American government to suspend military aid to Guatemala and, after a drawn-out investigation which cast little light on their motives, five soldiers were convicted of the murder in September 1992. Others involved have managed to evade capture and their commanding officer, Captain Hugo Contreras, escaped from jail shortly after his arrest. Carole fought the case for years and remains at the finca.

*Finca Ixobel* is a supremely beautiful and relaxing place, where you can swim in the pond, walk in the forest, dodge the resident "attack" Macaws and stuff yourself stupid with healthy home-grown food. There are **hikes** into the jungle, horse-riding trips, rafting, four-wheel-drive jungle jaunts, and short excursions to nearby caves. Accommodation is in attractive bungalows with private bath (④), regular rooms (②/③), or dorms (②), and there's also camping and hammock space (US$3) and tree houses (②). You run up a tab for accommodation, food and drink, paying when you leave – which can be a rude awakening. To get to the finca, ask the bus driver to drop you at the gate (marked by a large sign), from where it's a fifteen-minute walk through the pine trees; after dark, it's probably safest to head for the *Fonda Ixobel 2* restaurant (see above) in Poptún and they'll call a taxi (US$3–4) to drop you off.

# Flores

**FLORES**, the capital of Petén, has an easy pace and a sedate, old-world atmosphere diametrically opposite to the commerce and bustle that typifies most towns in Petén. Its genteel cobbled streets, ageing houses and twin-domed church are set on a small island in Lago de Petén Itzá, connected to the mainland by a short (manmade) causeway. The frontier mentality lies just across the water in **SANTA ELENA**, a chaotic, featureless town that's dusty in the dry season and mud-bound during the rains.

The **lake** was a natural choice for settlement, and its shores were heavily populated in Maya times, with the capital of the Itzá, **Tayasal**, occupying the island that was to become modern Flores. Cortés passed through here in 1525, on his way south to Honduras, and left behind a sick horse which he promised to send for later. A horse-worshipping cult started as a result, and later visitors were sacrificed to the equine deity. Tayasal was eventually destroyed by Martín de Ursúa and an army of 235 in 1697. For the entire colonial period (and indeed up to the 1960s) Flores languished in virtual isolation, having more contact with neighbouring Belize than with the capital. Today, despite the steady flow of tourists passing through en route to Tikal, the town retains an urbane air. It has little to detain you and is small enough to explore in an hour or so, but it does offer a spectacular lakeside location and some attractive places to stay.

## Arrival and information

Arriving by **bus** from Guatemala City or Belize, you'll be dropped off within a few blocks of the causeway to Flores. The **airport** is 3km east of the causeway; taxis into town charge around US$2. **Local buses** cover the route, crossing the causeway about every ten minutes, but they entail a time-consuming change halfway; returning to the airport, they leave from the Flores end of the causeway every twenty minutes or so.

There's an Inguat desk in the airport's arrivals hall (daily 7am–noon & 3-6pm; ☎926 0533), with reasonable maps and good **information** available in English; in the departure area, the Banco de Quetzal will cash travellers' cheques and change dollars or quetzales at good rates. There's another Inguat office on the plaza in Flores (Mon–Sat 8am–4.30pm; ☎926 0669), where the helpful staff will most likely direct you across the plaza to **CINCAP** (Mon–Fri 9am–1pm & 2–6pm; ☎926 0718), a very useful resource centre with more detailed maps, books and leaflets, and exhibitions on historical and contemporary life in Petén. This is also the production office of *Destination Petén*, a free monthly listings and **information magazine**, available at most hotels and travel agencies. If you're planning to go on a trip to remote parts of the Maya Biosphere Reserve, check with **ProPetén** on Calle Central (Mon–Fri 8am–5pm; ☎926 1370, fax 926 0495, *propeten@guate.net*) for current information on route conditions, accommodation and guides. They also do **organized trips**, including the "Scarlet Macaw Trail", a five-day expedition by truck, horse and boat along rivers and through primary forest, taking in the remote ruins of El Perú and the largest concentration of scarlet macaws in northern Central America.

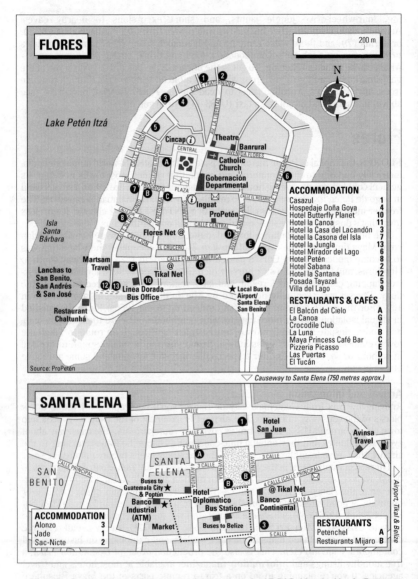

**FLORES**

Lake Petén Itzá

Isla Santa Bárbara

Cincap ℹ
Theatre
Banrural
CENTRAL
Catholic Church
Gobernación Departmental
Inguat ℹ
ProPetén
Flores Net @

Martsam Travel
Tikal Net @
Línea Dorada Bus Office

Lanchas to San Benito, San Andrés & San José

Restaurant Chaltunhá

★ Local Bus to Airport/ Santa Elena/ San Benito

0        200 m

N

**ACCOMMODATION**

| | |
|---|---|
| Casazul | 1 |
| Hospedaje Doña Goya | 4 |
| Hotel Butterfly Planet | 10 |
| Hotel la Canoa | 11 |
| Hotel la Casa del Lacandón | 3 |
| Hotel la Casona del Isla | 7 |
| Hotel la Jungla | 13 |
| Hotel Mirador del Lago | 6 |
| Hotel Petén | 8 |
| Hotel Sabana | 2 |
| Hotel la Santana | 12 |
| Posada Tayazal | 5 |
| Villa del Lago | 9 |

**RESTAURANTS & CAFÉS**

| | |
|---|---|
| El Balcón del Cielo | A |
| La Canoa | G |
| Crocodile Club | F |
| La Luna | B |
| Maya Princess Café Bar | C |
| Pizzeria Picasso | D |
| Las Puertas | E |
| El Tucán | H |

Source: ProPetén

▽ *Causeway to Santa Elena (750 metres approx.)*

**SANTA ELENA**

1 CALLE
1 CALLE A
Hotel San Juan
2 CALLE
SANTA ELENA
3 CALLE
Avinsa Travel
Buses to Guatemala City ★ & Poptún
Hotel Diplomatico
Banco Industrial (ATM)
Bus Station
@ Tikal Net
Banco Continental
Market
Buses to Belize

SAN BENITO

▷ *Airport, Tikal & Belize*

**ACCOMMODATION**

| | |
|---|---|
| Alonzo | 3 |
| Jade | 1 |
| Sac-Nicte | 2 |

**RESTAURANTS**

| | |
|---|---|
| Petenchel | A |
| Restaurants Mijaro | B |

If you're interested in doing some **voluntary work**, ARCAS (*Asociación de Rescate y Conservación de Vida Silvestre*), the Wildlife Conservation and Rescue Association (☎926 2022, *arcaspeten@intelnet.net.gt*), runs a rescue service for animals taken illegally as pets from the forests and always needs volunteers. The work, while rewarding, can be very demanding and you'll need to sign up for at least a week (US$50 per person). You can obtain information from their office in Santa Elena, two blocks south of Telgua.

## Accommodation

Accommodation in Flores/Santa Elena has undergone a boom in recent years and the sheer number of new **hotels** keeps prices competitive. There are several good budget places in Flores itself, making it unnecessary to stay in noisier and dirtier Santa Elena unless your budget is extremely tight.

### FLORES

**La Casa del Lacandón**, on the lakeshore, Calle Fraternidad (☎926 3592). Good new hotel with a selection of accommodation, all with private bath. The downstairs rooms are clean and offer reasonable value, but the upstairs rooms (especially 101 and 105 with stunning lake views) are larger and more attractive. ③.

**Casazul**, close to the northern tip of the island (☎926 1138). Stylishly converted colonial-style mansion house with light, tastefully decorated rooms, all with two double beds, wooden furniture, fridges and a/c. ⑤.

**Hospedaje Doña Goya**, at the north end of the island (☎926-3538). Excellent family-run budget guest house. Clean, light rooms with fans, some with private bath; the ones at the front have balconies. Also offers a book exchange, a roof-top terrace with hammocks and trips to nearby caves. Good rates for single travellers. ②.

**Hotel Butterfly Planet**, near the Linea Dorada office (☎926-0357, *martsam@guate.net*). Clean, inexpensive rooms with shared cold-water bath. Run by Benedicto Grijalva of Martsam Travel, so very good for information and tours. ②.

**Hotel la Casona de la Isla**, Calle 30 de Junio (☎ & fax 926-0593, *www.corpetur.com*). The one with the arresting citrus and powder-blue paint job. Attractive, modern rooms with private bath and a/c, swimming pool and spectacular sunset views from the terrace bar-restaurant. ⑤.

**Hotel la Jungla**, in the southwest corner of the island (☎926 0634). The best value in this price range, with gleaming tiled floors and private baths with hot water. Also has rooftop views over the town and lake and a good restaurant. ③.

**Hotel Mirador del Lago**, Calle 15 de Septiembre (☎926-3276). Easily the best just-above-budget hotel in Flores, with well-furnished rooms with two beds, private bath and fan. Friendly owner Mimi Salguero (who speaks a little English) keeps the lobby fridge stocked with beer and soft drinks, and has tables on a lakeshore terrace at which to enjoy them. Great sunset views from the roof. ③.

**Hotel Sabana**, at the northern tip of the island (☎ & fax 926 1248, *www.sabanahotel.com*). Large modern place with a small pool and nice lake views, especially from the restaurant. All the 28 rooms have a/c and cable TV and represent good value. ⑤.

**Hotel Santana**, in the southwest corner of Flores (☎9260492, fax 9260662). Recently modernized three-storey building with a small pool and patio overlooking the lake. Very comfortable, spotless rooms with fan and private bath; first-floor rooms have private lakeside terraces and a/c. ⑤.

**Posada Tayazal**, Calle la Unión near the *Doña Goya* (☎ & fax 926 0568). Well-run budget hotel with decent basic rooms, some with private bath. Shared bathrooms have hot water. Roof terrace, information service and tours to Tikal. ②.

### SANTA ELENA

**Hotel Alonzo**, 6 Av 4–99 (☎926 0105). Reasonable budget rooms, some with balconies and a few with private hot- or cold-water bath (the shared bathroom is grubby). There's also a restaurant and a public telephone. ②/③.

**Hotel Jade**, 6 Avenida. A backpackers' stronghold. Shambolic but the cheapest place in town. ①.

**Hotel Sac-Nicte**, 1 C 4–45 (☎ & fax 926 0092). Clean rooms with fan and private shower; second-floor rooms have views of the lake. ②.

## Eating and drinking

Flores unquestionably offers the most cosmopolitan dining scene in Petén and there are a number of good restaurants, many with delightful lakeside views, though prices are a little higher than elsewhere in Guatemala. Santa Elena has a very limited selection of comedores so even if you're staying here you may want to cross the causeway for a little more atmosphere. Many restaurants here also serve **wild game**, often listed on menus as *comida silvestre*. Virtually all this has been taken illegally from reserves and you should avoid ordering items such as *tepescuintle* (paca, a large relation of the guinea-pig), *venado* (deer), or *coche de monte* (peccary, or wild pig).

## FLORES

**La Canoa**, Calle Centro América. Popular, good-value place, serving pasta, great soups, and some vegetarian and Guatemalan food, as well as excellent breakfasts.

**Crocodile Club**, Calle Centro América, near Martsam Travel and under the same ownership. Really good, filling meals (some vegetarian) and bar snacks in a friendly atmosphere. Music, movies, book exchange and information.

**La Luna**, at the far end of Calle 30 de Junio. The best restaurant in town, though not that expensive, set in a wonderfully atmospheric old building. Meat, fish and pasta, plus home-made soup and a few vegetarian dishes. It doesn't serve wild game. Also great for an espresso.

**Pizzeria Picasso**, across the street from the *Tucán* and run by the same family (☎926-0637). Great pizza served under cooling breezes from the ceiling fans, and they will deliver.

**Las Puertas**, signposted on Calle Santa Ana. Paint-splattered walls and live music as well as very good pasta and healthy breakfasts. Worth it for the atmosphere.

**Maya Princess Café Bar**, Avenida Reforma. An interesting creative international menu – teriyaki chicken, salad with basil leaves – and a sociable vibe make this a deservedly popular place. Movies shown at 4pm and 9pm daily, moderate prices.

**El Tucán**, a few metres east of the causeway, on the waterfront but reached from Calle Centro America. Good fish, enormous chef's salads, great Mexican food and the best waterside terrace in Flores, but prices are higher than they used to be and there's wild game on the menu.

## SANTA ELENA

**Mijaro**, two locations; one on the road from the causeway, the other round the corner on Calle Principal. The best Guatemalan restaurants in Santa Elena, with good food at local prices and a daily special. You can usually leave luggage here while you look for a room.

**Restaurant Petenchel**, 2 Calle, past the park. Simple, good food. The nicest place to eat within two blocks of the main street and you can leave your luggage here.

## Listings

**Banks and currency exchange** Most banks in Santa Elena will change cash dollars but the Banco Continental on Calle Principal in Santa Elena, at the junction of the road to the causeway (Mon–Sat 8.30am–8pm), has the best rates. For Visa credit/debit card cash advances use Banco Industrial (24-hr ATM), for Mastercard transactions use Banco G&T Continental. You can also change dollars and cash travellers' cheques at one of the recommended travel agents, below.

**Car and bike rental** Several firms, including Budget, Hertz and Koka, operate from the airport. All offer cars, minibuses and jeeps, with prices from around US$65 a day for a jeep. Bikes can be rented from Martsam Travel, Flores, for US$1.25/3225 per hour (daily 7am–7pm; ☎ & fax 926 0494).

**Doctor** Centro Medico Maya, 4 Avenida near 3 Calle in Santa Elena, down the street by the *Hotel Diplomatico* (☎926-0180), is helpful and professional, though no English is spoken.

**Language schools** San Andrés and San José, two very attractive villages on the north shore of the lake, both have good Spanish schools and, since few of the villagers speak English, are excellent places to learn and practise the language. Official rates (around US$170 a week for lessons, food and lodging) may seem more expensive than schools in Antigua or Xela, in highland Guatemala, but you may get a discount if you contact the school directly or ask one of the recommended travel agents (below) to call for you – they won't charge you extra for this. The Eco Escuela in San Andrés (☎928-8106, *ecoescuela@guate.net*) is larger and has been established longer than the Escuela Bio-Itzá in San José (☎928-8142, *bioitza@guate.net*), but the instruction in the latter is just as good and San José is arguably the prettier village. Lanchas for the villages leave regularly from Flores, and there are buses from Santa Elena.

**Laundry** Lavandería Amelia, behind CINCAP in Flores; Lavandería Emanuel on 6 Avenida in Santa Elena.

**Post office** Two doors away from the Inguat office in Flores; on Calle Principal, two blocks east of the *Banco Continental*, in Santa Elena (Mon–Fri 8am–4.30pm).

**Telephones and email** Telgua is in Santa Elena on 5 C, but you're better off using Tikal Net, at 4 C and 6 Av, for all phone, fax and Internet facilities; they also have another branch in Flores at Calle Centro America (daily 8.30am–10.30pm).

**Travel agents and tour operators** Every hotel in Flores – and a good many in Santa Elena – seems to be offering tours, but most can simply sell you minibus trips to Tikal or bus and plane tickets. The best travel agent in Flores is Martsam Travel (☎ & fax 926-3225, *martsam@guate.net*), at the western end of Calle Centro America; the owners speak English, run a daily trip to Yaxhá (p.472) and know Belize well. Avinsa (☎929-0808,*www.tikaltravel.com*), a few blocks east along Calle Principal in Santa Elena, arranges first-class tours throughout Guatemala and the entire Maya region, and is the only agent able to issue international airline tickets beyond Mexico or Belize; staff speak English and German. Evolution Adventures (☎926 0633, *evolution@internetdetelgua.com.gt*), off Calle Centro America, opposite Tikal Net, offers overnight backpacking trips to the more remote ruins of the Maya Biosphere Reserve, such as El Perú, Río Azul and El Mirador, formerly very difficult to reach on your own; it's owned by a Canadian, David Jackaman. Eco Maya, at Calle 30 de Junio in Flores (☎926 1363 *www.ecomaya.com*), is also recommended for trips to remote ruins including El Zotz and Mirador and the Scarlet Macaw trail inside the Laguna del Tigre reserve. The *Hotel San Juan* travel agency in Santa Elena is not recommended.

# Around Flores

If you have a few hours to spare in Flores, the most obvious excursion is a **trip on the lake**. Boatmen can take you around a circuit that takes in a mirador, a small ruin on the peninsula opposite and the **Peténcito zoo** (daily 8am–5pm), 3km east of Santa Elena, with its small collection of sluggish local wildlife, and pause for a swim along the way. Beware the concrete waterslide by the zoo – it's caused at least one death. Boatmen loiter behind the *Hotel Yum Kax* or around the start of the causeway. If you'd rather paddle around under your own steam you can rent a canoe for around US$2 an hour.

Of the numerous **caves** in the hills behind Santa Elena, the most accessible is **Aktun Kan** (daily 8am–5pm; US$1.20). Simply follow the Flores causeway through Santa Elena, turn left when it forks in front of a small hill, and then take the first right. Otherwise known as *La Cueva de la Serpiente*, the cave is the legendary home of a huge snake. The guard may explain some of the bizarre names given to the various shapes inside, some of which resemble animals and even a marimba.

## San Andrés and San José

Though accessible by bus and boat, the traditional villages of **San Andrés** and **San José**, across the lake from Flores, have until recently received few visitors. Sloping steeply up from the shore, the streets are lined with one-storey buildings, some of palmetto sticks and thatch, some coated with plaster and others with brightly painted concrete. Pigs and chickens wander freely. **Getting to the villages** is best achieved by using the lanchas (US$0.50 to San Andrés; US$0.75 to San José) that leave when full from the beach next to the *Hotel Santana* in Flores and from **San Benito**, a suburb of Santa Elena. A chartered *expreso* from Flores or San Benito will cost around US$9. Regular morning **buses** leave for San Andrés from the market in Santa Elena; if they don't continue to San José, it's an easy 2km walk downhill. Lanchas return throughout the day at regular intervals until 5pm.

Most outsiders in **SAN ANDRÉS** are students at the **Eco-Escuela de Español** (see "Listings", opposite), the longest-established language school in Petén. Since nobody in the village speaks English, a course here is an excellent opportunity to immerse yourself in Spanish without distractions, though it may be daunting for absolute beginners. There are currently no hospedajes in the village, but 3km to the west is the attractive *Hotel Nitún* (☎201 0759, fax 926 0807, *www.nitun.com*; ⑤ including transport from Flores), with full-board **accommodation** in thatched stone cabañas with hardwood floors and private bathrooms and a restaurant serving superb food. *Hotel Nitún* is the base for Monkey Eco Tours (same contact details) which organizes expeditions to remote archeological sites.

**SAN JOSÉ**, perched above a lovely bay, just 2km east along the shore from San Andrés, is even more relaxed than its neighbour and it too has a language school, the Bio-Itzá Spanish School (see "Listings", p.454). The village is undergoing something of a cultural revival: Itzá, the pre-conquest Maya tongue, is being taught in the school, and you'll see signs in the language dotted all around. Over the hill beyond the village is a secluded rocky beach where there's a shelter to sling a hammock and a couple of cabins to rent.

Beyond San José a signed track on the left leads 4km to the Classic period **ruins of Motúl** (free). The site is fairly spread out and little visited (though there should be a caretaker about), with four plazas, stelae and pyramids. It's a secluded spot, ideal for bird-watching, and probably best visited by bicycle from either of the villages – either borrow one from a villager or rent a bike in Flores.

# El Remate

On the eastern shore of Lago de Petén Itzá, 30km from Santa Elena on the road to Tikal, **EL REMATE** offers a pleasant alternative to staying in Flores. It's a quiet, friendly village, growing in popularity as a convenient base for visits to Tikal. **Getting to El Remate** is easy: every minibus to Tikal passes through the village, or catch any bus heading for the Belize border, get off at the village of Ixlú (also called El Cruce) and it's a 2km walk down the Tikal road. **Returning to Flores**, three local buses pass through between 5.30am and 8am (you can check the latest schedule at *La Casa de Don David*) and a swarm of minibuses from Tikal also ply the route.

On the north shore of the lake, 3km along the dirt road that heads west from the centre of El Remate, the **Biotopo Cerro Cahuí** (daily; US$3.50) is a six-and-a-half-square-kilometre wildlife conservation area comprising lakeshore, ponds and some of the best examples of undisturbed tropical forest in Petén. The smallest and most accessible of Petén's reserves, it contains a rich diversity of plants and animals and is especially recommended for bird-watchers. There are hiking trails, a couple of small ruins and two thatched miradores on the hill above the lake; pick up maps and information at the gate where you sign in, close to the *El Gringo Perdido* hotel.

There's lots to explore in the rich tropical environment around El Remate, including boats tours of the eastern end of the lakeshore operated by the *Casa de Don David*. Plenty of places will also rent you a canoe for a dollar an hour.

## Accommodation and eating

Most of the places listed here have a distinctive charm and they're fairly well spaced, with no sense of overcrowding. There are a few simple comedores offering inexpensive Guatemalan food, and most of the hotels also provide meals. Accommodation options are listed in the order you approach them from Puente Ixlú.

**Camping Sal Itzá**, 100m down a signed track opposite the lakeshore right at the beginning of the village. Simple stick-and-thatch cabins and camping on a steep hillside with lake views. Run by a very friendly family, headed by Juan and Rita, who'll cook tasty local food on request. ②.

**El Mirador del Duende**, high above the lake, reached by a stairway cut into the cliff (*miraduende@hotmail.com*). An incredible collection of globular whitewashed stucco cabañas decorated with Maya glyphs, plus space for hammocks and tents. There's a wonderful chill-out terrace overlooking the lake and a restaurant serving cheap vegetarian food. ②.

**La Mansión del Pajaro Serpiente**, just below *El Mirador del Duende* (☎ & fax 926 4. *nature@ietravel.com*). The most comfortable accommodation on the road to Tikal. Stone-built ai. thatched two-storey cabañas in a tropical garden and smaller rooms, all with superb lake views. Annoyingly, the owners fluctuate their prices according to demand, so bargain at quiet times of the year. Good food and a small swimming pool. ④–⑤.

**Hotel Ixchel**, just off the Tikal road close to the junction. Simple but fairly comfortable wood cabins, run by a very friendly local family. ②.

**Casa de Bruno's Place**, just past the *Ixchel*, at the junction. Four basic, functional rooms with shared bath, behind the village store. ②.

**La Casa de Don David**, 300m beyond *La Mansión*, right on the junction (☎306-2190,*www.lacasade-dondavid.com*). Comfortable, spacious and secure wooden bungalows and rooms with private hot-water bath, set in grassy grounds just back from the lakeshore. Owners David and Rosa Kuhn offer great hospitality and home cooking. David is a mine of information about Petén, and can change money, arrange trips, and sell bus tickets for Belize and Guatemala City; the staff know the times of local buses. There are usually a couple of bikes for guests to borrow. ④.

**Casa Mobego**, 500m down the road to Cerro Cahuí on the right. Good budget deal right by the lake. Simple, well-constructed stick-and-thatch cabañas, plus camping, canoe rental, a good, inexpensive restaurant and swimming. ②.

**Casa de Doña Tonita**, 800m down the road to Cerro Cahuí on the right. Four basic clapboard rooms, built high above the lake, with great views. The owner also runs a pleasant thatched-roofed restaurant next door with vegetarian food and snacks. ②.

**El Gringo Perdido**, on the north shore, 3km from *Don David's* (☎ & fax 334 2305, *ecoadventure@mail2.guate.net*). Long-established place in a supremely tranquil setting offering rooms with bath, a mosquito-netted bunk, good-value basic cabañas and camping (US$3 per person). The restaurant is less impressive. Guided canoe tours available. ③–⑤.

**Hotel Camino Real Tikal**, beyond Cerro Cahuí, 5km from the Tikal highway (in Guatemala City ☎926 0207, *www.caminor@infovia.com.gt*). Luxury option in extensive lakeside grounds with excellent views of the lake and a private beach. Rooms are a bit unimaginative and corporate, with attendant luxury trappings like buggies and a souvenir shop. Free use of kayaks and a guided tour of the Biotopo Cerro Cahuí. US$132 for a double. ⑨.

# Tikal

Towering above the rainforest, **Tikal** is possibly the most magnificent of all Maya ruins. The site is dominated by five enormous temples, steep-sided limestone pyramids that rise up to over 60m from the forest floor, while around them are literally thousands of other structures, many semi-strangled by giant roots and still hidden beneath mounds of earth. The site itself is deep in the jungle of the **Parque Nacional Tikal**, a protected area of some 370 square kilometres on the edge of the even larger Maya Biosphere Reserve and adjoining another large *biotopo*. The

Tikal emblem glyphs

trees around the ruins are home to hundreds of species including howler and spider monkeys, toucans and parakeets. The sheer scale of the place is overwhelming and its atmosphere spellbinding. Whether you can spare as little as an hour or as long as a week, it's always worth the trip.

Plane and bus schedules are designed to make it easy to visit the ruins as a day-trip from Flores or Guatemala City, but if you can spare the time it's well worth **staying overnight**, partly because you'll need the extra time to do justice to the ruins themselves but, more importantly, to spend dawn and dusk at the site, when the forest canopy bursts into a frenzy of sound and activity. The air fills with the screech of toucans and the roar of howler monkeys, while flocks of parakeets wheel around the temples and bats launch themselves into the night. With a bit of luck you might even see a grey fox sneak across one of the plazas.

## Arrival and information

The best way to reach the ruins is in one of the **tourist minibuses** that meet flights from the capital and are operated by just about every hotel in Flores and Santa Elena, starting at 4am to catch the sunrise. In addition a **local bus** leaves the market at 1pm, passing the _Hotel San Juan_ and arriving at Tikal about two hours later; it then continues to Uaxactún (see p.464), returning to Santa Elena at 5am. If you're travelling from Belize to Tikal, there is no need to go all the way to Flores; get off instead at **Puente Ixlú** – the three-way junction at the eastern end of Lago de Petén Itzá – to change buses. The local bus from Santa Elena to Tikal and Uaxactún passes at about 2pm and there are passing minibuses all day long, at their most frequent in the mornings.

**Entrance** to the national park costs US$6.40 a day (payable every day you stay at the site; if you arrive after 3pm you'll be given a ticket for the next day). The ruins are **open** daily from 6am to 6pm; extensions to 8pm can be obtained from the _inspectoría_ (7am–noon & 2–5pm), a small white hut to the left of the entrance to the ruins.

At the entrance, between the _Jungle Lodge_ and _Jaguar Inn_ hotels (see below), the one-room **Museo Tikal** (Mon–Fri 9am–5pm, Sat & Sun 9am–4pm; US$1.30) houses some of the artefacts found in the ruins, including jewellery, ceramics, obsidian eccentric flints, the jade jewellery found in tumba 116 and the magnificent Stela 31, which shows the Tikal ruler Stormy Sky bearing a jaguar head belt and a jade necklace. There's a spectacular **reconstruction of Hasaw Chan K'awil's tomb**, one of the richest ever found in the Maya world, containing 180 worked jade items in the form of bracelets, anklets, necklaces and earplugs, and delicately incised bones, including the famous carving depicting deities paddling canoes bearing the dead to the underworld.

There are a **post office**, shops and **visitor centre**, where you'll find an overpriced café-restaurant, souvenir stalls as well as the **Museo Lítico** (same hours as Museo Tikal; free) where there are nineteen more stelae, though they are very poorly labelled and there is no supplementary information in English. Two **books** of note are usually available: William Coe's _Tikal: A Handbook to the Ancient Maya Ruins_ is the best guide to the site, while _The Birds of Tikal_, although by no means comprehensive, is useful for identifying some of the hundreds of species you might come across as you wander round.

A **licensed guide** to show you the site (US$40 for a 4hr tour) is an extremely worthwhile investment if you can afford it. Many, including Eulogio López García and José Luis Morales Monzón, speak excellent English, and they all know the site really well. You'll find them waiting for business by the visitor centre and the _inspectoría_ gate.

## Accommodation, eating and drinking

There are three **hotels** at the ruins, all of them fairly expensive and not especially good value, though they offer discounts out of season. The largest and most luxurious is the _Jungle Lodge_ (in Guatemala City ☎ 476 8775, fax 476 0294, _www.junglelodge.com_; ④/⑤), which offers good bungalow accommodation with two double beds but no a/c, and some pretty comfortable "budget" rooms which lack private baths but are often booked up, plus a restaurant and a pool. Next door is the overpriced _Jaguar Inn_ (☎926 0002; fax 926 2413, _www.jaguartikal.com_ ⑤), with nine bungalows with little verandahs, camping (US$3.20 per person) but no pool. Close by, the _Tikal Inn_ (☎926 0065, fax 594 6944, _tikalinn@internetdetelgua.com.gt_; ⑤) is a better bet, with nice thatched bungalows, pleasant rooms and a glorious swimming pool. Alternatively, for US$4.80 you can **camp** or sling a **hammock** under one of the thatched shelters in a cleared space used as a campsite. Hammocks and mosquito nets (essential in the wet season) can sometimes be rented from the camping *administración* – or ask at *Jaguar Inn*. At the entrance to the campsite there's a shower block, but water is sporadic. It is illegal to camp or sleep out within the ruins.

The three simple **comedores** at the entrance to the ruins and a couple more inside offer a limited menu of traditional Guatemalan specialities – eggs, beans, grilled meat and chicken. For more extensive and expensive menus, there's an adequate restaurant in the *Jaguar Inn*. It's essential to buy some water before setting out, though cold drinks are sold at a number of spots within the ruins.

## The rise and fall of Tikal

According to the latest archeological evidence, the first occupants of Tikal arrived around 900 BC, during the **Middle Preclassic**, making the site amongst the oldest Maya settlements. They were probably attracted by its position above the surrounding seasonal swamps and by the availability of flint for making tools and weapons. It's also one of the few cities where we know the name used by the people who lived there; they called their city **Mutul** — "knot of hair" — found in the city's emblem glyph, which depicts the rear view of a head, with what appears to be a knotted headband around it. The first definite evidence of buildings dates from 500 BC, and by about 200 BC ceremonial structures had emerged, including the original version of the **North Acropolis**.

Two hundred years later, at around the time of Christ, the **Great Plaza** had begun to take shape and Tikal was already established as a major site with a large permanent population. Despite development and sophisticated architecture, Tikal remained very much a secondary centre, dominated, along with the rest of the area, by **El Mirador**, a massive city about 65km to the north (see p.466).

The closing years of the **Preclassic** era (250–300AD) were marked by the eruption of the Ilopango volcano in El Salvador, which smothered huge areas of Guatemala in a thick layer of volcanic ash. Trade routes were disrupted and the ensuing years saw the decline and abandonment of El Mirador, creating a power vacuum disputed bitterly between the cities of Tikal and Uaxactún. Tikal eventually won under the inspired leadership of Toh Chac Ich'ak, **Great Jaguar Paw**. Tikal's warriors overran Uaxactún, enabling Tikal to dominate central Petén for much of the next five hundred years. This extended period of prosperity saw the city's population grow to somewhere between 50,000 and 100,000, spreading to cover an area of around thirty square kilometres. Crucial to this success were Tikal's alliances with the powerful cities of Kaminaljuyú (near present-day Guatemala City) and Teotihuacán (to the north of modern Mexico City); stelae and paintings from the period show that Tikal's elite adopted Teotihuacán styles of clothing, pottery and weaponry. In the middle of the sixth century, however, Tikal suffered a huge setback. Already weakened by upheavals in central Mexico, where Teotihuacán was in decline, the city now faced major challenges from the east, where the city of **Caracol** (see p.273) was emerging as a major regional power, and from the north where **Calakmul** (see p.102) was becoming a Maya "superpower". In an apparent attempt to subdue a potential rival, **Double Bird**, the ruler of Tikal, launched an attack (known as an "axe war") on Caracol and its ambitious leader, Yahaw-te, **Lord Water**, in 556 AD. Despite capturing and sacrificing a noble from Caracol, Double Bird's strategy was only temporarily successful; in 562 AD Lord Water hit back in a devastating "star war", which crushed Tikal and almost certainly sacrificed Double Bird. The victors stamped their authority over the humiliated nobles of Tikal, smashing stelae, desecrating tombs and destroying written records, ushering in a 130-year "hiatus" during which no inscribed monuments were erected and Tikal was overshadowed by Caracol, supported by its powerful ally, Calakmul.

Towards the end of the seventh century, however, Caracol's stranglehold had begun to weaken and Tikal gradually started to recover its lost power. Under the formidable

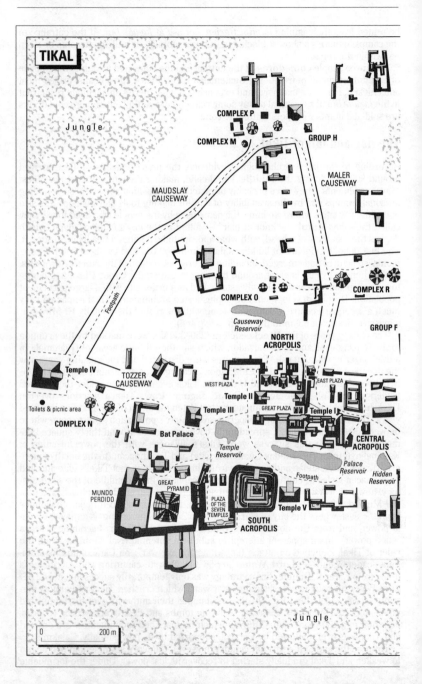

TIKAL

Jungle

COMPLEX P

COMPLEX M

GROUP H

MALER
CAUSEWAY

MAUDSLAY
CAUSEWAY

Footpath

COMPLEX O

COMPLEX R

Causeway
Reservoir

GROUP F

NORTH
ACROPOLIS

Temple IV

TOZZER
CAUSEWAY

WEST PLAZA

EAST PLAZA

Toilets & picnic area

Temple II

GREAT PLAZA

Temple I

COMPLEX N

Temple III

Bat Palace

Temple
Reservoir

Footpath

CENTRAL
ACROPOLIS

Palace
Reservoir

Hidden
Reservoir

MUNDO
PERDIDO

GREAT
PYRAMID

PLAZA
OF THE
SEVEN
TEMPLES

Temple V

SOUTH
ACROPOLIS

Jungle

0        200 m

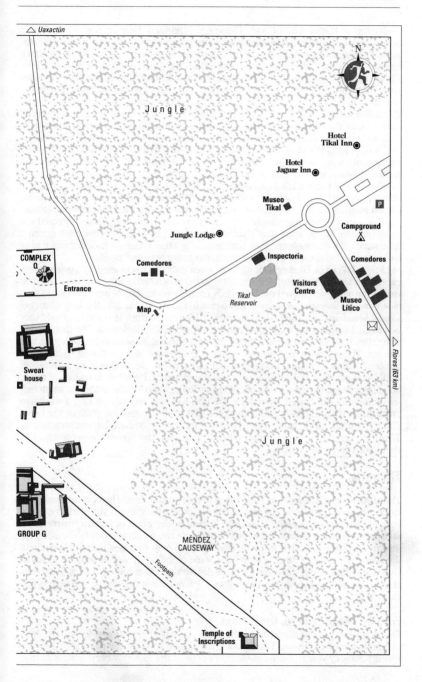

leadership of Hasaw Chan K'awil, **Heavenly Standard Bearer**, who reigned from 682—723 AD, the main ceremonial areas were reclaimed from the desecration suffered at the hands of Caracol. By 695 AD, Tikal was powerful enough to launch an attack against Calakmul, capturing and executing its king, Yich'ak K'ak or **Fiery Claw/Jaguar Paw**, and severely weakening the alliance against Tikal. The following year, Hasaw Chan K'awil repeated his astonishing coup by capturing **Split Earth**, the new king of Calakmul, and Tikal regained its position among the most important of Petén cities. Hasaw Chan K'awil's leadership gave birth to a revitalized and powerful ruling dynasty: in the hundred years following his death Tikal's five main temples were built and his son, Yik'in Chan K'awil or **Divine Sunset Lord** (who ascended the throne in 734 AD), had his father's body entombed in the magnificent **Temple I**. Temples and monuments were still under construction until at least 869 AD, when Tikal's last recorded date is inscribed on Stela 24.

What brought about Tikal's final **downfall** remains a mystery, but what is certain is that around 900 AD almost the entire lowland Maya civilization collapsed. Possible causes range from an earthquake to popular uprising, with the latest theories indicating that an environmental disaster caused by overpopulation may have triggered the disintegration. We do know that Tikal was abandoned by the end of the tenth century. Afterwards, the site was used from time to time by other groups, who worshipped here and repositioned many of the stelae, but it was never occupied again.

Little is known of Tikal again until 1848, when it was **rediscovered** by a government expedition led by Modesto Méndez. Later in the nineteenth century a Swiss scientist visited the site and removed the beautifully carved wooden lintels from the tops of temples 1 and 4 – they are currently in a museum in Basel – and in 1881 the English archeologist Maudslay took the first photographs of the ruins. Until 1951 the site could only be reached on horseback and the ruins remained mostly uncleared. The Guatemalan army then built an airstrip, paving the way for a cultural invasion of archeologists and tourists. The gargantuan project to excavate and restore the site started in 1956, and involved teams from the University of Pennsylvania and Guatemala's Institute of Anthropology. Most of the major work was completed by 1984, but thousands of minor buildings remain buried in roots, shoots and rubble. There's little doubt that an incredible amount is still buried around the site however – as recently as 1996 a workman unearthed a stela (Stela 40, dating from 468 AD) while mowing the grass on the Great Plaza. A ten-year project to restore Temple 5 (at 58m the second highest structure at Tikal) is currently being co-ordinated with help from the Spanish government, and should be completed by 2007.

# The ruins

The sheer scale of the ruins at Tikal can at first seem daunting. The **central area**, with its five main temples, forms by far the most impressive section; if you start to explore beyond this you can ramble seemingly forever in the maze of smaller, **unrestored structures** and complexes. Compared to the scale and magnificence of the main area, they're not that impressive, but armed with a good map (the best is in Coe's guide to the ruins), it can be exciting to search for some of the rarely visited outlying sections. Don't even think about exploring the more distant structures without a map; every year at least one tourist gets lost in the jungle. Tikal is certain to exhaust you before you exhaust it.

## From the entrance to the Great Plaza

Following the path to the right of the **map** you pass **Complexes Q and R**, twin pyramids built by **Chitam**, Tikal's last known ruler, to mark the passing of a *katum* (twenty 360-day years). Set to one side is a copy of the superbly carved Stela 22 (the original is now in the Museo Lítico, inside the visitor centre), the glyph carvings on it recording the ascension to the throne in 768 AD of Tikal's last known ruler, **Chitam**, portrayed in full regalia, complete with a sweeping headress and staff of authority. Bearing to the left after Complex R you approach the **East Plaza**; in its southeast corner stands an imposing temple, beneath which were found the remains of several severed heads, the victims of human sacrifice. Behind the plaza is the **sweat house**, which may have been similar to those used by highland Maya today. It's thought that Maya priests would take a sweat bath in order to cleanse themselves before conducting religious rituals.

From here a few short steps bring you to the **Great Plaza**, the heart of the ancient city. Surrounded by four massive structures, this was the focus of ceremonial and religious activity at Tikal for around a thousand years. Beneath the grass lie four layers of paving, the oldest of which dates from about 150 BC and the most recent from 700 AD. **Temple 1**, towering 44m above the plaza, is the hallmark of Tikal – it's also known as the Temple of the Grand Jaguar because of the jaguar carved in its door lintel (now in a museum in Basel). This is the temple built as a burial monument to contain the magnificent **tomb of Hasaw Chan K'awil** (682–721 AD) by his son and successor Yik'in Chan K'awil. Within the tomb at the temple's core, the skeleton was found facing north, surrounded by an assortment of jade, pearls, seashells and also stingray spines, which were used in bloody body-piercing rituals. A reconstruction of the tomb (tumba 116) is on show in the Museo Tikal.

Standing opposite, like a squat version of Temple 1, is **Temple 2**, known as the Temple of the Masks for the two grotesque masks, now heavily eroded, that flank the central stairway. As yet no tomb has been found beneath this temple, which now stands 38m high, although with its roof comb intact it would have equalled Temple 1. It's an easy climb up the staircase to the top and the view, almost level with the forest canopy, is incredible, with the great plaza spread out below.

The **North Acropolis**, which fills the whole north side of the Great Plaza, is one of the most complex structures in the entire Maya world. In true Maya style it was built and rebuilt on top of itself, and beneath the twelve temples that can be seen today are the remains of about a hundred other structures. As early as 100 BC the Maya had constructed elaborate platforms supporting temples and tombs here. Archeologists have removed some of the surface to reveal these earlier structures, including two four-metre-high **masks**. One facing the plaza, protected by a thatched roof, is clearly visible; the other can be reached by following the dark passageway to the side – you'll need a torch. In front of the North Acropolis are two lines of **stelae** carved with images of Tikal's ruling elite, with circular altars at their bases, all of which were originally painted a brilliant red. These and other stelae throughout the site bear the marks of **ritual defacement**, carried out when one ruler replaced another to erase any latent powers that the image may have retained.

## The Central Acropolis and Temple 5

On the other side of the plaza is the **Central Acropolis**, a maze of tiny interconnecting rooms and stairways built around six smallish courtyards. The buildings here are usually referred to as palaces rather than temples, although their precise use remains a mystery. Possibilities include law courts, temporary retreats, administrative centres, and homes for Tikal's elite. Behind the acropolis is the palace reservoir, which was fed with rainwater by a series of channels from all over the city. Further behind the Central Acropolis is the 58-metre-high **Temple 5**, which supports a single tiny room at the top thought to be a mortuary shrine to an unknown ruler. The temple is currently the subject of a huge restoration project, due to be completed by around 2007, when the view from the top will be superb, with a great profile of Temple 1 and a side view of the central plaza.

## From the West Plaza to Temple 4

Behind Temple 2 is the **West Plaza**, dominated by a large Late Classic temple on the north side, and scattered with various altars and stelae. From here the Tozzer Causeway – one of the raised routes that connected the main parts of the city – leads west to **Temple 3** (55m), covered in jungle vegetation. A fragment of Stela 24, found at the base of the temple, dates it at 810 AD. Around the back of the temple is a huge palace complex, of which only the **Bat Palace** has been restored. At the end of the Tozzer Causeway is **Temple 4**, the tallest of all the Tikal structures at a massive 64m. Built in 741 AD, it is thought by some archeologists to be the resting place of the ruler **Yik'in Chan K'awil**, whose image was depicted on wooden lintels built into the top of the temple. Twin ladders, one for the ascent, the other for the descent, attached to the sides of the temple delineate the route. Slow and exhausting as the climb is, one of the finest views of the whole site awaits. All around you the forest canopy stretches out to the horizon, interrupted only by the great roof combs of the other temples.

## The Mundo Perdido, the Plaza of the Seven Temples and the Temple of the Inscriptions

To the south of the Central Acropolis, reached by a trail from Temple 3, you'll find the **Plaza of the Seven Temples**, which forms part of a complex dating back to before Christ. There's an unusual triple ball court on the north side of the plaza, and to the east is the unexcavated South Acropolis. To the west, the **Mundo Perdido**, or Lost World, is another magical and very distinct section of the site with its own ambience and architecture. Little is known about the ruins in this part of the site, but archeologists hope that further research will help to explain the early history of Tikal. The main feature is the **great pyramid**, a 32-metre-high structure whose surface hides four earlier versions, the first dating from 500 BC. The top of the pyramid offers awesome views towards Temple 4 and the Great Plaza and makes an excellent base for the visual dramatics of sunrise or sunset.

Finally, there's the **Temple of the Inscriptions**, reached along the Méndez Causeway from the East Plaza behind Temple 1. The temple (only discovered in 1951) is about 1km from the plaza. It's famous for its 12m roof comb, at the back of which is a huge but rather faint hieroglyphic text.

# Uaxactún and the far north

Away to the north of Tikal, lost in a sea of jungle, are several other very substantial **ruins** – unrestored and for the most part uncleared, but with their own unique atmosphere. The village and ruins of **Uaxactún** lie 24km north of Tikal, strung out by the side of a disused airstrip. With two places to stay, several comedores and a daily bus to Santa Elena, the village is an ideal jumping-off point for the more remote sites of **El Zotz** and **Río Azul**, where the bulk of the temples are coated in an anarchic tangle of vegetation and only the tallest roof combs are visible. **Dirt tracks** go as far as Río Azul and El Zotz, though doubtless they'll soon be reached by road. For the moment, however, they remain well beyond the reach of the average visitor – perfect if you're in search of an adventure and want to see a virtually untouched Maya site.

## Uaxactún

**UAXACTÚN** is substantially smaller than Tikal, but thought to date from the same era. During the Preclassic period Uaxactún and Tikal coexisted in relative harmony, dominated by El Mirador, but by the first century AD, with El Mirador in decline, a fierce rivalry ignited between Tikal and Uaxactún. The two finally clashed in 378 AD when Tikal's warriors conquered Uaxactún, forcing it to accept subordinate status.

The overall impact of Uaxactún may be a little disappointing after the grandeur of Tikal, but you'll probably have the site to yourself, giving you the chance to soak up the atmosphere. The most interesting buildings are in **Group E**, east of the airstrip, where three reconstructed temples, built side by side, are arranged to function as an observatory. Viewed from the top of a fourth temple, the sun rises behind the north temple on the longest day of the year and behind the southern one on the shortest day. Beneath one of these temples the famous **E-VII** was unearthed, once thought to date back to 2000BC, though a much later date is now accepted. The original pyramid had a simple staircase up the front, flanked by two stucco masks, and post holes in the top suggest that it may have been covered by a thatched shelter. Over on the other side of the airstrip is **Group A**, a series of larger temples and residential compounds, some of them reconstructed, and some impressive stelae.

## Practicalities

A **bus** from Flores passes through Tikal en route for Uaxactún at around 3.30pm; alternatively, you could take one of the **tours** run by a number of companies based in Flores. **Staying** overnight you have two options: the basic *EcoCampamento* (☎926 0077 in Flores; rooms ②) has tents and hammocks (US$3 per person), protected by mosquito nets, under a thatched shelter; the welcoming *Campamento Ecológico El Chiclero* (☎926 1033, fax 926 1095 in Flores; US$10 per person) offers clean rooms without bath, or you can camp or sling up a hammock for US$2.50 a head. Owner Heria Herrera also organizes four-wheel-drive trips to Río Azul, and prepares excellent food.

Uaxactún's **guide association** has a small **information office** at the end of the airstrip and will arrange **camping trips** to any of the remote northern sites, into the jungle or east to Nakúm and Yaxhá. Equipment is carried on horseback and the price (US$30 per person per day for a group of three or more) includes a guide, horses, camping gear and food. Check at CINCAP or ProPetén in Flores for advice and help with putting together excursions, or contact Evolution Adventures (see p.455).

# El Zotz

Thirty kilometres west of Uaxactún, along a rough jeep track sometimes passable in the dry season (by four-wheel drive) is **El Zotz**, a large Maya site set in its own *biotopo* reserve adjoining the Tikal national park. To **get there** you can rent vehicles in Uaxactún, or hire a packhorse, guide, food and camping equipment from Uaxactún's guide association. After about four hours' walk – almost halfway – you come to **Santa Cruz**, where you can camp if necessary. At the site itself you'll be welcomed by the guards who look after the *biotopo* headquarters. You can camp here and, with permission, use their kitchen and drinking water; remember to bring some food to share with the guides.

Totally unrestored and smothered by vegetation, El Zotz has been systematically looted, although there are now guards on duty all year round. Zotz means "bat" in Maya and each evening at dusk you'll see tens, perhaps hundreds, of thousands of **bats** of several species emerge from a cave near the campsite. It's especially impressive in the moonlight, the beating wings sounding like a river flowing over rapids – one of the most remarkable natural sights in Petén.

Walking on, it takes about four and a half hours to get to **Cruce dos Aguadas**, a crossroads village on the bus route between Santa Elena and Carmelita. Here you'll find shops and the *Comedor Patojas*, where they'll let you sling a hammock or camp. Northwards, the road goes to Carmelita for El Mirador; there's also a track westwards towards El Perú, though this is not passable in the rainy season.

# Río Azul

The remote site of **Río Azul**, almost on the tripartite border where Guatemala, Belize and Mexico meet, was only rediscovered in 1962. The city and its suburbs had a population of around five thousand and probably reached a peak in the Preclassic era, but remained an important site well into the Classic period. Although totally unrestored, the core of the site is similar to a small-scale Tikal, with the tallest temple (AIII) standing some 47m above the forest floor, surfacing above the treetops and giving magnificent views across the jungle.

Several incredible **tombs** have been unearthed here, lined with white plaster and painted with vivid red glyphs. Tomb 19 is thought to have contained the remains of one of the sons of Stormy Sky, Tikal's great early Classic expansionist ruler (who ruled Tikal shortly after it conquered Uaxactún), suggesting that the city may have been founded by Tikal to consolidate the borders of its empire. Nearby tombs contained bodies of warriors dressed in clothing typical of Teotihuacán in central Mexico – further supporting evidence of links between Tikal and the mighty ancient city.

Extensive **looting** occurred after the site's discovery, with a gang of up to eighty men plundering the tombs and removing some of the finest murals in the Maya world once the archeological teams had retreated to Flores in the rainy season. Río Azul supplied the international market with unique treasures including some incredible green jade masks and pendants. Mercifully, despite its chamber being looted in 1981, Tomb 1's walls remain almost intact. Today there are two resident guards.

The **road** that connects Tikal and Uaxactún continues for another 95km north to Río Azul. This route is only passable in the dry season, and can be covered by four-wheel-drives in as little as four hours, depending on the conditions. **Walking** or on **horseback** it's four days each way – three at a push. Trips can be arranged through *El Chiclero* in Uaxactún or through ProPetén and CINCAP or a number of agents in Flores. Once you arrive at Río Azul you'll be welcome to **stay** at the guard's camp (bring some supplies).

# El Mirador

**El Mirador** is perhaps the most exotic and mysterious of all Petén's Maya sites. Still buried in the forest, this massive city matches Tikal's scale, and may even surpass it. Rediscovered in 1926, it dates from an earlier period than Tikal, flourishing between 150 BC and 150 AD, and was almost certainly the first great city in the Maya World. It was unquestionably the dominant city in Petén, occupying a commanding position above the rainforest, at an altitude of 250m, and was home to tens of thousands of Maya. Little archeological work has been done here but it's clear that the site represents the peak of Preclassic Maya culture, which was far more sophisticated than was once believed.

The core of the site covers some sixteen square kilometres, stretching between two massive pyramids that face each other across the forest. The site's western side is marked by the massive **Tigre Complex**, made up of a huge single pyramid flanked by two smaller structures, a triadic design that's characteristic of El Mirador's architecture. The base of this complex alone would cover around three football fields, while the height of the 2000-year-old main pyramid touches 70m, equivalent to an eighteen-storey building and making the structure the tallest anywhere in the Maya world. In front of the Tigre Complex is El Mirador's sacred hub: a long narrow plaza, the **Central Acropolis**, and a row of smaller buildings. Burial chambers unearthed in this central section contained the bodies of priests and noblemen, surrounded by the obsidian lancets and stingray spines used to pierce the penis, ears and tongue in ritual bloodletting ceremonies. The spilling of blood was seen by the Maya as a method of summoning and sustaining the gods, and was clearly common at all the great ceremonial centres.

To the south of the Tigre Complex is the **Monos Complex**, another triadic structure and plaza, named after the resident howler monkeys. To the north the **León**

**pyramid** and the **Casabel Complex** mark the edge of the site. Heading away to the east, the Puleston Causeway runs to the smaller East Group, the largest of which (about 2km from the Tigre Complex) is the **Danta Complex**. This is another triadic structure, rising in three stages to a height just below that of the Tigre pyramid, but with an even better view since it was built on higher land.

The area **around El Mirador** is riddled with smaller Maya sites, and as you look out across the forest from the top of either of the main temples you can see others rising above the horizon on all sides – including the giant Calakmul in Mexico (see p.102). Among the most accessible are **Nakbé**, some 10km to the southeast, with origins as early as 1000 BC, probably predating all other Maya sites in the area. Some initial excavation work has been done at Nakbé, uncovering several pyramids from as early as 600 BC, some reaching 45m in height. A huge Maya mask (5m by 8m) was also found in September 1992, and doubtless much more will follow. Far Horizons run expeditions to Nakbé; see "Basics" p.5 for details.

**El Tintal**, a massive site 21km to the southwest of El Mirador, was connected by a causeway to its neighbour, and the ruins, though severely looted, make an ideal campsite. Climb to the top of the largest pyramid and there are spectacular views, including El Mirador in the distance.

**Getting to** El Mirador is a substantial undertaking, involving a rough 60km bus or pick-up journey from Santa Elena to **Carmelita**, a chicle- and *xate*-gathering centre, followed by two days of hard jungle hiking – you'll need a horse to carry your food and equipment. The journey – impossibly muddy in the rainy season – is best attempted from mid-January to August; February to April is the driest period. It offers an exceptional chance to see virtually untouched forest, and perhaps some of the creatures that inhabit it. EcoMaya (see p.455) offers five-day **tours** (around US$200 for two people) from Flores, including guide, packhorse and digs in Carmelita, or you can travel **independently**, arranging a guide in Carmelita (about US$30 a day) who will then organize packhorse, food, water and camping gear for you – ask for Luís Morales, president of the Tourist Committee, who can sort out guides for the trip. You should definitely bring some supplies for the guards, who spend forty days at a time in the forest, subsisting on beans and tortillas. Whether you take a tour or go independently, you're advised to examine the information and maps at ProPetén and CINCAP first.

To **get to** Carmelita there's a daily bus at 1pm from Santa Elena via San Andrés (see p.455) and Cruce Dos Aguadas (see p.465). There's basic but clean **accommodation** at the *Campamento Nakbé* (②), 1.5km before the village, where the large thatched shelters have mosquito nets and hammocks, or, if you have your own tent, you can **camp** (US$2 per person). For a good feed, visit the *Comedor Pepe Toño* in the centre of the village, run by Brenda Zapata, who is a mine of information about the area and can introduce you to the local guides.

# Sayaxché and around

Southwest of Flores, on a lazy bend in the Río Pasión, the easygoing frontier town of **SAYAXCHÉ** makes an ideal base for exploring the surrounding forest and its huge collection of archeological remains. The town is the supply centre for a vast surrounding area that is being steadily cleared and colonized. The complex network of rivers and swamps that cuts through the forested wilderness here has been an important trade route since Maya times, and there are several interesting ruins in the area. Upstream is **Ceibal**, a small but beautiful site in a wonderful jungle setting; to the south is **Lago de Petexbatún**, on the shores of which are the small ruins of **Dos Pilas** and **Aguateca**. Both sites offer great opportunities to wander in the forest and watch the wildlife.

## Sayaxché practicalities

**Getting to Sayaxché** from Flores is very straightforward, with several Pinita **buses** (5.30am, 8am, 10am, 1pm & 4pm; 2hr) and one Del Rosio service (5am) plying the fairly smooth 62km dirt road. At other times hitching a ride in a **pick-up** is not too difficult, or there are a number of travel agencies offering day tours (around US$30) from Flores. A ferry takes you over the Río Pasión, directly opposite Sayaxché.

**Hotels** in Sayaxché are on the basic side. The *Guayacán* (☎926 6111; ③), right beside the river, is the first you come to, with plain functional rooms, some with private bath, and lovely sunset views from the terrace. For a cheaper room, head right from the dock to the friendly *Hotel Posada Segura* (②) which has decent, clean rooms, some with private bath; alternatively, head left down the street above the *Guayacan* to the basic but cheap *Hospedaje Mayapan* (①) where you may be able to rent a **bike** for visiting Ceibal. There are plenty of reasonable places to **eat**, the best being the *Restaurant Yaxkin* (closes 8pm), which is a little pricey, though the portions are huge. There is also decent food at *Guayacan* and at *La Montaña*, 100m south on the same street, a restaurant owned by the knowledgeable and helpful Julián Mariona, who can arrange **trips** to the nearby ruins (around US$40 a day). Plenty of **boatmen** are eager to take you up- or downriver, though they tend to see all tourists as walking cash-dispensers and quote prices in dollars. Try Pedro Méndez Requena of Viajes Don Pedro (☎ & fax 928 6109), who offers **tours** of the area from his office on the riverfront. You can change travellers' cheques at Banora, a block up from the *Guayacan*.

# The ruins of Ceibal

The most accessible and impressive of the sites near Sayaxché is **Ceibal**, which you can reach by land or river. It's easy enough to make it there and back in an afternoon **by boat**; haggle with the boatmen at the waterfront and you can expect to pay around US$40 (for up to six people). The beautiful hour-long boat trip is followed by a thirty-minute hike uphill through towering rainforest to the ruins. **By road**, Ceibal is just 17km from Sayaxché. Any transport heading south out of town towards Cruce del Pato passes the entrance track to the site, from where it's an 8km walk through fields and then jungle to the ruins. Travel agents in Flores also run day-trips to Ceibal (around US$30 per person); see p.455 for recommended companies.

Surrounded by forest and shaded by huge ceiba trees, **the ruins** of Ceibal are a mixture of cleared open plazas and untamed jungle. Though many of the largest temples lie buried under mounds, Ceibal does have some outstanding carving, well preserved by the use of hard stone. The two main plazas are dotted with lovely **stelae**, centred around two low platforms. During the Classic period Ceibal was a relatively minor site, but it grew rapidly between 830 and 930 AD, apparently after falling under the control of colonists from what is now Mexico, becoming a large lowland site, with an estimated population of around ten thousand. Outside influence is clearly visible in the carving here: speech scrolls, straight noses, waist-length hair and serpent motifs are all decidedly non-Maya. The monkey-faced Stela 2 is particularly striking, beyond which is Stela 14, another impressive sculpture straight ahead down the path. If you turn right here and walk for ten minutes you'll reach the only other restored part of the site, set superbly in a clearing in the forest – an unmissable massive circular stone platform which was either an altar or **observation** deck for astronomy.

# Lago de Petexbatún: Aguateca and Dos Pilas

A similar distance to the south of Sayaxché is **Lago de Petexbatún**, a spectacular expanse of water ringed by dense forest and containing plentiful supplies of snook, bass, alligator and freshwater turtle. The shores of the lake abound with wildlife and Maya remains and, though the ruins themselves are small and unrestored, their sheer number suggests that the lake was an important trading centre for the Maya. **Aguateca**, perched on a high outcrop on the southern tip of the lake, is the most accessible site (although it's the furthest from Sayaxché) as a boat can get you to within twenty minutes' walk of it.

Encompassed by dense tropical forest and with superb views of the lake, Aguateca has a magical atmosphere. Though looters damaged some structures here in 2000, you can clearly make out the temples and plazas, dotted with well-preserved stelae. The carving is superbly executed, the images including rulers, captives, hummingbirds, pineapples and pelicans. Aguateca is also the site of the only known **bridge** in the Maya world, which crosses a narrow gash in the hillside, but although it's unique it's not that impressive. If you ask the guards who live here, they may give you an enthusiastic and well-informed tour of the site, and if you want to **stay** they'll find some space for you to sling a hammock or pitch a tent – bring along a mosquito net and some food.

Slightly closer to Sayaxché is **Dos Pilas**, another unreconstructed site, buried in the jungle to the west of the lake. Dos Pilas was the centre of a formidable empire in the early part of the eighth century, with a population approaching ten thousand. The ruins are quite unusual, as the major structures are grouped in an east–west linear pattern. Around the central plaza are some tremendous stelae, altars and four **hieroglyphic stairways** decorated with glyphs and figures.

To **get to Dos Pilas** from Sayaxché, it's a 45-minute speedboat trip (or up to 3hr in a cargo boat) to the *Posada El Caribe* (☎928 6114, fax 928 6168; ⑦ full board) with clean, screened cabins, good food and boat trips to Aguateca, situated at the northern tip of the lake and then a further 12km trek on foot to the ruins. About 7km from the lake you pass the small site of **Arroyo de Piedra**, where you'll find a plaza and two fairly well-preserved stelae. It may also be possible to get to both sites **by mule** (or even truck) during the dry months.

## South to the Ixcán

South of Sayaxché the road skirts the edge of the **Parque Nacional Ceibal**, at first slicing through a stretch of jungle, then through a flat, degraded land of scrub, lone tree stumps, cattle pasture and thatched cabañas full of indigenous families. These Q'eqchi', some returning refugees, attempt to eke out a meagre existence in this poor, largely treeless landscape. Half an hour before **Cruce del Pato** (see p.447), where the road splits, the magnificent bulk of the Cuchumatanes mountain range comes into view, the looming, forested peaks rising abruptly from the plain. A Del Rosio bus runs down this road to **Playitas** every morning.

# Routes to Mexico

There are a number of possible routes **into Mexico** from Petén, all of which offer a sense of adventure and a glimpse of the rainforest – and involve shuttling between buses, boats and immigration posts. However, travellers should bear in mind that at the time of writing, Mexican border officials were only giving **two-week visas** to travellers entering the state of Chiapas from Guatemala, due to the armed conflict in the region.

### From Sayaxché to Benemérito

Downriver from Sayaxché, the **Río Pasión** snakes its way through an area of forest, swamp and small settlements to **Pipiles**, which marks the point where the rivers Salinas and Pasión merge to form the Usumacinta. All boats stop here for **immigra-**

**tion**, and exit stamps can be obtained. Not far from Pipiles is the small Maya site of **Altar de los Sacrificios**, commanding an important river junction. This is one of the oldest sites in Petén, but these days there's not much to see beyond a solitary stela. Following the **Usumacinta** downstream you arrive at **Benemérito** in Mexico (see p.150), a sprawling frontier town at the end of a dirt road from Palenque. It's about US$8–10 for this eight-hour trip, though cargo boats can take a couple of days to get this far. There are basic hotels and restaurants in Benemérito and you can head on to Yaxchilán from here directly by boat or, much more cheaply, by bus to Frontera Corozal (where there are basic bedrooms and camping) and then by boat.

## From Bethel to Frontera Corozal

The cheapest and most straightforward route to Mexico is along the rough road to **BETHEL** on the Río Usumacinta, where there is a Guatemalan **immigration** post. Three buses a day leave Flores for Bethel (5am, 8am & 1pm; 4hr), passing the El Subín junction north of Sayaxché about a couple of hours later. At Bethel it's relatively easy to find a lancha heading downstream to Frontera Corozal (around US$7, more if there are a shortage of passengers; 30min); however, it's usually possible to get off the bus, obtain your exit stamp in Bethel and continue on the same bus for a further 12km to the tiny settlement of **Téchnica**, where you can cross the Usumacinta for just US$0.70, to Corozal on the opposite bank. At the time of writing there's no accommodation or other facilities in Téchnica.

If you need to stay, Bethel itself is a pleasant village where you can **camp** above the riverbank and there are several **comedores** and shops. The **Bethel ruins**, 1.5km from the village, are today little more than tree-covered mounds, but there's an excellent **eco-campamento** here called the *Posada Maya*, with hammocks (☎801 1799; ①), tents (including mattresses and clean sheets) under thatched shelters (US$6 per person), and wooden cabins (US$9 per person) on top of a wooded cliff high above the river.

Over the border in Frontera Corozal (see p.148) there is an **immigration post**, plus some comedores and very basic hotels. From here there are regular **buses**, shared minibuses and tour buses to Palenque until 3pm (4hr). For further adventure, the spectacular ruins of **Yaxchilán** (see p.149), grouped around a great loop in the Usumacinta, are 15km away; **hiring a boat** for this beautiful trip costs around US$60 return.

## El Naranjo to La Palma

A less popular and more expensive route **from Flores to Mexico** takes you by a partly paved road to **EL NARANJO** (several buses a day until 2.30pm; 4hr). El Naranjo is a rough spot, consisting of little more than an army base, an **immigration** post, where you'll be asked for a "leaving tax" of around US$5, stores (offering poor exchange rates), comedores and basic hotels. The best place **to stay** is the friendly, family-run *Posada San Pedro* across the river (☎926 1276 in Flores; ③). The other places in town are pretty filthy. The river trip down the San Pedro starts here; there's usually a **boat** (US$20 per person; 4hr) for Mexico at around 1pm, returning from La Palma at 8am. Your first port of call is the Mexican immigration post, about an hour away, and beyond that is the small riverside village of **La Palma** in Mexico (see p.189). La Palma has basic rooms to rent and bus connections to Tenosique (last bus 5pm).

## Piedras Negras

On the Guatemalan side of the Usumacinta, downstream from Yaxchilán, the ruins of **Piedras Negras** are some of the most inaccessible and least visited of all the major Maya ruins. Though many of the very best carvings are on display in the Museo Nacional de Arqueología y Etnología in Guatemala City, where they're a great deal easier to see, there's still plenty to experience on site. Piedras Negras, whose name

Piedras Negras glyph

refers to the stones lining the river bank here, was closely allied with Yaxchilán and probably under its rule at various times.

Upon arrival, the most immediately impressive monument is a large rock jutting over the riverbank with a carving of a male seated figure presenting a bundle to a female figure. This was once surrounded by glyphs, now badly eroded and best seen at night with a torch held at a low angle. Continuing up the hill, across plazas and over the ruins of buildings, you get some idea of the city's size. Several buildings are comparatively well preserved, particularly the **sweat baths**, used for ritual purification. The most imposing of all is the **Acropolis**, a huge complex of rooms, passages and courtyards towering 100m above the riverbank. A **megalithic stairway** led down to the river at one time, doubtless a humbling sight to visitors (and captives) before the forest invaded the city. Another intriguing sight is a huge double-headed turtle glyph carved on a rock overhanging a small valley. This is a reference to the end of a *katun*; inside the main glyph is a giant representation of the day sign Ahau (which also means Lord), recalling the myth of the birth of the maize god. During research carried out at Piedras Negras in the 1930s, the artist and epigrapher Tatiana Proskouriakoff noticed that dates carved on monuments corresponded approximately to a human life span, indicating that the glyphs might refer to events in one person's lifetime, possibly the rulers of the city. Rejected for decades by the archeological establishment, her theory was later proved correct.

Traditionally, the presence of FAR guerrillas in the region protected the ruins from systematic looting – neither looters nor the army dared enter. Now that the guerrillas have gone and access from the Mexican bank is becoming easier, it remains to be seen how long Piedras Negras can maintain its relatively untouched state. The site is currently being researched by a joint American-Guatemalan team of Maya academics – the first serious investigation of Piedras Negras since 1939.

There's no easy way to **get to** Piedras Negras, as the site is only accessible by boat. Several tour operators run trips down the Usumacinta, with the best-organized being Maya Expeditions (see p.340), a specialist white-water rafting operation based in Guatemala City.

# From Flores to Belize

The hundred kilometres from Flores to the border with Belize take you through another sparsely inhabited section of Petén, a journey of around two and a half hours by bus down a pretty decent road that's paved most of the way. If you catch the 5am express service you can even make it straight through to Chetumal, in Mexico, the same day. Along the way the bus passes through **Ixlú** (see p.356), halfway between Tikal and Flores, so if you're coming directly from the site or El Remate you can pick up a ride there.

## Lago de Yaxhá and the ruins of Nakúm

About halfway between Puente Ixlú and the border is **Lago de Yaxhá**, a shallow limestone depression ringed by dense rainforest and home to two isolated Maya sites: Yaxhá and Topoxté. The turn-off is clearly signposted and the bus driver will stop if you ask. If you haven't arranged accommodation at *El Sombrero* (see below) then you'll probably be faced with a sweltering two-hour walk to get there, though there is some traffic to and from the village of La Máquina, 2km before the lakes. Just before you reach the lakes you pass a **control post** where you may be asked to sign in. From here it's 3km to the site: head along the road between the lakes then turn left (signed) for Yaxhá.

**Yaxhá**, covering several square kilometres of a ridge overlooking the lake, is primarily a Classic period city. The early history of the site is unclear due to a lack of inscriptions, though the sheer scale of the ruins (only Tikal and El Mirador are larger in Guatemala) confirm it was undoubtedly a major player in the central Maya region. Although some restoration has been completed, don't expect the manicured splendour of Tikal. What you can count on, though, is real atmosphere as you try to discover the many features still half hidden by the forest. The site is open daily (8am–5pm) and **entrance** is free at the time of writing; if you're not on a guided trip then one of the guardians will show you around for a small tip. The ruins are spread out over nine plazas and around five hundred structures have been mapped so far,

Yaxhá emblem glyph

including several huge pyramids and large acropolis complexes. The tallest and most impressive pyramid, Structure 216, 250m northeast of the entrance, rises in tiers to a height of over 30m; the recent restoration enables you to climb to the top for spectacular views over the forest and lake.

**Topoxté**, a much smaller site on an island close to the west shore of the lake, is best reached by boat from *El Sombrero*. There is a 4km trail to a spot opposite the island but you still have to get over to it – and large crocodiles inhabit the lake. The structures you see are not on the scale of those at Yaxhá, and date mainly from the Late Postclassic, though the site has been occupied since Preclassic times. Work is in progress to restore some structures. Several tour operators in Flores offer trips to Yaxhá and Topoxté (see p.455).

If you want to **stay** nearby, the wonderful, solar-powered *Campamento El Sombrero* (☎926 5229, fax 926 5198, *sombrero@guate.net*; ④), 200m from the road on the south side of the lake, has thatched rooms in wooden jungle lodges and space for **camping**; the Italian-born owner, Gabriela Moretti, can arrange boat trips on the lake and horseback riding; she'll pick you up from the bus stop if you've called in advance. There's another *campamento*, run by locals on behalf of Inguat, on the far side of the lake, below Yaxhá, where you can **pitch a tent** or sling a hammock beneath a thatched shelter for free.

The unrestored **ruins of Nakúm**, a somewhat larger site, are about 20km north of Lago de Yaxhá, though the road is rarely passable so you'll probably have to walk. The most impressive structure is the residential-style palace, which has forty rooms and is similar to the North Acropolis at Tikal. There are two guards here who will show you where to camp or put up a hammock. It's also possible to **walk to Tikal** in a day from Nakúm (around 25km), though you'll need to persuade a guard to act as a **guide**, or bring one with you – speak to Inguat or see CINCAP in Flores.

## The border: Melchor de Mencos

Despite the differences between Guatemala and Belize, border formalities are fairly straightforward: you'll probably be asked for a small "departure tax" of US$1 to leave Guatemala, though there is officially no fee. **Moneychangers** will pester you on either side of the border – most give a fair rate. There's also a **bank** (Mon–Fri 8.30am–6pm) just beyond the immigration building, next to the *Hotel Frontera Palace* (☎ & fax 926 5196; ④), which has rooms in pleasant thatched cabins, hot water and a restaurant.

Buses to the border from Flores/Santa Elena leave from the marketplace in Santa Elena eight times daily between 5am and 6pm. Mundo Maya also operates a 5am **express service**, leaving from their offices on Calle Principal in Santa Elena, to Belize City (5hr; US$20) and on to Chetumal (8hr; US$35) where it connects with a luxury Mexican bus to Cancún (5hr 30min, US$9). The *Hotel San Juan* operates a similar express bus service, leaving at 5am. Buses leave **for Belize City** every hour or so (3hr) right from the border. Indeed, most actually begin their journey from the market in Melchor; for other destinations you may have to take a shared taxi to Benque Viejo or to San Ignacio (US$2 per person; 20min).

# travel details

## Buses

**Agua Blanca** to: Guatemala City (3 daily; 5hr).

**Chiquimula** to: El Florido (hourly between 6am–4pm; 1hr 30min); Esquipulas (every 15 min; 1hr); Guatemala City (14 daily; 3hr 30min); Ipala (11 daily; 1hr); Puerto Barrios (10 daily; 3hr).

**Cobán** to: Cahabón (4 daily; 4hr); El Estor (10 daily; 8hr); Fray Bartolomé de Las Casas (5 daily; 7hr); Guatemala City (30 daily; 4–5hr);Lanquín (4 daily; 3hr); San Cristóbal Verapaz (hourly; 45min); San Pedro Carchá (every 15 min; 20min); Senahú (3 daily; 7hr); Tactic (hourly; 45min), Uspantán (3 daily; 5hr).

**Cubulco** to: Guatemala City via El Chol (1 daily; 9hr); Guatemala City via la Cumbre (5 daily; 5hr 30min); Rabinal (hourly; 30min); Salamá (hourly; 1hr 30min).

**Esquipulas** to: Aguacaliente for Honduras (every 30 min; 30min) and for El Salvador (every 30min; 1hr); Chiquimula (every 15min; 1hr); Guatemala City (hourly 2am–6pm; 4hr).

**Flores** to: Belize City (2 daily; 5hr); Bethel (3 daily; 5hr); Carmelita (1 daily; 4hr); Chetumal (2 daily; 9hr); Cruce del Pato (2 daily; 4hr); El Naranjo (8 daily; 4–5hr);Guatemala City (30 daily; 8–10 hr); Melchor de Mencos (10 daily; 2hr 30min); Sayaxché (6 daily; 2hr); Tikal (1 daily; 2hr); Uaxactún (1 daily; 3hr).

**Poptún** to: Flores (around 30 daily; 2hr); Río Dulce (around 30 daily; 2hr 30min).

**Puerto Barrios** to: Chiquimula (10 daily; 3hr); Esquipulas (4 daily;4hr); Guatemala City (18 daily; 5hr); Honduras border (every 30 mins; 1hr).

**Salamá** to: Cubulco (hourly; 1hr 30min); Guatemala City (hourly; 3hr 30min); Rabinal (hourly; 1hr).

**San Pedro Carchá** to: Cobán (every 15min; 20min); Fray Bartolomé de Las Casas (5 daily; 6hr 30min); Raxrujá via Sebol (2 daily; 7 hr); Uspantán via Cobán (2 daily; 5hr).

**Rabinal** to: Cubulco (hourly; 30min); Guatemala City via El Chol (1 daily; 8 hr); Guatemala City via La Cumbre (hourly; 4hr 30min); Salamá (hourly; 1hr).

**Sayaxché** to: Cruce de Pato (2 daily; 2hr); Flores (6 daily; 2hr).

**Tikal** to: Flores (1 daily; 2hr), plus numerous minibuses (1hr); Uaxactún (1 daily; 3hr).

## Pick-ups

**Cobán** to: Playa Grande via Laguna Lachuá (1 or 2 early morning most days; around 8hr); Chisec (2 daily, 3hr).

**Raxrujá** to: Cruce del Pato: first pick-up early morning to village of Canleche (1hr), second pick-up to Cruce del Pato (20min).

## Boats

**El Naranjo** to: La Palma, Mexico (daily; 1pm).

**Sayaxché** to: Benemérito, Mexico: a trading boat leaves most days (at least 12hr, could be much longer); rented speedboats take 2hr 30min–3hr.

**Flores/San Benito** to: San Andrés: boats (25min) leave when full, in daylight hours only.

**Puerto Barrios** to: Lívingston: ferry twice daily at 10am and 5pm (1hr 30min; US$1.50), plus speedboats (approx hourly; 45min); Punta Gorda, Belize daily at 10am and 2pm (1hr 30min).

**Lívingston** to: Río Dulce (several daily around 8am; around 3hr); Puerto Barrios (5am & 2pm; 1hr 30min); Punta Gorda, Belize (Tues & Fri 8am, minimum 4 people; 1hr); Omoa, Honduras (minimum 6 people; 2hr 30min).

**Río Dulce** to: Guatemala City (Fri, Sat, Sun; 1hr 20min).

**Sayaxché** to: Rancho el Caribe on the Río Petexbatún: there should be a daily boat (2hr).

## Planes

**Cobán** to: Guatemala City (daily; 30min); Fray Bartolomé de Las Casas and Playa Grande (irregular flights).

**Flores** to: Guatemala City (10 daily; 50min); Belize City (4 daily; 30min); Cancún (1 daily); Palenque (3 weekly; 40min); Chetumal (3 weekly; 45min).

**Puerto Barrios** to: Guatemala City (daily; 1hr).

You can also charter flights to Uaxactún, Dos Lagunas, El Naranjo, Sayaxché, Poptún, Río Dulce, Lívingston and to airports in Mexico and Honduras.

# PART FIVE

# HONDURAS & EL SALVADOR

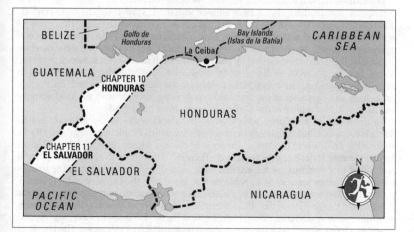

BELIZE

Golfo de Honduras

Bay Islands (Islas de la Bahía)

CARIBBEAN SEA

La Ceiba

GUATEMALA

CHAPTER 10 HONDURAS

HONDURAS

CHAPTER 11 EL SALVADOR

EL SALVADOR

PACIFIC OCEAN

NICARAGUA

N

# HONDURAS & EL SALVADOR

L ying at the southernmost fringe of the old Maya empire, Honduras and El Salvador seem, at first glance, to have little to recommend them to visitors. This book just covers the Maya regions of these two countries, a slice of mountainous land bordering Guatemala. Boasting only a handful of archeological sites, which pale considerably in comparison with those in Mexico and Guatemala, this part of Central America is better known for civil war, turbulence and abject poverty. Foreign visitors here are relatively few, stopping off only to visit **Copán**, before heading on to the **Bay Islands** – Roatán, Guanaja and Utila – a string of cayes with fantastic diving opportunities. Yet those who spend longer in the region find themselves swayed by the breathtaking scenery and the friendliness of the people who inhabit it. Travelling here is not easy, but making the effort to do so is well worth it.

**Honduras**, the original Banana Republic, is more renowned for staggering levels of corruption than anything else. A close alliance with the US prevented the bitter conflicts that beset its neighbours in the 1980s, but has not succeeded in alleviating the country's acute **economic and social problems**. After Nicaragua, this is Latin America's second poorest nation, with levels of poverty that can be disturbing to witness, a situation exasperated by the destruction caused by Hurricanne Mitch in 1998. Yet the open generosity and genuine friendliness displayed by those who have little else are what leave an enduring impression. The country and people are wonderfully diverse, with the rugged landscapes and character of the highlands contrasting strongly with the vivid scenery and laid-back atmosphere of the Caribbean north coast and islands.

To the south of Honduras, tucked along the Pacific edge of the isthmus, lies **El Salvador**, the smallest country in Central America, which is chiefly remembered for its devastating **civil war** in the 1980s. Throughout the lost decade, atrocity followed atrocity in a seemingly unstoppable escalation. Then in 1992, with both sides having fought each other to a standstill, peace accords were signed, and the attention of the world's press moved elsewhere, while El Salvador was faced with the complex task of rebuilding itself. Today, few tourists visit the country, deterred by an ever-present reputation for violence and danger. Those that do, however, are often overwhelmed by the sheer beauty of the country, stretching from lush, tropical Pacific lowlands to sweeping rugged mountain chains, dotted with the omnipresent cones of extinct volcanoes. The people of El Salvador are some of the most engaging and interesting in the region. With a well-deserved reputation for hard work and business acumen, they live life with a vigour that would be hard to match, and confront the dangers of a still uncertain future head on.

## A brief history of Honduras

Before the arrival of the Spanish, Honduras was populated by a number of different tribes, of whom the Maya are the best documented. Archeologists believe that **Maya settlers** began moving south into the Río Copán valley from around 1000 BC. Construction of the city of **Copán** began around 100 AD and by the time of the founding of the royal dynasty in 426 AD, Copán exerted control as far north as the Valle de Sula, east to Lago Yojoa and west into what is now Guatemala. Home to the governing and religious elite, and supporting a total population of around 28,000, the city was the pre-eminent Maya centre for scientific and artistic development. When, for reasons which are not entirely clear, Maya civilization began to collapse around 900 AD, Copán was abandoned, although the area it previously controlled remained inhabited.

**Columbus** landed on the island of Guanaja on July 30, 1502, during his fourth and final voyage, before exploring the Central American coastline visible on the horizon. Sailing east along the coast, the fleet first stopped at Punta Caxinas, close to present-day Trujillo, where the first Catholic Mass in Latin America was held on August 14, 1502. A further twenty years elapsed before the conquistadors returned to take possession of the new territory, with the first **Spanish settlement**, Triunfo de la Cruz on the Bahía de Tela, founded in 1524 by Cristóbal de Olid.

With Honduras under control, the Spanish began to focus their attention on the interior of the country, largely because of the inhospitable climate of the coastal settlements and their vulnerability to pirate attacks. The discovery of **gold** in the Valle de Comayagua in 1539, and **silver** around Tegucigalpa over the following forty years, seemed to promise untold riches. For the indigenous inhabitants, the consolidation of Spanish power was catastrophic. Contemporary population records are notoriously inaccurate, but from an estimated 400,000 in 1524, the population had probably fallen as low as 15,000 by 1571. Those who survived the diseases of the Old World were enslaved and either shipped overseas or sent to the mines. Social structures collapsed and communities were forcibly dispersed, with the most affected peoples being the highland tribes, since they had most contact with the colonists. Incredibly, considering their impact, the number of colonists numbered fewer than 300 throughout the seventeenth century.

For the Spanish, the steep **decline in population** was, above all, a severe hindrance to economic development. Though, at their peak, the mines provided a comfortable living for their owners, from the seventeenth century onwards the labour shortage made working deeper seams impracticable, and profits dropped sharply as a result. By the early nineteenth century, Honduras was an **economy in crisis**: mining was virtually defunct and a series of severe droughts hit both agriculture and livestock. Society was sharply divided, with a narrow layer of the relatively wealthy – state functionaries, merchants, a handful of mine- and hacienda-owners – above the poor mass of Mestizo and indigenous peoples. There was no middle class, nor any kind of unifying national infrastructure, and by the time of independence in 1821, Honduras still had no national printing press, newspapers or university.

News of **independence** reached Honduras on September 28, 1821, and the provinces of Central America declared themselves an independent republic on July 1, 1823, only to plunge almost immediately into civil war. The Honduran Francisco Morazán, elected president of the republic in 1830, was unable to persuade even his own countrymen of the potential of a united republic. Faced repeatedly with uprisings he was unable to crush, Morazán resigned in 1839, when Honduras and Nicaragua went to war against El Salvador. The Central American Republic was finished, and the five independent republics, among them the **Republic of Honduras**, came into existence.

The newly independent country stumbled through successive political and economic crises, much of it occasioned by rivalry between Liberal and Conservative political forces. Not until 1876 did the country begin to assume the aspects of a modern state, under the premiership of **Dr Marco Aurelio Soto**, a Liberal, and his successor Luis Bográn. These two men reformed the judiciary, Church and armed forces and put into place unified communications and education infrastructures. Believing that foreign capital was the key to economic development, **foreign investment** by US, British and European companies was encouraged. This developed industries, but crucially allowed most of the country's resources to be controlled by foreign concerns. In the banana industry, for example, three companies – United Fruit, Vacarro Bros (later Standard Fruit) and the Cuyamel Fruit Company (bought out by United Fruit in 1929) – soon became dominant, all but wiping out small-scale producers. Government concessions allowed the companies to steadily

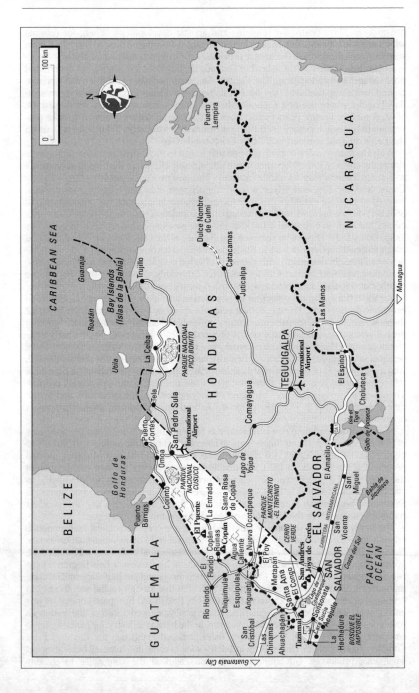

increase their holdings, which, by 1924, amounted to half a million acres of land on the north coast and control of seventy percent of Honduras's total exports, with subsequent expansion into and control of railways, energy and banking sectors and substantial political influence. A succession of weak and shortlived governments struggled to keep control in the face of the dominant interests of the fruit companies and, behind them, the US, along the virtually autonomous north coast.

Over the next thirty years, the foundations of the modern state were laid and a new national cohesion was formed, with a central bank, a public service and increased export. A **coup** in October 1956 introduced the **military** as a new element into the hierarchy of power, with the 1957 constitution giving the armed forces the right to disregard governmental action they regarded as unconstitutional. In October 1963, a second coup installed Colonel Oswaldo López Arellano as provisional president, and during his first period of office one of the more bizarre conflicts of modern Central America occurred, the so-called **"Football War"**. The conflict stemmed from tensions generated by a steady rise in illegal migration of campesinos from El Salvador into Honduras in search of land. The two countries began a series of qualifying matches for the 1970 World Cup, and at the second match, won 3–0 by El Salvador, spectators booed the Honduran national anthem and attacked visiting Honduran fans. On July 14, 1969, the Salvadorean army bombed targets within Honduras and advanced into Honduran territory. After three days, around two thousand deaths and a complete rupture of diplomatic relations, the Organization of American States (OAS) negotiated a ceasefire and established a three kilometre-wide demilitarized zone along the border. Only in 1992 did both sides accept an International Court of Justice ruling demarcating the border in its current location.

Another coup restored López to power in December 1972. His attempted new industrialization programme was – given the by now endemic **corruption** at senior levels of government, in the military and in business – a recipe for disaster; millions of dollars of national and international loans and aid money were siphoned off to private bank accounts. Forced from office through the **"Bananagate"**, López succeeded in April 1975 by Colonel Juan Melgar Castro. During his tenure and that (1978–81) of his successor General Policarpo Paz García, agrarian reform slowed to a trickle, repression of civil rights and freedom of speech increased, and corruption among military and government personnel grew to almost laughable levels.

Following the **Sandinista revolution** in Nicaragua in July 1979, Honduras found itself at the centre of US geo-political strategy – the "fourth border of the US". Honduras became the focus for the US-backed Contra war in Nicaragua, accepting in return over US$1.5bn of direct economic and military aid during the 1980s. Domestically, the relationship between the military and government grew ever closer. **Human rights** violations rose alarmingly, with the army implicated in at least 184 "disappearances" of activists from labour organizations and peace movements. In 1984, army officers, increasingly anxious over Alvarez's actions, forced him into exile. Honduras's role in US affairs diminished after Reagan left office and both the Contra war and the civil war in El Salvador were resolved, focusing attention on the country's worsening economic and social problems. Under **Rafael Leonardo Callejas** (in office 1989–93), neo-Liberal austerity measures were introduced, leading to a sharp rise in poverty levels, and although jurisdiction over legal and government affairs was slowly wrestled back from the military, human rights abuses were still common. In 1993, the widely respected Liberal candidate, businessman turned politician **Carlos Roberto Reina**, was elected president, on a platform of engineering moral renewal through tackling governmental and business corruption. Though acting successfully on the most overt cases, he was not able to prevent the economy sliding further into recession, or to halt a steadily worsening spiral of social instability, affecting the north coast in particular.

**Carlos Flores Facussé** took office in January 1998 and immediately set about trying to reduce Honduras's massive international debt, organizing a series of meetings with the IMF and World Bank. Though Flores had been elected with a campaign pledge to reverse the cycle of deepening poverty and social despair through investment and a programme of national conciliation, he largely maintained the free-market economics of his predecessors. Corporation tax was slashed and sweeping privatization plans were proposed in an austerity package formulated to gain debt relief, while sales tax was hiked from 7 to 12 per cent.

But just as these policies were being implemented, and before debt relief had been granted, **Hurricane Mitch** began brewing offshore in October 1998. The category five hurricane first battered Guanaja, laying siege to the Bay Island for three days before ripping across mainland Honduras, unleashing colossal volumes of rainfall in an apocalyptic trail across the country. After provoking landslides and storm surges that killed over a thousand people in the capital Tegucigalpa, Mitch pursued an erratic path back across Honduras, triggering devastating mud slides and floods in Nicaragua and along the path of the Ríos Chamelecón and Ulúa from the Western highlands to San Pedro Sula. Though the final death toll will never be known, it's estimated that Mitch killed over 7,000 people in Honduras, 4,000 in Nicaragua and around 400 in Guatemala and El Salvador. Thousands more remain unaccounted for.

President Carlos Flores declared that Mitch had set Honduras back fifty years and the world's media reported a cataclysmic picture of damage and devastation. These initial assessments looked over-pessimistic, as the nation – aided by teams from all over the world – steadily pulled itself together again, quickly patching up much of the key infrastructure. A year after the hurricane, all the main highways were open and most of the hundred bridges damaged by Mitch had been patched up or rebuilt, and tourists were returning.

Yet reconstruction aside, it quickly became clear that Mitch had seriously exacerbated the nation's fundamental weaknesses and inequalities. The **economy** remains critically weak and almost totally dependent on inward investment, which chiefly goes into the *maquila* garment-assembly factories of the north. This industry, dominated by Korean and US companies, enjoys tax-free status and pays notoriously poor wages, while prestige technology companies opt to settle in stable Costa Rica where the workforce is well-educated. **Crime rates** have soared since Mitch, as violent gangs settle turf wars in the streets of San Pedro Sula and cocaine trafficking has become a key industry. The discredited police force retain a reputation for systematic corruption and have been implicated in the widespread killing of street children in the large cities – the charity *Casa Alianza* reported the extra-judicial killing of 673 Honduran children and teenagers between January 1998 and March 2001.

As the December 2001 elections approached, life for most Hondurans remained a struggle in a country gripped by poverty and lack of opportunity. The key campaign issues are likely to reflect this, with unemployment, the state of the economy and law and order being uppermost in people's minds. The new president will also have to renegotiate Honduras' massive external debt, and implement fundamental developmental changes in co-ordination with the numerous international organizations that have settled in Honduras after Mitch.

## A brief history of El Salvador

The first settled peoples of El Salvador were **the Maya**, who had arrived in the territory by at least 1200 BC, and from 500 BC had developed several large settlements in the west and centre of the country. During the Classic period (300–900 AD), important cities developed and thrived at San Andrés, Tazumal, Cara Sucia and Quelepa, though these cities were abandoned around 900 AD, when the Maya empire began to crumble. During the early Postclassic period (900–1200 AD), a succession of Nahuatl-speaking groups, known as Pipils, began to migrate south from Mexico. Final waves of Nahuatl speakers arrived in the thirteenth and fourteenth centuries.

After an exploratory visit by Andrés Niño in May 1522, **the Spanish** arrived in force in El Salvador in June 1524. Pedro de Alvarado, commanding a force of around 250 Spanish and 5000 indigenous soldiers, entered what is now the department of Ahuachapán from Guatemala. Initial progress was slow – it is thought that the Pipil forces were up to twice as large as those of the Spanish – and domination of western El Salvador was secured only in April 1528. Only in 1538 was the Spanish hold upon the whole of the territory secure.

During the colonial rule, the conquistadors established the *encomienda* system and developed **haciendas** for those Spaniards wishing to take advantage of the abundant agricultural resources. Basalm and cocoa became increasingly important export crops, with a huge demand from Europe. However, from the early eighteenth century, there was growing demand for *añil* (indigo), and landowners rejected cocoa in favour of producing this superior dye. By the mid-eighteenth century, indigo had become the primary export crop, with the main beneficiaries being the hacienda owners and *comerciantes* – the middle men handling the sale and shipping. El Salvador became a rigidly stratified society, whose European elite consisted of the small number of Spanish-born Crown functionaries and priests and a few hundred Creole (Latin American-born) hacienda owners and *comerciantes*; of available agricultural land, around half was held in private haciendas. The vast majority of the population, Mestizo and indigenous, existed at subsistence level, cultivating maize.

Following independence in 1841 El Salvador was in an almost perpetual state of turmoil as rival Liberals and Conservatives battled for power. Not until the presidency of Rafael Zaldívar did the country achieve any measure of stability. Economically, the production of coffee became the driving force from 1860 onwards, fuelled by the collapse in demand for indigo and the growing popularity of coffee on the tables of Europe and North America. This **coffee boom** created the conditions for the development of a "coffee elite" and land became concentrated into fewer and fewer hands – a tiny but powerful oligarchy, with three quarters of all land eventually held by less than two percent of the population. The oligarchy monopolized coffee production and trade, extending its interests into other agricultural sectors, industry and finance. Over the next decades, until a military coup in 1898, private interests were the motivating force behind all changes in government, but in the first decades of the twentieth century, the coffee boom also brought relative economic stability and consolidation of the state. Transport links, including railways, and a communications system were put into place, education expanded and a functioning civil judicial system established. At the same time, it was a period of deepening social polarization. The elite dominated business and the state machine, while the vast majority lived in the most basic of conditions. Despite regular elections, democracy was a concept in name only, with the bulk of the population excluded from both the political process and the profits from coffee. Growing civil violence was dealt with by increasing repression from the government.

Plans for democratic development set in place by President Bosque at his election in 1927 were brought to an abrupt end by the **Wall Street Crash** in 1929, which decimated the market in coffee, the crop that generated 95 percent of El Salvador's total exports. Worst affected by the collapse were the landless poor, whose living conditions deteriorated appallingly. **Social unrest** was exacerbated by growing repression, and on the night of January 22, 1932, thousands of campesinos rebelled. Armed mainly with machetes, they attacked military installations and haciendas in the west of the country, assassinating hundreds of civilians including government functionaries. Mainly because plans to rebel had been publicly widely known in the days before the event, government forces rapidly quashed the rebellion and the ringleaders were arrested and later executed.

The scale of government action in the wake of the failed rebellion was unprecedented in the history of the country. The army, the police, the *guardia nacional* and the private forces of the hacienda owners engaged in a week-long orgy of killing. During "La Matanza" (the massacre), as it became known, anyone suspected of connections to the rebellion, anyone wearing indigenous dress or anyone simply perceived to be guilty was shot. In some cases, whole villages disappeared. The death toll was estimated at up to 30,000 people, although the government itself insisted that only two thousand were killed. For El Salvador's indigenous population, the effects of the massacre went far beyond the immediate death toll: it became suspect to be identified as *indio* (Indian) and, as a result, traditional dress, language and customs largely disappeared.

The rebellion and its bloody aftermath ushered in a era of **military rule** as the oligarchy, desperate to defend its interests, handed political power to the army while retaining economic control. For the next fifty years, the two groups worked together in a symbiotic relationship. Successive groups of military officers assumed power, usually removed from office by coup and counter-coup while the economic business of state was handled by the oligarchy, who relied on the army to protect its interests.

After World War II, the economy diversified into production of sugar, cotton and beef for export. Profits and benefits deriving from this expansion remained firmly in the hands of the oligarchy, while the vast majority of the population had no access to land. The census of 1971 recorded that 64 percent of agricultural land was held by four percent of landowners. A downturn in external markets in the 1970s again led to a steep deterioration, followed by growing, militant pressure for change. The elections of 1972, won by the Christian Democratic Party (PDC) advocating a peaceful road to reform, should have heralded this change. The army, however, installed its own candidate, Colonel Arturo Molina, exiled Duarte and other opposition leaders, and cracked down on trade union and reform activists.

Throughout the 1970s repression continued. In 1977, news programmes around the world showed footage of the army firing upon unarmed civilians during a protest in front of the cathedral in central San Salvador; up to three hundred died. In 1980, Archbishop Oscar Romero was assassinated on the orders of a serving army officer, Roberto D'Aubuisson. Though preliminary reforms were implemented and agreement secured for a transfer of power from military to civilian hands, these were insufficient to halt a deepening cycle of extra-judicial violence. Many were convinced that change could only come through violence. At both ends of the spectrum far-right paramilitary death squads and left-wing guerrilla groups began to mobilize.

In October 1980, the formal integration of all the left-wing guerrilla organizations led to the foundation of the Frente Faribundo Martí de Liberación Nacional (**FMLN**). Three months later, in January 1981, the FMLN launched its first general offensive, gaining territory in the eastern and northern departments of the country and forcing the government into defensive action. The newly-installed US Reagan administration began to pump aid to the government, to expand and to equip fighting forces. Despite this, however, the army remained hampered by insufficient organization, leadership and endemic corruption, unable to confront the guerrillas' ambush tactics and targeted attacks. During the course of the war, 80,000 people were killed and more than 500,000 fled the country as refugees. Against a background of continuing fighting, the promised transfer of power from military to civilian hands was completed, with parliamentary elections in 1982 and a new constitution introduced in 1983. The FMLN, however, remained outside the political process and sporadic attempts at peace talks foundered upon the seemingly irresolvable demands for fundamental changes in the role and structure of the army.

Widely perceived as incompetent and corrupt, Duarte was succeeded in 1989 by Alfredo Cristiani, candidate of the right-wing Alianza Republicana Nacionalista (**ARENA**) party founded by Roberto D'Aubuisson. The FMLN renewed offensives against the government, most spectacularly during its "final offensive" of November

1989 when areas of major cities, including San Salvador, were occupied. In turn, the death squads and the military intensified their activities. Suspected FMLN sympathizers, trade unionists and Church activists were intimidated and assassinated.

In April 1990, representatives of both the FMLN and the government, under the chairmanship of the UN, took part in a series of negotiations that would eventually lead to peace. **The Chapultepec Accords**, signed on January 16, 1992, were followed on February 1 by a formal ceasefire. The FMLN agreed to the demobilization of its forces, the government to a purge of the armed forces and reduction in their size. A land transfer programme, expected to transfer ten percent of agricultural land to demobilized combatants and refugees, was inaugurated, and a tripartite commission, including the government, workers and private sector, was set up to formulate further social and economic policies. On December 15, 1992, the day the FMLN registered as an official political party, the civil war was formally ended.

Recovery from the brutalization of civil war has been slow and the consolidation of **democracy** a troubled process. The protracted dissolution of the warring armies and a lengthy delay in establishing the new civil police force created a security vacuum across the country in the first two postwar years. Many disaffected former combatants remained on the fringes of society, unemployment soared and the circulation of firearms in society went unchecked. Delinquency, crime and civil violence ensued and have plagued the country ever since.

The first **post-war elections** held in March 1994 resulted in Armando Calderón Sol of the ARENA party assuming the presidency. The new government pursued a neo-liberal, free-market economic policy and privatized large sectors of the economy, including the controversial sale of Antel, the state telecommunications company. However, **dissatisfaction** increased, primarily because of the government's failure to comply with the Chapultepec Accords and widespread accusations of fraud and corruption. Members of the armed forces accused of human rights abuses were offered amnesty or early retirement rather than prosecution, while former war combatants from both sides remained marginalized. The cost of living rose, poverty increased and unemployment reached an unprecedented level. Much of the foreign aid, donations and grants received were used to rebuild the nation's shattered infrastructure, but very little was channelled towards job creation projects, and critics berated the lack of a clearly-defined, strategic long term national plan. Large scale privatization further concentrated wealth in the hands of the elite and increased prices for consumers. The profound divisions in society – that originally led to civil war – grew wider than ever.

The FMLN's perceived failure in the 1994 elections was followed by a fractious split between the "orthodox" and "reformist" factions of the party. Its fortunes were revived by impressive results across the country in the March 1997 **municipal elections**, including winning the prized mayoral seat of the capital, San Salvador. Yet failure to build on these results would divide the FMLN still further, and its indecision over selecting a candidate for the March 1999 **presidential elections** led to an easy victory for ARENA's Francisco Flores. Only forty percent of the electorate turned out to vote, evidence of popular contempt for politicians of both major parties and frustration at the speed of economic reform.

Much of the country, though, concentrated on the hardships of daily life rather than going to the polls. **Hurricane Mitch** had hit the country in October 1998, killing 374 and rendering 56,000 people homeless. The government's response was slow and much of the international effort was focused on harder hit neighbours, Honduras and Nicaragua. Infrastructure was destroyed and agricultural output, badly affected the previous year by **El Niño**, was severely damaged. Natural disaster was again exacerbating El Salvador's man-made woes.

The economy slowed post-1995 and a new **sales tax** was levied on a selection of basic commodities, inciting a national strike. A report by the Universidad de Centroamérica

(UCA), in March 2000, listed El Salvador as one of the most violent countries in Latin America, with widespread gang warfare, narcotrafficking and civil violence. A spate of kidnapping of businessmen and women for ransom has gone largely unchecked, and the small talk of the nation became littered with the term *delincuencia*.

The economy failed to grow sufficiently at the turn of the millennium despite a healthy, and very profitable, banking sector. Always the most industrialized of the Central American economies, El Salvador's economy had also developed a strong *maquiladora* sector, whereby manufactured goods are produced specifically for export. This sector helped build export markets, but relies on cheap Salvadorean labour and does not produce any goods for domestic consumption. The domestic economy remains heavily **underwritten** – to the annual tune of US$1.3 billion - by Salvadorans working abroad, primarily in the USA, who send money home to their families. In June 2000, the Flores government signed **a free trade agreement** with Mexico, Guatemala and Honduras to stimulate economic growth. President Flores also gained parliamentary approval for a highly controversial US military training base in El Salvador. Approved on the agreement that the base would be used solely to fight drug trafficking, Salvadorans were suspicious of US military intervention returning to their domestic affairs.

The FMLN again scored heavy victories in the March 2000 **legislative elections**, taking 31 of the 84 seats available in the national assembly. ARENA won only 29 seats, but the right wing maintained its ruling majority through a coalition with the Partido de Conciliación Nacional (PCN) winning fourteen seats. At the turn of 2000 rumours spread that the Flores government was considering **dollarizing** the economy in order to attract overseas investment and stimulate domestic growth. Such an event seemed unlikely, until **November 2000** when the historic announcement was made. **La Ley de Integración Monetaria** was passed, despite FMLN abstention, by the Asamblea Nacional on 30 November 2000 rubber stamping El Salvador as the third Latin American nation to officially embrace the "greenback". As from 1 January 2001, El Salvador has operated a dual currency system with all goods and services priced in both US dollars and Salvadoran colones. The Salvadoran colón now has a limited shelf life and will be slowly withdrawn from circulation; as from 2003 El Salvador will be a fully functioning dollar economy.

Barely thirteen days into the new year, however, El Salvador was struck by a devastating **earthquake** measuring 7.7 on the Richter scale. Although the **epicentre** of the quake was offshore in the Pacific ocean powerful tremors were felt across Central America from southern Mexico to Panama. El Salvador bore the brunt of this act of natural destruction; 800 people were killed, over 60,000 homes were destroyed and damage to roads, buildings and infrastructure was widespread. Exactly one month later a second powerful earthquake, centred near the eastern city of San Vicente, killed a further 250 and five days later a third earthquake, with its epicentre near the capital San Salvador, exacerbated the massive damage and destruction across the country. As El Salvador entered into its tenth year of post-war peace, these earthquakes represented a monstrous national tragedy that did incalculable damage to the process of restructuring the nation's shattered post-war economy and society.

# CHAPTER TEN

# HONDURAS

N orthwestern Honduras offers some of the country's most spectacular tourist attractions, including Copán, one of the finest sites of the Maya world, and the glorious white beaches of the Bay Islands, the country's most visited destination. Added to these, the inspiring, untouched natural beauty of the country and the open generosity and friendliness of the people make this a fascinating and enjoyable region to visit.

**Copán** is the site that most people head for first, just a short distance from the Guatemalan border. The buildings may not be able to match Tikal or Chichén Itzá in terms of sheer scale, but the architecture, especially the carvings and stelae, are outstanding. Further north, **San Pedro Sula**, Honduras's second city, is a useful transport hub and an excellent base for exploring one of the country's finest cloudforest reserves, the **Parque Nacional el Cusuco**. Ecotourism is becoming an increasingly important niche sector in the nation's economy, and an increasing number of Hondurans are becoming aware of the role the country's extensive network of **national parks** and reserves plays in protecting irreplaceable natural resources. The remoter parts of the parks host an astonishing array of flora and fauna, amid some of the finest stretches of virgin **cloud-** and **tropical forest** in Central America.

The lively coastal town of **La Ceiba** is a convenient stop-off en route to the Bay Islands; if you've time to stay a while, there are also some good beaches just outside the town and one of the most accessible cloudforest reserves in the country: **Pico Bonito**. Less than 60km from the north coast are the **Bay Islands** – Roatán, Guanaja and Utila – where idyllic palm-fringed beaches and clear, Caribbean waters make for the ultimate in beach holidays and provide world-class snorkelling and diving.

## Into Honduras from Guatemala

The quiet Guatemala–Honduras border post of **El Florido** (open daily 6am–6pm) is 57km from Chiquimula, a quick dash along a smooth paved highway through spectacular thinly populated mountain scenery. Second-class buses leave every thirty minutes for the border (6am–4.30pm; 1hr 15min). The crossing here is straightforward, with backpackers en route to and from the ruins forming most of the traffic. Officially there's no fee to leave Guatemala but border guards may try to charge you a US$1 or so to leave the country, while the Hondurans usually ask for another US$1 to enter their country, though the official entry charge is US$0.50. Most nationalities **do not need a visa** to enter Honduras (see Basics p.17). If you do, and you're entering Honduras only to visit

## ACCOMMODATION PRICE CODES

All the accommodation listed in this book has been categorized into one of nine price bands, as set out below. The prices quoted are in US dollars and refer to the cheapest room available for two people sharing in high season.

| | | |
|---|---|---|
| ① under US$5 | ④ US$15–25 | ⑦ US$60–80 |
| ② US$5–10 | ⑤ US$25–40 | ⑧ US$80–100 |
| ③ US$10–15 | ⑥ US$40–60 | ⑨ over US$100 |

Copán, and intend to re-enter Guatemala almost immediately, ask the Honduran guards for a temporary entrance stamp. This is given to you on a separate piece of paper, thus keeping your Guatemalan visa valid. There's a **bank**, Banrural (Mon–Fri 8am–4pm, Sat 9am–1pm), a kilometre west of the border (inside Guatemala) that will change travellers' cheques and cash dollars, or you can deal with the ever-present moneychangers at the border post who handle dollars, lempiras and quetzales at pretty fair rates. From El Florido, **pick-ups** run when full (about every thirty minutes) to the town of Copán Ruinas, taking around twenty minutes; the last leaves around 5.45pm. Heading into Guatemala, the last bus leaves El Florido at 4pm, though it's sensible to cross as early in the day as possible to ensure onward connections in Guatemala.

# Copán and around

Twelve kilometres east of the Guatemalan border crossing of El Florido, in the serene, rolling landscape of Honduras's western highlands, lies the ancient city of **Copán**.

One of the most impressive of all the Maya sites, its pre-eminence derives not from size – it's less imposing than Tikal or Chichén Itzá – but from the overwhelming legacy of artistic craftsmanship that has survived here over hundreds of years. Not surprisingly, the site is heavily promoted by the Honduran government and tour operators, and now ranks as the second most visited spot in the country after the Bay Islands.

Copán emblem glyph

## Copán Ruinas: the town

The archeological site of Copán lies one kilometre south of the small town of **COPÁN RUINAS**, generally simply referred to as Copán, a charming place of steep cobbled streets and red-tiled roofs, set among lush green hills. Despite the weekly influx of hundreds of visitors, which now contributes a large part of the town's income, it has managed to remain largely unspoilt and genuinely friendly. Many travellers are seduced by Copán's delightfully relaxed atmosphere, clean air and rural setting, and end up spending longer here than planned – studying Spanish, eating and drinking well, or exploring the region's other minor sites, hot springs and beautiful countryside.

Half a day spent walking around Copán is enough to take in virtually all of the town's attractions. The **plaza**, the parque central – lined with banks, municipal structures and an attractive, whitewashed baroque-style church – was originally designed and built by visiting archeologists Tatiana Proskouriakoff and Gustav Stromsvik. Unfortunately the simple elegance of the original layout, which followed classical Spanish lines, has been spoilt somewhat by grandiose remodelling initiatives, including a series of sweeping pillars and arches, unleashed by a local mayor in the last few years. It does remain a popular place to kill time however, its benches filled with cowboy-booted farmhands and camera-touting visitors in the late afternoon.

On the west side of the plaza, and somewhat eclipsed by the new sculpture museum at the site itself, though still worth a visit, is the **Museo Regional de Arqueología** (Mon–Sat 8am–4pm; US$2). Displayed inside are some highly impressive Maya carvings collected from the Copán region, including Altars T and U which are rich with glyphs and **Stela B**, depicting the ruler Waxaklajuun Ub'aah K'awiil (Eighteen Rabbit) and some remarkable intricately detailed eccentric flints – ornamental oddities with seven interlocking heads carved from obsidian. There are two remarkable **tombs**, including the remains of a female shaman, complete with jade jewellery and the skulls of a puma, deer, and two human sacrificial victims. The other tomb (10J-45) of an early Classic period ruler of Copán was only discovered in 1999 during road building work.

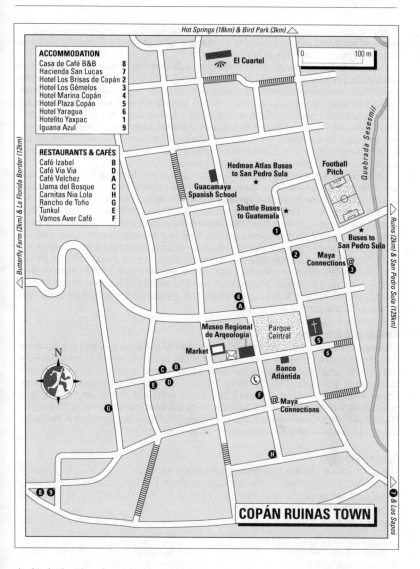

Hot Springs (18km) & Bird Park (3km)

**ACCOMMODATION**
| | |
|---|---|
| Casa de Café B&B | 8 |
| Hacienda San Lucas | 7 |
| Hotel Los Brisas de Copán | 2 |
| Hotel Los Gémelos | 3 |
| Hotel Marina Copán | 4 |
| Hotel Plaza Copán | 5 |
| Hotel Yaragua | 6 |
| Hotelito Yaxpac | 1 |
| Iguana Azul | 9 |

**RESTAURANTS & CAFÉS**
| | |
|---|---|
| Café Izabel | B |
| Café Via Via | D |
| Café Velchez | A |
| Llama del Bosque | C |
| Carnitas Nia Lola | H |
| Rancho de Toño | G |
| Tunkul | E |
| Vamos Aver Café | F |

El Cuartel

0    100 m

Butterfly Farm (2km) & La Florida Border (12km)

Quebrada Sesesmil

Hedman Atlas Buses to San Pedro Sula

Football Pitch

Guacamaya Spanish School

Shuttle Buses to Guatemala

Buses to San Pedro Sula

Maya Connections

Ruins (2km) & San Pedro Sula (125km)

Museo Regional de Arqeología

Parque Central

Market

Banco Atlántida

Maya Connections

N

COPÁN RUINAS TOWN

7 & Los Sapos

Archeologists found a vaulted burial chamber, dating from the sixth century, where the leader, whose identity is yet unknown, was buried with numerous ceramics and two large carved jade pectoral pieces.

Just behind the museum, the tiny municipal **market** is worth a browse (turn right beyond the post office) or, for a wonderful view over the town and surrounding countryside, walk north from the parque central for about five blocks to *el cuartel*, the old military barracks up the hill. Catering to the growing tourist trade are a number of new **souvenir shops** on or close to the parque central, selling ceramic, wood and leather crafts from the region and elsewhere in the country; all are broadly similar in terms of price and range. Tabacos y Recuerdos, next to the *La Posada* hotel, has a wide selection of Honduran cigars.

On the outskirts of town, a twenty-minute walk from the plaza along the road to Guatemala, Enchanted Wings (daily 8.30am–5pm; US$5) is a small screened **butterfly park** which spills down a riverside, owned by an English enthusiast and his Honduran wife. Unfortunately, Copán's cool winter nights periodically wipe out some of the forty or so specimens – many of which are collected from the steamier tropical environs of the north coast – so you may not find an abundance of butterflies, though look out for the speckled brown "giant owl" and the scarlet-and-yellow "helicopter", two of the hardier species. Butterflies hatch in the morning hours, so if you plan to go to the centre, it's best to time your visit accordingly if you can.

On the other side of town, 3km north of the plaza, a new **bird park** is set to open in late 2001, with macaws and toucans to admire. If you continue along this road for another 15km you come to some **hot springs** (US$0.75), set in lush highland scenery dotted with coffee fincas and patches of pine forests. Once there you can either wallow around in man-made pools or head to the source via a short trail where cool river water and near boiling-hot spring waters combine. Your best bet to **get to** the *aguas termales* is to hitch a ride on a passing pick-up, which are reasonably frequent from outside the *Hotel Paty* in Copán and also pass the bird park; expect to pay around a US$1 for the ride, which takes about 50 minutes. Don't leave it any later than 3.30pm if you're planning to hitch back to Copán. Alternatively, speak to one of Copán's tour operators (see Listings p.490); Yaragua Tours can arrange a half-day pick-up trip at 2pm for US$10 per person for a minimum of four people.

## Arrival and information

**Pick-ups** from the border at El Florido enter town from the west, running up to circle the parque central. Buses from other destinations in Honduras enter town from the east, by the small football field. The **post office** is just behind the museum while Hondutel is just south of the plaza. There's an excellent community **website** (*www.copanruinas*.com) where you'll find useful hotel and restaurant listings, local news and links; you can choose between several **internet** cafés in town, including two branches of Maya Connections; one is just south of the plaza and the other is inside the *Hotel Los Gémelos* – rates hover around US$5 an hour.

## Accommodation

Many of the town's **hotels** have undergone refits to attract the ever-booming organized tour market, joining a swathe of new mid-range places and keeping prices competitive. There's not too much choice at the budget end of the market, however, where places fill up quickly at busy times of the year.

**Casa de Café B&B**, at the southwest edge of town, overlooking the Río Copán valley (☎651 4620, fax 651 4623, *www.todomundo.com/casadecafe*). A charming place, with a fabulous garden where you could lie in a hammock and enjoy the views all day. Ten comfortable, airy rooms all with wood panelling and nice individual touches, private bathrooms and steaming hot water. A huge ranch-style breakfast is included and there's free coffee all day, plus a library and TV. ⑥.

**Hacienda San Lucas**, 1.8 km south of the plaza (☎651 4106, *sanlucas@copanruinas.com*). Wonderful converted farmhouse accommodation and camping set in the hills south of Copán, with startling views over the valley. Restaurant with excellent home-cooked food; plus horse riding, and hiking trails to the Los Sapos site. Breakfast is included. ⑥.

**Hotel Brisas de Copán**, one block north of the parque central (☎651 4118). Twenty-two very clean, though slightly soulless, good-sized rooms, all with bath, hot water and TV. There's parking and a terrace bar is planned. ④.

**Hotel Los Gémelos**, close to the bus stop (☎651 4077). Backpackers' stronghold, still going strong. Very friendly place, with basic but spotless rooms, all with shared bath. The family provide hot water if enough people ask, and also run the adjacent Maya Communications Internet café. ②.

**Hotel Plaza Copán** on the east side of the plaza (☎651 4508, fax 651 4039, *placopan@netsys.hn*). Twenty-one good-value rooms, some overlooking the square and all with a/c and cable TV; plus there's a small kidney-shaped pool. ⑥.

**Hotel Marina Copán**, just northwest of the plaza (☎651 4070, fax 651 4477, *hmarina@netsys.hn*). The most luxurious place in town by a long shot. Stylish rooms all have a/c and TV, and there's a small pool, a sauna, a gym and a bar on site. ⑨.

**Hotel Yaragua**, half a block east of the plaza (☎651 4050). Two floors of smallish but comfortable rooms, set around a verdant little courtyard, all with good-quality double beds and cable TV. Excellent value for this category. ④.

**Hotelito Yaxpac**, a block north of the plaza (☎651 4025). Four good-value, simple, clean rooms, all with private bath and some with little balconies, run by a friendly family. ②.

**Iguana Azul**, next to the *Casa de Café* and under the same ownership (☎651 4620, fax 651 4623, *www.todomundo.com /iguanaazul/index.html*). The definitive budget choice with three private double rooms and two very pleasant dormitories, all with shared bath and decent mattresses. Pretty garden, communal area and laundry facilities, plus great travel information. Dorms ①, doubles ②–③.

## Eating and drinking

Copán has a wide range of places to **eat** and **drink**, many of them catering specifically to the tourist market, and standards are usually very high with generous portions and good service. Virtually all restaurants stop serving at 10pm.

**Café Izabel**, one block west of the plaza. Unpretentious comedor serving a range of well-prepared local dishes; the vegetable soup is particularly good.

**Café Via Via**, two blocks west of the plaza. Belgian-owned establishment with a nice little streetside terrace and magazines to browse through. Good sandwiches, breakfasts, pancakes and omelettes.

**Café Velchez**, northwest corner of the parque. Pleasant European-style café, serving good but fairly pricey coffees, juices and licuados, alcoholic drinks (including wine by the glass), cakes and light meals. There's a cigar bar upstairs where the tables are good for people-watching.

**Carnitas Nia Lola**, two blocks south of the plaza. The most atmospheric place in town. Highly popular, locally owned restaurant-bar on two levels, serving large portions of delicious grilled and barbecued meats, plus vegetarian dishes, at reasonable prices. Equally popular as a bar venue, there's an early-evening happy hour and always a good mix of locals and visitors.

**Llama del Bosque**, two blocks west of the parque. Slightly old-fashioned restaurant with a wide menu including local breakfasts, meat and chicken dishes, baleadas and snacks.

**Rancho de Toño**, two blocks west of the plaza. Vast new *palapa*-style restaurant, specializing in fresh fish. Huge portions, friendly service and not too expensive.

**Tunkul Bar and Restaurant**, across from the *Llama del Bosque*. Busy garden restaurant-bar with good food (including burritos, vegetarian dishes and near-legendary garlic chicken), lively music and a happy hour (8–9pm).

**Vamos a Ver Café**, one block south of the parque. Busy Dutch-owned garden café, popular with travellers, with delicious homemade soups, sandwiches and snacks.

## Listings

**Banks** Banco Atlántida in the plaza will change travellers' cheques, cash dollars and quetzales (at poor rates) and give advances on Visa cards.

**Book exchange** Justo a Tiempo, two blocks southwest of the plaza (Mon–Sat 7.30am–5.30pm); the friendly American owner also offers great cakes and coffee.

**Immigration** The *Migración* office is on the west side of the plaza next to the museum (Mon–Fri 7am–4pm).

**Language schools** Copán is an excellent place to study, with two Spanish schools to choose between, though it's a more expensive learning centre than in Guatemala – four hours of classes plus full family-based accommodation and meals costs US$175 a week. Guacamaya (☎ & fax 651 4360, *www.guacamaya.com*), three blocks north of the plaza, has the better reputation, while Ixbalanque (☎ & fax 651 4432, *ixbalan@hn2.com*), a block and a half just west of the plaza, is also worth considering.

**Laundry** Justo a Tiempo, two blocks southwest of the plaza (Mon–Sat 7.30am–5.30pm).

**Shuttle buses** Contact Monarcas (☎651 4361), two blocks north of the plaza, for direct shuttles to Guatemala City and Antigua (US$25 per person).

**Tour operators** Go Native Tours (☎651 4432, *ixbalanqu@hn2.com*), a block and a half west of the plaza, and Yaragua Tours (☎ & fax 651 4050, *yaraguatours@hotmail.com*), half a block east of the plaza, both offer similarly priced tours. Trips include the hot springs (US$10 per person), horse riding (from US$15 for 3hr), the Finca El Cisne coffee farm (US$30) and the El Rubi waterfall (US$15 per person), and a spectacular local cave, the Cueva el Boquerón (US$70 for the trip). Xukpi Tours (☎651 4435) is an excellent specialist bird-watching outfit run by the very knowledgeable guide Jorge Barraza.

## Copán: a brief history of the ruins

Once the most important **city-state** on the southern fringes of the Maya world Copán was largely cut off from all other cities except **Quiriguá**, 64km to the north in Guatemala (see p.420). Archeologists now believe that settlers began moving into the Río Copán valley from around 1400 BC, taking advantage of the rich agricultural potential of the land, although construction of the city is not thought to have begun until around 100 AD.

Copán remained a small, isolated settlement until the arrival of an outsider, **Yak K'uk Mo'** (Great Sun First Quetzal Macaw), in 426 AD, the warrior–shaman founder of the 400-year royal dynasty. It's unclear whether he was from either Teotihuacan, the Mesoamerican superpower, or Tikal (which was under strong Teotihuacan influence at the time), but Yak K'uk Mo' established the basic layout of the city. An intense cult of veneration, first established by his son **Popol Hol**, was continued by subsequent members of the dynasty – fifteen generations of his descendants were still asserting their lineage to Copán's enduringly charismatic founder.

Little is known about the next seven kings that followed Popol Hol, but in 553 AD the **golden era** of Copán began with the accession to the throne of **Moon Jaguar**, who constructed the magnificent Rosalila temple, now buried beneath Temple 16. The city thrived through the reigns of **Smoke Serpent** (578–628 AD), **Smoke Jaguar** (628–695 AD) and **Eighteen Rabbit** (695–738 AD) as the great fertility of the Copán region was exploited and wealth amassed from control of the jade trade along the Río Motagua. These resources and periods of stable, long-lasting governments allowed for unprecedented political and social growth as the population boomed to around 28,000 by 760 AD, the highest urban density in the entire Maya region.

Ambitious reconstruction of the city continued throughout this era, utilizing local andesite, a fine-grained, even-textured volcanic rock that was easily quarried and particularly suited to detailed carving, as well as substantial local limestone beds ideal for stucco production. The highly artistic carved relief style for which Copán is famous developed, reaching a pinnacle during the reign of Eighteen Rabbit – whose image is depicted on many of the site's magnificent stelae and who also oversaw the construction of the Great Plaza, the final version of the ball court and Temple 22 in the East Court.

Following the audacious capture and decapitation of Eighteen Rabbit by Quiriguá's Cauac Sky, construction at Copán came to a complete halt for seventeen years, possibly indicating a period of subjugation by its former vassal state. The royal dynasty managed to regroup after the ambush attack at the hands of Quiriguá, however, to flourish gloriously, albeit briefly again. **Smoke Shell** (749–763 AD) completed the construction of the **Hieroglyphic Stairway**, one of the most impressive pieces of Maya architecture, in an

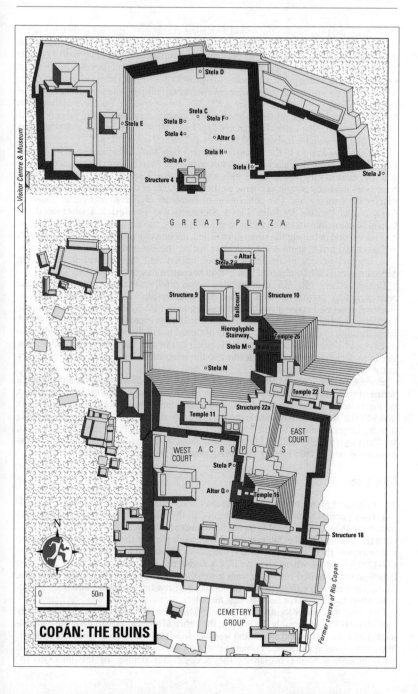

COPÁN: THE RUINS

effort designed to symbolize the revival. Optimism continued during the early years of the ruler **Yax Pasah** (763–820 AD), Smoke Shell's son, who commissioned **Altar Q**, which illustrates the entire dynasty from its beginning, and completed the final version of **Temple 16**, which towers over the site, around 776 AD. Towards the end of his rule, the rot set in: skeletal remains indicate that the decline was provoked by inadequate food resources, due to population pressures and subsequent environmental collapse. The seventeenth and final ruler, **Ukit Took'**, assumed the throne in 822 AD – two years after Yax Pasah is thought to have died – but his reign proved to be miserably inauspicious. Poignantly, the only monument to his reign, Altar L, which attempted to link his rule with the dynasty, was never completed, as if the sculptor had downed his tools and walked out on the job.

The site was known to the Spanish, although they took little interest in it. A court official, Don Diego de Palacios, in a letter written in March 1576, mentions the ruins of a magnificent city "constructed with such skill that it seems that they could never have been made by people as coarse as the inhabitants of this province". Not until the nineteenth century and the publication of *Incidents of Travel in Central America, Chiapas and Yucatán* by **John Lloyd Stephens** and **Frederick Catherwood** did Copán become known to the wider world. Stephens, the then acting US ambassador, had succeeded in buying the ruins in 1839 and, accompanied by Catherwood, a British architect and artist, spent several weeks clearing the site and mapping the buildings. The instant success of the book on publication and the interest it sparked in Mesoamerican culture ensured that Copán became a magnet for archeologists.

British archeologist **Alfred Maudslay** began a full-scale mapping, excavation and reconstruction project in 1891 under the sponsorship of the Peabody Museum, Harvard. A second major investigation was begun in 1935 by the Washington Carnegie Institute, which involved diverting the Río Copán to prevent it carving into the site. A breakthrough in understanding, not only of Copán but of the whole Maya World, came in 1959 and 1960, when archeologists Heinrich Berlin and Tatiana Proskouriakoff first began to decipher **hieroglyphs**, leading to the realization that they record the history of the cities and the dynasties.

Since 1977, the Instituto Hondureño de Antropología e Historia has been running a series of projects with the help of archeologists from around the world. Copán is now perhaps the best understood of all Maya cities, and a series of tunnelling projects beneath the Acropolis have unearthed remarkable discoveries including the Rosalila temple, buried beneath Temple 16, in 1989, which is now open to the public. In 1993, the Papagayo temple, built by Popol Hol and dedicated to his father Yax K'uk Mo', was uncovered, and in 1998 further burrowing unveiled the tomb of the founder himself.

## The site

The ruins lie 1.5km east of town, a pleasant fifteen-minute walk along a raised footpath that runs parallel to the highway. Entrance to the site (daily 8am–4pm; US$10, also includes Las Sepultras ruins) is through the **visitor centre** on the left-hand side of the car park, where a small exhibition explains Copán's place in the Maya World. Inside the visitor centre there's a **ticket office** (access to the archeological tunnels is an extra US$12) and a desk where you can hire a registered site guide (US$10 for 2hr) – an excellent investment if you really want to get the most out of Copán. On the other side of the car park is a **cafeteria**, serving drinks and reasonable meals, and a small souvenir shop (with print but no slide film for sale).

Opposite the visitor centre, the terrific **Museum of Mayan Sculpture** (daily 8am–4pm; US$5) is arguably the finest in the entire Maya region with a tremendous collection of stelae, altars and panels and well-labelled explanations in English and Spanish. You enter through a dramatic entrance doorway, resembling the jaws of a serpent, and pass through a tunnel (signifying the passage into *xibalba*, or the underworld).

Dominating the museum is a full-scale, flamboyantly painted replica of the magnificent **Rosalila Temple**, built by Moon Jaguar in 571 and discovered intact under Temple 16. A vast crimson and jade coloured mask of the Sun God, depicted with wings out-stretched, forms the main facade of the temple. Other ground-floor exhibits concentrate upon aspects of Maya beliefs and cosmology, while the upper floor houses many of the finest original sculptures from the Copán valley, comprehensively displaying the ability and skill of the Maya craftsmen.

From the museum it's a 200m walk east to the **warden's gate**, the entrance to the site proper, where your ticket will be checked and where there are usually several squabbling macaws to greet your arrival – these are tame and sleep in cages by the gate at night.

## The Great Plaza

Straight through the avenue of trees lies the **Great Plaza**, a rectangular three-hectare arena strewn with the magnificently carved and exceptionally well-preserved stelae that are Copán's outstanding features. Initially, the visual impact of this grassy expanse may seem a little underwhelming: the first structure you see is **Stucture 4**, a modest-ly sized pyramid-temple, while the stepped buildings bordering the northern end of the plaza are low and unremarkable. This part of the Great Plaza was once a public place, the stepped sides bordered by a densely populated residential area. The grandest build-ings are confined to the monumental temples that border the southern section of the plaza, rising to form the Acropolis, the domain of the ruling and religious elite.

Dotted all around are Copán's famed **stelae** and altars, made from the local andesite. Most of the stelae represent **Eighteen Rabbit**, Copán's "King of the Arts" (Stelae A, B, C, D, F, H and 4). **Stela A**, dating from 731 AD, has incredibly deep carving, although the faces are now eroded; its sides include a total of 52 glyphs, translating into a famous inscription that includes the emblem glyphs of the four great cities of Copán, Palenque, Tikal and Calakmul – a text designed to show that Eighteen Rabbit saw his city as a piv-otal power in the Maya world. **Stela B** depicts a slightly oriental-looking Eighteen Rabbit, bearing a turban-like headdress that's intertwined with twin macaws, while his hands support a bar motif, a symbol designed to show the ruler holding up the sky. **Stela C** (730 AD) is one of the earliest stones to have faces on both sides and, like many of the central stelae, it has an altar at its base, carved in the shape of a turtle. Two rulers are represented here: facing the turtle (a symbol of longevity) is Eighteen Rabbit's father, Smoke Jaguar, who lived well into his eighties, while on other side is Eighteen Rabbit himself. **Stela H**, perhaps the most impressively executed of all the sculptures, shows Eighteen Rabbit wearing the latticed skirt of the Maize God, his wrists weighed down with jewellery, while the face of the "divine lord" is crowned with a stunning headdress.

South of Structure 4, as you head towards the Acropolis, is the I-shaped **ball court**, one of the largest and most elaborate of the Classic period, and one of the few Maya courts still to have a paved floor. It was completed in 738 AD, just four months before Eighteen Rabbit's demise at the hands of Quiriguá, and beneath it lie two previous ver-sions. Like its predecessors, the court was dedicated to the great macaw deity, and both sloping sides of the court are lined with three sculptured macaw heads. The rooms that line the sides of the court, overlooking the playing area, were probably used by priests and members of the elite as they observed the ritual of the game.

Pressed up against the ball court, protected by a vast canvas cover, is the famed **Hieroglyphic Stairway**, perhaps the most astonishing monument of all. The stairway, which takes up the entire western face of the Temple 26 pyramid, is made up of some 72 stone steps; every block is carved to form part of the glyphic sequence – around 2200 glyph blocks in all. It forms the longest known Maya hieroglyphic text, but, unfor-tunately, attempted reconstruction by early archeologists left the sequence so jumbled that a complete interpretation is still some way off. It is known that the stairway was initiated to record the dynastic history of the city. Some of the lower steps were first put in place by Eighteen Rabbit in 710 AD, while Smoke Shell rearranged and completed most of the sequences in an effort to reassert the city's dignity and strength in 755 AD. At the base of the stairway the badly weathered **Stela M** depicts Smoke Shell and records a solar eclipse in 756 AD.

Adjacent to the Hieroglyphic Stairway, and towering over the extreme southern end of the plaza, are the vertiginous steps of **Temple 11**, also known as the Temple of the Inscriptions. The temple was constructed by Smoke Shell, who is thought to have been buried beneath the structure, though no tomb has yet been found. At its base, **Stela N** (761 AD) represents Smoke Shell, another classic piece of Copán carving, with portraits on the two main faces of the stela and glyphs down the sides. The depth of the relief has protected the nooks and crannies, and in some of these you can still see flakes of paint; originally the carvings and buildings would have been painted in a whole range of bright colours, but for some reason only the red has survived.

## The Acropolis

From the southwestern corner edge of the plaza, a trail runs past some original drainage ducts and then stone steps climb steeply up the side of Temple 11, to a soaring cluster of temples, dubbed the **Acropolis**. This lofty inner sanctum of the city was the reserve of royalty, nobles and priests, the political and ceremonial core where religious rituals were enacted, sacrifices performed and rulers entombed. The whole structure grew in size over four hundred years, the temples growing higher and higher as larger structures were built over the remains of early buildings. A warren of excavating tunnels, some open to the public, bore through the vast bulk of the Acropolis to these structures including the Rosalila temple and several tombs. From the summit of Temple 11, beside a giant ceiba tree, a tree held sacred to the Maya, there's a panoramic view of the site below, over the ball court and Great Plaza to the green hills beyond.

A few metres east of Temple 11 are the **Mat House** (Structure 22A), a governmental building distinguished by its upper interlocking stone mat weave-like patterns; and **Temple 22**, which boasts some superbly intricate stonework around the door frames. Constructed under Eighteen Rabbit, Temple 22 functioned as a "sacred mountain" where the elite would perform religious blood-letting ceremonies. Above the door is the body of a double-headed snake, its heads resting on two figures, which in turn are supported by skulls. The decoration here is unique in the southern Maya region, with only the Yucatán sites such as Kabáh and Chicanna having carvings of comparable quality.

Below Temple 22 are the stepped sides of the **East Court**, a graceful plaza which also bears elaborate carvings, including life-sized jaguar heads, with hollow eyes which would have once held pieces of jade or polished obsidian. In the middle of the western staircase, flanked by the jaguars, is a rectangular Venus mask, carved in superb deep relief. Rising over the court and dominating the Acropolis, **Temple 16** is the tallest structure in Copán, a 30-metre pyramid completed by the 16th ruler, Yax Pasaj, in 776 AD. In order to build Temple 16 Yax Pasaj had to build on top of the **Rosalila temple**, a project which was undertaken with extraordinary, and atypical, care not to destroy the earlier temple – generally, it was Maya custom to ritually deface or destroy obsolete temples or stelae. The temple served as a centre for worship during the reign of Smoke Serpent, or Butz'Chan, Copán's eleventh ruler (578–628 AD), a period that marked the apogee of political, social and artistic growth, so the discovery of the Rosalila has been one of the most exciting finds of recent years. You can now view the brilliant original facade of the buried temple by entering through a short **tunnel** – an unforgettable, if costly at US$12, experience, as it may be sealed again in future years. The admission price does at least include access to two further tunnels, which extend below the East Plaza past some early cosmological stucco carvings – including a huge macaw mask – more buried temple facades and crypts including the Galindo tomb.

At the southern end of the East Court is **Structure 18**, a small square building with four carved panels, and the burial place of Yax Pasaj in AD 821. The diminutive scale of the structure reveals how quickly decline set in, and the militaristic nature of the panels reflective of the troubled times. The tomb was empty when excavated by archeologists and is thought to have been looted on a number of occasions. From Structure 18 there's a terrific perspective of the valley, over the Río Copán, which eroded the eastern buildings of the Acropolis over the centuries until its path was diverted by early archeologists. South of Structure 18, the **Cemetery Group** was once thought to have been a burial site, though it's now known to have been a residential complex, and home to the ruling elite. To date, however, little work has been done on this part of the ruins.

The second plaza of the Acropolis, the **West Court**, is confined by the south side of Temple 11, which has eight small doorways, and Temple 16. **Altar Q**, at the base of Temple 16, is the court's most famous feature and an astonishing monument of ancestral symbolism. Carved in 776 AD, it celebrates Yax Pasaj's accession to the throne on July 2, 763. The top of the altar is carved with six hieroglyphic blocks, while the sides are decorated with sixteen cross-legged figures, all seated on cushions, who represent previous rulers of Copán. All are pointing towards a portrait of Yax Pasaj which shows him receiving a ceremonial staff from the city's first ruler, Yax K'uk Mo', thereby endorsing Yax Pasaj's right to rule. Behind the altar is a small crypt, discovered to contain the remains of a macaw and fifteen big cats, sacrificed in honour of his ancestors when the altar was inaugurated.

## Las Sepultras

Two kilometres east of Copán via the highway is the smaller site of **Las Sepultras** (daily 8am–4pm; entrance on the same ticket as for Copán), the focus of much archeological interest in recent years because of the information it provides on daily domestic life in Maya times. Eighteen of some forty residential compounds at the site have been excavated, yielding one hundred buildings that would have been inhabited by the elite. Smaller compounds on the edge of the site are thought to have housed young princes, as well as concubines and servants. It was customary to bury the nobility close to their residences, and around the compounds more than 250 tombs have been excavated, allowing insights into the Maya way of life. Given the number of women found in the tombs it seems likely that they practised polygamy. One of the most interesting finds – the tomb of a priest or shaman, dating from around 450 AD – is on display in the museum in Copán Ruinas.

# Around Copán

There are a couple of places within easy reach of Copán that make an extra day or two's stay here worthwhile. Closest is the small Maya site of **Los Sapos**, a delightful walk south from town. Ten kilometres or so in the opposite direction, the picturesque waterfall of **El Rubí** is the perfect spot for a picnic. Copán is also a convenient spot to cross over into Guatemala, with the **El Florido** border crossing just 12km to the west.

**Los Sapos**, dating from the same era as Copán, is set in the hills to the south of town, less than an hour's gentle walk away. The site, whose name derives from a rock carved in the shape of a frog, is thought to have been a place where Maya women came to bear children; unfortunately, though, time and weather have eroded much of the carving. To get there, follow the main road south out of town, turn left onto a dirt track just past the river bridge and follow this as it begins to climb gently into the hills, past the *Hacienda San Lucas* farmhouse hotel (see p.488). The views across the tobacco fields of the river valley are beautiful, and there are plenty of spots for swimming along the way.

Pick-ups leave Copán regularly throughout the day for the peaceful town of **Santa Rita**, 9km northeast. At the river bridge, just before entering the town, a path leads up to **El Rubí**, a pretty double waterfall on the Río Copán, about 2km away. Surrounded by shady woods, this is the perfect spot for a swim in the clear, cold water, followed by a picnic. Follow the path as it climbs along and above the right-hand bank of the river for about twenty minutes; just past a steep stretch and small bend to the right, the narrow path running down through the pasture on the left leads to a pool and high rock, on the other side of which is El Rubí.

## Leaving Copán: north to San Pedro Sula

Direct luxury air-conditioned Hedman Atlas **buses** (☎651 4106) leave Copán for San Pedro Sula daily at 2pm (2hr 45min) from their terminal two blocks north of the plaza, in the *Hacienda San Lucas* information centre; the company are also planning to run two more daily departures. Two other bus companies, Gama and Casarola, also run less expensive direct and non-direct services to San Pedro Sula; while slower local buses run every two hours to La Entrada from where there are plenty of connections to San Pedro Sula. The journey along CA-11, winding its way through lightly wooded mountains and fertile pasture lands, is undeniably scenic until you inevitably find yourself passing through **LA ENTRADA**, a distinctly unlikeable junction town 55km northeast of Copán. La Entrada's only redeeming feature is its proximity to the small site of El Puente (see below), though if you get stuck here, *Hotel San Carlos* (☎898 5228; ④), at the junction of CA-11 and CA-4, is the best of the available **accommodation**.

### El Puente

Breaking the journey in La Entrada gives you a chance to visit the archeological site of **El Puente** (daily 8am–4pm; US$5); a signed turn on CA-11 4km before La Entrada gives access to the site, 6km away. Opened in 1994, El Puente has few visitors, which makes its location – amid the grassy fields flanking the Río Chinamito – all the more enjoyable, although after the glories of Copán, the scale of the site is inevitably disappointing.

Once a sizeable **Maya** settlement, dating back to the Late Classic period and under the authority of Copán, El Puente contains more than two hundred structures. To date, only a small number in the centre have been excavated, including religious buildings and structures for the use of the elite, built around what was the main plaza. The most important of these (Structure 1) is an eleven-metre-high, six-stepped pyramid, oriented east–west and thought to be a funerary temple; the long, lower pyramid along its lower edge contains burial chambers. The small **museum** at the entrance to the park, about 1km from the restorations, has an informative exhibition on the site itself and on Maya culture in general.

No public transport runs up the road to the site, but hitching is considered safe; traffic is more frequent in the mornings. A round-trip taxi fare from La Entrada will cost around US$10, including an hour at the ruins.

# San Pedro Sula

Honduras's second city, and the country's economic focus, **SAN PEDRO SULA** sprawls across the fertile Valle de Sula, at the foot of the Merendón mountain chain, just an hour from the coast. Flat and uninspiring to look at, and for most of the year uncomfortably hot and humid, this is not a city for sightseeing. However, it's the transport hub for northern and western Honduras, making a stay here, however short, usually unavoidable. On a more positive note, in terms of **facilities**, San Pedro ranks alongside the capital, Tegucigalpa, with its own international airport, foreign consulates, and a

# SAN PEDRO SULA

## ACCOMMODATION
| | |
|---|---|
| Ambassador | 12 |
| Bolívar | 1 |
| Gran Hotel Conquistador | 6 |
| Ejecutive Real del Valle | 9 |
| Gran Hotel San Pedro | 7 |
| Gran Hotel Sula | 3 |
| Holiday Inn | 2 |
| Hotel Ejecutivo | 4 |
| Hotel Internacional Palace | 5 |
| Hotel Palmira | 11 |
| Hotel San José | 10 |
| Hotel Terraza | 8 |

## BUSES
| | |
|---|---|
| Buses to La Ceiba | a |
| Buses to Puerto Cortés | c |
| Buses to Copán | b |
| Buses to Agua Caliente | d |

## RESTAURANTS, CAFÉS & CYBERCAFÉS
| | |
|---|---|
| Café Pamplona | E |
| Cafetería Mayan Way | F |
| Don Udo's | A |
| Espresso Americano/Hondusoft | D |
| Gedeón cybercafé | B |
| Italian Grill Café | G |
| Pizzería Italia | C |
| Restaurante Las Tejas | H |

Puerto Cortés

Metro Plaza Mall

Fundacion Ecología Fasquelle Exhibition Hall

Mercado de Artesanías Guamilito

Estadio Francisco Morazán

Multicines Plaza

Cine Géminis

Centro Cultural Sampedraño

Museo de Arqueología e Historia

Credomatic

Parque Central

Cathedral

Train Station

Mercado Municipal

Multiplaza Mall

Airport

AVENIDA CIRCUNVALACIÓN

0    500 m

wide range of hotels, restaurants and shopping outlets, so that travellers coming from the north rarely need to visit the capital. If you do choose to stick around for a day or two, it's not difficult to organize a trip out to one of the country's finest **cloudforest reserves**, the Parque Nacional Cusuco (see p.501).

One of the first Spanish settlements in the country, founded by Pedro de Alvadaro in 1536, today's San Pedro bears almost no trace of its pre-twentieth-century incarnation. Burnt out by French corsairs in 1660 and virtually abandoned during a yellow fever epidemic in 1892, the city struggled to maintain a population of more than five thousand; today only a few wooden buildings remain as proof of its long past. Its fortunes began to rise with the growth of the **banana** industry in the late nineteenth century, when the city rapidly cemented its role as Honduras's commercial centre. With its outer reaches continuing to sprout factories, many of them foreign-owned, and a population currently in the region of 600,000, San Pedro today ranks as one of the fastest-growing cities in Central America.

## Arrival and information

The **Aeropuerto Internacional Villeda Morales**, the point of entry for both domestic and international flights, including daily flights to and from the Bay Islands via La Ceiba, lies 12km southeast of the city. As yet, there is no public transport between the airport and the city centre; **taxis** charge around US$8. **Buses** arrive at their own separate terminals, most within a few blocks of each other in central San Pedro.

San Pedro's regular **grid layout** makes navigation easy: avenidas run north–south and calles east–west, numbered in ascending order from the central 1 Avenida and 1 Calle, which intersect two blocks east of the cathedral. The city is further divided into **quadrants**, whose labels – southwest (SO), southeast (SE), northwest (NO) and northeast (NE) – are always used in directions. The bus terminals, many hotels and the main commercial area are in the southwest sector, close to the centre. Running west from the parque central, 1 Calle is also known as the Blvd Morazán for the first twelve blocks until it meets the **Av Circunvalación** ring road, which separates the city centre from San Pedro's wealthiest residential districts; this is where many of the more upmarket restaurants are located. Beyond the Circunvalación, 1 Calle becomes Blvd los Próceres.

## Accommodation

San Pedro's **accommodation** ranges from a spate of new four- and five-star luxury hotels, including a *Holiday Inn* and *Camino Real*, to sleazy, dollar-a-night dives. Expect to pay at least US$12 for an acceptable double room with bath in a secure hotel; double that, and TV and air conditioning become standard. The area south of the market can get rough at night, and although foreigners are unlikely to be targeted, it is not really a place to be wandering around after dark.

**Ambassador**, 7 C & 5 Av SO (☎557 6825, fax 557 5860). Reasonably comfortable rooms, all with bath and a/c. Not a particularly pleasant area at night, but convenient for many of the bus terminals. ④.

**Bolívar**, 2 C & 2 Av NO (☎553 3224, fax 553 4823). Good-value hotel in a central location with an upmarket feel about it. The large rooms all have bath, a/c and TV. Downstairs there is a small pool and terrace, and a rather characterless bar and restaurant. ⑤.

**Ejecutive Real del Valle**, Edificio Maria Emilia, 6 Av, 4–5 C SO (☎553 0366). A comfortable place with a welcoming atmosphere. The front door is always kept locked. All rooms have a/c, bath, hot water and TV. ④.

**Gran Hotel Conquistador**, 2 C SO, 7–8 Av (☎552 7605). Small and very friendly place, four blocks west of the parque central. Rooms are small but clean and all have bath, a/c and TV. ⑤.

**Gran Hotel San Pedro**, 3 C, 1–2 Av SO (☎553 1513, fax 553 1655). Large, rambling place that's popular with travellers. The choice of rooms ranges from basic ones with shared bath to reasonably spacious options with large beds, private bath, a/c and TV. ②–④.

**Gran Hotel Sula**, 1 C O, at the parque central (☎552 9999, fax 552 7000, *www.intertel.hn/tourism/gransula*). Venerable city landmark set in an excellent location in the main square where the business-class rooms have everything you would expect for the price, including balconies with views over the city. Small pool, 24–hour café and restaurant. ⑧.

**Holiday Inn**, 1 C, 10–11 Av (☎550 8080, fax 550 5353, *www.holiday-inn-sps.com*) New luxury block set in a pleasant residential area. Classy, commodious rooms, many with wonderful views, all with huge beds. Special weekend and corporate rates available. ⑧.

**Hotel Ejecutivo**, 10 Av & 2 C SO (☎552 4289, fax 552 5868). Well-run mid-range hotel, located in a quiet residential area, a ten-minute walk from the centre. Large rooms all have two double beds, a/c, bathrooms with power showers, and TV; the price includes a simple breakfast. Slightly cheaper rooms are available in a second block directly opposite. ⑤–⑥.

**Hotel Internacional Palace**, 8 Av, 3 C SO (☎550 3838, fax 550 0969, *www.intertel.hn/tourism/palace*). Refurbished hotel offering high-level accommodation at reasonable prices. All rooms have bath, hot water, a/c and TV. The rooftop pool and bar are a good place to cool off. ⑥.

**Hotel Palmira** 6 C, 6–7 Av SO. Conveniently located beside the Casarola bus terminal for Copán, this is a basic but cleanish place where all the rooms have private bathrooms; some also have a/c. ②–③.

**Hotel San José**, 6 Av, 5–6 C SO (☎557 1208). One of the better hotels in the lower price range. Clean, good-sized rooms with bath and a choice of fan or a/c. ②.

**Hotel Terraza**, 6 Av, 4–5 C SO (☎550 3108). Safe, good value and convenient for the centre and bus terminals. Rooms all have bath and hot water, some with a/c, and the café downstairs serves decent breakfasts. ③–④.

# The City

**Parque Barahona**, or the parque central, large and recently repaved, is the focus of the city centre, teeming with vendors, shoe-shine boys, moneychangers and general malcontents. On its eastern edge, the colonial-style **Catedral Municipal** was actually only completed in the mid-1950s; facing it across the parque is the unremarkable Palacio Muncipal, home to the city administration.

San Pedro has few tourist attractions, but one place that is worth a visit is the **Museo de Arqueología e Historia**, a few blocks north of the parque at 3 Av, 4 C NO (Wed–Mon 9am–4.15pm; US$0.65). The museum's collection (mostly labelled in Spanish only) of pre-Columbian sculptures, ceramics and other artefacts, the majority recovered from the Sula valley, outline the development of civilization in the region from 1500 BC onwards; weaponry and paintings from the colonial period continue the theme. While you're in this area, check out what's on at the **Centro Cultural Sampedrano**, 3 C, 3–4 Av NO (☎553 3911), which regularly hosts concerts and plays. A block southeast at 1 C and 7 Av (above *Pizzería Italia*) is the ecological foundation **Fundación Ecologista Hector Rodrigo Pastor Fasquelle** (☎552 1014 or 557 6598; Mon–Fri 8am–noon & 1–5pm, Sat 8am–noon), which is an excellent resource centre with information about the ecology of Honduras. Displays feature pictorial and written explanations of the development of cloudforests and the wildlife encountered in the country's varied habitats, including the nearby Parque Nacional de Cusuco (for details of Cusuco's **information** office, see p.502).

San Pedro has a good selection of places to buy **handicrafts** produced throughout the country. Ten or so blocks northwest of the parque central, the **Mercado Guamilito**, 9 Av, 6–7 C NO, is an indoor market with numerous stalls selling hammocks, ceramics, leatherwork and wooden goods. If you can carry them, the cotton hammocks are a good buy; gentle bartering should get you better prices. A couple of shops on the Calle Peatonal, just off the parque central, sell similar stuff, though prices are higher and the range not as wide. For the more eclectically minded, Le Merendón, a taxi ride out of the centre at 18 Av, 6 C SO, is a thatch-roofed display area–cum–beer garden, with an offbeat selection of works from artisans around the country; look out for the huge straw animals and the ceramic garden decorations. Danilo's, a couple of streets away at 18 Av B, 9 C SO, is an outlet for one of the best leather goods producers in the country, selling excellent-value bags, purses and belts, among other items. Finally, the vast general market, the **mercado municipal**, is between 4–5 Av SO and 5–6 C SO, though stalls spill onto the streets around for several blocks.

# Eating, drinking and entertainment

As you'd expect in such a business-oriented city there's a good selection of **places to eat** and a diverse range of evening entertainment. The more down-to-earth places can be found in the centre, while the Av Circunvalación, south of 1 C, is the so-called Zona Viva, the place to go for upmarket restaurants, bars and clubs. There's a number of modern multi-screen **cinemas** – including the Multicines Plaza de Sula at 10 Av and 4 C NO, Cine Tropicana, at 2 C, 7 Av SO, and the Cine Géminis, 1 C, 12 Av NO – all are within easy walking distance of the centre, and show new US films and the occasional Latin American offering.

## Cafés and restaurants

**Café Pamplona**, parque central. Always crowded with locals, this place has 70s' kitsch decor, an extensive menu, decent coffee and reasonable prices. Don't expect too much in the way of service but soak up the noisy atmosphere (closes 8pm).

**Café Skandia**, in the *Gran Hotel Sula*. Air-conditioned and open 24hr, the *Skandia* is something of a San Pedro institution, offering sandwiches, light meals and snacks, which are not as expensive as you might expect.

**Cafetería Mayan Way**, 6 Av, 4–5 C SO, next to *Hotel Terraza*. Slightly sleazy, but popular with travellers for the good breakfasts, set lunches and daily specials at down-to-earth prices. Open until 2am Fri and Sat.

**Don Udo's**, 1 C, 20 Av SO (☎552 5225). Dutch-owned restaurant that's held to be one of the city's finest, offering a broad range of European (including carpaccio) and local dishes and a decent wine list. Prices are not cheap, but worth it for a splurge; expect to pay from US$15 a head for a full meal with wine. Sunday brunches are less formal. Mon–Sat evenings, Sun 10am–2pm.

**Espresso Americano**, just west of the parque central on 3 C SO. Modern *Starbucks*-style coffee house with good mochas, cappuccinos, and even frappaccinos.

**Italian Grill Café**, 8 C, 16 Av SO (☎552 1770). Authentic Italian place where the generously sized pasta dishes include a side salad and focaccia bread; there's olive oil and balsamic vinegar for seasoning. Suprisingly moderate prices, though wines are expensive. Closed Sun.

**Pizzería Italia**, 1 C, 7 Av NO. Cosy little place with wonderful timewarp furnishings, serving good pizza (around US$4) and a small selection of pasta dishes (around US$5).

**Restaurante Las Tejas**, Av Circunvalación, 9 C SO. Popular place for Honduran-style lunch and dinner, with a wide selection of well-prepared seafood, as well as meat and chicken dishes.

**Shauky's Place**, 18 Av, 8 C SO. Now moved from the outskirts of the city, this easy-going bar and restaurant has tables set around an open-air gravelled garden. Delicious steak and meat dishes costing around US$7 and a few vegetarian choices too. Mon–Sat from 4pm.

## Bars and clubs

After dark, the best bet for a cheap drink in the central zone is to start out at the *Mayan Way* (see above) or *Johnny's*, by the market, an idiosyncratic spirits-only bar, where locals go to shoot the breeze to the accompaniment of 1950s be-bop. Out in the suburbs *Frog's Sports Bar*, Blvd los Próceres, 19–20 C SO, has pool tables and giant TV screens.

Clubbers should head for either *Henry's* or *Confetti's* in the Zona Viva for Latino pop and Euro dance while *El Quijote* at 11 C, 3–4 SO is probably the most exclusive place in town, attracting a flash, label-conscious crowd.

## Listings

**Airlines** American Airlines, Centro Comercial Firenze, 16 Av, 2 C (☎558 0518 or 558 0521, fax 558 0527); British Airways, Edificio Sempe, Carretera a Chamelecon (☎556 6952 or 552 3942, fax 556 8764); Continental, Plaza Versalles, Av Circunvalación (☎557 4141), and at the airport (☎668 3208); COPA, *Gran Hotel Sula* (☎550 5586); Iberia, Edificio Quiroz 2C, 1–2 Av (☎557 5311, fax 553 4297), airport (☎668 3218); Isleña, Edifico Trejo Merlo, 7 Av, 1–2 C (☎ & fax 552 8322); Sosa, 8 Av, 1 C SO (☎550 6545), airport (☎668 3223); Grupo Taca, Av Cirunvalación & 13 Av NO (☎550 5262), airport (☎668 3333).

**American Express** Agencia de Viajes Mundirama, Edificio Martinez Valenzuela, 2 C, 2–3 Av SO (☎553 1193, fax 557 9022).

**Banks and exchange** Banco Atlántida has a number of branches in the downtown area, including a branch in the parque central, for exchange and Visa advances; Banco de Occidente, 6 Av, 2–3 C SO, changes cash and travellers' cheques; Credomatic, 5 Av, 1–2 C NO, advances cash on Visa and Mastercard.

**Bookshops** The cigar shop in the *Gran Hotel Sula* has a small assortment of English-language fiction, books on Honduras and US magazines and newspapers.

**Car rental** Avis, Blvd Morazán 58 (☎552 2872); Budget, Aeropuerto Villeda Morales (☎566 2267, fax 553 3411); Dollar, 3 Av 3–4 C NO (☎552 7626); Molinari, *Gran Hotel Sula* (☎553 2639, fax 552 2704) and at the airport (☎566 2580).

**Consulates** Belize, Km 5, road to Puerto Cortés (☎551 0124, fax 551 1740); El Salvador, 6th floor, Edificio Rivera, 3 C, 5–6 Av SO (☎553 3604; Mon–Fri 9am–noon & 2–3.30pm); Guatemala, 8 C, 5–6 Av NO (☎553 3560; Mon–Fri 8.30am–2pm); Mexico, 2 C, 20 Av SO, 205 (☎553 2604; Mon–Fri 8.30–11.30am); Netherlands, Plaza Venecia 14 Av, 7–8 C SO (☎552 9724); UK, 13 Av, 11–12 C SO, No 62 (☎557 2046; Mon–Fri 9am–noon).

**Immigration** Direcion General de Migración, Calle Peatonal, above the Moreira Honduras souvenir shop (☎553 3728; Mon–Fri 8am–4pm).

**Internet** The number of cybercafés in town is growing rapidly. Hondusoft is the most central, on the first floor of the Edificio Gran Via, just south of the parque central on c/Peatonal; rates are just $2 an hour. On the west side of town, Gedeón, Local 1A, Plaza GMC, 6 Av Norte, 2–3 C NO, is very well set up, with rows of gleaming imac machines; rates are US$2.65 an hour.

**Laundry** Lavandería Express 9 Av, 3 C NO (Mon–Sat 8am–5pm).

**Medical care** Emergency department at Clínica Bendaña, Av Circunvalación, 9–10 C SO (☎553 1618).

**Police** ☎552 3128.

**Post office** At 9 C, 3 Av SO (Mon–Fri 7.30am–8pm, Sat 7.30am–12.30pm).

**Telephone office** Hondutel, at 4 C, 4 Av SO, is open 24hr; fax service is available 8am–5pm. Gedeón (see Internet above) have web phone call facilities.

**Travel agents and tours** Agencia de Viajes Mundirama, Edificio Martinez Valenzuela, 2 C, 2–3 Av SO (☎553 0192, fax 557 9022), is efficient and well organized for booking or changing international air tickets. Transmundo de Sula, 5 Av, 4 C NO (☎550 1140), is also a reputable company. Mesoamérica Travel, Edificio Picadelli, 11C, 2–3 Av (☎557 0332, fax 557 6886, *www.mesoamerica-travel.com*), is an excellent tour agency with trips to reserves including Punta Sal near Tela and Cusuco, and the Bay Islands; Maya Tropic Tours based in the *Gran Hotel Sula* (☎557 8830, *may-att@netsy*.hn) also offer trips to Copán and Cusuco.

## Around San Pedro: Parque Nacional de Cusuco

Only 20km or so west of San Pedro in the Sierra del Merendón, the stunning **Parque Nacional de Cusuco** (daily 6am–5pm; US$10) supports an abundant range of animal and plant life, much of it rare and threatened. Though inevitably affected by the proximity of human settlement, Cusuco is still a joy to visit and not too difficult to reach from San Pedro. To see as much as possible, the best plan is to arrive in the afternoon, camp overnight and walk the trails early in the morning.

The lower reaches of the park have long been inhabited and were heavily logged during the 1950s, contributing to disastrous floods during the 1970s, while there were serious landslides after Hurricane Mitch in 1998. Here the mixed pine and broadleaf forest is secondary regrowth. At around 1800m the **cloudforest** begins, its dense oaks and liquidambars reaching to 40m in some places, stacked over avocados and palms, all supporting mosses, vines, orchids and numerous species of heliconias, recognizable by the red or orange brackets holding the blossoms. Studies carried out in the park in 1992–95 revealed the existence of at least seventeen species of plant hitherto unknown in Honduras.

Four **trails**, ranging between 1km and 2.5km, have been laid out among the lower sections of cloudforest (there is no access to the highest, steepest sections of the reserve), taking you through a hushed world of dense, dripping, multi-layered vegetation. If you're incredibly lucky, you might spot the reserve's namesake, the *cusuco* (armadillo), as well as salamanders, monkeys and even a jaguar, but the dazzling range of birdlife is likely to be more rewarding in terms of sightings. Quetzals can be spotted from April to June, and trogons, kites and woodpeckers are among the more numerous of the hundred-plus species of bird living here.

### Park practicalities

Cusuco is managed by the Fundación Ecologista Hector Rodrigo Pastor Fasquelle, whose office is above the *Pizzería Italia*, 1 C, 7 Av NO, in San Pedro Sula (☎552 1014 or 557 6598). Information leaflets are usually available and they can also advise on getting to the reserve. The main point of **access** is via the small town of **COFRADÍA**, 18km southwest of San Pedro off CA-4. From here, a dirt road continues for another 26km to the village of **BUENOS AIRES**, 5km beyond which is the park **visitor centre**. Getting there independently is time-consuming: you need to take a westbound bus to Santa Rosa de Copán, alighting in the village of Cofradía (1hr), and then wait for onward transport. Other options include renting a car – a 4WD can make the whole journey in about two hours, depending on the state of the road – or taking a tour from San Pedro (see opposite). At the visitor centre there are displays on the wildlife, trail maps, a dormitory (①) and a campsite.

### Moving on from San Pedro Sula

There are frequent bus departures from San Pedro for cities inland and all destinations along the north coast (see below). If you're heading **for the Bay Islands** (see p.510) by road you'll need to travel via La Ceiba on either a Catisa-Tupsa bus from 2 Av 5–6 C SO (☎552 1042) who run twelve standard direct buses, or with one of two air-conditioned luxury bus companies: Viana at Av Circunvalación, 200m from *Wendy's* (☎556 9261), have two daily departures while Hedman Atlas at 3 C & 8Av NO (☎553-1361) have three daily departures.

# The northwest coast: Omoa to the Guatemalan border

North of San Pedro Sula, Highway CA-5 clears the edges of the city to run through the flat agricultural lands of the Sula valley, amidst lush, tropical scenery. After 60km the four lane highway reaches the coast at **PUERTO CORTÉS**, Honduras's main port, where the unstinting heat and dilapidated wooden buildings merely add to the rough and ready feel of the place. There is nothing here to entice you to stop but *Hotel El*

*Centro* at 3Av, just west of the plaza (☎665 1160; ② & ④), has basic but serviceable singles and doubles, some with cable TV and private bathrooms, while *Hotel Villa Capri*, close to the docks at 1C and 2 Av (☎665 6136, fax 665 6139, *villa-capri@lemaco.hn*; ⑦), has the best rooms in town, all with a/c.

Three companies run **buses** between San Pedro Sula and Puerto Cortés including Citul, whose offices are at 6 Av, 7–8 C SO in San Pedro, the most reliable operator; they have services every thirty minutes between 6am and 6pm, and the journey time is one hour. The Citul terminal in Puerto Cortés is a block north of the main plaza at 4 Av and 4C with **immigration** (Mon–Fri 8am–noon and 1–5pm; ☎665 0582), conveniently placed close by at 5 Av and 4 C, a further block to the north. To **change money**, head for Banco Atlántida (Mon–Fri 8.30am–5pm, Sat 9am–1.30pm) on the south side of the plaza, or to the market just to the west where the largest shoe stall owner changes dollars at fair rates. You can check **email** from Plaza Marinakys at 2 Av and 6 C (Mon–Sat 8am–6.30pm), two blocks east of the plaza.

**Moving on** from Puerto Cortés, there are buses to Corinto, for **Guatemala**, every hour and a half (8am–3.30pm; 4hr) and hourly connections to Omoa (1hr); buses leave from the Transportes Citral terminal on 3 C a block west of the plaza. It's also possible to travel from Puerto Cortés by fast skiff, the *Gulf Cruza*, to **Belize**, a weekly trip that leaves on Mondays at 10 am from the old bridge at La Laguna, 3km south of the town centre. The boat trip takes around seven hours to get to Belize City (US$75) via immigration at the banana dock at Big Creek for immigration and Placencia (2pm, US$50). For more information and the latest schedules and prices call ☎665 1200 or ☎665 5556.

# Omoa

Spreading inland from a deep bay, at the point where the mountains of the Sierra de Omoa meet the Caribbean, the fishing village of **OMOA** has become increasingly popular in recent years, with travellers coming here for a couple of days' total relaxation. At one time strategically important in the defence of the Spanish colonies against marauding British pirates, today the village dozes lethargically under the heat of the Caribbean sun. Its one outstanding sight, the restored **Fortaleza de San Fernando de Omoa** (Mon–Fri 8am–4pm, Sat & Sun 9am–5pm; US$1.30), stands mute witness to this colourful history. Now isolated amidst tropical greenery a kilometre from the coast, beached as the sea has receded over the centuries, the triangular fort was originally intended to protect the port of Puerto Barrios in Guatemala. Work began in 1759 but was never fully completed, due to a combination of bureaucratic inefficiency, problems with materials and labour shortage. The steadily weakening Spanish authorities then suffered the ignominy of witnessing the fortress temporarily occupied by British and Miskito military forces in October 1779.

The rather narrow village **beach**, lined with colourful fishing boats, offers stunning views west across the curve of the bay and the mountain backdrop. At weekends hordes of day-trippers turn up and it's often too crowded for comfort. Better swimming can be had by walking five minutes or so out of the village in either direction, while fifteen minutes around the headland to the east is a much wider, usually emptier expanse of beach.

## Practicalities

**Buses** between Puerto Cortés and Corinto pass the southern end of the village, close to the **immigration** office (in theory, daily 8am–5pm though often unmanned) which is right on the highway. The coast and hotels are 2km away to the north, past the fortress and the **Hondutel** office on the way.

Rising numbers of foreign tourists have led to the opening of a handful of reasonably comfortable **places to stay**. Heading towards the beach from the highway, you'll come to the Swiss-run *Roli's Place* (☎ and fax 658 9082, *RG@yaxpactours.com*; ②), an excellent budget base with camping (US$2 per person) and mosquito-screened dormitories (US$3.50 per person) where there's also **internet** access for US$5.80 per hour. Close to the seafront, *Pia's Place* (☎658 9076; ②) is a new place run by a friendly long-term *gringa* resident which offers basic clean rooms and dormitory accommodation (US$3 per person). Next door, by the waterfront, the comfortable *Bahía de Omoa* (☎ 658 9076; ④) is also run by Pia, with large, modern rooms, all with private bath and a/c. Pia also organizes snorkelling trips to the spectacular Sapadillo cayes, in Belizean waters north-west of Omoa, when there's sufficient demand. For a good feed head to the *Botín del Suizo* restaurant for European and local dishes or one of the **champas** on the beach-front – small, palm-thatched restaurants serving well-cooked seafood and other dishes. Try the clean and friendly *Fisherman's Hut*, or *Champa Virginia*, where a substantial meal costs US$3–4.

Moving on from Omoa to **Guatemala** it's an excruciatingly slow and bumpy bus ride southwest to the town of **Corinto**, 2km from the border. Buses run every hour and a half along this route which is steadily being patched up after Mitch wiped out all the bridges in 1998. Currently it takes up to three hours to cover the (flat !) 50km to Corinto though as the road improves and the bridges are rebuilt, the journey time will be cut. Corinto currently has an **immigration** office (daily 8am–5.30pm) though a new joint Guatemalan–Honduran customs and immigration point is due to open at the border itself (2km north of town) in 2003. Currently, frequent pick-ups shuttle to and from the border, from where you catch a minibus (every thirty minutes) over the new Arizona bridge, along a new paved road which crosses the Río Motagua. Minibuses pass though the village of Entre Ríos, for Guatemalan immigration, to Puerto Barrios, an hour from the Honduras border.

If you're pressed for time, adventurous souls can charter a lancha from Omoa to make the two-hour, invariably very wet, boat journey over to Lívingston in **Guatemala**. Ask around in the guest houses or the *Botín del Suizo* for a captain; the price is around US$260 for the trip, which can be divided among up to ten people.

# La Ceiba

One hundred and ninety kilometres east along the coast from San Pedro Sula, steamy **LA CEIBA**, the lively capital of the department of Atlántida, is in many ways one of the more approachable Honduran cities. Though the town is completely bereft of architec-tural interest and its sandy beaches are strewn with garbage, it does at least enjoy a stunning setting beneath the backdrop of the steep, green slopes of the Cordillera Nombre de Dios. The city is bustling and self-assured by day, with a cosmopolitan mix of inhabitants including the large Garífuna community, but it's the night that's really celebrated in Ceiba, when visitors and locals gather to sample the city's throbbing dance scene. Things really come to a head during La Ceiba's **Carnaval** in the third week of May, when 200,000 revellers descend on the town.

La Ceiba owes its existence to the **banana** industry: the Vaccaro Bros (later Standard Fruit and now Dole) first laid plantations in the area in 1899 and set up their company headquarters in town in 1905. Although fruit is no longer shipped out through La Ceiba, the plantations are still important to the local economy, with crops of pineap-ple and African palm now as significant as bananas.

Though for many travellers Ceiba, as it's generally known, is no more than a stop-off en route to the Bay Islands (see p.510), there are some good beaches just 10km or so outside town. Alternatively, with more time and a little planning – or the services of a tour operator – you can explore the cloudforest of the nearby Parque Nacional Pico Bonito or the mangrove swamps of the Refugio Vida Silvestre (see p.510).

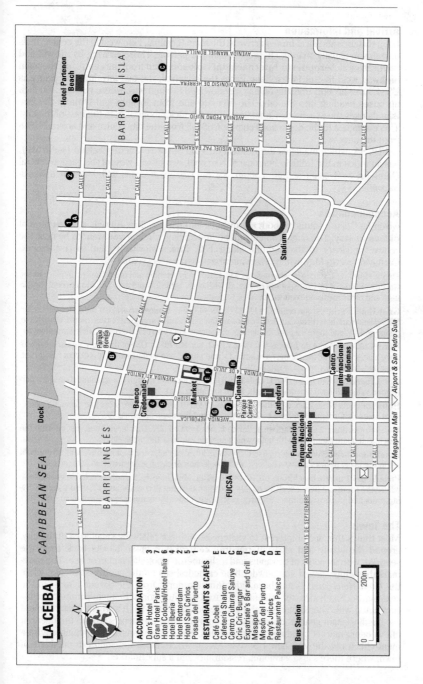

## Arrival and information

Long-distance and local **buses** arrive at the main terminal, 2km west of the centre; taxis downtown, usually shared, charge US$0.50 per person. Those arriving by **air** will find themselves at **Aeropuerto Internacional Golosón**, 9km from the centre, off the main highway west to San Pedro Sula. From the terminal, the taxi fare into the centre is US$4.50, or around US$3 if you flag one down on the highway, where you can also pick up buses heading into the city. The **ferry** to and from **Roatán** and **Utila** in the Bay Islands uses the Muelle de Cabotaje municipal dock, about 5km to the east of the city. There's no bus to the dock; taxis charge US$4–5 from the city centre and around US$8 from the airport.

**FUCSA**, which manages the Refugio de Vida Silvestre Cuero y Salado (see p.510), has an office in the Edificio Ferrocarril Nacional, two blocks west of the parque central (Mon–Fri 8–11.30am & 1.30–4.30pm, Sat 8–11.30am; ☎ & fax 443 0329, *fucsa@laceiba.com*).

## Accommodation

Given La Ceiba's status, as both a provincial and party centre, there is a wide range of **places to stay**. The only problem will be in deciding whether you want to be near the centre, or closer to the nightlife along 1 C. Prices inevitably tend to rise around Carnaval time in May, when reserving ahead becomes essential.

**Dan's Hotel**, C 3, Barrio la Isla (☎ & fax 443 4219). Very friendly and quiet family-run place in the Garífuna barrio of La Isla. Spotless rooms, all with bath, cable TV and a/c. The owners cook breakfasts and other meals on request. ④.

**Gran Hotel Paris**, parque central (☎443 2391, fax 443 1614, *www.granhotelparis.com*). Recently refurbished landmark hotel in an excellent location on the main plaza. Large comfortable rooms, all with a/c, phone and TV, and there's a pool, a quiet bar, restaurant and cybercafé. Excellent value for money. ⑥.

**Hotel Colonial**, Av 14 de Julio, 6–7 C (☎443 1953, fax 443 1955). One of the more upmarket downtown places where all the rooms have bath, TV and phone, and facilities include a decent restaurant, a bar and, bizarrely enough, a sauna. ⑤.

**Hotel Iberia**, Av San Isidro, 5–6 C (☎443 0401). Noisy location though the spacious rooms are fairly good value: all have two double beds, bath, a/c and TV. ③.

**Hotel Italia**, Av 14 de Julio, next to the *Colonial* (☎443 0150). Rooms are large and clean, but somewhat sparsely furnished; all have baths, however, and the place is secure. ②.

**Hotel Rotterdam**, 1 C, Av Barahona, Barrio la Isla (☎443 0321). Dutch-run hotel, just up from the beach. Adequate rooms, all with bath, which are fair value for the price. ②.

**Hotel San Carlos**, Av San Isidro, 5–6 C (☎443 0330). Well-run, very popular travellers' stronghold set in the heart of town above a bakery, with a selection of clean, safe rooms, all with fans. ②.

**Posada del Puerto**, beachfront, off 1C (☎440 0030). Very homely, friendly beachside guesthouse where the rooms all have excellent quality beds and pleasant decor, a/c and TV. Also a guests' living room and kitchen, and there's a large restaurant, under the same management, next door. ⑤.

## The Town

Most things that are of interest to visitors lie within a relatively small area of the city, around the shady and pleasant **parque central**, six or so blocks back from the seafront, with its pools of terrapins and a slumberous-looking caiman or two. The unremarkable whitewashed and powder-blue cathedral sits on the southeast corner, while the *Gran Hotel Paris* is northern side. Running north from the parque almost to the seafront, Av San Isidro, Av Atlántida and Av 14 de Julio form the main commercial district, lined with shops, banks and a couple of supermarkets. It's worth a look around the bustling main general **market** which sprawls along the streets around the decrepit old wooden, market building on Av Atlántida. For a more sanitized shopping environment check out the vast new US–style Megaplaza **mall** on the southern outskirts of town, where there's also a cinema, restaurants and a supermarket.

Night action takes place along 1 C, which parallels the length of the seafront. Nicknamed the "Zona Viva" due to the preponderance of bars and clubs, 1 C extends west from the old dock and over the river estuary into **Barrio la Isla**, a quieter residential district, mainly home to Garífuna, once it leaves the seafront. All the **beaches** within the city limits are, sadly, too polluted and dirty for even the most desperate to want to brave the rough water. Better by far is to head east to the much cleaner beaches a few kilometres out of town (see p.509).

## Eating, drinking and entertainment

Not for nothing does La Ceiba have a reputation as the place to party. The **Zona Viva** hums most nights of the week, though weekends are really explosive, with a profusion of places to drink and get down. A hedonistic local crowd, plus a steady trickle of tourists and a growing number of resident ex-pats, both in front of and behind the bar, have helped to create a buoyant atmosphere. While the range of **places to eat** is not that extensive, it's not impossible to find good Honduran and international food, though restaurants generally stop serving at around 10pm. There's a **cinema** just east of the parque central on 8 C, and two screens at the Cines Milenium in the Megaplaza south of town (you'll need a taxi) for the usual subtitled Hollywood fare.

If you can make it, the most exciting time to be in La Ceiba is during **Carnaval**, a week-long bash held every May to celebrate the city's patron saint, San Isidro. Dances and street events in various barrios around town culminate in an afternoon parade on the third Saturday of the month. Led by a float carrying the Carnaval Queen, the parade moves slowly down the gaudily decked Av San Isidro. Bands on stages placed along the avenida then compete to outplay each other throughout the evening and into the early hours. The 200,000 or so partygoers who attend Carnaval every year flock between the stages and the clubs on 1 C where the dancing continues until dawn.

### *RESTAURANTS AND CAFÉS*

**Café Cobel**, 7 C, Av San Isidro. A fast-turnaround place serving breakfasts and lunch, mainly to office workers. The food is good, as are the juices, and the portions large.

**Café Tropical**, Av Atlántida, 4–5 C. Cheerful café serving from early morning to around 10pm. Good pollo frito features heavily in the daily set menus.

**Cafeteria Shalom** inside a small mall on 7C, between Av Atlántida and Av 14 de Julio. Perhaps the most unexpected find in La Ceiba, this is a superb Israeli–owned canteen serving delicious Middle Eastern food including falafel, kebabs and stuffed peppers. Excellent lunch buffet special for US$2.25. Open daily 7am–8pm.

**La Casa**, 9 C, Av San Isidro–Av 14 de Julio. Centrally located comedor, with tables set around an open patio. Wide range of Honduran food, with buffet–style eating for around US$1.50 a head.

**Centro Cultural Satuye**, 4 C, Av Herrera, Barrio la Isla. Light-hearted and informal Garífuna restaurant. Loud live music in the evenings.

**Cric Cric Burger**, Av 14 de Julio, 3 C. Good burgers, steak sandwiches and other snacks are served to the accompaniment of very loud music. The side tables are a good place to watch comings and goings in the street.

**Expatriate's Bar and Grill**, 12 C, two blocks east of Av San Isidro. Airy, North-American-owned thatched bar with a good range of excellent vegetarian dishes, grilled chicken and fish and barbecued ribs. Welcoming atmosphere and popular with resident foreigners, so it's a good source of local information. Mon & Thurs–Sun 4pm–midnight.

**Masapán** 7C, between Av la República and Av San Isidro. Consistently popular self-service cafeteria, open 24-hour, with a cheap buffet of Honduran and American-style food.

**Mesón del Puerto**, on the seafront, just off 1C, Barrio La Isla. Excellent but pricey beachside restaurant with delicious menu of grilled meats, including *parrillada*; professional service.

**Paty's Juices**, 14 de Julio, 6–7C. Friendly family-owned place ideal for rich, delicious and inexpensive fresh juices, licuados and fruit salads.

**Restaurante Palace**, Av 14 de Julio, 8 C. Big barn of a place serving pretty good, fairly authentic Chinese dishes.

## BARS AND CLUBS

**African Dance**, 1 C, two blocks east of the river, Barrio la Isla. A Garífuna dance hall, with live punta, plus some latin and reggae, with dancing most nights of the week.

**Cherry's**, on the beach, at the end of Av 14 de Julio. A popular club, open all week and packed at the weekend. Plays a mixture of Latin American rhythms, reggae and country music.

**El Mussol**, 1C, 7 blocks from the bridge in Barrio la Isla. Probably the smartest club in the Zona Viva, with drink prices a little higher than in other venues.

**Safari**, just over the river in Barrio la Isla. Another popular club, attracting a predominantly local crowd.

**Scape's**, just over the river in Barrio la Isla. Lively beachfront bar, with food, pool tables and a dancefloor.

## Listings

**Airlines** On the parque central are Isleña (☎443 0179), Sosa (☎443 1399) and Taca (☎443 1912); all three also have ticket desks at the airport, as do Rollins Air (☎443 2177) and Cayman Airways (☎440 0863).

**Banks** Banco Ficahsa, for travellers' cheques, is just west of the parque central on 8C, while Credomatic, Av San Isidro, 5–6 C, is the place for Visa and Mastercard cash advances.

**Book exchange** The Rain Forest store, C la Julia, off 9 C (☎443 2917), always has a reasonable stock.

**Car rental** Molinari, *Gran Hotel Paris* (☎443 2391, fax 443 0055).

**Hospital** Hospital Euro Honduras, 1C, Av Atlántida, Barrio el Centro (☎443 0244), is a modern well-equipped private hospital, with 24-hour emergency clinic and English- and German-speaking staff.

**Immigration** Av 14 Julio, 1–2 C (Mon–Fri 8am–noon & 2–4pm; ☎442 0638).

**Internet** There are several cybercafés in La Ceiba including the efficient Hondusoft on the upper floor of the Centro Comercial Panyotti shopping mall at 7C between Av Atlántida and Av 14 de Julio (Mon–Fri 8am–8pm, Sat 8am–6pm), with fast connection rates for US$3.50 an hour, plus internet phone dial-ups. Intercon at Av San Isidro, 6–7 C (Mon–Sat 8am–8pm, Sun 9am–7pm), is another reliable place, also with Telnet, where rates are US$3 an hour.

**Language school** Centro Internacional de Idiomas, Av San Isidro, 12–13 (☎ & fax 440 1557, *www.worldwide.edu/honduras/cici*), is a good Spanish school with a/c classrooms. Rates are US$220 weekly for four hours of one-to-one tuition and homestay, including all meals.

**Laundry** Lavandería Super Clean, 16 C, Av San Isidro.

**Police** ☎441 0795 or 199.

**Post office** Av Morazán and 13 C, south of the parque.

**Telephones** Hondutel, at Av Ramón Rosa, 5–6 C, is open 24hr; or use the internet cafés (see above) for internet phone dial-ups.

**Travel agent** Paso Travel Service, Av San Isidro, 11–12 C (☎443 3186).

**Tour operators** For trekking trips to Pico Bonito (see opposite) and white-water rafting on the Río Cangrejal, there are several excellent companies: try La Moskitia Ecoaventuras, Parque Bonilla, Av 14 de Julio at 1 C (☎442 0104, *www.honduras.com/moskita*); Euro Honduras Tours, Av Atlántida at 1 C (☎443 3874, *eurohonduras@caribe.net*); Jungle River Rafting, Av Miguel Paz Barahona, Barrio la Isla (☎440 1268, *jungle@laceiba.com*); or Ríos Honduras (☎995 6925, *www.paddlehonduras*.com).

# Around La Ceiba

The broad sandy **beaches** and clean water at Playa de Perú and the village of Sambo Creek are easy to reach as day-trips from the city; both are a short distance east along the coast. A trip to explore the **cloudforest** within the Parque Nacional Pico Bonito requires

## CRIME AND DRUGS ON THE NORTH COAST

Increasing use of **drugs** has led to a significant rise in **crime** rates along the north coast. Muggings, bag-snatchings and personal attacks have all been reported and while the chances are that nothing will happen to you, it's sensible to take some precautions. Make sure you are never visibly carrying large amounts of cash, or expensive-looking bags or cameras; avoid walking around the centre of town late at night; and never go onto the beaches after dark – advice that holds for the whole of the north coast.

more planning, although the eastern edge of the reserve, formed by the Río Cangrejal, is more easily accessible, offering opportunities for swimming and white-water **rafting**.

### The beaches: Playa de Perú and Sambo Creek

Ten kilometres east of the city, **Playa de Perú** is a wide sweep of clean sand that's popular at weekends. Any bus running east up the coast will drop you at the turn-off on the highway, from where it's a fifteen-minute walk to the beach. About 2km past the turning for Playa de Perú, on the Río María, there's a series of **waterfalls** and **natural pools** set in lush, shady forest. A path leads from Río María village on the highway, winding through the hills along the left bank of the river. It takes around thirty minutes to walk to the first cascade and pool; some sections are muddy and a bit of a scramble during the wet season.

There are further deserted expanses of white sand at the friendly Garífuna village of **SAMBO CREEK**, 8km beyond Río María. You can eat excellent fresh fish at a couple of good restaurants in the village and there's also either cheap beds at the basic *Hotel Hermanos Avila* (①) or more comfortable accommodation at the new *Hotel la Canadien* (☎440 2099, fax 440 2097; ④), which has pleasant rooms, a great beachside plot and a pool. Olanchito or Jutiapa buses from La Ceiba will drop you at the turn-off to Sambo Creek on the highway, a couple of kilometres from the village; slower buses run all the way to the village centre from La Ceiba's terminal every 45 minutes.

### Parque Nacional Pico Bonito

Directly south of La Ceiba, the Cordillera Nombre de Dios shelters the **Parque Nacional Pico Bonito** (daily 6am–4pm; US$6), a remote expanse of tropical broadleaf forest, cloudforest and – in its southern reaches, above the Río Aguan valley – pine forest. Taking its name from the awe-inspiring bulk of Pico Bonito (2435m) itself, the park is the source of twenty rivers, including the Zacate, Bonito and Cangrejal, which cascade majestically down the steep, thickly covered slopes, and it provides sanctuary for an abundance of wildlife including armadillos, howler and spider monkeys, pumas and tigrillos. This abundance is due in large part to the inaccessibility of much of the park. The lower fringes are the most easily penetrable, with a small number of trails laid out through the dense greenery. The easiest place to get into the park is via the grounds of the *Lodge at Pico Bonito* (☎440 0388, *www .picobonito.com*; ⑧–⑨), a world–class **jungle lodge** with amazing bungalow accommodation, gourmet cuisine, a pool and a sublime setting in the foothills of the forest reserve. To **get there** head for the village of **Los Pinos**, 12km from La Ceiba on the Tela highway, and the hotel is signposted, 3km away up a dirt side road. Trails from *The Lodge* snake up through the tree cover to a lookout from where Utila is visible, and down to beautiful river bathing pools. Tour companies in La Ceiba operate day- and overnight trips to Pico Bonito, from around US$40 per person (see opposite).

Just below *The Lodge* are two further attractions. Finca Mariposa (US$5) is a **butterfly park**, signposted 600m from the hotel, where there are more than 40 species to examine in a large screened garden house. A further 2km from the butterfly park, but better reached from a one-kilometre-long dirt road from Los Pinos, AMARAS (☎443 3824, *fupnapib@ kaceiba*.com; US$2) is a small **wildlife refuge centre** run by Ricardo Steiner, a Honduran eco-activist. The centre takes in monkeys, big cats (including jaguar), macaws and parrots confiscated from traffickers and previously kept as pets, and prepares them for release back in to the wild, where possible – volunteers are needed and visitors welcome.

The **Río Cangrejal**, forming the eastern boundary of the park, boasts some of the best Class III and IV rapids in Central America; **white-water rafting** and **kayaking** trips are organized by some of the tour companies listed on p.508. There are also some magnificent swimming spots, backed by gorgeous mountain scenery, along the river valley. It's tricky to get to the river under your own steam, but you could contact the German-owned Omega Rafting (☎440 0334, *omegatours@laceiba*.com), who run a small **hotel** (②) geared for eco-travellers on the banks of the Cangrejal – transport from La Ceiba, full board and a day spent either trekking, horse riding or rafting costs US$50 per person.

### Refugio de Vida Silvestre Cuero y Salado

Thirty kilometres west from La Ceiba, the **Refugio de Vida Silvestre Cuero y Salado** (daily 7am–4pm; US$10) is one of the last substantial remnants of wetlands and mangrove swamp along the north coast. The reserve is home to a large number of animal and bird species, many of which are endangered, including manatees, jaguars, howler and white-faced monkeys, sea turtles, hawks and seasonal influxes of migratory birds. Though nominally protected since 1987, the edges of the reserve are under constant pressure from local farmers wanting to drain the land for new pastures.

The best way to see the reserve is to take a **guided tour**, not least because the guides know the spots where you're likely to see some wildlife. FUCSA, the body that manages the reserve, has an office in La Ceiba (see p.506) and organizes regular tours (US$18 per boat), which you need to book in advance. They also run a small **campsite** at the reserve, and have tents for hire (US$7) which can sleep four.

To get to the reserve **independently**, catch one of the hourly buses from La Ceiba's terminal to the village of La Unión, 20km or so west. From here, you can either make your way on foot through the fruit plantations – it takes around an hour and a half to walk the 8km – or travel by *burra*, a flat, poled railcar (locals charge between US$6–10, depending on numbers, to shunt you along the tracks). The last bus back to La Ceiba leaves La Unión mid-afternoon.

# The Bay Islands

Strung in a gentle curve less than 60km off the north coast of Honduras, the **Bay Islands (Islas de la Bahía)**, with their clear, calm waters and abundant marine life, are the country's main tourist attraction. Resting along a coral reef, the islands are a perfect destination for cheap diving, sailing and fishing; less active visitors can sling a hammock and relax in the shade on the many palm-fringed, soft-sand beaches. Comprising three main islands and some 65 smaller cayes, this sweeping 125-kilometre island chain lies on the **Bonacca Ridge**, an underwater extension of the mainland Sierra de Omoa mountain range. **Roatán** is the largest and most developed of the islands, while **Guanaja**, to the east, is an upmarket resort destination with some wonderful dive sites, and **Utila**, the closest to the mainland, is a target for budget travellers from all over the world.

Even old hands get excited about **diving** the waters around the Bay Islands, where lizard fish and toadfish dart by, scarcely distinguishable from the coral, eagle rays glide through the water like huge birds flying through the air, and parrotfish chomp steadily

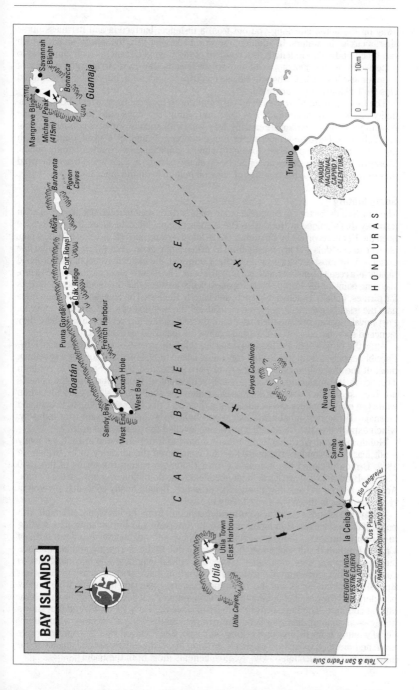

**BAY ISLANDS**

N

10km
0

Savannah Bight
Mangrove Bight
Bonacca
*Guanaja*
Michael Peak
(415m)

Barbareta
Pigeon Cayes
Morat
Port Royal
Oak Ridge
Punta Gorda
French Harbour
*Roatán*
Sandy Bay
Coxen Hole
West End
West Bay

Trujillo
PARQUE NACIONAL CAPIRO Y CALENTURA

H O N D U R A S

C A R I B B E A N   S E A

*Cayos Cochinos*

Nueva Armenia

Sambo Creek

La Ceiba
Río Cangrejal
Los Pinos
PARQUE NACIONAL PICO BONITO

*Utila*
Utila Town
(East Harbour)
Utila Cayes

REFUGIO DE VIDA SILVESTRE CUERO Y SALADO

▽ Tela & San Pedro Sula

away on the coral; checking you out from a distance, barracuda and harmless nurse sharks circle the waters. In addition, the world's largest fish, the **whale shark**, which can reach up to 16m in length, is a resident of the Cayman Trench which plummets to impervious depths just north of the arc of islands. It's most frequently spotted in October and November, when dive boats run trips to look for it, but can be encountered close to Utilan waters year round.

The **best time to visit** the islands is from March to September, when the water visibility is good, and the weather is clear and sunny; the rains start in October, while November and December are usually very wet, with squally showers continuing until late February. Daytime temperatures range between 25 and 29°C year round, though the heat is rarely oppressive, thanks to almost constant east–southeast trade winds. **Mosquitoes** and **sandflies** are endemic on all the islands, at their worst when the wind dies down; at night lavish coatings of baby oil help to keep the latter away.

## Some history

The Bay Islands' history of conquest, pirate raids and constant immigration has resulted in a society that's unique in Honduras. The islands' original inhabitants are thought to have been the **Pech**, recorded by Columbus on his fourth voyage in 1502 as being a "robust people who adore idols and live mostly from a certain white grain from which they make fine bread and the most perfect beer". After the **Conquest**, the indigenous population dropped rapidly as a result of enslavement and forced labour. The islands' strategic location, as a provisioning point for the Europe-bound Spanish fleets, ensured that they soon became targets for **pirates**, initially Dutch and French, and latterly English. The Spanish decision to evacuate the islands, eventually achieved in 1650, left the way open for the pirates to move in. Port Royal, Roatán, became their base until the mid-eighteenth century, from where they launched sporadic attacks on ships and against the mainland settlements.

After the pirates left, Roatán was deserted until the arrival of the **Garífuna** in 1797. Forcibly expelled from the British-controlled island of St Vincent following a rebellion, most of the three-thousand-strong group were persuaded by the Spanish to settle in Trujillo on the mainland, leaving a small settlement at Punta Gorda on the island's north coast. Further waves of settlers came after the abolition of slavery in 1830, when white Cayman Islanders and freed slaves arrived on Utila, later spreading to Roatán and Guanaja. These new inhabitants fished and built up a very successful fruit industry, which exported to the US – until a hurricane levelled the plantations in 1877.

Honduras acquired rights to the islands following **independence** in 1821, yet many – not least the islanders themselves – still considered the territory to be British. In 1852, Britain declared the islands a Crown Colony, breaking the terms of the 1850 Clayton-Bulwer Treaty, an agreement not to exercise dominion over any part of Central America. Forced to back down under US pressure, Britain finally conceded sovereignty to Honduras in the Wyke-Cruz Treaty of 1859.

Today, the islands retain their **cultural** distinction from the mainland, although with both Spanish-speaking Hondurans and North American and European ex-pats settling in growing numbers, there is ongoing re-shaping and adaptation. A unique form of **Creole English** is still spoken on the street, but due to the increasing number of mainlanders migrating here, Spanish – always the official language – is becoming just as common. This government-encouraged migration has sparked tensions between English–speaking locals and the Latino newcomers, especially in Roatán where many islanders feel they are being swamped by land–hungry outsiders with whom they have little in common. The huge growth in tourism since the early 1990s, a trend that shows no signs of abating, has also been controversial as the islands' income, which traditionally came from fishing or working on cargo ships and oil rigs, is coming to rely more and more on tourism. Concern is growing about the environmental impact of the industry and the question of who, exactly, benefits most from the boom.

## Getting to the islands

The growth in tourism to the islands over the past few years means that all three are served by several daily flights from the mainland and both Utila and Roatán have daily boat connections with the coastal city of **La Ceiba** (see p.504).

Most travellers use the excellent scheduled **ferry service** leaving La Ceiba daily for Utila (1hr, US$12 one way) at 9.30am and for Roatán (2hr, US$13 one way) daily at 3pm. **Flying** to the islands is also uncomplicated, with locals treating the twin-propeller light aircraft almost like buses; tickets are very cheap and standarized by the Honduran government – there are no price variations between airlines. There are over twenty flights a day to Roatán (30min, US$20), four daily to Utila (20min, US$17) and five daily to Guanaja (40min, US$33) from La Ceiba. Availability is very rarely a problem, and you can buy your tickets on the spot at the airport, though you should book ahead in the peak holiday seasons (Christmas–Easter and August). All internal flights from San Pedro Sula (1hr) and Tegucigalpa (1hr) are via a quick stopover in La Ceiba. Schedules change at short notice and flights are sometimes cancelled altogether; bear in mind there might be delays to your arrival and, more crucially, departure. The domestic **airlines**, Isleña, Taca and Sosa, have offices on the central square in La Ceiba and at the airport; all also fly to San Pedro Sula and Tegucigalpa. Another internal carrier, Rollins Air, also has an office at the airport.

**From Belize**, the easiest way to get to the Bay Islands is **to fly** to Roatán with Taca (US$274 return). Alternatively, you can go by **boat** from Belize City or Placencia (see p.298) to **Puerto Cortés**, in Honduras and then continue by bus to La Ceiba via San Pedro Sula (see p.496).

There are also several **international flights** to Roatán: Taca operate one direct return flight a week from Houston, Miami and New Orleans; call their office in Roatán on ☎445 1387 for the latest schedules.

# Utila

Smallest of the three main Bay Islands, **UTILA** is a key destination for budget travellers intent on learning to **dive** at some of the cheapest prices in the world. Even if you don't want to don tanks, the superb waters around the island offer great swimming and snorkelling possibilities. Utila is still the cheapest island, with the cost of living only slightly higher than on the mainland, although prices are gradually rising. Life is laid-back and people are on the whole friendly; crimes against tourists are very rare, though watch out for the periodic dancehall brawl. As elsewhere, respect local customs in dress and don't walk around in your bathing suit. Note also that drinking from glass bottles on the street is prohibited.

## Arrival and information

All boats **dock** in the centre of **Utila Town** (also known as East Harbour), a large, curved harbour that's the island's only settlement and home to the vast majority of its 2000-strong population. The island's main road, a twenty-minute walk end to end, runs along the seafront from The Point in the east to Sandy Bay in the west. A new airport is currently being hacked out of the jungle 3km north of Utila Town, at the end of the island's second main road, **Cola de Mico Road**, which heads inland from the dock; until it opens, sometime in 2002 if the necessary finances materialize, all planes land at a dirt **airstrip** in The Point.

Wherever you arrive, you'll be met by representatives from the dive schools with **maps** and information on special offers. Many schools offer free accommodation during their courses, but it's worth checking out the various options before signing up. For more objective **information**, the Utila branch of BICA (Bay Islands' Conservation Association) has a visitor and information office on the main street east of the dock, though its opening hours are erratic (usually Mon–Fri 9am–noon and a couple of hours in the afternoon).

Everything in town is within easy walking distance; it takes around twenty minutes to stroll from the airstrip to the far western end. **Bikes** can be rented from Delco, next to Henderson's grocery store, just west of the dock, the *Mango Café* (see p.516) and other places around town. Rates start at US$2 a day for an old bike, around US$5 for a decent mountain bike (not that you'll need it). Some locals use four-wheeled motorbikes to get around and occasionally pick up hitchers.

## Accommodation

Utila has more than 25 affordable guest houses and hotels, and a profusion of rooms for rent; there's always somewhere available, even at Christmas and Easter. Most of the dive schools have links with a hostel, so that enrolment on a scuba course gets you a few free or discounted nights' accommodation. Everywhere is within walking distance of the dock and airstrip, and the accommodation listed below is in the order that you come to it, walking west along the road from the airstrip. There are no designated places to **camp** except on the cayes.

### FROM THE AIRSTRIP TO THE MAIN DOCK

**Sharkey's Reef Hotel**, behind *Sharkey's Reef Restaurant*, close to the airstrip (☎425 3212; hjackson@hondutel.hn). Set in a peaceful garden, the rooms all have a/c, private bathrooms and cable TV, and some have kitchens. There's also a terrace with great views over the lagoon. ⑤–⑥.

**Trudy's** (☎425 3103). A popular place with large, clean rooms, and you can swim from the dock at the back. ①.

**Cooper's Inn** (☎425 3184). One of the best budget places on the island, with clean, basic rooms and friendly management. ①.

**Rubi's Inn**, two minutes' walk from the dock (☎425 3240). Very clean, with airy rooms and views over the water; kitchen facilities are available. ①.

### COLA DE MICO ROAD

**Blueberry Hill**, just beyond Thompson's bakery, on the opposite side of the road (☎425 3141). Characterful cabins with basic cooking facilities, run by friendly owners, but ear plugs are essential at weekends when the *Bucket 'o' Blood* bar opposite fires up. ①.

**Mango Inn**, five minutes' walk up the road (☎425 3335, www.mango-inn.com). A beautiful, well-run place, timber-built in Caribbean style and set in shady gardens. It has a range of rooms, from a/c, thatched bungalows to pleasant dorms. Also has a book exchange and laundry service, and the attached *Mango Café* is a lively spot serving good food. Dorms ①, rooms ③, bungalows ④, but all rates are at least halved if you dive with the associated Utila Dive Center.

### SANDY BAY

**Tropical Hotel**, opposite Hondutel telephone office (no phone). Very popular backpackers' stronghold, the small functional rooms all have fans and there's a communal kitchen. ①.

**Utila Lodge**, behind Hondutel (☎425 3143, ulodge@hondutel.hn). The *Lodge* offers comfortable a/c rooms that are almost exclusively occupied by divers signed up on weekly packages ($735 per person including all meals). It has its own dock and the owners can arrange fishing trips. ⑨.

**Seaside Inn**, opposite Gunter's Dive Shop (☎425 3150). A reasonable place, with plain but clean rooms (some with private bath), plus small apartments. ①–②.

**Margaritaville Beach Hotel**, ten minutes' walk west of the dock (☎425 3266). Tranquil seafront location well away from the main dock, with large, airy rooms, all with private bath. ②.

## Diving

Most visitors come to Utila specifically for the **diving**, attracted by the low prices, the clarity of water and the abundant marine life. Even in winter, the water is generally calm; common sightings include nurse and hammerhead sharks, turtles, parrotfish, stingrays, porcupine fish and an increasing number of dolphins. On the north coast of the island, Blackish Point and Duppy Waters are both excellent sites, while on the south coast, the best spots are Black Coral Wall and Pretty Bush. The good schools will be happy to spend time talking to you about the merits of the various sites.

Rather than signing up with the first dive school representative who approaches you, it's worth spending a morning walking around checking out all the schools. **Price** is not really a consideration, with the dozen or so dive shops all charging around US$140 for a three- to five-day PADI course; advanced and divemaster courses are also on offer, as are fun dives, from US$12. **Safety** is a more pertinent issue: for peace of mind, you should make sure that you understand – and get along with – the instructors, many of whom speak a number of languages. Also, before signing up, check that classes have no more than six people, that the equipment is well maintained and that all boats have working oxygen and a first-aid kit. Anyone with asthma or ear problems should not be allowed to dive. A worthwhile investment is the diving **insurance** sold by BICA for US$3 a day, which covers you for medical treatment in an emergency.

**Recommended schools** include the Utila Dive Centre (*www.utiladivecentre.com*) on the road between the dock and the dirt airstrip; Gunter's Dive Shop (*ecomar@hondutel.hn*), two minutes' walk west of the dock, which also rents out sea kayaks; Alton's (*altons@hondutel.hn*), two minutes' walk west of the airstrip; and Underwater Vision (*tamara@psi.net.hn*), opposite *Trudy's*. Salty Dog's, a minute's walk west of the dock, has **underwater photography** equipment for rent, and many of the dive shops also rent out **snorkelling** equipment for around $10 a day.

It is important to bear in mind that the coral reef dies every time it is touched. BICA has been installing buoys on each of the sites to prevent boats anchoring on the reef and all the reputable schools will use these.

## Swimming, snorkelling and walking

The best swimming near town is at the **Blue Bayou**, a twenty-minute walk west of the centre, where you can bathe in chest-deep water and snorkel further out; there's a US$1 charge to use the area, which also boasts a small sandy beach and rickety wooden pier where you can sunbathe in peace away from the sandflies, and a food stand selling snacks and beers. Hammocks are slung in the shade of coconut trees and there's snorkelling gear available for rent (US$1.50 per hour). Blue Bayou is also the site of the **Utila Sea Turtle Conservation Project**, a privately run scheme set up with support from BICA, where Hawksbill and Loggerhead turtle eggs are incubated, the hatchlings fed and then released; visitors are welcome. East of town, **Airport Beach,** at the end of the dirt airstrip, offers good snorkelling just offshore (though access is more difficult) as does the little reef beyond the **lighthouse**. The path from the end of the airstrip up the east coast of the island leads to a couple of small coves – the second is good for swimming and sunbathing – though all the land around here is currently up for sale. Five minutes beyond the coves, you'll come to the **Ironshores**, a mile-long stretch of low volcanic cliffs with lava tunnels cutting down to the water.

Another pleasant walk or cycle ride (about 5km) is along the Cola de Mico Road across the island to **Pumpkin Hill** and beach, about an hour's walk from East Harbour, passing the new airport. The 82-metre hill, the eroded crest of an extinct volcano, gives good views over the island and across to the mainland and the dark bulk of Pico Bonito (see p.509). Down on the beach, lava rocks cascade into the sea, forming underwater caves – there's good snorkelling here when the water is calm, though it's not safe to free dive down into the caves.

## The Cayes

**Utila Cayes** – eleven tiny outcrops strung along the southwestern edge of the island – were designated a wildlife refuge in 1992. **Suc Suc** (or Jewel) **Caye** and **Pigeon Caye**, connected by a narrow causeway, are both inhabited, and the pace of life here is slower even than in Utila. Small launches regularly shuttle between Suc Suc and Utila (US$1), or can be rented to take you across for a day's snorkelling, if you have your own equipment. *Vicky's Rooms* on Suc Suc (①) offers basic **accommodation**, and there are a couple of reasonable restaurants and a good fish market.

**Water Caye**, a blissful stretch of white sand, coconut palms, pellucid water and a small coral reef, is even more idyllic for the absence of sandflies. Camping is allowed (bring all your food, equipment for a campfire and water), and a caretaker turns up every day to collect US$1 for use of the island (hammocks are an extra $1 to rent). Water Caye is also the ultimate desert-island venue for occasional full moon parties and a spectacular annual two-day July rave, with European house and techno DJs, organized by Sunjam and the *Mango Inn* (see *www.sunjam.com* for information). **Transport** to the caye is organized during such events; at other times, dive boats will often drop you off on their way to the north coast for a small fee, or you can ask the owner of the *Bundu Café* (see below).

## Eating

**Lobster** and **fish** are obviously staples on the islands, along with the usual rice, beans and chicken. With the tourists, however, have also come **European and American foods** – pasta, pizza, burgers, pancakes and granola. Since most things have to be brought in by boat, **prices** are higher than on the mainland: main courses start at around US$4, and beers cost at least US$1. For eating on the cheap, head for the evening stalls on the road by the dock, which do a thriving trade in *baleadas*. Note that many of the restaurants stop serving at around 10pm.

**Bundu Café**, on the main street, east of the dock. Serves European-style breakfasts and lunches and lassi-style milkshakes. Also offers a book exchange.

**Captain Jack's**, five minutes' walk west of the dock. Dutch–Utilan owned café-restaurant serving excellent-value lunches including burritos and sandwiches, freshly squeezed orange juice, and delicious dinners including fish cakes and grilled kingfish steaks.

**Cross Creek**, at the Point. Superb Caribbean cooking, majoring in flavoursome pan-fried fish and seafood, from one of Utila's best chefs, in a quiet spot beside the lagoon. Fairly expensive, around $10 a head with a drink.

**Delaney's Island Kitchen**, three minutes east of the dock. Simple, well-executed island cooking, plus a few Western dishes like pasta.

**Golden Rose**, two minutes west of the dock. Good-value Caribbean and Honduran dishes, popular with dive instructors and locals.

**Jade Seahorse**, on Cola de Mico Road. Serves great breakfasts and *licuados*, and good seafood.

**Mango Café**, in the *Mango Inn*. A popular place with an interesting selection of tasty well-presented European food, espresso and cappuccino, and a lively bar. Closed Mon.

**Mermaid's Corner**, at *Rubi's Inn*. There's a great atmosphere in this popular pasta and pizza restaurant, though service can be very slow.

**RJs**, at the Point, beside the bridge. Gregarious atmosphere and famous for its excellent meat and fish barbecues, *RJs* is very popular with dive crews and students.

**Thompson's Bakery**, Cola de Mico Road. Near-legendary place to hang out, read, drink coffee and meet other travellers, while sampling the good-value breakfasts, or range of daily baked goods – try the johnny cakes.

## Nightlife

Despite its tiny population, Utila is a fearsomely hedonistic party island. The hottest place in town for travellers is the *Coco Loco Bar,* just west of the dock, which draws a lively bunch of party heads with its extended happy hour and regular house, techno and reggae parties. *Casino*, by the dock, attracts a more local crowd with thundering reggae and a dash of salsa and merengue. During the rest of the week, the *Mango Café* is a popular spot for cheap beer and a quiet drink, while the *Bucket 'o' Blood*, very close by on Cola de Mico Road, boasts a bombastic sound system but fewer drinkers. Further along the Cola de Mico road towards the new airport, the huge open-air *Bar in da Bush* can get very lively at weekends.

## Listings

**Airlines** Tickets for Sosa and Rollins, covering domestic routes in Honduras, can be purchased in the captain's office by the dock.

**Banks** Banco Atlántida and Bancahsa, both close to the dock, exchange money and offer advances on Visa cards (Mon–Fri 8–11.30am & 1.30–4pm, Sat 8–11.30am); or try Henderson's store just to the west at other times.

**Bicycles** can be rented for around $5 a day from Delco, just west of the dock, or from the *Mango Café*.

**Books** The *Bundu Café*, on the main street, east of the dock, has a book exchange.

**Doctor** The Community Medical Center, two minutes west of the dock (Mon–Fri 8am–noon).

**Immigration office** is next to Hondutel in Sandy Bay (Mon–Fri 9am–noon & 2–4.30pm).

**Internet** Two minutes west of the dock, Bay Island Computer Services (*bicomput@hondutel.com*) offers internet access for $12 an hour, and also discounted international calls.

**Port office** In the large building in the main dock (Mon–Fri 8.30am–noon & 2–5pm, Sat 8.30am–noon).

**Post office** Also in the large building in the main dock (Mon–Fri 9am–noon & 2–4.30pm, Sat 9–11.30am).

**Telephones** Best rates for international calls are at Bay Island Computer Services (see under "Internet", above) and the Reef Cinema. Avoid the Hondutel office, next to the immigration office, where the rates are extortionate.

**Travel agents** Tropical Travel and Utila Tour Travel Center, both east of the dock on the airstrip road, can confirm and book flights to La Ceiba, and elsewhere in Central America.

# Roatán

Some 50km from La Ceiba, **Roatán** is the largest of the Bay Islands, a curving ridged hump almost 50km long and 5km across at its widest point. Geared towards tourism at the upper end of the scale, the island's accommodation mostly comes in the form of all-in luxury **resort packages**, although there are some good deals to be found all along the price scale. Like Utila, Roatán is a superb **diving** destination, but also offers some great hiking, as well as the chance to do nothing except laze on a beach. **Coxen Hole** is the island's commercial centre, while **West End** is the place to head for absolute relaxation.

## Arrival and getting around

Regular flights from La Ceiba and occasionally further afield land at the **airport**, on the road to French Harbour, 3km from Coxen Hole – the main town on the south side of the island. A taxi to West End costs $10, or you could walk to the road and wait for one of the public minibuses which head to Coxen Hole every 20 minutes or so (L.10; US$0.70) and catch another connection there. There are an information desk, a hotel reservation desk, car rental agencies and a bank at the airport. The **ferry dock** is in the centre of Coxen Hole.

A paved road runs west–east along the island connecting the major communities. **Minibuses** leave regularly from Main Street in Coxen Hole, heading west to Sandy Bay and West End (every 20min until late afternoon) and east to Brick Bay, French Harbour, Oak Ridge and Punta Gorda (every 30min or so until late afternoon); fares are L.10–15 (US$0.70–1). However, if you really want to explore, you'll need to **rent a car** or **motorbike**. In addition to the agencies at the airport, Sandy Bay Rent-a-Car (☎445 1710, fax 445 1711) has offices at Sandy Bay and West End, where you can rent jeeps for $45 per day, and motorbikes for $25 a day.

## Coxen Hole

**Coxen Hole** (aka Roatán Town) itself is dusty and run-down and most visitors come here only to change money or shop. All of the town's practical facilities and most shops are on a hundred-metre stretch of Main Street, near where the buses stop. For tourist **information**, pick up a copy of the *Coconut Telegraph*, a magazine about the island and its events from the Cooper Building; you'll find the headquarters of BICA (Mon–Fri 9am–noon & 2–5pm) here as well, where you can obtain detail about Roatán's flora and fauna. For **changing travellers' cheques**, dollars and cash advances on Visa cards, try Bancahsa, or Credomatic. The **immigration office** and the **post office** are both near the small square on Main Street, while **Hondutel** (for telephones) is behind Bancahsa. HB Warren is the largest **supermarket** on the island and there's a small, not too impressive general **market**, just behind Main Street. The island's best set-up **internet** café, Paradise Computers (Mon–Fri 9am–5pm, Sat 9am–1pm), is a five-minute walk from the centre of town on the road to West End, and though rates are very high (around $12 an hour) the epic cappuccinos and delicious carrot cake help compensate a little.

Although it's unlikely unless you have a very early flight, you can **stay** here at the *Hotel Cayview*, on Main Street (☎445 1222; ⑤), with comfortable rooms with a/c and private baths, while the *Hotel El Paso* (☎445 1367; ④), nearby on the same street, has clean rooms, but communal bathrooms. There are a number of cheap comedores, serving standard Honduran **food**, while *Qué Tal Cafe*, on Thicket Street, just past Paradise Computers, serves European-style breakfasts and snacks – Librería Casi Todo, in the same building, is the best place for secondhand **books**.

## Sandy Bay

Midway between Coxen Hole and West End, **SANDY BAY** is an unassuming community with a number of interesting attractions. The **Institute for Marine Sciences** (Sun–Tues & Thurs–Sat 9am–5pm; $3), based at *Antony's Key Resort* (see below), has exhibitions on the marine life and geology of the islands and a museum with useful information on local history and archeology. You can also watch daily bottle-nosed dolphin shows (Mon, Tues, Thurs & Fri 10am & 4pm, Sat & Sun 10am, 1pm & 4pm; $4), and dive or snorkel with the dolphins ($100 and $75 respectively; must be booked in advance, ☎445 1327). Across the road from the institute, several short nature trails weave through the jungle at the **Carambola Botanical Gardens** (daily 8am–5pm; $3), a riot of beautiful flowers, lush ferns and tropical trees. Twenty minutes' walk from the gardens up Monte Carambola you come to the **Iguana Wall**, a section of cliff that's a breeding ground for iguanas and parrots. From the top of the mountain you can see across to Utila on clear days. Bordering the gardens, Sandy Bay's newest attraction is the **Tropical Treasures Bird Park** (Mon–Sat 10am–5pm; $5, children $3), with toucans, parrots and scarlet macaws kept in spacious aviaries to admire – the entrance fee includes a guided tour.

There are several places **to stay** in the Sandy Bay area, all of which are clearly signposted, including the attractive *Beth's Hostel* (☎445 1266; ④) and *Oceanside Inn* (☎445 1552; ⑥), with large rooms and a good restaurant; and three dive resorts, the best of which is *Antony's Key Resort* (☎445 1003, fax 445 1140, *www.anthonys-key.com*; weekly packages from $600), one of the smartest places on the island, with cabins set among the trees and on a small caye. Popular places **to eat** include *Rick's American Café*, set on the hillside above the road, serving giant US-style burgers, and *Monkey Lala*, next door, offering superb seafood.

## West End

With its calm waters and incredible soft white beaches, **West End**, 14km from Coxen Hole, makes the most of its ideal setting, gearing itself mainly towards independent travellers on all budgets with a good selection of attractive accommodation. Set in the

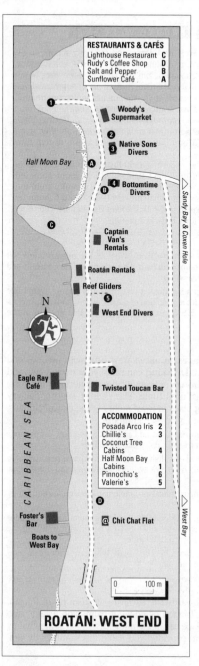

**RESTAURANTS & CAFÉS**
| | |
|---|---|
| Lighthouse Restaurant | C |
| Rudy's Coffee Shop | D |
| Salt and Pepper | B |
| Sunflower Café | A |

Woody's Supermarket
Native Sons Divers
Bottomtime Divers
Captain Van's Rentals
Roatán Rentals
Reef Gliders
West End Divers
Twisted Toucan Bar
Eagle Ray Café

△ Sandy Bay & Coxen Hole

Half Moon Bay

**ACCOMMODATION**
| | |
|---|---|
| Posada Arco Iris | 2 |
| Chillie's | 3 |
| Coconut Tree Cabins | 4 |
| Half Moon Bay Cabins | 1 |
| Pinnochio's | 6 |
| Valerie's | 5 |

Foster's Bar
@ Chit Chat Flat

△ West Bay

Boats to West Bay

*C A R I B B E A N   S E A*

N

0    100 m

**ROATÁN: WEST END**

southwest corner of the island, round a shallow bay, the village has retained a laid-back charm, and the gathering pace of tourist development has done little to dent the locals' friendliness.

The paved road from Coxen Hole finishes at the northern end of the community, not far from **Half Moon Bay**, a beautifully sheltered sandy beach, ringed with hotels. Turning to the south at the end of the paved road from Coxen Hole, a sandy track runs alongside the water's edge through the heart of West End, passing a merry bunch of guest houses, bars and restaurants, set between patches of coconut palms. Try Roatán Rentals at the north of West End or Sandy Bay Rent-a-Car close by for **car rental**, or Captain Van's Rentals for a bicycle, moped or motorbike (though their rates are pricey). The sole **internet** café, *Chit Chat Flat*, located towards the southern end of West End, charges $12 an hour for pretty lethargic connections.

### ACCOMMODATION

Most of the accommodation in West End and Half Moon Bay is charmingly individualistic. During low season (April–July and September–mid-December) heavy discounts are available, particularly for longer stays.

**Posada Arco Iris**, Half Moon Bay (☎445 1264, *http://roatanet.com/scuba/posada.htm*). Excellent, imaginatively furnished, spacious rooms, studios and apartments, all with fridges and hammocks and some with a/c, set in attractive gardens just off the beach. ④–⑥.

**Chillie's** Half Moon Bay (☎445 1214, *mermaid@globalnet.hn*) Very well set-up, English–Honduran-owned backpackers' stronghold, with dorm beds and private rooms, a kitchen and camping available. Also home to Native Sons Divers. ③.

**Coconut Tree Cabins**, at the entrance to the village (☎445 1648, *www.coconuttree.com*). Comfortable, spacious cabins all with covered porches, fridges and hot water. ⑤–⑥.

**Half Moon Bay Cabins**, Half Moon Bay (☎445 1075). Upmarket place with a lively restaurant and bar. Secluded cabins scattered around wooded grounds, close to the water's edge; all have fan or a/c. ⑤.

**Pinnochio's** (☎445 1481, fax 445 1008, *pinocchio69@bigfoot.com*). West End wooden building, set on a small hill above the village, with clean, airy rooms with bath. The owners are very friendly and there's a good restaurant downstairs (reviewed below). ⑤.

**Valerie's**, about 100m along West End, then up a signposted dirt track (no phone). Venerable love-it-or-hate-it West End chaotic boho set up with a profusion of quirky accommodation, including two trailer-style rooms and a large dorm (US$5 per person); guests also get use of the kitchen. ②–③.

## EATING AND DRINKING

There is a more than adequate range of **places to eat** in West End, with fish, seafood and pasta featuring heavily on many menus. **Drinking** can drain your pocket fast, and it's best to seek out the half-price **happy hours** at many of the restaurants and bars; starting at around 4.30pm, many of them last until 10pm. The *Twisted Toucan*, halfway along the seafront, is usually the happening place in town most nights, except Fridays, when everyone heads to *Foster's* for the weekly reggae jump up.

**Lighthouse Restaurant**, close to the seafront between West End and Half Moon Bay. Big portions of reasonably priced Caribbean food served up in friendly, diner-like surrounds.

**Pinocchio's**, close to the centre of West End. Well-established as one of the finest restaurants in West End with an eclectic range of creative, but fairly pricey, European meat and fish dishes. Closed Wed.

**Rudy's Coffee Stop** Legendary breakfasts of banana pancakes, omelettes, fresh coffee and juices. Closed Sun.

**Salt and Pepper**, at the entrance to the village. A wide-ranging gourmet menu, which includes French, Japanese and Thai dishes. Expect to pay upwards of US$10 a head, with wine, but the relaxed atmosphere and excellent cooking make it worth the money.

**Sunflower Café**, close to the centre of Half Moon Bay. Cheerful North American–owned café serving delicious omelettes, bagels and muffins. Open 7am–3pm only.

## West Bay

Two kilometres southwest of West End, towards the extreme western tip of Roatán, **West Bay** is a stunning white sand beach, fringed by coconut palms and leading into crystal-clear water. The tranquillity of the place has been mildly disrupted somewhat by a rash of cabaña and hotel construction, but provided you avoid the sandflies by sunbathing on the jetties, it's still a sublime place to relax and enjoy the Caribbean. There's decent snorkelling at the southern end of the beach, though the once pristine reef has suffered in recent years from increasing river run-off and the close attentions of unsupervised day-trippers.

It's a pleasant forty-five-minute stroll south along the beach and over a few rock outcrops from West End to **reach** West Bay; alternatively, you can take one of the small launches that leave *Foster's Restaurant* regularly – the last one returns around 7pm (9pm in high season). A dirt road also runs here: from West End, head up the road to Coxen Hole and take the first turning on the right. If you want **to stay**, the Swiss-owned *Bananarama* (☎992 9679, *www.roatanet.com/bananarama*; ⑤) has comfortable little wood cabins with mosquito nets and 24-hour hot water, while for something really luxurious, head for the Canadian-owned *Island Pearl Resort* (☎991 1858,*www.roatanpearl.com*; ⑨), which boasts stunning, two-storey houses equipped with kitchens and hot tubs plus a gourmet restaurant set in a spacious beachside plot. Both hotels have good in-house dive schools.

## Eastern Roatán

From Coxen Hole, the paved road runs northeast past the small secluded cove of **Brick Bay** to **FRENCH HARBOUR**, a busy fishing port and the island's second largest town. More attractive than Coxen Hole and less run-down, it's a lively place **to stay** for a couple of days, and all the accommodation is right in the centre. *Harbour View Hotel* (☎455 5390; ④) has reasonable rooms with bath and hot water, while the more upmarket *Buccaneer Hotel* (☎455 5032; ⑥) has a pool and a large wooden deck overlooking the water. The best place **to eat** is *Gio's*, by the Credomatic building on the waterfront, where you can dine on excellent but pricey seafood; for more local fare, try *Pat's Place*, 50m further on.

From French Harbour the road cuts inland along a central ridge to give superb views of both the north and south coasts of the island. After about 14km it reaches **OAK RIDGE**, an attractive fishing port with wooden houses strung along its harbour. There are some nice unspoiled beaches to the east of town, accessible by launches from the main dock. The best place **to stay** is the clean and pleasant *Hotel San José* (☎435 2328; ③–④), on a small caye a short distance across the water from the dock. Launches run from the main dock to the caye on demand (US$0.50). Some 5km from Oak Ridge, on the northern coast of the island, **PUNTA GORDA** is the oldest Garífuna community in Honduras. Today it's a slightly dilapidated little port with no historical buildings, though the very basic *Los Cincos Hermanos* (②) offers fairly clean **rooms** and has an attached comedor.

From the end of the paved road at Punta Gorda, a dirt track, accessible to vehicles, continues east along the island, passing the turn-off for the secluded **Paya Beach** after around 1.5km, where there's a new dive hotel, the pleasant little *Paya Beach Resort* (☎924 2220, *www.payabay.com*; ⑦ including all meals). A further 5km or so along here is **Camp Bay Beach**, an idyllic undeveloped stretch of white sand and coconut palms, though there are plots of land for sale here so things may change soon. The road ends at the village of **PORT ROYAL**, on the southern edge of the island, where the faint remains of a fort built by the English can be seen on a caye offshore. The village lies in the **Port Royal Park and Wildlife Reserve**, the largest refuge on the island, set up in 1978 in an attempt to protect endangered species such as the yellow-naped parrot, as well as the watershed for eastern Roatán.

The eastern tip of Roatán is made up of mangrove swamps, with a small island, **Morat**, just offshore. Beyond is **Barbareta**, another caye, and one that has retained much of its virgin forest cover. The *Barbareta Beach Resort* runs inclusive packages, from US$220 for three nights, with diving, windsurfing, hiking, mountain biking and fishing tours available (in USA ☎888/450 3483). The reef around Barbareta and the nearby **Pigeon Cayes** offers good snorkelling; launches can be hired to reach these islands from Oak Ridge, for around US$35 for a return trip.

# Guanaja

The easternmost Bay Island, **Guanaja** was the most beautiful, densely forested and undeveloped of them all until **Hurricane Mitch** laid siege to it, lashing the land with winds of up to 300kph during a 50-hour period in October 1998. Though buildings have been patched up and reforestation projects have been implemented, the landscape will take decades to recover. The hilly main island of Guanaja, some 25km long and up to four kilometres wide, is divided by a narrow canal and is very thinly populated – the only villages of any substance on the main island are **Savannah Bight** (on the east coast) and **Mangrove Bight** (on the north coast). Most of Guanaja's 12,000 inhabitants live in **Bonacca** or **Guanaja Town**, a crowded settlement that sits on a small caye a few hundred metres offshore. It's here that you'll find the island's shops, as well as the bulk of the reasonably priced accommodation. The only way to get between the two islands is by water taxi, which adds both to the atmosphere and to the cost of living.

## Arrival and information

Guanaja **airstrip** is on the main island, next to the canal. Aside from a couple of dirt tracks there are no roads, and the main form of transport is small launches. Boats from the main dock in Bonacca meet all flights and rides can be hitched on private boats to Mangrove Bight for a nominal fee. There are no scheduled **boat** services to Guanaja from the mainland, but regular cargo ships sail to the island from La Ceiba and other ports in Honduras.

Virtually all the houses in Bonacca are built on stilts – vestiges of early settlement by the Cayman islanders – the buildings clinging to wooden causeways over the canals, many of which have now been filled in. The main causeway, running for about 500m east–west along the caye with a maze of small passages branching off it, is where you'll find all the shops, **banks** and businesses. You can change dollars, travellers' cheques and get cash advances at Bancahsa, to the right of the dock (Mon–Fri 8–11.30am & 1.30–4pm, Sat 8–11.30am only).

## Accommodation

Most of the hotels on Guanaja are luxury all-inclusive dive resorts offering weekly packages; but in Bonacca you'll find a small number of mid-range hotels – though none of these are particularly good value for money. Construction work is due to start in late 2001 on a spectacular new luxury resort, co-owned by Hollywood actor Christopher Lambert, on the north side of the island, though it's not likely to be finished for several years.

### *BONACCA*

**Hotel Miller**, halfway along the main causeway (☎453 4327). The building is slightly rundown, but the rooms are in reasonable condition. Most have hot water and, for a little extra, a/c and cable TV. ④.

**Hotel Rosario**, opposite the *Hotel Miller* (☎453 4240). A modern building, with comfortable rooms, all with private bath, a/c and TV. ④.

**Hotel Nights Inn**, at the extreme western end of the causeway (☎453 4465). New family-run place with very clean and comfortable, fairly spacious rooms, all with cable TV and a/c. ⑤.

### *BIG ISLAND*

**Bayman Bay Club**, on the north side of the island (☎991 0281, *bayman@caribe.hn* ). Large, well-spaced, pleasantly furnished cabins set on a wooded hillside above a small beach. Packages including dives and all meals cost US$700–750 a week per person.

**The Island House Resort**, on the north side of the island (fax 453 4146). Pleasant accommodation in large house run by a friendly islander dive instructor, close to several expanses of beautiful beach. Room with full board (⑥); full board and diving (⑦).

**Posada del Sol**, on the south side of the island (☎ & fax 453 4186, *posadadelsol@aol.com*). Stylish cabins are scattered around sixty acres of ground, and the amenities here include pool, tennis courts, sea kayaks and snorkelling equipment. From US$775 per person for an all-inclusive dive package.

## Around the island

Though Guanaja's Caribbean pine forests were flattened by Mitch, there's still some decent **hiking** across the island. A wonderful trail leads from Mangrove Bight up to **Michael's Peak**, the highest point of the entire Bay Islands (412m) and down to Sandy Bay on the south coast, affording stunning views of Guanaja, Bonacca and the surrounding reef. Fit walkers can do the trail in a day, though you can camp on the summit, provided you bring your own provisions. Some of the island's finest white sand **beaches** are around the rocky headland of **Michael's Rock**, near the *Island House Resort* on the north coast, with good snorkelling close to the shore. **Diving** is excellent all around the main island, but particularly off the small cayes to the east, and at Black Rocks, off the northern tip of the main island, where there's an underwater coral canyon. To get to these sites you'll have to contact one of the hotel-based dive schools: the *Island Dive Resort* usually has the best rates, at around US$70 for two dives including equipment. **Fishing** and **snorkelling** can be fixed with local boatmen who charge US$10–15 to take you out on the water. In many areas, however, the reef is close enough to swim to if you have your own snorkel gear.

## Eating and drinking

There are several **restaurants** in Bonacca, most of which stay open till around 9pm and close on Sundays. None is particularly cheap, however, as most of the supplies have to be shipped in from the mainland. In Bonacca itself, try *Bonacca's Garden*, halfway along the main causeway, or the *Best Stop*, next to the basketball court, for snacks, cakes and yummy sticky buns. The funkiest **bar** in town is *Nit's Bar*, just east of the main dock, where the clapboard walls shake to classic reggae sounds, while you'll find Guanaja's best margaritas at the air-conditioned bar *The End of the World* on the main causeway.

# Cayos Cochinos

Lying 17km offshore from the mainland, the **Cayos Cochinos (Hog Islands)** comprise two, thickly wooded main islands – **Cochino Grande** and **Cochino Pequeño** – and thirteen cayes, all of them privately owned. The small amount of effort it takes to get here is well worth it for a few days' utter tranquillity. Fringed by a reef, the whole area has been designated a marine reserve, with anchoring on the reef and commercial fishing both strictly prohibited. The US Smithsonian Institute, which manages the reserve, has a research station on Cochino Pequeño. The hills are studded with hardwood forests, palms and cactus, and Cochino Grande has a number of trails across its interior, and a small peak rising to 145m.

Organized **accommodation** on the islands is limited to the *Plantation Beach Resort* on Cochino Grande (☎442 0974, *www.plantationbeachresort.com*), which does weekly dive packages for around US$800, including all meals and three dives a day; they collect guests by launch from the Muralla de Cabotaje dock in La Ceiba (Saturday; US$75 return). It can be more rewarding, however, to stay in the traditional Garífuna fishing village of **CHACHAUATE** on Lower Monitor Caye, south of Cochino Grande. Here, the villagers have allocated a hut for visitors to sling their hammocks for a minimal charge, and will cook meals for you. Basic groceries are available in the village, though you should bring water and your main food supplies with you from the mainland.

Unless you're staying at the *Plantation Beach*, the only way to the Cayos is to charter a boat from the Muelle de Cabotaje dock at La Ceiba (US$60–80 return for up to six people) but be sure to bargain hard, or from the Garífuna village of **Nueva Armenia**, (around US$40 return for a charter) 40km east of La Ceiba. One bus a day runs to Nueva Armenia (2hr) from La Ceiba; more frequent buses to Trujillo, Tocoa and Olanchito all pass through Jutiapa, 8km inland from Nueva Armenia, from where you can hitch or walk. There is a basic hotel (①) in Nueva Armenia and a few simple eating places.

## travel details

### Buses

**Copán** to: El Florido (approx every 30min; 20min); La Entrada (every 45min; 1hr 30min); San Pedro Sula (4–6 daily; 2hr 45min); Antigua and Guatemala City (1–2 shuttle buses daily; 7hr).

**La Ceiba** to: Nueva Armenia (11am; 2hr); San Pedro Sula (14 daily; 3hr).

**La Entrada** to: San Pedro Sula (every 30min, 1hr 30 min; four direct services a day, 1hr).

**San Pedro Sula** to: Copán (4–6 daily; 3hr); La Ceiba (14 daily; 3hr).

### Flights

**La Ceiba** to: Roatán (20 daily); Utila (4 daily); Guanaja (5 daily); San Pedro Sula (5 daily); Gran Cayman (2 weekly, Mon and Fri); Miami (2–3 daily).

**San Pedro Sula** to: La Ceiba (5 daily) Roatán (4 daily via La Ceiba); Belize City (1 daily); San Salvador (1 daily); Miami (2–3 daily); Houston (1 daily); Mexico City (1 daily).

### Boats

MV Galaxy runs daily between La Ceiba and Roatán (2hr, US$13) and Utila (1hr, US$12).

**La Ceiba** to: Roatán 3pm.

**Roatán** to: La Ceiba 7am.

**La Ceiba** to: Utila 9.30am.

**Utila** to: La Ceiba 11.30am.

**Puerto Cortés** to: Belize City, Mon at 10am, calling at Big Creek and Placencia.

# CHAPTER ELEVEN

# EL SALVADOR

I n western El Salvador you'll find beautiful mountain scenery, relaxing towns and Maya ruins, and, edging the Pacific, some of the cleanest and most remote beaches of the region. Easily accessed from Guatemala through several border crossings, this area offers a perfect introduction to the rest of the country for travellers. **The Pacific coast** is a sweep of remote, sandy, tropical beaches, many of which boast fine surf, backed by fertile coastal lowlands. Towns and villages all along the coast are linked by the **Carretera Littoral**, the main paved highway. This is a beautifully scenic route with the slopes of the Cordillera de Apaneca rising to the north and rolling green pasture lands to the south. Public transport runs regularly to many places, but private transport is the best way to reach some of the more remote and beautiful beaches. While there are clusters of **tourist facilities** here and there, don't expect the facilities of international resorts. Instead, the beauty of this part of the country lies in relaxing on clean beaches or spending time in the relatively undisturbed fishing villages of the coast.

Travelling east along the coast from the Guatemalan border, you'll encounter the popular, scenic beaches of **Los Cóbanos** and **Barra de Santiago**. To really get off the beaten track, though, you can visit the remote forest reserve of **Bosque El Imposible**, while the small city of **Sonsonate** is the first major stop with accommodation, banks and restaurants. From Sonsonate, buses leave regularly for the capital San Salvador and for Ahuachapán, Santa Ana and other points north.

More muted than in the north, the **landscapes** of western El Salvador also offer a perfect introduction to the country. Soft mountain chains edge back from the valleys, which are dominated by the dull, green expanses of the coffee plantations that bring the area its wealth. Spared from the most violent hardships of the 1980s conflict, the friendly towns and cities here are more amenable to visitors than in many places, and a relatively well-developed tourist infrastructure makes travelling fairly easy.

The joy of this part of the country exists largely in soaking up the atmosphere. The mountain towns of **Apaneca** and **Juayúa**, located along the scenic **Ruta de las Flores**, and the unflustered city of **Ahuachapán** are perfect for a few days spent relaxing, perhaps taking a gentle hike through the countryside; not far from the border with Guatemala, Ahuachapán in particular is a great little place to acclimatize yourself to El Salvador. The larger city of **Santa Ana** is a mellow contrast to the capital, with the nearby peaks of **Cerro Verde**, **Volcán Santa Ana** and **Volcán Izalco**, the stunning crater lake of **Lago de Coatepeque** and the pre-Columbian site of **Tazumal** short hops away. Hard by the border, the accommodating little town of **Metapán** gives access to the **Bosque Montecristo**, where hiking trails weave through some of the most remote and preciously preserved cloudforest in this part of the world.

## East from Guatemala

The Pacific Coast border crossing between Guatemala and El Salvador is at **La Hachadura**, a busy crossing used by the international buses heading from Talismán, on the Mexican/Guatemalan border, to San Salvador. There is a small hospedaje on the Guatemalan side and the crossing is regularly served by buses from Escuintla and Guatemala City. There is no tax for entry to El Salvador; neither are there any banks, however there are plenty of **moneychangers** hanging around eager for your business. Remember though, that US dollars are now legal tender in El Salvador so if you are carrying some with you it won't be necessary to change money at the border. If, however, you only have Guatemalan quetzales it is worth getting rid of them here as it gets increasingly difficult to do so the further away you are from the border. The closest accommodation to the border on the El Salvador side is in the city of **Sonsonate**, 46km and a two-hour bus journey away, so it's wise to try and cross by early afternoon at the latest.

# Cara Sucia and Bosque El Imposible

The first point of any interest once over the border is **CARA SUCIA**, a small village some 10km from La Hachadura on the Carretera Littoral. Dusty and somewhat bedraggled as it stretches along the highway, the village is chiefly important for its vicinity to the **archeological site** of Cara Sucia and one of El Salvador's greatest hidden glories, the forest reserve of **Bosque El Imposible**.

The Cara Sucia **archeological site**, lying 1km or so south of the highway, was in its heyday a substantial **Maya settlement** made wealthy by trade in salt. However, for those who have come straight from the glories of Guatemala, be prepared – as so often in El Salvador – for some disappointment. The challenge here involves engaging in a little detective work as you attempt to gain some idea of what the original settlement might have looked like from what little has been rescued. Initial excavations at Cara Sucia uncovered a number of structures including two ball courts, but today, all work has been halted in the ever hopeful anticipation of new funds arriving. However, it makes for a very peaceful place for a picnic, and the walk to the site is very relaxing. There is no public **transport** to the site; from the crossroads 50m before the bridge at the western end of the village, take the road leading right, opposite *Comedor Nohemy*, and walk for about twenty minutes until you reach the Cooperativa Cara Sucia buildings on the right. Ask the guard to let you through and follow the track round the buildings, taking the right-hand fork to the ruins.

## Bosque El Imposible

The road leading right at the crossroads in Cara Sucia provides access to one of El Salvador's least-known natural gems, the forest reserve of **Bosque El Imposible**, so-called because of the difficulty of traversing the mountain tracks to get into it. Covering over 31 square kilometres and rising through three climatic zones across the Cordillera de Apaneca, **El Imposible** is almost unique in the deforested, ecological disaster zone that is El Salvador today, being one of the last remaining examples of the tropical forest that covered this part of Mesoamerica in pre-Columbian times. It is also the source of eight rivers, some of which play an important role in sustaining the mangrove swamps along the coast. The reserve contains more than 400 species of trees and 1600 species of plants, some of which are unique to the area. Birdwatchers may glimpse some of the more than 300 species, including the emerald toucan, trogons, hummingbirds and eagles, while the park provides a secure habitat for a diverse range of animals, including anteaters, the white-tailed deer, ocelots, the tigrillo and more than 500 different species of butterfly.

**Getting to El Imposible** without a private vehicle is time-consuming and most people make their own way or join up with a tour; try Salvador Tours, *saltours@es.com.sv*. The reserve is managed by a non-governmental organization, **SalvaNatura** (77a Av Nte 304, Col Escalón, San Salvador; ☎263 1111, fax 263 3516, *salvanatura@saltel.net*, *www.salvanatura.org*), from whom you need to apply for written permission to enter at least one week in advance; an **entrance fee** of US$6 is required before permission is given to enter the park. Once you reach the park the only money you should need to pay is if you wish to hire a guide. Salva Natura also have a small office in the nearby village of **San Francisco Menéndez**, the main point of access for the reserve, and if you're very persuasive, you may be able to get permission to enter the reserve from there. The turning for San Francisco Menéndez is on the highway 4km past Cara Sucia; some pick-ups run from Cara Sucia to the entrance – be prepared to leave early and negotiate the price. Another entrance to the park is at **Desvio Ahuachapío**, halfway between the Sonsonate–Acajutla road and Cara Sucia. This sector of the park is called San Benito and there is a small community, **Caserío San Miguelito**, with tiendas selling artesanías and the *Comedor La Montaña* serving snacks and meals. As yet, there is no formal provision for **staying** in the reserve, though SalvaNatura is planning to build a hotel and campground in a nearby village; call them for details (see above).

## The coast to Acajutla

Some 17km or so southeast of Cara Sucia is one of El Salvador's most remote and cleanest beaches, **Playa Barra de Santiago**. Long, wide and usually empty, it lies beside a small mangrove estuary, fringed on one side with palm trees and lapped on the other by the Pacific. A rough road, 10km past Cara Sucia, runs the 7km from the highway to the estuary, from where you should bargain with a fishing boat to take you across to the fishing village of Barra de Santiago, where the beach starts. Irregular buses leave the village in the morning for the city of Sonsonate; otherwise your only hope is to wait for one of the sporadic pick-ups.

Fifteen kilometres further east along the highway and another dirt road turning to the left, at the hamlet of Metalío, you'll reach a turning to **Playa de Metalío**, a couple of kilometres away. Another palm-fringed expanse of sand – in this case more grey than golden – the beach is deserted during the week but, because of its greater accessibility, busy at weekends. Its beauty is periodically marred by the refuse washed up from the port of Acajutla, just east down the coast.

Historically important for being the site of Pedro de Alvarado's first encounter with the Pipils in 1524, **ACAJUTLA** today is a hot, seedy and distinctly edgy place. The major town on this section of the coast, it lies 4km from the Carretera Littoral at the end of a spur road. Though Salvadoreans flock here at weekends, it has little to recommend it to tourists and staying inland in Sonsonate is a far better option. If you do decide to come here, buses run from Sonsonate to Acajutla every half-hour, stopping to pick up passengers from coastal highway buses at the junction.

## Sonsonate and south

The main focal point of the western coastal region of El Salvador is the small, flat and invariably hot city of **SONSONATE**. Though lying 18km or so inland, it is a place you will inevitably have to pass through. Set in rich tobacco, coconut and cattle-ranching country, Sonsonate – "the city of the coconuts" – is a bustling, commercial place with little of tourist interest. Much of the city was badly damaged by the January 2001 earthquake. However, it does offer the first decent accommodation on the way to or from the border, and if you're in El Salvador at the end of January, it's worth making an effort to be here for the annual festival of **Verbena de Sonsonate**, when a host of music and drama performances are laid on. Even more colourful are the Easter celebrations during Holy Week, **Semana Santa**, when crowds flock to join the street processions and intricate pictures are drawn in coloured sawdust on the pavements. Sonsonate is also the **transport hub** for connections to the western beaches, the mountain town of Apeneca and the city of Santa Ana (see p.532).

**Buses** arrive at the main terminal, on C 15 de Septiembre, seven blocks east of the centre, and fifteen minutes' walk to the parque central. Of the limited **accommodation** in the centre, the *Hotel Orbe* on Av Fray Mucci Sur and 4a C Ote, two blocks east of the parque, has reasonably clean rooms with private bath (☎451 1416; ②). *Hotel Modelo* on the corner of C Obispo Marroquin and 10a Av Sur (on the main street between the bus terminal and parque) has nice clean rooms with TV, a/c and en-suite bath, noisy by day but quiet at night (☎451 1679; ③). The best option, however, is the *Hotel Agape*, set in beautiful gardens on the outskirts of town 2km along the road to San Salvador (take bus 53A or 53J from crossroads by the bus terminal and ask driver to let you off outside the hotel), with comfortably furnished rooms (☎451 1456; ④). There are a number of **restaurants** along this road, and in the centre a row of comedores overlooks the river by the rather attractive white bridge, on 4a Av Nte.

Moving on from Sonsonate, **buses** run regularly for San Salvador, or north across the Cordillera de Apaneca to the cities of Ahuachapán and Santa Ana. The latter is the best base for visiting the Maya sites of Tazumal, San Andrés and Joya de Cerén.

### Los Cóbanos and Los Remedios

**Los Cóbanos**, 25km due south of Sonsonate, is a favourite beach for Salvadorean holiday makers and consequently somewhat crowded at weekends. Although rather rocky, this pretty, gently curved beach makes a nice contrast to the lengthy, broad expanses of sand that one normally associates with the Pacific coast; here the sea is gentle and the swimming good. There are a couple of places with **cabañas** for rent, of which *Solimar* (②) is the nicest, although it's closed during the week. Set slightly back from the seafront, the *Mar y Plata* (②) is slightly run-down, though if you are here midweek you'll have it virtually to yourself. A number of small shacks serve fresh fish and other **meals**. If you walk round the headland and over the rocks at the west end of the small bay, you'll come to the quieter beach of **Los Remedios**.

Bus #257 leaves Sonsonate every hour for Los Cóbanos until early evening and there are also occasional direct buses from San Salvador; the last bus back to Sonsonate leaves the beach at 5pm.

# The Cordillera de Apaneca to Ahuachapán

Stretching east for more than 70km from the Guatemalan border, the **Cordillera Apaneca-Ilamatepec** is a glorious range of mountains, patchworked coffee plantations and acres of pine forests set by day under a clear, golden light. The village of **NAHUIZALCO**, set on the southern edge of the range about 10km north of Sonsonate (see p.527), marks the beginning of the **Ruta de las Flores**, which traces a line up to the village of **Concepción de Ataco** and was so named because of the abundant white coffee flowers visible during May and the wild flowers that embroider the hills and valleys from October to February. The town thrives on the manufacture of wicker, with workshops lining the main street. Some of the pieces, such as baskets, are small enough to take home; gentle bargaining is acceptable. There is also an intriguing nightly market where fruit and vegetables are sold by candlelight.

Beyond Nahuizalco, the air cools and freshens as the road winds its way up into the mountains proper; there are superb vistas down to Sonsonate and across the plains to the coast. Fourteen kilometres from Sonsonate is **SALCOATITÁN**, a sleepy little mountain village with the small clean *Hotel Oasis* (②), a couple of simple places to eat and some beautiful hikes in the surrounding area. Two kilometres further on down a spur road is the neighbouring town of **JUAYÚA** (pronounced "hwai-oo-a"). Here the magnificent **Templo del Señor de Juayúa**, built in 1955 in colonial style, and with stained-glass windows depicting the saints, houses the **Black Christ of Juayúa**, carved by Quiro Cataño, sculptor of the Black Christ of Esquipulas in Guatemala (see p.433). Consequently the town is something of a pilgrimage site, particularly during the January festival, and has recently begun to develop its tourism potential, with a couple of small hotels and restaurants opening up and an actively developing tourism agency, Juayutur (☎452 2002, *juayutur@navegante.com.sv*). **Accommodation** is available at the *Casa de Huéspedes de Doña Mercedes*, a cheerful place with comfortable rooms, hot water and cable TV, busy at weekends and holidays (2a Av Sur at 6a C Ote 3–6; ☎452 2287; ④). *Alojamiento Las Azaleas* is more basic but clean and has a decent restaurant (C Merceditas Cáceres Ote at 2a Av Sur; ☎452 2383; ③). Of the **places to eat**, *La Calera* on the parque serves good coffee, cakes and light meals.

## Apaneca and the Laguna Verde

A short leg further along the road from Salcoatitán is another quiet, charming mountain town, **APANECA**, founded by Pedro de Alvarado in the mid-sixteenth century and earmarked as a National Area of Tourist Interest in 1996. Popular with weekend visitors, and home to one of the best-known restaurants in the country, drawing wealthy San Salvadoreans and foreign residents alike, the town nonetheless retains an air of friendly tranquillity. During the week, you're likely to have the place – and the exquisite mountain scenery – to yourself. To **stay**, you could try one of two new hostels – supported by the national tourism agency, CORSATUR – located at each end of the town and both well signposted from the parque: *Hostal Rural Las Orquídeas* (☎433 0061; ③, bookings required at weekends) has four clean, simple rooms with hot water, and breakfast available, while *Hostal Rural Las Ninfas* is very similar. The best-quality accommodation on offer is at the *Cabañas de Apaneca,* with twelve comfortable wood cabins set in lush gardens overlooking the mountain slopes, and a good on-site restaurant (☎450 5106, fax 450 5137; ⑥; reserve restaurant at weekends and holidays). The best place to **eat**, however, is *La Cocina de mi Abuela* (Sat & Sun only 11.30am–5pm; ☎450 5203, ext 301), housed in a beautifully decorated colonial-era house. The nicest tables are on the covered verandah at the back, affording scenic views. Fresh lake fish will set you back about US$8, and you can also get lasagne, meat and chicken. *Restaurante Fonda Lamatepec*, near *Cabañas de Apaneca*, also serves excellent, if pricey, cuisine in a fine setting. Otherwise, eating options in town are limited to the row of friendly little comedores opposite the church. The town is easily accessible by **bus** from both Sonsonate (see p.527; 1hr 30min) and Ahuachapán (1hr) if you decide to come for the day or just for a meal.

### Laguna Verde

There is little to do in Apaneca itself, but it's an enjoyable, not too strenuous walk through woods and fincas to the **Laguna Verde**, a small crater lake 4km to the northeast of town. Fringed by reeds and set amid mist-clad pine slopes, the lake is a popular destination, and at the weekends you're likely to share the path with numerous families and walking groups.

From the highway on the edge of town, follow the dirt road to the right of the Jardín de Flores garden centre, which winds up and round the mountain, passing several fincas and a couple of small hamlets, overlooked by the weekend retreats of wealthy San Salvadoreans. An enjoyable short cut is to walk up the dried-up stream bed through the woods, which links the bends of the road. This is quite a scramble, though, and it's easy to get lost – ask directions from anyone you meet. The hamlet just above the lake, reached after about ninety minutes, has sweeping views on clear days. The white city sheltering in the valley below is Ahuachapán, while to the north the peak of Cerro Artilleria on the Guatemalan border is visible. The grassy slopes around the lake make a good spot for a picnic and you can also swim here. Closer to town, to the north, the smaller, less impressive **Laguna Las Ninfas** is an easy forest walk of about 45 minutes.

# Ahuachapán and around

From Apaneca the road winds 10km down to the city of **AHUACHAPÁN**. This area, and the lands further north, are some of the oldest inhabited regions of what is today El Salvador, due in large part to the extremely fertile soil. Artefacts found in the region date back to the first Maya around 1200 BC. Ahuachapán is also one of the oldest Spanish settlements in the country, achieving city status in 1862, and has generally been a place of quiet bourgeois comfort; two attacks by Guatemalan troops – in 1863 and 1864 – were both firmly repulsed. In the early twentieth century the British visitor Percy Martin noted: "The people as a whole seemed to me to be very well-to-do and evidences of refinement and solid comfort were to be met with on all sides . . . I was also impressed with the absence of the usual number of drinking shops, of which I counted scarcely more than six in the whole town. The town is a quiet, sleepy and eminently peaceful place of residence where one might dream away one's life contentedly enough." Today the city's main industry is geothermal electricity generation, at one time supplying seventy percent of the country's grid; consequently there are usually a number of European and Japanese technicians stationed here.

To get **to Guatemala** from here, a reasonably good and very scenic road runs the 20km or so to the border just past **Las Chinamas**; local buses leave every fifteen minutes, taking about an hour. International buses from Santa Ana (see p.532) also pass through at about 5.30am. There is no ticket office: stand on 6a C Pte more or less opposite the *Hotel San José* to flag down the buses. On the Guatemalan side, buses run from Valle Nuevo to Guatemala City. Heading northeast from Ahuachapán, the road winds down through the last spurs of the Cordillera to **Chalchuapa**, situated on a scenic broad plain, that contains the archeological site of Tazumal. It's an easy trip from either Ahuachapán or Santa Ana.

## Arrival and accommodation

**Buses** arrive at the terminal on Av Commercial, 10a–12a C Pte, eight blocks from the parque central. Two main streets, 2a Av Nte and Av Francisco Menéndez, run parallel from the bus terminal to the cathedral on the parque. **Telecom** is 3a C Pte and 2a Av Sur by the parque, while the **post office** is at 4a C Ote and 1a Av Nte. Banco Cuscatlán and Ahorromet Scotiabank are on Av Francisco Menéndez and C Gerardo Barrios, and Banco de Comercio is on the corner of 4a C Pte and Av Francisco Menéndez. **Internet** facilities are available at Cybercafe Cupac, Av Francisco Menéndez and 1a C Pte (US$2.20 per hour). Two supermarkets, De Todo and Despensa Familiar, are located by the bus terminal.

Of the **accommodation**, *La Casa Blanca*, on 2a Av Nte at C Barrios a couple of blocks from the parque, is housed in a well-decorated colonial building; the large, clean rooms all have bath and TV. The restaurant, set around a small courtyard, is slightly overpriced but good for sitting with a coffee or a beer (☎443 1505, fax 443 1503; ④). For those on a budget, *Hotel San José* on 6a C Pte between Av Commercial and 2a Av Nte, close to the market, has clean, if dark, rooms (☎443 1820; ③). The nicest place to stay, however, is *Hotel el Parador*, 2km out of town on the road to the Guatemalan border post (Las Chinamas). All rooms have bath, hot water and TV; there's a restaurant (10am–9pm) and a small pool open to the public (☎443 0331; ⑤).

## The city and around

Apart from its quiet, gently fading streets, and the lively daily **market** around the bus station, the main things to see in Ahuachapán are its **churches**. From the parque central, the imposing white edifice of the **Iglesia Parroquia de Nuestra Señora de la Asunción** dominates the centre of the city and acts as the focus for the annual fiesta in the first week of February. The spare 1950s-built **El Calvario**, with a fine, carved crucifix, is on 6a C Pte at 2a Av Nte.

Immediately south of the city, the hump of **Cerro Ataco** is a not too difficult, safe climb of about two hours; follow 2a Av Sur out of town and pick any one of the small paths going up to the summit. The body of water visible to the northwest, off the road to Las Chinamas, is the **Lago de Llano**, a small, lily-fringed lake fished extensively by locals. It's a thirty-minute stroll along the main road from the centre of town to the lake, or you can catch bus #60 to the rather depressing village of Las Brisas, set 2km back from the highway and about 500m from the lake shore; buses leave regularly from the market.

Some 5km east of town near the hamlet of El Barro, the **ausoles**, or geysers, form the basis of the local geothermal industry. The plumes of steam forced up from the earth hang impressively over the lush green vegetation and bright red soil, and look particularly stunning in the golden light of the early morning sun.

## Eating and drinking

Like most Salvadorean provincial cities, Ahuachapán is not overly blessed with **places to eat**. All restaurants tend to close relatively early, around 9pm, except for the *El Parador*, *El Paso* and *La Posada* restaurants, in a row on the Las Chinamas road. These serve meat and seafood standards, and occasionally have live music at the weekends. In the centre, *Tacos el Zocalo* and *Jardín de China*, next door to each other on 1a Av Sur at 1a C Ote and with the same owner, offer Ahuachapán's version of Mexican and Chinese cuisine respectively; both are relaxed places, good for a drink as well as a meal. *La Estancia*, housed in a rather run-down white building on 1a Av Sur at C Barrios, has well-prepared standards at average prices. *Pollo Campero*, part of a reliable fried-chicken chain, is at 3a C Pte and Av Francisco Menéndez, while *Mixta "S"*, 2a Av Sur by the parque, is a fast-food place with a range of simple meals, snacks and juices. For sitting and people-watching, stands in the parque serve coffee and snacks.

# Tacuba

About 15km from Ahuachapán, and sitting at the foot of **Parque Nacional El Imposible**, is the mountain village of **TACUBA**. An important settlement existed here long before the Spaniards arrived, and strong folkloric and traditional village traditions remain. Although the village is very quiet, with little to do, Tacuba makes a fine base for exploring the nearby mountains and valleys. The winding, scenic bus journey from Ahuachapán offers fantastic views of coffee plantations and the mountains of El Imposible. Nearby are some wonderful waterfalls and the ruins of one of the largest colonial churches in the country. There are few **places to stay** other than private lodgings, however *La Cabaña de Tacuba* (☎417 4332; ⑥, bookings recommended) is a shining light. Recently completed, and set amid manicured palm tree gardens, the hotel offers a fine range of accommodation, including large double rooms and suites. The price includes three meals and the owner, Señora Julieta Menéndez, will supply information on nature trails and hiking in the area.

## Chalchuapa and Tazumal

In addition to its faded but beautiful colonial church, **CHALCHUAPA** contains the most important site in El Salvador, **Tazumal** (Tues–Sun 9am–5pm; US$3). The ruins are, by comparison with sites in Honduras and Guatemala, rather small, although they do have their own, impressive beauty. **Buses** drop off at a small plaza a few blocks from the centre of Chalchuapa, from where you walk uphill for about four blocks and turn left at the sign; there is nowhere to stay. An informative (Spanish-language) museum at the site explains the development of the civilizations and displays artefacts discovered during excavations. Nearby the ruins of **El Trapiche** and **Casa Blanca** are currently being excavated but at the time of writing were yet to open to the public.

What is now the town of Chalchuapa was the seat of power for a strong and thriving Maya population from 900 BC onwards. The inhabitants produced "Usulutan" ceramics, key items of commerce in the Maya zone, and also controlled the trade in obsidian from Guatemala. This early society was literate – evidence suggests that they had both calendar and writing systems – and highly stratified, and artefacts indicate strong links with Olmec civilizations in Mexico. The catastrophic eruption of Volcán Ilopango in around 250 AD, which covered an area of 10,000 square kilometres in ash, did not affect Chalchuapa as badly as the central zone of the country; the area was quickly repopulated and Tazumal gradually became the main settlement.

Of the nine structures identified here, only two remain in reasonable condition, with a third partially excavated; the rest have been destroyed by the expansion of the town. The central, largest structure – a stepped ceremonial platform, influenced by the style of Teotihuacán in Mexico – dates back to the Classic period (300–900 AD). Altogether, thirteen different building stages took place over 750 years, mostly during the Late Classic period (600–900 AD), and beneath the structure are traces of a platform dating back to between 100 and 200 AD. Originally a number of smaller temples were attached to the main structure. At the base of its northern edge, a number of tombs (Late Classic period) have yielded artefacts such as Tiquisate ware from Guatemala, jade jewellery, items for religious rites and a flask containing powdered iron oxide. This last was used for decorating a ceremonial stone *hacha* or head, used during ball games. The ball court itself lay on the southern edge of the structure.

Tazumal was abandoned around the end of the ninth century, at the collapse of the Classic Maya culture. Unusually for abandoned Maya cities, however, immigrating Pipils (a Nahuatl-speaking group, migrants from Mexico around the tenth century AD, who established themselves in west, northwest and central El Salvador) then occupied the site. Structure 2, to the west of the main platform, is a Pipil pyramid dating back to the Early Postclassic period (900–1200 AD). The new residents also constructed another ball court, to the northwest corner of the site. Tazumal was finally abandoned around 1200 AD, with the focus of settlement in the area moving towards the centre of the current town.

Past Chalchuapa, the road runs for a further 10km, flanked by serene, green coffee plantations, before intersecting with the Carretera Interamericana (CA-1). Head northwest here and you reach the Guatemalan border at San Cristóbal. Continue straight on, however, for a couple of kilometres further if Santa Ana is your destination.

# Santa Ana

Self-possessed **SANTA ANA**, the second most important city in El Salvador, lies in a superb location in the Cihautehuacán valley. Surrounded by green peaks, with the slope of Volcán Santa Ana rising to the southwest, the gently decaying colonial streets exude a certain bourgeois complacency. Far mellower than San Salvador and regarding itself as above the unseemly commercial bustle of both the capital and San Miguel, El

Salvador's third city, it makes a very good and relatively relaxed introduction to El Salvador's "big town" life. Pleasures here, though, are very low-key, consisting in the main of admiring the handful of grandiose buildings or simply walking the streets soaking up the atmosphere. Easy day-trips away are the natural attractions of **Lago de Coatepeque**, the forest reserve of **Cerro Verde** and the summit of the volcanoes **Santa Ana** and **Izalco**, as well as the sites of **San Andrés** and **Joya de Cerén**.

## Some history

The conquistadors passed through the valley soon after their arrival in El Salvador, discovering a Pipil town of about three thousand inhabitants more or less where Santa Ana now stands. A Spanish settlement, however, was not founded until July 1569, when the disgraced Bishop Bernardino de Villapando arrived in the valley, en route from Guatemala. Commenting on the beauty and fertility of the area, he ordered work to begin on a church dedicated to **Nuestra Señora de Santa Ana**, the saint of the day of his arrival. This, completed in 1576, was on the site where the cathedral now stands, but was destroyed in the early twentieth century to make way for the new building. The settlement grew relatively quickly; a census of 1770 records that the population was almost as large as San Salvador at the time, made up of 589 Spanish and ladino families, and 138 indigenous families.

Ranching and agriculture, particularly sugar cane and latterly coffee, contributed to the city's wealth, and by the end of the nineteenth century Santa Ana was secure in its position of second city in El Salvador, numbering around 30,000 inhabitants. Buildings that befitted the city's perceived status, such as the theatre and cathedral, sprang up. Today, with a population of over 200,000, the city retains an air of restrained, provincial calm, generally only ruptured during the **July fiesta**, when a host of events brings the streets to life.

## Arrival and information

**Buses** arrive at the main terminal on 10a Av Sur between 13a and 15a C Pte, nine or so blocks southwest of the central district; city bus #51 runs to the centre from the terminal, or you can walk it in about fifteen minutes. International buses to and from Guatemala City use the small Melva International terminal on 25a C Pte between 6–8a Av Sur. **Telecom** is on C Libertad at 5a Av Sur, just down from the parque central and the **post office** on 7a C Pte between Av Independencia and 2a Av Sur. **Banks**, which cluster around 2a Av Nte behind the Alcaldía, include Banco de Comercio, Banco Agrícola, Banco Salvadoreño and Banco Hipotecario; Banco Cuscatlán is on the corner of 3a C Pte and Av Independencia. There's a small, mainly fruit and vegetable market around the bus terminal; the larger **Mercado Central**, on 8a Av Sur, between 1a–3a C Pte, burned down in October 2000, but a temporary replacement is now in operation. There is also a La Despensa de Don Juan supermarket on the parque, while a new Metrocentro shopping centre, with shops, restaurants and banks, has opened at the entrance into town; buses running to and from San Salvador pass by the entrance.

## Accommodation

Santa Ana's second-city status is not reflected in its range of **accommodation**, although there are a couple of reasonably comfortable hotels, one convenient for the bus terminal and the other closer to the general market. This area, around 8a and 10a Av Sur, has a concentration of cheap and basic places to stay, but it is not recommended to walk around here alone at night. As in all Salvadorean cities, street lighting is extremely weak, and this is considered to be one of the rougher parts of the city. The hotels listed below, however, are acceptable to stay in.

**Hotel La Libertad**, 4a C Ote at 1a Av Nte (☎440 2358). Perhaps the nicest budget place in the city with clean, basic rooms, some with bath, and in a great location right by the cathedral; bring your own padlock for the doors. ②.

**Hotel Livingston**, 10a Av Sur between 7a and 9a C Pte (☎440 1801, fax 447 0435). Safe, but rooms are small and box-like with shared baths. ②.

**Hotel Maya**, 11a C Ote at 11a Av Sur (☎441 3612). Another good, secure place, with motel style rooms, some with bath; a 20min walk from the centre. ④.

**Hospedaje Tikal**, 10a Av Sur between C Jos Mariano Menoez and 11 C Pte between 5a–7a C Pte (☎440 4127). Small, basic rooms, but clean and well run. ①–②.

**Hotel Sahara**, 3a C Pte between 8a and 10a Av Sur (☎ & fax 447 8865, *hotel_sahara@yahoo.com*). The city's best, with large comfortable rooms, good service, bar and a restaurant open until 10pm. ⑥.

**International Hotel Inn**, 25a C Pte and 10a Av Sur (☎440 0810, fax 440 0804). Convenient for the bus terminal and international buses. The rooms are rather small but comfortable, all with TV and bath. Watch out for the cockroaches. ④.

## The City

The heart of Santa Ana is the **Parque Libertad**, a neatly laid-out plaza with a gaggle of food kiosks and a small bandstand, where people gather to sit and chat in the early evenings. The main intersection (Av Independencia Sur/Nte and C Libertad Pte/Ote) skirts its southwest corner. On the eastern edge of the parque is the magnificent **Cathedral**, an imposing neo-Gothic edifice completed in 1905. Inside, brick arches soar upwards and side chapels, some containing images dating back four hundred years and originally contained in the first church on the site, line the walls to the altar. Inset into the walls are plaques from local worshippers giving thanks to various saints for miracles performed. On the northern edge of the plaza, the **Teatro Nacional**, completed in classic Renaissance style in 1910, was funded by taxes on local dignitaries. Once the proud home of the country's leading theatre companies, the building became a movie theatre before falling into disuse. Facing the cathedral on the western edge of the plaza is the **Alcaldía**, another fine Renaissance-style piece of architecture. The largest city hall of its type when it was built, the facade is lavishly decorated in a style that travel writer Paul Theroux noted as the "colonnaded opulence of a ducal palace".

Another important church, **El Calvario**, five blocks west of the parque on 10a Av Nte by Parque Menéndez, is now in ruins as a result of the January 2001 earthquake, although there are plans to reconstruct it. Completed in 1885, the building has already been destroyed and rebuilt twice. South of the central parque, on 1a Av Sur, sits the **Parroquia de Nuestra Señora del Carmen**, built in 1822; in 1871 it was briefly occupied by peasants from the area around Volcán Santa Ana, who, spurred on by Guatemalan president Rafael Carrera's calls for the indigenous peoples to reclaim their land, ran riot through the city. After the uprising fizzled out, those who refused to give themselves up were hunted through the mountains and killed.

## Eating and entertainment

Santa Ana has a reasonable number of moderately priced places to **eat** around the centre; nightlife, however, is not high on the city's list of priorities. Most restaurants tend to shut around 10pm, even at the weekends. The **cinema** on C Libertad at 3a Av Sur is virtually the only place to go after nightfall; it shows standard first-run Hollywood films, subtitled.

**Café Cappuchino**, Av Independencia at C Libertad Pte. A relaxed, leafy café just off the plaza, serving coffees, good juices, beers and simple meals (daily until 8pm).

**Café Fiesta**, 1a C Pte and 1a Av Sur. Large indoor restaurant with high ceiling and loud music. Serves cheap and cheerful lunches.

**Cafetería Central**, 2a Av Sur between 1a and 3a C Pte. Good for large breakfasts and cheap lunches.

**Cafetin El Ciclista**, corner of 2a Av Sur between 3a and 5a C Pte. Lunches and set meals, popular with locals.

**K'y'Jau**, C Libertad between 4a and 6a Av Sur. Popular restaurant, serving large portions of authentic Chinese food.

**Los Horcones**, next to the cathedral on Parque Libertad. The best views in the city, with seats on the open terrace facing over the cathedral and the plaza. The usual standards are well prepared and the juices are great.

**Kiko's Pizza**, Av Independencia between 7a and 9a C Pte. Huge pizzas: the regular size is more than enough for two.

**Los Patios**, 21a C Pte between Av Independencia and 2a Av Sur. One of the smartest places in the city, serving good meals in a nice courtyard setting at reasonable prices.

**El Tucan Gourmet**, Av Independencia Sur 33, fine, but not cheap, meat and seafood dishes.

# Around Santa Ana

West from Santa Ana, the three **volcanic peaks** of Cerro Verde, Santa Ana and Izalco together form a concise, living example of geological evolution. The oldest, **Cerro Verde**, is now a softened, densely vegetated mountain harbouring a national park. **Volcán Santa Ana**, nominally active, has cultivated lower slopes giving way to the bare lava of the summit, while juvenile **Volcán Izalco**, one of the youngest volcanoes in the world, is an almost perfectly bare lava cone. The tranquil beauty of the collapsed crater lake of **Lago de Coatepeque**, just a few kilometres east of the three peaks, makes it a very popular spot, especially at weekends.

Some 30km southeast from Santa Ana, just off the Carretera Interamericana, lie two of the most important archeological excavations in El Salvador, the Maya sites of **San Andrés** and **Joya de Cerén**. Around an hour's bus journey from Santa Ana, both can easily be visited in a day-trip from the city.

## Cerro Verde

From the El Congo junction, 15km southeast of Santa Ana, a narrow road winds up through the coffee plantations, maize fields and pine woods of the ancient volcano Cerro Verde to the **Parque Nacional Cerro Verde**. Lying 2000m above sea-level on what was the crater of the long-extinct volcano, this is the most accessible reserve in the country; consequently you're unlikely to be able to walk the short trails in solitude, particularly at the weekends. The dense, mature forest shelters numerous species of **plants** including pinabetes and more than fifty types of orchids. Animal life tends to stay out of sight; most likely to be spotted are **birds**, including the native xara – with a shimmering blue body and black head – hummingbirds and toucans. Armadillos, deer and cuzuco are also sheltered in the park.

Cerro Verde is relatively well managed with clear trails and lookouts over Volcán Santa Ana and, far below, Lago de Coatepeque. However, the large numbers of visitors it receives cannot help but make an impact and there are increasing calls for the management to be taken out of the hands of the government tourist service and be given to a private organization. From the entrance gate (daily until 5.30pm; US$0.60) a short track leads up to the car park, to the left of which is a small orchid garden. The main trail, the **sendero natural**, leads from the top of the car park, looping clockwise through the reserve. Despite the weekend crowds this is an enjoyable walk of around 45 minutes through the green calm of the forest. Smaller trails branching through the trees are variously closed off for conservation work.

By the car park are basic **cabañas** (①), although you have to bring your own food and water; check with the wardens as to where you can pitch a **tent**. The *Hotel del la Montaña,* which lies just by the car park, was originally a government-run luxury resort, built to take advantage of the superb views of the stark, black cone of Volcán Izalco. Closed for refurbishment in 1997, there are as yet no indications as to when it will reopen.

Unless you're driving, **getting to Cerro Verde** requires a bit of planning, so it's probably worth hiring a taxi for a few hours (around US$30–40). Otherwise, three buses a day run directly from Santa Ana to the car park, the last leaving the city mid-afternoon (1hr 30min). The last bus back leaves from the car park at 5pm, but only runs as far as El Congo. Buses to Sonsonate pass the turn-off to the park, 14km from the entrance, from where you have to walk.

## Volcán Santa Ana

From a signed turn about ten minutes into the *sendero natural*, a path branches down to the left, leading eventually to the summit of the mighty **Volcán Santa Ana**, known also as "Llamatepec" or "father hill". The highest volcanic peak in the country at 2365m, Santa Ana is still considered active, although it hasn't erupted since the early twentieth century. The process of reforestation is far less advanced here than in Cerro Verde, and the outlines of the volcano far starker.

The walk to the summit takes two or three hours altogether. Heading downhill from the signed turn for about twenty minutes brings you to the Finca San Blas; the path continues past here and begins to wind up though woodlands. After about 45 minutes, the gradient gets steeper and woodland cover gives way to rock and, towards the summit, lava. Three newer craters sit inside the older larger one, which takes about an hour to circumnavigate, and at the bottom of the newest crater is a small, green sulphur lake.

## Volcán Izalco

Just below the Cerro Verde is a lookout west over the visually stunning **Volcán Izalco**. Beginning as a small hole in the ground in 1770, the volcano was formed when lava began to pour continuously over the next two centuries. Clearly visible from the ocean, the "lighthouse of the Pacific" was used by sailors to navigate by until the volcano finally stopped erupting in the 1960s. Looming up from the breast of a hill, the bleak, black volcanic cone of the 1900-metre Izalco is a startling and spectacular contrast to the green slopes on which you're standing. It is possible to walk up Izalco, although locals advise against it, particularly alone, as robberies are not unknown. Local police can occasionally be persuaded to escort groups of five or more. A marked trail leads from the lookout down for about thirty minutes to a saddle between the two volcanoes. From here it takes at least an hour to climb the completely bare slopes of volcanic scree to the summit.

## Lago de Coatepeque

East from the El Congo junction (15km from Santa Ana), a winding branch road descends 3km to the stunning crater lake of **Lago de Coatepeque**, shadowed by the three peaks. The bus ride descends down the winding road towards the stunning deep blue waters, fed by natural hot springs, and the *mirador* (ask the driver to let you off here, although it is some distance from the lake's edge – try to hitch or wait for the next bus) yields fine panoramic, camera-friendly vistas. Inevitably the lake is a popular weekend destination, both for the rich and not so rich; much of the shore is bounded by private houses and access to the water is difficult. Follow the road round to the left when it reaches the lake and you come to *Hotel Torremolinos* (☎446 9437; ⑤), which charges a small fee for day use of a semi-public beach; you can also rent boats. The **rooms** in the hotel are large and clean, but much nicer is the *Hotel de Lago* (☎446 9511; ⑤) just up the road, with large, shady gardens and a restaurant overlooking the lake. An excellent budget choice is *Amacuilco* (②), on the main road just before *Hotel Torremolinos*, a relaxed, lovingly decorated hostel located at the water's edge, and with a purpose-built pier café over the lake; the hostel offers shared rooms, free use of a canoe and information on diving and jetskiing.

Buses leave Santa Ana every thirty minutes for the lake, running past the two hotels and the hostel. If heading onwards from the lake **to San Salvador**, take the Santa Ana bus as far as the El Congo junction, from where you can walk down the slip road to the main highway and catch any passing bus running from Santa Ana to the capital.

## San Andrés and Joya de Cerén

Set among rolling fertile agricultural land, the site of **San Andrés** (Tues–Sun 9am–4pm; US$3) is initially visually disappointing, being much smaller than sites in Guatemala or Honduras. Nonetheless, it is one of the largest pre-Columbian sites in El Salvador, originally covering around three and a half square kilometres and supporting a population of about 12,000. The site reached its peak in the Late Classic era, between around 650 and 900 AD, establishing itself as the regional capital for the settlements in the Zapotitán valley.

Only sections of the ceremonial centre have been excavated and the remains of seven major structures are visible; sadly, these have been preserved with the help of concrete, spoiling their beauty somewhat and visibly driving home the message that large amounts of cash are a necessity in the preservation of sites like this. Ruins from what would have been the surrounding residential districts, still visible up to fifty years ago, have now also been lost to farming activity. However, you can wander freely around the site, and it is a popular spot for picnicking families at the weekends. The informative museum (labelling in Spanish only) has a small replica of what the site would have looked like in its prime.

Of what is on view, the **Acropolis** (or south plaza) forms the major part of the centre, a raised platform supporting a number of pyramids and annexes. Structure 1, on the south edge, was a temple and on its north face are the remains of an altar. Access to these pyramids was restricted to the governing elite, whose living quarters (Los Aposentos) lay along the north and west edges of the acropolis; the bases of two of these have been reconstructed. The pyramids along the east edge of the acropolis were possibly burial chambers. North of the acropolis lay another plaza, used for markets and communal events. The largest pyramid (Structure 5) lies on the eastern edge of this plaza, but has not yet been excavated. Following the collapse of the Maya empire from around 900 AD, San Andrés was not taken over by incoming Pipils, although the remains of a small farm dating from the Early Postclassic era (900–1200 AD) have been found close to Los Aposentos.

Any San Salvador-bound bus will drop you off on the highway at the marked access road to the site, from where it is about five minutes' walk to the entrance. If you wish to visit **Joya de Cerén** (Tues–Sun 9am–4pm; US$3), continue on the bus for a further 5km to a junction on the left marked for the town of San Juan Opico. The site was originally a prosperous Maya village, supporting its population in a style far superior to that enjoyed by many Salvadoreans today. Around 600 AD, however, the village was destroyed in a volcanic eruption, and lava from this and subsequent eruptions buried the site under up to five metres of ash until its accidental discovery in 1976. Those accustomed to the imposing, ceremonial edifices of the sites in Guatemala will initially be sorely disappointed, yet Joya de Cerén, known as the "Pompeii of the Americas" because of its well-preserved state, was designated a World Heritage Site in 1993; its importance comes from the wealth of detail provided about the daily lives of the Maya.

To date, eighteen structures have been discovered, of which ten have so far been excavated. These include houses, storage rooms and one believed to be used for religious rituals or communal events; not all are open to the public, however. Artefacts found at the site, including jars containing petrified beans, utensils and ceramics, and the discovery of gardens for growing a wide range of plants including maize, beans, agave and chiles has helped to confirm a picture of this society as well organized and stable, relatively wealthy and with networks of trade links throughout the Central American isthmus. Archeologists are continuing to study the area and hope to develop the site further as both a tourist facility and educational centre. There is a small but informative **museum** at the site, detailing the development of the Maya empire and outlining the course of excavations, though there's no English labelling.

It is possible to walk between San Andrés and Joya de Cerén, but you shouldn't attempt it alone. A path leads across the fields behind San Andrés, emerging about 4km northeast at an old rail track and abandoned station, just off the San Juan Opico road. From here it is a further 3km or so to Joya de Cerén.

# Santa Ana to San Cristóbal and the Guatemalan border

At the junction with the road from Chalchuapa, the Carretera Interamericana heads northwest for 30km, through the small town of **Candalería de la Frontera** and on through gentle, green rolling countryside to the Guatemalan border at **San Cristóbal**. There are frequent buses from Santa Ana (1hr) to the crossing, which is efficient and not too busy, and has no exit or entry charges. There is no bank at the border, but numerous moneychangers offer reasonable rates for dollars, colones and quetzales. On the Guatemalan side, buses run to Asunción Mita, with connections to Guatemala City.

## From Santa Ana to Metapán

Leaving Santa Ana, CA-12 heads north through agricultural plains and badly deforested hills, becoming wilder after it passes through the dusty town of **Texistepeque**, once a pre-Columbian Pok'omam settlement, and a Spanish town from 1556. Sixteen kilometres further on, at the hamlet of Desagüe, a dirt road leads 2km or so to serene **Lago de Güija**, surrounded by low hills; Río Ostía, flowing through the lake, forms the border with Guatemala. On the **Las Figuras** arm of land – accessible on foot during the dry season – stretching out on the left side of the lakeshore are a number of faint pre-Columbian rock carvings; the area around the lakeshore was populated exclusively by indigenous groups until well into the seventeenth century. You can rent boats from here to the small island of **La Tipa** in the lake.

Ten kilometres beyond the lake, the small town of **METAPÁN** is scenically set on the edge of the mountains of the Cordillera Metapán-Alotepeque, which run east along the border with Honduras. Having survived a number of setbacks, including two devastating fires which nearly destroyed the town, Metapán was one of only four communities which supported Delgado's first call for independence in 1811; rioting citizens opened the jail and attacked representatives of the Spanish Crown. These days it is a charming, friendly and forward-thinking town, if slumbering for the most part beneath the sun. Here the **Iglesia de la Parroquia**, completed in 1743, is considered to be one of El Salvador's finest colonial churches, with a beautifully preserved facade. Inside, the main altar is flanked by small pieces worked in silver from a local mine, while the ornately decorated cupola features paintings of SS Gregory, Augustine, Ambrose and Jerome.

Metapán boasts a few decent **hotels**, among them the comfortable *Hotel San José* (☎442 0556; ④), on the edge of town by the bus terminal a few blocks from the centre, with comfortable rooms all with bath and TV, and a restaurant open until 9pm. Next door is a De Todo supermarket. A few doors along is the new and well-managed *Hotel y Restaurante Centroamérica* (☎442 0066; ②–③) which has simple rooms and a small restaurant serving all meals. In town, the friendly *Hotel Christina* (☎442 0044; ②–③), on 4a Av Sur and C 15 de Septiembre, has a range of good, clean rooms with and without bath, some of which have hot water and TV. More basic is the *Hospedaje Central* on 2a Av Nte at C 15 de Septiembre in the centre of town (②). For **eating**, a number of good comedores line 2a C Pte, including *Panadería y Pupusería Elizabeth*, dishing up good *pupusas* from late afternoon onwards, and *Comedor La Esperanza*, which serves excellent breakfasts and lunches; further down the street are *Chicken Bell* and *Pollo Master*, which both offer good-quality fried chicken and fast food. Of the number of **banks** in town, Banco Salvadoreño is located on the park, Banco de Comercio is at Av Ignacio Gomez and C 15 de Septiembre and Banco Cuscatlán is on the corner of 3a C Pte and Av Dr Isidro Menéndez.

# Around Metapán: Bosque Montecristo

The main reason for staying in Metapán is for access to the international reserve of **Bosque Montecristo**. Established in 1986, with funding received from, among others, the European Union, the reserve rises through two climatic zones and is managed as part of the **El Trifinio International Biosphere**, administered by the governments of El Salvador, Honduras and Guatemala. The reserve centres on the **Cerro Montecristo** (2418m), at whose summit the borders of the three countries converge.

In the higher reaches of Montecristo, beginning at around 2100m, there are twelve square kilometres of **virgin cloudforest**. Orchids and pinabetes, typical of cloudforests, thrive in the climatic conditions of an average annual rainfall of two metres and a hundred percent humidity. Huge oaks, pines and cypresses, some towering to over 20m, swathed in creepers, lichens and mosses, form a dense canopy preventing sunlight from reaching the forest floor. The numerous species of wildlife – though they tend to be shy of humans – include mountain foxes, howler and spider monkeys and the occasional jaguar. The abundant birdlife includes quetzals, hummingbirds, striped owl and Elliot's colibri. On the lower slopes of the reserve, the forest cover is mainly mixed pine and broadleaf woods, much of it secondary growth, replanted since the early 1970s; acute deforestation and consequent severe flooding had provided the impetus for the creation of a reserve. This lower zone is inhabited, with a fragile equilibrium being reached between the demands of the people who live here and those of conservation.

## Getting to Montecristo

The untouched beauty of the upper heights of Montecristo is due in large part to its remoteness; the only road in is a dirt track running northeast from Metapán. If you're driving (4-wheel drive necessary), the road from Metapán branches right off the highway just before the *Hotel San José*. You're not allowed to enter on foot. Occasional pickups also make the journey; otherwise you'll have to arrange transport at the hotel or the market. Montecristo is managed by the **National Parks and Wildlife Service** at MAG (Col Santa Lucía, El Matazano, Ilopango; ☎227 0622), from whom authorization should be sought to enter. Again, as in the case of El Imposible, if you're fixing this up by phone, you'll need to be persistent. Note that the cloudforest is **closed** to visitors from May to October and that there is an **entrance fee** of US$1.50, payable in advance to the NPWS.

The park entrance is 5km from Metapán; after another 2km you come to the Hacienda San José, or *Casco Colonial*, where the wardens are based and where you will need to register. From here the road continues for another 14km before reaching **Los Planes** (1890m), Some 16km inside the park are a **tourist centre**, a well-organized recreation area with a small restaurant, camping area and the wondrous **Jardín de Cien Años** orchid garden. If **camping**, bring food and water.

From Los Planes a marked trail leads to **Punto Trifinio**, the summit of Cerro Montecristo, where the three countries meet. Walking straight to the summit will take around three hours; the path leads through the cloudforest, however, and you can branch off in any direction (be careful not to get lost). You must bring warm clothing and good footwear. Trails also lead from just below Los Planes to the peaks of Cerro el Brujo and Cerro Miramundo.

## Crossing into Guatemala: north to Anguiatú

Regular buses (around 30min) make the 13km trip from Metapán along CA-12 to **Anguiatú** and the **Guatemalan border**. This is the most convenient crossing if you're heading for Esquipulas in Guatemala (see p.433), and the formalities are straightforward. If coming in the other direction, note that the last bus to Metapán leaves at 6.30pm. There are no banks, but lots of moneychangers.

## travel details

### Buses

**Ahuachapán** to: Chalchuapa (#210, every 15min until 6pm; 1hr); Las Chinamas (#263, every 15min until 5.30pm; 1hr); Santa Ana (#210, every 15min until 6pm; 1hr 30min).

**La Hachadura** to: Sonsonate (#259, every 10min until 6.30pm; 2hr).

**Metapán** to: Anguiatú (#211A, every 30min until 6.30pm; 30min).

**Santa Ana** to: Cerro Verde (#248 to Sonsonate runs via the car park; 3 daily; 1hr 30min); Chalchuapa (#277, #218, every 10 min; 40min); Lago Coatepeque (#220 ("El Lago"), every 30min until 5.30pm; 1hr); Metapán (#235, every 30min until 6.30pm; 1hr 30min); San Andrés (#201 every 15min until 6pm; 1hr; for Joya de Cerén take the same bus to the junction for San Juan Opico and change); San Cristóbal (#236 every 15min until 5.30pm; 50min).

**Sonsonate** to: Acajutla (#207, #215a, #252, every 10min until 7pm; 30min); Ahuachapán (#249, every 30min until 5.30pm; 2hr 30min); Apaneca (#249, every 30min until 5.30pm; 1hr 45min); Barra de Santiago (#285, 1 daily; 1hr 30min); Cerro Verde (take the Santa Ana bus #216, which passes the turn-off; 1hr 30min); Juayúa (#249, every 30min until 5.30pm; 1hr 30min); La Hachadura (#259, every 10min until 5.30pm, passing the access roads for Metalío and Barra de Santiago and running through Cara Sucia, 2hr; or #286, via San Francisco Menéndez, 4 daily, 2hr 30min); Los Cóbanos (#257, hourly until 5pm; 45min); Nahuizalco (#249, every 30min until 5.30pm; 30min); Salcoatitán (#249, every 30min until 5.30pm; 1hr 15min); Santa Ana (#216, every 15min until 5.45pm; 2hr).

### International buses

**Santa Ana** to: Guatemala City (Melva International, 25a C Pte, 6a–8a Av Sur; ☎440 1608; buy ticket one day in advance) hourly from 5.30am to 4 pm (4–6hr).

# CHRONOLOGY: THE MAYA

**c. 20,000 BC–10,000 BC**     **Paleo-Indian culture (also called Lithic or Early Hunter periods)**.

Several waves of hunter-gatherers from Asia cross the Bering land bridge into the American continent, though some scholars believe they may also have a maritime route, using boats.

**c.10,000 BC**     **Clovis culture**.

Worked stone projectile points – first identified at Clovis, New Mexico – used to hunt large herbivores, including mammoths, found at many sites in North and Central America.

**c.6000 BC–1800 BC**     **Archaic (Proto-Maya) period**.

General warming of the climate following the retreat of northern ice sheets. The Pacific littoral region between Chiapas and western El Salvador is the most intensely inhabited area of the Maya world, though there are well-established villages and trade routes throughout the region. Villagers farm maize and beans, catch fish and make pottery. Clay figures discovered from this period may be the first religious artefacts. A Proto-Maya language is thought to have been spoken.

August 13, 3114 BC     **13.0.0.0.0. 4 Ahau 8 Kumk'u**.

Mythical starting date of current "**Great Cycle**", the creation of the present world; due to end on December 21, 2012.

**1800 BC–250 AD**     **Preclassic (or Formative) period**.

The **Olmec** culture, the first emergent civilization of Mesoamerica in the Maya region, brings an early calendar and new gods. Trade in jade, salt and cacao increases between villages, and by the end of the period, the central region is developing very quickly, making pottery, and establishing the first substantial buildings.

1700 BC     Olmec civilization emerges on Gulf coast of Mexico, just outside the Maya region.

1400 BC     First settlement in Copán valley.

c.1000 BC     Early architectural platforms constructed at **Cuello** in Belize.

1000–300 BC     **Middle Preclassic**

Relatively sophisticated building construction at Nakbé in northern Petén. Many of the earliest foundations of the central region's sites could also have originated in this period. Olmec, then Izapa cultures, dominate southern Gulf of Mexico and Pacific coasts.

750 BC     **Nakbé** is flourishing. Possibly the very first Maya "city", it is dominated by eighteen-metre-high temples. Maya culture eclipses Olmec influence in Petén.

500 BC     First evidence of buildings at **Tikal**.

400 BC     **Olmec** cultural influence wanes throughout the region. Izapan artistic styles start to influence the south.

| | |
|---|---|
| 300 BC–250 AD | **Late Preclassic.** Early development of the foundations of Maya civilization: calendar, writing, architectural design and sophisticated artistic style. Monumental temple cities emerge. Causeways (*sacbes*) are built and trade links flourish. Evidence of enormous constructions in the Yucatán emerge: temple foundations at **Edzná** and canals and moat systems at **Yaxuná**. |
| 300 BC | Nakbé temples rebuilt to 45-metre height and colossal stucco masks constructed. Early building work at **El Mirador**. |
| 200 BC | **Miraflores culture** thrives on Pacific coast and Guatemalan highlands, centred at **Kaminaljuyú**; elaborate stelae carved. First ceremonial structures built at **Tikal**, **Uaxactún** and possibly **Calakmul**. |
| 150 BC | The first great Maya city-state, **El Mirador**, emerges; seventy-metre-high temples are built, framed by giant masks. |
| 36 BC | First known Long Count date, corresponding to 7 December 36 BC inscribed on Stela 2 at **Chiapa de Corzo**, Chiapas, though outside the Maya area at the time. |
| c.1 AD | Major pyramids, platforms and giant stucco masks constructed at Uaxactún, Tikal and Cerros, but the region is dominated by El Mirador. Emergence of Teotihuacán in Mexico. |
| 36 AD | First known Maya Long Count date, on Stela 1 at **El Baúl** on Pacific coast. |
| 150 AD | **El Mirador** abandoned, possibly due to disease or environmental collapse; rise of **Calakmul**. |
| 199 AD | Earliest recorded use of Long Count date in central region. |
| 250 AD | **Kaminaljuyú** all but abandoned. |
| **250—600 AD** | **Early Classic period.**<br>Maya region and much of Mexico influenced, or even dominated, by the great metropolis of Teotihuacán, north of modern-day Mexico City. Dated inscriptions emerge in the lowlands. Elaborate carved stelae erected throughout central region after 435 AD. Extensive trade network along Caribbean coast between Yucatán and Honduras. |
| 292 AD | Stela 29 carved at **Tikal**, with Long Count calendar date. |
| c. 359 AD | Yoaat B'alam I (Progenitor Jaguar) becomes first king of **Yaxchilián**. |
| 378 AD | Siyaj K'ak' (Lord Fire-Born), probably from **Teotihuacán**, ejects (and probably kills) **Tikal's** ruler Chak Tok Ich'aak (Great Burning Claw) and defeats **Uaxactún** with a new weapon, the *atlatl* (spearthrower). A new dynasty rules the Maya; most existing monuments are destroyed. |
| 400 AD | Guatemalan highlands under Teotihuacán control; **Kaminaljuyú** rebuilt in its style. |
| 426 AD | Yax K'uk Mo' (Great-Sun First Quetzal Macaw), probably from Teotihuacán, founds dynasty at **Copán.** |
| 435 AD | Completion of Baktun 8 (9.0.0.0.0). Population of **Copán** rises and building work accelerates. |

| | |
|---|---|
| c. 460 AD | Moon Skull of **Yaxchilán** captures ruler A of Piedras Negras. |
| c 514 AD | Warriors from **Piedras Negras** return home with prisoners from Yaxchilán, including the king, Knot-eye Jaguar I (probably *joy b'alam* – "Tied Jaguar"). |
| 526 AD | Skull-Mahk´ina II ascends the throne of **Yaxchilán**. |
| 534–593 AD | **Middle Classic hiatus**: dearth of stelae carving and building throughout central region except at **Caracol**. |
| 537 AD | Skull-Mahk´ina II involved in a conflict with Stone Hand Jaguar of Calakmul, killing one of his sub-lords. |
| 546 AD | Tuun K'ab' Hix (Stone Hand Jaguar) of Calakmul presides over the accession of Aj Wosal (Double Comb) at **Naranjo**. |
| 550 AD | **Becan** first occupied. |
| 556 AD | Wak Chan K'awil (Double Bird) of **Tikal** (537–562 AD) enacts an "axe war" against **Caracol**. |
| 562 AD | Yajaw Te' K'inich II (Lord Water) of **Caracol** retaliates in concert with Sky Witness of **Calakmul**; no new monuments are raised at Tikal for 130 years and Calakmul becomes regional superpower. |
| c. 600 AD | Collapse of Teotihuacán. Population density in core Maya region reaches an estimated 965 people per square kilometre. **Uxmal** first occupied. |
| **600–800 AD** | **Late Classic period** |
| | Golden age of the Maya, as civilization reaches intellectual and artistic peak and numerous powerful city-states emerge in central region, though the mighty superpowers of **Calakmul** and **Tikal** dominate. Monumental construction of temples, plazas, pyramids and palaces. Puuc, Río Bec and Chenes cities all flourish in northern area; spectacular construction throughout the Maya world. |
| 611 AD | Scroll Serpent of **Calakmul** attacks Palenque and destroys the city centre. |
| 615 AD | K'inich Hanaab Pakal (Great Sun Shield) begins 68-year reign at **Palenque**. |
| 624 AD | Warriors from **Piedras Negras** capture several nobles from Palenque and the unlocated site of Sak Tz'i. |
| 626 AD | K'an II of **Caracol** attacks Naranjo. More attacks follow in 627 AD and 631 AD. Yuknoom Head, new ruler of Calakmul, joins in on the last attack, seizing the city. |
| 628 AD | Smoke Imix's (Ruler 12) 67-year reign begins at **Copán**. |
| 636 AD | Yuknoom Ch'een II's ("The Great") 50-year reign begins at **Calakmul**. |
| 645 AD | B'alaj Chan K'awil (Flint Sky) begins reign of first king of **Dos Pilas**. |
| 657 AD | Yuknoom the Great of **Calakmul** attacks Tikal, whose ruler Nuun Ujol Chaak (Shield Skull) takes refuge in Palenque. |
| 659 AD | Nuun Ujol Chaak of **Tikal** wins in battle against Yaxchilán, probably launched from his exile. |

| | |
|---|---|
| 672 AD | Nuun Ujol Chaak of **Tikal** returns from exile, launches a "star war" against **Dos Pilas** and takes it. B'alaj Chan K'awil takes refuge (probably in Calakmul). In 677 AD he returns to Dos Pilas, and in 679 AD he captures and kills Nuun Ujol Chaak in a final clash. |
| 681 AD | Itzamnaaj B'alam II (Shield Jaguar) begins 60-year reign at **Yaxchilán**. |
| 682 AD | Hasaw Chan K'awill (Heavenly Standard Bearer) begins 52-year reign at **Tikal** and achieves its resurgence in a series of successful military campaigns against Calakmul and vast construction projects. Flint Sky of **Dos Pilas** sends his daughter Lady Six Sky to **Naranjo** to re-establish the royal house there. |
| 683 AD | Pakal buried at **Palenque**; succeeded by his son Chan Bahlum. A panel in Palenque describes Chan Bahlum's attack on **Toniná** in 687 AD, resulting in disappearance of Tonina's Ruler II. |
| 693 AD | K'ak Tilaw Chan Chaak (Smoking Squirrel), new ruler of **Naranjo**, retaliates against **Caracol** by repeatedly attacking its allies, Ucanal (693 AD and 698 AD), Yaxhá (710 AD) and Sacnab (711 AD). |
| 695 AD | Smoke Imix of Copán dies; succeeded by Waxaklajuun Ub'aah K'awil ("Eighteen Rabbit"). Hasaw Chan K`awil of **Tikal** captures Yich'aak K'ak (Fiery Claw) of **Calakmul**, breaking its power. |
| c700 AD | **Yaxchilán** dominates the Usumacinta region. Population of Caracol estimated at over 100,000. Structure 1 at **Río Bec** built. |
| 711 AD | K'inich B'aaknal Chaak (Great Sun Bone Place Rain God) of **Toniná** attacks Palenque and captures its king, K'an Joy Chitam (Precious/Yellow Tied Peccary). |
| 734 AD | Hasaw Chan K`awil of **Tikal** dies; succeeded by his son, Yik'in Chan K'awill (Sunset Sacred Lord). He organizes Tikal's attacks on **El Perú** (743 AD) and on **Naranjo** (in 744 AD). These are the last recorded "star war events" in Petén. |
| 735 AD | Ruler 3 of **Dos Pilas** captures Yich'aak B'alam (Jaguar Claw) of **Seibal**; Seibal was to remain subjected for the next 60 years. |
| 738 AD | **Copán's** Waxaklajuun Ub'aah K'awil killed by K'ak Tiliw Chan (Cauac Sky) of **Quiriguá**, a subordinate city. No monuments are built at Copán for 17 years; the city never fully recovers its former power. |

| c.750 AD | Population peaks in central region. Temples I, II and V built at **Tikal**. |
|---|---|
| 755 AD | Yaxun Balam IV (Bird Jaguar IV) of **Yaxchilán** captures Jewelled Skull of the unlocated site of Sanab'Huk'ay. |
| c.760 AD | **Xpujil**'s Structure 1 and **Chicanná**'s Structure 2 built. |
| c.790 AD | **Bonampak** murals painted, but site abandoned shortly afterwards. **Dos Pilas** overrun. End of the *katun* celebrated across the Maya world with carved stelae. |
| 795 AD | Ruler 7 of **Piedras Negras** captures the lords of **Pomoná**. |
| **800–910 AD** | **Terminal Classic**. |
| | Overpopulation and intense agricultural cultivation in region, possibly leading to environmental collapse. **Seibal** flourishes briefly in isolation. Most main cities almost abandoned by 900 AD except in the northern area and in Belize, where trade continues along the rivers and coast. |
| 808 AD | Skull Mahk'ina III of **Yaxchilán** captures ruler 7 of **Piedras Negras**, ending Classic Maya culture in the upper Usumacinta region. |
| 810 AD | Dark Sun builds Temple III, the last of **Tikal's** temple pyramids. Last dated inscription at **Quiriguá**. |
| 830 AD | Completion of Baktun 9. |
| 849 AD | Jewelled K'awil of **Tikal** witnesses the **Seibal** ruler's commemoration of the katun (10.1.0.0.0). Five stelae erected in Toltec/Maya style. |
| c.860 AD | Population of central region down to a third of previous level. |
| 869 AD | Last recorded date at **Tikal**. |
| c.900 AD | **Uxmal** and **Chichén Itzá** abandoned. |
| 909 AD | Erection of the last stela in Maya region at **Toniná**.(to commemorate the Katun ending 10.4.0.0.0) |
| 910—c.1530 AD | **Postclassic period** |
| 910—1200 AD | **Early Postclassic**.  Maya collapse sees cities abandoned throughout the region. The **Toltec** from Central Mexico invade Yucatán, bringing a new religious cult and architectural styles such as the *Chacmool*. Itzá influence replaces Toltec. |
| 1100 AD | The Toltec invade Puuc hills. |
| 1200 AD | **Chichén Itzá** reoccupied by Toltec; new construction begins. Itzá driven from Campeche coast. |
| 1200—1500 AD | **Late Postclassic**. Toltec influence fades in Yucatán, and Itzá invade. Later years see Yucatán divided into sixteen small states. Cobá and Tulum thrive. |
| c.1250 AD | Toltec enter Guatemala. **Utatlán** founded. |
| c.1270 AD | Itzá establish **Mayapán**; in 1283 AD it becomes capital of Yucatán. |
| c.1450 AD | Itzá establish **Tayasal** (also called Noh Petén, "Great Island") on Lago Petén Itzá. |

| | |
|---|---|
| 1450 AD | Quiché state dominates warring highlands. |
| 1470 AD | Cakchiquel throw off Quiché control and found their capital at **Iximché**. |
| 1500 AD | Continual conflict in Guatemalan highlands between the main tribal groups. |
| 1511 AD | Spanish sailors, including Gonzalo Guerrero and Gerónimo de Aguilar, are shipwrecked on the southern coast of Yucatán. |
| 1519 AD | **Cortés** lands in Cozumel. Aguilar joins him, becoming an interpreter; Guerrero remains, becoming a Maya war leader. |
| 1521 AD | Aztec capital of **Tenochtitlán** falls to Spanish under Cortés. |
| 1523 AD | Alvarado arrives in Guatemala. Establishes capital at Iximché in 1524. |
| 1525 AD | Cortés passes through unconquered Itzá territory on his way to Honduras. |
| 1697 AD | Itzá capital of **Tayasal**, the last independent Maya kingdom, falls to Spanish under Martín de Ursúa. |

# THE MAYA ACHIEVEMENT

**For some three thousand years before the arrival of the Spanish, Maya civilization dominated Mesoamerica, leaving behind some of the most impressive architecture in the entire continent. The scale and grandeur of some Maya cities, such as El Mirador, built around 100 BC, was greater than those of anything that existed in Europe at the time, and the artistry and splendour of Maya civilization at the height of the Classic era arguably eclipsed those of its Old World contemporaries. The Maya culture was complex and sophisticated, fostering the highest standards of engineering, astronomy, stone carving and mathematics, as well as an intricate writing system.**

To appreciate all this you have to see for yourself the remains of the great centres. Despite centuries of neglect, abuse and the throttling attentions of the jungle, they are still astounding – the biggest temple-pyramids tower up to seventy metres above the forest floor, well above the jungle canopy. Stone monuments, however, leave much of the story untold, and there is still a great deal that we have to learn about Maya civilization. What follows is the briefest of introductions to the subject, hopefully just enough to whet your appetite for the immense volumes that have been written on it; some of these are listed in "Books" on p.579.

## THE MAYA SOCIETY

By the Early Classic period, the Maya cities had become organized into a hierarchy of power, with cities such as Kaminaljuyú, Tikal and Calakmul dominating vast areas and controlling the smaller sites through a complex structure of **alliances**. The cities jostled for power and influence, occasionally erupting into open warfare, which was also partly fuelled by the need for sacrificial victims. The distance between the larger sites averaged around 30km, and between these were myriad smaller settlements, religious centres and residential groups. The structure of the alliances can be traced through the use of emblem glyphs. Only the glyphs of the main centres are used in isolation, while the names of smaller sites are used in conjunction with those of their larger patrons. Of all the myriad Classic cities, the dominant ones were clearly Tikal, Calakmul, Palenque, Copán, Caracol, Piedras Negras, Naranjo, Dos Pilas and Yaxchilán. Trade, marriages and warfare between the large centres were commonplace as the cities were bound up in an endless round of competition and conflict.

By the Late Classic period, **population densities** across a broad swathe of territory in the central region were as high as 965 people per square kilometre – an extraordinarily high figure, equivalent to densities in rural China today. It's thought there were strict divisions between the classes, with perhaps eighty percent being preoccupied with intensive cultivation to feed these vast numbers. The peasant farmers, who were at the bottom of the social scale, also provided the labour necessary to construct the monumental temples that decorate the centre of every city (the Maya did not have the wheel) as well as perform regular "military service" duties. Even in the suburbs where the peasants lived, there are complexes of religious structures with simple, small-scale temples where ceremonies took place.

While the remains of the great Maya sites are a testament to the scale and sophistication of Maya civilization, they offer little insight into daily life in Maya times. To reconstruct the lives of the **ordinary Maya** archeologists have turned to the smaller residential groups that surround the main sites, littered with the remains of household utensils, pottery, bones and farming tools. These groups are made up of simple structures made of poles and wattle-and-daub, each of which was home to a single family. The groups as a whole probably housed an extended family, who would have farmed and hunted together and may well have specialized in some trade or craft. The people living in these groups were commoners, their lives largely dependent on agriculture. Maize, beans, cacao, squash, chiles and fruit trees were cultivated in raised and irrigated fields, while wild fruits were harvested from the surrounding forest. It's not certain whether the land was privately or communally owned.

Until the 1960s, Mayanists had long shared the view that the ordinary Maya were ruled by a scholarly astronomer-priest elite, who were preoccupied with religious devotion and the study of calendrics and the stars. They were thought to be men of reason, with no time for the barbarity of war and conquest, and were often compared to the ancient Greeks. However, this early utopian vision could not have been further from the truth: the decipherment of Maya glyphs has proved that the Maya rulers were primarily concerned with the glories of battle and conquest and preserving their royal bloodlines; human sacrifice and blood-letting rituals were also a pivotal part of elite Maya society. The rulers considered themselves to be god-humans and thought that the line of royal accession could only be achieved by sacred validation in the form of human **blood-letting** (see p.552).

There were two **elite classes**: *ahau* and *cahal*, who between them probably made up two or three percent of the population. The *ahau* title was reserved exclusively for the ruler and extremely close blood relatives – the top echelon of Maya society; membership could only be inherited. One step down was the *cahal* class, most of whom would have shared bloodlines with the *ahau*. The *cahal* were mainly governors of subsidiary settlements which were under the control of the dominant city-state and their status was always subordinate to the *ahau*. Although *cahal* lords commissioned their own stelae, the inscriptions always declared loyalty to the regional ruler.

The rulers lived close to the ceremonial centre of the Maya city, in imposing palaces, though the rooms were limited in size because the Maya never mastered the use of the arch. Palaces doubled as administrative centres and were used for official receptions for visiting dignitaries, with strategically positioned thrones where the ruler would preside over religious ceremonies.

The "**middle class**" of Maya society consisted of a professional class (*ah na:ab*) of architects, senior scribes (*ah tz'ib*), sculptors, bureaucrats and master artisans, some of whom were also titled, and probably young princes and important court performers. Priests and shamans can also be included in this middle class, though, surprisingly, no title for the priesthood has yet been recognized. It's possible that not giving the priests a title may have been a method used by a fearful ruler to limit their influence. Through their knowledge of calendrics and supernatural prophecies, the priests were also relied upon to divine the appropriate time to plant and harvest crops.

There's no doubt that **women** played an influential role in Maya society, and in the late Classic period there were even some women rulers – Lady Ahpo Katun at Piedras Negras, Lady Ahpo-Hel at Palenque and a Lady Six Sky at Naranjo. Women also presided at court and were given prestigious titles – Lady Cahal of Bonampak, for example. More frequently, however, as in Europe, dynasties were allied and enhanced by the marriage of royal women between cities. One of the best documented strategic marriages occurred after the great southern city of Copán had suffered the humiliation of having its leader captured and sacrificed by upstart local rival Quiriguá in 738 AD – a royal marriage was arranged with a noblewoman from Palenque over 500km away.

Maya **agriculture** was continuously adapting to the needs of the developing society, and the early practice of slash and burn was soon replaced by more intensive and sophisticated methods to meet the needs of a growing population. Some of the land was terraced, drained or irrigated in order to improve its fertility and ensure that fields didn't have to lie fallow for long periods, and the capture of water became crucial to the success of a site. This was especially true in the more arid Yucatán peninsula where utilizing natural underground sinkholes (*cenotes*) and the construction of man-made wells were critical to survival.

The large lowland cities, today hemmed in by the forest, were once surrounded by open fields, canals and residential compounds, while slash-and-burn agriculture probably continued in marginal and outlying areas. Agriculture became a preoccupation, with the ordinary Maya trading at least some of their food in markets, although all households still had a kitchen garden where they grew herbs and fruit.

Maize has always been the basis of the Maya **diet**, in ancient times as much as it is today. Once harvested it was made into *saka*, a cornmeal gruel, which was eaten with chile as the first meal of the day. During the day labourers ate a mixture of corn dough and water, and we know that tamales were also a popular speciality. The main meal, eaten in the evenings, would have been similarly maize-based, although it may well have included meat and vegetables. As a supplement to this simple diet, deer, peccary, wild turkeys, duck, pigeons and quail were all hunted with bows and arrows or blowguns. The Maya also made use of dogs, for both hunting and eating. Fish were also eaten, and the remains of fish hooks and nets have been found in some sites, while there is evidence that those living on the coast traded dried fish far inland. As well as food, the forest provided firewood, and cotton was cultivated to be dyed with natural colours and then spun into cloth.

## THE MAYA CALENDAR

One of the cornerstones of Maya thinking was an obsession with **time**. For both practical and mystical reasons the Maya developed a highly sophisticated understanding of arithmetics, calendrics and astronomy, all of which they believed gave them the power to understand and predict events. All great occasions were interpreted on the basis of the Maya calendar, and it was this precise understanding of time that gave the ruling elite its authority. The majority of the carvings, on temples and stelae, record the exact date at which rulers were born, ascended to power and died.

The basis of all Maya **calculation** was the vigesimal counting system, which used multiples of twenty. All figures were written using a combination of three symbols – a shell to denote zero, a dot for one and a bar for five – which you can still see on many stelae. When calculating calendrical systems the Maya used a slightly different notation known as the head-variant system, in which each number from one to twenty was represented by a deity, whose head was used to represent the number.

When it comes to the Maya **calendar** things start to get a little more complicated as a number of different counting systems were used, depending on the reason the date was being calculated. The basic unit of the Maya calendar was the day, or *kin*, followed by the *uinal*, a group of twenty days roughly equivalent to our month; but at the next level things start to get more complex as the Maya marked the passing of time in three distinct ways. The **260-day almanac** (16 *uinals*) was used to calculate the timing of ceremonial events. Each day was associated with a particular deity that had strong influence over those born on that

particular day. This calendar wasn't divided into months but had 260 distinct day names. (This system is still in use among some Kaqchikel and Mam Maya who name their children according to its structure and celebrate fiestas according to its dictates.) A second calendar, the so-called "**vague year**" or *haab*, was made up of 18 *uinals* and five *kins*, a total of 365 days, making it a close approximation of the solar year. These two calendars weren't used in isolation but operated in parallel so that once every 52 years the new day of the solar year coincided with the same day in the 260-day almanac, a meeting that was regarded as very powerful and marked the start of a new era.

Finally the Maya had another system for marking the passing of history, which is used on dedicatory monuments. The system, known as the **long count**, is based on the great cycle of 13 *baktuns* (a period of 5128 years). The current period dates from August 13, 3114 BC and is destined to come to an end on December 21, 2012. The dates in this system simply record the number of days that have elapsed since the start of the current great cycle, a task that calls for ten different numbers – recording the equivalent of years, decades, centuries etc. In later years the Maya sculptors obviously tired of this exhaustive process and opted instead for the short count, an abbreviated version.

## ASTRONOMY

Alongside their fascination with time, the Maya were obsessed with the sky and devoted much time and energy to unravelling its patterns. Several large sites such as Copán, Uaxactún and Chichén Itzá have **observatories** carefully aligned with solar and lunar sequences.

The Maya showed a great understanding of **astronomy** and with their 365-day "vague year" were just half a day out in their calculations of the solar year, while at Copán, towards the end of the seventh century AD, Maya astronomers had calculated the lunar cycle at 29.53020 days,

## MAYA TIME: THE UNITS

| | |
|---|---|
| 1 *kin* = 24 hours | 20 *baktun* = 1 *pictun*, or 2,880,000 days |
| 20 *kins* = 1 *uinal*, or 20 days | 20 *pictuns* = 1 *calabtun*, or 57,600,000 days |
| 18 *uinals* = 1 *tun*, or 360 days | 20 *calabtuns* = 1 *kinchiltun*, or 1,152,000,000 days |
| 20 *tuns* = 1 *katun*, or 7200 days | 20 *kinchiltuns* = 1 *alautun*, or 23,040,000,000 days |
| 20 *katuns* = 1 *baktun*, or 144,000 days | |

## RITUAL BLOODLETTING AND THE MAYA

**Ritual bloodletting** was a fundamental part of Maya religious life, practised by all strata of Maya society. It took many forms, from cursory self-inflicted blood offerings to elaborate ceremonies involving the mass sacrifice of captive kings and enemy warriors. The Maya modelled their lives according to a vision of the cosmos, and within this arena, human actions could affect the future, auspiciously or otherwise. Pivotal to this vision was the concept that blood spilling helped repay man's debt to the gods, who had endowed the gift of life.

The K'iche' Maya creation story, the **Popol Vuh**, tells of the creation, destruction and re-creation of previous imperfect worlds before their own was made. Earlier races had been conceived and then destroyed for failing to praise their creators, the gods. Finally the Maya people were made by mixing ground maize, the region's food staple, with the sacrificial blood of the gods. Consumed by the omnipresent fear that the world could again be destroyed, the Maya sought to appease the gods and ensure continued prosperity through bloodletting.

First practised by the **Olmec**, Mesoamerica's "mother culture", more than 3000 years ago, bloodletting continued until the arrival of the conquistadors. Among the early Maya, ritual blood offerings were primarily concerned with renewal and agricultural fertility, closely linked to creation mythology.

Later in the Classic period, with increasing social complexity and proven agricultural reliability, bloodletting may have become more related to the shifting concerns of the day, including warfare and political alliances. The practice later grew to apocalyptic degrees of carnage among the **Aztecs**, horrifying the Spanish, whose chronicler Diego Duran describes the sacrifice of 80,000 victims at the rededication of the Templo Mayor in their capital.

As well as direct representations of the sacrificial act, the Maya developed a symbolic iconography of bloodletting, so that the smallest motif, such as three knotted bands or smoke scrolls, could express blood sacrifice. Maya bloodletting iconography had its roots in Olmec art, including the elaborate vision quest serpent, depicted in the eighth century Yaxchilán lintels, which grew from the corpus of Olmec serpentine motifs. Through their wealth and control of resources, the Maya nobility recorded their actions through the use of non-perishable artistic mediums. The fact that depictions of bloodletting were chosen for preservation on **stone**, a costly and laborious medium, confirms its religious, social and political significance.

A common bloodletting ritual may have consisted of cutting the earlobes, cheeks, thighs or other fleshy parts of the body and collecting the blood to burn, or sprinkling it directly on a shrine or idol. Undertaken for numerous reasons – to

not too far off our current estimate of 29.53059. In the Dresden Codex their calculations extend to the 405 lunations over a period of 11,960 days, as part of a pattern that set out to predict eclipses. At the same time they had calculated with astonishing accuracy the movements of Venus, Mars and perhaps Mercury. Venus was of particular importance to the Maya as they linked its presence with success in war, and there are several stelae that record the appearance of Venus prompting the decision to attack.

## RELIGION

Maya **cosmology** is far from straightforward as at every stage an idea is balanced by its opposite and each part of the universe is made up of many layers. To the Maya this is the third version of the earth, the previous two having been destroyed by deluges. The current version is a flat surface, with four corners, each associated with a certain colour; white for north, red for east, yellow for

south and black for west, with green at the centre. Above this the sky is supported by four trees, each a different colour and species, which are also sometimes depicted as gods, known as *Bacabs*. At its centre the sky is supported by a ceiba tree. Above the sky is a heaven of thirteen layers, each of which has its own god, while the very top layer is overseen by an owl. Other attested models of the world include that of a turtle (the land) floating on the sea. However, it was the underworld, *Xibalbá*, the "Place of Fright", which was of greater importance to most Maya, as it was in this direction that they passed after death, on their way to the place of rest. The nine layers of hell were guarded by the "Lords of the Night", and deep caves were thought to connect with the underworld.

Woven into this universe the Maya recognized an incredible array of **gods**. Every divinity had four manifestations based upon colour and direction and many also had counterparts in the underworld and consorts of the opposite bless a journey, the planting of crops, or the passing of a family member – these rites may have been performed individually or by an entire community, accompanied by prayers, the sacrifice of animals and the burning of copal incense.

**Elite bloodletting rituals** often took place at important or auspicious occasions: during accession ceremonies, at the birth of an heir, to mark the passing of a calendar round, in times of war, drought or disease, and to ensure regeneration and prosperity. Bloodletting also served as a rite of passage, or the individual quest for a prophetic vision and communication with the gods, providing access to the spiritual world.

There seem to have been two main **auto-sacrificial rituals** practised by the Maya elite. These were not undertaken lightly and carried severe physical and psychological repercussions. As part of a larger ceremony, the actual act of letting blood may have been preceded by days of preparation, meditation, fasting, sexual abstinence and bodily purification with sweat baths. A male rite was to draw blood by pricking the penis with either a stingray spine, obsidian lancet or flint knife. The second rite, piercing the tongue, was probably practised by both sexes although is most famously illustrated by Lady Xoc in the **Yaxchilán lintels**, now housed in the British Museum. The blood offering was then soaked into bark paper and collected in ceremonial bowls to be burnt as a presentation and petition to the Gods.

The Maya also practised bloodletting in the form of **captive sacrifice**, a highly ceremonial affair in which prolonged death and torture were features – gruesomely depicted in the Bonampak murals. Prisoners then either faced death by decapitation, or by having their heart removed. Hearts were then burnt as an offering to the gods, while decapitated heads might be displayed on a skull-rack.

Maya **warfare** often reflected the need for ritual bloodletting, as warriors frequently sought to capture alive rulers of rival cities, who would then be imprisoned and sacrificed at a later date. The soaring temples of the city centre then served as ceremonial theatres for elaborate religious rituals, allowing victories to be proclaimed to the entire community. Sacrificial victims would have been especially important to mark the accession of a new ruler, the bloodletting adding legitimacy to the king and affirming his power.

Blood offerings were integral to ancient Amerindian life, a tradition passed on from the Olmec to the Maya and then on to the Aztec. Bloodletting developed from culture to culture through material and ideological exchange but always retained its central elements – links to the supernatural, mythical origins and a vital connection with the continued prosperity of mankind and mother earth.

*Simone Clifford-Jaeger*

sex. In addition to this there was an extensive array of patron deities, each associated with a particular trade or particular class. Every activity from suicide to sex had its representative in the Maya pantheon.

## RELIGIOUS RITUAL

The combined complexity of the Maya pantheon and calendar gave every day a particular significance, and the ancient Maya were bound up in a demanding **cycle of religious ritual**. The main purpose of ritual was the procurement of success by appealing to the right god at the right time and in the right way. As every event, from planting to childbirth, was associated with a particular divinity, all of the main events in daily life demanded some kind of religious ritual and for the most important of these the Maya staged elaborate ceremonies.

While each ceremony had its own format there's a certain pattern that binds them all. The correct day was carefully chosen by priestly divination, and for several days beforehand the participants fasted and remained abstinent. The main ceremony was dominated by the expulsion of all evil spirits, the burning of incense before the idols, a sacrifice (either animal or human), and bloodletting.

In divination rituals, used to foretell the pattern of future events or account for the cause of past events, the elite used various **drugs** to achieve altered states of consciousness. Perhaps the most obvious of these was alcohol, either made from fermented maize or a combination of honey and the bark of the balnche tree. Wild tobacco, which is considerably stronger than the modern domesticated version, was also smoked. The Maya also used a range of hallucinogenic mushrooms, all of which were appropriately named, but none more so than the *xibalbaj obox*, "underworld mushroom", and the *k'aizalah obox*, "lost judgement mushroom".

# THE MAYA TODAY

**Despite the suggestions of numerous New Age books on the secrets of the "Ancient Maya", neither the Maya nor their traditional beliefs have vanished. Like most of the indigenous people of America, they have survived, though few peoples in the world can have been more persecuted. Since the Spanish Conquest in 1524, they have endured continuous subjugation under a feudal system, the banning of their religion and compulsory conversion to Christianity, and the shattering of their culture.**

These ravages left the twentieth-century Maya people as scattered and introspective tribal communities, divided into two geographical groups – the Highland Maya of Guatemala and Chiapas, and the Lowland Maya of Eastern Mexico, Guatemala and Belize – with little communication between them. However, in the 1980s and 1990s, the savage persecution and widespread killing of the Highland Maya began to foment a new solidarity between the two groups and a new sense of nationhood. This bore literary fruit when Rigoberta Menchú, a survivor of the army's worst excesses and the daughter of an assassinated Maya community leader, published her autobiography in 1983, subtitled "Asi Me Nacio La Conciencia" (This is How my Consciousness was Born). Her Nobel Peace Prize, awarded in 1992, brought international attention to the Maya and, for the first time, Maya voices were heard in the United Nations.

## MAYA IDENTITY: A POLITICAL ISSUE

It is a great paradox that in terms of physical characteristics and associated genetic make-up, there is little to separate an indigenous Mexican or Central American from most ladinos. Though most of the people today known as Maya are descendants of the ancient Maya, so too are the majority of the region's non-indigenous people. Some anthropologists have claimed that cultural criteria and language are the things that distinguish Maya from non-Maya, but even in the Maya heartlands of the Yucatán, Chiapas and highland Guatemala, only a minority of Maya men wear indigenous dress, and many speak perfect Spanish. Ultimately, though, the question of indigenous identity is a political and not an anthropological problem. People should be able to define themselves, yet, since the Conquest, the Maya have only been defined by people other than themselves. An official explained the system used in Guatemalan censuses in the 1980s as follows: "We ask the subject's neighbours if they're indigenous, then consider dress, language, and general socio-economic condition." Today, however, as Maya are becoming more politically aware, they are beginning to see themselves differently. "We need to recover not only our own identity, but the right to define that identity ourselves. It should not be left to some European or North American academic," proclaims Alberto Esquit, a Guatemalan Maya activist in *The Maya of Guatemala* by Phillip Wearne.

In Guatemala, a sense of what it is to be Maya is becoming increasingly widespread and the definition of this is known as **Mayanidad**. It is difficult to express exactly what this encapsulates, but a few elements of it can be gleaned from Rigoberta Menchú's autobiography and from *Perpectivas y Propuestas de los Pueblos Mayas de Guatemala* (Views and Proposals of the Maya People of Guatemala), prepared by the Fundación Vicente Menchú of Guatemala. Mayanidad is primarily characterized by a **devotion to the land**, not for private ownership – an idea which arrived with the Spanish – but for communal sharing. "We never think of taking all for ourselves and leaving our brothers and sisters with nothing," explained one Maya. Other characteristics are **traditional forms of dress**, which express symbolic meanings, and the **consumption of maize** as the basic element of a staple diet, prepared in the form of tortillas baked by hand on a comal.

The ceremonies and symbols of what is essentially a **holistic religion**, administered by a shamanic priest, are another important element. This concentrates on the sacredness of the earth, which is seen as a mother constantly providing for us, and of the sun, seen as a father channelling life energy to the earth. Religion also involves a symbolic link between **cardinal points**, colour and the livelihood of the Maya people; the burning of **incense**, **ritual dance** and the practice of traditional **shamanic healing**; and a set of **mythological stories** involving patterns in the sky and features of the landscape. Religion touches every aspect of life, including **social decision-making**, a process that relies on consensus: "In order

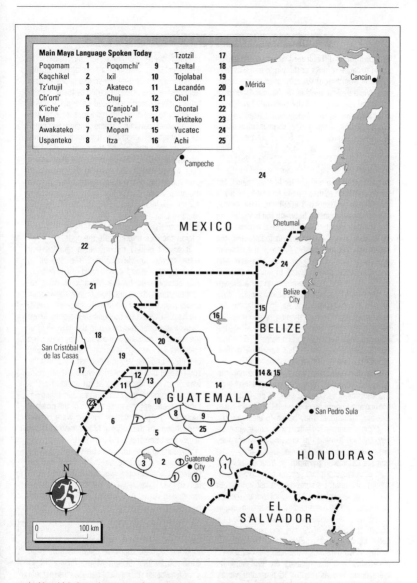

**Main Maya Language Spoken Today**

| | | | |
|---|---|---|---|
| Poqomam | 1 | Poqomchi' | 9 |
| Kaqchikel | 2 | Ixil | 10 |
| Tz'utujil | 3 | Akateco | 11 |
| Ch'orti' | 4 | Chuj | 12 |
| K'iche' | 5 | Q'anjob'al | 13 |
| Mam | 6 | Q'eqchi' | 14 |
| Awakateko | 7 | Mopan | 15 |
| Uspanteko | 8 | Itza | 16 |

| | |
|---|---|
| Tzotzíl | 17 |
| Tzeltal | 18 |
| Tojolabal | 19 |
| Lacandón | 20 |
| Chol | 21 |
| Chontal | 22 |
| Tektiteko | 23 |
| Yucatec | 24 |
| Achi | 25 |

to decide which day to have a meeting we look at the calendar and search for a good day which will augur well for our deliberations. Before an important meeting we prepare our hearts with a Maya ceremony. After that we are ready to share our problems and ideas, ready to listen to all and to try and understand what each has to say. Later we

have a period of conciliation to enable us to reach a commonly held position."

Recent archeological work has shown that a vast number of these beliefs and traditions were held and practised by the Maya's pre-Columbian ancestors, further enabling modern Maya to reclaim their heritage.

## MAYA SPIRITUALITY AND SHAMANISM

**Shamanism** is difficult for Westerners to understand because it looks at the world in a way very different from that of Western science or philosophy. While science teaches us that our experience of ourself is a product of the material of which we are made, so that our thoughts, for example, are the properties of our brains, shamanism teaches that our thoughts and our brains are manifestations of a deeper inner reality which lies behind our experience of ourselves as thinkers: the material world is an aspect of the spiritual, not vice versa. This is true not just for human beings, but for everything animate and inanimate, from a crocodile to a mountain. The primordial forces that control the relationship between the material and the spiritual (death, life, time), are the gods.

Human beings are crucial in maintaining the balance in this relationship between the material and the spiritual. Their agent is the **shaman**, who abandons body and thoughts to enter a state of trance. He or she then journeys into the archetypal spirit world, redressing imbalances which manifest in the material world as, for instance, disease or drought. If the shaman is successful in altering the spirit world to favourably affect the material, then his activity must be paid for so that the balance is preserved. Thus **sacrifice** is often required before or after a shamanic ritual.

This shamanic legacy was adapted and elaborated by the great civilization that preceded the Maya, the **Olmecs**. The Olmecs were to pre-Columbian Mexico and Central America what the Greeks are to Western civilization. They began to elaborate the precepts of shamanism into a more complex mythology, building a replica of the volcano where they believed the world was created by the gods – the first pre-Columbian **pyramid**. In front of this they built a rectangular plaza, where rituals were conducted, and near it a sunken court decorated with water plants, symbolic of the spirit world. The city was ruled over by a shamanic king, sometimes portrayed in carved stelae, who administered the rituals and the politics of the city and propitiated the gods through human sacrifice or ritual bloodletting.

The Maya pyramids were also seen as sacred mountains, and the temples on their summits were conceived as mouths to the spirit world. Like everything else in the shamanic world, these mountains were spiritually alive, and the Maya symbolized this by carving the mouths of mountain spirits known as **"Witz"** monsters around the temple doors (most dramatically at Chicanná, Hormiguero and the Chenes sites), or on their sides (for example, at Tikal). These mountain temples were administered by priests or shamanic kings who had a special relationship with the spirit world – their source of power. This relationship was often indicated by the representation of entwined feathered serpents in close proximity to depictions of the Maya lords on stelae or other carvings. These "vision serpents" were symbolic conduits for souls travelling between the material and the spirit world. They are also portrayed rearing up in front of people in deep trance states, and opening their mouths to emit the heads of the dead or other beings from the other world – as in the famous lintel of Lady Xoc of Yaxchilán, now in the British Museum in London. Like the Olmec rulers, the Maya lords also practised bloodletting (see p.552) and human sacrifice to propitiate the gods.

It wasn't merely the mountain temples that were sacred in Maya cities. The spaces in between were used for prolonged rituals or festivals administered by the Maya lords, who re-enacted the myths of creation, ritually transferring power from the spirit world to the material; a modern parallel would be Catholic sacraments. Maya myths were often played out in the movement of the stars; the passage of the Milky Way across the night sky, for instance, was symbolic of the raising of a great tree (the World Tree) that separates the spirit world and the material world. Architecture was often oriented to the astral bodies for this reason and buildings were arranged in triangular form to represent the three stones of the **cosmic hearth** – the place where humans were cooked into creation by the Lords of Maize, marked in the sky by the three stars of Orion's Belt.

The famous pre-Columbian **ball game** also had ritual significance. Like the sunken court of the Olmecs, the ball court was decorated with symbols of the border between the material and spirit world, and within it, teams of players competed, re-enacting a game played by the Hero Twins, mythological characters who defeated the Lords of Death, then rescuing their parents, the Lords of Maize, who went on to create the present world.

Many of these shamanic traditions have been preserved by the modern Maya. Yucatec Maya *xmen* (shamans) still mediate between the material and spiritual worlds when they invoke the spirit of rain, the god Chac, during times of drought. The Maya of San Lorenzo Zinacantán still venerate the spirits of the mountains that overlook their valley home, and all over the Maya World communities still affirm the myths of creation in elaborate annual festivals and celebrations.

## A HISTORY OF THE MODERN MAYA

More than any other factor, it was the political events of the 1980s and 1990s in Guatemala and across the border in Mexico's Chiapas state that were crucial in establishing a new sense of Maya solidarity and, subsequently, identity. Both conflicts were part of the age-old problem of **land distribution**. After they conquered Mexico and Central America, the Spanish, who were forbidden from enslaving the native population by the Catholic Church and the Reyes Católicos, Fernando and Isabel, sought other means of controlling the people. The result was the "**hacienda system**", whereby the indigenous communities were broken up and the villagers resettled on the edges of huge estates owned by colonists from Spain, many of whom were little more than peasants themselves, from the poorest regions of the country, such as Extremadura and Castilla La Mancha. The landowners then rented small plots of land to the indigenous people at rates that were sufficiently high to ensure that they were always owed a little money, paid back in the form of labour on the hacienda estates. After independence, this system was perpetuated, and even today in the twenty-first century most of the peasants of Latin America are controlled in this way. In Guatemala, the successors to the haciendas are the coastal coffee and sugarcane **fincas**, to which Highland Maya peasants, unable to sustain a living on their poor lands in the mountains, are ferried at harvest time. In Mexico, huge farms are run by wealthy estate owners, known in Chiapas as *caciques*. In the Yucatán, however, fewer Maya labour under debt peonage as the plantations that produced *henequen* (sisal) collapsed with the introduction of nylon. This domination by the landowners looked as if it would continue indefinitely, until two factors brought it to a head in the 1980s: Catholic Liberation Theology and the threatened or actual appropriation of the little communal land worked by the Maya.

**Liberation Theology** was conceived in 1967 at a conference of South American bishops in Medellín Colombia, who decided that the Church's priority should be to help the poor, rather than the rich. The theology demanded a "**preferential option for the poor**" through the erosion of unjust class structures and the establishment of base communities to empower both the urban and rural poor at a grass-roots level, by addressing their basic needs and teaching them about their rights.

This new theology spread quickly throughout Latin America. In Guatemala, it was practised by **Catholic Action**, a movement that taught the Maya about the root causes of their poverty and gave them a belief that they could change the unjust social structure that perpetuated it. However, there were often brutal consequences for its practitioners, and countless priests were murdered throughout the 1980s by US-backed or -installed military regimes, paranoid about Communism. In El Salvador, **Archbishop Romero** was shot dead while denouncing the exploitation of the poor to his parishioners during a sermon. In Mexico, the bishop of San Cristóbal de las Casas in Chiapas, **Samuel Ruiz**, was dubbed "the red bishop" by Mexico's political dictatorship, the PRI, and blamed by them for fomenting the Zapatista movement.

Liberation Theology helped the Highland Maya of Guatemala and Chiapas to understand why they were poor, but when threats to take away the little land still worked by the Maya followed, they provoked first resistance and then insurrection.

### ETHNIC CLEANSING IN GUATEMALA

The 1970s and 1980s saw increased tension in the Guatemalan highlands as wealthy ladinos and agro-businesses targeted Maya **communal lands** for intensive farming.

Land has been confiscated from the Maya ever since the Conquest: tourists visiting Guatemala City invariably pass along Avenida La Reforma, named in commemoration of a "reform" which abolished Maya ownership of communal lands in the nineteenth century. The revolts which followed this decision, which were crushed with characteristic brutality, were mirrored one hundred years later. This time, however, the Maya communities, consolidated by the work of Catholic Action, began to resist.

During the recession of the 1970s, growing numbers of urban Maya had taken leading roles in unions and community groups, and as Highland Maya began to journey to the capital to protest their land rights and hire lawyers to defend their land, these groups met and exchanged ideas. Recognizing their joint aims and concerns, they began to work together more closely. However, they were met with repression, combined with the failure of the corrupt legal system and the government to address their demands. As the Maya protested more forcefully, the repression increased. According to an Oxfam report, the mutilated, dismembered and sexually abused bodies of 168 community leaders were found by or returned to Maya villagers between February 1976 and February 1977.

After **General Lucas García** came to power in a blatantly rigged election, the violence increased. Troops opened fire on a group of seven hundred peaceful demonstrators in **Panzós** in 1978, and death squads were given a free hand to rape, torture and kill potential "subversives". Maya villagers, becoming increasingly desperate, began to look for protection elsewhere. Inspired by the Cuban Revolution, **guerrilla groups**, such as **ORPA** (the Organization of the People in Arms) and **EGP** (the Guerrilla Army of the Poor) had been working amongst tribal groups in the highlands since the early 1970s and, by the end of the decade, frightened Maya were joining them in droves, hoping for protection from the brutalities of the army. The guerrillas, however, were ladino Marxists, with little interest in the Maya except as a means to bring about a proletarian revolution. By the early 1980s the split between ladinos and indigenous people in the guerrilla movements was at crisis point and increasing numbers of Maya felt that the guerrillas, too, had failed them. While the guerrillas fled to the mountains, villagers were left to face the army guns – and the systematic brutality of Guatemala's dictator, born-again Christian **General Ríos Montt**, who claimed his power "by God's Will".

Montt pledged to eradicate the guerrillas and set about a programme of ethnic cleansing – **The National Plan of Security and Development** – which would involve "changes in the basic structure of the state". The army was briefed and given maps with the positions of villages marked with pins. Under operation **"preventative terror"**, the villages with pink or yellow pins were burnt to the ground and the fleeing populations relocated in **model villages** and given the choice of being fed or killed. Those who chose to be fed were then organized into "civilian patrols" headed by military commissioners, whose job was to spy out possible subversives and fight against the guerrillas. The aim was to force the Maya to become ladinos and blur their identity by mixing the various communities.

Operation **"scorched earth"** dealt with those villages marked with red pins. After resident ladinos and landowners had been persuaded to leave "for their own safety" (because the army had been instructed to allow no survivors), troops swept through these highland villages, burning homes, destroying everything they could find and killing villagers as they fled. In the ensuing carnage, up to forty percent of some tribal groups were wiped out, and millions of displaced people who had somehow survived fled across the border to Mexico or chanced their luck in the mountains.

This method of reconquering the Maya through suppression, murder and relocation was continued by Montt's successor, **General Victores**, and the army, backed by civilian president, **Vinicio Cerezo**. Culturally, the scorched earth programme seemed devastating, but by the late 1980s, it became clear that it had in fact heightened **Maya self-awareness**, rather than subsumed it. Maya people came to regard themselves not merely as members of different tribes but as a people with a common heritage and traditions. The repression continued under **President Serrano**, who sanctioned death squads and extra-judicial killings, but could not prevent the formation of the **Mutual Support Group** (GAM) which, despite the assassination of a number of its leaders, worked to bring international attention to Guatemala's appalling human rights scandals. In 1990, villagers in Santiago Atitlán expelled the army after troops had murdered thirteen people, inspiring other highland villages to demand the closure of military bases. Two years later, when Spanish and Latin American politicians organized lavish celebrations to commemorate the 500-year anniversary of Columbus's "discovery" of the Americas, Maya leaders made clear their community had nothing to rejoice about, and organized protest marches in the capital. An alternative Quincentenary conference, dedicated to the world's indigenous people, was held in Quetzaltenango, attended by indigenous leaders from all over the world. Later in the same year the strengthening indigenous rights movement was given a massive boost when the K'iche' Maya activist **Rigoberta Menchú** won the Nobel Peace Prize.

In 1996 the new government of **Álvaro Arzú** moved decisively to end the civil war, signing **Peace Accords** with the guerrilla groups. One of the key components of the settlement was a pledge to help indigenous Guatemalans via a programme of reform for the Maya, including encouraging education in native tongues, greater political participation and the preservation of sacred areas. Though hundreds of new Maya language schools have opened across the country, efforts to bring the Maya into the political mainstream suffered a serious setback when the electorate rejected proposed changes to the Guatemalan constitution in a 1999 referendum. Disturbingly, the turnout was weakest in Maya areas, as the community who stood to gain most from the constitutional change failed or chose not to vote. The reasons for this electoral debacle were complex, but the apathy only served to highlight the size of the task ahead – for many Maya voting remains an alien concept, something that ladinos do to support a ladino-dominated state which they feel they have little or no stake in.

The other key part of the Peace Accords, the **UN-presided Truth Commission** report into Civil War atrocities and human rights, condemned the military for the vast majority of the killings. As some ninety percent of the 150,000 dead and 50,000 "disappeared" were Maya, indigenous leaders (including Rigoberta Menchú, who lost many family members) have campaigned hard to charge the perpetrators of the violence for genocide in both Guatemalan and international courts. By August 2001 it seemed the accused – including ex-presidents Lucas García and Ríos Montt – would avoid prosecution, though there was increasing public pressure from the indigenous community to bring army officers, indicted with war crimes and massacres, to justice.

Though Guatemala's Maya remain poor and marginalized, with 75 percent illiteracy and the lowest life expectancy in the western hemisphere, there are unmistakable signs of a cultural reawakening and assertiveness. So far the little that they have gained, they have paid for dearly; yet as Rigoberta Menchú herself puts it: "After so many years of struggle, this period seems to be the end of five hundred years of injustice, five hundred years of night. We are moving into the light of a new era for our peoples. After so many years of waiting for a new dawn, we believe our voices will make themselves heard..."

## OPPRESSION AND INSURRECTION IN CHIAPAS

On January 1, 1994, the day the **North American Free Trade Agreement** (NAFTA) took effect, a predominantly Maya militia wearing balaclavas occupied several cities in Chiapas, including the capital, **San Cristóbal de las Casas**, proclaiming *Basta Ya!* (That's Enough!) to the government. Calling themselves the **Zapatista Army of National Liberation (EZLN)**, they were, like their Guatemalan counterparts, protesting against debt peonage and the further erosion of indigenous land rights.

Emiliano **Zapata**, from whom the Zapatistas take their name, was a guerrilla leader in the Mexican Revolution of 1910, determined to dismantle the hacienda system and redistribute land to the indigenous community. Though Zapata's dream was never fully realized, **Article 27** of the 1917 Constitution provided for the allocation of communal holdings — known as **ejidos** — to campesinos and indigenous people. Though still owned by the state, the *ejidos* were held in common, usually within village communities. In the early 1990s, however, **President Carlos Salinas** decided to modernize the Mexican economy in preparation for NAFTA: Article 27 was repealed and the *ejidos* were up for grabs.

It is hardly surprising, then, that the reinstatement of Article 27 was, and still is, one of the Zapatistas' key demands. The state's perception of the uprising, as well as the continuing response to it, was neatly expressed by a cartoon which appeared in the Mexican press shortly after the Zapatistas had made their demands. A detained Maya stands in front of a police official who says, "So, you don't speak Spanish? First charge then, treason."

Initially, the Mexican army reacted to the Zapatista/Maya rebellion with a use of force only exceeded by their Guatemalan counterparts. After expelling foreign journalists, they bombed Maya villages regarded as EZLN strongholds, murdered captured civilians suspected of being sympathizers and began a campaign of terror. Long hidden from the outside world, the repressive side of the Mexican state – together with the plight of the nation's indigenous people – were suddenly front-page news. Salinas called a cease-fire and began negotiations.

**Manuel Camacho Solis** was appointed Commissioner for Peace and Reconciliation in Chiapas, while the mysterious, balaclava-clad, pipe-smoking **Subcomandante Marcos** spoke for the EZLN. In an intermediary role was **Samuel Ruíz**, bishop of San Cristóbal de las Casas and a respected campaigner for indigenous rights. Some **concessions** were offered to the Zapatistas and they retreated for lengthy consultation with their communities. Although the rebellion directly affected only part of Chiapas, Maya groups, who had long backed other political parties, denounced the PRI, accusing it of vote-rigging and of supporting the corrupt *caciques* (landowners), who kept them in bonded labour. By May, peasants had occupied nineteen municipal headquarters, and by June, over three hundred farms had been seized from *caciques*. In July, the EZLN reported that the communities had overwhelmingly rejected the proposals; the cease-fire, however, still held.

In the **August 1994 elections**, the PRI managed to hang on to not only national power, but also the governership of Chiapas. Though there are peasants within Chiapas who strongly support the PRI, the state election was almost certainly a fraud, and, in protest, the defeated opposition candidate, **Amado Avendaño Figueroa**, declared himself "rebel governor". Half the municipalities in the state backed him, refusing to pay taxes to the government, and the EZLN warned that if the PRI candidate assumed power in Chiapas then they would call an end to their truce. When the new president, **Ernesto Zedillo**, attended the inauguration of the governor of Chiapas the Zapatista response was immediate. Without firing a shot, the guerrillas penetrated the army cordon and consolidated their political base from four municipalities to 35. Shortly afterwards, again undetected and without any gunfire, they retreated to the mountains, where they began a long (and continuing) stand-off with the government.

The army responded in 1995 by launching an offensive and revealing that Subcomandante Marcos was, in fact, **Rafael Sebastián Guillén Vicente**, a professor of communications from Mexico City and a former Sandinista brigadier. Exercising the military option was a high-risk strategy for Zedillo, and one that didn't really come off: the EZLN enjoyed considerable public sympathy, especially in view of their largely non-violent methods. Even unmasking Marcos failed to affect his popularity – indeed, cries of "Guillén for president" became common at opposition rallies. In a rapid U-turn, the government called off the army and set up **new negotiations**.

These proved to be even more protracted than the 1994 talks but eventually resulted in the **San Andrés Accords on Rights and Indigenous Cultures** (named for the village near San Cristóbal where they took place), signed in February 1996. The Accords guaranteed indigenous representation in national and state legislatures, but their implementation would require constitutional and legislative changes which Zedillo failed to push through Congress. Relations between the Zapatistas and the government negotiators, characterized by mutual distrust, were strained to breaking point, and in September the EZLN suspended further peace talks.

In the lengthy period of negotiation the small enclaves liberated from the wealthy landowners by the Zapatistas were left to successfully govern their own. The Maya have introduced traditional systems of social organization, administration of justice and agricultural production, and though the government in Mexico City insists that the Zapatistas have made life worse for the Maya, things are very different on the ground. Michael McCaughan, a British journalist who visited the villages in June 1998, described what he saw: "The peasant farmers . . . seem bewildered by the fulfilment of a centuries-old dream . . . there is a new confidence. Indian men and women used to walk with heads bowed; now they look you in the eye and discuss world politics."

In April 1997, Human Rights Watch published a report exposing state responsibility for mounting rural violence against pro-Zapatista Maya in Chiapas, and against other indigenous peoples and campesinos, unhappy with their exploitation at the hands of rich landowners throughout Mexico. They concluded not only that the PRI had failed to bring local *caciques* to justice, but that they had supported **paramilitary groups** known as **guardias blancas** (white guards, paid for by *caciques* to protect private property and the political infrastructure which they support).

Political neglect, accompanied by a remorseless increase of the military presence on the Zapatistas' perimeter, appeared also to give the paramilitary groups even greater freedom to operate, further escalating the level of violence. This culminated in the December 1997 **massacre at Acteal**: 45 displaced Tzotíl Indians, 36 of them women and children, were murdered by paramilitary forces linked to PRI officials in Chiapas. The killings brought world-wide condemnation. Zedillo announced an official investigation to show that the federal government writ still ran in Chiapas, and ordered the arrest of those suspected of taking part in the massacre.

The few changes that occurred after Acteal were little more than window-dressing and the extra troops sent to Chiapas, ostensibly to stop more paramilitary killings, failed to prevent further violence and intimidation of Zapatista supporters. The army even entered Zapatista strongholds on the pretext of searching for paramilitary arms and began to move against the autonomous municipalities set up by the Zapatistas. This betrayal of the principles of a negotiated settlement finally provoked Bishop Ruiz to resign from his role as mediator in June 1998. Negotiations broke down completely and the tension rose even higher when the Chiapas governor **Roberto Albores Guillén** described the autonomous municipalities as "the greatest threat to democracy" in Mexico and pledged to dismantle them. Foreign journalists were expelled and 60,000 troops, paramilitaries and police, now under army control, surrounded and destroyed several Zapatista villages.

In a landmark victory on July 2, 2000, **Vicente Fox**, the PAN candidate (during his campaign he had famously promised to resolve the Chiapas problem "in fifteen minutes"), was elected president and inaugurated in December that year. Not only was he the first democratically elected opposition candidate to have taken office, it was the end of seven decades of PRI rule.

Three months after Fox's inauguration, the so-called **"Zapatour"**, headed by Subcomandante Marcos and 23 fellow *comandantes*, set off from Chiapas and proceeded up to Mexico City with all the style and presence of a rock tour. Thousands of people lined the route to wave them on through their month-long journey, with the procession attracting international media attention. On March 28, 2001, the masked rebel commanders arrived in the capital and addressed Mexico's congress, demanding, in eloquent, emotional speeches, the release of all Zapatistas held prisoner since the Chiapas uprising began in 1994, that troops be withdrawn from the state, and that a bill be passed guaranteeing the political and cultural rights of

the country's ten million indigenous Mexicans.

Although a symbolic success for both the rebel group and Fox – demonstrating that he means business and will go to ground-breaking lengths to achieve peace within Mexico – many observers saw the victories as fairly hollow. Although the Zapatistas were allowed to present their case in Congress, there is still a long way to go before a lasting agreement on the validity and nature of indigenous rights in Mexico is achieved.

## THE YUCATEC MAYA

Until recently, the least persecuted Maya group were those of Mexico's Yucatán peninsula. After the collapse of the market in *henequen* (used for making high-quality rope) earlier this century, the Maya who had until that point been subjugated under a system of debt peonage were more or less left to their own devices. The Yucatán became a quiet backwater and Mérida didn't even have road connections to the rest of Mexico. In the 1960s, though, the government decided to transform **Cancún**, a Maya fishing village, into a major tourist resort.

There is something distasteful about the way in which Maya images are used to sell dream holidays to package tourists destined for Cancún. Pictures of cute, sanitized Maya children smile from brochures and billboards welcoming visitors to the Maya world, and vast ugly hotels mimic the designs of their ancestors' temples. Though a few commendable ecotourism projects, particularly in Campeche state, are attempting to channel a little money to the Maya, most of this new-found wealth doesn't reach them; instead it falls into the pockets of the wealthy ladino landowning group who have for so long exploited them.

That aside, the Yucatán is still a healthier area for the Maya than almost any other in the Maya world. Maya children are not allowed to learn their own language in schools, for example, but mass tourism has thankfully yet to oust the majority of the peninsula's villagers. Many still grow maize on milpas and continue to practise traditional lifestyles. Maya **xmen** (shamans) operate throughout the peninsula, even in larger centres like Ticul and Mérida, though they are most concentrated in the countryside, particularly around the important spiritual centre of **Felipe Carillo Puerto** in Quintana Roo.

## THE MAYA OF BELIZE

The **Maya** in Belize are from three groups – the Yucatec, Mopan and Kekchí (Q'eqchi, in Guatemala) – and make up around eleven percent of the population. Many of the ancestors of the **Yucatec** Maya entered Belize to escape the fighting in the Caste Wars and most were soon acculturated into the Mestizo way of life as small farmers. The **Mopan** Maya came to Belize in the 1880s and settled in the hills of Toledo and the area of Benque Viejo in the west. The **Kekchí**, from the area around Cobán in Guatemala (where most of their ethnic group still live), began to arrive around the same time, to work in cacao plantations in southern Belize.

Following the conquest of Yucatán many of the Maya in the northern half of Belize were under some form of Spanish control in one of nine mission towns. Others were enslaved and sent to Spanish colonies in the Caribbean and some were even captured and sold as slaves by British pirates; the remainder fled to the forests.

When the Mopan and **Kekchí** arrived in the south the British colonial administration allowed them to stay within designated **reservation areas**, on land still owned by the government. Currently this comprises about 300 square kilometres in the Toledo District, but even that is under threat. According to Belize law, only protected areas are closed to loggers; "Indian Reservations" are not, and since the Maya do not actually own the land, the government continues to brush aside Maya demands for title to the land they live on, arguing that land in Belize cannot be divided along ethnic lines.

In September 1995, the Belize government granted a licence to a Malaysian company to log the Maya reservation land. Logging began in 1996, in **Conejo Landing**. Bulldozers moved in, pushing down almost everything in their path, despite government assurances that only larger trees were to be selected for logging, and turning the Maya's principal source of drinking water into mud soup. In 1997 the bulldozers headed for the **Hinchasones** and **Xpichilha** reservations, where their "selective logging" resulted in floods that devastated Maya milpas and wrecked homes. Although Maya protests were initially rebuffed, the government did suspend some logging licences, partly from fear of adverse international publicity aimed at a country which was trying to promote itself as an "ecotourism" destination, but some logging still continues.

In the absence of any accurate government maps of their lands, the villagers, with cartographic expertise from the University of Berkeley, produced an illustrated **Maya Atlas** in 1997 (see "Books" p.000), a beautiful book with plans of every village and information about each community's culture and traditions. As one community leader explained: "Through our Atlas, our voices can be heard as we relate the history of our villages, as we describe our culture and way of life. Our aim is to protect our unique way of life and have indigenous rights respected. We believe our Atlas will help press our claim for legal rights to our land".

The Maya have taken their cause to an international level, following Rigoberta Menchú's example, lobbying the **United Nations** and international NGOs, with some success. International funding agencies have agreed not to release loans for proposed road projects unless Maya concerns are met, but tensions remain. The paving of the Southern Highway and a proposal to pave the road through the Maya villages to the Guatemalan border, creating an international highway, threatens to exacerbate the situation by making access to these areas even easier, encouraging land settlers. New roads will mean an increase in land prices and the Maya of Toledo, who are still largely dependent on subsistence agriculture, fear they will be pushed further into the margins of the Belizean economy unless they own the land they live on.

## THE FUTURE

The indigenous peoples of the Americas have faced a stark choice since the time of the Conquest – assimilate or accept oppression. For five hundred years many have chosen the path of oppression and been marginalized by their rulers, who called them **Indians**, after Columbus's mistake. "Mexicans make no connection between their Aztec ancestors and the poor Indian selling vegetables on the pavement," notes a member of the country's National Indigenous Institute. "For most . . . one represents historic pride, the other contemporary shame."

Today, however "Indian" has become a pejorative term, and awareness of Native American culture, philosophy and rights is increasing. For over a decade, the UN Working Group on Indigenous Peoples has been drawing up a

**EZLN**, *www.ezln.org* Website dedicated to the Zapatistas.

**Foundation for Human Rights in Guatemala**, 4554 N Broadway Ave, Chicago IL 60640 (☎773/250-3407, *www.fhrg.org*). Charitable group that publish regular news and human rights updates and a free newsletter.

**Institute of Maya Studies**, 3280 South Miami Ave, Miami, FL 33129 (☎305/666-0779, *www.mayastudies.org*). Respected institution with an extensive research library and regular events and lectures. Membership (from US$30 annually) includes a monthly newsletter.

**Maya – The Guatemalan Indian Centre**, 94 Wandsworth Bridge Rd, London SW6 2TF, UK (*www.maya.org.uk*, ☎020/7371 5291). Superb resource centre run by one of Europe's foremost Mayanists, the venue for regular talks and exhibitions. There's also a world-class textile collection and an extensive library and video archive, though they don't provide tourist information. Membership is £5 annually.

**Mesoweb**, *www.mesoweb.com* Excellent website, mainly concentrating on the ancient Maya, but with some contemporary content.

**Mexico Solidarity Network**, 4834 N Springfield, Chicago, IL 60625 (☎773/583-7728, *www.mexicosolidarity.org*). Coalition of over 80 organizations dedicated to improving human rights and democracy in Mexico.

**The Rigoberta Menchú Tum Foundation**, *www.rigobertamenchu.org* Rigoberta Menchú's homepage detailing the work of her organization and providing links to other sites.

**Mundo Maya**, *www.mayadiscovery.com* Informative site, rich with features on all things Maya.

**Human Rights Watch**, *www.hrw.org* and offices in USA at 350 5th Ave, 34th floor, NY 10118-3299 (☎212/290-4700, *hrwnyc@hrw.org*), and in the UK at 33 Islington High St, London N1 9LH (☎020/7713 1995, *hrw@hrw.org*). Large organization that produces excellent, concise annual country reports and regular features monitoring human rights in the region.

**Minority Rights Group**, 379 Brixton Rd, London SW9 7DE (☎020/7978 9498, *www.minorityrights.org*). Publishers of useful background leaflet *The Maya of Guatemala* by Philip Wearne, plus analysis and news summaries of issues affecting indigenous people.

**Yax Te' Foundation**, 3520 Coolheights Dr, Rancho Palos Verdes, CA 90275-6231 (☎ & fax 310/377-8763, *www.yaxte.org*). US-based Maya publishers, with an extensive catalogue and excellent links from their website.

draft declaration on the rights of the world's indigenous peoples. However, as the story of the Maya illustrates, this is occurring alongside continued and vigorous oppression by the descendants of the conquerors. Nonetheless, the Maya are optimistic, and their spirit, it seems, is indestructible. "Little by little we are moving forward," claims Rigoberta Menchú. "We have carried on a broad struggle for many years, and many people, many stalwart hearts in many parts of the world have accompanied us. We have always said that solidarity is a product of consciousness, a product of love, of love for life and for other people."

# LANDSCAPE
# AND WILDLIFE

The countries of the Maya World embrace an astonishingly diverse collection of environments, ranging from the world's second longest coral reef along the Caribbean coast, through the lowland rainforests of Mesoamerica and the upland pine forests of the Guatemalan highlands, to the exposed volcanic peaks of Guatemala, and down to mangrove lagoons on the sweltering Pacific coast. The region's wildlife is, if anything, even more varied than might be expected, due to the location of this region at the northern end of the land bridge between the temperate life zones to the north (the Nearctic) and the Neotropics to the south, and there are a number of local endemic species – found nowhere else in the world.

This diversity of habitats makes the Maya World an ideal location for wildlife enthusiasts and, though the main reason for visiting the **archeological sites** may be to understand more about the ancient Maya, the sites themselves also provide a vital refuge for the plants and animals of the region. This section aims to provide a general overview of the main ecosystems of the Maya World and give examples of some of the flora and fauna you might find there.

## LANDSCAPE

The distinct geographical and climatic patterns found in any region create a series of **biomes** (life zones or habitats), each with its own characteristic flora and fauna. These are effectively an ecological map, with temperature and rainfall being the main co-ordinates. The range of elevation found in the countries of the Maya World means there are around ten biomes: from subtropical dry forest on the northwest coast of Yucatán to tropical montane forest found on the highest slopes of the volcanoes. Some of the main ones are covered below.

## YUCATÁN AND THE GULF COAST LOWLANDS

The **Yucatán peninsula** is a limestone plateau, generally low-lying but gradually increasing in elevation from north to south. Although rainfall is plentiful, the dry season is more pronounced in the extreme northwest, and precipitation also gradually increases from north to south. Due to the permeable nature of limestone there is almost no surface water: most rain immediately soaks through and dissolves the rock, creating a **subterranean drainage** system, with great underground rivers flowing through caverns, and often entering the sea just offshore in upwellings of fresh water. Inland, **sinkholes** (cenotes) are formed when a cave roof collapses, where the water level is many metres below the surface of the land. In the north the vegetation is predominantly dry, tangled scrub and bush, although large areas have been cleared for cultivation. To the south are lusher subtropical forests, where the effects of agriculture are less obvious and the dense forest of **acacia**, **albizias**, **gumbo limbo** and **ceiba** is in parts almost impenetrable. The **sapodilla** tree grows here too, and **chicle**, used in the preparation of chewing gum, is harvested from its latex.

The **Gulf of Mexico coast** is low-lying and marshy in the north and west (protected in the Río Lagartos and Celestún national parks), giving way to a swampy, alluvial plain in Tabasco. Dotted with lagoons and crossed by the lower reaches of the Usumacinta, the Grijalva and a number of other rivers, the plain drains a huge volume of water from the Chiapas and Guatemalan highlands. Here much of the original rainforest has disappeared, replaced by banana plantations and cattle pasture; the climate is also ideal for cacao, grown here for thousands of years to produce chocolate.

## THE TROPICAL RAINFORESTS

Between north-central Yucatán and the northern foothills of the central highlands, and from the Gulf of Mexico to the Caribbean coast, the natural vegetation is either **tropical moist forest** or, with average temperatures of 24ºC and annual rainfall over 2000mm on some lower mountain slopes and coastal locations, true tropical rainforest. Formerly, this forest would have covered the whole of the region outlined above, but under pressure from agriculture and logging much of it has been reduced to a central "core", comprising southern Campeche and Quintana Roo, northern Petén, western and south-central Belize and the Lacandón forest of Chiapas. This area is still sufficiently large to support the whole range of wildlife described in the following section, and indeed much of it is under official protection in reserves and national parks, though their edges are constantly being nibbled away.

So diverse is the forest that scientists have identified seventy different forest types here, dependent on factors including (but not limited to) soil category, elevation and distance from the coast. However, it is the **broadleaved**, usually deciduous, trees, palms and vines which form the tropical rainforest (or moist forest) once the right conditions of temperature and moisture are met. The rainforest is characterized by the presence of several layers (though these will probably not be obvious from the ground), often connected by lianas and creepers: the **canopy**, perhaps 30–60m high, through which individual **emergent** trees rise; the **understorey** typically 10–20m high; and the **shrub** or ground layer. Many trees have only shallow tap roots, so **buttress roots**, flaring out from the trunk up to 6m above the ground, provide extra support.

The combination of a year-round growing season, plenty of moisture and millions of years of evolution has produced a unique environment. While temperate forests tend to be dominated by a few species – fir, oak or beech, for example – diversity characterizes the tropical forest. Each species is specifically adapted to fit into a particular ecological niche, where it receives a precise amount of light and moisture. It's a **biological storehouse** that has yet to be fully explored, although it has already yielded some astonishing discoveries. Steroid hormones, such as cortisone, and diosgenin, the active ingredient in birth control pills, were developed from wild yams found in these forests; and tetrodoxin, which is derived from a species of frog, is an anaesthetic 160,000 times stronger than cocaine.

Despite its size and diversity the forest is surprisingly **fragile**. It forms a closed system in which nutrients are continuously recycled and decaying plant matter fuels new growth. The forest floor is a spongy mass of roots, mosses and fungi, in which nutrients are broken down with the assistance of insects, bacteria and other micro-organisms, and chemical decay, before being released to the waiting roots and fresh seedlings. The thick canopy prevents much light reaching the forest floor, ensuring that the soil remains damp but warm – a hotbed of decomposition. The death of a large tree prompts a flurry of growth as new light reaches the forest floor, but once the trees are removed the soil is highly vulnerable, deprived of its main source of fertility. Exposed to the harsh tropical sun and direct rainfall, an area of cleared forest soon becomes prone to flooding and drought. Recently cleared land will contain enough nutrients for a few years of good growth, but its fertility declines rapidly. If the trees are stripped from a large area, soil erosion will silt the rivers and parched soils will disrupt local rainfall patterns. In its undisturbed state, however, the forest is superbly beautiful and is home to an incredible range of wildlife.

## THE HIGHLANDS

The **highlands** occupy a broad region south of the main rainforest belt, stretching continuously from western Chiapas through the western and eastern highlands of Guatemala to the Maya Mountains of Belize. In Mexico the non-volcanic **Sierra Madre de Chiapas** runs parallel to the coast, forming a steep barrier between 2500–2900m high to routes inland. Its sharp escarpments create a vast rain shadow, contributing to the relative aridity of the central depression of Chiapas.

The Sierras continue through Guatemala and into El Salvador as a chain of 33 **volcanoes**, each peak within view of the next, beginning with Tacaná at over 4000m, straddling the Mexico–Guatemala border, right through to Izalco in El Salvador, the highest being **Tajumulco** at 4220m, just inside Guatemala. There are also three active cones: **Fuego**, **Pacaya** and **Santiaguito**, all of which belch sulphurous fumes, volcanic ash and the occasional fountain of molten rock. Beneath the surface their subterranean fires heat the bedrock, resulting in a number of **hot springs**.

On the northern side of the Sierra Madre and the volcanic ridge are the **central valleys** of the highlands, a complex mixture of sweeping bowls, steep-sided valleys, open plateaus and jagged peaks. This central area is home to the highland Maya population and all the available land is intensively farmed, with hillsides carved into workable terraces and portioned up into a patchwork of small fields. Traditionally, the land is rotated between milpa (slash-and-burn) fields and a fallow period, but in most areas it's now under constant pressure; the fertility of the soil is virtually exhausted and only with the assistance of fertilizer can it still produce a worthwhile crop. The pressure on land is immense and each generation is forced to farm more marginal territory. This is particularly evident in some areas of Alta Verapaz in Guatemala, where planting on steep hillsides causes the exposed soil to be washed into the valley below.

Some areas remain off-limits to farmers, however: the peaks of the volcanoes, protected as national parks, are too steep to plant, and vast tracts of the highlands are still **forested**, with pine trees dominating, intermixed with oak, cedar and fir. At the higher elevations (2000–3000m) and under the right conditions **tropical montane forests** occur in isolated patches, some of which can be described as **cloudforests**. This scarce habitat features some evergreen trees, with branches draped in thick mosses, bromeliads and vines, and is home to one of the region's rarest and most spectacular birds, the resplendent **quetzal**, found in the cloudforests of Chiapas' Sierra Madre and the Verapaces of Guatemala. Heading on to the north, the land rises to form several **mountain ranges**, the largest of which is the **Sierra de los Cuchumatanes**, a massive chain of granite peaks that reach a height of 3790m above Huehuetenango; further to the east there are several smaller ranges such as the Sierra de Chuacús, the Sierra de las Minas and the Sierra de Chama. The high peaks support stunted trees and open grassland, used for grazing sheep and cattle, but are too cold for maize and most other crops.

## THE CARIBBEAN COAST AND THE BARRIER REEF

The unique environment of the **Caribbean Barrier Reef** is an almost continuous chain of **coral** beginning just south of Cancún and running 600km to the far south of Belize and the Bay Islands of Honduras. East of the barrier reef are the only four **atolls** in the Caribbean: roughly oval-shaped reefs rising from the seabed surrounding a central lagoon. The largest, **Banco Chinchorro**, off the coast of southern Quintana Roo, is still infrequently visited; the others (relatively more accessible) are in Belize. All are either proposed protected areas or already under some form of protection as national parks or marine reserves; **Glover's Reef** is considered by scientists to be the best developed and the most pristine atoll in the Caribbean. **Offshore islands**, from Isla Contoy in the north, down through Isla Mujeres and **Cozumel** (off Quintana Roo) and Belize's hundreds of **cayes**, south to the **Bay Islands**, all have their own coral reefs and provide superb wildlife refuges, home to several endemic species.

Immediately inland from the coast and on the cayes, occupying slightly higher ground, the **littoral forest** is characterized by salt-tolerant plants, often with tough, waxy leaves which help conserve water. Species include red and white **gumbo limbo**, black **poisonwood**, **zericote**, **palmetto** and of course the **coconut**, which typifies Caribbean beaches, though it's not actually a native. The littoral forest supports a very high density of fauna, especially migrating birds, due to the succession of fruits and seeds, yet, due to its location, it also faces very high development pressure.

The shoreline is still largely covered with **mangroves**, which play an important economic role, not merely as nurseries for commercial fish species but also for their stabilization of the shoreline and their ability to absorb the force of hurricanes: each kilometre of mangrove shoreline is valued at several thousand dollars per year. The cutting down of mangroves, particularly on the cayes, exposes the land to the full force of the sea and can mean the end of a small and unstable island. The dominant species of the coastal fringe is the **red mangrove**, although in due course it undermines its own environment by consolidating the sea bed until it becomes more suitable for the less salt-tolerant black and white mangroves. The basis of the shoreline food chain is the nutrient-rich mud, held in place by the mangroves, whose roots are home to **oysters** and **sponges**. In the shallows, "meadows" of **seagrass beds** provide nurseries for many fish and invertebrates, and pasture for conch, manatees and turtles. The extensive root system of seagrasses also protects beaches from erosion by holding the fragments of sand and coral together.

The reef is a world of astounding beauty, where fish and coral come in every imaginable colour. The corals look like a brilliant underwater forest, but in fact each coral is composed of colonies of individual **polyps**, feeding off plankton wafting past in the current. There are basically two types of coral: the hard, calcareous, reef-building corals, such as **brain coral** and **elkhorn coral** (known scientifically as the **hydrocorals**; 74 species), and the soft corals such as **sea fans** and **feather plumes** (the **ococorals**; 36 species). On the reefs you'll find the **chalice sponge**, which is a garish pink, the appropriately named **fire coral**, the delicate **feather-star crinoid** and the **apartment sponge**, a tall thin tube with lots of small holes in it.

In 1995 a major **coral reef bleaching** event occurred throughout the Caribbean. Coral bleaching occurs when the coral polyp loses some or all of the symbiotic **microalgae** (zooxanthellae) which live in its cells. This usually happens in response to stress, the most common cause of which is a period of above average sea temperatures, and it appears that the increased occurrence of coral bleaching is an indication of global warming.

## THE PACIFIC COAST

The **Pacific coastline** is marked by a thin strip of grey or black volcanic sand, pounded by the surf. The **beach** itself mainly takes the form of large sandbanks, dotted with palm trees, which are ideal nesting sites for marine turtles. Behind these and before the mainland proper, **lagoons** and mangrove swamps create a maze of waterways that are an ideal breeding ground for young fish, waterfowl and a range of small mammals. Between the shore and the foothills of the highlands, the humid **coastal plain** is a fertile, intensively farmed area. The volcanic and alluvial soils here are ideal for cultivating sugar cane, cotton and palm oil, and for rubber plantations and cattle ranches. There's little land that remains untouched by the hand of commercial agriculture so it's hard to imagine what this must once have looked like, but it was almost certainly very similar to Petén – a mixture of savannah and rainforest supporting a rich array of wildlife.

Approaching the highlands, the volcanic soils, high rainfall and good drainage conspire to make it ideal for growing **coffee**, and it's here that Mexico, Guatemala and El Salvador produce excellent crops, with rows of olive-green bushes ranked beneath shady trees. Where the land is unsuitable for coffee, lush tropical forest still grows, clinging to the hills. As you head up into the highlands, through deeply cleft valleys, you pass through some of this superb forest, dripping with moss-covered vines, bromeliads and orchids.

## WILDLIFE

With far more species of plants and animals than the whole of North America, the Maya World is a paradise for visiting naturalists, above all for **botanists** and **bird-watchers**, with over 4500 species of flowering plants and over six hundred bird species. **Mammals**, too, are very diverse, ranging from the **jaguar**, the largest land predator, to tiny forest shrews, though both are equally elusive. The most common sighting is likely to be of **bats**, which make up almost half of all mammal species here. To give a complete listing of even the main species in each animal family, and the places you're likely to find them, would be impossible, so the ones mentioned below are necessarily just a small sample.

If you are keen on **seeing wildlife**, or even signs of it, there are a few things you can do to improve your chances. First, consider buying a specialist **wildlife guide** (see p.581 for a selection) and bring it along. Second, stay in or near one of the **protected areas**. This might sound obvious, but all too often tourists are taken into a nature reserve during the day, when many animals are resting in the shade, in order to spend a few hours wandering about in the heat before trundling back to a hotel in the town. Nothing can increase your chances of spotting wildlife more than spending a whole day and a night in a reserve. Thus, the golden rule is never go on a day-trip to a reserve if you can spend the night there. Although many of the jungle lodges used by tour companies are very expensive, there are usually some budget options not far away. Finally, whether you're on an organized tour or travelling alone, go on a trail with a recommended **local guide**: you'll see more wildlife and glean more astonishing facts about the forest ecosystems under their guidance than you ever could alone.

Dozens of wildlife sites, national parks and reserves are covered in this guide. Some of the best, covering a range of habitats and which have several nearby accommodation choices, include: in Quintana Roo, the **Si'an Ka'an Biosphere Reserve**; in Chiapas, the **Montes Azules Biosphere Reserve**; in Guatemala, **Parque Nacional Tikal** and the Biotopo Mario Dary (the **Quetzal Reserve**); and in Belize, **Crooked Tree Wildlife Sanctuary** and the **Cockscomb Basin Wildlife Sanctuary**.

## BIRDS

**Birdlife** is plentiful throughout the entire region. At many archeological sites, birding is unrivalled and local specialities include **chestnut-headed oropendola**, **scaled ant pitta**, **white-whiskered puffbird**, **slaty-tailed trogon**, **green shrike vireo** and **masked tanager**. You'll also see flocks of screeching **parrots**, including **red-lored**, **white-fronted** and **yellow-headed Aztec parakeets** and perhaps even the magnificent **scarlet macaw**. Many of the huge variety of **hummingbirds** can be seen from the decks of jungle lodges or along village trails; overhead, the ever-present black and turkey **vultures** (zopilote) will be circling and in the forests you might be lucky and see the larger and more strikingly coloured **king vulture**. The forest is also home to three species of **toucan**: the collared aracari, the emerald toucanet and the keel-billed toucan – in some parks you can even see all three in one tree.

One particularly interesting lowland species is the **oropendola**, a large oriole which builds a long woven nest that hangs from trees and telephone wires. They tend to nest in colonies and a single tree might support fifty nests. You'll probably notice the nests more than the birds, but they thrive everywhere. Particularly striking also are the brilliantly coloured **trogons**, including Guatemala's national bird, the resplendent **quetzal**. This magnificent bird once inhabited the cloudforests from Chiapas to Costa Rica but, since the days of the Maya when it was hunted for its fantastic green tailfeathers, which snake behind it through the air as it flies, quetzal numbers have been significantly reduced and its current status is severely endangered. In Chiapas it is protected in the El Triunfo Biosphere Reserve, and in Guatemala in the Biotopo de Quetzal in Baja Verapaz (see p.437).

As the top predators in many places, **raptors** are often indicative of the overall health of a particular ecosystem. In the wetlands and on the coast **ospreys** are very common, and you'll often see them swooping on a fish and maybe even feeding their chicks. **Snail kites** are frequently seen on tree stumps along slow-moving rivers and, as its name implies, the **roadside hawk** is often seen sitting on fence posts along rural roads. The Mountain Pine Ridge of Belize is the habitat of the rare **orange-breasted falcon**; its very similar cousin, the **bat falcon**, is more widespread. The largest raptors, such as the **harpy eagle**, the **solitary eagle**, the **black and white hawk eagle** and the **ornate hawk eagle**, are rarely seen, but with perseverance and luck they may be spotted in remote protected forests. In the trees and on the ground, amongst the dense vegetation, it is also possible to see the larger game birds, such as **curassow**, **crested guan**, **chachalaca** and the splendidly coloured **ocellated turkey** – rare in most places but common at Tikal.

The abundant **freshwater wetlands**, rivers and **coastal lagoons** provide both feeding and breeding grounds for a huge variety of aquatic birds and are wonderful places for bird-watching; you're likely to see more species in and around these habitats than anywhere else. There are several species of kingfisher: the **belted kingfisher**, the region's largest, is one of the most common, as is the smallest, the **pygmy kingfisher**. Members of the heron family include **tri-coloured herons**, **boat-billed herons**, **great egret**, **white ibis**, **roseate spoonbill**, and in some areas **wood storks** and **jabiru storks** – the last is the largest flying bird in the Americas. Other wetland birds include the **sungrebe**, **spotted rail**, **ruddy crake**, **northern jacana**, often seen stepping delicately on lily pads, and the **anhinga** – a cormorant-like bird which captures fish by spearing them with its dagger-like bill.

The northern edge of the Yucatán Peninsula is famous for its fabulous collection of **migrating birds**, on their way to or from the eastern seaboard of North America, and its most famous residents are the large flocks of **greater flamingo**. Offshore, **Cozumel**, Mexico's largest island, provides some rewarding opportunities to sight seabirds such as **royal** and **Caspian terns**, **black skimmer** and **Mexican sheartails**. Inland, the sparse woodland provides shelter for many typical endemics, such as the **Caribbean dove**, **lesser nighthawk**, **Yucatán vireo**, **Cozumel vireo**, **bananaquit** and a variety of **tanagers**. **Half Moon Caye**, right out on the eastern edge of Lighthouse Reef, Belize's outermost atoll, is a wildlife reserve designed to protect a breeding colony of four thousand **red-footed boobies**. Here you'll also see **frigate birds**, **brown pelicans**, **mangrove warblers** and **white-crowned pigeons**.

## MAMMALS

Although mammals are widespread, they are almost always elusive, and your best chance of seeing them is at the bigger reserves and archeological sites, where they may have lost some of their fear of humans. At many forest sites you'll almost certainly see **howler** or **spider monkeys**, and at Bermudian Landing in the lower Belize River valley (see p.215), you're almost guaranteed close-up views of troops of black howler monkeys – and you'll certainly hear the famous deep-throated roar of the males.

The largest land animal in the region is **Baird's tapir**, weighing up to 300kg, and usually found near water. Tapirs are endangered throughout most of their range but are not rare in Belize – though you're not likely to see one without a guide. Two species of peccary (New World wild pigs), the **collared** and the **white-lipped**, wander the forest floors in large groups, seeking out roots and palm nuts. The smaller herbivores include the **paca**, a rodent about the size of a piglet, which is hunted everywhere for food. It goes under several other names – tepescuintle, agouti and, in Belize, gibnut. You'll often see **coati**, inquisitive and intelligent members of the raccoon family, foraging in the leaf litter around the ruins with their long snouts, usually in family groups. Coatis and small **grey foxes** are frequently seen at Tikal, and in many places you can see **opossums** or **armadillos**.

Five species of wild cats are found in the region, though most are now rare outside the protected areas. **Jaguars** formerly ranged widely over the whole region, but the densest population is found in the lower elevation forests in the central area. **Pumas** usually keep to remote highland and lowland forests; less rare but still uncommon are the much smaller **ocelot** and the **margay**, which is about the size

of a large domestic cat. The **jaguarundi** is the smallest and commonest of the wild cats, and you might spot one on a trail as it hunts during the day.

The coastal zone is home to the **West Indian manatee**, which can reach 4m in length and weigh up to 450kg. These placid and shy creatures move between the freshwater lagoons and the open sea. They were once hunted for their meat but are now protected and the places where they congregate have become tourist attractions. Belize has the largest manatee population in the Caribbean, estimated at between three hundred and seven hundred individuals. Dolphins are frequently seen just offshore, mostly the **Atlantic bottle-nosed dolphin**, though further out large schools of the smaller **spotted dolphin** are sometimes found.

## REPTILES AND AMPHIBIANS

Reptiles might not be high on anyone's list of reasons to visit the Maya World, but they are plentiful and some are spectacular, even beautiful. Take a trip along almost any river and you'll see **green iguanas**; their very similar cousin the **spiny-tailed iguana** is very common at archeological sites in Yucatán. Even the small ones look like miniature dinosaurs and the big ones appear very fearsome, but they're all vegetarians. Other **lizards** are very common and you'll often see **geckos** lurking on a wall or ceiling hunting flies, or gaze in astonishment as a **basilisk** dashes upright across a creek or lagoon; hence its name in Belize – the "Jesus Christ lizard". Drift quietly along a river and you'll see **mud turtles** or **Central American river turtles** sunning themselves on logs.

Along the lower courses of rivers draining to the Gulf coast and the Caribbean are **Morelet's crocodiles**, which are common in almost any body of water, and not dangerous to humans unless they are very large – at least 3m long – but heed the warnings of locals if they advise against swimming in a particular lagoon. Previously hunted almost to extinction, they have made a remarkable comeback since being protected, and are now frequently spotted in Belize, Petén and Tabasco. The **caiman** is a smaller cousin, found in lagoons on the Pacific coast. The largest and rarest of the crocodilians is the **American salt-water crocodile**, found in places along the Yucatán coast, but probably most numerous on Turneffe Atoll in Belize.

Although there are at least 65 species of **snake** in the region, only a few are venomous and you're actually unlikely to see any snakes at all. One of the commonest is the **boa constrictor**, which is also the largest, growing up to 4m, though it poses no threat to humans. Others you might see are **coral snakes** (which are venomous) and **false coral snakes** (which are not); in theory they're easily distinguished by noting the arrangement of adjacent colours in the stripes, but it's best to admire all snakes from a distance unless you're an expert.

At night in the forest you'll hear the characteristic chorus of frog mating calls and you'll frequently find the **red-eyed tree frog** – a beautiful pale green creature about the size of the top joint of your thumb – in your shower in any rustic cabin. Less appealing perhaps are the giant **marine toads**, the largest toad in the Americas, weighing in at up to 1kg and growing to over 20cm. Like most frogs and toads it has toxic glands and the toxin of the marine toad has hallucinogenic properties – a property the ancient Maya exploited in their ceremonies by licking these glands and interpreting the resultant visions.

Three species of **marine turtle**, the **loggerhead**, the **green** and the **hawksbill**, inhabit the Caribbean Barrier Reef, nesting on isolated beaches, particularly on the atolls, but they are seen infrequently as they are still hunted for food. Recent changes in legislation and international agreements have provided them with greater protection, however, and **volunteers** are needed to patrol nesting beaches; see "Voluntary Work" on p.49 and "Conservation Organizations" on p.572 for details.

## FISH

The Caribbean Barrier Reef is home to an incredible range of fish, including **angel-** and **parrotfish**, several species of **stingrays** and **sharks** (the most common are the relatively harmless nurse shark), **conger** and **moray eels**, **spotted goatfish**, and small striped **sergeant-major**. The sea and islands are also home to **grouper**, **barracuda**, **marlin** and the magnificent **sailfish**. **Whale sharks**, the largest fish in the world, gather in large numbers off southern Belize and the Bay Islands to gorge on **snapper** and **grouper** eggs. The reef has been harvested for millennia, catching manatees and turtles as well as fish, but these days the **spiny lobster** and **queen conch** are the main catch, most of which are exported to the US. In the last two decades the fishing industry has been booming and the numbers of both of these have now gone into decline.

## INSECTS

Finally, one thing you'll realize pretty soon in the region is that you're never far from an **insect** of some sort. Mostly you'll be trying to avoid them or even destroy them, particularly the common (though by no means ever-present) **mosquitoes** and **sandflies**. Some of the most beautiful insects, however, are the **butterflies**, which you'll frequently see feeding in clouds at the edges of puddles on trails. The caterpillars, too, are fascinating – and sometimes enormous. The largest and most spectacular are the members of the morpho family, of which the **blue morpho**, found in lowland forests, is a gorgeous electric blue. There are many more you can see on a visit to one of a growing number of **butterfly exhibits** in the region, particularly in Belize.

**Ants** are the most numerous insects on the planet; something you can well believe on any walk in the forest here. The most impressive are perhaps **army ants**, with the whole colony ranging through the forest in a narrow column, voraciously hunting for insects. Don't be misled by the horror movies – they can't overpower you and rip the flesh from your bones – though they will give you a nasty bite if you get too close. People in rural areas welcome a visit as the ants will clear pests from their houses. **Leafcutter ants** have regular trails through the forest along which they carry sections of leaves often much larger than their bodies – the source of their alternative name, "parasol ants". The leaves are not food for the ants, but provide a growing medium for a unique type of **fungus** which the ants do eat. Evolution has linked ant and fungus, and neither can now survive without the other. **Spiders** (not strictly insects but arachnids) are also very common: take a walk at night with a flashlight anywhere in the countryside and you'll see the beam reflected back by the eyes of dozens of **wolf spiders**. **Tarantulas**, too, are found everywhere – and they really are as big as your hand. The sharp fangs look dangerous but tarantulas won't bite unless they're severely provoked.

# CONSERVATION AND ECOTOURISM

Today the astonishing natural and cultural diversity of the Maya world is facing an unprecedented and undeniable crisis. Pressure from local companies and foreign multinationals to exploit its natural resources, combined with rapid population growth, both causes and accelerates degradation of the environment. The guilty parties are not just those logging the tropical forests, extracting oil or clearing the land for agriculture: one of the largest single problems now affecting many areas of natural beauty is the expansion of the tourist industry. Beginning with the planning of Cancún in the late 1960s, and eagerly and speedily emulated in forms large and small throughout the region, tourism was originally envisaged as a relatively easy source of foreign exchange and an engine to power growth in an undeveloped area – virtually no consideration was given at the outset to the environmental consequences of this policy.

Economically, at least as far as GDP's bottom line goes, tourism has been phenomenally successful. It's the largest civil industry in the world and the largest single source of foreign exchange over most of the area covered by this book. Most people, in the tourist industry and elsewhere, are more concerned with meeting immediate financial needs than with environmental issues. Tourists, however, are high consumers of clean water, fuel and disposable products – items often not available to or affordable by local people. Building hotels in coastal areas destroys mangroves, divers and snorkellers trample coral reefs and demand seafood dinners, and speeding boats disturb feeding manatees and flamingoes. Few places in the region have effective waste treatment, and most sewage goes either directly into the sea or ground water, or via highly inefficient septic tanks; solid wastes are dumped in festering open landfills.

The rise of foreign tourism to the Maya region has coincided with a general heightening of concern for the environment, most evident among the educated middle classes of the developed world – the very people who have recently acquired the means and inclination to travel to tropical destinations. At the same time alarming evidence of rainforest destruction raises the demand that something be done to save the forests. This desire for preservation of "nature" as a pristine wilderness is seen by some as a new form of imperialism, where "solutions" to new problems are proposed and imposed by Northern environmentalists, without regard to the needs of often impoverished local people.

More recently though, emphasis has focused on finding an acceptable balance between conservation and development. And, since tourism now plays an ever-increasing role in the region's economy, it's coupled to this Holy Grail of "sustainable development" in the thoroughly postmodern concept of "**ecotourism**" – difficult to define and even more difficult to demonstrate – but eagerly sought as a seal of approval and often appropriated indiscriminately.

## CONSERVATION STRATEGIES

Over the past few decades all the governments of the region have begun to address environmental problems. Conservation and **environmental legislation** has been enacted, ministries responsible for its implementation have been created, and an often bewildering array of protected areas have been declared. In all too many cases, though, these governmental initiatives are poorly funded and many of the parks and reserves exist only on paper. As the number of relatively natural areas declines, however, there is an increasing level of effectiveness by the organizations responsible for the management of protected areas. And, since government budget allocations are frequently inadequate to fully meet the needs of conservation (and it's hard to see how they ever could be in developing countries), funds and expertise are increasingly available from aid budgets from the developed countries and from local and international **non-governmental organizations (NGOs)**; some of the most prominent are listed on the box on p.572.

Unfortunately, there is no scope here to describe and evaluate all the differing designations of protected areas which exist throughout the Maya region. Each nation has its own definitions and the level of protection afforded by

## CONSERVATION ORGANIZATIONS ACTIVE IN THE MAYA WORLD

The organizations below are some of the largest conservation NGOs in the world, undertaking a vast range of conservation tasks, including planning and management at the highest levels. All also support training and ecotourism projects in the areas where they work and they also may operate **volunteer programmes** in conjunction with partner NGOs in the region. They publish numerous books and papers and their websites will provide a huge amount of information.

### INTERNATIONAL ORGANIZATIONS

**Conservation International** (*www.conservation.org*). A very large organization, with the largest conservation presence in the Maya world, working primarily in the Montes Azules, El Triunfo and Maya biosphere reserves.

**The Nature Conservancy** (*http://nature.org*). Another large conservation NGO working throughout the region, including projects to establish community-based tourism in southern Belize, Petén and Chiapas.

**Wildlife Conservation Society** (*www.wcs.org*). Formerly the New York Zoological Society, WCS is currently involved in efforts to establish the Mesoamerican Biological Corridor; it's also active in many other terrestrial and marine conservation projects throughout Central America.

**The Worldwide Fund for Nature** (*www.panda.org*). Funds projects to support local conservation NGOs throughout the region, including at Calakmul in Mexico, Gladden Spit in Belize and around Cobán in Guatemala.

### IN BELIZE

**The Belize Audubon Society** (*www.belizeaudubon.org*). The pre-eminent conservation organization in Belize, with responsibility for managing many of the country's reserves. Also publishes books, guides and fact sheets on the reserves and provides useful information for travellers on visiting them.

**The Belize Zoo and Tropical Education Center** (see p.252, *www.belizezoo.org*). A well-deserved reputation for native species conservation and education. The Belize Zoo and the ZOOMAT in Tuxtla, Chiapas (see p.166), are the best zoos in the Maya World and a visit to either is highly recommended.

**Green Reef** (*www.ambergriscaye.com*). Dedicated to the promotion of sustainable use and conservation of Belize's coastal resources, particularly on Ambergris Caye; also runs educational programmes and can accept volunteers.

**The Siwa-Ban Foundation** (see p.244, *sbf@btl.net*). Helped establish the Caye Caulker Forest and Marine Reserve (see p.240); accepts self-funded volunteers to work on educational projects and biological surveys.

**The Toledo Institute for Environment and Develpoment (TIDE)** (*www.belizeecotours.org*). Based in Punta Gorda in the far south of Belize, TIDE works to promote alternative sources of income for local people, including training nature guides. Also co-manages Paynes Creek national park and Port Honduras marine reserve.

**The Wildlife Care Center of Belize** (*wildlifecarecenter@yahoo.com*). Runs a rehabilitation centre for confiscated and rescued native wildlife. Also has training opportunities for self-funded students and volunteers who'll need to commit for at least a month.

### IN MEXICO

**Amigos de Si'an Ka'an** (*www.cancun.com/siankaan/*). A leading non-profit organization running superb guided tours into the Si'an Ka'an Biosphere Reserve (see p.128). Revenues are used

national park status, for example, will often vary as much within a country as between countries. Generally though, major archeological sites will be located within a national park or an archeological reserve, and in some cases these parks may also be a part of a much larger protected area, such as a biosphere reserve (see box, p.575).

**Mexico** boasts more than 125,000 square kilometres of protected area, the vast majority of which are managed under the auspices of the Ministry of Environment and Natural Resouces, SEMARNAT, whose website *www.semarnat.gob.mx* has links covering all areas within its jurisdiction. Many of Mexico's largest and most biodiverse reserves are in the Maya region but overall only fifteen percent of the country's protected areas are federally owned; many designated reserves are on lands owned by communities or municipalities.

Recent additions to **Belize's** already impressive network of reserves mean that over forty for conservation projects and local education programmes, stressing the importance of sustainable use of resources.

**Pronatura** (*www.pronatura.org.mx*). Another well-organized group dedicated to the conservation of Mexico's protected areas, with branches in Yucatán, Chiapas and Campeche. Currently involved with projects in Río Lagartos, Celestún and the Calakmul Biosphere Reserve and is actively involved in environmental management, community development, research and environmental education.

## IN GUATEMALA

**Alianza Verde** (Green Alliance, *www.greendeal .org*). Based in CINCAP, Flores (see p.451), and supported by Conservation International, this is a consortium of ecotourism operators and conservation organizations, working closely with Guatemala's National Protected Areas Commission (CONAP) and ProPetén (see below), focusing primarily on sustainable development in the Maya Biosphere Reserve. It is developing "Green Deal", a code of practice and certification for ecotourism businesses.

**Centre for Conservation Studies (CECON)**. A department of Guatemala's University of San Carlos, with head offices at the Botanical Garden in Guatemala City (see p.334). CECON manages and conducts scientific research in all seven of the nations' *biotopos*. These are often the best-protected areas within reserves, such as El Zotz near Tikal, Monterrico on the Pacific coast and the Biotopo del Quetzal in Baja Verapaz. Others are in very remote areas and there's usually some basic accommodation for visitors.

**Defensores de la Naturaleza** (*www.defensores .org*). Excellent group successfully combining conservation with sustainable tourism in the Biotopo Sierra de las Minas and the Bocas de Polochic Wildlife Reserve (see p.431); currently beginning a new project in the vast Sierra de Lacandón national park in western Petén, which contains the greatest biodiversity in Guatemala.

**Fundary** (*www.guate.net/fundarymanabique*). Working with communities in the Punta Manabique Reserve (see. p.424) to establish sustainable tourism in this *biotopo* on Guatemala's Caribbean coast. Volunteers (preferably with a background in biology or ecotourism) are needed to patrol marine turtle nesting beaches, undertake manatee and dolphin observation and work in the iguana and parrot reserves.

**Proyecto Eco-Quetzal**, 2a C 14–36, Zona 1, Cobán, (☎952-1047, *bidaspeq@guate.net*). Long-established NGO, with a successful record in protecting the forests around Cobán by offering economic alternatives to indigenous people, including excellent ecotourism projects in remote areas led by Q'eqchi' Maya guides.

**ProPetén** (see p.451). Funded largely by Conservation International (above), this is the largest NGO in Petén, working on numerous conservation and resource management projects in the Maya Biosphere Reserve.

## IN EL SALVADOR

**SalvaNatura** (see p.527). An NGO working to safeguard the few remaining areas of natural beauty in El Salvador, including Bosque Imposible (see p.526), the largest protected area in the country. The group recently launched an environmental education and community development programme.

## IN HONDURAS

**Bay Islands Conservation Association (BICA)** (see p.513, ☎445-1424, in US 1- 800/227-3483). A well-organized environmental group based on Roatán, involved with establishing and managing marine parks in the Bay Islands.

percent of its territory is under some form of legal protection, gaining the country international recognition as one of the most conservation-aware nations of the Americas. Belize also leads the way in developing **co-management agreements** between the government departments responsible for the nation's conservation strategy and well-organized local NGOs to draw up and implement management plans for several reserves. Belize is currently the only country in the region which levies a completely transparent **conservation fee** (currently US$3.75) on all visitors. Known as the Protected Areas Conservation Trust (PACT, *www.pactbelize.org*), the revenue generated is divided among the government departments and NGOs responsible for conservation and protected area management.

**Guatemala's** most important piece of conservation legislation, the **Protected Areas Law**, was enacted in 1989, in the wake of international reaction to satellite pictures of the extensive deforestation in Mexico, adjacent to the Petén rainforest. The Maya Biosphere Reserve, encompassing 16,000 square kilometres of northern Petén, was established as a direct result of this law, and forms the core element of what conservationists call "**The Maya Forest**" – the largest remaining tract of forest in Mesoamerica. This is a contiguous expanse of protected areas, stretching from the Montes Azules and Calakmul biosphere reserves in Mexico, across the whole of Petén, to the system of forest reserves in Belize reaching to the Caribbean coast.

**Honduras** suffers from rapid deforestation and soil erosion and the first environmental law was passed only in 1993. In recent years environmental groups have formed to jointly administer some of the country's protected areas and parks and to tackle issues from both a local and a national perspective. There are now over a hundred biological reserves and protected areas, though the more critical environmentalists have described these as nothing more than "paper parks" and claim that the government has not shown the political will nor given the financial backing to curb the destruction of the forest by multinational timber companies.

Smallest of the five Maya World nations, **El Salvador** has the highest population density and the most degraded environment in Central America. Intensive cultivation of the land for cash crops, urban pressures and civil war have been responsible for the depletion of much of the country's original forest. The country also suffers from serious water pollution and soil erosion. Its first serious environmental legislation, **the Law of the Environment**, was only passed in 1998, yet El Salvador's fledgling environmental movement regards it as progressive and ambitious, and even the business community has given it a guarded welcome.

Each country has either proposals for or has implemented a **National System of Protected Areas** – the actual name may vary slightly – with the aim of conserving viable examples of all ecosystems within their boundaries. Progress has been most noticeable on a co-operative level, with most countries signatories to several **international conservation agreements**, including the **Ramsar Convention**, to protect wetlands of international importance, the **Convention on Biodiversity and the Protection of Natural Areas**, and the **Convention on International Trade in Endangered Species (CITES)**. Belize has by far the largest area of marine reserves, and all countries except El Salvador (with no Caribbean coast) have signed the **Mesoamerican Coral Reef System Initiative** (the Tulum Declaration), to promote conservation of the Caribbean Barrier Reef they share. Eventually it is hoped that this will lead to a continuous network of marine reserves from Yucatán to Honduras, and many of Belize's marine reserves have also been declared **World Heritage Sites**.

By 1992, when the region's civil and guerrilla wars were all but over, all the Central American nations established the **Central American Commission for Environment and Development (CCAD)**, with the aim of providing a regional framework to promote and sustain co-operation between the emerging democratic governments. An overriding priority is to encourage regional agreements on biodiversity and sustainable development, an aspiration demonstrated in the recent launch of the **Mesoamerican Biological Corridor**. This is an ambitious proposal to establish a connected system of protected areas stretching from central Mexico to Panama – linked by the **Mesoamerican Trail**, a hiking, cycling and kayaking route mainly following the Caribbean coast. For updates on these projects visit *www.biomeso.org* and *www.mesosenderos.org*.

## ECOTOURISM

Nature tourism, or **ecotourism**, now represents the fastest growing sector of the industry, and the tourist industries of the Maya World have embraced the concept – or at least the term – enthusiastically. The rationale behind ecotourism is that revenue from visitors to places of conservation or cultural interest can be successfully channelled into protecting the natural resources of the sites they come to visit. Ideally, it is community-based tourism, benefiting local people by providing them with greater economic incentives in safeguarding their environment than in damaging it. It should also minimize the harmful effects of tourism on the natural environment, and better still, promote conservation.

A workable, universally recognized **definition** is difficult to pin down, and there is a fundamental contradiction in encouraging ever greater numbers of tourists to visit a particular site while

## BIOSPHERE RESERVES

**Biosphere reserves** are one example of protected area status worth exploring, as the designation covers many of the largest protected areas in the region, including the **Calakmul**, **Montes Azules** and **Sian Ka'an** biosphere reserves in Mexico, and the **Maya Biosphere Reserve** in Guatemala. Belize has no areas designated as biosphere reserves but the **Rio Bravo Conservation Area** is managed under the same principles. Biosphere reserves should have an area of at least 100 square kilometres, and contain at least one ecosystem not significantly altered by human activity; new communities are not permitted to be established within their boundaries. They generally also contain endemic species (found nowhere else) or species threatened or in danger of extinction.

According to UNESCO, where the concept originated in 1968, the aim of biosphere reserves is to provide "the link between conservation of biodiversity and the development needs of local communities". Ideally, they are divided into three zones, each with different ecological functions, potential uses and management structures: an outer **buffer** (or transition) **zone**, where the emphasis is on sustainable rural development aimed at relieving pressure on the inner zones; beyond this is a **multiple use zone**, where sustainable extraction of renewable resources takes place, and a strictly protected **core zone**, designated for conservation and scientific research, with no extractive use permitted. As ecotourism may meet some of the economic needs of local communities, there are some (admittedly too few) viable examples of the theory being put into practice in all such reserves mentioned in the guide.

And, provided management plans are well designed and properly implemented, their core zones may meet real conservation objectives.

Huge sums of foreign aid, mainly from the USA but also from Europe and Japan, have flooded into a multitude of projects in the biosphere reserves. The aid money is designed to supplement government conservation budgets and in some cases it forms by far the largest component. Funds are usually funnelled into local NGOs through the giant international NGOs, with very mixed results. Although there have been some successes, such as training guides and providing basic tourist infrastructure in **Carmelita** (for El Mirador) and at **Lacanhá**, (near Bonampak), many projects, such as a guides' co-operative at Uaxactún, collapsed when the aid funding ran out. Often the sheer number of NGOs in the same place, each claiming "jurisdiction" over a particular area, results in complex duplication of efforts and resources. Sustainable development has become a multinational industry, often of more benefit to the conservation professionals than to the communities living in the biosphere reserves. There's little doubt, however, that without this level of international pressure and funding many biosphere reserves would be degraded even more rapidly than they are at present – and the Maya Biosphere Reserve would never have been created in the first place. Ecotourism initiatives in and around the biospheres and other reserves may well offer the best chances of combining development and conservation in the region. Lessons have been learned from past mistakes and most governments and NGOs are working towards an integrated system of conservation management.

expecting (or hoping) that this will also ensure its protection. Until a common definition is arrived at, and guidelines set out for ecotourism objectives, anyone regarding him/herself as an ecotourist will have to judge whether a project is using market interest in all things "green" to make a quick profit or is genuinely involved in conservation. However, an increasing number of people desire – demand even – that their visit minimizes environmental damage, making a deliberate choice to take "low-impact" tours which also promote cultural exchange.

Whatever its benefits, ecotourism is not a panacea for all the deep-rooted environmental and social problems that mass tourism has

created over the years. Previously untouched areas with delicately balanced physical and cultural environments are being "discovered" and sometimes overwhelmed by visitors. All tourism comes at a price in terms of environmental degradation, and no matter how aware we may be, the sheer presence of visitors can have a damaging effect on the natural environment and local culture. Perhaps the biggest problem is the misuse of the term itself. As a relatively new destination for international tourism, the Maya World suffers from the hijacking of the "eco" prefix – to the extent that hotel chains are describing new resorts as "ecological" without defining what this

## SETTING ECOTOURISM STANDARDS IN THE MAYA WORLD

Although there are no truly national or international bodies which set universally recognized standards for certifying ecotourism businesses, there are some organizations and associations worth mentioning. Planeta (*www.planeta.com*), superbly designed, with excellent and relevant links, founded by prolific author and journalist Ron Mader, is by far the best resource for information and analysis on all aspects of environmental and ecotourism issues in Mexico and Central America. On the site (compiled from contributors) is a condensed summary of criteria that must be met to satisfy most definitions of ecotourism:

    it includes meaningful community participation;

    it provides for conservation measures;

    it is profitable and can sustain itself.

### Mexico

Asociación Méxicana de Turismo de Aventura y Ecoturismo (Amtave, *www.amtave.com*). Amtave is a group of about fifty travel providers with various interpretations of ecotourism; several operate in the Maya area of Mexico.

### Belize

The Belize Ecotourism Association (BETA, *www.belizenet.com/beta*). A small but growing band of hotels and other tourism businesses attempting to set environmental and ecotourism standards for the industry. The Toledo Ecotourism Association in Punta Gorda (see p.308) is a group comprising mainly Maya communities encouraging good practice in ecotourism in the far south of Belize.

### Guatemala

Asociación Ecoturismo Guatemala (*www.ecoturismoguatemala.org*). Works with various government institutions and the private sector in policy planning to develop ecotourism projects, including management, marketing and guide training, and in sourcing funding and low-interest loans for small tourism businesses. Members agree to a detailed Code of Ethics (likely to be widely adopted) which, if properly implemented, will advance the objectives and status of ecotourism in the country.

means. Luxury cabaña complexes are advertised as "resembling a Maya village" – though guests could question how many authentic Maya villages contain golf courses, marinas and swimming pools. Many companies have taken advantage of this new niche in the market to sell more or less the same old tourism product, repackaged under the "eco" label – a practice that some environmentalists have termed **eco-exploitation**.

## THE FUTURE

Although conservation measures are being actively addressed as regional integration moves forward on all fronts, demands for development are increasing. The recently announced Plan Puebla – following hard on the heels of the launch of the Mesoamerican Biological Corridor (see above) – is a far-reaching project to "modernize" the economy of the whole area from southern Mexico to Panama. New roads, hydroelectric plants and industrial development are planned, bringing the benefits of globalization to a region on the periphery of North American prosperity. Petroleum extraction already damages protected areas in southern Chiapas and

northwestern Petén and plans are already advanced to develop oilfields in the northeastern area of the Maya Biosphere Reserve and in the Calakmul Biosphere Reserve in Mexico. One highly controversial aspect of this plan is a proposal to push a paved highway through the forest north from Tikal to connect with the road to Cancún, devastating several of the most valuable and remote protected areas in the region.

In order to counter such well-funded proposals environmentalists throughout the region are becoming increasingly better organized, and often participating in setting out national conservation policy. One of the most innovative and successful conservation management policies has been to enable people living in and around reserves to have a real say in how protected areas can benefit them. With support and training from more experienced NGOs, local groups draw up co-management plans in accordance with conservation objectives. They may have input into a reserve's budget allocation, set entry fees, license guides and provide accommodation for visitors. It's likely that declaring a reserve has deprived local people of a valuable food resource, by banning or placing restriction on hunting or fishing for example; if participation in co-management schemes can be seen to provide a reliable income those involved are more likely to be supportive in continuing protected area status.

Although concerned visitors can check if the hotel they stay in or tour company they use are members of an accredited ecotourism association, there's still the question of who verifies the principles of the association itself – who can certify the certifiers? As the tourist industry moves closer to setting out guidelines which clarify an acceptable definition of ecotourism, community-based tourism will play an important part in taking conservation and development in the Maya World into the twenty-first century.

# BOOKS

Until recently the Maya World has provoked limited literary attention, but the armed confrontations of the 1980s, the struggles for Maya rights in the 1990s and recent advances in Maya epigraphy and archeology have seen an upsurge in the number of publications. However, there are no books currently available that take a contemporaneous look at politics in the Maya World as a whole – books are divided between those covering Central America as a region or individual countries, though many of the travel-based accounts delve fairly deeply into the subject.

For the less mainstream, and especially for **contemporary Latin America**, there are a few useful specialist sources. **In the UK** the Latin America Bureau (LAB), 1 Amwell St, London EC1R 1UL (*www.lab.org.uk*), publishes books covering all aspects of the region's society, current affairs and politics. In London you can freely visit **Canning House Library** (see p.26 for details), which has the UK's largest publicly accessible collection of books and periodicals on Latin America, though you have to be a member to take books out and receive the twice-yearly Bulletin, a review of recently published books on Latin America. **In the US** the Inter-Hemispheric Resource Center (*www.irc-online.org*) produces a wide range of contemporary publications on US-Mexico relations and on Latin America in general.

Below, books covering the Maya World and Central America are listed first, followed by sections on each country. Publishers are given in the format UK/US; where only one publisher is listed, this covers both the UK and US, unless specified.

## TRAVEL AND IMPRESSIONS

**Fabío Bourbon** *The Lost Cities of the Maya: The Life and Art of Frederick Catherwood* (Swan Hill, UK). The only complete colour reproductions available in a recent book of Frederick Catherwood's amazing paintings of Maya cities lost in the jungle as he travelled around Yucatán and Central America 160 years ago with the adventurer and diplomat John Lloyd Stevens (see below). It was Catherwood's eye for detail and superb artistic skill as much as Stevens's writing which stimulated and sustained the tremendous public interest in the ancient Maya, though Catherwood's role had in many ways previously been neglected.

**Simon Calder** *The Panamericana* (Vacation Work). Prolific writer, broadcaster and veteran backpackper Calder travels the entire Carretera Panamericana – The Pan-American Highway – from the Texas border to Yaviza in Panamá. An enormously funny and candid guide to the route and places just off it, it's also packed with practical information and wry observation; the diagrams of border crossings are particularly useful.

**Peter Canby** *Heart of the Sky – Travels Among the Maya* (HarperCollins). The author treads a familiar path through the Maya World, encountering an interesting collection of ex-pats, Mayanists, priests, Guatemala City's idle rich and a female shaman. Though not as erudite as Ronald Wright's masterful account (see below), it's still an accessible and informative read.

**Anthony Daniels** *Sweet Waist of America* (Arrow/Trafalgar Square; o/p). A delight to read. Daniels takes a refreshingly even-handed approach to Guatemala and comes up with a fascinating cocktail of people and politics, discarding the stereotypes that litter most books on Central America.

**Peter Ford** *Tekkin a Waalk along the Miskito Coast* (Flamingo Press). Ford gives himself the task of walking along the Caribbean coast from Belize to Panamá in the mid-1980s. A nice tale, with snippets of information on Garífuna, Bay Islander and Miskito history, and contemporary development.

**Thomas Gage** *Travels in the New World* (University of Oklahoma Press). Unusual account of a Dominican friar's travels through Mexico and Central America between 1635 and 1637, including some fascinating insights into colonial life, as well as some great attacks on the greed and pomposity of the Catholic Church abroad.

**Aldous Huxley** *Beyond the Mexique Bay* (Flamingo, UK). Huxley's travels took him, in 1934, from Belize through Guatemala to Mexico; swept on by his fascination for history and religion, he sprouted bizarre theories on everything he saw. Some great descriptions of Maya sites and culture, with superb one-liners summing up people and places. Some editions are illustrated with some interesting photographs of the ruins, people and markets.

**Patrick Marnham** *So Far From God* (Penguin). A saddened and vaguely right-wing account of Marnham's travels through the Americas from the US to Nicaragua (missing out Belize), including a fair chunk in the Maya region. Dotted with amusing anecdotes and interesting observations, the book's descriptions are dominated by the civil wars in Guatemala and El Salvador.

**Nigel Pride** *A Butterfly Sings to Pacaya* (Constable; o/p). An account of the author's travels, accompanied by his wife and four-year-old son, south from the US border in a jeep, heading through Mexico, Belize and Guatemala. A large section of the book is set in Maya areas, and it is illustrated by the author's drawings of people and animals. Though the travels took place over 25 years ago, the pleasures and privations they experience rarely appear dated.

**John Lloyd Stephens** *Incidents of Travel in Central America, Chiapas, and Yucatán* (Dover/Prentice Hall). Stephens was a classic nineteenth-century traveller. Acting as American ambassador to Central America, he indulged his own enthusiasm for archeology; while the republics fought it out among themselves, he was wading through the jungle stumbling across ancient cities. His journals, written with superb Victorian pomposity punctuated with sudden waves of enthusiasm, make great reading. Some editions include fantastic illustrations by Catherwood of the ruins overgrown with tropical rainforest (see *The Lost Cities of the Maya*, above).

**Ronald Wright** *Time Among the Maya* (Grove, US). A vivid and sympathetic account of travels from Belize through Guatemala, Chiapas and Yucatán, meeting the Maya and exploring their obsession with time. The book's twin points of interest are the ancient Maya and the violence of the 1970s and 1980s. The author's knowledge is evident in the superb historical insight he imparts throughout the book, and it's still one of the very best travel books on the area.

## ANCIENT MAYA CIVILIZATION

**Michael Coe** *The Maya* (Thames & Hudson). Now in its sixth edition, this clear and comprehensive introduction to Maya archeology is certainly the best on offer. Coe has also written several more weighty, academic volumes. His *Breaking the Maya Code* (Penguin/Thames & Hudson), a very personal history of the decipherment of the glyphs, owes much to the fact that Coe was present at many of the most important meetings leading to the breakthrough. This book demonstrates that the glyphs did actually reproduce Maya speech. *The Art of the Maya Scribe* (Thames & Hudson), written with Justin Kerr, developer of "rollout" photography — a technique enabling the viewer to see the whole surface of a cylindrical vessel — is a wonderfully illustrated history of Maya writing which also takes the reader on a journey through the Maya universe and mythology via the astonishingly skillful calligraphy of the Maya artists themselves.

**T. Patrick Culbert** *Maya Civilization* (Smithsonian Press in US). Well-structured introduction to the subject written by a prominent Mayanist, which includes the latest theories on the collapse of the Classic civilization; colour illustrations and photographs throughout. *Classic Maya Political History* (Cambridge University Press), edited by the same author, is far more academic in tone and content.

**M.S. Edmonson** (translator) *The Book of Chilam Balam of Chumayel* (Agean, US, o/p). The *Chilam Balam* is a recollection of Maya history and myth, recorded by the Spanish after the Conquest. Although the style is not easy, it's one of the few insights into the Maya view of the world.

**William L. Fash** *Scribes, Warriors and Kings* (Thames & Hudson). The definitive guide to the ruins of Copán with the complete historical background, superb maps and lavishly adorned with drawings and photographs.

**Grant D. Jones** *The Conquest of the Last Maya Kingdom* (Stanford University Press). A massive academic tome that's also a fascinating history of the Itzá Maya and a gripping tale of how the Spanish entered and finally defeated the last independent Maya kingdom, at Tayasal (Nojpetén), site of present-day Flores, Guatemala.

**Simon Martin and Nikolai Grube** ,*Chronicle of the Maya Kings and Queens* (Thames & Hudson). The dynastic records of eleven major Maya kingdoms including Palenque, Tikal, Caracol and Copán are brought to life by two of the foremost experts in Maya hieroglyphic writing, frequently describing their own ground-breaking discoveries. By far the best recent book on the Maya, with the best maps of each site and superb photographs and drawings.

**Mary Ellen Miller** *The Art of Mesoamerica: From Olmec to Aztec* (Thames & Hudson). An excellent, wonderfully illustrated survey of the artisanship of the ancient cultures of Mexico, whose work reflects the sophistication of their civilizations. Miller is the acknowledged expert on Mayan and Mesoamerican art (especially the Bonampak murals) and her more recent *Maya Art and Architecture* (Thames & Hudson) provides fascinating and well-illustrated background reading on dozens of Maya sites.

**Mary Ellen Miller and Karl Taube** *The Gods and Symbols of Ancient Mexico and the Maya: An Illustrated Dictionary of Mesoamerican Religion* (Thames & Hudson). A superb modern reference tool for studying ancient Mesoamerica, written by two leading scholars. Taube's *Aztec and Maya Myths* (British Museum Press) is perfect as a short accessible introduction to the region's mythology.

**Jeremy A. Sabloff** *The Cities of Ancient Mexico* (Thames & Hudson). The best introduction to ancient Mexico currently available. In *The New Archaeology and the Ancient Maya* (Scientific American Library) Sabloff explains the "revolution" which has taken place in Maya archeology since the 1960s, overturning many firmly held beliefs and assumptions on the nature of Maya society, and stating how the study of archeology relates to current environmental problems.

**Linda Schele and David Freidel (et al)**. The authors, in the forefront of the "new archeology", have been personally responsible for decoding many of the glyphs. While the writing style, which frequently includes "recreations" of scenes inspired by their discoveries, is controversial, it has nevertheless inspired a devoted following. *A Forest of Kings: The Untold Story of the Ancient Maya* (Quill, US), in conjunction with *The Blood of Kings* by Linda Schele and Mary Miller, shows that, far from

being governed by peaceful astronomer-priests, the ancient Maya were ruled by hereditary kings, lived in populous, aggressive city-states, and engaged in a continuous entanglement of alliances and war. *The Maya Cosmos* (Quill, US) by Schele, Freidel and Joy Parker, is perhaps more difficult to read, dense with copious notes, but continues to examine Maya ritual and religion in a unique and far-reaching way. *The Code of Kings* (Scribner, US), written in collaboration with Peter Matthews and illustrated with Justin Kerr's famous "rollout" photography of Maya ceramics, examines in detail the significance of the monuments at selected Maya sites. Her last book – Linda Schele died in April 1998 – and a classic of epigraphic interpretation.

**Peter Schmidt, Mercedes de la Garza and Enrique Nalda** (eds) *Maya Civilization* (Thames & Hudson). Monumental collaborative effort, with sections written by many prominent Mayanists, lusciously presented with over 600 colour images of some breathtaking Maya art. The scholarly text is also impressive, with important contributions on the importance of Calakmul to the Classic Maya history and sea trade routes along the Yucatán coast.

**Robert J. Sharer**, *The Ancient Maya* (Stanford University). The classic, comprehensive account of Maya civilization, now in a completely revised and much more readable fifth edition, yet as authoritative as ever. Required reading for archeology students, it provides a fascinating reference for the non-expert. Also worth reading and even more accessible is his *Daily Life in Maya Civilization* (Greenwood, US).

**Michael Smith and Marilyn A. Masson** *The Ancient Civilizations of Mesoamerica* (Blackwell, UK). Authoritative and absorbing book which includes most of the latest findings and explores theoretical concepts with in-depth studies of selected sites. Ideal background reading for field school students.

**Barbara L. Stark and Philip J. Arnold** (eds) *The Myth of Quetzalcoatl* (John Hopkins University Press). This remarkable and highly readable academic book sifts through archeological evidence of the cult of Quetzalcoatl, the Plumed Serpent (Kukulkan to the Maya), from Mexico, Guatemala, El Salvador, and Nicaragua, showing how the myth diffused throughout Mesoamerica.

**Dennis Tedlock** (translator) *The Popol Vuh* (Scribner/Touchstone). The epic poem of the K'iche' Maya of Guatemala, written shortly after the Conquest and intended to preserve the tribe's knowledge of its history. It's an amazing swirl of ancient mythological characters and their wandering through the K'iche' highlands, tracing K'iche' ancestry back to the beginning. Though there are other versions, Tedlock's is the definitive publication.

**J. Eric S. Thompson** *The Rise and Fall of the Maya Civilization* (University of Oklahoma). A major authority on the ancient Maya during his lifetime, Thompson produced many academic studies, of which this is one of the more approachable. Although recent researchers have overturned many of Thompson's theories, his work provided the inspiration for the postwar surge of interest in the Maya and he remains a respected figure. Thompson also wrote *The Maya of Belize – Historical Chapters Since Columbus* (Cubola, Belize), an interesting study of the Maya there in the first two centuries of Spanish colonial rule. It's a little-researched area of Belizean history and casts some light on the groups that weren't immediately conquered by the Spanish.

## WILDLIFE AND THE ENVIRONMENT

**Les Betelsky** *Tropical Mexico* and *Belize and Northern Guatemala*; new titles in the *Ecotraveller's Wildlife Guide* series (Academic Press). Although other, specialist wildlife guides may cover their own subjects in more detail, these are the only reasonably comprehensive single-volume guides to the mammals, birds, reptiles, amphibians and marine life of the regions they cover. Helpfully, the illustration of each creature is given opposite its description, avoiding confusing page-flicking; worth bringing on a trip.

**Louise H. Emmons** *Neotropical Rainforest Mammals* (University of Chicago). Supported by François Feer's colour illustrations, this highly informative book is written by experts for non-scientists. Local and scientific names are given, along with plenty of interesting snippets. Emmons is also the principal author of *The Cockscomb Basin Wildlife Sanctuary* (Producciones de la Hamaca, Belize; Orang-Utan Press, US), a comprehensive guide to the history, flora and fauna of Belize's Jaguar Reserve.

**Steve Howell and Sophie Webb** *The Birds of Mexico and Northern Central America* (Oxford University Press). A tremendous work, the result of years of research, this is the definitive book on the region's birds. Essential for all serious birders.

**C. Kaplan** *Coral Reefs of the Caribbean and Florida* (Houghton Mifflin). Useful handbook on the abundant undersea wildlife of the Atlantic coast of the Maya world.

**John C. Kricher** *A Neotropical Companion* (Princeton University Press). Subtitled "An Introduction to the Animals, Plants and Ecosystems of the New World Tropics", this contains an amazing amount of valuable information for nature lovers. Researched mainly in Central America, so there's plenty that's directly relevant.

**Alan Rabinowitz** *Jaguar* (Arbor House, UK). Account of the author's experiences studying jaguars in Belize for the New York Zoological Society in the early 1980s. Rabinowitz was instrumental in the establishment of the Jaguar Reserve in 1984.

**Joel Simon** *Endangered Mexico* (Sierra Club). Eloquent and compelling study documenting the environmental crisis facing Mexico at the start of the twenty-first century. Accurate and very moving, it's essential reading for those wanting to know how and why the crisis exists – and why no one can offer solutions.

**David Rains Wallace** *The Monkey's Bridge* (Sierra Club). When the Panama Land Bridge formed between North and South America, three million years ago, plants and animals surged back and forth across it in an evolutionary intermingling that created one of the world's richest natural environments. This engaging account of Central America's role as an evolutionary link between the two continents cleverly interweaves natural history, human history, travel writing and personal reflection.

## OTHER GUIDEBOOKS

In **Mexico** the best and most complete series of guides is that published by Guías Panorama – they have small books on all the main archeological sites, as well as more general titles ranging from *Wild Flowers of Mexico* to *Pancho Villa – Truth and Legend*.

**Andrew Coe** *Archaeological Mexico* (Moon). Accurate and very informative cultural interpretation and detailed accounts of 52 sites throughout the country, with almost half the book devoted to the Maya region; written by the son of the great Mayanist Michael Coe. Worth carrying on a trip through the area.

**William Coe** *Tikal: A Handbook to the Ancient Maya Ruins*. Superbly detailed account of the site, usually available at the ruins. The detailed map of the main area is essential for in-depth exploration.

**Byron Foster** (ed) *Warlords and Maize Men – A Guide to the Maya Sites of Belize* (Cubola, Belize). An excellent handbook to fifteen of the most accessible sites in Belize, compiled by the Association for Belizean Archaeology and the Belize Department of Archaeology; a new edition is planned.

**Bruce Hunter** *A Guide to Ancient Maya Ruins* (University of Oklahoma Press). Useful accompaniment to all the major sites in the Maya World, though many of the more obscure ruins are omitted.

**Freya Rauscher** *Cruising Guide to Belize & Mexico's Caribbean Coast* (Wescott Cove Publishing, US). Although aimed primarily at yachting visitors, this very detailed book offers fascinating insights into the entire Barrier Reef as far south as Guatemala, with great details on the cayes of Belize. You'll find it in some island resorts and on larger dive boats.

**Joyce Kelly** Kelly's books in the *Archaeological Guide* series (all University of Oklahoma Press) are detailed and practical guides to dozens of sites, from the crowded to the remote. All have excellent photographs and accurate maps. The "star ratings" – based on a site's archeological importance, degree of restoration and accessibility – may affront purists, but they do a valuable opinion on how worthwhile a particular visit might be. *Mexico's Yucatán Peninsula* is an essential purchase for real exploration of the Mexico's Maya ruins and includes over 90 sites and eight museums. *Northern Central America* covers 38 Maya sites and 25 museums in Guatemala, Belize, Honduras and El Salvador, and is an indispensable companion for anyone travelling through these countries. Her latest title, *Central and Southern Mexico*, covers 70 sites and 60 museums, from La Quemada south of Zacatecas, to Izapa, almost on the Guatemalan border, and is the best yet.

**Richard Perry** *Maya Missions* and *More Maya Missions* (Espadaña Press, US). Specialist titles, ideal for travellers who want more information on ecclesiastical architecture than most guidebooks can provide; both are illustrated by the author's simple but beautiful drawings. The first title covers colonial Yucatán, the second deals with Chiapas; you can find them in tourist bookshops in the areas they cover.

## CENTRAL AMERICAN HISTORY AND POLITICS

**Sebastian Cayetano** *Garífuna History, Language & Culture of Belize, Central America & the Caribbean* (Angelus Press, Belize). A brief, simply written history of the Garífuna. Mainly aimed at children, it also mentions the great changes the Garífuna (or Garinagu) are experiencing as they adapt to modern life.

**Peter Dale-Scott and Jonathan Marshall** *Cocaine Politics: Drugs, Armies and the CIA in Central America* (University of California). Polemical but well-researched exposé of CIA involvement in cocaine trafficking and political oppression in Central America in the 1980s. Reveals the truth behind the Iran–Contra scandal and gives the lie to the rhetoric of the war on drugs.

**James Dunkerley** *Power in the Isthmus* and *The Pacification of Central America* (Norton/Verso). Detailed accounts of the region's politics (excluding Belize) that offer a good study of recent events, particularly the region's civil wars, albeit in academic style. Well researched with plenty of statistics and charts.

**Susan C. Stonch** (ed) *Endangered Peoples of Latin America* (Greenwood, US). For a book covering the whole continent there's a surprising amount of information on Mexico and Central America, with a disturbing analysis of why tourism and new environmental and conservation laws can exclude local people from their own land and resources. Chapters documenting how the Maya of Quintana Roo are overwhelmed by the explosive growth of tourism and the successful struggle of the English-speaking Bay Islanders to be recognized as an indigenous group in Honduras present just two of the contemporary problems facing the people of the region.

**William Weinberg** *War on the Land: Ecology and Politics in Central America* (Zed Books/ Humanities Press). The author tells a story of intertwining conflicts and causes between conservation (and to a small extent ecotourism), land rights and politics in the individual Central American countries in a volume that deftly straddles the gap between academic interest and the general reader.

**Ralph Lee Woodward Jr** *Central America: A Nation Divided* (Oxford University Press). More readable than Dunkerley (see above), this is probably the best book for a general summary of the Central American situation, despite its daft title.

## MEXICO

The sources below are all entertaining and/or important references: more standard general histories include Henry Bamford Parkes' *History of Mexico* (Houghton Mifflin); *Fire and Blood: a History of Mexico* by T.R. Fehrenbach (Replica); *The Course of Mexican History* by Michael Meyer, William Sherman and Susan Deeds(OUP); and *Mexico in Crisis* by Judith Hellman (Holmes & Meier).

### HISTORY, POLITICS AND SOCIETY

**Quetzil E. Casteñeda** *In the Museum of Maya Culture: Touring Chichén Itzá* (University of Minnesota). An anthropological study of contemporary Maya culture which, although heavily theoretical in places, examines the relationships between the Mexican government, the Maya of Yucatán and the tourists who come to visit the ruins of their ancestors and buy souvenirs from them in a concise, accessible style.

**Inga Clendinnen** *Ambivalent Conquests: Maya and Spaniard in Yucatán 1517 to 1570* (CUP). A product of meticulous research which documents the methods and consequences of the Spanish Conquest of the Yucatán. The ambivalence in the title reflects doubts about the effectiveness of the Conquest in subjugating the Maya, and the book provides insights into post-conquest rebellions: over three hundred years after the Conquest the Maya rose in revolt during the Caste Wars, and almost succeeded in driving out their white overlords, while in January 1994, Maya peasants in Chiapas stunned the world and severely embarrassed the Mexican government by briefly capturing and controlling cities in the southeastern area of the state.

**Don E. Dumond** *The Machete and the Cross* (University of Nebraska). Diligent research and analysis make this by far the best study of the

Caste Wars of Yucatán since Nelson Reed's classic book.

**Bernal Díaz** *The Conquest of New Spain*, translated by J.M. Cohen (Viking). This abridged version is the best available of Díaz's classic *Historia Verdadera de la Conquista de la Nueva España*. Díaz, having been on two earlier expeditions to Mexico, accompanied Cortés throughout his campaign of Conquest, and this magnificent eye-witness account still makes compulsive reading.

**Brian Hamnett** *A Concise History of Mexico* (CUP) Begins with a brief examination of contemporary issues and then jumps back to the time of the Olmecs. A combined chronological and thematic approach is used to analyse the social and political history of Mexico from then up to the 1990s. Being concise, some fairly large chunks of history are glossed over, but various key events and issues are explored in greater detail and this makes for a very good general introduction.

**Gary H.Gossen** *Telling Maya Tales* (Routledge). A sympathetic and inspirational compilation of the cosmology, creation myths, poetry and everyday life of the Tzotzíl Maya from San Juan Chamula, Chiapas, written by an anthropologist who's lived and studied there since the mid-1960s. Wonderful cultural insight without in any way demeaning or patronizing the people portrayed.

**Guiomar Rovira** *Women of Maize* (LAB). Rovira, a Mexican journalist, witnessed the Zapatista uprising in Chiapas on New Year's Day 1994. This book, which interweaves narrative, history and the personal recollections of numerous women involved in the rebellion, provides an extraordinary insight into the lives of indigenous people. The women interviewed reflect on how their previously traditional lifestyles were transformed when they joined up with the Zapatista National Liberation Army and gained access to education and other opportunities they'd never even dreamt of.

**John Ross** *Rebellion from the Roots* (Common Courage Press, US). A fascinating early account of the build-up to and first months of the 1994 Zapatista rebellion, and still the definitive book on the subject. Ross's reporting style provides a really detailed and informative background, showing the uprising was no surprise to the Mexican army. He's also the author of *Mexico in Focus* (LAB/Interlink), a short but authoritative guide to modern Mexican society, politics and culture – worth reading before a visit.

**Chloë Sayer** *The Arts and Crafts of Mexico* (Thames & Hudson/Chronicle). Sayer is the author of numerous books on Mexican arts, crafts and associated subjects (see below); all of them worth reading. *The Skeleton at the Feast* (University of Texas), written with Elizabeth Carmichael, is a wonderful, superbly illustrated insight into attitudes to death and the dead in Mexico.

## FICTION

**Tony Cartano** *After the Conquest* (Secker & Warburg, o/p). An extraordinary fictional account of a fictional author who believes he is B. Traven's son and sets out to discover the truth about his father (see below). A psychological thriller which is also full of Mexican history and politics.

**Carlos Fuentes** *The Death of Artemio Cruz* (Penguin/ Atlantic/Noonday), *The Old Gringo* (Noonday). Fuentes is by far the best-known Mexican writer outside Mexico, influenced by Mariano Azuela and Juan Rulfo, and an early exponent of "magical realism.". In *The Death of Artemio Cruz*, the hero, a rich and powerful man on his deathbed, looks back over his life and loves, from an idealist youth in the Revolution through disillusion to corruption and power; in many ways an indictment of modern Mexican society. More recently, *The Crystal Frontier* (Bloomsbury/Farrar, Strauss & Giroux) is a collection of stories examining the way personal contacts colour Mexicans' experiences of their unequal relationship with the US.

**Graham Greene** *The Power and the Glory* (Penguin). Inspired by his investigative travels, this story of a doomed whisky priest on the run from the authorities makes a great yarn. It was a wonderful movie too.

**Malcolm Lowry** *Under the Volcano* (Pan/NAL-Dutton). A classic since its publication, Lowry's account of the last day in the life of the British consul in Cuernavaca – passed in a mescal-induced haze – is totally brilliant. His *Dark as the Grave Wherein my Friend is Laid* is also based on his Mexican experiences.

**Juan Rulfo** *Pedro Páramo* (Serpent's Tail/Grove Atlantic). Widely regarded as the greatest Mexican novel of the twentieth century and a precursor of magic realism. The living

and spirit worlds mesh when, at the dying behest of his mother, the narrator visits the deserted village haunted by the memory of his brutal patriarch father, Pedro Páramo. Dark, depressing and initially confusing but ultimately very rewarding. Rulfo's short-story collection *The Burning Plain and Other Stories* (University of Texas), is rated by Gabriel García Marquez as the best in Latin America.

**B. Traven** Traven wrote a whole series of compelling novels set in Mexico. Among the best known are *Treasure of the Sierra Madre* (Prion/Hill & Wang) and *The Death Ship* (L Hill Books), but of more direct interest if you're travelling in Chiaps are such works as *The Bridge in the Jungle* and the six books in the Jungle series: *Government, The Carreta, March to the Monteria, Trozas, The Rebellion of the Hanged* and *General from the Jungle* (all Allison & Busby/I R Dee, some o/p). These latter all deal with the state of the peasantry and the growth of Revolutionary feeling in the last years of the Díaz dictatorship, and if at times they're overly polemical, as a whole they're enthralling.

## BELIZE

### HISTORY, POLITICS AND SOCIETY

**Rosita Arvigo with Nadia Epstein** *Sastun*. A rare glimpse into the life and work of a Maya *curandero*, the late Elijio Panti of San Antonio, Belize. Dr Arvigo has ensured the survival of many generations of accumulated healing knowledge, and this book is a testimony to both her perseverance in becoming accepted by Mr Panti and the cultural wisdom of the indigenous people. Arvigo has also written and co-authored several other books on traditional medicine in Belize, including *Rainforest Remedies*.

**The Maya Atlas** (North Atlantic Books, Berkley). As much a collection of personal accounts compiled by the contemporary Maya of southern Belize as it is a geography book, this is a fascinating co-production between university researchers and the Maya of Toledo. Trained by Berkely cartographers, teams of villagers surveyed their lands, completed a census and then wrote a history of each community. The regional maps accurately show the position of each village and drawings and photographs show scenes from everyday life. Available in Belize from the Toledo Maya Cultural Council, PO Box 104, Punta Gorda, Belize.

**Tom Barry and Dylan Vernon** *Inside Belize* (Resource Center in US). Excellent summary of the social economic and political affairs, published in 1995.

**Gerald S. Koop** *Pioneer Years in Belize* (Country Graphics, Belize). A history of the Mennonites in Belize, written in a style as stolid and practical as the lives of the pioneers themselves. A good read nonetheless.

**Ian Peedle** *Belize in Focus* (LAB, UK/Resource Center, US). A recent addition to this excellent series: an up-to-date, easily digested overview of Belizean society and politics. Worth taking along if you're there for more than a few days.

**Assad Shoman** *Thirteen Chapters of a History of Belize* (Angelus Press, Belize). A long overdue treatment of the country's history written by a Belizean who's not afraid to examine colonial myths with a detailed and rational analysis. Primarily a school textbook, but the style will not alienate non-student readers. Shoman, active in politics both before and since independence, also wrote *Party Politics in Belize*, a short but highly detailed account of the development of party politics in the country.

**Ann Sutherland**, *The Making of Belize: Globalization in the Margins* (Bergin and Garvey, US). A recent study of cultural and economic changes in Belize, based on the author's experiences as a visitor and her observations as an anthropologist. The result is an enjoyable mixture of academic research, anecdotal insights and strong, even controversial, opinion. Sutherland reserves her strongest criticism for conservationists, whom she castigates as "eco-colonialists [who] totally disregard the interests of the Belizean people".

**Colville Young**, *Creole Proverbs of Belize* (Cubola, Belize). A wonderful compilation of oral folk-wisdom from Belize, written by the present governor general, who's also a distinguished linguist. Each saying or proverb is written in Creole, translated into English, and then has its meaning explained. A primer for street life.

## FICTION, POETRY AND AUTOBIOGRAPHY

**Zee Edgell** *Beka Lamb* (Heinemann). A young girl's account of growing up in Belize in the 1950s, in which the problems of adolescence are described alongside those of the Belizean independence movement. The book also explores everyday life in the colony, describing the powerful structure of matriarchal society and the influence of the Catholic Church. *In Times Like These* (Heinemann) is a semi-autobiographical account of personal and political intrigue set in the months leading up to Belize's independence.

**Zoila Ellis** *On Heroes, Lizards and Passion* (Cubola, Belize). Seven short stories written by a Belizean woman with a deep understanding of her country's people and their culture.

**Felicia Hernandez** *Those Ridiculous Years* (Cubola, Belize). A short autobiographical book about growing up in Dangriga in the 1960s.

**Emory King** *Belize 1798* (Tropical Books, Belize). Rip-roaring historical novel peopled by the characters involved in the Battle of St George's Caye. King's enthusiasm for his country's history is supported by meticulous research in archives on both sides of the Atlantic. Wonderful holiday reading. His first book *Hey Dad, This is Belize*, a hilarious account of family life in Belize, became something of a minor classic and was followed up with *I Spent it all in Belize*, an anthology of witty, lightly satirical articles gently but effectively pricking the pomposity of officialdom.

**Carlos Ledson Miller** *Belize – A Novel* (Xlibris, US). Fast-paced historical saga of a Central American father and his two sons – one American and one Belizean – who struggle against a forbidding land, and often with each other. The story opens in 1961, on the eve of Hurricane Hattie, then transports the reader across forty years from the unrest of colonial British Honduras to the turbulence of present-day Belize.

**Shots From The Heart** (Cubola, Belize). Slim anthology of the work of three young Belizean poets: Yasser Musa, Kiren Shoman and Simone Waight. Evocative imagery and perceptive comment relate experiences of a changing society. Musa's *Belize City Poem* (published separately) is a sharply observed, at times vitriolic, commentary on the impact of the simultaneous arrival of independence and US-dominated television on Belizean society.

## GUATEMALA

### HISTORY, POLITICS AND SOCIETY

**Edward F Fisher and R McKenna Brown** (eds)*Maya Cultural Activism in Guatemala* (University of Texas Press). Effectual summary of the indigenous movement in Guatemala, with strong chapters on clothing and identity and the revival of interest in Maya language and hieroglyphic writing.

**Jim Handy** *Gift of the Devil* (South End Press in US). Excellent history of Guatemala, concise and readable with a sharp focus on the Maya population and the brief period of socialist government. Now a little dated, but if you're interested in the historical background behind the civil war then this is the book to read. By no means objective, it sets out to expose the development of oppression and to point the finger at those responsible.

**Rigoberta Menchú** *Rigoberta Menchú – An Indian Woman in Guatemala* and *Crossing Borders* (Verso/Norton). Momentous story of one of Latin America's most remarkable women, Nobel Peace Prize winner Rigoberta Menchú. The first volume is a horrific account of family life in the Maya highlands, recording how Menchú's family were targeted, terrorized and murdered by the military. The book also reveals much concerning K'iche' Maya cultural traditions and the enormous gulf between ladino and indigenous society in Guatemala. The second volume is more optimistic, documenting Menchú's life in exile in Mexico, her work at the United Nations fighting for indigenous people and her return to Guatemala. Though Menchú's courage and determination are undeniable, serious doubts have since arisen concerning the accuracy of her story recounted in the first book, best read with David Stoll's biography (see below).

**Víctor Perera** *Unfinished Conquest* (University of California Press). Superb, extremely readable account of the civil war tragedy, plus comprehensive attention to the political, social and economic inequalities affecting the author's native country. Immaculately researched, the book's strength comes from the extensive interviews with both ordinary and influential Guatemalans and incisive analysis of recent history. The best introduction to the subject.

**Jean-Marie Simon** *Eternal Spring – Eternal Tyranny* (Norton). Of all the books on human rights in Guatemala, this is the one that speaks with the utmost clarity. Combining the highest standards in photography with crisp text, there's no attempt to persuade you – the facts are allowed to speak for themselves, which they do with amazing strength. If you want to know what happened in Guatemala over the last twenty years or so there is no better book. Again, Simon clearly takes sides, aligning herself with the revolutionary left: there's no mention of any abuses committed by the guerrillas.

**David Stoll** *Rigoberta Menchú and the Story of All Poor Guatemalans* (Westview Press). Iconoclastic biography, based on painstaking research and testimony, that delivers a formidable broadside against considerable pieces of the Menchú story.

### FICTION

**Miguel Ángel Asturias** *Hombres de Maíz* (Macmillan). Guatemala's most famous author, Nobel Prize winner Asturias, is deeply indebted to Guatemalan history and culture in his work. "Men of Maize" is generally regarded as his masterpiece, classically Latin American in its magic realist style, and bound up in the complexity of indigenous culture. His other works include *El Señor Presidente*, a grotesque portrayal of social chaos and dictatorial rule, based on Asturias's own experience; *El Papa Verde*, which explores the murky world of the United Fruit Company; and *Weekend en Guatemala*, describing the downfall of the Arbenz government.

**Francisco Goldman** *The Long Night of White Chickens* (Faber and Faber). Drawing on the stylistic complexity of Latin American fiction, this novel tells the tale of a young Guatemalan orphan who flees to Boston, US, and works as a maid. When she finally returns home to Guatemala City she is murdered. It's a tremendously interesting and ambitious story, flavoured with all the bitterness and beauty of Guatemala's natural and political landscape. The novel inspired the film *Men With Guns*.

**Gaspar Pedro Gonzáles** *A Mayan Life* (Yax Te' Press, US). Absorbing story of the personal and cultural difficulties affecting a Q'anjob'al Maya from the Cuchumatanes mountains. The conflict between indigenous and ladino values becomes acutely evident as the central character seeks a higher education. Rich in ethnological detail and highly autobiographical, the book claims to be the first novel ever written by a Maya writer.

## HONDURAS

### HISTORY, POLITICS AND SOCIETY
**Donald Schulz and Deborah Sundloff Schulz** (Westview Press). Superbly readable,

exhaustive account of modern Honduran history, concentrating on US involvement in the 1980s, and the Contras.

**William V. Davidson** *Historical Geography of the Bay Islands, Honduras* (South University Press, US). A study of physical and cultural geographical development of the islands. Useful for pieces of interesting background information.

## FICTION

**Paul Theroux** *The Mosquito Coast* (Penguin). Well-known tale of the collapse of a man in the steaming heat of Mosquitia. Though entertaining, Theroux only touches upon a remote corner of Honduras and the novel does little to enlighten the reader about the country as a whole. The movie, with Harrison Ford and Helen Mirren, was filmed in Belize.

**Guillermo Yuscarán** is the pen name of expatriate William Lewis, a long-time resident of Honduras. His novels and short stories – including *Blue Pariah* and *Points of Light* –illustrating contemporary Honduran life can be bought (Spanish and English-language; Nuevo Sol, Tegucigalpa) in bookshops in Tegucigalpa, San Pedro Sula and Roatán.

## SPECIALIST GUIDES

**Sharon Collins** *Diving and Snorkeling Roatán and Honduras' Bay Islands* (Lonely Planet). Covers many of the main dive sites in Utila and Roatán, though the Guanajá content is a little sketchy.

## EL SALVADOR

## HISTORY, POLITICS AND SOCIETY

**Robert Armstrong and Janet Shenk** *El Salvador: The Face of Revolution*. Accessible history of the root causes and development of the civil war of the 1980s.

**Charles Clements** *Witness to War* (Bantam Press). Fascinating account of a year spent working in the guerrilla zone of Guazapa in the early 1980s by a volunteer US doctor. A vivid portrayal of how the civil war affected a spe-

cific area, which allows the reader a greater insight into what conditions were like across El Salvador.

**Larry Dowell and Mark Deinner** *El Salvador* (Norton). Evocative and compelling collection of photographs taken during 1986, sharply delineating the progress of the civil war and its impact.

**Kevin Murray and Tom Barry** *El Salvador –a Country Guide* (Resource Center). Concise study of contemporary political, economic and social affairs, with historical background, detailing the initiatives made in the years following the 1992 peace accords.

## FICTION AND POETRY

**Roque Dalton** *Taberna y Otras Lugares; Poemas Clandestinas and Pobrecito Poeta que era Yo.* Perhaps the most famous Salvadorean poet, Dalton was also a journalist and revolutionary, and in constant open conflict with successive governments. Born in 1935, he was imprisoned and exiled on various occasions, always returning to the land of his birth. He was a member of the People's Revolutionary Army (ERP) in the early 1970s, along with founder members of the FMLN. After differences of opinion led to his departing the movement he was assassinated on ERP orders in May 1975 near Guazapa; his death remains a landmark in Salvadorean literary history and still remains unsolved. *Taberna y Otras Lugares* and *Poemas Clandestinas* are both collections of poetry, while *Pobrecito Poeta que era Yo* is a novella.

**Mirrors of War** (Zed Books). Wide-ranging collection of modern poetry and prose by Salvadorean writers, focusing on the causes and impact of the civil war.

**Salarrué** *Eso y Más, Cuentos de Barro* and *La Espada y Otras Narraciones*. Born Salvador Salazar Arrué in 1899, Salarrué was a writer, painter and commentator, and is one of the most widely known Salvadorean writers. His short stories and novellas focus upon the lives and realities of campesinos and non-metropolites.

# LANGUAGE

There are over thirty languages spoken in the Maya World, but the *lingua franca* is Spanish, except in Belize and the Bay Islands of Honduras where English predominates. Almost everyone will speak some Spanish (even Belizean creoles), though it must be remembered it is the first language of perhaps only seventy percent of the region's people. In the Guatemalan highlands it's a second language for almost everyone and both locals and travellers struggle with grammar and verbs.

It is possible to survive speaking little or no Spanish if you confine yourself to the more touristy areas but you'll be in for a frustrating time – and if you plan to get off the beaten path some Spanish is essential. Just learning some basic conversational terms will open lots of doors, help prevent misunderstandings and enable you to bargain much more effectively. Simply learning the numbers will help immeasurably in hotels, restaurants, shops and at the marketplace. Many people choose to study Spanish in the Maya region (see p.000), as it's undoubtedly an excellent place to learn and courses are priced extremely competively.

## SPANISH

The good news is that the Spanish spoken in Latin America is generally spoken much less rapidly and is much easier to decipher than in the rapid-fire, lispy intonations of Castile and Andalucía. Gone is the soft s, replaced by a crisp and clear version, and there's no need to learn the second person plural (*vosotros*) endings – they're not used in Latin America. People are generally incredibly patient, and you'll find the locals very willing to make an effort to understand you. Once you get going you'll find that Spanish is one of the easiest languages to pick up – most of the complicated words are derived from Latin and are very similar in English and Spanish.

The rules of **pronunciation** are pretty straightforward once you get to know them, and strictly observed. An acute accent means that the stress falls on the accented syllable. Unless there's an **accent**, words ending in d, l, r and z are stressed on the last syllable, all others on the second last. All **vowels** are pure and short.

**A** somewhere between the "A" sound of back and that of father.

**E** as in get.

**I** as in police.

**O** as in hot.

**U** as in rule.

**C** is soft before E and I, hard otherwise: *cerca* is pronounced serka.

**G** works the same way, a guttural "H" sound (like the *ch* in loch) before E or I, a hard G elsewhere – *gigante* becomes higante.

**H** is always silent.

**J** the same sound as a guttural G: *jamón* is pronounced hamon.

**LL** sounds like an English Y: *tortilla* is pronounced torteeya.

**N** is as in English unless it has a tilde (accent) over it, when it becomes NY: *mañana* sounds like manyana.

**QU** is pronounced like an English K.

**R** is rolled, RR doubly so.

**V** sounds more like B, *vino* becoming beano.

**X** in the Maya world is pronounced SH – *Xela* is pronounced shela.

**Z** is the same as a soft C, so *cerveza* becomes servesa.

Below is a list of a few essential words and phrases (and see pp.37–39 for food lists), though if you're travelling for any length of time a dictionary and a **phrasebook** are worthwhile investments: the *Rough Guide to Mexican Spanish* is the best practical guide for the region. When choosing a **dictionary** it's better to buy a Latin American one – the University of Chicago version (Pocket Books) is good. When using a dictionary, remember that in Spanish CH, LL, and Ñ count as separate letters and are listed after the Cs, Ls, and Ns respectively.

## A SPANISH LANGUAGE GUIDE

### BASICS

| | | | |
|---|---|---|---|
| Yes, No | *Sí, No* | Open, Closed | *Abierto/a, Cerrado/a* |
| Please, Thank you | *Por favor, Gracias* | With, Without | *Con, Sin* |
| Where?, When? | *¿Dónde?, ¿Cuándo?* | Good, Bad | *Buen(o)/a, Mal(o)/a* |
| What?, How much? | *¿Qué?, ¿Cuánto?* | Big, Small | *Gran(de), Pequeño/a* |
| Here, There | *Aquí, Allí* | More, Less | *Más, Menos* |
| This, That | *Este, Eso* | Today, Tomorrow | *Hoy, Mañana* |
| Now, Later | *Ahora, Más tarde* | Yesterday | *Ayer* |

### GREETINGS AND RESPONSES

| | | | |
|---|---|---|---|
| Hello, Goodbye | *Hola, Adiós* | What (did you say)? | *¿Mande?* |
| Good morning | *Buenos días* | My name is . . . | *Me llamo . . .* |
| Good afternoon/night | *Buenas tardes/noches* | What's your name? | *¿Cómo se llama usted?* |
| See you later | *Hasta luego* | I am English | *Soy/inglés(a)* |
| Sorry | *Lo siento/discúlpeme* | American | *americano (a)* |
| Excuse me | *Con permiso/perdón* | Australian | *australiano(a)* |
| How are you? | *¿Cómo está (usted)?* | British | *británico* |
| I (don't) understand | *(No) Entiendo* | Canadian | *canadiense* |
| Could you speak more slowly? | *¿Podría hablar más lento?* | Dutch | *holandés (a)* |
| | | Irish | *irlandés(a)* |
| Not at all/You're welcome | *De nada* | from New Zealand | *neozelandés(a)* |
| | | Scottish | *escosés(a)* |
| Do you speak English? | *¿Habla (usted) inglés?* | South African | *sudafricano(a)* |
| I don't speak Spanish | *(No) Hablo Español* | Welsh | *galés(a)* |

### NEEDS – HOTELS AND TRANSPORT

| | | | |
|---|---|---|---|
| I want | *Quiero* | Is there a hotel nearby? | *¿Hay un hotel aquí cerca?* |
| I'd like | *Quisiera* | How do I get to . . . ? | *¿Por dónde se va a . . .?* |
| Do you know . . . ? | *¿Sabe . . . ?* | Left, right, straight on | *Izquierda, derecha, derecho* |
| I don't know | *No sé* | | |
| There is (is there)? | *(¿)Hay(?)* | Where is . . . ? | *¿Dónde está . . . ?* |
| Give me . . . (one like that) | *Deme . . . (uno así)* | . . . the bus station | *. . . el terminal de camionetas* |
| Do you have . . . ? | *¿Tiene . . . ?* | . . . the nearest bank | *. . . el banco más cercano* |
| . . . the time | *. . . la hora* | | |
| . . . a room | *. . . un cuarto* | . . . the post office | *. . . el correo/la oficina de correos* |
| . . . with two beds/ double bed | *. . . con dos camas/ cama matrimonial* | | |
| It's for one person (two people) | *Es para una persona (dos personas)* | . . . the toilet | *. . . el baño/sanitario* |
| | | Where does the bus to . . . leave from? | *¿De dónde sale la camioneta para . . . ?* |
| . . . for one night (one week) | *. . . para una noche (una semana)* | | |
| It's fine, how much is it? | *¿Está bien, cuánto es?* | I'd like a (return) ticket to . . . | *Quisiera un boleto (de ida y vuelta) para . . .* |
| It's too expensive | *Es demasiado caro* | What time does it leave (arrive in . . . )? | *¿A qué hora sale (llega en . . . )?* |
| Don't you have anything cheaper? | *¿No tiene algo más barato?* | | |
| Can one . . . ? | *¿Se puede . . . ?* | What is there to eat? | *¿Qué hay para comer?* |
| . . . camp (near) here? | *¿ . . . acampar aquí (cerca)?* | What's that? | *¿Qué es eso?* |
| | | What's this called in Spanish? | *¿Cómo se llama este en Español?* |

*continued overleaf*

## A SPANISH LANGUAGE GUIDE contd

### NUMBERS AND DAYS

| | | | | | |
|---|---|---|---|---|---|
| 0 | *cero* | 22 | *veintidós* | first | *primero/a* |
| 1 | *un/uno/una* | 30 | *treinta* | second | *segundo/a* |
| 2 | *dos* | 31 | *treinta y uno* | third | *tercero/a* |
| 3 | *tres* | 40 | *cuarenta* | fourth | *cuarto/a* |
| 4 | *cuatro* | 50 | *cincuenta* | fifth | *quinto/a* |
| 5 | *cinco* | 60 | *sesenta* | sixth | *sexto/a* |
| 6 | *seis* | 70 | *setenta* | seventh | *séptimo/a* |
| 7 | *siete* | 80 | *ochenta* | eighth | *octavo/a* |
| 8 | *ocho* | 90 | *noventa* | ninth | *noveno/a* |
| 9 | *nueve* | 100 | *cien* | tenth | *décimo/a* |
| 10 | *diez* | 101 | *ciento uno* | | |
| 11 | *once* | 200 | *doscientos* | Monday | *lunes* |
| 12 | *doce* | 201 | *doscientos uno* | Tuesday | *martes* |
| 13 | *trece* | 500 | *quinientos* | Wednesday | *miércoles* |
| 14 | *catorce* | 1000 | *mil* | Thursday | *jueves* |
| 15 | *quince* | 2000 | *dos mil* | Friday | *viernes* |
| 16 | *dieciséis* | 1000000 | *un millión* | Saturday | *sábado* |
| 20 | *veinte* | 1999 | *mil novocientos* | Sunday | *domingo* |
| 21 | *veintiuno* | | *noventa y nueve* | | |

## ENGLISH

The English spoken in Belize and the Honduran Bay Islands is delightfully melodic, unmistakably Caribbean in rhythm and tone and sounds very similar to Jamaican patois. Initially this rich **Creole** dialect is difficult to understand – you will be able to pick up familiar phrases and expressions but complete comprehension is just out of reach. Creole is loosely based on English, but also uses elements of French, Spanish, African and Maya languages. Fortunately, almost everyone who speaks Creole also learns standard English at school, so they can dilute the patois if necessary. Here's a brief taster of some simple phrases.

*Bad ting neda gat owna* – Bad things never have owners.

*Betta belly burst than good bikkle waste* – It's better that the belly bursts than good victuals go to waste.

*Cow no business eena haas gylop* – Cows have no business in a horse race.

For more words of wisdom, there are usually copies of *Creole Proverbs of Belize* available in Belize City.

## MAYA LANGUAGES

After years of state-backed *castellanización* programmes when Spanish was the only language of tuition and Maya schoolchildren were left virtual classroom spectators, a network of Maya schools has now been established, with hundreds alone in Q'eqchi' areas of Guatemala. A strong indigenous cultural movement has now developed throughout the region, intent on preserving the dozens of different Maya languages still spoken (for a comprehensive map see p.000). Because the Maya birthrate is much higher than the ladino, there is now every chance that the main languages like K'iche', Yucateca and Mam will survive, though the fate of the more isolated tongues is far from secure.

If you're planning an extended stay in a remote indigenous region to do development work, it's extremely helpful to learn a little of the local language first. There are a number of language schools (see pp.351, 401, 443) where you can **study a Maya language** and pick up the essentials. The Yax Te' Foundation (see Maya resources box in Contexts), devoted to promoting and supporting Maya culture and language, has an excellent website from where you can purchase study material and dictionaries.

Maya words do not easily translate into Spanish (or English) so you may see the same place spelt in different ways: *K'umarkaaj* can be spelt *K'umarcaah* or even *Gumarcaj*. Nearly all Maya words are pronounced stressing the final syllable, which is often accented: Atitlán is A-tit-LAN, Calakmul is Ca-lak-MUL.

C is always hard like a K, unlike Spanish.
J is a guttural H, as in Spanish.
U like a W at the beginnning of a word and like an OO in the middle of a word – Uaxactún is pronounced washaktoon.
X sounds like SH – *Xela* is pronounced shela.

# GLOSSARY

**AGUARDIENTE** Raw alcohol made from sugar cane.

**AGUAS** Bottled fizzy drinks such as Coca Cola, Sprite or Pepsi.

**ALCALDE** Mayor.

**ALDEA** Small settlement.

**ALTIPLANO** Highland area of western Guatemala.

**AYUNTAMIENTO** Town hall.

**BALEADA** Stuffed tortilla street snack (Honduras only).

**BARRANCA** Steep-sided ravine.

**BARRIO** Neighbourhood or district.

**BAYMEN** Early white settlers in Belize.

**BIOTOPO** Protected area of national ecological interest, usually with limited tourist access.

**BRUJO** Maya priest able to communicate with the spirit world.

**KAQCHIKEL** Indigenous highland group occupying an area between Guatemala City and Lago de Atitlán, who, historically, collaborated with the conquistadors to defeat their rivals the K'iche' and Tz'utujil.

**CAMIONETA** Second-class bus in Guatemala. Small truck or van in other parts of Latin America.

**CANTINA** A hard-drinking bar where the machismo and beer run freely.

**CENOTE** Large natural wells found in the Yucatán that connect with the water table via a network of drains in the limestone. Also used for ceremonial purposes.

**CHAC** Maya rain god.

**CHAPÍN** Nickname for a Guatemalan.

**CHICLE** Sapodilla tree sap from which chewing gum is made.

**CLASSIC** Period during which ancient Maya civilization was at its height, usually given as 300–900 AD.

**CODEX** Maya manuscript made from the bark of the fig tree and written in hieroglyphs. Most were destroyed by the Spanish, but a copy of the Dresden Codex can be found in the Popol Vuh museum in Guatemala City (see p.334).

**COFRADÍA** Religious brotherhood dedicated to the protection of a particular saint. These groups form the basis of religious and civil hierarchy in traditional Guatemalan society and combine Catholic and pagan practices.

**COLECTIVO** Collective minibus transport, usually more expensive than the bus.

**COLONIA** City suburb.

**COMEDOR** Basic restaurant, usually with just one or two things on the menu. Always the cheapest place to eat.

**CORTE** Traditional Maya skirt, often elaborately embroidered.

**COSTUMBRE** Traditional customs of the highland Maya, usually of religious and cultural significance. Often refers to traditions that owe more to paganism than Catholicism.

**CREOLE** Belizeans of mixed Afro-Caribbean descent.

**CUADRA** Street block.

**DON/DOÑA** Sir/Madam. Mostly used to address a professional person or employer.

**EFECTIVO** Cash.

**EVANGÉLICO** Christian evangelist or fundamentalist; often missionaries. Used to denote numerous Protestant sects seeking converts.

**EZLN** The Zapatista Army of National Liberation, lead by Subcomandante Marcos and active in Chiapas since 1994 (see pp.139 & 559).

**FERIA** Fair.

**FINCA** Plantation-style farm.

**GARÍFUNA** Black Carib group with a unique language and strong African heritage living in village communities along the Caribbean coast between Belize and Nicaragua.

**GRINGO/GRINGA** Any white-skinned foreigner, but particularly North Americans. Not necessarily a term of abuse.

**HENEQUEN** Fibre from the agave (sisal) plant, grown in Yucatán and Guatemala to make rope.

**HOSPEDAJE** Small basic hotel.

**HUIPIL** A Maya woman's traditional blouse, usually woven or embroidered. In Guatemala and Chiapas most indigenous villages still have a unique design.

**INDÍGENA** Indigenous person of Maya descent.

**ÍNDIO/A** Racially abusive term to describe someone of Maya descent. The word *indito/a* is equally offensive.

**INGUAT** Guatemalan tourist board.

**ITZÁ** Tribal group who constructed Chichén Itzá; small pockets still live near Flores, in Petén, and continue to speak the Itza language.

**I.V.A.** Sales tax.

**IXIL** Highland group grouped around the three towns of Guatemala's Ixil triangle – Nebaj, Chajul and San Juan Cotzal.

**K'ICHE'** Largest of the Guatemalan Maya tribes, centred on the town of Santa Cruz del Quiché. Their ancient capital is close by at Utatlán.

**KUKULCÁN** The Maya name for Quetzalcoatl, the plumed serpent. The most powerful, enigmatic and widespread of all the gods.

**LADINO** A vague term – at its most specific defining someone of mixed Spanish and indigenous blood, but more commonly used to describe a person of "Western" culture, or one who dresses in "Western" style, be they pure blood Maya or mixed blood.

**LICUADO** Blended fruit juice made with water or milk.

**MAM** Maya group occupying the far west part of Guatemala's highlands, around Huehuetenango.

**MARIMBA** Huge xylophone-like instrument used in traditional music. Also signifies the style of music played on this instrument.

**MAYA** General term for the large tribal group who inhabited Guatemala, southeastern Mexico, Belize, western Honduras and a slice of El Salvador since the earliest times, and still do.

**MESTIZO** Person of mixed native and Spanish blood.

**METATE** Flat stone for grinding maize into flour.

**MIGRACIÓN** Immigration office.

**MILPA** Maize field, usually cleared by slash and burn.

**MINUGUA** United Nations mission in Guatemala to oversee the peace process.

**MIRADOR** Lookout point.

**NATURAL** Another term for an indigenous person.

**PALAPA** Thatched palm-leaf hut.

**PENSIÓN** Simple hotel.

**PILA** Font or wash basin; either domestic or communal.

**PISTO** Guatemalan slang for cash.

**PIPIL** Indigenous tribal group which occupied much of the Guatemalan Pacific coast at the time of the Conquest. Only their art survives, around the town of Santa Lucía Cotzumalguapa.

**POPOL VUH** The K'iche' Maya's epic story of the creation and history of their people (see p.552).

**POSTCLASSIC** Period between the decline of Maya civilization and the arrival of the Spanish, 900–1530 AD.

**PRECLASSIC** Archeological era preceding the blooming of Maya civilization, usually given as 1500 BC–300 AD.

**PULLMAN** Fast and comfortable bus, usually an old Greyhound.

**PUNTA ROCK** The music of the Garífuna.

**Q'EQCHI'** Guatemalan Maya tribal group spread across a large area around Cobán, the Verapaces highlands, Lago de Izabal, the Petén and southern Belize where they are known as Kekchí.

**SIERRA** Mountain range.

**TECÚN UMÁN** Last king of the K'iche' tribe, defeated in battle by Alvarado.

**TEMPORADA** Season. *La temporada de lluvia* is the rainy season.

**TEOTIHUACÁN** First major urban power in Mesoamerica, just north of today's Mexico City, that dominated the Maya region until the mid-Classic era.

**TIENDA** Shop.

**TÍPICA** Literally "typical". Guatemalan-made clothes woven from multicoloured textiles, usually geared towards the Western customer. Also used to describe a local dish - *comida típica*.

**TRAJE** Traditional Maya costume.

**TZOLKIN** The Maya's 260-day calendar that acts as an almanac and horoscope.

**TZUTE** Headcloth or scarf worn as a part of traditional Maya costume.

**TZ'UTUJIL** Indigenous tribal group occupying the land to the south of Lago de Atitlán.

**XATE** Decorative palm leaves harvested in the Petén for export to the US, to be used in flower arrangements.

**ZÓCALO** The main plaza in any Mexican town.

## MAYA ARCHITECTURAL TERMS

**ALTAR** Elaborately carved altars, often of a cylindrical design, were grouped round the fringes of the main plaza. Used to record historical events, they probably also functioned as sacrificial stones. Some of the most fascinating are at Caracol (see pp.273–275). See also **zoomorph**.

**BALL COURT** Narrow, stone-flagged rectangular court with banked sides where the Maya ball game was played. The courts symbolized a stage between the real and supernatural worlds and for the ball players it could be a game of life and death – losers were sometimes sacrificed. The ball court at Chichén Itzá (see p.88) is 90m long but most are around 30m.

**CHAC MOOL** Reclining stone figure of Toltec origin that probably functioned as a sacrificial stone altar. Found from central Mexico to El Salvador but best-known examples are at Chichén Itzá.

**CHENES** Yucatecan Maya architectural style, related to the Puuc. The ruins of Hochob and Dzibilnocac (see pp.100 & 101) are good examples, with highly stylized temple facades.

**CHULTÚN** Man-made cistern lined with plaster, common in the Puuc region.

**CORBEL VAULT** "False arch" where each stone slightly overlaps the one below. A relatively primitive technique which severely limits the width of doorways and interiors. The Labná arch (see p.81) is particularly beautiful.

**GLYPH** Element in Maya writing, roughly the equivalent of a letter or phrase; used to record historical events. Some glyphs are phonetic, while others represent an entire description or concept as in Chinese characters. Dominant Classic and Postclassic sites had unique emblem glyphs; some like Copán used several.

**LINTEL** Top block of stone or wood above a doorway or window, often carved to record important events and dates. Those from Yaxchilán (see p.149) are especially well executed.

**MURAL** Painted scene used to illustrate aspects of Maya life, mostly famously at Bonampak (see p.146) where there are stupendous images of processions, dances and ceremonies.

**PALACE** Maya palaces occupied prominent locations near the ceremonial heart of the city, usually resting on low platforms, and almost certainly housed the royal elite. There are particularly striking palaces at Palenque, Cancuén, Sayil, Kabáh, and Uxmal.

**PUUC** Architectural style of the Puuc hills 80km south of Mérida. Typified by classically proportioned buildings, rich with columns and arches and decorated with mosaic friezes of geometric patterns (see pp.77–83).

**PUTÚN** Style dominant at Ceibal in central Petén (see p.468), exhibiting strong Mexican characteristics.

**RÍO BEC** Style typified by long buildings with matching towers and narrow roof combs; found at the ruins of Becán, Chicanná and Río Bec itself (see p.102).

**ROOF COMB** Decorative top crest on stone temples, possibly intended to enhance verticality. Originally painted in arresting colours and often framed by giant stucco figures.

**SACBÉ** Paved Maya road or raised causeway near the centre of Maya cities. Probably designed for ceremonial processions and to save rulers from sloshing through the lowland marshes. *Sacbés* were also trade routes and there are hundreds of kilometres still evident in the Yucatán and northern Petén today.

**STELA** Free-standing, often exquisitely carved stone monument. Decorating major Maya sites, stelae fulfilled a sacred and political role commemorating historical events. Among the largest and most impressive are the ones at Quiriguá (see p.420) and Copán (see pp.486–495).

**TEMPLE** Monumental stone structure of pivotal religious significance built in the ceremonial heart of a city, usually with a pyramid-shaped base and topped with a narrow room or two used for secretive ceremonies and bloody sacrifices. Those at Tikal (see pp.457–464) and El Mirador (see p.466) reach over 60m, while Calakmul (see p.102) is the bulkiest.

**TOLTEC** Style of the central Mexican tribal group who invaded parts of the Maya region from the Yucatán to El Salvador. Many of the major buildings at Chichén Itzá are typically Toltec.

**ZOOMORPH** Spectacular stone altar intricately carved with animal images and glyphs. Peculiar to Quiriguá (see p.402), though similar altars exist in Izapa.